SHORT STORY INDEX

Supplement 1950-1954

SHORT STORY INDEX

Supplement 1950-1954

AN INDEX TO 9,575 STORIES IN 549 COLLECTIONS

Compiled by

DOROTHY E. COOK
ESTELLE A. FIDELL

NEW YORK
THE H. W. WILSON COMPANY
1956

Published 1956

Second printing 1963

Third printing 1971

Printed in the U.S.A.

International Standard Book Number 0-8242-0385-2

Library of Congress Card No. (53-8991)

25161

PREFACE

This supplement to the SHORT STORY INDEX covers the years 1950-1954 and indexes 9,575 stories in 549 collections. In style it basically follows the pattern set up by the compilers for the basic volume of the SHORT STORY INDEX, but with certain changes which the publishers hope will represent improvements.

The innovations in this Supplement are three-fold:

1. **Type:** There has been a substitution of larger 8 point type for the former 6 point type.

2. **Capitalization:** To avoid confusion in distinguishing subjects from authors, the use of all-capital letters in this volume is reserved for subject entries only; authors' names are given in boldface with conventional capitalization.

3. **Directory of Publishers:** A list of the publishers from whom the books indexed may be obtained has been added following the "List of Collections Indexed".

It is hoped that the next supplement covering the years 1955-1959 will be published in the Fall of 1960.

Sincere thanks are extended to various members of the staff who assisted in the work, especially to Mrs. Loretta Devine and Mrs. Agnes Bryceland.

August 1956

DOROTHY E. COOK
ESTELLE A. FIDELL

Directions for Use

Part 1 of this Index is in dictionary form with author, title, and subject entries in one alphabet. Part 2 is a list of the collections indexed. Part 3 is a directory of publishers. The following directions apply to Part 1.

Author Entry. This entry gives the full name of the author, years of birth and death, whenever ascertainable, title of story, author and title of collection or collections in which the story is found. It may be recognized by the boldface type, *not* in capital letters.

Sample entry:

> **Faulkner, William,** 1897-
> Spotted horses
> Gordon, C. and Tate, A. eds. House of
> fiction

This means that the short story by William Faulkner "Spotted horses" appears in the collection entitled "House of fiction" edited by C. Gordon and A. Tate. For fuller information about "House of fiction" consult the "List of Collections Indexed," under Gordon, C.

Title Entry. This entry is used primarily to identify the author under whose name the full information will be given. Only the first word of each title entry is in boldface type.

Sample entry:

> **Spotted** horses. Faulkner, W.

Subject Entry. All stories in this Index dealing in whole or in part with a particular subject are listed under that subject. Such entries are in capital letters, in boldface type.

Sample entry:

> **HORSES**
> Faulkner, W. Spotted horses

In some collections all the stories may deal with the same subject. In such cases the entry under that subject indicates the editor or author and title of the collection, followed by the number of stories, rather than the listing of the individual stories.

Sample entry:

> **HORSES**
> Foote, J. T. Hoofbeats; 13 stories

The phrase "13 stories" identifies this type of entry.

SHORT STORY INDEX
Supplement 1950-1954

PART I

Author, title, subject index to short stories

ABANDONED CHILDREN. See Foundlings; Orphans

ABANDONED SHIPS. See Ships, Abandoned

ABDUCTION. See Disappearances; Kidnapping

Abduction of Abner Greer. Bond, N. S.

Abdullah, Achmed, 1881-1945
McCarthy hunts peace
American boy (Periodical) American boy anthology

ABEL (BIBLICAL CHARACTER)
Feild, B. How Abel slew Cain

Abernathy, Robert, 1924-
Heritage
Conklin, G. ed. Omnibus of science fiction
Peril of the blue world
Wollheim, D. A. comp. Flight into space

Able to Zebra. Tucker, W.

ABNORMAL CHILDREN. See Children, Abnormal and backward

ABOLITION OF SLAVERY. See Slavery

ABORTION
Lowry, R. J. C. For girlhood and for love

About my sons. Ferrone, J. R.

About Shorty. Gellhorn, M. E.

Above the clouds. Sommerfield, J.

Above the river. Williams, W. C.

Abraham. Kierkegaard, S. A.

ABRAHAM, THE PATRIARCH
Kierkegaard, S. A. Abraham

Abrahams, William
Interpretation of dreams
Story (Periodical) Story; no. 2

Abraham's glory. Davies, R.

Abramovich, Solomon Jacob. See Abramowitz, Shalom Jacob

Abramowitz, Shalom Jacob, 1836-1917
The calf
Howe, I. and Greenberg, E. eds. Treasury of Yiddish stories
Same as: Little calf
The exchange
Leftwich, J. ed. Yisröel. 1952 ed.
How the Czar fooled Montefiore
Ausubel, N. ed. Treasury of Jewish humor
Little calf
Ausubel, N. ed. Treasury of Jewish humor
Same as: The calf

Absalom. Kuttner, H.

Absence of Mr Glass. Chesterton, G. K.

Absent hat pin. Hitchens, D. B.

ABSENT-MINDEDNESS
Munro, H. H. Louise
Thurber, J. Secret life of Walter Mitty

Absent-mindedness in a parish choir. Hardy, T.

Absolution. Fitzgerald, F. S. K.

Absolutism. Johnston, N. F.

The **academy.** Asch, S.

ACADIANS IN LOUISIANA
Jackson, C. T. Horse of Hurricane Reef

Accident. Christie, A. M.

The **accident.** Williams, W. C.

ACCIDENTAL SHOOTING. See Hunting—Accidents

ACCIDENTS
Aldrich, T. B. Marjorie Daw
Bennett, P. Fugitive from the mind
Boyle, K. Maiden, maiden
Ervine, St J. G. The mountain
Greene, G. Basement room
Hopkinson, H. T. Mountain madness
Humphrey, W. Man with a family
O'Donovan, M. Vanity
Phillips, A. Presence in the grove
Poe, E. A. Angel of the odd
Young, E. H. The stream
See also Accidents, Industrial Aeronautics—Accidents; Automobiles—Accidents; Hunting—Accidents

ACCIDENTS, AIRPLANE. See Aeronautics—Accidents

ACCIDENTS, INDUSTRIAL
Di Donato, P. Christ in concrete

According to the landmarks. Claudy, C. H.

According to their lights. Porter, W. S.

Account rendered. Harvey, W. F.

ACCOUNTANTS
Collier, J. Midnight blue

Acheson, Edward Goodrich, 1856-1931
Big shot
This week magazine. This week's short-short stories

Achievement of the cat. Munro, H. H.

Ackerman, Forrest J.
Mute question
Crossen, K. F. ed. Adventures in tomorrow

ACROBATICS. See Acrobats and acrobatism

ACROBATS AND ACROBATISM
Alexander, S. Part of the act
Constiner, M. Lady and the tumblers
Maugham, W. S. Gigolo and Gigolette

Across Siberia. Chekhov, A. P.

Across the sea. Verga, G.

Act of contrition. Smith, J. E.

Act of faith. Shaw, I.

Act of God. Tobin, R. L.

Action. Montague, C. E.

Action in Prague. Doty, W. L.

Action off Formosa. Holmes, W. J.

Action on Azura. Osborne, R.

Actor and the alibi. Chesterton, G. K.

ACTORS
Benson, T. Man with the phoney tin foot
Bernstein, D. Death of an actor
Brophy, B. His wife survived him
Collier, J. Gavin O'Leary
Hughes, L. Trouble with the angels
Jackson, C. R. Romeo
Porter, W. S. Duplicity of Hargraves
Porter, W. S. The rathskeller and the
rose
Porter, W. S. Song and the sergeant
Porter, W. S. Strictly business
Schulberg, B. W. Typical gesture of
Colonel Duggan
Villiers de l'Isle-Adam, J. M. M. P. A.
comte de. Desire to be a man
See also Actresses; Moving picture
actors and actresses

ACTORS, MOVING PICTURE. See
Moving picture actors and actresses

The **actress.** Winslow, T. S.

ACTRESSES
Collier, J. Gavin O'Leary
Collier, J. Pictures in the fire
Collier, J. Youth from Vienna
Coward, N. P. Ashes of roses
Coward, N. P. Star quality
Felder, D. F. Purple hat
Merrick, L. Doll in the pink silk dress
Porter, W. S. The memento
Porter, W. S. The rathskeller and the
rose
Porter, W. S. Song and the sergeant
Porter, W. S. Strictly business
Ullman, J. R. Hello darling
Waltari, M. T. Before the twilight of the
gods
Waltari, M. T. Moonscape
Winslow, T. S. The actress
Winslow, T. S. Technique
Zangwill, L. Prelude to a pint of bitter

ACTRESSES, MOVING PICTURE. See
Moving picture actors and actresses

Ad Astra. Faulkner, W.

Adalantado of the Seven Cities. Irving, W.

Adam, Villiers de l'Isle. See Villiers de
l'Isle-Adam, Jean Marie Mathias
Philippe Auguste, comte de

Adam. Powell, D.

Adam and Eve. Friedman, S.

Adam and I. Kristol, I.

Adams, Bertram Martin, 1879-
The foreigner
Cooper, A. C. ed. Modern short stories

Adams, Bill, pseud. See Adams, Bertram
Martin

Adams, James Douglas, 1875-
Cap'n Ezra, privateer; excerpt
Fenner, P. R. comp. Pirates, pirates,
pirates

Adam's death. Boyle, K.

Adamson, Rigmore
Music lesson
Weaver, R. and James, H. eds. Ca-
nadian short stories

Addison, Joseph, 1672-1719
Vision of Mirzah
Cerf, B. A. and Moriarty, H. C. eds.
Anthology of famous British stories

Ade, George, 1866-1944
Effie Whittlesy
Burrell, J. A. and Cerf, B. A. eds. An-
thology of famous American stories

ADIRONDACK MOUNTAINS
Warner, C. D. A-hunting of the deer

Adjustment of nature. Porter, W. S.

Adler, Jacob, 1877-
Bluff, a story of the depression
Ausubel, N. ed. Treasury of Jewish
humor
My Pinya
Ausubel, N. ed. Treasury of Jewish
humor
Yente Telebende
Ausubel, N. ed. Treasury of Jewish
humor

Adler, Warren, 1927-
Other people
American vanguard, 1950
Polka dot dress
Wolfe, D. M. ed. Which grain will grow

ADMINISTRATORS. See Civil service

The **admiral.** Porter, W. S.

ADMIRALS
Porter, W. S. The admiral
Porter, W. S. Flag paramount

Admiral's inspection. Jameson, M.

ADOLESCENCE
Cousins, M. White kid gloves
Daly, M. Sixteen
De Meyer, J. Boy crazy
Dostoevskii, F. M. Little hero
Eicher, E. But not Jeff
Fisher, D. C. Sunset at sixteen
Fisher, D. F. C. Sex education
Fitzgerald, F. S. K. Bernice bobs her
hair
Furman, A. L. ed. Teen-age sea stories;
13 stories
Jackson, M. W. The stepmother
Kaufman, A. First love
Laurence, M. Uncertain flowering
McFarland, W. K. comp. Then it hap-
pened; 21 stories
McLaren, F. C. Date with Dora
Murphy, R. You've got to learn
Roberts, D. The girl on the lake
Schweitzer, G. Kid brother
Seventeen (Periodical) Nineteen from
Seventeen; 19 stories
Stowe, A. comp. It's a date; 10 stories
Strain, F. B. But you don't understand;
12 stories

ADOLESCENCE—*Continued*
Strong, P. N. Running dark
Summers, J. L. Open season; 11 stories
Thompson, T. Jolly
ADOLESCENTS. See Adolescence
ADOPTED CHILDREN. See Foster children
ADOPTION. See Foster children
Adrian. Munro. H. H.
The **adulteress.** Fleg, E.
ADULTERY. See Marriage problems
Advent. Gunnarson, G.
Adventure. Anderson, S.
The **adventure.** Lagerkvist, P. F.
Adventure of Baron Munchausen. Martin, J.
Adventure of Foulkes Rath. Doyle, A. C.
Adventure of Ricoletti of the club foot. Derleth, A. W.
Adventure of the Abbas ruby. Doyle, A. C.
Adventure of the Beryl Coronet. Doyle, Sir A. C.
Adventure of the black baronet. Doyle, A. C. and Carr, J. D.
Adventure of the Black Narcissus. Derleth, A. W.
Adventure of the blue carbuncle. Doyle, Sir A. C.
Adventure of the broken chessman. Derleth, A. W.
Adventure of the Camberwell beauty. Derleth, A. W.
Adventure of the circular room. Derleth, A. W.
Adventure of the Clapham cook. Christie, A. M.
Adventure of the Copper Beeches. Doyle, Sir A. C.
Adventure of the Dark Angels. Doyle, A. C.
Adventure of the Dauphin's doll. Queen, E. pseud.
Adventure of the dead cat. Queen, E. pseud.
Adventure of the Deptford horror. Doyle, A. C.
Adventure of the dog in the manger. Derleth, A. W.
Adventure of the emperor's dice. Queen, E. pseud.
Adventure of the engineer's thumb. Doyle, Sir A. C.
Adventure of the fallen angel. Queen, E. pseud.
Adventure of the five royal coachmen. Derleth, A. W.
Adventure of the German student. Irving, W.
Adventure of the Gettysburg bugle. Queen, E. pseud.
Adventure of the gold hunter. Doyle, A. C. and Carr, J. D.
Adventure of the Highgate miracle. Doyle, A. C. and Carr, J. D.
Adventure of the ides of Michael Magoon. Queen. E. pseud.

Adventure of the inner circle. Queen, E. pseud.
Adventure of the kind Mr Smith. Locke, W. J.
Adventure of the lost locomotive. Derleth, A. W.
Adventure of the medical finger. Queen, E. pseud.
Adventure of the needle's eye. Queen, E. pseud.
Adventure of the noble bachelor. Doyle, Sir A. C.
Adventure of the one-penny black. Queen, E. pseud.
Adventure of the paralytic mendicant. Derleth, A. W.
Adventure of the perfect husband. Derleth, A. W.
Adventure of the President's half disme. Queen, E. pseud.
Adventure of the proper comma. Derleth, A. W.
Adventure of the purloined periapt. Derleth, A. W.
Adventure of the red widow. Doyle, A. C.
Adventure of the remarkable worm. Derleth, A. W.
Adventure of the Rydberg numbers. Derleth, A. W.
Adventure of the sealed room. Doyle, A. C. and Carr, J. D.
Adventure of the seven clocks. Doyle, A. C. and Carr, J. D.
Adventure of the six silver spiders. Derleth, A. W.
Adventure of the speckled band. Doyle, Sir A. C.
Adventure of the telltale bottle. Queen, E. pseud.
Adventure of the three R's. Queen, E. pseud.
Adventure of the Tottenham werewolf. Derleth, A. W.
Adventure of the two women. Doyle, A. C.
Adventure of the wax gamblers. Doyle, A. C. and Carr, J. D.
Adventure on Lone Gulch Trail. Reynolds, H. M. G. C.
Adventure with a dog. Muir, J.
An **adventure** with a dog and a glacier. Muir, J.
The **adventurer.** Kornbluth, C. M.
ADVENTURES, INTERPLANETARY. See Interplanetary voyages
Adventures of Hershel Summerwind. Manger, I.
Adventures of Shamrock Jolnes. Porter, W. S.
ADVERTISING
Aspinwall, M. Thundering Hurd
Crossen, K. F. Things of distinction
Munro, H. H. Filboid Studge, the story of a mouse that helped
Olds, H. D. Vic's Orr Kid
Platt, G. Play the field alone
Porter, W. S. Green door
See also Publicity

Aegean storm. Cicellis, K.

Æpyornis Island. Wells, H. G.

AERONAUTICS
Jensen, P. ed. Fireside book of flying stories; 19 stories
Marcus, P. Tip the green earth
Verral, C. S. Itch to win
Wells, H. G. Argonauts of the air
Wells, H. G. Filmer
See also Air pilots

Accidents
Aumonier, S. Source of irritation
La Farge, O. Old century's river
Newhouse, E. Close your eyes
Sansom, W. Small world

Flights
Angell, R. Flight through the dark
Coward, N. P. This time to-morrow
De Vries, P. We don't know
Doyle, Sir A. C. Horror of the heights
Gellhorn, M. E. Miami-New York
Jackson, C. R. The outlander
Litten, F. N. Blackout over Cleveland

AERONAUTICS, MILITARY
Nordhoff, C. B. and Hall, J. N. School for combat
O'Connell, R. B. You'll never mind
See also European War, 1914-1918—Aerial operations; World War, 1939-1945—Aerial operations

Aesop. Simak, C. D.

AESTHETICS. See Esthetics

Affair at St Albans. Sass, H. R.

Affair at the Victory Ball. Christie, A. M.

Affair of honor. Hutchins, M. P. M.

Affair of the wayward jeep. Mauldin, W. H.

Affair on Jacklight Creek. Hendryx, J. B.

L'**affaire** foul tip. Brookhouser, F.

AFRICA
Conrad, J. Heart of darkness
Hemingway, E. Snows of Kilimanjaro
Waldeck, T. J. Igongo elephants

Native races
Elliott, G. P. Faq'
Fletcher, I. White leopard
Hughes, L. African morning
Lessing, D. M. Old Chief Mshlanga

AFRICA, NORTH
Bowles, P. F. By the water
Bowles, P. F. Delicate prey
Bowles, P. F. Tea on the mountain

AFRICA, SOUTH
Annixter, P. pseud. The lynching
Cloete, S. Silence of Mr Prendegast
Gordimer, N. Soft voice of the serpent, and other stories; 21 stories
Krige, U. The coffin
Krige, U. The dream
Lessing, D. M. This was the Old Chief's country; 10 stories
Marshall, E. Hill people

African morning. Hughes, L.

AFRICAN TRIBES. See Africa—Native races; also names of individual tribes, e.g. Kafirs (Africa people); Zulus; etc.

After all I did for Israel. Levin, M.

After Holbein. Wharton, E. N. J.

After-hours visitor. Tazewell, C.

After-image. Caldwell, E.

AFTER LIFE. See Future life

After school. Erskine, L. Y.

After the hay-makin'. Schwarz, C. J.

After the storm. Hemingway, E.

After the theatre. Chekhov, A. P.

After twenty years. Porter, W. S.

After you, my dear Alphonse. Jackson, S.

Afternoon. Sansom, W.

Afternoon hunt with the Tantivity hounds. Surtees, R. S.

Afternoon in the life of Father Burrell. Lieberman, R.

Afternoon miracle. Porter, W. S.

Afternoon of a faun. Ferber, E.

Afternoon sun. Willingham, C.

Afterthought. Fyfe, H. B.

Against orders. Claudy, C. H.

Age of love. Kjelgaard, B.

Age of romance. Bentham, J.

AGED. See Old age

Agee, James, 1909-
Mother's tale
Best American short stories, 1953

Agnon, Samuel Joseph, 1888-
Jack-of-all-trades
Ausubel, N. ed. Treasury of Jewish humor
Jewish cat
Ausubel, N. ed. Treasury of Jewish humor
Sabbathai
Leftwich, J. ed. Yisröel. 1952 ed.
Story of the cantor
Ausubel, N. ed. Treasury of Jewish humor

AGNOSTICS. See Atheism

AGRICULTURE. See Farm life

Ah the university. Collier, J.

Ah, woe is me. Gordimer, N.

Ah Wong. Travers, P. L.

Ahasuerus. See Xerses I, King of Persia

The **Aherns.** Corkery, D.

A-hunting of the deer. Warner, C. D.

Aiken, Conrad Potter, 1889-
The anniversary
Aiken, C. P. Short stories
Bachelor supper
Aiken, C. P. Short stories
Bow down, Isaac!
Aiken, C. P. Short stories
Bring! Bring!
Aiken, C. P. Short stories
By my troth, Nerissa!
Aiken, C. P. Short stories
Dark city
Aiken, C. P. Short stories
The disciple
Aiken, C. P. Short stories
Farewell! Farewell! Farewell!
Aiken, C. P. Short stories
Field of flowers
Aiken, C. P. Short stories

Aiken, Conrad P.—*Continued*
Fish supper
  Aiken, C. P. Short stories
Gehenna
  Aiken, C. P. Short stories
Hello, Tib
  Aiken, C. P. Short stories
Hey, Taxi!
  Aiken, C. P. Short stories
I love you very dearly
  Aiken, C. P. Short stories
Impulse
  Aiken, C. P. Short stories
Last visit
  Aiken, C. P. Short stories
Life isn't a short story
  Aiken, C. P. Short stories
Man alone at lunch
  Aiken, C. P. Short stories
Mr Arcularis
  Aiken, C. P. Short stories
  Fabricant, N. D. and Werner, H. eds.
    World's best doctor stories
Night before prohibition
  Aiken, C. P. Short stories
Pair of Vikings
  Aiken, C. P. Short stories
Round by round
  Aiken, C. P. Short stories
Silent snow, secret snow
  Aiken, C. P. Short stories
  Burrell, J. A. and Cerf, B. A. eds. An-
    thology of famous American stories
  Schorer, M. ed. The story
Smith and Jones
  Aiken, C. P. Short stories
Spider, spider
  Aiken, C. P. Short stories
State of mind
  Aiken, C. P. Short stories
Strange moonlight
  Aiken, C. P. Short stories
  Ludwig, J. B. and Poirier, W. R. eds.
    Stories, British and American
Thistledown
  Aiken, C. P. Short stories
Your obituary, well written
  Aiken, C. P. Short stories
  Blodgett, H. W. ed. Story survey
AIR PILOTS
  Bellah, J. W. Fear
  Dodson, D. B. The let-down
  Harvey, W. F. Flying out of Mrs Bar-
    nard Hollis
  Jackson, C. R. The outlander
  Jenkins, W. F. Search in the mist
  Knapp, S. E. Clipped wings
  Litten, F. N. Blackout over Cleveland
  Litten, F. N. Winner's money
  Mowat, F. Woman he left to die
  Redman, B. R. Ground mist
  Wells, H. G. Little mother up the
    Mörderberg
  Woolley, R. The pupil
  Youd, C. Christmas tree
AIR RAIDS
  Sansom, W. Building alive
  Sansom, W. Journey into smoke
AIR TRAVEL. See Aeronautics—Flights
AIRCRAFT CARRIERS. See Airplane car-
  riers
AIRPLANE ACCIDENTS. See Aero-
  nautics—Accidents

AIRPLANE CARRIERS
  Beach, E. L. Archerfish
AIRPLANE RACING
  Litten, F. N. Winner's money
AIRPLANES
Accidents
  See Aeronautics—Accidents
AIRPLANES, HOSPITAL
  Bates, H. E. Time expired
AIRPLANES, MILITARY
  Moore, W. Flying Dutchman
  Stocker, J. S. I rode a tornado
    See also Aeronautics, Military
Ajax of Ajax. Pearson, M.
Akeley, Carl Ethan, 1864-1926
  Elephant
    Andrews, R. C. ed. My favorite stories
    of the great outdoors
AKIBA BEN JOSEPH, 50-132
  Cohn, E. Legend of Rabbi Akiba
Akutagawa, Ryūnosuke, 1892-1927
  The dragon
    Akutagawa, R. Rashomon, and other
    stories
  In a grove
    Akutagawa, R. Rashomon, and **other**
    stories
  Kesa and Morito
    Akutagawa, R. Rashomon, and other
    stories
  The martyr
    Akutagawa, R. Rashomon, and other
    stories
  Rashomon
    Akutagawa, R. Rashomon, and other
    stories
  Yam gruel
    Akutagawa, R. Rashomon, and other
    stories
ALABAMA
  Bierce, A. Occurrence at Owl Creek
  bridge
Alabarce, Arturo Souto. See Souto Alabarce,
  Arturo
Alabaster, Mary Ellen
  The tide
    Stanford short stories, 1951
Alabaster hand. Munby, A. N. L.
Aladdin. Arabian nights
Alarcon, Pedro Antonio de, 1833-1891
  Guardian angel
    Fremantle, A. J. ed. Mothers
  The prophecy
    De Onís, H. ed. Spanish stories and
    tales
Alas, Leopoldo, 1852-1901
  Cock of Socrates
    De Onís, H. ed. Spanish stories and
    tales
Alas, all thinking! Bates, H.
ALASKA
  Annixter, P. pseud. Kadiak
  Carrighar, S. Marooned children
  Cooke, A. A. One missing
  Davis, A. L. The Klondiker
  Muir, J. An adventure with a dog and a
  glacier

Albee, George Sumner
Pink organdie
Story (Periodical) Story; no. 2
The top
Story (Periodical) Story; no. 3

Albert knows his place. Moore, M.

Albino and Darling Jill. Caldwell, E.

Albrizio, Gene
The bereft
Southern review. Anthology of stories from the Southern review

Alch, Alan Howard
Night to howl
Story (Periodical) Story; no. 3

Alchemist's secret. Gordon, A.

Alcoholic case. Fitzgerald, F. S. K.

ALCOHOLISM
Aswell, J. R. Shadow of evil
Calisher, H. In Greenwich there are many gravelled walks
Felder, D. F. Purple hat
Fitzgerald, F. S. K. Babylon revisited
Maugham, W. S. The pool
Parker, D. R. Big blonde
Russell, J. Jetsam
Walsh, M. Sword of Yung Lo
See also Drunkards

Aldrich, Bess (Streeter) 1881-1954
Another brought gifts
Cooper, A. C. ed. Modern short stories
Bid the tapers twinkle
Lohan, R. and Lohan, M. eds. New Christmas treasury
Day of retaliation
Aldrich, B. S. The Bess Streeter Aldrich reader
The dreams are real
Brentano, F. ed. The word lives on
How far is it to Hollywood?
Aldrich, B. S. The Bess Streeter Aldrich reader
Juno's swans
Aldrich, B. S. The Bess Streeter Aldrich reader
Welcome home, Hal!
Aldrich, B. S. The Bess Streeter Aldrich reader
Will the romance be the same?
Aldrich, B. S. The Bess Streeter Aldrich reader

Aldrich, Thomas Bailey, 1836-1907
How we astonished the Rivermouthians
Davis, C. B. ed. Eyes of boyhood
Marjorie Daw
Burrell, J. A. and Cerf, B. A. eds. Anthology of famous American stories
Cuff, R. P. ed. American short story survey
Fabricant, N. D. and Werner, H. eds. World's best doctor stories
Lamb, L. ed. Family book of best loved short stories
Struggle for life
Christ, H. I. and Shostak, J. eds. Short stories

Aleichem, Sholom, pseud. See Rabinowitz, Shalom

Alex acquires some dust. Hendryx, J. B.

Alexander, Charles, 1897-
As a dog should
Bloch, M. ed. Favorite dog stories

Alexander, David
And on the third day
Mystery Writers of America, inc. Maiden murders

Alexander, Sidney, 1912-
Part of the act
Heilman, R. B. ed. Modern short stories

Alexander, W.
One leg too many
Conklin, G. ed. Big book of science fiction

Alexander Botts goes underground. Upson, W. H.

Alexander Botts vs. the income tax. Upson, W. H.

Alexander the bait. Klass, P.

Alexander to the park. Johnson, J. W.

ALFRED THE GREAT, KING OF ENGLAND, 849-901
Bolton, I. M. Saint for Wessex

Algebra. Yushkevich, S. S.

ALGONQUIAN INDIANS
Garner, H. One, two, three little Indians

Algren, Nelson, 1909-
Captain is impaled
Prize stories of 1950
He swung and he missed
Ribalow, H. U. ed. World's greatest boxing stories
How the devil came down Division Street
Best of the Best American short stories
So help me
Ribalow, H. U. ed. These your children

Ali Baba and the forty horse-power. Bergengruen, W.

Alias All-American. Chute, B. J.

Alibi Ike. Lardner, R. W.

ALIBIS
Fischer, B. Nobody's business

Alice's pint. Davies, R.

Alien. Del Rey, L.

The **alien.** McConnell, W.

Alien corn. Maugham, W. S.

ALIENS
Boyle, K. Wanderer

Alive—alive oh! Sitwell, Sir O. bart.

All alone again. Cooke, A. A.

All brothers are men. Beck, W.

All gold cañon. London, J.

All good Bems. Brown, F.

All Hallows. De La Mare, W. J.

All horse players die broke. Runyon, D.

All in one day. Florence, G. L.

All kind of pep. Caldwell, E.

All of God's children got shoes. Schoenfeld, H.

All on a winter's night. Strong, A.

All problems are simple. Seager, A.

All roads. Farnsworth, M.

All saints. Bowen, E.

All that glitters. Pratt, F. and De Camp, L. S.
All that glitters. Propes, A.
All the dead pilots. Faulkner, W.
All the little jokers. Parker, J. R.
All the time in the world. Clarke, A. C.
All the town's talking. Schulberg, B. W.
All the way to the moon. Quentin, P. pseud.
All the years of her life. Callaghan, M.
All they do is talk. Newhouse, E.
All things are nothing to me. Farrell, J. T.
Allan, Glenn, 1901-
Kentucky line-up
Creamer, J. B. comp. Twenty-two stories about horses and men
Allan, Ted, 1916-
Lies my father told me
Weaver, R. and James, H. eds. Canadian short stories
Allan Franklin. Rossiter, H. D.
Allard, Pat
Lucky star
Furman, A. L. ed. Teen-age horse stories
Allegheny. Foote, J. T.
ALLEGORIES
Benét, S. V. Johnny Pye and the Fool-killer
Cohn, E. Remains of virtue
Forster, E. M. Other side of the hedge
Gide, A. P. G. Theseus
Hawthorne, N. Celestial railroad
Hawthorne, N. Maypole of Merry Mount
Kafka, F. Hunger-artist
Kafka, F. Hunter Gracchus
Lagerkvist, P. F. Myth of mankind
Peretz, I. L. Pious cat
Quiroga, H. The fatherland
Sansom, W. From the water junction
Simak, C. D. The answers
Allen, Edward, and Kelley, Francis Beverly, 1905-
Public enemies
Fenner, P. R. comp. Elephants, elephants, elephants
ALLEN, ETHAN, 1737-1789
Allen, M. P. In the name of the Great Jehovah and the Continental Congress
Allen, Grant, 1848-1899
Pausodyne
Derleth, A. W. ed. Beyond time & space
Allen, Hervey, 1889-1949
Surgery at Aquila
Fabricant, N. D. and Werner, H. eds. World's best doctor stories
Allen, James Lane, 1849-1925
King Solomon of Kentucky
Summers, H. S. ed. Kentucky story
Allen, Margaret
Her gift
Elmquist, R. M. ed. Fifty years of Christmas
Allen, Merritt Parmelee, 1892-1954
Camel into eagle
Fenner, P. R. comp. Giggle box
Chariots away
Boy's life (Periodical) Boys' life Adventure stories

In the name of the Great Jehovah and the Continental Congress
Fenner, P. R. comp. Yankee Doodle
Second race
Fenner, P. R. comp. Indians, Indians, Indians
Two chests of treasure
Fenner, P. R. comp. Pirates, pirates, pirates
Furman, A. L. ed. Teen-age sea stories
Yoo hoo! Mudhen!
Fenner, P. R. comp. Fun! Fun! Fun!
Allen High's youth problem. Erdman, L. G.
ALLERGY
La Farge, O. No, my darling daughter
ALLIGATORS
Annixter, P. pseud. Dragon rider
Allingham, Margery, 1904-
The Lieabout
Mystery Writers of America, inc. Crooks' tour
One morning they'll hang him
Queen, E. pseud. ed. Queen's awards: 5th ser.
Tall story
Queen, E. pseud. ed. Ellery Queen's awards: 9th ser.
ALMANACS
Bester, A. Of time and Third Avenue
Almond tree. De La Mare, W. J.
Almost like dead. Goldman, A.
Alone in shark waters. Kruse, J.
Alone Men. McHugh, V.
Alone the stranger passes Komroff, M.
Alpert, Hollis
The change
Seventeen (Periodical) The Seventeen reader
ALPS
Bruhl, E. Great match
Maupassant, G. de. The inn
ALPS, FRENCH
Boyle, K. Wanderer
Knowlton, E. Petite première in the Mont Blanc Massif
ALPS, SWISS
Montague, C. E. Action
ALSACE
Daudet, A. Last class
Alson, Lawrence, 1920-
Lieutenant's laundry
American vanguard, 1950
The altar. Sheckley, R.
Altar at midnight. Kornbluth, C. M.
Altar cloth. Lyon, K.
Altar of the dead. James, H.
Alte Bobbe. Angoff, C.
Always a bridesmaid. Kober, A.
Always good for a belly laugh. Glen, E.
Always Reddy. Henry, M.
Always trust a cop. Cohen, O. R.
Am I blue? Ullman, J. R.
Amateur night in Harlem. Davis, G.

AMATEUR THEATRICALS
Gordimer, N. The amateurs
Grimson, M. S. When TV came to the backwoods
Munro, H. H. Peace offering
See also College and school drama

The **amateurs**. Gordimer, N.

Amazing lady. Clark, A. A. G.

The **Amazon**. Leskov, N. S.

The **ambassadors**. White, W. A. P.

Ambassadors from Venus. Crossen, K. F.

The **ambassadress**. Auchincloss, L.

AMBITION
Anderson, S. The egg
Fitzgerald, F. S. K. Winter dreams
Grimson, M. S. Eureca cottage

Ambition. Bade, W. L.

Ambitious guest. Hawthorne, N.

Ambitious violet. Gibran, K.

AMBULANCES
Porter, W. S. Comedy in rubber
Stuart, J. Competition at Slush Creek

AMBULANCES, AIR. See Airplanes, Hospital

American dream girl Farrell, J. T.

American girl looks at Europe. Grimson, M. S.

AMERICAN INDIANS. See Indians of Central America; Indians of Mexico; Indians of North America; Indians of South America; also names of individual tribes or nations

American me. Griffith, B. W.

AMERICAN SOLDIERS. See Soldiers, American

Americanization of Shadrach Cohen. Block, R. E.

Americans all. Foley, M.

AMERICANS IN AFRICA
Ullman, J. R. Between you and I

AMERICANS IN BALI
Benson, T. Funeral feast

AMERICANS IN BRAZIL
Seager, A. Quitandinha

AMERICANS IN ENGLAND
Arlen, M. Gentleman from America
Collins, W. Miss Bertha and the Yankee
James, H. Author of Beltraffio
Montague, M. P. England to America
Salinger, J. D. For Esmé—with love and squalor

AMERICANS IN EUROPE
Auchincloss, L. The ambassadress
Grimson, M. S. American girl looks at Europe
James, H. Daisy Miller
Lawrence, D. H. Things
McCarthy, M. T. The cicerone
Maugham, W. S. Wash-tub

AMERICANS IN FIJI ISLANDS
Michener, J. A. Mynah birds
Vandercook, J. W. Pretending makes it so

AMERICANS IN FRANCE
Boyd, T. A. Responsibility
Brookhouser, F. Not that kind of a deal
Farrell, J. T. Fritz
Farrell, J. T. I want to go home
Farrell, J. T. Love affairs in Paris
Fitzgerald, F. S. K. Babylon revisited
James, H. Bundle of letters
Miller, M. B. Ruth and Irma
Wharton, E. N. J. Madame de Treymes

AMERICANS IN GERMANY
Boyle, K. Soldier ran away
Putnam, C. Old acrobat and the ruined city
Schmidt, C. F. Ancestral voices
Stafford, J. Echo and the nemesis
Stafford, J. The nemesis
Stafford, J. Winter's tale

AMERICANS IN GREAT BRITAIN. See Americans in England

AMERICANS IN HAITI
Rattner, J. Haitian incident

AMERICANS IN ITALY
Bunin, I. A. Gentleman from San Francisco
De La Roche, M. Quartet
Lowry, R. J. Law and order
Maugham, W. S. Woman of fifty
Miller, A. Monte Saint Angelo
Tennyson, H. Home leave

AMERICANS IN JAPAN
Christopher, R. Jishin
Conrad, R. E. Call of the street
Wincelberg, S. The conqueror

AMERICANS IN KOREA
Winter, A. B. Party dress

AMERICANS IN MEXICO
Gordon, E. E. Value of the dollar
Quentin, P. pseud. Love comes to Miss Lucy

AMERICANS IN NEW GUINEA
Ullman, J. R. Am I blue?

AMERICANS IN NEW ZEALAND
Michener, J. A. Until they sail

AMERICANS IN PALESTINE
Lewisohn, L. Holy Land

AMERICANS IN PARIS. See Americans in France

AMERICANS IN PORTUGAL
Saroyan, W. The Assyrian

AMERICANS IN RUSSIA
McKelway, St C. Russian who wanted to be friends
Maugham, W. S. Mr Harrington's washing

AMERICANS IN SHANGHAI
Patterson, R. Babe

AMERICANS IN THE SOUTH SEA ISLANDS
Maugham, W. S. Fall of Edward Barnard
Michener, J. A. Mr Morgan

AMERICANS IN THE WEST INDIES
Goldsmith, G. Tender to the ship

Amethyst cross. Freeman, K.

AMISH MENNONITES. See Mennonites

AMNESIA
Blackburn, R. H. Clay dish
Du Maurier, D. Split second
Munro, H. H. Holiday task
Porter, W. S. Rambles in Aphasia
Among the trees. Fuchs, A. M.
Among those presents. Price, E. B.
Amorous ghost. Bagnold, E.
AMOS, THE PROPHET
Wilson, D. C. Priest and prophet at Bethel
Amour dure. Paget, V.
AMPUTATION
Maupasant, G. de. At sea
AMPUTEES. See Cripples
AMSTERDAM. See Netherlands—Amsterdam
Amsterdam: The angel's eye. Charteris, L.
The **amulet.** Raddall, T. H.
AMUSEMENT PARKS
Whittemore, R. The Stutz and the tub
Amy Foster. Conrad, J.
Ancestral amethyst. Pratt, F. and De Camp, L. S.
Ancestral voices. Schmidt, C. F.
ANCESTRY. See Heredity
The **anchor.** Seligsohn, I. J.
Anchor man. Strong, P. N.
Anchor me in mire. Kaufman, A.
Ancient brain. Stangland, A. G.
Ancient gentility. Williams, W. C.
Ancient history and low hurdles. Saroyan, W.
And be merry. . . MacLean, K.
And Delilah. Paterson, N.
And it comes out here. Del Rey, L.
And Jacob called. Sultan, S.
And lo! The bird. Bond, N. S.
And now farewell. Summers, J. L.
And on the third day. Alexander, D.
And someday to Mars. Long, F. B.
And the Dean was happy. Carter, R. G.
"And the goose hangs high." Hendryx, J. B.
And the moon be still as bright. Bradbury, R.
And the walls came tumbling down. . . Harris, J. B.
And then he wept. Pinski, D.
And then there were none. Russell, E. F.
ANDALUSIA. See Spain—Andalusia
ANDERSEN, HANS CHRISTIAN, 1805-1875
Yates, E. Enshrined in the heart
Andersen Nexø, Martin. See Nexø, Martin Andersen
Anderson, Dillon, 1906-
The auction
Collier's, the national weekly. Collier's best

Forty years of firewood
Peery, W. W. ed. 21 Texas short stories
Anderson, Esther Victoria, 1892-
Old Tom O'Grady of Shay Ranch
Anderson, E. V. Six tales for all the family
Phantom Hall
Anderson, E. V. Six tales for all the family
Rib steak
Anderson, E. V. Six tales for all the family
Smell of smoke
Anderson, E. V. Six tales for all the family
Tapestry extravaganza
Anderson, E. V. Six tales for all the family
Wildy's secret revealer
Anderson, E. V. Six tales for all the family
Anderson, Merrill
Fog and the saints
Story (Periodical) Story; no. 1
Anderson, Poul, 1926-
Butch
Derleth, A. W. ed. Time to come
Double-dyed villains
Greenberg, M. ed. Travelers of space
Flight to forever
Year's best science fiction novels, 1952
Genius
Bleiler, E. F. and Dikty, T. E. eds. Science fiction omnibus: The best science fiction stories, 1949, 1950
Helping hand
Conklin, G. ed. Possible worlds of science fiction
Inside earth
Galaxy science fiction magazine. Galaxy reader of science fiction
Interloper
Derleth, A. W. ed. The outer reaches
Last monster
Lesser, M. A. ed. Looking forward
Sam Hall
Conklin, G. ed. Science-fiction thinking machines
The tinkler
Derleth, A. W. ed. World of tomorrow
Anderson, Poul, 1926- **and Dickson, Gordon**
Trespass
Best science fiction stories: 1951
Anderson, Sherwood, 1876-1941
Adventure
Stegner, W. E.; Scowcroft, R. and Ilyin, B. eds. Writer's art
Death in the woods
Davis, R. G. ed. Ten modern masters
Drink
Greene, J. I. and Abbell, E. eds. Stories of sudden truth
The egg
Davis, R. G. ed. Ten modern masters
Schorer, M. ed. The story
Hands
Cory, D. W. pseud. comp. 21 variations on a theme

Anderson, Sherwood—*Continued*
I want to know why
Burrell, J. A. and Cerf, B. A. eds. Anthology of famous American stories
Ludwig, J. B. and Poirier, W. R. eds. Stories, British and American
Shaw, H. and Bement, D. Reading the short story
I'm a fool
Best of the Best American short stories, 1915-1950
Burrell, J. A. and Cerf, B. A. eds. Anthology of famous American stories
Davis, R. G. ed. Ten modern masters
Day, A. G. ed. Greatest American short stories
Millett, F. B. ed. Reading fiction
"Queer"
Forester, N. ed. American poetry and prose. 1952 ed.
Seeds
West, R. B. and Stallman, R. W. eds. Art of modern fiction
Sophistication
Blodgett, H. W. ed. Story survey
Schramm, W. L. ed. Great short stories
Waite, H. O. and Atkinson, B. P. eds. Literature for our time
Andreev, Leonid Nikolaevich, 1871-1919
Love and betrayal
Selden, R. ed. Ways of God and men
On the day of the crucifixion
Brentano, F. ed. The word lives on
Andrews, Mary Raymond (Shipman) 1865?-1936
Counsel assigned
Scribner treasury
Perfect tribute
Scribner treasury
Andrew's father. Krimsky, J.
Andreyev, Leonid. See Andreev, Leonid Nikolaevich
ANDROS, SIR EDMUND, 1637-1714
Hawthorne, N. Gray champion
Andy Munroe's funeral. Davis, S. P.
ANESTHETICS
Harvey, W. F. Account rendered
Angel of the odd. Poe, E. A.
Angel was a Yankee. Benét, S. V.
Angel with purple hair. Paul, H.
Angela. Farrell, J. T.
Angela was eighteen. Wakelee, L.
Angelic angleworm. Brown, F.
Angell, Roger, 1920-
Fight through the dark
Best American short stories, 1951
ANGELS
Benét, S. V. Angel was a Yankee
Collier, J. Fallen star
Collier, J. Hell hath no fury
Connolly, M. Reason for Ann
De La Mare, W. J. The trumpet
Angel's egg. Pangborn, E.
Angels in Chayder. Golding, L.
Angels in the jets. Bixby, J.
Angharad. Ready, W. B.
Angie Lee's fortune. Winslow, T. S.

ANGLING. See Fishing
Angram folly. Bentley, P. E.
Anglo-Saxons of Auxierville. Stuart, J.
Angoff, Charles, 1902-
Alte Bobbe
Ribalow, H. U. ed. This land, these people
Where did yesterday go?
Best American short stories, 1950
Angry lions, lazy lions. Baro, G.
Angus MacAuliffe and the gowden tooch. Tanner, C. R.
Animal-cracker plot. De Camp, L. S.
ANIMAL INTELLIGENCE
Williams, J. H. Elephant intelligence
ANIMAL SOUNDS. See Sound production of animals
ANIMAL TRAINERS. See Animals—Training
ANIMALS
Bottome, P. Man and beast; 5 stories
Harris, J. C. Wonderful Tar-Baby story
Heinlein, R. A. Jerry was a man
Kipling, R. Elephant's child
Lesser, M. Black Eyes and the daily grind
Seton, E. T. Wild animals I have known; 8 stories
Williams, R. Head-hunters
See also names of individual animals

Training

Bottome, P. Caesar's wife's ear
Bottome, P. Henry
Mukerji, D. G. Kari the elephant
Richards, D. Training Alice and Congo
Waldeck, T. J. Evil one

Treatment

Buck, F. Elephant midget
Lang, D. An elephant never forgets
ANIMALS, IMAGINARY. See Animals, Mythical
ANIMALS, MYTHICAL
Cartmill, C. Huge beast
De Camp, L. S. Blue giraffe
Harvey, W. F. Beast with five fingers
Samachson, J. Country doctor
Waldo, E. H. The hurkle is a happy beast
Wellman, M. W. Dhoh
Wells, H. G. Sea raiders
Williams, R. Head hunters
See also Dragons
ANIMALS, PREHISTORIC
De Camp, L. S. Employment
Ann Lee's. Bowen, E.
Anna was bad. Boxer, J.
ANNAM. See Indo-China, French
ANNAPOLIS NAVAL ACADEMY. See United States. Naval Academy, Annapolis
Anne's terrible good nature. Lucas, E. V.
Annett, Ronald Ross, 1895-
Gentle like a cyclone
Creamer, J. B. comp. Twenty-two stories about horses and men
Dennis, W. ed. Palomino and other horses

Annett, William S. 1928-
The relic
Weaver, R. and James, H. eds. Canadian short stories
The **anniversary.** Aiken, C. P.
Annixter, Paul, pseud.
Brought to cover
Annixter, P. pseud. Brought to cover
Dragon rider
Annixter, P. pseud. Brought to cover
First ally
Annixter, P. pseud. Brought to cover
Hunting coat
Annixter, P. pseud. Brought to cover
Kadiak
Annixter, P. pseud. Brought to cover
Ketch dog
Annixter, P. pseud. Brought to cover
Last lobo
Annixter, P. pseud. Brought to cover
Loose tiger
Annixter, P. pseud. Brought to cover
The lynching
Annixter, P. pseud. Brought to cover
Old Hook 'n' Eye
Annixter, P. pseud. Brought to cover
Orchids and crocodiles
Annixter, P. pseud. Brought to cover
Secret of Coon Castle
Annixter, P. pseud. Brought to cover
The swordsman
Annixter, P. pseud. Brought to cover
White possum
Annixter, P. pseud. Brought to cover
With the greatest of ease
Annixter, P. pseud. Brought to cover
Anomaly of the empty man. White, W. A. P.
The **anonymous.** Clark, W. Van T.
Another American tragedy. Collier, J.
Another brought gifts. Aldrich, B. S.
Another part of the sky. Gordimer, N.
Another quiet bye with Mr Jorrocks. Surtees R. S.
Another worry. Cooke, A. A.
Ansky, S. pseud. See Rappoport, Solomon
Answer. Brown, F.
Answer. Stubbs, H. C.
Answer is nothing. Barker, A. L.
The **answers.** Simak, C. D.
Ant and the eye. Oliver, C.
Ant and the grasshopper. Maugham, W. S.
ANTARCTIC REGIONS
Heard, G. Wingless victory
See also Arctic regions
ANTHROPOLOGISTS
Brackett, L. Last days of Shandakor
Gardner, M. Island of five colors
Michener, J. A. The fossickers
ANTI-GRAVITATION. See Gravity
ANTIPATHIES. See Prejudices and antipathies
ANTIQUE DEALERS
De La Mare, W. J. The talisman
ANTISEMITISM. See Jews

ANTS
Beebe, W. Home town of the army ants
Jenkins, W. F. Doomsday deferred
Wells, H. G. Empire of the ants
The **ants.** Snow, W. W.
Any more at home like you? Oliver, C.
Any pain, peril or danger. Claudy, C. H.
Any way race. Person, W. T.
Anything new on the strangler? Ullman, J. M.
APACHE INDIANS
DeVries, M. Stage to Yuma
Apage Satanas. Koestler, A.
APARTMENT HOUSES
Cheever, J. The superintendent
Horwitz, J. The burial
Horwitz, J. The conspirators
Horwitz, J. Generations of man
The **ape.** Pritchett, V. S.
APES
Kafka, F. Report to an academy
Pritchett, V. S. The ape
See also Baboons; Chimpanzees; Gorillas; Monkeys; Orang-utangs
The **apostate.** Milburn, G.
Apostolides, Alex, 1923- See Clifton, M. jt. auth.
Apparition of Mrs Veal. Defoe, D.
APPARITIONS. See Ghosts; Hallucinations and illusions
Appearance and reality. Maugham, W. S.
Appell, George C.
Calculated risk
Argosy (Periodical) Argosy Book of adventure stories
APPENDECTOMY. See Appendicitis
APPENDICITIS
Gray, D. Ting-a-ling
Shaw, I. Faith at sea
Appendicitis. Tennyson, H.
Appet, Nelson, 1910-
The prophet
American vanguard, 1950
Ribalow, H. U. ed. These your children
The test
American vanguard, 1952
Apple for Mom. Pace, J.
Apple seed and apple thorn. Enright, E.
Apple tree. Du Maurier, D.
Apple-tree. Galsworthy, J.
Apple-tree table. Melville, H.
APPLE TREES
Clayton, J. B. White circle
See also Trees
Appleton, Victor, pseud.
Sky ride—a Tom Swift story
Jensen, P. ed. Fireside book of flying stories
Appointment in tomorrow. Leiber, F.
The **appraisal.** Schorr, Z.
Apprentice thief. MacManus, S.
APPRENTICES
Chekhov, A. P. Vanka
Appropriate measures. Chekhov, A. P.

APRIL FOOL'S DAY
Dostoevskiĭ, F. M. Polzunkov
April is the cruelest month. Berger, T. L.
April witch. Bradbury, R.
AQUARIUMS
Clark, W. Van T. Fish who could close his eyes
Arabella, the third. Eggleston, M. W.
ARABIA
Ashkenazi, T. The miserly emir
Graham, R. B. C. Faith
ARABIAN NIGHTS
Aladdin; or the wonderful lamp
Cody, S. ed. Greatest stories and how they were written

Characters from
Poe, E. A. Thousand-and-second tale of Scheherazade
ARABS
Dunsany, E. J. M. D. P. 18th baron. Story of land and sea
Tennyson, H. In the desert
ARABS IN PALESTINE
Stinetorf, L. A. Refugee village
Araby. Joyce, J.
ARAPAHO INDIANS
Cook, K. Ba-ee
Ararat. Henderson, Z.
Arcadia recalled. Johnson, J. W.
ARCHEOLOGISTS
Wharton, E. N. J. A bottle of Perrier
Archerfish. Beach, E. L.
Archibald, J. William, 1918-
Ernestine in Dominica
Story (Periodical) Story no. 3
ARCHITECTS
De Vries, P. Today and today
Porter, W. S. Witches' loaves
ARCTIC REGIONS
Stefánsson, V. Seal hunting
See also Antarctic regions
Are you run-down, tired— Rosmond, B. and Lake, L. M.
Are you too late, or was I too early. Collier, J.
Arena. Brown, F.
Arfon. Davies, R.
ARGENTINE REPUBLIC

19th century
Hudson, W. H. Story of a piebald horse
Buenos Aires
Cancela, A. Life and death of a hero
Argonauts of the air. Wells, H. G.
Argument with death. O'Rourke, F.
Arico, Victor, 1912-
Civil rights
Arico, V. The knight returns, and other stories
Double bliss
Arico, V. The knight returns, and other stories
His great decision
Arico, V. The knight returns, and other **stories**

Knight returns
Arico, V. The knight returns, and other stories
Merchant's monument
Arico, V. The knight returns, and other stories
Pelican and the lyre bird
Arico, V. The knight returns, and other stories
The promotion
Arico, V. The knight returns, and other stories
The rebel
Arico, V. The knight returns, and other stories
To punish the offender
Arico, V. The knight returns, and other stories
Tomorrow you're sentenced
Arico, V. The knight returns, and other stories
Trusting snakes
Arico, V. The knight returns, and other stories
Water canteen
Arico, V. The knight returns, and other stories
ARISTOCRACY

England
Maugham, W. S. Lord Mountdrago
France
Balzac, H. de. Other Diane
Italy
Gobineau, J. A. comte de. Red handkerchief
Japan
Akutagawa, R. Yam gruel
Russia
Sobol, A. M. Last expedition of Baron Feuhbel-Feuhtzenau
Aristocracy versus hash. Porter, W. S.
The **aristocrat.** Zoshchenko, M. M.
Arkansas. Weeks, R.
Arlen, Michael, 1895-1956
Cavalier of the streets
Cerf, B. A. and Moriarty, H. C. eds. Anthology of famous British stories
Gentleman from America
Davenport, B. ed. Ghostly tales to be told
Arm of Mrs Egan. Harvey, W. F.
Armageddon. Brown, F.
ARMED FORCES. See Soldiers; also names of countries with subdivision Army
ARMENIANS IN THE UNITED STATES
Saroyan, W. My cousin Dikran, the orator
Saroyan, W. Summer of the beautiful white horse
Saroyan, W. Theological student
Armistice. Tennyson, H.
ARMS AND ARMOR
Sheckley, R. Last weapon
Armstrong, Anthony, pseud. See Willis, Anthony Armstrong

Armstrong, Charlotte, 1905-
  The enemy
    Queen, E. pseud. ed. Queen's awards:
      6th ser.
  Laugh it off
    Queen, E. pseud. ed. The Queen's
      awards: 8th ser.
Armstrong, Matt
  A filly owns a fella!
    Furman, A. L. ed. Teen-age horse stor-
      ies
ARMY AIR FORCES. See United States.
  Army Air Forces
ARMY ANTS. See Ants
Arnold, Maxwell, 1919-
  Cannibal pot
    Stanford short stories, 1950
Aronson, Robert
  Seaworthy
    Furman, A. L. ed. Teen-age dog stories
Arnow, Harriette Louisa (Simpson) 1908-
  Washerwoman's day
    Southern review. Anthology of stories
      from the Southern review
Arrhenius horror. Miller, P. S.
The arrow. Morley, C. D.
Arrow of heaven. Chesterton, G. K.
ARSON
  Collier, J. Great possibilities
  Faulkner, W. Barn burning
  Waugh, E. Love among the ruins
      See also Fires
ARSONISTS. See Arson
Art and the bronco. Porter, W. S.
ART COLLECTORS
  Zweig, S. Invisible collection
Art colony. Boyle, K.
ART CRITICS
  Werfel, F. Saverio's secret
      See also Critics
ART DEALERS
  Lawrence, D. H. Lovely lady
  Zweig, S. Invisible collection
  Zweig, S. Unseen collection
ART GALLERIES AND MUSEUMS
  Munro, H. H. Reginald on the Academy
ART OBJECTS

Collectors
      See Art collectors
ART SCHOOLS
  Brenner, L. Revolt
  Salinger, J. D. De Daumier-Smith's blue
    period
Artful Mr Glencannon. Gilpatric, G.
ARTHUR, KING
  Malory, Sir T. Marvellous adventure of
    the sword
Arthur, Robert
  Big money
    Mystery Writers of America, inc.
      Four-&-twenty bloodhounds
  Change of address
    Mystery Writers of America, inc. But-
      cher, baker, murder-maker
  Evolution's end
    Crossen, K. F. ed. Adventures in tomor-
      row

  MWA murder
    Mystery Writers of America, inc.
      Crooks' tour
  Man in the morgue
    Mystery Writers of America, inc.
      20 great tales of murder
  Postpaid to Paradise
    Magazine of fantasy and science fiction.
      Best from Fantasy and science fiction;
      [1st ser]
  Wheel of time
    Brown, F. and Reynolds, M. eds.
      Science-fiction carnival
Arthur Aronymus. Lasker-Schüler, E.
ARTIFICIAL LIMBS
  Alexander, W. One leg too many
  Davies, R. Benefit concert
  Wolfe, B. Self portrait
The artist. Kaplan, R.
Artist at home. Faulkner, W.
ARTIST LIFE
  Boyle, K. Art colony
  Humphrey, W.. The fauve
  James, H. Tree of knowledge
  Porter, W. S. Extradited from Bohemia
  Porter, W. S. Last leaf
  Porter, W. S. Service of love
ARTISTS
  Collier, J. Night! Youth! Paris! And the
    moon
  Hill, M. Y. Sea anchor
      See also Architects; Illustrators;
    Painters; Sculptors
Artist's life. Powell, D.
ARTISTS' MODELS
  James, H. Real thing
As a dog should. Alexander, C.
As benefits forgot. Corkery, D.
"As handsome does."** Eames, G. T.
As I am, you will be. Friedman, B. H.
As never was. Miller, P. S.
As ye sow— Fisher, D. F. C.
The ascent. West, R. B.
Ascent to heaven. Rudnicki, A.
Asch, Nathan, 1902-
  Inland, western sea
    Best American short stories, 1951
    Greene, J. I. and Abell, E. eds. Stories
      of sudden truth
Asch, Shalom, 1880-
  The academy
    Ausubel, N. ed. Treasury of Jewish
      humor
  Duty to live
    Fremantle, A. J. ed. Mothers
  "I will send thee"
    Selden, R. ed. Ways of God and men
  Into thy hands
    Brentano, F. ed. The word lives on
  Kola Road
    Leftwich, J. ed. Yisröel, 1952 ed.
    Same as: Kola Street
  Kola Street
    Howe, I. and Greenberg, E. eds. Treas-
      ury of Yiddish stories
    Same as: Kola Road
  Mama
    Ungar, F. ed. To mother with love

Asch, Shalom—*Continued*
Quiet garden spot
Howe, I. and Greenberg, E. eds. Treasury of Yiddish stories
Sanctification of the Name
Howe, I. and Greenberg, E. eds. Treasury of Yiddish stories

Asch, Sholem. See Asch, Shalom

Asem. Goldsmith, O.

Ashabranner, Brent
Genius of Strap Buckner
Western Writers of America. Holsters and heroes

Ashby, Richard
Master race
Sloane, W. M. ed. Space, space, space

Ashes. Fairbanks, D.

Ashes for the wind. Téllez, H.

Ashes of roses. Coward, N. P.

Ashes of the ages and eternal fire. Gibran, K.

Ashford, Daisy
A proposale
McFarland, W. K. comp. Then it happened

Ashkenazi, Touvia, 1904-
Miserly Emir
Story (Periodical) Story; no. 1

Ashkenazy, Irvin
Pop's boy
Ribalow, H. U. ed. World's greatest boxing stories

Ashley, Elizabeth L. 1926-
Aunt Lil
American vanguard, 1953
In another image
American vanguard, 1952

Asimov, Isaac, 1920-
Belief
Merril, J. ed. Beyond the barriers of space and time
"Breeds there a man. . . ?"
Derleth, A. W. ed. Beachheads in space
Bridle and saddle
Greenberg, M. ed. Men against the stars
C chute
Galaxy science fiction magazine. Second Galaxy reader of science fiction
Catch that rabbit
Asimov, I. I, robot
Christmas on Ganymede
Crossen, K. F. ed. Adventures in tomorrow
Death sentence
Derleth, A. W. ed. The outer reaches
Escape!
Asimov, I. I, robot
Evidence
Asimov, I. I, robot
Evitable conflict
Asimov, I. I, robot
Homo Sol
Conklin, G. ed. Omnibus of science fiction
Hostess
Galaxy science fiction magazine. Galaxy reader of science fiction
"In a good cause—"
Healy, R. J. ed. New tales of space and time

It's such a beautiful day
Star science fiction stories no. 3
Liar!
Asimov, I. I, robot
Little lost robot
Asimov, I. I, robot
Misbegotten missionary
Heinlein, R. A. ed. Tomorrow, the stars
Mother Earth
Greenberg, M. ed. Journey to infinity
Nightfall
Astounding science fiction (Periodical)
Astounding science fiction anthology
No connection
Bleiler, E. F. and Dikty, T. E. eds. Science fiction omnibus: The best science fiction stories, 1949, 1950
"Nobody here but. . ."
Star science fiction stories [no. 1]
Not final
Conklin, G. ed. Possible worlds of science fiction
The pause
Derleth, A. W. ed. Time to come
Reason
Asimov, I. I, robot
Robbie
Asimov, I. I, robot
Conklin, G. ed. Science-fiction thinking machines
Red Queen's race
Pratt, F. ed. World of wonder
Runaround
Asimov, I. I, robot
Sally
Abell, E. ed. American accent
Trends
Greenberg, M. ed. Man against the stars
Victory unintentional
Lesser, M. A. ed. Looking forward
What if. . .
Conklin, G. ed. Science-fiction adventures in dimension

Ask me anything. Knight, D.

Ask me no more. Beck, W.

Asleep in Armageddon. Bradbury, R.

Aspern papers. James, H.

Asphodel. Welty, E.

Aspinwall, Marguerite
Night before Christmas
American girl (Periodical) Christmas all year 'round
Secret closet
Furman, A. L. ed. Everygirls mystery stories
Snowbound Christmas
American girl (Periodical) Christmas all year 'round
Thundering Hurd
Furman, A. L. ed. Everygirls career stories

Asquith, Lady Cynthia Mary Evelyn (Charteris) 1887-
One grave too few
Asquith, Lady C. M. E. C. ed. Book of modern ghosts

ASSASSINATION
Gobineau, J. A. comte de. Red handkerchief

An assemblage of husbands and wives.
Lewis, S.
ASSES AND MULES
Allen, M. P. Chariots away
Bonner, P. H. Mollie
Caldwell, E. Meddlesome Jack
Untermeyer, L. Donkey of God
Verga, G. Saint Joseph's ass
Assessor of success. Porter, W. S.
The assignation. Poe, E. A.
Assignment to Aldebaran. Crossen, K. F.
The Assyrian. Saroyan, W.
ASSYRIANS
Saroyan, W. The Assyrian
Asteroid of fear. Gallun, R. Z.
Asteroid of gold. Simak, C. D.
Asters for Teddie. Spettigue, D.
Astral plane—land of dreams. Ekbergh, I. D.
ASTROLOGERS
Verral, C. S. Itch to win
ASTRONOMERS
Pearson, M. and Corwin, C. Mask of
Demeter
Wells, H. G. The star
ASTRONOMICAL OBSERVATORIES
Wells, H. G. In the Avu observatory
Aswell, James R. 1906-
Shadow of evil
Best American short stories, 1950
Asylum. Van Vogt, A. E.
At arms with Morpheus. Porter, W. S.
At Fish Rapids. Hendryx, J. B.
At Mrs Farrelly's. Carroll, J. W.
At no extra cost. Phillips, P.
At Paso Rojo. Bowles, P. F.
At sea. Maupassant, G. de
At the bay. Mansfield, K.
At the crossroads. Grimson, M. S.
At the end of the passage. Kipling, R
At the front. Williams, W. C.
At the landing. Welty, E.
At the rainbow's end. London, J.
Atavism of John Tom Little Bear. Porter,
W. S.
ATHEISM
Bloomgarden, S. Share of paradise
Steele, W. D. Man who saw through
heaven
The atheist. Claudy, C. H.
Atheist's mass. Balzac, H. de
Athens, Greece, 1942. Gregory, V. K.
Atherton, Gertrude Franklin (Horn) 1857-
1948
Pearls of Loreto
Burrell, J. A. and Cerf, B. A. eds. An-
thology of famous American stories
ATHLETES
Doty, W. L. College star
Farrell, J. T. Yellow streak
ATHLETICS. See Athletes; Sports
Atkinson, Benjamin P. See Waite, H. O.
jt. ed.

ATLANTIS
Doyle, Sir A. C. Maracot Deep
Plato. Plato's Atlantis
Smith, E. E. Atlantis
Atlantis. Smith E. E.
Atlantis, Plato's. Plato
ATLAS MOUNTAINS
Elliott, G. P. Faq'
Atmospherics. Harvey, W. F.
ATOLLS
Michener, J. A. Mr Morgan
ATOMIC BOMB
Wylie, P. Smuggled atom bomb
ATOMIC ENERGY
Asimov, I. "Breeds there a man. . .?"
Doar, G. Outer limit
Heinlein, R. A. Blowups happen
Piper, H. B. Operation RSVP
Van Vogt, A. E. Dormant
ATOMIC POWER. See Atomic energy
ATONEMENT
Kompert, L. Silent woman
The attack. Coatsworth, E. J.
The attacker. Wolson, M.
Attitude. Stubbs, H. C.
Attitudes. Farmer, P. J.
Auchincloss, Louis, 1917-
The ambassadress
Auchincloss, L. Injustice collectors
Billy and the gargoyles
Auchincloss, L. Romantic egoists
Edification of Marianne
Auchincloss, L. Injustice collectors
Evolution of Lorna Treadway
Auchincloss, L. Romantic egoists
Fall of a sparrow
Auchincloss, L. Injustice collectors
Finish, good lady
Auchincloss, L. Injustice collectors
Fortune of Arleus Kane
Auchincloss, L. Romantic egoists
Gemlike flame
Auchincloss, L. Romantic egoists
Great world and Timothy Colt
Auchincloss, L. Romantic egoists
Greg's peg
Auchincloss, L. Injustice collectors
Legends of Henry Everett
Auchincloss, L. Romantic egoists
Loyalty up and loyalty down
Auchincloss, L. Romantic egoists
Maud
Auchincloss, L. Injustice collectors
The miracle
Auchincloss, L. Injustice collectors
Unholy three
Auchincloss, L. Injustice collectors
Wally
Auchincloss, L. Romantic egoists
The auction. Anderson, D.
Audition. Powell, D.
AUDUBON, JOHN JAMES, 1785-1851
Welty, E. Still moment
Auerbach, Berthold, 1812-1882
Hansjorg and his pipe
Leftwich, J. ed. Yisröel. 1952 ed.
Aufwiedersehen abend. Boyle, K.
August afternoon. Caldwell, E.

August heat. Harvey, W. F.
August tenth. Jones, R. S.
Augustine, Saint, Bp. of Hippo, 354-430
  Monica's son
    Fremantle, A. J. ed. Mothers
Augustus and spring tonic. Henderson, Le G.
Augustus meets his first Indian. Henderson, Le G.
Augustus, pirate. Henderson, Le G.
Aumonier, Stacy, 1887-1928
  Source of irritation
    Cerf, B. A. and Moriarty, H. C. eds. Anthology of famous British stories
Aunt Esther's galoshes. Rosenberg, E. C.
Aunt Lil. Ashley, E. L.
Aunt Rose's ghost story. Yaffe, J.
Aunt Suzanne. McLaverty, M.
Auntie Bissel. Suckow, R.
Auntimay. De La Roche, M.
AUNTS
  Auchincloss, L. Unholy three
  Ballard, J. C. Mountain summer
  Beck, W. Years brought to an end
  De La Mare, W. J. Seaton's aunt
  De La Roche, M. Auntimay
  Macauley, R. The wishbone
  McLaverty, M. Aunt Suzanne
  Miller, C. Gentle season
  Munro, H. H. Way to the dairy
  Rosenberg, E. C. Aunt Esther's galoshes
  Waltari, M. T. Moonscape
  Watson, J. His mother's sermon
  Wesely, D. Week of roses
AURELIUS ANTONINUS, MARCUS, EMPEROR OF ROME, 121-180
  Cohn, E. Rabbi and emperor
Aurevilly, Jules Amédée Barbey d'. See Barbey d' Aurevilly, Jules Amédée
Aurora's Angus. Mannzen, D.
Austin, Mary
  Green bough
    Selden, R. ed. Ways of God and men
AUSTRALIANS IN ENGLAND
  Edginton, H. M. Purple and fine linen
AUSTRIA
  Boyle, K. White horses of Vienna
The **author.** Johnson, J. W.
Author of Beltraffio. James, H.
AUTHORS
  Aiken, C. P. Life isn't a short story
  Aiken, C. P. Your obituary, well written
  Beck, W. Edge of doom
  Benét, S. V. No visitors
  Borges, J. L. Secret miracle
  Brookhouser, F. Young man from yesterday
  Brown, F. All good bems
  Chekhov, A. P. The skit
  Collier, J. Collaboration
  Collier, J. Pictures in the fire
  Collier, J. Variation on a theme
  De La Roche, M. Boy in the house
  Farrell, J. T. John Hitchcock
  Farrell, J. T. The martyr
  Farrell, J. T. Power of literature
  Fitzgerald, F. S. K. Financing Finnegan
  Fletcher, V. Coda to a writers' conference

  Gregutt, H. C. Climb for the big ones
  Gregutt, H. C. The secret
  Harvey, W. F. Habeas Corpus Club
  Hemingway, E. Snows of Kilimanjaro
  Jackson, C. R. The outlander
  James, H. Author of Beltraffio
  James, H. Death of the lion
  James, H. Middle years
  Jarrell, R. Gertrude and Sidney
  Johnson, J. W. The author
  Karchmer, S. N. Fistful of Alamo heroes
  Keller, D. H. Creation unforgivable
  Keller, D. H. Literary corkscrew
  Kipling, R. "Finest story in the world"
  Lawrence, D. H. Two blue birds
  Lewis, S. Post-mortem murder
  Mann, T. Weary hour
  Maugham, W. S. Creature impulse
  Maugham, W. S. Human element
  Maugham, W. S. Round dozen
  Maugham, W. S. Social sense
  Maugham, W. S. Voice of the turtle
  Mitchell, J. Professor Sea Gull
  Munro, H. H. Mark
  Newhouse, E. Irving
  Porter, W. S. Dinner at—
  Porter, W. S. Dog and the playlet
  Porter, W. S. Plutonian fire
  Porter, W. S. Proof of the pudding
  Porter, W. S. Sacrifice hit
  Porter, W. S. Sound and fury
  Porter, W. S. Sparrows in Madison Square
  Saroyan, W. The Assyrian
  Saroyan, W. Cocktail party
  Saroyan, W. Cold day
  Schulberg, B. W. Note on the literary life
  Shultz, W. H. Oreste
  Sutro, A. Bread on the waters
  Tucker, W. "MCMLV"
  Walpole, Sir H. Mr Oddy
  Walsh, M. Thomasheen James and the dictation machine
  Waugh, E. Excursion in reality
  Waugh, E. Work suspended
  West, J. Breach of promise
  Willingham, C. Record of a man
    See also Children as authors; Dramatists; Journalists; Poets; also names of individual authors
AUTOBIOGRAPHICAL STORIES
  Feuchtwanger, L. Balance sheet of my life
  Karchmer, S. N. Fistful of Alamo heroes
  McCarthy, M. T. The blackguard
  McCarthy, M. T. Yonder peasant, who is he?
AUTOMATA
  Asimov, I. I, robot; 9 stories
  Asimov, I. "Nobody here but. . ."
  Asimov, I. Sally
  Asimov, I. Victory unintentional
  Binder, E. I, robot
  Bradbury, R. Marionettes, inc.
  Breuer, M. J. Man with the strange head
  Curtis, B. Peculiar people
  Del Rey, L. Helen O'Loy
  Del Rey, L. Instinct
  Del Rey, L. Into thy hands
  Fyfe, H. B. Manners of the age
  Gallun, R. Z. Old Faithful
  Gault, W. C. Made to measure
  Greenberg, M. ed. Robot and the man
  Highstone, H. A. Frankenstein—unlimited

AUTOMATA—*Continued*
Jacobi, C. Gentleman is an Epwa
Jameson, M. Pride
Jenkins, W. F. Logic named Joe
Jenkins, W. F. The wabbler
Keller, D. H. Psychophonic nurse
Keller, D. H. Yeast men
Klass, P. Child's play
Knight, D. Ask me anything
Kuttner, H. Deadlock
Kuttner, H. Open secret
La Farge, O. John the revelator
Leiber, F. Appointment in tomorrow
Miller, W. M. Izzard and the membrane
Saroyan, W. Mr Mechano
Van Vogt, A. E. Automaton
Van Vogt, A. E. Fulfillment
Wolfe, B. Self portrait

Automata: I. Wright, S. F.

Automata: II. Wright, S. F.

Automata: III. Wright, S. F.

Automaton. Van Vogt, A. A.

AUTOMOBILE ACCIDENTS. See Automobiles—Accidents

AUTOMOBILE DRIVERS
Farnsworth, M. All roads
Felsen, G. Hot rod; condensation
Felsen, G. Trenton in thirty minutes
Floherty, J. J. Duel at 70 miles an hour
Jackson, C. R. Sunday drive
Mauldin, W. H. Affair of the wayward jeep
Rhodes, W. P. Women will out
Roberts, R. M. Follow that car

AUTOMOBILE DRIVING. See Automobile drivers

AUTOMOBILE INDUSTRY AND TRADE. See Automobiles

AUTOMOBILE RACES
Campbell, Sir M. Won by inches!
Gault, W. C. Brick road to glory
Gault, W. C. Dirt-track thunder
Gault, W. C. Thunder Road
Purdy, K. W. Change of plan
White, W. Too big a dream

Automobile that wouldn't run. Caldwell, E.

AUTOMOBILES
Asimov, I. Sally
Carter, M. First car
Hauser, M. L. Calling all cars
Keller, D. H. Living machine
Mauldin, W. H. Affair of the wayward jeep
Moore, G. M. Two for a ride
Petrov, V. "Get a horse, comrade"
Roberts, R. M. Yellow convertible
Walker, T. The wonderful automobile

Accidents
Beck, W. Edge of doom
Demott, B. H. Sense that in the scene delights
Hanlon, B. Crushed orchid
Harvey, W. F. Dead of night
Murdock, R. M. Stop, look, listen
Neville, K. Bettyann
Priestley, J. B. Guest of honour
Saintsbury, E. B. Bread upon the waters

Seligsohn, I. J. The anchor
Ward, F. Kill and run
Willingham, C. Afternoon sun

Touring
Beck, W. Detour in the dark
Duke, O. Struttin' with some barbecue
Horgan, P. Peach stone

Trailers
Anderson, D. Forty years of firewood

Autre temps. Wharton, E. N. J.

Autumn. Strindberg, A.

Autumn bloom. Steele, W. D.

Autumn courtship. Caldwell, E.

Autumn cricket. Dunsany, E. J. M. D. P. 18th baron

Autumn leaves. Merochnik, M.

AVALANCHES
Purcell, D. Rider of the avalanche

AVARICE
Clemens, S. L. Man that corrupted Hadleyburg
Tolstoi, L. N. Graf. Three arshins of land

Ave, amor, morituri te salutant. George, W. L.

The **avenging.** Lord, J.

Avenging angels. Doyle, Sir A. C.

Avenging chance. Cox, A. B.

AVIATION. See Aeronautics

AVIATORS. See Air pilots

AVIATRIXES. See Air pilots

AVIGNON. See France Provincial and rural—Avignon

Avrom the cobbler. Reisin, A.

The **awakening.** Babel', I. E.

The **awakening.** Corkery, D.

The **award.** Monn, A.

Away! Away! Boyd, J.

Aycock, Roger D.
Problem on Balak
Galaxy science fiction magazine. Second Galaxy reader of science fiction
Unwelcome tenant
Merril, J. ed. Beyond human ken

Azuela, Mariano, 1873-1952
Under dogs
Burnett, W. ed. World's best

B

B+M—planet 4. Heard, G.

Baa-baa, black sheep. Earley, S. B.

Babb, Sanora
Wild flower
Best American short stories, 1950

Babe. Patterson, R.

Babel, Isaac Immanuelovich. See Babel', Isaak Emmanuilovich

Babel', Isaak Emmanuilovich, 1894-
  The awakening
    Ausubel, N. ed. Treasury of Jewish
      humor
  In Odessa
    Ausubel, N. ed. Treasury of Jewish
      humor
  The King
    Guerney, B. G. comp. New Russian
      stories
  Rabbi's son
    Leftwich, J. ed. Yisröel. 1952 ed.
Babes in the jungle. Porter, W. S.
Babes in the wood. O'Donovan, M.
Babette. Maupassant, G. de
BABIES. See Children
Babikoff, Vladimir, 1907-
  Day of rest
    American vanguard, 1950
BABOONS
  Annixter, P. pseud. The lynching
Babs and Phill who eloped. Strain, F. B.
Babus of Nayanjore. Tagore, Sir R.
Baby buntings. Squires, R.
Baby killer. Elliott, R. B.
Baby on Neptune. Harris, C. W. and
    Breuer, M. J.
Baby party. Fitzgerald, F. S. K.
Baby sitter for Christmas. Cousins, M.
Baby sitter vs. Ronnie. Johnson, H.
BABY SITTERS
  De Vries, P. They also sit
  Johnson, H. Baby sitter vs. Ronnie
Babylon revisited. Fitzgerald, F. S. K.
Bachelor supper. Aiken, C. P.
BACH, JOHANN SEBASTIAN, 1685-1750
  Brachvogel, A. E. Christmas at the Bachs'
BACHELORS
  Bates, H. E. Little farm
  Bowen, E. The lover
  Bowen, E. New house
  Huysmans, J. K. Monsieur Folantin
  Melville, H. Paradise of bachelors
Bachelor's death. Schnitzler, A.
Back again. Schuyler, W.
Back drawing-room. Bowen, E.
Back for Christmas. Collier, J.
Back of beyond. Maugham, W. S.
Back on the road. Caldwell, E.
Back there in the grass. Morris, G.
Back to Julie. Wilson, R.
Back to school. Doty, W. L.
Back to the beginning. Robertson, J. H.
Back to the land—Oregon, 1907. Davis,
  H. L.
Back to the sea. Pincherle, A.
Back to Treasure Island. Calahan, H. A.
Back where I had never been. McNulty, J.
Backfire. Rocklynne, R.
The background. Munro, H. H.
Backward, turn backward. Davis, D. S.
Backyard ballgame. Farrell, J. T.

Bacon, Francis, viscount St Albans, 1561-
  1626
  New Atlantis
    Derleth, A. W. ed. Beyond time &
      space
BACTERIAL WARFARE
  Jenkins, W. F. Symbiosis
  Robertson, M. Battle of the monsters
BACTERIOLOGISTS
  Wells, H. G. Stolen bacillus
Bad boy from Brooklyn. Seide, M.
Bad corner. Van Doren, M.
Bad day for sales. Leiber, F.
Bad dreams. Taylor, P. H.
Bad man passes on. Hendryx, J. B.
Bad man reaches Halfaday. Hendryx, J. B.
Bad year. Cheshire, G.
Bade, William L.
  Ambition
    Conklin, G. ed. Science-fiction adven-
      tures in dimension
Badge of policeman O'Roon. Porter, W. S.
BADGERS
  Kafka, F. The burrow
Ba-ee. Cook, K.
The bag. Munro, H. H.
Bag of silver. Bentley, P. E.
Bagnold, Enid
  Amorous ghost
    Carrington, H. ed. Week-end book of
      ghost stories
Bailey, Albert Edward, 1871-
  Jimmy finds a plan
    Elmquist, R. M. ed. Fifty years of
      Christmas
Bailiffs at Framley. Trollope, A.
Bair, Tom
  Falcon's nest
    Burnett, W. and Burnett, H. S. eds.
      Sextet
Bait for a tiger. Walker, D. H.
Bait from McGillicudy. Wylie, P.
Baker, Denys Val
  Beautiful house
    Story (Periodical) Story; no. 1
Baker, Dorothy (Dodds) 1907-
  Little white cat
    Joseph, M. ed. Best cat stories
  Summer
    New writing (Periodical) Best stories
Baker, Frank, 1908-
  Blessed are the clean of heart; they shall
    see God
    Baker, F. Blessed are they
  Blessed are the merciful; they shall obtain
    mercy
    Baker, F. Blessed are they
  Blessed are the patient; they shall inherit
    the land
    Baker, F. Blessed are they
  Blessed are the peace-makers; they shall
    be counted the children of God
    Baker, F. Blessed are they
  Blessed are the poor in spirit; the king-
    dom of heaven is theirs
    Baker, F. Blessed are they

Baker, Frank—_Continued_
Blessed are those who hunger and thirst for holiness; they shall have their fill
Baker, F. Blessed are they
Blessed are those who mourn; they shall be comforted
Baker, F. Blessed are they
Blessed are those who suffer persecution in the cause of right; the kingdom of heaven is theirs
Baker, F. Blessed are they
Baker, Ray Stannard, 1870-1946
A day of pleasant bread
Brentano, F. ed. The word lives on
Lohan, R. and Lohan, M. eds. New Christmas treasury
Baker Street irregulars. Doyle, Sir A. C.
BAKERIES AND BAKERS
Gorky, M. Twenty-six and one
Greene, H. I. Bread and snow
Horwitz, J. The strudel
Porter, W. S. Witches' loaves
Shneur, Z. The girl
Baker's daughter. Bianco, M. W.
BAKING. See Bakeries and bakers
Balance. Christopher, J.
Balance his, swing yours. Stegner, W. E.
Balance sheet of my life. Feuchtwanger, L.
Balch, Glenn, 1902-
Price on Hide-rack
American boy (Periodical) American boy anthology
Balchin, Nigel, 1908-
Now we are broke, my dear
Saturday evening post (Periodical) Saturday evening post stories, 1950
The **balcony.** Milne, A. A.
Baldwin, Hanson Weightman, 1903-
R. M. S. Titanic
McFee, W. ed. Great sea stories of modern times
Baldwin, James, 1841-1925
Broiefort, the black Arabian
Dennis, W. ed. Palomino and other horses
BALKAN STATES
Munro, H. H. Cupboard of the yesterdays
Munro, H. H. Purple of the Balkan Kings
Ball, Max Waite
Case of the wooden bowls
Bachelor, J. M.; Henry, R. L. and Salisbury, R. eds. Current thinking and writing; 2d ser.
Ball-of-fat. Maupassant, G. de
Ballad of the sad café. McCullers, C. S.
Ballantyne, Thomas A.
Reunion at evening
American vanguard, 1952
Ballard, James Clarence, 1921-
Mountain summer
Best American short stories, 1953
BALLET
Woody, R. L. J. Cue for Connie
Woody, R. L. J. Second chance
See also Dancers; Dancing
BALLET DANCERS. See Ballet
BALLOON ASCENSIONS. See Balloons

Balloon hoax. Poe, E. A.
BALLOONS
Ekbergh, I. D. Up in a balloon
Poe, E. A. Balloon hoax
Poe, E. A. Mellonta Tauta
Poe, E. A. Unparalleled adventure of one Hans Pfaall
Repton, H. From a private mad-house
BALLS (PARTIES) See Parties
Balm of Gilead. Caldwell, E.
Balmer, Edwin, 1883- **and Wylie, Philip,** 1902-
When worlds collide; excerpts
Kuebler, H. W. ed. Treasury of science fiction classics
Balzac, Honoré de, 1799-1850
Atheist's mass
Fabricant, N. D. and Werner, H. eds. World's best doctor stories
Mother's letter
Ungar, F. ed. To mother with love
Old maid
Dupee, F. W. ed. Great French short novels
Other Diane
Geist, S. ed. French stories and tales
Passion in the desert
Blodgett, H. W. ed. Story survey
Cody, S. ed. Greatest stories and how they were written
Lamb, L. ed. Family book of best loved short stories
Neider, C. ed. Great short stories from the world's literature
Bamberg, Robert Douglas
Cave of warm winds
Hathaway, B. and Sessions, J. A. eds. Writers for tomorrow. 2d ser.
BANANA
Porter, W. S. Day we celebrate
Band concert. Jackson, C. R.
BANDITS. See Brigands and robbers
BANDS (MUSIC)
O'Donovan, M. Orpheus and his lute
See also Musicians
Bandy. Miers, E. S.
Banér, Skulda Vanadis, 1899-
Good dog forward
Cavanna, B. ed. Pick of the litter
Same as: "Good girl—forward!"
"Good girl—forward!"
American girl (Periodical) On my honor
Same as: Good dog forward
Bang on the head. Seager, A.
BANGKOK. See Thailand—Bangkok
Bangs, John Kendrick, 1862-1922
Water ghost of Harrowby Hall
Fenner, P. R. comp. Ghosts, ghosts, ghosts
BANK CLERKS. See Clerks
BANK ROBBERS
Aldrich, B. S. How far is it to Hollywood?
Frazee, S. Fire killer
Muheim, H. Dusty drawer
Bank that broke the man at Monte Carlo. Sansom, W.

BANKERS
Collins, W. Fauntleroy
Davis, R. H. Wasted day
Porter, W. S. Friends in San Rosario
Porter, W. S. Guardian of the accolade
Waltari, M. T. Tie from Paris
See also Banks and banking; Capitalists and financiers

BANKS AND BANKING
MacDonald, J. D. The miniature
Nadir, I. M. My first deposit
See also Bankers

Banquet and a half. Hays, L.

Bantien, Alvin M.
Emergency
Oberfirst, R. ed. 1952 anthology of best original short-shorts

Baptism of some importance. Becker, S. D.

Baptist hymnal. Miner, M. S.

The **baptizing.** Ingraham, J. H.

Bar-Nothing's happy birthday. Cunningham, E.

Bar sinister. Davis, R. H.

BARBARIANS. See Man, Prehistoric

BARBARITIES. See War

Barbecue. Runyon, D.

Barbèd rose. Guest, A.

Barber, Alfred, 1922-
The caught
American vanguard, 1952

BARBERS
Lardner, R. W. Haircut
Schaefer, J. W. Leander Frailey

Barber's clever wife. Steele, F. A.

Barbey d' Aurévilly, Jules Amédée, 1808-1889
Happiness in crime
Dupee, F. W. ed. Great French short novels

Barbour, Ralph Henry, 1870-1944
"Hoot!" said the owl
American boy (Periodical) American boy anthology

BARCELONA. See Spain—Barcelona

Bargain in brimstone. Oursler, F.

Barker, A. L. 1919-
Answer is nothing
Barker, A. L. Novelette; with other stories
Domini
Barker, A. L. Novelette; with other stories
The freak
Barker, A. L. Novelette; with other stories
Heartbreak
Barker, A. L. Novelette; with other stories
Jane Dore—dear childe
Barker, A. L. Novelette; with other stories
Novelette
Barker, A. L. Novelette; with other stories
Pringle
Barker, A. L. Novelette; with other stories
Romney
Barker, A. L. Novelette; with other stories
Story of Mathias
Barker, A. L. Novelette; with other stories
Variations on a theme of rain
Barker, A. L. Novelette; with other stories
Villain as a young boy
Barker, A. L. Novelette; with other stories

Barker, Squire Omar, 1894-
Man in the hard hat
Western Writers of America. Holsters and heroes

Barlow, Thomas
Sudden heart
Saturday evening post (Periodical) Saturday evening post stories, 1950

Barn burning. Faulkner, W.

Barnard, Leslie Gordon, 1890-
Dancing bear
Pacey, D. ed. Book of Canadian stories
Four men and a box
This week magazine. This week's short-short stories

Barney. Stanton, W.

Barney whose life was "all work and no play." Strain, F. B.

BARNUM, PHINEAS TAYLOR, 1810-1891
Benét, S. V. Angel was a Yankee

Baro, Gene
Angry lions, lazy lions
Story (Periodical) Story no. 2

Baroja y Nessi, Pío, 1872-
Cabbages of the cemetery
De Onís, H. ed. Spanish stories and tales

BARONS. See Aristocracy

Barr, James, pseud.
Bottom of the cloud
Barr, J. pseud. Derricks
First you take a live goat
Barr, J. pseud. Derricks
Good kid
Barr, J. pseud. Derricks
Hanging fire
Barr, J. pseud. Derricks
Spur piece
Barr, J. pseud. Derricks
Success story
Barr, J. pseud. Derricks
Tryout
Barr, J. pseud. Derricks

Barrie, Sir James Matthew, bart. 1860-1937
Courting of T'nowhead's Bell
Cerf, B. A. and Moriarty, H. C. eds. Anthology of famous British stories
Farewell Miss Julie Logan
Scribner treasury
The last night
Brentano, F. ed. The word lives on
Making of a minister
Neider, C. ed. Men of the high calling

Barrier of dread. Merril, J.

Barring the weight. Ready, W. B.

The **barrister.** Milne, A. A.

Barry, Jerome, 1894-
    Fourth degree
        Mystery Writers of America, inc.
        Maiden murders
BARS. See Hotels, taverns, etc.
Barsetshire. Trollope, A.
Barsetshire worthy—Archdeacon Grantly.
    Trollope, A.
BARTENDERS
    Jenkin, P. A. Cool million
    Saroyan, W. Third day after Christmas
Bartholomew Arnold; or, After the war is
    over. Stein, G.
"Bartimeus," pseud. See Ritchie, Lewis An-
    selm da Costa
Bartleby. Melville, H.
Bartleby the scrivener. Melville, H.
Basch, Monika
    Second act
        Hathaway, B. and Sessions, J. A. eds.
        Writers for tomorrow. 2d ser.
BASEBALL
    Bateman, A. Diamond horseshoes
    Bradbury, R. Big black and white game
    Breslin, H. Bat and a prayer
    Brookhouser, F. L'affaire foul tip
    Brubaker, H. Milk pitcher
    Coombs, C. I. Saga of Sleepy Mugoon
    Cox, W. R. Pinch hitter
    Dailey, J. The rookie
    Erin, B. Don't jinx the pitcher
    Fenner, P. R. Crack of the bat; 10 stories.
    Fontaine, R. L. God hit a home run
    Furman, A. L. ed. Teen-age stories of
        the diamond; 13 stories
    Gallery, D. V. Hokey-Pocus McGee
    Gallico, P. W. Summer dream
    Garber, R. S. ed. Baseball reader; 25
        stories
    Hillger, E. H. Lomax pitching
    Holder, W. Storm over second
    Katkov, N. Charlie Baseball
    Lowry, R. Little baseball world
    Miers, E. S. Kid who beat the Dodgers
    Montross, L. Nine ladies vs fate
    Oblinger, M. Jackpot vs Yellowstrike
    O'Rourke, F. Greatest victory, and other
        baseball stories; 12 stories
    O'Rourke, F. The heavenly world series,
        and other baseball stories; 9 stories
    Rutt, E. Canary from Cuba
    Sandberg, H. W. Kid from Shingle Creek
    Schram, W. L. Horse that played third
        base for Brooklyn
    Schramm, W. L. My kingdom for Jones
    Siegel, L. Lay it down, Ziggy!
    Temple, W. H. Most unusual season
    Ullman, J. R. I seen 'em go
    Van Loan, C. E. Mister Conley
    West, C. Smoke ball kid
    Young, S. We won't be needing you, Al
Baseball Hattie. Runyon, D.
The basement. Largerkvist, P. F.
Basement room. Greene, G.
BASKETBALL
    Bee, C. F. Freeze the ball
    Charnley, M. V. Brodie horns in
    Chute, B. J. Five captains
    Chute, B. J. Four-ring circus

Chute, B. J. Kid brother
Coombs, C. I. Hardwood hazard
Coombs, C. I. Part time hoopster
Farrell, J. T. Tournament star
Gartner, J. Left-hand stuff
Jackson, M. W. The hero
Larsen, D. Freeze-out
Miers, E. S. No heroes wanted
Person, W. T. "I play basketball"
Person, W. T. Long-Shot Porter
Peterson, G. M. Sophomore forward
Phillips, J. A. Fast break
Pierrot, G. P. Sheriton turnabout
Roberts, R. M. The fix
Stoakes, H. R. Turtles played the hares
Temple, W. H. Record-breaker
Wilner, H. Whistle and the heroes
BASQUES
    Baroja y Nessi, P. Cabbages of the ceme-
    tery
Bat. Meader, S. W.
Bat and a prayer. Breslin, H.
Bat Eye Cantrill. Hendryx, J. B.
Bateman, Arnold
    Diamond horseshoes
        Boys' life (Periodical) Boys' life Adven-
        ture stories
    Gus the gloom
        Furman, A. L. ed. Teen-age stories of
        the diamond
    Rig ship for diving
        Furman, A. L. ed. Teen-age sea stories
    Submarine jitters
        Furman, A. L. ed. Teen-age sea stories
Bates, Harry
    Alas, all thinking!
        Bleiler, E. F. and Dikty, T. E. eds.
        ' Imagination unlimited
    Death of a sensitive
        Moskowitz, S. comp. Editor's choice in
        science fiction
Bates, Herbert Ernest, 1905-
    Bedfordshire clanger
        Bates, H. E. Colonel Julian, and other
        stories
    Christmas song
        Bates, H. E. Colonel Julian, and other
        stories
    Colonel Julian
        Bates, H. E. Colonel Julian, and other
        stories
    The flag
        Bates, H. E. Colonel Julian, and other
        stories
    The frontier
        Bates, H. E. Colonel Julian, and other
        stories
    Girl called Peter
        Bates, H. E. Colonel Julian, and other
        stories
    Joe Johnson
        Bates, H. E. Colonel Julian, and other
        stories
    The lighthouse
        Bates, H. E. Colonel Julian, and other
        stories
    Little farm
        Bates, H. E. Colonel Julian, and other
        stories

Bates, Herbert E.—*Continued*
  Major of Hussars
    Bates, H. E. Colonel Julian, and other
      stories
  Mrs Vincent
    Bates, H. E. Colonel Julian, and other
      stories
  No more the nightingales
    Bates, H. E. Colonel Julian, and other
      stories
  The park
    Bates, H. E. Colonel Julian, and other
      stories
  Sugar for the horse
    Bates, H. E. Colonel Julian, and other
      stories
  Time expired
    Bates, H. E. Colonel Julian, and other
      stories
Bates, Ralph, 1899-
  Forty-third division
    Cerf, B. A. and Moriarty, H. C. eds.
      Anthology of famous British stories
  Wailing precipice
    Talbot, D. ed. Treasury of mountaineer-
      ing stories
The **bath.** O'Flaherty, L.
BATHING BEACHES
  Beck, W. Far whistle
BATHS, TURKISH
  Munro, H. H. The Recessional
BATHYSPHERE
  Jenkins, W. F. De profundis
Battle in the moonlight. Ellsberg, E.
Battle of Finney's Ford. West, J.
Battle of life. Dickens, C.
Battle of the marten and the porcupine.
  Reid, M.
Battle of the monsters. Robertson, M.
Battle of the S . . . S. Elliott, B.
Battle royal. O'Rourke, F.
Battle with a whale. Davies, W. M.
Battle with the bees. Stuart, J.
BATTLES
  Coolidge, O. E. Prefect of Jerusalem
    See also names of particular battles
Baudelaire, Charles Pierre, 1821-1867
  Death of a hero
    Geist, S. ed. French stories and tales
  The rope
    Geist, S. ed. French stories and tales
Bauer, Florence Anne (Marvyne)
  The waters of Bethesda
    Brentano, F. ed. The word lives on
Bauer, Gladys V.
  Scared
    Furman, A. L. ed. Everygirls mystery
      stories
Baum, Vicki, 1888-
  Old house
    Leftwich, J. ed. Yisröel. 1952 ed.
Bayou bait. White, L. T.
BAYOUS
  Grau, S. A. Joshua
BAZAARS. See Fairs
Bazán, Emilia Pardo. See Pardo Bazan,
  Emilia, condesa de

Be nice to Mr Campbell. Lowry, R. J. C.
Be present at our table, Lord. Saroyan, W.
Beach, Edward Latimer, 1918-
  Archerfish
    Fenner, P. R. comp. Speed, speed, speed
    McFee, W. ed. Great sea stories of
      modern times
  Wahoo
    Fenner, P. R. comp. Stories of the sea
Beach of Falesá. Stevenson, R. L.
Beach squatter. Davis, H. L.
BEACHCOMBERS
  Russell, J. Jetsam
Beachcroft, Thomas Owen, 1902-
  Erne from the coast
    Certner, S. and Henry, G. H. eds. Short
      stories for our times
    Christ, H. I. and Shostak, J. eds. Short
      stories
  The eyes
    Cerf, B. A. and Moriarty, H. C. eds.
      Anthology of famous British stories
  Old Hard
    Schorer, M. ed. The story
Beachead in Bohemia. Marsh, W. N.
Beachhead. Simak, C. D.
Beaconsfield, Benjamin Disraeli, 1st earl of,
  1804-1881
  Ixion in heaven
    Leftwich, J. ed. Yisröel 1952 ed.
Beal, Forrest
  Bertie the uninvited
    Dachs, D. ed. Treasury of sports humor
Beanstalk. Blish, J.
The **bear.** Faulkner, W.
Bear and the hunter's step-son
  Pacey, D. ed Book of Canadian stories
Bear hunt. Faulkner, W.
Bear that thought he was a dog. Roberts,
  Sir C. G. D.
BEARS
  Annixter, P. pseud. Kadiak
  Barnard, L. C. Dancing bear
  Burke, N. Polar night
  Caldwell, E. Hamrick's polar bear
  Faulkner, W. The bear
  Grimson, M. S. King of the north woods
  Kahanovich, P. From my estates
  Kjelgaard, J. A. Blood on the ice
  Roberts, Sir C. G. D. Thirteen bears;
    13 stories
  Schaefer, J. W. Something lost
  Stuart, J. No hero
  West, R. B. Last of the grizzly bears
Beast from 20,000 fathoms. Bradbury, R.
Beast in the jungle. James, H.
Beast of Bourbon. Pratt, F. and De Camp,
  L. S.
Beast with five fingers. Harvey, W. F.
BEATITUDES
  Baker, F. Blessed are they; 8 stories
Beau: the dog who served two masters.
  Little, G. W.
Beauclerk, Helen De Vere
  Miracle of the vineyard
    Selden, R. ed. Ways of God and men

Beaumont, Charles, 1929-
  Beautiful woman
    Wollheim, D. A. 'ed. Prize science fic-
      tion
  Keeper of the dream
    Derleth, A. W. ed. Time to come
Beaumont, Gerald, 1886-1926
  The crab
    Graber, R. S. ed. Baseball reader
Beautiful, beautiful, beautiful! Freidman, S.
Beautiful house. Baker, D. V.
Beautiful night for Orion. Clay, R.
Beautiful tree. Sangster, M. E.
Beautiful woman. Beaumont, C.
BEAUTY. See Esthetics
BEAUTY, PERSONAL
  Beaumont, C. Beautiful woman
  Brush, K. I. Good Wednesday
Beauty and the diamond ring. Moore, J. P.
BEAUTY SHOPS
  Olds, H. D. Susan steps out
  Pratt, F. and De Camp, L. S. More than
    skin deep
  Welty, E. Petrified man
  Winslow, T. S. Fur flies
BEAVERS
  Mills, E. A. My beaver pal
Because of little apples. Chekhov, A. P.
Because she was like me. Schweitzer, G.
Beck, V. J.
  Night boat from Barcelona
    Story (Periodical) Story; no. 2
Beck, Warren
  All brothers are men
    Beck, W. Far whistle, and other stories
  Ask me no more
    Beck, W. Far whistle, and other stories
  Blue sash
    Best of the Best American short stories,
      1915-1950
  The child is father
    Beck, W. Far whistle, and other stories
  Clean platter
    Beck, W. Far whistle, and other stories
  Detour in the dark
    Beck, W. Far whistle, and other stories
  Edge of doom
    Beck, W. Far whistle, and other stories
    Best American short stories, 1950
  Far whistle
    Beck, W. Far whistle, and other stories
  Felix
    Beck, W. Far whistle, and other stories
  Men working
    Beck, W. Far whistle, and other stories
  No continuing city
    Beck, W. Far whistle, and other stories
  Shadow of turning
    Abell, E. ed. American accent
    Beck, W. Far whistle, and other stories
  Verdict of innocence
    Beck, W. Far whistle, and other stories
  Years brought to an end
    Beck, W. Far whistle, and other stories
Becker, Stephen D. 1927-
  Baptism of some importance
    Story (Periodical) Story; no. 4
  Town mouse
    Best American short stories, 1953

Beckoning sea. Mandel, G.
Becky's Christmas turkey. Skinner, C. L.
Bedford-Jones, Henry, 1887-1949
  Thirteen men
    Bluebook (Periodical) Best sea stories
      from Bluebook
Bedford-Jones, Henry, 1887-1949 **and Wil-
    liams, L. B.**
  Yellow Ship
    Bluebook (Periodical) Best sea stories
      from Bluebook
Bedfordshire clanger. Bates, H. E.
BEDS
  Collins, W. Terribly strange bed
Bee, Clair Francis, 1900-
  Freeze the ball
    Herzberg, M. J. comp. Treasure chest
      of sport stories
BEE. See Bees
Beebe, William, 1877-
  Home town of the army ants
    Andrews, R. C. ed. My favorite stories
      of the great outdoors
Beep. Blish, J.
Beer, Thomas, 1889-1940
  Tact
    Burrell, J. A. and Cerf, B. A. eds. An-
      thology of famous American stories
BEER
  Rabinowitz, S. My brother Eliyahu's drink
Beerbohm, Sir Max, 1872-1956
  Happy hypocrite
    Cerf, B. A. and Moriarty, H. C. eds.
      Anthology of famous British stories
BEES
  Gray, W. H. Bees from Borneo
  Stuart, J. Battle with the bees
  Wilson, R. M. Cyprian bees
Bees from Borneo. Gray, W. H.
BEETLES
  Poe, E. A. The gold-bug
Before its time. Dolbier, M.
Before the burning of Rome. Blackburn,
    E. R.
Before the flood. Milne, A. A.
Before the party. Maugham, W. S.
Before the races. DeJong, D. C.
Before the throne of beauty. Gibran, K.
Before the twilight of the gods. Waltari,
    M. T.
The **beggar.** Chekov, A. P.
Beggar-woman of Locarno. Kleist, H. von
BEGGARS
  Benét, S. V. Bishop's beggar
  Bunin, I. A. Evening in spring
  Chekov, A. P. The beggar
  Lagerkvist, P. F. The basement
  Maugham, W. S. The bum
  Munro, H. H. Dusk
  Munro, H. H. The romancers
  Steinberg, Y. Reb Anshel the golden
      See also Tramps
The **beggars.** O'Flaherty, L.
Begin again. Boyle, K.
Beginning of a story. Taylor, E.

Behind the garment. Gibran, K.

Behind the plate. Strong, P. N.

Behold it was a dream. Broughton, R.

Bekir and his dog, Aslan. Ekrem, S.

BELGIANS IN GERMANY
Sansom, W. How Claeys died

Belief. Asimov, I.

BELIEF AND DOUBT. See Faith

Bell, Vereen McNeill, 1911-1944
Brag dog
Cavanna, B. ed. Pick of the litter
Dog man
American boy (Periodical) American
boy anthology
Tarpon!
American boy (Periodical) American
boy Adventure stories

Bell-ringer of Angel's. Harte, B.

The **bell-tower.** Melville, H.

Bella Fleace gave a party. Waugh, E.

Bellah, James Warner, 1899-
Fear
Jensen, P. ed. Fireside book of flying
stories

Bellamy, Edward, 1850-1898
Blindman's world
Derleth, A. W. ed. Beyond time & space

Bella's got a fella. Kober, A.

Belle Monahan. Cawley, C. C.

Bellevue days. McNulty, J.

Bellow, Saul, 1915-
Sermon by Doctor Pep
Best American short stories, 1950

BELL-RINGERS. See Bells and bell-ringers

The **bells.** Innis, M. E. Q.

BELLS AND BELL-RINGERS
Melville, H. The bell-tower
Poe, E. A. Devil in the belfry

Below Cape Horn. Marmur, J.

Bement, Douglas, 1898-1943. See Shaw, H.
jt. auth.

Bench of desolation. James, H.

Bench warmer. Chute, B. J.

Benchley, Nathaniel, 1915-
Mrs Crocker's mutiny
This week magazine. This week's short-
short stories

Benchley, Robert Charles, 1889-1945
Score in the stands
Graber, R. S. ed. Baseball reader
Tooth, the whole tooth, and nothing but
the tooth
Fenner, P. R. comp. Fun! Fun! Fun!
Watching baseball
Graber, R. S. ed. Baseball reader

Bend down, indeed! Melnick, C. R.

Bendrodt, James Charles
Butch
Bendrodt, J. C. Of men, dogs and horses
Chowsie
Bendrodt, J. C. Of men, dogs and horses
Irish lad
Bendrodt, J. C. Of men, dogs and horses
Spike
Bendrodt, J. C. Of men, dogs and horses

Valiant lady
Bendrodt, J. C. Of men, dogs and horses
Zaimis
Bendrodt, J. C. Of men, dogs and horses

Benediction. Chou, S.

Benefield, Barry, 1883-
Christmas Eve's Day
Lohan, R. and Lohan, M. eds. New
Christmas treasury
Incident at Boiling Springs
Peery, W. W. ed. 21 Texas short stories

Benefield, John Barry. See Benefield, Barry

Benefit concert. Davies, R.

Benefit of clergy. Marshall, E.

Benefit of clergy. Russell, B. A. W. R. 3d
earl

Benefits of American life. Farrell, J. T.

Benét, Laura
Horseshoe nails
Story parade (Periodical) Adventure
stories

Benét, Stephen Vincent, 1898-1943
Angel was a Yankee
Merril, J. ed. Beyond human ken
Bishop's beggar
Neider, C. ed. Men of the high calling
Blood of the martyrs
Lass, A. H. and Horowitz, A. eds.
Stories for youth
By the waters of Babylon
Schramm, W. L. ed. Great short stories
Devil and Daniel Webster
Blaustein, A. P. ed. Fiction goes to
court
Day, A. G. ed. Greatest American short
stories
Fenner, P. R. comp. Ghosts, ghosts,
ghosts
First-prize stories, 1919-1954
Shaw, H. and Bement, D. Reading the
short story
Stauffer, R. M.; Cunningham, W. H. and
Sullivan, C. J. eds. Adventures in
modern literature
End to dreams
First-prize stories, 1919-1954
Freedom's a hard-bought thing
First-prize stories, 1919-1954
Johnny Pye and the Fool-killer
Davis, C. B. ed. Eyes of boyhood
No visitors
Fabricant, N. D. and Werner, H. eds.
World's best doctor stories
Sobbin' women
Certner, S. and Henry, G. H. eds. Short
stories for our times
Tooth for Paul Revere
Lynskey, W. C. ed. Reading modern
fiction

BENEVOLENCE. See Charity

BENGAL. See India--Bengal

Benighted savage. Jackson, C. R.

Benito Cereno. Melville, H.

Benjamin, Irwin Eugene, 1927-
Do-gooder
American vanguard, 1953

Bennett, Arnold, 1867-1931
Mary with the high hand
  Cerf, B. A. and Moriarty, H. C. eds.
    Anthology of famous British stories
Bennett, Keith
Rocketeers have shaggy ears
  Greenberg, M. ed. Travelers of space
Bennett, Kem, 1919-
Death at attention
  Strang, R. M. and Roberts, R. M. eds.
    Teen-age tales v2
The soothsayer
  Magazine of fantasy and science fiction.
    Best from Fantasy and science fiction;
    2d ser.
Bennett, Myra E.
Hornet's nest
  Lantz, J. E. ed. Stories of Christian
    living
Bennett, Peggy, 1925-
Death under the hawthornes
  Best American short stories, 1950
  Prize stories of 1950
Fugitive from the mind
  Best American short stories, 1951
Bennett, Richard, 1899-
Strange little piper
  Story parade (Periodical) Adventure
    stories
Bennett, Russell H. 1896-
Rancher's horse
  Dennis, W. ed. Palomino and other
    horses
Bennett, Stephen
Girls are so helpless
  Furman, A. L. ed. Everygirls career
    stories
Benny and the bird-dogs. Rawlings, M. K.
Benny and the Tar-Baby. Watson, J. C.
Benowitz, Elliott, 1930-
Rush hour
  Wolfe, D. M. ed. Which grain will grow
Benson, Ben
Killer in the house
  Mystery Writers of America, inc.
    Butcher, baker, murder-maker
Benson, Sally, 1900-
The overcoat
  Lass, A. H. and Horowitz, A. eds.
    Stories for youth
  Shaw, H. and Bement, D. Reading the
    short story
Benson, Stella, 1892-1933
Man who missed the bus
  Lynskey, W. C. ed. Reading modern
    fiction
Story coldly told
  Short, R. W. and Sewall, R. B. eds.
    Short stories for study. 1950 ed.
Benson, Theodora, 1906-
Bones of A. T. Stewart
  Benson, T. Man from the tunnel, and
    other stories
Childishness of Mr. Mountfort
  Benson, T. Man from the tunnel, and
    other stories
Door marked exit
  Benson, T. Man from the tunnel, and
    other stories

Frog and the lion
  Benson, T. Man from the tunnel, and
    other stories
Funeral feast
  Benson, T. Man from the tunnel, and
    other stories
Golden fish
  Benson, T. Man from the tunnel, and
    other stories
Harry was good to the girls
  Benson, T. Man from the tunnel, and
    other stories
In the fourth ward
  Benson, T. Man from the tunnel, and
    other stories
Lion and the prey
  Benson, T. Man from the tunnel, and
    other stories
Long time ago
  Benson, T. Man from the tunnel, and
    other stories
Man from the tunnel
  Benson, T. Man from the tunnel, and
    other stories
Man with the phoney tin foot
  Benson, T. Man from the tunnel, and
    other stories
Nice fright
  Benson, T. Man from the tunnel, and
    other stories
Not by bread alone
  Benson, T. Man from the tunnel, and
    other stories
Shakespeare's elderly bore
  Benson, T. Man from the tunnel, and
    other stories
To-morrow is another day
  Benson, T. Man from the tunnel, and
    other stories
White cock
  Benson, T. Man from the tunnel, and
    other stories
White sea monkey
  Benson, T. Man from the tunnel, and
    other stories
Yes-girl
  Benson, T. Man from the tunnel, and
    other stories
Bensusan, Samuel Levy, 1872-
Death
  Leftwich, J. ed. Yisröel, 1952 ed.
Bent, James F.
Team man
  Furman, A. L. ed. Teen-age stories of
    the diamond
Bentham, Josephine
Age of romance
  Stowe, A. comp. It's a date
Bentley, Edmund Clerihew, 1875-1956
Clever cockatoo
  Bond, R. T. ed. Handbook for poisoners
Bentley, Phyllis Eleanor, 1894-
Angram folly
  Bentley, P. E. Panorama
Bag of silver
  Bentley, P. E. Panorama
Case in Chancery
  Bentley, P. E. Panorama
Everything under control
  Bentley, P. E. Panorama
Great lady
  Bentley, P. E. Panorama

Bentley, Phyllis E.—*Continued*
One night in Bradford
Bentley, P. E. Panorama
The sun and the hedge
Bentley, P. E. Panorama

BEQUESTS. See Inheritance and succession; Wills

The **bereaved.** Brookhouser, F.

The **bereft.** Albrizio, G.

Berenice. Poe, E. A.

Berg, Louis, 1900-
Nasty Kupperman and the Ku Klux Klan
Ribalow, H. U. ed. This land, these people

Berge, B
The lovely green boat
Best American short stories, 1952

Bergelson, David, 1884-
Citizen Woli Brenner
Leftwich, J. ed. Yisröel, 1952 ed.
In a backwoods town
Howe, I. and Greenberg, E. eds. Treasury of Yiddish stories
The squash
Ausubel, N. ed. Treasury of Jewish humor

Bergengruen, Werner, 1892-
Ali Baba and the forty horse-power
Bergengruen, W. Last Captain of Horse
Concerning muskets
Bergengruen, W. Last Captain of Horse
Easter Greeting
Bergengruen, W. Last Captain of Horse
Eye cure
Bergengruen, W. Last Captain of Horse
Giorgio and Martino
Bergengruen, W. Last Captain of Horse
The knight
Bergengruen, W. Last Captain of Horse
Lykin's sleigh-ride
Bergengruen, W. Last Captain of Horse
Magnanimity contest
Bergengruen, W. Last Captain of Horse
Marshal and his secretary
Bergengruen, W. Last Captain of Horse
Old Hussar
Bergengruen, W. Last Captain of Horse
On presenting arms
Bergengruen, W. Last Captain of Horse
Orban twins
Bergengruen, W. Last Captain of Horse
Pupsik
Bergengruen, W. Last Captain of Horse
Royal game
Bergengruen, W. Last Captain of Horse
Sand doctor
Bergengruen, W. Last Captain of Horse
The sentry
Bergengruen, W. Last Captain of Horse
Shining fools
Bergengruen, W. Last Captain of Horse
Stabenhaüser
Bergengruen, W. Last Captain of Horse
Trivulzio and the King
Bergengruen, W. Last Captain of Horse
When Riga was evacuated
Bergengruen, W. Last Captain of Horse

Berger, T. L.
April is the cruelest month
American vanguard, 1950
Child's play
Wolfe, D. M. ed. Which grain will grow

Berkeley, Anthony, pseud. See Cox, Anthony Berkeley

Berkshire comedy. Seager, A.

Berman, Hannah, 1890-
Horse thief
Leftwich, J. ed. Yisröel. 1952 ed.

Bernice bobs her hair. Fitzgerald, F. S. K.

Bernstein, David, 1915-
Death of an actor
Ribalow, H. U. ed. This land, these people

Bernstein, Herman, 1876-1935
Greatest funeral in the world
Leftwich, J. ed. Yisröel. 1952 ed.

Berom. Berryman, J.

Berry, John
New shoes
Prize stories of 1950

Berry patch. Stegner, W. E.

Berryman, John, 1914-
Berom
Bleiler, E. F. and Dikty, T. E. eds. Imagination unlimited
Imaginary Jew
Swallow, A. ed. Anchor in the sea
Space rating
Conklin, G. ed. Possible worlds of science fiction

Bertie the uninvited. Beal, F.

Bertie's Christmas Eve. Munro, H. H.

Berto, Giuseppe
Lull at Cassino
Berto, G. Works of God, and other stories
Need to die
Berto, G. Works of God, and other stories
War passed over us
Berto, G. Works of God, and other stories
Works of God
Berto, G. Works of God, and other stories

Beside still waters. Sheckley, R.

Beside the Shalimar. Marshall, E.

Best foot forward. Wright, F. F.

Best of breed. Taber, G. B.

Best of everything. Ellin, S.

Best position. O'Rourke, F.

Best riding and roping. James, W.

Best sea stories from Bluebook. Bluebook (Periodical)

Best-seller. Porter, W. S.

Bester, Alfred, 1913-
Disappearing act
Star science fiction stories, no. 2
5,271,009
Pohl, F. ed. Assignment in tomorrow
Hobson's choice
Magazine of fantasy and science fiction. Best from Fantasy and science fiction; 2d ser.

Bester, Alfred—*Continued*
Oddy and Id
Best science fiction stories: 1951
Of time and Third Avenue
Best science fiction stories: 1952
Star light, star bright
Magazine of fantasy and science fiction.
Best from Fantasy and science fiction;
3d ser.
Time is the traitor
Best science-fiction stories: 1954
The **bet** Chekhov, A. P.
Bet the wild queen! Fox, N. A.
Betelgeuse Bridge. Klass, P.
Bethmoora. Dunsany, E. J. M. D. P. 18th
baron
The **betrayers.** Ellin, S.
BETROTHALS
Beer, T. Tact
Hatvany, L. báró. Bondy, jr.
Maugham, W. S. The escape
Maugham, W. S. Fall of Edward Barnard
Newell, V. S. My Julie
O'Donovan, M. Sorcerer's apprentice
O'Donovan, M. Torrent damned
Zangwill, L. Prelude to a pint of bitter

Better mousetrap. Pratt, F. and De Camp,
L. S.

BETTING. See Gambling; Wagers

Betting Scotchman
Cerf, B A. and Moriarty, H. C. eds.
Anthology of famous British stories

Betts, Doris
Child so fair
Betts, D. Gentle insurrection, and other
stories
End of Henry Fribble
Betts, D. Gentle insurrection, and other
stories
Family album
Betts, D. Gentle insurrection, and other
stories
Gentle insurrection
Betts, D. Gentle insurrection, and other
stories
Mark of distinction
Betts, D. Gentle insurrection, and other
stories
Miss Parker possessed
Betts, D. Gentle insurrection, and other
stories
Mr Shawn and Father Scott
Betts, D. Gentle insurrection, and other
stories
Sense of humor
Betts, D. Gentle insurrection, and other
stories
Serpents and doves
Betts, D. Gentle insurrection, and other
stories
The sword
Betts, D. Gentle insurrection, and other
stories
Sympathetic visitor
Betts, D. Gentle insurrection, and other
stories
Very old are beautiful
Betts, D. Gentle insurrection, and other
stories

Bettyann. Neville, K.
Between rounds. Porter, W. S.
Between the acts. Woolf, V. S.
Between the porch and the altar. Stafford, J.
Between you and I. Ullman, J. R.
Bewilderment of Snake McKoy. Spain, N.
Bexar scrip no. 2692. Porter, W. S.
Beyle, Marie Henri, 1783-1842
Mina de Vanghel
Geist, S. ed. French stories and tales
Vanina Vanini
Dupee, F. W. ed. Great French short
novels
Beyond. Faulkner, W.
Beyond Bedlam. Guin, W.
Beyond infinity. Carr, R. S.
Beyond price. Cave, H. B.
Beyond the Black River. Howard, R. E.
Beyond the frontier. Johnson, D. M.
Beyond the glass mountain. Stegner, W. E.
Beyond the grave. Frank, H.
Beyond the Singing Flame. Smith, C. A.
Bezique of death. Johns, V. P.
Bialik, Chaim Nachman. See Bialik, Hayyim
Nahman
Bialik, Elisa
Horse called Pete
Dennis, W. ed. Palomino and other
horses
Bialik, Hayyim Nahman, 1873-1934
King David's cave
Leftwich, J. ed. Yisröel. 1952 ed.
Short Friday
Ausubel, N. ed. Treasury of Jewish
humor

Bianca's hands. Waldo, E. H.

Bianco, Margery (Williams) 1880-1944
Baker's daughter
Fenner, P. R. comp. Fools and funny
fellows
See also Bowman, J. C. jt. auth.

BIBLE IN LITERATURE
Selden, R. ed. Ways of God and man;
24 stories

BIBLICAL CHARACTERS
Frischman, D. Sinai

BIBLICAL STORIES
Hazaz, C. Bridegroom of blood

Bid the tapers twinkle. Aldrich, B. S.

Bierce, Ambrose, 1842-1914?
Boarded window
Burrell, J. A. and Cerf, B. A. eds. An-
thology of famous American stories
Damned thing
Kuebler, H. W. ed. Treasury of sci-
ence fiction classics
Moonlit road
Conklin, G. and Conklin, L. T. eds.
Supernatural reader
Moxon's master
Conklin, G. ed. Science-fiction thinking
machines
Occurrence at Owl Creek bridge
Burrell, J. A. and Cerf, B. A. eds.
Anthology of famous American stories

Bierce, Ambrose—Occurrence at Owl Creek
  bridge—*Continued*
    Day, A. G. ed. Greatest American short
    stories
    One of the missing
      Blodgett, H. W. ed. Story survey. 1953
      ed.
Big bed. Monchek, B.
Big black and white game. Bradbury, R.
Big blonde. Parker, D. R.
Big Bones rides alone. Cheley, F. R.
Big Boy Blues. Runyon, D.
Big Buck. Caldwell, E.
Big career. Schlichter, E. W.
Big Chlorinda, happy Chlorinda. Lowrey,
  P. H.
Big crop of millet. Caldwell, E.
Big Dan Reilly. O'Higgins, H. J.
Big day. Bonner, P. H.
Big Doc's girl. Medearis, M.
Big Ed. Spilo, R.
Big engine. Hayes, W. E.
Big enough for a horse. Van Doren, M.
Big grey picnic. Muheim, H.
Big heart. Vogau, B. A.
Big holiday. Leiber, F.
Big hunger. Miller, W. M.
Big Jack Small. Gally, J. W.
Big Jeff. Farrell, J. T.
Big meeting. Hughes, L.
Big mistake. Caldwell, E.
Big money. Arthur, R.
Big red house on Hope Street. Connolly,
  M.
Big shot. Acheson, E. G.
Big shot. Chute, B. J.
Big shot. Dresser, D.
Big shoulders. Runyon, D.
The big splash. Miers, E. S.
Big succeh. Reisin, A.
Big train. Foote, J. T.
Big trip up yonder. Vonnegut, K.
Big umbrella. Runyon, D.
BIGAMY
  Maugham, W. S. Round dozen
Bigger they come! Buckingham, N.
Biggest doll in the house. Modell, M.
Biggest flounder. Rendina, L. J. C.
Bigland, Eileen
  Lass with the delicate air
    Asquith, Lady C. M. E. C. ed. Book
    of modern ghosts
BILLIARDS
  Munro, H. H. Fate
Billie's fire. Prentice, H.
BILLS, LEGISLATIVE. See Legislation
Bill's eyes. Campbell, W. E. M.
Billy and the gargoyles. Auchincloss, L.
Billy Budd, foretopman. Melville, H.
Billy had a system. Holland, M.
Billy the Bastard. Newhouse, E.

Binder, Eando
  Conquest of life
    Margulies, L. and Friend, O. J. eds.
    From off this world
  I, robot
    Moskowitz, S. comp. Editor's choice
    in science fiction
Bingo. Seton, E. T.
Bini and Bettine. Kneale, N.
BIOGRAPHERS
  Tarkington, B. Walterson
    See also Authors
Biography project. Dell, D.
Biological experiment. Keller, K. H.
BIOLOGISTS
  Steinbeck, J. Snake of one's own
Bird, Will Richard, 1891-
  Movies come to Gull Point
    Pacey, D. ed. Book of Canadian stories
BIRD DEALERS. See Birds
BIRD HUNTERS
  Jewett, S. O. White heron
Bird life. Willingham, C.
Bird of Bagdad. Porter, W. S.
Bird of omen. Marshall, E.
Bird of Paradise. Marshall, E.
Bird of prey. Collier, J.
Bird song. Goss, J. M.
Birdie, come back. Van Doren, M.
BIRDS
  Burroughs, J. Sharp eyes
  De Vries, P. We don't know
  Du Maurier, D. The birds
  Kulbak, M. Munie the bird dealer
  Maugham, W. S. Princess September
  Squires, R. Baby bunting
    See also names of particular birds:
    Eagles; Parrots; etc.
BIRDS, EXTINCT
  Wells, H. G. Æpyornis island
The birds. Du Maurier, D.
The birds. Van Doren, M.
Birds of passage Nexø, M. A.
Birds on the western front. Munro, H. H.
Birmingham, Stephen G. 1929-
  Reappearance
    Story (Periodical) Story; no. 4
Birth. Cronin, A. J.
Birth of a man. Gorky, M.
Birth of a salesman. Wodehouse, P. G.
BIRTH OF CHILDREN. See Childbirth
Birthday of the Infanta. Wilde, O.
BIRTHDAY PARTIES. See Birthdays
BIRTHDAYS
  Clark, W. Van T. Watchful gods
  Cunningham, E. Bar-Nothing's happy
    birthday
  Grimson, M. S. Happy birthday to you
The birthplace. James, H.
Birthright. Kohn, P. A.

Bishop, Leonard, 1922-
Crazy Hymie and the nickel
American vanguard, 1950
Grass, milk, and children
Wolfe, D. M. ed. Which grain will grow
Bishop sends his inhibition. Trollope, A.
BISHOPS
Tolstoĭ, L. N. Graf. Three hermits
BISHOPS, CATHOLIC
Benét, S. V. Bishop's beggar
O'Donovan, M. Vanity
See also Catholic priests
Bishop's beggar. Benét, S. V.
Bishop's fool. Lewis, W.
Bitter dawn. Bonner, P. H.
Bitter farce. Schwartz, D.
Bitter trail. DeRosso, H. A.
Bitter wall. Ferrone, J. R.
Bixby, Jerome, 1923-
Angels in the jets
Pohl, F. ed. Assignment in tomorrow
It's a good life
Star science fiction stories, no. 2
Page and player
Norton, A. M. ed. Space pioneers
Bjørnson, Bjørnstjerne, 1832-1910
The brothers
Stauffer, R. M.; Cunningham, W. H.
and Sullivan, C. J. eds. Adventures
in modern literature
How the mountain was clad
Andrews, R. C. ed. My favorite stories
of the great outdoors
Black ball. De Camp, L. S. and Pratt, F.
Black ball. Pratt, F. and De Camp, L. S.
Black Bat. Miers, E. S.
Black bile. Rossiter, H. D.
Black brassard. Sheppard, J.
Black bread. Verga, G.
Black cabinet. Carr, J. D.
Black cat. Poe, E. A.
Black devil, mainly. Paterson, N.
Black Eyes and the daily grind. Lesser, M.
Black Falcon. Sperry, A.
Black flag. Powell, F.
Black god's kiss. Moore, C. L.
Black god's shadow. Moore, C. L.
Black horse. Kjelgaard, J. A.
Black John buys a York boat. Hendryx,
J. B.
Black John chats with Corporal Downey.
Hendryx, J. B.
Black John delivers a deed. Hendryx, J. B.
Black John departs for Dawson. Hendryx,
J. B.
Black John does some checking. Hendryx,
J. B.
Black John gets a tip. Hendryx, J. B.
Black John goes to Dawson. Hendryx, J. B.
Black John goes to Fortymile. Hendryx,
J. B.
Black John holds a conference. Hendryx,
J. B.

Black John makes a purchase. Hendryx,
J. B.
Black John sells his York boat. Hendryx,
J. B.
Black John talks with the goose. Hendryx,
J. B.
Black John wins a bet. Hendryx, J. B.
Black Lamars. Mowery, W. B.
Black ledger. Queen, E. pseud.
Black lie. Sandy, S.
Black magician. Coolidge, O. E.
BLACK MARKETS
Housesold, G. Brandy for the parson
Putnam, C. Old acrobat and the ruined
city
BLACK MASS
Irwin, M. E. F. Earlier service
Black music. Faulkner, W.
Black pits of Luna. Heinlein, R. A.
Black prince. Grau, S. A.
Black road. Steele, W. D.
Black seal. Machen, A.
Black star passes. Campbell, J. W.
Black Storm. Hinkle, T. C.
Black Swamp. Roberts, Sir C. G. D.
Black thirst. Moore, C. L.
Black water blues. Culver, M.
Blackbeard. Malcolmson, A. B.
Blackberry winter. Warren, R. P.
Blackburn, Ernest Richard, 1926-
Before the burning of Rome
Blackburn, E. R. The swaying elms, and
other stories
Christiane the Huguenot
Blackburn, E. R. The swaying elms, and
other stories
Galatians 2:20
Blackburn, E. R. The swaying elms, and
other stories
Good win
Blackburn, E. R. The swaying elms, and
other stories
Jerome of Prague
Blackburn, E. R. The swaying elms, and
other stories
Last king
Blackburn, E. R. The swaying elms, and
other stories
Missed train
Blackburn, E. R. The swaying elms, and
other stories
Mission door
Blackburn, E. R. The swaying elms, and
other stories
Story of Pompeii
Blackburn, E. R. The swaying elms, and
other stories
Sunrise
Blackburn, E. R. The swaying elms, and
other stories
Swaying elms
Blackburn, E. R. The swaying elms, and
other stories
Walk for me
Blackburn, E. R. The swaying elms, and
other stories

Blackburn, Robert Harold, 1919-
Clay dish
Weaver, R. and James, H. eds. Canadian short stories
The **blackguard.** McCarthy, M. T.
Blackjack bargainer. Porter, W. S.
BLACKMAIL
Arlen, M. Cavalier of the streets
Brandon, W. Party to blackmail
Collins, W. Stolen letter
Doyle, Sir A. C. Scandal in Bohemia
Elston, A. V. Blackmail
Munro, H. H. Treasure-ship
Porter, W. S. Remnants of the code
Queen, E. pseud. Money talks
Queen, E. pseud. Sound of blackmail
Blackmail. Elston, A. V.
Blackout over Cleveland. Litten, F. N.
BLACKSMITHS
Cunningham, J. M. Iron rose
Blackwood, Algernon, 1869-1951
Psychical invasion
Carrington, H. ed. Week-end book of ghost stories
Roman remains
Derleth, A. W. ed. Night's yawning peal
Valley of the beasts
Cerf, B. A. and Moriarty, H. C. eds. Anthology of famous British stories
The Wendigo
Davenport, B. ed. Ghostly tales to be told
Bland, Edith (Nesbit) 1858-1924
Digging for treasure
Fenner, P. R. comp. Fun! Fun! Fun!
The pavilion
Conklin, G. and Conklin, L. T. eds. Supernatural reader
The **blanket.** Brooke, J.
The **blanket.** Dell, F.
Blast of the book. Chesterton, G. K.
Bleeding heart. Stafford, J.
Blessed are the clean of heart; they shall see God. Baker, F.
Blessed are the merciful; they shall obtain mercy. Baker, F.
Blessed are the patient; they shall inherit the land. Baker, F.
Blessed are the peace-makers; they shall be counted the children of God. Baker, F.
Blessed are the poor in spirit; the kingdom of heaven is theirs. Baker, F.
Blessed are those who hunger and thirst for holiness; they shall have their fill. Baker, F.
Blessed are those who mourn; they shall be comforted. Baker, F.
Blessed are those who suffer persecution in the cause of right; the kingdom of heaven is theirs. Baker, F.
Blessed event. Sellars, M.
The **blight.** Cox, A. J.
BLIND
Baum, V. Old house
Campbell, W. E. M. Bill's eyes
Corkery, D. Storm struck
Edmonds, W. D. Blind Eve
Kipling, R. 'They'
Lawrence, D. H. Blind man
Schisgall, O. Eyes in the dark
Schnitzler, A. Blind Geronimo and his brother
Taylor, E. Spry old character
Wells, H. G. Country of the blind
Zweig, S. Invisible collection
Zweig, S. Unseen collection
Blind alley. Jameson, M.
Blind Eve. Edmonds, W. D.
Blind Geronimo and his brother. Schnitzler, A.
Blind man. Lawrence, D. H.
Blind man, the deaf man, and the donkey. Frere, M. E. I.
Blind man's buff. Jameson, M.
Blind man's holiday. Porter, W. S.
Blind spot. Munro, H. H.
Blinding of André Maloche. Mowat, F.
Blinding shadows. Wandrei, D.
Blindman's world. Bellamy, E.
BLINDNESS. See Blind
Blish, James
Beanstalk
Crossen, K. F. ed. Future tense
Beep
Sloane, W. M. ed. Stories for tomorrow
The box
Conklin, G. ed. Omnibus of science fiction
FYI
Star science fiction stories, no. 2
Mistake inside
Pratt, F. ed. World of wonder
Okie
Sloane, W. M. ed. Stories for tomorrow
Solar plexus
Merril, J. ed. Beyond human ken
Surface tension
Galaxy science fiction magazine. Second Galaxy reader of science fiction
Year's best science fiction novels, 1953
Bliss. Mansfield, K.
Blister. Foote, J. T.
Blixen, Karen, 1885-
The pearls
Burnett, W. ed. World's best
Bloch, Alan
Men are different
Conklin, G. ed. Science-fiction thinking machines
Bloch, Jean Richard, 1884-1947
Heresy of the water taps
Ausubel, N. ed. Treasury of Jewish humor
Leftwich, J. ed. Yisröel. 1952 ed.
Bloch, Robert, 1914-
Fear planet
Derleth, A. W. ed. Far boundaries
Man who collected Poe
Derleth, A. W. ed. Night's yawning peal
Blochman, Lawrence Goldtree, 1900-
Brood of evil
Best detective stories of the year— 1950
Blochman, L. G. Diagnosis: homicide

Blochman, Lawrence G.—*Continued*
But the patient died
  Blochman, L. G. Diagnosis: homicide
Calendar girl
  Best detective stories of the year—1953
Catfish story
  Blochman, L. G. Diagnosis: homicide
Deadly back-fire
  Blochman, L. G. Diagnosis: homicide
Diagnosis deferred
  Blochman, L. G. Diagnosis: homicide
Fifty-carat jinx
  Mystery Writers of America, inc. Maiden murders
Half-naked truth
  Blochman, L. G. Diagnosis: homicide
Jimat of Dorland
  Mystery Writers of America, inc. Crooks' tour
Kiss of Kandahar
  Best detective stories of the year—1952
Phantom cry-baby
  Blochman, L. G. Diagnosis: homicide
Riviera renegade
  Mystery Writers of America, inc. 20 great tales of murder
Rum for dinner
  Blochman, L. G. Diagnosis: homicide
Zarapore beat
  Mystery Writers of America, inc. Four-&-twenty bloodhounds

Block, Rudolph Edgar, 1870-1940
Americanization of Shadrach Cohen
  Ribalow, H. U. ed. These your children

Blockade runner. Jameson, M.

Blond dog. Stoumen, L. C.

Blond mink. Runyon, D.

Blonde nurse. Walsh, T.

Blood-feud of Toad-Water. Munro, H. H.

Blood is a bright shadow. Moseley, H.

Blood of the martyrs. Benét, S. V.

Blood on the ice. Kjelgaard, J. A.

Blood will tell. Marquis, D.

Bloodhound. Boyd, J.

BLOODHOUNDS
Boyd, J. Bloodhound

Bloodstained beach. Marmur, J.

Bloodstock. Irwin, M. E. F.

Bloomfield, Howard, 1900-
Murder tavern
  Argosy (Periodical) Argosy Book of adventure stories
Pirate and the gamecock
  Argosy (Periodical) Argosy Book of sea stories
The trap
  Cuff, R. P. ed. American short story survey

Bloomgarden, Solomon, 1870-
Share of paradise
  Ausubel, N. ed. Treasury of Jewish humor
Zoology
  Ausubel, N. ed. Treasury of Jewish humor

Blossom on the yew. Dawkins, M. L.

"**Blow** up with the brig!" Collins, W.

Blowing up a train. Lawrence, T. E.

Blowups happen. Heinlein, R. A.

Blue, Edna, 1901-
Nothing overwhelms Giuseppe
  Bachelor, J. M.; Henry, R. L. and Salisbury, R. eds. Current thinking and writing; 2d ser.

Blue Boy. Caldwell, E.

Blue brocade. Hill, M. Y.

Blue carbuncle. Doyle, Sir A. C.

Blue charm. Bonner, P. H.

Blue cross. Chesterton, G. K.

Blue flag. Hill, K.

Blue giraffe. De Camp, L. S.

Blue hat. Elliott, H. S.

Blue Hotel. Crane, S.

Blue hyacinths. Powell, D.

BLUE JAYS
Clemens, S. L. Jim Baker's blue-jay yarn

Blue murder. Steele, W. D.

Blue ribbon. Woolrich, C.

Blue ribbon event. Carter, R. G.

Blue sash. Beck, W.

Blue-winged teal. Stegner, W. E.

Bluff. Adler, J.

Boa constrictor and rabbit. Chekhov, A. P.

Boar-pig. Munro, H. H.

Board of Inland Revenue v. Haddock. Herbert, Sir A. P.

Boarded window. Bierce, A.

BOARDERS. See Boarding houses

BOARDING HOUSES
Barker, A. L. Pringle
Carroll, J. W. At Mrs Farrelly's
Chekhov, A. P. The lodger
De La Roche, M. Widow Cruse
Jackson, C. R. Sleeper awakened
Leiper, G. B. The magnolias
Porter, W. S. Aristocracy versus hash
Porter, W. S. Between rounds
Porter, W. S. Furnished room
Porter, W. S. Skylight room
Porter, W. S. Third ingredient
  See also Hotels, taverns, etc.

BOARDING SCHOOLS. See School life

BOARS
Annixter, P. pseud. Brought to cover

Boat journey. Shackleton, Sir E. H.

BOAT RACES
Coombs, C. I. River challenge
  See also Rowing; Yacht racing

The **boats.** Crawford, C.

BOATS AND BOATING
Clark, W. Van T. The rapids
Loring, S. M. Eel-trap
Michel, E. Moon tide
  See also House boats; Motorboats; River boats; Submarine boats

BOAZ
Fineman, I. In the fields of Boaz

BOB SLEDS. See Tobogganing

Bobo and the Christmas spirit. Price, E. B.

Boccaccio, Giovanni, 1313-1375
  Patient Griselda
    Cody, S. ed. Greatest stories, and how
    they were written
Body of an American. Dos Passos, J. R.
Body-snatcher. Stevenson, R. L.
BODY-SNATCHING
  Harvey, W. F. No body
BODY WEIGHT CONTROL. See Corpulence
BOERS. See Africa, South
BOHEMIAN LIFE. See Artist life
BOHEMIANS IN THE UNITED STATES. See Czechoslovakians in the United States
Boiler room. Sansom, W.
Bojer, Johan, 1872-
  A letter to Klaus Brock
    Brentano, F. ed. The word lives on
BOLSHEVISM. See Communism—Russia
Bolt from the blue. Broun, H. C.
Bolté, Mary, 1921-
  End of the depression
    Best American short stories, 1951
    Greene, J. I. and Abell, E. eds. Stories of sudden truth
Bolton, Isabel, pseud. See Miller, Mary Britton
Bolton, Ivy May, 1879-
  Saint for Wessex
    Hazeltine, A. I. comp. Selected stories for teen-agers
The **bombardier.** Gallico, P. W.
BOMBARDMENT
  Macfarlan, A. A. Camp at Saint Adrien
Bombers' night. Fabyan, E.
BOMBS. See Projectiles
The **bombshop.** O'Faoláin, S.
Bon-Bon. Poe, E. A.
Bond, Nelson Slade, 1908-
  Abduction of Abner Greer
    Brown, F. and Reynolds, M. eds. Science-fiction carnival
  And lo! The bird
    Derleth, A. W. ed. Far boundaries
  Conquerors' isle
    Pratt, F. ed. World of wonder
  Day we celebrate
    Conklin, G. ed. Possible worlds of science fiction
  The sportsman
    Creamer, J. B. comp. Twenty-two stories about horses and men
  Steady like a rock
    Dachs, D. ed. Treasury of sports humor
  This is the land
    Derleth, A. W. ed. The outer reaches
  To people a new world
    Derleth, A. W. ed. Beachheads in space
Bond. Karchmer, S.
Bondarenko, William Carl, 1921-
  Job well done
    American vanguard, 1953
Bondy, jr. Hatvany, L. báró
Bones for Davy Jones. Commings, J.

Bones of A. T. Stewart. Benson, T.
The **bonesetter.** Walsh, M.
Bonham, Frank
  Burn him out
    Argosy (Periodical) Book of adventure stories
  I'll take the high road
    Western Writers of America. Holsters and heroes
  One ride too many
    Western Writers of America. Bad men and good
Bonham, Margaret
  Fine place for the cat
    Joseph, M. ed. Best cat stories
Bonnaffon, Anne
  Quick shoots
    Wolfe, D. M. ed. Which grain will grow
Bonner, Nicholas
  Mr Mitts
    Thinker's digest (Periodical) Spoiled priest, and other stories
Bonner, Paul Hyde, 1893-
  Big day
    Bonner, P. H. Glorious mornings
  Bitter dawn
    Bonner, P. H. Glorious mornings
  Blue charm
    Bonner, P. H. Glorious mornings
  Caddis hatch
    Bonner, P. H. Glorious mornings
  Foul is fair
    Bonner, P. H. Glorious mornings
  Made to measure
    Bonner, P. H. Glorious mornings
  Mollie
    Bonner, P. H. Glorious mornings
  Pump house key
    Bonner, P. H. Glorious mornings
  Rajah's Rock
    Bonner, P. H. Glorious mornings
  Stalker & Co.
    Bonner, P. H. Glorious mornings
  The triumph
    Bonner, P. H. Glorious mornings
  Velia
    Bonner, P. H. Glorious mornings
Bontemps. Whitmore, S.
Bontsha the Silent. Peretz, I. L.
The **book.** Irwin, M. E. F.
Book-bag. Maugham, W. S.
BOOK SALESMEN. See Booksellers and bookselling
Booker, Adria E.
  Box-car to castle
    Booker, A. E. Was it too late? & other stories
  Rancher of the hills
    Booker, A. E. Was it too late? & other stories
  Second Christmas
    Booker, A. E. Was it too late? & other stories
  That others might live
    Booker, A. E. Was it too late? & other stories
  Was it too late?
    Booker, A. E. Was it too late? & other stories

Booker, Simeon
She never knew
Ford, N. A. and Faggett, H. L. eds.
Best short stories by Afro-American
writers (1925-1950)

BOOKKEEPERS. See Accountants

BOOKS
Milne, A. A. Rise and fall of Mortimer
Scrivens
Porter, W. S. Best-seller
Tunkel, J. The gift
Yates, E. Enshrined in the heart

BOOKS AND READING
Hall, E. G. Callie of Crooked Creek
P'u Sung-ling. The bookworm

BOOKSELLERS AND BOOKSELLING
Abramowitz, S. J. The exchange
Lagerkvist, P. F. God's little traveling
salesman
Munro, H. H. Mark

BOOKSHOPS. See Booksellers and bookselling

The **bookworm.** P'u Sung-ling

Boomerang. Russell, E. F.

BOONE, DANIEL, 1734-1820
Fast, H. M. Tall hunter

BOOTBLACKS
Brookhouser, F. You aim so high

BOOTH, JOHN WILKES, 1838-1865
Carr, J. D. Black cabinet

Booth, Maud Ballington (Charlesworth)
1865-1948
Christ's tree
Elmquist, R. M. ed. Fifty years to
Christmas

BOOTLEGGING. See Liquor traffic

BOOTS AND SHOES
Porter, W. S. Ships
Porter, W. S. Shoes
See also Shoemakers

Boots, who made the Princess say, "That's
a story." Dasent, Sir G. W.

Borden, Mary, 1886-
In Nazareth
Selden, R. ed. Ways of God and men

BORES (PERSONS)
Cotterell, G. Delicate warning
Munro, H. H. Defensive diamond

BORES (TIDAL PHENOMENA) See
Tidal waves

Borges, Jorge Luis, 1900-
Secret miracle
De Onís, H. ed. Spanish stories and
tales

Born killer. Davis, D. S.

Born of man and woman. Matheson, R.

BORNEO. See Dutch East Indies—Borneo

BORROWING
Jackson, C. R. Money
Maugham, W. S. Ant and the grass-
hopper

Boscombe Valley mystery. Doyle, Sir A. C.

Bosher, E. F.
Too much Hugo
Furman, A. L. ed. Teen-age dog stories

Bosis, Lauro de, 1901-1931?
Story of my death
Jensen, P. ed. Fireside book of flying
stories

BOSTON. See Massachusetts—Boston

Bottle imp. Stevenson, R. L.

Bottle of Perrier. Wharton, E. N. J.

Bottle party. Collier, J.

Bottom of the cloud. Barr, J. pseud.

Bottome, Phyllis, 1884-
Caesar's wife's ear
Bottome, P. Man and beast
Dark Blue
Bottome, P. Man and beast
Henry
Bottome, P. Man and beast
Liqueur glass
Bond, R. T. ed. Handbook for poisoners
A pair
Bottome, P. Man and beast
Pink medicine
Bottome, P. Man and beast
Splendid fellow
Talbot, D. ed. Treasury of mountaineer-
ing stories

Botts and the brink of disaster. Upson,
W. H.

Botts and the jet-propelled tractor. Upson,
W. H.

Botts bogs down. Upson, W. H.

Botts cleans out the parts department. Upson,
W. H.

Botts discovers uranium. Upson, W. H.

Botts gets a new job. Upson, W. H.

Botts makes magic. Upson, W. H.

Boucher, Anthony, pseud. See White, William Anthony Parker

Bound for the bottom. Wallace, J. F.

Bow down, Isaac! Aiken, C. P.

Bowen, Elizabeth, 1899-
All saints
Bowen, E. Early stories
Ann Lee's
Bowen, E. Early stories
Back drawing-room
Bowen, E. Early stories
Breakfast
Bowen, E. Early stories
Cat jumps
Ludwig, J. B. and Poirier, W. R. eds.
Stories, British and American
Charity
Bowen, E. Early stories
Cherry soul
Magazine of fantasy and science fiction.
Best from Fantasy and science fiction;
2d ser.
Coming home
Bowen, E. Early stories
The confidante
Bowen, E. Early stories
The contessina
Bowen, E. Early stories
Daffodils
Bowen, E. Early stories

Bowen, Elizabeth—*Continued*
Demon lover
Gordon, C. and Tate, A. eds. House of
fiction
Lynskey, W. C. ed. Reading modern
fiction
Easter **egg** party
Burnett, W. ed. World's best
Evil that men do—
Bowen, E. Early stories
Hand in glove
Asquith, Lady C. M. E. C. ed. Book of
modern ghosts
Her table spread
O'Faoláin, S. The short story
Human habitation
Bowen, E. Early stories
The lover
Bowen, E. Early stories
Lunch
Bowen, E. Early stories
Making arrangements
Bowen, E. Early stories
Mrs Windermere
Bowen, E. Early stories
Mysterious Kôr
New writing (Periodical) Best stories
New house
Bowen, E. Early stories
The parrot
Bowen, E. Early stories
Recent photograph
Bowen, E. Early stories
Requiescat
Bowen, E. Early stories
The return
Bowen, E. Early stories
The secession
Bowen, E. Early stories
Shadowy third
Bowen, E. Early stories
The storm
Bowen, E. Early stories
Sunday evening
Bowen, E. Early stories
The visitor
Bowen, E. Early stories
Bowen, Robert Owen, 1920-
Other river
Best American short stories, 1952
Bower of roses. Forester, C. S.
Bowes-Lyon, Susannah Sarah, 1920-
Harum Scarum; the life story of a horse
Dennis, W. ed. Palomino and other
horses
The **bowl.** De La Mare, W. J.
The **bowl.** Fitzgerald, F. S. K.
Bowles, Paul Frederic, 1911-
At Paso Rojo
Bowles, P. F. Delicate prey, and other
stories
By the water
Bowles, P. F. Delicate prey, and other
stories
Lynskey W. C. ed. Reading modern
fiction
Call at Corazón
Bowles, P. F. Delicate prey, and other
stories

Circular valley
Bowles, P. F. Delicate prey, and other
stories
Delicate prey
Bowles, P. F. Delicate prey, and other
stories
Distant episode
Bowles, P. F. Delicate prey, and other
stories
The echo
Bowles, P. F. Delicate prey, and other
stories
Fourth day out from Santa Cruz
Bowles, P. F. Delicate prey, and other
stories
How many midnights
Bowles, P. F. Delicate prey, and other
stories
Pages from Cold Point
Bowles, P. F. Delicate prey, and other
stories
Cory D. W. pseud. comp. 21 variations
on a theme
Pastor Dowe at Tacaté
Best American short stories, 1950
Bowles, P. F. Delicate prey, and other
stories
The scorpion
Bowles, P. F. Delicate prey, and other
stories
Señor Ong and Señor Ha
Bowles, P. F. Delicate prey, and other
stories
Tea on the mountain
Bowles, P. F. Delicate prey, and other
stories
Thousand days for Mokhtar
Bowles, P. F. Delicate prey, and other
stories
Under the sky
Bowles, P. F. Delicate prey, and other
stories
Ludwig, J. B. and Poirier, W. R. eds.
Stories, British and American
You are not I
Bowles, P. F. Delicate prey, and other
stories
Bowman, James Cloyd, 1880-
First war party
Fenner, P. R. comp. Indians, Indians,
Indians
**Bowman, James Cloyd, 1880- and Bianco,
Margery (Williams) 1880-1944**
Wise men of Holmola
Fenner, P. R. comp. Fools and funny
fellows
The **box.** Blish, J.
Box-car to castle. Booker, A. E.
Box of ginger. Calisher, H.
Box score battle. Worthington, J.
Boxer, Jack, 1909-
Anna was bad
Wolfe, D. M. ed. Which grain will grow
Boxer: old. Sylvester, H.
BOXERS. See Boxing
BOXING
Dachs, D. Speaking of characters
Fay, W. Lady says murder
Fay, W. Murder the bum
Gallico, P. W. Melee of the Mages

BOXING—*Continued*
Griffith, R. Jingle bells
Hemingway, E. Fifty grand
Johnston, N. F. Absolution
Lanham, E. M. Listen to me, boy
Lardner, J. Sudden attack of heartbreak
London, J. Piece of steak
Maxwell, J. A. Fighter
Merson, B. Cross-up
Parker, D. F. Passing of the first floor
    back
Philips, J. P. Man who had no friends
Porter, W. S. Hygeia at the Solito
Queen, E. pseud. Matter of seconds
Ribalow, H. U. ed. World's greatest box-
    ing stories; 18 stories
Runyon, D. Leopard's spots
Schulberg, B. W. Crowd pleaser
Schulberg, B. W. Meal ticket
Schulberg, B. W. Memory in white
Schulberg, B. W. Pride of Tony Colucci
Switzer, R. Death of a prize fighter
    See also Fighting, Hand-to-hand

Boy and a dog. Singmaster, E.

Boy bites man. Shulman, M.

Boy crazy. De Meyer, J.

Boy in the house. De La Roche, M.

Boy in the mirror. Summers, J. L.

Boy in the summer sun. Schorer, M.

BOY SCOUTS
Long, E. W. Green match
Macfarlan, A. A. Camp at Saint Adrien
Strong, P. N. Shantyboat pirate
Strong, P. N. Trail of the whiffle-poof

Boy who drew cats. Hearn, L.

Boy who gave his dog away. Rawlings, C. A.

Boy who ran away. Jackson, C. R.

Boy who went away. Moll, E.

Boy who wrote 'no.' Lord, J.

Boy with a trumpet. Davies, R.

Boy with the innocent eyes. Kandel, L.

BOYCOTTS
Bergelson, D. In a backwoods town

Boyd, James, 1888-1944
Away! Away!
    Boyd, J. Old pines, and other stories
Bloodhound
    Boyd, J. Old pines, and other stories
Civic crisis
    Boyd, J. Old pines, and other stories
Elms and Fair Oaks
    Boyd, J. Old pines, and other stories
    Jones, K. M. ed. New Confederate short
        stories
Fiesta
    Boyd, J. Old pines, and other stories
Flat town
    Boyd, J. Old pines, and other stories
Gizzard of a scientist
    Boyd, J. Old pines, and other stories
Lookout
    Bachelor, J. M.; Henry, R. L. and
        Salisbury, R. eds. Current thinking
        and writing; 2d ser.
Old pines
    Boyd, J. Old pines, and other stories

Shiftless
    Boyd, J. Old pines, and other stories
Verse on the window
    Boyd, J. Old pines, and other stories

Boyd, Thomas Alexander, 1898-1935
Responsibility
    Shaw, H. and Bement, D. Reading the
        short story

Boyle, Kay, 1903-
Adam's death
    Boyle, K. Smoking mountain
Art colony
    Millett, F. B. Reading fiction
Aufwiedersehen abend
    Boyle, K. Smoking mountain
Begin again
    Boyle, K. Smoking mountain
Bridegroom's body
    Southern review. Anthology of stories
        from the Southern review
Cabaret
    Boyle, K. Smoking mountain
Crazy hunter
    Ludwig, R. M. and Perry, M. B. eds.
        Nine short novels
The criminal
    Boyle, K. Smoking mountain
Defeat
    First-prize stories, 1919-1954
Diagnosis of a selfish lady
    Saturday evening post (Periodical) Sat-
        urday evening post stories, 1952
Disgrace to the family
    Saturday evening post (Periodical) Sat-
        urday evening post stories, 1950
Effigy of war
    Heilman, R. B. ed. Modern short stories
Fife's house
    Boyle, K. Smoking mountain
Frankfurt in our blood
    Boyle, K. Smoking mountain
His idea of a mother
    West, R. B. and Stallman, R. W. eds.
        Art of modern fiction
Home
    Boyle, K. Smoking mountain
Keep your pity
    Barrows, H. ed. 15 stories
The lost
    Best American short stories, 1952
    Boyle, K. Smoking mountain
Lovers of gain
    Bachelor, J. M.; Henry, R. L. and Salis-
        bury, R. eds. Current thinking and
        writing; 2d ser.
    Boyle, K. Smoking mountain
Maiden, maiden
    Talbot, D. ed. Treasury of mountaineer-
        ing stories
Natives don't cry
    Felheim, M.; Newman, F. B. and Stein-
        hoff, W. R. eds. Modern short stories
Nothing ever breaks except the heart
    Best of the Best American short stories,
        1915-1950
Soldier ran away
    Saturday evening post (Periodical) Sat-
        urday evening post stories, 1953
Summer evening
    Boyle, K. Smoking mountain
    Prize stories of 1950

Boyle, Kay—*Continued*
They weren't going to die
Lynskey, W. C. ed. Reading modern fiction
Wanderer
Swallow, A. ed. Anchor in the sea
White horses of Vienna
First-prize stories, 1919-1954

Boylston, Helen (Dore) 1895-
Stuff of dreams
Eaton, H. T. ed. Short stories

BOYS
Adler, J. My Pinya
Aiken, C. P. Silent snow, secret snow
Aiken, C. P. Strange moonlight
Allen, M. P. Yoo hoo! Mudhen!
Bennett, P. Death under the hawthornes
Bennett, P. Fugitive from the mind
Boyle, K. His idea of a mother
Casper, L. Sense of direction
Chekhov, A. P. Vanka
Clark, W. Van T. Watchful gods
Clayton, J. B. White circle
Crane, S. The fight
Crane, S. His new mittens
Cuevas, E. Lock the doors, lock the windows
Davis, R. H. Tree toad
De La Roche, M. Boy in the house
Dostoevskiĭ, F. M. Heavenly Christmas tree
Doty, W. L. Silver cross
Eisenberg, F. Roof sitter
Ewald, C. My little boy
Fitzgerald, F. S. K. Captured shadow
Fitzgerald, F. S. K. Freshest boy
Fitzgerald, F. S. K. Scandal detectives
Goldman, A. Almost like dead
Goodman, J. C. Kingdom of Gordon
Granberry, E. P. Trip to Czardis
Grau, S. A. Joshua
Greene, G. Basement room
Harte, B. How Santa Claus came to Simpson's Bar
Heyert, M. New kid
Johnson, D. M. Prairie kid
Kipling, R. Tods' amendment
Krige, U. The dream
Lagerkvist, P. F. Guest of reality
McCourt, E. A. White mustang
Mann, T. Fight between Jappe and Do Escobar
Miller, C. Gentle season
Modell, J. Day in the sun
Monchek, B. Big bed
Nadir, I. M. My first love
Nuhn, F. Ten
O'Donovan, M. Face of evil
O'Donovan, M. Man of the house
O'Donovan, M. Masculine protest
Paterson, R. Slowpoke
Porter, K. A. Downward path to wisdom
Porter, W. S. Ransom of Red Chief
Rossiter, H. D. How dear to my heart
Salinger, J. D. Down at the dinghy
Sansom, W. From the water junction
Saroyan, W. Parsley garden
Saroyan, W. Pheasant hunter
Saroyan, W. The plot
Saroyan, W. Resurrection of a life
Schweitzer, G. Kid brother

Seide, M. Bad boy from Brooklyn
Stegner, W. E. Butcher bird
Steinbeck, J. Red pony
Street, J. H. Weep no more, My Lady
Tarkington, B. "Little gentleman"
Taylor, P. H. Two ladies in retirement
Ware, L. Phantom of the bridge
Watson, J. C. Benny and the Tar-Baby
Wilbur, R. Game of catch
Wilson, A. Necessity's child
Wolfe, T. Lost boy
See also Adolescence; Children

BOYS' CLUBS
Salinger, J. D. Laughing man

Boy's will. Quentin, P. pseud.

Boys will be boys. Cobb, I. S.

Boz, pseud. See Dickens, Charles

Brace, Gerald Warner, 1901-
Deep water man
Blodgett, H. W. ed. Story survey. 1953 ed.

Brachvogel, Albert Emil, 1824-1878
Christmas at the Bachs'
Lohan, R. and Lohan, M. eds. New Christmas treasury

Brackett, Leigh
Enchantress of Venus
Margulies, L. and Friend, O. J. eds. Giant anthology of science fiction
Last days of Shandakor
Wollheim, D. A. ed. Prize science fiction
Retreat to the stars
Crossen, K. F. ed. Adventures in tomorrow

Bradbury, Ray, 1920-
And the moon be still as bright
Bleiler, E. F. and Dikty, T. E. eds. Science fiction omnibus: The best science fiction stories, 1949, 1950
April witch
Bradbury, R. Golden apples of the sun
Asleep in Armageddon
Conklin, G. ed. Possible worlds of science fiction
Beast from 20,000 fathoms
Saturday evening post (Periodical) Saturday evening post stories, 1951
Big black and white game
Bradbury, R. Golden apples of the sun
The city
Bradbury, R. Illustrated man
Concrete mixer
Bradbury, R. Illustrated man
Dwellers in silence
Best science fiction stories: 1950
Bleiler, E. F. and Dikty, T. E. eds. Science fiction omnibus: The best science fiction stories, 1949, 1950
Embroidery
Bradbury, R. Golden apples of the sun
En la noche
Bradbury, R. Golden apples of the sun
The exiles
Bradbury, R. Illustrated man
Derleth, A. W. ed. Beyond time & space
Fire balloons
Bradbury, R. Illustrated man
Flying machine
Bradbury, R. Golden apples of the sun

Bradbury, Ray—*Continued*
Fog horn
  Bradbury, R. Golden apples of the sun
Forever and the earth
  Conklin, G. ed. Big book of science
    fiction
The fox and the forest
  Bradbury, R. Illustrated man
  Same as: Fox in the forest
Fox in the forest
  Best science fiction stories: 1951
  Same as: The fox and the forest
Fruit at the bottom of the bowl
  Bradbury, R. Golden apples of the sun
Garbage collector
  Bradbury, R. Golden apples of the sun
Golden apples of the sun
  Bradbury, R. Golden apples of the sun
Golden kite, the silver wind
  Bradbury, R. Golden apples of the sun
Great fire
  Bradbury, R. Golden apples of the sun
  Seventeen (Periodical) Nineteen from
    Seventeen
Great wide world over there
  Bradbury, R. Golden apples of the sun
Hail and farewell
  Bradbury, R. Golden apples of the sun
Here there be tygers
  Healy, R. J. ed. New tales of space and
    time
The highway
  Bradbury, R. Illustrated man
Holiday
  Derleth, A. W. ed. Far boundaries
I see you never
  Bradbury, R. Golden apples of the sun
The illustrated man
  Bradbury, R. Illustrated man
In this sign
  Lesser, M. A. ed. Looking forward
Invisible boy
  Bradbury, R. Golden apples of the sun
Kaleidoscope
  Bradbury, R. Illustrated man
  Conklin, G. ed. Omnibus of science
    fiction
King of the gray spaces
  Wollheim, D. A. comp. Every boy's
    book of science-fiction
Last night of the world
  Bradbury, R. Illustrated world
A little journey
  Galaxy science fiction magazine. Ga-
    laxy reader of science fiction
Long rain
  Bradbury, R. Illustrated man
The man
  Best science fiction stories: 1950
  Bleiler, E. F. and Dikty, T. E. eds.
    Science fiction omnibus: The best
    science fiction stories, 1949, 1950
  Bradbury, R. Illustrated man
Marionettes, inc.
  Bradbury, R. Illustrated man
Mars is heaven
  Bleiler, E. F. and Dikty, T. E. eds.
    Science fiction omnibus: The best
    science fiction stories, 1949, 1950
The meadow
  Bradbury, R. Golden apples of the sun

Million-year picnic
  Pratt, F. ed. World of wonder
The murderer
  Bradbury, R. Golden apples of the sun
Naming of names
  Startling stories (Periodical) Best
    from Startling stories
Night meeting
  Conklin, G. ed. Science-fiction adven-
    tures in dimension
No particular night or morning
  Bradbury, R. Illustrated man
The one who waits
  Derleth, A. W. ed. Far boundaries
Other foot
  Best American short stories, 1952
  Bradbury, R. Illustrated man
The pedestrian
  Best science fiction stories: 1952
  Bradbury, R. Golden apples of the sun
Powerhouse
  Bradbury, R. Golden apples of the sun
Referent
  Bleiler, E. F. and Dikty, T. E. eds.
    Imagination unlimited
The rocket
  Bradbury, R. Illustrated man
Rocket man
  Bradbury, R. Illustrated man
Scent of sarsaparilla
  Sloane, W. M. ed. Stories for tomorrow
  Star science fiction stories [no. 1]
Shape of things
  Greenberg, M. ed. Travelers of space
The smile
  Derleth, A. W. ed. Worlds of tomorrow
Sound of thunder
  Bradbury, R. Golden apples of the sun
Strawberry window
  Star science fiction stories, no. 3
Subterfuge
  Pohl, F. ed. Assignment in tomorrow
Sun and shadow
  Bradbury, R. Golden apples of the sun
There will come soft rains
  Crossen, K. F. ed. Adventures in to-
    morrow
Tombling day
  Conklin, G. and Conklin, L. T. eds.
    Supernatural reader
The veldt
  Bradbury, R. Illustrated man
  Merril, J. ed. Beyond the barriers of
    space and time
The visitor
  Bradbury, R. Illustrated man
The wilderness
  Bradbury, R. Golden apples of the sun
  Sloane, W. M. ed. Stories for tomorrow
World the children made
  Saturday evening post (Periodical)
    Saturday evening post stories, 1950
Ylla
  Derleth, A. W. ed. The outer reaches
Zero hour
  Bradbury, R. Illustrated man
Bradford, Roark, 1896-1948
Child of God
  First-prize stories, 1919-1954
Stratagem of Joshua
  Selden, R. ed. Ways of God and men

Bradley, Mary (Hastings)
  Show window
    Stowe, A. comp. It's a date
Brag dog. Bell, V. M.
BRAGGING. See Pride and vanity
BRAHMANS
  Kipling, R. Miracle of Purun Bhagat
Brahmin Beachhead. Hale, N.
BRAHMINS. See Brahmans
BRAIN SURGERY. See Surgery
BRAINS, MECHANICAL. See Automata
Brake happy. Coombs, C. I.
Bramley is so bracing. Wodehouse, P. G.
Brand, Max, pseud.
  Dust storm
    Meredith, S. ed. Bar 2
  The king
    This week magazine. This week's short-
      short stories
  Wine on the desert
    Christ, H. I. and Shostak, J. eds. Short
      stories
Brandel, Marc, 1919-
  Hasty act
    This week magazine. This week's short-
      short stories
BRANDING
  Warren, W. S. The branding
The branding. Warren, W. S.
Brandon, William
  Chiltipiquin
    Creamer, J. B. comp. Twenty-two sto-
      ries about horses and men
  College queen
    This week magazine. This week's short-
      short stories
  Ghost lode
    Meredith, S. ed. Bar 1: roundup of best
      western stories
  Party to blackmail
    This week magazine. This week's short-
      short stories
Brandt, Wolfgang Ernst Langewiesche- See
    Langewiesche-Brandt, Wolfgang Ernst
Brandy for the parson. Household, G.
Brannon, William T.
  Perfect secretary
    Mystery Writers of America, inc. Four-
      &-twenty bloodhounds
Brave new world. Huxley, A. L.
BRAVERY. See Courage
BRAZIL
  Annixter, P. pseud. Orchids and croco-
      diles
  Ullman, J. R. Island of the blue macaws
  Wells, H. G. Empire of the ants

        Rio de Janeiro
  Seager, A. Quitandinha
BREACH OF PROMISE
  Harte, B. Colonel Starbottle for the plain-
      tiff
Breach of promise. West, J.
BREAD
  Porter, W. S. Unknown quantity
Bread and Butter miss. Munro, H. H.

Bread and snow. Greene, H. I.
Bread on the waters. Sutro, A.
Bread upon the waters. Saintsbury, E. B.
The break. Jackson, C. R.
Break in the chain. Doyle, Sir A. C.
Breakdown. Williamson, J.
Breakfast. Bowen, E.
Breakfast in bed. Finney, J.
BREAKFASTS
  Bowen, E. Breakfast
Breaking point. Schulberg, B. W.
Breaking strain. Clarke, A. C.
Brecht, Harold Walton, 1899-
  Vienna roast
    Shaw, H. and Bement, D. Reading the
      short story
Breck, Vivian, pseud. See Breckenfeld,
    Vivian Gurney
Breckenfeld, Vivian Gurney
  Touch of Arab
    American girl (Periodical) Favorite
      stories
Bred for battle. Runyon, D.
"Breeds there a man. . . ?" Asimov, I.
Brement, Marshall, 1932-
  Youth
    American vanguard 1953
Brenner, Leah, 1915-
  Discovery
    Brenner, L. Artist grows up in Mexico
  Drunken lizard
    Brenner, L. Artist grows up in Mexico
  Ghost's shoes
    Brenner, L. Artist grows up in Mexico
  Little general
    Brenner, L. Artist grows up in Mexico
  Merchant of art
    Brenner, L. Artist grows up in Mexico
  Moon magic
    Brenner, L. Artist grows up in Mexico
  Revolt
    Brenner, L. Artist grows up in Mexico
Brentano, Clemens Maria, 1778-1842
  Picnic of Mores the cat
    Pick, R. ed. German stories and tales
  Story of the just Casper and the fair
      Annie
    Lange, V. ed. Great German short
      novels and stories
Breslin, Howard, 1912-
  Bat and a prayer
    Dachs, D. ed. Treasury of sports humor
Bretherton, Vivian Rosamond
  Love me, love my car
    Stowe, A. comp. It's a date
Bretnor, Reginald
  Gnurrs come from the voodvork out
    Best science fiction stories, 1951
  Little Anton
    Healy, R. J. ed. New tales of space and
      time
  Maybe just a little one
    Magazine of fantasy and science fiction.
      Best from Fantasy and science fic-
      tion; 3d ser.

Breuer, Bessie, 1893-
  Home is a place
    Stegner, W. E.; Scowcroft, R. and Ilyin,
      B. eds. Writer's art
Breuer, Miles J.
  Gostak and the doshes
    Conklin, G. ed. Science-fiction adven-
      tures in dimension
  Man with the strange head
    Conklin, G. ed. Big book of science
      fiction
        See also Harris, C. W. jt. auth.
BRIBERY
  Dostoevskiĭ, F. M. Polzunkov
  Munro, H. H. Boar-pig
Brick, John, 1922-
  The captives
    Brick, J. They ran for their lives
  Message for Uncle Billy
    Brick, J. They ran for their lives
  Rifleman's run
    Brick, J. They ran for their lives
Brick road to glory. Gault, W. C.
Brickdust row. Porter, W. S.
Bridal night. O'Donovan, M.
Bridal party. Fitzgerald, F. S. K.
The bride. Wohl, S.
Bride comes to Yellow Sky. Crane, S.
Bride of the man-horse. Dunsany, E. J. M.
  D. P. 18th baron
Bridegroom of blood. Hazaz, C.
Bridegroom on the scaffold. Cohan, A. E.
Bridegroom's body. Boyle, K.
BRIDES. See Husband and wife
Bride's bed. Gibran, K.
BRIDGE (GAME)
  Dahl, R. My ladylove, my dove
  Maugham, W. S. Three fat women of
    Antibes
BRIDGES
  Dresser, D. Extradition
  Ware, L. Phantom of the bridge
Bridget's burden. Eggleston, M. W.
The bridle. Keller, D. H.
Bridle and saddle. Asimov, I.
Brief début of Tildy. Porter, W. S.
Brier, Howard Maxwell, 1903-
  Newspaper man
    American boy (Periodical) American boy
      Adventure stories
  Sky hook
    Boys' life (Periodical) Boys' life Adven-
      ture stories
  Thoroughbred
    Harper, W comp. Dog show
  Yogi's dark horse
    Strang, R. M. and Roberts, R. M. eds.
      Teen-age tales; bk 1
BRIGANDS AND ROBBERS
  Alarcón, P. A. de. The prophecy
  Chekhov, A. P. The dream
  Porter, W. S. Hiding of Black Bill
  Porter, W. S. Holding up a train
  Porter, W. S. Roads we take
        See also Bank robbers; Thieves
Brigands in Snuggletop Woods. Weeks, R.

Bright and morning. Parker, G.
Bright day. Grau, S. A.
Brightness falls from the air. Seabright, I.
Brim Beauvais. Stein, G.
Brimstone Bill. Jameson, M.
Bring! Bring! Aiken, C. P.
Brink, Carol (Ryrie) 1895-
  Massacree!
    Fenner, P. R. comp. Indians, Indians,
      Indians
Brink of darkness. Winters, Y.
BRITISH. See English
BRITISH COLUMBIA. See Canada—Brit-
  ish Columbia
BRITISH NAVY. See Great Britain. Navy
BRITISH SOLDIERS. See Soldiers, Brit-
  ish
Bro, Margueritte (Harmon) 1894-
  It had to happen
    McFarland, W. K. comp. Then it hap-
      pened
BROADWAY, NEW YORK (CITY) See
  New York (City)—Manhattan
Broadway incident. Runyon, D.
Broch, Hermann, 1886-1951
  Zerline, the old servant girl
    Pick, R. ed. German stories and tales
Brod, Max, 1884-
  Death is a passing weakness
    Leftwich, J. ed. Yisröel. 1952 ed.
Brodie horns in. Charnley, M. V.
The brogue. Munro, H. H.
Broiefort, the black Arabian. Baldwin, J.
Broken fan. De La Roche, M.
Broken leg. Stern, J.
BROKERS
  Kornbluth, C. M. Dominoes
  Porter, W. S. Romance of a busy broker
Bromfield, Louis, 1896-1956
  Great façade
    Grayson, C. ed. Fourth round
  Sugar camp
    Andrews, R. C. ed. My favorite stories
      of the great outdoors
  Tabloid news
    Queen, E. pseud. ed. Literature of
      crime
BRONCO-BUSTERS. See Cowboys
Brondfield, Jerome
  That's my boy
    Herzberg, M. J. comp. Treasure chest
      of sport stories
Bronson, Wilfred Swancourt, 1894-
  Brush with the enemy
    Fenner, P. R. comp. Indians, Indians,
      Indians
Bronx oracle. Kober, A.
BRONX PARK. See New York (City)
  Zoological Park
Bronze thing. Newhouse, E.
Bronzes of Martel Greer. Winslow, T. S.
The brooch. Faulkner, W.
Brood of evil. Blochman, L. G.
Brooke, Jocelyn, 1908-
  The blanket
    New writing (Periodical) Best stories

Brookhouser, Frank, 1912-
L'affaire foul tip
Brookhouser, F. She made the big town! And other stories
The bereaved
Brookhouser, F. She made the big town! And other stories
Easter egg
Brookhouser, F. She made the big town! And other stories
Certner, S. and Henry, G. H. eds. Short stories for our times
Epilogue in the blues for Joey
Brookhouser, F. She made the big town! And other stories
Grave digger and Biggie Doone
Brookhouser, F. She made the big town! And other stories
Inn was promise
Brookhouser, F. She made the big town! And other stories
Life, going by
Brookhouser, F. She made the big town! And other stories
Little boy blues
Brookhouser, F. She made the big town! And other stories
Love that is lost
Brookhouser, F. She made the big town! And other stories
Mr Timothy and the model
Brookhouser, F. She made the big town! And other stories
My father and the circus
Brookhouser, F. She made the big town! And other stories
Not that kind of a deal
Brookhouser, F. She made the big town! And other stories
Pierre
Brookhouser, F. She made the big town! And other stories
Say that Jimmy kissed me
Brookhouser, F. She made the big town! And other stories
She did not cry at all
Brookhouser, F. She made the big town! And other stories
She made the big town!
Brookhouser, F. She made the big town! And other stories
Snake woman and the preacher's wife
Brookhouser, F. She made the big town! And other stories
Triumph with bells and laughter
Brookhouser, F. She made the big town! And other stories
You aim so high
Brookhouser, F. She made the big town! And other stories
Young man from yesterday
Brookhouser, F. She made the big town! And other stories

BROOKLYN. See New York (City)— Brooklyn

BROOKLYN. BASEBALL CLUB (NATIONAL LEAGUE)
Heuman, W. There are broken hearts in Brooklyn
See also Baseball

BROOKLYN DODGERS. See Brooklyn. Baseball Club (National League)

Brooks, Collin, 1893-
Possession on completion
Asquith, Lady C. M. E. C. ed. Book of modern ghosts
Brooks, Graham
Devil's tail
Story (Periodical) Story; no. 1
Brooks, Walter Rollin, 1886-
Jimmy takes vanishing lessons
Fenner, P. R. comp. Ghosts, ghosts, ghosts
Broomsticks. De La Mare, W. J.
Brophy, Brigid, 1929-
Crown princess
Brophy, B. Crown princess & other stories
Financial world
Brophy, B. Crown princess & other stories
Fordie
Brophy, B. Crown princess & other stories
His wife survived him
Brophy, B. Crown princess & other stories
Late afternoon of a faun
Brophy, B. Crown princess & other stories
Mrs Mandford's drawing-room
Brophy, B. Crown princess & other stories
Broster, Dorothy Kathleen, 1877-1950
Couching at the door
Carrington, H. ed. Week-end book of ghost stories
Davenport, B. ed. Ghostly tales to be told
Brother Bascombe is annoyed. Claudy, C. H.
Brother Boniface. Lavin, M.
Brother Willie. Hendryx, J. B.
A brotherhood. Swinton, A.
BROTHERS
Ballard, J. C. Mountain summer
Barker, A. L. Romney
Bennett, A. Mary with the high hand
Bergengruen, W. The knight
Bjørnson, B. The brothers
Coward, N. P. A richer dust
Farrell, J. T. Two brothers
Fitzgerald, F. S. K. Family in the wind
Garber, G. The gun on the wall
Grinnell, D. pseud. Extending the holdings
Hopkinson, H. T. Mountain madness
Johnson, D. M. War shirt
Lerner, M. The brothers
Maugham, W. S. Ant and the grasshopper
Maupassant, G. de. At sea
Newhouse, E. My brother's second funeral
Parsons, E. Not a soul will come along
Pratt, F. and De Camp, L. S. My brother's keeper
Putman, C. The wounded
Schnitzler, A. Blind Geronimo and his brother
Tucker, W. My brother's wife
Two brothers
Van Doren, M. In what far country

BROTHERS—*Continued*
   Walsh, M. Sword of Yung Lo
   Waugh, E. Winner takes all
   West, J. Shivaree before breakfast
      See also Brothers and sisters
The **brothers.** Bjørnson, B.
The **brothers.** Lerner, M.
BROTHERS AND SISTERS
   Auchincloss, L. The ambassadress
   Benefield, B. Christmas Eve's Day
   Cooke, A. A. Four of a kind
   Howarth, J. The novitiate
   Lamkin, S. Comes a day
   Maugham, W. S. Book-bag
   Pasinetti, P. M. Family history
   Porter, K. A. The grave
   Stifter, A. Rock crystal
   Tarkington, B. Walterson
   Van Doren, M. Four brothers
   Williams, T. Resemblance between a violin
     case and a coffin
      See also Brothers; Children; Sisters
Brothers beyond the void. Fairman, P. W.
BROTHERS-IN-LAW
   Maltz, A. Happiest man on earth
   Walsh, M. Quiet man
Brother's keeper. Steele, W. D.
Brothers of the yoke. Roberts, Sir C. G. D.
Brought to cover. Annixter, P. pseud.
Broughton, Rhoda, 1840-1920
   Behold it was a dream
     Merril, J. ed. Beyond the barriers of
     space and time
Broun, Heywood Campbell, 1888-1939
   Bolt from the blue
     Graber, R. S. ed. Baseball reader
   Even to Judas
     Brentano, F. ed. The word lives on
   Fifty-first dragon
     Lass, A. H. and Horowitz, A. eds.
     Stories for youth
   Frankincense and myrrh
     Brentano, F. ed. The word lives on
   Trials of a ballplayer's wife
     Graber, R. S. ed. Baseball reader
   We, too, are bidden
     Brentano, F. ed. The word lives on
Brown, Bill
   Medicine dancer
     Merril, J. ed. Beyond the barriers of
     space and time
   Star ducks
     Best science fiction stories: 1951
Brown, E. Leigh, 1877-
   Hero
     Oberfirst, R. ed. 1954 anthology of best
     original short-shorts
Brown, Fredric, 1906-
   All good Bems
     Brown, F. Space on my hands
   Angelic angleworm
     Brown, F. Angels and spaceships
   Answer
     Brown, F. Angels and spaceships
   Arena
     Conklin, G. ed. Big book of science
     fiction
   Armageddon
     Brown, F. Angels and spaceships

Cain
   Brown, F. Mostly murder
Come and go mad
   Brown, F. Space on my hands
Crisis, 1999
   Best detective stories of the year—1950
   Brown, F. Space on my hands
Cry silence
   Brown, F. Mostly murder
Daisies
   Brown, F. Angels and spaceships
Dangerous people
   Brown, F. Mostly murder
Daymare
   Brown, F. Space on my hands
Death of Riley
   Brown, F. Mostly murder
Don't look behind you
   Brown, F. Mostly murder
Etaoin Shrdlu
   Brown, F. Angels and spaceships
   Pratt, F. ed. World of wonder
Four blind men
   Brown, F. Mostly murder
Gateway to darkness
   Margulies, L. and Friend, O. J. eds.
     Giant anthology of science fiction
Greatest poem ever written
   Brown, F. Mostly murder
Hall of mirrors
   Pohl, F. ed. Assignment in tomorrow
Hat trick
   Brown, F. Angels and spaceships
Honeymoon in hell
   Galaxy science fiction magazine. Galaxy
     reader of science fiction
I'll cut your throat again, Kathleen
   Brown, F. Mostly murder
Knock
   Bleiler, E. F. and Dikty, T. E. eds.
     Science fiction omnibus: the best
     science fiction stories, 1949, 1950
   Brown, F. Space on my hands
Last Martian
   Best science fiction stories: 1951
   Galaxy science fiction magazine. Galaxy
     reader of science fiction
Laughing butcher
   Brown, F. Mostly murder
Letter to a phoenix
   Brown, F. Angels and spaceships
   Greenberg, M. ed. Journey to infinity
Little apple hard to peel
   Brown, F. Mostly murder
Little white lye
   Brown, F. Mostly murder
Miss Darkness
   Brown, F. Mostly murder
Mr Smith kicks the bucket
   Mystery Writers of America, inc. Four-
     &-twenty bloodhounds
Motive goes round and round
   Brown, F. Mostly murder
Mouse
   Best science fiction stories: 1950
   Bleiler, E. F. and Dikty, T. E. eds.
     Science fiction omnibus: the best sci-
     ence fiction stories, 1949, 1950
Night the world ended
   Brown, F. Mostly murder
Nose of Don Aristide
   Brown, F. Mostly murder
Nothing Sirius
   Brown, F. Space on my hands

Brown, Fredric—*Continued*
Paradox lost
Brown, F. and Reynolds, M. eds. Science-fiction carnival
Pattern
Brown, F. Angels and spaceships
Pi in the sky
Brown, F. Space on my hands
Placet is a crazy place
Brown, F. Angels and spaceships
Greenberg, M. ed. Travelers of space
Politeness
Brown, F. Angels and spaceships
Preposterous
Brown, F. Angels and spaceships
Reconciliation
Brown, F. Angels and spaceships
Search
Brown, F. Angels and spaceships
Sentence
Brown, F. Angels and spaceships
Solipsist
Brown, F. Angels and spaceships
Something green
Brown, F. Space on my hands
Star mouse
Brown, F. Space on my hands
This way out
Brown, F. Mostly murder
Town wanted
Brown, F. Mostly murder
Voice behind him
Brown, F. Mostly murder
The waveries
Brown, F. Angels and spaceships
Conklin, G. ed. Invaders of earth
The weapon
Conklin, G. ed. Omnibus of science fiction
Mystery Writers of America, inc. Crooks' tour
Yehudi principle
Brown, F. Angels and spaceships
See also Reynolds, M. jt. auth.

Brown, George, 1931-
One in a million
Oberfirst, R. ed. 1954 anthology of best original short-shorts

Brown, John, 1810-1882
Rab and his friends
Cerf, B. A. and Moriarty, H. C. eds. Anthology of famous British stories

Brown, Kenneth Irving, 1896-
Christmas guest
Lohan, R. and Lohan, M. eds. New Christmas treasury

Brown, Margery (Finn) 1913-
Orders for Korea
Saturday evening post (Periodical) Saturday evening post stories, 1952

Brown, Martha Evelyn
Red hat
Ford, N. A. and Faggett, H. L. eds. Best short stories by Afro-American writers (1925-1950)

Brown, Will C.
Duel in Captive Valley
Meredith, S. ed. Bar 2

Brown cap. Van Doren, M.

Brown of Calaveras. Harte, B.

Brown Wolf. London, J.

Browne, John Ross, 1817-1875
Peep at Washoe
Emrich, D. ed. Comstock bonanza

Browning, John S.
Burning bright
Greenberg, M. ed. Robot and the man

Brubaker, Howard, 1882-
The milk pitcher
Cooper, A. C. ed. Modern short stories
Dachs, D. ed. Treasury of sports humor

Bruce, J. Campbell
Rescuer extraordinary
McFee, W. ed. Great sea stories of modern times

Bruce, Stanley, 1914-
Farewell to crime
Oberfirst, R. ed. 1952 anthology of best original short-shorts

Bruggen, Carry (de Haan) van, 1881-1932
Seder night
Leftwich, J. ed. Yisröel. 1952 ed.

Bruhl, Étienne, 1898-
Great match
Talbot, D. ed. Treasury of mountaineering stories

Brumbaugh, Florence
Helpful Henry
Story parade (Periodical) Adventure stories

BRUNN (PREHISTORIC TRIBE) See Man, Prehistoric

Brunner, K. Houston
Thou good and faithful
Norton, A. M. ed. Space pioneers

Brush, Katharine Ingham, 1902-1952
Football girl
Dachs, D. ed. Treasury of sports humor
Good Wednesday
Shaw, H. and Bement, D. Reading the short story
Night club
Bogorad, S. N. and Tevithick, J. eds. College miscellany
Burrell, J. A. and Cerf, B. A. eds. Anthology of famous American stories

Brush fire. Cain, J. M.

BRUSH FIRES. See Fires

Brush with the enemy. Bronson, W. S.

Brushwood boy. Kipling, R.

The **brute.** Conrad, J.

Brute's Christmas. Henderson, D.

Bubbles. Steele, W. D.

BUBONIC PLAGUE. See Plague

BUCCANEERS. See Pirates

Buchan, John, 1st baron Tweedsmuir, 1875-1940
An extract from the journal of Father Duplessis
Brentano, F. ed. The word lives on
Kings of Orion
Cerf, B. A. and Moriarty, H. C. eds. Anthology of famous British stories
Space
Derleth, A. W. ed. Beyond time & space

Buck, Frank, 1882-1950
  Elephant midget
    Fenner, P. R. comp. Elephants, elephants, elephants
  Elephants!
    Fenner, P. R. comp. Elephants, elephants, elephants
Buck, Pearl (Sydenstricker) 1892-
  Good river
    Eaton, H. T. ed. Short stories
  Man's foes
    Certner, S. and Henry, G. H. eds. Short stories for our times
  Old demon
    Lass, A. H. and Horowitz, A. eds. Stories for youth
  One named Jesus
    Brentano, F. ed. The word lives on
  Ransom
    Queen, E. pseud. ed. Literature of crime
Buck Fanshaw's funeral. Clemens, S. L.
Buck in the hills. Clark, W. Van T.
Buckingham, Nash, 1880-
  Bigger they come!
    Buckingham, N. Hallowed years
  Carry me back
    Buckingham, N. Hallowed years
  Comin' twenty-one
    Buckingham, N. Hallowed years
  Cricket field
    Buckingham, N. Hallowed years
  Death stalked the spring-stand!
    Buckingham, N. Hallowed years
  Hallowed years
    Buckingham, N. Hallowed years
  The high sign
    Buckingham, N. Hallowed years
  Lady
    Buckingham, N. Hallowed years
  Remember. . .
    Buckingham, N. Hallowed years
  Snake-eyes! !
    Buckingham, N. Hallowed years
  Tight place
    Buckingham, N. Hallowed years
  "When time who steals our years away!"
    Buckingham, N. Hallowed years
The buckpasser. Kahler, H. M.
BUDDHIST PRIESTS
  Holland, R. S. Cobra's hood
The buddies. Farrell, J. T.
Budding explorer. Robin, R.
BUDGETS, PERSONAL
  Verner, C. Meddlin' Papa
Budrys, Algis J.
  Congruent people
    Star science fiction stories, no. 2
  Frightened tree
    Pohl, F. ed. Assignment in tomorrow
BUENOS AIRES. See Argentine Republic—Buenos Aires
Buffalo and Injuns. Sperry, A.
Buffalo dance. Meigs, C. L.
Buffalo wallow. Jackson, C. T.
The buffalos. Williams, W. C.
Bugles blow retreat. Dowdey, C.
Buglesong. Stegner, W. E.
Building alive. Sansom, W.

Built up logically. Schoenfeld, H.
The bull. Munro, H. H.
Bullard reflects. Jameson, M.
Bulletin board. Canine, W.
Bullets for Bouquet. Doyle, F. C.
BULLFIGHTERS AND BULLFIGHTING
  Hemingway, E. Capital of the world
Bullfrog hunt. Macfarlan, A. A.
BULLFROGS. See Frogs
BULLS
  Bottome, P. Dark Blue
  Munro, H. H. The bull
  Munro, H. H. Stalled ox
  Stuart, J. To market, to market
  See also Cattle
The bully. Reaney, J. C.
Bulwer-Lytton, Edward George Earle Lytton, 1st baron Lytton. See Lytton, Edward George Earle Lytton Bulwer-Lytton, 1st baron
The bum. Maugham, W. S.
Bum: wearer of the Silver Shield. Little, G. W.
BUMS. See Tramps
Bundle of letters. James, H.
Bunin, Ivan Alekseevich, 1870-1953
  Dry valley
    Rahv, P. ed. Great Russian short novels
  Evening in spring
    Neider, C. ed. Great short stories from the world's literature
  Gentleman from San Francisco
    Burnett, W. ed. World's best
    Schorer, M. ed. The story
    West, R. B. and Stallman, R. W. eds. Art of modern fiction
Bunker Mouse. Greene, F. S.
Bunn, Harriet F.
  Sophy's Christmas dinner
    American girl (Periodical) Christmas all year 'round
Bunner, Henry Cuyler, 1855-1896
  Infidelity of Zenobia
    Fabricant, N. D. and Werner, H. eds. World's best doctor stories
  Love-letters of Smith
    Cuff, R. P. ed. American short story survey
  Story of a New York house
    Scribner treasury
  Two churches of 'Quawket
    Blodgett, H. W. ed. Story survey. 1953 ed.
    Eaton, H. T. ed. Short stories
    Neider, C. ed. Men of the high calling
Bunner sisters. Wharton, E. N. J.
BUNYAN, PAUL
  Rounds, G. Knute, the giant bullsnake
  Rounds, G. Paul goes hunting
Burden of guilt. Hawkins, J. and Hawkins, W.
Burden of loveliness. Williams, W. C.
Burdick, Eugene L.
  Log the man dead
    McFee, W. ed. Great sea stories of modern times

Burdick's last battle. Thompson, T.
Bureau of slick tricks. Fyfe, H. B.
The **bureaucrat.** Jameson, M.
Burge McCall. Runyon, D.
Burgess, Gelett, 1866-1951
  Ghost-extinguisher
    Carrington, H. ed. Week-end book of ghost stories
BURGLARS. See Theft; Thieves
BURIAL. See Burials at sea; Catacombs; The dead; Funeral rites and ceremonies
BURIAL, PREMATURE
  Aldrich, T. B. Struggle for life
  Irving, C. Buried alive
  Poe, E. A. Fall of the House of Usher
  Poe, E. A. Premature burial
The **burial.** Horwitz, J.
Burial of the guns. Page, T. N.
BURIALS AT SEA
  Conrad, J. The nigger of the Narcissus
  Maugham, W. S. P. & O.
BURIED ALIVE. See Burial, Premature
Buried alive. Irving, C.
Buried treasure. Porter, W. S.
Burke, Norah, 1907-
  Polar night
    Story (Periodical) Story; no. 4
Burke, Thomas, 1887-1945
  Chink and the child
    Cerf, B. A. and Moriarty, H. C. eds. Anthology of famous British stories
  Hands of Mr Ottermole
    Lynskey, W. C. ed. Reading modern fiction
  Johnson looked back
    Davenport, B. ed. Ghostly tales to be told
Burks, Arthur J. 1898-
  The captive
    Story (Periodical) Story; no. 1
BURMA
  Marshall, E. Elephant remembers
  Marshall, E. Heart of Little Shikara
  Swinton, A. Courage
Burman, Ben Lucien, 1895-
  Children of Noah
    Summers, H. S. ed. Kentucky story
Burn him out. Bonham, F.
Burned chair. Rinehart, M. R.
Burnet, Dana, 1888-
  Shattered dream
    Saturday evening post (Periodical) Saturday evening post stories, 1952
  Vision of Henry Whipple
    Saturday evening post (Periodical) Saturday evening post stories, 1951
  Why did he leave me?
    Saturday evening post (Periodical) Saturday evening post stories, 1953
Burnett, Hallie Southgate, 1908-
  The burning
    Story (Periodical) Story; no. 3
Burnett, Whit, 1899-
  Suffer the little children
    Story (Periodical) Story; no. 2

Burnett, William Riley, 1899-
  Dressing-up
    First-prize stories, 1919-1954
The **burning.** Burnett, H. S.
The **burning.** Welty, E.
Burning bright. Browning, J. S.
Burning cactus. Spender, S.
Burning of Egliswyl. Wedekind, F.
Burns, John Horne, 1916-1953
  Momma
    Cory, D. W. pseud. comp. 21 variations on a theme
BURR, AARON, 1756-1836
  Welty, E. First love
Burrage, Alfred McLelland, 1889-
  The waxwork
    Certner, S. and Henry, G. H. eds. Short stories for our times
    Christ, H. I. and Shostak, J. eds. Short stories
BURROS
  Clark, W. Van T. Indian well
  Grey, Z. Tappan's burro
    See also Asses and mules
Burroughs, John, 1837-1921
  Sharp eyes
    Andrews, R. C. ed. My favorite stories of the great outdoors
The **burrow.** Kafka, F.
Burt, Maxwell Struthers, 1882-1954
  Each in his generation
    First-prize stories, 1919-1954
  Rope and the bulldog
    American boy (Periodical) American boy Adventure stories
BURYING GROUNDS. See Cemeteries
BUS DRIVERS
  Lamberton, L. Sleet storm
BUSES. See Motor buses
Bush, Geoffrey, 1929-
  Great reckoning in a little room
    Best American short stories, 1954
Bush medicine. O'Meara, W.
Busher's letters home. Lardner, R. W.
BUSINESS
  De La Mare, W. J. Lispet, Lispett and Vaine
  Kahler, H. M. The buckpasser
  Street, J. L. Mr Bisbee's princess
  Thurber, J. Catbird seat
  Van Doren, M. Miss Swallow
    See also Bankers; Capitalists and financiers; Merchants; also the names of particular businesses, e.g. Real estate business

  Unscrupulous methods
  Kersh, G. One way of getting a hundred pounds
Business, as usual. Reynolds, M.
BUSINESS DEPRESSION, 1929
  Bolté, M. End of the depression
Business of killing. Leiber, F.
Business proposition. Hendryx, J. B.
Busman's holiday. Young, F. B.
But not Jeff. Eicher, E.
But the patient died. Blochman, L. G

But without horns. Page, N. W.
Butch. Anderson, P.
Butch. Bendrodt, J. C.
Butcher bird. Stegner, W. E.
Butcher to the queen, Walsh, M.
The **butcherbirds.** Patt, E.
BUTCHERS
    Anderson, E. V. Rib steak
    Bergelson, D. In a backwoods town
    Caldwell, E. Man who looked like himself
    Caldwell, E. Saturday afternoon
    Cavanaugh, J. P. The lamb
    Suhl, Y. Saved by the sale
Butler, Ellis Parker, 1869-1937
    Too much horse
        American boy (Periodical) American boy
        anthology
Butler, Mabel
    Mr Sweeney
        Oberfirst, R. ed. 1954 anthology of best
        original short-shorts
BUTLERS. See Servants—Butlers
The **butterfly.** Van Doren, M.
Butterworth, Hezekiah, 1839-1905
    My grandmother's grandmother's Christ-
    mas candle
        Lohan, R. and Lohan, M. eds. New
        Christmas treasury
Buyer from Cactus City. Porter, W. S.
BUYERS OF DRESSES
    Porter, W. S. Buyer from Cactus City
By appointment. Steele, W. D.
By courier. Porter, W. S.
By his bootstraps. Heinlein, R. A.
By Jupiter. Elam, R. M.
By my troth, Nerissa! Aiken, C. P.
By one, by two, and by three. King-Hall, S.
"**By** the sea." Jackson, C. R.
By the water. Bowles, P. F.
By the waters of Babylon. Benét, S. V.
By the waters of Babylon. Goudge, E.
By these presents. Kuttner, H.
By virtue of circumference. Van Dresser, P.
By way of a Christmas card. Eggleston,
    M. W.
'**Bye,** 'bye, Bluebeard. Shore, V. B.
Bye-day with Mr Jorrocks. Surtees, R. S.
Byézhin Meadow. Turgenev, I. S.
Byrd, Sigman
    Old man's bride
        Saturday evening post (Periodical) Sat-
        urday evening post stories, 1950
Byrne, Donn, 1889-1928
    Rivers of Damascus
        Cerf, B. A. and Moriarty, H. C. eds.
        Anthology of famous British stories
    Tale of James Carabine
        Ribalow, H. U. ed. World's greatest
        boxing stories
The **bystander.** La Farge, O.
Byzantine omelette. Munro, H. H.

C

C chute. Asimov, I.
C.Y.E. McCarthy, M. T.
CAB DRIVERS
    Chekhov, A. P. Grief
    Kantor, M. Fabulous cabman
    Porter, W. S. From the cabby's seat
    Ullman, J. R. White night
CABALA
    Peretz, I. L. Cabalists
Cabalists. Peretz, I. L.
Caballero's way. Porter, W. S.
Cabaret. Boyle, K.
CABARETS. See Music halls (Variety
    theaters, cabarets, etc.); Night clubs
CABBAGES
    Poe, E. A. Devil in the belfry
Cabbages of the cemetery. Baroja y Nessi,
    P.
Cabell, James Branch, 1879-
    Porcelain cups
        Burrell, J. A. and Cerf, B. A. eds. An-
        thology of famous American stories
Cabin boy. Knight, D.
Cabin door. Roberts, Sir C. G. D.
Cable, George Washington, 1844-1925
    Madame Delphine
        Scribner treasury
The **Cabuliwallah.** Tagore, R.
The **cactus.** Porter, W. S.
Caddis hatch. Bonner, P. H.
CAESAR, CAIUS JULIUS
    Wilder, T. N. From a journal-letter of
    Julius Caesar
Caesar's wife's ear. Bottome, P.
Café in Jaffa. Gellhorn, M. E.
CAFÉS. See Restaurants, lunchrooms, etc.
CAIN (BIBLICAL CHARACTER)
    Feild, B. How Abel slew Cain
Cain, James Mallahan, 1892-
    Brush fire
        Grayson, C. ed. Fourth round
Cain, Jeanette, 1924-
    Fantasy
        Wolfe, D. M. ed. Which grain will
        grow
Cain. Brown, F.
CAJUNS. See Acadians in Louisiana
CAKES. See Food
Calahan, Harold Augustus, 1899-
    Back to Treasure Island; excerpt
        Fenner, P. R. comp. Pirates, pirates,
        pirates
Calculated risk. Appell, G. C.
Calculation of N'bambwe. Kneale, N.
Caldwell, Erskine, 1903-
    After-image
        Caldwell, E. Complete stories
    Albino and Darling Jill
        Caldwell, E. Humorous side of Erskine
        Caldwell
    All kind of pep
        Caldwell, E. Humorous side of Erskine
        Caldwell

Caldwell, Erskine—*Continued*
August afternoon
  Caldwell, E. Complete stories
Automobile that wouldn't run
  Caldwell, E. Complete stories
Autumn courtship
  Caldwell, E. Complete stories
Back on the road
  Caldwell, E. Complete stories
  Caldwell, E. Courting of Susie Brown
Balm of Gilead
  Caldwell, E. Complete stories
  Caldwell, E. Courting of Susie Brown
  Caldwell, E. Humorous side of Erskine
    Caldwell
Big Buck
  Caldwell, E. Complete stories
  Caldwell, E. Courting of Susie Brown
  Caldwell, E. Humorous side of Erskine
    Caldwell
Big crop of millet
  Caldwell, E. Humorous side of Erskine
    Caldwell
Big mistake
  Caldwell, E. Humorous side of Erskine
    Caldwell
Blue Boy
  Caldwell, E. Complete stories
Candy-man Beechum
  Caldwell, E. Complete stories
Carnival
  Caldwell, E. Complete stories
Cold winter
  Caldwell, E. Complete stories
Corduroy pants
  Caldwell, E. Complete stories
Country full of Swedes
  Caldwell, E. Complete stories
  Caldwell, E. Humorous side of Erskine
    Caldwell
Courting of Susie Brown
  Caldwell, E. Complete stories
  Caldwell, E. Courting of Susie Brown
Crown-fire
  Caldwell, E. Complete stories
Daughter
  Caldwell, E. Complete stories
  Short, R. W. and Sewall, R. B. eds.
    Short stories for study. 1950 ed.
Day the presidential candidate came to
    Ciudad Tamaulipas
  Caldwell, E. Complete stories
  Caldwell, E. Courting of Susie Brown
Day's wooing
  Caldwell, E. Complete stories
  Caldwell, E. Humorous side of Erskine
    Caldwell
Doggone Douthits
  Caldwell, E. Humorous side of Erskine
    Caldwell
Dorothy
  Caldwell, E. Complete stories
The dream
  Caldwell, E. Complete stories
Empty room
  Caldwell, E. Complete stories
End of Christy Tucker
  Caldwell, E. Complete stories
  Caldwell, E. Courting of Susie Brown
Evelyn and the rest of us
  Caldwell, E. Complete stories
Evening in Nuevo Leon
  Caldwell, E. Complete stories
  Caldwell, E. Courting of Susie Brown

First autumn
  Caldwell, E. Complete stories
Fly in the coffin
  Caldwell, E. Complete stories
Girl Ellen
  Caldwell, E. Complete stories
Gold-fever
  Caldwell, E. Humorous side of Erskine
    Caldwell
Grass fire
  Caldwell, E. Complete stories
Growing season
  Caldwell, E. Complete stories
Hamrick's polar bear
  Caldwell, E. Complete stories
Handy
  Caldwell, E. Complete stories
  Caldwell, E. Courting of Susie Brown
Here and today
  Caldwell, E. Complete stories
  Caldwell, E. Courting of Susie Brown
Honeymoon
  Caldwell, E. Complete stories
  Caldwell, E. Humorous side of Erskine
    Caldwell
Horse thief
  Best of the Best American short stories,
    1915-1950
  Caldwell, E. Complete stories
Indian summer
  Caldwell, E. Complete stories
It happened like this
  Caldwell, E. Complete stories
Joe Craddock's old woman
  Caldwell, E. Complete stories
John the Indian and George Hopkins
  Caldwell, E. Complete stories
  Caldwell, E. Humorous side of Erskine
    Caldwell
Kathyanne and the piggy bank
  Caldwell, E. Humorous side of Erskine
    Caldwell
Kneel to the rising sun
  Burrell, J. A. and Cerf, B. A. eds. An-
    thology of famous American stories
  Caldwell, E. Complete stories
Knife to cut the corn bread with
  Caldwell, E. Complete stories
Lonely day
  Caldwell, E. Complete stories
Mamma's little girl
  Caldwell, E. Complete stories
Man and woman
  Caldwell, E. Complete stories
Man who looked like himself
  Caldwell, E. Complete stories
Martha Jean
  Caldwell, E. Complete stories
Masses of men
  Caldwell, E. Complete stories
Mating of Marjorie
  Caldwell, E. Complete stories
Maud Island
  Caldwell, E. Complete stories
Meddlesome Jack
  Caldwell, E. Complete stories
Medicine man
  Caldwell, E. Complete stories
Memorandum
  Caldwell, E. Complete stories
Midsummer passion
  Caldwell, E. Complete stories

Caldwell, Erskine—*Continued*
Midwinter guest
  Caldwell, E. Complete stories
  Caldwell, E. Courting of Susie Brown
Molly Cotton-Tail
  Caldwell, E. Complete stories
My autumn courtship
  Caldwell, E. Humorous side of Erskine
    Caldwell
My old man
  Caldwell, E. Humorous side of Erskine
    Caldwell
Negro in the well
  Caldwell, E. Complete stories
New cabin
  Caldwell, E. Complete stories
Nine dollars' worth of mumble
  Caldwell, E. Complete stories
Over the Green Mountains
  Caldwell, E. Complete stories
People v. Abe Lathan, colored
  Caldwell, E. Complete stories
  Caldwell, E. Courting of Susie Brown
People's choice
  Caldwell, E. Complete stories
Picking cotton
  Caldwell, E. Complete stories
The picture
  Caldwell, E. Complete stories
Priming the well
  Caldwell, E. Complete stories
Rachel
  Caldwell, E. Complete stories
Return to Lavinia
  Caldwell, E. Complete stories
Romantically inclined
  Caldwell, E. Humorous side of Erskine
    Caldwell
The rumor
  Caldwell, E. Complete stories
Runaway
  Caldwell, E. Complete stories
Sack of turnips
  Caldwell, E. Humorous side of Erskine
    Caldwell
Saturday afternoon
  Caldwell, E. Complete stories
Savannah River payday
  Caldwell, E. Complete stories
The shooting
  Caldwell, E. Complete stories
Sick horse
  Caldwell, E. Complete stories
  Caldwell, E. Courting of Susie Brown
Slow death
  Caldwell, E. Complete stories
Small day
  Caldwell, E. Complete stories
Snacker
  Caldwell, E. Complete stories
Spence cooperates
  Caldwell, E. Humorous side of Erskine
    Caldwell
Squire Dinwiddy
  Caldwell, E. Complete stories
  Caldwell, E. Courting of Susie Brown
Strawberry season
  Caldwell, E. Complete stories
Summer accident
  Caldwell, E. Complete stories
  Caldwell, E. Courting of Susie Brown
The sunfield
  Caldwell, E. Complete stories
Swell-looking girl
  Caldwell, E. Complete stories
Ten thousand blueberry crates
  Caldwell, E. Complete stories
  Caldwell, E. Humorous side of Erskine
    Caldwell
Thunderstorm
  Caldwell, E. Complete stories
  Caldwell, E. Courting of Susie Brown
Uncle Henry's love nest
  Caldwell, E. Complete stories
Uncle Jeff
  Caldwell, E. Complete stories
  Caldwell, E. Courting of Susie Brown
Very late spring
  Caldwell, E. Complete stories
The visitor
  Caldwell, E. Complete stories
Walnut hunt
  Caldwell, E. Complete stories
Warm river
  Caldwell, E. Complete stories
  Greene, J. I. and Abell, E. eds. Stories
    of sudden truth
We are looking at you, Agnes
  Caldwell, E. Complete stories
Where the girls were different
  Caldwell, E. Complete stories
  Caldwell, E. Humorous side of Erskine
    Caldwell
Wild flowers
  Caldwell, E. Complete stories
The windfall
  Caldwell, E. Complete stories
  Caldwell, E. Courting of Susie Brown
Woman in the house
  Caldwell, E. Complete stories
Yellow girl
  Burnett, W. ed. World's best
  Caldwell, E. Complete stories

Caleb Thumble returns to Barchester. Trollope, A.

Caleb's ark. Davies, R.

Calendar girl. Blochman, L. G.

CALF. See Cattle

The **calf.** Abramowitz, S. J.

Calico shoes. Farrell, J. T.

CALIFORNIA

1846-1900

Harte, B. Outcasts of Poker Flat
Harte, B. Tennessee's partner

20th century

Leighton, M. C. Legacy of Canyon John
Steinbeck, J. The chrysanthemums

Fresno

Saroyan, W. Cornet players
Saroyan, W. The foreigner

Hollywood

Brand, M. pseud. The king
Schulberg, B. My Christmas carol

Monterey

Atherton, G. F. H. Pearls of Loreto

CALIFORNIA RANCH LIFE. See Ranch
life—California

Caliph and the cad. Porter, W. S.

Caliph, cupid and the clock. Porter, W. S.

Calisher, Hortense, 1911-
Box of ginger
Calisher, H. In the absence of angels
Heartburn
Calisher, H. In the absence of angels
In Greenwich there are many gravelled
walks
Best American short stories, 1951
Calisher, H. In the absence of angels
In the absence of angels
Calisher, H. In the absence of angels
Letitia, emeritus
Calisher, H. In the absence of angels
Middle drawer
Calisher, H. In the absence of angels
Night riders of Northville
Calisher, H. In the absence of angels
Old stock
Calisher, H. In the absence of angels
One of the chosen
Calisher, H. In the absence of angels
Ribalow, H. U. ed. These your children
Point of departure
Calisher, H. In the absence of angels
Pool of narcissus
Calisher, H. In the absence of angels
Sound of waiting
Calisher, H. In the absence of angels
The watchers
Calisher, H. In the absence of angels
Woman who was everybody
Calisher, H. In the absence of angels
Wreath for Miss Totten
Best American short stories, 1952
Calisher, H. In the absence of angels
The **call.** Laurence, B.
Call at Corazón. Bowles, P. F.
Call it courage. Sperry, A.
Call loan. Porter, W. S.
Call of the blood. Cervantes Saavedra, M. de
Call of the street. Conrad, R. E.
Call of the tame. Porter, W. S.
Call on the President. Runyon, D.
Call this land home. Haycox, E.
Callaghan, Morley Edward, 1903-
All the years of her life
Certner, S. and Henry, G. H. eds. Short
stories for our times
Lass, A. H. and Horowitz, A. eds.
Stories for youth
Father and son
Pacey, D. ed. Book of Canadian stories
Luke Baldwin's vow
Furman, A. L. ed. Teen-age dog stories
Rigmarole
Burnett, W. ed. World's best
Callie of Crooked Creek. Hall, E. G.
Calling all cars. Hauser, M. L.
Calling of the lop-horned bull. Roberts, Sir
C. G. D.
Calloway's code. Porter, W. S.
Calmahain. Wall, J. W.
CALVES. See Cattle
Calvin, the cat. Warner, C. D.
CALVINISM
De Vries, P. Good boy
De Vries, P. Tulip
Calvo, Lino Novás. See Novás Calvo, Lino

**CAMBRIDGE, ENGLAND. UNIVER-
SITY**
Levy, A. Cohen of Trinity
Camel into eagle. Allen, M. P.
The **cameleers.** Curtis, K.
CAMORRA
Conrad, J. Il conde
Camouflage. Kuttner, H.
Camp, Lyon Sprague de. See De Camp,
Lyon Sprague
Camp at Saint Adrien. Macfarlan, A. A.
CAMP-MEETINGS
Hughes, L. Big meeting
Steele, W. D. Man and boy
The **campaign.** Horwitz, J.
Campaigning cowpoke. Gray, C.
Campanella, Giovanni Domenico. See Cam-
panella, Tommasi
Campanella, Tommasi
City of the sun
Derleth, A. W. ed. Beyond time & space
Campbell, John Wood, 1910-
Black star passes
Campbell, J. W. Black star passes
Cloak of Aesir
Campbell, J. W. Cloak of Aesir
The escape
Campbell, J. W. Cloak of Aesir
Forgetfulness
Campbell, J. W. Cloak of Aesir
The invaders
Campbell, J. W. Cloak of Aesir
The machine
Campbell, J. W. Cloak of Aesir
Out of the night
Campbell, J. W. Cloak of Aesir
Piracy preferred
Campbell, J. W. Black star passes
Rebellion
Campbell, J. W. Cloak of Aesir
Solarite
Campbell, J. W. Black star passes
Campbell, Sir Malcolm, 1885-
Won by inches!
Fenner, P. R. comp. Speed, speed, speed
Campbell, William Edward March, 1894-1954
Bill's eyes
Fabricant, N. D. and Werner, H. eds.
World's best doctor stories
I broke my back on a rosebud
Greene, J. I. and Abell, E. eds. Stories
of sudden truth
Personal letter
Heilman, R. B. ed. Modern short stories
Sum in addition
Shaw, H. and Bement, D. Reading the
short story
CAMPING
Chute, B. J. Too close to nature
Macfarlan, A. A. Campfire adventure
stories; 8 stories
White, S. E. On lying awake at night
See also Outdoor life
CAMPS, SUMMER
Auchincloss, L. Edification of Marianne
Camus, Albert, 1913-
Sentence of death
Burnett, W. ed. World's best

Can all this grandeur perish? Farrell, J. T.
Can of paint. Van Vogt, A. E.

CANADA
Pacey, D. ed. Book of Canadian stories; 30 stories
Weaver, R. and James, H. eds. Canadian short stories; 24 stories

British Columbia
McConnell, W. Totem
Mayse, A. Midnight Mike

Montreal
Waddington, P. Street that got mislaid

New Brunswick
Garner, H. One mile of ice

Northwest Territories
Hendryx, J. B. Intrigue on Halfaday Creek; 28 stories
Mowat, F. Woman he left to die

Ontario
Garner, H. One, two, three little Indians

Quebec (Province)
Allan, T. Lies my father told me
Macfarlan, A. A. Moose boy
Marshall, J. Old woman
Thériault, Y. Jeannette

Toronto
Seton, E. T. Silverspot: the story of a crow

CANADA. ROYAL CANADIAN MOUNTED POLICE
Erskine, L. Y. Mystery at Moon Lake
Mowery, W. B. Sagas of the Mounted Police; 8 stories

Canaday, John Edwin, 1907-
Three strips of flesh
Mystery Writers of America, inc. Four-&-twenty bloodhounds

CANADIAN MOUNTED POLICE. See Canada. Royal Canadian Mounted Police

Canary from Cuba. Rutt, E.

Cancel all I said. Collier, J.

Cancela, Arturo, 1892-
Life and death of a hero
De Onís, H. ed. Spanish stories and tales

CANCER (DISEASE)
McCoy, E. The cape

A candle in Vienna. Cronin, A. J.

CANDLEMAKERS. See Candles

CANDLES
Howard, H. Dipping of the candlemaker

Candy from Fairyland. Farrell, J. T.

Candy-man Beechum. Caldwell, E.

Canfield, Dorothy. See Fisher, Dorothea Frances (Canfield)

Canine, William, 1922-
Bulletin board
Story (Periodical) Story; no. 3
The clematis
Story (Periodical) Story; no. 4

Cannibal pot. Arnold, M.

CANNIBALISM
Harris, J. B. Survival
Rabinowitz, S. The pair

Canning, Victor, 1911-
Man who hated time
This week magazine. This week's short-short stories
Mystery of Kela Ouai
Best detective stories of the year—1953
Never trust a lady
This week magazine. This week's short-short stories
The smuggler
Best detective stories of the year—1952
This week magazine. This week's short-short stories

Cannon, James J.
Gambler's sad saga
Dachs, D. ed. Treasury of sports humor

Cannon, Jimmy. See Cannon, James, J.

CANNONS. See Ordnance

Canossa. Munro, H. H.

Can't cross Jordan by myself. Steele, W. D.

Can't slip any drugs to sisters on Fifth Avenue. McNulty, J.

Canticle of the sun. Goudge, E.

CANTORS
Agnon, S. J. Story of the cantor
Dick, I. M. Two strangers came to town
Peretz, I. L. Ne'ilah in Gehenna

Cantrill remains on Halfaday. Hendryx, J. B.

The canyon flowers. Gordon, C. W.

Canzoneri, Robert
Survival
Story (Periodical) Story; no. 2

The cape. McCoy, E.

Cape Race. De La Mare, W. J.

CAPITAL AND LABOR. See Labor and laboring classes

Capital of the world. Hemingway, E.

CAPITAL PUNISHMENT
Chekhov, A. The bet

CAPITALISTS AND FINANCIERS
Brophy, B. Financial world
Porter, W. S. Night in New Arabia
Porter, W. S. Unknown quantity

Cap'n Ezra, privateer. Adams, J. D.

Capote, Truman, 1924-
House of flowers
Greene, J. I. and Abell, E. eds. Stories of sudden truth
Prize stories of 1951
Shut a final door
First-prize stories, 1919-1954

Cappy: the pride of Engine Company 65. Little, G. W.

Capra. Wall, J. W.

CAPRI
Maugham, W. S. Lotus eater
Maugham, W. S. Mayhew
Wells, H. G. Dream of Armageddon

Captain Burle. Zola, E.

Captain Dalgety returns. Whistler, L.

Captain is impaled. Algren, N.

Captain Kidder. Sandberg, H. W.

Captain Kit. Vetter, M. M.

Captain Murderer. Dickens, C.

Captain of the "Ullswater." Roberts, M.

Captain returns. Hill, J. H.

Captain's doll. Lawrence, D. H.

CAPTAINS, ENGLISH. See Great Britain
—Army

CAPTAINS OF SHIPS. See Shipmasters

Captain's prisoner. Clements, C. J.

The captive. Burks, A. J.

The captive. Gordon, C.

Captive audience. Griffith, A. W.

Captive heart. Vance, C.

The captives. Brick, J.

CAPTIVES OF INDIANS. See Indians of
North America—Captivities

Capture of a brig. Meader, S. W.

Captured shadow. Fitzgerald, F. S. K.

CARBONARI
Beyle, M. H. Vanina Vanini

CARBONATED BEVERAGES
Parker, J. R. All the little jokers

Carcassonne. Faulkner, W.

CARD GAMES. See Cards

CARD-SHARPERS. See Gambling

Cardboard box. Doyle, Sir A. C.

Cardiac suture. Weiss, E.

Cardozo, Nancy
Hundred years from now
Seventeen (Periodical) Nineteen from
Seventeen
Unborn ghosts
Best American short stories, 1952

CARDS
Chekhov, A. P. Vint

Career of Augurt Nimrodtk. Willingham, C.

Carelessness. Chekhov, A. P.

Caretaker. Schmitz, J. H.

Carey, Ernestine Moller (Gilbreth) See Gilbreth, F. B. jt. auth.

CARIB INDIANS
Brown, K. I. Christmas guest

Caricature. Rydberg, E.

CARICATURISTS. See Cartoonists

Carlson, Esther, 1921?-
Museum piece
Pratt, F. ed. World of wonder

Carman, Kathleen
The debt
Thinker's digest (Peroidical) Spoiled
priest, and other stories

Carmer, Carl Lamson, 1893-
Mr Sims and Henry
Strang, R. M. and Roberts, R. M. eds.
Teen-age tales v 1
See also Del Rey, L. jt. ed.

Carmi. Karp, D. B.

CARNIVAL
Caldwell, E. Carnival
Collier, J. Sleeping Beauty
Hall, J. B. Spot in history

Carnival. Caldwell, E.

CAROUSEL. See Merry-go-rounds

CARPENTERS
Schaefer, J. W. Hugo Kertchak, builder
Van Doren, M. Three carpenters

Carpenter's daughter. Coolidge, O. E.

Carr, Albert H. Zolotkoff, 1902-
Case of catnapping
Queen, E. pseud. ed. Ellery Queen's
awards: 9th ser.
If a body. . .
Queen, E. pseud, ed. Queen's awards:
8th ser.
Murder at City Hall
Queen, E. pseud. ed. Queen's awards:
6th ser.
Trial of John Nobody
Queen, E. pseud. ed. Queen's awards:
5th ser.
Tyger! Tyger!
Queen, E. pseud. ed. Queen's awards:
7th ser.

Carr, Dickson. See Carr, John Dickson

Carr, John Dickson, 1905-
Black cabinet
Mystery Writers of America inc. 20
great tales of murder
Clue of the red wig
Carr, J. D. The third bullet, and other
stories
Footprint in the sky
Christ, H. I. and Shostak, J. eds. Short
stories
Gentleman from Paris
Best detective stories of the year—1951
Carr, J. D. The third bullet, and other
stories
Queen, E. pseud. ed. Queen's awards:
5th ser.
House in Goblin Wood
Carr, J. D. The third bullet, and other
stories
Locked room
Carr, J. D. The third bullet, and other
stories
Proverbial murder
Carr, J. D. The third bullet, and other
stories
The third bullet
Carr, J. D. The third bullet, and other
stories
Wrong problem
Carr, J. D. The third bullet, and other
stories
Mystery Writers of America, inc. Four-
&-twenty bloodhounds
See also Doyle, A. C. jt. auth.

Carr, Robert Spencer, 1909-
Beyond infinity
Carr, R. S. Beyond infinity
Dictator's double
Saturday evening post (Periodical) Sat-
urday day evening post stories, 1952
Easter eggs
Best science fiction stories: 1950
Bleiler, E. F. and Dikty, T. E. eds. Sci-
ence fiction omnibus: The best science
fiction stories, 1949, 1950
Morning star
Carr, R. S. Beyond infinity

Carr, Robert S.—*Continued*
Mutation
Carr, R. S. Beyond infinity
Those men from Mars
Carr, R. S. Beyond infinity
Carrighar, Sally
Marooned children
Saturday evening post (Periodical) Saturday evening post stories, 1953
Carrington, Hereward, 1880-
The escape
Carrington, H. ed. Week-end book of ghost stories
The miracle
Carrington, H. ed. Week-end book of ghost stories
rroll, **Joseph W.** 1911-
At Mrs Farrelly's
Best American short stories, 1953
Matthew and the lace curtain
Collier's, the national weekly. Collier's best
Prefect of discipline
Gable, M. Sister, ed. Many-colored fleece
Carry me back. Buckingham, N.
Carse, Robert, 1903-
Sailor's pay
Furman, A. L. ed. Teen-age sea stories
Carson poker incident. Davis, S. P.
Carter, Marjorie
First car
Strang, R. M. and Roberts, R. M. eds. Teen-age tales v 1
Carter, Paul
Ounce of prevention
Derleth, A. W. ed. Far boundaries
Carter, Russell Gordon, 1892-
And the Dean was happy
Lantz, J. E. ed. Stories of Christian living
Blue ribbon event
Owen, F. ed. Teen-age victory parade
Future captain
Lantz, J. E. ed. Stories of Christian living
High-pressure stuff
Strang, R. M. and Roberts, R. M. eds. Teen-age tales v 1
Parachute warning
Strang, R. M. and Roberts, R. M. eds. Teen-age tales v 2
Tea from the brigantine
Fenner, P. R. comp. Yankee Doodle
Cartmill, Cleve
Green cat
Derleth, A. W. ed. The outer reaches
Huge beast
Magazine of fantasy and science fiction. Best of Fantasy and science fiction; [1st ser]
Number nine
Jenkins, W. F. ed. Great stories of science fiction
Overthrow
Greenberg, M. ed. Journey to infinity
You can't say that
Healy, R. J. ed. New tales of space and travel
CARTOONISTS
Ryberg, E. Caricature

artur, **Peter,** pseud.
The mist
Conklin, G. ed. Science-fiction adventures in dimension
Carver, Charles, 1915-
Hanging Hollow
Peery, W. W. ed. 21 Texas short stories
Twenty floors up
This week magazine. This week's short-short stories
CARVING WOOD. See Wood carving
Case in Chancery. Bentley, P. E.
Case of catnapping. Carr, A. H. Z.
Case of Charles Dexter Ward. Lovecraft, H. P.
Case of General Ople and Lady Camper. Meredith, G.
Case of identity. Doyle, Sir A. C.
Case of Karen Smith. Shore, V. B.
Case of myopia. Henderson, S. E.
Case of the irate witness. Gardner, E. S.
Case of the psychoanalyst. Strasser, S.
Case of the southpaw spy. Schneider, G. W.
Case of the wooden bowls. Ball, M. W.
Casey, Marian (Whinery)
First harpist
American girl (Periodical) On my honor
Cash, M. L.
Hangover
Oberfirst, R. ed. 1954 anthology of best original short-shorts
Cash and carry guy. Holder, W.
Cask of Amontillado. Poe, E. A.
Casper, Leonard, 1923-
Deep country part
Stanford short stories, 1953
Sense of direction
Best American short stories, 1951
Prize stories of 1951
Cassill, R. V. 1919-
Larchmoor is not the world
Best American short stories, 1951
Greene, J. I. and Abell, E. eds. Stories of sudden truth
Life of the sleeping beauty
Best American short stories, 1953
War in the air
Prize stories, 1954
Castaway. Chandler, A. B.
Castaway. Williams, R. M.
CASTAWAYS. See Shipwrecks and castaways
Castle Rackrent. Edgeworth, M.
Casual affair. Maugham, W. S.
Casual incident. Farrell, J. T.
Casualty. Lowry, R. J. C.
The **cat.** Colette, S. G.
The **cat.** Freeman, M. E. W.
Cat and Custard-pot day with the Handlcy Cross. Surtees, R. S.
Cat-eyed woman. Reese, J. H.
Cat jumps. Bowen, E.
Cat nipped. Schaefer, J. W.
Cat that would not die. Marshall, E.

Cat up a tree. Sansom, W.
CATACOMBS
Poe, E. A. Cask of Amontillado
Catalonian night. Morand, P.
CATASTROPHES. See Accidents
Catbird seat. Thurber, J.
The catch. Gordimer, N.
Catch that Martian. Knight, D.
Catch that rabbit. Asimov, I.
Category Phoenix. Ellanby, B.
CATERPILLARS
Edmonds, W. D. Death of Red Peril
Catfish story. Blochman, L. G.
CATHEDRALS AND CATHEDRAL LIFE
De La Mare, W. J. All Hallows
Douglas, L. C. Dean Harcourt
Cather, Willa Sibert, 1873-1947
Neighbor Rosicky
Foerster, N. ed. American poetry and prose. 1952 ed.
Schramm, W. L. ed. Great short stories
Stauffer, R. M.; Cunningham, W. H. and Sullivan, C. J. eds. Adventures in modern literature
Paul's case
Burrell, J. A. and Cerf, B. A. eds. Anthology of famous American stories
Day, A. G. ed. Greatest American short stories
Lynskey, W. C. ed. Reading modern fiction
Queen, E. pseud. ed. Literature of crime
CATHOLIC CHURCH. See Catholic faith
CATHOLIC FAITH
Balzac, H. de. Atheist's mass
Daudet, A. Father Gaucher's elixir
Doty, W. L. Action in Prague
Doty, W. L. Father Murray's first failure
Doty, W. L. Rectory parlor
Doty, W. L. Silver cross
Fitzgerald, F. S. K. Absolution
Freemantle, A. J. ed. Mothers; 18 stories
Gable, M. Sister, ed. Many-colored fleece; 24 stories
Greene, G. Hint of an explanation
Lieberman, R. Heaven is so high; 13 stories
O'Donovan, M. Custom of the country
O'Donovan, M. Face of evil
O'Donovan, M. My first Protestant
Paget, V. Virgin of the Seven Daggers
Thinker's digest (Periodical)
Spoiled priest, and other stories; 46 stories
CATHOLIC PRIESTS
Becker, S. D. Baptism of some importance
Betts, D. Mr Shawn and Father Scott
Bloch, J. R. Heresy of the water taps
Cable, G. W. Madame Delphine
Chesterton, G. K. Blue cross
Connolly, M. Seminary Hill
Doty, W. L. Back to school
Doty, W. L. The fisherman
Gautier, T. Clarimonde
Gordon, A. Devil and Father Francisco
Goudge, E. Icon on the wall
Goudge, E. Three gray men
Harte, B. Knight-errant of the foothills

Horgan, P. Devil in the desert
Joyce, J. The sisters
Lemelin, R. Stations of the Cross
Lieberman, R. Indiscretions of Father Lawrence
Lieberman, R. Matter of time
O'Donovan, M. The frying-pan
O'Donovan, M. The miracle
O'Donovan, M. Old faith
O'Donovan, M. The sentry
O'Donovan, M. The shepherds
O'Donovan, M. Vanity
Powers, J. F. Death of a favorite
Powers, J. F. The forks
Powers, J. F. Lions, harts, leaping does
Powers, J. F. Prince of Darkness
Pratt, F. and De Camp, L. S. Palimpsest of St Augustine
Robinson, L. W. Ruin of soul
Sheehan, P. A. Spoiled priest
Van Doren, M. Father O'Connell
Verga, G. His Reverence
Voorhees, M. B. Robe and the sword
Werfel, F. V. Third commandment
Wilde, O. Priest and the acolyte
CATS
Agnon, S. J. Jewish cat
Aiken, C. P. Hello, Tib
Boylston, H. D. Stuff of dreams
Brentano, C. M. Picnic of Mores the cat
Carr, A. H. Z. Case of catnapping
Cartmill, C. Green cat
Ekbergh, I. D. Lost cat
Ekbergh, I. D. Toozee the puss
Fabre, J. H. C. Story of my cats
Freeman, M. E. W. The cat
Hearn, L. Boy who drew cats
Howe, D. White kitten
Humphrey, W. Sister
Joseph, M. ed. Best cat stories; 17 stories
Marmur, J. Mad Island
Munro, H. H. Achievement of the cat
Munro, H. H. Tobermory
Pangborn, E. Mrrrar
Peretz, I. L. Pious cat
Phillpotts, E. "Hey diddle diddle, the cat . . ."
Pirandello, L. House of agony
Poe, E. A. The black cat
Runyon, D. Johnny One-Eye
Steele, W. D. Bubbles
Steele, W. D. Yellow cat
Taber, G. B. Never a dull moment
The cat's-paw. Ellin, S.
CATSKILL MOUNTAINS
Irving, W. Rip Van Winkle
CATTLE
Abramowitz, S. J. The calf
Abramowitz, S. J. Little calf
Agee, J. Mother's tale
Cheshire, G. Bad year
Davies, R. Conflict in Morfa
Evans, E. E. The shed
Herbert, Sir A. P. Board of Inland Revenue v. Haddock
Mannzen, D. Aurora's Angus
See also Branding; Bulls
CATTLE DRIVES
Scott, Sir W. Two drovers
Cattle raid on Cooley. Ready, W. B.
Cattle rustlers. James, W.

CATTLE THIEVES
James, W. Cattle rustlers

Caudill, Rebecca, 1899-
Fern Barrie's new plans
Hazeltine, A. I. comp. Selected stories
for teen-agers

The **caught**. Barber, A.

Caught. Porter, W. S.

Causey, James, 1924-
Teething ring
Galaxy science fiction magazine. Second Galaxy reader of science fiction

Cavalier of the streets. Arlen, M.

Cavalleria rusticana. Verga, G.

Cavanaugh, James Patrick, 1922-
The lamb
American vanguard, 1953
Martha's yesterdays
American vanguard, 1952

Cavanna, Betty, 1909-
Puppy business
American girl (Periodical) Favorite stories
Furman, A. L. ed. Teen-age dog stories

Cave, Hugh Barnett, 1910-
Beyond price
Certner, S. and Henry, G. H. eds. Short stories for our times
Peril of the river
This week magazine. This week's short-short stories
Two were left
Strang, R. M. and Roberts, R. M. eds. Teen-age tales v2

Cave of warm winds. Bamberg, R. D.

Caveat emptor. Pratt, F. and De Camp, L. S.

Cawley, Clifford Comer
Belle Monahan
Cawley, C. C. No trip like this, and other stories
Grunion run
Cawley, C. C. No trip like this, and other stories
The lost
Cawley, C. C. No trip like this, and other stories
No trip like this
Cawley, C. C. No trip like this, and other stories
When day is done
Cawley, C. C. No trip like this, and other stories

Celebrated jumping frog of Calaveras County. Clemens, S. L.

The **celebration**. De La Roche, M.

CELEBRITIES
Saphir, M. G. A conquest

Celeste. Merochnik, M.

Celestial omnibus. Forster, E. M.

Celestial railroad. Hawthorne, N.

Cellmate. Waldo, E. H.

CEMETERIES
Jackson, C. R. Sunday drive
Johnson, H. It happened to me
Porter, K. A. The grave

Cemetery bait. Runyon, D.

Censored, the goat. Stong, P. D.

CENSUS
Horwitz, J. New York

Census. Simak, C. D.

Centaur in brass. Faulkner, W.

CENTAURS
Dunsany, E. J. M. D. P. 18th baron. Bride of the man-horse

CEPHALONIA. See Ionian Islands

Cervantes, Miguel de. See Cervantes Saavedra, Miguel de

Cervantes Saavedra, Miguel de, 1547-1616
Call of the blood
De Onís, H. ed. Spanish stories and tales

CEYLON
Buck, F. Elephants!

Chadwick, Ann
Smith
Joseph, M. ed. Best cat stories

Chaikin, N. G.
Climate of the family
Best American short stories, 1952

Chains. Kneale, N.

Chair of philanthromathematics. Porter, W. S.

The **challenge**. Newcomb, C.

The **challenge**. O'Flaherty, L.

The **challenge**. Vandercook, J. W.

Chalmers, Bea
The contest
Furman, A. L. ed. Everygirls career stories

Chamberlain, George Agnew, 1879-
Monarch the bum
Creamer, J. B. comp. Twenty-two stories about horses and men

Chamberlain, William
Chaplain of Company C
Saturday evening post (Periodical) Saturday evening post stories, 1951

Chambers, Robert William, 1865-1933
Demoiselle d'Ys
Moskowitz, S. comp. Editor's choice in science fiction

Chambers, Ruth E.
Jinx ship
Furman, A. L. ed. Everygirls mystery stories

The **Champ**. Ish-Kishor, S.

Champagne for the old lady. Sitwell, Sir O. bart.

Champion. Lardner, R. W.

The **champion**. Stuart, J.

Champion comes home. Taber, G. B.

Champion of the weather. Porter, W. S.

The **champions**. Hager, M.

CHANCE
Hawthorne, N. David Swan
Johnson, D. M. Warrior's exile
Norris, K. T. What happened to Alanna
Porter, W. S. Phoebe
Pratt, F. and De Camp, L. S. Eve of St John

Chance for adventure. Shulman, M.

Chandler, A. Bertram
  Castaway
    Conklin, G. ed. Science-fiction adventures in dimension
  False dawn
    Greenberg, M. ed. Journey to infinity
  Giant killer
    Pratt, F. ed. World of wonder
  Ship from nowhere
    Argosy (Periodical) Argosy Book of sea stories
Chandler, Raymond, 1888-
  I'll be waiting
    Grayson, C. ed. Fourth round
    Mystery Writers of America, inc. Butcher, baker, murder-maker
The change. Alpert, H.
Change of address. Arthur, R.
Change of air. Gold, I.
Change of pitchers. Patten, G.
Change of plan. Purdy, K. W.
Change of station. Haycox, E.
CHANNEL ISLANDS
  Goudge, E. Doing good
  Goudge, E. Midnight in the stable
Channel 10. Hatch, E.
Chaparral Christmas gift. Porter, W. S.
Chaparral prince. Porter, W. S.
Chaplain of Company C. Chamberlain, W.
CHAPLAINS. See Clergy
The Chaplet. Munro, H. H.
Chaplin, Sid
  Pigeon cree
    New writing (Periodical) Best stories
Chapman, Warren, 1917-
  Where Teetee Wood lies cold and dead
    Stanford short stories, 1951
Chapo—the faker. James, W.
Char on raven's bench. Holwerda, F.
Character of dogs. Stevenson, R. L.
CHARACTERS, LITERARY. See Literary characters
Charcoal burners. Krige, U.
Chariots away. Allen, M. P.
CHARITIES
  Crane, S. Men in the storm
  Francis, O. Ladies call on Mr Pussick
CHARITY
  Benét, S. V. Bishop's beggar
  Goudge, E. Doing good
  Grebanier, B. D. N. Life began today
  Mansfield, K. Cup of tea
Charity. Bowen, E.
Charity ward. Tracy, D.
Charles. Jackson, S.
Charles and Charlemagne. Sitwell, Sir O. bart.
Charles Husson. Verlaine, P. M.
CHARLESTON. See South Carolina—Charleston
Charlie Baseball. Katkov, N.
CHARMS
  Jacobs, W. S. Monkey's paw

Charnley, Mitchell Vaughn, 1898-
  Brodie horns in
    Herzberg, M. J. comp. Treasure chest of sport stories
Chartered rowboat. Millar, B.
Charteris, Leslie, 1907-
  Amsterdam: The angel's eye
    Charteris, L. The Saint in Europe
  Dawn
    Charteris, L. Second Saint omnibus
  Jeannine
    Charteris, L. Second Saint omnibus
  Juan-les-pins: the Spanish cow
    Charteris, L. The Saint in Europe
  Judith
    Charteris, L. Second Saint omnibus
  Lucerne: The loaded tourist
    Charteris, L. The Saint in Europe
  Man who liked ants
    Charteris, L. Second Saint omnibus
  Masked angel
    Charteris, L. Second Saint omnibus
  Palm Springs
    Charteris, L. Second Saint omnibus
  Paris: The covetous headsman
    Charteris, L. The Saint in Europe
  Revolution racket
    Best detective stories of the year—1954
  The Rhine: The Rhine maiden
    Charteris, L. The Saint in Europe
  Rome: The Latin touch
    Charteris, L. The Saint in Europe
  Sizzling saboteur
    Charteris, L. Second Saint omnibus
  Star producers
    Charteris, L. Second Saint omnibus
  Teresa
    Charteris, L. Second Saint omnibus
  Tirol: The golden journey
    Charteris, L. The Saint in Europe
  Wicked cousin
    Charteris, L. Second Saint omnibus
Chase, Francis
  General from the Pentagon
    Saturday evening post (Periodical) Saturday evening post stories, 1953
Chase, Margaret
  I hate a dumpy woman
    Collier's the national weekly. Collier's best
Chase, Mary Ellen, 1887-
  Reuben's courtship
    Brentano, F. ed. The word lives on
  Salesmanship
    Shaw, H. and Bement, D. Reading the short story
The chaser. Collier, J.
Chastity
  Lin, Y. ed. Famous Chinese short stories
Château of missing men. Simenon, G.
Chatter-stick sermon. Faggett, H. L.
Chaucer, Geoffrey, 1340?-1400
  Pardoner's tale
    Cerf, B. A. and Moriarty, H. C. eds. Anthology of famous British stories
CHAUFFEURS. See Servants—Chauffeurs
The cheapjack. O'Donovan, M.
The cheat. Jackson, C. R.

CHEATING. See Swindlers and swindling

Cheerful tortoise. Hall, J. N.

Cheerio. Powell, D.

Cheery soul. Bowen, E.

Cheever, John, 1912-
  The children
    Cheever, J. Enormous radio, and other
      stories
  Christmas is a sad season for the poor
    Cheever, J. Enormous radio, and other
      stories
  Clancy in the Tower of Babel
    Cheever, J. Enormous radio, and other
      stories
  The cure
    Cheever, J. Enormous radio, and other
      stories
  Enormous radio
    Best of the Best American short stories,
      1915-1950
    Cheever, J. Enormous radio, and other
      stories
  Goodbye, my brother
    Cheever, J. Enormous radio, and other
      stories
  The Hartleys
    Cheever, J. Enormous radio, and other
      stories
  O city of broken dreams
    Cheever, J. Enormous radio, and other
      stories
  Pot of gold
    Cheever, J. Enormous radio, and other
      stories
    Greene, J. I. and Abell, E. eds. Stories
      of sudden truth
    Prize stories 1951
  Season of divorce
    Best American short stories, 1951
    Cheever, J. Enormous radio, and other
      stories
  Summer farmer
    Cheever, J. Enormous radio, and other
      stories
  The superintendent
    Cheever, J. Enormous radio, and other
      stories
  Sutton Place story
    Cheever, J. Enormous radio, and other
      stories
  Torch song
    Cheever, J. Enormous radio, and other
      stories
  Vega
    Prize stories of 1950

CHEFS. See Servants—Cooks

Chekhov, Anton Pavlovich, 1860-1904
  Across Siberia
    Chekhov, A. P. Unknown Chekhov
  After the theatre
    Davis, R. G. ed. Ten modern masters
  Appropriate measures
    Chekhov, A. P. Woman in the case, and
      other stories
  Because of little apples
    Chekhov, A. P. Unknown Chekhov
  The beggar
    Schramm, W. L. ed. Great short stories
  The bet
    Thinker's digest (Periodical) Spoiled
      priest, and other stories

Boa constrictor and rabbit
    Chekhov, A. P. Unknown Chekhov
    Chekhov, A. P. Woman in the case, and
      other stories
Carelessness
    Fabricant, N. D. and Werner, H. eds.
      World's best doctor stories
Chorus girl
    Barrows, H. ed. 15 stories
La Cigale
    West, R. B. and Stallman, R. W. eds.
      Art of modern fiction
De-composition
    Chekhov, A. P. Unknown Chekhov
The diplomat
    Chekhov, A. P. Woman in the case, and
      other stories
Disagreeable experience
    Chekhov, A. P. Woman in the case, and
      other stories
The dream; a Christmas story
    Chekhov, A. P. Woman in the case, and
      other stories
Drowning
    Chekhov, A. P. Unknown Chekhov
Enemies
    Fabricant, N. D. and Werner, H. eds.
      World's best doctor stories
Eve of the the trial; the defendant's story
    Chekhov, A. P. Woman in the case, and
      other stories
A fragment
    Chekhov, A. P. Unknown Chekhov
Good news
    Chekhov, A. P. Unknown Chekhov
Gooseberries
    Felheim, M.; Newman, F. B. and Stein-
      hoff, W. R. eds. Modern short stories
    O'Faoláin, S. The short story
    Schorer, M. ed. The story
    Short, R. W. and Sewall, R. B. eds.
      Short stories for study. 1950 ed.
Grief
    Blodgett, H. W. ed. Story survey.
      1953 ed.
The guest
    Chekhov, A. P. Woman in the case, and
      other stories
His first appearance
    Chekhov, A. P. Woman in the case, and
      other stories
History of a business enterprise
    Chekhov, A. P. Woman in the case, and
      other stories
Holy simplicity
    Chekhov, A. P. Woman in the case,
      and other stories
    Same as: Saintly simplicity
Hydrophobia
    Chekhov, A. P. Unknown Chekhov
In exile
    Stegner, W. E.; Scowcroft, R. and
      Ilyin, B. eds. Writer's art
The lodger
    Chekhov, A. P. Unknown Chekhov
    Chekhov, A. P. Woman in the case,
      and other stories
The mask
    Chekhov, A. P. Woman in the case,
      and other stories
Moscow hypocrites
    Chekhov, A. P. Unknown Chekhov

Chekhov, Anton P.—*Continued*
Mutual superiority
Chekhov, A. P. Woman in the case,
and other stories
New villa
Lynskey, W. C. ed. Reading modern
fiction
On the harmful effects of tobacco; final
version
Chekhov, A. P. Unknown Chekhov
On the harmful effects of tobacco; first
version
Chekhov, A. P. Unknown Chekhov
On the road
Gordon, C. and Tate, A. eds. House
of fiction
Same as: On the way
On the way
Stegner, W. E.; Scowcroft, R. and
Ilyin, B. eds. Writer's art
Same as: On the road
One man's meat
Chekhov, A. P. Woman in the case,
and other stories
Other people's misfortune
Chekhov, A. P. Unknown Chekhov
Same as: Other people's trouble
Other people's trouble
Chekhov, A. P. Woman in the case,
and other stories
Same as: Other people's misfortune
Out of sheer boredom; a holiday love
story
Chekhov, A. P. Woman in the case,
and other stories
Peasants
Chekhov, A. P. Unknown Chekhov
Perpetuum mobile
Chekhov, A. P. Unknown Chekhov
Reporter's dream
Chekhov, A. P. Woman in the case,
and other stories
Saintly simplicity
Chekhov, A. P. Unknown Chekhov
Same as: Holy simplicity
The schoolmistress
Barrows, H. ed. 15 stories
75,000
Chekhov, A. P. Woman in the case,
and other stories
Sinister night
Chekhov, A. P. Woman in the case,
and other stories
The skit
Chekhov, A. P. Unknown Chekhov
Tædium vitæ
Chekhov, A. P. Woman in the case,
and other stories
Three Annas
Cody, S. ed. Greatest stories and how
they were written
Two in one
Chekhov, A. P. Unknown Chekhov
Two of a kind
Chekhov, A. P. Unknown Chekhov
Unpleasant incident
Chekhov, A. P. Woman in the case,
and other stories
Same as: An unpleasantness
An unpleasantness
Chekhov, A. P. Unknown Chekhov
Same as: Unpleasant incident

Vanka
Bogorad, S. N. and Trevithick, J. eds.
College miscellany
Neider, C. ed. Great short stories
Neider, C. ed. Great short stories from
the world's literature
Verotchka
Lamb, L. ed. Family book of best
loved short stories
Village Elder
Chekhov, A. P. Unknown Chekhov
Vint
Chekhov, A. P. Unknown Chekhov
Visit to friends
Chekhov, A. P. Unknown Chekhov
Chekhov, A. P. Woman in the case,
and other stories
Ward no. 6
Neider, C. ed. Short novels of the
masters
Rahv, P. ed. Great Russian short
novels
Woman in the case
Chekhov, A. P. Woman in the case,
and other stories
Women make trouble
Chekhov, A. P. Unknown Chekhov
Worse and worse
Chekhov, A. P. Unknown Chekhov
Yegor's story; excerpt from "The Island
of Sakhalin"
Chekhov, A. P. Unknown Chekhov
Cheley, Frank Hobart, 1889-
Big Bones rides alone
Furman, A. L. ed. Teen-age horse
stories
Chelsea cat. Kitchin, C. H. B.
Chemist and druggist. Harvey, W. F.
CHEMISTS
Harvey, W. F. Chemist and druggist
O'Donovan, M. Torrent damned
Ch'en Hsüan-Yu, fl. 8th century
Chienniang
Lin, Y. ed. Famous Chinese short
stories
Ch'engshih, T'uan. See T'uan Ch'engshih
Cherchez la femme. Porter, W. S.
Cherchez la frame. Rice, C. and Palmer, S.
Chéri. Colette, S. G.
CHEROKEE INDIANS
Porter, W. S. Atavism of John Tom
Little Bear
Porter, W. S. He also serves
Cheshire, Giff
Bad year
Western Writers of America. Holsters
and horses
Strangers in the evening
Western Writers of America. Bad men
and good
Chesnutt, Charles Waddell, 1856-1932
Wife of his youth
Dreer, H. ed. American literature by
Negro authors
CHESS
Aiken, C. P. The disciple
Bergengruen, W. Royal game
Dunsany, E. J. M. D. P. 18th baron.
Three sailors' gambit

CHESS—*Continued*
Elin, S. Fool's mate
Nemerov, H. and Johnson, W. R. Exchange of men

Chesterton, Gilbert Keith, 1874-1936
Absence of Mr Glass
Chesterton, G. K. Father Brown omnibus. 1951 ed.
Actor and the alibi
Chesterton, G. K. Father Brown omnibus. 1951 ed.
Arrow of heaven
Chesterton, G. K. Father Brown omnibus. 1951 ed.
Blast of the book
Chesterton, G. K. Father Brown omnibus. 1951 ed.
Blue cross
Chesterton, G. K. Father Brown omnibus. 1951 ed.
Neider, C. ed. Men of the high calling
Chief mourner of Marne
Chesterton, G. K. Father Brown omnibus. 1951 ed.
Crime of the Communist
Chesterton, G. K. Father Brown omnibus. 1951 ed.
Curse of the golden cross
Chesterton, G. K. Father Brown omnibus. 1951 ed.
Dagger with wings
Chesterton, G. K. Father Brown omnibus. 1951 ed.
Doom of the Darnaways
Chesterton, G. K. Father Brown omnibus. 1951 ed.
Duel of Dr Hirsch
Chesterton, G. K. Father Brown omnibus. 1951 ed.
Eye of Apollo
Chesterton, G. K. Father Brown omnibus. 1951 ed.
Fairy tale of Father Brown
Chesterton, G. K. Father Brown omnibus. 1951 ed.
Flying stars
Chesterton, G. K. Father Brown omnibus. 1951 ed.
Ghost of Gideon Wise
Chesterton, G. K. Father Brown omnibus. 1951 ed.
God of the gongs
Chesterton, G. K. Father Brown omnibus. 1951 ed.
Green man
Chesterton, G. K. Father Brown omnibus. 1951 ed.
Hammer of God
Cerf, B. A. and Moriarty, H. C. eds. Anthology of famous British stories
Chesterton, G. K. Father Brown omnibus. 1951 ed.
Head of Cæsar
Chesterton, G. K. Father Brown omnibus. 1951 ed.
Honour of Israel Gow
Chesterton, G. K. Father Brown omnibus. 1951 ed.
Insoluble problem
Chesterton, G. K. Father Brown omnibus. 1951 ed.

Invisible man
Chesterton, G. K. Father Brown omnibus. 1951 ed.
Christ, H. I. and Shostak, J. eds. Short stories
Man in the passage
Chesterton, G. K. Father Brown omnibus. 1951 ed.
Man with two beards
Chesterton, G. K. Father Brown omnibus. 1951 ed.
Miracle of Moon Crescent
Chesterton, G. K. Father Brown omnibus. 1951 ed.
Mirror of the magistrate
Chesterton, G. K. Father Brown omnibus. 1951 ed.
Mistake of the machine
Chesterton, G. K. Father Brown omnibus. 1951 ed.
Oracle of the dog
Chesterton, G. K. Father Brown omnibus. 1951 ed.
Paradise of thieves
Chesterton, G. K. Father Brown omnibus. 1951 ed.
Perishing of the pendragons
Chesterton, G. K. Father Brown omnibus. 1951 ed.
Point of a pin
Chesterton, G. K. Father Brown omnibus. 1951 ed.
Purple wig
Chesterton, G. K. Father Brown omnibus. 1951 ed.
Pursuit of Mr Blue
Chesterton, G. K. Father Brown omnibus. 1951 ed.
Queer feet
Chesterton, G. K. Father Brown omnibus. 1951 ed.
Quick one
Bond, R. T. ed. Handbook for poisoners
Chesterton, G. K. Father Brown omnibus. 1951 ed.
Red moon of Meru
Chesterton, G. K. Father Brown omnibus. 1951 ed.
Resurrection of Father Brown
Chesterton, G. K. Father Brown omnibus. 1951 ed.
Salad of Colonel Cray
Chesterton, G. K. Father Brown omnibus. 1951 ed.
Scandal of Father Brown
Chesterton, G. K. Father Brown omnibus. 1951 ed.
Secret garden
Chesterton, G. K. Father Brown omnibus. 1951 ed.
Secret of Father Brown
Chesterton, G. K. Father Brown omnibus. 1951 ed.
Secret of Flambeau
Chesterton, G. K. Father Brown omnibus. 1951 ed.
Sign of Prince Saradine
Chesterton, G. K. Father Brown omnibus. 1951 ed.
Sign of the broken sword
Chesterton, G. K. Father Brown omnibus. 1951 ed.

Chesterton, Gilbert K.—_Continued_
Song of the flying fish
Chesterton, G. K. Father Brown omnibus. 1951 ed.
Strange crime of John Boulnois
Chesterton, G. K. Father Brown omnibus. 1951 ed.
Three tools of death
Chesterton, G. K. Father Brown omnibus. 1951 ed.
Vampire of the village
Chesterton, G. K. Father Brown omnibus. 1951 ed.
Vanishing of Vaudrey
Chesterton, G. K. Father Brown omnibus. 1951 ed.
Worst crime in the world
Chesterton, G. K. Father Brown omnibus. 1951 ed.
Wrong shape
Chesterton, G. K. Father Brown omnibus. 1951 ed.

Chestor, Rui, pseud. See Courtier, Sidney Hobson

CHESTS (FURNITURE)
De La Mare, W. J. The riddle

CHEYENNE INDIANS
Johnson, D. M. Scars of honor
Johnson, D. M. War shirt
Lane, C. D. River dragon

CHICAGO. See Illinois—Chicago

Chichester, Francis Charles, 1901-
Palm Island plane factory
Jensen, P. ed. Fireside book of flying stories

Chicken dinner. Ullman, J. R.

Chicken on the wind. King, M. P.

CHICKENS. See Poultry

Chico and the badman. Thompson, T.

Chidester, Ann, 1919-
Mrs Ketting and Clark Gable
Prize stories of 1950
Wood smoke
Best American short stories, 1952

Chief mourner of Marne. Chesterton, G. K.

Chief operator. Ward, E. S. P.

Chienniang. Ch'en Hsüan-yu

Child, Charles B.
Inspector had a habit
Best detective stories of the year—1950

CHILD AUTHORS. See Children as authors

Child by Chronos. Harness, C. L.

The **child** is father. Beck, W.

CHILD MARRIAGE
Goodwin, R. V. Going home

Child missing! Queen, E. pseud.

CHILD MURDER. See Infanticide

CHILD MUSICIANS. See Children as musicians

Child of God. Bradford, R.

Child of God. O'Flaherty, L.

Child of void. St Clair, M.

CHILD PRODIGIES. See Children, Gifted

CHILD PSYCHOLOGY. See Children

Child so fair. Betts, D.

Child that walked at night. O'Meara, W.

Child wore a pink sweater. MacDonald, D.

CHILDBIRTH
Balzac, H. de. Mother's letter
Becker, S. D. Baptism of some importance
Cronin, A. J. Birth
Ferrara, J. Figurine of love
Gorki, M. Birth of a man
Irwin, M. E. F. The doctor
Taylor, E. Light of day
Vaughn, G. Tornado

Childhood of a leader. Sartre, J. P.

Childish thing. Metcalfe, J.

Childishness of Mr Mountfort. Benson, T.

CHILDREN
Aiken, C. P. Strange moonlight
Alexander, S. Part of the act
Betts, D. Sense of humor
Birmingham, S. G. Reappearance
Bolté, M. End of the depression
Carrighar, S. Marooned children
Dann, L. One summer afternoon
Evans, E. E. The shed
Faulkner, W. That evening sun
Friedman, S. Adam and Eve
Goudge, E. Doing good
Goudge, E. Midnight in the stable
Horwitz, J. Cup of tea
Ivanov, V. V. The kid
Kipling, R. Toomai of the elephants
Lagerkvist, P. F. Children's campaign
Mansfield, K. Doll's house
Munro, H. H. Lumber-room
Munro, H. H. Morlvera
Munro, H. H. The penance
Munro, H. H. The quest
Rabinowitz, S. Page from the Song of Songs
Russell, E. F. I am nothing
Salinger, J. D. For Esmé—with love and squalor
Schorer, M. What we don't know hurts us
Seaver, J. Kingdom in the corn
Stewart, R. The promise
Taylor, P. H. Bad dreams
Waldeck, T. J. Evil one
Wilson, H. L. Wrong twin
Wolfe, D. M. ed. Which grain will grow; 35 stories
Yoss, N. Children learn so fast
Zugsmith, L. Room in the world
See also Boys; Girls

Diseases
Williams, W. C. Use of force

CHILDREN, ABNORMAL AND BACKWARD
Davies, R. Arfon
Fitzgerald, F. S. K. Curious case of Benjamin Button
Kuttner, H. When the bough breaks
Rosaire, F. Pod of a weed

CHILDREN, CRIPPLED. See Cripples

CHILDREN, DEFORMED. See Children, Abnormal and backward

CHILDREN, GIFTED
Clifton, M. Star, Bright
De Vries, P. Tulip
Humphrey, W. Report cards
Huxley, A. L. Young Archimedes
Kuttner, H. Absalom

CHILDREN, GIFTED—*Continued*
Salinger, J. D. Teddy
Shiras, W. H. In hiding
Shiras, W. H. Opening doors

CHILDREN, LOST
Cheever, J. Sutton Place story
Heinlein, R. A. Black pits of Luna
Porter, W. S. Atavism of John Tom Little Bear
Porter, W. S. Church with an overshot wheel
Saroyan, W. Third day after Christmas
Van Doren, M. Rescue

CHILDREN, SICK
Colette, S. G. Sick child

The **children**. Cheever, J.

Children. Corkery, D.

CHILDREN AND PARENTS. See Parent and child

Children are bored on Sunday. Stafford, J.

CHILDREN AS AUTHORS
Ashford, D. A proposale
Waugh, E. Curse of the horse race

CHILDREN AS MUSICIANS
McCullers, C. S. Wunderkind

Children learn so fast. Yoss, N.

Children of Noah. Burman, B. L.

Children of Old Somebody. Goyen, W.

Children of Ruth. Elliott, G. P.

Children of Set. Coolidge, O. E.

Children of the times. Farrell, J. T.

Children's campaign. Lagerkvist, P. F.

Children's day with Mr Jovey Jessop's hounds. Surtees, R. S.

Children's hour. Keith, E.

CHILDREN'S PARTIES
Bowen, E. Easter egg party
Holland, W. Billy had a system
Munro, H. H. The strategist
See also Birthdays; Parties

Children's room. Jones, R. F.

Child's day. West, J.

Child's dream of a star. Dickens, C.

Child's play. Berger, T. L.

Child's play. Klass, P.

CHILE
Conrad, J. Gaspar Ruiz

Chiltipiquin. Brandon, W.

The **chimes**. Dickens, C.

CHIMES AND CHIMING. See Bells and bell-ringers

CHIMNEYS
Melville, H. I and my chimney

CHIMPANZEES
Leinster, M. Keyhole

Chin, Yuen. See Yuen Chin

CHINA
Dunsany, E. J. M. D. P. 18th baron. East and West
Lin, Y. ed. Famous Chinese short stories; 20 stories

1900-date
Buck, P. S. Good river
Buck, P. S. Old demon
Buck, P. S. One named Jesus

Chou, S. Benediction
Shen, T. Little Flute

Hangchow
Mrs White

Hong Kong
Small, S. H. Stalking shadow

Legends and folk tales
See Legends and folk tales—China

Shanghai
Patterson, R. Babe

China run. Paterson, N.

Chinese dagger. Small, S. H.

CHINESE IN AUSTRALIA
Travers, P. L. Ah Wong

CHINESE IN ENGLAND
Burke, T. Chink and the child

CHINESE IN INDO-CHINA
Payne, P. S. R. Red mountain

CHINESE IN MONGOLIA
Vogau, B. A. Big heart

CHINESE IN THE UNITED STATES
Ekbergh, I. D. Mysterious Chinese mandrake
Harte, B. Wan Lee, the pagan
Small, S. H. Chinese dagger

Ching, Ching, Chinaman. Steele, W. D.

The **Chink**. Stegner, W. E.

Chink and the child. Burke, T.

Chinn, Laurene Chambers
Spelling bee
Bachelor, J. M.; Henry, R. L. and Salisbury, R. eds. Current thinking and writing; 2d ser.

Chinoiserie. McCloy, H.

Chip off the old block. Stegner, W. E.

CHIPMUNKS
Van Doren, M. Lady over the wall

CHIPPEWA INDIANS
Macfarlan, A. A. Moose boy

CHIVALRY
Bergengruen, W. Shining fools
See also Knights and knighthood

The **choice**. Wharton, E. N. J.

Choice of the litter. Lull, R.

Choice of weapons. Newhouse, E.

CHOIRMASTERS
Chekhov, A. P. Worse and worse

CHOIRS (MUSIC)
Hardy, T. Absent-mindedness in a parish choir

CHOLERA
Allen, J. L. King Solomon of Kentucky
Kipling, R. Without benefit of clergy
See also Epidemics

Chop-sticks. Chrisman, A. B.

Chore for a spaceman. Sheldon, W.

Chorus girl. Chekhov, A. P.

Chou, Shu-jên, 1881-1936
Benediction
Neider, C. ed. Great short stories from the world's literature

Chowsie. Bendrodt, J. C.

Chrisman, Arthur Bowie, 1889-1953
  Chop-sticks
    Fenner, P. R. comp. Fools and funny fellows

Christ in concrete. Di Donato, P.

CHRISTENINGS
  De La Mare, W. J. The bowl
  Hardy, T. Three strangers

CHRISTIAN LIFE
  Blackburn, E. R. Swaying elms
  Lantz, J. E. ed. Stories of Christian living; 18 stories

CHRISTIAN SCIENCE
  Munro, H. H. The quest

Christiane the Huguenot. Blackburn, E. R.

Christie, Agatha (Miller) 1891-
  Accident
    Bond, R. T. ed. Handbook for poisoners
  Adventure of the Clapham cook
    Christie, A. M. Under dog, and other stories
  Affair at the Victory Ball
    Christie, A. M. Under dog, and other stories
  Cornish mystery
    Christie, A. M. Under dog, and other stories
  King of clubs
    Christie, A. M. Under dog, and other stories
  Last séance
    Merril, J. ed. Beyond the barriers of space and time
  Lemesurier inheritance
    Christie, A. M. Under dog, and other stories
  Market Basing mystery
    Christie, A. M. Under dog, and other stories
  Plymouth Express
    Christie, A. M. Under dog, and other stories
  Submarine plans
    Christie, A. M. Under dog, and other stories
  Under dog
    Christie, A. M. Under dog, and other stories

CHRISTMAS
  Aldrich, B. S. Another brought gifts
  American girl (Periodical) Christmas all year 'round; 25 stories
  Baker, R. S. A day of pleasant bread
  Broun, H. C. Even to Judas
  Cheever, J. Christmas is a sad season for the poor
  Cooke, A. Christmas Eve; 3 stories
  Cousins, M. Christmas gift; 8 stories
  Cousins, M. Uncle Edgar and the reluctant saint
  Dickens, C. Christmas carol
  Dickens, C. Christmas stories; 3 stories
  Dostoevskii, F. M. Heavenly Christmas tree
  Eggleston, M. W. Red stocking, and other Christmas stories; 20 stories
  Elliot, I. Christmas is a time for great things

  Elmquist, R. M. ed. Fifty years of Christmas; 16 stories
  Foster, M. Present for Christmas
  Goodman, P. Iddings Clark
  Goudge, E. Reward of faith; 8 stories
  Grimson, M. S. Christmas story
  Grimson, M. S. Gather up the pieces
  Harte, B. How Santa Claus came to Simpson's Bar
  Henderson, D. Brute's Christmas
  Hertlein, R. P. G. Christmas
  Irwin, M. E. F. Mistletoe
  Krige, U. Christmas box
  Locke, W. J. Wise men of Trehenna
  Lohan, R. and Lohan, M. eds. New Christmas treasury; 27 stories
  Mathews, M. Tough little Christmas story
  Miller, A. D. Plum pudding and mince pie
  Morley, C. D. Home again
  Munro, H. H. Bertie's Christmas Eve
  Porter, W. S. Chaparral Christmas gift
  Porter, W. S. Christmas by injunction
  Porter, W. S. Compliments of the season
  Porter, W. S. Gift of the magi
  Porter, W. S. Whistling Dick's Christmas stocking
  Puzo, M. Last Christmas
  Sawyer, R. Fiddler, play fast, play faster
  Schubert, P. White Elk
  Schulberg, B. W. My Christmas carol
  Stifter, A. Rock crystal
  Taber, G. B. Christmas gift
  Van Dyke, H. First Christmas tree
  Van Paassen, P. Uncle Kees protests
  Wall, J. W. Christmas story
  Weber, L. M. Christmas thaw
  Wiggin, K. D. S. The Ruggleses go to a Christmas party
    See also Jesus Christ—Nativity

Christmas angel. Eggleston, M. W.

Christmas anyhow. Hill, M. Y.

Christmas at Polly Moran's. Gregutt, H. C.

Christmas at the Bachs'. Brachvogel, A. E.

Christmas at Thunder Gap. Wright, K. O.

Christmas box. Krige, U.

Christmas by injunction. Porter, W. S.

Christmas carol. Davis, S. P.

Christmas carol. Dickens, C.

Christmas cherries. Gray, E. J.

Christmas Day in the workhouse. Wilson, A.

Christmas Eve. Cooke, A.

Christmas Eve in a lumber camp. Gordon, C. W.

Christmas Eve, one-three. Cooke, A.

Christmas every day. Howells, W. D.

Christmas Eve's Day. Benefield, B.

Christmas game. Munby, A. N. L.

Christmas gift. Powys, T. F.

Christmas gift. Taber, G. B.

A **Christmas** gift for father. Eggleston, M. W.

CHRISTMAS GIFTS. See Christmas; Gifts

Christmas guest. Brown, K. I.

Christmas in Carthage. Gilbertson, M. G.
Christmas is a sad season for the poor. Cheever, J.
Christmas is a time for great things. Elliot, I.
Christmas meeting. Timperley, R.
Christmas morning. O'Donovan, M.
Christmas on Ganymede. Asimov, I.
Christmas party. Milne, A. A.
Christmas rose. Fitzsimmons, B. J.
Christmas shadrach. Stockton, F. R.
Christmas skis. Miers, E. S.
Christmas solo. Eggleston, M. W.
Christmas song. Bates, H. E.
CHRISTMAS STORIES. See Christmas
Christmas story. Grimson, M. S.
Christmas story. Wall, J. W.
Christmas thaw. Weber, L. M.
Christmas tree. Youd, C.
Christmas tree and a wedding. Dostoevskiĭ, F. M.
CHRISTMAS TREES
  Goudge, E. Legend of the first Christmas tree
  Grimson, M. S. Christmas story
  Hale, L. P. Peterkins' Christmas tree
  Van Dyke, H. First Christmas tree
Christmas visitor. Eggleston, M. W.
Christopher, John, 1922-
  Balance
    Best science fiction stories: 1952
  Man of destiny
    Galaxy science fiction magazine. Galaxy reader of science fiction
    Lesser, M. A. ed. Looking forward
  Socrates
    Merril, J. ed. Beyond human ken
    Sloane, W. M. ed. Stories for tomorrow
Christopher, Robert, 1924-
  Jishin
    Best American short stories, 1950
Christowe, Stoyan, 1898-
  My grandfather's eyes
    Certner, S. and Henry, G. H. eds. Short stories for our times
Christ's tree. Booth, M. B. C.
Chromium helmet. Waldo, E. H.
The chronicler. Van Vogt, A. E.
The chronoclasm. Harris, J. B.
Chronokinesis of Jonathan Hull. White, W. A. P.
The chrysanthemums. Steinbeck, J.
CHURCH ATTENDANCE
  Bennett, P. Fugitive from the mind
  Hawthorne, N. Sunday at home
  Irwin, M. E. F. Earlier service
CHURCH SCHOOLS
  Doty, W. L. Parochial school
Church with an overshot-wheel. Porter, W. S.
CHURCHES
  Bunner, H. C. Two churches of 'Quawket
  Faulkner, W. Shingles for the Lord

  Hall, J. B. In the time of demonstration
  Lemelin, R. Stations of the Cross
  Melville, H. Temple first
Churchyard yew. LeFanu, J. S.
CHURCHYARDS. See Cemeteries
Chute, Beatrice Joy, 1913-
  Alias All-American
    Chute, B. J. Teen-age sports parade
  Bench warmer
    Boys' life (Periodical) Boys' life Adventure stories
  Big shot
    Chute, B. J. Teen-age sports parade
  Double fault
    Chute, B. J. Teen-age sports parade
  Doubles or nothing
    Owen, F. ed. Teen-age victory parade
  Dumb bunny
    Fenner, P. R. comp. Crack of the bat
  Fall guy
    Owen, F. ed. Teen-age winter sports stories
  Five captains
    Chute, B. J. Teen-age sports parade
  Four-ring circus
    Owen, F. ed. Teen-age winter sports stories
  Kid brother
    Herzberg, M. J. comp. Treasure chest of sport stories
  Magnificent merger
    Chute, B. J. Teen-age sports parade
  Master mind
    Chute, B. J. Teen-age sports parade
  Really important person
    Certner, S. and Henry, G. H. eds. Short stories for our times
  Red Pepper
    Chute, B. J. Teen-age sports parade
  Ski high
    Chute, B. J. Teen-age sports parade
  Thank you, Dr Russell
    Certner, S. and Henry, G. H. eds. Short stories for our times
  Too close to nature
    Chute, B. J. Teen-age sports parade
  Triple threat
    Chute, B. J. Teen-age sports parade
  The winner
    Chute, B. J. Teen-age sports parade
Chute, Verne, 1917-
  Never trust the obvious
    Mystery Writers of America, inc. Four-&-twenty bloodhounds
Ciancimino, Helen. See Gregutt, Helen Ciancimino
Cicellis, Kay
  Aegean storm
    Cicellis, K. Easy way
  Easy way
    Cicellis, K. Easy way
  The excursion
    Cicellis, K. Easy way
  Hungry man
    Cicellis, K. Easy way
  Miracles of the Saint
    Cicellis, K. Easy way
  No admittance
    Cicellis, K. Easy way
  Recovery
    Cicellis, K. Easy way

Cicellis, Kay—*Continued*
  Turn of the tide
    Cicellis, K. Easy way
  Twisted branch
    Cicellis, K. Easy way
  Visit to a neighbor
    Cicellis, K. Easy way
The **cicerone**. McCarthy, M. T.
La **Cigale**. Chekhov, A. P.
CIGARETTES. See Smoking
CIGARS. See Smoking
Cinderella. T'uan Ch'engshih
Cinderella's sister. Stern, G. B.
CIPHER AND TELEGRAPH CODES
  Poe, E. A. The gold-bug
  Porter, W. S. Calloway's code
Circular valley. Bowles, P. F.
Circumstance. Spofford, H. E. P.
CIRCUS
  Alexander, S. Part of the act
  Allen, E. and Kelley, F. B. Public enemies
  Annixter, P. pseud. With the greatest of
    ease
  Benson, T. Frog and the lion
  Brookhouser, F. My father and the circus
  Brookhouser, F. Snake woman and the
    preacher's wife
  Lang, D. An elephant never forgets
  Maier, H. World outside
  Welty, E. Keela, the outcast Indian
    maiden
      See also Acrobats and acrobatism;
  Carnival
CIRCUS PERFORMERS. See Circus
CITIES, IMAGINARY. See Imaginary
  cities
CITIES AND TOWNS
  Blish, J. Okie
  Lewis, S. An assemblage of husbands
    and wives
  Peretz, I. L. Dead town
  Porter, W. S. Municipal report
  Porter, W. S. Pride of the cities
  Tucker, L. Cubic city
      See also Ghost towns
Citizen Woli Brenner. Bergelson, D.
The **citizner**. Zara, L.
The **city**. Bradbury, R.
The **city**. Horwitz, J.
City. Simak, C. D.
CITY LIFE. See Cities and towns
City of dreadful night. Porter, W. S.
City of Singing Flame. Smith, C. A.
City of the angels. Davidson, S.
City of the dead. Gibran, K.
City of the sun. Campanella, T.
City underground. Thibaudeau, C.
City wise. Greenfield, I.
Civic crisis. Boyd, J.
CIVIL LIBERTY. See Liberty
Civil rights. Arico, V.
CIVIL SERVICE
  Maugham, W. S. Casual affair
  Maugham, W. S. Door of opportunity

  Maugham, W. S. Mackintosh
  Maugham, W. S. The outstation
  Waddington, P. Street that got mislaid
CIVIL WAR (SPAIN) See Spain—20th
  century—Civil War, 1936-1939
CIVIL WAR (UNITED STATES). See
  United States—19th century—Civil
  War
Civil War. Sholokhov, M. A.
Clair de lune. Schneider, G. W.
CLAIRVOYANCE
  Porter, W. S. Fifth wheel
  Wells, H. G. Crystal egg
  Winslow, T. S. Odd old lady
      See also Fortune telling; Mind read-
  ing
Clancy in the Tower of Babel. Cheever, J.
CLARE. See Ireland—Clare
Clarimonde. Gautier, T.
Clarion call. Porter, W. S.
Clark, Alfred Alexander Gordon, 1900-
  Amazing lady
    This week magazine. This week's
      short-short stories
  Murderer's luck
    Best detective stories of the year—1952
CLARK, GEORGE ROGERS, 1752-1818
  Gulick, G. C. Waters of Manitou
Clark, Walter Van Tilburg, 1909-
  The anonymous
    Clark, W. Van T. Watchful gods, and
      other stories
  Buck in the hills
    Clark, W. Van T. Watchful gods, and
      other stories
  Fish who could close his eyes
    Clark, W. Van T. Watchful gods, and
      other stories
  Hook
    Clark, W. Van T. Watchful gods, and
      other stories
    Lynskey, W. C. ed. Reading modern fic-
      tion
  Indian well
    Andrews, R. C. ed. My favorite stories
      of the great outdoors
    Clark, W. Van T. Watchful gods, and
      other stories
  Portable phonograph
    Bogorad, S. N. and Trevithick, J. eds.
      College miscellany
    Burrell, J. A. and Cerf, B. A. eds. An-
      thology of famous American stories
    Clark, W. Van T. Watchful gods, and
      other stories
    Crossen, K. F. ed. Adventures in to-
      morrow
    Felheim, M.; Newman, F. B. and Stein-
      hoff, W. R. eds. Modern short sto-
      ries
    Schorer, M. ed. The story
    Stegner, W. E.; Scowcroft, R. and
      Ilyin, B. eds. Writer's art
    West, R. B. and Stallman, R. W. eds.
      Art of modern fiction
  The pretender
    Meredith, S. ed. Bar 3
  The rapids
    Clark, W. Van T. Watchful gods, and
      other stories

Clark, Walter Van T.—*Continued*
Watchful gods
  Clark, W. Van T. Watchful gods, and other stories
Why don't you look where you're going?
  Clark, W. Van T. Watchful gods, and other stories
Wind and the snow of winter
  Best of the Best American short stories, 1915-1950
  Clark, W. Van T. Watchful gods, and other stories
  First-prize stories, 1919-1954
  Ludwig, J. B. and Poirier, W. R. eds. Stories, British and American

Clarke, Arthur Charles, 1917-
All the time in the world
  Wollheim, D. A. ed. Prize science fiction
Breaking strain
  Clarke, A. C. Expedition to earth
Deep range
  Star science fiction stories, no. 3
Exile of the eons
  Clarke, A. C. Expedition to earth
Expedition to earth
  Clarke, A. C. Expedition to earth
Fires within
  Derleth, A. W. ed. Worlds of tomorrow
Forgotten enemy
  Sloane, W. M. ed. Stories for tomorrow
Hide and seek
  Clarke, A. C. Expedition to earth
  Sloane, W. M. ed. Space, space, space
History lesson
  Clarke, A. C. Expedition to earth
  Conklin, G. ed. Omnibus of science fiction
"If I forget thee, oh Earth. . ."
  Clarke, A. C. Expedition to earth
Inheritance
  Clarke, A. C. Expedition to earth
Loophole
  Clarke, A. C. Expedition to earth
Nine billion names of God
  Sloane, W. M. ed. Stories for tomorrow
  Star science fiction stories [no. 1]
No morning after
  Derleth, A. W. ed. Time to come
Second dawn
  Clarke, A. C. Expedition to earth
Seeker of the sphinx
  Year's best science fiction novels, 1952
The sentinel
  Clarke, A. C. Expedition to earth
Superiority
  Clarke, A. C. Expedition to earth
  Derleth, A. W. ed. Worlds of tomorrow
Thirty seconds—thirty days
  Startling stories (Periodical) Best from Startling stories
Transience
  Lesser, M. A. ed. Looking forward
Walk in the dark
  Conklin, G. ed. Possible worlds of science fiction
Wall of darkness
  Moskowitz, S. comp. Editor's choice in science fiction

Clash by night. Kuttner, H.

Class. Foote, J. T.
CLASS DISTINCTION
  Mansfield, K. Doll's house
Claud's dog. Dahl, R.
Claudy, Carl Harry, 1879-
According to the landmarks
  Claudy, C. H. These were brethren
Against orders
  Claudy, C. H. These were brethren
Any pain, peril or danger
  Claudy, C. H. These were brethren
The atheist
  Claudy, C. H. These were brethren
Brother Bascombe is annoyed
  Claudy, C. H. These were brethren
Diary of a hard-boiled noble
  Claudy, C. H. These were brethren
Due and timely warning
  Claudy, C. H. These were brethren
For a master's wages
  Claudy, C. H. These were brethren
Fourth point
  Claudy, C. H. These were brethren
Gentle Masonic way
  Claudy, C. H. These were brethren
Greater love hath no man than this
  Claudy, C. H. These were brethren
He told it to the judge
  Claudy, C. H. These were brethren
Helmet of Pluto
  American boy (Periodical) American boy Adventure stories
Hidden riches of secret places
  Claudy, C. H. These were brethren
High finance
  Claudy, C. H. These were brethren
Land of No Shadow
  Del Rey, L.; Matschat, C. H. and Carmer, C. L. eds. Year after tomorrow
Long arm
  Claudy, C. H. These were brethren
Master minds of Mars
  Del Rey, L.; Matschat, C. H. and Carmer, C. L. eds. Year after tomorrow
Mystery
  Claudy, C. H. These were brethren
Not blotted
  Claudy, C. H. These were brethren
Plumbers
  Claudy, C. H. These were brethren
Three dollars
  Claudy, C. H. These were brethren
To entertain strangers
  Claudy, C. H. These were brethren
Tongue of beast
  Del Rey, L.; Matschat, C. H. and Carmer, C. L. eds. Year after tomorrow
Two pillars blight
  Claudy, C. H. These were brethren
Was it murder?
  Claudy, C. H. These were brethren
Witnesses
  Claudy, C. H. These were brethren
Yellow streak
  Claudy, C. H. These were brethren

Claustrophobia. Goodloe, A. C.

Clay, Richard, 1915-
Beautiful night for Orion
  Best American short stories, 1954
Very sharp for jagging
  Prize stories 1954

Clay. Joyce, J.
Clay dish. Blackburn, R. H.
Clayton, John Bell, 1906-1955
  Ride a pale ghost into night and time
    Jones, K. M. New Confederate short
    stories
  White circle
    First-prize stories, 1919-1954
Clean platter. Beck, W.
Clean well-lighted place. Hemingway, E.
CLEANING WOMEN. See Servants—
  Cleaning women
Clearing in the sky. Stuart, J.
The clematis. Canine, W.
Clemens, Samuel Langhorne, 1835-1910
  Buck Fanshaw's funeral
    Emrich, D. ed. Comstock bonanza
    Foerster, N. ed. American poetry and
    prose. 1952 ed.
  Celebrated jumping frog of Calaveras
  County
    Burrell, J. A. and Cerf, B. A. eds. An-
    thology of famous American stories
    Day, A. G. ed. Greatest American
    short stories
    Foerster, N. ed. American poetry and
    prose. 1952 ed.
    Lamb, L. ed. Family book of best
    loved short stories
  Concerning notaries
    Emrich, D. ed. Comstock bonanza
  Dog's tale
    Neider, C. ed. Great short stories from
    the world's literature
  Eve's diary
    Selden, R. ed. Ways of God and men
  Jim Baker's blue-jay yarn
    Andrews, R. C. ed. My favorite stories
    of the great outdoors
  Latest sensation (II)
    Emrich, D. ed. Comstock bonanza
  Man that corrupted Hadleyburg
    Burrell, J. A. and Cerf, B. A. eds. An-
    thology of famous American stories
    Foerster, N. ed. American poetry and
    prose. 1952 ed.
  Mr Skae's item
    Emrich, D. ed. Comstock bonanza
  My bloody massacre (I)
    Emrich, D. ed. Comstock bonanza
  My late senatorial secretaryship
    Emrich, D. ed. Comstock bonanza
  My platonic sweetheart
    Blodgett, H. W. ed. Story survey.
    1953 ed.
  Mysterious stranger
    Ludwig, R. M. and Perry, M. B. eds.
    Nine short novels
  Petrified man (I-II)
    Emrich, D. ed. Comstock bonanza
  Stolen white elephant
    Queen, E. pseud. ed. Literature of
    crime
  Wings
    Brentano, F. ed. The word lives on
Clement, Hal, pseud. See Stubbs, Harry
  Clement
Clements, Calvin J.
  Captain's prisoner
    Argosy (Periodical) Argosy Book of
    sea stories

Keep off the rail!
  Argosy (Periodical) Argosy Book of
  sports stories
Cleo. Runyon, D.
CLERGY
  Barrie, Sir J. M. bart. Farewell Miss
    Julie Logan
  Betts, D. Family album
  Bloch, J. R. Heresy of the water taps
  Bowles, P. F. Pastor Dowe at Tacaté
  Bunner, M. C. Two churches of 'Quawket
  Clemens, S. L. Buck Fanshaw's funeral
  Davies, R. Conflict in Morfa
  Gally, J. W. Big Jack Small
  Galsworthy, J. Manna
  Goodman, J. C. Kingdom of Gordon
  Hale, E. E. My double, and how he undid
    me
  Harvey, W. F. Vicar's web
  Hawthorne, N. Minister's black veil
  Munro, H. H. Lost sanjak
  Neider, C. ed. Men of the high calling;
    14 stories
  Russell, B. A. W. R. 3d earl. Benefit of
    clergy
  Schaefer, J. W. Takes a real man. . .
  Steele, W. D. Ching, Ching, Chinaman
  Street, J. H. The old, old story
  Thomason, J. W. Preacher goes to Texas
  Watson, J. His mother's sermon
  Wolfe, T. Portrait of Bascom Hawke
CLERGY, ANGLICAN AND EPISCO-
  PAL
  Queen, E. pseud. Witch of Times Square
  Van Paassen, P. The unsaid prayer
CLERGY, CATHOLIC. See Catholic priests
Clerical error. Cozzens, J. G.
CLERKS
  Golding, L. Doomington wanderer
  Joyce, J. Counterparts
  Moore, G. Clerk's quest
Clerk's quest. Moore, G.
CLEVELAND, GROVER, PRESIDENT
  U.S. 1837-1908
  Porter, W. S. Snapshot at the President
Clever cockatoo. Bentley, E. C.
Clever Elsa. Grimm, J. L. K. and Grimm,
  W. K.
Clever Manka. Fillmore, P. H.
The cliff. Sansom, W.
Cliff dance. Thompson, H.
Clifton, Mark, 1906-
  The conqueror
    Best science-fiction stories: 1953
    Conklin, G. ed. Omnibus of science fic-
    tion
  Star Bright
    Galaxy science fiction magazine. Second
    Galaxy reader of science fiction
    Wollheim, D. A. ed. Prize science fiction
  What have I done?
    Merril, J. ed. Beyond human ken
Clifton, Mark, 1906- and Apostolides, Alex,
  1923-
  Crazy Joey
    Merril, J. ed. Beyond the barriers of
    space and time

Clifton, M. and Apostolides, A.—*Continued*
What thin partitions
Best science-fiction stories: 1954
Moskowitz, S. comp. Editor's choice in
science fiction
Climate of the family. Chaikin, N. G.
Climb for the big ones. Gregutt, H. C.
Climbing for goats. White, S. E.
Clingerman, Mildred
Minister without portfolio
Conklin, G. ed. Invaders of earth
Sloane, W. M. ed. Stories for tomorrow
Stair trick
Magazine of fantasy and science fiction.
Best from Fantasy and science fiction;
2d ser.
The **clinic.** Waldo, E. H.
Clipped wings. Knapp, S. E.
CLIPPER SHIPS. See Sailing vessels
Cloak of Aesir. Campbell, J. W.
Clochette. Maupassant, G. de
CLOCKMAKERS. See Clocks and watches
CLOCKS AND WATCHES
Canning, V. Man who hated time
De La Mare, W. J. The talisman
Farrell, J. T. Willie Collins
Haliburton, T. C. Sam Slick the clock-
maker
Platt, G. Very false alarm
Cloete, Stuart, 1897-
Silence of Mr Prendegast
Esquire (Periodical) Girls from Esquire
Clog dance for a dead farce. Kneale, N.
Close your eyes. Newhouse, E.
Closed cabinet
Davenport, B. ed. Tales to be told in
the dark
Closed door. Guest, A.
Closed shop. Maugham, W. S.
Closed trophy room. Marshall, E.
CLOTHING AND DRESS
Gordimer, N. The talisman
Porter, W. S. From each according to his
ability
Porter, W. S. Purple dress
Woolf, V. S. New dress
Clouds on the Circle-P. Haycox, E.
Clovis on parental responsibilities. Munro,
H. H.
Clovis on the alleged romance of business.
Munro, H. H.
CLUBS
Dunsany, E. J. M. D. P. 18th baron. Ex-
iles' Club
Whitney, P. A. Lucky 'leven
Clue of the red wig. Carr, J. D.
Clues of the tattooed man & the broken leg.
Rawson, C.
Clumpy who was all arms and legs. Strain,
F. B.
Clyde. Farrell, J. T.
COACHING (ATHLETICS)
Scott, V. Don't run, don't pass

COAL MINES AND MINING
Wales
Davies, R. Boy with a trumpet, and other
selected short stories; 20 stories
Coaly-bay the outlaw horse. Seton, E. T.
Coat for St Patrick's Day. Ready, W. B.
Coates, Robert Myron, 1897-
The need
Best American short stories, 1953
Coatsworth, Elizabeth Jane, 1893-
The attack
Fenner, P. R. comp. Indians, Indians,
Indians
Forgotten island
Story parade (Periodical) Adventure
stories
Patchy
Story parade (Periodical) Adventure
stories
Peddler's cart
Fenner, P. R. comp. Yankee Doodle
Race in the wilderness
Fenner, P R. comp. Yankee Doodle
Cobb, Irvin Shrewsbury, 1876-1944
Boys will be boys
Best of the Best American short stories,
1915-1950
Blaustein, A. P ed. Fiction goes to
court
Occurrence up a side street
Bond, R. T. ed. Handbook for poisoners
Snake doctor
First-prize stories, 1919-1954
Summers, H. S. ed. Kentucky story
Cobbler, cobbler, mend my shoe. Maxtone
Graham, J. A.
COBBLERS. See Shoemakers
Coblentz, Catherine (Cate) 1897-1951
Dog who chose a prince
Fenner, P. R. comp. Dogs, dogs, dogs
Montgomery the loyalest
Harper, W. comp. Dog show
Coblentz, Stanton Arthur, 1896-
Sunward
Wollheim, D. A. comp. Flight into space
COBRAS. See Snakes
Cobra's hood. Holland, R. S.
The **cobweb.** Munro, H. H.
COCHISE, APACHE CHIEF, d. 1874
L'Amour, L. Gift of Cochise
Cochran, Ruth Gilbert, 1893-
Present for Elly
American girl (Periodical) Christmas all
year 'round
Sally steps in
Furman, A. L. ed. Everygirls mystery
stories
Cock-a-doodle-doo! Melville, H.
COCK FIGHTING
Benson, T. White cock
Foote, J. T. Fowl disaster
Wolfert, I. The indomitable
See also Roosters
Cock of Socrates. Alas, L.
COCKATOOS
Cottrell, D. M. Pit in the jungle

Cockburn, Claud, 1904-
  Total recall
    Best detective stories of the year—1952
COCKNEY DIALECT. See Dialect sto-
  ries—English—Cockney
Cockrell, Eustace Williams
  Keyhole artist
    This week magazine. This week's short-
    short stories
COCKROACHES
  Babikoff, V. Day of rest
  Bates, H. Death of a sensitive
  Gilpatric, G. Mr Glencannon and the ail-
    ing cockroach
  Zamiatin, E. I. God
COCKS. See Cock fighting; Poultry; Roost-
  ers
COCKTAIL PARTIES. See Parties
Cocktail party. Saroyan, W.
Coda to a writers' conference. Fletcher, V.
The code. Moore, C. L.
CODES, TELEGRAPH. See Cipher and
  telegraph codes
Coffin, Robert Peter Tristram, 1892-1955
  Seraph in the apple tree
    Hazeltine, A. I. comp. Selected stories
    for teen-agers
The coffin. Krige, U.
COFFINS
  Krige, U. The coffin
  Pirandello, L. Reserved coffin
  Poe, E. A. Oblong box
Coggins, Frank
  The killer
    Ford, N. A. and Faggett, H. L. eds.
    Best short stories by Afro-American
    writers (1925-1950)
Cogswell, Theodore R.
  Minimum sentence
    Galaxy science fiction magazine. Second
    Galaxy reader of science fiction
  Specter general
    Norton, A. M. ed. Space service
  Wall around the world
    Merril, J. ed. Beyond the barriers of
    space and time
Cohan, Alfred E. 1920-
  Bridegroom on the scaffold
    American vanguard, 1950
Cohen, Octavus Roy, 1891-
  Always trust a cop
    Queen, E. pseud. ed. Queen's awards;
    7th ser.
  Florian Slappey—private eye
    Best detective stories of the year—1951
  Law and the profits
    Blaustein, A. P. ed. Fiction goes to
    court
  Once upon a crime
    Best detective stories of the year—1952
  Toot for a toot
    Moskowitz, S. ed. Great railroad sto-
    ries of the world
Cohen of Trinity. Levy, A.
Cohn, Edgar A. 1927-
  The present
    American vanguard, 1953

Cohn, Emil, 1881-1948
  Given years
    Cohn, E. Stories and fantasies from the
    Jewish past
  Honi ha-Maeggel
    Cohn, E. Stories and fantasies from the
    Jewish past
  It looks like justice
    Cohn, E. Stories and fantasies from the
    Jewish past
  Legend of Rabbi Akiba
    Cohn, E. Stories and fantasies from the
    Jewish past
  Rabban Gamaliel
    Cohn, E. Stories and fantasies from the
    Jewish past
  Rabbi and emperor
    Cohn, E. Stories and fantasies from the
    Jewish past
  Rebellious tree
    Cohn, E. Stories and fantasies from
    the Jewish past
  Remains of virtue
    Cohn, E. Stories and fantasies from
    the Jewish past
  Simha of Worms
    Cohn, E. Stories and fantasies from
    the Jewish past
  Waters of Shiloah
    Cohn, E. Stories and fantasies from
    the Jewish past
A coincidence. Farrell, J. T.
Cold day. Saroyan, W.
Cold front. Stubbs, H. C.
Cold money. Queen, E. pseud.
Cold potato. De Vries, P.
Cold war. Neville, K.
Cold water and cherry pie. O'Rourke, F.
Cold winds of Adesta. Flanagan, T.
Cold winter. Caldwell, E.
Cold world. Williams, W. C.
Coleman comes back. Emery, R. G.
Colette, Sidonie Gabrielle, 1873-1954
  The cat
    Colette, S. G. Short novels of Colette
  Chéri
    Colette, S. G. Short novels of Colette
  Duo
    Colette, S. G. Short novels of Colette
  Indulgent husband
    Colette, S. G. Short novels of Colette
  Last of Chéri
    Colette, S. G. Short novels of Colette
  Other one
    Colette, S. G. Short novels of Colette
  Sick child
    Gordon, C. and Tate, A. eds. House
    of fiction
Collaboration. Collier, J.
COLLABORATIONISTS. See Treason
Colladay, Morrison M.
  Planetoid of doom
    Conklin, G. ed. Big book of science
    fiction
The collar. Irwin, M. E. F.
The collector. Heard, G.
The collectors. Dewey, G. G. and Dan-
  cey, M.

COLLEGE ALUMNI
Calisher, H. One of the chosen
Farrell, J. T. Virginians are coming

COLLEGE AND SCHOOL DRAMA
Fitzgerald, F. S. K. Captured shadow
See also Amateur theatricals

COLLEGE LIFE

United States

Beck, W. Ask me no more
Boyd, J. Elms and Fair Oaks
Brandon, W. College queen
Caldwell, E. Snacker
Fitzgerald, F. S. K. Woman with a past
Milburn, G. Student in economics
Parker, J. R. Domino method
Porter, W. S. Chair of philanthro-
    mathematics
Rydberg, E. Little genius
Seager, A. All problems are simple
Seager, A. Bang on the head
Shulman, M. The many loves of Dobie
    Gillis; 11 stories
Willingham, C. Wilby spirit

College marriage. Woodward, G. B.

COLLEGE SPORTS. See Sports

College queen. Brandon, W.

College star. Doty, W. L.

Collier, John, 1901-
Ah the university
    Collier, J. Fancies and goodnights
Another American tragedy
    Collier, J. Fancies and goodnights
    Fabricant, N. D. and Werner, H. eds.
    World's best doctor stories
Are you too late or was I too early
    Collier, J. Fancies and goodnights
Back for Christmas
    Collier, J. Fancies and goodnights
Bird of prey
    Collier, J. Fancies and goodnights
    Conklin, G. and Conklin, L. T. eds.
    Supernatural reader
Bottle party
    Carrington, H. ed. Week-end book of
        ghost stories
    Collier, J. Fancies and goodnights
Cancel all I said
    Collier, J. Fancies and goodnights
The chaser
    Collier, J. Fancies and goodnights
Collaboration
    Collier, J. Fancies and goodnights
De mortuis
    Collier, J. Fancies and goodnights
The Devil, George and Rosie
    Collier, J. Fancies and goodnights
Evening primrose
    Collier, J. Fancies and goodnights
Fallen star
    Collier, J. Fancies and goodnights
Frog prince
    Collier, J. Fancies and goodnights
Gavin O'Leary
    Collier, J. Fancies and goodnights
Great possibilities
    Collier, J. Fancies and goodnights
Green thoughts
    Collier, J. Fancies and goodnights

Halfway to Hell
    Collier, J. Fancies and goodnights
Hell hath no fury
    Collier, J. Fancies and goodnights
If youth knew if age could
    Collier, J. Fancies and goodnights
In the cards
    Collier, J. Fancies and goodnights
Incident on a lake
    Collier, J. Fancies and goodnights
Interpretation of a dream
    Collier, J. Fancies and goodnights
    Merril, J. ed. Beyond the barriers of
        space and time
Invisible dove dancer of Strathpheen Is-
    land
    Collier, J. Fancies and goodnights
Lady on the grey
    Collier, J. Fancies and goodnights
Little memento
    Collier, J. Fancies and goodnights
Mary
    Collier, J. Fancies and goodnights
Midnight blue
    Collier, J. Fancies and goodnights
Night! Youth! Paris! And the moon
    Collier, J. Fancies and goodnights
Old acquaintance
    Collier, J. Fancies and goodnights
Over insurance
    Collier, J. Fancies and goodnights
Pictures in the fire
    Collier, J. Fancies and goodnights
Possession of Angela Bradshaw
    Collier, J. Fancies and goodnights
Right side
    Collier, J. Fancies and goodnights
Romance lingers, adventure lives
    Collier, J. Fancies and goodnights
Rope enough
    Collier, J. Fancies and goodnights
Season of mists
    Collier, J. Fancies and goodnights
Sleeping Beauty
    Collier, J. Fancies and goodnights
Special delivery
    Collier, J. Fancies and goodnights
Spring fever
    Collier, J. Fancies and goodnights
Squirrels have bright eyes
    Collier, J. Fancies and goodnights
Steel cat
    Collier, J. Fancies and goodnights
Three Bears Cottage
    Collier, J. Fancies and goodnights
Thus I refute Beelzy
    Collier, J. Fancies and goodnights
    Davenport, B. ed. Tales to be told in
        the dark
    Millett, F. B. ed. Reading fiction
Touch of nutmeg makes it
    Collier, J. Fancies and goodnights
Variation on a theme
    Collier, J. Fancies and goodnights
Wet Saturday
    Collier, J. Fancies and goodnights
Witch's money
    Collier, J. Fancies and goodnights
Without benefit of Galsworthy
    Collier, J. Fancies and goodnights
Youth from Vienna
    Collier, J. Fancies and goodnights

Collins, Wilkie, 1824-1889
  'Blow up with the brig!'
    Collins, W. Tales of suspense
    Eaton, H. T. ed. Short stories
  Dead hand
    Collins, W. Tales of suspense
  Dream-woman
    Collins, W. Tales of suspense
  Fauntleroy
    Collins, W. Tales of suspense
  Lady of Glenwith Grange
    Collins, W. Tales of suspense
  Miss Bertha and the Yankee
    Collins, W. Tales of suspense
  Mr Lepel and the housekeeper
    Collins, W. Tales of suspense
  Mr Policeman and the cook
    Collins, W. Tales of suspense
  Stolen letter
    Collins, W. Tales of suspense
  Terribly strange bed
    Blodgett, H. W. ed. Story survey.
      1953 ed.
    Collins, W. Tales of suspense
COLLISIONS, RAILROAD. See Railroads
  —Accidents
Colloquy of Monos and Una. Poe, E. A.
COLOMBIA
  Tablanca, L. Country girl
The **colonel.** Doty, W. L.
Colonel Julian. Bates, H. E.
Colonel Starbottle for the plaintiff. Harte, B.
Colonel's lady. Maugham, W. S.
Color out of space Lovecraft, H. P.
COLORADO
  Gardiner, D. Not a lick of sense
Colored girls of Passenack—old and new.
  Williams, W. C.
COLORED PEOPLE. See Negroes
Colossus. Wandrei, D.
The **colt.** Stegner, W. E.
COLUMBUS, CHRISTOPHER, 1446?-1506
  Walsh, M. Mission sermon
Columbus was a dope. Heinlein, R. A.
Combat with the octopus. Hugo, V. M.
  comte
The **combination.** Van Doren, M.
Come again another day. Newhouse, E.
Come and go mad. Brown, F.
Come back, my love. Walsh, M.
Come fly with me. De La Roche, M.
Come on, Wagon! Henderson, Z.
The **comeback.** Powell, D.
Comedy cop. Farrell, J. T.
Comedy entombed: 1930. Williams, W. C.
Comedy in rubber. Porter, W. S.
Comes a day. Lamkin, S.
The **Comet.** Derieux, S. A.
Comfort, Alexander, 1920-
  Martyrdom of the house
    Felheim, M.; Newman, F. B. and Stein-
    hoff, W. R. eds. Modern short stories
Comfort and joy. Glen, M. A.
Comfort and joy. Hill, J. H.

Comin' twenty-one. Buckingham, N.
Coming attraction. Leiber, F.
Coming down the mountain. Stuart, J.
Coming home. Bowen, E.
Coming of Lad. Terhune, A. P.
Coming of the white man
  Pacey, D. ed. Book of Canadian stories
Coming-out of Maggie. Porter, W. S.
Command. Kahn, B. I.
Command performance. Miller, W. M.
COMMANDMENTS, TEN
  Hurston, Z. N. The tablets of the law
COMMENCEMENTS
  Toole, K. Short space
  Van Doren, M. Truth about Sylvanus
Comments of Moung Ka. Munro, H. H.
COMMERCIAL TRAVELERS
  Campbell, W. E. M. Sum in addition
  Harte, B. Dick Boyle's business card
  Munro, H. H. The background
    See also Salesmen and salesmanship
Commings, Joseph
  Bones for Davy Jones
    Mystery Writers of America, inc.
    Crooks' tour
  Death by black magic
    Mystery Writers of America, inc. Four-
    &-twenty bloodhounds
Common confusion. Kafka, F.
Common denominator. MacDonald, J. D.
Common meter. Fisher, R.
Commonplace story. Gordimer, N.
COMMUNION. See Lord's Supper
COMMUNISM
  Shaw, I. Sailor off the Bremen
      Czechoslovak Republic
  Doty, W. L. Action in Prague
      Russia
  Fraerman, R. I. The expedition
  Frank, P. Those wily Americans
  Yakovlev, A. S. The wizard
      United States
  Cheever, J. Vega
  Farrell, J. T. The martyr
  Farrell, J. T. The renegade
  Fiedler, L. A. Fear of innocence
  Greenfield, R. Way of a traitor
  Lowry, R. J. C. Defense in University
    City
  Wallace, R. Secret weapon of Joe Smith
COMMUTERS
  Dahl, R. Galloping Foxley
  Humphrey, W. Last husband
COMPANIONS. See Servants—Companions
COMPETITION
  Ball, M. W. Case of the wooden bowls
Competition. Hull, E. M.
Competition at Slush Creek. Stuart, J.
Competitors. Rosenfeld, J.
Compleat werewolf. White, W. A. P.
Complete life of John Hopkins. Porter, W. S.
Completely automatic. Waldo, E. H.
Compliments of the author. Kuttner, H.

Compliments of the season. Porter, W. S.
Compline. Sullivan, R.
COMPOSERS. See Musicians—Composers
COMPULSORY MILITARY SERVICE.
    See Military service, Compulsory
Comstock, Henry B.
    Fish wagon
        Fenner, P. R. comp. Speed, speed, speed
Con Cregan's legacy. Lever, C. J.
CONCENTRATION CAMPS
    Forester, C. S. Evidence
    Forester, C. S. Head and the feet
    Forester, C. S. Miriam's miracle
        See also World War, 1939-1945—
    Prisoners and prisons
Concerning discoveries. Grimson, M. S.
Concerning muskets. Bergengruen, W.
Concerning notaries. Clemens, S. L.
CONCERTS
    Davies, R. Benefit concert
    Schmidt, C. F. Ancestral voices
The conclusion. Doyle, Sir A. C.
CONCORD. See Massachusetts—Concord
Concrete experience. Gilpatrick, E.
Concrete mixer. Bradbury, R.
CONCRETE WORKERS
    Di Donato, P. Christ in concrete
Il Conde. Conrad, J.
CONDEMNED PRISONERS. See Prison-
    ers and prisons
Conditionally human. Miller, W. M.
CONDORS
    Leighton, M. C. Legacy of Canyon John
CONDUCT OF LIFE
    Walpole, Sir H. The life and death of a
    crisis
Cones. Long, F. B.
CONEY ISLAND
    Porter, W. S. Brickdust row
    Porter, W. S. Greater Coney
CONFEDERACY. See Confederate States
    of America
CONFEDERATE STATES OF AMER-
    ICA
    Waldron, W. If Lincoln had yielded
        See also Southern States; United
    States—19th century—Civil War
Army
    Page, T. N. Burial of the guns
CONFESSION
    Smith, J. E. Act of contrition
CONFESSION (CATHOLIC)
    Fitzgerald, F. S. K. Absolution
    Lieberman, R. Afternoon in the life of
        Father Burrell
    O'Donovan, M. First confession
Confessions of a humorist. Porter, W. S.
The confidante. Bowen, E.
CONFIRMATION
    Irwin, M. E. F. Earlier service
Conflict in Morfa. Davies, R.
Conflict is joined. White, R.

Conflicting passions. Sykes, C.
Confusion of sentiment. Zweig, S.
CONGO, BELGIAN
Uganda
    Akeley, C. E. Elephant
Congo cargo. Flynn, T. T.
CONGRESSES AND CONVENTIONS
    Wilson, E. Mrs Golightly and the first
    convention
Congruent people. Budrys, A. J.
The conjurer. Hamos, G.
CONJURING
    Brown, F. Armageddon
    Rawson, C. Off the face of the earth
        See also Magic
Conklin, Lucy Tempkin. See Conklin, G. jt.
    ed.
CONNECTICUT
20th century
    Bennett, P. Death under the hawthornes
Connell, Evan S. 1924-
    I came from yonder mountain
        Prize stories of 1951
Connell, John, pseud. See Robertson, John
    Henry
Connelly, Marc. See Connelly, Marcus Cook
Connelly, Marcus Cook, 1890-
    Coroner's inquest
        Blaustein, A. P. ed. Fiction goes to
        court
Conner, Rearden, 1905-
    Long pike
        Story (Periodical) Story; no. 1
The connoisseur. De La Mare, W. J.
Connolly, James Brendan, 1868-
    The trawler
        Scribner treasury
Connolly, Myles, 1897-
    Big red house on Hope Street
        Connolly, M. Reason for Ann, and other
        stories
    Love, Tomi
        Connolly, M. Reason for Ann, and other
        stories
    Natural causes
        Connolly, M. Reason for Ann, and other
        stories
    Pigeon from St Bartholomew's
        Connolly, M. Reason for Ann, and other
        stories
    Reason for Ann
        Connolly, M. Reason for Ann, and other
        stories
    Seminary Hill
        Connolly, M. Reason for Ann, and other
        stories
Connor, Ralph, pseud. See Gordon, Charles
    William
The conqueror. Clifton, M.
The conqueror. Seager, A.
The conqueror. Wincelberg, S.
The conquerors. Malraux, A.
Conquerors' isle. Bond, N. S.
A conquest. Saphir, M. G.
Conquest. White, W. A. P.

Conquest of life. Binder, E.
Conquest of two worlds. Hamilton, E.
El conquistador. Doyle, T. L.
Conrad, Joseph, 1857-1924
　Amy Foster
　　Schorer, M. ed. The story
　The brute
　　Conrad, J. Tales of land and sea
　Il Conde
　　Conrad, J. Tales of land and sea
　The duel
　　Conrad, J. Tales of land and sea
　End of the tether
　　Conrad, J. Tales of land and sea
　Freya of the Seven Isles
　　Conrad, J. Tales of land and sea
　Gaspar Ruiz
　　Conrad, J. Tales of land and sea
　Heart of darkness
　　Conrad, J. Tales of land and sea
　　Ludwig, J. B. and Poirier, W. R. eds.
　　　Stories, British and American
　　Ludwig, R. M. and Perry, M. B. eds.
　　　Nine short novels
　　Short, R. W. and Sewall, R. B. eds.
　　　Short stories for study. 1950 ed.
　Initiation
　　Andrews, R. C. ed. My favorite stories
　　　of the great outdoors
　The lagoon
　　Millett, F. B. ed. Reading fiction
　Nigger of the Narcissus
　　Conrad, J. Tales of land and sea
　Secret sharer
　　Connolly, C. ed. Great English short
　　　novels
　　Conrad, J. Tales of land and sea
　　Davis, R. G. ed. Ten modern masters
　　Lamb, L. ed. Family book of best loved
　　　short stories
　　Lynskey, W. C. ed. Reading modern
　　　fiction
　　McFee, W. ed. Great sea stories of
　　　modern times
　　Schramm, W. L. ed. Great short stories
　　Waite, H. O. and Atkinson, B. P. eds.
　　　Literature for our time
　　West, R. B. and Stallman, R. W. eds.
　　　Art of modern fiction
　The shadow-line
　　Conrad, J. Tales of land and sea
　Typhoon
　　Conrad, J. Tales of land and sea
　Youth
　　Cerf, B. A. and Moriarty, H. C. eds.
　　　Anthology of famous British stories
　　Conrad, J. Tales of land and sea
　　Davis, R. G. ed. Ten modern masters
Conrad, Robert E. 1928-
　Call of the street
　　Oberfirst, R. ed. 1952 anthology of best
　　　original short-shorts

CONSCIENCE
　Kuttner, H. Private eye
　Maugham, W. S. Lord Mountdrago
　Nordau, M. S. Share in the hereafter
　Poe, E. A. William Wilson
　Stevenson, R. L. Markheim
　Villiers de l'Isle-Adam, J. M. M. P. A.
　　comte de. Desire to be a man

Conscience in art. Porter, W. S.
Conscience of the court. Hurston, Z. N.
CONSCIENTIOUS OBJECTORS
　Ullman, J. R. Presumed lost
CONSCRIPTION. See Military service,
　　Compulsory
Consider courage. Van Doren, M.
Considine, Bob. See Considine, Robert Ber-
　　nard
Considine, Robert Bernard, 1906-
　How Babe got his name
　　Fenner, P. R. comp. Crack of the bat
CONSPIRACIES
　Porter, W. S. Ruler of men
The conspirators. Horwitz, J.
Constable of Lone Sioux. Mowery, W. B.
CONSTANTINOPLE. See Turkey—Con-
　　stantinople
Constiner, Merle
　Lady and the tumblers
　　Argosy (Periodical) Argosy Book of
　　　adventure stories
The consul. Davis, R. H.
The consul. Maugham, W. S.
CONSULS
　Davis, R. H. The consul
　Maugham, W. S. The consul
　Porter, W. S. Cupid's exile number two
　Porter, W. S. Lotus and the bottle
　Porter, W. S. Phonograph and the graft
　Porter, W. S. Remnants of the code
　Porter, W. S. Ships
　Porter, W. S. Shoes
　　　See also Diplomatic life
CONSUMPTION (DISEASE) See Tuber-
　　culosis
Contact, incorporated. Osborne, R.
Contagion. MacLean, K.
The contessina. Bowen, E.
The contest. Chalmers, B.
Continent makers. De Camp, L. S.
Continuation of the reminiscences of John
　　Watson, M. D. Doyle, Sir A. C.
Contradictory case. Philips, J. P.
Contraption. Simak, C. D.
CONVALESCENT HOMES. See Hos-
　　pitals, Convalescent
CONVENT LIFE
　Lieberman, R. Heaven is so high; 13
　　stories
CONVENT SCHOOLS
　Connolly, M. Big red house on Hope
　　Street
　MacMahon, B. Corn was springing
CONVENTIONS. See Congresses and con-
　　ventions
Conversation in Prague. Stern, D.
Conversation of Eiros and Charmion. Poe,
　　E. A.
CONVERSION
　Blackburn, E. R. Good win
　Bradbury, R. Powerhouse
　De La Roche, M. Word for Coffey
　Maupassant, G. de. My uncle Sosthenes
　Oursler, F. Bargain in brimstone

Conversion of Willie Heaps. Garner, H.

The **convert**. Shaw, I.

CONVERTS, CATHOLIC
O'Donovan, M. Custom of the country
O'Donovan, M. My first Protestant

CONVICT SHIPS. See Prison ships

CONVICTS
Chekhov, A. P. Yegor's story
Faulkner, W. Old man
> *See also* Convicts, Escaped; Prisoners and prisons

CONVICTS, ESCAPED
Arico, V. His great decision
Collins, W. Lady of Glenwith Grange
Ekbergh, I. D. Lady's maid
Hardy, T. Three strangers
Jackson, C. R. The break
Moreau, L. The face
Paul, L. No more trouble for Jedwick
Rader, P. Tabby cat
Russell, J. Fourth man

Coo-Cullen. Ready, W. B.

Coo-Cullen growing up. Ready, W. B.

Cook, Kathryn
Ba-ee
  Furman, A. L. ed. Teen-age horse stories

Cook-runner. Household, G.

Cooke, Alistair, 1908-
Christmas Eve
  Lohan, R. and Lohan, M. eds. New Christmas treasury
Christmas Eve, one-three
  Cooke, A. Christmas Eve

Cooke, Arthur A.
All alone again
  Cooke, A. A. Beguile
Another worry
  Cooke, A. A. Beguile
Disappointed, but
  Cooke, A. A. Beguile
For the love of a race horse
  Cooke, A. A. Beguile
Four of a kind
  Cooke, A. A. Beguile
Goose and the gander
  Cooke, A. A. Beguile
The Grace Mansion
  Cooke, A. A. Beguile
In exchange for poverty
  Cooke, A. A. Beguile
My own brother
  Cooke, A. A. Beguile
My own son
  Cooke, A. A. Beguile
N.R.A. for a dollar
  Cooke, A. A. Beguile
One missing
  Cooke, A. A. Beguile
The prey
  Cooke, A. A. Beguile
Returning good for evil
  Cooke, A. A. Beguile
Scum of the earth
  Cooke, A. A. Beguile
Three links
  Cooke, A. A. Beguile

Two peas in a pod
  Cooke, A. A. Beguile
A wasted life
  Cooke, A. A. Beguile

Cooke, Charles, 1904-
Nothing can change it
  Fabricant, N. D. and Werner, H. eds. World's best doctor stories

COOKERY
Porter, W. S. Third ingredient
Pratt, F. and De Camp, L. S. Green thumb
Rogow, L. That certain flavor
Saphir, M. G. Gastronomy of the Jews
> *See also* Bakeries and bakers

Cookie. Taylor, P. H.

COOKS. See Servants—Cooks

Cooky: the heroic dog who wasn't brave. Little, G. W.

Cool million. Jenkin, P. A.

Coolidge, Olivia E.
Black magician
  Coolidge, O. E. Egyptian adventures
Carpenter's daughter
  Coolidge, O. E. Egyptian adventures
Children of Set
  Coolidge, O. E. Egyptian adventures
Escape from Kosseir
  Coolidge, O. E. Egyptian adventures
Feast of Cats
  Coolidge, O. E. Egyptian adventures
First-born
  Coolidge, O. E. Egyptian adventures
Judgment of the gods
  Coolidge, O. E. Egyptian adventures
Little Pharaoh
  Coolidge, O. E. Egyptian adventures
Luck charm
  Coolidge, O. E. Egyptian adventures
Prefect of Jerusalem
  Coolidge, O. E. Egyptian adventures
The tree
  Coolidge, O. E. Egyptian adventures
Unquiet spirit
  Coolidge, O. E. Egyptian adventures

Coombs, Charles Ira, 1914-
Brake happy
  Coombs, C. I. Teen-age champion sports stories
Downhill dilemma
  Coombs, C. I. Teen-age champion sports stories
Fielder's choice
  Furman, A. L. ed. Teen-age stories of the diamond
Four fathom fury
  Coombs, C. I. Teen-age champion sports stories
Freeze out
  Coombs, C. I. Teen-age champion sports stories
Hardwood hazard
  Coombs, C. I. Teen-age champion sports stories
Headline halfback
  Coombs, C. I. Teen-age champion sports stories
Hillbilly halfback
  Coombs, C. I. Teen-age champion sports stories

Coombs, Charles I.—*Continued*
  Ice ostrich
    Coombs, C. I. Teen-age champion sports
      stories
  Lucky stick
    Coombs, C. I. Teen-age champion sports
      stories
  Millie's big story
    Furman, A. L. ed. Everygirls career
      stories
  Net nemesis
    Coombs, C. I. Teen-age champion sports
      stories
  Newton man
    Coombs, C. I. Teen-age champion sports
      stories
  Nose for news
    Furman, A. L. ed. Everygirls career
      stories
  Part time hoopster
    Coombs, C. I. Teen-age champion sports
      stories
  River challenge
    Coombs, C. I. Teen-age champion sports
      stories
  Saga of Sleepy Mugoon
    Coombs, C. I. Teen-age champion sports
      stories
  Silent wings
    Coombs, C. I. Teen-age champion sports
      stories
  Strictly big league
    Furman A. L. ed. Teen-age stories of
      the diamond
  Unlucky number
    Coombs, C. I. Teen-age champion sports
      stories
  Varsity vaulter
    Coombs, C. I. Teen-age champion sports
      stories
  Water bug
    Coombs, C. I. Teen-age champion sports
      stories

Co-operate—or else. Van Vogt, A. E.

Cooter James. Schaefer, J. W.

Cop and the anthem. Porter, W. S.

Cop-killer. Stout, R.

Coppard, Alfred Edgar, 1878-
  Fifty pounds
    Heilman, R. B. ed. Modern short stories
  Handsome lady
    Blodgett, H. W. ed. Story survey.
      1953 ed.
  The higgler
    Cerf, B. A. and Moriarty, H. C. eds.
      Anthology of famous British stories
  Piffingcap
    Conklin, G. and Conklin, L. T. eds.
      Supernatural reader

Coppel, Alfred, 1921-
  The dreamer
    Best science-fiction stories: 1953
  The exile
    Sloane, W. M. ed. Stories for tomorrow
  The Peacemaker
    Wollheim D. A. ed. Prize science fiction

Coppock, Charles, 1906-
  Pirate gold
    Fenner, P. R. comp. Pirates, pirates,
      pirates

Cop's gift. Stout, R.

Copy girl. Hillman, G. M.

Coquette. Horwitz, M.

Corazón. Pattullo, G.

Corduroy pants. Caldwell, E.

Corkery, Daniel, 1878-
  The Aherns
    Corkery, D. The wager, and other
      stories
  As benefits forgot
    Corkery, D. The wager, and other
      stories
  The awakening
    Corkery, D. The wager, and other
      stories
  Children
    Corkery, D. The wager, and other
      stories
  Emptied sack
    Corkery, D. The wager, and other
      stories
  Lilac tree
    Corkery, D. The wager, and other
      stories
  On the heights
    Corkery, D. The wager, and other
      stories
  Ploughing of the leaca
    Corkery, D. The wager, and other
      stories
  The return
    Corkery, D. The wager, and other
      stories
  Rock-of-the-mass
    Corkery, D. The wager, and other
      stories
  The stones
    Corkery, D. The wager, and other
      stories
  Storm struck
    Corkery, D. The wager, and other
      stories
  Unfinished symphony
    Corkery, D. The wager, and other
      stories
  Vanity
    Corkery, D. The wager, and other
      stories
  Vision
    Corkery, D. The wager, and other
      stories
  The wager
    Corkery, D. The wager, and other sto-
      ries

CORN
  Giono, J. Corn dies

Corn dies. Giono, J.

Corn was springing. MacMahon, B.

CORNET PLAYERS. See Musicians—
    Cornet players

Cornet players. Saroyan, W.

CORNETISTS. See Musicians—Cornet
    players

Cornier, Vincent
  O time in your flight
    Queen, E. pseud. ed. Queen's awards:
      6th ser.

Cornish mystery. Christie, A. M.

CORNWALL. See England, Provincial and
    rural—Cornwall

Coroner de luxe. McDaniel, R.
Coroner's inquest. Connelly, M. C.
Coroner's inquest. Hendryx, J. B.
Corporal Downey appears on Halfaday. Hendryx, J. B.
Corporal Downey gets a tip. Hendryx, J. B.
Corporal Downey makes an arrest. Hendryx, J. B.
Corporal Downey states his case. Hendryx, J. B.
Corporal Downey visits Halfaday. Hendryx, J. B.
Corporal Hardy. Danielson, R. E.
Corporal Nat. Mowery, W. B.
CORPSES. See The dead
CORPULENCE
  Maugham, W. S. Three fat women of Antibes
  Stafford, J. The nemesis
  Wells, H. G. Truth about Pyecraft
Corpus delectable. Pratt, F. and De Camp, L. S.
Corpus delicti. Post, M. D.
CORRESPONDENCE. See Letters, Stories about
CORRUPTION (IN POLITICS)
  Brookhouser, F. A life, going by
  Faulkner, W. Monk
CORSICA
  Mérimée, P. Mateo Falcone
  Russell, B. A. W. R. 3d earl. Corsican ordeal of Miss X
  Sansom, W. My little robins
Corsican ordeal of Miss X. Russell, B. A. W. R. 3d earl
CORSICANS
  Maugham, W. S. French Joe
Corwin, Cecil. See Pearson, M. jt. auth.
Cosmic jackpot. Smith, G. O.
COSMOGONY, BIBLICAL. See Creation
Cosmopolite in a café. Porter, W. S.
COSSACKS
  Porter, W. S. Foreign policy of company 99
Cost of living. Sheckley, R.
Costa Rican counterpoint. Stettner, S.
Costly outing. Maupassant, G. de
COTTAGES, SUMMER. See Summer homes
Cotterell, Geoffrey, 1919-
  Delicate warning
    This week magazine. This week's short-short stories
COTTON
  Kidd, H. L. Low road go down
Cottrell, Dorothy (Wilkinson) 1902-
  Pit in the jungle
    Saturday evening post (Periodical) Saturday evening post stories, 1951
  Sharks were hungry
    Argosy (Periodical) Argosy Book of adventure stories
Couch, Sir Arthur Thomas Quiller. See Quiller-Couch, Sir Arthur Thomas

Couching at the door. Broster, D. K.
COUGARS. See Pumas
Counsel assigned. Andrews, M. R. S.
Counsel for Œdipus. O'Donovan, M.
Counselman, Mary Elizabeth
  Tree's wife
    Conklin, G. and Conklin, L. T. eds. Supernatural reader
COUNSELS. See Law and lawyers
Count and the wedding guest. Porter, W. S.
Count Magnus. James, M. R.
Counter charm. Phillips, P.
Counter-transference. Temple, W. F.
COUNTERFEITERS
  Agnon, S. J. Sabbathai
  Porter, W. S. One dollar's worth
Counterparts. Joyce, J.
Country doctor. Kafka, F.
Country doctor. Marquis, D.
Country doctor. Samachson, J.
Country excursion. Maupassant, G. de
Country full of Swedes. Caldwell, E.
Country gentleman. Irwin, M. E. F.
Country girl. Tablanca, L.
COUNTRY LIFE

New England
  Cheever, J. Summer farmer

Poland
  Bergelson, D. In a backwoods town
  Singer, I. J. Sand

United States
  Baker, R. S. Day of pleasant bread
  Steele, W. D. Black road
Country love story. Stafford, J.
Country of elusion. Porter, W. S.
Country of the blind. Wells, H. G.
Country rain. Williams, W. C.
COUNTY KERRY. See Ireland—County Kerry
Couple next door. Millar, M.
Couple of old-timers. Newhouse, E.
Coupling, J. J. pseud.
  Mr Kincaid's pasts
    Merril, J. ed. Beyond the barriers of space and time
  Period piece
    Bleiler, E. F. and Dikty, T. E. eds. Science fiction omnibus: The best science fiction stories, 1949, 1950
COURAGE
  Faulkner, W. Turnabout
  Humphrey, W. The shell
  Kirtland, A. Trial by fire
  Munro, H. H. Easter egg
  Porter, W. S. Afternoon miracle
    See also Cowardice; Heroes
Courage. Carrington, H. ed.
Courage. Irwin, M. E. F.
Courage. Swinton, A.
Courage and the power. Van Doren, M.

Cournos, John, 1881-
The samovar
Leftwich, J. ed. Yisröel. 1952 ed.
Course of true love. Kober, A.
COURT MARTIAL. See Courts martial
and courts of inquiry
COURT-ROOM SCENES. See Trials
Courtesy. Simak, C. D.
Courtesy of the road. Morriss, M.
The **courthouse.** Faulkner, W.
Courtier, Sidney Hobson
Run for your life
Argosy (Periodical) Argosy Book of
adventure stories
Courtin' on Cutshin. Fox, J.
Courting of Miss Darlie Blanche. Knox, J.
Courting of Sister Wisby. Jewett, S. O.
Courting of Susie Brown. Caldwell, E.
Courting of T'nowhead's Bell. Barrie, Sir
J. M. bart.

COURTS AND COURTIERS

England

Cabell, J. B. Porcelain cups

France

Bergengruen, W. Trivulzio and the King

Italy

Paget, V. Amour dure
Paget, V. Prince Alberic and the Snake
Lady

Russia

Tynīanov, I. N. Second Lieutenant Likewise

**COURTS MARTIAL AND COURTS OF
INQUIRY**
Hale, E. E. Man without a country
Kipling, R. 'Love-o'-women'
Melville, H. Billy Budd, foretopman
Voorhees, M. B. Robe and the sword

COURTSHIP
Barrie, Sir J. M. bart. Courting of T'now-
head's Bell
Caldwell, E. Autumn courtship
Collins, W. Miss Bertha and the Yankee
Ekbergh, I. D. Courtship of Lydia
Faulkner, W. A courtship
Fox, J. Courtin' on Cutshin
Irwin, M. E. F. Mistletoe
Irwin, M. E. F. Where beauty lies
Miller, C. Gentle season
O'Donovan, M. Lady of the sagas
Upson, W. H. Quiet wedding
A **courtship.** Faulkner, W.
Courtship deferred. Kober, A.
Courtship of Lydia. Ekbergh, I. D.
Cousin Phillis. Gaskell, E. C. S.
Cousin Teresa. Munro, H. H.
Cousins, Margaret, 1905-
Baby sitter for Christmas
Cousins, M. Christmas gift
Fifty-dollar bottle
Cousins, M. Christmas gift
Homemade miracle
Cousins, M. Christmas gift
Inconstant star
Cousins, M. Christmas gift

Poor black sheep
Cousins, M. Christmas gift
Santa Claus and the Tenth Avenue kid
Cousins, M. Christmas gift
She didn't like people
Furman, A. L. ed. Teen-age dog stories
Small world
Cousins, M. Christmas gift
Uncle Edgar and the reluctant saint
Peery, W. W. ed. 21 Texas short stories
White kid gloves
Cousins, M. Christmas gift
Lohan, R. and Lohan, M. eds. New
Christmas treasury

COUSINS
Davies, R. Pleasures of the table
Lawrence, D. H. Lovely lady
Livesay, D. Glass house
Saroyan, W. Summer of the beautiful
white horse
Schorr, Z. Her rich American cousin
Wharton, E. N. J. The old maid

Coventry. Heinlein, R. A.

Coward, Noël Pierce, 1899-
Ashes of roses
Coward, N. P. Star quality
Mr and Mrs Edgehill
Coward, N. P. Star quality
Richer dust
Coward, N. P. Star quality
Star quality
Coward, N. P. Star quality
Stop me if you've heard it
Coward, N. P. Star quality
This time to-morrow
Coward, N. P. Star quality

COWARDICE
Crane, S. Red badge of courage
Hemingway, E. Short happy life of
Francis Macomber
Jackson, C. R. Boy who ran away
Maugham, W. S. Door of opportunity
Maugham, W. S. Yellow streak

COWBOYS
Bonham, F. One ride too many
Burtis, T. Rope and the bulldog
Erskine, L. Y. Horses and men
Fenner, P. R. comp. Cowboys, cowboys,
cowboys; 17 stories
Fleming, J. S. Ride 'im Chick Norris!
James, W. Will James' Book of cowboy
stories; 15 stories
Pattullo, G. Corazón
Payne, S. With an O X herd
Porter, W. S. Art and the bronco
Porter, W. S. Last of the troubadours
Porter, W. S. The Marquis and Miss
Sally
Souto Alabarce, A. Coyote 13
Wister, O. Journey in search of Christ-
mas
Wood, K. Workaday cowboy
See also Ranch life; The West;
Western stories

Cowpony's prize. Davis, L. R.

COWRIE ISLAND
Coward, N. P. Mr and Mrs Edgehill

COWS. See Cattle

Cox, Anthony Berkeley, 1893-
Avenging chance
Bond, R. T. ed. Handbook for poisoners
Cox, Arthur Jean, 1929-
The blight
Derleth, A. W. ed. Time to come
Cox, Irving
Hole in the sky
Derleth, A. W. ed. Time to come
Like gods they came
Sloane, W. M. ed. Space, space, space
Cox, William R.
Pinch hitter
Argosy (Periodical) Argosy Book of sports stories
Coxe, George Harmon, 1901-
Death certificate
Mystery Writers of America, inc. Four-&-twenty bloodhounds
Doctor takes a case
Mystery Writers of America, inc. 20 great tales of murder
Coyote 13. Souto Alabarce, A.
COYOTES
Clark, W. Van T. The pretender
Souto Alabarce, A. Coyote 13

Cozzens, James Gould, 1903-
Clerical error
Queen, E. pseud. ed. Literature of crime
Men running
Grayson, C. ed. Fourth round
Jones, K. M. ed. New Confederate short stories
Total stranger
First-prize stories, 1919-1954

The **crab.** Beaumont, G.

CRAB FISHERIES. See Shell-fish fisheries

Crabfroth. Sansom, W.

Crane, Robert, pseud. See Glemser, Bernard

Crane, Stephen, 1871-1900
Blue Hotel
Crane, S. Stephen Crane: an omnibus
Foerster, N. ed. American poetry and prose. 1952 ed.
Lynskey, W. C. ed. Reading modern fiction
Bride comes to Yellow Sky
Crane, S. Stephen Crane: an omnibus
Schorer, M. ed. The story
Episode of war
Crane, S. Stephen Crane: an omnibus
Experiment in misery
Crane, S. Stephen Crane: an omnibus
The fight
Davis, C. B. ed. Eyes of boyhood
George's mother
Crane, S. Stephen Crane: an omnibus
Gray sleeve
Lamb, L. ed. Family book of best loved short stories
His new mittens
Crane, S. Stephen Crane: an omnibus
The knife
Crane, S. Stephen Crane: an omnibus
Maggie: a girl of the streets
Crane, S. Stephen Crane: an omnibus
Men in the storm
Crane, S. Stephen Crane: an omnibus

Mystery of heroism
Crane, S. Stephen Crane: an omnibus
Open boat
Barrows, H. ed. 15 stories
Burrell, J. A. and Cerf, B. A. eds. Anthology of famous American stories
Crane, S. Stephen Crane: an omnibus
Day, A. G. ed. Greatest American short stories
Gordon, C. and Tate, A. eds. House of fiction
Schramm, W. L. ed. Great short stories
West, R. B. and Stallman, R. W. eds. Art of modern fiction
Red badge of courage
Ludwig, R. M. and Perry, M. B. eds. Nine short novels
Upturned face
Crane, S. Stephen Crane: an omnibus
Short, R. W. and Sewall, R. B. eds. Short stories for study. 1950 ed.
CRATES, OF THEBES
Schwob, M. Crates
Crawford, Constance
The boats
Stanford short stories, 1952
Crawford, Elizabeth, and Dalmas, Herbert
Rush-hour romance
This week magazine. This week's short-short stories
Crawford, Francis Marion, 1854-1909
For the blood is the life
Conklin, G. and Conklin, L. T. eds. Supernatural reader
Screaming skull
Davenport, B. ed. Ghostly tales to be told

Crawford's consistency. James, H.

Crazy hunter. Boyle, K.

Crazy Hymie and the nickel. Bishop, L.

Crazy Joey. Clifton, M. and Apostolides, A.

Crazy over horse mackerel. Wylie, P.

Crazy Sunday. Fitzgerald, F. S. K.

CREATION
Del Rey, L. Into thy hands

Creation unforgivable. Keller, D. H.

Creative impulse. Maugham, W. S.

The **creatures.** De La Mare, W. J.

Credle, Ellis, 1902-
Mary Lou's Christmas
Story parade (Periodical) Adventure stories
Pudding that broke up the preaching
Fenner, P. R. comp. Fun! Fun! Fun!
Tall tale from the high hills
Fenner, P. R. comp. Fun! Fun! Fun!

CREMATION
Fairbanks, D. Ashes

Crémieux, Benjamin, 1888-
The traveller
Leftwich, J. ed. Yisröel. 1952 ed.

Cremona violin. Hoffmann, E. T. A.

Crevasse. Faulkner, W.

Cricket boy. P'u Sung-ling

Cricket field. Buckingham, N.

Cricket on the hearth. Dickens, C.

CRICKETS (INSECTS)
P'u Sung-ling. Cricket boy
CRIME AND CRIMINALS
Aiken, C. P. Smith and Jones
Buckingham, N. Death stalked the spring-stand!
Chekhov, A. P. Yegor's story
Connolly, M. Big red house on Hope Street
Frazee, S. Graveyard shift
Maugham, W. S. Episode
Milton, M. E. Favor granted
Moore, G. M. Two for a ride
Peacock, W. S. Night in the warehouse
Porter, W. S. Clarion call
Pratt, F. and De Camp, L. S. Ancestral amethyst
Queen, E. pseud. ed. Literature of crime; 26 stories
Rath, I. E. Longest day I live
Sheehan, D. V. Get-away boy
Sinclair, J. L. Killer and the pit
Taubes, F. Trouble on 98th Street
Zoshchenko, M. M. Sleuth-hound
See also Convicts; Murder stories; Mystery and detective stories; and names of particular crimes, e.g. Embezzlement; Theft; Treason; etc.
Crime of the Communist. Chesterton, G. K.
CRIMEAN WAR, 1853-1856
Rappoport, S. Moses Montefiore
The **criminal.** Boyle, K.
The **criminal.** Gibran, K.
CRIMINALS. See Crime and criminals
Crip, come home! Thomas, R.
CRIPPLES
Blackburn, E. R. Walk for me
Butler, M. Mr Sweeney
Campbell, W. E. M. I broke my back on a rosebud
Jones, J. Two legs for the two of us
Lagerkvist, P. F. The basement
Lowry, R. Little baseball world
Schulberg, B. W. Road to recovery
Upshaw, N. Love smelled of vanilla
Crisis. Grendon, E.
Crisis in Utopia. Knight, N. L.
Crisis, 1999. Brown, F.
Crispin's way. Downey, H.
Critchell, Laurence Sanford, 1918-
Loyalty check
Best Army short stories, 1950
Critical factor. Stubbs, H. C.
The **"critter."** Terhune, A. P.
The **critters.** Long, F. B.
Crockett, Samuel Rutherford, 1860-1914
Reverend John Smith prepares his sermon
Neider, C. ed. Men of the high calling
Stickit minister
Neider, C. ed. Men of the high calling
Crocodile tears. Gilpatric, G.
CROCODILES
Annixter, P. pseud. Orchids and crocodiles
Kipling, R. Elephant's child
See also Alligators
CRO-MAGNON. See Man, Prehistoric

CROMWELL, ELIZABETH (BOUR-CHIER) fl. 17th century
Irwin, M. E. F. Mrs Oliver Cromwell
Cronin, Archibald Joseph, 1896-
Birth
Burnett, W. ed. World's best
A candle in Vienna
Brentano, F. ed. The word lives on
Crooked arm. Meader, S. W.
Crooked man. Doyle, Sir A. C.
CROQUET
Williams, T. Three players of a summer game
Crosbie starts his honeymoon. Trollope, A.
Cross, John A.
Hunch that clicked
Oberfirst, R. ed. 1952 anthology of best original short-shorts
Railroad tangle
Oberfirst, R. ed. 1954 anthology of best original short-shorts
Cross, Joseph, pseud. See Nemerov, Howard, and Johnson, William R.
Cross, Mary Ann (Evans) See Eliot, George, pseud.
Cross buns for Friday. Johnson, R.
Cross currents. Munro, H. H.
CROSS-EXAMINATION. See Trials
The **cross**-up. Merson, B.
Crossen, Kendell Foster, 1910-
Ambassadors from Venus
Derleth, A. W. ed. Beachheads in space
Assignment to Aldebaran
Year's best science fiction novels, 1954
Restricted clientele
Crossen, K. F. ed. Adventures in tomorrow
Things of distinction
Crossen, K. F. ed. Future tense
Too late for murder
Mystery Writers of America, inc. Four-&-twenty bloodhounds
CROW INDIANS
Gulick, G. C. Rendezvous romance
Johnson, D. M. Man called Horse
Johnson, D. M. The unbeliever
Crowbar Captain. Patrick, J.
Crowd pleaser. Schulberg, B. W.
Crowell, Chester Theodore, 1888-1941
The stoic
Peery, W. W. ed. 21 Texas short stories
Crown-fire. Caldwell, E.
Crown princess. Brophy, B.
Crowning glory. Newby, P. H.
Crowning glory. Paterson, N.
CROWS
Seton, E. T. Silverspot
Crucible of power. Williamson, J.
Crucifixus Etiam. Miller, W. M.
"Cruel and barbarous treatment." McCarthy, M. T.
CRUELTY
Grimson, M. S. At the crossroads
Sergîeev-Tsenskii, S. N. Man you couldn't kill
Shneur, Z. The girl

CRUELTY TO ANIMALS. See Animals—
Treatment
Cruise. Waugh, E.
Cruises in the sun. Curtis, K.
Crump, Irving, 1887-
Dead men on parade
Fenner, P. R. comp. Ghosts, ghosts,
ghosts
Little guy
Boys' life (Periodical) Boys' life Adventure stories
Pirate island
Furman, A. L. ed. Teen-age sea stories
Two-bits of traffic C
Furman, A. L. ed. Teen-age horse
stories
Crunch catches one. Wylie, P.
Crushed orchid. Hanlon, B.
Cry deep, cry still. Haycox, E.
Cry of the graves. Gibran, K.
Cry silence. Brown F.
CRYPTOGRAPHY
Poe, E. A. Gold bug
See also Ciphers and telegraph codes
Crystal egg. Wells, H. G.
CRYSTAL GAZING. See Clairvoyance
Crystal stream. Rudnicki, A.
Cub-hunting with Mr Neville's hounds. Surtees, R. S.
Cubic city. Tucker, L.
Cue for Connie. Woody, R. L. J.
Cuevas, Ernesto, 1923-
Lock the doors, lock the windows
Weaver, R. and James, H. eds. Canadian short stories
Culture. Household, G.
Culture. Shelton, J.
Culver, Monty, 1929-
Black water blues
Prize stories of 1951
CUMBERLAND MOUNTAINS. See Kentucky—Cumberland Mountains
Cummings, Ray
Girl in the golden atom
Margulies, L. and Friend, O. J. eds.
Giant anthology of science fiction
Gravity professor
Wollheim, D. A. comp. Every boy's
book of science-fiction
Cunningham, Eugene, 1896-
Bar-Nothing's happy birthday
Peery, W. W. ed. 21 Texas short stories
Cunningham, John M.
Iron rose
Western Writers of America. Holsters
and heroes
Tin star
Western Writers of America. Bad men
and good
Cunninghame Graham, Robert Bontine. See
Graham, Robert Bontine Cunninghame
Cup of tea. Horwitz, J.
Cup of tea. Mansfield, K.
Cupboard of the yesterdays. Munro, H. H.
Cupid à la carte. Porter, W. S.

Cupid wags his tail. Faggett, H. L.
Cupid's exile number two. Porter, W. S.
Curates. See Clergy
Curate's friend. Forster, E. M.
Curbstone philosophy. Farrell, J. T.
The **cure.** Cheever, J.
The **cure.** Kuttner, H.
Cure for lumbago. Van Loan, C.
Curious case of Benjamin Button. Fitzgerald,
F. S. K.
Curle, Richard, 1883-
Suppressed edition
Derleth, A. W. ed. Night's yawning
peal
Curling, Jonathan
Restless rest-house
Asquith, Lady C. M. E. C. ed. Book of
modern ghosts
Curly-beard. Tu Kwang-t'ing
Curly maple. Knox, J.
Curphey's follower. Kneale, N.
Curry, Peggy (Simpson)
Osage Girl
Creamer, J. B. comp. Twenty-two stories about horses and men
Curse of the golden cross. Chesterton, G. K.
Curse of the horse race. Waugh, E.
CURSES
Harvey, W. F. Arm of Mrs Egan
Peretz, I. L. Devotion without end
CURSES, FAMILY
Closed cabinet
Curtain of green. Welty, E.
Curtis, Betsy, 1917-
Peculiar people
Best science fiction stories: 1952
Curtis, Kent
The cameleers
Curtis, K. Cruises in the sun
Cruises in the sun
Curtis, K. Cruises in the sun
Drumbeaters Island
Curtis, K. Cruises in the sun
Curtis, Maxine
Navy blue and bold
Seventeen (Periodical) The Seventeen
reader
Sleek sixteen
Seventeen (Periodical) Nineteen from
Seventeen
Stowe, A. comp. It's a date
Curtiss, Philip Everett, 1885-
Eight-dollar pup
Cavanna, B. ed. Pick of the litter
Curwood, James Oliver, 1878-1927
Kazan
Bloch, M. ed. Favorite dog stories
Cush gets a toothache. Hendryx, J. B.
Cush takes inventory. Hendryx, J. B.
Custom of the country. Haycox, E.
Custom of the country. O'Donovan, M.
Cut yourself a slice of show. Kaufman, W.
Cuter Malone turns down a deal. Hendryx,
J. B.

Cuthbert, Chester D.
Sublime vigil
Moskowitz, S. comp. Editor's choice in
science fiction
Cutler, J. Linwood
Fire-boy of Dunsoon
Story parade (Periodical) Adventure
stories
CYBERNETICS. See Automata
Cycle of Manhattan. Winslow, T. S.
Cyclists' raid. Rooney, F.
Cyclops, Heard, G.
Cynthia who was afraid not to pet. Strain,
F. B.
Cyprian bees. Wilson, R. M.
Czech dog. Hardy, W. G.
CZECHOSLOVAKIANS IN TAHITI
Hall, J. N. Haunted island
**CZECHOSLOVAKIANS IN THE
UNITED STATES**
Cather, W. S. Neighbour Rosicky

D

DP! Kuttner, H.
Dachs, David, 1922-
Speaking of characters
Dachs, D. ed. Treasury of sports humor
Daffodils. Bowen, E.
Dagger with wings. Chesterton, G. K.
Daggle-Tail. Lavin, M.
Daguio, Amador T. 1912-
Wedding dance
Stanford short stories, 1953
Dahl, Roald, 1916-
Claud's dog
Dahl, R. Someone like you
Death of an old man
Jensen, P. ed. Fireside book of flying
stories
Dip in the pool
Dahl, R. Someone like you
Galloping Foxley
Dahl, R. Someone like you
Great automatic grammatisator
Dahl, R. Someone like you
Lamb to the slaughter
Dahl, R. Someone like you
Man from the south
Dahl, R. Someone like you
My lady love, my dove
· Dahl, R. Someone like you
Neck
Dahl, R. Someone like you
Nunc dimittis
Dahl, R. Someone like you
Poison
Dahl, R. Someone like you
Skin
Dahl, R. Someone like you
The soldier
Dahl, R. Someone like you
Someone like you
Jensen, P. ed. Fireside book of flying
stories

Sound machine
Dahl, R. Someone like you
Taste
Dahl, R. Someone like you
Grayson, C. ed. Fourth round
The wish
Dahl, R. Someone like you
DAHLIAS
Clifton, M. The conqueror
Dailey, Jim
The rookie
Herzberg, M. J. comp. Treasure chest
of sport stories
DAIRYING
Brubaker, H. Milk pitcher
See also Farm life
Daisies. Brown, F.
Daisy Miller. James, H.
DAKOTA INDIANS
Johnson, D. M. Flame on the frontier
Johnson, D. M. Journey to the fort
Meigs, C. L. Buffalo dance
Dalmas, Herbert. See Crawford, E. jt. auth.
Daly, Maureen, 1921-
Sixteen
Lass, A. H. and Horowitz, A. eds.
Stories for youth
Thinker's digest (Periodical) Spoiled
priest, and other stories
Dames and ethics. Kaufman, W.
Damned thing. Bierce, A.
Damsel with a dulcimer. Ferguson, M.
Dance for the devil. McCourt, E. A.
DANCE HALLS
Benson, T. Harry was good to the girls
DANCE MARATHONS
McCoy, H. They shoot horses, don't they?
Dance of a new world. MacDonald, J. D.
Dance of the dead. Matheson, R.
DANCE ORCHESTRA. See Orchestra
Dance with the devil. Emmons, B.
DANCES. See Dancing
DANCES (PARTIES) See Parties
Dancey, Max, 1916-. See Dewey, G. G. jt.
auth.
DANCING
Ekbergh, I. D. Pink Ballerina
Fitzgerald, F. S. K. Woman with a past
Galsworthy, J. Salta pro nobis
Lansing, E. C. H. There's something
about you
Maupassant, G. de. Minuet
Porter, W. S. Unprofitable servant
Ullman, J. R. White night
Willingham, C. Career of Augurt Nim-
rodtk
See also Ballet
Dancing bear. Barnard, L. G.
Dandy: the funny-looking dog. Little, G. W.
Danger by candlelight. Macfarlan, A. A.
Danger wears two faces. Kaplan, A. H.
Dangerous ice. Young, S.
Dangerous people. Brown, F.
Daniel, Hawthorne, 1890-
Shores of Tripoli
Furman, A. L. ed. Teen-age sea stories

Danielson, Richard Ely, 1885-
  Corporal Hardy
    Cooper, A. C. ed. Modern short stories
  The quid pro quo
    Bachelor, J. M.; Henry, R. L. and
      Salisbury, R. eds. Current thinking
      and writing; 2d ser.
Dann, Lois, 1922-
  One summer afternoon
    American vanguard, 1950
Dannay, Frederic, 1905- **and Lee, Manfred
      Bennington,** 1905- See Queen, Ellery,
      pseud.
Danny Hagan's blind spot. Gilmour, W.
Danse Macabre. Strong, L. A. G.
Danse pseudomacabre. Williams, W. C.
Darcy in the Land of Youth. O'Donovan, M.
The **dare.** Schulberg, B. W.
Daring young man on the flying trapeze.
      Saroyan, W.
Dark Blue. Bottome, P.
Dark city. Aiken, C. P.
Dark horses. Harvey, W. F.
Dark interlude. McClure, J.
Dark interlude. Reynolds, M. and Brown,
      F.
Dark knight. Doty, W. L.
Dark night of Ramón Yendía. Novás Calvo,
      L.
Dark nuptial. Locke, R. D.
Dark red chrysanthemum. Thorne, A.
Dark walk. Taylor, P. H.
Darkness in Paris. Remarque, E. M.
Darling, Frederick
  The drag
    Story (Periodical) Story; no. 3
Darwick, Richard, 1928-
  Mother and son
    American vanguard, 1950
DARWINISM. See Evolution
Dasent, Sir George Webbe, 1817-1896
  Boots, who made the Princess say, "That's
      a story"
    Fenner, P. R. comp. Fools and funny
      stories
Date to remember. Temple, W. F.
Date with Dora. McLaren, F. C.
Date with Janie. Roberts, R. M.
Date with Ricky. Emery, A.
Daudet, Alphonse, 1840-1897
  Death of the Dauphin
    Schramm, W. L. ed. Great short stories
  Father Gaucher's elixir
    O'Faoláin, S. The short story
  Last class
    Eaton, H. T. ed. Short stories
  M. Seguin's goat
    Blodgett, H. W. ed. Story survey.
      1953 ed.
Daughter. Caldwell, E.
DAUGHTERS. See Fathers and daughters;
      Mothers and daughters; Parent and
      child
Daughters of earth. Merril, J.
Daughters of the late colonel. Mansfield, K.

Dauphin, Death of the. Daudet, A.
DAVID, KING OF ISRAEL
  Schmitt, G. David and Bathsheba
David and Bathsheba. Schmitt, G.
David Swan. Hawthorne, N.
Davidson, Sue
  City of the angels
    Stanford short stories, 1951
  The rivals
    Stanford short stories, 1951
Davies, Rhys, 1903-
  Abraham's glory
    Davies, R. Boy with a trumpet, and
      other selected short stories
  Alice's pint
    Davies, R. Boy with a trumpet, and
      other selected short stories
  Arfon
    Davies, R. Boy with a trumpet, and
      other selected short stories
  Benefit concert
    Davies, R. Boy with a trumpet, and
      other selected short stories
  Boy with a trumpet
    Davies, R. Boy with a trumpet, and
      other selected short stories
  Caleb's ark
    Davies, R. Boy with a trumpet, and
      other selected short stories
  Conflict in Morfa
    Davies, R. Boy with a trumpet, and
      other selected short stories
  Dilemma of Catherine Fuchsias
    Davies, R. Boy with a trumpet, and
      other selected short stories
  The farm
    Davies, R. Boy with a trumpet, and
      other selected short stories
  Fashion plate
    Davies, R. Boy with a trumpet, and
      other selected short stories
  Foolish one
    Davies, R. Boy with a trumpet, and
      other selected short stories
  Gents only
    Davies, R. Boy with a trumpet, and
      other selected short stories
  Human condition
    Davies, R. Boy with a trumpet, and
      other selected short stories
  Mourning for Ianto
    Davies, R. Boy with a trumpet, and
      other selected short stories
  Nightgown
    Davies, R. Boy with a trumpet, and
      other selected short stories
  Pleasures of the table
    Davies, R. Boy with a trumpet, and
      other selected short stories
  Resurrection
    Davies, R. Boy with a trumpet, and
      other selected short stories
  River, flow gently
    Davies, R. Boy with a trumpet, and
      other selected short stories
  The sisters
    Davies, R. Boy with a trumpet, and
      other selected short stories
  Two friends
    Davies, R. Boy with a trumpet, and
      other selected short stories

Davies, Valentine, 1905-
Great King Kelly
Graber, R. S. ed. Baseball reader
Davies, William Morris, 1814?-1890
Battle with a whale
Andrews, R. C. ed. My favorite stories
of the great outdoors
Davis, Alice Lee
First disciple
Elmquist, R. M. ed. Fifty years to
Christmas
The Klondiker
Oberfirst, R. ed. 1954 anthology of best
original short-shorts
Davis, Chan
Letter to Ellen
Conklin, G. ed. Science-fiction thinking
machines
Davis, Dorothy Salisbury
Backward, turn backward
Queen, E. pseud. ed. Ellery Queen's
awards: 9th ser.
Born killer
Queen, E. pseud. ed. The Queen's
awards: 8th ser.
Spring fever
Queen, E. pseud. ed. Queen's awards:
7th ser.
Davis, Franklin Milton, 1918-
Five Alls
Best Army short stories, 1950
Davis, Gene
Amateur night in Harlem
Ford, N. A. and Faggett, H. L. eds.
Best short stories by Afro-American
writers (1925-1950)
Davis, Harold Lenoir, 1896-
Back to the land—Oregon, 1907
Davis, H. L. Team bells woke me, and
other stories
Beach squatter
Davis, H. L. Team bells woke me, and
other stories
Extra gang
Davis, H. L. Team bells woke me, and
other stories
Flying switch
Davis, H. L. Team bells woke me, and
other stories
Homestead orchard
Davis, H. L. Team bells woke me, and
other stories
Old man Isbell's wife
Davis, H. L. Team bells woke me, and
other stories
Open winter
Davis, H. L. Team bells woke me, and
other stories
Shiloh's water's
Davis, H. L. Team bells woke me, and
other stories
Stubborn spearmen
Davis, H. L. Team bells woke me, and
other stories
Team bells woke me
Davis, H. L. Team bells woke me, and
other stories
Town in eastern Oregon
Davis, H. L. Team bells woke me, and
other stories

Vanishing wolf
Davis, H. L. Team bells woke me, and
other stories
World of little doves
Davis, H. L. Team bells woke me, and
other stories
Davis, Lavinia (Riker) 1909-
Cowpony's prize
Fenner, P. R. comp. Cowboys, cowboys,
cowboys
Feeling for human interest
Furman, A. L. ed. Everygirls career
stories
Davis, Richard Harding, 1864-1916
Bar sinister
Burrell, J. A. and Cerf, B. A. eds. An-
thology of famous American stories
Scribner treasury
The consul
Scribner treasury
The deserter
Scribner treasury
In the fog
Lamb, L. ed. Family book of best loved
short stories
Wasted day
Blaustein, A. P. ed. Fiction goes to
court
Davis, Robert, 1881-1949
Ne-nu-ka
Fenner, P. R. comp. Dogs, dogs, dogs
Davis, Robert Hobart, 1869-1942
Tree toad
Davis, C. B. ed. Eyes of boyhood
Davis, Samuel Post, 1850-1918
Andy Munroe's funeral
Emrich, D. ed. Comstock bonanza
Carson poker incident
Emrich, D. ed. Comstock bonanza
Christmas carol
Emrich, D. ed. Comstock bonanza
Mystery of the Savage sump
Emrich, D. ed. Comstock bonanza
Sage-brush chief
Emrich, D. ed. Comstock bonanza
Stock chapter
Emrich, D. ed. Comstock bonanza
Dawkins, Mary Lucile, 1927-
Blossom on the yew
Stanford short stories, 1953
Dawn. Charteris, L.
Dawn of another day. Williams, W. C.
Dawn of remembered spring. Stuart, J.
Daxbr baxbr. Smith, E. E.
Day, Clarence Shepard, 1874-1935
Noblest instrument
Lass, A. H. and Horowitz, A. eds.
Stories for youth
Day after tomorrow. Powell, D.
Day at the zoo. Farrell, J. T.
Day before. Newhouse, E.
Day he got fired. Lowry, R. J. C.
Day in a woman's life. Kaye-Smith, S.
Day in Hit-im-and Hold-im-shire. Surtees,
R. S.
Day in New York. Montross, L. S.
Day in the sun. Modell, J.
Day in town. Haycox, E.

Day of pleasant bread. Baker, R. S.
Day of rest. Babikoff, V.
Day of retaliation. Aldrich, B. S.
Day of the cipher. Walker, A.
Day of the dance. Kiley, N. C.
Day of the last rock fight. Whitehill, J.
Day papa died. Neiman, S.
Day resurgent. Porter, W. S.
Day the flag fell. Elam, R. M.
Day the presidential candidate came to Ciudad Tamaulipas. Caldwell, E.
Day we celebrate. Bond, N. S.
Day we celebrate. Porter, W. S.
Day with Hard-and Sharp hounds. Surtees, R. S.
Daymare. Brown, F.
Days and nights. Rein, H. E.
Day's pleasure. Heseltine, N.
Day's wait. Hemingway, E.
Day's wooing. Caldwell, E.
Day's work. Porter, K. A.
De bello Gallico. Keller, W. A.
De mortuis. Collier, J.
De profundis. Jenkins, W. F.
De profundis. Kuttner, H.
DEACONS
  Caldwell, E. People's choice
THE DEAD
  Lagerkvist, P. F. Eternal smile
  Poe, E. A. Colloquy of Monos and Una
  Poe, E. A. Conversation of Eiros and Charmion
  Poe, E. A. King Pest
  Rabinowitz, S. Eternal life
  Wells, H. G. The Plattner story
  See also Death
The **dead.** Joyce, J.
Dead end. MacFarlane, W.
Dead hand. Collins, W.
Dead heat. Sitwell, Sir O. bart
Dead men on parade. Crump, I.
Dead of night. Harvey W. F.
Dead planet. Hamilton, E.
Dead run. Wallace, W. J.
Dead town. Peretz, I. L.
Dead woman. Keller, D. H.
Deadline. Haycox, E.
Deadlock. Kuttner, H.
Deadly back-fire. Blochman, L. G.
Deadly host. Jones, R. F.
Deadly north face. Ullman, J. R.
DEAF AND DUMB
  Garrold, R. P. Man's hands
  Miller, C. Gentle season
  Seabright, I. The listening child
  Welty, E. The key
DEAF-MUTES. See Deaf and dumb
Deal in wheat. Norris, F.
Dean Harcourt. Douglas, L. C.
Dear Devil. Russell, E. F.
Dear Diary. Matheson, R.

"**Dear** mother..." Marotta, G.
Dear Pen Pal. Van Vogt, A. E.
Dear Sister Sadie. Winslow, T. S.
Deasy, Mary, 1914-
  Morning sun
    Best American short stories, 1953
DEATH
  Aiken, C. P. Strange moonlight
  Albrizio, G. The bereft
  Aldrich, B. S. The dreams are real
  Betts, D. The sword
  Casper, L. Sense of direction
  Grau, S. A. One summer
  Greene, G. Second death
  Harvey, W. F. August heat
  James, H. Beast in the jungle
  Joyce, J. The sisters
  Lagerkvist, P. F. Guest of reality
  Myers, H. Pale sergeant
  Neiman, S. Day papa died
  Opatoshu, J. Eternal wedding gown
  Pasinetti, P. M. Family history
  Pirandello, L. Horse in the moon
  Powers, J. F. Lions, harts, leaping does
  Reymont, W. S. Twilight
  Sansom, W. Little room
  Seide, M. Bad boy form Brooklyn
  Steele, W. D. Fe-fi-fo-fum
  Taylor, E. Beginning of a story
  Taylor, E. First death of her life
  Taylor, P. H. Their losses
  Tolstoǐ, L. N. Graf. Death of Iván Ilých
  Valle-Inclán, R. del. My sister Antonia
  Waldo, E. H. What dead men tell
    See also; The dead; Immortality, Physical
Death. Bensusan, S. L.
DEATH, APPARENT
  Davies, R. Resurrection
  Maupassant, G. de. Family affair
    See also Burial, Premature
Death at attention. Bennett, K.
DEATH BED SCENES. See Deathbed scenes
Death by black magic. Commings, J.
Death certificate. Coxe, G. H.
Death drag. Faulkner, W.
Death—in the bag. Snow, W.
Death in the family. Froscher, W.
Death in the house. Lincoln, V. E.
Death in the pass. Sjögren, E.
Death in the woods. Anderson, S.
Death in Venice. Mann, T.
Death is a passing weakness. Brod, M.
Death of a bachelor. Schnitzler, A.
Death of a centenarian. De La Roche, M.
Death of a favorite. Powers, J. F.
Death of a god. Sitwell, Sir O. bart
Death of a hero. Baudelaire, C. P.
Death of a prize fighter. Switzer, R.
Death of a sensitive. Bates, H.
Death of a traveling salesman. Welty, E.
Death of an actor. Bernstein, D.
Death of an old man. Dahl, R.
Death of Baldy. Sansom, W.

Death of Iván Ilých. Tolstoĭ, L. N. Graf
Death of Judas. Komroff, M.
Death of Pierce. Fay, S.
Death of Red Peril. Edmonds, W. D.
Death of Riley. Brown, F.
Death of the Dauphin. Daudet, A.
Death of the glen. Stewart, G. R.
Death of the lion. James, H.
Death of the moon. Phillips, A. M.
Death of the Zulu. Krige, U.
Death of Uncle Andy. Knox, J.
Death sentence. Asimov, I.
Death stalked the spring-stand! Bucking-
   ham, N.
Death under the hawthornes. Bennett, P.
DEATHBED SCENES
   Bennett, A. Mary with the high hand
   Daudet, A. Death of the Dauphin
   Eliot, G. pseud. Lifted veil
   Lytle, A. N. Jericho, Jericho, Jericho
   Poe, E. A. Facts in the case of M.
      Valdemar
   Poe, E. A. Ligeia
   Porter, W. S. Lord Oakhurst's curse
   Turgenev, I. S. District doctor
   Watson, J. Story of Dr MacLure
   Whitmore, S. Bontemps
   Zangwill, I. Sabbath breaker
Death's eye view. MacDonald, J. D.
The **debt.** Carman, K.
Debt of honor. Household, G.
DEBTS
   Shaw, I. Triumph of justice
   Thomson, E. W. Privilege of the limits
DECALOGUE. See Commandments, Ten
De Camp, Lyon Sprague, 1907-
   Animal-cracker plot
      De Camp, L. S. Continent makers, and
      other tales of the Viagens
   Blue giraffe
      Pratt, F. ed. World of wonder
   Continent makers
      De Camp, L. S. Continent makers, and
      other tales of the Viagens
   Employment
      Bleiler, E. F. and Dikty, T. E. eds.
      Imagination unlimited
   The exalted
      Astounding science fiction (Periodical)
      Astounding science fiction anthology
   Finished
      De Camp, L. S. Continent makers, and
      other tales of the Viagens
   Galton whistle
      De Camp, L. S. Continent makers, and
      other tales of the Viagens
   Git along
      De Camp, L. S. Continent makers, and
      other tales of the Viagens
      Derleth, A. W. ed. The outer reaches
   Hyperpilosity
      Conklin, G. ed. Omnibus of science
      fiction
   Inspector's teeth
      De Camp, L. S. Continent makers, and
      other tales of the Viagens
   Ordeal of Professor Klein
      Derleth, A. W. ed. Beachheads in space

   Perpetual motion
      De Camp, L. S. Continent makers, and
      other tales of the Viagens
   Summer wear
      Best science fiction stories: 1951
      De Camp, L. S. Continent makers, and
      other tales of the Viagens
De Camp, Lyon Sprague, 1907- **and Pratt,
   Fletcher,** 1897-1956
   Black ball
      Magazine of fantasy and science fiction.
      Best from Fantasy and science fiction;
      2d ser.
   Gavagan's bar
      Magazine of fantasy and science fiction.
      Best from Fantasy and science fiction;
      [1st ser.]
   Untimely toper
      Magazine of fantasy and science fiction.
      Best from Fantasy and science fiction;
      3d ser.
      See also Pratt, F. jt. auth.
DECATUR, STEPHEN, 1779-1820
   Daniel, H. Shores of Tripoli
DECEIT. See Truthfulness and falsehood
DECEPTION. See Hoaxes
Decision. O'Rourke, F.
Decision for spring. Summers, J. L.
Declaration of independence. Wright, F. F.
De-composition. Chekhov, A. P.
De Courcy, Dorothy, and De Courcy, John
   Rat race
      Conklin, G. ed. Big book of science
      fiction
De Courcy, John. See De Courcy, D. jt.
   auth.
De Daumier-Smith's blue period. Salinger,
   J. D.
Dee, Roger, pseud. See Aycock, Roger D.
Deed of entail. Hoffmann, E. T. A.
Deenie. Powell, D.
Deep country part. Casper, L.
Deep range. Clarke, A. C.
Deep water man. Brace, G. W.
DEER
   Rawlings, C. A. Flash of lightning
   Schulberg, B. W. Our white deer
   Seton, E. T. Trail of the Sandhill Stag
DEER HUNTING
   Bonner, P. H. Stalker & Co.
   Clark, W. Van T. Buck in the hills
   Warner, C. D. A-hunting of the deer
Defeat. Boyle, K.
Defeat. Sitwell, Sir O. bart
Defeat of the city. Porter, W. S.
The **defeated.** Gordimer, N.
DEFECTIVES AND DELINQUENTS
   Cather, W. S. Paul's case
Defender of the faith. Doty, W. L.
Defense. Van Vogt, A. E.
Defense in University City. Lowry, R. J. C.
Defense mechanism. MacLean, K.
Defensive diamond. Munro, H. H.

Defoe, Daniel, 1661?-1731
Apparition of Mrs Veal
  Cerf, B. A. and Moriarty H. C. eds.
    Anthology of famous British stories
  Same as: True relation of the apparition
    of one Mrs Veal
Friendly demon
  Magazine of fantasy and science fiction.
    Best from Fantasy and science fiction;
    [1st ser.]
True relation of the apparition of one
  Mrs Veal
  Neider, C. ed. Great short stories from
    the world's literature
  Same as: Apparition of Mrs Veal

DeFord, Miriam Allen, 1888-
The oleander
  Bond, R. T. ed. Handbook for poisoners
Throwback
  Crossen, K. F. ed. Future tense

DEFORMITIES
Chandler, A. B. Giant killer
Fitzgerald, F. S. K. Curious case of
  Benjamin Button
Merril, J. That only a mother
Sayres, W. C. Olaf the magnificent
Welty, E. Petrified man
      See also Face—Abnormities and
    deformities

DeJong, David Cornel, 1905-
Before the races
  Oberfirst, R. ed. 1954 anthology of best
    original short-shorts
Preparations for the night
  Swallow, A. ed. Anchor in the sea

De La Mare, Walter John, 1873-1956
All Hollows
  De La Mare, W. J. Collected tales
Almond tree
  De La Mare, W. J. Collected tales
The bowl
  De La Mare, W. J. Collected tales
Broomsticks
  Joseph, M. ed. Best cat stories
Cape Race
  De La Mare, W. J. Collected tales
The connoisseur
  De La Mare, W. J. Collected tales
The creature
  De La Mare, W. J. Collected tales
The guardian
  Asquith, Lady C. M. E. C. ed. Book of
    modern ghosts
Ideal craftsman
  De La Mare, W. J. Collected tales
  Queen, E. pseud. ed. Literature of crime
In the forest
  De La Mare, W. J. Collected tales
Lispet, Lispett and Vaine
  De La Mare, W. J. Collected tales
Miss Duveen
  De La Mare, W. J. Collected tales
Missing
  De La Mare, W. J. Collected tales
The nap
  Blodgett, H. W. ed. Story survey.
    1953 ed.
  De La Mare, W. J. Collected tales
The orgy: an idyll
  De La Mare, W. J. Collected tales

Physic
  De La Mare, W. J. Collected tales
The riddle
  De La Mare, W. J. Collected tales
Seaton's aunt
  De La Mare, W. J. Collected tales
Strangers and pilgrims
  De La Mare, W. J. Collected tales
The talisman
  De La Mare, W. J. Collected tales
Three friends
  De La Mare, W. J. Collected tales
The tree
  De La Mare, W. J. Collected tales
The trumpet
  De La Mare, W. J. Collected tales
The vats
  De La Mare, W. J. Collected tales
The wharf
  De La Mare, W. J. Collected tales
Willows
  De La Mare, W. J. Collected tales

De La Roche, Mazo, 1885-
Auntimay
  De La Roche, M. Boy in the house, and
    other stories
Boy in the house
  De La Roche, M. Boy in the house, and
    other stories
Broken fan
  De La Roche, M. Boy in the house, and
    other stories
The celebration
  De La Roche, M. Boy in the house, and
    other stories
Come fly with me
  Pacey, D. ed. Book of Canadian stories
Death of a centenarian
  Burnett, W. ed. World's best
Patient Miss Peel
  De La Roche, M. Boy in the house, and
    other stories
Quartet
  De La Roche, M. Boy in the house, and
    other stories
Submissive wife
  De La Roche, M. Boy in the house, and
    other stories
"Twa kings"
  De La Roche, M. Boy in the house, and
    other stories
Widow Cruse
  De La Roche, M. Boy in the house, and
    other stories
Word for Coffey
  De La Roche, M. Boy in the house, and
    other stories

De La Torre, Lillian, 1902-
Disappearing servant wench
  Mystery Writers of America, inc. Four-
    &-twenty bloodhounds
Second sight of Dr Sam: Johnson
  Mystery Writers of America, inc.
    Maiden murders
Stroke of thirteen
  Queen, E. pseud, ed. Queen's awards:
    8th ser.

Delavigne, Jean François Casimir, 1792-1843
Up the garret stairs
  Carrington, H. ed. Week-end book of
    ghost stories

Delayed decision. O'Rourke, F.

Deledda, Grazia, 1871-1936
Two miracles
Fremantle, A. J. ed. Mothers
Delicate female. Whitney, P. A.
Delicate prey. Bowles, P. F.
Delicate warning. Cotterell, G.
DELICATESSEN STORES. See Food
stores
Delilah and the space-rigger. Heinlein, R. A.
Dell, Dudley
Biography project
Galaxy science fiction magazine. Galaxy
reader of science fiction
Dell, Floyd, 1887-
The blanket
Christ, H. I. and Shostak, J. eds. Short
stories
Dell'archiprete, Ruby
Good girl
American vanguard, 1950
Del Rey, Lester, 1915-
Alien
Star science fiction stories, no. 3
And it comes out here
Conklin, G. ed. Science-fiction adven-
tures in dimension
Helen O'Loy
Merril, J. ed. Beyond human ken
Pohl, F. ed. Assignment in tomorrow
Idealist
Star science fiction stories [no. 1]
Instinct
Conklin, G. ed. Omnibus of science
fiction
Into thy hands
Greenberg, M. ed. Robot and the man
Lesser, M. A. ed. Looking forward
Kindness
Del Rey, L.; Matschat, C. H. and
Carmer, C. L. eds. Year after to-
morrow
Luck of Ignatz
Del Rey, L.; Matschat, C. H. and
Carmer, C. L. eds. Year after to-
morrow
The monster
Heinlein, R. A. ed. Tomorrow, the stars
Over the top
Astounding science fiction (Periodical)
Astounding science fiction anthology
Pound of cure
Star science fiction stories, no. 2
Though dreamers die
Greenberg, M. ed. Robot and the man
Wings of night
Conklin, G. ed. Big book of science
fiction
"The years draw nigh"
Derleth, A. W. ed. Beachheads in space
Delta interlude. Newman, R. S.
DeLynn, Leslie, 1922-
How I came to love the smell of a bar-
room
Wolfe, D. M. ed. Which grain will grow
De Maupassant, Guy. See Maupassant,
Guy de
De Meyer, John
Boy crazy
Saturday evening post (Periodical)
Saturday evening post stories, 1953

Deming, Richard
For value received
Best detective stories of the year—1953
Hanging fire
Meredith, S. ed. Bar 2
Mugger murder
Best detective stories of the year—1953
DEMOCRACY
Munro, H. H. Comments of Moung Ka
Porter, W. S. Sociology in serge and
straw
Rinehart, M. R. One hour of glory
Saroyan, W. Ancient history and low
hurdles
Demoiselle d'Ys. Chambers, R. W.
Demon lover. Bowen, E.
DEMONOLOGY. See Devil
DEMONS. See Devil
The **demons.** Sheckley, R.
Demotion. Locke, R. D.
DeMott, Benjamin Haile
Sense that in the scene delights
Best American short stories, 1954
Dempsey, David K. 1914-
Hope chest
Story (Periodical) Story; no. 3
Denicoff Marvin
Winter detail
Story (Periodical) Story; no. 3
DENMARK
Nexø, M. A. Birds of passage
DENTISTS
Benchley, R. C. The tooth, the whole
tooth, and nothing but the tooth
Lewis, S. Land
Vickers, R. Man with the sneer
DEPARTMENT STORES
Calisher, H. Woman who was everybody
Collier, J. Evening primrose
Porter, W. S. Lickpenny lover
Porter, W. S. Trimmed lamp
Departmental case. Porter, W. S.
DEPRESSION. See Business depression,
1929
De profundis. Jenkins, W. F.
De Quille, Dan, pseud. See Wright, William
De Quincey, Thomas, 1785-1859
Savannah-al-mar
Neider, C. ed. Great short stories from
the world's literature
The **derelict.** Tomlinson, H. M.
Derieux, Samuel Arthur, 1881-1922
The Comet
Bloch, M. ed. Favorite dog stories
Derleth August William, 1909-
Adventure of Ricoletti of the club foot
Derleth, A. W. Memoirs of Solar Pons
Adventure of the Black Narcissus
Mystery Writers of America, inc.
Maiden murders
Adventure of the broken chessman
Derleth, A. W. Memoirs of Solar Pons
Adventure of the Camberwell beauty
Derleth, A. W. Three problems for
Solar Pons
Adventure of the circular room
Derleth, A. W. Memoirs of Solar Pons

Derleth, August W.—*Continued*
Adventure of the dog in the manger
  Derleth, A. W. Memoirs of Solar Pons
Adventure of the five royal coachmen
  Derleth, A. W. Memoirs of Solar Pons
Adventure of the lost locomotive
  Derleth, A. W. Memoirs of Solar Pons
Adventure of the paralytic mendicant
  Derleth, A. W. Memoirs of Solar Pons
Adventure of the perfect husband
  Derleth, A. W. Memoirs of Solar Pons
Adventure of the proper comma
  Derleth, A. W. Memoirs of Solar Pons
Adventure of the purloined periapt
  Mystery Writers of America, inc. Four-
    & twenty bloodhounds
Adventure of the remarkable worm
  Derleth, A. W. Three problems for
    Solar Pons
Adventure of the Rydberg numbers
  Derleth, A. W. Three problems for
    Solar Pons
Adventure of the six silver spiders
  Derleth, A. W. Memoirs of Solar Pons
Adventure of the Tottenham werewolf
  Derleth, A. W. Memoirs of Solar Pons
The lonesome place
  Derleth, A. W. ed. Night's yawning
    peal
McIlvaine's star
  Derleth, A. W. ed. Worlds of tomorrow
  Wollheim, D. A. ed. Prize science
    fiction
Sheraton mirror
  Cuff, R. P. ed. American short story
    survey
The telescope
  Story (Periodical) Story; no. 2
DeRosso, H. A.
  Bitter trail
    Meredith, S. ed. Bar 3
Des takes a holiday. Wylie, P.
Descendant of kings. Williams, W. C.
Descent into the maelström. Poe, E. A.
Desert fire. O'Meara, W.
DESERT ISLANDS
  Wells, H. G. Æpyornis Island
Desert orchid. Reese, J. H.
DESERTED HOUSES. See Houses, De-
  serted
Deserted mine. Sawyer, R.
The **deserter.** Davis, R. H.
The **deserter.** Klass, P.
Desertion. Simak, C. D.
DESERTION, MILITARY
  Davis, R. H. The deserter
DESERTION AND NON-SUPPORT
  Hawthorne, N. Wakefield
  Winslow, T. S. Mrs Wilson's husband
    goes for a swim
DESERTS
  Brand, M. pseud. Wine on the desert
  Clark, W. Van T. Indian well
  Grey, Z. Tappan's burro
  Prado, P. Laugh in the desert
Desire to be a man. Villiers de l'Isle-Adam,
  J. M. M. P. A. comte de

De Soto, Hernando. See Soto, Hernando
  de
DESPERADOES. See Outlaws
Desperate journey. Gunn, N. M.
DESPOTISM
  Hawthorne, N. Gray champion
Desrick on Yandro. Wellman, M. W.
De Stendhal, pseud. See Beyle, Marie Henri
Destiny strikes back. Whitley, C. M.
Destiny times three. Leiber, F.
DESTRUCTION OF EARTH. See Earth,
  Destruction of
**DETECTIVE AND MYSTERY STO-
  RIES.** See Mystery and detective
  stories
Detective detector. Porter, W. S.
DETECTIVES
  Alcazar, Doctor. See stories by Mac-
    Donald, P.
  Arnold, Shadrack. See stories by Chute, V.
  Banner, Brooks Urban. See stories by
    Commings, J.
  Bell, Adam. See stories by Carr, J. D.
  Brown, Father. See stories by Chesterton,
    G. K.
  Burgess, James. See stories by Brannon,
    W. T.
  Campion, Albert. See stories by Alling-
    ham, M.
  Chafik, Chafik J. See stories by Child,
    C. B.
  Coffee, Dr Daniel Webster. See stories
    by Blochman, L. G.
  Death, Mortimer, See stories by Crossen,
    K. F.
  Duffy, Detective Henry. See stories by
    Hayward, J. L.
  Dupin, C. Auguste. See stories by Poe,
    E. A.
  Fell, Gideon. See stories by Carr, J. D.
  Finney, Mary. See stories by Canaday,
    J. E.
  Forsythe, Wade II. See stories by Rine-
    hart, M. R.
  Gryce, Ebenezer. See stories by Green,
    A. K.
  Gurney, Cap. See stories by Brown, F.
  Hazlerigg, Chief Inspector. See stories by
    Gilbert, M. F.
  Holmes, Sherlock. See stories by Doyle.
    Sir A. C.
  Holmes, Sherlock. See stories by Doyle,
    A. C. and Carr, J. D.
  Joad, Bela. See stories by Brown, F.
  Johnson, Dr Samuel. See stories by De
    La Torre, L.
  Jolnes, Shamrock. See stories by Porter,
    W. S.
  Jordan, Scott. See stories by Masur,
    H. Q.
  Liddell, Johnny. See stories by Kane, F.
  Luke, Charley. See stories by Alling-
    ham, M.
  Lupin, Arsène. See stories by LeBlanc, M.
  MacDonald, Lieutenant. See stories by
    White, W. A. P.
  McGarry, Dan. See stories by Taylor, M.
  Magruder, Inspector John Bankhead. See
    stories by Prince, J. and Prince, H.

DETECTIVES—*Continued*

Maigret, Inspector. See stories by Simenon, G.

Malone, John J. See stories by Rice, C.

March, Colonel. See stories by Carr, J. D.

Marquis, Colonel. See stories by Carr, J. D.

Marshall, John Conger. See stories by Knipscheer, J. M. W.

Marshall, Suzanne Willet. See stories by Knipscheer, J. M. W.

Mason, Perry. See stories by Gardner, E. S.

Merlini, the great. See stories by Rawson, C.

Merrivale, Sir Henry. See stories by Carr, J. D.

Murdock, Rachel. See stories by Hitchens, D. B.

Noble, Nicholas. See stories by White, W. A. P.

O'Reilly, Terrence Patrick. See stories by Blochman, L. G.

Paris, Detective-Inspector Wade. See stories by Benson, B.

Parker, Sergeant Nels. See stories by Deming, R.

Pedley, Benjamin Tilmon. See stories by Winchell, P.

Pettit, Don Aristide. See stories by Brown, F.

Piper, Inspector Oscar. See stories by Palmer, S.

Poggioli, Professor Henry. See stories by Stribling, T. S.

Poirot, Hercule. See stories by Christie, A. M.

Pons, Solar. See stories by Derleth, A. W.

Pym, Mrs. See stories by Morland, N.

Queen, Ellery. See stories by Queen, E. pseud.

"The Saint." See stories by Charteris, L.

Shayne, Michael. See stories by Dresser, D.

Slappey, Florian. See stories by Cohen, O. R.

Smith, Henry. See stories by Brown, F.

Standish, Dr Paul. See stories by Coxe, G. H.

Stevens, Gavin. See stories by Faulkner, W.

Templar, Simon. See stories by Charteris, L.

Thinking machine. See stories by Futrelle, J.

Tictocq. See stories by Porter, W. S.

Trant, Timothy Tregaskis. See stories by Quentin, P. pseud.

Trent, Philip Marsham. See stories by Bentley, W. C.

Troy, Haila Rogers. See stories by Roos, K. pseud.

Troy, Jeff. See stories by Roos, K. pseud.

Valentin, Aristide. See stories by Chesterton, G. K.

Willets, Sheriff Andrew. See stories by Davis, D. S.

Withers, Miss Hildegarde. See stories by Palmer, S.

Wolfe, Nero. See stories by Stout, R.

Detour in the dark. Beck, W.

Detour to Calcutta. Marshall, E.

DETOURS. See Automobile drivers

Detzer, Karl William, 1891-
Surfman number nine
American boy (Periodical) American boy Adventure stories

Deutsch, A. J.
Subway named Mobius
Conklin, G. ed. Omnibus of science fiction

Deutsch, Lajos Hatvany-. See Hatvany Lajos, báró

DEVIL

Benét, S. V. Devil and Daniel Webster
Betts, D. Serpents and doves
Brooks, G. The devil's tail
Clemens, S. L. Mysterious stranger
Collier, J. The Devil, George and Rosie
Collier, J. Fallen star
Collier, J. Hell hath no fury
Collier, J. Possession of Angela Bradshaw
Collier, J. Right side
Defoe, D. The friendly demon
Dickens, C. The rat that could speak
Elliott, B. Devil was sick
Grau, S. A. Black prince
Hawthorne, N. Ethan Brand
Hawthorne, N. Young Goodman Brown
Horgan, P. Devil in the desert
Irving, W. Devil and Tom Walker
Irwin, M. E. F. The book
James, M. R. Count Magnus
Jameson, M. Blind alley
Kuttner, H. By these presents
Lagerkvist, P. F. Lift that went down into hell
Poe, E. A. Bon-Bon
Poe, E. A. Devil in the belfry
Poe, E. A. Never bet the Devil your head
Stevenson, R. L. Bottle imp
Tolstoï, A. N. Graf. Fusty Devil
Van Doren, M. Satan's best girl
See also Hell

The **devil.** Maupassant, G. de

Devil and Daniel Webster. Benét, S. V.

Devil and Father Francisco. Gordon, A.

The **devil** and Tom Walker. Irving, W.

DEVIL FISH. See Octopus

The **Devil,** George and Rosie. Collier, J.

Devil in the belfry. Poe, E. A.

Devil in the desert. Horgan, P.

Devil of a fellow. Steele, W. D.

Devil on Salvation Bluff. Kuttner, H.

Devil on wheels. Winchell, P.

Devil was sick. Elliott, B.

Devil's autograph. Munby, A. N. L.

Devil's henchman. Jenkins, W. F.

Devil's tail. Brooks, G.

Devin, Bernard, 1928-
The rattle
American vanguard, 1953

Devlin. Ready, W. B.

DEVONSHIRE. See England, Provincial and rural—Devonshire

Devotion without end. Peretz, I. L.

Devries, Marvin
    Stage to Yuma
        Saturday evening post (Periodical)
        Saturday evening post stories, 1953

De Vries, Peter
    Cold potato
        De Vries, P. No but I saw the movie
    Different cultural levels eat here
        De Vries, P. No but I saw the movie
    Double or nothing
        De Vries, P. No but I saw the movie
    Every leave that falls
        De Vries, P. No but I saw the movie
    Flesh and the devil
        De Vries, P. No but I saw the movie
    From there to infinity
        De Vries, P. No but I saw the movie
    Good boy
        De Vries, P. No but I saw the movie
    Household words
        De Vries, P. No but I saw the movie
    How can I leave thee?
        De Vries, P. No but I saw the movie
    I don't want to go
        De Vries, P. No but I saw the movie
    If he hollers let him holler
        De Vries, P. No but I saw the movie
    If the shoe hurts
        De Vries, P. No but I saw the movie
    Jam today
        De Vries, P. No but I saw the movie
    Let 'em eat cook
        De Vries, P. No but I saw the movie
    Life among the winesaps
        De Vries, P. No but I saw the movie
    One
        De Vries, P. No but I saw the movie
    Open house
        De Vries, P. No but I saw the movie
    Overture
        De Vries, P. No but I saw the movie
    Pygmalion
        De Vries, P. No but I saw the movie
    Requiem for a noun
        De Vries, P. No but I saw the movie
    Scene
        De Vries, P. No but I saw the movie
    They also sit
        De Vries, P. No but I saw the movie
    Through a glass darkly
        De Vries, P. No but I saw the movie
    Today and today
        De Vries, P. No but I saw the movie
    Touch and go
        De Vries, P. No but I saw the movie
    Tulip
        De Vries, P. No but I saw the movie
    We don't know
        De Vries, P. No but I saw the movie
    You and who else?
        De Vries, P. No but I saw the movie

De Wets come to Kloof Grange. Lessing,
    D. M.

Dewey, G. Gordon, 1916-
    The tooth
        Magazine of fantasy and science fiction.
        Best from Fantasy and science fiction;
        2d ser.

Dewey, G. Gordon, 1916- and **Dancey, Max,**
    1916-
    The collectors
        Best science-fiction stories: 1954

Dhoh. Wellman, M. W.

DIABETES
    Shapiro, L. Journeying through the milky
    way

DIABETICS. See Diabetes

Diagnosis deferred. Blochman, L. G.

Diagnosis of a selfish lady. Boyle, K.

DIALECT STORIES

Cockney
    See Dialect stories—English—Cock-
    ney

English—Cockney
Kipling, R. On Greenhow Hill
Munro, H. H. Morlvera

English—Devonshire
Phillpotts, E. "Hey diddle diddle, the
    cat. . ."

English—Yorkshire
Knight, E. M. Flying Yorkshireman

Irish
Kipling, R. Incarnation of Krishna Mul-
    vaney
Lover, S. The gridiron
Walsh, M. Thomasheen James and the
    dictation machine

Jewish
Kober, A. Bella, Bella kissed a fella;
    15 stories

Middle West
Clemens, S. E. Celebrated jumping frog
    of Calaveras County
Garland, H. Under the lion's paw

Mountain whites (Southern States)
Hall, E. G. Callie of Crooked Creek
Harris, G. W. Sut Lovingood; 8 stories
Porter, W. S. Whirligig of life
Still, J. Master time

Negro
Cohen, O. R. Law and the profits
Harris, J. C. Wonderful Tar-Baby story
Paul, L. No more trouble for Jedwick
Rice, A. C. H. Hoodooed

New England
Benét, S. V. Devil and Daniel Webster
Freeman, M. E. W. Revolt of "Mother"
Jewett, S. O. Courting of Sister Wisby
Slosson, A. T. Fishin' Jimmy

Scotch
Barrie, Sir J. M. bart. Courting of T'now-
    head's Bell
Crockett, S. R. Reverend John Smith
    prepares his sermon
Crockett, S. R. Stickit minister
Gilpatric, G. Last Glencannon omnibus;
    10 stories
Watson, J. Story of Dr MacLure

DIALECT STORIES—*Continued*

Southern

Dowdey, C. Bugles blow Retreat
Fox, J. Courtin' on Cutshin
Furman, L. Experience on the dress line
Granberry, E. P. Trip to Czardis
Kidd, H. L. Low road go down
Pratt, F. and De Camp, L. S. Stone of the sages
Rawlings, M. K. Benny and the bird-dogs
Rawlings, M. K. Gal young un
Smith, E. V. Prelude

Southwestern

Cunningham, E. Bar-Nothing's happy birthday
Watson, J. C. Benny and the Tar-Baby

Texas

See Dialect stories—Southwestern

Western

Clemens, S. L. Buck Fanshaw's funeral
Harte, B. Mrs Skaggs's husbands
Meredith, S. ed. Bar 2; 12 stories

Yiddish

See Dialect stories—Jewish

A dialogue. Walsh, M.

Diamant, Gertrude, 1901-
Snows of Bardonechhia
Queen, E. pseud. ed. Queen's awards: 7th ser.

Diamond as big as the Ritz. Fitzgerald, F. S. K.

Diamond horseshoes. Bateman, A.

Diamond lens. O'Brien, F.-J.

Diamond necklace. Maupassant, G. de

Diamond of Kali. Porter, W. S.

DIAMONDS
Fitzgerald, F. S. K. Diamond as big as the Ritz
Porter, W. S. Diamond of Kali

DIARIES (STORIES IN DIARY FORM)
Barrie, Sir J. M. bart. Farewell Miss Julie Logan
Clifton, M. Star, Bright
Collier, J. Evening primrose
Maupassant, G. de. Diary of a madman
Maupassant, G. de. The Horla
Paget, V. Amour dure
Shute, H. A. "Sequil" - or, Things whitch aint finished in the first
Wolfe, B. Self portrait

DIARIES, STORIES ABOUT
Chekhov, A. P. A fragment
Elston, A. V. Last day of my life
Willingham, C. Secret journal

Diary of a hard-boiled noble. Claudy, C. H.

Diary of a madman. Maupassant, G. de

DICE, See Gambling

Dick, Isaac Meier, 1807?-1893
Two strangers came to town
Ausubel, N. ed. Treasury of Jewish humor

Dick, Philip K. 1928-
Foster, you're dead
Star science fiction stories, no. 3

Golden man
Merril, J. ed. Beyond the barriers of space and time
Jon's world
Derleth, A. W. ed. Time to come
Second variety
Year's best science fiction novels, 1954

Dick Boyle's busines card. Harte, B.

Dickens, Charles, 1812-1870
Battle of life
Dickens, C. Christmas books
Captain Murderer
Davenport, B. ed. Ghostly tales to be told
Child's dream of a star
Cody, S. ed. Greatest stories and how they were written
The chimes
Dickens, C. Christmas books
Dickens, C. Christmas stories
Christmas carol
Cerf, B. A. and Moriarty, H. C. eds. Anthology of famous British stories
Cody, S. ed. Greatest stories and how they were written
Dickens, C. Christmas books
Dickens, C. Christmas stories
Lamb, L. ed. Family book of best loved short stories
Cricket on the hearth
Dickens, C. Christmas books
Dickens, C. Christmas stories
Haunted man
Dickens, C. Christmas books
Hunted down
Queen, E. pseud. ed. Literature of crime
Rat that could speak
Magazine of fantasy and science fiction. Best from Fantasy and science fiction; [1st ser.]
The signal-man
Blodgett, H. W. ed. Story survey. 1953 ed.
Moskowitz, S. ed. Great railroad stories of the world

About

Walpole, Sir H. Mr Huffam

Dickinson, Hugh
Reluctant hangman
Gable, M. Sister, ed. Many-colored fleece

Dickson, Carter, pseud. See Carr, John Dickson

Dickson, Gordon R.
Listen
Wollheim, D. A. ed. Prize science fiction
Lulungomeena
Lesser, M. A. ed. Looking forward
Steel brother
Norton, A. M. ed. Space service
See also Anderson, P. jt. auth.

Dickson, Helen, pseud. See Reynolds, Helen Mary Greenwood (Campbell)

Dicky. Porter, W. S.

DICTAPHONES
Walsh, M. Thomasheen James and the dictation machine

DICTATION MACHINES. See Dictaphones

DICTATORS
Benét, S. V. Blood of the martyrs
Kohnbluth, C. M. Marching morons

Dictator's double. Carr, R. S.

Did he touch you? Gatty, L.

Diderot, Denis, 1713-1784
Rameau's nephew
Dupee, F. W. ed. Great French short
novels

Di Donato, Pietro, 1911-
Christ in concrete
Best of the Best American short stories,
1915-1950

Die, Maestro, die! Waldo, E. H.

Different cultural levels eat here. De
Vries, P.

Difficult man. Williams, W. C.

Digging for treasure. Bland, E. N.

Digging our own graves. Farrell, J. T.

Dignity, a springer spaniel. Meek, S. St P.

Dilemma of Catherine Fuchsias. Davies, R.

Dilemma of Grampa Dubois. Lipman, C.
and Lipman, M.

Dill pickle. Mansfield, K.

Dime brings you success. Pratt, F. and De
Camp, L. S.

Diminishing draft. Kaempffert, W. B.

DINERS. See Restaurants, lunch rooms,
etc.

Dinesen, Isak, pseud. See Blixen, Karen

Dingle, Aylward Edward, 1874-
Owner's interest
Bluebook (Periodical) Best sea stories
from Bluebook

Dingle, Captain. See Dingle, Aylward Edward

DINING. See Dinners

Dinner at—. Porter, W. S.

DINNERS
Aiken, C. P. Fish supper
Bowen, E. Her table spread
Ekbergh, I. D. Katherine the clown
Farrell, J. T. Romantic interlude in the
life of Willie Collins
Humphrey, W. Quail for Mr Forester
Huysmans, J. K. Monsieur Folantin
Mallea, E. Pillars of society
Maugham, W. S. The luncheon
Munro, H. H. Phantom luncheon
Runyon, D. Piece of pie
Seager, A. Second wedding

Dinnis, Enid Maud, 1873-1942
The intervener
Thinker's digest (Periodical) Spoiled
priest, and other stories
No-man's Danny
Thinker's digest (Periodical) Spoiled
priest, and other stories
The peacemaker
Thinker's digest (Periodical) Spoiled
priest, and other stories

Dionea. Paget, V.

Dip in the pool. Dahl, R.

Diplomacy in Hollywood. Kaufman, W.

The diplomat. Chekhov, A. P.

DIPLOMATIC LIFE
Maugham, W. S. His Excellency
Piper, H. B. He walked around the
horses
See also Consuls

DIPLOMATS. See Diplomatic life

Dipping of the candlemaker. Howard, H.

Dirt-track thunder. Gault, W. C.

DISABLED. See Cripples

Disabled soldier. Goldsmith, O.

Disagreeable experience. Chekhov, A. P.

Disappearance of Crispina Umberleigh.
Munro, H. H.

DISAPPEARANCES
Cuthbert, C. D. Sublime vigil
De La Mare, W. J. Missing
Hawthorne, N. Wakefield
Huckabay, M. B. Ghost of Sam Bates
Kaempffert, W. B. Diminishing draft
MacDonald, P. Private—keep out
Munro, H. H. Disappearance of Crispina
Umberleigh
Porter, W. S. Renaissance at Charleroi
Porter, W. S. Strange story
Richter, C. Sinister journey
Sherwood, R. E. "Extra! Extra!"
Wells, H. G. The Plattner story
Winslow, T. S. Bronzes of Martel Greer
Woolrich, C. Wait for me downstairs
See also Invisibility

Disappearing act. Bester, A.

Disappearing act. Matheson, R.

Disappearing servant wench. De La
Torre, L.

Disappointed, but. Cooke, A. A.

DISASTERS
Colladay, M. M. Planetoid of doom
McMorrow, T. Mr Murphy of New York
See also Accidents; Fires; Floods;
Shipwrecks and castaways; Storms

The disciple. Aiken, C. P.

DISCIPLINE
Doty, W. L. Back to school

Discord makers. Reynolds, M.

Discounters of money. Porter, W. S.

Discovery. Brenner, L.

DISEASES
MacLean, K. Contagion
See also names of diseases, e.g.
Malaria

DISFIGUREMENTS. See Face—Abnormities
and deformities

Disgrace to the family. Boyle, K.

Disguise. Wollheim, D. A.

DISGUISES. See Impersonations

DISHONESTY. See Honesty

The disinherited. Pagano, J.

DISMISSAL OF EMPLOYEES. See Employees, Dismissal of

Disorder and early sorrow. Mann, T.

DISORDERS OF PERSONALITY. See
Personality, Disorders of

Dispatch to the general. Haycox, E.

"Disperse, ye rebels!" Forbes, E.

Displaced persons. Sansom, W.

The **dispossessed.** Sullivan, R.
Disraeli, Benjamin. See Beaconsfield, Benjamin Disraeli, 1st earl of
Distant episode. Bowles, P. F.
DISTILLING, ILLICIT
    Rawlings, M. K. Gal young un
DISTINCTION, CLASS. See Class distinction
Distressing tale of Thangobrind the jeweller. Dunsany, E. J. M. D. P. 18th baron
District doctor. Turgenev, I. S.
Ditzen, Rudolf, 1893-1947
    Fifty marks
        Lohan, R. and Lohan, M. eds. New Christmas treasury
Diversion. Ullman, J. R.
Divine, Arthur Durham, 1904-
    Thirty minutes to zero
        Saturday evening post (Periodical) Saturday evening post stories, 1953
Divine, David, pseud. See Divine, Arthur Durham
DIVINE HEALING. See Christian science; Faith cure; Miracles
DIVING
    Coombs, C. I. Water bug
    Maugham, W. S. Gigolo and gigolette
    Miers, E. S. Big splash
    Reck, F. M. Diving fool
DIVING, SUBMARINE
    Crump. I. Dead men on parade
    Doyle, Sir A. C. Maracot Deep
    Hemingway, E. After the storm
    Rieseberg, H. E. I dive for treasure
    Wells, H. G. In the abyss
        See also Skin diving
Diving fool. Reck, F. M.
DIVORCE
    Connolly, M. Natural causes
    Doty, W. L. Rectory parlor
    Grau, S. A. Fever flower
    McCarthy, M. T. "Cruel and barbarous treatment"
    McCullers, C. S. The sojourner
    Maugham, W. S. Closed shop
    Munro, H. H. Unkindest blow
    O'Donovan, M. Father and son
    Patterson, E. G. Homecoming
    Porter, W. S. Hypotheses of failure
    Porter, W. S. Whirligig of life
    Stewart, R. The promise
    Stranger's note
    Tarkington, B. Rennie Peddigoe
    Wharton, E. N. J. Autres temps
    Wharton, E. N. J. Madame De Treymes
    Wharton, E. N. J. The other two
    Winslow, T. S. Hotel dog
        See also Marriage problems
Divorce in Naples. Faulkner, W.
DIVORCÉES. See Divorce
Dixon, Edwina Streeter
    Pa sees again
        Ford, N. A. and Faggett, H. L. eds. Best short stories by Afro-American writers (1925-1950)
Do-gooder. Benjamin, I. E.
Do you like it here? O'Hara, J.

Do you remember Mary? Kutner, N.
Doar, Graham
    Outer limit
        Conklin, G. ed. Big book of science fiction
Dobie, James Frank, 1888-
    Midas on a goatskin
        Peery, W. W. ed. 21 Texas short stories
The **doctor.** Irwin, M. E. F.
Dr Fillgrave refuses a fee. Trollope, A.
Doctor Hanray's second chance. Richter, C.
Dr Heidegger's experiment. Hawthorne, N.
The **doctor,** his wife, and the clock. Green, A. K.
Doctor-know-it-all. Gág, W.
Dr Lu-Mie. Kruse, C. B.
Doctor Mallory. Hart, A.
Dr Martino. Faulkner, W.
Dr Ox's experiment. Verne, J.
Doctor takes a case. Coxe, G. H.
DOCTORS. See Dentists; Physicians
Doctors of death. Thompson, T.
Dodge, John Everett
    Headwall tempo
        Owen, F. ed. Teen-age winter sports stories
DODGERS. See Brooklyn. Baseball club (National League)
Dodson, Daniel B. 1918-
    The let-down
        Story (Periodical) Story; no. 1
Doestoevsky, Feodor. See Dostoevskiĭ, Feodor Mikhailovich
Dog and the playlet. Porter, W. S.
Dog Andrew. Train, A. C.
Dog days. Jones, M. P. jr.
Dog died first. Fischer, B.
Dog for Miss Boo. Runbeck, M. L.
Dog in the double bottoms. White, R.
Dog man. Bell, V. M.
DOG SHOWS
    Davis, R. H. Bar sinister
    Taber, G. B. Best of breed
    Taber, G. B. Top Hat goes to town
    Taber, G. B. You can't buy a dog
Dog that sounded like a fire siren. Lull, R.
Dog who chose a prince. Coblentz, C. C.
Doggone Douthits. Caldwell, E.
DOGS
    Anderson, E. V. Old Tom O'Grady of Shay Ranch
    Annixter, P. pseud. First ally
    Annixter, P. pseud. Hunting cost
    Annixter, P. pseud. Ketch dog
    Balch, G. Price on Hide-rack
    Bell, V. M. Dog man
    Bendrodt, J. C. Butch
    Bendrodt, J. C. Chowsie
    Blish, J. Beanstalk
    Bloch, M. ed. Favorite dog stories; 14 stories
    Bottome, P. Pink medicine
    Brown, J. Rab and his friends
    Buckingham, N. Cricket field
    Buckingham, N. Hallowed years

DOGS—*Continued*
Buckingham, N. Lady
Buckingham, N. "When time who steals our years away!"
Cavanna, B. ed. Pick of the litter; 14 stories
Cavanna, B. Puppy business
Cave, H. B. Two were left
Christopher, J. Socrates
Clemens, S. L. Dog's tale
Cooke, A. A. N.R.A. for a dollar
Davis, R. H. Bar sinister
Ebner von Eschenbach, M. freifrau. Krambambuli
Edmonds, W. D. Honor of the county
Farrell, J. T. Lib
Faulkner, W. The hound
Fenner, P. R. comp. Dogs dogs, dogs; 14 stories
Ford, C. Man of his own
Furman, A. L. ed. Teen-age dog stories; 14 stories
Gally, J. W. Hualapi
Gipson, F. B. My kind of a man
Gold, H. L. Matter of form
Guthrie, A. B. Ebbie
Hardy, W. G. Czech dog
Harper, W. comp. Dog show; 16 stories
Henderson, D. Brute's Christmas
Hoffman, E. On trial
Jenkins, W. F. Propagandist
Kafka, F. Investigations of a dog
Kantor, M. That Greek dog
Kantor, M. Voice of Bugle Ann
Knight, E. M. Lassie Come-Home
Lincoln, V. E. Death in the house
Little, G. W. True stories of heroic dogs; 16 stories
London, J. Brown Wolf
Lull, R. Dog that sounded like a fire siren
Mayse, A. Midnight Mike
Moll, E. Boy who went away
Morley, C. D. Home again
Muir, J. An adventure with a dog and a glacier
Munro, H. H. Louis
Nicola, H. B. Two on trial
Porter, W. S. Memoirs of a yellow dog
Porter, W. S. Ulysses and the dogman
Rabinowitz, S. Rabchik, a Jewish dog
Rawlings, M. K. Benny and the bird-dogs
Seton, E. T. Bingo
Seton, E. T. Wully
Stevenson, R. L. Character of dogs
Spiegel, I. Ghetto dog
Street, J. H. Weep no more, My Lady
Taber, G. B. When dogs meet people; 12 stories
Terhune, A. P. Hero
Terhune, A. P. One minute longer
Train, A. C. Dog Andrew
Vetter, M. M. Fool dog
Waldo, E. H. Tiny and the monster
Waugh, E. On guard
Welsh, M. Thomasheen James goes to the dogs
West, M. T. Hector
Winslow, T. S. Hotel dog
Winslow, T. S. Lamb chop for the little dog

Dog's dog. Kjelgaard, J. A.

Dog's tale. Clemens, S. L.
Doing good. Goudge, E.
Dolbier, Maurice
Before its time
Fenner, P. R. comp. Fun! Fun! Fun!
The **doll.** Pain, B. E. O.
DOLL HOUSES
Mansfield, K. Doll's house
Doll in the pink silk dress. Merrick, L.
Dollar bill. Van Doren, M.
DOLLS
Lawrence, D. H. Captain's doll
Lowry, R. J. C. Skyblue lady
Munro, H. H. Morlvera
Pain, B. E. O. The doll
Porter, W. S. Compliments of the season
Doll's house. Mansfield, K.
Domain of Arnheim. Poe. E. A.
Domestic dilemma. McCullers, C. S.
DOMESTIC ECONOMY. See Home economics
Domini. Barker, A. L.
Domino method. Parker, J. R.
Dominoes. Kornbluth, C. M.
Don Juan (Retired) O'Donovan, M.
Don Juan's temptation. O'Donovan, M.
Don Licciu Papa. Verga, G.
Donahoe, Edward, 1900-
Head by Scopas
West, R. B. and Stallman, R. W. eds. Art of modern fiction
Madness in the heart
Southern review. Anthology of stories from the Southern review
Donato, Pietro di. See Di Donato, Pietro
Donkey of God. Untermeyer, L.
DONKEYS. See Asses and mules
Donn-Byrne, Brian Oswald. See Byrne, Donn
Donnelly, Richard, 1929-
The secret
American vanguard, 1952
Don't jinx the pitcher. Erin, B.
Don't live in the past. Knight, D.
Don't look behind you. Brown, F.
Don't run, don't pass. Scott, V.
Dooley and the children's hour. Peterson, C. A.
Doolittles depart from Halfaday. Hendryx, J. B.
Doom of the Darnaways. Chesterton, G. K.
Doomington wanderer. Golding, L.
DOOMSDAY. See Judgment Day
Doomsday deferred. Jenkins, W. F.
The **door.** Keller, D. H.
Door between. Wyckoff, J.
Door marked exit. Benson, T.
Door of opportunity. Maugham, W. S.
Door of unrest. Porter, W. S.
The **doorbell.** Keller, D. H.
Doowinkle, Attorney. Klingsberg, H. M.

Doremus, John, 1920-
The whistle
Wolfe, D. M. ed. Which grain will grow

Dormant. Van Vogt, A. E.

Dorothy. Caldwell, E.

Dorrance, Ward Allison, 1904-
Stop on the way to Texas
Best American short stories, 1954

Dos Passos, John Roderigo, 1896-
Body of an American
Burrell, J. A. and Cerf, B. A. eds.
Anthology of famous American stories

Dostoevskiĭ, Fedor Mikhaĭlovich, 1821-1881
Christmas tree and a wedding
Dostoevskiĭ, F. M. White nights, and
other stories
Eternal husband
Rahv, P. ed. Great Russian short novels
Faint heart
Dostoevskiĭ, F. M. White nights, and
other stories
Father Zossima's duel
Hazeltine, A. I. comp. Selected stories
for teen-agers
Heavenly Christmas tree
Neider, C. ed. Great short stories from
the world's literature
Little hero
Dostoevskiĭ, F. M. White nights, and
other stories
Mr Prohartchin
Dostoevskiĭ, F. M. White nights, and
other stories
Notes from underground
Dostoevskiĭ, F. M. White nights, and
other stories
Neider, C. ed. Short novels of the
masters
Peasant Marey
Short, R. W. and Benson, R. B. eds.
Short stories for study. 1950 ed.
Polzunkov
Dostoevskiĭ, F. M. White nights, and
other stories
White nights
Dostoevskiĭ, F. M. White nights, and
other stories

Doty, William Lodewick, 1919-
Action in Prague
Doty, W. L. Stories for discussion
Back to school
Doty, W. L. Stories for discussion
College star
Doty, W. L. Stories for discussion
The colonel
Doty, W. L. Stories for discussion
Dark knight
Doty, W. L. Stories for discussion
Defender of the faith
Doty, W. L. Stories for discussion
Father Murray's first failure
Doty, W. L. Stories for discussion
The fisherman
Doty, W. L. Stories for discussion
Greatest of these
Doty, W. L. Stories for discussion
Maggie Winthrop
Doty, W. L. Stories for discussion
Man with the monocle
Doty, W. L. Stories for discussion

Mr Dee and the middle-man
Doty, W. L. Stories for discussion
Parochial school
Doty, W. L. Stories for discussion
Pittsburgh special
Doty, W. L. Stories for discussion
Rectory parlor
Doty, W. L. Stories for discussion
Silver cross
Doty, W. L. Stories for discussion
Welcome home
Doty, W. L. Stories for discussion

Double bliss. Arico, V.

Double corner, Stegner, W. E.

Double cross. Marshall, E.

Double-dyed deceiver. Porter, W. S.

Double-dyed villains. Anderson, P.

Double exposure. Hecht, B.

Double fault. Chute, B. J.

Double image. Vickers, R.

Double or nothing. De Vries, P.

Double your money. Queen, E. pseud.

Doubles or nothing. Chute, B. J.

Doubles or nothing. Reeve, J.

Dougherty's eye-opener. Porter, W. S.

Doughnut jockey. Fennel, E.

DOUGHNUTS
McCloskey, R. The doughnuts

The **doughnuts.** McCloskey, R.

Doughty, LeGarde S.
The firebird
Best American short stories, 1954

Douglas, John Scott, 1905-
Water broncs
Fenner, P. R. comp. Speed, speed, speed

Douglas, Lloyd Cassel, 1877-1951
Dean Harcourt
Neider, C. ed. Men of the high calling
Pentecost
Brentano, F. ed. The word lives on

Dovbish, Bella, 1898-
White light
American vanguard, 1952

Dove of God. Schneider, G. W.

DOVES. See Pigeons

Dowdey, Clifford, 1904-
Bugles blow retreat
Jones, K. M. ed. New Confederate
short stories

Down at the dinghy. Salinger, J. D.

Down from the mountains. Parker, J. R.

"**Down** pens" Munro, H. H.

Downey, Fairfax Davis, 1893-
Stand to horse
Furman, A. L. ed. Teen-age horse
stories

Downey, Harris
Crispin's way
Best American short stories, 1953
The hunters
Best American short stories, 1951
First-prize stories, 1919-1954
Greene, J. I. and Abell, E. ed. Stories
of sudden truth
Prize stories of 1951

Downhill dilemma. Coombs, C. I.
Downing, J. Hyatt, 1888-
Man needs a horse
Dennis, W. ed. Palomino and other
horses
Downward path to wisdom. Porter, K. A.
Doyle, Adrian Conan, 1910-1955
Adventure of Foulkes Rath
Doyle, A. C. and Carr, J. D. Exploits
of Sherlock Holmes
Adventure of the Abbas ruby
Doyle, A. C. and Carr, J. D. Exploits
of Sherlock Holmes
Adventure of the Dark Angels
Doyle, A. C. and Carr, J. D. Exploits
of Sherlock Holmes
Adventure of the Deptford horror
Doyle, A. C. and Carr, J. D. Exploits
of Sherlock Holmes
Adventure of the red widow
Doyle, A. C. and Carr, J. D. Exploits
of Sherlock Holmes
Adventure of the two women
Doyle, A. C. and Carr, J. D. Exploits
of Sherlock Holmes
Doyle, Adrian Conan, 1910-1955, **and Carr,
John Dickson,** 1905-
Adventure of the black baronet
Doyle, A. C. and Carr, J. D. Exploits
of Sherlock Holmes
Adventure of the gold hunter
Doyle, A. C. and Carr, J. D. Exploits
of Sherlock Holmes
Adventure of the Highgate miracle
Doyle, A. C. and Carr, J. D. Exploits of
Sherlock Holmes
Adventure of the sealed room
Doyle, A. C. and Carr, J. D. Exploits
of Sherlock Holmes
Adventure of the seven clocks
Doyle, A. C. and Carr, J. D. Exploits
of Sherlock Holmes
Adventure of the wax gamblers
Doyle, A. C. and Carr, J. D. Exploits
of Sherlock Holmes
Doyle, Sir Arthur Conan, 1859-1930
Adventure of the Beryl Coronet
Doyle, Sir A. C. Adventures of Sherlock
Holmes
Adventure of the blue carbuncle
Doyle, Sir A. C. Adventures of Sherlock
Holmes
Same as: Blue carbuncle
Adventure of the Copper Beeches
Doyle, Sir A. C. Adventures of Sherlock
Holmes
Adventure of the engineer's thumb
Doyle, Sir A. C. Adventures of Sherlock
Holmes
Adventure of the noble bachelor
Doyle, Sir A. C. Adventures of Sherlock
Holmes
Adventure of the speckled band
Doyle, Sir A. C. Adventures of Sherlock
Holmes
Cerf, B. A. and Moriarty, H. C. eds.
Anthology of famous British stories
Christ, H. I. and Shostak, J. eds. Short
stories
Lamb, L. ed. Family book of best loved
short stories
Same as: Speckled band

Avenging angels
Doyle, Sir A. C. Adventures of Sherlock
Holmes
Baker Street irregulars
Doyle, Sir A. C. Adventures of Sherlock
Holmes
Blue carbuncle
Doyle, Sir A. C. Sherlock Holmes
Same as: Adventures of the blue car-
buncle
Boscombe Valley mystery
Doyle, Sir A. C. Adventures of Sherlock
Holmes
Doyle, Sir A. C. Book of Sherlock
Holmes
Break in the chain
Doyle, Sir A. C. Adventures of Sherlock
Holmes
Cardboard box
Doyle, Sir A. C. Adventures of Sherlock
Holmes
Case of identity
Doyle, Sir A. C. Adventures of Sherlock
Holmes
Doyle, Sir A. C. Book of Sherlock
Holmes
The conclusion
Doyle, Sir A. C. Adventures of Sherlock
Holmes
Continuation of the reminiscences of John
Watson, M. D.
Doyle, Sir A. C. Adventures of Sherlock
Holmes
Crooked man
Doyle, Sir A. C. Adventures of Sherlock
Holmes
Empty house
Doyle, Sir A. C. Sherlock Holmes
End of the Islander
Doyle, Sir A. C. Adventures of Sherlock
Holmes
Episode of the barrel
Doyle, Sir A. C. Adventures of Sherlock
Holmes
Final problem
Doyle, Sir A. C. Adventures of Sherlock
Holmes
Five orange pips
Doyle, Sir A. C. Adventures of Sherlock
Holmes
Flight for life
Doyle, Sir A. C. Adventures of Sherlock
Holmes
Flower of Utah
Doyle, Sir A. C. Adventures of Sherlock
Holmes
The "Gloria Scott"
Doyle, Sir A. C. Adventures of Sherlock
Holmes
Great Agra treasure
Doyle, Sir A. C. Adventures of Sherlock
Holmes
Greek interpreter
Doyle, Sir A. C. Adventures of Sherlock
Holmes
Doyle, Sir A. C. Sherlock Holmes
His last bow
Doyle, Sir A. C. Sherlock Holmes
Horror of the heights
Jensen, P. ed. Fireside book of flying
stories

Doyle, Sir Arthur C.—*Continued*
In quest of a solution
Doyle, Sir A. C. Adventures of Sherlock
Holmes
John Ferrier talks with the prophet
Doyle, Sir A. C. Adventures of Sherlock
Holmes
Lauriston Gardens mystery
Doyle, Sir A. C. Adventures of Sherlock
Holmes
Light in the darkness
Doyle, Sir A. C. Adventures of Sherlock
Holmes
Man with the twisted lip
Doyle, Sir A. C. Adventures of Sherlock
Holmes
Maracot Deep
Kuebler, H. W. ed. Treasury of science
fiction classics
Missing three-quarter
Doyle, Sir A. C. Sherlock Holmes
Mr Sherlock Holmes
Doyle, Sir A. C. Adventures of Sherlock
Holmes
Musgrave ritual
Doyle, Sir A. C. Adventures of Sherlock
Holmes
Naval treaty
Doyle, Sir A. C. Adventures of Sherlock
Holmes
Doyle, Sir A. C. Sherlock Holmes
On the great alkali plain
Doyle, Sir A. C. Adventures of Sherlock
Holmes
Our advertisement brings a visitor
Doyle, Sir A. C. Adventures of Sherlock
Holmes
Red-Headed League
Doyle, Sir A. C. Adventures of Sherlock
Holmes
Doyle, Sir A. C. Book of Sherlock
Holmes
Doyle, Sir A. C. Sherlock Holmes
Schramm, W. L. ed. Great short stories
Reigate squires
Doyle, Sir A. C. Adventures of Sherlock
Holmes
Resident patient
Doyle, Sir A. C. Adventures of Sherlock
Holmes
Scandal in Bohemia
Doyle, Sir A. C. Adventures of Sherlock
Holmes
Doyle, Sir A. C. Book of Sherlock
Holmes
Doyle, Sir A. C. Sherlock Holmes
Science of deduction
Doyle, Sir A. C. Adventures of Sherlock
Holmes
Sherlock Holmes gives a demonstration
Doyle, Sir A. C. Adventures of Sherlock
Holmes
Sign of the four
Doyle, Sir A. C. Book of Sherlock
Holmes
Doyle, Sir A. C. Sherlock Holmes
Silver Blaze
Doyle, Sir A. C. Adventures of Sherlock
Holmes
Doyle, Sir A. C. Sherlock Holmes

Speckled band
Doyle, Sir A. C. Sherlock Holmes
Same as: Adventure of the speckled
band
Statement of the case
Doyle, Sir A. C. Adventures of Sherlock
Holmes
Stockbroker's clerk
Doyle, Sir A. C. Adventures of Sherlock
Holmes
Story of the bald-headed man
Doyle, Sir A. C. Adventures of Sherlock
Holmes
Strange story of Jonathan Small
Doyle, Sir A. C. Adventures of Sherlock
Holmes
A study in scarlet
Doyle, Sir A. C. Book of Sherlock
Holmes
Tobias Gregson shows what he can do
Doyle, Sir A. C. Adventures of Sherlock
Holmes
Tragedy of Pondicherry Lodge
Doyle, Sir A. C. Adventures of Sherlock
Holmes
What John Rance had to tell
Doyle, Sir A. C. Adventures of Sher-
lock Holmes
Yellow face
Doyle, Sir A. C. Adventures of Sherlock
Holmes
Doyle, Fredric Clyde
Bullets for Bouquet
Hazeltine, A. I. comp. Selected stories
for teen-agers
Doyle, Louis, 1920-
Go to the ant
Wolfe, D. M. ed. Which grain will grow
Doyle, Thomas L.
El conquistador
Stanford short stories, 1950
DRAFT, MILITARY. See Military service,
Compulsory
The **drag.** Darling, F.
Drago, Harry Sinclair, 1888-
Long winter
Western Writers of America. Bad men
and good
Sagebrush champion
Furman, A. L. ed. Teen-age horse stories
The **dragon.** Akutagawa, R.
Dragon! Everett, E. W.
Dragon rider. Annixter, P. pseud.
DRAGONS
Akutagawa, R. The dragon
Grahame, K. Reluctant dragon
DRAMATISTS
Cheever, J. O city of broken dreams
Saroyan, W. Poet at home
Winslow, T. S. Technique
The **dream.** Caldwell, E.
The **dream.** Chekhov, A. P.
The **dream.** Krige, U.
The **dream.** Maugham, W. S.
The **dream.** Porter, W. S.
The **dream.** Van Doren, M.
Dream of Armageddon. Wells, H. G.
Dream of drums. Sullivan, R.

Dream-woman. Collins, W.
The **dreamer**. Coppel, A.
The **dreamer**. Munro, H. H.
DREAMS
Aikens, C. P. Mr Arcularis
Benét, S. V. End to dreams
Bowles, P. F Thousand days for Mokhtar
Caldwell, E. The dream
Chekhov, A. P. Reporter's dream
Clemens, S. L. My platonic sweetheart
Clemens, S. L. Mysterious stranger
Collier, J. Interpretation of a dream
Collier, J. Midnight blue
Collins, W. Dream-woman
Curry, P. S. Osage Girl
De La Mare, W. J. Three friends
De La Mare, W. J. The wharf
Ekbergh, I. D. Astral plane—land of dreams
Fitzgerald, F. S. K. Winter dreams
Hawthorne, N. Celestial railroad
James, H. Great good place
Johnson, D. M. Warrior's exile
Kipling, R. Brushwood Boy
Maugham, W. S. The dream
Maugham, W. S. Lord Mountdrago
Moore, C. L. Scarlet dream
Myers, H. Pale sergeant
Nourse, A. E. Nightmare brother
Poe, E. A. Angel of the odd
Poe, E. A. Domain of Arnheim
Poe, E. A. Tale of the Ragged Mountains
Porter, W. S. The dream
Robin, R. Pleasant dreams
Schoenfeld, B. C. Eagle and the cheetah
Schwartz, D. In dreams begin responsibilities
Van Doren, M. The dream
Van Doren, M. Grandison and son
Waldo, E. H. Chromium helmet
Wells, H. G. Dream of Armageddon
Wilson, L. Not quite Martin
The **dreams** are real. Aldrich, B. S.
Dreams are sacred. Phillips, P.
Dream's end. Kuttner, H.
Dreiser, Theodore, 1871-1945
Lost Phoebe
Burrell, J. A. and Cerf, B. A. eds. Anthology of famous American stories
Day, A. G. ed. Greatest American short stories
Foerster, N. ed. American poetry and prose. 1952 ed.
Schramm, W. L. ed. Great short stories
Dress for Kitty. Grove, E.
Dress of white silk. Matheson, R.
Dresser, Daniel
White army
Wollheim, D. A. comp. Every boy's book of science-fiction
Dresser, Davis, 1904-
Big shot
Mystery writers of America, inc. Crooks' tour
Extradition
Mystery Writers of America, inc. Butcher, baker, murder-maker
Michael Shayne as I know him
Mystery Writers of America, inc. Four-&-twenty bloodhounds
You killed Elizabeth
Mystery Writers of America, inc. 20 great tales of murder
Dresser, Peter van. See Van Dresser, Peter
DRESSES. See Clothing and dress
Dressing-up. Burnett, W. R.
DRESSMAKERS
Furman, L. Experience on the dress line
DREYFUS, ALFRED, 1859-1935
Rabinowitz, S. Dreyfus in Kasrilevke
Dreyfus in Kasrilevke. Rabinowitz, S.
Drezmal Grace I.
Little Mohammed and Egypt's king
Best Army short stories, 1950
Drink. Anderson, S.
Drinkard, Ivey Noah
Mission for baby
Oberfirst, R. ed. 1952 anthology of best original short-shorts
DRIVERS. See Teamsters
DRIVERS, AUTOMOBILE. See Automobile drivers
Driver's seat. Queen, E. pseud.
Drop in the bucket. Fisher, D. F. C.
Drop of pure liquid. Willingham, C.
Droste-Hülshoff, Annette Elizabeth, Freiin von, 1797-1848
Jews' beech tree
Lange, V. ed. Great German short novels and stories
DROUGHTS
Güiraldes, R. Old ranch
Wilson, J. W. Grass grown again
DROWNING
Welty, E. Wide net
Wharton, E. N. J. The choice
Drowning. Chekhov, A. P.
DRUGS
Smith, C. A. Plutonian drug
Wells, H. G. New accelerator
Drumbeaters Island. Curtis, K.
DRUMMERS. See Commercial travelers
Drums in the fog. Holland, R. S.
Drums of the fore and aft. Kipling, R.
The **drunkard.** O'Donovan, M.
DRUNKARDS
Algren, N. How the devil came down Division Street
Benjamin, I. E. Do-gooder
Bunin, I. A. Evening in spring
De Vries, P. Every leave that falls
Fitzgerald, F. S. K. Alcoholic case
Hughes, L. On the way home
Li Kung-tso. Drunkard's dream
Maugham, W. S. Before the party
Porter, K. A. Day's work
Porter, W. S. Blackjack bargainer
Porter, W. S. Rubaiyat of a Scotch highball
Stuart, J. Woman in the house
Van Doren, M. Birdie, come back
See also Alcoholism
Drunkard's dream. Li Kung-tso

Drunken lizard. Brenner, L.
DRUNKENNESS. See Alcoholism; Drunkards

Dry September. Faulkner, W.
Dry valley. Bunin, I. A.
DUAL PERSONALITY
Dostoevskiĭ, F. M. Notes from underground
Guin, W. Beyond Bedlam
Lincoln, V. E. No evidence
Stevenson, R. L. Strange case of Dr Jekyll and Mr Hyde
Wharton, E. N. J. After Holbein
DUBLIN. See Ireland—Dublin

Du Bose, Virginia G.
Full cycle
Oberfirst, R. ed. 1954 anthology of best original short-shorts
Duc de L'Omelette. Poe, E. A.
Duchess and the jeweller. Woolf, V. S.
DUCK SHOOTING
Bonner, P. H. Bitter dawn
Buckingham, N. Comin' twenty-one
Buckingham, N. High sign
Lowrey, P. H. Too young to have a gun
Lytle, A. N. The guide
Stegner, W. E. Blue-winged teal
See also Game and game birds
DUCKS
McLaverty, M. Wild duck's nest
Due and timely warning. Claudy, C. H.
Due process. Miner, H.
The **duel.** Conrad, J.
The **duel.** Maupassant, G. de
The **duel.** Porter, W. S.
Duel at 70 miles an hour. Floherty, J. J.
Duel in Captive Valley. Brown, W. C.
Duel of Dr Hirsch. Chesterton, G. K.
DUELING
Collins, W. Miss Bertha and the Yankee
Dostoevskiĭ, F. M. Father Zossima's duel
Harte, B. Passage in the life of Mr John Oakhurst
Maupassant, G. de. The duel
Verga, G. Cavalleria rusticana
DUELS. See Dueling
Dueña for a day. Von Hagen, C. I. B.
Duke, Osborn
Struttin' with some barbecue
Best American short stories, 1953
The **Duke** entertains. Trollope, A.
Duke: the gun-shy watchdog. Little, G. W.
Dumas in Hollywood. Kaufman, W.
Du Maurier, Daphne, 1907-
Apple tree
Du Maurier, D. Kiss me again, stranger
The birds
Du Maurier, D. Kiss me again, stranger
Kiss me again, stranger
Du Maurier, D. Kiss me again, stranger
Little photographer
Du Maurier, D. Kiss me again, stranger
Monte Verità
Du Maurier, D. Kiss me again, stranger

No motive
Du Maurier, D. Kiss me again, stranger
Old man
Du Maurier, D. Kiss me again, stranger
Split second
Du Maurier, D. Kiss me again, stranger
DUMB. See Deaf and dumb
Dumb-animal. Sitwell, Sir O. bart.
Dumb bunny. Chute, B. J.
Dumb waiter. Miller, W. M.
Dumbest man in the army. Sneider, V. J.
DUMMIES. See Models, Fashion
Dunbar, Olivia Howard, 1873-1953
Shell of sense
Carrington, H. ed. Week-end book of ghost stories
Dunbar, Paul Laurence, 1872-1906
Strength of Gideon
Dreer, H. ed. American literature by Negro authors
Duncan, Norman, 1871-1916
Fruits of toil
Pacey, D. ed. Book of Canadian stories
Dune roller. May, J.
DUNGEONS. See Prisoners and prisons
Dunkerley, Arthur Charles. See Oxenham, John
Dunne, Finley Peter, 1867-1936
Mr Dooley on athletics
Dachs, D. ed. Treasury of sports humor
Dunsany, Edward John Moreton Drax Plunkett, 18th baron, 1878-
Autumn cricket
Asquith, Lady C. M. E. C. ed. Book of modern ghosts
Bethmoora
Dunsany, E. J. M. D. P. 18th baron. Sword of Welleran, and other tales of enchantment
Bride of the man-horse
Dunsany, E. J. M. D. P. 18th baron. Sword of Welleran, and other tales of enchantment
Distressing tale of Thangobrind the jeweller
Dunsany, E. J. M. D. P. 18th baron. Sword of Welleran, and other tales of enchantment
East and West
Dunsany, E. J. M. D. P. 18th baron. Sword of Welleran, and other tales of enchantment
Exiles' club
Dunsany, E. J. M. D. P. 18th baron. Sword of Welleran, and other tales of enchantment
The hen
Dunsany, E. J. M. D. P. 18th baron. Sword of Welleran, and other tales of enchantment
Idle days on the Yan
Dunsany, E. J. M. D. P. 18th baron. Sword of Welleran, and other tales of enchantment
Kith of the Elf-folk
Dunsany, E. J. M. D. P. 18th baron. Sword of Welleran, and other tales of enchantment

Dunsany, Edward J. M. D. P. 18th baron
—*Continued*
Memory machine
This week magazine. This week's short-
short stories
Most dangerous man in the world
Queen, E. pseud. ed. Queen's awards:
6th ser.
Poltarnees, Beholder of Ocean
Dunsany, E. J. M. D. P. 18th baron.
Sword of Welleran, and other tales
of enchantment
The return
Dunsany, E. J. M. D. P. 18th baron.
Sword of Welleran, and other tales
of enchantment
The sign
Derleth, A. W. ed. Night's yawning peal
Story of land and sea
Dunsany, E. J. M. D. P. 18th baron.
Sword of Welleran, and other tales
of enchantment
Sword of Welleran
Cerf, B. A. and Moriarty, H. C. eds.
Anthology of famous British stories
Dunsany, E. J. M. D. P. 18th baron.
Sword of Welleran, and other tales
of enchantment
Thirteen at table
Conklin, G. and Conklin, L. T. eds.
Supernatural reader
Three sailors' gambit
Dunsany, E. J. M. D. P. 18th baron.
Sword of Welleran, and other tales
of enchantment
Two bottles of relish
Davenport, B. ed. Tales to be told in
the dark
Widow Flynn's apple tree
Dunsany, E. J. M. D. P. 18th baron.
Sword of Welleran, and other tales
of enchantment
Wonderful window
Dunsany, E. J. M. D. P. 18th baron.
Sword of Welleran, and other tales
of enchantment

Dunsing, Dee May
Vireo's song
Fenner, P. R. comp. Yankee Doodle

Duo. Colette, S. G.

Duplicity of Hargraves. Porter, W. S.

Duranty, Walter, 1884-
The parrot
First-prize stories, 1919-1954

Dusk. Munro, H. H.

Dust storm. Brand, M. pseud.

Dusty drawer. Muheim, H.

DUTCH EAST INDIES
Annixter, P. pseud. Loose tiger
Benson, T. Golden fish
Benson, T. Yes-girl
Maugham, W. S. Vessel of wrath

Borneo
Blochman, L. G. Jimat of Dorland
Maugham, W. S. Before the party
Maugham, W. S. Force of circumstance
Maugham, W. S. Neil MacAdam

Maugham, W. S. The outstation
Maugham, W. S. Yellow streak

Java
Benson, T. White sea monkey
DUTCH IN BORNEO
Maugham, W. S. End of the flight
DUTCH IN SOUTH AFRICA. See Africa,
South
DUTCH IN THE EAST INDIES
Maugham, W. S. Four Dutchmen
DUTCH IN THE UNITED STATES
Irving, W. Legend of Sleepy Hollow
Irving, W. Rip Van Winkle
Duty to live. Asch, S.
Duvoisin, Roger Antoine, 1904-
Three sneezes
Fenner, P. R. comp. Fools and funny
fellows
DWARFS
Connelly, M. C. Coroner's inquest
Newhouse, E. Gorgeous number
Wilde, O. Birthday of the Infanta
Dwellers in silence. Bradbury, R.
DWELLINGS. See Houses
Dworzan, Helene L. 1925-
Husband for Bluma
American vanguard, 1953
Dyalhis, Nictzin
When the green star waned
Derleth, A. W. ed. Beyond time & space
Dye, Charles
Syndrome Johnny
Galaxy science fiction magazine. Galaxy
reader of science fiction
Dyer, Walter Alden, 1878-1943
Gulliver the Great
Fenner, P. R. comp. Dogs, dogs, dogs
Harper, W. comp. Dog show
DYING. See Death
Dying man. Rudnicki, A.
DYING SCENES. See Deathbed scenes

E

E for effort. Sherred, T. L.
E pluribus unicorn. Waldo, E. H.
E S P. See Thought-transference
Each in his generation. Burt, M. S.
The **eagle.** Newhouse, E.
Eagle and the cheetah. Schoenfeld, B. C.
EAGLES
Beachcroft, T. O. Erne from the coast
Roberts, Sir C. G. D. "The young ravens
that call upon him"
Sass, H. R. Gray Eagle
Eames, Genevieve Torrey
". . . as handsome does"
Fenner, P. R. comp. Dogs, dogs, dogs
Earley, Stephen B.
Baa-baa, black sheep
Gable, M. Sister, ed. Many-colored fleece
Earlier service. Irwin, M. E. F.

EARTH
Clarke, A. C. Fires within
EARTH, DESTRUCTION OF
Balmer, E. and Wylie, P. When worlds collide
Carr, R. S. Mutation
Cox, I. Like gods they came
Dyalhis, N. When the green star waned
Hubbard, L. R. When shadows fall
Keller, D. H. The Star
Kornbluth, C. M. Silly season
Page, N. W. But without horns
Russell, E. F. Dear Devil
Van Vogt, A. E. The monster
Wandrei, D. Infinity zero
See also End of the world
Earth-bound. Grimson, M. S.
Earthquake in Chile. Kleist, H. von
East and West. Dunsany, E. J. M. D. P. 18th baron
EAST SIDE. See New York (City)—East Side
EASTER
Connolly, M. Pigeon from St Bartholomew's
Munro, H. H. Easter egg
Porter, W. S. Day resurgent
Taber, G. B. Man at the gate
Taylor, M. McGarry joins the Easter parade
Easter egg. Brookhouser, F.
Easter egg. Munro, H. H.
Easter egg party. Bowen, E.
Easter eggs. Carr, R. S.
Easter Greeting. Bergengruen, W.
Easter of the soul. Porter, W. S.
Easy day for a lady. Ullman, J. R.
Easy going man. O'Rourke, F.
Easy way. Cicellis, K.
EATING CONTESTS. See Dinners
Eating days. Shapiro, L.
Eaton, C. E.
Motion of forgetfulness is slow
Best American short stories, 1952
Ebbie. Guthrie, A. B.
Eberhart, Mignon (Good) 1899-
Wagstaff pearls
Best detective stories of the year—1953
Ebner-Eschenbach, Marie von. See Ebner von Eschenbach, Marie, Freifrau
Ebner von Eschenbach, Marie, Freifrau, 1830-1916
Krambambuli
Pick, R. ed. German stories and tales
Ebony elephant. Lawson, E.
Eça de Queiroz, José Maria, 1845-1900
Woman taken in adultery
Selden, R. ed. Ways of God and men
The echo. Bowles, P. F.
Echo and the nemesis. Stafford, J.
ECUADOR
Wells, H. G. Country of the blind
Ed Walsh pitches a no-hit game. Farrell, J. T.

Eddy, C. M.
Loved dead
Derleth, A. W. ed. Night's yawning peal
EDEN
Clemens, S. L. Eve's diary
Lagerkvist, P. F. Paradise
Edge of doom. Beck, W.
Edgeworth, Maria, 1767-1849
Castle Rackrent
Connolly, C. ed. Great English short novels
Edginton, Helen Marion, 1883-
Purple and fine linen
Cerf, B. A. and Moriarty, H. C. eds. Anthology of famous British stories
Edginton, May. See Edginton, Helen Marion
Edification of Marianne. Auchincloss, L.
EDISON, THOMAS ALVA, 1847-1931
Serviss, G. P. Edison's conquest of Mars
Edison's conquest of Mars. Serviss, G. P.
Editha. Howells, W. D.
EDITORS. See Journalists
Edmée. Zhabotinskiĭ, V. E.
Edmonds, Walter Dumaux, 1903-
Blind Eve
Blodgett, H. W. ed. Story survey. 1953 ed.
Death of Red Peril
Christ, H. I. and Shostak, J. eds. Short stories
Honor of the county
Grayson, C. ed. Fourth round
Judge
Cuff, R. P. ed. American short story survey
EDUCATION
Asch, S. The academy
Higbee, A. R. Words for John Willie
Rabinowitz, S. Gy-ma-na-si-a
See also School life; Teachers
Education in the world state. Huxley, A. L.
Edwards, Dolton
Meihem in ce klasrum
Astounding science fiction (Periodical)
Astounding science fiction anthology
Eel by the tail. Lang, A. K.
The eel-trap. Loring, S. M.
EELS
Loring, S. M. The eel-trap
Millay, E. St V. Murder in the Fishing Cat
Effie Whittlesy. Ade, G.
Effigy of war. Boyle, K.
The egg. Anderson, S.
Egg farm. Lee, U.
Egg from the sky. Hunt, F. C.
Eggleston, Margaret (White) 1878-
Arabella, the third
Eggleston, M. W. Red stocking, and other Christmas stories
Bridget's burden
Eggleston, M. W. Red stocking, and other Christmas stories
By way of a Christmas card
Eggleston, M. W. Red stocking, and other Christmas stories

Eggleston, Margaret W.—*Continued*
Christmas angel
  Eggleston, M. W. Red stocking, and
    other Christmas stories
A Christmas gift for father
  Eggleston, M. W. Red stocking, and
    other Christmas stories
Christmas solo
  Eggleston, M. W. Red stocking, and
    other Christmas stories
Christmas visitor
  Eggleston, M. W. Red stocking, and
    other Christmas stories
Gift of the wise man
  Eggleston, M. W. Red stocking, and
    other Christmas stories
In the patchwork quilt
  Eggleston, M. W. Red stocking, and
    other Christmas stories
Indian's Christmas gift
  Eggleston, M. W. Red stocking, and
    other Christmas stories
Love gift
  Eggleston, M. W. Red stocking, and
    other Christmas stories
Mother's Christmas present
  Eggleston, M. W. Red stocking, and
    other Christmas stories
On Christmas Day
  Eggleston, M. W. Red stocking, and
    other Christmas stories
Peter's Christmas present
  Eggleston, M. W. Red stocking, and
    other Christmas stories
Red stocking
  Eggleston, M. W. Red stocking, and
    other Christmas stories
Smile box
  Eggleston, M. W. Red stocking, and
    other Christmas stories
Smiling lady
  Eggleston, M. W. Red stocking, and
    other Christmas stories
The thief
  Eggleston, M. W. Red stocking, and
    other Christmas stories
Uncle David's Christmas
  Eggleston, M. W. Red stocking, and
    other Christmas stories
When Santa helped
  Eggleston, M. W. Red stocking, and
    other Christmas stories

EGGS
Anderson, S. The egg

Ego machine. Kuttner, H.

EGOISM
Aleksander, I. The Landrath
Auchincloss, L. Romantic egoists; 8 stories
Mansfield, K. Dill pickle
Maugham, W. S. Door of opportunity

EGYPT

To 640
Coolidge, O. E. Egyptian adventures; 12
  stories

1882-date
Shaw, I. Walking wounded
Wall, J. W. Capra

Cairo
Tennyson, H. Appendicitis

Kings and rulers
Drezmal, G. I. Little Mohammed and
  Egypt's king

EGYPTIAN SLAVES. See Slavery—Egypt

Ehrenburg, Il'IA Grigor'evich, 1891-
The storm; excerpts
  Burnett, W. ed. World's best

Eichelberger, Rosa (Kohler)
On Christmas Eve
  Furman, A. L. ed. Everygirls career
    stories

Eicher, Elizabeth
But not Jeff
  American girl (Periodical) Favorite
    stories

Eichrodt, John
Nadia Devereux
  Burnett, W. and Burnett, H. S. eds.
    Sextet

Eight-dollar pup. Curtiss, P. E.

Eighty-yard run. Shaw, I.

Eighty years old. Grimson, M. S.

EIRE. See Ireland

Eisenberg, Frances, 1912-
Roof sitter
  Eaton, H. T. ed. Short stories

Ekbergh, Ida Diana
Astral plane—land of dreams
  Ekbergh, I. D. Mysterious Chinese
    mandrake, and other stories
Courtship of Lydia
  Ekbergh, I. D. Mysterious Chinese
    mandrake, and other stories
Gentleman from India
  Ekbergh, I. D. Mysterious Chinese
    mandrake, and other stories
Hindu Yogi science of breath
  Ekbergh, I. D. Mysterious Chinese
    mandrake, and other stories
Katherine the clown
  Ekbergh, I. D. Mysterious Chinese
    mandrake, and other stories
Lady's maid
  Ekbergh, I. D. Mysterious Chinese
    mandrake, and other stories
Lost cat
  Ekbergh, I. D. Mysterious Chinese
    mandrake, and other stories
Lure of perfume
  Ekbergh, I. D. Mysterious Chinese
    mandrake, and other stories
Matron in distress
  Ekbergh, I. D. Mysterious Chinese
    mandrake, and other stories
Mysterious Chinese mandrake
  Ekbergh, I. D. Mysterious Chinese
    mandrake, and other stories
Pink ballerina
  Ekbergh, I. D. Mysterious Chinese
    mandrake, and other stories
Strange story
  Ekbergh, I. D. Mysterious Chinese
    mandrake, and other stories
Toozee the puss
  Ekbergh, I. D. Mysterious Chinese
    mandrake, and other stories

Ekbergh, Ida D.—*Continued*
Up in a balloon
Ekbergh, I. D. Mysterious Chinese mandrake, and other stories
White silk gloves
Ekbergh, I. D. Mysterious Chinese mandrake, and other stories
Ekrem, Selma
Bekir and his dog, Aslan
Furman, A. L. ed. Teen-age dog stories
Elaine's hope. Levine, T. M.
Elam, Richard M.
By Jupiter
Elam, R. M. Teen-age science fiction stories
Day the flag fell
Elam, R. M. Teen-age science fiction stories
Hands across the deep
Elam, R. M. Teen-age science fiction stories
Iron moon
Elam, R. M. Teen-age science fiction stories
Lunar trap
Elam, R. M. Teen-age science fiction stories
Project ocean floor
Elam, R. M. Teen-age science fiction stories
Red sands
Elam, R. M. Teen-age science fiction stories
Sol's little brother
Elam, R. M. Teen-age science fiction stories
Strange men
Elam, R. M. Teen-age science fiction stories
Venusway
Elam, R. M. Teen-age science fiction stories
What time is it?
Elam, R. M. Teen-age science fiction stories
ELECTIONS
Munro, H. H. Hyacinth

Corrupt practices
Stuart, J. Thirty-two votes before breakfast
Elegy for Alma's Aunt Amy. Suckow, R.
Eleonora. Poe, E. A.
Elephant. Akeley, C. E.
Elephant adventure. Mukerji, D. G.
ELEPHANT DRIVERS. See Mahouts
Elephant intelligence. Williams, J. H.
Elephant midget. Buck, F.
Elephant never forgets. Lang, D.
Elephant remembers. Marshall, E.
ELEPHANTS
Akeley, C. E. Elephant
Bunner, H. C. Infidelity of Zenobia
Clemens, W. L. Stolen white elephant
Fenner, P. R. comp. Elephants, elephants, elephants; 14 stories
Kipling, R. Moti Guj—mutineer
Marshall, E. Elephant remembers

Elephants. Buck, F.
Elephant's child. Kipling, R.
Elephas frumenti. Pratt, F. and De Camp, L. S.
ELEVATOR OPERATORS
Cheever, J. Christmas is a sad season for the poor
Lanning, G. Old Turkey Neck
ELEVATORS
Carver, C. Twenty floors up
Elias, Alice, 1925-
Jarka
American vanguard, 1950
Eliot, George, pseud.
In the prison
Brentano, F. ed. The word lives on
Lifted veil
Connolly, C. ed. Great English short novels
Eliot, George Fielding, 1894-
Uncertain weapon
Bluebook (Periodical) Best sea stories from Bluebook
ELK
Munro, H. H. The elk
Poe, E. A. The elk
See also Deer
The **elk.** Munro, H. H.
The **elk.** Poe, E. A.
Elkins, Evelyn
The no-counts
Furman, A. L. ed. Teen-age dog stories
Ellanby, Boyd
Category Phoenix
Year's best science fiction novels, 1953
Ellin, Stanley, 1917?-
Best of everything
Queen, E. pseud. ed. Queen's awards: 7th ser.
The betrayers
Mystery Writers of America, inc. Butcher, baker, murder-maker
Queen, E. pseud, ed. Queen's awards: 8th ser.
The cat's-paw
Best detective stories of the year—1950
Fool's mate
Queen, E. pseud. ed. Queen's awards: 6th ser.
House party
Queen, E. pseud. ed. Ellery Queen's awards: 9th ser.
Orderly world of Mr Appleby
Best detective stories of the year—1951
Queen, E. pseud. ed. Queen's awards: 5th ser.
Specialty of the house
Mystery Writers of America, inc. Maiden murders
Elliot, Ian
Christmas is a time for great things
Hathaway, B. and Sessions, J. A. eds. Writers for tomorrow. 2d ser.
Elliott, Bruce, 1914-
Battle of the S . . . S
Crossen, K. F. ed. Future tense
Devil was sick
Crossen, K. F. ed. Adventures in tomorrow

Elliott, Bruce—*Continued*
  Fearsome fable
    Magazine of fantasy and science fiction.
      Best from Fantasy and science fiction;
      [1st ser]
Elliott, George P. 1918-
  Children of Ruth
    Best American short stories, 1952
  Family matter
    Prize stories, 1954
  Faq'
    Best American short stories, 1953
  The NRACP
    Best American short stories, 1950
Elliott, Helen S.
  Blue hat
    Oberfirst, R. ed. 1952 anthology of best
      original short-shorts
Elliott, Rose Bedrick
  Baby killer
    Crossen, K. F. ed. Future tense
Ellis, Mary Hamrick
  The invitation
    Strang, R. M. and Roberts, R. M. eds.
      Teen-age tales v2
Ellsberg, Edward, 1891-
  Battle in the moonlight
    Fenner, P. R. comp. Yankee Doodle
Elly. Faulkner, W.
Elms and Fair Oaks. Boyd, J.
ELOPEMENTS
  Maugham, W. S. Creative impulse
  Porter, W. S. Love-philtre of Ikey Schoen-
    stein
Elsewhen. Heinlein, R. A.
Elsie in New York. Porter, W. S.
Elston, Allan Vaughan, 1887-
  Blackmail
    Best detective stories of the year—1950
  Last day of my life
    Best detective stories of the year—1952
Eltha. Suckow, R.
Elvie Burdette. Schaefer, J. W.
Emancipation of Billy. Porter, W. S.
EMBEZZLEMENT
  Harte, B. Postmistress of Laurel Run
  Lewis, S. Willow walk
  Stevenson, R. L. Pavilion on the links
Embroidery. Bradbury, R.
Emergency. Bantien, A. M.
Emergency landing. Williams, R.
Emery, Anne, 1907-
  Date with Ricky
    American girl (Periodical) On my honor
Emery, Guy. See Emery, Russell Guy
Emery, Russell Guy, 1908-
  Coleman comes back
    Fenner, P. R. comp. Crack of the bat
Eminence. Suckow, R.
Emmet Dutrow. Schaefer, J. W.
Emmons, Betsy
  Dance with the devil
    Seventeen (Periodical) The Seventeen
      reader
Empire of the ants. Wells, H. G.

EMPLOYEES, DISMISSAL OF
  Lowry, R. J. C. Day he got fired
Employment. De Camp, L. S.
Emptied sack. Corkery, D.
Empty holster. Thompson, T.
Empty house. Doyle, Sir A. C.
Empty room. Caldwell, E.
En la noche. Bradbury, R.
The Encantados; or, Enchanted Isles. Mel-
  ville, H.
Enchanted forest. Leiber, F.
Enchanted kiss. Porter, W. S.
Enchanted profile. Porter, W. S.
Enchanted village. Van Vogt, A. E.
Enchantress of Venus. Brackett, L.
Encounter in the mist. Munby, A. N. L.
Encounter with the Queen of Bothnya.
  Yaffe, J.
End of a dream. Stewart, O.
End of Christie Tucker. Caldwell, E.
End of Coo-Cullen. Ready, W. B.
End of Henry Fribble. Betts, D.
End of her rope. Heide, H. J.
End of the depression. Bolté, M.
End of the flight. Maugham, W. S.
End of the game. Patten, G.
End of the Islander. Doyle, Sir A. C.
End of the line. Hawkins, J. and Hawk-
  ins, W.
End of the line. Schmitz, J. H.
End of the tether. Conrad, J.
End of the tunnel. Gordimer, N.
END OF THE WORLD
  Bradbury, R. Last night of the world
  Brown, F. Knock
  Clark, W. Van T. Portable phonograph
  Clarke, A. C. Forgotten enemy
  Knight, D. Not with a bang
  Poe, E. A. Conversation of Eiros and
    Charmion
    See also Earth, Destruction of
End to dreams. Benét, S. V.
ENDECOTT, JOHN, 1589-1665
  Hawthorne, N. Endicott and the Red
    Cross
Enderby and the sleeping beauty. Kneale, N.
Enders, Gordon Bandy
  Kismet and the nomad woman
    Best Army short stories, 1950
Endicott, John. See Endecott, John
Endicott and the Red Cross. Hawthorne, N.
Endowment policy. Kuttner, H.
Enemies. Chekhov, A. P.
Enemies in space. Grunert, K.
The enemy. Armstrong, C.
Enemy planet. Gallery, D. V.
ENGAGEMENTS. See Betrothals
Engine and the flare. Van Doren, M.
ENGINEERS
  Beck, W. Far whistle
  Dresser, D. Extradition
    See also Railroad engineers

England, George Allan, 1877-1936
  Prize cargo
    Bluebook (Periodical) Best sea stories
    from Bluebook
ENGLAND
            16th century
Evans, T. M. Gentlemen of valor
            19th century
Dickens, C. See all stories by this author
James, H. Great good place
            Invasions
Hardy, T. Tradition of 1804
            London
Morley, C. D. The arrow
        London—16th century
Irwin, I. H. Spring flight
        London—19th century
Melville, H. Rich man's crumbs
Melville, H. Temple second
        London—20th century
Lewis, W. Rotting Hill; 9 stories
Maugham, W. S. Jane
Maugham, W. S. Virtue
Smith, L. P. 'Ivanhoe'
Waugh, E. Work suspended
ENGLAND, PROVINCIAL AND RURAL
Aiken, C. P. Pair of Vikings
Boyle, K. Bridegroom's body
Irwin, M. E. F. Courage
Kipling, R. 'They'
Kipling, R. Village that voted the earth
  was flat
Lawrence, D. H. Shades of spring
Maugham, W. S. Home
Maugham, W. S. Round dozen
Surtees, R. S. Hunting scenes; 26 stories
Taylor, E. I live in a world of make-
  believe
Taylor, E. Shadows of the world
Taylor, E. Swan-moving
Trollope, A. Bedside Barsetshire; 26
  stories
Waugh, E. Englishman's home
Waugh, E. Period piece
Waugh, E. Winner takes all
            Cornwall
Tregarthen, J. C. Great run
Trollope, A. Malachi's Cove
            Devonshire
Galsworthy, J. The apple tree
            Essex
Harvey, W. F. Euphemia witchmaid
            Yorkshire
Bentley, P. E. Panorama; 7 stories
Knight, E. M. Lassie Come-Home
England to America. Montague, M. P.
English, Thelma
  Troubled water
    Wolfe, D. M. ed. Which grain will grow
ENGLISH DIALECT STORIES. See
  Dialect stories—English
ENGLISH IN AFRICA
  Conrad, J. Heart of darkness
De Camp, L. S. Blue giraffe
Laurence, M. Uncertain flowering
Stern, J. Man who was loved
ENGLISH IN AFRICA, EAST
  Buchan, J. 1st baron Tweedsmuir. Kings
  of Orion
ENGLISH IN ASIA MINOR
  Maugham, W. S. In a strange land
ENGLISH IN BORNEO
  Maugham, W. S. Before the party
  Maugham, W. S. Flotsam and jetsam
  Maugham, W. S. Force of circumstance
  Maugham, W. S. The outstation
  Maugham, W. S. Virtue
  Maugham, W. S. Yellow streak
ENGLISH IN BURMA
  Maugham, W. S. Mabel
  Maugham, W. S. Masterson
ENGLISH IN CAPRI
  Maugham, W. S. Lotus eater
ENGLISH IN CHINA
  Maugham, W. S. The consul
  Maugham, W. S. The taipan
ENGLISH IN DUTCH EAST INDIES
  Benson, T. Yes-girl
ENGLISH IN EGYPT
  Shaw, I. Walking wounded
ENGLISH IN GERMANY
  Piper, H. B. He walked around the horses
ENGLISH IN INDIA
  Forster, E. M. The trial
  Kipling, R. At the end of the passage
  Kipling, R. Man who was
  Kipling, R. Mark of the beast
  Kipling, R. On Greenhow Hill
  Kipling, R. Tods' amendment
  Kipling, R. Tomb of his ancestors
  Kipling, R. William the Conqueror
  Kipling, R. Without benefit of clergy
  Weston, C. Forest of the night
ENGLISH IN INDO-CHINA, FRENCH
  Maugham, W. S. Mirage
ENGLISH IN IRELAND
  Irwin, M. E. F. Bloodstock
  Irwin, M. E. F. Country gentleman
  O'Donovan, M. Custom of the country
ENGLISH IN MALAY ARCHIPELAGO
  Maugham, W. S. Back of beyond
  Maugham, W. S. Casual affair
ENGLISH IN MALAY PENINSULA
  Maugham, W. S. Door of opportunity
  Maugham, W. S. Footprints in the jungle
ENGLISH IN MONGOLIA
  Vogau, B. A. Big heart
ENGLISH IN OCEANICA
  Coward, N. P. Mr and Mrs Edgehill
ENGLISH IN RUSSIA
  Munro, H. H. Reginald in Russia
ENGLISH IN SAMOA
  Maugham, W. S. Mackintosh
  Maugham, W. S. The pool
ENGLISH IN SPAIN
  Maugham, W. S. Happy man
ENGLISH IN SWITZERLAND
  Ervine, St J. G. The mountain
  Maugham, W. S. Miss King
ENGLISH IN THE RIVIERA
  Maugham, W. S. Lion's skin

ENGLISH IN THE UNITED STATES
Evans, T. M. Transients
McCall, M. C. Fraternity
ENGLISH NAVY. See Great Britain. Navy
ENGLISH POLITICS. See Politics—England
ENGLISH SOLDIERS. See Soldiers—British
Englishman's home. Waugh, E.
ENOCH ARDEN STORIES
Morrison, A. That brute Simmons
Porter, W. S. Thing's the play
Sherwood, R. E. "Extra! Extra!"
See also Disappearances
Enormous radio. Cheever, J.
Enormous room. Gold, H. L. and Krepps, R. W.
Enormous window. Styron, W.
Enough. Schulberg, B. W.
Enright, Elizabeth, 1909-
Apple seed and apple thorn
Best American short stories, 1954
First face
Best American short stories, 1952
The sardillion
Prize stories of 1950
Temperate zone
Best American short stories, 1951
Enshrined in the heart. Yates, E.
Ensign Carson, USCGR. Lane, G. C.
Ensign Weasel. Schulberg, B. W.
ENTOMBMENT. See Burial, Premature
The envelope. Taylor, C. L.
Environment. Geier, C. S.
Envy. Olyesha, I. K.
EPIDEMICS
Simak, C. D. Courtesy
EPIGRAMS
De Vries, P. One
EPILEPTICS
Poe, E. A. Berenice
Epilogue in the blues for Joey. Brookhouser, F.
Episode. Maugham, W. S.
Episode at the Honeypot. Van Doren, M.
Episode—1880. Haycox, E.
Episode in the life of the Marshal de Bassompieere. Hofmannsthal, H. H. Edler von
Episode of the barrel. Doyle, Sir A. C.
Episode of war. Crane, S.
Episode on Dhee Minor. Walton, H.
Erdman, Loula Grace
Allen High's youth problem
Strang, R. M. and Roberts, R. M. eds. Teen-age tales v 1
Medal for Becky
American girl (Periodical) On my honor
There was a star
Elmquist, R. M. ed. Fifty years to Christmas
ERIE CANAL
Edmonds, W. D. Blind Eve

Erin, Bill, 1918-
Don't jinx the pitcher
Argosy (Periodical) Argosy Book of sports stories
Quiet morning
Meredith, S. ed. Bar 3
Ermine, Will, pseud. See Drago, Harry Sinclair
Erne from the coast. Beachcroft, T. O.
Ernenwein, Leslie Charles, 1900-
Trail hand
Western Writers of America. Bad men and good
ERNES. See Eagles
Ernestine in Dominica. Archibald, J. W.
Ernst, Paul
Microscopic giants
Margulies, L. and Friend, O. J. eds. From off this world
"Nothing happens on the moon"
Conklin, G. ed. Omnibus of science fiction
Thing in the pond
Stauffer, R. M.; Cunningham, W. H. and Sullivan, C. J. eds. Adventures in modern literature
Erostratus. Sartre, J. P.
ERRORS
Brandel, M. Hasty act
Erskine, Laurie York, 1894-
After school
American boy (Periodical) American boy anthology
Horses and men
American boy (Periodical) American boy Adventure stories
Mystery at Moon Lake
Strang, R. M. and Roberts, R. M. eds. Teen-age tales v 1
Mystery of Mike
Boys' life (Periodical) Boys' life Adventure stories
Ervine, St John Greer, 1883-
The mountain
Talbot, D. ed. Treasury of mountaineering stories
Escape! Asimov, I.
The escape. Campbell, J. W.
The escape. Carrington, H.
The escape. Hendryx, J. B.
The escape. Maugham, W. S.
Escape from Kosseir. Coolidge, O. E.
Escape from Pharaoh. Hurston, Z. N.
ESCAPED CONVICTS. See Convicts, Escaped
ESCAPES
Brick, J. Message for Uncle Billy
Brick, J. Rifleman's run
Carrington, H. The escape
Conrad, J. Secret sharer
Coolidge, O. E. Escape from Kosseir
Corkery, D. On the heights
Futrelle, J. Problem of Cell 13
Hardy, T. Three strangers
Hilton, J. Twilight of the wise
Martyr, W. Sleeping draft
Wassermann, J. Lukardis
Woods, W. Free man

ESKIMOS
  Carrighar, S. Marooned children
  Cave, H. B. Two were left
  Mowat, F. Lost in the barren lands
  Mowat, F. Woman he left to die
  Mowery, W. B. Mannikin talk
  Porter, W. S. Ferry of unfulfilment
  Roberts, Sir C. G. D. On the roof of the
    world
  Stefánsson, V. Seal hunting
  Sullivan, A. Salving of Pyack
Esmé. Munro, H. H.
ESPIONAGE. See Spies
ESPRITU SANTO
  Michener, J. A. The good life
Essence of strawberry. Kneale, N.
ESSEX, ENGLAND. See England, Pro-
  vincial and rural—Essex
The essrig. Ogus, A. D.
Estate and trespass. Hall, J. B.
Estate of Alice V. Gregg. Parker, J. R.
ESTATES. See Houses; Real property
Estes, Eleanor, 1906-
  Trainload of soldiers; excerpt from "Rufus
    M"
    Fenner, P. R. comp. Giggle box
ESTHETICS
  Lieberman, E. Thing of beauty
Etaoin Shrdlu. Brown, F.
Eternal husband. Dostoevskiĭ, F. M.
ETERNAL LIFE. See Immortality;
  Longevity
Eternal life. Rabinowitz, S.
Eternal man. Sharp, D. D.
Eternal rectangle. Willingham, C.
Eternal smile. Lagerkvist, P. F.
Eternal triangle. O'Donovan, M.
Eternal wedding gown. Opatoshu, J.
Eternity lost. Simak, C. D.
Ethan Brand. Hawthorne, N.
Ethics of pig. Porter, W. S.
ETHROG
  Ogus, A. D. The essrig
Etnier, Elizabeth (Jax) 1911-
  The willow
    Aswell, M. L. W. ed. New short novels
Eupepsia. Willingham, C.
Euphemia witchmaid. Harvey, W. F.
Eureca cottage. Grimson, M. S.
EUROPEAN WAR, 1914-1918
  Auchincloss, L. Maud
  Aumonier, S. Source of irritation
  Hemingway, E. Now I lay me
  Munro, H. H. Birds on the western front
  Munro, H. H. Square egg

Aerial operations

  Bellah, J. W. Fear
  Nordhoff, C. B. and Hall, J. N. In
    pyjamas

France

  Boyd, T. A. Responsibility

Italy

  Hemingway, E. In another country
  Hemingway, E. Way you'll never be

Medical and sanitary affairs

  Scott, H. S. Sister

Russia

  Bergengruen, W. When Riga was evacu-
    ated

Secret service

  Maugham, W. S. Giulia Lazzari
  Maugham, W. S. Hairless Mexican
  Maugham, W. S. The traitor
  Noyes, A. Uncle Hyacinth
Eustis, Helen, 1916-
  Rider on the pale horse
    Saturday evening post (Periodical)
      Saturday evening post stories, 1950
Evans, Edward Everett, 1893-
  The shed
    Sloane, W. M. ed. Stories for tomorrow
Evans, Hubert Reginald, 1892-
  Ghost-town dog
    Harper, W. comp. Dog show
Evans, Thomas M. 1881-
  Gentlemen of valor
    Evans, T. M. Gentlemen of valor, and
      other stories
  The salesman
    Evans, T. M. Gentlemen of valor, and
      other stories
  Transients
    Evans, T. M. Gentlemen of valor, and
      other stories
Eve and the sea serpent. Wylie, P.
Eve enters. Van de Water, F. F.
Eve of St John. Pratt, F. and De Camp,
  L. S.
Eve of the trial. Chekhov, A. P.
Evelyn and the rest of us. Caldwell, E.
Even to Judas. Brown, H. C.
**EVENING AND CONTINUATION
  SCHOOLS**
  Rosten, L. C. Mr K*A*P*L*A*N the
    Magnificent
Evening in Nuevo Leon. Caldwell, E.
Evening in spring. Bunin, I. A.
Evening primrose. Collier, J.
EVENING SCHOOLS. See Evening and
  continuation schools
Evenings at home. Hardwick, E.
An evening's entertainment. Haycox, E.
Evensong. Waldron, D.
Eventide of the feast. Gibran, K.
Ever been to Brooklyn? Newhouse, E.
EVEREST, MOUNT
  Jenks, A. No way down
Everett, Ethel Walton
  Dragon!
    Story parade (Periodical) Adventure
      stories
Every day is ladies' day. Powell, D.
Every leave that falls. De Vries, P.
Everybody loves my baby. Shulman, M.
Everything under control. Bentley, P. E.
Eve's diary. Clemens, S. L.
EVICTION
  Thompson, T. Shore for the sinking

The **eviction**. O'Flaherty, L.
Evidence. Asimov, I.
Evidence. Forester, C. S.
Evidence is high proof. Stuart, J.
EVIL. See Good and evil
Evil angel. Lagerkvist, P. F.
Evil one. Waldeck, T. J.
Evil that men do— Bowen, E.
Evitable conflict. Asimov, I.
EVOLUTION
  Blish, J. Beanstalk
  Hamilton, E. Man who evolved
  Heard, G. Cyclops
  Shiras, W. H. In hiding
Evolution of Lorna Treadway. Auchincloss, L.
Evolution's end. Arthur, R.
Ewald, Carl, 1856-1908
  My little boy
    Scribner treasury
Ex machina. Kuttner, H.
Exact science of matrimony. Porter, W. S.
The **exalted**. De Camp, L. S.
EXAMINATIONS
  Phillips, P. Plagiarist
Excelsior. Wodehouse, P. G.
Excepting Mrs Pentherby. Munro, H. H.
The **exchange**. Abramowitz, S. J.
EXCHANGE OF IDENTITY. See Dual personality; Impersonations
Exchange of men. Nemerov, H. and Johnson, W. R.
Excitement in Ergo. Willingham, C.
EX-CONVICTS
  Porter, W. S. Retrieved reformation
  Rawlings, M. K. The pardon
The **excursion**. Cicellis, K.
The **excursion**. Kneale, N.
Excursion in reality. Waugh, E.
EXECUTIONS AND EXECUTIONERS
  Bierce, A. Occurrence at Owl Creek bridge
  Borges, J. L. Secret miracle
  Deasy, M. Morning sun
  Granberry, E. Trip to Czardis
  Kafka, F. In the penal colony
  Maugham, W. S. Man with the scar
  Maugham, W. S. Official position
  O'Donovan, M. Guests of the nation
  Porter, W. S. The dream
    See also Hanging
EXHUMATION
  Caldwell, E. John the Indian and George Hopkins
  Nordau, M. S. Share in the hereafter
The **exile**. Coppel, A.
Exile. Gellhorn, M. E.
Exile. Hamilton, E.
Exile of the eons. Clarke, A. C.
Exiled from earth. Merwin, S.
EXILES
  Chekhov, A. P. In exile
    See also Refugees

The **exiles**. Bradbury, R.
Exiles' club. Dunsany, E. J. M. D. P. 18th baron
Exit. Tucker, W.
Exit line. Merwin, S.
Exit the professor. Kuttner, H.
The **expedition**. Fraerman, R. I.
Expedition polychrome. Winter, J. A.
Expedition to earth. Clarke, A. C.
Expensive Mr Botts. Upson, W. H.
Experience on the dress line. Furman, L.
Experiment. Rogers, K.
Experiment in crime. Wylie, P.
Experiment in misery. Crane, S.
Experimental world. Lagerkvist, P. F.
EXPERIMENTS, SCIENTIFIC
  Verne, J. Dr Ox's experiment
The **expert**. Wylie, P.
Extending the holdings. Grinnell, D. pseud.
EXTORTION. See Blackmail
"**Extra! Extra!**" Sherwood, R. E.
Extra gang. Davis, H. L.
EXTRA-SENSORY PERCEPTION. See Thought-transference
An **extract** from the journal of Father Duplessis. Buchan, J. 1st baron Tweedsmuir
Extradited from Bohemia. Porter, W. S.
EXTRADITION
  Porter, W. S. Theory and the hound
Extradition. Dresser, D.
Eye cure. Bergengruen, W.
An **eye** for an eye. White, R.
Eye man. Sansom, W.
Eye of Apollo. Chesterton, G. K.
EYES
  Sansom, W. Eye man
The **eyes**. Beachcroft, T. O.
Eyes in the dark. Schisgall, O.
Eyes of boyhood. Davis, C. B.
Eyre, Katherine (Wigmore) 1901-
  Spurs for Antonia
    Fenner, P. R. comp. Cowboys, cowboys, cowboys

F

F— Matheson, R.
FYI. Blish, J.
Fable of the good lion. Hemingway, E.
FABLES
  Hemingway, E. Fable of the good lion
Fabre, Jean Henri Casimer, 1823-1915
  Story of my cats
    Andrews, R. C. ed. My favorite stories of the great outdoors
Fabulous cabman. Kantor, M.
Fabyan, Evelyn
  Bombers' night
    Asquith, Lady C. M. E. C. ed. Book of modern ghosts

FACE
    Abnormities and deformities
Donahoe, E. Head by Scopas
Grimson, M. S. Story of Paula
Maugham, W. S. Man with the scar
The **face.** Moreau, L.
Face behind the bar. Stern, J.
Face is familiar but— Shulman, M.
Face of evil. O'Donovan, M.
Face of Hollywood. Schulberg, B. W.
Face of stone. Williams, W. C.
Face of the poor. Graham, M. C.
FACTORIES
  Kaplan, R. The artist
  O'Donovan, M. Darcy in the Land of
    Youth
  O'Donovan, M. Jerome
FACTORY WORKERS. See Factories
Facts about the hyacinthes. Van Doren, M.
Facts in the case of M. Valdemar. Poe,
  E. A.
Facts of life. Maugham, W. S.
Faggett, Harry Lee, 1911-
  Chatter-stick sermon
    Ford, N. A. and Faggett, H. L. eds.
      Best short stories by Afro-American
      writers (1925-1950)
  Cupid wags his tail
    Ford, N. A. and Faggett, H. L. eds.
      Best short stories by Afro-American
      writers (1925-1950)
  Goldfish bowl
    Ford, N. A. and Faggett, H. L. eds.
      Best short stories by Afro-American
      writers (1925-1950)
The **failure.** Taylor, K. H.
Faint heart. Dostoevskiĭ, F. M.
Fairbanks, Douglas, 1909-
  Ashes
    Grayson, C. ed. Fourth round
FAIRIES
  Collier, J. Bottle party
  Kuttner, H. Gnome there was
  Munro, H. H. Saint and the Goblin
  Walsh, M. Come back, my love
    See also Fantasies; Legends and
  folk tales; Supernatural phenomena
Fairman, Paul W.
  Brothers beyond the void
    Derleth, A. W. ed. Worlds of tomorrow
FAIRS
  Grimson, M. S. Grandma goes to the Fair
  Joyce, J. Araby
  Van Doren, M. Dollar bill
Fairy tale of Father Brown. Chesterton,
  G. K.
FAIRY TALES. See Fairies; Fantasies;
  Legends and folk tales
FAITH
  Cronin, A. J. A candle in Vienna
  Eliot, G. pseud. In the prison
  Grimson, M. S. Gather up the pieces
  Llewellyn, R. Faith to be healed
  Melville, H. The **sermon**
Faith. Graham, R. B. C.

Faith at sea. Shaw, I.
FAITH CURE
  Hughes, L. Tain't so
FAITH HEALING. See Faith cure
Faith, hope and charity. Grimson, M. S.
Faith to be healed. Llewellyn, R.
FAITHFULNESS
  Hurston, Z. N. Conscience of the court
FAKES. See Swindlers and swindling
FALCONRY
  Chambers, R. W. Demoiselle d'Ys
FALCONS
  Bair, T. Falcon's nest
Falcon's nest. Bair, T.
Fall guy. Chute, B. J.
Fall of a sparrow. Auchincloss, L.
Fall of Edward Barnard. Maugham, W. S.
Fall of the House of Usher. Poe, E. A.
Fallada, Hans, pseud. See Ditzen, Rudolf
Fallen star. Collier, J.
FALLS. See Accidents
FALSE ACCUSATION
  Maupassant, G. de. The string
  Stoumen, L. C. The blond dog
False dawn. Chandler, A. B.
False gems. Maupassant, G. de
FALSEHOOD. See Truthfulness and false-
  hood
FAMILY. See Family life
Family affair. Maupassant, G. de
Family album. Betts, D.
FAMILY CHRONICLES
  Bunner, H. C. Story of a New York house
  Van Doren, M. One of the Garretsons
    See also Family life
Family history. Pasinetti, P. M.
Family in the wind. Fitzgerald, F. S. K.
FAMILY LIFE
  Aiken, C. P. Dark city
  Aldrich, B. S. Will the romance be the
    same?
  Allan, T. Lies my father told me
  Asch, S. The academy
  Barrie, Sir J. M. bart. The last night
  Betts, D. Family album
  Bolté, M. End of the depression
  Cheever, J. Goodbye, my brother
  Chekhov, A. P. Two of a kind
  De La Roche, M. The celebration
  Elliott, G. P. Family matter
  Enright, E. Temperate zone
  Freedman, D. Mendel Marantz—genius
  Gilbreth, F. B. and Carey, E. M. C.
    Pygmalion
  Grau, S. A. Miss Yellow Eyes
  Grimson, M. S. Eureca cottage
  Hauser, M. L. Calling all cars
  Hayes, H. M. Jenny takes a holiday
  Hertlein, R. P. G. Christmas
  Hill, M. Y. Sea anchor
  Humphrey, W. Sister
  Jones, R. F. Farthest horizon
  Krige, U. The dream
  Lagerkvist, P. F. Guest of reality
  Lamkin, S. Comes a day
  Lloyd, B. B. Forgotten greeting cards

FAMILY LIFE—*Continued*
  Macauley, R. The wishbone
  McCullers, C. S. Domestic dilemma
  Mann, T. Disorder and early sorrow
  Mathews, M. Tough little Christmas story
  O'Donovan, M. Little mother
  O'Donovan, M. Mad Lomasneys
  O'Donovan, M. Sense of responsibility
  Porter, K. A. Old mortality
  Rosenfeld, J. Competitors
  Saroyan, W. Mr Mechano
  Taber, G. B. Honey and the home front
  Taylor, P. H. Sky line
  Trilling, L. Other Margaret
  Van Doren, M. One of hers
  Verga, G. Black bread
  Weissenberg, I. M. Father and the boys
  Welty, E. Why I live at the P.O.
  Wilson, A. Rex imperator
  Winslow, T. S. Cycle of Manhattan
      See also Children; Family chronicles;
      Fathers; Grandfathers; Grandmothers;
      Mothers

Family man. Moore, I. S.

Family matter. Elliott, G. P.

FAMILY REUNIONS
  Cooke, A. A. Three links
  Hardwick, E. Evenings at home

FAMINES
  Gibbs, Sir P. H. Stranger in the village
  Gregory, V. E. Athens, Greece, 1942
  Kipling, R. William the Conqueror

Fancy woman. Taylor, P. H.

FANTASIES
  Anderson, E. V. Phantom Hall
  Arabian nights. Aladdin
  Benét, S. V. By the waters of Babylon
  Bradbury, R. April witch
  Brown, F. Angels and spaceships; 17
    stories
  Brown, F. Etaoin Shrdlu
  Clarke, A. C. Wall of darkness
  Cohn, E. Stories and fantasies from the
    Jewish past; 10 stories
  Colette, S. G. Sick child
  Collier, J. Bottle party
  Collier, J. The Devil, George and Rosie
  Collier, J. Fallen star
  Collier, J. Green thoughts
  Collier, J. Halfway to Hell
  Collier, J. Hell hath no fury
  Collier, J. Thus I refute Beelzy
  Connolly, M. Reason for Ann
  De Camp, L. S. Blue giraffe
  Dickens, C. Child's dream of a star
  Dunsany, E. J. M. D. P. 18th baron. Beth-
    moora
  Dunsany, E. J. M. D. P. 18th baron. Dis-
    tressing tale of Thangobrind the
    jeweller
  Dunsany, E. J. M. D. P. 18th baron. Idle
    days of the Yan
  Dunsany, E. J. M. D. P. 18th baron. Kith
    of the Elf-folk
  Dunsany, E. J. D. P. 18th baron. Sword
    of Welleran
  Dunsany, E. J. M. D. P. 18th baron. Widow
    Flynn's apple tree
  Eustis, H. Rider on the pale horse
  Fenner, P. R. Fools and funny fellows; 21
    stories

  Fitzgerald, F. S. K. Diamond as big as
    the Ritz
  Forster, E. M. Celestial omnibus
  Forster, E. M. Mr Andrews
  Forster, E. M. Other side of the hedge
  Hause, M. Turn off the moon
  Hawthorne, N. David Swan
  Heard, G. Great fog
  Heinlein, R. A. Our fair city
  Hoffmann, E. T. A. History of Krakatuk
  Howard, R. E. Coming of Conan; 7 stories
  Howard, R. E. King Conan; 5 stories
  Howard, R. E. Sword of Conan; 4 stories
  Kafka, F. The metamorphosis
  Kahanovich, P. From my estates
  Kirkland, J. Wall of fire
  Lagerkvist, P. F. Lift that went down into
    hell
  Li Fu-yen. Lodging for the night
  Li Fu-yen. Matrimony Inn
  Li Kung-tso. Drunkard's dream
  Masefield, J. Western islands
  Maugham, W. S. Princess September
  Morris, G. Back there in the grass
  Mott, F. L. Phantom fliver
  Peretz, I. L. Bontsha the silent
  Peretz, I. L. Ne'ilah in Gehenna
  Poe, E. A. Ligeia
  Porter, W. S. Roads of destiny
  Pritchett, V. S. The ape
  Procter, M. No place for magic
  Stockton, F. R. Lady or the tiger?
  Tagore, Sir R. Hungry stones
  Thackeray, W. M. Sultan stork
  Traven, B. pseud. Third guest
  Van Doren, M. Princess who couldn't say
    yes
  Van Doren, M. Tall one
  Van Doren, M. Three carpenters
  Van Doren, M. Witch of Ramoth
  Walpole, Sir H. Mr Huffam
      See also Fairies; Ghosts; Hallucina-
      tions and illusions; Legends and folk
      tales; Science fiction; Supernatural
      phenomena

Fantasy. Cain, J.

Faq'. Elliot, G.

The **far** and the near. Wolfe, T.

Far below. Johnson, R. B.

Far Centaurus. Van Vogt, A. E.

Far whistle. Beck, W.

Farcical history of Richard Greenow. Huxley, A. L.

A **farewell.** Schnitzler, A.

Farewell! Farewell! Farewell! Aiken, C. P.

Farewell, hon. Willingham, C.

Farewell Miss Julie Logan. Barrie, Sir J. M.
  bart.

Farewell, sweet love. Heath, P.

Farewell to crime. Bruce, S.

Farewell to Eden. Waldo, E. H.

Farjeon, Eleanor, 1881-
  Spooner
    Asquith, Lady C. M. E. C. ed. Book of
    modern ghosts

Farley, Ralph Milne, pseud. See Hoar, Roger
  Sherman

Farley, Walter, 1915-
  The storm
    Strang, R. M. and Roberts, R. M. eds.
      Teen-age tales v 1
The farm. Davies, R.
FARM LIFE
  Bates, H. E. Little farm
  Glaspell, S. Jury of her peers
  Graham, M. C. Face of the poor
  Grimson, M. S. When Dan came home
  Humphrey, W. Man with a family
  Love, P. H. Jersey heifer
  Porter, W. S. Defeat of the city
  Stull, P. Growing pains

        Arkansas
  Weeks, R. Arkansas

        Ireland
  Corkery, D. Rock-of-the-mass
  O'Donovan, M. Uprooted

        Kansas
  Le Sueur, M. Persephone

        Middle West
  Cather, W. S. Neighbour Rosicky
  Garland, H. Under the lion's paw
  Johnson, J. W. Arcadia recalled

        Nebraska
  Aldrich, B. S. Day of retaliation

        New England
  Aiken, C. P. Bow down, Isaac!
  Freeman, M. E. W. Revolt of "Mother"

        Russia
  Chekhov, A. P. Gooseberries

        Sicily
  Verga, G. The gentry

        Tennessee
  Warren, R. P. Blackberry winter

        Vermont
  Lewis, S. Land

        Wales
  Davies, R. The farm

        The West
  Babb, S. Wild flower

FARM TENANCY. See Tenant farming

Farmer, Philip José
  Attitudes
    Magazine of fantasy and science fiction.
      Best from Fantasy and science fiction;
      3d ser.
  Mother
    Pohl, F. ed. Assignment in tomorrow

FARMERS. See Farm life

Farmer's wife. Maupassant, G. de

Farnsworth, Mona
  All roads
    Moskowitz, S. comp. Editor's choice in
      science fiction

Farrell, James Thomas, 1904-
  All things are nothing to me
    Farrell, J. T. Short stories
  American dream girl
    Farrell, J. T. American dream girl

Angela
  Farrell, J. T. Short stories
Backyard ballgame
  Graber, R. S. ed. Baseball reader
Benefits of American life
  Farrell, J. T. Short stories
Big Jeff
  Farrell, J. T. Short stories
The buddies
  Farrell, J. T. Short stories
Calico shoes
  Farrell, J. T. Short stories
Can all this grandeur perish?
  Farrell, J. T. Short stories
Candy from Fairyland
  Farrell, J. T. American dream girl
Casual incident
  Cory, D. W. pseud. comp. 21 variations
    on a theme
  Farrell, J. T. Short stories
Children of the times
  Farrell, J. T. Short stories
Clyde
  Farrell, J. T. Short stories
A coincidence
  Farrell, J. T. American dream girl
Comedy cop
  Farrell, J. T. Short stories
Curbstone philosophy
  Farrell, J. T. Short stories
Day at the zoo
  Farrell, J. T. American dream girl
Digging our own graves
  Farrell, J. T. American dream girl
Ed Walsh pitches a no-hit game
  Graber, R. S. ed. Baseball reader
Fastest runner on Sixty-first Street
  Farrell, J. T. American dream girl
Footnote
  Farrell, J. T. Short stories
For white men only
  Farrell, J. T. Short stories
Fritz
  Farrell, J. T. Further short stories
Front-page story
  Farrell, J. T. Short stories
Game in the park
  Graber, R. S. ed. Baseball reader
Girls at the Sphinx
  Farrell, J. T. American dream girl
Guillotine party
  Farrell, J. T. Short stories
Have I got sun in my eyes?
  Farrell, J. T. American dream girl
Helen I love you
  Farrell, J. T. Short stories
Hell of a good time
  Farrell, J. T. Short stories
Honey, we'll be brave
  Farrell, J. T. Short stories
I want to go home
  Farrell, J. T. American dream girl
In accents of death!
  Farrell, J. T. Short stories
In City Hall Square
  Farrell, J. T. Short stories
Jim O'Neill
  Farrell, J. T. Short stories
John Hitchcock
  Farrell, J. T. Further short stories
Johnny's old man
  Farrell, J. T. American dream girl

Farrell, James T.—*Continued*
Jo-Jo
  Farrell, J. T. Short stories
Just boys
  Farrell, J. T. Short stories
Lib
  Farrell, J. T. Further short stories
Literary love
  Farrell, J. T. American dream girl
Little blond fellow
  Farrell, J. T. Short stories
Looking 'em over
  Farrell, J. T. Short stories
Love affair in Paris
  Farrell, J. T. American dream girl
The martyr
  Farrell, J. T. American dream girl
Mary O'Reilley
  Farrell, J. T. Short stories
Meet the girls!
  Farrell, J. T. Short stories
Mendel and his wife
  Farrell, J. T. Short stories
Merry Clouters
  Farrell, J. T. Short stories
Milly and the porker
  Farrell, J. T. American dream girl
Mr Lunkhead, the banker
  Farrell, J. T. Short stories
A misunderstanding
  Farrell, J. T. American dream girl
My friend the doctor
  Fabricant, N. D. and Werner, H. eds.
    World's best doctor stories
Noble guy
  Farrell, J. T. Short stories
Nostalgia
  Farrell, J. T. Short stories
Open road
  Farrell, J. T. Short stories
Oratory contest
  Farrell, J. T. Short stories
Paris scene: 1931
  Farrell, J. T. Further short stories
Power of literature
  Farrell, J. T. Further short stories
Practical joke
  Farrell, J. T. Short stories
Precinct captain
  Farrell, J. T. Short stories
The Professor
  Farrell, J. T. Short stories
The renegade
  Farrell, J. T. American dream girl
Reverend Father Gilhooley
  Farrell, J. T. Short stories
Romantic interlude in the life of Willie
    Collins
  Farrell, J. T. American dream girl
The scarecrow
  Farrell, J. T. Short stories
The scoop
  Farrell, J. T. Short stories
Seventeen
  Farrell, J. T. Short stories
Soap
  Farrell, J. T. Short stories
Spring evening
  Farrell, J. T. Short stories
Studs
  Farrell, J. T. Short stories
Summer morning in Dublin in 1938
  Farrell, J. T. Further short stories

Summer tryout
  Farrell, J. T. American dream girl
Sunday
  Farrell, J. T. Short stories
Thanksgiving spirit
  Farrell, J. T. Short stories
Tournament star
  Farrell, J. T. Further short stories
Twenty-five bucks
  Farrell, J. T. Short stories
  Ribalow, H. U. ed. World's greatest
    boxing stories
Two brothers
  Farrell, J. T. Further short stories
Two sisters
  Farrell, J. T. Short stories
Virginians are coming
  Farrell, J. T. Further short stories
Wake of Patsy McLaughlin
  Farrell, J. T. American dream girl
Wanted: a chauffeur
  Farrell, J. T. Short stories
Wedding bells will ring so merrily
  Farrell, J. T. Short stories
Well, that's that
  Farrell, J. T. Short stories
When boyhood dreams come true
  Farrell, J. T. Further short stories
Willie Collins
  Farrell, J. T. Further short stories
Workout in the park
  Graber, R. S. ed. Baseball reader
Yellow streak
  Farrell, J. T. American dream girl

Farthest horizon. Jones, R. F.

Farwell, Mabel Brown
  Let yourself go
    Lantz, J. E. ed. Stories of Christian
    living

Fascinating stranger. Fessier, M.

FASCISM
  Mann, T. Mario and the magician
  Silone, I. The trap
    See also National socialism

FASHION
  Porter, W. S. From each according to his
    ability

FASHION MODELS. See Models, Fashion
  (Persons)

Fashion plate. Davies, R.

Fast, Howard Melvin, 1914-
  Tall hunter
    Fenner, P. R. comp. Yankee Doodle
  Where are your guns?
    Ribalow, H. U. ed. This land, these
    people

Fast break. Phillips, J. A.

Fast falls the eventide. Russell, E. F.

Fastest runner on Sixty-first Street. Farrell, J. T.

FAT. See Corpulence

Fat cat. Quentin, P. pseud.

Fat of the cat. Keller, G.

Fat of the land. Yezierska, A.

Fatal red hair. Snow, W.

FATALISM. See Fate and fatalism

Fate. Munro, H. H.

FATE AND FATALISM
Harvey, W. F. August heat
Father and I. Lagerkvist, P. F.
Father and son. Callaghan, M.
Father and son. O'Donovan, M.
Father and the boys. Weissenberg, I. M.
Father Christmas. McLaverty, M.
Father comes home. Welshimer, H.
Father Gaucher's elixir. Daudet, A.
Father Murray's first failure. Doty, W. L.
Father O'Connell. Van Doren, M.
Father Zossima's duel. Dostoevskiĭ, F. M.

The **fatherland**. Quiroga, H.

FATHERS
Caldwell, E. First autumn
Corkery, D. Emptied sack
Davies, R. Abraham's glory
De La Mare, W. J. The nap
Elliott, G. P. Family matter
Marquand, J. P. Yoicks—and away
Mathews, M. Tough little Christmas story
Michener, J. A. The story
Newhouse, E. Seventy thousand dollars
Putman, C. News from Troy
Stuart, J. Clearing in the sky
Verner, C. Meddlin' Papa
    See also Fathers and daughters;
Fathers and sons

FATHERS AND DAUGHTERS
Aiken, C. P. I love you very dearly
Brown, G. One in a million
Cancela, A. Life and death of a hero
Cheever, J. The Hartleys
Dell'Archiprete, R. Good girl
Donahoe, E. Madness in the heart
Dovbish, B. White light
Fitzgerald, F. S. K. Babylon revisited
Hawthorne, N. Rappaccini's daughter
Miner, M. S. Jocelyn
Newhouse, E. The eagle
Newhouse, E. New Year's Day
Newhouse, E. The wolf
Rabinowitz, S. Hodel
Robinson, R. S. Mango tree
Schulberg, B. W. Short digest of a long novel
Thériault, Y. Jeannette
Trilling, L. Other Margaret
Unamuno y Jugo, M. de. Solitude
Winn, J. Hungry sister

FATHERS AND SONS
Anderson, S. "Queer"
Appet, N. The test
Auchincloss, L. The miracle
Beachcroft, T. O. Erne from the coast
Beck, W. Detour in the dark
Beck, W. Far whistle
Betts, D. The sword
Block, R. E. Americanization of Shadrach Cohen
Bowles, P. F. Pages from Cold Point
Boyle, K. Soldier ran away
Bradbury, R. Rocket man
Burnett, W. Suffer the children
Callagan, M. Father and son
Casper, L. Sense of direction
Chekhov, A. P. Holy simplicity
Chekhov, A. P. Saintly simplicity
Collier, J. Ah the university

Collier, J. Thus I refute Beelzy
Connolly, M. Love, Tomi
Corkery, D. Vision
Cozzens, J. G. Total stranger
De La Mare, W. J. Almond tree
Ewald, C. My little boy
Faulkner, W. Barn burning
Goodman, J. C. Kingdom of Gordon
Goudsmit, S. Romantic boy
Hemingway, E. My old man
Horwitz, M. Coquette
Horwitz, J. Generations of man
Kafka, F. The judgment
Lagerkvist, P. F. Father and I
Lanham, E. M. Listen to me, boy
Levine, S. Gift for a birthday
Loveridge, G. Latter end
Mabry, T. D. Indian feather
Maupassant, G. de. Hautot, father and son
Mérimée, P. Mateo Falcone
Milburn, G. The apostate
Newhouse, E. War for Tony
O'Donovan, M. Father and son
Reisin, A. Tuition for the rebbe
Saroyan, W. Pheasant hunter
Schaefer, J. W. Harvey Kendall
Schoenfeld, B. C. Eagle and the cheetah
Scott, W. R. My father doesn't like me
Sherman, R. Now there is peace
Stafford, J. A reunion
Stegner, W. E. Blue-winged teal
Stull, P. Growing pains
Taylor, K. Pale green fishes
Taylor, P. H. Porte-cochere
Thibaudeau, C. City underground
Thurber, J. More alarms at night
Ullman, J. R. Visitation
Van Doren, M. Grandison and son
Van Doren, M. Rich, poor, and indifferent
    See also Parent and child

FATHERS-IN-LAW
Goyen, W. White rooster
Waltari, M. T. Tie from Paris

Faulkner, William, 1897-
Ad Astra
    Faulkner, W. Collected stories
All the dead pilots
    Faulkner, W. Collected stories
Artist at home
    Faulkner, W. Collected stories
Barn burning
    Faulkner, W. Collected stories
    Faulkner, W. Faulkner reader
    First-prize stories, 1919-1954
The bear
    Day, A. G. ed. Greatest American short stories
    Faulkner, W. Faulkner reader
    Ludwig, R. M. and Perry, M. B. eds. Nine short novels
    Schramm, W. L. ed. Great short stories
    Short, R. W. and Sewall, R. B. eds. Short stories for study. 1950 ed.
    Waite, H. O. and Atkinson, B. P. eds. Literature for our time
Bear hunt
    Faulkner, W. Collected stories
Beyond
    Faulkner, W. Collected stories
Black music
    Faulkner, W. Collected stories
The brooch
    Faulkner, W. Collected stories

Faulkner, William—*Continued*

Carcassonne
Faulkner, W. Collected stories
Centaur in brass
Faulkner, W. Collected stories
The courthouse
Faulkner, W. Faulkner reader
A courtship
Faulkner, W. Collected stories
First-prize stories, 1919-1954
Crevasse
Faulkner, W. Collected stories
Death drag
Faulkner, W. Collected stories
Divorce in Naples
Faulkner, W. Collected stories
Dr Martino
Faulkner, W. Collected stories
Dry September
Davis, R. G. ed. Ten modern masters
Faulkner, W. Collected stories
Faulkner, W. Faulkner reader
Lynskey, W. C. ed. Reading modern fiction
Elly
Faulkner, W. Collected stories
Fox hunt
Faulkner, W. Collected stories
Golden land
Faulkner, W. Collected stories
Hair
Faulkner, W. Collected stories
Hand upon the waters
Best of the Best American short stories, 1915-1950
Honor
Faulkner, W. Collected stories
The hound
Bogorad, S. N. and Trevithick, J. eds. College miscellany
A justice
Faulkner, W. Collected stories
Faulkner, W. Faulkner reader
The leg
Faulkner, W. Collected stories
Lo!
Faulkner, W. Collected stories
Mistral
Faulkner, W. Collected stories
Monk
Queen, E. pseud. ed. Literature of crime
Mountain victory
Faulkner, W. Collected stories
Mule in the yard
Faulkner, W. Collected stories
My Grandmother Millard and General Bedford Forrest and the Battle of Harrykin Creek
Faulkner, W. Collected stories
Name for the city
Prize stories of 1951
Odor of verbena
Faulkner, W. Faulkner reader
Old man
Faulkner, W. Faulkner reader
Old people
Davis, R. G. ed. Ten modern masters
Schorer, M. ed. The story
Pennsylvania Station
Faulkner, W. Collected stories
Percy Grimm
Faulkner, W. Faulkner reader

Red leaves
Faulkner, W. Collected stories
Rose for Emily
Burrell, J. A. and Cerf, B. A. eds. Anthology of famous American stories
Faulkner, W. Collected stories
Faulkner, W. Faulkner reader
Foerster, N. ed. American poetry and prose. 1952 ed.
West, R. B. and Stallman, R. W. eds. Art of modern fiction
Shall not perish
Faulkner, W. Collected stories
Shingles for the Lord
Faulkner, W. Collected stories
Faulkner, W. Faulkner reader
Slouch
Farrell, J. T. American dream girl
Spotted horses
Faulkner, W. Faulkner reader
Felheim, M.; Newman, F. B. and Steinhoff, W. R. eds. Modern short stories
Gordon, C. and Tate, A. eds. House of fiction
Ludwig, J. B. and Poirier, W. R. eds. Stories, British and American
Sunday morning at the Compsons
Burnett, W. ed. World's best
Tall men
Faulkner, W. Collected stories
That evening sun
Blodgett, H. W. ed. Story survey. 1953 ed.
Faulkner, W. Collected stories
Faulkner, W. Faulkner reader
Heilman, R. B. ed. Modern short stories
Same as: That evening sun go down
That evening sun go down
Neider, C. ed. Great short stories from the world's literature
Same as: That evening sun
That will be fine
Faulkner, W. Collected stories
There was a queen
Faulkner, W. Collected stories
Tomorrow
Blaustein, A. P. ed. Fiction goes to court
Turnabout
Faulkner, W. Collected stories
Faulkner, W. Faulkner reader
Jensen, P. ed. Fireside book of flying stories
Two soldiers
Faulkner, W. Collected stories
Uncle Willy
Faulkner, W. Collected stories
Victory
Faulkner, W. Collected stories
Was
Davis, R. G. ed. Ten modern masters
Millett, F. B. ed. Reading fiction
Wash
Faulkner, W. Collected stories
Faulkner, W. Faulkner reader

Fauntleroy. Collins, W.

Faust, Frederick, 1892-1944. See Brand, M. pseud.

The **fauve.** Humphrey, W.

Favicchio, John
  Three buttonholes
    Oberfirst, R. ed. 1954 anthology of best
    original short-shorts
Favor granted. Milton, M. E.
Fay, Sarah, 1924-
  Death of Pierce
    Stanford short stories, 1952
Fay, William, 1872-1947
  Lady says murder
    Argosy (Periodical) Argosy Book of
    sports stories
  Murder the bum!
    Herzberg, M. J. comp. Treasure chest
    of sport stories
  A nice, clean job
    Best detective stories of the year—1950
  Touchdown crazy
    Herzberg, M. J. comp. Treasure chest
    of sport stories
Fe-fi-fo-fum. Steele, W. D.
FEAR
  Clark, W. Van T. The pretender
  Faulkner, W. That evening sun
  Hergesheimer, J. Wild oranges
  Keller, D. H. Thing in the cellar
  Kipling, R. At the end of the passage
  Maugham, W. S. End of the flight
  Maupassant, G. de. The duel
  Maupassant, G. de. The Horla
  Poe, E. A. Fall of the House of Usher
  Rath, I. E. Longest day I live
  Sansom, W. Little fears
  Sansom, W. Vertical ladder
    See also Cowardice
Fear. Bellah, J. W.
Fear of innocence. Fiedler, L. A.
Fear planet. Bloch, R.
Fearsome fable. Elliott, B.
Feast of Cats. Coolidge, O. E.
Feast of Nemesis. Munro, H. H.
FEAST OF TABERNACLES. See Sukkoth
Feathers. Sullivan, R.
Feathers. Van Vechten, C.
FEBRUARY
  Grimson, M. S. Leap year
FEEBLE-MINDED
  Hall, J. B. In the time of demonstrations
  Kuehn, S. The hunt
  Lardner, R. W. Haircut
  Welty, E. Lily Daw and the three ladies
    See also Idiocy
Feeling for human interest. Davis, L. R.
Feeney, Thomas Butler
  Whiter than snow
    Thinker's digest (Periodical) Spoiled
    priest, and other stories
Feet of clay. Wodehouse, P. G.
Feet on the ground. Powell, D.
Feild, Bruce
  How Abel slew Cain
    Dachs, D. ed. Treasury of sports humor
Felder, Dora Fishman, 1917-
  Purple hat
    American vanguard, 1953
  Time for silence
    American vanguard, 1953

Felix. Beck, W.
Felsen, Gregor, 1916-
  Horatio
    Seventeen (Periodical) Nineteen from
    Seventeen
  Hot rod; condensation
    Strang, R. M. and Roberts, R. M. eds.
    Teen-age tales v2
  Trenton in thirty minutes
    Fenner, P. R. comp. Speed, speed, speed
Felsen, Henry Gregor. See Felsen, Gregor
Feminine wiles. Williams, R. E.
FENCES
  Betts, D. Mark of distinction
FENCING
  Lewis, R. Roman holiday
Fennel, Erik
  Doughnut jockey
    Bleiler, E. F. and Dikty, T. E. eds. Sci-
    ence fiction omnibus: The best science
    fiction stories, 1949, 1950
Fenton, Edward, 1917-
  Gun shy
    Fenner, P. R. comp. Dogs, dogs, dogs
Fenton, Frank, 1904- and Petracca, Joseph
  Tolliver's travels
    Healy, R. J. ed. New tales of space and
    time
Ferber, Edna, 1887-
  Afternoon of a faun
    Burrell, J. A. and Cerf, B. A. eds. An-
    thology of famous American stories
  Old lady Mandle
    Ungar, F. ed. To mother with love
  Old man Minick
    Leftwich, J. ed. Yisröel. 1952 ed.
Ferguson, Malcolm
  Damsel with a dulcimer
    Derleth, A. W. ed. Night's yawning peal
Fern Barrie's new plans. Caudill, R.
Ferrara, Jackie, 1930?-
  Figurine of love
    American vanguard, 1953
FERRETS
  Munro, H. H. Sredni Vashtar
Ferrone, John R.
  About my sons
    Stanford short stories, 1952
  Bitter wall
    Stanford short stories, 1951
  Her own people
    Stanford short stories, 1952
  Rise of Lorenzo Villari
    Stanford short stories, 1953
Ferry of fulfilment. Porter, W. S.
Fessenden's worlds. Hamilton, E.
Fessier, Michael, 1903-
  Fascinating stranger
    Jenkins, W. F. ed. Great stories of sci-
    ence fiction
  Man-taming woman
    Meredith, S. ed. Bar 2
  That's what happened to me
    Christ, H. I. and Shostak, J. eds. Short
    stories
FESTIVALS
  Boyd, J. Fiesta
  Buck, F. Elephants!

FESTIVALS—*Continued*
Coolidge, O. E. Feast of Cats
Hawthorne, N. Maypole of Merry Mount
Feuchtwanger, Lion, 1884-
Balance sheet of my life
Ausubel, N. ed. Treasury of Jewish humor
Mendel Hirsch
Leftwich, J. ed. Yisröel. 1952 ed.
FEUDS
Bergengruen, W. Magnanimity contest
Drinkard, I. N. Mission for baby
Kantor, M. Life in her hands
Munro, H. H. The interlopers
Porter, W. S. Blackjack bargainer
Porter, W. S. Squaring the circle
Porter, W. S. Technical error
Stuart, J. Land of our enemies
Stuart, J. When mountain men make peace
Trollope, A. Malachi's Cove
Van Doren, M. Not a natural man
Fever flower. Grau, S. A.
Fickle fortune. Porter, W. S.
FICTITIOUS ANIMALS. See Animals, Mythical
The **fiddler.** Melville, H.
Fiddler, play fast, play faster. Sawyer, R.
Fiedler, Leslie A. 1917-
Fear of innocence
Best American short stories, 1950
Field, Rachel Lyman, 1894-1942
A woman of virtue
Brentano, F. ed. The word lives on
Field, S. S. 1906-
Good-by to Cap'm John
Southern review. Anthology of stories from the Southern review
Field of flowers. Aiken, C. P.
FIELD SPORTS. See Hunting; Track athletics
Field study. Phillips, P.
FIELD TRIALS. See Dogs
Fielder's choice. Coombs, C. I.
Fielding, Edward
Fountain of youth
This week magazine. This week's short-short stories
Fields of wheat. Lynch, J. A.
FIENDS. See Crime and criminals
Fiesta. Boyd, J.
FIESTAS. See Festivals
Fife's house. Boyle, K.
Fifteen. Sherman, D.
Fifth commandment. Hutchins, M. P. M.
Fifth friend. Kjelgaard, J. A.
Fifth wheel. Porter, W. S.
Fifty-carat jinx. Blochman, L. G.
Fifty-dollar bottle. Cousins, M.
Fifty-first dragon. Broun, H. C.
Fifty-four, forty and fight. Wylie, P.
Fifty grand. Hemingway, E.
Fifty marks. Ditzen, R.
Fifty pounds. Coppard, A. E.
Fifty yard dash. Saroyan, W.

FIG
Sultan, S. Fugue of the fig tree
The **fight.** Crane, S.
Fight between Jappe and Do Escobar, Mann, T.
Fight number twenty-five. Stuart, J.
Fighter. Maxwell, J. A.
FIGHTING. See Boxing; Dueling; Fighting, Hand-to-hand
FIGHTING, HAND-TO-HAND
Crane, S. Blue Hotel
Crane, S. The fight
Mahoney, W. B. Wrong guy
Mann, T. Fight between Jappe and Do Escobar
Modell, J. Day in the sun
O'Flaherty, L. The challenge
Sansom, W. Boiler room
Walsh, M. Quiet man
Fighting finish. Lacy, M.
Figurine of love. Ferrara, J.
FIJI ISLANDS
Michener, J. A. Mynah birds
Filboid Studge, the story of a mouse that helped. Munro, H. H.
Filial sentiments of a parracide. Proust, M.
Fillmore, Parker Hoysted, 1878-1944
Clever Manka
Fenner, P. R. comp. Fools and funny fellows
Mary, Mary, so contrary
Fenner, P. R. comp. Fools and funny fellows
A **filly** owns a fella! Armstrong, M.
Film library. Van Vogt, A. E.
Filmer. Wells, H. G.
Final command. Van Vogt, A. E.
Final embarrassment. Williams, W. C.
Final problem. Doyle, Sir A. C.
Finality unlimited. Wandrei, D.
Financial world. Brophy, B.
FINANCIERS. See Capitalists and financiers
Financing Finnegan. Fitzgerald, F. S. K.
Find the woman. Millar, K.
Findlay, D. K.
Suicide on skis
Herzberg, M. J. comp. Treasure chest of sport stories
Fine place for the cat. Bonham, M.
Fineman, Irving, 1893-
In the fields of Boaz
Selden, R. ed. Ways of God and men
Interview with Ahashuerus
Ausubel, N. ed. Treasury of Jewish humor
Finest story in the world. Kipling, R.
Finger, Charles Joseph, 1871-1941
Na-Ha the fighter
Hazeltine, A. I. comp. Selected stories for teen-agers
Yankee captain in Patagonia
Fenner, P. R. comp. Pirates, pirates pirates
Finger man. Prince, J. and Prince, H.
Fingers of fear. MacDonald, P.

Finish, good lady. Auchincloss, L.
Finished. De Camp, L. S.
FINLAND
20th century
Sillanpää, F. E. Night of the harvest festival
Waltari, M. T. Moonscape
Finney, Jack, 1912?-
Breakfast in bed
Collier's, the national weekly. Collier's best
I'm scared
Heinlein, R. A. ed. Tomorrow, the stars
Third level
Magazine of fantasy and science fiction
Best from Fantasy and science fiction; 2d ser.
FIRE
London, J. To build a fire
Fire and the sword. Robinson, F. M.
Fire balloons. Bradbury, R.
Fire-boy of Dunsoon. Cutler, J. L.
FIRE EXTINCTION. See Firemen
Fire in the bush. Warwick, J.
Fire killer. Frazee, S.
FIREARMS
Bonner, P. H. Made to measure
The firebird. Doughty, LeG. S.
Fireboat style. Gallister, M. pseud.
FIREMEN
Brier, H. M. Sky hook
Gallister, M. pseud. Fireboat style
Porter, W. S. Foreign policy of Company 99
Sansom, W. In the morning
Sansom, W. Journey into smoke
See also Fire extinction; Fires
FIREMEN, RAILROAD. See Railroads—Employees
FIRES
Caldwell, E. Grass fire
Kirtland, A. Trial by fire
Newell, A. S. Grandpop comes home
Strong, J. Hired man
Vickers, R. Man with the sneer
Walton, H. Episode on Dhee Minor
Warwick, J. Fire in the bush
Welty, E. The burning
FIRES (AT SEA)
Conrad, J. Youth
Floherty, J. J. Sea afire
FIRES, FOREST. See Forest fires
Fires within. Clarke, A. C.
Firewater. Klass, P.
First ally. Annixter, P. pseud.
First autumn. Caldwell, E.
First blood. Household, G.
First-born. Coolidge, O. E.
First car. Carter, M.
First Christmas tree. Van Dyke, H.
First confession. O'Donovan, M.
First contact. Jenkins, W. F.

First death of her life. Taylor, E.
First disciple. Davis, A. L.
First face. Enright, E.
First Fourth in White Pine. Hart, F.
First harpist. Casey, M. W.
First love. Kaufman, A.
First love. O'Donovan, M.
First love. Turgenev, I. S.
First love. Welty, E.
First sad facts. Stein, M.
First stone. Mason, G. S.
First war party. Bowman, J. C.
First you take a live goat. Barr, J. pseud.
Fischer, Bruno, 1908-
Dog died first
Best detective stories of the year—1950
My Aunt Celia
Mystery Writers of America, inc. Butcher, baker, murder-maker
Nobody's business
Mystery Writers of America, inc. Crooks' tour
Fish, Horace, 1885-
Wrists on the door
Thinker's digest (Periodical) Spoiled priest, and other stories
FISH. See Fishes
Fish are such liars. Pertwee, R.
Fish bites man. Wylie, P.
Fish supper. Aiken, C. P.
Fish wagon. Comstock, H. B.
Fish who could close his eyes. Clark, W. Van T.
Fisher, Dorothea Frances (Canfield) 1879-
As ye sow—
Brentano, F. ed. The word lives on
Lohan, R. and Lohan, M. eds. New Christmas treasury
Drop in the bucket
Burnett, W. ed. World's best
Flint and fire
Stegner, W. E.; Scowcroft, R. and Ilyin, B. eds. Writer's art
Forgotten mother
Ungar, F. ed. To mother with love
Sex education
Best of the Best American short stories, 1915-1950
Sunset at sixteen
Hazeltine, A. I. comp. Selected stories for teen-agers
Witch doctor
McFarland, W. K. comp. Then it happened
Fisher, Philip M.
Lights
Conklin, G. and Conklin, L. T. eds. Supernatural reader
Fisher, Rudolph, 1897-1934
Common meter
Ford, N. A. and Fagget, H. L. eds. Best short stories by Afro-American writers (1925-1950)

The fisherman. Doty, W. L.
Fisherman's luck. Matthews, R. D.
FISHERMEN
  Canning, V. The smuggler
  Connolly, J. B. The trawler
  Maugham, W. S. Salvatore
  Maupassant, G. de. At sea
  Mayse, A. Midnight Mike
  Peretz, I. L. Miracle on the sea
  Poe, E. A. Descent into the maelström
  Thériault, Y. Jeannette
  Ullman, J. R. Pau
  Watkins, R. H. Offshore
  Welty, E. At the landing
    See also Fishing

Fishers of the air. Roberts, Sir C. G. D.

FISHES
  Conner, R. The long pike
  Gordimer, N. The catch
  Li Fu-yen. Man who became a fish
  Pertwee, R. Fish are such liars
  Walsh, M. Honest fisherman

Fishin' Jimmy. Slosson, A. T.

FISHING
  Beal, F. Bertie, the uninvited
  Bonner, P. H. Blue charm
  Bonner, P. H. Caddis hatch
  Bonner, P. H. Foul is fair
  Bonner, P. H. Rajah's Rock
  Bonner, P. H. Velia
  Ford, C. Trout widows
  Gordon, A. Sea devil
  Gordon, C. Old Red
  Grau, S. A. Joshua
  Keith, S. Siren of hope
  Macfarlan, A. A. Tackle buster
  Perrault, E. G. Silver King
  Person, W. T. Monster of Blue-Hole Lake
  Person, W. T. Won by a tail
  Sherman, H. M. Porky, the outboarder
  Slosson, A. T. Fishin' Jimmy
  Spiller, B. L. Net profit
  Verga, G. Ugly weather
  Walsh, M. Honest fisherman
  Watkins, R. H. Offshore
  Welty, E. Wide net
  Wylie, P. Best of Crunch and Des; 21
    stories
  Wylie, P. Sporting blood
  Wylie, P. Way of all fish
    See also Fishermen

Fishing excursion. Maupassant, G. de

Fishman, Joseph Fulling
  Old Calamity tries a bluff
    Mystery Writers of America, inc.
    Maiden murders

Fisk Fogle. Van Doren, M.

FIST FIGHTING. See Fighting, Hand-to-
  hand

Fistful of Alamo heroes. Karchmer, S.

Fitt, Mary, pseud. See Freeman, Kathleen

The fittest. MacLean, K.

Fitts, Henry K.
  Rattlesnake Trail
    Owen, F. ed. Teen-age winter sports
    stories

Fitzgerald, Bill
  Iron maiden
    Best Army short stories, 1950
Fitzgerald, Francis Scott Key, 1896-1940
  Absolution
    Fitzgerald, F. S. K. Stories
  Alcoholic case
    Fitzgerald, F. S. K. Stories
  Baby party
    Fitzgerald, F. S. K. Stories
  Babylon revisited
    Bogorad, S. N. and Trevithick, J. eds.
    College miscellany
    Fitzgerald, F. S. K. Stories
    Foerster, N. ed. American poetry and
    prose. 1952 ed.
    Ludwig, J. B. and Poirier, W. R. eds.
    Stories, British and American
  Bernice bobs her hair
    Fitzgerald, F. S. K. Stories
  The bowl
    Grayson, C. ed. Fourth round
  Bridal party
    Fitzgerald, F. S. K. Stories
  Captured shadow
    Fitzgerald, F. S. K. Stories
  Crazy Sunday
    Fitzgerald, F. S. K. Stories
  Curious case of Benjamin Button
    Kuebler, H. W. ed. Treasury of science
    fiction classics
  Diamond as big as the Ritz
    Fitzgerald, F. S. K. Stories
  Family in the wind
    Fitzgerald, F. S. K. Stories
  Financing Finnegan
    Fitzgerald, F. S. K. Stories
  Freshest boy
    Blodgett, H. W. ed. Story survey.
    1953 ed.
    Fitzgerald, F. S. K. Stories
    Schorer, M. ed. The story
  Ice palace
    Fitzgerald, F. S. K. Stories
  Jelly-bean
    Shaw, H. and Bement, D. Reading the
    short story
  Last of the belles
    Fitzgerald, F. S. K. Stories
    Lynskey, W. C. ed. Reading modern
    fiction
  Long way out
    Fitzgerald, F. S. K. Stories
  Lost decade
    Fitzgerald, F. S. K. Stories
  Magnetism
    Fitzgerald, F. S. K. Stories
  May Day
    Fitzgerald, F. S. K. Stories
  Pat Hobby himself: a patriotic short
    Fitzgerald, F. S. K. Stories
  Pat Hobby himself: two old-timers
    Fitzgerald, F. S. K. Stories
  Rich boy
    Burrell, J. A. and Cerf, B. A. eds.
    Anthology of famous American stories
    Fitzgerald, F. S. K. Stories
    Waite, H. O. and Atkinson, B. P. eds.
    Literature for our time
  Rough crossing
    Fitzgerald, F. S. K. Stories
  Scandal detectives
    Fitzgerald, F. S. K. Stories

Fitzgerald, Francis S. K.—*Continued*
  "The sensible thing"
    Fitzgerald, F. S. K. Stories
  Three hours between planes
    Fitzgerald, F. S. K. Stories
  Two wrongs
    Fitzgerald, F. S. K. Stories
  Winter dreams
    Fitzgerald, F. S. K. Stories
  Woman from Twenty-One
    Esquire (Periodical) Girls from Esquire
  Woman with a past
    Fitzgerald, F. S. K. Stories

Fitzsimmons, Betty Jung
  Christmas rose
    Elmquist, R. M. ed. Fifty years to
      Christmas

Five Alls. Davis, F. M.

Five captains. Chute, B. J.

5,271,009. Bester, A.

Five orange pips. Doyle, Sir A. C.

Five parts of summer. Littledale, H. A.

Five wives of Fergus O'Malley. Maguire,
  R. A.

Five years in the Marmalade. Krepps, R. W.

The fix. Roberts, R. M.

The flag. Bates, H. E.

Flag paramount. Porter, W. S.

Flagman Thiel. Hauptmann, G. J. R.

FLAGMEN. See Railroads—Employees

FLAGS
  Hart, F. First Fourth in White Pine
  Porter, W. S. Flag paramount

Flame on the frontier. Johnson, D. M.

Flanagan, Thomas
  Cold winds of Adesta
    Queen, E. pseud. ed. Queen's awards:
      7th ser.

Flash of lightning. Rawlings, C. A.

FLASHBACKS. See Retrospective stories

Flashing spikes. O'Rourke, F.

Flat town. Boyd, J.

Flaubert, Gustave, 1821-1880
  Legend of St Julian the Hospitaller
    Dupee, F. W. ed. Great French short
      novels
    Neider, C. ed. Great short stories from
      the world's literature
  Simple heart
    Geist, S. ed. French stories and tales
    Gordon, C. and Tate, A. eds. House of
      fiction
    Neider, C. ed. Short novels of the
      masters

Flaw. MacDonald, J. D.

The flea. Sawyer, R.

FLEAS
  Collier, J. Gavin O'Leary

Fleg, Edmond, 1874-
  The adulteress
    Leftwich, J. ed. Yisröel. 1952 ed.
  Solomon the King
    Selden, R. ed. Ways of God and men

Fleming, Joseph S.
  Ride 'im Chick Norris
    Furman, A. L. ed. Teen-age horse
      stories

Flesh and the devil. De Vries, P.

Fletcher, Grace Nies
  Texas Christmas 1872
    Elmquist, R. M. ed. Fifty years of
      Christmas

Fletcher, Inglis (Clark) 1888-
  White leopard
    American boy (Periodical) American
      boy Adventure stories

Fletcher, Vivian, 1913-
  Coda to a writers' conference
    Story (Periodical) Story; no. 4

FLIERS. See Air pilots

FLIES
  Pirandello, L. The fly
  Porges, A. The flies

FLIGHT
  Bradbury, R. Flying machine
  Jenkins, W. F. Historical note
  Keller, D. H. Flying fool
  Knight, E. M. Flying Yorkshireman
  Lieberman, R. Sister Innocent and the
    useful miracle
  Stapledon, W. O. Flying men
  Tale of a chemist

Flight for life. Doyle, Sir A. C.

Flight into Egypt. Rosegger, P.

Flight south. Seager, A.

Flight that failed. Hull, E. M.

Flight through the dark. Angell, R.

Flight to forever. Anderson, P.

Flimsy walls. Parker, C. W.

Flint and fire. Fisher, D. F. C.

Flo. Kneale, N.

Floherty, John Joseph, 1882-
  Duel at 70 miles an hour
    Fenner, P. R. comp. Speed, speed, speed
  Sea afire
    Fenner, J. J. comp. Stories of the sea

The flood. Parker, Sir G. bart.

FLOODS
  Becker, S. D. Baptism of some importance
  Brace, G. W. Deep water man
  Burman, B. L. Children of Noah
  Cave, H. B. Peril of the river
  Harte, B. High-water mark
  Kantor, M. Life in her hands
  MacDonald, P. Man out of the rain
  Marquis, D. Country doctor
  Munro, H. H. The guests
  Welty, E. At the landing

Flora, Fletcher
  Torrid zone
    Queen, E. pseud. ed. Queen's awards:
      7th ser.

Florence, Gordon Louis, 1915-
  All in one day
    Oberfirst, R. ed. 1954 anthology of best
      original short-shorts

FLORENCE. See Italy—Florence

Florian Slappey—private eye. Cohen, O. R.

FLORICULTURE. See Gardens and gardening

FLORIDA
Curtis, K. Cruises in the sun; 3 stories
Granberry, E. Trip to Czardis
Rawlings, M. K. Benny and the bird-dogs
Rawlings, M. K. Gal young un
Rinehart, M. R. Murder and the south wind

St. Petersburg
Lardner, R. W. Golden honeymoon

Flotsam and jetsam. Maugham, W. S.

The flower. Rugel, M.

FLOWER GARDENING. See Gardens and gardening

Flower of Utah. Doyle, Sir A. C.

Flowering Judas. Porter, K. A.

Flowering of the strange orchid. See Wells, H. G. Strange orchid

FLOWERS. See Gardens and gardening; also names of particular flowers, e.g. Orchids

Flowers for an angel. Morland, N.

Flowers for Marjorie. Welty, E.

Fluffy. Waldo, E. H.

Flute-player. O'Flaherty, L.

FLUTE PLAYERS. See Musicians—Flute players

Fluted arrow. Mowery, W. B.

The fly. Pirandello, L.

The fly. Porges, A.

Fly away home. Jackson, R. B.

Fly chaser. Sherman, H. M.

Fly in the coffin. Caldwell, E.

FLYERS. See Air pilots

Flying Cloud in the Roaring Forties. Sperry, A.

Flying Dutchman. Moore, W.

Flying fool. Keller, D. H.

Flying machine. Bradbury, R.

Flying men. Stapledon, W. O.

Flying out of Mrs Barnard Hollis. Harvey, W. F.

FLYING SAUCERS
Doar, G. Outer limit
Holmes, K. Man who rode the saucer

Flying stars. Chesterton, G. K.

Flying switch. Davis, H. L.

Flying Yorkshireman. Knight, E. M.

Flynn, Thomas Theodore, 1902-
Congo cargo
Argosy (Periodical) Argosy Book of sea stories

FOG
Heard, G. Great fog
Porter, W. S. Fog in Santone

Fog and the saints. Anderson, M.

Fog horn. Bradbury, R.

FOG HORNS
Bradbury, R. Fog horn

Fog in Santone. Porter, W. S.

Foggy. Hall, D.

Foley, Martha
Americans all
Lantz, J. E. ed. Stories of Christian living
Glory, glory, hallelujah
Ribalow, H. U. ed. World's greatest boxing stories

Foley, Teresa
Sam and the dean
Story (Periodical) Story; no. 1

FOLK TALES. See Legends and folk tales

FOLKLORE. See Legends and folk tales

Follow that car. Roberts, R. M.

Fonger, Hilary
Ripeness of the time
Seventeen (Periodical) Nineteen from Seventeen

Fontaine, Robert Louis, 1912?-
God hit a home run
Dachs, D. ed. Treasury of sports humor
How do you say good-bye?
McFarland, W. K. comp. Then it happened

FOOD
Hays, L. Banquet and a half
Huysmans, J. K. Monsieur Folantin
Maugham, W. S. The luncheon
Munro, H. H. Blind spot
Munro, H. H. The Chaplet
Munro, H. H. Quail seed
Nadir, I. M. Nuttose and protose
Nadir, I. M. Ruined by success
Renard, J. Spoiled cake
    See also Bread; Breakfasts; Dinners and Dining

Fool about a horse. Santee, R.

Fool dog. Vetter, M. M.

The fool-killer. Porter, W. S.

Foolish one. Davies, R.

Foolproof frame-up. Klingsberg, H. M.

FOOLS AND JESTERS
Baudelaire, C. P. Death of a hero
Benét, S. V. Johnny Pye and the fool killer
Poe, E. A. Hop-Frog

Fool's mate. Ellin, S.

FOOTBALL
Brondfield, J. That's my boy
Brush, K. I. Football girl
Chute, B. J. Alias All-American
Chute, B. J. Bench warmer
Chute, B. J. Big shot
Chute, B. J. Master mind
Coombs, C. I. Headline halfback
Coombs, C. I. Hillbilly halfback
Coombs, C. I. Newton man
Coombs, C. I. Unlucky number
Fay, W. Touchdown crazy
Fitzgerald, F. S. K. The bowl
Heinz, W. C. Man's game
Heyliger, W. Man who wouldn't break
Herndon, B. Run, iron man
Holder, W. Cash and carry guy
Johnson, H. She'll be sorry
Miers, E. S. Scrub cure
Platt, G. Touchdown for Rex
Runyon, D. Hold 'em Yale

FOOTBALL—*Continued*
  Shaw, I. Eighty-yard run
  Sylvester, H. Return of the hero
  Tunis, J. R. Ronald leaves the Academy
  Young, S. Maloney's last stand
Football girl. Brush, K. I.
Foote, John Taintor, 1881-1950
  Allegheny
    Bloch, M. ed. Favorite dog stories
  Big train
    Foote, J. T. Hoofbeats
  Blister
    Foote, J. T. Hoofbeats
  Class
    Creamer, J. B. comp. Twenty-two
      stories about horses and men
    Foote, J. T. Hoofbeats
  Fowl disaster
    Foote, J. T. Hoofbeats
  Look of eagles
    Foote, J. T. Hoofbeats
    Herzberg, M. J. comp. Treasure chest of
      sport stories
  Old pastures
    Foote, J. T. Hoofbeats
  Ole man Sanford
    Foote, J. T. Hoofbeats
  Salvation
    Foote, J. T. Hoofbeats
  Shame on you
    Foote, J. T. Hoofbeats
  Spirit dope
    Foote, J. T. Hoofbeats
  Tip in time
    Foote, J. T. Hoofbeats
  Très Jolie
    Foote, J. T. Hoofbeats
  Two ringers
    Creamer, J. B. comp. Twenty-two
      stories about horses and men
    Foote, J. T. Hoofbeats
Foote, Shelby, 1916-
  Ride out
    Aswell, M. L. W. ed. New short novels
Footnote. Farrell, J. T.
Footprint in the sky. Carr, J. D.
Footprints in the jungle. Maugham, W. S.
For a horse. James, W.
For a master's wages. Claudy, C. H.
For Esmé—with love and squalor. Salinger,
  J. D.
For girlhood and for love. Lowry, R. J. C.
For love of a man. London, J.
For men only. Wilsey, R. G.
For military merit. Lukert, E. P.
For the blood is the life. Crawford, F. M.
For the duration of the war. Munro, H. H.
For the honor of XDY. Kahmann, M. C.
For the last time. Jordan, G.
For the love of a race horse. Cooke, A. A.
For the public. Kahn, B. I.
For the sake of freedom. James, W.
For the want of a cigarette. Schneider,
  G. W.

For they know not what they do. Steele,
  W. D.
For this is Christmas Day. Sangster, M. E.
For value received. Deming, R.
For white men only. Farrell, J. T.
Foran, John P.
  The kiss-off
    Best detective stories of the year—1952
Forbes, Esther, 1894-
  "Disperse, ye rebels!"
    Fenner, P. R. comp. Yankee Doodle
Forbidden buzzards. Munro, H. H.
Force of circumstance. Maugham, W. S.
Ford, Corey, 1902-
  Man of his own
    This week magazine. This week's short-
      short stories
  Slipstream
    Bloch, M. ed. Favorite dog stories
  Snake dance
    Lass, A. H. and Horowitz, A. eds.
      Stories for youth
  Trout widows
    Dachs, D. ed. Treasury of sports humor
Ford, James Lauren, 1854-1928
  Spiritualist's tale
    Carrington, H. ed. Week-end book of
      ghost stories
Ford, Nick Aaron, 1904-
  Let the church roll on
    Ford, N. A. and Faggett, H. L. eds.
      Best short stories by Afro-American
      writers (1925-1950)
  Majesty of the law
    Ford, N. A. and Faggett, H. L. eds.
      Best short stories by Afro-American
      writers (1925-1950)
  No room in the inn
    Ford, N. A. and Faggett, H. L. eds.
      Best short stories by Afro-American
      writers (1925-1950)
  One way to victory
    Ford, N. A. and Faggett, H. L. eds.
      Best short stories by Afro-American
      writers (1925-1950)
Fordie. Brophy, B.
Forecast. Jones. R. F.
FOREIGN CORRESPONDENTS. See
  Journalists
FOREIGN LEGION (FRENCH ARMY)
  Miller, W. H. Message to the Camel Corps
Foreign policy of Company 99. Porter, W. S.
FOREIGN SERVICE. See Civil service
The **foreigner.** Adams, B. M.
The **foreigner.** Saroyan, W.
Forest of the night. Weston, C. G.
FOREST FIRES
  Anderson, E. V. Smell of smoke
  Cain, J. M. Brush fire
  Carter, R. G. Parachute warning
  Roberts, Sir C. G. D. Gauntlet of fire
  Stewart, G. R. Death of the glen
Forest of the South. Gordon, C.
Forester, Cecil Scott, 1899-
  Bower of roses
    Forester, C. S. The nightmare

Forester, Cecil S.—*Continued*
Evidence
  Forester, C. S. The nightmare
Head and the feet
  Forester, C. S. The nightmare
Hornblower and Noah's ark
  Forester, C. S. Mr Midshipman Hornblower
Hornblower and the cargo of rice
  Forester, C. S. Mr Midshipman Hornblower
Hornblower and the even chance
  Forester, C. S. Mr Midshipman Hornblower
Hornblower and the examination for lieutenant
  Forester, C. S. Mr Midshipman Hornblower
Hornblower and the man who felt queer
  Forester, C. S. Mr Midshipman Hornblower
Hornblower and the man who saw God
  Forester, C. S. Mr Midshipman Hornblower
Hornblower and the penalty of failure
  Forester, C. S. Mr Midshipman Hornblower
Hornblower and the Spanish galleys
  Forester, C. S. Mr Midshipman Hornblower
Hornblower, the Duchess, and the Devil
  Forester, C. S. Mr Midshipman Hornblower
Hornblower, the frogs, and the lobsters
  Forester, C. S. Mr Midshipman Hornblower
The hostage
  Forester, C. S. The nightmare
Indecision
  Forester, C. S. The nightmare
Letters in evidence
  Queen, E. pseud. ed. Literature of crime
Man whose wishes came true
  Queen, E. pseud. ed. Queen's awards: 6th ser.
Miriam's miracle
  Forester, C. S. The nightmare
Physiology of fear
  Forester, C. S. The nightmare
To be given to God
  Forester, C. S. The nightmare
The unbelievable
  Forester, C. S. The nightmare
Wandering Gentile
  Forester, C. S. The nightmare

FORESTERS
Munro, H. H. The interlopers

FORESTS AND FORESTRY
Hudson, W. H. Mysterious forest
Van Vogt, A. E. Process

Forever and the earth. Bradbury, R.

Forever Florida. Gizycka, F.

Forewarned. Munro, H. H.

FORGERY
Collins, W. Fauntleroy

FORGERY OF WORKS OF ART
Harvey, W. F. Old masters

Forget-me-not. Temple, W. F.

Forgetfulness. Campbell, J. W.

FORGIVENESS
Goudge, E. Canticle of the sun

Forgiveness of Tenchu Taen. Kummer, F. A.

Forgotten. Miller, P. S.

Forgotten enemy. Clarke, A. C.

Forgotten greeting cards. Lloyd, B. B.

Forgotten island. Coatsworth, E. J.

Forgotten mother. Fisher, D. F. C.

Forgotten world. Hamilton, E.

The **forks.** Powers, J. F.

Forster, Edward Morgan, 1879-
Celestial omnibus
  Cerf, B. A. and Moriarty, H. C. eds. Anthology of famous British stories
  Ludwig, J. B. and Poirier, W. R. eds. Stories, British and American
  Shaw, H. and Bement, D. Reading the short story
Curate's friend
  Conklin, G. and Conklin, L. T. eds. Supernatural reader
Machine stops
  Felheim, M.; Newman, F. B. and Steinhoff, W. R. eds. Modern short stories
  Kuebler, H. W. ed. Treasury of science fiction classics
  Waite, H. O. and Atkinson, B. P. eds. Literature for our time
Mr Andrews
  Heilman, R. B. ed. Modern short stories
Other side of the hedge
  Ludwig, J. B. and Poirier, W. R. eds. Stories, British and American
  Lynskey, W. C. ed. Reading modern fiction
The trial
  Burnett, W. ed. World's best

Fortune of Arleus Kane. Auchincloss, L.

FORTUNE-TELLING
Collier, J. In the cards
Porter, W. S. Tobin's palm
Van Doren, M. Consider courage
Winslow, T. S. Angie Lee's fortune

Forty-third division. Bates, R.

Forty years of firewood. Anderson, D.

The **fossickers.** Michener, J. A.

Foster, Bennett
Outlaws are in town
  Meredith, S. ed. Bar 2

Foster, Constance Jackson, 1899-
It's a man's world
  Stowe, A. comp. It's a date

Foster, Michael, 1904-
Later
  Thinker's digest (Periodical) Spoiled priest, and other stories
Present for Christmas
  Saturday evening post (Periodical) Saturday evening post stories, 1951

FOSTER CHILDREN
Annett, W. S. The relic
Cooke, A. A. Returning good for evil
Devin, B. The rattle
Ringwood, G. P. Little ghost

FOSTER CHILDREN—*Continued*
Rosenberg, E. Happy one
Stevenson, R. L. Treasure of Franchard
Wharton, E. N. J. Mission of Jane
See also Foundlings; Orphans

Foster, you're dead. Dick, P. K.

Foul is fair. Bonner, P. H.

Found out. Haycox, E.

FOUNDLINGS
Goyen, W. Pore Perrie

FOUNTAIN OF YOUTH. See Rejuvenation

Fountain of youth. Fielding, E.

Four blind men. Brown, F.

Four bottles of beer. Williams, W. C.

Four brothers. Van Doren, M.

Four-dimensional roller-press. Olsen, B.

Four Dutchmen. Maugham, W. S.

Four fathom fury. Coombs, C. I.

Four freedoms. Newhouse, E.

Four in one. Knight, D.

Four meetings. James, H.

Four men and a box. Barnard, L. G.

Four-minute mile. Rackowe, A.

Four of a kind. Cooke, A. A.

Four-poster. Munby, A. N. L.

Four-ring circus. Chute, B. J.

The fourflusher. Perry, G. S.

Fournier, Alain, 1886-1914
Miracle of the farmer's wife
Fremantle, A. J. ed. Mothers

Fourth day out from Santa Cruz. Bowles, P. F.

Fourth degree. Barry, J.

FOURTH DIMENSION
Jenkins, W. F. Sidewise in time
Kuttner, H. Time locker
Olsen, B. Four-dimensional roller-press
Fourth-dimensional demonstrator. Jenkins, W. F.

Fourth dynasty. Winterbotham, R. R.

Fourth in Salvador. Porter, W. S.

Fourth man. Russell, J.

FOURTH OF JULY CELEBRATIONS
Hart, F. First Fourth in White Pine
Porter, W. S. Fourth in Salvador

Fourth point. Claudy, C. H.

Fowl disaster. Foote, J. T.

Fowler, Bertram Baynes, 1893-
Some can't take it
Eaton, H. T. ed. Short stories

Fox, James M. pseud. See Knipscheer, James M. W.

Fox, John, 1862-1919
Courtin' on Cutshin
Summers, H. S. ed. Kentucky story
Knight of the Cumberland
Scribner treasury

Fox, Monroe L. 1914?-
Seeing eye dog
Bloch, M. ed. Favorite dog stories

Fox, Norman Arnold, 1911-
Bet the wild queen!
Western Writers of America. Bad men and good
Only the dead ride proudly
Western Writers of America. Holsters and heroes

The fox. Lawrence, D. H.

The fox and the forest. Bradbury, R.

Fox hunt. Faulkner, W.

FOX HUNTING
Boyd, J. Away! Away!
Caldwell, E. Negro in the well
Faulkner, W. Fox hunt
Kantor, M. Voice of Bugle Ann
McCauley, M. C. Li'l Reynard
Munro, H. H. The bag
Munro, H. H. Esmé
Somerville, E. A. O. and Martin, V. F. Philippa's fox-hunt
Surtees, R. S. Hunting scenes; 26 stories
Tregarthen, J. C. Great run
Williamson, H. Trapper's mates

Fox in the forest. Bradbury, R.

"Fox-in-the-morning." Porter, W. S.

Fox in the Pennine Hills. Proctor, M.

FOXES
Kjelgaard, J. A. Blood on the ice
Lawrence, D. H. The fox
Seton, E. T. Springfield fox
Tregarthen, J. C. Great run

Foxhole in Washington. Schulberg, B. W.

Foxholes of Mars. Leiber, E.

Fraerman, Ruvim Isaevich
The expedition
Guerney, B. G. comp. New Russian stories

A fragment. Chekhov, A. P.

France, Anatole, 1844-1924
Manuscript of a village doctor
Blodgett, H. W. ed. Story survey. 1953 ed.
Our lady's juggler
Lamb, L. ed. Family book of best loved stories
Procurator of Judæa
Selden, R. ed. Ways of God and men

FRANCE
15th century
Stevenson, R. L. Sire de Malétroit's door
16th century
Chambers, R. W. Demoiselle d'Ys
Lewis, J. Wife of Martin Guerre
17th century
Blackburn, E. R. Christiane the Huguenot
18th century—1789-1799
Irving, W. Adventure of the German student
1870-1940
Macfarlan, A. A. Camp at Saint Adrien
1940-1945
Macfarlan, A. A. Danger by candlelight
Avignon
See France, Provincial and rural—Avignon

FRANCE—*Continued*

Marseilles

Collier, J. If youth knew if age could

Paris

Charteris, L. Paris: The covetous headsman

Paris—15th century

Stevenson, R. L. Lodging for the night

Paris—20th century

Collier, J. Old acquaintance
Crémieux, B. The traveller
Farrell, J. T. Paris scene: 1931
Fitzgerald, F. S. K. Babylon revisited
Maugham, W. S. Appearance and reality

Provence

See France, Provincial and rural—Provence

Pyrénees-Orientales

See France, Provincial and rural—

FRANCE, PROVINCIAL AND RURAL

Becker, S. D. Baptism of some importance
Maugham, W. S. The unconquered

Avignon

Fabre, J. H. C. Story of my cats

Provence

Daudet, A. M. Seguin's goat

Pyrénees-Orientales

Collier, J. Witch's money

Franchise. Neville, K.

FRANCIS I, KING OF FRANCE, 1494-1547

Bergengruen, W. Trivulzio and the King

FRANCIS OF ASSISI, SAINT, 1182-1226

Untermeyer, L. Donkey of God

Francis, Owen, 1898-
Ladies call on Mr Pussick
Blodgett, H. W. ed. Story survey. 1953 ed.

Francis cures the leper. White, H. C.

FRANCISCANS

Powers, J. F. Lions, harts, leaping does

FRANCO-GERMAN WAR, 1870-1871

Maupassant, G. de. La Mère Sauvage

FRANCO-PRUSSIAN WAR. See Franco-German War, 1870-1871

Frank, Hans
Beyond the grave
Ungar, F. ed. To mother with love

Frank, Pat, 1908-
The madman
Argosy (Periodical) Argosy Book of adventure stories
Those wily Americans
This week magazine. This week's short-short stories

Frank, Waldo David, 1889-
Under the dome
Leftwich, J. ed. Yisröel. 1952 ed.
Same as: Under the dome: Aleph
Under the dome: Aleph
Ribalow, H. U. ed. This land, these people
Same as: Under the dome

Frank and honest. Upson, W. H.

Frank takes a brother's privilege. Trollope, A.

Frankau, Gilbert, 1884-1952
An outlier from his tribe
Leftwich, J. ed. Yisröel. 1952 ed.

Frankau, Pamela, 1908-
Jezebel covets a vineyard
Selden, R. ed. Ways of God and men

Frankenstein—unlimited. Highstone, H. A.

Frankfurt in our blood. Boyle, K.

Frankie the newspaperman. Williams, W. C.

Frankincense and myrrh. Broun, H. C.

Franklin, George Cory, 1872-
Snip; the dog that became a coyote
Harper, W. comp. Dog show

Franzos, Karl Emil, 1848-1904
Saviour of the people
Leftwich, J. ed. Yisröel. 1952 ed.
Shylock in Czernowitz
Ausubel, N. ed. Treasury of Jewish humor

FRATERNITIES. See Greek letter societies

Fraternity. McCall, M. C.

A fratricide. Kafka, F.

FRAUD

Annett, W. S. The relic
Collier, J. Sleeping Beauty
Russell, B. A. W. R. 3d earl. Infraredioscope
Stout, R. Cop's gift
See also Swindlers and swindling

Fraudulent skunk. Guthrie, A. B.

Frazee, Steve
Fire killer
Meredith, S. ed. Bar 2
Graveyard shift
Best detective stories of the year—1954
Great medicine
Meredith, S. ed. Bar 3
Luck of Riley
Western Writers of America. Holsters and heroes
Man at Gantt's Place
Meredith, S. ed. Bar 1 roundup of best western stories
My brother down there
Best American short stories, 1954
Queen, E. pseud, ed. Queen's awards: 8th ser.

The freak. Barker, A. L.

FREAKS. See Deformities

Free as the air. Keller, D. H.

Free Joe and the rest of the world. Harris, J. C.

Free man. Woods, W.

Freedman, David, 1898-1936
Mendel Marantz—genius
Ausubel, N. ed. Treasury of Jewish humor

FREEDOM. See Liberty

Freedom. O'Donovan, M.

Freedom. Sabin, E. L.

Freedom's a hard-bought thing. Benét, S. V.

Freeman, Kathleen, 1897-
Amethyst cross
Asquith, Lady C. M. E. C. ed. Book of modern ghosts
Freeman, Mary Eleanor (Wilkins) 1852-1930
The cat
Andrews, R. C. ed. My favorite stories of the great outdoors
New England nun
Burrell, J. A. and Cerf, B. A. eds. Anthology of famous American stories
Revolt of "Mother"
Cuff, R. P. ed. American short story survey
Ungar, F. ed. To mother with love
Freeman, Richard Austin, 1862-1943
Rex v. Burnaby
Bond, R. T. ed. Handbook for poisoners
FREEMASONS
Claudy, C. H. These were brethren; 24 stories
Maupassant, G. de. My uncle Sosthenes
FREETHINKERS. See Atheism
Freeze out. Coombs, C. I.
Freeze-out. Larsen, D.
Freeze the ball. Bee, C. F.
Freighted hour. Lieberman, R.
FREIGHTS AND FREIGHTERS
Stevens, J. Jerkline
French, Frank C.
Stick up
Oberfirst, R. ed. 1952 anthology of best original short-shorts
FRENCH ACADIANS. See Acadians in Louisiana
FRENCH ALPS. See Alps, French
FRENCH ARISTOCRACY. See Aristocracy—France
FRENCH COURTIERS. See Courts and courtiers—France
FRENCH GUIANA
Maugham, W. S. Man with a conscience
Maugham, W. S. Official position
FRENCH IN AFRICA
Balzac, H. de. Passion in the desert
FRENCH IN THE SOUTH SEAS
Michener, J. A. The good life
FRENCH IN THE UNITED STATES
Field, R. L. A woman of virtue
Horwitz, M. Coquette
Whitney, P. A. Lucky 'leven
FRENCH INDO-CHINA. See Indo-China, French
French Joe. Maugham, W. S.
Frere, Marie. See Frere, Mary Eliza Isabella
Frere, Mary Eliza Isabella, 1845-1911
Blind man, the deaf man, and the donkey
Fenner, P. R. comp. Fools and funny fellows
The jackal and the alligator
Fenner, P. R. comp. Fools and funny fellows
Fresh and open sky. Sullivan, R.
Fresh snow. Humphrey, W.
Freshest boy. Fitzgerald, F. S. K.

FRESNO. See California—Fresno
Freya of the Seven Isles. Conrad, J.
Friedman, Bernard Harper
As I am, you will be
Hathaway, B. and Sessions, J. A. eds. Writers for tomorrow. 2d ser.
Friedman, Stuart, 1913-
Beautiful, beautiful, beautiful!
Derleth, A. W. ed. Worlds of tomorrow
Friedman, Sylvia
Adam and Eve
American vanguard, 1950
Friend, Oscar Jerome, 1897-
Impossible highway
Jenkins, W. F. ed. Great stories of science fiction
Friend in need. Maugham, W. S.
Friend in the closet. Kesten, H.
Friend of Buck Hollister. Raine, W. M.
Friend of the family. McCarthy, M. T.
Friend of the family. Wilson, R.
Friend to man. Kornbluth, C. M.
Friendly call. Porter, W. S.
Friendly demon. Defoe, D.
FRIENDS. See Friendship
FRIENDS, SOCIETY OF
Lewis, M. Well of anger
West, J. The illumination
West, J. Shivaree before breakfast
Friends in San Rosario. Porter, W. S.
FRIENDSHIP
Aldrich, B. S. Juno's swans
Beck, W. No continuing city
Davies, R. Two friends
Galbraith, N. F. To have and to lose
Gomberg, V. G. Glaciers
Harte, B. Left out on Lone Star Mountain
Harte, B. Tennessee's partner
London, J. Shadow and the flash
Maupassant, G. de. Two friends
O'Donovan, M. A romantic
Patton, F. G. The game
Porter, W. S. After twenty years
Porter, W. S. Friendly call
Porter, W. S. Telemachus, friend
Porter, W. S. Trimmed lamp
Young, E. H. The stream
Friendship's due. Sitwell, Sir O. bart.
FRIGHT. See Fear
Frightened tree. Budrys, A. J.
Frightened wife. Rinehart, M. R.
Frischman, David, 1865?-1922
Sinai
Leftwich, J. ed. Yisröel. 1952 ed.
Frishman, David. See Frischman, David
Frison-Roche, Roger, 1906-
Their kingdom
Talbot, D. ed. Treasury of mountaineering stories
Fritz. Farrell, J. T.
Frog and the lion. Benson, T.
Frog prince. Collier, J.
FROGS
Clemens, S. L. Celebrated jumping frog of Calaveras County
Macfarlan, A. A. Bullfrog hunt

From a journal-letter of Julius Caesar. Wilder, T. N.

From a private mad-house. Repton, H.

From beyond. Lovecraft, H. P.

From each according to his ability. Porter, W. S.

From morning till night. Hutchins, M. P. M.

From my estates. Kahanovich, P.

From the cabby's seat. Porter, W. S.

From the water junction. Sansom, W.

From there to infinity. De Vries, P.

From what a Litvak makes a living. Tunkel, J.

Front-page story. Farrell, J. T.

The frontier. Bates, H. E.

FRONTIER AND PIONEER LIFE
Johnson, D. M. Indian country; 11 stories

Alabama
Vines, H. Ginsing gatherers

Illinois
Wellman, M. W. Tall Bram of Little Pigeon

Kentucky
Webber, E. M. Passage to Kentucky

Nevada
Clemens, S. L. My bloody massacre (I)
Emrich, D. ed. Comstock bonanza; 21 stories

New England
Hawthorne, N. Roger Malvin's burial

North Dakota
Wood, F. G. Turkey-red

Ohio
Bierce, A. Boarded window

The West
Schaefer, J. W. The pioneers; 11 stories

Froscher, Wingate
Death in the family
Best American short stories, 1953

Frost, Frances Mary, 1905-
Heart being perished
Certner, S. and Henry, G. H. eds. Short stories for our times

Frost, Lesley
Very mischief
Fenner, P. R. comp. Giggle box

Frost-giant's daughter. Howard, R. E.

Frozen truth. Gally, J. W.

Fru Holm. Karmel, I.

Frug, Simon Samuel, 1860-1917
Last kopeck
Ausubel, N. ed. Treasury of Jewish humor
Leftwich, J. ed. Yisröel. 1952 ed.

Fruit at the bottom of the bowl. Bradbury, R.

Fruits of toil. Duncan, N.

Frying-pan. O'Donovan, M.

Fuchs, Abraham Moses, 1890-
Among the trees
Leftwich, J. ed. Yisröel. 1952 ed.

Fugitive from the mind. Bennett, P.

FUGITIVE SLAVES. See Slavery—Fugitive slaves

FUGITIVES
Novás Calvo, L. Dark night of Ramón Yendía
Procter, M. Fox in the Pennine Hills
See also Convicts, Escaped

Fugue for harmonicas. Seager, A.

Fugue of the fig tree. Sultan, S.

Fulfillment. Van Vogt, A. E.

Full circle. Matheson, R.

Full cycle. Du Bose, V. G.

Fultz, Dessa M.
Snowshoe Thompson
Story parade (Periodical) Adventure stories

Fulvous yellow. Kauffmann, S.

FUND RAISING
Cohen, O. R. Law and the profits

Funeral feast. Benson, T.

FUNERAL RITES AND CEREMONIES
Arnow, H. L. S. Washerwoman's day
Bernstein, H. Greatest funeral in the world
Betts, D. Sense of humor
Bunner, H. C. Two churches of 'Quawket
Caldwell, E. Fly in the coffin
Clemens, S. L. Buck Fanshaw's funeral
Coolidge, O. E. Unquiet spirit
Crane, S. Upturned face
Davies, R. Human condition
Davies, R. Mourning for Ianto
Davis, S. P. Andy Munroe's funeral
Farrell, J. T. Wake of Patsy McLaughlin
Johnson, D. M. Man who shot Liberty Valance
Newhouse, E. My brother's second funeral
Sheppard, J. Black brassard
Spettigue, D. Asters for Teddie
Watson, J. Story of Dr. MacLure
Weissenberg, I. M. Mazel tov
See also Funeral orations

Jewish
Gordimer, N. Watcher of the dead
Klein, J. M. Yisgadel

FUNGI
Pratt, F. and Ruby, B. F. Thing in the woods

Fur. Munro, H. H.

Fur flies. Winslow, T. S.

FUR TRAPPERS. See Trappers

FURLOUGHS. See Soldiers—Furloughs

Furman, Lucy, 1870-
Experience on the dress line
Summers, H. S. ed. Kentucky story

FURNACES
De Vries, P. I don't want to go

Furnas, Joseph Chamberlain, 1905-
Laocoön complex
Merril, J. ed. Beyond the barriers of space and time

Furnished room. Porter, W. S.

FURNITURE. See specific articles of furniture, e.g. Sofas

Fusty Devil. Tolstoi, A. N.

Futrelle, Jacques, 1875-1912
Problem of Cell 13
  Christ, H. I. and Shostak, J. eds. Short stories

FUTURE, STORIES OF THE
Asimov, I. "In a good cause—"
Best science fiction stories: 1950; 13 stories
Bradbury, R. Forever and the earth
Bradbury, R. King of the gray spaces
Bradbury, R. The pedestrian
Bradbury, R. Referent
Bradbury, R. The wilderness
Brown, F. Crisis, 1999
Campbell, J. W. Cloak of Aesir; 7 stories
Cartmill, C. You can't say that
Clarke, A. C. Expedition to earth; 11 stories
Conklin, G. ed. Omnibus of science fiction; 42 stories
Crossen, K. F. ed. Adventures in tomorrow; 15 stories
De Camp, L. S. Continent makers, and other tales of the Viagens; 8 stories
Derleth, A. W. ed. Beachheads in space; 14 stories
Derleth, A. W. ed. Far boundaries; 20 stories
Derleth, A. W. ed. The outer reaches; 17 stories
Derleth, A. W. ed. Worlds of tomorrow; 19 stories
Fenton, F. and Petracca, J. Tolliver's travels
Frank, P. The madman
Galaxy science fiction magazine. Galaxy reader of science fiction; 33 stories
Gallery, D. V. Enemy planet
Greenberg, M. comp. Five science fiction novels; 5 stories
Greenberg, M. ed. Journey to infinity; 12 stories
Greenberg, M. ed. Men against the stars; 12 stories
Grendon, E. Crisis
Heinlein, R. A. Green hills of earth
Heinlein, R. A. Man who sold the moon; 6 stories
Huxley, A. L. Brave new world
Huxley, A. L. Education in the world state
Jameson, M. Bullard of the space patrol; 7 stories
Keller, D. H. Biological experiment
Keller, D. H. Free as the air
Kornbluth, C. M. Marching morons
Leiber, F. Moon is green
Lesser, M. A. ed. Looking forward; 20 stories
MacDonald, J. D. The miniature
Margulies, L. and Friend, O. J. eds. From off this world; 18 stories
Merril, J. Barrier of dread
Van Vogt, A. E. The seesaw
Verne, J. In the year 2889

Waugh, E. Love among the ruins
Wells, H. G. Story of the days to come
White, W. A. P. Quest for Saint Aquin
  See also Science fiction

Future captain. Carter, R. G.
FUTURE LIFE
Clemens, S. L. Wings
Milne, A. A. The balcony
Stephens, J. The threepenny-piece
  See also Heaven

FUTURE TIME. See Time
Fu-yen, Li. See Li Fu-Yen
Fuzzy things. Hitchens, D. B.
Fyfe, H. B.
Afterthought
  Merril, J. ed. Beyond human ken
Bureau of slick tricks
  Greenberg, M. ed. Travelers of space
Implode and peddle
  Norton, A. M. ed. Space service
In value deceived
  Conklin, G. ed. Possible worlds of science fiction
  Sloane, W. M. ed. Stories for tomorrow
Locked out
  Greenberg, M. ed. Men against the stars
Manners of the age
  Conklin, G. ed. Omnibus of science fiction
Moonwalk
  Norton, A. M. ed. Space pioneers
Protected species
  Astounding science fiction (Periodical)
  Astounding science fiction anthology
Ransom
  Magazine of fantasy and science fiction. Best from Fantasy and science fiction; 2d ser.
Star-linked
  Norton, A. M. ed. Space service
Well-oiled machine
  Brown, F. and Reynolds, M. eds. Science-fiction carnival

G

Gable type. Herbert, F. H.
Gabriel-Ernest. Munro, H. H.
Gabrielle de Bergerac. James, H.
Gadget had a ghost. Jenkins, W. F.
Gág, Wanda, 1893-1946
Doctor-know-it-all
  Fenner, P. R. comp. Fools and funny fellows
Gone is gone
  Fenner, P. R. comp. Fools and funny fellows
Gainfort, Phyllis, 1924-
The pact
  Wolfe, D. M. ed. Which grain will grow
Gal young un. Rawlings, M. K.
Gala programme. Munro, H. H.
Galahad, Sir
Malory, Sir T. Marvellous adventure of the sword

GALAPAGOS ISLANDS
Melville, H. The encantadas or enchanted isles
Galatians 2:20. Blackburn, E. R.
Galbraith, N. F.
To have and to lose
Oberfirst, R. ed. 1954 anthology of best original short-shorts
Gale, Zona, 1874-1938
Human
Lohan, R. and Lohan, M. eds. New Christmas treasury
GALICIA. See Poland
Gallegher plus. Kuttner, H.
Gallegos, Rómulo, 1884-
Man of character
De Onís, H. ed. Spanish stories and tales
Gallery, David Vincent, 1901-
Enemy planet
Grayson, C. ed. Fourth round
Hokey-Pocus McGee
Argosy (Periodical) Argosy Book of sports stories
Gallery-shy. Gault, W. C.
Gallico, Paul William, 1897-
The bombardier
Eaton, H. T. ed. Short stories
McKabe
Grayson, C. ed Fourth round
Man who hated people
Saturday evening post (Periodical) Saturday evening post stories, 1950
Melee of the Mages
Dachs, D. ed. Treasury of sports humor
Secret ingredient
Saturday evening post (Periodical) Saturday evening post stories, 1952
Summer dream
Bachelor, J. M.; Henry, R. L. and Salisbury, R. eds. Current thinking and writing; 2d ser.
"When in doubt—wash"
Joseph, M. ed. Best cat stories
Gallister, Michael, pseud.
Fireboat style
Bluebook (Periodical) Best sea stories from Bluebook
Galloping Foxley. Dahl, R.
Gallun, Raymond Z.
Asteroid of fear
Norton, A. M. ed. Space pioneers
Old Faithful
Bleiler, E. F. and Dikty, T. E. eds. Imagination unlimited
Operation pumice
Conklin, G. ed. Possible worlds of science fiction
Return of a legend
Norton, A. M. ed. Space service
The scarab
Conklin, G. ed. Science-fiction thinking machines
Trail blazer
Norton, A. M. ed. Space pioneers
Gally, James W. 1828-1891
Big Jack Small
Emrich, D. ed. Comstock bonanza
Frozen truth
Emrich, D. ed. Comstock bonanza

Hualapi
Emrich, D. ed. Comstock bonanza
Spirits
Emrich, D. ed. Comstock bonanza
Galsworthy, John, 1867-1933
Apple-tree
Cerf, B. A. and Moriarty, H. C. eds. Anthology of famous British stories
Scribner treasury
The juryman
Blaustein, A. P. ed. Fiction goes to court
Queen, E. pseud. ed. Literature of crime
Manna
Short, R. W. and Sewall, R. B. eds. Short stories for study. 1950 ed.
Quality
Lass, A. H. and Horowitz, A. eds. Stories for youth
Shaw, H. and Bement, D. Reading the short story
Salta pro nobis
Blodgett, H. W. ed. Story survey. 1953 ed.
Timber
Schramm, W. L. ed. Great short stories
Ultima Thule
Cooper, A. C. ed. Modern short stories
Galton whistle. De Camp, L. S.
Galway Bay. O'Flaherty, L.
GAMALIEL I
Cohn, E. Rabban Gamaliel
Gambler, the nun, and the radio, Hemingway, E.
GAMBLERS. See Gambling
Gambler's Club. Queen, E. pseud.
Gambler's sad saga. Cannon, J. J.
GAMBLING
Blackburn, E. R. Last king
Cannon, J. J. Gambler's sad saga
Collier, J. Ah the university
Collins, W. Terribly strange bed
Cooke, A. A. The Grace Mansion
Crane, S. Blue Hotel
Doty, W. L. Pittsburgh special
Fitzgerald, B. Iron maiden
Fitzgerald, F. S. K. Jelly-bean
Fox, N. A. Bet the wild queen!
Frazee, S. Luck of Riley
Harte, B. Brown of Calaveras
Harte, B. Outcasts of Poker Flat
Harte, B. Passage in the life of Mr John Oakhurst
Harte, B. Protégée of Jack Hamlin's
Lawrence, D. H. Rocking-horse winner
Maugham, W. S. Facts of life
Maugham, W. S. Raw material
Munro, H. H. The stake
Munro, H. H. Way to the dairy
Nordau, M. S. Share in the hereafter
Porter, W. S. Suite homes and their romance
Queen, E. pseud. Gambler's Club
Saroyan, W. The Assyrian
Taylor, E. Oasis of gaiety
Woodward, G. B. College marriage
See also Lotteries; Wagers
The game. Patton, F. G.

GAME AND GAME BIRDS
Buckingham, N. Remember...
Gordon, C. Last day in the field
    See also Birds; Duck shooting;
Grouse hunting; Hunting
GAME BIRDS. See Game and game birds
Game chickens. Seager, A.
Game cock. McLaverty, M.
GAME COCKS. See Roosters; Cock fight-
ing
Game for blondes. MacDonald, J. D.
Game grows hotter. Patten, G.
GAME HUNTING. See Hunting
Game in the park. Farrell, J. T.
Game of catch. Wilbur, R.
GAME PROTECTION
Buckingham, N. Bigger they come!
Buckingham, N. High sign
Buckingham, N. Tight place
Ebner von Eschenbach, M. Freifrau. Kram-
bambuli
GAMEKEEPERS. See Game protection
GAMES
Harvey, W. F. Vicar's web
Munro, H. H. Reginald's Christmas revel
Munro, H. H. The strategist
Munro, H. H. Touch of realism
GANGS
Newhouse, E. The Mentocrats
GANGSTERS
Babel', I. E. In Odessa
Babel', I. E. The King
Burnett, W. R. Dressing-up
Hemingway, E. The killers
Kirch, J. A. Murder for two
La Farge, O. The bystander
Porter, W. S. Vanity and some sables
Runyon, D. Sense of humor
Gannett, Ruth Stiles, 1923-
Some of father's adventures
    Fenner, P. R. comp. Giggle box
Gannon, S. Anna
Me and Joe
    Oberfirst, R. ed. 1954 anthology of best
original short-shorts
GARAGE WORKERS
Ferber, E. Afternoon of a faun
Fowler, B. B. Some can't take it
Jones, R. F. Tools of the trade
Garbage collector. Bradbury, R.
Garber, Gladys, 1919-
Gun on the wall
    Story (Periodical) Story; no. 2
GARDEN PARTIES
Mansfield, K. Garden-party
Munro, H. H. Boar-pig
Munro, H. H. Reginald
Garden-party. Mansfield, K.
The **gardener.** St Clair, M.
GARDENING. See Gardens and garden-
ing
GARDENS AND GARDENING
Hawthorne, N. Rappaccini's daughter
Livesay, D. Glass house
Munro, H. H. Occasional garden

Parker, J. R. Monks revel at Winkton
Steinbeck, J. The chrysanthemums
Welty, E. Curtain of green
Gardiner, Dorothy, 1894-
Not a lick of sense
    Mystery Writers of America, inc.
Crooks' tour
Gardner, Erle Stanley, 1889-
Case of the irate witness
    Best detective stories of the year—1954
    Blaustein, A. P. ed. Fiction goes to
court
Gardner, Martin, 1914-
Island of five colors
    Crossen, K. F. ed. Future tense
No-sided professor
    Magazine of fantasy and science fiction.
Best from Fantasy and science fiction;
[1st ser.]
Thang
    Bleiler, E. F. and Dikty, T. E. eds. Sci-
ence fiction omnibus: The best science
fiction stories, 1949, 1950
Gardner, Thomas S.
Last woman
    Margulies, L. and Friend, O. J. eds.
From off this world
Gardner, W. W.
Many are the brave
    Lantz, J. E. ed. Stories of Christian
living
Garland, Hamlin, 1860-1940
Mrs Ripley's trip
    Blodgett, H. W. ed. Story survey.
1953 ed.
Return of a private
    Burrell, J. A. and Cerf, B. A. eds. An-
thology of famous American stories
Under the lion's paw
    Foerster, N. ed. American poetry and
prose. 1952 ed.
Garner, Hugh, 1913-
Conversion of Willie Heaps
    Best American short stories, 1952
One mile of ice
    Weaver, R. and James, H. eds. Canadian
short stories
One, two, three little Indians
    Weaver, R. and James, H. eds. Canadian
short stories
Garrigue, Jean
The snowfall
    Swallow, A. ed. Anchor in the sea
Garrold, Richard Philip, 1874-1920
Man's hand
    Thinker's digest (Periodical) Spoiled
priest, and other stories
Garthwaite, Marion (Hook) 1893-
Riding the Pony Express
    Fenner, P. R. comp. Yankee Doodle
Gartner, John
Jug Leg Kelley
    Owen, F. ed. Teen-age winter sports
stories
Left-hand stuff
    Owen, F. ed. Teen-age winter sports
stories

Gaskell, Elizabeth Cleghorn (Stevenson)
1810-1865
Cousin Phillis
Connolly, C. ed. Great English short
novels
The half-brothers
Cerf, B. A. and Moriarty, H. C. eds.
Anthology of famous British stories
Ungar, F. ed. To mother with love
Gaspar Ruiz. Conrad, J.
Gastronomy of the Jews. Saphir, M. G.
Gates, Doris, 1901-
Seventh pup
Harper, W. comp. Dog show
Gateway to darkness. Brown, F.
Gather up the pieces. Grimson, M. S.
Gatty, Lin
Did he touch you?
Hathaway, B. and Sessions, J. A. eds.
Writers for tomorrow. 2d ser.
Gault, William Campbell
Brick road to glory
Argosy (Periodical) Argosy Book of
sports stories
Dirt-track thunder
Argosy (Periodical) Argosy Book of
sports stories
Gallery-shy
Argosy (Periodical) Argosy Book of
sports stories
Made to measure
Galaxy science fiction magazine. Galaxy
reader of science fiction
Marksman
Mystery Writers of America, inc.
Maiden murders
Thunder Road
Fenner, P. R. comp. Speed, speed, speed
Gauntlet of fire. Roberts, Sir C. G. D.
Gautier, Théophile, 1811-1872
Clarimonde
Carrington, H. ed. Week-end book of
ghost stories
Gavagan's bar. De Camp, L. S. and Pratt, F.
Gavin O'Leary. Collier, J.
Geer, Elizabeth, 1927-
Genoese street song
American vanguard, 1952
GEESE
Dunsany, E. J. M. D. P. 18th baron.
Widow Flynn's apple tree
Rosenfeld, J. Sick goose
GEHENNA. See Hell
Gehenna. Aiken, C. P.
Gehrig, Henry Louis, 1903-1941
Graham, F. Joining the Yankees
Geier, Chester S.
Environment
Conklin, G. ed. Omnibus of science fic-
tion
Gellhorn, Martha Ellis, 1908-
About Shorty
Esquire (Periodical) Girls from Esquire
Gellhorn, M. E. Honeyed peace
Café in Jaffa
Gellhorn, M. E. Honeyed peace
Exile
Gellhorn, M. E. Honeyed peace

The German
Gellhorn, M. E. Honeyed peace
Honeyed peace
Gellhorn, M. E. Honeyed peace
Miami-New York
Gellhorn, M. E. Honeyed peace
Psychiatrist of one's own
Gellhorn, M. E. Honeyed peace
Venus ascendant
Gellhorn, M. E. Honeyed peace
Voyage forme la jeunesse
Gellhorn, M. E. Honeyed peace
Weekend at Grimsby
Best American short stories, 1952
Gellhorn, M. E. Honeyed peace
Gemlike flame. Auchincloss, L.
General from the Pentagon. Chase, F.
General Pingley. Schaefer, J. W.
General Washington's pig. Hale, E. E.
GENERALS
Chase, F. General from the Pentagon
Generation of Noah. Klass, P.
Generations of man. Horwitz, J.
GENEROSITY
Goudge, E. Doing good
Generous wine. Schmitz, E.
GENETICS. See Evolution
Genial check-capped ghosts. Gilpatric, G.
GENII. See Jinn
GENIUS
Babel', I. E. Awakening
Christopher, J. Balance
France, A. Manuscript of a village doctor
Mann, T. Death in Venice
See also Children, Gifted
Genius. Anderson, P.
Genius of Strap Buckner. Ashabranner, B.
Genoese street song. Geer, E.
Gentle insurrection. Betts, D.
Gentle like a cyclone. Annett, R. R.
Gentle Masonic way. Claudy, C. H.
Gentle season. Miller, C.
Gentleman and the tiger. Marshall, E.
Gentleman from America. Arlen, M.
Gentleman from India. Ekbergh, I. D.
Gentleman from Paris. Carr, J. D.
Gentleman from San Francisco. Bunin, I. A.
Gentleman is an Epwa. Jacobi, C.
Gentlemen, be seated. Heinlein, R. A.
Gentlemen of valor. Evans, T. M.
Gentlemen—the Queen! Tucker, W.
The **gentry.** Verga, G.
Gents only. Davies, R.
GEORGE, SAINT
Grahame, K. Reluctant dragon
**GEORGE V, KING OF GREAT BRIT-
AIN,** 1865-1936
Jubilee
De La Roche, M. "Twa kings"
George, Walter Lionel, 1882-1926
Ave, amor, morituri te salutant
Leftwich, J. ed. Yisröel. 1952 ed.
George Ingram pays his debt. Hendryx, J. B.

George's mother. Crane, S.
GEORGETOWN, MARYLAND. See Maryland—Georgetown
GEORGIA
Fitzgerald, F. S. K. Jelly-bean
Fitzgerald, F. S. K. Last of the belles
Harris, J. C. Free Joe and the rest of the world
Georgia's ruling. Porter, W. S.
Gerahty, Digby George
Six months more to live
Saturday evening post (Periodical) Saturday evening post stories, 1952
The **German.** Gellhorn, M. E.
German Harry. Maugham, W. S.
GERMAN LEGENDS. See Legends and folk tales—Germany
GERMAN OFFICERS. See Germany—Army
GERMAN SOLDIERS. See Soldiers, German
GERMANS IN FRANCE
Boyle, K. Defeat
Farrell, J. T. Fritz
GERMANS IN ITALY
Mann, T. Death in Venice
Paget, V. Amour dure
GERMANS IN NETHERLANDS
Hebel, J. P. Kannitverstan
GERMANS IN NORWAY
Lyon, K. Altar cloth
GERMANS IN SWITZERLAND
Ullman, J. R. Mountains of the Axis
GERMANS IN THE UNITED STATES
Aldrich, B. S. Day of retaliation
Gellhorn, M. E. Exile
GERMANY
8th century
Van Dyke, H. First Christmas tree
14th century
Roth, C. The martyr
18th century
Auerbach, B. Hansjorg and his pipe
1918-date
Boyle, K. Smoking mountain; 11 stories
Ditzen, R. Fifty marks
Forester, C. S. The nightmare; 10 stories
Putnam, C. Old acrobat and the ruined city
Stafford, J. Winter's tale
Van Vogt, A. E. Secret unattainable
Army
Forester, C. S. Indecision
Lawrence, D. H. Prussian officer
Waltari, M. T. Before the twilight of the gods
Heidelberg
Stafford, J. The nemesis
Nuremberg
Saphir, M. G. A conquest
Gertrude and Sidney. Jarrell, R.
"**Get** a horse, comrade." Petrov, V.
Get-away boy. Sheehan, D. V.

Getting quick rich. Papashvily, G. and Papashvily, H. W.
Ghetto dog. Spiegel, I.
Ghost. Kuttner, H.
Ghost and flesh, water and dirt. Goyen, W.
Ghost-extinguisher. Burgess, G.
Ghost lode. Brandon, W.
Ghost of a chance. Porter, W. S.
Ghost of General Jackson. Moody, M. H.
Ghost of Gideon Wise. Chesterton, G. K.
Ghost of Gillin Run. Mowery, W. B.
Ghost of me. White, W. A. P.
Ghost of Sam Bates. Huckabay, M. B.
Ghost runner. Miers, E. S.
GHOST SHIPS
Poe, E. A. Ms. found in a bottle
Steele, W. D. Yellow cat
Wetjen, A. R. Ship of silence
See also Ships
GHOST STORIES. See Ghosts
Ghost-town dog. Evans, H. R.
GHOST WRITING. See Writing, Automatic
Ghostly rental. James, H.
GHOSTS
Addison, J. Vision of Mirzah
Anderson, E. V. Phantom Hall
Asquith, Lady C. M. E. C. Book of modern ghosts; 20 stories
Bergengruen, W. Pupsik
Bierce, A. Damned thing
Bowen, E. Cat jumps
Bowen, E. Demon lover
Boyd, J. Verse on the window
Buckingham, N. Cricket field
Carrington, H. ed. Week-end book of ghost stories; 20 stories
Collier, J. Are you too late or was I too early
Conklin, G. and Conklin, L. T. eds. Supernatural reader; 27 stories
Coolidge, O. E. Unquiet spirit
Davenport, B. ed. Ghostly tales to be told; 16 stories
Davenport, B. ed. Tales to be told in the dark; 13 stories
Defoe, D. Apparition of Mrs Veal
Defoe, D. True relation of the apparition of one Mrs Veal
De La Mare, W. J. All Hallows
De La Mare, W. J. Seaton's aunt
De La Mare, W. J. Strangers and pilgrims
Derleth, A. W. ed. Night's yawning peal; 15 stories
Derleth, A. W. Sheraton mirror
Dickens, C. Christmas carol
Dickens, C. The signal-man
Dunsany, E. J. M. D. P. 18th baron. The return
Fenner, P. R. comp. Ghosts, ghosts, ghosts; 15 stories
Goyen, W. Ghost and flesh; 8 stories
Hawthorne, N. Gray champion
Irving, W. Legend of Sleepy Hollow
James, H. Ghostly rental
James, H. Jolly corner
Jealousy
Kipling, R. 'They'

GHOSTS—*Continued*
Kleist, H. von. Beggar-woman of Locarno
Kuttner, H. Ghost
Lytton, E. G. E. L. B-L. 1st baron. House and the brain
Maugham, W. S. Man from Glasgow
Merochnik, M. Influence
Miers, E. S. Ghost runner
Munby, A. N. L. Alabaster hand and other stories; 14 stories
Munro, H. H. The hedgehog
Munro, H. H. Laura
Paget, V. Wicked voice
Poe, E. A. King Pest
Porter, W. S. Ghost of a chance
Priestley, J. B. Uncle Phil on TV
P'u Sung-ling. Jojo
Quiller-Couch, Sir A. T. Roll-call of the reef
Sansom, W. Saving grace
Steele, W. D. Can't cross Jordan by myself
Stevenson, R. L. Thrawn Janet
Tucker, W. Tourist trade
Van Doren, M. The key
Van Doren, M. No thunder, no lightning
Van Doren, M. Twentieth floor
Van Doren, M. Witch of Ramoth
Wells, H. G. Inexperienced ghost
Weston, C. G. Man in gray
Wharton, E. N. J. The lady's maid's bell
Winslow, T. S. Rudolph
    See also Hallucinations and illusions; Supernatural phenomena

Ghost's shoes. Brenner, L.

GI story. Queen, E. pseud.

Giant Finn MacCool. Ready, W. B.

Giant killer. Chandler, A. B.

GIANTS
Blish, J. Beanstalk
Chandler, A. B. Giant killer

GIBBONS
Annixter, P. pseud. With the greatest of ease

Gibbs, Angelica
The test
    Lass, A. H. and Horowitz, A. eds. Stories for youth

Gibbs, Sir Philip Hamilton, 1877-
Stranger in the village
    Cerf, B. A. and Moriarty, H. C. eds. Anthology of famous British stories

Gibran, Kahlil, 1886-1931
Ambitious violet
    Gibran, K. Treasury of Kahlil Gibran
Ashes of the ages and eternal fire
    Gibran, K. Treasury of Kahlil Gibran
Before the throne of beauty
    Gibran, K. Treasury of Kahlil Gibran
Behind the garment
    Gibran, K. Treasury of Kahlil Gibran
Bride's bed
    Gibran, K. Treasury of Kahlil Gibran
City of the dead
    Gibran, K. Treasury of Kahlil Gibran
The criminal
    Gibran, K. Treasury of Kahlil Gibran
Cry of the graves
    Gibran, K. Treasury of Kahlil Gibran

Eventide of the feast
    Gibran, K. Treasury of Kahlil Gibran
Grave digger
    Gibran, K. Treasury of Kahlil Gibran
Honeyed poison
    Gibran, K. Treasury of Kahlil Gibran
John the madman
    Gibran, K. Treasury of Kahlil Gibran
Khalil the heretic
    Gibran, K. Treasury of Kahlil Gibran
Last supper
    Selden, R. ed. Ways of God and men
Lonely poet
    Gibran, K. Treasury of Kahlil Gibran
Madame Rose Hanie
    Gibran, K. Treasury of Kahlil Gibran
The mermaids
    Gibran, K. Treasury of Kahlil Gibran
Rafca, the bride of Cana
    Brentano, F. ed. The word lives on
Satan
    Gibran, K. Treasury of Kahlil Gibran
Secrets of the heart
    Gibran, K. Treasury of Kahlil Gibran
The tempest
    Gibran, K. Treasury of Kahlil Gibran
Two infants
    Gibran, K. Treasury of Kahlil Gibran
Two wishes
    Gibran, K. Treasury of Kahlil Gibran
Widow and her son
    Gibran, K. Treasury of Kahlil Gibran
Yesterday and today
    Gibran, K. Treasury of Kahlil Gibran

Gidé, Andre Paul Guillaume, 1869-1951
My mother
    Neider, C. ed. Great short stories from the world's literature
Theseus
    Geist, S. ed. French stories and tales
The gift
    Ausubel, N. ed. Treasury of Jewish humor

The gift. Steinbeck, J.

The gift. Tunkel, J.

Gift for a birthday. Levine, S.

Gift of Cochise. L'Amour, L.

Gift of God. Pratt, F. and De Camp, L. S.

Gift of love. Jackson, D. V. S.

Gift of the emperor. Katz, L.

Gift of the Magi. Porter, W. S.

Gift of the wise man. Eggleston, M. W.

GIFTED CHILDREN. See Children, Gifted

GIFTS
Clemens, S. L. Man that corrupted Hadleyburg
Gordimer, N. Present for a good girl
Munro, H. H. "Down pens"
Munro, H. H. Fur
Munro, H. H. Reginald on Christmas presents
Robinson, F. M. Santa Claus planet

Gigolo and gigolette. Maugham, W. S.

Gilbert, Kenneth, 1889-
Jungle brothers
    American boy (Periodical) American boy Adventure stories

Gilbert, Kenneth—*Continued*
Old man of the mountains
American boy (Periodical) American boy
Adventure stories
Pool of adventure
American boy (Periodical) American boy
Anthology

Gilbert, Michael Frances, 1912-
Modus operandi
Mystery Writers of America, inc.
Butcher, baker, murder-maker
Source seven
Mystery Writers of America, inc.
Crooks' tour

Gilbert, Nan, pseud. See Gilbertson, Mildred
Geiger

Gilbertson, Mildred Geiger
Christmas in Carthage
American girl (Periodical) Christmas all
year 'round
American girl (Periodical) On my honor

**Gilbreth, Frank Bunker, 1911- and Carey,
Ernestine Moller (Gilbreth) 1908-**
Orphans in uniform
Fenner, P. R. comp. Fun! Fun! Fun!
Pygmalion
McFarland, W. K. comp. Then it hap-
pened

Gilford, C. B.
Heaven can wait
Queen, E. pseud, ed. Queen's awards:
8th ser.

Gill, Brendan, 1914-
The knife
Gable, M. Sister, ed. Many-colored fleece
Night bus to Atlanta
Esquire (Periodical) Girls from Esquire

Gill, Tom, 1891-
Jungle war
Fremantle, A. J. ed. Mothers

**Gilman, Charlotte (Perkins) Stetson, 1860-
1935**
Yellow wall-paper
Davenport, B. ed. Ghostly tales to be
told

Gilmour, William, 1924?-
Danny Hagan's blind spot
American vanguard, 1950

Gilpatric, Guy, 1896-1950
Artful Mr Glencannon
Gilpatric, G. Last Glencannon omnibus
Crocodile tears
Gilpatric, G. Last Glencannon omnibus
Genial check-capped ghosts
Jensen, P. ed. Fireside book of flying
stories
Glasgow fantom
Gilpatric, G. Last Glencannon omnibus
Glencannon collection
Gilpatric, G. Last Glencannon omnibus
Home stretch
Gilpatric, G. Last Glencannon omnibus
Masked monster
Gilpatric, G. Last Glencannon omnibus
Mr Glencannon and the ailing cockroach
Gilpatric, G. Last Glencannon omnibus
Monkey business at Gibraltar
Gilpatric, G. Last Glencannon omnibus
Souse of the border
Gilpatric, G. Last Glencannon omnibus
Where early fa's the dew
Gilpatric, G. Last Glencannon omnibus
Wing walker
Jensen, P. ed. Fireside book of flying
stories

Gilpatrick, Elsie
Concrete experience
Oberfirst, R. ed. 1952 anthology of best
original short-shorts

Gimpel the fool. Singer, I. B.

Gin comes in bottles. Pratt, F. and De
Camp, L. S.

Gingerbread. Wahl, B.

Ginsing gatherers. Vines, H.

Gioconda smile. Huxley, A. L.

Giono, Jean, 1895-
Corn dies
Short, R. W. and Sewall, R. B. eds.
Short stories for study. 1950 ed.

Giorgio and Martino. Bergengruen, W.

GIPSIES
Alarcón, P. A. de. The prophecy
Mulhoffer, D. B. Last year

Gipson, Fred Benjamin, 1908-
My kind of a man
Peery, W. W. ed. 21 Texas short sto-
ries

"Girl." Porter, W. S.

The **girl.** Shneur, Z.

Girl and the graft. Porter, W. S.

Girl and the habit. Porter, W. S.

Girl called Peter. Bates, H. E.

Girl Ellen. Caldwell, E.

Girl in the golden atom. Cummings, R.

Girl next door. Sullivan, R.

Girl on horseback. Ullman, J. R.

Girl on the bus. Sansom, W.

Girl on the lake. Roberts, D.

Girl overboard. Quentin, P. pseud.

Girl who had to get married. Newhouse, E.

Girl who married a monster. White,
W. A. P.

Girl who wasn't wanted. McNeil, S.

Girl with a pimply face. Williams, W. C.

Girl with the flaxen hair. Grau, S. A.

GIRLS
Aldrich, B. S. How far is it to Hollywood?
Aldrich, B. S. Juno's swans
American girl (Periodical) Favorite sto-
ries; 21 stories
American girl (Periodical) On my honor;
20 stories
Gustafson, R. The pigeon
Harte, B. M'liss
McFarland, W. K. comp. Then it hap-
pened; 21 stories
Parker, J. R. Katrina
Quentin, P. pseud. Witness for the pros-
ecution
Sansom, W. Something terrible, some-
thing lovely
Schwartz, R. A. Shoes of bright green
leather
Stowe, A. comp. It's a date; 10 stories
See also Brothers and sisters; Chil-
dren; Parent and child

Girls are so helpless. Bennett, S.
Girls at the Sphinx. Farrell, J. T.
GIRLS' CLUBS
  Doty, W. L. Father Murray's first failure
Girls from Earth. Robinson, F. M.
Girls in black. Winslow, T. S.
Gissing, George, 1857-1903
  Pig and whistle
    Blodgett, H. W. ed. Story survey.
    1953 ed.
Git along. De Camp, L. S.
'Git or git got.' Wolfert, I.
Giulia Lazzari. Maugham, W. S.
Give my love to Maggie. Van Ness, L.
Given years. Cohn, E.
Gizycka, Felicia, 1905-
  Forever Florida
    Story (Periodical) Story; no. 3
Gizzard of a scientist. Boyd, J.
GLACIERS
  Muir, J. An adventure with a dog and a
    glacier
Glaciers. Gomberg, V. G.
GLADNESS. See Happiness
The glads. Powell, D.
GLANDERS (DISEASE)
  Pirandello, L. The fly
Glasgow fantom. Gilpatric, G.
Glaspell, Susan, 1882-1948
  Jury of her peers
    Burrell, J. A. and Cerf, B. A. eds.
    Anthology of famous American stories
Glass boy. Summers, J. L.
Glass eye. Russell, E. F.
Glass house. Livesay, D.
Glass of milk. Rojas, M.
Glass of orange juice. Reynolds, Q. J.
Glass of tea. Tunkel, J.
Glass wall. Lincoln, V. E.
Glassman, Baruch, 1893-
  Tarnished gold
    Leftwich, J. ed. Yisröel. 1952 ed.
Glatstein, Jacob, 1896-
  The return
    Howe, I. and Greenberg, E. eds. Treas-
    ury of Yiddish stories
Gleeb for earth. Schafhauser, C.
Gleeps. Miller, P. S.
Glemser, Bernard, 1908-
  Purple fields
    Star science fiction stories, no. 2
Glen, Enid
  Always good for a belly laugh
    Best American short stories, 1952
Glen, Mary Avery
  Comfort and joy
    American girl (Periodical) Christmas all
    year 'round
GLIDERS (AERONAUTICS)
  Coombs, C. I. Silent wings
  Hallstead, W. F. Thunder and the wise
    guy
Gliding gulfs and going people. Sansom, W.
The "Gloria Scott." Doyle, Sir A. C.

Glory, glory, hallelujah. Foley, M.
GLOVES
  Ekbergh, I. D. White silk gloves
Glow-worm. Sitwell, Sir O. bart.
Glückel of Hamelin. See Hameln, Glückel of
Gnome there was. Kuttner, H.
GNOMES. See Fairies
Gnurrs come from the voodvork out. Bret-
  nor, R.
Go to the ant. Doyle, L.
GOATS
  Caldwell, E. My old man
  Daudet, A. M. Seguin's goat
  Hinton, J. Mediators to the goatherd
  Kilcrin, I. Star buck
  O'Flaherty, L. Wild goat's kid
  Stong, P. D. Censored, the goat
  Tolstoï, A. N. Graf. Fusty Devil
    See also Rocky Mountain goats
Gobineau, Joseph Arthur, comte de, 1816-
  1882
  Red handkerchief
    Geist, S. ed. French stories and tales
GOBLINS. See Fairies
GOD
  Brown, F. Search
  De Quincey, T. Savannah-la-mar
  Horowitz, E. God's agents have beards
  Lagerkvist, P. F. Paradise
  Rilke, R. M. The stranger
  Temple, W. F. Forget-me-not
God. Zamiatin, E. I.
God and Daphne. Kneale, N.
God and the angry men. Johnston, N. F.
God and the little cat. Jepson, S.
God has no wife. Van Doren, M.
God hit a home run. Fontaine, R. L.
God in the bowl. Howard, R. E.
God is good to a Jew. Hecht, B.
God of the gongs. Chesterton, G. K.
God wheel. Keller, D. H.
Godchaux, Elma, d. 1941
  Horn that called Bambine
    Southern review. Anthology of stories
    from the Southern review
Godfrey, Peter
  Lady and the dragon
    Queen, E. pseud. ed. Queen's awards:
    5th ser.
GODS
  Beaconsfield, B. D. 1st earl of. Ixion in
    heaven
God's agents have beards. Horowitz, E.
Gods in exile. Heine, H.
God's little traveling salesman. Lagerkvist,
  P. F.
Godwin, Francis, Bp. of Hereford, 1562-1633
  Man in the moone
    Derleth, A. W. ed. Beyond time & space
Goethe, Johann Wolfgang von, 1749-1832
  Sorrows of Young Werther
    Lange, V. ed. Great German short
    novels and stories

        About
  Bergengruen, W. On presenting arms

Gogol', Nikolaĭ Vasil'evich, 1809-1852
Old-world landowners
Gordon, C. and Tate, A. eds. House of fiction
The overcoat
Rahv, P. ed. Great Russian short novels
Goin' to town. Stegner, W. E.
Going home. Goodwin, R. V.
Gold, Herbert, 1924-
Mirror and Mr Sneeves
Story (Periodical) Story; no. 3
The witch
Prize stories, 1954
Gold, Horace L.
Man with English
Star science fiction stories ₍no. 1₎
Matter of form
Conklin, G. ed. Big book of science fiction
Pohl, F. ed. Assignment in tomorrow
Perfect murder
Conklin, G. ed. Science-fiction adventures in dimension
Gold, Horace L. and Krepps, Robert Wilson, 1919-
Enormous room
Year's best science fiction novels, 1954
Gold, Ivan, 1932-
Change of air
Best American short stories, 1954
Gold, Michael, 1894-
Mushrooms in Bronx Park
Ausubel, N. ed. Treasury of Jewish humor
Sam Kravitz, that thief
Ausubel, N. ed. Treasury of Jewish humor
Gold, Zachary
Spring over Brooklyn
Stauffer, R. M.; Cunningham, W. H. and Sullivan, C. J. eds. Adventures in modern literature
The **gold** bug. Poe, E. A.
Gold-fever. Caldwell, E.
Gold mine in the sky. Williams, H. L.
GOLD MINES AND MINING
Davis, A. L. The Klondiker
London, J. All-gold cañon
London, J. Too much gold
Mowery, W. B. Long shadow
See also Mines and mining
Gold of Caxamalca. Wassermann, J.
Gold that glittered. Porter, W. S.
Golden apples of the sun. Bradbury, R.
Golden arm. Jacobs, J.
Golden bough. Keller, D. H.
Golden egg. Waldo, E. H.
Golden fish. Benson, T.
Golden honeymoon. Lardner, R. W.
Golden kite, the silver wind. Bradbury, R.
Golden land. Faulkner, W.
Golden man. Dick, P. K.
Golden pitcher. Gunterman, B. L.
Golden pot. Hoffmann, E. T. A.
Golden wedding. Suckow, R.
Goldfish bowl. Faggett, H. L.

Goldilocks. Waltari, M. T.
Golding, Louis, 1895-
Angels in Chayder
Ausubel, N. ed. Treasury of Jewish humor
Doomington wanderer
Leftwich, J. ed. Yisröel. 1952 ed.
Goldman, Alvin, 1927-
Almost like dead
Weaver, R. and James, H. eds. Canadian short stories
Goldsmith, Gloria, 1925-
Tender to the ship
American vanguard, 1953
Goldsmith, Oliver, 1728-1774
Asem
Cerf, B. A. and Moriarty, H. C. eds. Anthology of famous British stories
Disabled soldier
Ludwig, J. B. and Poirier, W. R. eds. Stories, British and American
Neider, C. ed. Great short stories from the world's literature
Goldsmith, Ruth M. 1919-
Yankee exodus
Best science-fiction stories: 1954
Goldstone, H.
Virtuoso
Conklin, G. ed. Science-fiction thinking machines
The **golem.** Peretz, I. L.
GOLF
Bond, N. S. Steady like a rock
Field, S. S. Good-by to Cap'm John
Gault, W. C. Gallery-shy
Miers, E. S. Skeedunk Special
Person, W. T. Pony Porter swing
Train, A. Mr Tutt collects a bet
Van Loan, C. Cure for lumbago
Gomberg, Vladimïr Germanovich, 1894-
Glaciers
Talbot, D. ed. Treasury of mountaineering stories
Gomez. Kornbluth, C. M.
GONDOLIERS
Sansom, W. Miss Haines and the gondolier
Gone is gone. Gág, W.
Gonzalez, N. V. M.
Morning star
Stanford short stories, 1950
Warm hand
Stanford short stories, 1950
Good, Edward, 1885-
Salt for the soul
Leftwich, J. ed. Yisröel. 1952 ed.
GOOD AND EVIL
Hawthorne, N. Great Stone Face
Hawthorne, N. Young Goodman Brown
Maugham, W. S. Judgment seat
O'Donovan, M. Face of evil
Russell, B. A. W. R. 3d earl. Satan in the suburbs
Stevenson, R. L. Markheim
Good Anna. Stein, G.
Good boy. De Vries, P.
Good-by, Debbie. McDowell, D.
Good-by to Cap'm John. Field, S. S.

Good-by to Miss Stoddard's. Pultz, C.
Good dog forward. Banér, S. V.
Good girl. Dell'Archiprete, R.
"**Good** girl—forward!" Banér, S. V.
Good kid. Barr, J. pseud.
The **good** life. Michener, J. A.
Good marriage. Haycox, E.
Good-natured slob. Williams, W. C.
Good news. Chekhov, A. P.
Good night, Mr James. Simak, C. D.
Good old days. Williams, W. C.
Good people of Milton. Schwartz, R. H.
Good provider. Gross, M.
Good river. Buck, P. S.
GOOD SAMARITAN (PARABLE)
  Goudge, E. Doing good
Good thing to know. Van Doren, M
Good Wednesday. Brush, K. I.
Good-willer. Plumb, B.
Good win. Blackburn, E. R.
Goodbye forever. Rice, C.
Good-bye, Ilha! Manning, L.
Goodbye, my brother. Cheever, J.
Goodloe, Abbie Carter, 1867-
  Claustrophobia
    Thinker's digest (Periodical) Spoiled
    priest, and other stories
Goodly creatures. Kornbluth, C. M.
Goodman, J. Carol
  Kingdom of Gordon
    Best American short stories, 1951
Goodman, Joseph T. 1838-1917
  "Trumpet" comes to Pickeye!
    Emrich, D. ed. Comstock bonanza
Goodman, Paul, 1916-
  Iddings Clark
    Horizon (Periodical) Golden Horizon
  Memorial synagogue
    Ribalow, H. U. ed. This land, these
    people
Goodridge Roberts, Theodore, 1877-1953
  White wolf
    Pacey, D. ed. Book of Canadian stories
Goodwin, Ruth V.
  Going home
    Abell, E. ed. American accent
GOOSE. See Geese
Goose and the gander. Cooke, A. A.
Gooseberries. Chekhov, A. P.
GOPHERS
  Howarth, J. The novitiate
Gordimer, Nadine
  Ah, woe is me
    Gordimer, N. Soft voice of the serpent,
    and other stories
  The amateurs
    Gordimer, N. Soft voice of the serpent,
    and other stories
  Another part of the sky
    Gordimer, N. Soft voice of the serpent,
    and other stories
  The catch
    Gordimer, N. Soft voice of the serpent,
    and other stories

  Commonplace story
    Gordimer, N. Soft voice of the serpent,
    and other stories
  The defeated
    Gordimer, N. Soft voice of the serpent,
    and other stories
  End of the tunnel
    Gordimer, N. Soft voice of the serpent,
    and other stories
  Hour and the years
    Gordimer, N. Soft voice of the serpent,
    and other stories
  In the beginning
    Gordimer, N. Soft voice of the serpent,
    and other stories
  Is there nowhere else where we can meet?
    Gordimer, N. Soft voice of the serpent,
    and other stories
  Kindest thing to do
    Gordimer, N. Soft voice of the serpent,
    and other stories
  Monday is better than Sunday
    Gordimer, N. Soft voice of the serpent,
    and other stories
  Present for a good girl
    Gordimer, N. Soft voice of the serpent,
    and other stories
  The prisoner
    Gordimer, N. Soft voice of the serpent,
    and other stories
  Soft voice of the serpent
    Gordimer, N. Soft voice of the serpent,
    and other stories
  The talisman
    Gordimer, N. Soft voice of the serpent,
    and other stories
  Train from Rhodesia
    Gordimer, N. Soft voice of the serpent,
    and other stories
  Treasures of the sea
    Gordimer, N. Soft voice of the serpent,
    and other stories
  Umbilical cord
    Gordimer, N. Soft voice of the serpent,
    and other stories
  La vie Bohème
    Gordimer, N. Soft voice of the serpent,
    and other stories
  Watcher of the dead
    Gordimer, N. Soft voice of the serpent,
    and other stories
Gordon, Arthur, 1912-
  Alchemist's secret
    This week magazine. This week's short-
    short stories
  Devil and Father Francisco
    This week magazine. This week's short-
    short stories
  Kiss for the Lieutenant
    This week magazine. This week's short-
    short stories
  Old Ironpuss
    Saturday evening post (Periodical)
    Saturday evening post stories, 1951
  Sea devil
    Saturday evening post (Periodical)
    Saturday evening post stories, 1953
Gordon, Caroline, 1895-
  The captive
    Lynskey, W. C. ed. Reading modern
    fiction

Gordan, Caroline—*Continued*
  Forest of the South
    Jones, K. M. ed. New Confederate short
      stories
  Her quaint honour
    West, R. B. and Stallman, R. W. eds.
      Art of modern fiction
  Last day in the field
    Heilman, R. B. ed. Modern short sto-
      ries
  Old Red
    Summers, H. S. ed. Kentucky story
Gordon, Charles Monroe, 1857-1946
  Christmas Eve in a lumber camp
    Elmquist, R. M. ed. Fifty years of
      Christmas
Gordon, Charles William, 1860-1937
  The canyon flowers
    Brentano, F. ed. The word lives on
Gordon, Ethel (Edison)
  Value of the dollar
    Best American short stories, 1951
Gorge of the Churels. Wakefield, H. R.
Gorgeous number. Newhouse, E.
GORILLAS
  Collier, J. Variation on a theme
Gorki, Maxim, pseud. See Gorky, Maxim
Gorky, Maxim, 1868-1936
  Birth of a man
    Fremantle, A. J. ed. Mothers
  Might of motherhood
    Ungar, F. ed. To mother with love
  On the way
    Guerney, B. G. comp. New Russian
      stories
  One autumn night
    Blodgett, H. W. ed. Story survey.
      1953 ed.
    Short, R. W. and Sewall, R. B. eds.
      Short stories for study. 1950 ed.
  Twenty-six and one
    Cody, S. ed. Greatest stories and how
      they were written
Gorska, Halina, d. 1943
  Prince Godfrey frees mountain dwellers
    and little shepherds from a savage
    werewolf and from witches
    Fenner, P. R. comp. Ghosts, ghosts,
      ghosts
Goss, John Mayo, 1892-
  Bird song
    First-prize stories, 1919-1954
GOSSIP
  Brush, K. I. Good Wednesday
  Hawthorne, N. Mr Higginbotham's catas-
    trophe
  Welty, E. Petrified man
Gostak and the doshes. Breuer, M. J.
Goudge, Elizabeth, 1900-
  By the waters of Babylon
    Goudge, E. Reward of faith
  Canticle of the sun
    Goudge, E. Reward of faith
  Doing good
    Brentano, F. ed. The word lives on
  Icon on the wall
    Goudge, E. Reward of faith
  Legend of the first Christmas tree
    Goudge, E. Reward of faith
  Midnight in the stable
    Lohan, R. and Lohan, M. eds. New
      Christmas treasury
  Reward of faith
    Goudge, E. Reward of faith
  Son-of-David
    Goudge, E. Reward of faith
  Three gray men
    Goudge, E. Reward of faith
  Well of the star
    Goudge, E. Reward of faith
Goudsmit, Samuel, 1884-
  Romantic boy
    Leftwich, J. ed. Yisröel. 1952 ed.
GOVERNESSES
  Birmingham, S. G. Reappearance
  Maugham, W. S. String of beads
GOVERNMENT EMPLOYEES. See Civil
  service
Governor Warburton's right-hand man.
  Stuart, J.
Goyen, William, 1918-
  Children of Old Somebody
    Goyen, W. Ghost and flesh
  Ghost and flesh, water and dirt
    Goyen, W. Ghost and flesh
  Grasshopper's burden
    Goyen, W. Ghost and flesh
  Her breath upon the windowpane
    Best American short stories, 1951
    Peery, W. W. ed. 21 Texas short stories
  Letter in the cedarchest
    Goyen, W. Ghost and flesh
  Nests in a stone image
    Goyen, W. Ghost and flesh
  Pore Perrie
    Goyen, W. Ghost and flesh
  Shape of light
    Goyen, W. Ghost and flesh
  White rooster
    Goyen, W. Ghost and flesh
    Ludwig, J. B. and Poirier, W. R. eds.
      Stories, British and American
Grace, Skinner, 1922-
  Nice little girl
    Wolfe, D. M. ed. Which grain will grow
Grace Crawley and the Archdeacon. Trol-
  lope, A.
The **Grace** Mansion. Cooke, A. A.
GRACES. See Prayers
Grade, Chaim, 1910-
  My quarrel with Hersh Rasseyner
    Howe, I. and Greenberg, E. eds. Treas-
      ury of Yiddish stories
GRADUATIONS. See Commencements
Graham, Frank, 1893-
  Joining the Yankees
    Fenner, P. R. comp. Crack of the bat
Graham, Margaret (Collier) 1850-1910
  Face of the poor
    Cooper, A. C. ed. Modern short stories
Graham, Robert Bontine Cunninghame,
  1852-1936
  Faith
    Cerf, B. A. and Moriarty, H. C. eds.
      Anthology of famous British stories
Grahame, Kenneth, 1859-1932
  Reluctant dragon
    Fenner, P. R. comp. Fun! Fun! Fun!

GRAMOPHONE. See Phonograph

The gramophone. Wendroff, Z.

GRANADA. See Spain—Granada

Granberg, Bill
  Hi, sailor!
    Fenner, P. R. comp. Stories of the sea

Granberry, Edwin Phillips, 1897-
  Trip to Czardis
    Blodgett, H. W. ed. Story survey.
      1953 ed.
    Shaw, H. and Bement, D. Reading the
      short story

Grand march. Powell, D.

Grand prize. Newcomb, C.

GRANDCHILDREN
  Betts, D. Child so fair

GRANDFATHERS
  Beck, W. Verdict of innocence
  Clay, R. Very sharp for jagging
  Cohn, E. A. The present
  Dell, F. The blanket
  Goyen, W. White rooster
  Jenkins, W. F. Little terror
  Newell, A. S. Grandpop comes home
  Overholser, W. D. Patriarch of Gunsight
    Flat
  Rinehart, M. R. One hour of glory
  Steinbeck, J. Leader of the people
  Van Doren, M. The pair
  Van Doren, M. Wild wet place

Grandfather's tale. Schneider, G. W.

Grandison and son. Van Doren, M.

Grandma. Winslow, T. S.

Grandma goes to the Fair. Grimson, M. S.

GRANDMOTHERS
  Aiken, C. P. Last visit
  Grimson, M. S. Grandma goes to the Fair
  Kensinger, F. R. Sense of destination
  O'Donovan, M. First confession
  Pendergast, C. The picnic
  Poe, E. A. The spectacles
  Riter, F. Sense of destination
  Somerville, E. A. Œ. and Martin, V. F.
    Trinket's colt
  Van Doren, M. Wild wet place
  Winslow, T. S. Grandma
  Winslow, T. S. Odd old lady

GRANDPARENTS. See Grandfathers;
  Grandmothers

Grandpop comes home. Newell, A. S.

Grant, George Hook, 1896-
  The hurricane
    Bluebook (Periodical) Best sea stories
      from Bluebook

Grass fire. Caldwell, E.

Grass grow again. Wilson, J. W.

Grass, milk, and children. Bishop, L.

Grass on the other side. Smith, L.

Grasshopper a burden. Thompson, L.

Grasshopper's burden. Goyen, W.

GRATITUDE
  Schwarz, F. C. Serpent's tooth
  Shaw, I. Faith at sea

Grau, Shirley Ann
  Black prince
    Grau, S. A. Black prince, and other
      stories

Bright day
  Grau, S. A. Black prince, and other
    stories
Fever flower
  Grau, S. A. Black prince, and other
    stories
Girl with the flaxen hair
  Grau, S. A. Black prince, and other
    stories
Joshua
  Grau, S. A. Black prince, and other
    stories
Miss Yellow Eyes
  Grau, S. A. Black prince, and other
    stories
One summer
  Grau, S. A. Black prince, and other
    stories
Way of a man
  Grau, S. A. Black prince, and other
    stories
White girl, fine girl
  Grau, S. A. Black prince, and other
    stories

The grave. Porter, K. A.

Grave digger. Gibran, K.

Grave digger and Biggie Doone. Brookhouser, F.

GRAVE ROBBERS
  Coolidge, O. E. Black magician

GRAVEDIGGERS
  Farrell, J. T. Digging our own graves

Graves, Robert, 1895-
  The shout
    Magazine of fantasy and science fiction.
      Best from Fantasy and science fiction;
      2d ser.

GRAVES. See Cemeteries; Funeral rites
  and ceremonies

Graveyard shift. Frazee, S.

GRAVEYARDS. See Cemeteries

GRAVITY
  Clifton, M. and Apostolides, A. What thin
    partitions
  Cummings, R. Gravity professor
  Jones, R. F. Noise level

Gravity professor. Cummings, R.

Gray, Clark
  Campaigning cowpoke
    Meredith, S. ed. Bar 1 roundup of best
      western stories

Gray, David, 1870-
  His first race
    Creamer, J. B. comp. Twenty-two
      stories about horses and men
  Ting-a-ling
    Creamer, J. B. comp. Twenty-two
      stories about horses and men

Gray, Elizabeth Janet, 1902-
  Christmas cherries
    Story parade (Periodical) Adventure
      stories

Gray, Will H.
  Bees from Borneo
    Conklin, G. ed. Omnibus of science fic-
      tion

Gray champion. Hawthorne, N.

Gray goose. Steele, W. D.

Gray sleeve. Crane, S.
Grayson, David, pseud. See Baker, Ray
  Stannard
Great Agra treasure. Doyle, Sir A. C.
Great automatic grammatisator. Dahl, R.
GREAT BRITAIN
  See also England; Ireland; Scotland

Army

Betting Scotchman
Irwin, M. E. F. Country gentleman
Kipling, R. Drums of the fore and aft
Kipling, R. Man who was
Swinton, A. A brotherhood
Ullman, J. R. Diversion

Invasions

See England—Invasions

Navy

Divine, A. D. Thirty minutes to zero
Melville, H. Billy Budd, foretopman

Royal Air Force

Stanley, J. B. Matter of spelling
Great cold. Long, F. B.
Great day. Sargeson, F.
Great deal of weather. Van Doren, M.
Great disciple. Ready, W. B.
Great engine. Van Vogt, A. E.
Great façade. Bromfield, L.
Great fire. Bradbury, R.
Great fog. Heard, G.
Great good place. James, H.
GREAT GRANDMOTHERS
  Angoff, C. Alte Bobbe
Great judge. Van Vogt, A. E.
Great King Kelly. Davies, V.
Great lady. Bentley, P. E.
Great match. Bruhl, É.
Great medicine. Frazee, S.
Great pancake record. Johnson, O. M.
Great possibilities. Collier, J.
Great reckoning in a little room. Bush, G.
Great run. Tregarthen, J. C.
Great run with the F.H.H. Surtees, R. S.
Great Stefan Konecki. Rudnicki, A.
Great Stone Face. Hawthorne, N.
GREAT WALL OF CHINA
  Kafka, F. Great wall of China
Great whirring of wings. Keene, D.
Great wide world over there. Bradbury, R.
Great world and Timothy Colt. Auchin-
  closs, L.
Greater Coney. Porter, W. S.
Greater love. Winston, H.
Greater love hath no man than this. Claudy,
  C. H.
Greatest funeral in the world. Bernstein, H.
Greatest man in the world. Thurber, J.
Greatest poem ever written. Brown, F.
Greatest Tertian. White, W. A. P.
Greatest victory. O'Rourke, F.

Grebanier, Bernard David N. 1903-
  Life began today
    Story (Periodical) Story; no. 2
Greco, Emily
  Real friend
    American vanguard, 1952
GREECE
  Mitchison, N. M. H. Take back your bay
    wreath

Athens

Miller, P. S. Status quondam
GREED. See Misers
Greek interpreter. Doyle, Sir A. C.
GREEK LETTER SOCIETIES
  Beck, W. All brothers are men
  De Camp, L. S. The inspector's teeth
  Hogan, A. Sorority
GREEKS IN THE UNITED STATES
  Kantor, M. That Greek dog
Green, Anna Katharine, 1846-1935
  The doctor, his wife, and the clock
    Cuff, R. P. ed. American short story
    survey
Green, H. Gordon, 1912-
  Man who waved the flag
    Lantz, J. E. ed. Stories of Christian
    living
Green, Henry, pseud.
  Mr Jonas
    New writing (Periodical) Best stories
Green-and-gold string. MacDonald, P.
Green bough. Austin, M.
Green cat. Cartmill, C.
Green door. Porter, W. S.
Green hills of earth. Heinlein, R. A.
Green man. Chesterton, G. K.
Green match. Long, E. W.
Green tendrils. Van Luik, C.
Green thoughts. Collier, J.
Green thumb. Pratt, F. and De Camp, L. S.
Green torture. Hilliard, A. R.
Greene, Frederick Stuart, 1870-
  Bunker Mouse
    Thinker's digest (Periodical) Spoiled
    priest, and other stories
Greene, Graham, 1904-
  Basement room
    Heilman, R. B. ed. Modern short sto-
    ries
    Schorer, M. ed. The story
  Hint of an explanation
    Burnett, W. ed. World's best
    Gable, M. Sister, ed. Many-colored
    fleece
  Men at work
    New writing (Periodical) Best stories
  Second death
    Lynskey, W. C. ed. Reading modern
    fiction
Greene, Henry Irving, 1920-
  Bread and snow
    American vanguard, 1950
Greenfield, Irving, 1928-
  City wise
    American vanguard, 1952

Greenfield, Robert, 1911-
Jonathan Harrow
American vanguard, 1953
Way of a traitor
American vanguard, 1950
GREENWICH VILLAGE. See New York
(City)—Greenwich Village
The **greeting.** Sitwell, Sir O. bart.
Gregory, Vahan Krikorian, 1927-
Athens, Greece, 1942
Best American short stories, 1953
Greg's peg. Auchincloss, L.
Gregutt, Helen Ciancimino
Christmas at Polly Moran's
American girl (Periodical) Christmas
all year 'round
Climb for the big ones
Furman, A. L. ed Everygirls career
stories
Jam session at Abby's
American girl (Periodical) Favorite sto-
ries
The secret
Furman, A. L. ed Everygirls career
stories
There isn't time now
McFarland, W. K. comp. Then it hap-
pened
Victory
American girl (Periodical) On my honor
GRENADA. See Spain—Granada
Grendon, Edward
Crisis
Conklin, G. ed. Invaders of earth
Trip one
Sloane, W. M. ed. Space, space, space
Grendon, Stephen, 1909-
Mr George
Derleth, A. W. ed. Night's yawning peal
Mrs. Manifold
Conklin, G. and Conklin, L. T. eds.
Supernatural reader
Open, sesame!
Derleth, A. W. ed. Far boundaries
Song of the pewee
Derleth, A. W. ed. Far boundaries
Gresham, William Lindsay
Star gypsies
Magazine of fantasy and science fiction.
Best from Fantasy and science fiction;
3d ser.
Grey, Zane, 1872-1939
Old Well-Well
Graber, R. S. ed. Baseball reader
The rube
Graber, R. S. ed. Baseball reader
Tappan's burro
Andrews, R. C. ed. My favorite stories
of the great outdoors
Grey eagle. Sass, H. R.
Grey ones. Priestley, J. B.
Grey seagull. O'Flaherty, L.
GRIDDLE CAKES
Porter, W. S. Pimienta pancakes
The **gridiron.** Lover, S.
GRIEF. See Joy and sorrow
Grief. Chekhov, A. P.

Griffin, John Howard, 1920-
Miss Henrietta Briggs and her metamor-
phosis
Story (Periodical) Story; no. 3
Griffith, Ann Warren
Captive audience
Magazine of fantasy and science fiction.
Best from Fantasy and science fiction;
3d ser.
Zeritsky's law
Conklin, G. ed. Omnibus of science fic-
tion
Griffith, Beatrice Winston
American me
Seventeen (Periodical) Nineteen from
Seventeen
Griffith, Robert
Jingle bells
Dachs, D. ed. Treasury of sports humor
**Grimm, Jakob Ludwig Karl, 1785-1863, and
Grimm, Wilhelm Karl, 1786-1859**
Clever Elsa
Fenner, P. R. comp. Fools and funny
fellows
Grimm, Wilhelm Karl, 1786-1859. See
Grimm, J. L. K. jt. auth.
Grimson, Marie S.
American girl looks at Europe
Grimson, M. S. At the crossroads, and
other stories and sketches
At the crossroads
Grimson, M. S. At the crossroads, and
other stories and sketches
Christmas story
Grimson, M. S. At the crossroads, and
other stories and sketches
Concerning discoveries
Grimson, M. S. At the crossroads, and
other stories and sketches
Earth-bound
Grimson, M. S. At the crossroads, and
other stories and sketches
Eighty years old
Grimson, M. S. At the crossroads, and
other stories and sketches
Eureca cottage
Grimson, M. S. At the crossroads, and
other stories and sketches
Faith, hope and charity
Grimson, M. S. At the crossroads, and
other stories and sketches
Gather up the pieces
Grimson, M. S. At the crossroads, and
other stories and sketches
Grandma goes to the Fair
Grimson, M. S. At the crossroads, and
other stories and sketches
Happy birthday to you
Grimson, M. S. At the crossroads, and
other stories and sketches
It never fails
Grimson, M. S. At the crossroads, and
other stories and sketches
King of the north woods
Grimson, M. S. At the crossroads, and
other stories and sketches
Leap year
Grimson, M. S. At the crossroads, and
other stories and sketches

Grimson, Marie S.—*Continued*
  Leif goes west
    Grimson, M. S. At the crossroads, and
      other stories and sketches
  Norway
    Grimson, M. S. At the crossroads, and
      other stories and sketches
  Regarding monuments
    Grimson, M. S. At the crossroads, and
      other stories and sketches
  Story of Paula
    Grimson, M. S. At the crossroads, and
      other stories and sketches
  When Dan came home
    Grimson, M. S. At the crossroads, and
      other stories and sketches
  When TV came to the backwoods
    Grimson, M. S. At the crossroads, and
      other stories and sketches
  Who is my neighbor?
    Grimson, M. S. At the crossroads, and
      other stories and sketches
  Will and a way
    Grimson, M. S. At the crossroads, and
      other stories and sketches
  Won and lost
    Grimson, M. S. At the crossroads, and
      other stories and sketches

Grinevskiĭ, Aleksandr Stepanovich, 1880-1932
  The ratcatcher
    Guerney, B. G. comp. New Russian
      stories

Grinnell, David, pseud.
  Extending the holdings
    Best science fiction stories: 1952
  Malice aforethought
    Merril, J. ed. Beyond the barriers of
      space and time
  Rag thing
    Conklin, G. ed. Omnibus of science fic-
      tion
  Top secret
    Conklin, G. ed. Invaders of earth

Gronowicz, Antoni, 1913-
  Mania-head-in-the-clouds
    Hazeltine, A. I. comp. Selected stories
      for teen-agers

Groseclose, Elgin Earl, 1899-
  The healing of the lepers
    Brentano, F. ed. The word lives on

Gross, Marion
  Good provider
    Conklin, G. ed. Science-fiction adven-
      tures in dimension

Grosskopf, Edward K. 1920-
  Tea for Tamahara
    Oberfirst, R. ed. 1952 anthology of best
      original short-shorts——

Ground mist. Redman, B. R.

GROUSE HUNTING
  Bonner, P. H. Big day

Grove, Edgar
  Dress for Kitty
    Story (Periodical) Story; no. 2

Grove, Frederick Philip, 1872-1948
  Snow
    Pacey, D. ed. Book of Canadian stories

Grove, Walt, 1921-
  Man who flew into a rage
    Collier's, the national weekly. Collier's
      best

Growing pains. Stull, P.

Growing season. Caldwell, E.

Grunert, Karl, 1865-1907
  Enemies in space
    Conklin, G. ed. Invaders of space

Grunion run. Cawley, C. C.

GUADALCANAL
  Michener, J. A. The story

GUADALUPE, OUR LADY OF
  Steinbeck, J. Miracle of Tepayac

GUARD DUTY
  Bergengruen, W. The sentry
  O'Donovan, M. The sentry

The **guardian**. De La Mare, W. J.

The **guardian**. Robertson, F. C.

Guardian angel. Alarcon, P. A. de.

Guardian angel. Willingham, C.

Guardian of the accolade. Porter, W. S.

GUARDIANS
  Harte, B. Protégé of Jack Hamlin's
  Harte, B. Ward of Colonel Starbottle's

Guardians of Parnassus. Russell, B. A. W. R.
      3d earl

GUAYANA INDIANS
  Hudson, W. H. Mysterious forest

Guest, Anna, 1913?-
  Barbèd rose
    American vanguard, 1953
  Closed door
    American vanguard, 1952

The **guest**. Chekhov, A. P.

Guest of honour. Priestley, J. B.

Guest of reality. Lagerkvist, P. F.

GUESTS
  Bowen, E. The visitor
  Hawthorne, N. Ambitious guest
  Munro, H. H. The hen
  Parker, J. R. Joy, joy, joy!
  Parker, J. R. Lower Mississippi
  Parker, J. R. Red carpet
  Rabinowitz, S. Passover guest

The **guests**. Munro, H. H.

Guests of the nation. O'Donovan, M.

The **guide**. Lytle, A. N.

GUIDES (HUNTING)
  La Farge, O. Old century's river
  Mowery, W. B. Man-killer

Guillotine party. Farrell, J. T.

Guilty. Hurst, F.

"**Guilty** party." Porter, W. S.

Guilty witness. Hershman, M.

Guin, Wyman
  Beyond Bedlam
    Galaxy science fiction magazine. Galazy
      reader of science fiction
  Trigger tide
    Conklin, G. ed. Omnibus of science fic-
      tion

Guinea pig. McKenney, R.

Guinevere for everybody. Williamson, J.

Guiney, Louise Imogen, 1861-1920
The provider
Fremantle, A. J. ed. Mothers
Guinness, Alec
Money for jam
New writing (Periodical) Best stories
Güiraldes, Ricardo, 1886-1927
Old ranch
De Onís, H. ed. Spanish stories and tales
Gulf. Heinlein, R. A.
Gulick, Bill. See Gulick, Grover C.
Gulick, Grover C. 1916-
Rendezvous romance
Western Writers of America. Bad men
and good
Squaw fever
Meredith, S. ed. Bar 2
Two-faced promise
Meredith, S. ed. Bar 1 roundup of best
western stories
Waters of Manitou
Western Writers of America. Holsters
and heroes
Gulliver the Great. Dyer, W. A.
Gun job. Thompson, T.
Gun on the wall. Garber, G.
Gun shy. Fenton, E.
Gunn, James E.
The misogynist
Galaxy science fiction magazine. Sec-
ond Galaxy reader of science fiction
Gunn, Neil Miller, 1891-
Desperate journey
Saturday evening post (Periodical) Sat-
urday evening post stories, 1952
Gunnarson, Gunnar, 1889-
Advent
Brentano, F. ed. The word lives on
The **gunny.** Turner, R.
GUNS. See Firearms
Gunterman, Bertha L.
Golden pitcher
Fenner, P. R. comp. Ghosts, ghosts,
ghosts
Gurnard, Joseph
Poets' excursion
New Writing (Periodical) Best stories
Gus the gloom. Bateman, A.
Gust of wind. Hill, J. H.
Gustafson, Ralph, 1909-
The pigeon
Best American short stories, 1950
Guthrie, Alfred Bertram, 1901-
Ebbie
Abell, E. ed. American accent
Summers, H. S. ed. Kentucky story
Fraudulent skunk
Meredith, S. ed. Bar I roundup of best
western stories
Gutman, Chaim, 1887-
No enemy of his
Ausubel, N. ed. Treasury of Jewish
humor
Real customers
Ausubel, N. ed. Treasury of Jewish
humor

Gy-ma-na-si-a. Rabinowitz, S.
GYMNASTS. See Acrobats and acrobatism
GYPSIES. See Gipsies

H

Haardt, Sara Powell, 1898-1935
Little white girl
Thinker's digest (Periodical) Spoiled
priest, and other stories
Habeas Corpus Club. Harvey, W. F.
Hadji Murad. Tolstoĭ, L. N. Graf
Hagedorn, Herman, 1882-
Hour of stars
Elmquist, R. M. ed. Fifty years of
Christmas
Hager, Mark
The champions
Fenner, P. R. comp. Dogs, dogs, dogs
Hail, Steve
Taste of command
Argosy (Periodical) Argosy Book of
sea stories
Hail and farewell. Bradbury, R.
"**Hail,** brother and farewell." Karchmer, S.
Hail fellow well met. Herron, E.
HAIR
De Camp, L. S. Hyperpilosity
Fitzgerald, F. S. K. Bernice bobs her hair
Hauser, M. The mouse
Maupassant, G. de. One phase of love
Porter, W. S. Gift of the Magi
Hair. Faulkner, W.
HAIR DRESSERS. See Barbers; Beauty,
Personal
Hair shirt. Vickers, R.
Haircut. Lardner, R. W.
Hairless Mexican. Maugham, W. S.
HAITI
Capote, T. House of flowers
Litten, F. N. Tell it to the Marines

Port-Au-Prince
Rattner, J. Haitian incident
Haitian incident. Rattner, J.
Halberdier of the Little Rheinschloss. Por-
ter, W. S.
Hale, Edward Everett, 1822-1909
General Washington's pig
Eaton, H. T. ed. Short stories
Man without a country
Burrell, J. A. and Cerf, B. A. eds. An-
thology of famous American stories
My double, and how he undid me
Cuff, R. P. ed. American short story
survey
Hale, Lucretia Peabody, 1820-1900
Peterkins' Christmas tree
Fenner, P. R. comp. Fools and funny
fellows
Hale, Nancy, 1908-
No one my grief can tell
Blodgett, H. W. ed. Story survey.
1953 ed.

Hale, Nathan
Brahmin Beachhead
Best American short stories, 1952
Half-brothers. Gaskell, E. C. S.
HALF-CASTES
Maugham, W. S. Yellow streak
Half-naked truth. Blochman, L. G.
HALF-SISTERS
Rinehart, M. R. If only it were yesterday
Halfway to Hell. Collier, J.
Haliburton, Thomas Chandler, 1796-1865
Sam Slick the clockmaker
Pacey, D. ed. Book of Canadian stories
Hall, Desmond
Pickles and pearls
Argosy (Periodical) Argosy Book of
adventure stories
Hall, Douglass
Foggy
Ford, N. A. and Faggett, H. L. eds.
Best short stories by Afro-American
writers (1925-1950)
Hall, Esther Greenacre
Callie of Crooked Creek
American girl (Periodical) Favorite sto-
ries
Hall, James B.
Estate and trespass: a Gothic story
Prize stories, 1954
In the time of demonstrations
Prize stories of 1951
Spot in history
Best American short stories, 1953
Hall, James Norman, 1887-1951
Cheerful tortoise
McFee, W. ed. Great sea stories of
modern times
Haunted island
Saturday evening post (Periodical)
Saturday evening post stories, 1950
See also Nordhoff, C. B. jt. auth.
Hall, Stephen. See King-Hall, Stephen
Hall of mirrors. Brown, F.
Hallack, Cecily, 1898-1938
Wretched old capitalist
Thinker's digest (Periodical) Spoiled
priest, and other stories
Halladay, Velma, 1919?-
One-beautiful Ellie
Oberfirst, R. ed. 1952 anthology of best
original short-shorts
Halliday, Brett, pseud. See Dresser, Davis
Hallinan, Nancy, 1921-
Limbo
American vanguard, 1950
Hallowed years. Buckingham, N.
Hallstead, William F.
Space Lane cadet
Fenner, P. R. comp. Speed, speed, speed
Thunder and the wise guy
Fenner, P. R. comp. Speed, speed, speed
Hallucination orbit. Macgregor, J. M.
HALLUCINATIONS AND ILLUSIONS
Dreiser, T. Lost Phoebe
Gellhorn, M. E. Psychiatrist of one's own
Hurst, F. Guilty
Maugham, W. S. The taipan

Miller, W. M. Little creeps
Munro, H. H. Soul of Laploshka
Nelson, A. Narapoia
Poe, E. A. Ligeia
Poe, E. A. The sphinx
Priestley, J. B. Grey ones
Richter, C. Doctor Hanray's second
chance
Thurber, J. The whip-poor-will
Wells, H. G. Remarkable case of David-
son's eyes
See also Ghosts
Halper, Albert, 1904-
My mother's love story
Ribalow, H. U. ed. These your children
Hameiri, Avigdor, 1890-
Three Halutzot
Leftwich, J. ed. Yisröel. 1952 ed.
Hamelyn, Glückel of, 1646-1724
A story
Leftwich, J. ed. Yisröel. 1952 ed.
Hamilton, Edmond, 1904-
Conquest of two worlds
Wollheim, D. A. comp. Every boy's
book of science-fiction
Dead planet
Derleth, A. W. ed. Worlds of tomorrow
Exile
Lesser, M. A. ed. Looking forward
Fessenden's worlds
Derleth, A. W. ed. Beyond time & space
Forgotten world
Margulies, L. and Friend, O. J. eds.
Giant anthology of science fiction
Man who evolved
Margulies, L. and Friend, O. J. eds.
From off this world
What's it like out there?
Startling stories (Periodical) Best from
Startling stories
Hamilton, Roland T.
Symbol of courage
Ford, N. A. Faggett, H. L. eds. Best
short stories by Afro-American writers
(1925-1950)
Hammer of God. Chesterton, G. K.
Hammett, Dashiell, 1894-
His brother's keeper
Ribalow, H. U. ed. World's greatest
boxing stories
Hammond, Keith, pseud. See Kuttner,
Henry
Hamos, George
The conjurer
Story (Periodical) Story; no. 3
Hamrick's polar bear. Caldwell, E.
Hamsun, Knut, 1859-1952
Wonderful new machine
Burnett, W. ed. World's best
HAND
Maupassant, G. de. The hand
Hand in glove. Bowen, E.
Hand of God. Keeler, H. S.
The **hand** that riles the world. Porter, W. S.
HAND-TO-HAND-FIGHTING. See Fight-
ing, Hand-to-hand
Hand upon the waters. Faulkner, W.
Handbook of Hymen. Porter, W. S.

Hands. Anderson, S.
Hands across the deep. Elam, R. M.
Hands across the sea. Williams, W. C.
Hands of Mr Ottermole. Burke, T.
Handsome lady. Coppard, A. E.
Handy. Caldwell, E.
HANGCHOW. See China—Hangchow
HANGING
    Baudelaire, C. P. The rope
    Bierce, A. Occurrence at Owl Creek
        bridge
    Bradford, R. Child of God
    Carver, C. Hanging Hollow
    Harte, B. Tennessee's partner
    Lagerkvist, P. F. The hangman
Hanging fire. Barr, J. pseud.
Hanging fire. Deming, R.
Hanging Hollow. Carver, C.
HANGINGS (EXECUTIONS). See Hang-
    ing
The hangman. Lagerkvist, P. F.
HANGMEN. See Hanging
Hangover. Cash, M. L.
Hanlon, Brooke
    Crushed orchid
        Saturday evening post (Periodical)
        Saturday evening post stories, 1950
Hannibal's elephants. Powers, A.
HANSEN'S DISEASE. See Leprosy
Hansjorg and his pipe. Auerbach, B.
HANUKKAH (FEAST OF LIGHTS)
    Peretz, I. L. Little Hanukkah lamp
Happiest creature. Williamson, J.
Happiest man on earth. Maltz, A.
HAPPINESS
    Maugham, W. S. Happy man
    Maupassant, G. de. Happiness
Happiness in crime. Barbey d'Aurevilly,
    J. A.
Happy birthday to you. Grimson, M. S.
Happy couple. Maugham, W. S.
Happy ending. Kuttner, H.
Happy failure. Melville, H.
Happy hypocrite. Beerbohm, Sir M.
Happy man. Maugham, W. S.
Happy New Year. Sansom, W.
Happy New Year, kamerades! Lowry,
    R. J. C.
Happy one. Rosenberg, E.
The harbinger. Porter, W. S.
Hard day. Parker, J. R.
Hard-luck diggings. Kuttner, H.
HARDWARE STORES
    De Vries, P. Household words
Hardwick, Elizabeth, 1916-
    Evenings at home
        Summers, H. S. ed. Kentucky story
Hardwood hazard. Coombs, C. I.
Hardy, Thomas, 1840-1928
    Absent-mindedness in a parish choir
        Ludwig, J. B. and Poirier, W. R. eds.
        Stories, British and American

Son's veto
    Fremantle, A. J. ed. Mothers
Three strangers
    Bogorad, S. N. and Trevithick, J. eds.
        College miscellany
    Cerf, B. A. and Moriarty, H. C. eds.
        Anthology of famous British stories
    Short, R. W. and Sewall, R. B. eds.
        Short stories for study. 1950 ed.
Tony Kytes, the arch-deceiver
    Blodgett, H. W. ed. Story survey.
        1953 ed.
Tradition of 1804
    Barrows, H. ed. 15 stories
Tragedy of two ambitions
    Felheim, M.; Newman, F. B. and Stein-
        hoff, W. R. eds. Modern short stories

Hardy, William George, 1896-
Czech dog
    Pacey, D. ed. Book of Canadian stories

The Hardys. Humphrey, W.

Hare, Cyril, pseud. See Clark, Alfred Alex-
    ander Gordon

Harlem tragedy. Porter, W. S.

The harmonizer. Van Vogt, A. E.

Harmony. Lardner, R. W.

Harnden, Ruth Peabody
Rebellion
    Prize stories, 1954

Harness, Charles L.
Child by Chronos
    Magazine of fantasy and science fiction.
        Best from Fantasy and science fiction;
        3d ser.
New reality
    Best science fiction stories: 1951

HARNESS RACING. See Horse racing

Harrington, Dennis
Trouble with the union
    Gable, M. Sister, ed. Many-colored fleece

Harris, Clare Winger, 1891- and Breuer,
    Miles, J.
Baby on Neptune
    Wollheim, D. A. comp. Flight into space

Harris, George Washington, 1814-1869
In the family bosom
    Harris, G. W. Sut lovingood
Second view of the family bosom
    Harris, G. W. Sut Lovingood
Sut and the Burns family
    Harris, G. W. Sut Lovingood
Sut as a boy
    Harris, G. W. Sut Lovingood
Sut meets the law
    Harris, G. W. Sut Lovingood
Sut on the national scene
    Harris, G. W. Sut Lovingood
Sut sets certain individuals right
    Harris, G. W. Sut Lovingood
Sut takes on the whole world
    Harris, G. W. Sut Lovingood

Harris, Joel Chandler, 1848-1908
Free Joe and the rest of the world
    Scribner treasury
Wonderful Tar-Baby story
    Day, A. G. ed. Greatest American short
        stories

Harris, John Beynon, 1903-
And the walls came tumbling down. . .
Derleth, A. W. ed. Beachheads in space
The chronoclasm
Star science fiction stories [no. 1]
Jizzle
Magazine of fantasy and science fiction.
Best from Fantasy and science fiction;
2d ser.
Meteor
Derleth, A. W. ed. Beachheads in space
Perforce to dream
Merril, J. ed. Beyond the barriers of
space and time
Pillar to post
Galaxy science fiction magazine. Second
Galaxy reader of science fiction
Survival
Best science-fiction stories: 1953
Technical slip
Derleth, A. W. ed. Night's yawning peal
Time to rest
Derleth, A. W. ed. Far boundaries
Harrison, Henry Sydnor, 1880-1930
Miss Hinch
Cuff, R. P. ed. American short story
survey
Shaw, H. and Bement, D. Reading the
short story
Harry was good to the girls. Benson, T.
Hart, Alan, 1890-
Doctor Mallory
Fabricant, N. D. and Werner, H. eds.
World's best doctor stories
Hart, Fred, d. 1897
First Fourth in White Pine
Emrich, D. ed. Comstock bonanza
Hart, James S.
The traitor
Conklin, G. and Conklin, L. T. eds.
Supernatural reader
Harte, Bret, 1836-1902
Bell-ringer of Angel's
Harte, B. Best of Bret Harte
Brown of Calaveras
Harte, B. Best of Bret Harte
Colonel Starbottle for the plaintiff
Harte, B. Best of Bret Harte
Dick Boyle's business card
Harte, B. Best of Bret Harte
Harte, B. Bret Harte's stories of the
old West
High-water mark
Harte, B. Best of Bret Harte
Harte, B. Bret Harte's stories of the
old West
How Santa Claus came to Simpson's Bar
Harte, B. Best of Bret Harte
Harte, B. Bret Harte's stories of the
old West
Idyll of Red Gulch
Harte, B. Best of Bret Harte
Ingénue of the Sierras
Harte, B. Best of Bret Harte
Harte, B. Bret Harte's stories of the
old West
Knight-errant of the foothills
Harte, B. Bret Harte's stories of the
old West
Left out on Lone Star Mountain
Harte, B. Best of Bret Harte

Luck of Roaring Camp
Harte, B. Best of Bret Harte
Harte, B. Bret Harte's stories of the
old West
Miggles
Harte, B. Best of Bret Harte
Harte, B. Bret Harte's stories of the
old West
Mrs Skaggs's husbands
Harte, B. Best of Bret Harte
M'liss
Harte, B. Bret Harte's stories of the
old West
Outcasts of Poker Flat
Burrell, J. A. and Cerf, B. A. eds. An-
thology of famous American stories
Cody, S. ed. Greatest stories and how
they were written
Cuff, R. P. ed. American short story
survey
Day, A. G. ed. Greatest American short
stories
Foerster, N. ed. American poetry and
prose. 1952 ed.
Harte, B. Best of Bret Harte
Harte, B. Bret Harte's stories of the
old West
Lamb, L. ed. Family book of best loved
short stories
Schramm, W. L. ed. Great short stories
Passage in the life of Mr John Oakhurst
Harte, B. Best of Bret Harte
Post mistress of Laurel Run
Harte, B. Best of Bret Harte
Prosper's "old mother"
Eaton, H. T. ed. Short stories
Protégée of Jack Hamlin's
Harte, B. Best of Bret Harte
Tennessee's partner
Blodgett, H. W. ed. Story survey.
1953 ed.
Harte, B. Best of Bret Harte
Harte, B. Bret Harte's stories of the
old West
Wan Lee, the pagan
Harte, B. Best of Bret Harte
Ward of Colonel Starbottle's
Harte, B. Bret Harte's stories of the
old West
Yellow dog
Block, M. ed. Favorite dog stories
Harte, Francis Bret. See Harte, Bret
Hartley, Leslie Poles, 1895-
W. S.
Asquith, Lady C. M. E. C. ed. Book of
modern ghosts
The **Hartleys.** Cheever, J.
Harum Scarum; the life story of a horse.
Bowes-Lyon, S. S.
Harvest. Morrison, J.
The **harvest.** Upshaw, H.
HARVESTING
Giono, J. Corn dies
Harvey, William Fryer, 1885-1937
Account rendered
Harvey, W. F. Arm of Mrs Egan, and
other strange stories
Arm of Mrs Egan
Harvey, W. F. Arm of Mrs Egan, and
other strange stories

Harvey, William F.—*Continued*
Atmospherics
  Harvey, W. F. Arm of Mrs Egan, and
    other strange stories
August heat
  Carrington, H. ed. Week-end book of
    ghost stories
  Christ, H. I. and Shostak, J. eds. Short
    stories
  Davenport, B. ed. Ghostly tales to be
    told
Beast with five fingers
  Davenport, B. ed. Tales to be told in
    the dark
Chemist and druggist
  Harvey, W. F. Arm of Mrs Egan, and
    other strange stories
Dark horses
  Harvey, W. F. Arm of Mrs Egan, and
    other strange stories
Dead of night
  Harvey, W. F. Arm of Mrs Egan, and
    other strange stories
Euphemia witchmaid
  Harvey, W. F. Arm of Mrs Egan, and
    other strange stories
Flying out of Mrs Barnard Hollis
  Harvey, W. F. Arm of Mrs Egan, and
    other strange stories
Habeas Corpus Club
  Harvey, W. F. Arm of Mrs Egan, and
    other strange stories
The lake
  Harvey, W. F. Arm of Mrs Egan, and
    other strange stories
Long road
  Harvey, W. F. Arm of Mrs Egan, and
    other strange stories
Mishandled
  Harvey, W. F. Arm of Mrs Egan, and
    other strange stories
No body
  Harvey, W. F. Arm of Mrs Egan, and
    other strange stories
Old masters
  Harvey, W. F. Arm of Mrs Egan, and
    other strange stories
Ripe for development
  Harvey, W. F. Arm of Mrs Egan, and
    other strange stories
Vicar's web
  Harvey, W. F. Arm of Mrs Egan, and
    other strange stories
Harvey Kendall. Schaefer, J. W.
Harwood, Kitty
Papa's going bye-bye
  Queen, E. pseud. ed. Queen's awards:
    7th ser.
Hasas, Haïm, 1897-
Bridegroom of blood
  Leftwich, J. ed. Yisröel. 1952 ed.
Hasley, Lucile
Little girls
  Gable, M. Sister, ed. Many-colored fleece
Hasty act. Brandel, M.
Hat trick. Brown, F.
Hat trick. Muller, C. G.
Hatch, Eric, 1901-
Channel 10
  This week magazine. This week's
    short-short stories

HATS
Crossen, K. F. Things of distinction
Porter, W. S. Red roses of Tonia
Rabinowitz, S. On account of a hat
Taylor, M. McGarry joins the Easter
    parade
Welty, E. Purple hat
Hatvany, Lajos, báró, 1880-
Bondy, jr.
  Ausubel, N. ed. Treasury of Jewish
    humor
Haunted hollow. Mowery, W. B.
HAUNTED HOUSES. See Ghosts
Haunted island. Hall, J. N.
Haunted man. Dickens, C.
Haunted wreck. Henderson, Le G.
**Hauptmann, Gerhart Johann Robert, 1862-
    1946**
Flagman Thiel
  Lange, V. ed. Great German short
    novels and stories
  Moskowitz, S. ed. Great railroad stories
    of the world
Hause, Mary
Turn off the moon
  Oberfirst, R. ed. 1952 anthology of best
    original short-shorts
Hauser, Margaret Louise, 1909-
Calling all cars
  Strang, R. M. and Roberts, R. M. eds.
    Teen-age tales v2
Hauser, Marianne, 1920-
The mouse
  Best American short stories, 1950
Hautot, father and son. Maupassant, G. de
Hautot Senior & Hautot Junior. Maupassant,
    G. de
Have a heart, lady! Lamson, R. R.
Have I got sun in my eyes? Farrell, J. T.
HAWAIIAN ISLANDS
Marquand, J. P. You can't do that
Maugham, W. S. Honolulu
Stern, J. Travellers' tears
Stevenson, R. L. Bottle imp
Stevenson, R. L. Isle of voices
Ullman, J. R. Pau
Ullman, J. R. Silver sword
**Hawkins, John, 1910- and Hawkins, Ward,
    1912-**
Burden of guilt
  Best detective stories of the year—1951
End of the line
  Saturday evening post (Periodical) Sat-
    urday evening post stories, 1952
Killer is loose
  Best detective stories of the year—1954
Love song in a honky-tonk
  Saturday evening post (Periodical) Sat-
    urday evening post stories, 1951
**Hawkins, Ward, 1912- See Hawkins, J. jt.
    auth.**
HAWKS
Clark, W. Van T. Hook
Hawthorne, Nathaniel, 1804-1864
Ambitious guest
  Day, A. G. ed. Greatest American short
    stories
  Hawthorne, N. Best of Hawthorne

Hawthorne, Nathaniel—*Continued*
Celestial railroad
Hawthorne, N. Best of Hawthorne
David Swan
Foerster, N. ed. American poetry and
prose. 1952 ed.
Dr Heidegger's experiment
Christ, H. I. and Shostak, J. eds. Short
stories
Endicott and the Red Cross
Foerster, N. ed. American poetry and
prose. 1952 ed.
Ethan Brand
Barrows, H. ed. 15 stories
Foerster, N. ed. American poetry and
prose. 1952 ed.
Hawthorne, N. Best of Hawthorne
Gray Champion
Hawthorne, N. Best of Hawthorne
Neider, C. ed. Great short stories from
the world's literature
Great Stone Face
Burrell, J. A. and Cerf, B. A. eds.
Anthology of famous American stories
Cody, S. ed. Greatest stories and how
they were written
Cuff, R. P. ed. American short story
survey
Maypole of Merry Mount
Foerster, N. ed. American poetry and
prose. 1952 ed.
Minister's black veil
Foerster, N. ed. American poetry and
prose. 1952 ed.
Hawthorne, N. Best of Hawthorne
Neider, C. ed. Men of high calling
Mr Higginbotham's catastrophe
Blodgett, H. W. ed. Story survey.
1953 ed.
Rappaccini's daughter
Bond, R. T. ed. Handbook for poisoners
Burrell, J. A. and Cerf, B. A. eds. An-
thology of famous American stories
Foerster, N. ed. American poetry and
prose. 1952 ed.
Hawthorne, N. Best of Hawthorne
Lamb, L. ed. Family book of best loved
short stories
Schramm, W. L. ed. Great short stories
West, R. B. and Stallman, R. W. eds.
Art of modern fiction
Roger Malvin's burial
Hawthorne, N. Best of Hawthorne
Scarlet letter
Hawthorne, N. Best of Hawthorne
Sunday at home
Hawthorne, N. Best of Hawthorne
Wakefield
Ludwig, J. B. and Poirier, W. R. eds.
Stories, British and American
Wives of the dead
Hawthorne, N. Best of Hawthorne
Young Goodman Brown
Foerster, N. ed. American poetry and
prose. 1952 ed.
Gordon, C. and Tate, A. eds. House of
fiction
Hawthorne, N. Best of Hawthorne

Haycox, Ernest, 1899-1950
Call this land home
Haycox, E. Pioneer loves

Change of station
Haycox, E. By rope and lead
Clouds on the Circle-P
Haycox, E. Outlaw
Cry deep, cry still
Haycox, E. Pioneer loves
Custom of the country
Haycox, E. Pioneer loves
Day in town
Haycox, E. Pioneer loves
Deadline
Haycox, E. Rough justice
Dispatch to the general
Meredith, S. ed. Bar 3
Episode—1880
Haycox, E. Rough justice
An evening's entertainment
Haycox, E. Outlaw
Found out
Haycox, E. Outlaw
Good marriage
Haycox, E. Pioneer loves
Inscrutable man
Haycox, E. Rough justice
Land rush
Haycox, E. By rope and lead
Last draw
Haycox, E. Outlaw
Lonesome ride
Haycox, E. Rough justice
Meredith, S. ed. Bar 1 roundup of best
western stories
Man with a past
Haycox, E. Outlaw
Mrs Benson
Haycox, E. Rough justice
Night on Don Jaime Street
Haycox, E. Rough justice
No time for dreams
Haycox, E. Pioneer loves
Odd chance
Haycox, E. Outlaw
Oh, lovely land
Haycox, E. By rope and lead
Quarter section on Dullknife Creek
Haycox, E. Pioneer loves
Question of blood
Haycox, E. By rope and lead
Ride the river
Haycox, E. Outlaw
Scout detail
Haycox, E. By rope and lead
Meredith, S. ed. Bar 2
Smoky in the west
Haycox, E. Pioneer loves
Stage station
Haycox, E. Outlaw
Stage to Lordsburg
Haycox, E. By rope and lead
The stranger
Haycox, E. Outlaw
Tactical maneuver
Haycox, E. By rope and lead
Tavern at Powell's Ferry
Haycox, E. Pioneer loves
To the limit
Haycox, E. Outlaw
Toll bridge
Haycox, E. Rough justice
Violent interlude
Haycox, E. By rope and lead
Water hole
Haycox, E. Rough justice

Haycox, Ernest—*Continued*
Weight of command
Haycox, E. By rope and lead
Wild Jack Rhett
Haycox, E. Rough justice
HAYDEN PLANETARIUM (NEW YORK CITY)
Beck, W. Shadow of turning
Hayes, Hazel M.
Jenny takes a holiday
Oberfirst, R. ed. 1952 anthology of best original short-shorts
Hayes, Nelson
Weaning of Laura Wade
Story (Periodical) Story; no. 2
Hayes, William Edward
Big engine
Moskowitz, S. ed. Great railroad stories of the world
HAY-FEVER
Canine, W. The clematis
Hays, Lee
Banquet and a half
Queen, E. pseud. ed. Ellery Queen's awards: 9th ser.
Haywood, Carolyn, 1898-
Little Eddie goes to town
Fenner, P. R. comp. Giggle box
Prize corn chowder
Fenner, P. R. comp. Giggle box
Haywood, John L.
Heat spell
Queen, E. pseud. ed. Ellery Queen's awards: 9th ser.
Hazaz, Hayyim. See Hasas, Haïm
Hazlitt, William, 1778-1830
Liber amoris
Connolly, C. ed. Great English short novels
He also serves. Porter, W. S.
He don't plant cotton. Powers, J. F.
He sought to know God. Hobart, A. T. N.
He swung and he missed. Algren, N.
He told it to the judge. Claudy, C. H.
He walked around the horses. Piper, H. B.
He who laughs last. Miers, E. S.
He who woos and runs away. Kober, A.
He wouldn't be a Jew, by an Elder of Zion
Ausubel, N. ed. Treasury of Jewish humor
Head, Gay, pseud. See Hauser, Margaret Louise
Head, Matthew, pseud. See Canaday, John Edwin
Head and the feet. Forester, C. S.
Head by Scopas. Donahoe, E.
The **head-hunter.** Porter, W. S.
Head-hunters. Williams, R.
Head of Cæsar. Chesterton, G. K.
Headley, Elizabeth (Cavanna) See Cavanna, Betty
Headline halfback. Coombs, C. I.
Headwall tempo. Dodge, J. E.
Heagney, Harold Jerome, 1890-
Madame Jeanne De Chantal
Fremantle, A. J. ed. Mothers

Healing of the lepers. Groseclose, E. E.
HEALTH RESORTS, WATERING-PLACES, ETC.
Hearn, L. The storm
Healthiest girl in town. Stafford, J.
Heard, Gerald, 1889-
B+M—planet 4
Healy, R. J. ed. New tales of space and time
The collector
Magazine of fantasy and science fiction. Best from Fantasy and science fiction, 1952
Cyclops
Crossen, K. F. ed. Future tense
Great fog
Heilman, R. B. ed. Modern short stories
The swap
Conklin, G. and Conklin, L. T. eds. Supernatural reader
Wingless victory
Derleth, A. W. ed. Beyond time & space
Heard, Henry Fitzgerald. See Heard, Gerald
Hearn, Lafcadio, 1850-1904
Boy who drew cats
Burrell, J. A. and Cerf, B. A. eds. Anthology of famous American stories
Mujina
Davenport, B. ed. Tales to be told in the dark
The storm
Andrews, R. C. ed. My favorite stories of the great outdoors
HEART

Diseases

Cather, W. S. Neighbour Rosicky
Maugham, W. S. Louise
Heart being perished. Frost, F. M.
Heart in the mouth. Household, G.
Heart of darkness. Conrad, J.
Heart of elm. Wilson, A.
Heart of Lily Long. Marshall, E.
Heart of Little Shikara. Marshall, E.
Heartbreak. Barker, A. L.
Heartburn. Calisher, H.
Hearts and crosses. Porter, W. S.
Hearts and hands. Porter, W. S.
Heart's reason. Mallea, E.
Heat spell. Hayward, J. L.
Heath, Priscilla
Farewell, sweet love
Best American short stories, 1954
Heathcott, Mary
Neil's girl
Story (Periodical) Story; no. 4
Heather wine. Walsh, M.
Heatter, Basil, 1918-
Island happy
Saturday evening post (Periodical) Saturday evening post stories, 1950
HEAVEN
Bradford, R. Child of God
Clemens, S. L. Wings
Forster, E. M. Mr Andrews
Temple, W. F. Forget-me-not
See also Future life

Heaven can wait. Gilford, C. B.
Heaven in my hand. Humphreys, A. L.
Heaven to hell. Hughes, L.
Heavenly Christmas tree. Dostoevskiĭ, F. M.
Heavenly world series. O'Rourke, F.
Heavyside Hunt: The new Master's first day. Surtees, R. S.
Heavyside Hunt again: The lady whipper-in. Surtees, R. S.
Hebel, Johann Peter, 1760-1826
  The hussar
    Pick, R. ed. German stories and tales
  Kannitverstan
    Pick, R. ed. German stories and tales
  Unexpected reunion
    Pick, R. ed. German stories and tales
Hébert, Anne
  House on the esplanade
    Best American short stories, 1954
HEBREWS. See Jews
Hecht, Ben, 1893-
  Double exposure
    Best detective stories of the year—1950
  God is good to a Jew
    Ribalow, H. U. ed. These your children
  Miracle of the fifteen murderers
    Fabricant, N. D. and Werner, H. eds. World's best doctor stories
  Swindler's luck
    Grayson, C. ed. Fourth round
Hector. West, M. P.
Hedenstjerna, Alfred von
  A mother
    Ungar, F. ed. To mother with love
The **hedgehog.** Munro, H. H.
Heggen, Thomas, 1919-1949
  Night watch
    Stegner, W. E.; Scowcroft, R. and Ilyin, B. eds. Writer's art
Heide, Helen J.
  End of her rope
    Oberfirst, R. ed. 1952 anthology of best original short-shorts
HEIDELBERG. See Germany—Heidelberg
Heijermans, Herman, 1864-1924
  Shabbes-soup
    Ausubel, N. ed. Treasury of Jewish humor
Heimann, Moritz, 1868-1925
  Message that failed
    Pick, R. ed. German stories and tales
Heine, Heinrich, 1797-1856
  Gods in exile
    Lange, V. ed. Great German short novels and stories
  Seder night
    Leftwich, J. ed. Yisröel. 1952 ed.
    Same as: Tale of olden time
  Tale of olden time
    Neider, C. ed. Great short stories from the world's literature
    Same as: Seder night
Heinlein, Robert Anson, 1907-
  Black pits of Luna
    Conklin, G. ed. Possible worlds of science fiction
    Heinlein, R. A. Green hills of earth

  Blowups happen
    Astounding science fiction (Periodical) Astounding science fiction anthology
    Heinlein, R. A. Man who sold the moon
  By his bootstraps
    Margulies, L. and Friend, O. J. eds. Giant anthology of science fiction
  Columbus was a dope
    Greenberg, M. ed. Travelers of space
  Coventry
    Heinlein, R. A. Revolt in 2100
  Delilah and the space-rigger
    Heinlein, R. A. Green hills of earth
  Elsewhen
    Heinlein, R. A. Assignment in eternity
  Gentlemen, be seated
    Heinlein, R. A. Green hills of earth
  Green hills of earth
    Heinlein, R. A. Green hills of earth
  Gulf
    Heinlein, R. A. Assignment in eternity
  "If this goes on-"
    Heinlein, R. A. Revolt in 2100
  "It's great to be back"
    Heinlein, R. A. Green hills of earth
  Jerry was a man
    Heinlein, R. A. Assignment in eternity
  "Let there be light"
    Heinlein, R. A. Man who sold the moon
  Life-line
    Heinlein, R. A. Man who sold the moon
  Logic of empire
    Heinlein, R. A. Green hills of earth
  Long watch
    Derleth, A. W. ed. Beyond time & space
    Heinlein, R. A. Green hills of earth
  Lost legacy
    Heinlein, R. A. Assignment in eternity
  Man who sold the moon
    Heinlein, R. A. Man who sold the moon
  Misfit
    Heinlein, R. A. Revolt in 2100
  Ordeal in space
    Heinlein, R. A. Green hills of earth
  Our fair city
    Merril, J. ed. Beyond human ken
  Requiem
    Heinlein, R. A. Man who sold the moon
  Roads must roll
    Heinlein, R. A. Man who sold the moon
  Space jockey
    Heinlein, R. A. Green hills of earth
  They
    Pratt, F. ed. World of wonder
  Water is for washing
    Argosy (Periodical) Argosy Book of adventure stories
  "—We also walk dogs"
    Heinlein, R. A. Green hills of earth
  Year of the jackpot
    Galaxy science fiction magazine. Second Galaxy reader of science fiction
Heinz, W. C.
  Man's game
    Herzberg, M. J. comp. Treasure chest of sport stories
Heir apparent. Moore, C. L.
Heir unapparent. Van Vogt, A. E.
HEIRS. See Inheritance and succession
Helen, I love you. Farrell, J. T.
Helen O'Loy. Del Rey, L.

Helfer, Harold
Sea serpent of Spoonville Beach
Story (Periodical) Story; no. 4
Strange notion
Story (Periodical) Story; no. 1
HELL
Collier, J. Devil, George and Rosie
Lagerkvist, P. F. Lift that went down
into hell
Munro, H. H. Infernal Parliament
Peretz, I. L. Ne'ilah in Gehenna
Hell hath no fury. Collier, J.
Hell of a good time. Farrell, J. T.
Hello darling. Ullman, J. R.
Hello, Tib. Aiken, C. P.
Helmet of Pluto. Claudy, C. H.
Help gets the legs. Hutchins, M. P. M.
Helpful Henry. Brumbaugh, F.
Helping hand. Anderson, P.
Helping the other fellow. Porter, W. S.
Helvick, James, pseud. See Cockburn, Claud
Hemingway, Ernest, 1898-
After the storm
Blodgett, H. W. ed. Story survey.
1953 ed.
Grayson, C. ed. Fourth round
Hemingway, E. Hemingway reader
Capital of the world
Hemingway, E. Hemingway reader
Clean, well-lighted place
Heilman, R. B. ed. Modern short stories
Hemingway, E. Hemingway reader
Schorer, M. ed. The story
Day's wait
Davis, C. B. ed. Eyes of boyhood
Fable of the good lion
Hemingway, E. Hemingway reader
Fifty grand
Hemingway, E. Hemingway reader
Ribalow, H. U. ed. World's greatest
boxing stories
Gambler, the nun, and the radio
Burrell, J. A. and Cerf, B. A. eds.
Anthology of famous American stories
In another country
Davis, R. G. ed. Ten modern masters
Ludwig, J. B. and Poirier, W. R. eds.
Stories, British and American
Shaw, H. and Bement, D. Reading the
short story
Short, R. W. and Sewall, R. B. eds.
Short stories for study. 1950 ed.
The killers
Burrell, J. A. and Cerf, B. A. eds.
Anthology of famous American stories
Foerster, N. ed. American poetry and
prose. 1952 ed.
Lamb, L. ed. Family book of best loved
short stories
Queen, E. pseud. ed. Literature of
crime
Short, R. W. and Sewall, R. B. eds.
Short stories for study. 1950 ed.
Light of the world
Hemingway, E. Hemingway reader
O'Faoláin, S. The short story
My old man
Best of the Best American short stories,
1915-1950
Davis, R. G. ed. Ten modern masters

Now I lay me
Barrows, H. ed. 15 stories
Schramm, W. L. ed. Great short stories
Old man at the bridge
Hemingway, E. Hemingway reader
Short happy life of Francis Macomber
Davis, R. G. ed. Ten modern masters
Hemingway, E. Hemingway reader
West, R. B. and Stallman, R. W. eds.
Art of modern fiction
Snows of Kilimanjaro
Burnett, W. ed. World's best
Foerster, N. ed. American poetry and
prose. 1952 ed.
Gordon, C. and Tate, A. eds. House of
fiction
Hemingway, E. Hemingway reader
Lynskey, W. C. ed. Reading modern fic-
tion
Neider, C. ed. Great short stories from
the world's literature
Waite, H. O. and Atkinson, B. P. eds.
Literature for our time
Three-day blow
Millett, F. B. ed. Reading fiction
Way you'll never be
Hemingway, E. Hemingway reader
The hen. Dunsany, E. J. M. D. P. 18th
baron
The hen. Munro, H. H.
Henderson, Dion, 1921-
Brute's Christmas
Strang, R. M. and Roberts, R. M. eds.
Teen-age tales v 1
Henderson, Le Grand, 1901-
Augustus and spring tonic
Fenner, P. R. comp. Giggle box
Augustus meets his first Indian
Fenner, P. R. comp. Indians, Indians,
Indians
Augustus, pirate
Fenner, P. R. comp. Pirates, pirates,
pirates
Haunted wreck
Story parade (Periodical) Adventure
stories
Henderson, Stephen E.
Case of myopia
Lantz, J. E. ed. Stories of Christian
living
Henderson, Zenna, 1917-
Ararat
Best science-fiction stories: 1953
Come on, Wagon!
Magazine of fantasy and science fiction.
Best from Fantasy and science fiction;
2d ser.
You know what, teacher?
Queen, E. pseud. ed. Ellery Queen's
awards: 9th ser.
Hendryx, James Beardsley, 1880-
Affair on Jacklight Creek
American boy (Periodical) American
boy anthology
Alex acquires some dust
Hendryx, J. B. Intrigue on Halfaday
Creek
"And the goose hangs high"
Hendryx, J. B. Intrigue on Halfaday
Creek

Hendryx, James B.—*Continued*
At Fish Rapids
  Hendryx, J. B. Murder on Halfaday
  Creek
Bad man passes on
  Hendryx, J. B. Intrigue on Halfaday
  Creek
Bad man reaches Halfaday
  Hendryx, J. B. Intrigue on Halfaday
  Creek
Bat Eye Cantrill
  Hendryx, J. B. Murder on Halfaday
  Creek
Black John buys a York boat
  Hendryx, J. B. Intrigue on Halfaday
  Creek
Black John chats with Corporal Downey
  Hendryx, J. B. Murder on Halfaday
  Creek
Black John delivers a deed
  Hendryx, J. B. Intrigue on Halfaday
  Creek
Black John departs for Dawson
  Hendryx, J. B. Murder on Halfaday
  Creek
Black John does some checking
  Hendryx, J. B. Intrigue on Halfaday
  Creek
Black John gets a tip
  Hendryx, J. B. Intrigue on Halfaday
  Creek
Black John goes to Dawson
  Hendryx, J. B. Intrigue on Halfaday
  Creek
Black John goes to Fortymile
  Hendryx, J. B. Murder on Halfaday
  Creek
Black John holds a conference
  Hendryx, J. B. Intrigue on Halfaday
  Creek
Black John makes a purchase
  Hendryx, J. B. Murder on Halfaday
  Creek
Black John sells his York boat
  Hendryx, J. B. Intrigue on Halfaday
  Creek
Black John talks with the goose
  Hendryx, J. B. Intrigue on Halfaday
  Creek
Black John wins a bet
  Hendryx, J. B. Murder on Halfaday
  Creek
Brother Willie
  Hendryx, J. B. Murder on Halfaday
  Creek
Business proposition
  Hendryx, J. B. Murder on Halfaday
  Creek
Cantrill remains on Halfaday
  Hendryx, J. B. Murder on Halfaday
  Creek
Coroner's inquest
  Hendryx, J. B. Intrigue on Halfaday
  Creek
Corporal Downey appears on Halfaday
  Hendryx, J. B. Intrigue on Halfaday
  Creek
Corporal Downey gets a tip
  Hendryx, J. B. Murder on Halfaday
  Creek
Corporal Downey makes an arrest; 2 sto-
  ries

Hendryx, J. B. Murder on Halfaday
  Creek
Corporal Downey states his case
  Hendryx, J. B. Intrigue on Halfaday
  Creek
Corporal Downey visits Halfaday
  Hendryx, J. B. Murder on Halfaday
  Creek
Cush gets a toothache
  Hendryx, J. B. Murder on Halfaday
  Creek
Cush takes inventory
  Hendryx, J. B. Murder on Halfaday
  Creek
Cuter Malone turns down a deal
  Hendryx, J. B. Intrigue on Halfaday
  Creek
Doolittles depart from Halfaday
  Hendryx, J. B. Murder on Halfaday
  Creek
The escape
  Hendryx, J. B. Intrigue on Halfaday
  Creek
George Ingram pays his debt
  Hendryx, J. B. Murder on Halfaday
  Creek
Hines and Heatherly explain the deal
  Hendryx, J. B. Intrigue on Halfaday
  Creek
In Cushing's saloon
  Hendryx, J. B. Murder on Halfaday
  Creek
Introducing Pete Collins
  Hendryx, J. B. Intrigue on Halfaday
  Creek
Joe Smiley collects a reward
  Hendryx, J. B. Murder on Halfaday
  Creek
Joe Smiley shows up on Halfaday
  Hendryx, J. B. Murder on Halfaday
  Creek
Man who couldn't remember
  Hendryx, J. B. Murder on Halfaday
  Creek
Man with the glass eye
  Hendryx, J. B. Intrigue on Halfaday
  Creek
Miners' meetin'
  Hendryx, J. B. Intrigue on Halfaday
  Creek
  Hendryx, J. B. Murder on Halfaday
  Creek
One-armed John finds a corpse
  Hendryx, J. B. Intrigue on Halfaday
  Creek
One-armed John voices a threat
  Hendryx, J. B. Intrigue on Halfaday
  Creek
Package of big bills
  Hendryx, J. B. Murder on Halfaday
  Creek
Plan goes wrong
  Hendryx, J. B. Intrigue on Halfaday
  Creek
Plot backfires
  Hendryx, J. B. Murder on Halfaday
  Creek
Plot is hatched
  Hendryx, J. B. Murder on Halfaday
  Creek

Hendryx, James B.—*Continued*
Skin game
Hendryx, J. B. Murder on Halfaday Creek
Stranger arrives on Halfaday
Hendryx, J. B. Murder on Halfaday Creek
The surrender
Hendryx, J. B. Intrigue on Halfaday Creek
Trap is set
Hendryx, J. B. Murder on Halfaday Creek
Two men confer with Cuter Malone
Hendryx, J. B. Intrigue on Halfaday Creek
Unholy trio
Hendryx, J. B. Intrigue on Halfaday Creek
Wedding at Cushing's Fort
Hendryx, J. B. Intrigue on Halfaday Creek
William Henry VanBuren
Hendryx, J. B. Murder on Halfaday Creek
Willie craves action
Hendryx, J. B. Murder on Halfaday Creek

Henry, Marguerite, 1902-
Always Reddy
Fenner, P. R. comp. Dogs, dogs, dogs

Henry, O. pseud. See Porter, William Sydney

Henry. Bottome, P.

HENS. See Poultry

Her breath upon the windowpane. Goyen, W.

Her first ball. Mansfield, K.

Her gift. Allen, M.

Her own people. Ferrone, J. R.

Her quaint honour. Gordon, C.

Her rich American cousin. Schorr, Z.

Her table spread. Bowen, E.

Herbert, Sir Allan Patrick, 1890-
Board of Inland Revenue v. Haddock; Rex v. Haddock the Negotiable Cow
Blaustein, A. P. ed. Fiction goes to court

Herbert, Benson
World without
Margulies, L. and Friend, O. J. eds. From off this world

Herbert, Frederick Hugh, 1897-
Gable type
Stowe, A. comp. It's a date
We were just having fun
Esquire (Periodical) Girls from Esquire

Here and today. Caldwell, E.

Here, Putzi! Pratt, F. and De Camp, L. S.

Here there be tygers. Bradbury, R.

Here today, gone tomorrow. Powell, D.

HERESIES AND HERETICS
Bloch, J. R. Heresy of the water taps

Heresy of the water taps. Bloch, J. R.

HERETICS. See Heresies and heretics

Hergesheimer, Joseph, 1880-1954
Wild oranges
Burrell, J. A. and Cerf, B. A. eds. Anthology of famous American stories

Heritage. Abernathy, R.

Hermann the Irascible. Munro, H. H.

Hermit of Saturn's ring. Jones, N. R.

HERMITS
Maugham, W. S. German Harry
Porter, W. S. To him who waits
Tolstoi, L. N. Graf. Three hermits

Herndon, Booton
Run, iron man
Argosy (Periodical) Argosy Book of sports stories

Hero. Brown, E. L.

The hero. Jackson, M. W.

Hero. Terhune, A. P.

Hero returns. Montanelli, I.

HEROD ANTIPAS
Miró Ferrer, G. Herod Antipas

Herodes redivivus. Munby, A. N. L.

HEROES
Brown, E. L. Hero
Crane, S. Mystery of heroism
Jackson, C. R. The break
McLarn, J. C. Trackside grave
Montanelli, I. Hero returns
Ward, E. S. P. Chief operator

See also Courage

HEROINES. See Heroes

HEROISM. See Heroes

HERONS
Peattie, D. C. and Peattie, L. R. Weirwood marsh

Hero's death. Lagerkvist, P. F.

Herrick, Robert, 1868-1938
Master of the inn
Scribner treasury

Herron, Edwin
Hail fellow well met
Southern review. Anthology of stories from the Southern review

Herself. Pooler, J.

Hersey, John Richard, 1914-
Moment of judgment
Burnett, W. ed. World's best
Peggety's parcel of shortcomings
Greene, J. I. and Abell, E. eds. Stories of sudden truth
Prize stories of 1951

Hershman, Morris
Guilty witness
Mystery Writers of America, inc. Butcher, baker, murder-maker
Letter to the editor
Mystery Writers of America, inc. Crook's tour
Live bait
Mystery Writers of America, inc. 20 great tales of murder

Hertlein, Ruth (Wittek)
P. G. Christmas
American girl (Periodical) Christmas all year 'round
American girl (Periodical) Favorite stories

Herzl, Theodor, 1860-1904
  Thumbling and Sapling
    Leftwich, J. ed. Yisröel. 1952 ed.
Heseltine, Nigel, 1916-
  Day's pleasure
    Felheim, M.; Newman, F. B. and Stein-
      hoff, W. R. eds. Modern short stories
Hesse, Hermann, 1877-
  Within and without
    Burnett, W. ed. World's best
  Youth, beautiful youth
    Pick, R. ed. German stories and tales
Hester Lilly. Taylor, E.
Heuman, William
  There are broken hearts in Brooklyn
    Saturday evening post (Periodical) Sat-
      urday evening post stories, 1953
"Hey diddle diddle, the cat. . ." Phillpotts, E.
Hey, taxi! Aiken, C. P.
Hey wait for me. Williams, B.
Heyerdahl, Thor, 1914-
  Kon-Tiki reaches the South Sea Islands
    Fenner, P. R. comp. Stories of the sea
Heyert, Murray
  New kid
    Christ, H. I. and Shostak, J. eds. Short
      stories
Heyliger, William, 1884-
  Man who wouldn't break
    American boy (Periodical) American
      boy anthology
  Steelman's nerve
    Boys' life (Periodical) Boys life Adven-
      ture stories
  Too many crooks
    Furman, A. L. ed. Teen-age stories of
      the diamond
Hi, sailor! Granberg, B.
Hickey, H. B.
  Like a bird, like a fish
    Derleth, A. W. ed. Worlds of tomorrow
Hicks, Michael Allen
  The wake
    Story (Periodical) Story; no. 3
Hidden riches of secret places. Claudy,
  C. H.
Hide and seek. Clarke, A. C.
Hiding of Black Bill. Porter, W. S.
Higbee, Alma Robison
  Words for John Willie
    Hazeltine, A. I. comp. Selected stories
      for teen-agers
The higgler. Coppard, A. E.
High court. Kyd, T. pseud.
High finance. Claudy, C. H.
HIGH SCHOOL LIFE. See School life
HIGH SCHOOLS. See School life
The high sign. Buckingham, N.
High threshold. Nourse, A. E.
High victory. Lavender, D. S.
High-water mark. Harte, B.
Higher abdication. Porter, W. S.
Higher and higher. Marcus, P.
Higher pragmatism. Porter, W. S.

Highstone, Harold Alfred, 1901-
  Frankenstein—unlimited
    Derleth, A. W. ed. Far boundaries
The highway. Bradbury, R.
Highway. Lowndes, R. W.
HIGHWAYMEN. See Brigands and rob-
  bers
HIGHWAYS. See Roads
Hill, James H.
  Captain returns
    Ford, N. A. and Faggett, H. L. eds.
      Best short stories by Afro-American
      writers (1925-1950)
  Comfort and joy
    Ford, N. A. and Faggett, H. L. eds.
      Best short stories by Afro-American
      writers (1925-1950)
  Gust of wind
    Ford, N. A. and Faggett, H. L. eds.
      Best short stories by Afro-American
      writers (1925-1950)
Hill, Kay
  Blue flag
    Joseph, M. ed. Best cat stories
Hill, Marjorie (Yourd)
  Blue brocade
    American girl (Periodical) On my honor
  Christmas anyhow
    American girl (Periodical) Christmas
      all year 'round
  Sea anchor
    American girl (Periodical) Christmas
      all year 'round
    American girl (Periodical) Favorite
      stories
Hill people. Marshall, E.
Hillbilly halfback. Coombs, C. I.
Hillger, Elwood H.
  Lomax pitching
    Owen, F. ed. Teen-age victory parade
Hilliard, Alec Rowley, 1908-
  Green torture
    Margulies, L. and Friend, O. J. eds.
      From off this world
Hillman, Gordon Malherbe
  Copy girl
    McFarland, W. K. comp. Then it hap-
      pened
Hills of Donegal. Murtagh, L. D.
Hilton, James, 1900-1954
  Twilight of the wise
    Lohan, R. and Lohan, M. eds. New
      Christmas treasury
  The war years
    Brentano, F. ed. The word lives on
HIMALAYA MOUNTAINS
  Bottome, P. Splendid fellow
  Ullman, J. R. Top man
Hindsight. Williamson, J.
Hindu Yogi science of breath. Ekbergh,
  I. D.
HINDUS IN THE UNITED STATES
  Ekbergh, I. D. Gentleman from India
Hine, Alfred Blakelee, 1915-
  Kissing kind
    Collier's, the national weekly. Collier's
      best

Hines and Heatherly explain the deal. Hendryx, J. B.

Hinkle, Thomas Clark, 1876-1949
Black Storm
Dennis, W. ed. Palomino and other horses

Hint of an explanation. Greene, G.

Hinternhoff, John F.
Mutineers be hanged
Fenner, P. R. comp. Pirates, pirates, pirates
Furman, A. L. ed. Teen-age sea stories

Hinton, James, 1915-
Mediators to the goatherd
Southern review. Anthology of stories from the Southern review

HIRED GIRLS. See Servants—Hired girls

Hired man. Strong, J.

HIRED MEN. See Servants—Hired men

Hirshbein, Peretz, 1880-
Leftwich, J. ed. Yisröel. 1952 ed.

His brother's keeper. Hammett, D.

His Excellency. Maugham, W. S.

His first appearance. Chekhov, A. P.

His first race. Gray, D.

His great decision. Arico, V.

His idea of a mother. Boyle, K.

His last bow. Doyle, Sir A. C.

His mother. O'Higgins, H. J.

His mother's sermon. Watson, J.

His new mittens. Crane, S.

His Reverence. Verga, G.

His ship comes home. Sitwell, Sir O. bart.

His spurs. James, W.

His wife survived him. Brophy, B.

HISTORIANS
Auchincloss, L. Greg's peg
Maugham, W. S. Mayhew

Historical note. Jenkins, W. F.

History lesson. Clarke, A. C.

History of a business enterprise. Chekhov, A. P.

History of Krakatuk. Hoffmann, E. T. A.

The **hitch**-hikers. Welty, E.

Hitchens, Dolores (Birk) 1907-
Absent hat pin
Mystery Writers of America, inc. 20 great tales of murder
Fuzzy things
Mystery Writers of America, inc. Four-&-twenty bloodhounds

HITCHHIKERS
Barker, A. L. Villain as a young boy
Welty, E. Hitch-hikers

HITLER, ADOLF, 1889-1945
Forester, C. S. Wandering Gentile

Hoar, Roger Sherman
Liquid life
Jenkins, W. F. ed. Great stories of science fiction

HOAXES
Clemens, S. L. My bloody massacre (I)
Clemens, S. L. Petrified man (I-II)
Davis, R. H. In the fog
Dick, I. M. Two strangers came to town
Maugham, W. S. Winter cruise
Munro, H. H. Phantom luncheon
Poe, E. A. Balloon hoax
Poe, E. A. The spectacles
Poe, E. A. Unparalleled adventure of one Hans Pfaall
Porter, W. S. Double-dyed deceiver
Queen, E. pseud. Emperor's dice
Steinberg, Y. Reb Anshel the golden
See also Humor—Practical jokes

Hobart, Alice Tisdale (Nourse) 1882-
He sought to know God
Brentano, F. ed. The word lives on

Hobbies. Simak, C. D.

Hobbs, Augusta Kent
River pirates
American girl (Periodical) Favorite stories

Hobbyist. Russell, E. F.

HOBOES. See Tramps

Hobson's choice. Bester, A.

HOCKEY
Bendrodt, J. C. Spike
Coombs, C. I. Freeze out
Coombs, C. I. Ice ostrich
Coombs, C. I. Lucky stick
Kempton, K. P. Puck-eater
Muller, C. G. Hat trick
Sandberg, H. W. Captain Kidder
Sherman, H. M. Reeder, left defense
Young, S. Dangerous ice

Hodel. Rabinowitz, S.

Hodgson, William Hope, 1878-1918
Noise in the night
Derleth, A. W. ed. Beyond time & space

Hodkin, Ruth E.
Tomboy
Wolfe, D. M. ed. Which grain will grow

Hoffmann, Eleanor, 1895-
On trial
American girl (Periodical) On my honor
Polonaise
American girl (Periodical) Christmas all year 'round

Hoffmann, Ernst Theodor Amadeus, 1776-1822
Cremona violin
Lange, V. ed. Great German short novels and stories
Deed of entail
Hoffmann, E. T. A. Tales from Hoffmann
Golden pot
Hoffmann, E. T. A. Tales from Hoffmann
History of Krakatuk
Neider, C. ed. Great short stories from the world's literature
Mlle de Scudéri
Hoffmann, E. T. A. Tales from Hoffmann
The sandman
Hoffmann, E. T. A. Tales from Hoffmann
Story of Krespel
Hoffmann, E. T. A. Tales from Hoffmann

Hofmannsthal, Hugo Hofmann, Edler von,
  1874-1929
  Episode in the life of the Marshal de Bas-
    sompierre
    Pick, R. ed. German stories and tales
Hogan, Alice
  Sorority
    American girl (Periodical) On my
    honor
HOGS. See Swine
Hokey-Pocus McGee. Gallery, D. V.
Holberg, Lewis. See Holberg, Ludvig, baron
Holberg, Ludvig, baron, 1684-1754
  Tree men of Potu
    Derleth, A. W. ed. Beyond time & space
Hold back tomorrow. Neville, K.
Hold 'em Yale. Runyon, D.
Holder, William
  Cash and carry guy
    Argosy (Periodical) Argosy Book of
    sports stories
  Nitro ship
    Argosy (Periodical) Argosy Book of
    sea stories
  One guy, one gal, one island
    Argosy (Periodical) Argosy Book of
    adventure stories
  Storm over second
    Argosy (Periodical) Argosy Book of
    sports stories
Holding up a train. Porter W. S.
HOLDUPS. See Robbery
Hole, Lucy Ellen
  Prowler on the hill
    Oberfirst, R. ed. 1954 anthology of best
    original short-shorts
Hole in the moon. Seabright, I.
Hole in the sky. Cox, I.
Holenia, Alexander Maria Lernet- See
    Lernet-Holenia, Alexander Maria
Holiday. Bradbury, R.
Holiday house party. Vetter, M. M.
Holiday task. Munro, H. H.
HOLIDAYS. See names of particular holi-
    days; also Vacations
Holland, Marion
  Billy had a system
    Fenner, P. R. comp. Giggle box
Holland, Rupert Sargent, 1878-1952
  Cobra's hood
    Fenner, P. R. comp. Ghosts, ghosts,
    ghosts
  Drums in the fog
    Fenner, P. R. comp. Indians, Indians,
    Indians
  Pirates of Charles Town harbor
    Fenner, P. R. comp. Pirates, pirates,
    pirates
  Turn and turn about
    Fenner, P. R. comp. Pirates, pirates,
    pirates
HOLLYWOOD, CALIFORNIA. See Cali-
    fornia—Hollywood
Holmes, H. H. pseud. See White, William
    Anthony Parker

Holmes, Kenyon
  Man who rode the saucer
    Derleth, A. W. ed. Far boundaries
Holmes, Wilfred Jay, 1900-
  Action off Formosa
    Saturday evening post (Periodical)
    Saturday evening post stories, 1950
Holohan's hoist. McNamara, E.
Holt, Stephen, pseud. See Thompson, Harlan
Holtman, Alice, 1914-
  Min's God
    Wolfe, D. M. ed. Which grain will grow
Holwerda, Frank, 1908-
  Char on raven's bench
    Best American short stories, 1954
Holy door. O'Donovan, M.
HOLY LAND. See Palestine
Holy Land. Lewisohn, L.
Holy simplicity. Chekhov, A. P.
Home. Boyle, K.
Home. Hughes, L.
Home. Maugham, W. S.
Home again. Morley, C. D.
HOME COMING
  Arico, V. The knight returns
  Brookhouser, F. Young man from yester-
    day
  Garland, H. Return of a private
  Hesse, H. Youth, beautiful youth
  Markewich, R. Return to the Bronx
  Maugham, W. S. Home
  Newhouse, E. Pro and con
  Van Doren, M. Night at the Notch
HOME ECONOMICS
  Hope, M. R. Secret recipe
    See also Cookery
Home fires. Sullivan, R.
Home front. Stafford, J.
Home game. O'Rourke, F.
Home is a place. Breuer, B.
Home is in the heart. Nathan, R.
Home is the hunter. Kuttner, H.
Home is where the wreck is. Tucker, W.
Home stretch. Gilpatric, G.
Home to roost. Stout, R.
Home town of the army ants. Beebe, W.
Home tragedy. Verga, G.
HOMECOMING. See Home coming
Homecoming. Johns, V. P.
Homecoming. Nye, N. C.
Homecoming. Patterson, E. G.
Homeland. Wolf, M.
Homemade miracle. Cousins, M.
Homer and the lilies. West, J.
HOMES. See Houses
Homesick Buick. MacDonald, J. D.
Homesickness night. Kinau, R.
Homestead orchard. Davis, H. L.
Homicide House. Keene, D.
Homo Sol. Asimov, I.

HOMOSEXUALITY
Barr, J. pseud. Derricks; 7 stories
Cory, D. W. ed. 21 variations on a theme;
20 stories
Lowry, R. J. C. The victim
Maupassant, G. de. Paul's mistress
Honest fisherman. Walsh, M.
HONESTY
Lipman, C. and Lipman, M. Dilemma of
Grampa Dubois
Marquand, J. P. You can't do that
Porter, W. S. Masters of arts
Stern, R. G. Present for Minna
Honey and the home front. Taber, G. B.
Honey house. King, M. P.
Honey, we'll be brave. Farrell, J. T.
Honeyed peace. Gellhorn, M. E.
Honeyed poison. Gibran, K.
Honeymoon. Caldwell, E.
Honeymoon. Sullivan, R.
Honeymoon. Van Doren, M.
Honeymoon. Wincelberg, S.
Honeymoon in hell. Brown, F.
HONG KONG. See China—Hong Kong
Honi ha-Maeggel. Cohn, E.
HONOLULU. See Hawaiian Islands
Honolulu. Maugham, W. S.
Honor. Faulkner, W.
Honor of his house. Wyld Ospina, C.
Honor of the county. Edmonds, W. D.
Honour of Israel Gow. Chesterton, G. K.
Hoodooed. Rice, A. C. H.
Hook. Clark, W. Van T.
HOOKED RUGS. See Rugs, Hooked
Hooky line and sinker. Wylie, P.
"Hoot!" said the owl. Barbour, R. H.
Hop-Frog. Poe, E. A.
Hope, M. Russell
Secret recipe
Oberfirst, R. ed. 1951 anthology of best
original short-shorts
Hope chest. Dempsey, D. K.
HOPE CHESTS
Paget, V. Wedding chest
Hopkinson, Henry Thomas, 1905-
I have been drowned
New writing (Periodical) Best stories
Mountain madness
Talbot, D. ed. Treasury of mountaineer-
ing stories
Hopkinson, Tom. See Hopkinson, Henry
Thomas
Horace Chooney, M.D. West, J.
Horatio. Felsen, G.
Horgan, Paul, 1903-
Devil in the desert
Gable, M Sister, ed. Many-colored fleece
Saturday evening post (Periodical) Sat-
urday evening post stories, 1950
National honeymoon
Collier's, the national weekly. Collier's
best
Peach stone
Best of the Best American short stories,
1915-1950

The **Horla.** Maupassant, G. de
Hormones. Pratt, F.
Horn that called Bambine. Godchaux, E.
Hornblower and Noah's ark. Forester, C. S.
Hornblower and the cargo of rice. Forester,
C. S.
Hornblower and the even chance. Forester,
C. S.
Hornblower and the examination for lieuten-
ant. Forester, C. S.
Hornblower and the man who felt queer.
Forester, C. S.
Hornblower and the man who saw God.
Forester, C. S.
Hornblower and the penalty of failure. For-
ester, C. S.
Hornblower and the Spanish galleys. For-
ester, C. S.
Hornblower, the Duchess, and the Devil.
Forester, C. S.
Hornblower, the frogs, and the lobsters.
Forester, C. S.
HORNED TOADS
Porter, W. S. Jimmy Hayes and Muriel
Hornet's nest. Bennett, M. E.
Hornets of space. Starzl, R. F.
HOROSCOPES. See Astrologers
Horowitz, Emmanuel, 1910-
God's agents have beards
Ribalow, H. U. ed. These your children
Horror of the heights. Doyle, Sir A. C.
HORROR STORIES
Bierce, A. Boarded window
Blackwood, A. The Wendigo
Bowles, P. F. Distant episode
Bradbury, R. World the children made
Collier, J. Evening primrose
Collier, J. Green thoughts
Coppel, A. The exile
Crawford, F. M. Screaming skull
Davenport, B. ed. Tales to be told in the
dark; 13 stories
Doyle, Sir A. C. Adventure of the speckled
band
Eliot, G. pseud. Lifted veil
Faulkner, W. Rose for Emily
Gilman, C. P. S. Yellow wall-paper
Harris, J. B. Survival
Jacobs, W. S. Monkey's paw
James, H. Turn of the screw
Keller, D. H. Tiger cat
Keller, D. H. The worm
Kipling, R. Mark of the beast
Machen, A. White powder
Moore, C. L. Scarlet dream
Mudford, W. Iron shroud
Munby, A. N. L. Herodes redivivus
Parker, Sir G. bart. The flood
Poe, E. A. Berenice
Poe, E. A. Descent into the maelström
Poe, E. A. Fall of the house of Usher
Poe, E. A. Ligeia
Poe, E. A. Ms. found in a bottle
Poe, E. A. Morella
Poe, E. A. Pit and the pendulum
Poe, E. A. Tell-tale heart
Poe, E. A. William Wilson
Wakefield, H. W. Red Lodge

HORSE. See Horses
Horse called Pete. Bialk, E.
Horse dealer's daughter. Lawrence, D. H.
Horse drive. Martin, C. M.
Horse in the moon. Pirandello, L.
Horse of her own. Payne, S.
Horse of Hurricane Reef. Jackson, C. T.
HORSE RACING
  Anderson, S. I want to know why
  Anderson, S. I'm a fool
  Bendrodt, J. C. Irish lad
  Bendrodt, J. C. Valiant lady
  Byrne, D. Rivers of Damascus
  Chamberlain, G. A. Monarch the bum
  Clements, C. J. Keep off the rail!
  Cooke, A. A. For the love of a race horse
  Curry, P. S. Osage Girl
  DeJong, D. C. Before the races
  Foote, J. T. Class
  Foote, J. T. Hoofbeats; 13 stories
  Foote, J. T. Look of eagles
  Foote, J. T. Two ringers
  Gray, D. His first race
  Harvey, W. F. Dark horses
  Hemingway, E. My old man
  Irwin, M. E. F. Bloodstock
  Lawrence, D. H. Rocking-horse winner
  McKenney, J. Skycaptain
  Munro, H. H. Bread and Butter miss
  Munro, H. H. The Brogue
  Runyon, D. All horse players die broke
  Runyon, D. Snatching of Bookie Bob
  Sharp, M. Winning sequence
  Thompson, M. My brother who talked
    with horses
  Van Loan, C. E. Levelling with Elisha
  Van Loan, C. E. Playing even for
    Obadiah
  Winchell, P. Devil on wheels
HORSE SHOWS
  Allan, G. Kentucky line-up
  Newcomb, C. Grand prize
  Newcomb, E. Two for the show
Horse that played third base for Brooklyn.
  Schramm, W. L.
Horse thief. Berman, H.
Horse thief. Caldwell, E.
Horse thief. Opatovsky, J.
HORSE THIEVES
  Caldwell, E. Horse thief
  Loomis, N. M. Mustang trail to glory
  Opatovsky, J. Horse thief
  Somerville, E. A. Œ. and Martin, V. F.
    Trinket's colt
HORSE-TRADING
  Annett, R. R. Gentle like a cyclone
  Benefield, B. Incident at Boiling Springs
  Faulkner, W. Spotted horses
  Stuart, J. Horse trading Trembles
Horse-trading Trembles. Stuart, J.
HORSE TRAINING. See Horses
HORSEBACK RIDING. See Horseman-
  ship
HORSEMANSHIP
  Bond, N. S. The sportsman
  Bottome, P. A pair
  Erskine, L. Y. Horses and men

  Harnden, R. P. Rebellion
  James, W. Best riding and roping
  Lambert, J. Tall as the stars
HORSES
  Bates, H. E. Sugar for the horse
  Bendrodt, J. C. Irish lad
  Bendrodt, J. C. Valiant lady
  Bendrodt, J. C. Zaimis
  Bergengruen, W. Ali Baba and the forty
    horse-power
  Berman, H. Horse thief
  Bonham, F. I'll take the high road
  Bottome, P. A pair
  Breckenfeld, V. G. Touch of Arab
  Butler, E. P. Too much horse
  Caldwell, E. Sick horse
  Creamer, J. B. comp. Twenty-two stories
    about horses and men; 17 stories
  Davis, H. L. Open winter
  Dennis, W. Palomino and other horses
  Doyle, Sir A. C. Silver Blaze
  Drinkard, I. N. Mission for baby
  Farley, W. The storm
  Faulkner, W. Spotted horses
  Fenner, P. R. comp. Cowboys, cowboys,
    cowboys; 17 stories
  Foote, J. T. Hoofbeats; 13 stories
  Furman, A. L. ed. Teen-age horse sto-
    ries; 13 stories
  Hudson, W. H. Story of a piebald horse
  Jackson, C. T. Horse of Hurricane Reef
  James, W. Will James' Book of cowboy
    stories; 15 stories
  McCourt, E. A. White mustang
  McNulty, J. Where the grass, they say,
    is blue
  Miers, E. S. Bandy
  Miers, E. S. Black Bat
  Nason, L. H. Rodney
  O'Flaherty, L. Old hunter
  Pattullo, G. Corazón
  Reymont, W. S. Twilight
  Ross, S. The outlaw
  Runyon, D. Old Em's Kentucky home
  Saroyan, W. Summer of the beautiful
    white horse
  Schaefer, J. W. That Mark horse
  Seton, E. T. Pacing mustang
  Steele, W. D. Blue murder
  Steinbeck, J. The gift
  Steinbeck, J. Red pony
  Sture-Vasa, M. A. My friend Flicka
  Watson, J. C. Benny and the Tar-Baby
The horses. Stephens, J.
Horses and men. Erskine, L. Y.
Horseshoe nails. Benét, L.
Horseshoes. Lardner, R. W.
Horsie. Parker, D. R.
Horton, Philip
  What's in a corner
    Best American short stories, 1952
Horwitz, Julius, 1920-
  The burial
    Horwitz, J. The city
  The campaign
    Horwitz, J. The city
  The city
    Horwitz, J. The city
  The conspirators
    Horwitz, J. The city

Horwitz, Julius—*Continued*
  Cup of tea
    Horwitz, J. The city
  Generations of man
    Horwitz, J. The city
  If God makes you pretty
    Horwitz, J. The city
  The island
    Horwitz, J. The city
  Just love, love, sweet love
    Horwitz, J. The city
  Lunch
    Horwitz, J. The city
  The movers
    Horwitz, J. The city
  New York
    Horwitz, J. The city
  Old woman
    Horwitz, J. The city
  Poor people
    Horwitz, J The city
  The roof
    Horwitz, J The city
  The street
    Horwitz, J The city
  The strudel
    Horwitz, J The city
  The visitor
    Horwitz, J The city
  The voices
    Horwitz, J The city
Horwitz, Merle, 1930?-
  Coquette
    Oberfirst, R. ed. 1954 anthology of best
      original short-shorts
HOSEA, THE PROPHET
  Wilson, D. C. Priest and prophet at Bethel
HOSPITALITY
  Hawthorne, N. Ambitious guest
    See also Guests; Visiting
HOSPITALS, CONVALESCENT
  Karmel, I. Fru Holm
HOSPITALS AND SANATORIUMS
  Benét, S. V. No visitors
  Chekhov, A. P. An unpleasantness
  Conrad, R. E. Call of the street
  Gordon, A. Old Ironpuss
  Harvey, W. F. Dead of night
  Horwitz, J. Just love, love, sweet love
  Lansing, E. C. H. Touch of psychology
  McCarthy, M. T. Old men
  McNulty, J. Bellevue days
  Maugham, W. S. Sanatorium
  O'Donovan, M. Vanity
  Sansom, W. Eye man
  Seager, A. Pro arte
  Seager, A. The street
  Stafford, J. Interior castle
  Stern, J. Next door to death
The **hostage.** Forester, C. S.
Hostage. Stegner, W. E.
HOSTAGES
  Forester, C. S. The hostage
  O'Donovan, M. Guests of the nation
Hostages to Momus. Porter, W. S.
Hostess. Asimov, I.
Hot-collared mule. Stuart, J.
A **hot** dog on ice. Sherman, H. M.
Hot finish. Patten, G.

Hot rod. Felsen, G.
Hot time in the old town. Newhouse, E.
Hotel dog. Winslow, T. S.
Hotel François Ier. Stein, G.
HOTELS, TAVERNS, ETC.
  Aiken, C. P. The anniversary
  Beck, W. Clean platter
  Burns, J. H. Momma
  Crane, S. Blue Hotel
  Davies, R. River, flow gently
  Gally, J. W. Spirits
  Gissing, G. Pig and Whistle
  Harte, B. Miggles
  Herrick, R. Master of the inn
  Irving, W. Stout gentleman
  Jenkin, P. A. Cool million
  Lagerkvist, P. F. The hangman
  Mannix, E. New Year for Juicy
  Mansfield, K. Man without a temperament
  Maugham, W. S. In a strange land
  Millay, E. St V. Murder in the Fishing
    Cat
  Montross, L. S. Day in New York
  Moore, I. S. Family man
  Newhouse, E. Ten years on a desert
    island
  Porter, W. S. Enchanted profile
  Pratt, F. and De Camp, L. S. Tales from
    Gavagan's bar; 23 stories
  Sansom, W. Displaced persons
  Saroyan, W. Third day after Christmas
  Welty, E. Purple hat
The **hound.** Faulkner, W.
Hounds of Fate. Munro, H. H.
Hounds of spring. Parker, J. R.
Hour and the years. Gordimer, N.
Hour of stars. Hagedorn, H.
House and the brain. Lytton, E. G. E. L.
  B.-L. 1st baron
HOUSE BOATS
  Burman, B. L. Children of Noah
HOUSE CLEANING
  Aldrich, B. S. Will the romance be the
    same?
House dutiful. Klass, P.
HOUSE FLIES. See Flies
House in Goblin Wood. Carr, J. D.
House of agony. Pirandello, L.
House of flowers. Capote, T.
House of ocean born Mary. Lowndes, M. S.
House of the nightmare. White, E. L.
House on the esplanade. Hébert, A.
HOUSE PARTIES
  Bowen, E. Cat jumps
  Ellin, S. House party
  Munro, H. H. The elk
  Munro, H. H. Excepting Mrs Pentherby
  Munro, H. H. Matter of sentiment
  Munro, H. H. The oversight
  Munro, H. H. Reginald on house-parties
  Munro, H. H. Reginald's Christmas revel
House party. Ellin, S.
House that Johnny built. O'Donovan, M.
House that Nella lived in. Seely, M. H.
HOUSEBOATS. See House boats

Household, Geoffrey, 1900-
  Brandy for the parson
    Household, G. Tales of adventurers
  Cook-runner
    Household, G. Tales of adventurers
  Culture
    Household, G. Tales of adventurers
  Debt of honor
    Household, G. Tales of adventurers
  First blood
    Household, G. Tales of adventurers
  Heart in the mouth
    Household, G. Tales of adventurers
  The hut
    Household, G. Tales of adventurers
  Low water
    Household, G. Tales of adventurers
  The pejemuller
    Household, G. Tales of adventurers
  Picket lines of Marton Hevessy
    Household, G. Tales of adventurers
  Railroad harvest
    Household, G. Tales of adventurers
  Three kings
    Household, G. Tales of adventurers
  Woman in love
    Household, G. Tales of adventurers
HOUSEHOLD APPLIANCES
  Jakes, J. W. Machine
Household words. De Vries, P.
HOUSEKEEPERS. See Servants—House-
  keepers
HOUSEKEEPING. See Home economics
HOUSEMAIDS. See Servants—Maids
HOUSES
  Arthur, R. Change of address
  Baker, D. V. The beautiful house
  Bunner, H. C. Story of a New York
    house
  Chekhov, A. P. New villa
  Chekhov, A. P. Other people's misfor-
    tune
  De Vries, P. Today and today
  Grimson, M. S. Will and a way
  Humphrey, W. The Hardys
  Melville, H. The piazza
  Smith, L. P. 'Ivanhoe'
  Stettner, S. Summer place
HOUSES, APARTMENT. See Apartment
  houses
HOUSES, DESERTED
  Grinevskiĭ, A. S. The ratcatcher
HOUSES, HAUNTED. See Ghosts
HOUSTON. See Texas—Houston
How Abel slew Cain. Feild, B.
How Babe got his name. Considine, R. B.
How bad? How long? Van Doren, M.
How beautiful with shoes. Steele, W. D.
How Brother Aaron was saved. Knox, J.
How can I leave thee? De Vries, P.
How Claeys died. Sansom, W.
How dear to my heart. Rossiter, H. D.
How do you say good-bye? Fontaine, R. L.
How far is it to Hollywood? Aldrich, B. S.
How I came to love the smell of a bar-room.
  DeLynn, L.
How many midnights. Bowles, P. F.

How Old Stormalong captured Mocha Dick.
  Shapiro, I.
How old Timofei died singing. Rilke, R. M.
How Rezi baked motzas. Oesterreicher, A.
How Santa Claus came to Simpson's Bar.
  Harte, B.
How the Czar fooled Montefiore. Sforim,
  M. M.
How the devil came down Division Street.
  Algren, N.
How the good gifts were used by two.
  Pyle, H.
How the mountain was clad. Bjørnson, B.
How war came to Arcadia, N. Y. Jackson,
  C. R.
How we astonished the Rivermouthians.
  Aldrich, T. B.
Howard, Hayden
  Dipping of the candlemaker
    Queen, E. pseud. ed. Ellery Queen's
    awards: 9th ser.
Howard, Quentin R.
  Time for a change
    Oberfirst, R. ed. 1952 anthology of best
    original short-shorts
Howard, Robert Ervin, 1906-1936
  Beyond the Black River
    Howard, R. E. King Conan
  Frost-giant's daughter
    Howard, R. E. Coming of Conan
  God in the bowl
    Howard, R. E. Coming of Conan
  Jewels of Gwahlur
    Howard, R. E. King Conan
  Mirrors of Tuzun Thune
    Howard, R. E. Coming of Conan
  People of the black circle
    Howard, R. E. The sword of Conan
  Phoenix on the sword
    Howard, R. E. King Conan
  Pool of the black one
    Howard, R. E. The sword of Conan
  Queen of the Black Coast
    Howard, R. E. Coming of Conan
  Red nails
    Howard, R. E. The sword of Conan
  Rogues in the house
    Howard, R. E. Coming of Conan
  Scarlet citadel
    Howard, R. E. King Conan
  Shadow kingdom
    Howard, R. E. Coming of Conan
  Slithering shadow
    Howard, R. E. Sword of Conan
  Tower of the Elephant
    Howard, R. E. Coming of Conan
  Treasure of Tranicos
    Howard, R. E. King Conan
Howard, Wendell, 1891?-
  Last refuge of a scoundrel
    Howard, W. Last refuge of a scoundrel,
    and other stories
  The masterstroke
    Howard, W. Last refuge of a scoundrel,
    and other stories
  Put on the spot
    Howard, W. Last refuge of a scoundrel,
    and other stories

Howard, Wendell—*Continued*
The rainbow
Howard, W. Last refuge of a scoundrel, and other stories
Rude awakening
Howard, W. Last refuge of a scoundrel, and other stories
Howarth, Jean
The novitiate
Weaver, R. and James, H. eds. Canadian short stories
Howe, Diana, 1931-
White kitten
American vanguard, 1952
Howe, Joseph, 1804-1873
Locksmith of Philadelphia
Pacey, D. ed. Book of Canadian stories
Howells, William Dean, 1837-1920
Christmas every day
Lohan, R. and Lohan, M. eds. New Christmas treasury
Editha
Burrell, J. A. and Cerf, B. A. eds. Anthology of famous American stories
Ungar, F. ed. To mother with love
Howland, Rosemary
Magic night
McFarland, W. K. comp. Then it happened
Tonight will be different
Certner, S. and Henry, G. H. eds. Short stories for our times
How's that umpire? Wodehouse, P. G.
Hsieh Liang
Wolf of Chungshan
Lin, Y. ed. Famous Chinese short stories
Hsüan-Yu, Ch'en. See Ch'en Hsüan-yu
Hsün, Lu, pseud. See Chou, Shu-Jên
Hualapi. Gally, J. W.
The **hub.** MacDonald, P.
Hubbard, Lafayette Ronald, 1911-
When shadows fall
Greenberg, M. ed. Men against the stars
Hubbard, P. M.
Manuscript found in a vacuum
Magazine of fantasy and science fiction. Best from Fantasy and science fiction; 3d ser.
Huckabay, Mary Barrow
Ghost of Sam Bates
Oberfirst, R. ed. 1952 anthology of best original short-shorts
Huckabuck family and how they raised popcorn in Nebraska and quit and came back. Sandburg, C.
HUCKSTERS. See Peddlers and peddling
Huddling place. Simak, C. D.
Hudson, Alec, pseud. See Holmes, Wilfred Jay
Hudson, William Henry, 1841-1922
Mysterious forest
Andrews, R. C. ed. My favorite stories of the great outdoors
Story of a piebald horse
Cerf, B. A. and Moriarty, H. C. eds. Anthology of famous British stories

HUDSON RIVER
Irving, W. Legend of Sleepy Hollow
Huge beast. Cartmill, C.
Hughes, Langston, 1902-
African morning
Hughes, L. Laughing to keep from crying
Big meeting
Hughes, L. Laughing to keep from crying
Heaven to hell
Hughes, L. Laughing to keep from crying
Home
Gable, M. Sister, ed. Many-colored fleece
Little old spy
Hughes, L. Laughing to keep from crying
Mysterious Madame Shanghai
Hughes, L. Laughing to keep from crying
Name in the papers
Hughes, L. Laughing to keep from crying
Never room with a couple
Hughes, L. Laughing to keep from crying
On the road
Hughes, L. Laughing to keep from crying
On the way home
Hughes, L. Laughing to keep from crying
One Friday morning
Certner, S. and Henry, G. H. eds. Short stories for our times
Hughes, L. Laughing to keep from crying
Powder-white faces
Hughes, L. Laughing to keep from crying
Professor
Hughes, L. Laughing to keep from crying
Pushcart man
Hughes, L. Laughing to keep from crying
Rouge high
Hughes, L. Laughing to keep from crying
Sailor ashore
Hughes, L. Laughing to keep from crying
Saratoga rain
Hughes, L. Laughing to keep from crying
Slice him down
Hughes, L. Laughing to keep from crying
Something in common
Hughes, L. Laughing to keep from crying
Spanish blood
Hughes, L. Laughing to keep from crying
Tain't so
Hughes, L. Laughing to keep from crying
Tragedy at the Baths
Hughes, L. Laughing to keep from crying

Hughes, Langston—*Continued*
Trouble with the angels
Hughes, L. Laughing to keep from crying
Who's passing for who?
Hughes, L. Laughing to keep from crying
Why, you reckon?
Hughes, L. Laughing to keep from crying
Hughes, Richard Arthur Warren, 1900-
The stranger
Conklin, G. and Conklin, L. T. eds. Supernatural reader
Hugo, Victor Marie, comte, 1802-1885
Combat with the octopus
Andrews, R. C. ed. My favorite stories of the great outdoors
Hugo Kertchak, builder. Schaefer, J. W.
HUGUENOTS
Blackburn, E. R. Christiane the Huguenot
Hull, Edith Maude
Competition
Greenberg, M. ed. Men against the stars
Hull, Edna Mayne
Flight that failed
Conklin, G. ed. Science-fiction adventures in dimension
Hull down. Wylie, P.
Human. Gale, Z.
Human condition. Davies, R.
Human element. Maugham, W. S.
Human habitation. Bowen, E.
HUMAN RACE. See Man
Hume, Sue Tempest, 1915-
Shake hands with a murderer
Oberfirst, R. ed. 1954 anthology of best original short-shorts
Humiliation. Maupassant, G. de
HUMOR
Ausubel, N. ed. Treasury of Jewish humor; 82 stories
Chekhov, A. P. Woman in the case
Clemens, S. L. Celebrated jumping frog of Calaveras County
Cockrell, E. W. Keyhole artist
Dachs, D. ed. Treasury of sports humor; 36 stories
De Vries, P. Overture
Fenner, P. R. ed. Fools and funny fellows; 21 stories
Fenner, P. R. comp. Fun! Fun! Fun! 20 stories
Fenner, P. R. comp. Giggle box; 15 stories
Fessier, M. Man-taming woman
Hale, E. E. My double, and how he undid me
Hardy, T. Tony Kytes, the arch-deceiver
Harris, G. W. Sut Lovingood; 8 stories
Hersey, J. R. Peggety's parcel of shortcomings
Jackson, S. Charles
Kober, A. Bella, Bella kissed a fella; 15 stories
Mauldin, W. H. Affair of the wayward jeep
Mowery, W. B. Lamb and some slaughtering

Munro, H. H. Short stories of Saki; 134 stories
Munro, H. H. The storyteller
Pagano, J. Signor Santa
Porter, W. S. Confessions of a humorist
Porter, W. S. O. Henry's best stories; 25 stories
Rogow, L. Laziest man in Texas
Runyon, D. More guys and dolls; 34 stories
Schaefer, J. W. Leander Frailey
Stockton, F. R. Christmas shadrach
Surtees, R. S. Hunting scenes; 26 stories
Tarkington, B. "Little gentleman"
Thurber, J. More alarms at night
Thurber, J. Secret life of Walter Mitty
Tucker, W. Home is where the wreck is
Wodehouse, P. G. Jeeves and the song of songs
Wodehouse, P. G. Nothing serious; 10 stories
See also Improbable stories; Satire

Practical jokes
Betts, D. Sense of humor
Munro, H. H. Adrian
Munro, H. H. Bertie's Christmas Eve
Munro, H. H. The lull
Munro, H. H. Open window
Munro, H. H. She-wolf
Munro, H. H. Unrest-cure
Noyes, A. Uncle Hyacinth
Perry, G. S. The fourflusher
Porter, W. S. The Marquis and Miss Sally
Simpson, M. E. Practical joker

HUMOROUS STORIES. See Humor
Humphrey, William, 1924-
The fauve
Humphrey, W. Last husband, and other stories
Fresh snow
Humphrey, W. Last husband, and other stories
The Hardys
Humphrey, W. Last husband, and other stories
Prize stories of 1950
In sickness and health
Humphrey, W. Last husband, and other stories
Last husband
Humphrey, W. Last husband, and other stories
Man with a family
Humphrey, W. Last husband, and other stories
Quail for Mr Forester
Humphrey, W. Last husband, and other stories
Report cards
Humphrey, W. Last husband, and other stories
The shell
Humphrey, W. Last husband, and other stories
Sister
Humphrey, W. Last husband, and other stories
Humpty Dumpty had a great fall. Long, F. B.
Hunch that clicked. Cross, J. A.

HUNCHBACKS
Mann, T. Little Herr Friedemann
West, J. Breach of promise
Hundred years from now. Cardozo, N.
HUNGARIAN SOLDIERS. See Soldiers, Hungarian
HUNGARIANS IN THE UNITED STATES
Sinclair, J. pseud. Red necktie
Walden, A. E. So I'm home again
HUNGER
Maupassant, G. de. A vagabond
Rojas, M. Glass of milk
See also Famines
Hunger. Yezierska, A.
Hunger-artist. Kafka, F.
The hungry. Mann, T.
Hungry man. Cicellis, K.
Hungry sister. Winn, J.
Hungry stones. Tagore, Sir R.
Hunt, Finley C.
Egg from the sky
Hathaway, B. and Sessions, J. A. eds. Writers for tomorrow. 2d ser.
The hunt. Kuehn, S.
Hunted down. Dickens, C.
Hunter, Evan, 1926-
Small homicide
Best detective stories of the year—1954
Hunter Gracchus. Kafka, F.
The hunters. Downey, H.
HUNTING
Akeley, C. E. Elephant
Annixter, P. pseud. Dragon rider
Annixter, P. pseud. Hunting coat
Annixter, P. pseud. Kadiak
Annixter, P. pseud. Secret of Coon Castle
Blackwood, A. Valley of the beasts
Bond, N. S. The sportsman
Buck, F. Elephants!
Buckingham, N. Hallowed years; 12 stories
Caldwell, E. Molly-Cotton-Tail
Carrighar, S. Marooned childern
Faulkner, W. The bear
Faulkner, W. Old people
Flaubert, G. Legend of St Julian the Hospitaller
Gipson, F. B. My kind of a man
Gordon, C. Last day in the field
Hemingway, E. Short happy life of Francis Macomber
Humphrey, W. The shell
Marshall, E. Elephant remembers
Marshall, E. Heart of Little Shikara
Seton, E. T. Trail of the Sandhill stag
Stefánsson, V. Seal hunting
Stuart, J. Thanksgiving hunting
Waldeck, T. J. Igongo elephants
Williams, R. Head-hunters
See also Bird hunters; Deer hunting; Duck shooting; Fox hunting; Guides (Hunting); Shooting; Trappers

Accidents
Gray, D. His first race
Hunting coat. Annixter, P. pseud.

HUNTING DOGS. See Dogs
HUNTING GUIDES. See Guides (Hunting)
Hunting season. Robinson, F. M.
The huntress. Kaula, D.
The hurkle is a happy beast. Waldo, E. H.
The hurricane. Grant, G. H.
HURRICANES
Carse, R. Sailor's pay
Grant, G. H. The hurricane
Jackson, C. T. Horse of Hurricane Reef
Powell, F. Black flag
See also Storms
Hurry, hurry! Wilson, E.
Hurst, Fannie, 1889-
Guilty
Queen, E. pseud. ed. Literature of crime
Hurston, Zora Neale, 1901-
Conscience of the court
Saturday evening post (Periodical) Saturday evening post stories, 1950
Escape from Pharaoh
Seldon, R. ed. Ways of God and men
The tablets of the law
Brentano, F. ed. The word lives on
HUSBAND AND WIFE
Adler, J. Yente Telebende
Beck, W. The child is father
Benchley, N. Mrs Crocker's mutiny
Benson, S. The overcoat
Bergelson, D. The squash
Bottome, P. Pink medicine
Bowen, E. Evil that men do—
Bowen, E. Shadowy third
Bowles, P. F. Call at Corazón
Brookhouser, F. She did not cry at all
Caldwell, E. Here and today
Caldwell, E. Uncle Jeff
Callaghan, M. E. Rigmarole
Cave, H. B. Peril of the river
Cheever, J. Season of divorce
Chekhov, A. P. Three Annas
Cicellis, K. Aegean storm
Collier, J. Incident on a lake
Collier, J. Over insurance
Collier, J. Romance lingers, adventure lives
Collier, J. Three Bears Cottage
Collier, J. Youth from Vienna
Coward, N. P. Stop me if you've heard this
Davies, R. Foolish one
De La Roche, M. Submissive wife
De Vries, P. Cold potato
De Vries, P. Flesh and the devil
De Vries, P. Overture
De Vries, P. Scene
Howard, Q. R. Time for a change
Humphrey, W. The Hardys
Humphrey, W. In sickness and health
James, H. The liar
Juan Manuel, Infante of Castille. Man who married an ill-tempered wife
King, M. P. Chicken on the wind
Lagerkvist, P. F. Masquerade of souls
McCarthy, M. T. The weeds
MacDonald, J. D. I love you (occasionally)
Michener, J. A. The jungle
Munro, H. H. Reticence of Lady Anne

HUSBAND AND WIFE—*Continued*
　　Newhouse, E. Magic hour
　　Norris, H. Take her up tenderly
　　Parker, J. R. Tenth Street idyll
　　Pincherle, A. Back to the sea
　　Porter, W. S. Dougherty's eye-opener
　　Porter, W. S. The harbinger
　　Porter, W. S. Harlem tragedy
　　Porter, W. S. The pendulum
　　Prichard, R. Men and babies
　　Priestley, J. B. Night sequence
　　Pultz, C. Good-by to Miss Stoddard's
　　Rabinowitz, S. Menachem-Mendel, fortune
　　　　hunter
　　Schaefer, J. W. Prudence by name
　　Schulberg, B. W. Breaking point
　　Seager, A. Second wedding
　　Shapiro, L. Rebbe and the rebbetsin
　　Strindberg, A. Autumn
　　Taylor, P. H. Cookie
　　Thompson, L. Grasshopper a burden
　　Van Dyke, H. Wedding ring
　　Walsh, M. Come back, my love
　　Waugh, E. Tactical exercise
　　Welty, E. The key
　　Welty, E. The whistle
　　White, A. Moment of truth
　　Williams, R. E. Feminine wiles
　　Willingham, C. Guardian angel
　　Winslow, T. S. Mrs Wilson's husband
　　　　goes for a swim
　　Winslow, T. S. Other woman

Husband for Bluma. Dworzan, H. L.

HUSBANDS AND WIVES. See Husband
　and wife

The **hussar.** Hebel, J. P.

Hussar who loved three Jews. Molnar, F.

HUSSARS. See Soldiers, German

The **hut.** Household, G.

Hutchins, Maude Phelps (McVeigh)
　Affair of honor
　　Hutchins, M. P. M. Love is a pie
　Fifth commandment
　　Hutchins, M. P. M. Love is a pie
　From morning till night
　　Hutchins, M. P. M. Love is a pie
　Help gets the legs
　　Hutchins, M. P. M. Love is a pie
　Innocents
　　Hutchins, M. P. M. Love is a pie
　Les malheurs des mannequins
　　Hutchins, M. P. M. Love is a pie
　Soliloquy at dinner
　　Hutchins, M. P. M. Love is a pie
　Sweet girl graduate
　　Hutchins, M. P. M. Love is a pie
　A tale
　　Hutchins, M. P. M. Love is a pie
　What's in two names
　　Hutchins, M. P. M. Love is a pie

Huxley, Aldous Leonard, 1894-
　Brave new world; excerpts
　　Kuebler, H. W. ed. Treasury of science
　　　fiction classics
　Education in the world state
　　Waite, H. O. and Atkinson, B. P. eds.
　　　Literature for our time
　Farcical history of Richard Greenow
　　Connolly, C. ed. Great English short
　　　novels

Gioconda smile
　Cerf, B. A. and Moriarty, H. C. eds.
　　Anthology of famous British stories
　Heilman, R. B. ed. Modern short stories
　Queen, E. pseud. ed. Literature of crime
Nuns at luncheon
　Stegner, W. E.; Scowcroft, R. and Ilyin,
　　B. eds. Writer's art
Tillotson banquet
　Burnett, W. ed. World's best
Young Archimedes
　Short, R. W. and Sewall, R. B. eds.
　　Short stories for study. 1950 ed.
　Waite, H. O. and Atkinson, B. P. eds.
　　Literature for our time

Huysmans, Joris Karl, 1848-1907
　Monsieur Folantin
　　Geist, S. ed. French stories and tales

Hyacinth. Munro, H. H.

HYDROPHOBIA
　Chekhov, A. P. Hydrophobia
　Kipling, R. Mark of the beast

Hydrophobia. Chekhov, A. P.

HYENAS
　Munro, H. H. Esmé

Hygeia at the Solito. Porter, W. S.

Hyman, Mark
　The shepherd
　　Ford, N. A. and Faggett, H. L. eds.
　　　Best short stories by Afro-American
　　　writers (1925-1950)

Hyperpilosity. De Camp, L. S.

Hyperspherical basketball. Nearing, H.

HYPNOTISM
　Harvey, W. F. Long road
　Lytton, E. G. E. L. B.-L. 1st baron. House
　　and the brain
　Mann, T. Mario and the magician
　Poe, E. A. Facts in the case of M. Valde-
　　mar
　Poe, E. A. Mesmeric revelation
　Poe, E. A. Tales of the ragged mountains

Hypotheses of failure. Porter, W. S.

I

I am Edgar. Wexler, J.

I am not a stranger. Street, J. H.

I am nothing. Russell, E. F.

I and my chimney. Melville, H.

I broke my back on a rosebud. Campbell,
　W. E. M.

I came from yonder mountain. Connell, E. S.

I dive for treasure. Rieseberg, H. E.

I don't want to go. De Vries, P.

I hate a dumpy woman. Chase, M.

I have been drowned. Hopkinson, H. T.

I hope you'll understand. Newhouse, E.

I live in a world of make-believe. Taylor, E.

I love you (occasionally). MacDonald, J. D.

I love you very dearly. Aiken, C. P.

"**I** play basketball." Person, W. T.

I Puritani. Palacio Valdes, A.

I, robot. Binder, E.

I rode a tornado. Stocker, J.

I see you never. Bradbury, R.

I seen 'em go. Ullman, J. R.

I shall not be moved. Stewart, O.

I, the unspeakable. Sheldon, W.

I, Tobit. Van Doren, M.

I took thee, Constance. Le Berthon, T.

I turn pearl-diver. Nordhoff, C. B.

I want to go home. Farrell, J. T.

I want to know why. Anderson, S.

I will not abandon! Marmur, J.

"I will send thee." Asch, S.

ICE HOCKEY. See Hockey

Ice ostrich. Coombs, C. I.

Ice palace. Fitzgerald, F. S. K.

ICE SKATING. See Skating

ICELAND
Laxness, H. K. Icelandic pioneer

Icelandic pioneer. Laxness, H. K.

Icon on the wall. Goudge, E.

Iddings Clark. Goodman, P.

Idea of age. Taylor, E.

Ideal craftsman. De la Mare, W. J.

Ideal home. Powell, D.

IDEAL STATE. See Utopias

IDEALISM
Hawthorne, N. Great stone face
Lawrence, D. H. Things

Idealist. Del Rey, L.

The idealist. O'Donovan, M.

IDIOCY
Bishop, L. Crazy Hymie and the nickel
Wilson, A. Mummy to the rescue
See also Feeble-minded; Insanity

IDIOTS. See Feeble-minded; Idiocy

Idle days on the Yan. Dunsany, E. J. M. D.P. 18th baron

Idolater of Degas. Stern, J.

Idyll of Miss Sarah Brown. Runyon, D.

Idyll of Red Gulch. Harte, B.

Idyll through the looking-glass. Sitwell, Sir O. bart.

If a body. Carr, A. Z.

If God makes you pretty. Horwitz, J.

If he hollers let him holler. De Vries, P.

"If I forget thee, oh Earth. . ." Clarke, A. C.

If Lincoln had yielded. Waldron, W.

If not higher. Peretz, I. L.

If only it were yesterday. Rinehart, M. R.

If the shoe hurts. De Vries, P.

"If this goes on-" Heinlein, R. A.

If we could see. Meschi, E.

If you was a Molkin. Jenkins, W. F.

If you weel permit me. Vernam, G.

If youth knew, if age could. Collier, J.

Igongo elephants. Waldeck, T. J.

I'll be waiting. Chandler, R.

I'll cut your throat again, Kathleen. Brown, F.

I'll remember you. Summers, J. L.

I'll take the high road. Bonham, F.

ILLEGITIMACY
Cooke, A. A. Another worry
Davis, F. M. Five Alls
Maupassant, G. de. Simon's papa
O'Donovan, M. Lonely rock
Rinehart, M. R. The scandal
Waltari, M. T. Goldilocks
Wharton, E. N. J. The old maid

ILLICIT DISTILLING. See Distilling, Illicit

ILLINOIS

Chicago
Maugham, W. S. Fall of Edward Barnard
Taylor, P. H. Dark walk
Tucker, W. Street walker

ILLITERACY
Maugham, W. S. The verger
Porter, W. S. Schools and schools
Sandy, S. Black lie

ILLNESS
Aiken, C. P. Mr Arcularis
Bottome, P. Pink medicine
Hemingway, E. Day's wait
Humphrey, W. In sickness and health
Van Doren, M. The butterfly
Verga, G. Home tragedy
See also Invalids

The illumination. West, J.

The illusionaries. Russell, E. F.

ILLUSIONS. See Hallucinations and illusions

The illustrated man. Bradbury, R.

ILLUSTRATORS
James, H. Real thing

I'm a fool. Anderson, S.

I'm in a hurry. Upson, W. H.

I'm really fine. Schulberg, S.

I'm scared. Finney, J.

Image of the Lost Soul. Munro, H. H.

IMAGINARY ANIMALS. See Animals, Imaginary

IMAGINARY CITIES
De Quincey, T. Savannah-la-mar

Imaginary Jew. Berryman, J.

IMAGINARY KINGDOMS
Doyle, Sir A. C. Maracot deep
Dunsany, E. J. D. P. 18th baron. Sword of Welleran

IMAGINARY WARS AND BATTLES
Wells, H. G. Dream of Armageddon

IMBECILES. See Feeble-minded; Idiocy

IMITATIONS. See Impersonations

Immensee. Storm, T.

IMMIGRANTS
Francis, O. Ladies call on Mr Pussick
Meyer, E. L. When the aliens left
Schaefer, J. W. Hugo Kertchak, builder
See also French in the United States; Germans in the United States; etc.

Immodest maiden. Marshall, B.

Immortal orange. Shneur, Z.

Immortal woman. Tate, A.

IMMORTALITY
Rocklynne, R. Backfire
Sharp, D. D. Eternal man
Simak, C. D. Second childhood
Unamuno y Jugo, M. de. Saint Manuel
Bueno, martyr

IMMORTALITY, PHYSICAL
Pierce, J. A. Invariant
Porter, W. S. Door of unrest
Simak, C. D. Eternity lost
Simak, C. D. Second childhood

Imp of string. Van Doren, M.

Imp of the perverse. Poe, E. A.

Impacted man. Sheckley, R.

IMPERSONATIONS
Beerbohm, Sir M. Happy hypocrite
Beyle, M. H. Mina de Vanghel
Brod, M. Death is a passing weakness
Cockburn, C. Total recall
Collins, W. Lady of Glenwith Grange
Doyle, Sir A. C. Case of identity
Doyle, Sir A. C. Man with the twisted
lip
Ekbergh, I. D. Lady's maid
Hale, E. E. My double, and how he undid
me
Harrison, H. S. Miss Hinch
Harvey, W. F. Dark horses
Lewis, J. Wife of Martin Guerre
Locke, W. J. Adventure of the kind Mr
Smith
Maugham, W. S. Lion's skin
Maugham, W. S. Wash-tub
Munro, H. H. Hounds of Fate
Munro, H. H. Lost sanjak
Munro, H. H. Schartz-Metterklume meth-
od
Munro, H. H. Touch of realism
Poe, E. A. Oblong box
Porter, W. S. Double-dyed deceiver
Porter, W. S. Duplicity of Hargraves
Porter, W. S. Lost on dress parade
Porter, W. S. Midsummer masquerade
Porter, W. S. Reformation of Calliope
Porter, W. S. Thimble, thimble
Porter, W. S. Transients in Arcadia
Porter, W. S. While the auto waits
Vickers, R. Double image
Wells, H. G. Late Mr Elvesham

Implode and peddle. Fyfe, H. B.

Impossible highway. Friend, O. J.

Impossible play. O'Rourke, F.

IMPOSTERS. See Impersonations

IMPRESSMENT
Melville, H. Billy Budd, foretopman

IMPROBABLE STORIES
Ashabranner, B. Genius of Strap Buckner
Calisher, H. Heartburn
Carmer, C. L. Mr Sims and Henry
Credle, E. Tall tale from the high hills
Li Fu-yen. Man who became a fish
Li Fu-yen. The tiger
Munro, H. H. "Ministers of Grace"
Munro, H. H. Seventh pullet
Munro, H. H. Tobermory
Poe, E. A. Loss of breath
Pratt, F. and De Camp, L. S. Tales from
Gavagan's bar; 23 stories
Stockton, F. R. Widow's cruise

Impulse. Aiken, C. P.

Impulse. Russell, E. F.

In a backwoods town. Bergelson, D.

In a Bolshevist market-place. Yushkevich,
S. S.

In a dry country. Lyle, D.

In a glass darkly. Sullivan, R.

"**In** a good cause—" Asimov, I.

In a grove. Akutagawa, R.

In a strange land. Maugham, W. S.

In accents of death! Farrell, J. T.

In another country. Hemingway, E.

In another image. Ashley, E. L.

In City Hall Square. Farrell, J. T.

In Cushing's saloon. Hendryx, J. B.

In dreams begin responsibilities. Schwartz, D.

In exchange for poverty. Cooke, A. A.

In exile. Chekhov, A. P.

In Greenwich there are many gravelled
walks. Calisher, H.

In hiding. Shiras, W. H.

In Nazareth. Borden, M.

In Nazareth. Lagerlöf, S. O. L.

In northern waters. Williams, W. C.

In Odessa. Babel', I. E.

In pyjamas. Nordhoff, C. B. and Hall, J. N.

In quest of a solution. Doyle, Sir A. C.

In sickness and health. Humphrey, W.

In the absence of angels. Calisher, H.

In the abyss. Wells, H. G.

In the Avu observatory. Wells, H. G.

In the beginning. Gordimer, N.

In the borderland. Stockwell, J.

In the cards. Collier, J.

In the chair. Jackson, C. R.

In the days of our fathers. McClintic, W.

In the desert. Tennyson, H.

In the family bosom. Harris, G. W.

In the fields of Boaz. Fineman, I.

In the fog. Davis, R. H.

In the forest. De La Mare, W. J.

In the fourth ward. Benson, T.

In the French style. Shaw, I.

In the garden. Lincoln, V. E.

In the good old summer time. Miller, P. S.

In the moonlight. Maupassant, G. de

In the morning. Sansom, W.

In the name of the Great Jehovah and the
Continental Congress. Allen, M. P.

In the patchwork quilt. Eggleston, M. W.

In the penal colony. Kafka, F.

In the prison. Eliot, G. pseud.

In the scarlet star. Williamson, J.

In the time of demonstrations. Hall, J. B.

In the train. O'Donovan, M.

In the twilight. Stegner, W. E.

In the year 2889. Verne, J.

In this sign. Bradbury, R.

In time of calamity. Newhouse, E.

In value deceived. Fyfe, H. B.
In what far country. Van Doren, M.
Incarnation of Krishna Mulvaney. Kipling, R.

INCAS
Wassermann, J. Gold of Caxamalca

INCENDIARISM. See Arson

Incident at Boiling Springs. Benefield, B.
Incident on a lake. Collier, J.
Inclán, Ramón del Valle. See Valle-Inclán, Ramón del

INCOME TAX
Seager, A. Second wedding

Incompatibility. Sheehan, P. A.
Inconstant star. Cousins, M.
Incubation. MacDonald, J. D.
Indecision. Forester, C. S.

INDEPENDENCE DAY. See Fourth of July celebrations

INDIA
Annixter, P. pseud. Brought to cover
Collier, J. Rope enough
Marshall, E. Love stories of India; 15 stories

Bengal
Munro, H. H. Comments of Moung Ka

British occupation, 1765-1947
Kipling, R. At the end of the passage
Kipling, R. Drums of the fore and aft
Kipling, R. Incarnation of Krishna Mulvaney
Kipling, R. Man who was
Kipling, R. Man who would be king
Kipling, R. Tomb of his ancestors
Kipling, R. Toomai of the elephants
Kipling, R. William the Conqueror
Kipling, R. Without benefit of clergy
Mukerji, D. G. Elephant adventure
Tagore, Sir R. Hungry stones

Native races
Porter, W. S. Diamond of Kali
Swinton, A. A brotherhood
Tagore, Sir R. Babus of Nayanjore

Religion
Tagore, R. The Cabuliwallah

Indian feather. Mabry, T. D.
Indian fighter. Thompson, H.

INDIAN ROPE TRICK
Collier, J. Rope enough

Indian summer. Caldwell, E.
Indian summer of Dry Valley Johnson. Porter, W. S.

Indian well. Clark, W. Van T.

Indian's Christmas gift. Eggleston, M. W.

INDIANS IN THE FIJI ISLANDS
Michener, J. A. Mynah birds

INDIANS OF BRAZIL. See Indians of South America

INDIANS OF CANADA. See Indians of North America—Canada

INDIANS OF CENTRAL AMERICA
Clifton, M. The conqueror

INDIANS OF GUATEMALA. See Indians of Central America

INDIANS OF MEXICO
Brenner, L. An artist grows up in Mexico; 7 stories
Steinbeck, J. Miracle of Tepayac

INDIANS OF NORTH AMERICA
Anderson, D. Forty years of firewood
Butterworth, H. My grandmother's grandmother's Christmas candle
Coatsworth, E. J. Race in the wilderness
Fenner, P. R. comp. Indians, Indians, Indians; 16 stories
Frazee, S. Great medicine
Harte, B. Dick Boyle's business card
Haycox, E. Scout detail
London, J. Strength of the strong
Schaefer, J. W. Out of the past
   See also names of individual Indian tribes or nations: e.g. Apache Indians; Crow Indians; Dakota Indians; etc.

Canada
Mowery, W. B. The scout
Perrault, E. G. Silver King

Captivities
Brick, J. The captives
Brown, W. C. Duel in Captive Valley
Gordon, C. The captive
Johnson, D. M. Flame on the frontier
Johnson, D. M. Journey to the fort
Johnson, D. M. Man called Horse
Peattie, M. R. Red Fox
Rees, G. Rod of God
Smith, J. Life among the Indians

Children
Stafford, J. Summer day

Education
Clark, W. Van T. The anonymous

Legends
Bear and the hunter's step-son
Coming of the white man
Trickster and the old witch

Mississippi
Faulkner, W. A justice
Faulkner, W. Red leaves

Mythology
   See Indians of North America— Religion and mythology

Religion and mythology
Johnson, D. M. Scars of honor
Johnson, D. M. The unbeliever
Johnson, D. M. Warrior's exile

Wars
Fox, N. A. Only the dead ride proudly
Johnson, D. M. Beyond the frontier

INDIANS OF SOUTH AMERICA
Bowles, P. F. Pastor Dowe at Tacaté
Burks, A. J. The captive

Captivities
Erskine, L. Y. Mystery of Mike

Indiscretions of Father Lawrence. Lieberman, R.

INDO-CHINA, FRENCH
Payne, P. S. R. Red mountain

The indomitable blue. Wolfert, I.

Indulgent husband. Colette, S. G.

INDUSTRIAL ACCIDENTS. See Accidents, Industrial

INDUSTRIALISTS. See Capitalists and financiers

Inexperienced ghost. Wells, H. G.

INFANTICIDE
Hunter, E. Small homicide
James, H. Author of Beltraffio
Maugham, W. S. The unconquered
Renard, J. A romance

INFANTS. See Children

Infernal Parliament. Munro, H. H.

INFIDELITY. See Marriage problems

Infidelity of Zenobia. Bunner, H. C.

Infinity zero. Wandrei, D.

Influence. Merochnik, M.

The **infra**-medians. Wright, S. P.

The **infra**-redioscope. Russell, B. A. W. R. 3d earl

Ingénue of the Sierras. Harte, B.

Ingraham, Joseph Holt, 1809-1866
The baptizing
   Brentano, F. ed. The word lives on

Inheritance. Clarke, A. C.

INHERITANCE AND SUCCESSION
Caldwell, E. The windfall
Cobb, I. S. Boys will be boys
Collier, J. Incident on a lake
Coppard, A. E. Fifty pounds
Grau, S. A. Bright day
Harte, B. Mrs Skaggs's husbands
King, M. P. Chicken on the wind
Landa, M. J. Two legacies
Newhouse, E. Seventy thousand dollars
Platt, G. Very false alarm
Porter, W. S. One thousand dollars
Porter, W. S. Shocks of doom
Queen, E. pseud. Witch of Times Square
Shulman, M. Chance for adventure
Waugh, E. Period piece
Winslow, T. S. Angie Lee's fortune

Initiation. Conrad, J.

Initiation fee. Shallit, R.

Inland, western sea. Asch, N.

The **inn.** Maupassant, G. de

Inn was promise. Brookhouser, F.

Innis, Mary Emma (Quayle)
The bells
   Pacey, D. ed. Book of Canadian stories

Innocence of Reginald. Munro, H. H.

Innocents. Hutchins, M. P. M.

Innocents of Broadway. Porter, W. S.

INNS. See Hotels, taverns, etc.

Inquest. Williams, W. C.

INQUISITION
Poe, E. A. Pit and the pendulum

INSANE. See Insanity

The **insane.** Williams, W. C.

INSANE HOSPITALS
Goss, J. M. Bird song
Heinlein, R. A. They
Waugh, E. Mr Loveday's little outing

INSANITY
Aiken, C. P. Bow down, Isaac!
Aiken, C. P. Silent snow, secret snow
Becker, S. D. Town mouse
Bellow, S. Sermon by Doctor Pep
Benson, T. Man from the tunnel
Bowles, P. F. You are not I
Brod, M. Death is a passing weakness
Brown, F. Come and go mad
Chekhov, A. P. Ward no. 6
Collier, J. Special delivery
Dostoevskii, F. M. Faint heart
Farrell, J. T. A misunderstanding
Fitzgerald, F. S. K. Long way out
Harte, B. Mrs Skagg's husbands
Hauptmann, G. J. R. Flagman Thiel
Hergesheimer, J. Wild oranges
Huxley, A. L. Farcical history of Richard Greenow
Irving, W. Adventure of the German student
Jenkins, W. F. Strange case of John Kingman
Kuttner, H. De profundis
Kuttner, H. Dream's end
Leiber, F. Sanity
Lovecraft, H. P. Case of Charles Dexter Ward
Maupassant, G. de. Diary of a madman
Paget, V. Legend of Madame Krasinska
Peretz, I. L. Mad Talmudist
Poe, E. A. Fall of the house of Usher
Poe, E. A. System of Dr Tarr and Prof. Fether
Priestley, J. B. Grey ones
Salinger, J. D. Perfect day for bananafish
Sandoz, M. Y. On the verge; 4 stories
Sartre, J. P. The room
Schneider, R. Passing through Fieldsville
Steele, W. D. Bubbles
Steele, W. D. For they know not what they do
Steele, W. D. How beautiful with shoes
Still, J. Mrs Razor
Taylor, E. Sad garden
Temple, W. F. Counter-transference
Thompson, R. E. It's a nice day—Sunday
Waugh, E. Mr Loveday's little outing

The **inscription.** Munby, A. N. L.

Inscrutable man. Haycox, E.

INSECTS
Bretnor, R. Gnurrs come from voodvork out
Kafka, F. The metamorphosis
Melville, H. Apple-tree table
   See also names of particular insects: Ants; Bees; Beetles; etc.

Inside earth. Anderson, P.

Insoluble problem. Chesterton, G. K.

INSOMNIA
Hemingway, E. Now I lay me
Jackson, C. R. Sleeper awakened
Schmitz, E. Generous wine

Inspector had a habit. Child, C. B.

Inspector's teeth. De Camp, L. S.

Instinct. Del Rey, L.

INSTRUCTION. See Education

INSULTS
Chekhov, A. P. Worse and worse

INSURANCE
  Caldwell, E. Balm of Gilead
  Porter, W. S. Departmental case
INTELLIGENCE OF ANIMALS. See
    Animal intelligence
Interior castle. Stafford, J.
Interloper. Anderson, P.
The interlopers. Munro, H. H.
INTERMINGLED LIVES
  Asch, N. Inland, western sea
INTERNATIONAL INTRIGUE
  Charteris, L. Revolution racket
  Charteris, L. The Saint in Europe; 7
    stories
  Piper, H. B. Operation RSVP
INTERNATIONAL MARRIAGES
  James, H. Daisy Miller
  Spire, A. Rabbi and the siren
INTERNMENT CAMPS. See Concentra-
    tion camps
INTERNS. See Physicians
INTERPLANETARY VISITORS
  Abernathy, R. Peril of the blue world
  Anderson, P. Inside earth
  Ashby, R. Master race
  Asimov, I. Hostess
  Bradbury, R. Zero hour
  Brown, B. Star ducks
  Brown, F. The waveries
  Campbell, J. W. The invaders
  Cartmill, C. Green cat
  Clifton, M. What have I done?
  Clingerman, M. Minister without portfolio
  Conklin, G. ed. Invaders of earth; 21
    stories
  Fessier, M. Fascinating stranger
  Fyfe, H. B. Bureau of Slick Tricks
  Grendon, S. Open, sesame
  Harris, J. B. And the walls came tumbling
    down
  Harris, J. B. Meteor
  Heinlein, R. A. Gulf
  Hickey, H. B. Like a bird, like a fish
  Jacobs, S. Pilot and the bushman
  Knight, D. To serve man
  Krepps, R. W. Five years in the marma-
    lade
  Kuttner, H. Or else
  Leiber, F. Ship sails at midnight
  Lovecraft, H. P. Color out of space
  Lowndes, R. W. Highway
  Neville, K. Bettyann
  Oliver, C. Ant and the eye
  Reynolds, M. Isolationist
  Robinson, F. M. The hunting season
  Russell, E. F. Glass eye
  Sturgeon, T. Mewhu's jet
  Waldo, E. H. Rule of three
  Waldo, E. H. Unite and conquer
  White, W. A. P. Star dummy
  Williams, R. Emergency landing
  Williamson, J. Man from outside
INTERPLANETARY VOYAGES
  Anderson, P. Interloper
  Balmer, E. and Wylie, P. When worlds
    collide
  Berryman, J. Space rating
  Bradbury, R. Here there be tygers
  Bradbury, R. No particular night or
    morning

  Brown, F. Nothing Sirius
  Brown, F. Something green
  Campbell, J. W. Forgetfulness
  Carr, R. S. Beyond infinity
  Clarke, A. C. Breaking strain
  Crossen, K. F. ed. Adventures in tomor-
    row; 15 stories
  De Camp, L. S. Ordeal of Professor
    Klein
  Del Rey, L. Though dreamers die
  Fyfe, H. B. In value deceived
  Greenberg, M. ed. Men against the stars;
    12 stories
  Greenberg, M. ed. Travelers of space;
    14 stories
  Grinnell, D. pseud. Extending the hold-
    ings
  Hamilton, E. Conquest of two worlds
  Hamilton, E. Dead planet
  Harris, J. B. Survival
  Heinlein, R. A. Green hills of earth
  Holberg, L. baron. Three men of Potu
  Jenkins, W. F. Nobody saw the ship
  Jenkins, W. F. Propagandist
  Jenkins, W. F. Proxima centauri
  Klass, P. Alexander the bait
  Klass, P. Venus is a man's world
  Knight, D. Cabin boy
  Kornbluth, C. M. Altar at midnight
  Kuttner, H. Winner lose all
  Long, F. B. Two face
  Merril, J. Survival ship
  Poe, E. A. Unparalleled adventure of one
    Hans Pfaall
  Pratt, F. Roger Bacon formula
  Rocklynne, R. Jaywalker
  Serviss, G. P. Edison's conquest of Mars
  Simak, C. D. Asteroid of gold
  Sloane, W. M. ed. Space, space, space;
    10 stories
  Smith, C. A. Voyage to Sfanomoë
  Stapledon, W. O. Last terrestrials
  Starzl, R. F. Hornets of space
  Tucker, W. Home is where the wreck is
  Verne, J. Round the moon
  Waldo, E. H. Completely automatic
  Wandrei, D. Colossus
  Williamson, J. Through the purple cloud
  Wolf, M. Homeland
  Wollheim, D. A. comp. Flight into space;
    12 stories
INTERPLANETARY WARS
  De Courcy, D. and De Courcy, J. Rat
    race
Interpretation of a dream. Collier, J.
Interpretation of dreams. Abrahams, W.
INTER-RACIAL MARRIAGES
  Frankau, G. Outlier from his tribe
  Maugham, W. S. The consul
  Maugham, W. S. Mirage
  Maugham, W. S. The pool
  Merochnik, M. A saga
  Reynolds, M. and Brown, F. Dark inter-
    lude
INTERSTELLAR VISITORS. See Inter-
    planetary visitors
The intervener. Dinnis, E. M.
Intervention of providence. Parker, J. R.
The interview. Sykes, C.
Interview. Winslow, T. S.
Interview with Ahashuerus. Fineman, I.

Intimacy. Sartre, J. P.
Into the pit. Mann, T.
Into the web. Newell, D. M.
Into thy hands. Asch, S.
Into thy hands. Del Rey, L.
INTOLERANCE. See Race problems;
    Toleration
INTOXICATION. See Alcoholism; Drunk-
    ards
Introducing Pete Collins. Hendryx, J. B.
The invaders. Campbell, J. W.
The invaders. Macauley, R.
INVALIDS
    Aiken, C. P. Mr Arcularis
    Betts, D. Serpents and doves
    Harte, B. Miggles
    James, H. Middle years
    Mansfield, K. Man without a temperament
        See also Illness
Invariant. Pierce, J. A.
Invasion. Long, F. B.
INVENTIONS
    Anderson, E. V. Wildy's secret revealer
    Dahl, R. Great automatic grammatisator
    Melville, H. Happy failure
    Stockton, F. R. Tale of negative gravity
INVENTORS
    Brace, G. W. Deep water man
    Freedman, D. Mendel Marantz—genius
    Keller, D. H. Service first
Investigations of a dog. Kafka, F.
Invisible boy. Bradbury, R.
Invisible collection. Zweig, S.
Invisible dove dancer of Strathpheen Island.
    Collier, J.
Invisible man. Chesterton, G. K.
Invisible prisoner. LeBlanc, M.
Invisible shepherd. Krige, U.
INVISIBILITY
    Bradbury, R. Invisible boy
    Brooks, W. R. Jimmy takes vanishing
        lessons
    London, J. Shadow and the flash
The invitation. Ellis, M. H.
Ionian cycle. Klass, P.
IONIAN ISLANDS
    Cicellis, K. Miracles of the Saint
IRAN. See Persia
IRELAND
    Collier, J. Invisible dove dancer of Strath-
        pheen Island
    Corkery, D. The wager, and other stories;
        16 stories
    Waugh, E. Bella Fleace gave a party
        18th century
    Edgeworth, M. Castle Rackrent
        19th century
    Benson, T. Not by bread alone
    London, J. Samuel
    O'Donovan, M. Orpheus and his lute
    Yeats, W. B. Red Hanrahan
        20th century
    Irwin, M. E. F. The collar

    McLaverty, M. Game cock, and other
        stories; 12 stories
    McNulty, J. Back where I had never
        been
    O'Donovan, M. Majesty of the law
    O'Donovan, M. More stories; 29 stories
    O'Donovan, M. Traveller's samples; 14
        stories
    O'Donovan, M. Uprooted
    O'Flaherty, L. The challenge
    O'Hanlon, D. M. Life and death of a
        village
    Walsh, M. Son of a tinker; 9 stories
        Clare
    Collier, J. Lady on the grey
        County Kerry
    Walsh, M. Quiet man
        Dublin
    Farrell, J. T. Summer morning in Dublin
        in 1938
    Joyce, J. Araby
    Joyce, J. Ivy Day in the committee room
    Joyce, J. Little cloud
        Farm life
    See Farm life—Ireland
        Folklore
    See Legends and folk tales—Ireland
Irina, Aleksander
    The Landrath
        Guerney, B. G. comp. New Russian
        stories
Irish, William, pseud. See Woolrich,
    Cornell
Irish and the Jews and everybody else.
    Ready, W. B.
IRISH IN ENGLAND
    Irwin, M. E. F. Courage
    O'Donovan, M. Darcy in the Land of
        Youth
    O'Donovan, M. Jerome
    O'Donovan, M. Lonely rock
    O'Donovan, M. The sentry
    O'Donovan, M. Unapproved route
IRISH IN INDIA
    Kipling, R. Incarnation of Krishna Mul-
        vaney
Irish lad. Bendrodt, J. C.
IRON AND STEEL INDUSTRY
    Betts, D. Mark of distinction
Iron cross, first class. Schneider, G. W.
Iron maiden. Fitzgerald, B.
Iron moon. Elam, R. M.
Iron rose. Cunningham, J. M.
Iron shroud. Mudford, W.
Iron standard. Kuttner, H.
Irving, Cliff
    Buried alive
        Hathaway, B. and Sessions, J. A. eds.
        Writers for tomorrow. 2d ser.
Irving, Washington, 1783-1859
    Adalantado of the Seven Cities
        Cuff, R. P. ed. American short story
        survey
    Adventure of the German student
        Blodgett, H. W. ed. Story survey.
        1953 ed.

Irving, Washington—*Continued*
The devil and Tom Walker
Eaton, H. T. ed. Short stories
Legend of Sleepy Hollow
Burrell, J. A. and Cerf, B. A. eds.
Anthology of famous American stories
Foerster, N. ed. American poetry and
prose. 1952 ed.
Short, R. W. and Sewall, R. B. eds.
Short stories for study. 1950 ed.
Rip Van Winkle
Burrell, J. A. and Cerf, B. A. eds.
Anthology of famous American stories
Cody, S. ed. Greatest stories and how
they were written
Day, A. G. ed. Greatest American short
stories
Foerster, N. ed. American poetry and
prose. 1952 ed.
Lamb, L. ed. Family book of best loved
short stories
Stout gentleman
Neider, C. ed. Great short stories from
the world's literature

Irving. Newhouse, E.

Irwin, Inez (Haynes) 1873-
Spring flight
First-prize stories, 1919-1954

Irwin, John M.
Pennies from heaven
Seventeen (Periodical) The Seventeen
reader

Irwin, Margaret Emma Faith
Bloodstock
Irwin, M. E. F. Bloodstock, and other
stories
The book
Davenport, B. ed. Tales to be told in
the dark
Irwin, M. E. F. Bloodstock, and other
stories
The collar
Irwin, M. E. F. Bloodstock, and other
stories
Country gentleman
Irwin, M. E. F. Bloodstock, and other
stories
Courage
Irwin, M. E. F. Bloodstock, and other
stories
The doctor
Irwin, M. E. F. Bloodstock, and other
stories
Earlier service
Irwin, M. E. F. Bloodstock, and other
stories
Magazine of fantasy and science fiction.
Best from Fantasy and science fiction;
2d ser.
Mistletoe
Irwin, M. E. F. Bloodstock, and other
stories
Mrs Oliver Cromwell
Irwin, M. E. F. Bloodstock, and other
stories
Monsieur seeks a wife
Irwin, M. E. F. Bloodstock, and other
stories
Where beauty lies
Irwin, M. E. F. Bloodstock, and other
stories

Is there nowhere else where we can meet?
Gordimer, N.

Isaacson, Bernice Kavinoky, 1914-
Last bed
American vanguard, 1952
The onlooker
American vanguard, 1950

Isherwood, Christopher, 1904-
The Nowaks
New writing (Perioidcal) Best stories
On Ruegen Island
Cory, D. W. pseud. comp. 21 variations
on a theme

Ish-Kishor, Sulamith
The Champ
Strang, R. M. and Roberts, R. M. eds.
Teen-age tales v 1

The **island.** Horwitz, J.

Island happy. Heatter, B.

Island in the sky. Wellman, M. W.

Island of five colors. Gardner, M.

Island of ice. Waltari, M. T.

Island of the blue macaws. Ullman, J. R.

Island of the fay. Poe, E. A.

ISLANDS
Bloomfield, H. The trap
Collier, J. Invisible dove dancer of Strath-
pheen Island
Etnier, E. J. The willow
Gardner, M. Island of five colors
Hearn, L. The storm
Irving, W. Adalantado of the Seven Cities
Rousseau, J. J. Isle of St Peter
See also Desert islands

Isle-Adam, Villiers de l'. See Villiers de
l'Isle-Adam, Jean Marie Mathias
Philippe Auguste, comte de

ISLE OF MAN. See Man, Isle of

Isle of St Peter. Rousseau, J. J.

Isle of voices. Stevenson, R. L.

Isolationist. Reynolds, M.

ISRAEL
Tennyson, H. Land of my fathers

It ain't always the breaks. Kaufman, W.

It had to be. Pinski, D.

It had to happen. Bro, M. H.

It happened like this. Caldwell, E.

It happened to me. Johnson, H.

It looks like justice. Cohn, E.

It never fails. Grimson, M. S.

It wasn't syzygy. Waldo, E. H.

ITALIAN ARISTOCRACY. See Aristocracy—Italy

ITALIANS IN FRANCE
Boyle, K. Effigy of war

ITALIANS IN THE UNITED STATES
Blue, E. Nothing overwhelms Giuseppe
Malamud, B. The prison
Pagano, J. Signor Santa
Porter, W. S. Philistine in Bohemia
Shaw, I. Triumph of justice

ITALY
Paget, V. Amour dure
Paget, V. Wedding chest

14th century
Boccaccio, G. Patient Griselda

20th century
Mann, T. Mario and the magician
Maugham, W. S. Salvatore
Montanelli, I. Hero returns
Tennyson, H. Home leave

Florence
Huxley, A. L. Young Archimedes
Maugham, W. S. Woman of fifty

Naples
Burns, J. H. Momma

Padua
Hawthorne, N. Rappaccini's daughter

Pompeii
Blackburn, E. R. Story of Pompeii

Rome (City)
Charteris, L. Rome: The Latin touch
Paget, V. Seeker of pagan perfection
Wharton, E. N. J. Roman fever

Rome (City)—Ancient
See Rome

Venice
James, H. Aspern papers
Mann, T. Death in Venice
Poe, E. A. The assignation

Itch to win. Verral, C. S.

It's a good life. Bixby, J.

It's a man's world. Foster, C. J.

It's a nice day—Sunday. Thompson, R. E.

"It's great to be back." Heinlein, R. A.

It's such a beautiful day. Asimov, I.

It's such a nice day—Sunday. Thompson, R. E.

'Ivanhoe'. Smith, L. P.

Ivanov, Vsevolod Vîàcheslavovich, 1895?-
The kid
Guerney, B. G. comp. New Russian stories

IVY
Keller, D. H. Ivy war

Ivy Day in the committee room. Joyce, J.

Ivy war. Keller, D. H.

Ixion in heaven. Beaconsfield, B. D. 1st earl of

Izzard and the membrane. Miller, W. M.

J

Jabotinsky, Vladimir. See Zhabotïnskiĭ, Vladimir Evgen'evich

Jack-of-all-trades. Agnon, S. J.

The **jackal** and the alligator. Frere, M. A. I.

The **jackpot.** McNulty, J.

Jackpot vs. Yellowstrike. Oblinger, M.

JACKASSES. See Asses and mules

Jackson, Charles Reginald, 1903-
Band concert
Jackson, C. R. Sunnier side
Benighted savage
Jackson, C. R. Sunnier side
Boy who ran away
Jackson, C. R. Earthly creatures
The break
Jackson, C. R. Earthly creatures
"By the sea"
Jackson, C. R. Sunnier side
The cheat
Jackson, C. R. Earthly creatures
How war came to Arcadia, N. Y.
Jackson, C. R. Sunnier side
In the chair
Jackson, C. R. Sunnier side
Money
Jackson, C. R. Earthly creatures
Night visitor
Jackson, C. R. Sunnier side
Old men and boys
Jackson, C. R. Earthly creatures
The outlander
Jackson, C. R. Earthly creatures
Palm Sunday
Cory, D. W. pseud. comp. 21 variations on a theme
Jackson, C. R. Sunnier side
Parting at morning
Jackson, C. R. Earthly creatures
Rachel's summer
Jackson, C. R. Sunnier side
Romeo
Jackson, C. R. Earthly creatures
The sisters
Jackson, C. R. Sunnier side
Sleeper awakened
Jackson, C. R. Earthly creatures
Sophistication
Jackson, C. R. Sunnier side
Sunday drive
Jackson, C. R. Earthly creatures
Sunnier side
Jackson, C. R. Sunnier side
Tenting tonight
Jackson, C. R. Sunnier side

Jackson, Charles Tenney, 1874-
Buffalo wallow
Best American short stories, 1953
Horse of Hurricane Reef
Cuff, R. P. ed. American short story survey
Sea-horse of Grand Terre
Dennis, W. ed. Palomino and other horses

Jackson, Clive
Swordsmen of Varnis
Brown, F. and Reynolds, M. eds. Science-fiction carnival

Jackson, Dorothy V. S.
Gift of love
McFarland, W. K. comp. Then it happened
Seventeen (Periodical) Nineteen from Seventeen

Jackson, Margaret (Weymouth) 1895-
The hero
Christ, H. I. and Shostak, J. eds. Short stories

Jackson, Margaret W.—*Continued*
South toward home
    Eaton, H. T. ed. Short stories
The stepmother
    Lass, A. H. and Horowitz, A. eds.
    Stories for youth
Jackson, Roberts Brock
Fly away home
    Best American short stories, 1953
Jackson, Shirley, 1920-
After you, my dear Alphonse
    Felheim, M.; Newman, F. B. and Stein-
    hoff, W. R. eds. Modern short stories
Charles
    Stauffer, R. M.; Cunningham, W. H. and
    Sullivan, C. J. eds. Adventures in
    modern literature
The lottery
    Heilman, R. B. ed. Modern short stories
Summer people
    Best American short stories, 1951
JACKSON, THOMAS JONATHAN, 1824-
    1863
Moody, M. H. Ghost of General Jackson
Jacobi, Carl, 1908-
Gentleman is an Epwa
    Derleth, A. W. ed. Worlds of tomorrow
La Prello paper
    Derleth, A. W. ed. Night's yawning peal
Tepondicon
    Derleth, A. W. ed. Far boundaries
White pinnacle
    Derleth, A. W. ed. Time to come
Jacobs, Joseph, 1854-1916
Golden arm
    Fenner, P. R. comp. Ghosts, ghosts,
    ghosts
The tail
    Fenner, P. R. comp. Fools and funny
    fellows
Jacobs, Sylvia
Pilot and the bushman
    Galaxy science fiction magazine. Galaxy
    reader of science fiction
Jacobs, William Wymark, 1863-1943
Monkey's paw
    Cerf, B. A. and Moriarty, H. C. eds.
    Anthology of famous British stories
    Corrington, H. ed. Week-end book of
    ghost stories
    Davenport, B. ed. Ghostly tales to be
    told
Jacobson, Lee, E. 1924-
Last Saturday
    Wolfe, D. M. ed. Which grain will grow
Jade goddess
    Lin, Y. ed. Famous Chinese short stories
Jade ring. Norling, M. E.
JAGUARS
Gill, T. Jungle war
JAI ALAI
Sylvester, R. Last tanto
Jakes, John W. 1932-
Machine
    Best science-fiction stories: 1953
Jam session at Abby's. Gregutt, H. C.
JAM SESSIONS. See Jazz music
Jam today. De Vries, P.

JAMAICA
Powell, F. Black flag
JAMES I, KING OF GREAT BRITAIN,
    1566-1625
Evans, T. M. Gentlemen of valor
James, Daniel Lewis
Moon of delirium
    Conklin, G. ed. Possible worlds of sci-
    ence fiction
James, Henry, 1843-1916
Altar of the dead
    Stegner, W. E.; Scowcroft, R. and
    Ilyin, B. eds. Writer's art
Aspern papers
    James, H. Selected fiction
    Neider, C. ed. Short novels of the
    masters
Author of Beltraffio
    Burrell, J. A. and Cerf, B. A. eds.
    Anthology of famous American stories
Beast in the jungle
    Gordon, C. and Tate, A. eds. House of
    fiction
    James, H. Selected fiction
    James, H. Selected short stories
Bench of desolation
    Lynskey, W. C. ed. Reading modern
    fiction
The birthplace
    James, H. Selected short stories
Bundle of letters
    James, H. Selected short stories
Crawford's consistency
    James, H. Eight uncollected tales
Daisy Miller
    James, H. Selected fiction
Death of the lion
    Foerster, N. ed. American poetry and
    prose. 1952 ed.
    James, H. Selected short stories
Four meetings
    Felheim, M.; Newman, F. B. and Stein-
    hoff, W. R. eds. Modern short stories
Gabrielle de Bergerac
    James, H. Eight uncollected tales
Ghostly rental
    James, H. Eight uncollected tales
Great good place
    Neider, C. ed. Great short stories from
    the world's literature
Jolly corner
    James, H. Selected fiction
    James, H. Selected short stories
The liar
    West, R. B. and Stallman, R. W. eds.
    Art of modern fiction
Madame de Mauves
    Ludwig, R. M. and Perry, M. B. eds.
    Nine short novels
Middle years
    Davis, R. G. ed. Ten modern masters
    James, H. Selected short stories
My friend Bingham
    James, H. Eight uncollected tales
Osborne's revenge
    James, H. Eight uncollected tales
Paste
    Blodgett, H. W. ed. Story survey. 1953
    ed.
    Davis, R. G. ed. Ten modern masters
A problem
    James, H. Eight uncollected tales

James, Henry—*Continued*
  The pupil
    Cory, D. W. pseud. comp. 21 variations
      on a theme
    James, H. Selected fiction
    James, H. Selected short stories
    Short, R. W. and Sewall, R. B. eds.
      Short stories for study. 1950 ed.
  Real thing
    Burrell, J. A. and Cerf, B. A. eds. An-
      thology of famous American stories
    Foerster, N. ed. American poetry and
      prose. 1952 ed.
    James, H. Selected short stories
    Lamb, L. ed. Family book of best loved
      short stories
    O'Faoláin, S. The short story
  Story of a masterpiece
    James, H. Eight uncollected tales
  Story of a year
    James, H. Eight uncollected tales
  Tone of time
    Millett, F. B. ed. Reading fiction
  Tree of knowledge
    Davis, R. G. ed. Ten modern masters
  Turn of the screw
    Schorer, M. ed. The story
  Washington Square
    James, H. Selected fiction

James, Marquis, 1891-
  Stolen railroad train
    Moskowitz, S. ed. Great railroad stories
      of the world

James, Montague Rhodes, 1862-1936
  Count Magnus
    Davenport, B. ed. Ghostly tales to be
      told
  Lost hearts
    Conklin, G. and Conklin, L. T. eds.
      Supernatural reader
  The mezzotint
    Cerf, B. A. and Moriarty, H. C. eds.
      Anthology of famous British stories

James, Will, 1892-1942
  Best riding and roping
    James, W. Will James' Book of cowboy
      stories
  Cattle rustlers
    James, W. Will James' Book of cowboy
      stories
  Chapo—the faker
    Dennis, W. ed. Palomino and other
      horses
    James, W. Will James' Book of cowboy
      stories
  For a horse
    James, W. Will James' Book of cowboy
      stories
  For the sake of freedom
    James, W. Will James' Book of cowboy
      stories
  His spurs
    Fenner, P. R. comp. Cowboys, cowboys,
      cowboys
  Lone cowboy
    Fenner, P. R. comp. Cowboys, cowboys,
      cowboys
    James, W. Will James' Book of cowboy
      stories
  Makings of a cowhorse
    James, W. Will James' Book of cowboy
      stories
  Midnight
    Fenner, P. R. comp. Cowboys, cowboys,
      cowboys
  Narrow escape
    James, W. Will James' Book of cowboy
      stories
  On the dodge
    James, W. Will James' Book of cowboy
      stories
  On the drift
    James, W. Will James' Book of cowboy
      stories
  Once a cowboy
    James, W. Will James' Book of cowboy
      stories
  Silver mounted
    James, W. Will James' Book of cowboy
      stories
  Smoky, the range colt
    James, W. Will James' Book of cowboy
      stories
  When in Rome—
    James, W. Will James' Book of cowboy
      stories
  Winter months in a cow camp
    James, W. Will James' Book of cowboy
      stories

James A. Dukes. Willingham, C.

Jameson, Malcolm, 1891-1945
  Admiral's inspection
    Jameson, M. Bullard of the space patrol
  Blind alley
    Jenkins, W. F. ed. Great stories of sci-
      ence fiction
  Blind man's buff
    Bleiler, E. F. and Dikty, T. E. eds.
      Imagination unlimited
  Blockade runner
    Jameson, M. Bullard of the space patrol
  Brimstone Bill
    Jameson, M. Bullard of the space patrol
  Bullard reflects
    Jameson, M. Bullard of the space patrol
  The bureaucrat
    Jameson, M. Bullard of the space patrol
  Lilies of life
    Conklin, G. ed. Possible worlds of sci-
      ence fiction
  Orders
    Jameson, M. Bullard of the space patrol
  Pride
    Merril, J. ed. Beyond human ken
  White mutiny
    Jameson, M. Bullard of the space patrol

Jane. Maugham, W. S.

Jane. Willingham, C.

Jane Dore—dear childe. Barker, A. L.

JANITORS
  Sansom, W. Boiler room

JAPAN
  Akutagawa, R. Rashomon, and other
    stories; 6 stories
  Grosskopf, E. K. Tea for Tamahara
  Hearn, L. Boy who drew cats

Jarka. Elias, A.

Jarrell, Randall, 1914-
  Gertrude and Sidney
    Best American short stories, 1954

JAVA. See Dutch East Indies—Java

Jay Score. Russell, E. F.

Jaywalker. Rocklynne, R.

JAZZ MUSIC
De Vries, P. Jam today

JEALOUSY
Bowles, P. F. The echo
Porter, W. S. "Guilty party"
Rinehart, M. R. If only it were yesterday
Taylor, E. Hester Lilly
Van Doren, M. Fisk Fogle

Jealousy
Lin, Y. ed. Famous Chinese short stories

Jean Beicke. Williams, W. C.

Jeannette. Thériault, Y.

Jeannine. Charteris, L.

Jeep: the dog who came home. Little, G. W.

Jeeves and the song of songs. Wodehouse, P. G.

Jeff Peters as a personal magnet. Porter, W. S.

Jefferies, Richard, 1848-1887
Winds of heaven
Andrews, R. C. ed. My favorite stories of the great outdoors

Jelly-bean. Fitzgerald, F. S. K.

Jelly-fish. Keller, D. H.

Jenkin, Philip A. 1910-
Cool million
Story (Periodical) Story; no. 4

Jenkins, William Fitzgerald, 1896-
De profundis
Derleth, A. W. ed. Far boundaries
Jenkins, W. F. Sidewise in time, and other scientific adventures
Devil's henchman
Conklin, G. and Conklin, L. T. eds. Supernatural reader
Doomsday deferred
Best science fiction stories: 1950
Bleiler, E. F. and Dikty, T. E. eds. Science fiction omnibus: The best science fiction stories, 1949, 1950
First contact
Astounding science fiction (Periodical) Astounding science fiction anthology
Jensen, P. ed. Fireside book of flying stories
Sloane, W. M. ed. Stories for tomorrow
Fourth-dimensional demonstrator
Jenkins, W. F. Sidewise in time, and other scientific adventures
Gadget had a ghost
Year's best science fiction novels, 1953
Historical note
Astounding science fiction (Periodical) Astounding science fiction anthology
If you was a Molkin
Galaxy science fiction magazine. Galaxy reader of science fiction
The journey
Star science fiction stories [no. 1]
Keyhole
Heinlein, R. A. ed. Tomorrow, the stars
Life-work of Professor Muntz
Best science fiction stories: 1950
Bleiler, E. F. and Dikty, T. E. eds. Science fiction omnibus: the best science fiction stories, 1949, 1950

Little terror
Saturday evening post (Periodical) Saturday evening post stories, 1953
Logic named Joe
Brown, F. and Reynolds, M. eds. Science-fiction carnival
Jenkins, W. F. Sidewise in time, and other scientific adventures
Middle of the week after next
Best science-fiction stories: 1953
Conklin, G. ed. Science-fiction adventures in dimension
Nobody saw the ship
Conklin, G. ed. Big book of science fiction
Other now
Galaxy science fiction magazine. Galaxy reader of science fiction
Plague
Conklin, G. ed. Omnibus of science fiction
The plants
Greenberg, M. ed. Men against the stars
The power
Derleth, A. W. ed. The outer reaches
Jenkins, W. F. Sidewise in time, and other scientific adventures
Lesser, M. A. ed. Looking forward
Propagandist
Conklin, G. ed. Possible worlds of science fiction
Proxima centauri
Jenkins, W. F. Sidewise in time, and other scientific adventures
Search in the mist
Saturday evening post (Periodical) Saturday evening post stories, 1950
The sentimentalists
Year's best science fiction novels, 1954
Sidewise in time
Jenkins, W. F. Sidewise in time, and other scientific adventures
Strange case of John Kingman
Bleiler, E. F. and Dikty, T. E. eds. Science fiction omnibus: the best science fiction stories, 1949, 1950
Jenkins, W. F. ed. Great stories of science fiction
Symbiosis
Jenkins, W. F. ed. Great stories of science fiction
Things pass by
Margulies, L. and Friend, O. J. eds. Giant anthology of science fiction
This star shall be free
Conklin, G. ed. Invaders of earth
The wabbler
Merril, J. ed. Beyond human ken

Jenks, Almet, 1892-
No way down
Best American short stories, 1954

Jenny takes a holiday. Hayes, H. M.

Jepson, Selwyn, 1899-
God and the little cat
Joseph, M. ed. Best cat stories

JEREMIAH
Werfel, F. Jeremiah

Jeremy in the wind. Kneale, N.

Jeremy Rodock. Schaefer, J. W.

Jericho, Jericho, Jericho. Lytle, A. N.

Jerome. O'Donovan, M.
JEROME OF PRAGUE, d. 1415
  Blackburn, E. R. Jerome of Prague
Jerry. Meek, S. St P.
Jerry: the dog who refused to die. Little, G. W.
Jerry was a man. Heinlein, R. A.
Jersey, Guernsey, Alderney, Sark. Seager, A.
Jersey heifer. Love, P. H.
Jerusalem delivered. Zweig, A.
The jester. Klass, P.
JESTERS. See Fools and jesters
Jesting of Arlington Stringham. Munro, H. H.
Jesting pilot. Kuttner, H.
JESUITS
  O'Donovan, M. The miracle
JESUS CHRIST
  Austin, M. Green bough
  Eça de Queiroz, J. M. Woman taken in adultery
  Gibran, K. Rafca, the bride of Cana
  Goudge, E. By the waters of Babylon
  Ingraham, J. H. The baptizing
  Lagerlöf, S. O. L. In Nazareth
  Marie, consort of Ferdinand I, King of Rumania. What Vasile saw
  Oxenham, P. Of our meeting with Cousin John
  Rosegger, P. Flight into Egypt
  Rosegger, P. Of love and joy
  Van Dyke, H. Lost boy

     Crucifixion
Asch, S. Into thy hands

     Last Supper
See Lord's Supper

     Nativity
Beauclerk, H. De V. The miracle of the vineyard
Broun, H. C. We, too, are bidden
Oxenham, J. Their first meeting
Van Dyke, H. Other Wise Man

Jesus complex. Mohler, C.
JET PROPULSION. See Rocket ships
Jetsam. Russell, J.
JEWELERS
  Dunsany, E. J. M. D. P. 18th baron. Distressing tale of Thangobrind the jeweller
  Woolf, V. S. Duchess and the jeweller
JEWELRY
  James, H. Paste
  Maupassant, G. de. The jewels
  See also Necklaces
The jewels. Maupassant, G. de
Jewels of Gwahlur. Howard, R. E.
Jewett, Sarah Orne, 1849-1909
  Courting of Sister Wisby
    Burrell, J. A. and Cerf, B. A. eds. Anthology of famous American stories
  White heron
    Barrows, H. ed. 15 stories
Jewish cat. Agnon, S. J.

JEWISH DIALECT STORIES. See Dialect stories—Jewish
JEWISH QUESTION. See Jews
JEWISH RITES AND CEREMONIES. See Jews—Rites and ceremonies
JEWS
  Aiken, C. P. The disciple
  Ausubel, N. ed. Treasury of Jewish humor; 82 stories
  Berryman, J. Imaginary Jew
  Cohn, E. Stories and fantasies from the Jewish past; 10 stories
  Hecht, B. God is good to a Jew
  Heine, H. Tale of olden time
  Lincoln, V. E. Glass wall
  Ribalow, H. U. This land, these people; 24 stories
  Shaw, I. Act of faith
  Yushkevich, S. S. In a Bolshevist marketplace
  Zhabotĭnskiĭ, V. E. Edmée

     Persecutions
Asch, S. Duty to live
Asch, S. Kola Street
Asch, S. Santification of the Name
Cohn, E. Simhah of Worms
Feuchtwanger, L. Mendel Hirsch
Shapiro, L. White chalah
Shneur, Z. Revenge
Spiegel, I. Ghetto dog

     Religion
Glassman, B. Tarnished gold
Goldman, A. Almost like dead
Grade, C. My quarrel with Hersh Rasseyner
Klein, A. The Minyan
Reisin, A. Poor community
Singer, I. J. Repentance
  See also Rosh ha-Shanah; Yom Kippur

     Rites and ceremonies
Agnon, S. J. Sabbathai
Bruggen, C. de H. van. Seder night
Fleg, E. The adulteress
Heine, H. Tale of olden time
Ogus, A. D. Shofar blower of Lapinishok
Perl, P. Man in Israel
Rabinowitz, S. Passover guest
Rugel, M. The flower
Scheiner, F. Old man had four wives
Weidman, J. The Kinnehorrah

Jew's beech tree. Droste-Hülshoff, A. E. Freiin von
JEWS IN AUSTRIA
  Katz, L. Gift of the emperor
  Werfel, F. V. Third commandment
JEWS IN CANADA
  Allan, T. Lies my father told me
JEWS IN ENGLAND
  Frankau, G. Outlier from his tribe
  Golding, L. Angels in Chayder
  Golding, L. Doomington wanderer
  Kersh, G. One way of getting a hundred pounds
  Levy, A. Cohen of Trinity
  Maugham, W. S. Alien corn
  Rappoport, S. Moses Montefiore

JEWS IN ENGLAND—*Continued*
Zangwill, I. The luftmensch
Zangwill, I. Sabbath question in Sudminster
Zangwill, L. Prelude to a pint of bitter
JEWS IN FRANCE
Bloch, J. R. Heresy of the water taps
Tunkel, J. From what a Litvak makes a living
JEWS IN GERMANY
Baum, V. Old house
Cohn, E. Simhah of Worms
Feuchtwanger, L. Mendel Hirsch
Hameln, Glückel of. A story
Heine, H. Seder night
Heine, H. Tale of olden time
Kesten, H. Friend in the closet
Lasker-Schüler, E. Arthur Aronymus
Roth, C. The martyr
Sulkin, S. The plan
JEWS IN HUNGARY
Molnar, F. Hussar who loved three Jews
JEWS IN LITHUANIA
Shneur, Z. Immortal orange
JEWS IN NETHERLANDS
Peretz, I. L. Miracle on the sea
Praag, S. E. van. Weesperstraat
Tunkel, J. The gift
JEWS IN NEW YORK (CITY) See Jews in the United States—New York (City)
JEWS IN PALESTINE
Hirshbein, P. Tears on stones
Stinetorf, L. A. Refugee village
JEWS IN POLAND
Asch, S. Kola Road
Asch, S. Kola Street
Cohn, E. Given years
Franzos, K. E. Saviour of the people
Hersey, J. R. Moment of judgement
Rudnicki, A. Ascent to heaven; 4 stories
Tchernichowski, S. Shaatnez
JEWS IN RUSSIA
Abramowitz, S. J. The exchange
Angoff, C. Where did yesterday go?
Babel', I. E. Rabbi's son
Bergelson, D. Citizen Woli Brenner
Frug, S. S. Last kopek
Fuchs, A. M. Among the trees
Rabinowitz, S. Gy-ma-na-si-a
Rabinowitz, S. Passover in a village
Rappoport, S. Moses Montefiore
JEWS IN THE UNITED STATES
Appet, N. The prophet
Calisher, H. Old stock
Calisher, H. One of the chosen
Dworzan, H. L. Husband for Bluma
Glassman, B. Tarnished gold
Glatstein, J. The return
Katz, L. Technical expert
Ribalow, H. U. ed. These your children; 25 stories
Ribalow, H. U. This land, these people; 24 stories
Singer, I. B. Little shoemakers
Yezierska, A. Fat of the land

New York (City)

Calisher, H. The watchers
Gold, M. Sam Kravitz, that thief

Greenfield, R. Jonathan Harrow
Horwitz, J. The campaign
Horwitz, J. Cup of tea
Horwitz, J. Poor people
Horwitz, J. The strudel
Kober, A. Bella, Bella kissed a fella; 15 stories
Kober, A. Nobody can beat Freidkin's meats
Kobrin, L. Soul that mice nibbled up
Marcus, P. Higher and higher
Rosenberg, E. C. Aunt Esther's galoshes
Rosenberg, E. C. Mrs Rivkin grapples with the drama
Rothberg, A. A. Not with our fathers
Seide, M. Lady of my own
Shapiro, L. Journeying through the milky way
Suhl, Y. With the aid of the one above
Winslow, T. S. Cycle of Manhattan
Yaffe, J. Mom in the spring
Yaffe, J. Poor Cousin Evelyn; 9 stories
Yezierska, A. Fat of the land
JEZEBEL
Frankau, P. Jezebel covets a vineyard
Jezebel covets a vineyard. Frankau, P.
Jilting of Granny Weatherall. Porter, K. A.
Jim: a valiant Great dane. Little, G. W.
Jim Baker's blue-jay yarn. Clemens, S. L.
Jim O'Neill. Farrell, J. T.
Jimat of Dorland. Blochman, L. G.
Jimmy finds a plan. Bailey, A. E.
Jimmy Hayes and Muriel. Porter, W. S.
Jimmy rides the seal herd. Miers, E. S.
Jimmy Rose. Melville, H.
Jimmy takes vanishing lessons. Brooks, W. R.
Jimmy who thought he "inherited bad blood." Strain, F. B.
Jingle bells. Griffith, R.
Jingle wears his spurs. Sellard, D.
JINN
Arabian nights. Aladdin
Collier, J. Bottle party
Jinx man. Palmer, S.
Jinx ship. Chambers, R. E.
Jirel meets magic. Moore, C. L.
Jishin. Christopher, R.
JIU-JITSU
Clark, A. A. G. Amazing lady
Jizzle. Harris, J. B.
Job for the Macarone. Runyon, D.
The **job** is ended. Tucker, W.
Job well done. Bondarenko, W. C.
JOBLESS. See Unemployed
Job's tears. Still, J.
Jocelyn. Miner, M. S.
The **jockey.** McCullers, C. S.
JOCKEYS
Clements, C. J. Keep off the rail!
Hemingway, E. My old man
McCullers, C. S. The jockey
Van Loan, C. E. Levelling with Elisha
Joe Craddock's old woman. Caldwell, E.
Joe Johnson. Bates, H. E.

Joe Smiley collects a reward. Hendryx, J. B.
Joe Smiley shows up on Halfaday. Hendryx,
    J. B.
Joe Terrace. Runyon, D.
JOHN THE BAPTIST, SAINT
    Ingraham, J. H. The baptizing
    Oxenham, J. Of our meeting with Cousin
        John
John Ferrier talks with the Prophet. Doyle,
    Sir A. C.
John Hitchcock. Farrell, J. T.
John the Indian and George Hopkins. Cald-
    well, E.
John the madman. Gibran, K.
John the revelator. La Farge, O.
John Thomas's cube. Leimert, J.
Johnnie Poothers. Odger, C.
Johnny Eames does well. Trollope, A.
Johnny One-Eye. Runyon, D.
Johnny Pye and the Fool-killer. Benét, S. V.
Johnny's old man. Farrell, J. T.
Johns, Veronica Parker, 1907-
    Bezique of death
        Mystery Writers of America, inc. Mai-
            den murders
    Homecoming
        Queen, E. pseud. ed. Queen's awards:
            7th ser.
Johnson, Cynthia. See Schwarz, Cynthia
    Johnson
Johnson, Dorothy Marie, 1905-
    Beyond the frontier
        Johnson, D. M. Indian country
    Flame on the frontier
        Argosy (Periodical) Argosy Book of
            adventure stories
        Johnson, D. M. Indian country
    Journey to the fort
        Johnson, D. M. Indian country
        Meredith, S. ed. Bar 3
    Laugh in the face of danger
        Johnson, D. M. Indian country
    Man called Horse
        Johnson, D. M. Indian country
        Meredith, S. ed. Bar 1 roundup of best
            western stories
    Man who shot Liberty Valance
        Johnson, D. M. Indian country
    Prairie kid
        Johnson, D. M. Indian country
    Scars of honor
        Johnson, D. M. Indian country
    The unbeliever
        Johnson, D. M. Indian country
        Meredith, S. ed. Bar 2
    War shirt
        Johnson, D. M. Indian country
    Warrior's exile
        Johnson, D. M. Indian country
Johnson, Harold
    Baby sitter vs. Ronnie
        Strang, R. M. and Roberts, R. M. eds.
            Teen-age tales v 1
    It happened to me
        Strang, R. M. and Roberts, R. M. eds.
            Teen-age tales v 1

Rocky
    Strang, R. M. and Roberts, R. M. eds.
        Teen-age tales v2
She'll be sorry
    Strang, R. M. and Roberts, R. M. eds.
        Teen-age tales v2
Johnson, Josephine Winslow, 1910-
    Alexander to the park
        Felheim, M.; Newman, F. B. and Stein-
            hoff, W. R. eds. Modern short stories
    Arcadia recalled
        Blodgett, H. W. ed. Story survey. 1953
            ed.
    The author
        Best American short stories, 1950
    Mother's story
        Best American short stories, 1951
    Sorcerer's son
        Abell, E. ed. American accent
Johnson, Margaret Sweet, 1893-
    Rex of the Coast patrol
        Harper, W. comp. Dog show
Johnson, Martha, pseud. See Lansing, Elisa-
    beth Carleton (Hubbard)
Johnson, Owen McMahon, 1878-1952
    Great pancake record
        Burrell, J. A. and Cerf, B. A. eds.
            Anthology of famous American stories
    Varmint tries dissipation
        Fenner, P. R. comp. Fun! Fun! Fun!
Johnson, Robert Barbour
    Far below
        Moskowitz, S. comp. Editor's choice in
            science fiction
Johnson, Ruth
    Cross buns for Friday
        Ford, N. A. and Faggett, H. L. eds.
            Best short stories by Afro-American
            writers (1925-1950)
Johnson, William R. See Nemerov, H. jt.
    auth.
Johnson looked back. Burke, T.
Johnston, Northam F. 1921-
    Absolutism
        American vanguard, 1950
    God and the angry men
        American vanguard, 1952
Joining the Yankees. Graham, F.
Jo-Jo. Farrell, J. T.
Jojo. P'u Sung-ling
JOKES, PRACTICAL. See Humor—Prac-
    tical jokes
Jolly. Thompson, T.
Jolly corner. James, H.
JONAH (BIBLICAL CHARACTER)
    Melville, H. The sermon
    Nathan, R. Testing of Jonah
Jonah curse. Wallace, J. F.
Jonathan Harrow. Greenfield, R.
Jones, Henry Bedford- See Bedford-Jones,
    Henry
Jones, James, 1921-
    Two legs for the two of us
        Esquire (Periodical) Girls from Esquire
JONES, JOHN PAUL, 1747-1792
    Ellsberg, E. Battle in the moonlight

Jones, Louis Clark, 1908-
  Spooks of the valley
    Fenner, P. R. comp. Ghosts, ghosts,
      ghosts
Jones, Madison P. jr.
  Dog days
    Best American short stories, 1953
Jones, Neil R.
  Hermit of Saturn's ring
    Wollheim, D. A. comp. Flight into space
Jones, Raymond F. 1915-
  Children's room
    Jones, R. F. The toymaker
  Deadly host
    Jones, R. F. The toymaker
  Farthest horizon
    Norton, A. M. ed. Space pioneers
    Sloane, W. M. ed. Stories for tomorrow
  Forecast
    Jones, R. F. The toymaker
  Model shop
    Jones, R. F. The toymaker
  Noise level
    Sloane, W. M. ed. Stories for tomorrow
  Pete can fix it
    Conklin, G. ed. Science-fiction adven-
      tures in dimension
  Production test
    Lesser, M. A. ed. Looking forward
  Stone and a spear
    Conklin, G. ed. Omnibus of science fic-
      tion
  Tools of the trade
    Sloane, W. M. ed. Space, space, space
  The toymaker
    Jones, R. F. The toymaker
  Utility
    Jones, R. F. The toymaker
Jones, Ruby S.
  August tenth
    Oberfirst, R. ed. 1952 anthology of best
      original short-shorts
Jon's world. Dick, P. K.
Jordan, Gladys
  For the last time
    Oberfirst, R. ed. 1952 anthology of best
      original short-shorts
Jorrocks, John, pseud. See Surtees, Robert
    Smith
JOSEPH, THE PATRIARCH
  Mann, T. Into the pit
Josephine the singer; or, The Mouse Folk.
    Kafka, F.
JOSHUA (BIBLICAL CHARACTER)
  Bradford, R. Strategem of Joshua
Joshua. Grau, S. A.
Josiah Crawley at the Palace. Trollope, A.
Josiah Crawley charged with theft. Trollope,
    A.
Josiah Willett. Schaefer, J. W.
Josie who took things. Strain, F. B.
JOURNALISM. See Journalists
JOURNALISTS
  Aiken, C. P. Round by round
  Bowen, E. Recent photograph
  Brown, F. Night the world ended
  Brier, H. M. Newspaper man
  Carter, R. G. High-pressure stuff
  Chalmers, B. The contest
  Claudy, C. H. Helmet of Pluto
  Clemens, S. L. Mr Skae's item
  Clemens, S. L. My bloody massacre (I)
  Coombs, C. I. Millie's big story
  Coombs, C. I. Nose for news
  Coppard, A. E. Fifty pounds
  Davis, R. H. The deserter
  Fletcher, V. Coda to a writer's conference
  Gallico, P. W. McKabe
  Goodman, J. T. "Trumpet" comes to
      Pickeye!
  Grimson, M. S. Faith, hope and charity
  Hillman, G. M. Copy girl
  James, H. Death of the lion
  Joyce, J. Little cloud
  Kipling, R. Man who would be king
  Kipling, R. Village that voted the earth
      was flat
  Kirkland, J. Wall of fire
  Munro, H. H. Secret sin of Septimus
      Brope
  Munro, H. H. Yarkand manner
  Poe, E. A. X-ing a paragrab
  Porter, W. S. Calloway's code
  Priestley, J. B. The statues
  Schramm, W. L. My kingdom for Jones
  Tarkington, B. Walterson
  Taylor, S. W. Last voyage of the Unsink-
      able Sal
  Ullman, J. M. Anything new on the
      strangler?
  Verne, J. In the year 2889
  Waddell, R. You'd better be right!
  Wallace, R. Secret weapon of Joe Smith
  Waltari, M. T. Before the twilight of the
      gods
JOURNALS. See Diaries (Stories in diary
    form)
The journey. Jenkins, W. F.
Journey for Wilbur. Schnabel, J. F.
Journey into smoke. Sansom, W.
Journey to the fort. Johnson, D. M.
Journeying through the milky way. Shapiro,
    L.
JOURNEYS. See Travel
JOVIANS. See Jupiter (Planet)
JOY AND SORROW
  Berger, T. L. April is the cruelest month
  James, H. Altar of the dead
Joy, joy, joy! Parker, J. R.
Joyce, James, 1882-1941
  Araby
    Neider, C. ed. Great short stories from
      the world's literature
    Waite, H. O. and Atkinson, B. P. eds.
      Literature for our time
  Clay
    Lynskey, W. C. ed. Reading modern
      fiction
    Short, R. W. and Sewall, R. B. eds.
      Short stories for study. 1950 ed.
  Counterparts
    West, R. B. and Stallman, R. W. eds.
      Art of modern fiction

Joyce, James—*Continued*
  The dead
    Bogorad, S. N. and Trevithick, J. eds.
      College miscellany
    Cerf, B. A. and Moriarty, H. C. eds.
      Anthology of famous British stories
    Felheim, M.; Newman, F. B. and Steinhoff, W. R. eds. Modern short stories
    Gordon, C. and Tate, A. eds. House of fiction
    Ludwig, J. B. and Poirier, W. R. eds.
      Stories, British and American
    Neider, C. ed. Short novels of the masters
  Ivy Day in the committee room
    Stegner, W. E.; Scowcroft, R. and Ilyin, B. eds. Writer's art
  Little cloud
    Blodgett, H. W. ed. Story survey. 1953 ed.
    Heilman, R. B. ed. Modern short stories
    Schorer, M. ed. The story
  Painful case
    Barrows, H. ed. 15 stories
  The sisters
    Ludwig, J. B. and Poirier, W. R. eds.
      Stories, British and American

Juan-les-Pins: the Spanish cow. Charteris, L.
Juan Manuel, Infante of Castille, 1282-1347
  Man who married an ill-tempered wife
    De Onís, H. ed. Spanish stories and tales

JUDAISM. See Jews—Religion

Judas. O'Donovan, M.

JUDAS ISCARIOT
  Andreev, L. N. Love and betrayal
  Komroff, M. Death of Judas

Judas ram. Merwin, S.

Judas tree. Welch, D.

Judge. Edmonds, W. D.

JUDGES. See Law and lawyers

The **judgment.** Kafka, F.

JUDGMENT DAY
  Maugham, W. S. Judgment seat

Judgment night. Moore, C. L.

Judgment of Paris. Parker, J. R.

Judgment of the gods. Coolidge, O. E.

Judgment seat. Maugham, W. S.

Judith. Charteris, L.

Judkin of the parcels. Munro, H. H.

JUDO. See Jiu-jitsu

Jug Leg Kelley. Gartner, J.

JUGGLERS AND JUGGLING
  France, A. Our lady's juggler

JUGGLING. See Jugglers and juggling

Julie Romain. Maupassant, G. de

Julien. Zola, É.

JULIUS CAESAR. See Caesar, Caius Julius

JULY FOURTH. See Fourth of July celebrations

June recital. Welty, E.

The **jungle.** Michener, J. A.

Jungle brothers. Gilbert, K.

Jungle war. Gill, T.

JUNGLES
  Barnard, L. G. Four men and a box
  Conrad, J. Heart of darkness
  Cottrell, D. W. Pit in the jungle
  Gilbert, K. Jungle brothers
  Hudson, W. H. Mysterious forest
  Jenkins, W. F. Doomsday deferred
  Maugham, W. S. Neil MacAdam
  Mukerji, D. G. Kari the elephant
  Weston, C. Forest of the night

Junkyard. Simak, C. D.

Juno's swans. Aldrich, B. S.

JUPITER (PLANET)
  Asimov, I. Not final!
  Asimov, I. Victory unintentional
  Klass, P. The deserter
  Long, F. B. Red Storm on Jupiter
  Simak, C. D. Desertion

JURIES. See Trials

JURY DUTY. See Trials

Jury of her peers. Glaspell, S.

The **juryman.** Galsworthy, J.

Just a little havoc. Taber, G. B.

Just before the war with the Eskimos. Salinger, J. D.

Just boys. Farrell, J. T.

Just for you. Willard, H. W.

Just love, love, sweet love. Horwitz, J.

Justice, Donald, 1925-
  The lady
    Prize stories of 1950
    Stanford short stories, 1950
  Vineland's burning
    Prize stories, 1954

JUSTICE
  Bergengruen, W. Concerning muskets
  Lord, J. The avenging
  Stockton, F. R. Lady or the tiger?

A **justice.** Faulkner, W.

JUVENILE DELINQUENCY
  Callaghan, M. E. All the years of her life
  Cassill, R. V. War in the air
  Cather, W. S. Paul's case
  Connolly, M. Big red house on Hope Street
  Doty, W. L. Greatest of these
  Felsen, G. Trenton in thirty minutes
  Johnson, H. Rocky
  Lord, J. Boy who wrote 'no'

K

KABBALA. See Cabala

Kaddish. Taper, B.

Kadiak. Annixter, P. pseud.

Kaempffert, Waldemar Bernhard, 1877-
  Diminishing draft
    Conklin, G. ed. Big book of science fiction

KAFFIRS. See Kafirs (African people)

KAFIRS (AFRICAN PEOPLE)
  Millin, S. G. L. Why Adonis laughed. 1952 ed.

Kafka, Franz, 1883-1924
The burrow
  Kafka, F. Selected short stories
Common confusion
  Kafka, F. Selected short stories
Country doctor
  Kafka, F. Selected short stories
  Lange, V. ed. Great German short
    novels and stories
  Neider, C. ed. Great short stories from
    the world's literature
A fratricide
  Kafka, F. Selected short stories
Great wall of China
  Kafka, F. Selected short stories
Hunger artist
  Heilman, R. B. ed. Modern short stories
  Kafka, F. Selected short stories
  Millett, F. B. ed. Reading fiction
  West, R. B. and Stallman, R. W. eds.
    Art of modern fiction
Hunter Gracchus
  Gordon, C. and Tate, A. eds. House of
    fiction
  Kafka, F. Selected short stories
  Leftwich, J. ed. Yisröel. 1952 ed.
In the penal colony
  Kafka, F. Selected short stories
Investigations of a dog
  Kafka, F. Selected short stories
Josephine the singer; or, The Mouse Folk
  Kafka, F. Selected short stories
The judgment
  Felheim, M.; Newman, F. B. and Stein-
    hoff, W. R. eds. Modern short stories
  Kafka, F. Selected short stories
The metamorphosis
  Kafka, F. Selected short stories
  Ludwig, R. M. and Perry, M. B. eds.
    Nine short novels
  Neider, C. ed. Short novels of the
    masters
  Pick, R. ed. German stories and tales
  Pratt, F. ed. World of wonder
New advocate
  Kafka, F. Selected short stories
Old manuscript
  Kafka, F. Selected short stories
  Same as: Old page
Old page
  Lynskey, W. C. ed. Reading modern
    fiction
  Same as: Old manuscript
Report to an academy
  Kafka, F. Selected short stories

Kagawa, Toyohiko, 1888-
The last supper
  Brentano, F. ed. The word lives on

Kahanovich, Pinchas, 1884-
From my estates
  Leftwich, J. ed. Yisröel. 1952 ed

Kahler, Hugh MacNair, 1883-
The buckpasser
  Shaw, H. and Bement, D. Reading the
    short story

Kahmann, Mable (Chesley) 1901-
For the honor of XDY
  Story parade (Periodical) Adventure
    stories

Kahn, Bernard I.
Command
  Norton, A. M. ed. Space service
For the public
  Norton, A. M. ed. Space service
The **Kahn.** Wall, J. W.
Kaleidoscope. Bradbury, R.
Kalisman, Herbert H. 1920-
The stray
  American vanguard, 1950
Kandel, Lenore, 1932-
Boy with the innocent eyes
  American vanguard, 1953
Kane, Frank
Slay upon delivery
  Mystery Writers of America, inc.
    Four-&-twenty bloodhounds
KANGAROOS
  Jenkins, W. F. Fourth-dimensional demon-
    strator
Kannitverstan. Hebel, J. P.
KANSAS
                Farm life
      See Farm life—Kansas
Kantor, MacKinlay, 1904-
Fabulous cabman
  Saturday evening post (Periodical) Sat-
    urday evening post stories, 1950
Life in her hands
  Saturday evening post (Periodical) Sat-
    urday evening post stories, 1953
Man who had no eyes
  Certner, S. and Henry, G. H. eds. Short
    stories for our times
Papa Pierre's pipe
  This week magazine. This week's short-
    short stories
That Greek dog
  Lass, A. H. and Horowitz, A. eds.
    Stories for youth
Voice of Bugle Ann
  Andrews, R. C. ed. My favorite stories
    of the great outdoors
Yea, he did fly
  Grayson, C. ed. Fourth round
Kaplan, Alvin Harold, 1904-
Danger wears two faces
  Argosy (Periodical) Argosy Book of ad-
    venture stories
Kaplan, Ralph, 1917-
The artist
  Best American short stories, 1950
Night my brother came home
  Ribalow, H. U. ed. This land, these
    people
Karchmer, Sylvan, 1914-
Bond
  Ribalow, H. U. ed. These your children
Fistful of Alamo heroes
  Peery, W. W. ed. 21 Texas short stories
"Hail, brother and farewell"
  Best American short stories, 1950
Kari the elephant. Mukerji, D. G.
Karmel, Ilona, 1925-
Fru Holm
  Best American short stories, 1951
Karp, Deborah B. 1924-
Carmi
  Ribalow, H. U. ed. These your children

Katherine the clown. Ekbergh, I. D.
Kathyanne and the piggy bank. Caldwell, E.
Katkov, Norman, 1918-
  Charlie Baseball
    Argosy (Periodical) Argosy Book of
    sports stories
  Stop that fight!
    Ribalow, H. U. ed. World's greatest
    boxing stories
Katrina. Parker, J. R.
Katti's Galápagos Christmas. Von Hagen,
  C. I. B.
Katz, Leo, 1892-
  Gift of the emperor
    Ausubel, N. ed. Treasury of Jewish
    humor
  Technical expert
    Ausubel, N. ed. Treasury of Jewish
    humor
Katz, Shlomo
  Second Lieutenant, U.S.A. Res.
    Ribalow, H. U. ed. These your children
Kaufman, Alvin, 1925-
  Anchor me in mire
    American vanguard, 1950
Kaufman, Anne, 1917-
  First love
    American vanguard, 1953
Kaufman, Wolfe
  Cut yourself a slice of show
    Kaufman, W. Call me Nate
  Dames and ethics
    Kaufman, W. Call me Nate
  Diplomacy in Hollywood
    Kaufman, W. Call me Nate
  Dumas in Hollywood
    Kaufman, W. Call me Nate
  It ain't always the breaks
    Kaufman, W. Call me Nate
  Pity the poor producer
    Kaufman, W. Call me Nate
  Talking about writers
    Kaufman, W. Call me Nate
  That's picture business
    Kaufman, W. Call me Nate
  Three men on a nickel
    Kaufman, W. Call me Nate
  Wings of an angel
    Kaufman, W. Call me Nate
  You'll meet 'em all
    Kaufman, W. Call me Nate
Kauffmann, Stanley, 1916-
  Fulvous yellow
    Cory, D. W. pseud. comp. 21 variations
    on a theme
Kaula, David
  The huntress
    Hathaway, B. and Sessions, J. A. eds.
    Writers for tomorrow. 2d ser.
Kay uses the evidence. Lansing, E. C. H.
Kaye-Smith, Sheila, 1887-1956
  Day in a woman's life
    Cerf, B. A. and Moriarty, H. C. eds.
    Anthology of famous British stories
  The mockbeggar
    Blodgett, H. W. ed. Story survey.
    1953 ed.
Kazan. Curwood, J. O.
Keela, the outcast Indian maiden. Welty, E.

Keeler, Harry Stephen, 1890-
  Hand of God
    Mystery Writers of America, inc.
    20 great tales of murder
  Victim no. 5
    Mystery Writers of America, inc.
    Maiden murders
Keene, Day
  Great whirring of wings
    Mystery Writers of America, inc.
    Maiden murders
  Homicide House
    Mystery Writers of America, inc.
    Crooks' tour
  Remember the night
    Best detective stories of the year—1950
  "What so proudly we hail..."
    Conklin, G. ed. Science-fiction adven-
    tures in dimension
Keep off the rail! Clements, C. J.
Keep your pity. Boyle, K.
Keeper of the dream. Beaumont, C.
Keeper of the faith. Sienkiewicz, H.
Keith, Earl, 1926-
  Children's hour
    American vanguard, 1953
Keith, Sam
  Point of view
    Hathaway, B. and Sessions, J. A. eds.
    Writers for tomorrow. 2d ser.
  Siren of hope
    Hathaway, B. and Sessions, J. A. eds.
    Writers for tomorrow. 2d ser.
Kelland, Clarence Budington, 1881-
  Mark Tidd in the backwoods
    American boy (Periodical) American boy
    anthology
Kelleam, Joseph E. 1913-
  Rust
    Greenberg, M. ed. Robot and the man
Keller, David Henry, 1880-
  Biological experiment
    Keller, D. H. Tales from Underwood
  The bridle
    Keller, D. H. Tales from Underwood
  Creation unforgivable
    Keller, D. H. Tales from Underwood
  Dead woman
    Keller, D. H. Tales from Underwood
  The door
    Keller, D. H. Tales from Underwood
  The doorbell
    Conklin, G. ed. Omnibus of science fic-
    tion
    Keller, D. H. Tales from Underwood
  Flying fool
    Keller, D. H. Tales from Underwood
  Free as the air
    Keller, D. H. Tales from Underwood
  God wheel
    Keller, D. H. Tales from Underwood
  Golden bough
    Keller, D. H. Tales from Underwood
  Ivy war
    Keller, D. H. Tales from Underwood
  Jelly-fish
    Keller, D. H. Tales from Underwood
  Literary corkscrew
    Keller, D. H. Tales from Underwood
    Margulies, L. and Friend, O. J. eds.
    From off this world

Keller, David H.—*Continued*
Living machine
  Wollheim, D. A. comp. Every boy's
    book of science-fiction
Moon artist
  Keller, D. H. Tales from Underwood
Opium eater
  Keller, D. H. Tales from Underwood
Perfumed garden
  Keller, D. H. Tales from Underwood
Piece of linoleum
  Keller, D. H. Tales from Underwood
Psychophonic nurse
  Keller, D. H. Tales from Underwood
Revolt of the pedestrians
  Derleth, A. W. ed. Beyond time & space
  Keller, D. H. Tales from Underwood
Service first
  Derleth, A. W. ed. The outer reaches
The Star
  Derleth, A. W. ed. Beachheads in space
Thing in the cellar
  Conklin, G. and Conklin, L. T. eds.
    Supernatural reader
  Keller, D. H. Tales from Underwood
Tiger cat
  Keller, D. H. Tales from Underwood
The worm
  Keller, D. H. Tales from Underwood
Yeast men
  Keller, D. H. Tales from Underwood

Keller, Gottfried, 1819-1890
Fat of the cat
  Joseph, M. ed. Best cat stories
Little legend of the dance
  Pick, R. ed. German stories and tales
Naughty Saint Vitalis
  Lange, V. ed. Great German short
    novels and stories
Regula Amrain and her youngest son
  Fremantle, A. J. ed. Mothers
  Ungar, F. ed. To mother with love

Keller, William A. 1873-
De bello Gallico
  Wolfe, D. M. ed. Which grain will grow

Kelley, Francis Beverly, 1905- See Allen,
  E. jt. auth.

Kelly, Robert Glynn
Start in life
  Stanford short stories, 1950
Tiptoe all the way
  Stanford short stories, 1951

Kelsey, Alice (Geer)
Money from the sky
  Fenner, P. R. comp. Fools and funny
    fellows

Kempton, Kenneth Payson
Puck-eater
  Owen, F. ed. Teen-age winter sports
    stories

Kenig, Leo, 1889-
White shadow
  Leftwich, J. ed. Yisröel. 1952 ed.

Kennedy, Leo, 1907-
Priest in the family
  Pacey, D. ed. Book of Canadian stories

Kensinger, Faye Riter, 1910-
Sense of destination
  Prize stories of 1951

Kent, Charlotta Gilbert
Perpetua puts one over
  American girl (Periodical) Favorite
    stories
KENTON, SIMON, 1755-1836
  Webber, E. M. Passage to Kentucky
KENTUCKY
  Hall, E. G. Callie of Crooked Creek
  McNulty, J. Where the grass, they say,
    is blue
  Stuart, J. Woman in the house
  Summers, H. S. ed. Kentucky story; 15
    stories

Cumberland Mountains
  Fox, J. Knight of the Cumberland
Lexington
  Allen, J. L. King Solomon of Kentucky
Kentucky line-up. Allan, G.
Kepler, Johann, 1571-1630
Somnium: or the astronomy of the moon
  Derleth, A. W. ed. Beyond time & space
KERRY, COUNTY. See Ireland—County
  Kerry
Kersh, Gerald, 1909-
One way of getting a hundred pounds
  Ausubel, N. ed. Treasury of Jewish
    humor
Whatever happened to Corporal Cuckoo?
  Star science fiction stories, no. 3
Kesa and Morito. Akutagawa, R.
Kesten, Hermann, 1900-
Friend in the closet
  Pick, R. ed. German stories and tales
Ketch dog. Annixter, P. pseud.
Ketcham, Pauline
The mistake
  Oberfirst, R. ed. 1952 anthology of best
    original short-shorts
Ketchum, Philip, 1902-
Uncle Charlie
  Mystery Writers of America, inc.
    20 great tales of murder
Kew Gardens. Woolf, V. S.
The **key.** Van Doren, M.
The **key.** Welty, E.
Keyhole. Jenkins, W. F.
Keyhole artist. Cockrell, E. W.
Keystone feud. Scholz, J. V.
Khalil the heretic. Gibran, K.
The **kid.** Ivanov, V. V.
Kid brother. Chute, B. J.
Kid brother. Schweitzer, G.
Kid from Shingle Creek. Sandberg, H. W.
The **kid** who beat the Dodgers. Miers, E. S.
Kidd, Harry Lee, 1915-
Low road go down
  Peery, W. W. ed. 21 Texas short stories
KIDNAPPING
  Buck, P. S. Ransom
  Lord, M. Ransom note
  Paget, V. Wedding chest
  Porter, W. S. Hostages to Momus
  Porter, W. S. Ransom of Red Chief

KIDNAPPING—*Continued*
Queen, E. pseud. Child missing!
Runyon, D. Ransom . . . $1,000,000
Walsh, T. Blonde nurse
White monkey

Kierkegaard, Søren Aabye, 1813-1855
Abraham
Selden, R. ed. Ways of God and men

Kilcrin, Isabel
Star buck
McFarland, W. K. comp. Then it happened

Kiley, Norma Crawford
Day of the dance
Stanford short stories, 1953

Kill and run. Ward, F.

The **killer.** Coggins, F.

The **killer** and the pit. Sinclair, J. L.

Killer in the house. Benson, B.

Killer is loose. Hawkins, J. and Hawkins, W.

The **killers.** Hemingway, E.

Kinau, Rudolf, 1887-
Homesickness night
Lohan, R. and Lohan, M. eds. New Christmas treasury

Kind of scandal. Worthington, R.

Kindest thing to do. Gordimer, N.

KINDNESS
Grimson, M. S. It never fails

Kindness. Del Rey, L.

KINDNESS TO ANIMALS. See Animals
—Treatment

King, Mary Paula, 1909-
Chicken on the wind
Peery, W. W. ed. 21 Texas short stories
Honey house
Southern review. Anthology of stories from the Southern review

The **King.** Babel', I. E.

The **king.** Brand, M. pseud.

King and the Princess. O'Brien, J. S.

King David's cave. Bialik, H. N.

King-Hall, Stephen, 1893-
By one, by two, and by three
Davenport, B. ed. Tales to be told in the dark

King of clubs. Christie, A. M.

King of the gray spaces. Bradbury, R.

King of the north woods. Grimson, M. S.

King of thieves. Kuttner, H.

King Pest. Poe, E. A.

King Solomon of Kentucky. Allen, J. L.

Kingdom in the corn. Seaver, J.

Kingdom of Gordon. Goodman, J. C.

KINGDOMS, IMAGINARY. See Imaginary kingdoms

KINGS AND RULERS
Coolidge, O. E. Little Pharaoh
Doyle, Sir A. C. Scandal in Bohemia
Verga, G. So much for the King

King's English. Shulman, M.

Kings of Orion. Buchan, J. 1st baron Tweedsmuir

King's wishes. Sheckley, R.

The **Kinnehórrah.** Weidman, J.

Kipling, Rudyard, 1865-1936
At the end of the passage
Kipling, R. Maugham's choice of Kipling's best
Brushwood boy
Kipling, R. Maugham's choice of Kipling's best
Drums of the fore and aft
Cerf, B. A. and Moriarty, H. C. eds. Anthology of famous British stories
Elephant's child
Fenner, P. R. comp. Elephants, elephants, elephants
'Finest story in the world'
Kipling, R. Maugham's choice of Kipling's best
Pratt, F. ed. World of wonder
Incarnation of Krishna Mulvaney
Schramm, W. L. ed. Great short stories
Limitations of Pambé Serang
Queen, E. pseud. ed. Literature of crime
'Love-o'-women'
Kipling, R. Maugham's choice of Kipling's best
Man who was
Kipling, R. Maugham's choice of Kipling's best
Shaw, H. and Bement, D. Reading the short story
Man who would be king
Cerf, B. A. and Moriarty, H. C. eds. Anthology of famous British stories
Cody, S. ed. Greatest stories and how they were written
Kipling, R. Maugham's choice of Kipling's best
Lamb, L. ed. Family book of best loved short stories
Mark of the beast
Pratt, F. ed. World of wonder
Miracle of Purun Bhagat
Kipling, R. Maugham's choice of Kipling's best
Moti Guj—mutineer
Eaton, H. T. ed. Short stories
Mowgli's brothers
Kipling, R. Maugham's choice of Kipling's best
My own true ghost story
Carrington, H. ed. Week-end book of ghost stories
Fenner, P. R. comp. Ghosts, ghosts, ghosts
On Greenhow Hill
Gordon, C. and Tate, A. eds. House of fiction
Kipling, R. Maugham's choice of Kipling's best
Reingelder and the German flag
Bond, R. T. ed. Handbook for poisoners
'They'
Kipling, R. Maugham's choice of Kipling's best
Tods' amendment
Kipling, R. Maugham's choice of Kipling's best
Tomb of his ancestors
Kipling, R. Maugham's choice of Kipling's best
Toomai of the elephants
Fenner, P. R. comp. Elephants, elephants, elephants

Kipling, Rudyard—*Continued*
Village that voted the earth was flat
Kipling, R. Maugham's choice of Kipling's best
William the conqueror
Kipling, R. Maugham's choice of Kipling's best
'Wireless'
Kipling, R. Maugham's choice of Kipling's best
Without benefit of clergy
Kipling, R. Maugham's choice of Kipling's best

Kirch, James A.
Murder for two
Best detective stories of the year—1950
Till death do us part
Best detective stories of the year—1953

KIRGHIZ
Ivanov, V. V. The kid

Kirk, Ralph G. 1881-
To him who waits
Cavanna, B. ed. Pick of the litter

Kirkland, Jack, 1901-
Wall of fire
Moskowitz, S. comp. Editor's choice in science fiction

Kirtland, Ann
Trial by fire
Strang, R. M. and Roberts, R. M. eds. Teen-age tales v2

Kishor, Sulamith Ish- See Ish-Kishor, Sulamith

Kismet and the nomad woman. Enders, G. B.

The **kiss.** Sansom, W.

Kiss for the Lieutenant. Gordon, A.

Kiss me again, stranger. Du Maurier, D.

Kiss of Kandahar. Blochman, L. G.

The **kiss**-off. Foran, J. P.

Kissing kind. Hine, A. B.

Kitchin, Clifford Henry Benn, 1895-
Chelsea cat
Asquith, Lady C. M. E. C. ed. Book of modern ghosts

The **kite.** Maugham, W. S.

KITES
Maugham, W. S. The kite

Kith of the Elf-folk. Dunsany, E. J. M. D. P. 18th baron

KITTENS. See Cats

Kittura Remsberg. Schaefer, J. W.

Kitty, kitty, kitty. Pudney, J.

Kjelgaard, Betty
Age of love
This week magazine. This week's short-short stories
Black horse
Furman, A. L. ed. Teen-age horse stories
Blood on the ice
Boys' life (Periodical) Boys' life adventure stories
Dog's dog
Furman, A. L. ed. Teen-age dog stories
Fifth friend
Fenner, P. R. comp. Indians, Indians, Indians
Red's education
Fenner, P. R. comp. Dogs, dogs, dogs
Wilderness road
Fenner, P. R. comp. Indians, Indians, Indians

Klass, Philip, 1920-
Alexander the bait
Conklin, G. ed. Omnibus of science fiction
Betelgeuse Bridge
Galaxy science fiction magazine. Galaxy reader of science fiction
Heinlein, R. A. ed. Tomorrow, the stars
Child's play
Astounding science fiction (Periodical) Astounding science fiction anthology
Pratt, F. ed. World of wonder
The deserter
Star science fiction stories [no. 1]
Firewater
Year's best science fiction novels, 1953
Generation of Noah
Best science fiction stories: 1952
House dutiful
Merril, J. ed. Beyond human ken
Ionian cycle
Greenberg, M. ed. Travelers of space
The jester
Conklin, G. ed. Science-fiction thinking machines
Null-P
Derleth, A. W. ed. Worlds of tomorrow
Venus and the seven sexes
Brown, F. and Reynolds, M. eds. Science-fiction carnival
Venus is a man's world
Galaxy science fiction magazine. Galaxy reader of science fiction
"Will you walk a little faster?"
Conklin, G. ed. Invaders of earth

Klein, Alexander, 1918-
The Minyan
Ribalow, H. U. ed. This land, these people

Klein, Jenny Machlowitz
Yisgadal
Ribalow, H. U. ed. This land, these people

Kleist, Heinrich von, 1777-1811
Beggar-woman of Locarno
Neider, C. ed. Great short stories from the world's literature
Earthquake in Chile
Lange, V. ed. Great German short novels and stories

KLEPTOMANIA
Munro, H. H. Seven cream jugs

Kline, Otis Adelbert, 1891?-1946
Stolen centuries
Moskowitz, S. comp. Editor's choice in science fiction

Klingsberg, Harry M.
Doowinkle, Attorney
Blaustein, A. P. ed. Fiction goes to court
Foolproof frame-up
Best detective stories of the year—1951

Kloepfer, Marguerite
Skeleton of Mr Nethersoul
Seventeen (Periodical) Nineteen from Seventeen

KLONDIKE
  Hendryx, J. B. Murder on Halfaday
    Creek; 30 stories
  London, J. Sun-Dog Trail

The **Klondiker.** Davis, A. L.

Knapp, Sally Elizabeth, 1918-
  Clipped wings
    American girl (Periodical) Favorite
    stories

Knapsack of salvation. Langewiesche-Brandt,
  W. E.

Kneale, Nigel
  Bini and Bettine
    Kneale, N. Tomato Cain, and other
    stories
  Calculation of N'bambwe
    Kneale, N. Tomato Cain, and other
    stories
  Chains
    Kneale, N. Tomato Cain, and other
    stories
  Clog dance for a dead farce
    Kneale, N. Tomato Cain, and other
    stories
  Curphey's follower
    Kneale, N. Tomato Cain, and other
    stories
  Enderby and the sleeping beauty
    Kneale, N. Tomato Cain, and other
    stories
  Essence of strawberry
    Kneale, N. Tomato Cain, and other
    stories
  The excursion
    Kneale, N. Tomato Cain, and other
    stories
  Flo
    Kneale, N. Tomato Cain, and other
    stories
  God and Daphne
    Kneale, N. Tomato Cain, and other
    stories
  Jeremy in the wind
    Kneale, N. Tomato Cain, and other
    stories
  Lotus for Jamie
    Kneale, N. Tomato Cain, and other
    stories
  Minuke
    Conklin, G. and Conklin, L. T. eds.
    Supernatural reader
    Kneale, N. Tomato Cain, and other
    stories
  Mrs Mancini
    Kneale, N. Tomato Cain, and other
    stories
  Nature study
    Kneale, N. Tomato Cain, and other
    stories
  "Oh, mirror, mirror"
    Kneale, N. Tomato Cain, and other
    stories
  Patter of tiny feet
    Kneale, N. Tomato Cain, and other
    stories
  Peg
    Kneale, N. Tomato Cain, and other
    stories
  The photograph
    Kneale, N. Tomato Cain, and other
    stories

  The pond
    Kneale, N. Tomato Cain, and other
    stories
  Putting away of Uncle Quaggin
    Kneale, N. Tomato Cain, and other
    stories
    Stauffer, R. M.; Cunningham, W. H. and
    Sullivan, C. J. eds. Adventures in
    modern literature
  Quiet Mr Evans
    Kneale, N. Tomato Cain, and other
    stories
  The stocking
    Kneale, N. Tomato Cain, and other
    stories
  Tarroo-ushtey
    Kneale, N. Tomato Cain, and other
    stories
  They're scared, Mr Bradlaugh
    Kneale, N. Tomato Cain, and other
    stories
  Tomato Cain
    Kneale, N. Tomato Cain, and other
    stories
  Tootie and the cat licenses
    Kneale, N. Tomato Cain, and other
    stories
  Who—me, signor?
    Kneale, N. Tomato Cain, and other
    stories
  Zachary Crebbin's angel
    Kneale, N. Tomato Cain, and other
    stories

Kneel to the rising sun. Caldwell, E.

The **knife.** Crane, S.

The **knife.** Gill, B.

Knife of the times. Williams, W. C.

Knife to cut the corn bread with. Caldwell, E.

Knight, Damon
  Ask me anything
    Galaxy science fiction magazine. Galaxy
    reader of science fiction
  Cabin boy
    Galaxy science fiction magazine. Galaxy
    reader of science fiction
  Catch that Martian
    Conklin, G. ed. Omnibus of science fic-
    tion
  Don't live in the past
    Galaxy science fiction magazine. Galaxy
    reader of science fiction
  Four in one
    Galaxy science fiction magazine. Second
    Galaxy reader of science fiction
  Not with a bang
    Conklin, G. ed. Big book of science
    fiction
  To serve man
    Best science fiction stories: 1951

Knight, Eric Mowbray, 1897-1943
  Flying Yorkshireman
    Jensen, P. ed. Fireside book of flying
    stories
  Lassie Come-Home
    Andrews, R. C. ed. My favorite stories
    of the great outdoors
    Bloch, M. ed. Favorite dog stories
    Harper, W. comp. Dog show

Knight, Norman L.
Crisis in Utopia
Greenberg, M. comp. Five science fiction
novels
The **knight.** Bergengruen, W.
Knight-errant of the foothills. Harte, B.
Knight of the Cumberland. Fox, J.
The **knight** returns. Arico, V.
KNIGHTHOOD. See Knights and knight-
hood

KNIGHTS AND KNIGHTHOOD
Bergengruen, W. The knight
Bergengruen, W. Shining fools

Knipscheer, James M. W.
Start from scratch
Mystery Writers of America, inc. Four-
&-twenty bloodhounds

Knister, Raymond, 1899-1932
The strawstack
Pacey, D. ed. Book of Canadian stories

Knock. Brown, F.

Knowles, John
Turn with the sun
Story (Periodical) Story; no. 4

Knowlton, Elizabeth
Petite première in the Mont Blanc Massif
Talbot, D. ed. Treasury of mountaineer-
ing stories

Knox, Joe
Courting of Miss Darlie Blanche
Knox, J. Little Benders
Curly maple
Knox, J. Little Benders
Death of Uncle Andy
Knox, J. Little Benders
How Brother Aaron was saved
Knox, J. Little Benders
Little Ben
Knox, J. Little Benders
Little Ben's railroad
Knox, J. Little Benders
Magic touch
Knox, J. Little Benders
Mamma and the pot of gold
Knox, J. Little Benders
Man in the chimney corner
Knox, J. Little Benders
Miss Dulcie and the strange baby
Knox, J. Little Benders
Miss Emma Grisby
Knox, J. Little Benders
Miss Whipple and the Creekers
Knox, J. Little Benders
Mr Caleb Westly and the stranger
Knox, J. Little Benders
Morning I went to buy the horseshoe
Knox, J. Little Benders
Night Mamma told a bald-faced lie
Knox, J. Little Benders
Pete
Knox, J. Little Benders
Uncle Sod's birthday social
Knox, J. Little Benders

Knox, Ronald Arbuthnott, 1888-
Ruth
Thinker's digest (Periodical) Spoiled
priest, and other stories

Knute, the giant bullsnake. Rounds, G.

Kober, Arthur, 1900-
Always a bridesmaid
Kober, A. Bella, Bella kissed a fella
Bella's got a fella
Kober, A. Bella, Bella kissed a fella
Bronx oracle
Kober, A. Bella, Bella kissed a fella
Course of true love
Kober, A. Bella, Bella kissed a fella
Courtship deferred
Kober, A. Bella, Bella kissed a fella
He who woos and runs away
Kober, A. Bella, Bella kissed a fella
Letter from the Bronx
Ausubel, N. ed. Treasury of Jewish
humor
Life with mother
Kober, A. Bella, Bella kissed a fella
Nobody can beat Freidkin's meats
Ribalow, H. U. ed. This land, these
people
On (and off) the agenda
Kober, A. Bella, Bella kissed a fella
Other pebbles on the beach
Kober, A. Bella, Bella kissed a fella
Place in the sun
Kober, A. Bella, Bella kissed a fella
Return of the native
Kober, A. Bella, Bella kissed a fella
Suitor's white paper
Kober, A. Bella, Bella kissed a fella
Tête-à-tête
Kober, A. Bella, Bella kissed a fella
They shall inherit the earth
Kober, A. Bella, Bella kissed a fella
Time is out of joint
Kober, A. Bella, Bella kissed a fella

Kobold. Seager, A.

Kobrin, Leon, 1872-1946
Milchiger Synagogue and the blind
preacher
Ausubel, N. ed. Treasury of Jewish
humor
Soul that mice nibbled up
Ausubel, N. ed. Treasury of Jewish
humor
Temptation of Reb Mottel
Ausubel, N. ed. Treasury of Jewish
humor

Koestler, Arthur, 1905-
Apage Satanas
Burnett, W. ed. World's best

Kohn, Phyllis A. 1924-
Birthright
Wolfe, D. M. ed. Which grain will grow

Kola Road. Asch, S.

Kola Street. Asch, S.

Kolins, William F. 1926-
Years before anger
Wolfe, D. M. ed. Which grain will grow

Kompert, Leopold, 1822-1886
Silent woman
Leftwich, J. ed. Yisröel. 1952 ed.

Komroff, Manuel, 1890-
Alone the stranger passes
Brentano, F. ed. The word lives on
Death of Judas
Selden, R. ed. Ways of God and men

Komroff, Manuel—*Continued*
Light of the moon
Herzberg, M. J. comp. Treasure chest of
sport stories
Thousand-dollar bill
Certner, S. and Henry, G. H. eds. Short
stories for our times
Told in the stars
Brentano, F. ed. The word lives on
What is a miracle?
Lohan, R. and Lohan, M. eds. New
Christmas treasury

KONGO, BELGIAN. See Congo, Belgian

Kon-Tiki reaches the South Sea Islands.
Heyerdahl, T.

KOREAN WAR, 1950-1953
Burnet, D. Why did he leave me?
Chamberlain, W. Chaplain of Company C
Chase, F. General from the Pentagon
Landon, B. Advance party
Mauldin, W. H. Affair of the wayward
jeep
Sneider, V. J. A long way from home
Worden, W. L. Officers' girl

Kornbluth, Cyril M. 1923-
The adventurer
Pohl, F. ed. Assignment in tomorrow
Altar at midnight
Kornbluth, C. M. The explorers
Wollheim, D. A. ed. Prize science fiction
Dominoes
Star science fiction stories ₍no. 1₎
Friend to man
Kornbluth, C. M. The explorers
Gomez
Kornbluth, C. M. The explorers
Goodly creatures
Kornbluth, C. M. The explorers
Marching morons
Best science fiction stories: 1952
The mindworm
Best science fiction stories: 1951
Kornbluth, C. M. The explorers
Only thing we learn
Conklin, G. ed. Big book of science
fiction
The remorseful
Star science fiction stories, no. 2
Rocket of 1955
Kornbluth, C. M. The explorers
Silly season
Heinlein, R. A. ed. Tomorrow, the stars
That share of glory
Kornbluth, C. M. The explorers
Norton, A. M. ed. Space service
Thirteen o'clock
Kornbluth, C. M. The explorers
With these hands
Kornbluth, C. M. The explorers

Kovner, B. pseud. See Adler, Jacob

Krambambuli. Ebner von Eschenbach, M.
Freifrau

Krepps, Robert Wilson, 1919-
Five years in the Marmalade
Best science fiction stories: 1950
Bleiler, E. F. and Dikty, T. E. eds.
Science fiction omnibus: the best sci-
ence fiction stories, 1949, 1950
See also Gold, H. L. jt. auth.

Krige, Uys, 1910-
Charcoal burners
Krige, U. The dream and the desert
Christmas box
Krige, U. The dream and the desert
The coffin
Krige, U. The dream and the desert
Death of the Zulu
Krige, U. The dream and the desert
The dream
Krige, U. The dream and the desert
Invisible shepherd
Krige, U. The dream and the desert
La Miseria
Krige, U. The dream and the desert
Two Daumiers
Krige, U. The dream and the desert

Krimsky, Josephine, 1930-
Andrew's father
American vanguard, 1952

Kristol, Irving, 1920-
Adam and I
Ribalow, H. U. ed. These your children

Kruse, Clifton B.
Dr Lu-Mie
Wollheim, D. A. comp. Every boy's
book of science-fiction

Kruse, John
Alone in shark waters
McFee, W. ed. Great sea stories of
modern times

KU KLUX KLAN (1915-date)
Berg, L. Nasty Kupperman and the Ku
Klux Klan

Kubilius, Walter, 1918-
Other side
Best science fiction stories: 1952

Kubilius, Walter, 1918- **and Pratt, Fletcher,**
1897-1956
Second chance
Sloane, W. M. ed. Space, space, space

Kuehn, Susan, 1926-
The hunt
Prize stories of 1950
The searchers
Best American short stories, 1952
Stanford short stories, 1951

Kulbak, Moishe, 1896-
Munie the bird dealer
Howe, I. and Greenberg, E. eds. Treas-
ury of Yiddish stories

Kummer, Frederic Arnold, 1873-1943
Forgiveness of Tenchu Taen
Greenberg, M. ed. Travelers of space

Kutner, Nanette
Do you remember Mary?
McFarland, W. K. comp. Then it hap-
pened

Kuttner, Henry, 1914-
Absalom
Heinlein, R. A. ed. Tomorrow, the stars
By these presents
Kuttner, H. Ahead of time
Camouflage
Kuttner, H. Ahead of time
Clash by night
Astounding science fiction (Periodical)
Astounding science fiction anthology

Kuttner, Henry—*Continued*

Compliments of the author
Kuttner, H. Gnome there was, and other tales of science fiction and fantasy

The cure
Kuttner, H. Gnome there was, and other tales of science fiction and fantasy

DP!
Best science-fiction stories: 1954

De profundis
Kuttner, H. Ahead of time

Deadlock
Greenberg, M. ed. Robot and the man
Kuttner, H. Ahead of time

Devil on Salvation Bluff
Star science fiction stories, no. 3

Dream's end
Crossen, K. F. ed. Future tense

Ego machine
Brown, F. and Reynolds, M. eds. Science fiction carnival

Endowment policy
Conklin, G. ed. Science-fiction adventures in dimension

Ex machina
Bleiler, E. F. and Dikty, T. E. eds. Science fiction omnibus: the best science fiction stories, 1949, 1950
Kuttner, H. Robots have no tails

Exit the professor
Kuttner, H. Gnome there was, and other tales of science fiction and fantasy

Gallegher plus
Kuttner, H. Robots have no tails

Ghost
Kuttner, H. Ahead of time

Gnome there was
Kuttner, H. Gnome there was, and other tales of science fiction and fantasy
Merril, J. ed. Beyond human ken

Happy ending
Bleiler, E. F. and Dikty, T. E. eds. Science fiction omnibus: the best science fiction stories, 1949, 1950

Hard-luck diggings
Conklin, G. ed. Possible worlds of science fiction

Home is the hunter
Kuttner, H. Ahead of time

Iron standard
Greenberg, M. ed. Men against the stars

Jesting pilot
Kuttner, H. Gnome there was, and other tales of science fiction and fantasy

King of thieves
Lesser, M. A. ed. Looking forward

Line to tomorrow
Derleth, A. W. ed. Worlds of tomorrow

Margin for error
Conklin, G. ed. Big book of science fiction

Men of the ten books
Best science fiction stories: 1952

Mimsy were the borogoves
Kuttner, H. Gnome there was, and other tales of science fiction and fantasy

Noise
Startling stories (Periodical) Best from Startling stories

Open secret
Jenkins, W. F. ed. Great stories of science fiction

Or else
Kuttner, H. Ahead of time

Pile of trouble
Kuttner, H. Ahead of time

Private eye
Best science fiction stories: 1950
Bleiler, E. F. and Dikty, T. E. eds. Science fiction omnibus: the best science fiction stories, 1949, 1950

Proud robot
Kuttner, H. Robots have no tails

Rain check
Kuttner, H. Gnome there was, and other tales of science fiction and fantasy

See you later
Kuttner, H. Gnome there was, and other tales of science fiction and fantasy

Shock
Derleth, A. W. ed. The outer reaches
Kuttner, H. Ahead of time

Sword of tomorrow
Margulies, L. and Friend, O. J. eds. Giant anthology of science fiction

This is the house
Kuttner, H. Gnome there was, and other tales of science fiction and fantasy

Time locker
Kuttner, H. Robots have no tails

The Twonky
Kuttner, H. Gnome there was, and other tales of science fiction and fantasy

Voice of the lobster
Crossen, K. F. ed. Adventures in tomorrow

We kill people
Lesser, M. A. ed. Looking forward

What you need
Conklin, G. ed. Omnibus of science fiction
Kuttner, H. Gnome there was, and other science fiction and fantasy

When the bough breaks
Astounding science fiction (Periodical) Astounding science fiction anthology
Derleth, A. W. ed. Beyond time & space

When the earth lived
Margulies, L. and Friend, O. J. eds. From off this world

Winner lose all
Conklin, G. ed. Omnibus of science fiction

World is mine
Kuttner, H. Robots have no tails

Year day
Kuttner, H. Ahead of time

Kuttner, Henry, 1914- and Moore, Catherine Lucile, 1911-
Wild surmise
Star science fiction stories [no. 1]

KVASS. See Beer

Kyd, Thomas, pseud.
High court
Queen, E. pseud, ed. The Queen's awards: 8th ser.

L

La Mère Sauvage. Maupassant, G. de

LABOR AND LABORING CLASSES
Bergelson, D. In a backwoods town

Labyrinth. Willman, P.

Lacework Kid. Runyon, D.

Lacy, Ed
Right thing
Ford, N. A. and Faggett, H. L. eds.
Best short stories by Afro-American
writers (1925-1950)

Lacy, March
Fighting finish
Ford, N. A. and Faggett, H. L. eds.
Best short stories by Afro-American
writers (1925-1950)
No fools, no fun
Ford, N. A. and Faggett, H. L. eds.
Best short stories by Afro-American
writers (1925-1950)

LADDERS
Sansom, W. Vertical ladder

Ladies call on Mr Pussick. Francis, O.

LADIES' MAIDS. See Servants—Maids

Lady. Buckingham, N.

The **lady.** Justice, D.

Lady and the dragon. Godfrey, P.

Lady and the tumblers. Constiner, M.

Lady higher up. Porter, W. S.

Lady-killer. Steele, W. D.

Lady of Glenwith Grange. Collins, W.

Lady of my own. Seide, M.

Lady of the sagas. O'Donovan, M.

Lady on the grey. Collier, J.

Lady, or the tiger? Stockton, F. R.

Lady over the wall. Van Doren, M.

Lady says murder. Fay, W.

Lady walks. Powell, J.

Lady's maid. Ekbergh, I. D.

Lady's maid's bell. Wharton, E. N. J.

La Farge, Christopher, 1897-1956
Motet for two voices
Greene, J. I. and Abell, E. eds. Stories
of sudden truth

La Farge, Oliver, 1901-
The bystander
Best detective stories of the year—1954
John the revelator
Magazine of fantasy and science fiction.
Best from Fantasy and science fiction,
1952
No, my darling daughter
This week magazine. This week's short-
short stories
Old century's river
Best American short stories, 1951
Prize stories of 1951
Old men's plans
Grayson, C. ed. Fourth round
Woman hunt no good
Queen, E. pseud. ed. Queen's awards:
6th ser.

Lagerkvist, Pär Fabian, 1891-
The adventure
Lagerkvist, P. F. Eternal smile, and
other stories
The basement
Lagerkvist, P. F. Eternal smile, and
other stories
Children's campaign
Lagerkvist, P. F. Eternal smile, and
other stories
Eternal smile
Lagerkvist, P. F. Eternal smile, and
other stories
Evil angel
Lagerkvist, P. F. Eternal smile, and
other stories
Experimental world
Lagerkvist, P. F. Eternal smile, and
other stories
Father and I
Lagerkvist, P. F. Eternal smile, and
other stories
God's little traveling salesman
Lagerkvist, P. F. Eternal smile, and
other stories
Guest of reality
Lagerkvist, P. F. Eternal smile, and
other stories
The hangman
Lagerkvist, P. F. Eternal smile, and
other stories
Hero's death
Lagerkvist, P. F. Eternal smile, and
other stories
Lift that went down into hell
Lagerkvist, P. F. Eternal smile, and
other stories
Marriage feast
Lagerkvist, P. F. Eternal smile, and
other stories
Masquerade of souls
Lagerkvist, P. F. Eternal smile, and
other stories
Myth of mankind
Lagerkvist, P. F. Eternal smile, and
other stories
Paradise
Lagerkvist, P. F. Eternal smile, and
other stories
Princess and all the kingdom
Lagerkvist, P. F. Eternal smile, and
other stories
Saviour John
Lagerkvist, P. F. Eternal smile, and
other stories
Venerated bones
Lagerkvist, P. F. Eternal smile, and
other stories
Wave of Osiris
Lagerkvist, P. F. Eternal smile, and
other stories

Lagerlöf, Selma Ottiliana Lovisa, 1858-1940
In Nazareth
Brentano, F. ed. The word lives on
The outlaws
Neider, C. ed. Great short stories from
the world's literature

The **lagoon.** Conrad, J.

Laidlaw, Clara
Little black boys
Thinker's digest (Periodical) Spoiled
priest, and other stories

Lake, Leonard M. See Rosmond, B. jt. auth.

The lake. Harvey, W. F.

LAKE TAHOE
Davis, S. P. Mystery of the Savage sump

The lamb. Cavanaugh, J. P.

Lamb and some slaughtering. Mowery, W. B.

Lamb chop for the little dog. Winslow, T. S.

Lamb to the slaughter. Dahl, R.

Lambert, Janet
Tall as the stars
American girl (Periodical) Favorite stories

Lamberton, Louise, 1901-
Sleet storm
Cooper, A. C. ed. Modern short stories

LAMBS. See Sheep

The lament. O'Flaherty, L.

Lamkin, Speed, 1927-
Comes a day
Best American short stories, 1950
Prize stories of 1950

L'Amour, Louis, 1908-
Gift of Cochise
Meredith, S. ed. Bar 3

Lamp at noon. Ross, S.

LAMPS
Peretz, I. L. Little Hanukkah lamp

Lamson, Ruth Rankin
Have a heart, lady!
Cavanna, B. ed. Pick of the litter

Land. Lewis, S.

Land ironclads. Wells, H. G.

Land of my fathers. Tennyson, II.

Land of No Shadow. Claudy, C. H.

Land of our enemies. Stuart, J.

Land rush. Haycox, E.

LAND SPECULATION
Garland, H. Under the lion's paw

LAND TENURE
Porter, W. S. Bexar scrip no. 2692
Porter, W. S. Georgia's ruling
Tolstoï, L. N. Graf. Three arshins of land

LAND TITLES. See Land tenure

Landa, Myer Jack, 1874-
Two legacies
Leftwich, J. ed. Yisröel. 1952 ed.

The landing. Leshinsky, T.

LANDLORD AND TENANT
Edgeworth, M. Castle Rackrent
Parker, J. R. The millennium

Landon, Margaret Dorothea (Mortenson) 1903-
Reconciliation
Brentano, F. ed. The word lives on

Landor's cottage. Poe, E. A.

The Landrath. Irina, A.

Landscape with figures. Sansom, W.

LANDSLIDES
Hawthorne, N. Ambitious guest

Lane, Carl Daniel, 1899-
River dragon
Fenner, P. R. comp. Indians, Indians, Indians

Lane, George C.
Ensign Carson, USCGR
Furman, A. L. ed. Teen-age sea stories

Lang, Allan Kim
Eel by the tail
Conklin, G. ed. Invaders of earth

Lang, Don
Elephant never forgets
Fenner, P. R. comp. Elephants, elephants, elephants
Tramp, the sheep dog
Harper, W. comp. Dog show

Langewiesche-Brandt, Wolfgang Ernst, 1907-
Knapsack of salvation
Jensen, P. ed. Fireside book of flying stories
Three secrets of human flight
Jensen, P. ed. Fireside book of flying stories

LANGUAGE AND LANGUAGES
Berryman, J. Berom
Heinlein, R. A. Gulf

Lanham, Edwin Moultrie, 1904-
Listen to me, boy
Argosy (Periodical) Argosy Book of sports stories

Lanning, George, 1925-
Old Turkey Neck
Best American short stories, 1951

Lansing, Elisabeth Carleton (Hubbard) 1911-
Kay uses the evidence
Furman, A. L. ed. Everygirls mystery stories
There's something about you
American girl (Periodical) Favorite stories
Touch of psychology
American girl (Periodical) On my honor

Laocoön complex. Furnas, J. C.

LAPLAND
Sjogren, E. Death in the pass

La Prello paper. Jacobi, C.

Laputa. Swift, J.

Larchmoor is not the world. Cassill, R. V.

Lardner, John, 1912-
Sudden attack of heartbreak
Dachs, D. ed. Treasury of sports humor

Lardner, Ring Wilmer, 1885-1933
Alibi Ike
Graber, R. S. ed. Baseball reader
Busher's letters home
Graber, R. S. ed. Baseball reader
Champion
Ribalow, H. U. ed. World's greatest boxing stories
Golden honeymoon
Burrell, J. A. and Cerf, B. A. eds. Anthology of famous American stories
Scribner treasury
Haircut
Best of the Best American short stories, 1915-1950
Day, A. G. ed. Greatest American short stories
Gordon, C. and Tate, A. eds. House of fiction
Queen, E. pseud. ed. Literature of crime
Scribner treasury
Harmony
Graber, R. S. ed. Baseball reader

Lardner, Ring W.—*Continued*
  Horseshoes
    Dachs, D. ed. Treasury of sports humor
    Graber, R. S. ed. Baseball reader
  Some like them cold
    Burrell, J. A. and Cerf, B. A. eds.
      Anthology of famous American stories
    Stegner, W. E.; Scowcroft, R. and Ilyin,
      B. eds. Writer's art
  There are smiles
    Blodgett, H. W. ed. Story survey. 1953
    ed.
  Zone of quiet
    Lynskey, W. C. ed. Reading modern
    fiction
Larkspur again: A lawn meet at Rosemount
  Grange. Surtees, R. S.
Larkspur hounds: A morning with a bag-
  man. Surtees, R. S.
Larsen, David
  Freeze-out
    Owen, F. ed. Teen-age winter sports
    stories
Lasker-Schüler, Else, 1876-
  Arthur Aronymus; my father's story
    Leftwich, J. ed. Yisröel. 1952 ed.
Lass with the delicate air. Bigland, E.
Lassie Come-Home. Knight, E. M.
Last accounting. O'Rourke, F.
Last American. Mitchell, J. A.
Last bed. Isaacson, B. K.
Last Christmas Puzo, M.
Last cigarette. Roper, W.
Last class. Daudet, A.
Last day. Lieberman, R.
Last day. Matheson, R.
Last day at the office. Reese, J. H.
Last day in the field. Gordon, C.
Last day of all. Stanley, F. G.
Last day of my life. Elston, A. V.
Last days of M.G.B. 1087. Monsarrat, N.
Last days of Shandakor. Brackett, L.
Last draw. Haycox, E.
Last enemy. Piper, H. B.
Last expedition of Baron Feuhbel-Feuhtze-
  nau. Sobol, A. M.
Last hope. Reisin, A.
Last husband. Humphrey, W.
Last king. Blackburn, E. R.
Last kopek. Frug, S. S.
Last leaf. Porter, W. S.
Last-Light Channel. Lindquist, W.
Last lobo. Annixter, P. pseud.
Last Martian. Brown, F.
Last monster. Anderson, P.
The **last** night. Barrie, Sir J. M. bart.
Last night of the world. Bradbury, R.
Last of Chéri. Colette, S. G.
Last of the belles. Fitzgerald, F. S. K.
Last of the grizzly bears. West, R. B.
Last of the troubadours. Porter, W. S.
Last out. O'Rourke, F.
Last pitch. O'Rourke, F.
Last race. Sylvester, H

Last Rebel yell. Tolbert, F. X.
Last refuge of a scoundrel. Howard, W.
Last Saturday. Jacobson, L. E.
Last séance. Christie, A. M.
Last shot. O'Rourke, F.
LAST SUPPER. See Lord's supper
Last supper. Gibran, K.
The **last** supper. Kagawa, T.
Last tanto. Sylvester, R.
Last terrestrials. Stapledon, W. O.
Last time around. O'Rourke, F.
Last time up. O'Rourke, F.
Last visit. Aiken, C. P.
Last voyage of the Unsinkable Sal. Taylor,
  S. W.
Last weapon. Sheckley, R.
Last woman. Gardner, T. S.
Last year. Mulhoffer, D. B.
The **latchkey.** Schweitzer, G.
Late afternoon of a faun. Brophy, B.
Late Mr Elvesham. Wells, H. G.
Late night final. Russell, E. F.
Later. Foster, M.
Later than you think. Leiber, F.
Latest sensation (II) Clemens, S. L.
Latham, Philip, pseud. See Richardson,
  Robert Shirley
LA TRÉMOILLE, LOUIS II, DUC DE,
  1460-1525
  Lernet-Holenia, A. M. Mona Lisa
Latter end. Loveridge, G.
Laugh in the desert. Prado, P.
Laugh in the face of danger. Johnson, D. M.
Laugh it off. Armstrong, C.
Laughing butcher. Brown, F.
Laughing man. Salinger, J. D.
Launcelot, Sir
  Malory, Sir T. Marvellous adventure of
  the sword
Laura. Munro, H. H.
Laurence, Bethel
  The call
    Best American short stories, 1952
Laurence, Margaret, 1926-
  Uncertain flowering
    Story (Periodical) Story; no. 4
Lauriston Gardens mystery. Doyle, Sir
  A. C.
Lavender, David Sievert, 1910-
  High victory
    Boys' life (Periodical) Boys' life Ad-
    venture stories
Lavin, Mary, 1912-
  Brother Boniface
    Gable, M. Sister, ed. Many-colored
    fleece
  Daggle-Tail
    Cavanna, B. ed. Pick of the litter
LAW AND LAWYERS
  Andrews, M. R. S. Counsel assigned
  Auchincloss, L. Great world and Timo-
  thy Colt
  Auchincloss, L. Legends of Henry
  Everett

LAW AND LAWYERS—*Continued*
Auchincloss, L. Maud
Blaustein, A. P. ed. Fiction goes to court; 17 stories
Chekhov, A. P. His first appearance
Chekhov, A. P. Perpetuum mobile
Chekhov, A. P. Saintly simplicity
Chekhov, A. P. Village Elder
Chekhov, A. P. Visit to friends
Chekhov, A. P. Worse and worse
Collier, J. Great possibilities
Harte, B. Colonel Starbottle for the plaintiff
Klass, P. Child's play
McNeil, S. Girl who wasn't wanted
Melville, H. Bartlcby the scrivener
O'Donovan, M. Counsel for Œdipus
O'Donovan, M. Lady of the sagas
Pirandello, L. Reserved coffin
Porter, W. S. Emancipation of Billy
Porter, W. S. Hypotheses of failure
Salinger, J. D. Pretty mouth and green my eyes
Silone, I. Mr Aristotle
Verga, G. Don Licciu Papa
Weidman, J. Man inside

Law and order. Lowry, R. J.

Law and order. Porter, W. S.

Law and the profits. Cohen, O. R.

LAW CLERKS. See Law and lawyers

Lawlor, Harold
Silver highway
Conklin, G. and Conklin, L. T. eds. Supernatural reader

LAWN TENNIS. See Tennis

Lawrence, David Herbert, 1885-1930
Blind man
Blodgett, H. W. ed. Story survey. 1953 ed.
Captain's doll
West, R. B. and Stallman, R. W. eds. Art of modern fiction
The fox
Neider, C. ed. Short novels of the masters
Horse dealer's daughter
Schorer, M. ed. The story
Lovely lady
Heilman, R. B. ed. Modern short stories
Mother and daughter
Felheim, M.; Newman, F. B. and Steinhoff, W. R. eds. Modern short stories
Prussian officer
Cerf, B. A. and Moriarty, H. C. eds. Anthology of famous British stories
Cory, D. W. pseud. comp. 21 variations on a theme
Davis, R. G. ed. Ten modern masters
Rocking-horse winner
Davis, R. G. ed. Ten modern masters
Gordon, C. and Tate, A. eds. House of fiction
Ludwig, J. B. and Poirier, W. R. eds. Stories, British and American
Waite, H. O. and Atkinson, B. P. eds. Literature for our time
Shades of spring
Davis, R. G. ed. Ten modern masters
Shadow in the rose garden
Barrows, H. ed. 15 stories

Things
Ludwig, J. B. and Poirier, W. R. eds. Stories, British and American
Two blue birds
Neider, C. ed. Great short stories from the world's literature

Lawrence, Thomas Edward, 1888-1935
Blowing up a train
Moskowitz, S. ed. Great railroad stories of the world

Lawson, Edward
Ebony elephant
Ford, N. A. and Faggett, H. L. eds. Best short stories by Afro-American writers (1925-1950)

LAWSUITS. See Law and lawyers

LAWYERS. See Law and lawyers

Laxness, Halldor Kiljan, 1902-
Icelandic pioneer
Burnett, W. ed. World's best

Lay it down, Ziggy! Siegel, L.

Laziest man in Texas. Rogow, L.

LAZINESS
Fitzgerald, F. S. K. Jelly-bean

Leacock, Stephen, 1869-1944
Speculations of Jefferson Thorpe
Pacey, D. ed. Book of Canadian stories

Lead her like a pigeon. West, J.

Leader of the people. Steinbeck, J.

Leadington incident. Priestley, J. B.

Leaf thief. Saroyan, W.

Leander Frailey. Schaefer, J. W.

Leap for two lives. Whittemore, C. W.

Leap year. Grimson, M. S.

Learning's little tribute. Wilson, A.

Lebediger, Der. See Gutman, Chaim

Le Berthon, Ted
I took thee, Constance
Gable, M. Sister, ed. Many-colored fleece

Leblanc, Maurice, 1864-1941
Invisible prisoner
Stauffer, R. M.; Cunningham, W. H. and Sullivan, C. J. eds. Adventures in modern literature

The **lectern.** Munby, A. N. L.

LECTURERS. See Lectures and lecturing

LECTURES AND LECTURING
Pratt, F. and De Camp, L. S. When the night wind howls
Van Doren, M. Mrs Lancey

LECTURING. See Lectures and lecturing

Ledge on Bald Face. Roberts, Sir C. G. D.

Lee, Melicent (Humason) 1889-1943
Secret staircase
Story parade (Periodical) Adventure stories

Lee, Umphrey
Egg farm
Stanford short stories, 1952

Lee, Vernon, pseud. See Paget, Violet

Le Fanu, Joseph Sheridan, 1814-1873
Churchyard yew
Derleth, A. W. ed. Night's yawning peal
Room in the Dragon Volant
Connolly, C. ed. Great English short novels

Left-hand stuff. Gartner, J.
Left out on Lone Star Mountain. Harte, B.
The leg. Faulkner, W.
Leg man. Stewart, O.
LEGACIES. See Inheritance and succession
Legacy of Canyon John. Leighton, M. C.
Legal aid. O'Donovan, M.
LEGATIONS. See Diplomatic life
Legend of Madame Krasinska. Paget, V.
Legend of Rabbi Akiba. Cohn, E.
Legend of St Julian the Hospitaller. Flaubert, G.
Legend of Sleepy Hollow. Irving, W.
Legend of the first Christmas tree. Goudge, E.
Legend that walks like a man. Schulberg, B. W.
LEGENDS, JEWISH. See Legends and folk tales—Hebrew
LEGENDS AND FOLK TALES
Munro, H. H. Wolves of Cernogratz
Paget, V. Prince Alberic and the Snake Lady
Van Doren, M. The birds

China
Mrs White
T'uan Ch'engshih. Cinderella

France
Krige, U. Invisible shepherd

Germany
Hoffmann, E. T. A. History of Krakatuk
Keller, G. Little legend of the dance

Hebrew
Cohn, E. It looks like justice
Cohn, E. Legend of Rabbi Akiba
Cohn, E. Waters of Shiloah

Ireland
Corkery, D. Ploughing of the leaca

Japan
Akutagawa, R. The martyr

Negro
Harris, J. C. Wonderful Tar-Baby story

Norway
Bjørnson, B. How the mountain was clad

Portuguese
Krige, U. La Miseria

Russia
Tolstoĭ, L. N. Graf. Three hermits

South America
Finger, C. J. Na-Ha the fighter

Legends of Henry Everett. Auchincloss, L.
LEGISLATION
Kipling, R. Tods' amendment
Le Grand, pseud. See Henderson, Le Grand
Legs go first. Newhouse, E.
Lehmann, Rosamond, 1903-
Red-haired Miss Daintreys
New writing (Periodical) Best stories

Lehr, Wilson
No competition
Cory, D. W. pseud. comp. 21 variations on a theme
Leiber, Fritz, 1910-
Appointment in tomorrow
Best science fiction stories: 1952
Bad day for sales
Best science-fiction stories: 1954
Galaxy science fiction magazine. Second Galaxy reader of science fiction
Big holiday
Best science-fiction stories: 1954
Business of killing
Conklin, G. ed. Science-fiction adventures in dimension
Coming attraction
Best science fiction stories: 1951
Galaxy science fiction magazine. Galaxy reader of science fiction
Destiny times three
Greenberg, M. comp. Five science fiction novels
Enchanted forest
Derleth, A. W. ed. Worlds of tomorrow
Foxholes of Mars
Merril, J. ed. Beyond human ken
Later than you think
Derleth, A. W. ed. Far boundaries
Moon is green
Best science-fiction stories: 1953
Night he cried
Star science fiction stories [no. 1]
Pail of air
Galaxy science fiction magazine. Second Galaxy reader of science fiction
Norton, A. M. ed. Space pioneers
Poor superman
Heinlein, R. A. ed. Tomorrow, the stars
Sanity
Conklin, G. ed. Big book of science fiction
Ship sails at midnight
Derleth, A. W. ed. The outer reaches
Taboo
Greenberg, M. ed. Journey to infinity
Wanted—an enemy
Derleth, A. W. ed. Beyond time & space
LEIF ERICSSON, fl. 1000
Grimson, M. S. Leif goes west
Leif goes west. Grimson, M. S.
Leigh, Johanna, pseud. See Sayers, Dorothy Leigh
Leighton, Margaret (Carver) 1896-
Legacy of Canyon John
American girl (Periodical) Favorite stories
Spruce Point mystery
Furman, A. L. ed. Everygirls mystery stories
Leimert, John
John Thomas's cube
Conklin, G. ed. Omnibus of science fiction
Leiningen versus the ants. Stephenson, C.
Leinster, Murray, pseud. See Jenkins, William Fitzgerald
Leiper, Gudger Bart, 1921-
The magnolias
Prize stories of 1950

Lemelin, Roger, 1919-
Stations of the Cross
Weaver, R. and James, H. eds. Canadian short stories
Lemesurier inheritance. Christie, A. M.
Lena. Williams, W. C.
Lenore and the boys. Wright, H.
LEONARDO DA VINCI, 1452-1519
Lernet-Holenia, A. M. Mona Lisa
'Leopard' George. Lessing, D. M.
LEOPARDS
Balzac, H. de. Passion in the desert
Fletcher, I. White leopard
Leopard's spots. Runyon, D.
LEPERS. See Leprosy
LEPRECHAUNS
Pratt, F. and De Camp, L. S. All that glitters
The **Leprechauns.** Ready, W. B.
LEPROSY
Groseclose, E. E. The healing of the lepers
Kipling, R. Mark of the beast
White, H. C. Francis cures the leper
Lerner, Marvin, 1920?-
The brothers
Oberfirst, R. ed. 1954 anthology of best original short-stories
Lernet-Holenia, Alexander Maria, 1897-
Mona Lisa
Pick, R. ed. German stories and tales
Leshinsky, Tania
The landing
Story (Periodical) Story; no. 3
Leskov, Nikolaĭ Semenovich, 1831-1895
The Amazon
Rahv, P. ed. Great Russian short novels
Lesser, Milton A. 1928-
Black Eyes and the daily grind
Sloane, W. M. ed. Stories for tomorrow
Pen pal
Conklin, G. ed. Invaders of earth
Lessing, Bruno, pseud. See Block, Rudolph Edgar
Lessing, Doris May, 1919-
De Wets come to Kloof Grange
Lessing, D. M. This was the Old Chief's country
'Leopard' George
Lessing, D. M. This was the Old Chief's country
Little Tembi
Lessing, D. M. This was the Old Chief's country
No witchcraft for sale
Lessing, D. M. This was the Old Chief's country
The nuisance
Lessing, D. M. This was the Old Chief's country
Old Chief Mshlanga
Lessing, D. M. This was the Old Chief's country
Old John's place
Lessing, D. M. This was the Old Chief's country
Second hut
Lessing, D. M. This was the Old Chief's country
Sunrise on the veld
Lessing, D. M. This was the Old Chief's country
Winter in July
Lessing, D. M. This was the Old Chief's country
Lesson for Flying Goat. Verran, R.
Le Sueur, Meridel
Persephone
Swallow, A. ed. Anchor in the sea
The **let-down.** Dodson, D. B.
Let 'em eat cook. De Vries, P.
Let it rest. Patton, F. G.
Let me feel your pulse. Porter, W. S.
Let me go. Strong, L. A. G.
Let nothing you dismay. Sloane, W. M.
Let nothing you dismay. Wright, F. F.
Let the church roll on. Ford, N. A.
Let the wind blow. Vetter, M. M.
"Let there be light." Heinlein, R. A.
Let yourself go. Farwell, M. B.
Letitia, emeritus. Calisher, H.
The **letter.** Maugham, W. S.
The **letter.** Toland, S.
LETTER CARRIERS. See Postal service
Letter from the Bronx. Kober, A.
Letter in the cedarchest. Goyen, W.
Letter to a hostage. Saint Exupéry, A. de
Letter to a phoenix. Brown, F.
Letter to Ellen. Davis, C.
A **letter** to Klaus Brock. Bojer, J.
Letter to Mable. Streeter, E.
Letter to the Dean. Taber, G. B.
Letter to the editor. Hershman, M.
LETTER WRITERS
Silone, I. Mr Aristotle
LETTERS (STORIES IN LETTER FORM)
Aiken, C. P. I love you very dearly
Aldrich, T. B. Marjorie Daw
Bunner, H. C. Love-letters of Smith
Campbell, W. E. M. Personal letter
Chekhov, A. P. Vanka
Connolly, M. Natural causes
Elliott, G. P. The NRACP
Forester, C. S. Letters in evidence
James, H. Bundle of letters
Jenkins, W. F. The power
Kober, A. Letter from the Bronx
Lardner, R. W. Some like them cold
Milne, A. A. Rise and fall of Mortimer Scrivens
Munro, H. H. "Down pens"
Munro, H. H. Shock tactics
Paget, V. Dionea
Pasternak, B. L. Letters from Tula
Piper, H. B. Operation RSVP
Rabinowitz, S. Menachem-Mendel, fortune hunter
Upson, W. H. I'm in a hurry

LETTERS (STORIES IN LETTER FORM)—*Continued*
Waugh, E. Cruise
Whitehill, J. Day of the last rock fight
Winslow, T. S. Dear Sister Sadie
Wright, F. F. Declaration of independence
LETTERS, STORIES ABOUT
Collins, W. Stolen letter
McCarty, M. B. Your long black hair
Maugham, W. S. The letter
Poe, E. A. Purloined letter
Schnitzler, A. Death of a bachelor
Zangwill, I. The luftmensch
The **letters**. Swados, H.
Letters from Cairo. Miller, J. R.
Letters from Tula. Pasternak, B. L.
Letters in evidence. Forester, C. S.
Levelling with Elisha. Van Loan, C. E.
Lever, Charles James, 1806-1872
Con Cregan's legacy
Cerf, B. A. and Moriarty, H. C. eds. Anthology of famous British stories
Levin, Meyer, 1905-
After all I did for Israel
Ribalow, H. U. ed. These your children
Maurie finds his medium
Ribalow, H. U. ed. This land, these people
Levine, Samuel, 1907-
Gift for a birthday
American vanguard, 1952
Levine, Ted M.
Elaine's hope
Hathaway, B. and Sessions, J. A. eds. Writers for tomorrow. 2d ser.
LEVITATION. See Gravity
Levy, Amy, 1861-1889
Cohen of Trinity
Leftwich, J. ed. Yisröel. 1952 ed.
Lewis, Alun, 1915-1944
The raid
Barrows, H. ed. 15 stories
Ward 'O' 3 (b)
New writing (Periodical) Best stories
Lewis, Ethel G.
Portrait
Best American short stories, 1951
Lewis, Jack
Who's cribbing?
Startling stories (Periodical) Best from Startling stories
Lewis, Janet, 1899-
Wife of Martin Guerre
Swallow, A. ed. Anchor in the sea
Lewis, Morgan
Well of anger
Meredith, S. ed. Bar 1 roundup of best western stories
Lewis, Robert
Roman holiday
Herzberg, M. J. comp. Treasure chest of sport stories
Lewis, Sinclair, 1885-1951
An assemblage of husbands and wives
Burnett, W. ed. World's best
Land
Lamb, L. ed. Family book of best loved short stories

Stauffer, R. M.; Cunningham, W. H. and Sullivan, C. J. eds. Adventures in modern literature
Post-mortem murder
Queen, E. pseud. ed. Literature of crime
Willow walk
Grayson, C. ed. Fourth round
Young man Axelbrod
Thinker's digest (Periodical) Spoiled priest, and other stories
Lewis, Wyndham, 1886-
Bishop's fool
Lewis, W. Rotting Hill
Mr Patricks' toy shop
Lewis, W. Rotting Hill
My disciple
Lewis, W. Rotting Hill
My fellow traveller to Oxford
Lewis, W. Rotting Hill
Parents and horses
Lewis, W. Rotting Hill
Room without a telephone
Lewis, W. Rotting Hill
The rot
Lewis, W. Rotting Hill
Talking shop
Lewis, W. Rotting Hill
Time the tiger
Lewis, W. Rotting Hill
Lewisohn, Ludwig, 1882-1955
Holy Land
Leftwich, J. ed. Yisröel. 1952 ed.
Writ of divorcement
Ribalow, H. U. ed. This land, these people
LEXINGTON, KENTUCKY. See Kentucky—Lexington
Li, Guan-Yuen
My boy, my boy
Wolfe, D. M. ed. Which grain will grow
Li Fu-Yen, fl. 9th century
Lodging for the night
Lin, Y. ed. Famous Chinese short stories
Man who became a fish
Lin, Y. ed. Famous Chinese short stories
Matrimony Inn
Lin, Y. ed. Famous Chinese short stories
The tiger
Lin, Y. ed. Famous Chinese short stories
Li Kung-Tso, 770?-850?
Drunkard's dream
Lin, Y. ed. Famous Chinese short stories
Liang, Hsieh. See Hsieh, Liang
Liar! Asimov, I.
The **liar**. James, H.
LIARS
James, H. The liar
Munro, H. H. Defensive diamond
Lib. Farrell, J. T.
Liber amoris. Hazlitt, W.
LIBERTY
Benét, S. V. Freedom's a hard-bought thing

LIBERTY—*Continued*
  Quiroga, H. The fatherland
  Russell, E. F. And then there were none
  Woods, W. Free man
Liberty. Verga, G.
LIBERTY, STATUE OF. See Statue of
    Liberty, New York
Libin, Solomon, 1872-1955
  Schlemihlov's works
    Ausubel, N. ed. Treasury of Jewish
    humor
Libin, Z. See Libin, Solomon
LIBRARIANS
  Betts, D. Miss Parker possessed
  Munro, H. H. Story of St Vespaluus
  Pratt, F. and De Camp, L. S. No forward-
    ing address
  Walker, A. Day of the cipher
Lickpenny lover. Porter, W. S.
Lidin, Vladimir, pseud. See Gomberg, Vla-
    dimïr Germanovich
LIE DETECTORS AND DETECTION
  Brown, F. Crisis, 1999
The **Lieabout.** Allingham, M.
Lieber, Winifred M. 1919-
  Strange bed
    Wolfe, D. M. ed. Which grain will grow
Lieberman, Elias, 1883-
  Thing of beauty
    Thinker's digest (Periodical) Spoiled
    priest, and other stories
Lieberman, Rosalie
  Afternoon in the life of Father Burrell
    Lieberman, R. Heaven is so high
  Freighted hour
    Lieberman, R. Heaven is so high
  Indiscretions of Father Lawrence
    Lieberman, R. Heaven is so high
  Last day
    Lieberman, R. Heaven is so high
  Little business with Saint Bernard
    Lieberman, R. Heaven is so high
  Little loves of Sister Helen
    Lieberman, R. Heaven is so high
  Matter of time
    Lieberman, R. Heaven is so high
  Nuns' holiday
    Lieberman, R. Heaven is so high
  Reverend Mother and the foolish decision
    Lieberman, R. Heaven is so high
  Sister Innocent and the useful miracle
    Lieberman, R. Heaven is so high
  Strange event at St Brendan's
    Lieberman, R. Heaven is so high
  To the ringing of bells
    Lieberman, R. Heaven is so high
  Trouble at St Brendan's
    Lieberman, R. Heaven is so high
Lien Pu
  Madame D.
    Lin, Y. ed. Famous Chinese short sto-
    ries
Lies my father told me. Allen, T.
Lieutenant's laundry. Alson, L.
Life. O'Flaherty, L.
Life along the Passaic River. Williams,
    W. C.

Life among the Indians. Smith, J.
Life among the winesaps. De Vries, P.
The **life** and death of a crisis. Walpole,
    Sir H.
Life and death of a hero. Cancela, A.
Life and death of a village. O'Hanlon, D. M.
Life and death of George Wilson who was
    an extraordinary fine specimen. Pater-
    son, N.
Life began today. Grebanier, B. D. N.
Life begins at forty. Winston, H.
LIFE, CHRISTIAN. See Christian life
LIFE, FUTURE. See Future life
Life, going by. Brookhouser, F.
LIFE GUARDS. See Lifesaving
Life in her hands. Kantor, M.
Life isn't a short story. Aiken, C. P.
Life-line. Heinlein, R. A.
Life of Ma Parker. Mansfield, K.
Life of Riley. Sherman, R.
Life of the sleeping beauty. Cassill, R. V.
LIFE-SAVING. See Lifesaving
Life with mother. Kober, A.
Life-work of Professor Muntz. Jenkins,
    W. F.
Life you save may be your own. O'Con-
    nor, F.
Life's old sweet dream. Moffett, G.
LIFESAVING
  McKenney, R. Guinea pig
Lift that went down into hell. Lagerkvist,
    P. F.
Lifted veil. Eliot, G. pseud.
Ligeia. Poe, E. A.
LIGHT
  Heinlein, R. A. "Let there be light"
Light. O'Flaherty, L.
Light across the hill. Newhouse, E.
Light in France. Runyon, D.
Light in the darkness. Doyle, Sir A. C.
Light of day. Taylor, E.
Light of the moon. Komroff, M.
Light of the world. Hemingway, E.
Light tackle. Wylie, P.
Lighted candles. Shaw, H. O.
The **lighthouse.** Bates, H. E.
LIGHTNING CONDUCTORS
  Melville, H. Lightning-rod man
Lightning-rod man. Melville, H.
LIGHTNING RODS. See Lightning con-
    ductors
Lights. Fisher, P. M.
Like a bird, like a fish. Hickey, H. B.
Like gods they came. Cox, I.
Like son. Summers, J. L.
Like what? Van Doren, M.
Li'l Reynard. McCauley, M. C.
Lilac tree. Corkery, D.
Lilacs out of the dead land. O'Conaill, D.
Lilies of life. Jameson, M.
Lily Daw and the three ladies. **Welty, E.**

Limbo. Hallinan, N.
LIMBS, ARTIFICIAL. See Artificial limbs
LIME-KILNS
  Hawthorne, N. Ethan Brand
Limitations of Pambé Serang. Kipling, R.
Limiting factor. Simak, C. D.
LINCOLN, ABRAHAM, PRESIDENT U.S. 1809-1865
  Andrews, M. R. S. Counsel assigned
  Wellman, M. W. Tall Bram of Little Pigeon
Lincoln, Victoria Endicott, 1904-
  Death in the house
    Lincoln, V. E. Wild honey
  Glass wall
    Best American short stories, 1950
  In the garden
    Lincoln, V. E. Wild honey
  Lost in our wake, our archipelago
    Lincoln, V. E. Wild honey
  Lover's meeting
    Lincoln, V. E. Wild honey
  Make me real
    Lincoln, V. E. Wild honey
  Morning, a week before the crime
    Lincoln, V. E. Wild honey
  Morning wishes
    Lincoln, V. E. Wild honey
  No evidence
    Lincoln, V. E. Wild honey
  Now and again now
    Lincoln, V. E. Wild honey
  To live is to return
    Lincoln, V. E. Wild honey
  The understanding
    Lincoln, V. E. Wild honey
Linda who daydreamed. Strain, F. B.
Lindquist, Willis
  Last-Light Channel
    Strang, R. M. and Roberts, R. M. eds
      Teen-age tales v 1
  Striving after the wind
    Lantz, J. E. ed. Stories of Christian living
Line to tomorrow. Kuttner, H.
LINOTYPE. See Printers and printing
Lion and the prey. Benson, T.
LION TAMERS. See Animals—Training
LIONS
  Bottome, P. Caesar's wife's ear
  Hemingway, E. Fable of the good lion
  Hemingway, E. Short happy life of Francis Macomber
Lions, harts, leaping does. Powers, J. F.
Lion's mouth. Marlowe, S.
Lion's skin. Maugham, W. S.
Lipman, Clayre, and Lipman, Michel
  Dilemma of Grampa Dubois
    Mystery Writers of America, inc. Crooks' tour
  My last book
    Mystery Writers of America, inc. 20 great tales of murder
  Walking corpse
    Best detective stories of the year—1951
Lipman, Michel. See Lipman, C. jt. auth.
Lippincott, Joseph Wharton, 1887-
  Wilderness champion
    Harper, W. comp. Dog show

Lipsky, Eleazar, 1911-
  Quality of mercy
    Queen, E. pseud, ed. The Queen's awards: 8th ser.
  Stabbing in the streets
    Best detective stories of the year—1953
Liqueur glass. Bottome, P.
LIQUEURS. See Wine and wine making
Liquid life. Hoar, R. S.
LIQUOR TRAFFIC
  Grau, S. A. White girl, fine girl
LIQUORS
  Pratt, F. and De Camp, L. S. Gin comes in bottles
LISBON. See Portugal—Lisbon
Lispet, Lispett and Vaine. De La Mare, W. J.
Listen. Dickson, G. R.
Listen to me, boy. Lanham, E. M.
Listening child. Seabright, I.
LITERARY CHARACTERS
  Forster, E. M. Celestial omnibus
Literary corkscrew. Keller, D. H.
LITERARY CRITICS
  Fletcher, V. Coda to a writers' conference
  Gutman, C. No enemy of his
  James, H. Death of the lion
LITERARY FORGERIES AND MYSTI-FICATIONS
  Dahl, R. Great automatic grammatisator
  Munro, H. H. For the duration of the war
LITERARY LIFE
  Maugham, W. S. Creative impulse
Literary love. Farrell, J. T.
Litten, Frederick Nelson, 1885-1951
  Blackout over Cleveland
    American boy (Periodical) American boy Adventure stories
  Tell it to the Marines
    American boy (Periodical) American boy Adventure stories
  Winner's money
    American boy (Periodical) American boy anthology
Little, George Watson
  Beau: the dog who served two masters
    Little, G. W. True stories of heroic dogs
  Bum: wearer of the Silver Shield
    Little, G. W. True stories of heroic dogs
  Cappy: the pride of Engine Company 65
    Little, G. W. True stories of heroic dogs
  Cooky: the heroic dog who wasn't brave
    Little, G. W. True stories of heroic dogs
  Dandy: the funny-looking dog
    Little, G. W. True stories of heroic dogs
  Duke: the gun-shy watchdog
    Little, G. W. True stories of heroic dogs
  Jeep: the dog who came home
    Little, G. W. True stories of heroic dogs
  Jerry: the dog who refused to die
    Little, G. W. True stories of heroic dogs
  Jim: a valiant Great Dane
    Little, G. W. True stories of heroic dogs
  Mutt: the mongrel who knew no fear
    Little, G. W. True stories of heroic dogs
  Pal: the dog who trained himself
    Little, G. W. True stories of heroic dogs
  Queenie: the gallant-hearted collie
    Little, G. W. True stories of heroic dogs

Little, George W.—*Continued*
Rusty: the brave dog who lost his bark
Little, G. W. True stories of heroic dogs
Smoky: who twice saved his master's life
Little, G. W. True stories of heroic dogs
Tom: the friend of all boys
Little, G. W. True stories of heroic dogs
Trixie: the dog who did her duty
Little, G. W. True stories of heroic dogs
Little and unknown. Singmaster, E.
Little Anton. Bretnor, R.
Little apple hard to peel. Brown, F.
Little baseball world. Lowry, R. J. C.
Little Ben. Knox, J.
Little Ben's railroad. Knox, J.
LITTLE BIG HORN, BATTLE OF THE, 1876
Fox, N. A. Only the dead ride proudly
Little black boys. Laidlaw, C.
Little blond fellow. Farrell, J. T.
Little boy blues. Brookhouser, F.
Little Bubo. Willingham, C.
Little business with Saint Bernard. Lieberman, R.
Little calf. Abramowitz, S. J.
Little cask. Maupassant, G. de
Little cloud. Joyce, J.
Little companion. Wilson, A.
Little creeps. Miller, W. M.
Little dreams of Mr Morgan. Willingham, C.
Little Eddie goes to town. Haywood, C.
Little ewe lamb. Myers, R. H.
Little farm. Bates, H. E.
Little fears. Sansom, W.
Little Flute. Shen, T.
Little general. Brenner, L.
Little genius. Rydberg, E.
"Little gentleman." Tarkington, B.
Little ghost. Ringwood, G. P.
Little girls. Hasley, L.
Little Goat. Taber, G. B.
Little guy. Crump, I.
Little Hanukkah lamp. Peretz, I. L.
Little hero. Dostoevskiĭ, F. M.
Little Herr Friedemann. Mann, T.
Little house at Croix-Rousse. Simenon, G.
A **little** journey. Bradbury, R.
Little legend of the dance. Keller, G.
Little local color. Porter, W. S.
Little lost robot. Asimov, I.
Little loves of Sister Helen. Lieberman, R.
Little memento. Collier, J.
Little Mohammed and Egypt's king. Drezmal, G. I.
Little mother. O'Donovan, M.
Little mother up the Mörderberg. Wells, H. G.
Little old spy. Hughes, L.
Little Orvie's new dog Ralph. Tarkington, B.
Little Pharaoh. Coolidge, O. E.

Little photographer. Du Maurier, D.
Little Pinks. Runyon, D.
Little place. Van Doren, M.
Little red jungle. Siegel, B.
Little room. Sansom, W.
Little shoemakers. Singer, I. B.
Little sisters are such pests. Schweitzer, G.
"Little speck in garnered fruit." Porter, W. S.
Little talk about mobs. Porter, W. S.
Little Tembi. Lessing, D. M.
Little terror. Jenkins, W. F.
Little things like that. Vickers, R.
Little white cat. Baker, D. D.
Little white girl. Haardt, S. P.
Little white lye. Brown, F.
Littledale, Harold Alymer, 1927-
Five parts of summer
American vanguard, 1952
Live bait. Hershman, M.
Livesay, Dorothy, 1909-
Glass house
Best American short stories, 1951
Living machine. Keller, D. H.
Living torpedo. Yates, T.
Livvie. Welty, E.
Livvie is back. Welty, E.
Llewellyn, Richard
Faith to be healed
Brentano, F. ed. The word lives on
Lloyd, Bertha B.
Forgotten greeting cards
Oberfirst, R. ed. 1952 anthology of best original short-shorts
Lo! Faulkner, W.
The **loan.** Reisin, A.
LOANS
Porter, W. S. Call loan
Reisen, A. The loan
LOBBYING
Porter, W. S. Hand that riles the world
Lobo, the king of Currumpaw. Seton, E. T.
LOBOS. See Wolves
Lock the doors, lock the windows. Cuevas, E.
Locke, Robert Donald
Dark nuptial
Startling stories (Periodical) Best from Startling stories
Demotion
Wollheim, D. A. ed. Prize science fiction
Locke, William John, 1863-1930
Adventure of the kind Mr Smith
Cerf, B. A. and Moriarty, H. C. eds. Anthology of famous British stories
Wise men of Trehenna
Thinker's digest (Periodical) Spoiled priest, and other stories
Locked out. Fyfe, H. B.
Locked room. Carr, J. D.
LOCKOUTS. See Strikes and lockouts
Locksmith of Philadelphia. Howe, J.
LOCKSMITHS
Howe, J. Locksmith of Philadelphia

LOCUSTS
Gordimer, N. Soft voice of the serpent

The lodger. Chekhov, A. P.

Lodging for the night. Li Fu-yen

Lodging for the night. Stevenson, R. L.

LODGING HOUSES. See Boarding houses

LOG CABINS
Beck, W. Felix

Log of the "Evening Star." Noyes, A.

Log the man dead. Burdick, E. L.

LOGGERS. See Lumber industry

LOGGING. See Lumber industry

Logic named Joe. Jenkins, W. F.

Logic of empire. Heinlein, R. A.

Lomax pitching. Hillger, E. H.

London, Jack, 1876-1916
All-gold cañon
Schramm, W. L. ed. Great short stories
At the rainbow's end
London, J. Sun-Dog Trail and other
stories
Brown Wolf
London, J. Sun-Dog Trail and other
stories
For love of a man
Fenner, P. R. comp. Dogs, dogs, dogs
Love of life
London, J. Sun-Dog Trail and other
stories
Make westing
London, J. Sun-Dog Trail and other
stories
The Mexican
Ribalow, H. U. ed. World's greatest
boxing stories
Moon-face
London, J. Sun-Dog Trail and other
stories
Piece of steak
Christ, H. I. and Shostak, J. eds. Short
stories
Ribalow, H. U. ed. World's greatest
boxing stories
Raid on the oyster pirates
London, J. Sun-Dog Trail and other
stories
Samuel
Fremantle, A. J. ed. Mothers
Scarlet plague
Conklin, G. ed. Omnibus of science
fiction
Shadow of the flash
London, J. Sun-Dog Trail and other
stories
Son of the sun
London, J. Sun-Dog Trail and other
stories
Strength of the strong
London, J. Sun-Dog Trail and other
stories
Sun-Dog Trail
London, J. Sun-Dog Trail and other
stories
That spot
Bloch, M. ed. Favorite dog stories

To build a fire
Andrews, R. C. ed. My favorite stories
of the great outdoors
Burrell, J. A. and Cerf, B. A. eds. An-
thology of famous American stories
London, J. Sun-Dog Trail and other
stories
Too much gold
London, J. Sun-Dog Trail and other
stories

LONDON. See England—London
LONDON
Police
See Police—London

London night's entertainment. Sharp, M.

Lone cowboy. James, W.

LONELINESS
Capote, T. Shut a final door
Horwitz, J. The roof
Prado, P. Laugh in the desert

Lonely day. Caldwell, E.

Lonely heart. Runyon, D.

Lonely lives. O'Faoláin, S.

Lonely poet. Gibran, K.

Lonely reef. Swenson, E. P.

Lonely rock. O'Donovan, M.

Lonesome place. Derleth, A. W.

Lonesome ride. Haycox, E.

Lonesome road. Porter, W. S.

Long, Amelia Reynolds, 1904-
Reverse phylogeny
Conklin, G. ed. Science-fiction adven-
tures in dimension

Long, E. Waldo
Green match
Boys' life (Periodical) Boys' life Ad-
venture stories

Long, Frank Belknap, 1903-
And someday to Mars
Moskowitz, S. comp. Editor's choice
in science fiction
Cones
Conklin, G. ed. Possible worlds of
science fiction
The critters
Derleth, A. W. ed. The outer reaches
Great cold
Derleth, A. W. ed. Worlds of tomorrow
Humpty Dumpty had a great fall
Derleth, A. W. ed. Beyond time &
space
Invasion
Derleth, A. W. ed. Far boundaries
The Mercurian
Wollheim, D. A. comp. Flight into space
Red Storm on Jupiter
Wollheim, D. A. comp. Flight into space
To follow knowledge
Conklin, G. ed. Science-fiction adven-
tures in dimension
Two face
Best science fiction stories: 1951

Long arm. Claudy, C. H.

Long dawn. Loomis, N.

Long hot day. Zelver, P. F.

Long in populous city pent. Schorer, M.

Long journey. Sitwell, Sir O. bart.

Long pike. Conner, R.
Long rain. Bradbury, R.
Long road. Harvey, W. F.
Long road to Ummera. O'Donovan, M.
Long shadow. Mowery, W. B.
Long-shot Porter. Person, W. T.
Long time ago. Benson, T.
Long view. Pratt, F.
Long watch. Heinlein, R. A.
Long way from home. Sneider, V. J.
Long way out. Fitzgerald, F. S. K.
Long winter. Drago, H. S.
Long year. Summers, J. L.
Longest day I live. Rath, I. E.
LONGEVITY
   Binder, E. Conquest of life
Longstreet, Stephen, 1907-
   No peace with the sea
      Grayson, C. ed. Fourth round
Look after the strange girl. Priestley, J. B.
Look at the boats. McLaverty, M.
Look for the kid with the guts. O'Rourke, F.
Look of eagles. Foote, J. T.
Looking 'em over. Farrell, J. T.
LOOKING GLASSES. See Mirrors
Lookout. Boyd, J. jr.
Loomis, Noel M. 1905-
   Long dawn
      Conklin, G. ed. Big book of science
      fiction
   Mustang trail to glory
      Western Writers of America. Bad men
      and good
   The twilighters
      Meredith, S. ed. Bar 3
Loon laughs Macfarlan, A. A.
Loophole. Clarke, A. C.
Loose tiger. Annixter, P. pseud.
Lord, James
   Boy who wrote 'no'
      Horizon (Periodical) Golden Horizon
THE LORD. See God
Lord, Jonathan
   The avenging
      Meredith, S. ed. Bar 2
Lord, Mindret
   Ransom note
      Strang, R. M. and Roberts, R. M. eds.
      Teen-age tales v 1
Lord Mountdrago. Maugham, W. S.
Lord Oakhurst's curse. Porter, W. S.
Lord Scamperdale's finest day. Surtees,
   R. S.
LORD'S SUPPER
   Gibran, K. Last supper
   Greene, G. Hint of an explanation
   Kagawa, T. The last supper
Loring, Selden M.
   The eel-trap
      Owen, F. ed. Teen-age victory parade
Loss of breath. Poe, E. A.
The lost. Boyle, K.
The lost. Cawley, C. C.

Lost blend. Porter, W. S.
Lost boy. Van Dyke, H.
Lost boy. Wolfe, T.
Lost cat. Ekbergh, I. D.
LOST CHILDREN. See Children, Lost
Lost decade. Fitzgerald, F. S. K.
LOST GENERATION. See Youth
Lost god. Russell, J.
Lost hearts. James, M. R.
Lost in our wake, our archipelago. Lincoln,
   V. E.
Lost in the barren lands. Mowat, F.
Lost legacy. Heinlein, R. A.
Lost memory. Phillips, P.
Lost on dress parade. Porter, W. S.
LOST PERSONS. See Disappearences
Lost Phoebe. Dreiser, T.
Lost room. O'Brien, F.-J.
Lost sanjak. Munro, H. H.
Lost school bus. Sandoz, M.
Lost soldier. Whitmore, S.
Lost trail. Macfarlan, A. A.
Lot. Moore, W.
Lott, Davis Newton, 1913-
   Skipper played it safe
      Argosy (Periodical) Book of adventure
      stories
LOTTERIES
   Chekhov, A. P. 75,000
   Jackson, S. The lottery
   McNulty, J. The jackpot
The lottery. Jackson, S.
Lotus and the bottle. Porter, W. S.
Lotus eater. Maugham, W. S.
Lotus eaters. Weinbaum, S. G.
Lotus for Jamie. Kneale, N.
Lou Louder. Runyon, D.
Loud sing cuckoo. Weston, C.
LOUIS XII, KING OF FRANCE, 1462-
   1515
      Lernet-Holenia, A. M. Mona Lisa
Louis. Munro, H. H.
Louise. Maugham, W. S.
Louise. Munro, H. H.
LOUISIANA

New Orleans
   Cable, G. W. Madame Delphine
   Colladay, M. M. Planetoid of doom
Love, Peggy Harding, 1920-
   Jersey heifer
      Prize stories of 1951
Love. Maupassant, G. de
Love affair. Whitmore, S.
Love affair in Paris. Farrell, J. T.
Love among the ruins. Waugh, E.
Love and betrayal. Andreev, L. N.
Love-bird. Sitwell, Sir O. bart.
Love comes to Miss Lucy. Quentin, P.
   pseud.
Love gift. Eggleston, M. W.
Love is a fallacy. Shulman, M.

Love-letters of Smith. Bunner, H. C.
Love lies bleeding. MacDonald, P.
Love me, love my car. Bretherton, V. R.
The love-nest. Pratt, F. and De Camp, L. S.
'Love-o'-women'. Kipling, R.
Love of life. London, J.
Love of two chemists. Shulman, M.
Love on toast. Willingham, C.
Love-philtre of Ikey Schoenstein. Porter,
    W. S.
LOVE POTIONS
    Collier, J. The chaser
Love scene. Trollope, A.
Love smelled of vanilla. Upshaw, H.
Love song in a honky-tonk. Hawkins, J.
    and Hawkins, W.
Love story. Monig, C.
Love that is lost. Brookhouser, F.
Love, Tomi. Connolly, M.
Lovecraft, Howard Phillips, 1890-1937
    Case of Charles Dexter Ward
        Derleth, A. W. ed. Night's yawning peal
    Color out of space
        Conklin, G. ed. Omnibus of science fic-
        tion
    From beyond
        Derleth, A. W. ed. Worlds of tomorrow
Loved dead. Eddy, C. M. jr.
Lovely lady. Lawrence, D. H.
Lover, Samuel, 1797-1868
    The gridiron
        Cerf, B. A. and Moriarty, H. C. eds.
        Anthology of famous British stories
The **lover.** Bowen, E.
Lover and his lass. Rodgers, M. A.
Lover, when you're near me. Matheson, R.
Loveridge, George, 1904-
    Latter end
        Best American short stories, 1954
Lover's meeting. Lincoln, V. E.
Lovers' meeting. Sitwell, Sir O. bart.
Lovers of gain. Boyle, K.
Love's awakening. Maupassant, G. de
Low road go down. Kidd, H. L.
Low tide. Sitwell, Sir O. bart.
Low water. Household, G.
LOWER EAST SIDE. See New York
    (City)—East Side
Lower Mississippi is thicker than water.
    Parker, J. R.
Lowndes, Marion (Smith)
    House of ocean born Mary
        Fenner, P. R. comp. Ghosts, ghosts,
        ghosts
Lowndes, Robert W.
    Highway
        Lesser, M. A. ed. Looking forward
    Pride in his holsters
        Meredith, S. ed. Bar 1 roundup of best
        western stories

Lowrey, P. H.
    Big Chlorinda, happy Chlorinda
        Stanford short stories, 1950
    Too young to have a gun
        Prize stories, 1954
Lowry, Robert James Collas, 1919-
    Be nice to Mr Campbell
        Lowry, R. J. C. Happy New Year,
        kamerades!
        Prize stories of 1950
    Casualty
        Lowry, R. J. C. Happy New Year,
        kamerades!
    Day he got fired
        Lowry, R. J. C. Happy New Year,
        kamerades!
    Defense in University City
        Lowry, R. J. C. Happy New Year,
        kamerades!
    For girlhood and for love
        Lowry, R. J. C. Happy New Year,
        kamerades!
    Happy New Year, kamerades!
        Lowry, R. J. C. Happy New Year,
        kamerades!
    Law and order
        Horizon (Periodical) Golden Horizon
    Little baseball world
        Lass, A. H. and Horowitz, A. eds. Sto-
        ries for youth
        Lowry, R. J. C. Happy New Year,
        kamerades!
    Phistairus
        Lowry, R. J. C. Happy New Year,
        kamerades!
    Skyblue lady
        Lowry, R. J. C. Happy New Year,
        kamerades!
    The victim
        Lowry, R. J. C. Happy New Year,
        kamerades!
LOYALTY
    Critchell, L. S. Loyalty check
Loyalty check. Critchell, L. S.
Loyalty up and loyalty down. Auchincloss, L.
Lu Hsün, pseud. See Chou, Shu-jen
Lucas, Edward Verrall, 1868-1938
    Anne's terrible good nature
        Fenner, P. R. cmp. Giggle box
LUCERNE. See Switzerland—Lucerne
Lucerne: The loaded tourist. Charteris, L.
The **Luceys.** O'Donovan, M.
Lucian
    True history
        Derleth, A. W. ed. Beyond time & space
Lucian of Samosata. See Lucian
LUCK. See Chance
Luck. Steele, W. D.
Luck charm. Coolidge, O. E.
Luck of Ignatz. Del Rey, L.
Luck of Riley. Frazee, S.
Luck of Roaring Camp. Harte, B.
Lucky burglar. Maupassant, G. de
Lucky 'leven. Whitney, P. A.
Lucky Murdock. Van Doren, M.
Lucky star. Allard, P.
Lucky stick. Coombs, C. I.

The **luftmensch.** Zangwill, I.

Lukardis. Wassermann, J.

Luke Baldwin's vow. Callaghan, M. E.

Lukert, Edward P.
For military merit
Best Army short stories, 1950

Lull, Roderick, 1907?-
Choice of the litter
Cavanna, B. ed. Pick of the litter
Dog that sounded like a fire siren
This week magazine. This week's short-
short stories
No room in her heart
Saturday evening post (Periodical)
Saturday evening post stories, 1950

The **lull.** Munro, H. H.

Lull at Cassino. Berto, G.

Lulungomeena. Dickson, G. R.

LUMBER INDUSTRY
Galsworthy, J. Timber

LUMBERING. See Lumber industry

Lumber-room. Munro, H. H.

Lump of sugar. Queen, E. pseud.

Lumpkin, Grace
The treasure
Southern review. Anthology of stories
from the Southern review

Lunar trap. Elam, R. M.

LUNATIC ASYLUMS. See Insane hospitals

Lunch. Bowen, E.

Lunch. Horwitz, J.

The **luncheon.** Maugham, W. S.

LUNCHEONS. See Dinners

LUNCHROOMS. See Restaurants, lunchrooms, etc.

Lure of perfume. Ekbergh, I. D.

LYING. See Liars; Truthfulness and falsehood

Lykin's sleigh-ride. Bergengruen, W.

Lyle, David
In a dry country
Hathaway, B. and Sessions, J. A. eds.
Writers for tomorrow. 2d ser.
Open season
Hathaway, B. and Sessions, J. A. eds.
Writers for tomorrow. 2d ser.

Lynch, John A. 1922-
Fields of wheat
Stanford short stories, 1950

LYNCHING
Alexander, D. And on the third day
Caldwell, E. Saturday afternoon
Deming, R. Hanging fire
Faulkner, W. Dry September
Thompson, C. H. Posse
See also Hanging; Murder stories

The **lynching.** Annixter, P. pseud.

Lyon, Katherine
Altar cloth
Neider, C. ed. Men of the high calling

Lytle, Andrew Nelson, 1902-
The guide
Gordon, C. and Tate, A. eds. House of
fiction

Jericho, Jericho, Jericho
Southern review. Anthology of stories
from the Southern review

**Lytton, Edward George Earle Lytton Bul-
wer-Lyton, 1st baron,** 1803-1873
House and the brain
Cerf, B. A. and Moriarty, H. C. eds.
Anthology of famous British stories

M

M. Seguin's goat. Daudet, A.

"MCMLV." Tucker, W.

MWA murder. Arthur, R.

Mabel. Maugham, W. S.

Mabry, Thomas Dabney
Indian feather
First-prize stories, 1919-1954
Prize stories, 1954

MACARTHUR, MARY, 1930-1949
Kuttner, N. Do you remember Mary?

Macaulay, Rose
Whitewash
Asquith, Lady C. M. E. C. ed. Book of
modern ghosts

Macauley, Robie, 1919-
The invaders
Prize stories of 1951
The wishbone
Best American short stories, 1951

MACAWS. See Parrots

McCall, Mary Caldwell, 1904-
Fraternity
Eaton, H. T. ed. Short stories

McCarthy, Mary Therese, 1912-
The blackguard
McCarthy, M. T. Cast a cold eye
C.Y.E.
McCarthy, M. T. Cast a cold eye
The cicerone
McCarthy, M. T. Cast a cold eye
"Cruel and barbarous treatment"
Southern review. Anthology of stories
from the Southern review
Friend of the family
McCarthy, M. T. Cast a cold eye
Old men
McCarthy, M. T. Cast a cold eye
Unspoiled reaction
Felheim, M.; Newman, F. B. and Stein-
hoff, W. R. eds. Modern short stories
The weeds
McCarthy, M. T. Cast a cold eye
Yonder peasant, who is he?
McCarthy, M. T. Cast a cold eye

McCarthy hunts peace. Abdullah, A.

McCarty, Mary B.
Your long black hair
Oberfirst, R. ed. 1952 anthology of best
original short-shorts

McCauley, Mary Claire
Li'l Reynard
Thinker's digest (Periodical) Spoiled
priest, and other stories

McClintic, Winona
In the days of our fathers
Magazine of fantasy and science fiction.
Best from Fantasy and science fiction;
[1st ser]

McCloskey, Robert, 1914-
The doughnuts
Fenner, P. R. comp. Giggle box

McCloy, Helen
Chinoiserie
Mystery Writers of America, inc.
20 great tales of murder

McClure, Jane
Dark interlude
Queen, E. pseud. ed. Queen's awards:
7th ser.

McConnell, William, 1917-
The alien
Pacey, D. ed. Book of Canadian stories
Totem
Weaver, R. and James, H. eds. Canadian short stories

McCormick, H. P. See Reynolds, J. M. jt.
auth.

McCourt, Edward A. 1907-
Dance for the devil
Saturday evening post (Periodical) Saturday evening post stories, 1952
White mustang
Weaver, R. and James, H. eds. Canadian short stories

McCoy, Esther
The cape
Best American short stories, 1950

McCoy, Horace, 1897-
They shoot horses, don't they?
Grayson, C. ed. Fourth round

McCullers, Carson (Smith) 1917-
Ballad of the sad café
McCullers, C. S. Ballad of the sad café
Domestic dilemma
Abell, E. ed. American accent
McCullers, C. S. Ballad of the sad café
The jockey
McCullers, C. S. Ballad of the sad café
Madame Zilensky and the King of Finland
McCullers, C. S. Ballad of the sad café
The sojourner
McCullers, C. S. Ballad of the sad café
Prize stories of 1951
A tree. A rock. A cloud
McCullers, C. S. Ballad of the sad café
Wunderkind
McCullers, C. S. Ballad of the sad café

McDaniel, Ruel
Coroner de luxe
Blaustein, A. P. ed. Fiction goes to court

MacDonald, Dorothy
Child wore a pink sweater
Oberfirst, R. ed. 1954 anthology of best original short-shorts

MacDonald, John Dann, 1916-
Common denominator
Galaxy science fiction magazine. Galaxy reader of science fiction
Dance of a new world
Greenberg, M. ed. Journey to infinity
Death's eye view
Best detective stories of the year—1953
Flaw
Best science fiction stories: 1950
Bleiler, E. F. and Dikty, T. E. eds. Science fiction omnibus: the best science fiction stories, 1949, 1950
Game for blondes
Best science-fiction stories: 1953
Galaxy science fiction magazine. Second Galaxy reader of science fiction
Homesick Buick
Queen, E. pseud. ed. Queen's awards: 5th ser.
I love you (occasionally)
This week magazine This week's short-short stories
Incubation
Crossen, K. F. ed. Future tense
Mechanical answer
Greenberg, M. ed. Robot and the man
The miniature
Conklin, G. ed. Big book of science fiction
Ring around the redhead
Conklin, G. ed. Science-fiction adventures in dimension
Spectator sport
Conklin, G. ed. Omnibus of science fiction
Susceptibility
Galaxy science fiction magazine. Galaxy reader of science fiction

MacDonald, John Ross, pseud. See Miller, Kenneth

MacDonald, Philip
Fingers of fear
MacDonald, P. Something to hide
Green-and-gold string
MacDonald, P. Something to hide
The hub
Magazine of fantasy and science fiction.
Best from Fantasy and science fiction;
[1st ser]
Love lies bleeding
MacDonald, P. Something to hide
Queen, E. pseud. ed. Queen's awards: 5th ser.
Malice domestic
MacDonald, P. Something to hide
Man out of the rain
Queen, E. pseud. ed. Ellery Queen's awards: 9th ser.
Private—keep out
Pratt, F. ed. World of wonder
Something to hide
MacDonald, P. Something to hide
Wood-for-the-trees
MacDonald, P. Something to hide

MacDonald, Zillah Katherine
Shingle shack
Furman, A. L. ed. Everygirls mystery stories
Standing into danger
Furman, A. L. ed. Everygirls mystery stories

McDowell, Dorothy
Good-by, Debbie
Seventeen (Periodical) The Seventeen reader

Macfarlan, Allan A.
Bullfrog hunt
Macfarlan, A. A. Campfire adventure stories
Camp at Saint Adrien
Macfarlan, A. A. Campfire adventure stories
Danger by candlelight
Macfarlan, A. A. Campfire adventure stories
Loon laughs; mystery and adventure in Maine
Macfarlan, A. A. Campfire adventure stories
Lost trail
Macfarlan, A. A. Campfire adventure stories
Moose boy; adventures in the Canadian northwoods
Macfarlan, A. A. Campfire adventure stories
Swift Foot the hunter
Macfarlan, A. A. Campfire adventure stories
Tackle buster
Macfarlan, A. A. Campfire adventure stories
MacFarlane, Wallace
Dead end
Conklin, G. ed. Science-fiction thinking machines
McFee, William, 1881-
Reluctant hero
McFee, W. ed. Great sea stories of modern times
McGarry and the television frame-up. Taylor, M.
McGarry joins the Easter parade. Taylor, M.
McGivern, William P.
Sound of murder
Mystery writers of America, inc. Crooks' tour
Macgregor, James Murdoch
Hallucination orbit
Galaxy science fiction magazine. Second Galaxy reader of science fiction
One in three hundred
Best science-fiction stories: 1954
McGregor, R. J.
Perfect gentleman
Startling stories (Periodical) Best from Startling stories
McGregor affair. Rowland, S.
Machen, Arthur, 1863-1947
Black seal
Davenport, B. ed. Tales to be told in the dark
White people
Davenport, B. ed. Tales to be told in the dark
White powder
Davenport, B. ed. Ghostly tales to be told
The **machine.** Campbell, J. W.
Machine. Jakes, J. W.
Machine breaks down. Sitwell, Sir O. bart.
Machine stops. Forster, E. M.
MACHINERY AND MACHINISTS
Forster, E. M. Machine stops
Marshall, J. Old woman

MACHINISTS. See Machinery and machinists
McHugh, Vincent, 1904-
Alone Men
Argosy (Periodical) Argosy Book of sea stories
McIlvaine's star. Derleth, A. W.
McIntosh, J. T. pseud. See Macgregor, James Murdoch
Mackintosh. Maugham, W. S.
McKabe. Gallico, P. W.
McKay, Margaret Curtis
Thirty trips to Washington
American girl (Periodical) On my honor
McKelvey, Lynne, 1936-
The threshold
McFarland, W. K. comp. Then it happened
Seventeen (Periodical) Nineteen from Seventeen
McKelway, St Clair
Russian who wanted to be friends
Saturday evening post (Periodical) Saturday evening post stories, 1951
McKenney, John
Skycaptain
Creamer, J. B. comp. Twenty-two stories about horses and men
McKenney, Ruth, 1911-
Guinea pig
Dachs, D. ed. Treasury of sports humor
McLaren, Floris Clark, 1904-
Date with Dora
Weaver, R. and James, H. eds. Canadian short stories
MacLaren, Ian, pseud. See Watson, John
MacLaren-Ross, Julian
This mortal coil
Horizon (Periodical) Golden Horizon
McLarn, Jack Clinton
Trackside grave
Moskowitz, S. ed. Great railroad stories of the world
Yardmaster
Moskowitz, S. ed. Great railroad stories of the world
McLaverty, Michael
Aunt Suzanne
McLaverty, M. Game cock, and other stories
Father Christmas
McLaverty, M. Game cock, and other stories
Game cock
McLaverty, M. Game cock, and other stories
Look at the boats
McLaverty, M. Game cock, and other stories
The mother
McLaverty, M. Game cock, and other stories
Pigeons
McLaverty, M. Game cock, and other stories
Poteen maker
McLaverty, M. Game cock, and other stories

McLaverty, Michael—*Continued*
The prophet
  McLaverty, M. Game cock, and other
    stories
Road to the shore
  Gable, M. Sister, ed. Many-colored
    fleece
  McLaverty, M. Game cock, and other
    stories
The schooner
  McLaverty, M. Game cock, and other
    stories
White mare
  McLaverty, M. Game cock, and other
    stories
Wild duck's nest
  McLaverty, M. Game cock, and other
    stories

MacLean, Katherine
And be merry. . .
  Conklin, G. ed. Omnibus of science
    fiction
Contagion
  Best science fiction stories: 1951
  Conklin, G. ed. Possible worlds of sci-
    ence fiction
Defense mechanism
  Conklin, G. ed. Big book of science
    fiction
  Merril, J. ed. Beyond the barriers of
    space and time
The fittest
  Merril, J. ed. Beyond human ken
Pictures don't lie
  Conklin, G. ed. Invaders of earth
Snowball effect
  Galaxy science fiction magazine. Sec-
    ond Galaxy reader of science fiction

MacMahon, Bryan, 1909-
Corn was springing
  Ludwig, J. B. and Poirier, W. R. eds.
    Stories, British and American
Sing, Milo, sing
  Thinker's digest (Periodical) Spoiled
    priest, and other stories
Young Mari Li
  Gable, M. Sister, ed. Many-colored
    fleece

MacManus, Seumas, 1869-
Apprentice thief
  Fenner, P. R. comp. Fools and funny
    fellows

McMorrow, Thomas, 1886-
Mr Murphy of New York
  Conklin, G. ed. Big book of science fic-
    tion

McNamara, Ed
Holohan's hoist
  Story (Periodical) Story; no. 1

McNeil, Steve
Girl who wasn't wanted
  Saturday evening post (Periodical) Sat-
    urday evening post stories, 1953

McNulty, John, 1895-1956
Back where I had never been
  McNulty, J. Man gets around
Bellevue days
  McNulty, J. Man gets around
Can't slip any drugs to sisters on Fifth
    Avenue
  McNulty, J. Man gets around
The jackpot
  McNulty, J. Man gets around
Mrs Carmody's store
  McNulty, J. Man gets around
Müller with an umlaut
  McNulty, J. Man gets around
Overlooked lady
  McNulty, J. Man gets around
Slightly crocked
  McNulty, J. Man gets around
Television helps, but not very much
  McNulty, J. Man gets around
Third Avenue medicine
  McNulty, J. Man gets around
Where the grass, they say, is blue
  McNulty, J. Man gets around
Yellow-ball-in-the-side
  McNulty, J. Man gets around

Mac's masterpiece. O'Donovan, M.

Mad house. Matheson, R.

Mad Island. Marmur, J.

Mad Lomasneys. O'Donovan, M.

Mad Talmudist. Peretz, I. L.

Mad woman. Maupassant, G. de

Madame Bo-Peep, of the ranches. Porter,
  W. S.

Madame D. Lien Pu

Madame Delphine. Cable, G. W.

Madame de Mauves. James, H.

Madame de Treymes. Wharton, E. N. J.

Madame Jean De Chantal. Heagney, H. J.

Madame Parisse. Maupassant, G. de

Madame Rose Hanie. Gibran, K.

Madame Tellier's excursion. Maupassant, G.
  de

Madame Zilensky and the King of Finland.
  McCullers, C. S.

Madden, Harry T.
Not what she pretended
  Saturday evening post (Periodical) Sat-
    urday evening post stories, 1952

Made to measure. Bonner, P. H.

Made to measure. Gault, W. C.

Mlle de Scudéri. Hoffmann, E. T. A.

Mademoiselle Fifi. Maupassant, G. de

Madison Square Arabian night. Porter, W. S.

The madman. Frank, P.

MADNESS. See Insanity

Madness in the heart. Donahoe, E.

Maestro's magic wand. Schneider, G. W.

Maeterlinck, Maurice, 1862-1949
Massacre of the innocents
  Neider, C. ed. Great short stories from
    the world's literature

MAGAZINES. See Periodicals

Maggie: a girl of the streets. Crane, S.

Maggie Winthrop. Doty, W. L.

MAGI
Broun, H. C. Frankincense and myrrh
Goudge, E. Well of the star
Komroff, M. Told in the stars
Van Dyke, H. Other Wise Man

MAGIC
Bergengruen, W. Ali Baba and the forty horse-power
Blish, J. Mistake inside
Collier, J. Rope enough
Coolidge, O. E. Black magician
Coolidge, O. E. Children of Set
Mann, T. Magic and the magician
Procter, M. No place for magic
Wells, H. G. Magic shop
See also Conjuring

Magic at midnight. Tippett, J. S.
Magic circle. O'Rourke, F.
Magic hour. Newhouse, E.
Magic night. Howland, R.
Magic shop. Wells, H. G.
Magic touch. Knox, J.
MAGICIANS. See Conjuring; Magic
MAGISTRATES. See Law and lawyers
Magnanimity contest. Bergengruen, W.
Magnes, William D.
The vise
Story (Periodical) Story; no. 1
Magnetism. Fitzgerald, F. S. K.
Magnificent merger. Chute, B. J.
The magnolias. Leiper, G. B.
Maguire, R. A.
Five wives of Fergus O'Malley
Story (Periodical) Story; no. 3
Mahoney, William B.
Wrong guy
Lass, A. H. and Horowitz, A. eds. Stories for youth
MAHOUTS
Kipling, R. Moti Guj—mutineer
The maiden. Stafford, J.
Maiden, maiden. Boyle, K.
MAIDS. See Servants—Maids
Maier, Howard
Red dog
Cavanna, B. ed. Pick of the litter
Collier's, the national weekly. Collier's best
World outside
Best American short stories, 1950
MAIL CARRIERS. See Postal service
MAIL ORDER BUSINESS
Milburn, G. Wish nook
Mail starts. Skelton, C. L.
Main currents of American thought. Shaw, I.
MAINE
Auchincloss, L. Finish, good lady
Auchincloss, L. Greg's peg
Etnier, E. J. The willow
19th century
Hale, E. E. My double, and how he undid me
Spofford, H. E. P. Circumstance
20th century
Rawlings, C. A. Flash of lightning
Majesty of the law. Ford, N. A.
Majesty of the law. O'Donovan, M.
Major and Mrs Fletcher. Newhouse, E.

Major Burl. Schaefer, J. W.
Major of Hussars. Bates, H. E.
Make me real. Lincoln, V. E.
Make westing. London, J.
Makes the whole world kin. Porter, W. S.
Making arrangements. Bowen, E.
Making of a minister. Barrie, Sir J. M. bart.
Making of a New Yorker. Porter, W. S.
Makings of a cowhorse. James, W.
Malacca cane. Vigny, A. V. comte de
Malachi's Cove. Trollope, A.
Maladjusted classroom. Nearing, H.
Malamud, Bernard, 1914-
The prison
Best American short stories, 1951
MALARIA
Verga, G. Malaria
Malaria. Verga, G.
Maloney's last stand. Young, S.
Man-taming woman. Fessier, M.
MALAYA
Conrad, J. The lagoon
Maugham, W. S. Book-bag
Maugham, W. S. Door of opportunity
Maugham, W. S. Footprints in the jungle
Nelson, E. D. P. The St George ball
Malcolmson, Anne (Burnett) 1910-
Blackbeard
Fenner, P. R. comp. Pirates, pirates, pirates
Pecos Bill
Fenner, P. R. comp. Cowboys, cowboys, cowboys
MALEDICTIONS. See Curses
Les malheurs des mannequins. Hutchins, M. P. M.
Malice afterthought. Grinnell, D. pseud.
Malice domestic. MacDonald, P.
MALLARDS. See Ducks
Mallea, Eduardo, 1903-
Heart's reason
De Onís, H. ed. Spanish stories and tales
Pillars of society
Burnett, W. ed. World's best
Malory, Sir Thomas, 15th century
Marvellous adventure of the sword
Cerf, B. A. and Moriarty, H. C. eds. Anthology of famous British stories
Maloy, Lois, 1902-
Swift Thunder of the prairie
Fenner, P. R. comp. Indians, Indians, Indians
Malraux, André, 1895-
The conquerors
Dupee, F. W. ed. Great French short novels
Maltz, Albert, 1908-
Man on a road
Best of the Best American short stories, 1915-1950
Happiest man on earth
First-prize stories, 1919-1954
Mama. Asch, S.
Mama and the pot of gold. Knox, J.

Mama's little girl. Caldwell, E.
Mammon and the archer. Porter, W. S.
MAN
   Stapledon, W. O. Last terrestrials
MAN, ISLE OF
   Kneale, M. Putting away of Uncle Quag-
      gin
   Sawyer, R. Fiddler, play fast, play faster
MAN, MECHANICAL. See Automata
MAN, PREHISTORIC
   Annixter, P. pseud. First ally
   Howard, R. E. Coming of Conan; 7 stories
   Howard, R. E. King Conan; 5 stories
   Howard, R. E. Sword of Conan; 4 stories
   Loomis, N. Long dawn
   Macfarlan, A. A. Swift Foot the hunter
The man. Bradbury, R.
Man about town. Porter, W. S.
Man alone at lunch. Aiken, C. P.
Man and boy. Steele, W. D.
Man and woman. Caldwell, E.
Man at Gantt's Place. Frazee, S.
Man at the gate. Taber, G. B.
Man called Horse. Johnson, D. M.
Man from Glasgow. Maugham, W. S.
Man from Mars. Miller, P. S.
Man from outside. Williamson, J.
Man from the south. Dahl, R.
Man from the tunnel. Benson, T.
Man greatly beloved. Milne, A. A.
Man higher up. Porter, W. S.
Man in gray. Weston, C. G.
Man in Israel. Perl, P.
Man in the chimney corner. Knox, J.
Man in the hard hat. Barker, S. O.
Man in moon. Norton, H. A.
Man in the moon. Reynolds, M.
Man in the moone. Godwin, F.
Man in the morgue. Arthur, R.
Man in the passage. Chesterton, G. K.
Man in the velvet hat. Prince, J. and Prince,
   H.
Man inside. Weidman, J.
Man-killer. Mowery, W. B.
Man needs a horse. Downing, J. H.
Man of character. Gallegos, R.
Man of destiny. Christopher, J.
Man of his own. Ford, C.
Man of the crowd. Poe, E. A.
Man of the house. O'Donovan, M.
Man on a road. Maltz, A.
Man on Stormrift Mountain. Strong, P. N.
Man out of the rain. MacDonald, P.
Man that corrupted Hadleyburg. Clemens,
   S. L.
Man who became a fish. Li Fu-yen
Man who collected Poe. Bloch, R.
Man who confessed. Packard, F. L.
Man who could work miracles. Wells, H. G.
Man who couldn't remember. Hendryx, J. B.
Man who drove Strindberg mad. Sitwell,
   Sir O. bart.
Man who evolved. Hamilton, E.
Man who flew into a rage. Grove, W.
Man who had been around. Wylie, P.
Man who had died a lot. Van Doren, M.
Man who had no eyes. Kantor, M.
Man who had no friends. Philips, J. P.
Man who hated people. Gallico, P. W.
Man who hated time. Canning, V.
Man who invented sin. O'Faoláin, S.
Man who liked ants. Charteris, L.
Man who looked like himself. Caldwell, E.
Man who married an ill-tempered wife. Juan
   Manuel, Infante of Castille
Man who missed the bus. Benson, S.
Man who rode the saucer. Holmes, K.
Man who saw through heaven. Steele, W. D.
Man who shot Liberty Valance. Johnson,
   D. M.
Man who slept through the end of the world.
   Nadir, I. M.
Man who sold himself. O'Rourke, F.
Man who sold rope to the gnoles. Sea-
   bright, I.
Man who sold the moon. Heinlein, R. A.
Man who was. Kipling, R.
Man who was loved. Stern, J.
Man who wasn't there. Todd, R.
Man who waved the flag. Green, H. G.
Man who would be king. Kipling, R.
Man who wouldn't break. Heyliger, W.
Man whose wishes came true. Forester,
   C. S.
Man with a conscience. Maugham, W. S.
Man with a family. Humphrey, W.
Man with a past. Haycox, E.
Man with English. Gold, H. L.
Man with the glass eye. Hendryx, J. B.
Man with the monocle. Doty, W. L.
Man with the phoney tin foot. Benson, T.
Man with the scar. Maugham, W. S.
Man with the sneer. Vickers, R.
Man with the strange head, Breuer, M. J.
Man with the twisted lip. Doyle, Sir A. C.
Man with two beards. Chesterton, G. K.
Man without a country. Hale, E. E.
Man without a temperament. Mansfield, K.
Man you couldn't kill. Sergîeev-Tsenskiǐ,
   S. N.

Mandel, George, 1920-
   Beckoning sea
   American vanguard, 1950

MANDRAKE
   Ekbergh, I. D. Mysterious Chinese man-
      drake

Manger, Itzik, 1901-
   Adventures of Hershel Summerwind
      Howe, I. and Greenberg, E. eds. Treas-
      ury of Yiddish stories

Mango tree. Robinson, R. S.

MANHATTAN. See New York (City)—
Manhattan
Mania-head-in-the-clouds. Gronowicz, A.
MANIACS. See Insanity
MANICURISTS
Caldwell, E. We are looking at you,
Agnes
MANIKINS (FASHION MODELS) See
Models, Fashion (Persons)
Mann, Heinrich, 1871-1950
Three minute novel
Lange, V. ed. Great German short
novels and stories
Mann, Thomas, 1875-1955
Death in Venice
Lange, V. ed. Great German short
novels and stories
Neider, C. ed. Short novels of the
masters
Pick, R. ed. German stories and tales
Disorder and early sorrow
Davis, R. G. ed. Ten modern masters
Gordon, C. and Tate, A. eds. House of
fiction
Fight between Jappe and Do Escobar
Davis, R. G. ed. Ten modern masters
The hungry
Blodgett, H. W. ed. Story survey. 1953
ed.
Into the pit
Seldon, R. ed. Ways of God and men
Little Herr Friedemann
Davis, R. G. ed. Ten modern masters
West, R. B. and Stallman, R. W. eds.
Art of modern fiction
Mario and the magician
Felheim, M.; Newman, F. B. and Stein-
hoff, W. R. eds. Modern short stories
Heilman, R. B. ed. Modern short stories
Lynskey, W. C. ed. Reading modern
fiction
Short, R. W. and Sewall, R. B. eds.
Short stories for study. 1950 ed.
Masters of Buddenbrooks
Burnett, W. ed. World's best
Railway accident
Schorer, M. ed. The story
Tonio Kröger
Ludwig, R. M. and Perry, M. B. eds.
Nine short novels
Weary hour
Neider, C. ed. Great short stories from
the world's literature
Manna. Galsworthy, J.
Manna. Phillips, P.
Manners of the age. Fyfe, H. B.
Mannikin talk. Mowery, W. B.
Manning, Laurence
Good-bye, Ilha!
Merril, J. ed. Beyond human ken
Mannix, Edward, 1928-
New Year for Juicy
American vanguard, 1953
Mannzen, Don
Aurora's Angus
Oberfirst, R. ed. 1954 anthology of best
original short-shorts
Man's foes. Buck, P. S.
Man's game. Heinz, W. C.

Man's hand. Garrold, R. P.
Mansfield, Katherine, 1888-1923
At the bay
Stegner, W. E.; Scowcroft, R. and Ilyin,
B. eds. Writer's art.
Bliss
Heilman, R. B. ed. Modern short stories
Lynskey, W. C. ed. Reading modern
fiction
Cup of tea
Bogorad, S. N. and Trevithick, J. eds.
College miscellany
Shaw, H. and Bement, D. Reading the
short story
Daughters of the late colonel
West, R. B. and Stallman, R. W. eds.
Art of modern fiction
Dill pickle
Schramm, W. L. ed. Great short stories
Short, R. W. and Sewall, R. B. eds.
Short stories for study. 1950 ed.
Doll's house
Lamb, L. ed. Family book of best loved
short stories
Garden-party
Millett, F. B. ed. Reading fiction
Her first ball
Christ, H. I. and Shostak, J. eds. Short
stories
Felheim, M.; Newman, F. B. and Stein-
hoff, W. R. Modern short stories
Life of Ma Parker
Cerf, B. A. and Moriarty, H. C. eds.
Anthology of famous British stories
Stauffer, R. M.; Cunningham, W. H.
and Sullivan, C. J. eds. Adventures in
modern literature
Man without a temperament
Davis, R. G. ed. Ten modern masters
Pictures
Davis, R. G. ed. Ten modern masters
Taking the veil
Blodgett, H. W. ed. Story survey. 1953
ed.
Wind blows
Davis, R. G. ed. Ten modern masters
MANSLAUGHTER. See Assassination;
Crime and criminals; Murder stories;
Mystery and detective stories
Manuel, Juan. See Juan Manuel, Infante of
Castille
Ms. found in a bottle. Poe, E. A.
Manuscript found in a vacuum. Hubbard,
P. M.
Manuscript of a village doctor. France, A.
MANUSCRIPTS
James, H. Death of the lion
MANUSCRIPTS (PALIMPSESTS)
Pratt, F. and De Camp, L. S. Palimpsest
of St Augustine
Many are called. Van Doren, M.
Many are the brave. Gardner, W. W.
MAPLE SUGAR
Bromfield, L. Sugar camp
Mappined life. Munro, H. H.
Maracot Deep. Doyle, Sir A. C.
MARATHON DANCES. See Dance mara-
thons

MARBLE WORKERS. See Stone-cutters

March, William, pseud. See Campbell, William Edward March

Marche Militaire. Schneider, G. W.

Marching morons. Kornbluth, C. M.

MARCUS AURELIUS, EMPEROR OF ROME. See Aurelius Antoninus, Marcus, Emperor of Rome, 121-180

Marcus, Paul
Tip the green earth
This week magazine This week's short-short stories

Marcus, Pesach, 1896-
Higher and higher
Howe, I. and Greenberg, E. eds. Treasury of Yiddish stories

Margie passes. Shallit, J.

Margin for error. Kuttner, H.

Marguerite. Stein, G.

María Concepción. Porter, K. A.

Marie, Consort of Ferdinand I, King of Rumania, 1875-1938
What Vasile saw
Thinker's digest (Periodical) Spoiled priest, and other stories

MARIJUANA CIGARETTES. See Narcotics

Mario and the magician. Mann, T.

MARIONETTES. See Puppets and puppet plays

The marionettes. Porter, W. S.

Marionettes, inc. Bradbury, R.

Marjorie Daw. Aldrich, T. B.

Mark. Munro, H. H.

Mark of distinction. Betts, D.

Mark of the beast. Kipling, R.

Mark Robarts is adamant. Trollope, A.

Mark Robarts signs a bill. Trollope, A.

Mark Tidd in the backwoods. Kelland, C. B.

Mark Twain, pseud. See Clemens, Samuel Langhorne

Marker, Walter D.
Tree for two
Elmquist, R. M. ed. Fifty years to Christmas

Market Basing mystery. Christie, A. M.

Markewich, Robert, 1919-
Return to the Bronx
Ribalow, H. U. ed. This land, these people

Markfield, Wallace, 1926- Ph.D.
Ribalow, H. U. ed. These your children

Markheim. Stevenson, R. L.

Marksman. Gault, W. C.

MARLOWE, CHRISTOPHER, 1564-1593
Bush, G. Great reckoning in a little room
Cabell, J. B. Porcelain cups

Marlowe, Stephen
Lion's mouth
Lesser, M. A. ed. Looking forward

Marmur, Jacland, 1901-
Below Cape Horn
American boy (Periodical) American boy Adventure stories

Bloodstained beach
Saturday evening post (Periodical) Saturday evening post stories, 1952
I will not abandon!
Saturday evening post (Periodical) Saturday evening post stories, 1953
Mad Island
This week magazine. This week's short-short stories
Proved by the sea
Bluebook (Periodical) Best sea stories from Bluebook

Marooned children. Carrighar, S.

Marotta, Giuseppe, 1902-
"Dear mother. . ."
Fremantle, A. J. ed. Mothers
Ungar, F. ed. To mother with love

Marquand, John Phillips, 1924-
Yoicks—and away
Burnett, W. ed. World's best
You can't do that
Stauffer, R. M.; Cunningham, W. H. and Sullivan, C. J. eds. Adventures in modern literature

Marquis, Don, 1878-1937
Blood will tell
Cavanna, B. ed. Pick of the litter
Country doctor
Fabricant, N. D. and Werner, H. eds. World's best doctor stories

Marquis and Miss Sally. Porter, W. S.

Marquis de Fumerol. Maupassant, G. de

MARRIAGE
Dostoevskiĭ, F. M. Christmas tree and a wedding
Li Fu-yen. Matrimony Inn
Waugh, A. Wed, my darling daughter

MARRIAGE, MIXED
Johnson, D. M. Flame on the frontier

MARRIAGE, PROMISE OF. See Betrothals

MARRIAGE BROKERS
Dworzan, H. L. Husband for Bluma
Wendroff, Z. Statistics
Wendroff, Z. Two pleasures

Marriage feast. Lagerkvist, P. F.

MARRIAGE OF CHILDREN. See Child marriage

Marriage of convenience. Maugham, W. S.

MARRIAGE PROBLEMS
Balzac, H. de. Other Diane
Bergelson, D. In a backwoods town
Beyle, M. H. Mina de Vanghel
Broch, H. Zerline, the old servant girl
Chekhov, A. P. Boa constrictor and rabbit
Chekhov, A. P. La Cigale
Chekhov, A. P. Out of sheer boredom
Cloete, S. Silence of Mr Prendegast
De Vries, P. Double or nothing
De Vries, P. How can I leave thee?
De Vries, P. You and who else?
Ekbergh, I. D. Matron in distress
Gilpatrick, E. Concrete experience
Greene, G. Basement room
Halladay, V. Once-beautiful Ellie
Harte, B. Bell-ringer of Angel's
Harte, B. Brown of Calaveras
Harte, B. Passage in the life of Mr John Oakhurst

MARRIAGE PROBLEMS—*Continued*
Hatch, E. Channel 10
Horwitz, J. The movers
Humphrey, W. Last husband
Huxley, A. Gioconda smile
Jackson, C. R. The outlander
Jordan, G. For the last time
Kaye-Smith, S. The mockbeggar
Kulbak, M. Munie the bird dealer
La Farge, C. Motet for two voices
Laurence, M. Uncertain flowering
Lawrence, D. H. Captain's doll
Lawrence, D. H. Two blue birds
Lincoln, V. E. The understanding
Mallea, E. Heart's reason
Mansfield, K. Bliss
Maugham, W. S. Back of beyond
Maugham, W. S. Casual affair
Maugham, W. S. Colonel's lady
Maugham, W. S. Creative impulse
Maugham, W. S. Flotsam and jetsam
Maugham, W. S. Footprints in the jungle
Maugham, W. S. Force of circumstance
Maugham, W. S. His Excellency
Maugham, W. S. The kite
Maugham, W. S. P. & O.
Maugham, W. S. Point of honour
Maugham, W. S. The promise
Maugham, W. S. Social sense
Maugham, W. S. Virtue
Maugham, W. S. Woman of fifty
Maupassant, G. de. The jewels
Murrie, P. New beau
O'Donovan, M. Counsel for Œdipus
O'Donovan, M. The frying-pan
O'Donovan, M. Lonely rock
O'Donovan, M. Unapproved route
Parker, D. R. Big blonde
Porter, K. A. Day's work
Saintsbury, E. B. Bread upon the waters
Salinger, J. D. Pretty mouth and green my eyes
Sandy, S. Black lie
Sansom, W. The windows
Schnitzler, A. Bachelor's death
Schulberg, B. W. All the town's talking
Shaw, I. The convert
Singer, I. B. Gimpel the fool
Somerville, A. W. Tale of the old main line
Stettner, S. Summer place
Stone, W. J. Retribution
Stuart, J. The storm
Tarkington, B. Uncertain Molly Collicut
Verga, G. Cavalleria rusticana
Waltari, M. T. Tie from Paris
Waugh, E. Period piece
Wechsberg, J. New York is full of girls
Wharton, E. N. J. The choice
White, A. Moment of truth
Winslow, T. S. Fur flies
Winslow, T. S. Obsession
Winslow, T. S. Technique
See also Divorce; Husband and wife

Marriage that couldn't succeed. Richter, C.

Marry month of May. Porter, W. S.

MARS (PLANET)
Bellamy, E. Blindman's world
Brackett, L. Last days of Shandakor
Bradbury, R. Dwellers in silence
Bradbury, R. Fire balloons
Bradbury, R. Holiday
Bradbury, R. In this sign
Bradbury, R. Million-year picnic
Bradbury, R. One who waits
Bradbury, R. Other foot
Bradbury, R. Ylla
Carter, F. Ounce of prevention
Del Rey, L. "The years draw nigh"
Elam, R. M. Red sands
Fairman, P. W. Brothers beyond the void
Harris, J. B. Time to rest
Heard, G. B+M—planet 4
Kummer, F. A. Forgiveness of Tenchu Taen
Leiber, F. Foxholes of Mars
Leiber, F. Wanted—an enemy
Long, F. B. And someday to Mars
Serviss, G. P. Edison's conquest of Mars
Sheckley, R. Last weapon
Van Vogt, A. E. Enchanted village
Weinbaum, S. G. Martian odyssey
Weinbaum, S. G. Valley of dreams
White, W. A. P. Starbride
Williams, R. M. Red death of Mars
Williams, R. M. The seekers
Wolf, M. Homeland
See also Martians

Mars is heaven. Bradbury, R.

Marseilles. See France—Marseilles

Marsh, Willard N. 1922-
Beachhead in Bohemia
Best American short stories, 1953

Marshal and his secretary. Bergengruen, W.

Marshall, Bruce, 1899-
Immodest maiden
Saturday evening post (Periodical) Saturday evening post stories, 1951

Marshall, Edison, 1894-
Benefit of clergy
Marshall, E. Love stories of India
Beside the Shalimar
Marshall, E. Love stories of India
Bird of Omen
Marshall, E. Love stories of India
Bird of Paradise
Marshall, E. Love stories of India
Cat that would not die
Marshall, E. Love stories of India
Closed trophy room
Marshall, E. Love stories of India
Detour to Calcutta
Marshall, E. Love stories of India
Double cross
Marshall, E. Love stories of India
Elephant remembers
Andrews, R. C. ed. My favorite stories of the great outdoors
Marshall, E. Love stories of India
Gentleman and the tiger
Marshall, E. Love stories of India
Heart of Lily Long
Marshall, E. Love stories of India
Heart of Little Shikara
First-prize stories, 1919-1954
Masks off
Marshall, E. Love stories of India
Matter of honor
Marshall, E. Love stories of India
Pooja
Marshall, E. Love stories of India
Upturned card
Marshall, E. Love stories of India

Marshall, Elizabeth
Hill people
Best American short stories, 1953
Marshall, Joyce
Old woman
Weaver, R. and James, H. eds. Canadian short stories
Marshall, R. D.
Wrist watch and some ants
New writing (Periodical) Best stories
MARSHALS. See Sheriffs
MARSHES. See Swamps
Marsland, Anitra M.
Of shoes and ships
American girl (Periodical) On my honor
MARTENS
Reid, M. Battle of the marten and the porcupine
Martha Jean. Caldwell, E.
Martha's yesterdays. Cavanaugh, J. P.
Martian and the moron. Waldo, E. H.
Martian odyssey. Weinbaum, S. G.
MARTIANS
Bradbury, R. Concrete mixer
Brown, F. Last Martian
Brown, F. Mouse
Carr, R. S. Easter eggs
Carr, R. S. Those men from Mars
Curtis, B. Peculiar people
Grunert, K. Enemies in space
Jenkins, W. F. Nobody saw the ship
Knight, D. Catch that Martian
Long, F. B. Invasion
Miller, P. S. Man from Mars
Russell, E. F. Dear Devil
Stapledon, W. O. The Martians
Tucker, W. Gentlemen—the Queen!
Tucker, W. Job is ended
Tucker, W. Wayfaring strangers
Wells, H. G. Star begotten
White, W. A. P. The ambassadors
The **Martians.** Stapledon, W. O.
Martians and the Coys. Reynolds, M.
Martin, Charles Morris, 1891-
Horse drive
Fenner, P. R. comp. Cowboys, cowboys, cowboys
Martin, John
Adventure of Baron Munchausen
Fenner, P. R. comp. Fun! Fun! Fun!
Martin, Thomas H.
The switchboard
Best Army short stories, 1950
Martin, Violet Florence. See Somerville, E. A. O. jt. auth.
Martyr, Weston, 1885-
Sleeping draft
Cerf, B. A. and Moriarty, H. C. eds. Anthology of famous British stories
The **martyr.** Akutagawa, R.
The **martyr.** Farrell, J. T.
The **martyr.** Roth, C.
Martyrdom of the house. Comfort, A.
MARTYRS
Akutagawa, R. The martyr
The **marvel.** Smyth, E.

Marvellous adventure of the sword. Malory, Sir T.
Mary. Collier, J.
MARY, VIRGIN
Borden, M. In Nazareth
Güiraldes, R. Old ranch
Mary comes into money. Trollope, A.
Mary Lou's Christmas. Credle, E.
Mary, Mary, so contrary. Fillmore, P. H.
Mary O'Reilley. Farrell, J. T.
Mary with the high hand. Bennett, A.
MARYLAND

Georgetown
Tate, A. Immortal woman
Masculine principle. O'Donovan, M.
Masculine protest. O'Donovan, M.
Masefield, John, 1878-
Western islands
Cerf, B. A. and Moriarty, H. C. eds. Anthology of famous British stories
The **mask.** Chekhov, A. P.
Mask of Demeter. Pearson, M. and Corwin, C.
Masked angel. Charteris, L.
Masked monster. Gilpatric, G.
MASKS (FOR THE FACE)
Beerbohm, Sir M. Happy hypocrite
MASKS (PLAYS)
Hawthorne, N. Maypole of Merry Mount
Masks off. Marshall, E.
Mason, Grace (Sartwell) 1877-
First stone
Thinker's digest (Periodical) Spoiled priest, and other stories
Mason, Travis
Stood up
McFarland, W. K. comp. Then it happened
MASONRY (SECRET ORDER) See Freemasons
Masque of the Red Death. Poe, E. A.
Masquerade of souls. Lagerkvist, P. F.
MASQUERADES
Chekhov, A. P. The mask
Poe, E. A. Hop-Frog
Poe, E. A. Masque of the Red Death
MASQUES (PLAYS) See Masks (Plays)
MASS
Stafford, J. Between the porch and the altar
MASSACHUSETTS
Aiken, C. P. Last visit

18th century
Hawthorne, N. Wives of the dead

Boston—17th century
Hawthorne, N. Gray champion

Boston—20th century
Aiken, C. P. Night before prohibition

Concord
Thoreau, H. D. Winter at Walden

Nantucket
Strong, A. All on a winter's night

Massacre of the innocents. Maeterlinck, M.

Massacree! Brink, C. R.

MASSACRES
Maeterlinck, M. Massacre of the innocents
Verga, G. Liberty

Masses of men. Caldwell, E.

Master mind. Chute, B. J.

Master minds of Mars. Claudy, C. H.

Master of the inn. Herrick, R.

Master race. Ashby, R.

Master time. Still, J.

Masters of art. Porter, W. S.

Masters of Buddenbrooks. Mann, T.

Masterson. Maugham, W. S.

The **masterstroke.** Howard, W.

Masur, Harold Q. 1912-
Widow in waiting
Mystery Writers of America, inc.
Four-&-twenty bloodhounds

MATADORS. See Bullfighters and bullfighting

Match-maker. Munro, H. H.

MATCHMAKERS
Coolidge, O. E. Carpenter's daughter
Munro, H. H. Forbidden buzzards
Munro, H. H. The elk
See also Marriage brokers

Mateo Falcone. Mérimée, P.

Mathematical voodoo. Nearing, H.

MATHEMATICIANS
Jenkins, W. F. Sidewise in time

Mathematics of intelligence. Willingham, C.

Matheson, Richard, 1926-
Born of man and woman
Best science fiction stories: 1951
Matheson, R. Born of man and woman
Dance of the dead
Star science fiction stories, no. 3
Dear Diary
Matheson, R. Born of man and woman
Disappearing act
Matheson, R. Born of man and woman
Dress of white silk
Magazine of fantasy and science fiction.
Best from Fantasy and science fiction,
1952
Matheson, R. Born of man and woman
F—
Matheson, R. Born of man and woman
Full circle
Matheson, R. Born of man and woman
Last day
Best science-fiction stories: 1954
Lover, when you're near me
Best science-fiction stories: 1953
Galaxy science fiction magazine. Second
Galaxy reader of science fiction
Matheson, R. Born of man and woman
Mad house
Matheson, R. Born of man and woman
Return
Matheson, R. Born of man and woman
SRL ad
Brown, F. and Reynolds, M. eds. Sci-
ence-fiction carnival
Matheson, R. Born of man and woman

Shipshape home
Conklin, G. ed. Omnibus of science fic-
tion
Matheson, R. Born of man and woman
Third from the sun
Galaxy science fiction magazine. Galaxy
reader of science fiction
Matheson, R. Born of man and woman
Through channels
Matheson, R. Born of man and woman
To fit the crime
Matheson, R. Born of man and woman
The traveller
Matheson, R. Born of man and woman
The waker dreams
Galaxay science fiction magazine. Galaxy
reader of science fiction
The wedding
Matheson, R. Born of man and woman
Witch war
Best science fiction stories: 1952
Matheson, R. Born of man and woman

Mathews, Mack
Tough little Christmas story
Story (Periodical) Story; no. 4

Mating of a stamp collector. Thomason,
J. W.

Mating of Marjorie. Caldwell, E.

MATRIMONIAL AGENCIES. See Marriage brokers

Matrimony Inn. Li Fu-yen

Matron in distress. Ekbergh, I. D.

Matron of Ephesus. Petronius Arbiter

Matschat, Cecile (Hulse) See Del Rey, L.
jt. ed.

Matter of business. Maupassant, G. de

Matter of form. Gold, H. L.

Matter of honor. Marshall, E.

Matter of mean elevation. Porter, W. S.

Matter of seconds. Queen, E. pseud.

Matter of sentiment. Munro, H. H.

Matter of spelling. Stanley, J. B.

Matter of time. Lieberman, R.

Matter of vanity. Riter, F.

MATTERHORN
Mummery, A. F. The Matterhorn

The **Matterhorn.** Mummery, A. F.

Matthew and the lace curtain. Carroll, J. W.

Matthews, Ralph D.
Fisherman's luck
Ford, N. A. and Faggett, H. L. eds.
Best short stories by Afro-American
writers (1925-1950)

Maud. Auchincloss, L.

Maud Island. Caldwell, E.

Maugham, William Somerset, 1874-
Alien corn
Maugham, W. S. Complete short stories
v 1
Ant and the grasshopper
Maugham, W. S. Complete short stories
v2
Maugham, W. S. Encore
Appearance and reality
Maugham, W. S. Complete short stories
v2

Maugham, William S.—*Continued*

Back of beyond
　Maugham, W. S. Complete short stories
　v 1
Before the party
　Maugham, W. S. Complete short stories
　v 1
　Queen, E. pseud. ed. Literature of crime
Book-bag
　Maugham, W. S. Complete short stories
　v 1
The bum
　Maugham, W. S. Complete short stories
　v2
Casual affair
　Maugham, W. S. Complete short stories
　v2
Closed shop
　Maugham, W. S. Complete short stories
　v2
Colonel's lady
　Maugham, W. S. Complete short stories
　v2
The consul
　Maugham, W. S. Complete short stories
　v2
Creative impulse
　Maugham, W. S. Complete short stories
　v 1
Door of opportunity
　Felheim, M.; Newman, F. B. and Stein-
　　hoff, W. R. eds. Modern short stories
　Maugham, W. S. Complete short stories
　v 1
The dream
　Maugham, W. S. Complete short stories
　v2
End of the flight
　Maugham, W. S. Complete short stories
　v2
Episode
　Maugham, W. S. Complete short stories
　v2
The escape
　Maugham, W. S. Complete short stories
　v2
Facts of life
　Heilman, R. B. ed. Modern short stories
　Maugham, W. S. Complete short stories
　v2
Fall of Edward Barnard
　Maugham, W. S. Complete short stories
　v 1
Flotsam and jetsam
　Maugham, W. S. Complete short stories
　v2
Footprints in the jungle
　Maugham, W. S. Complete short stories
　v 1
Force of circumstance
　Maugham, W. S. Complete short stories
　v 1
Four Dutchmen
　Maugham, W. S. Complete short stories
　v2
French Joe
　Maugham, W. S. Complete short stories
　v2
Friend in need
　Maugham, W. S. Complete short stories
　v2

German Harry
　Maugham, W. S. Complete short stories
　v2
Gigolo and gigolette
　Maugham, W. S. Complete short stories
　v2
　Maugham, W. S. Encore
Giulia Lazzari
　Maugham, W. S. Complete short stories
　v 1
Hairless Mexican
　Maugham, W. S. Complete short stories
　v 1
Happy couple
　Maugham, W. S. Complete short stories
　v2
Happy man
　Maugham, W. S. Complete short stories
　v2
His Excellency
　Maugham, W. S. Complete short stories
　v 1
Home
　Maugham, W. S. Complete short stories
　v2
Honolulu
　Maugham, W. S. Complete short stories
　v 1
Human element
　Maugham, W. S. Complete short stories
　v 1
In a strange land
　Maugham, W. S. Complete short stories
　v2
Jane
　Maugham, W. S. Complete short stories
　v 1
Judgment seat
　Maugham, W. S. Complete short stories
　v2
The kite
　Maugham, W. S. Complete short stories
　v2
The letter
　Maugham, W. S. Complete short stories
　v 1
Lion's skin
　Maugham, W. S. Complete short stories
　v2
Lord Mountdrago
　Maugham, W. S. Complete short stories
　v2
Lotus eater
　Maugham, W. S. Complete short stories
　v2
　Schramm, W. L. ed. Great short stories
Louise
　Fabricant, N. D. and Werner, H. eds.
　　World's best doctor stories
　Maugham, W. S. Complete short stories
　v2
The luncheon
　Maugham, W. S. Complete short stories
　v2
Mabel
　Maugham, W. S. Complete short stories
　v2
Mackintosh
　Maugham, W. S. Complete short stories
　v 1
Man from Glasgow
　Maugham, W. S. Complete short stories
　v2

Maugham, William S.—*Continued*

Man with a conscience
  Maugham, W. S. Complete short stories
    v2

Man with the scar
  Maugham, W. S. Complete short stories
    v2

Marriage of convenience
  Maugham, W. S. Complete short stories
    v2

Masterson
  Maugham, W. S. Complete short stories
    v2

Mayhew
  Maugham, W. S. Complete short stories
    v2

Mirage
  Maugham, W. S. Complete short stories
    v2

Miss King
  Maugham, W. S. Complete short stories
    v 1

Mr Harrington's washing
  Maugham, W. S. Complete short stories
    v 1

Mr Know-All
  Davis, R. G. ed. Ten modern masters
  Maugham, W. S. Complete short stories
    v2
  Maugham, W. S. Trio

The mother
  Maugham, W. S. Complete short stories
    v2

Neil MacAdam
  Maugham, W. S. Complete short stories
    v 1

Official position
  Maugham, W. S. Complete short stories
    v2

The outstation
  Lynskey, W. C. ed. Reading modern
    fiction
  Maugham, W. S. Complete short stories
    v 1
  Stauffer, R. M.; Cunningham, W. H.
    and Sullivan, C. J. eds. Adventures in
    modern literature

P. & O.
  Maugham, W. S. Complete short stories
    v 1

The poet
  Maugham, W. S. Complete short stories
    v2

Point of honour
  Maugham, W. S. Complete short stories
    v2

The pool
  Maugham, W. S. Complete short stories
    v 1

Portrait of a gentleman
  Maugham, W. S. Complete short stories
    v2

Princess September
  Maugham, W. S. Complete short stories
    v2

The promise
  Maugham, W. S. Complete short stories
    v2

Rain
  Gordon, C. and Tate, A. eds. House of
    fiction
  Maugham, W. S. Complete short stories
    v 1

Raw material
  Maugham, W. S. Complete short stories
    v2

Red
  Cerf, B. A. and Moriarty, H. C. eds.
    Anthology of famous British stories
  Maugham, W. S. Complete short stories
    v 1

Romantic young lady
  Maugham, W. S. Complete short stories
    v2

Round dozen
  Maugham, W. S. Complete short stories
    v 1

Salvatore
  Maugham, W. S. Complete short stories
    v2

Sanatorium
  Maugham, W. S. Complete short stories
    v2
  Maugham, W. S. Trio

Social sense
  Maugham, W. S. Complete short stories
    v2

Straight flush
  Maugham, W. S. Complete short stories
    v2

String of beads
  Maugham, W. S. Complete short stories
    v2

The taipan
  Maugham, W. S. Complete short stories
    v2

Three fat women of Antibes
  Maugham, W. S. Complete short stories
    v2

The traitor
  Maugham, W. S. Complete short stories
    v 1

The treasure
  Maugham, W. S. Complete short stories
    v2

The unconquered
  Maugham, W. S. Complete short stories
    v2

The verger
  Maugham, W. S. Complete short stories
    v2
  Maugham, W. S. Trio

Vessel of wrath
  Maugham, W. S. Complete short stories
    v 1

Virtue
  Maugham, W. S. Complete short stories
    v 1

Voice of the turtle
  Maugham, W. S. Complete short stories
    v2

Wash-tub
  Maugham, W. S. Complete short stories
    v2

Winter cruise
  Maugham, W. S. Complete short stories
    v2
  Maugham, W. S. Encore

Woman of fifty
  Maugham, W. S. Complete short stories
    v2

Yellow streak
  Maugham, W. S. Complete short stories
    v 1

Mauldin, William Henry, 1921-
  Affair of the wayward jeep
    Saturday evening post (Periodical) Saturday evening post stories, 1953

Maupassant, Guy de, 1850-1893
  At sea
    Geist, S. ed. French stories and tales
  Babette
    Maupassant, G. de. Selected tales
  Ball-of-fat
    Maupassant, G. de. Selected tales
    Same as: Ball-of-tallow; Boule de suif; Tallow-ball
  Clochette
    Maupassant, G. de. Selected tales
    Same as: Bellflower
  Costly outing
    Maupassant, G. de. Selected tales
  Country excursion
    Maupassant, G. de. Selected tales
  The devil
    Maupassant, G. de. Selected tales
  Diamond necklace
    Maupassant, G. de. Selected tales
  Diary of a madman
    Maupassant, G. de. Selected tales
    Same as: A madman
  The duel
    Maupassant, G. de. Selected tales
    Same as: A coward
  False gems
    Maupassant, G. de. Selected tales
    Same as: The jewels
  Family affair
    Maupassant, G. de. Selected tales
    Same as: Family life
  Farmer's wife
    Maupassant, G. de. Selected tales
    Same as: The farmer
  Fishing excursion
    Maupassant, G. de. Selected tales
    Same as: Fishing party
  The hand
    Queen, E. pseud. ed. Literature of crime
    Same as: The Englishman
  Happiness
    Barrows, H. ed. 15 stories
  Hautot, father and son
    O'Faoláin, S. The short story
    Same as: Hautot Senior & Hautot Junior
  Hautot Senior & Hautot Junior
    Maupassant, G. de. Selected tales
    Same as: Hautot, father and son
  The Horla
    Maupassant, G. de. Selected tales
  Humiliation
    Maupassant, G. de. Selected tales
    Same as: Rose
  In the moonlight
    Maupassant, G. de. Selected tales
    Same as: Claire de lune; Moonlight
  The inn
    Schramm, W. L. ed. Great short stories
    Talbot, D. ed. Treasury of mountaineering stories
  The jewels
    Bogorad, S. N. and Trevithick, J. eds. College miscellany
    Davis, R. G. ed. Ten modern masters
    Same as: False gems
  Julie Romain
    Maupassant, G. de. Selected tales

  Little cask
    Maupassant, G. de. Selected tales
  Love
    Maupassant, G. de. Selected tales
    Schorer, M. ed. The story
  Love's awakening
    Maupassant, G. de. Selected tales
  Lucky burglar
    Maupassant, G. de. Selected tales
    Same as: The burglar
  Mad woman
    Maupassant, G. de. Selected tales
  Madame Parisse
    Maupassant, G. de. Selected tales
  Madame Tellier's excursion
    Maupassant, G. de. Selected tales
  Mademoiselle Fifi
    Maupassant, G. de. Selected tales
  Marquis de Fumerol
    Maupassant, G. de. Selected tales
  Matter of business
    Maupassant, G. de. Selected tales
  La Mère Sauvage
    West, R. B. and Stallman, R. W. eds. Art of modern fiction
    Same as: Mother Sauvage; Old Mother Sauvage
  Minuet
    Geist, S. ed. French stories and tales
    Same as: The dancers
  Moonlight
    Maupassant, G. de. Selected tales
    Same as: Claire de lune; In the moonlight
  Mother and son
    Ungar, F. ed. To mother with love
    Same as: Suspense
  My Uncle Sosthenes
    Maupassant, G. de. Selected tales
  The necklace
    Cody, S. ed. Greatest stories and how they were written
    Lamb, L. ed. Family book of best loved short stories
    Thinker's digest (Periodical) Spoiled priest, and other stories
  Normandy joke
    Maupassant, G. de. Selected tales
  Olive grove
    Maupassant, G. de. Selected tales
  One phase of love
    Maupassant, G. de. Selected tales
  Paul's mistress
    Cory, D. W. pseud. comp. 21 variations on a theme
  Piece of string
    Maupassant, G. de. Selected tales
    Same as: The string
  Saved
    Maupassant, G. de. Selected tales
  The signal
    Maupassant, G. de. Selected tales
    Same as: Playing with fire; The sign
  Simon's papa
    Maupassant, G. de. Selected tales
  The specter
    Maupassant, G. de. Selected tales
    Same as: The apparition; The spectre
  Story of a farm girl
    Gordon, C. and Tate, A. eds. House of fiction
    Maupassant, G. de. Selected tales

Maupassant, Guy de—*Continued*
The string
Cody, S. ed. Greatest stories and how
they were written
Same as: Piece of string
That pig of a Morin
Maupassant, G. de. Selected tales
Same as: That pig, Morin
Toine
Maupassant, G. de. Selected tales
Two friends
Blodgett, H. W. ed. Story survey. 1953
ed.
Two little soldiers
Maupassant, G. de. Selected tales
Same as: Little soldier
Ugly
Maupassant, G. de. Selected tales
The umbrella
Maupassant, G. de. Selected tales
A vagabond
Maupassant, G. de. Selected tales
Same as: The tramp
Vain beauty
Maupassant, G. de. Selected tales
The vendetta
Maupassant, G. de. Selected tales
Same as: Semillante
Was it a dream?
Maupassant, G. de. Selected tales
White wolf
Maupassant, G. de. Selected tales

Mauriac, François, 1885-
Thérèse and the doctor
Burnett, W. ed. World's best

Maurie finds his medium. Levin, M.

Maurois, André, 1885-
War against the moon
Conklin, G. ed. Omnibus of science
fiction

**Maxtone Graham, Joyce (Anstruther) 1901-
1953**
Cobbler, cobbler, mend my shoe
Fenner, P. R. comp. Ghosts, ghosts,
ghosts
Ugly sister
Magazine of fantasy and science fiction.
Best from Fantasy and science fiction;
2d ser.

Maxwell, James A. 1912-
Fighter
Prize stories, 1954

May, Julian
Dune roller
Bleiler, E. F. and Dikty, T. E. eds.
Imagination unlimited
Sloane, W. M. ed. Stories for tomorrow

MAY DAY
Hawthorne, N. Maypole of Merry Mount

May Day. Fitzgerald, F. S. K.

May the Temple be restored! Opatoshu, J.

Maybe a queen. Runyon, D.

Maybe just a little one. Bretnor, R.

Mayhew. Maugham, W. S.

MAYORS
Kafka, F. Hunter Gracchus

Maypole of Merry Mount. Hawthorne, N.

Mayse, Arthur
Midnight Mike
Saturday evening post (Periodical) Sat-
urday evening post stories, 1953
Sea gypsy
Saturday evening post (Periodical) Sat-
urday evening post stories, 1951

Mazel tov. Weissenberg, I. M.

Me and Joe. Gannon, S. A.

Me and my brother. Sykes, C.

Meader, Stephen Warren, 1892-
Bat
Fenner, P. R. comp. Pirates, pirates,
Capture of a brig
Fenner, P. R. comp. Pirates, pirates,
pirates
Crooked arm
Fenner, P. R. comp. Crack of the bat
Three hundred innings
Fenner, P. R. comp. Crack of the bat
Whaler 'round the Horn
Fenner, P. R. comp. Stories of the sea

The **meadow.** Bradbury, R.

Meal for the poor. Spector, M.

Meal ticket. Schulberg, B. W.

Mechanical answer. MacDonald, J. D.

MECHANICAL MEN. See Automata

Medal for Becky. Erdman, L. G.

Meddlesome Jack. Caldwell, E.

Meddlin' Papa. Verner, C.

Medearis, Mary, 1916?-
Big Doc's girl
McFarland, W. K. comp. Then it hap-
pened

Mediators to the goatherd. Hinton, J.

MEDICAL LIFE. See Physicians

MEDICAL RESEARCH
Lerner, M. The brothers

MEDICAL STUDENTS. See Physicians

Medicine dancer. Brown, B.

MEDICINE MAN
Porter, W. S. Jeff Peters as a personal
magnet

Medicine man. Caldwell, E.

**MEDICINES,   PATENT,   PROPRIE-
TARY, ETC.**
Caldwell, E. Medicine man
O'Donovan, M. Man of the house
Porter, W. S. Jeff Peters as a personal
magnet
Porter, W. S. Makes the whole world kin
Porter, W. S. "Next to reading matter"

MEDUSA (LEGEND)
Moore, C. L. Shambleau

Meek, Sterner St Paul, 1894-
Dignity, a springer spaniel
Harper, W. comp. Dog show
Jerry
Harper, W. comp. Dog show

Meet the girls! Farrell, J. T.

Megelhoffer theory. Taylor, M.

Meigs, Cornelia Lynde, 1884-
Buffalo dance
Fenner, P. R. comp. Indians, Indians,
Indians
Ship's cat
Story parade (Periodical) Adventure
stories

Meihem in ce klasrum. Edwards, D.

Melancholy Dane. Runyon, D.

Melee of the Mages. Gallico, P. W.

Mellonta Tauta. Poe, E. A.

Melnick, Carol Renner
  Bend down, indeed!
    Wolfe, D. M. ed. Which grain will grow

Melville, Herman, 1819-1891
  Apple-tree table
    Melville, H. Selected writings
  Bartleby
    Melville, H. Selected writings
    Same as: Bartleby the scrivener
  'Bartleby the scrivener
    Ludwig, J. B. and Poirier, W. R. eds.
      Stories, British and American
    Melville, H. Selected tales and poems
    Same as: Bartleby
  The bell-tower
    Melville, H. Selected tales and poems
    Melville, H. Selected writings
  Benito Cereno
    Foerster, N. ed. American poetry and
      prose. 1952 ed.
    Gordon, C. and Tate, A. eds. House of
      fiction
    Melville, H. Selected tales and poems
    Melville, H. Selected writings
    Neider, C. ed. Short novels of the
      masters
    West, R. B. and Stallman, R. W. eds.
      Art of modern fiction
  Billy Budd, foretopman
    Burrell, J. A. and Cerf, B. A. eds. An-
      thology of famous American stories
    Melville, H. Selected tales and poems
    Melville, H. Selected writings
  Cock-a-doodle-doo!
    Melville, H. Selected writings
  The Encantadas; or, Enchanted Isles
    Melville, H. Selected tales and poems
    Melville, H. Selected writings
  The fiddler
    Melville, H. Selected tales and poems
    Melville, H. Selected writings
  Happy failure: A story of the River Hud-
    son
    Melville, H. Selected writings
  I and my chimney
    Melville, H. Selected tales and poems
    Melville, H. Selected writings
  Jimmy Rose
    Melville, H. Selected tales and poems
    Melville, H. Selected writings
  Lightning-rod man
    Melville, H. Selected tales and poems
    Melville, H. Selected writings
  Paradise of bachelors
    Melville, H. Selected tales and poems
    Melville, H. Selected writings
  The piazza
    Melville, H. Selected writings
    Neider, C. ed. Great short stories from
      the world's literature
  Poor man's pudding
    Melville, H. Selected writings
  Rich man's crumbs
    Melville, H. Selected writings
  The sermon
    Brentano, F. ed. The word lives on
  Story of Toby
    Melville, H. Selected writings

  Tartarus of maids
    Melville, H. Selected tales and poems
    Melville, H. Selected writings
  Temple first
    Melville, H. Selected writings
  Temple second
    Melville, H. Selected writings

The **memento.** Porter, W. S.

Memento. Thompson, T.

A **memoir.** Suckow, R.

Memoirs of a ghost. Stonier, G. W.

Memoirs of a yellow dog. Porter, W. S.

Memorandum. Caldwell, E.

Memorial Eve. Suckow, R.

Memorial synagogue. Goodman, P.

Memory. Waldo, E. H.

A **memory.** Welty, E.

Memory in white. Schulberg, B. W.

Memory machine. Dunsany, E. J. M. D. P.
  18th baron

Men against the stars. Wellman, M. W.

Men and babies. Prichard, R.

Men are different. Bloch, A.

Men at work. Greene, G.

Men from the boys. Wilson, E.

Men in the storm. Crane, S.

Men of the ten books. Kuttner, H.

Men running. Cozzens, J. G.

Men working. Beck, W.

Menachem-Mendel, fortune hunter. Rabinowitz, S.

Mendel and his wife. Farrell, J. T.

Mendel Hirsch. Feuchtwanger, L.

Mendel Marantz—genius. Freedman, D.

MENINGITIS
  Beachcroft, T. O. The eyes

MENNONITES
  Lincoln, V. E. Morning wishes

MENSERVANTS. See Servants—Menservants

MENTAL ILLNESS. See Insanity; Neurasthenia

MENTAL INSTITUTIONS. See Insane
  hospitals

Mentiplay, Cedric R.
  Mutiny below
    Argosy (Periodical) Argosy Book of
      sea stories

The **Mentocrats.** Newhouse, E.

Merchant of art. Brenner, L.

MERCHANTS
  Caudill, R. Fern Barrie's new plans
  Chekhov, A. P. Moscow hypocrites
  Kuttner, H. What you need
  Zangwill, I. Sabbath question in Sud-
    minster

Merchant's monument. Arico, V.

The **Mercurian.** Long, F. B.

MERCURY (PLANET)
  Elam, R. M. Sol's little brother
  Long, F. B. Cones
  Long, F. B. The Mercurian

La **Mère** Sauvage. Maupassant, G. de

Meredith, George, 1828-1909
Case of General Ople and Lady Camper
Connolly, C. ed. Great English short
novels
Punishment of Shahpesh, the Persian, on
Khipil, the builder
Cerf, B. A. and Moriarty, H. C. eds.
Anthology of famous British stories
Mérimée, Prosper, 1803-1870
Mateo Falcone
Shaw, H. and Bement, D. Reading the
short story
The **mermaids.** Gibran, K.
Merochnik, Minnie, 1887-
Autumn leaves
Merochnik, M. Celeste, & other stories
Celeste
Merochnik, M. Celeste, & other stories
Influence
Merochnik, M. Celeste, & other stories
Prohibition
Merochnik, M. Celeste, & other stories
A saga
Merochnik, M. Celeste, & other stories
Merrick, Leonard, 1864-1939
Doll in the pink silk dress
Cerf, B. A. and Moriarty, H. C. eds.
Anthology of famous British stories
Merrie gentleman. Price, E. B.
Merril, Judith, 1923-
Barrier of dread
Greenberg, M. ed. Journey to infinity
Daughters of earth
Petrified planet
So proudly we hail
Star science fiction stories [no. 1]
Survival ship
Heinlein, R. A. ed. Tomorrow, the stars
That only a mother
Pratt, F. ed. World of wonder
Merriman, Henry Seton, pseud. See Scott,
Hugh Stowell
Merrittsville. Suckow, R.
Merry clouters. Farrell, J. T.
MERRY-GO-ROUNDS
Weissenberg, I. M. Father and the boys
Merry men. Stevenson, R. L.
Merson, Ben
The cross-up
Dachs, D. ed. Treasury of sports humor
Merwin, Sam, 1910-
Exiled from earth
Crossen, K. F. ed. Adventures in to-
morrow
Exit line
Conklin, G. ed. Possible worlds of sci-
ence fiction
Judas ram
Galaxy science fiction magazine. Galaxy
reader of science fiction
Meschi, Edward
If we could see
Ford, N. A. and Faggett, H. L. eds.
Best short stories by Afro-American
writers (1925-1950)
Mesdames Grantly and Proudie get together.
Trollope, A.
Mesmeric revelation. Poe, E. A.
MESMERISM. See Hypnotism

Message for Harold. Ullman, V.
Message for Uncle Billy. Brick, J.
Message that failed. Heimann, M.
Message to the Camel Corps. Miller, W. H.
The **messenger.** Sitwell, Sir O. bart.
MESSENGERS
Porter, W. S. By courier
MESSIAH
Frug, S. S. Last kopeck
METAMORPHOSIS
Kafka, F. The metamorphosis
Keller, D. H. The bridle
Mrs White
Smith, C. A. Metamorphosis of earth
Thackeray, W. M. Sultan stork
Tucker, W. My brother's wife
See also Supernatural phenomena
Metamorphosis. Kafka, F.
Metamorphosis of earth. Smith, C. A.
Metamorphosite. Russell, E. F.
Metcalfe, John, 1891-
Childish thing
Story (Periodical) Story; no. 2
Meteor. Harris, J. B.
Meteor. Powers, W. T.
Metzengerstein. Poe, E. A.
Metzker, Isaac, 1901-
To the new world
Howe, I. and Greenberg, E. eds. Treas-
ury of Yiddish stories
Mevorach, Jacob, 1915-
Telescope and the umbrella
American vanguard, 1952
Mewhu's jet. Sturgeon, T.
The **Mexican.** London, J.
MEXICAN BORDER
Brandon, W. Chiltipiquin
Porter, W. S. Caballero's way
MEXICANS IN ITALY
Maugham, W. S. Hairless Mexican
MEXICANS IN THE UNITED STATES
Bradbury, R. I see you never
Gilbertson, M. G. Christmas in Carthage
Hemingway, E. Gambler, the nun, and
the radio
Summers, J. L. Boy in the mirror
MEXICAN INDIANS. See Indians of
Mexico
MEXICO
Roper, W. Last cigarette
19th century
Porter, W. S. Matter of mean elevation
20th century
Azuela, M. Under dogs
Brenner, L. An artist grows up in Mex-
ico; 7 stories
Dresser, D. Big shot
Gordon, E. E. Value of the dollar
Hinton, J. Mediators to the goatherd
La Farge, O. Old century's river
Porter, K. A. Flowering Judas
Porter, K. A. María Concepción
Porter, W. S. Dicky

MEXICO—*Continued*

Presidents

Caldwell, E. Day the presidential candidate came to Ciudad Tamaulipas

Ranch life

See Ranch life—Mexico

Vera Cruz

Maugham, W. S. The bum

Meyer, Conrad Ferdinand, 1825-1898
Plautus in the convent
Lange, V. ed. Great German short novels and stories

Meyer, Ernest Louis, 1892-1952
When the aliens left
Lass, A. H. and Horowitz, A. eds. Stories for youth

Meyn, Marjorie. See Vetter, Marjorie (Meyn)

Meyouhas, Joseph
Noah the Prophet
Selden, R. ed. Ways of God and men

The **mezzotint.** James, M. R.

Miami-New York. Gellhorn, M. E.

MICE
Brown, F. Mouse
Brown, F. Star mouse
Collier, J. Steel cat
Hoffmann, E. T. A. History of Krakatuk
Kafka, F. Josephine the singer
Munro, H. H. The mouse

Michael Shayne as I know him. Dresser, D.

Michaëlis, Karin, 1872-1950
Teacher Jensen
Lohan, R. and Lohan, M. eds. New Christmas treasury

Michel, Ellison
Moon tide
Strang, R. M. and Roberts, R. M. eds. Teen-age tales v 1

Michener, James Albert, 1907-
The fossickers
Michener, J. A. Return to Paradise
The good life
Michener, J. A. Return to Paradise
The jungle
Michener, J. A. Return to Paradise
Milk run
Jensen, P. ed. Fireside book of flying stories
Mr Morgan
Michener, J. A. Return to Paradise
Mynah birds
Michener, J. A. Return to Paradise
Povenaa's daughter
Michener, J. A. Return to Paradise
The story
Michener, J. A. Return to Paradise
Until they sail
Michener, J. A. Return to Paradise

MICHIGAN
Macauley, R. The wishbone

Mickey. Weeks, E.

Microscopic giants. Ernst, P.

MICROSCOPE AND MICROSCOPY
O'Brien, F.-J. Diamond lens

Midas on a goatskin. Anderson, D.

MIDDLE AGE
Fielding, E. Fountain of youth
Taylor, E. Idea of age
Thompson, L. Grasshopper a burden
Waltari, M. T. Tie from Paris

Middle drawer. Calisher, H.

Middle of the week after next. Jenkins, W. F.

MIDDLE WEST
Beck, W. No continuing city

Farm life

See Farm life—Middle West

MIDDLE WESTERN DIALECT. See Dialect stories—Middle West

Middle years. James, H.

Middleton, Richard Barham, 1882-1911
Shepherd's boy
Magazine of fantasy and science fiction. Best from Fantasy and science fiction; 3d ser.

MIDGETS. See Dwarfs

Midnight. James, W.

Midnight blue. Collier, J.

Midnight in the stable. Goudge, E.

Midnight Mike. Mayse, A.

Midsummer knight's dream. Porter, W. S.

Midsummer masquerade. Porter, W. S.

Midsummer passion. Caldwell, E.

Midwinter guest. Caldwell, E.

Miers, Earl Schenck, 1910-
Bandy
Miers, E. S. The kid who beat the Dodgers, and other sports stories
The big splash
Miers, E. S. The kid who beat the Dodgers, and other sports stories
Black Bat
Miers, E. S. The kid who beat the Dodgers, and other sports stories
Christmas skis
Miers, E. S. The kid who beat the Dodgers, and other sports stories
Ghost runner
Miers, E. S. The kid who beat the Dodgers, and other sports stories
He who laughs last
Miers, E. S. The kid who beat the Dodgers, and other sports stories
Jimmy rides the seal herd
Miers, E. S. The kid who beat the Dodgers, and other sports stories
The kid who beat the Dodgers
Miers, E. S. The kid who beat the Dodgers, and other sports stories
No heroes wanted
Miers, E. S. The kid who beat the Dodgers, and other sports stories
Scrub cure
Miers, E. S. The kid who beat the Dodgers, and other sports stories
Skeedunk special
Miers, E. S. The kid who beat the Dodgers, and other sports stories
Weary Willie
Miers, E. S. The kid who beat the Dodgers, and other sports stories

Miggles. Harte, B.

Might of motherhood. Gorky, M.

Milburn, George, 1906-
The apostate
Heilman, R. B. ed. Modern short stories
Student in economics
Lass, A. H. and Horowitz, A. eds.
Stories for youth
Wish book
Southern review. Anthology of stories
from the Southern review
Milchiger Synagogue and the blind preacher.
Kobrin, L.
Miles, Mary K.
Sand fort
Stanford short stories, 1953
Miley Bennett. Schaefer, J. W.
MILITARY DESERTION. See Desertion,
Military
MILITARY LIFE. See Soldiers; also sub-
division Army under various countries,
e.g. Great Britain—Army
MILITARY SERVICE, COMPULSORY
Coolidge, O. E. Judgment of the gods
Franzos, K. E. Saviour of the people
The **milk** pitcher. Brubaker, H.
Milk run. Michener, J. A.
MILL WORKERS. See Iron and steel in-
dustry
Millar, Bruce, 1925-
Chartered rowboat
American vanguard, 1952
Millar, Kenneth, 1915-
Find the woman
Mystery Writers of America, inc. Maid-
en murders
Wild goose chase
Queen, E. pseud. ed. Ellery Queen's
awards: 9th ser.
Millar, Margaret, 1915-
Couple next door
Queen, E. pseud. ed. Ellery Queen's
awards: 9th ser.
Millay, Edna St Vincent, 1892-1950
Murder in the Fishing Cat
Queen, E. pseud. ed. Literature of crime
The **millennium.** Parker, J. R.
Miller, Alice (Duer) 1874-1942
Plum pudding and mince pie
Lamb, L. ed. Family book of best loved
short stories
Miller, Arthur, 1915-
Monte Saint Angelo
Greene, J. I. and Abell, E. eds. Stories
of sudden truth
Prize stories of 1951
Ribalow, H. U. ed. These your children
Miller, Charlotte, 1917-
Westfield House
American vanguard, 1952
Miller, Clyde
Gentle season
Aswell, M. L. W. ed. New short novels
Miller, James Robbins, 1915-
Letters from Cairo
Collier's, the national weekly. Collier's
best
Miller, Jean (Dupont)
Somebody else, not me
American girl (Periodical) Favorite
stories

Miller, Mary Britton, 1883-
Ruth and Irma
Cory, D. W. pseud. comp. 21 variations
on a theme
Miller, Peter Schuyler, 1912-
Arrhenius horror
Miller, P. S. The Titan
As never was
Miller, P. S. The Titan
Forgotten
Miller, P. S. The Titan
Gleeps
Miller, P. S. The Titan
In the good old summer time
Miller, P. S. The Titan
Man from Mars
Margulies, L. and Friend, O. J. eds.
From off this world
Old Man Mulligan
Miller, P. S. The Titan
Spawn
Miller, P. S. The Titan
Status quondam
Healy, R. J. ed. New tales of space and
time
The Titan
Miller, P. S. The Titan
Trouble on Tantalus
Greenberg, M. ed. Travelers of space
Miller, Walter M. 1923-
Big hunger
Wollheim, D. A. ed. Prize science fic-
tion
Command performance
Best science-fiction stories: 1953
Galaxy science fiction magazine. Second
Galaxy reader of science fiction
Conditionally human
Year's best science fiction novels, 1953
Crucifixus Etiam
Best science-fiction stories: 1954
Dumb waiter
Conklin, G. ed. Science-fiction thinking
machines
Izzard and the membrane
Year's best science fiction novels, 1952
Little creeps
Lesser, M. A. ed. Looking forward
No moon for me
Sloane, W. M. ed. Space, space, space
Wolf pack
Merril, J. ed. Beyond the barriers of
space and time
Miller, Warren Hastings, 1876-
Message to the Camel Corps
American boy (Periodical) American
boy Adventure stories
MILLERS
Porter, W. S. Church with an overshot-
wheel
Stevenson, R. L. Will 'o the mill
Millie's big story. Coombs, C. I.
Millin, Sarah Gertrude (Liebson) 1889-
Why Adonis laughed
Leftwich, J. ed. Yisröel. 1952 ed.
MILLINERS
Bowen, E. Ann Lee's
MILLINERY. See Hats
Million-to-one chance. Vickers, R.
Million-year picnic. Bradbury, R.

MILLIONAIRES
  Porter, W. S. Brickdust row
Mills, Enos Abijah, 1870-1922
  My beaver pal
    American boy (Periodical) American
    boy anthology
Milly and the porker. Farrell, J. T.
Milne, Alan Alexander, 1882-1956
  The balcony
    Milne, A. A. Table near the band
  The barrister
    Blaustein, A. P. ed. Fiction goes to
    court
  Before the flood
  ' Milne, A. A. Table near the band
  Christmas party
    Milne, A. A. Table near the band
  Man greatly beloved
    Milne, A. A. Table near the band
  Murder at eleven
    Milne, A. A. Table near the band
  Nearly perfect
    Best detective stories of the year—1951
  Portrait of Lydia
    Milne, A. A. Table near the band
  Prettiest girl in the room
    Milne, A. A. Table near the band
  Rattling good yarn
    Milne, A. A. Table near the band
  Rise and fall of Mortimer Scrivens
    Milne, A. A. Table near the band
  The river
    Milne, A. A. Table near the band
  Table near the band
    Milne, A. A. Table near the band
  Three dreams of Mr Findlater
    Milne, A. A. Table near the band
  Wibberley touch
    Milne, A. A. Table near the band
Milton, Marjorie E.
  Favor granted
    Oberfirst, R. ed. 1952 anthology of best
    original short-shorts
Mimsy were the borogroves. Kuttner, H.
Mina de Vanghel. Beyle, M. H.
Mind and body. Williams, W. C.
MIND CURE. See Christian Science; Faith
    cure
MIND READING
  Anderson, E. V. Wildy's secret revealer
  Kornbluth, C. M. The mindworm
    See also Clairvoyance
The mindworm. Kornbluth, C. M.
Mine enemy's dog. Williams, B. A.
Miner, Harry
  Due process
    Queen, E. pseud. ed. Ellery Queen's
    awards: 9th ser.
Miner, Marilyn Stuart
  Baptist hymnal
    American vanguard, 1952
  Jocelyn
    American vanguard, 1950
MINERS. See Mines and mining
Miners' meetin'. Hendryx, J. B.
MINES AND MINING
  Frazee, S. Luck of Riley
  Harte, B. Left out on Lone Star Mountain
  Harte, B. Mrs Skaggs's husbands

Hebel, J. P. Unexpected reunion
  Sawyer, R. Deserted mine
  Swinbank, G. New hat
    See also Gold mines and mining;
    Mining towns; Silver mines and min-
    ing
The miniature. MacDonald, J. D.
MINIATURE RAILROADS. See Rail-
    roads—Models
Minimum sentence. Cogswell, T. R.
MINING TOWNS
  Browne, J. R. Peep at Washoe
  Gally, J. W. Hualapi
  Harte, B. M'liss
  Porter, W. S. Christmas by injunction
Minister without portfolio. Clingerman, M.
MINISTERS. See Clergy
Minister's black veil. Hawthorne, N.
"Ministers of Grace" Munro, H. H.
MINISTERS OF THE GOSPEL. See
    Clergy
Minority report. Waldo, E. H.
Min's God. Holtman, A.
M'Intosh, J. T. pseud. See Macgregor, James
    Murdoch
Minuet. Maupassant, G. de
Minuke. Kneale, N.
The Minyan. Klein, A.
The miracle. Auchincloss, L.
The miracle. Carrington, H. ed.
The miracle. O'Donovan, M.
Miracle at Eastpoint. Ramsay, J.
Miracle of Moon Crescent. Chesterton, G. K.
Miracle of Purun Bhagat. Kipling, R.
Miracle of Tepayac. Steinbeck, J.
Miracle of the farmer's wife. Fournier, A.
Miracle of the fifteen murderers. Hecht, B.
Miracle of the vineyard. Beauclerk,
    H. De V.
Miracle on the sea. Peretz, I. L.
MIRACLE PLAYS. See Mysteries and
    miracle plays
MIRACLES
  Cicellis, K. Miracles of the Saint
  Deledda, G. Two miracles
  France, A. Our Lady's juggler
  Komroff, M. What is a miracle?
  Steinbeck, J. Miracle of Tepayac
  Wells, H. G. Man who could work mir-
    acles
Miracles of the Saint. Cicellis, K.
Miracles still happen. Wright, F. F.
Mirage. Maugham, W. S.
Miriam's miracle. Forester, C. S.
Miró Ferrer, Gabriel, 1879-1930
  Herod Antipas
    Selden, R. ed. Ways of God and men
Mirror and Mr Sneeves. Gold, H.
Mirror of the magistrate. Chesterton, G. K.
Mirrored room. Rinehart, A.
MIRRORS
  Derleth, A. W. Sheraton mirror
  Pooler, J. Herself

MIRRORS, MAGIC
Howard, R. E. Mirrors of Tuzun Thune
Mirrors of Tuzun Thune. Howard, R. E.
Misbegotten missionary. Asimov, I.
MISCEGNATION. See Inter-racial marriage
The miser. O'Donovan, M.
La Miseria. Krige, U.
Miserly Emir. Ashkenazi, T.
MISERS
Dostoevskiĭ, F. M. Mr Prohartchin
Porter, W. S. Enchanted profile
Tunkel, J. Glass of tea
Verga, G. Property
Miser's gold. Queen, E. pseud.
Misfit. Heinlein, R. A.
Mishandled. Harvey, W. F.
The misogynist. Gunn, J. E.
MISREPRESENTATION. See Fraud
Miss Ber. Parker, J. R.
Miss Bertha and the Yankee. Collins, W.
Miss Darkness. Brown, F.
Miss Dulcie and the strange baby. Knox, J.
Miss Duveen. De La Mare, W. J.
Miss Emma Grisby. Knox, J.
Miss Haines and the gondolier. Sansom, W.
Miss Henrietta Briggs and her metamorphosis. Griffin, J. H.
Miss Hinch. Harrison, H. S.
Miss King. Maugham, W. S.
Miss Paisley's cat. Vickers, R.
Miss Parker possessed. Betts, D.
Miss Swallow. Van Doren, M.
Miss Whipple and the Creekers. Knox, J.
Miss Yellow Eyes. Grau, S. A.
Missed train. Blackburn, E. R.
Misses Grant. Winslow, T. S.
Missing. De La Mare, W. J.
MISSING CHILDREN. See Children, Lost
Missing chord. Porter, W. S.
Missing one's coach
Derleth, A. W. ed. Far boundaries
MISSING PERSONS. See Disappearances
Missing three-quarter. Doyle, Sir A. C.
Mission door. Blackburn, E. R.
Mission for baby. Drinkard, I. N.
Mission of Jane. Wharton, E. N. J.
Mission sermon. Walsh, M.
Mission to Massachusetts. Parker, J. R.
MISSIONARIES
Bradbury, R. Fire balloons
Landon, M. D. M. Reconciliation
Maugham, W. S. Rain
Maugham, W. S. Vessel of wrath
Steele, W. D. Man who saw through heaven
MISSIONARIES, MEDICAL
Groseclose, E. E. The healing of the lepers
Hobart, A. T. N. He sought to know God
Missis Flinders. Slesinger, T.

MISSISSIPPI
Faulkner, W. Monk
Faulkner, W. Tomorrow
Welty, E. Golden apples; 7 stories
Welty, E. Why I live at the P.O.
Natchez Trace
Welty, E. First love
Welty, E. Livvie
Welty, E. Old Mr Marblehall
Welty, E. Still moment
MISSOURI
Johnson, J. W. Mother's story
Wolfe, T. Lost boy
The mist. Cartur, P. pseud.
The mistake. Ketcham, P.
Mistake inside. Blish, J.
Mistake of the machine. Chesterton, G. K.
MISTAKEN IDENTITY. See Impersonations
Mr and Mrs Edgehill. Coward, N. P.
Mr Andrews. Forster, E. M.
Mr Arcularis. Aiken, C. P.
Mr Aristotle. Silone, I.
Mr Birnbaum's little joke. Yaffe, J.
Mr Bisbee's princess. Street, J. L.
Mr Brisher's treasure. Wells, H. G.
Mr Britling writes until sunrise. Wells, H. G.
Mr Caleb Westly and the stranger. Knox, J.
Mr Carmody's safari. Rolland, K.
Mister Conley. Van Loan, C. E.
Mr Costello, hero. Waldo, E. H.
Mr Dee and the middle-man. Doty, W. I.
Mr Dooley on athletics. Dunne, F. P.
Mr Feldman. Yaffe, J.
Mr George. Grendon, S.
Mr Glencannon and the ailing cockroach. Gilpatric, G.
Mr Gregg and the occult. Parker, J. R.
Mr Harrington's washing. Maugham, W. S.
Mr Hasbrouck. Van Doren, M.
Mr Higginbotham's catastrophe. Hawthorne, N.
Mr Huffam. Walpole, Sir H.
Mr Jonas. Green, H. pseud.
Mr Jones goes to Bethlehem. Ramsey, H. B.
Mr K*A*P*L*A*N the Magnificent. Rosten, L. C.
Mr Kincaid's pasts. Coupling, J. J. pseud.
Mr Know-All. Maugham, W. S.
Mr Lepel and the housekeeper. Collins, W.
Mr Loveday's little outing. Waugh, E.
Mr Lunkhead, the banker. Farrell, J. T.
Mr Mechano. Saroyan, W.
Mr Mitts. Bonner, N.
Mr Moody. Wicklein, J. F.
Mr Morgan. Michener, J. A.
Mr Murphy of New York. McMorrow, T.
Mr Oddy. Walpole, Sir H.
Mr Patricks' toy shop. Lewis, W.
Mr Policeman and the cook. Collins, W.

Mr Pomponius Ego out with the Handley Cross. Surtees, R. S.

Mr Prohartchin. Dostoevskiĭ, F. M.

Mr Rabbi. Sandoz, M. Y.

Mr Shawn and Father Scott. Betts, D.

Mr Sherlock Holmes. Doyle, Sir A. C.

Mr Sims and Henry. Carmer, C. L.

Mr Skae's item. Clemens, S. L.

Mr Slope vanquished. Trollope, A.

Mr Smith kicks the bucket. Brown, F.

Mr Sponge's first day with the Flat Hat Hunt. Surtees, R. S.

Mr Sponge's first day with the Hanby. Surtees, R. S.

Mr Strenberry's tale. Priestley, J. B.

Mr Sweeney. Butler, M.

Mr Timothy and the model. Brookhouser, F.

Mr Tutt collects a bet. Train, A.

Mistletoe. Irwin, M. E. F.

Mistral. Faulkner, W.

Mrs Benson. Haycox, E.

Mrs Carmody's store. McNulty, J.

Mrs Crocker's mutiny. Benchley, N.

Mrs Golightly and the first convention. Wilson, E.

Mrs Ketting and Clark Gable. Chidester, A.

Mrs Kochinsky and the problem child. Osborne, M. H.

Mrs Lancey. Van Doren, M.

Mrs Mancini. Kneale, N.

Mrs Mandford's drawing-room. Brophy, B.

Mrs Manifold. Grendon, S.

Mrs Oliver Cromwell. Irwin, M. E. F.

Mrs Packletide's tiger. Munro, H. H.

Mrs Proudie goes too far. Trollope, A.

Mrs Proudie intervenes. Trollope, A.

Mrs Proudie vanquished. Trollope, A.

Mrs Razor. Still, J.

Mrs Ripley's trip. Garland, H.

Mrs Rivkin grapples with the drama. Rosenberg, E. C.

Mrs Skaggs's husbands. Harte, B.

Mrs Union Station. Welch, D.

Mrs Veal. Defoe, D.

Mrs Vincent. Bates, H. E.

Mrs Vogel and Ollie. Suckow, R.

Mrs White
Horizon (Periodical) Golden Horizon

Mrs Wilson's husband goes for a swim. Winslow, T. S.

Mrs Windermere. Bowen, E.

A misunderstanding. Farrell, J. T.

Mitchell, John Ames, 1845-1918
Last American
Derleth, A. W. ed. Far boundaries

Mitchell, Joseph, 1908-
Professor Sea Gull
Waite, H. O. and Atkinson, B. P. eds. Literature for our time

"Some bum might mistook me for a wrestler"
Dachs, D. ed. Treasury of sports humor

Mitchell, William Ormond, 1914-
Saint Sammy
Pacey, D. ed. Book of Canadian stories

Mitchison, Naomi Margaret (Haldane) 1897-
Take back your bay wreath
Cory, D. W. pseud. comp. 21 variations on a theme

Mitzie who was young for her age. Strain, F. B.

M'liss. Harte, B.

Mlle de Scudéri. Hoffmann, E. T. A.

Mock governor. Shulman, M.

The mockbeggar. Kaye-Smith, S.

Model of a judge. Samachson, J.

MODEL RAILROADS. See Railroads—Models

Model shop. Jones, R. F.

Modell, Jack
Day in the sun
American vanguard, 1950

Modell, Merriam, 1908-
Biggest doll in the house
Story (Periodical) Story; no. 3

MODELS, FASHION
Collier, J. Special delivery

MODELS, FASHION (PERSONS)
Farrell, J. T. American dream girl
Maugham, W. S. Appearance and reality

Modern rural sports. Porter, W. S.

Modest proposal. Stafford, J.

Modus operandi. Gilbert, M. F.

Moffett, George, 1920-
Life's old sweet dream
Burnett, W. and Burnett, H. S. eds. Sextet

MOHAMMEDANS
Graham, R. B. C. Faith

Mohler, Charles, 1913-
Jesus complex
Burnett, W. and Burnett, H. S. eds. Sextet

Moll, Elick, 1903-
Boy who went away
Saturday evening post (Periodical) Saturday evening post stories, 1951

Moller, Ernestine Carey (Gilbreth) 1908-
See Gilbreth, F. B. jt. auth.

Mollie. Bonner, P. H.

Molly Cotton-Tail. Caldwell, E.

Molnár, Ferenc, 1878-1952
Hussar who loved three Jews
Ausubel, N. ed. Treasury of Jewish humor

Mom in the spring. Yaffe, J.

Mom knows best. Yaffe, J.

Mom makes a bet. Yaffe, J.

Moment of judgment. Hersey, J. R.

Moment of truth. O'Rourke, F.

Moment of truth. White, A.

Moment of victory. Porter, W. S.

Moment without time. Rogers, J. T.

Momma. Burns, J. H.

Mona Lisa. Lernet-Holenia, A. M.

MONACO
Monte Carlo
Maugham, W. S. Facts of life
Monarch of Park Barren. Roberts, Sir C. G. D.
Monarch the bum. Chamberlain, G. A.
MONASTERY LIFE. See Monasticism and religious orders
MONASTICISM AND RELIGIOUS ORDERS
Daudet, A. Father Gaucher's elixir
See also Monks
Monchek, Barbara, 1924?-
Big bed
American vanguard, 1950
Monday come home. Rice, J. A.
Monday is better than Sunday. Gordimer, N.
MONEY
Porter, W. S. Tale of a tainted tenner
Money. Jackson, C. R.
Money for jam. Guinness, A.
Money from the sky. Kelsey, A. G.
Money maze. Porter, W. S.
MONEY RAISING. See Fund raising
Money talks. Queen, E. pseud.
MONGOLIA
Vogau, B. A. Big heart
Monica's son. Augustine, Saint, Bp. of Hippo
Monig, Christopher
Love story
Crossen, K. F. ed. Future tense
Monk. Faulkner, W.
Monkey business at Gibraltar. Gilpatric, G.
Monkey spirit. Poston, M. L.
MONKEYS
Gilbert, K. Jungle brothers
Munro, H. H. Remoulding of Groby Lington
Monkey's paw. Jacobs, W. W.
MONKS
Daudet, A. Father Gaucher's elixir
Dinnis, E. M. The peacemaker
Dostoevskiĭ, F. M. Father Zossima's duel
France, A. Our Lady's juggler
Goudge, E. Canticle of the sun
Porter, W. S. Robe of peace
Monks revel at Winkton. Parker, J. R.
Monn, Albert
The award
Ford, N. A. and Faggett, H. L. eds. Best short stories by Afro-American writers (1925-1950)
Our country
Ford, N. A. and Faggett, H. L. eds. Best short stories by Afro-American writers (1925-1950)
MONOLOGS
Akutagawa, R. Kesa and Morito
Chekhov, A. P. On the harmful effects of tobacco; first version
Chekhov, A. P. On the harmful effects of tobacco; final version

Furman, L. Experience on the dress line
Lardner, R. W. Haircut
Wolfe, T. Only the dead know Brooklyn
Willingham, C. Eternal rectangle
MONOPOLIES
Neville, K. Franchise
Porter, W. S. Octopus marooned
Monroe, Lyle, pseud. See Heinlein, Robert Anson
Monsarrat, Nicholas, 1910-
Last days of M.G.B. 1087
Saturday evening post (Periodical) Saturday evening post stories, 1952
Monsieur Folantin. Huysmans, J. K.
Monsieur seeks a wife. Irwin, M. E. F.
M. Seguin's goat. Daudet, A.
The monster. Del Rey, L.
The monster. Van Vogt, A. E.
Monster of Blue-Hole Lake. Person, W. T.
MONSTERS
Anderson, P. The tinkler
Blackwood, A. The Wendigo
Bradbury, R. Beast from 20,000 fathoms
Bradbury, R. Fog horn
Broster, D. K. Crouching at the door
Del Rey, L. The monster
Doyle, Sir A. C. Horror of the heights
Ernst, P. Thing in the pond
Matheson, R. Born of man and woman
May, J. Dune roller
Merwin, S. Exit line
Peretz, I. L. The golem
Pratt, F. and Ruby, B. F. Thing in the woods
Van Vogt, A. E. Vault of the beast
Wright, W. Washoe behemoth
See also Giants
The monsters. Sheckley, R.
MONT BLANC
Frison-Roche, R. Their kingdom
See also Alps, French
Montague, Charles Edward, 1867-1928
Action
Cerf, B. A. and Moriarty, H. C. eds. Anthology of famous British stories
Greene, J. I. and Abell, E. eds. Stories of sudden truth
Talbot, D. ed. Treasury of mountaineering stories
Montague, Margaret Prescott, 1878-
England to America
Cooper, A. C. ed. Modern short stories
First-prize stories, 1919-1954
MONTANA
Annixter, P. pseud. Last lobo
Johnson, D. M. Beyond the frontier
Johnson, D. M. Prairie kid
Montanelli, Indro, 1909-
Hero returns
This week magazine. This week's short-short stories
MONTE CARLO. See Monaco—Monte Carlo
Monte Saint Angelo. Miller, A.
Monte Verità. Du Maurier D.

MONTEFIORE, SIR MOSES, 1784-1885
Rappoport, S. Moses Montefiore
Rappoport, S. Two great men
Sforim, M. M. How the Czar fooled
Montefiore
MONTEREY, CALIFORNIA. See California—Monterey
Montgomery the loyalest. Coblentz, C. C.
MONTREAL. See Canada—Montreal
Montross, Lois (Seyster) 1897-
Day in New York
Blodgett, H. W. ed. Story survey. 1953
ed.
Montross, Lynn, 1895-
Nine ladies vs. fate
Dachs, D. ed. Treasury of sports humor
Moodie, Sussannah (Strickland) 1803-1885
Old Woodruff and his three wives
Pacey, D. ed. Book of Canadian stories
Moody, Minnie (Hite) 1900-
Ghost of General Jackson
Jones, K. M. ed. New Confederate short
stories
MOON
Clarke, A. C. The sentinel
Del Rey, L. Wings of night
Elam, R. M. Lunar trap
Ernst, P. "Nothing happens on the moon"
Gallun, R. Z. Operation Pumice
Godwin, F. Man in the moon
Heinlein, R. A. Black pits of Luna
Heinlein, R. A. Columbus was a dope
Heinlein, R. A. Green hills of earth; 10
stories
Heinlein, R. A. Man who sold the moon
Kepler, J. Somnium
Miller, W. M. No moon for me
Norton, H. A. Man in the moon
Phillips, A. M. Death of the moon
Repton, H. From a private mad-house
Reynolds, M. Man in the moon
Robinson, F. M. Reluctant heroes
Van Vogt, A. E. Defense
Verne, J. Round the moon
See also Science fiction
Moon artist. Keller, D. H.
Moon-face. London, J.
Moon is green. Leiber, F.
Moon lake. Welty, E.
Moon magic. Brenner, L.
Moon of delirium. James, D. L.
Moon tide. Michel, E.
Moonlight. Maupassant, G. de
Moonlight sonata. Woollcott, A.
Moonlit road. Bierce, A.
Moonscape. Waltari, M. T.
MOONSHINING. See Distilling, Illicit
Moonwalk. Fyfe, H. B.
Moore, Catherine Lucile, 1911-
Black god's kiss
Moore, C. L. Shambleau, and others
Black god's shadow
Moore, C. L. Shambleau, and others
Black thirst
Moore, C. L. Shambleau, and others
The code
Moore, C. L. Judgment night

Heir apparent
Moore, C. L. Judgment night
Jirel meets magic
Moore, C. L. Shambleau, and others
Judgment night
Moore, C. L. Judgment night
No woman born
Jenkins, W. F. ed. Great stories of science fiction
Paradise Street
Moore, C. L. Judgment night
Promised land
Moore, C. L. Judgment night
Scarlet dream
Crossen, K. F. ed. Future tense
Moore, C. L. Shambleau, and others
Shambleau
Crossen, K. F. ed. Adventures in to-morrow
Moore, C. L. Shambleau, and others
There shall be darkness
Greenberg, M. ed. Journey to infinity
Tree of life
Moore, C. L. Shambleau, and others
See also Kuttner, H. jt. auth.
Moore, David E. 1923-
Portrait
American vanguard, 1953
Moore, George, 1852-1933
Clerk's quest
Cerf, B. A. and Moriarty, H. C. eds.
Anthology of famous British stories
Moore, George M.
Two for a ride
Oberfirst, R. ed. 1954 anthology of best
original short-shorts
Moore, Ina Skrifvars
Family man
Oberfirst, R. ed. 1952 anthology of best
original short-shorts
Moore, John P.
Beauty and the diamond ring
Ford, N. A. and Faggett, H. L. eds.
Best short stories by Afro-American
writers (1925-1950)
Moore, Manning, 1914-
Albert knows his place
Wolfe, D. M. ed. Which grain will grow
Moore, Ward, 1903-
Flying Dutchman
Crossen, K. F. ed. Adventures in to-morrow
Lot
Best science-fiction stories: 1954
Magazine of fantasy and science fiction.
Best from Fantasy and science fiction;
3d ser.
Peacebringer
Conklin, G. ed. Big book of science fiction
We the people
Crossen, K. F. ed. Future tense
MOOSE
Annixter, P. pseud. Kadiak
Roberts, Sir C. G. D. Calling of the lop-horned bull
Roberts, Sir C. G. D. Monarch of Park
Barren
Moose boy. Macfarlan, A. A.

Morand, Paul, 1888-
Catalonian night
Dupee, F. W. ed. Great French short novels

Moravia, Alberto, pseud. See Pincherle, Alberto

More, Sir Thomas, 1478-1535
Utopia
Derleth, A. W. ed. Beyond time & space

More alarms at night. Thurber, J.

More like sisters. Winslow, T. S.

More than skin deep. Pratt, F. and De Camp, L. S.

Moreau, Louis, 1914-
The face
Southern review. Anthology of stories from the Southern review

Morehouse, Kathleen (Moore)
With the fog
Blodgett, H. W. ed. Story survey. 1953 ed.

Morella. Poe, E. A.

MORGAN, JOHN HUNT, 1825-1864
West, J. Battle of Finney's Ford

Morland, Nigel, 1905-
Flowers for an angel
Mystery writer's of America, inc. Crooks' tour
Queen, E. pseud. ed. Queen's awards: 6th ser.

Morley, Christopher Darlington, 1890-
The arrow
Burrell, J. A. and Cerf, B. A. eds. Anthology of American stories
Home again
Brentano, F. ed. The word lives on

Morlvera. Munro, H. H.

Morning, a week before the crime. Lincoln, V. E.

Morning I went to buy the horseshoe. Knox, J.

Morning star. Carr, R. S.

Morning star. Gonzalez, N. V. M.

Morning sun. Deasy, M.

Morning wishes. Lincoln, V. E.

Moroso, John Antonio, 1874-
Tierney meets a millionaire
American boy (Periodical) American boy anthology

MORPHINE, OVERDOSE OF
Porter, W. S. At arms with Morpheus

Morrill, George P.
One for O'Brien
Argosy (Periodical) Argosy Book of sea stories

Morris, Gouverneur, 1876-1947
Back there in the grass
Pratt, F. ed. World of wonder

Morrison, Arthur, 1863-1947
That brute Simmons
Cerf, B. A. and Moriarty, H. C. eds. Anthology of famous British stories

Morrison, Jack, 1922-
Harvest
Stanford short stories, 1952
Patchouly
Stanford short stories, 1951

Morrison, William, pseud. See Samachson, Joseph

Morrison, William Shepherd
The Sack
Heinlein, R. A. ed. Tomorrow, the stars

Morriss, Mack
Courtesy of the road
Collier's, the national weekly. Collier's best

MORTGAGES
Graham, M. C. Face of the poor

Mortimer. Van Doren, M.

MOSCOW. See Russia—Moscow

MOSCOW. UNIVERSITY
Chekhov, A. P. Good news

Moscow hypocrites. Chekhov, A. P.

Moseley, Howard, 1921-
Blood is a bright shadow
American vanguard, 1950

MOSES
Coolidge, O. E. First-born
Frischman, D. Sinai
Hurston, Z. N. Escape from Pharaoh
Hurston, Z. N. The tablets of the law

Moses Montefiore. Rappoport, S.

Mosquitoes of Arkansas. Weeks, R.

Most dangerous man in the world. Dunsany, E. J. M. D. P. 18th baron

Most unusual season. Temple, W. H.

Motet for two voices. La Farge, C.

Mother. Farmer, P. J.

A mother. Hedenstjerna, A. von

The mother. McLaverty, M.

The mother. Maugham, W. S.

The mother. Wiechert, E.

Mother and daughter. Lawrence, D. H.

Mother and son. Darwick, R.

Mother and son. Maupassant, G. de

Mother Earth. Asimov, I.

Mother of Angela Hogan. Norris, K. T.

MOTHERS
Baro, G. Angry lions, lazy lions
Betts, D. Very old are beautiful
Edginton, H. M. Purple and fine linen
Fisher, D. F. C. As ye sow—
Freeman, M. E. W. Revolt of "Mother"
Fremantle, A. J. ed. Mothers; 18 stories
Hale, N. No one my grief can tell
Harte, B. Prosper's "Old mother"
Horwitz, J. Old woman
Jackson, C. R. Parting at morning
McLaverty, M. The mother
Maupassant, G. de. La Mère Sauvage
Rugel, M. The flower
Taylor, E. "Taking mother out"
Ungar, F. ed. To mother with love; 18 stories
Winslow, T. S. Grandma
Yaffe, J. Mom in the spring
See also Grandmothers; Mothers and daughters; Mothers and sons; Mothers-in-law

MOTHERS AND DAUGHTERS
Albrizio, G. The bereft

MOTHERS AND DAUGHTERS—*Cont.*
Auchincloss, L. Finish, good lady
Barker, A. L. Domini
Bowen, E. Coming home
Cable, G. W. Madame Delphine
Calisher, H. Middle drawer
De Meyer, J. Boy crazy
Johnson, J. W. Mother's story
Karmel, I. Fru Holm
La Farge, O. No, my darling daughter
McDowell, D. Good-by, Debbie
Reid, C. B. Yellow leaf
Stewart, R. The promise
Taber, G. B. Letter to the Dean
Verga, G. Home tragedy
Waugh, A. Wed, my darling daughter
Winslow, T. S. More like sisters

MOTHERS AND SONS
Auchincloss, L. Greg's peg
Barrie, Sir J. M. bart. Making of a minister
Beck, W. Verdict of innocence
Beer, T. Tact
Calisher, H. In Greenwich there are many gravelled walks
Callaghan, M. All the years of her life
Chidester, A. Mrs Ketting and Clark Gable
Cicellis, K. Twisted branch
Crane, S. George's mother
Darwick, R. Mother and son
De La Mare, W. J. Physic
Froscher, W. Death in the family
Gide, A. P. G. My mother
Gordimer, N. Umbilical cord
Hardy, T. Son's veto
Heathcott, M. Neil's girl
Keller, G. Regula Amrain and her youngest son
Lawrence, D. H. Lovely lady
Lull, R. No room in her heart
Maugham, W. S. The mother
Miller, A. D. Plum pudding and mince pie
O'Donovan, M. Man of the house
Taylor, E. Red-letter day
Ungar, F. ed. To mother with love; 18 stories
Watson, J. His mother's sermon
Waugh, E. Winner takes all
Wells, H. G. Little mother up the Mörderberg
Wright, J. E. Pay night
Wyckoff, J. The door between

Mother's Christmas present. Eggleston, M. W.

MOTHERS-IN-LAW
Harvey, W. F. Atmospherics
Horwitz, J. The visitor
O'Donovan, M. Sense of responsibility
Seager, A. Sacrament
Verga, G. She-wolf

Mother's letter. Balzac, H. de

Mother's meeting. Ready, W. B.

Mothers of the north. Roberts, Sir C. G. D.

Mother's story. Johnson, J. W.

Mother's tale. Agee, J.

MOTHS
Kantor, M. Yea, he did fly

Moti Guj—mutineer. Kipling, R.

Motion of forgetfulness is slow. Eaton, C. E.

MOTION PICTURE ACTRESSES. See Moving picture actors and actresses

MOTION PICTURES. See Moving pictures

Motive goes round and round. Brown, F.

MOTOR BOATS. See Motorboats

MOTOR BUSES
Asch, N. Inland, western sea
Forster, E. M. Celestial omnibus
Gill, B. Night bus to Atlanta
Porter, L. S. Spendthrifts
Sandoz, M. Lost school bus
Spilo, R. Big Ed

MOTOR CARS. See Automobiles

MOTOR CYCLES. See Motorcycles

MOTORBOATS
Douglas, J. S. Water broncs
Sherman, H. M. Porky, the outboarder
Vetter, M. M. Captain Kit
See also Boats and boating

MOTORCYCLES
Aiken, C. P. Pair of Vikings
Jackson, R. B. Fly away home
Rooney, F. Cyclists' raid

Mott, Frank Luther, 1886-
Phantom flivver
Saturday evening post (Periodical)
Saturday evening post stories, 1950

MOUNT EVEREST. See Everest, Mount

The mountain. Ervine, St J. G.

MOUNTAIN CLIMBING. See Mountaineering

MOUNTAIN GOATS. See Rocky Mountain goats

MOUNTAIN LIONS. See Pumas

Mountain madness. Hopkinson, H. T.

Mountain summer. Ballard, J. C.

Mountain victory. Faulkner, W.

MOUNTAIN WHITES (SOUTHERN STATES)
Blackburn, E. R. Missed train
Connell, E. S. I came from yonder mountain
Fox, J. Knight of the Cumberland
Harris, G. W. Sut Lovingood; 8 stories
Morehouse, K. M. With the fog
Porter, W. S. Blackjack bargainer
Porter, W. S. Whirligig of life
Smith, E. V. Prelude
Still, J. Job's tears
Still, J. Master time
Strong, P. N. Man on Stormrift Mountain
Stuart, J. Clearing in the sky & other stories; 21 stories
See also Dialect stories—Mountain Whites (Southern States)

The mountaineer. Tucker, W.

MOUNTAINEERING
Du Maurier, D. Monte Verità
Kaplan, A. H. Danger wears two faces
Lavender, D. S. High victory
Montague, C. E. Action
Talbot, D. ed. Treasury of mountaineering stories; 19 stories

MOUNTAINEERING—*Continued*
Ullman, J. R. Deadly north face
Ullman, J. R. Easy day for a lady
Ullman, J. R. Mountains of the Axis
MOUNTAINS
Roberts, Sir C. G. D. Ledge on Bald Face
Mountains of the Axis. Ullman, J. R.
MOUNTED POLICE, CANADIAN. See Canada. Royal Canadian Mounted Police
Mourning for Ianto. Davies, R.
MOUSE. See Mice
Mouse. Brown, F.
The mouse. Hauser, M.
The mouse. Munro, H. H.
The mouse. O'Flaherty, L.
The movers. Horwitz, J.
MOVIE ACTRESSES. See Moving picture actors and actresses
Movies come to Gull Point. Bird, W. R.
MOVING (HOUSEHOLD GOODS)
Horwitz, J. The burial
Taylor, P. H. Dark walk
Moving finger. Wharton, E. N. J.
MOVING PICTURE ACTORS AND ACTRESSES
Brand, M. pseud. The king
Coward, N. P. A richer dust
Fitzgerald, F. S. K. Magnetism
Schweitzer, G. Because she was like me
Winslow, T. S. Interview
See also Actors; Actresses
MOVING PICTURE INDUSTRY. See Moving pictures
MOVING PICTURE PRODUCERS
Brand, M. pseud. The king
Collier, J. Cancel all I said
Schulberg, B. W. Table at Ciro's
MOVING PICTURE THEATERS
Beck, W. Men working
MOVING PICTURES
Bradbury, R. The meadow
Collier, J. Gavin O Leary
Collier, J. Pictures in the fire
De Vries, P. Scene
Elliott, B. Battle of the S . . . S
Fitzgerald, F. S. K. Crazy Sunday
Fitzgerald, F. S. K. Pat Hobby himself: a patriotic short
Fitzgerald, F. S. K. Pat Hobby himself: two old-timers
Schulberg, B. W. Face of Hollywood
Schulberg, B. W. Legend that walks like a man
Seager, A. Old man of the mountain
Sherred, T. L. E for effort
Van Vogt, A. E. Film library
Waugh, E. Excursion in reality
Willingham, C. Surface tension of molten metal

Mowat, Farley, 1920?-
Blinding of André Maloche
Saturday evening post (Periodical) Saturday evening post stories, 1952
Lost in the barren lands
Saturday evening post (Periodical) Saturday evening post stories, 1951

Woman he left to die
Saturday evening post (Periodical) Saturday evening post stories, 1953
Mowery, William Byron, 1899-
Black Lamars
Mowery, W. B. Tales of the Ozarks
Constable of Lone Sioux
Mowery, W. B. Sagas of the Mounted Police
Corporal Nat
Mowery, W. B. Sagas of the Mounted Police
Fluted arrow
Mowery, W. B. Tales of the Ozarks
Ghost of Gillin Run
Mowery, W. B. Tales of the Ozarks
Haunted hollow
Mowery, W. B. Tales of the Ozarks
Lamb and some slaughtering
Mowery, W. B. Sagas of the Mounted Police
Long shadow
Mowery, W. B. Sagas of the Mounted Police
Man-killer
Mystery Writers of America, inc. Butcher, baker, murder-maker
Mannikin talk
Mowery, W. B. Sagas of the Mounted Police
Outlaw trail
Mowery, W. B. Tales of the Ozarks
Relic of the Vikings
Mowery, W. B. Sagas of the Mounted Police
Rube and the racketeer
Mowery, W. B. Tales of the Ozarks
St Gabriel Zsbyski
Mowery, W. B. Sagas of the Mounted Police
Scalawag pup
Mowery, W. B. Tales of the Ozarks
The scout
Mowery, W. B. Sagas of the Mounted Police
'Seng hunter
Mowery, W. B. Tales of the Ozarks
Smoke tree
Mowery, W. B. Tales of the Ozarks
Mowgli's brothers. Kipling, R.
MOWING MACHINES
Hamsun, K. Wonderful new machine
Moxon's master. Bierce, A.
Mrrrar! Pangborn, E.
Mudford, William, 1782-1848
Iron shroud
Cerf, B. A. and Moriarty, H. C. eds. Anthology of famous British stories
Mugger murder. Deming, R.
MUHAMMEDANS. See Mohammedans
Muheim, Harry
Big grey picnic
Stanford short stories, 1950
Dusty drawer
Best detective stories of the year—1953
Muir, Jean
Pirate rat
Fenner, P. H. comp. Pirates, pirates, pirates

Muir, John, 1838-1914
Adventure with a dog
Bloch, M. ed. Favorite dog stories
An adventure with a dog and a glacier
Andrews, R. C. ed. My favorite stories
of the great outdoors

Mujina. Hearn, L.

Mukerji, Dhan Gopal, 1890-1936
Elephant adventure
Fenner, P. R. comp. Elephants, ele-
phants, elephants
Kari the elephant
Fenner, P. R. comp. Elephants, ele-
phants, elephants

Mulatto flair. Spencer, G.

MULATTOES
Cable, G. W. Madame Delphine

Mule in the yard. Faulkner, W.

Mule tracks. Newton, D. B.

MULES. See Asses and mules

Mulhoffer, Dorothy Barrie
Last year
Hathaway, B. and Sessions, J. A. eds.
Writers for tomorrow. 2d ser.

Muller, Charles G.
Hat trick
Herzberg, M. J. comp. Treasure chest
of sport stories
Owen, F. ed. Teen-age winter sports
stories

Müller with an umlaut. McNulty, J.

Mummery, Albert Frederick, 1855-1895
The Matterhorn
Talbot, D. ed. Treasury of mountaineer-
ing stories

MUMMIES
Brod, M. Death is a passing weakness

Mummy to the rescue. Wilson, A.

Munby, Alan Noel Latimer
Alabaster hand
Munby, A. N. L. Alabaster hand, and
other ghost stories
Christmas game
Munby, A. N. L. Alabaster hand, and
other ghost stories
Devil's autograph
Munby, A. N. L. Alabaster hand, and
other ghost stories
Encounter in the mist
Munby, A. N. L. Alabaster hand, and
other ghost stories
Four-poster
Munby, A. N. L. Alabaster hand, and
other ghost stories
Herodes redivivus
Munby, A. N. L. Alabaster hand, and
other ghost stories
The inscription
Munby, A. N. L. Alabaster hand, and
other ghost stories
The lectern
Munby, A. N. L. Alabaster hand, and
other ghost stories
Negro's head
Munby, A. N. L. Alabaster hand, and
other ghost stories
Number seventy-nine
Munby, A. N. L. Alabaster hand, and
other ghost stories

Topley Place sale
Munby, A. N. L. Alabaster hand, and
other ghost stories
Tregannet book of hours
Munby, A. N. L. Alabaster hand, and
other ghost stories
Tudor chimney
Munby, A. N. L. Alabaster hand, and
other ghost stories
White sack
Munby, A. N. L. Alabaster hand, and
other ghost stories

MUNCHAUSEN
Adventure. See Martin, J. Adventure of
Baron Munchausen

MUNICIPAL EMPLOYEES. See Civil
service

Municipal report. Porter, W. S.

MUNICIPALITIES. See Cities and towns

Munie the bird dealer. Kilbak, M.

Munro, Hector Hugh, 1870-1916
Achievement of the cat
Munro, H. H. Short stories of Saki
Adrian
Munro, H. H. Short stories of Saki
The background
Munro, H. H. Short stories of Saki
The bag
Munro, H. H. Short stories of Saki
Bertie's Christmas Eve
Munro, H. H. Short stories of Saki
Birds on the western front
Munro, H. H. Short stories of Saki
Blind spot
Munro, H. H. Short stories of Saki
Blood-feud of Toad-Water
Munro, H. H. Short stories of Saki
Boar-pig
Munro, H. H. Short stories of Saki
Bread and Butter miss
Munro, H. H. Short stories of Saki
The Brogue
Munro, H. H. Short stories of Saki
The bull
Munro, H. H. Short stories of Saki
Byzantine omelette
Munro, H. H. Short stories of Saki
Canossa
Munro, H. H. Short stories of Saki
The Chaplet
Munro, H. H. Short stories of Saki
Clovis on parental responsibilities
Munro, H. H. Short stories of Saki
Clovis on the alleged romance of business
Munro, H. H. Short stories of Saki
The cobweb
Munro, H. H. Short stories of Saki
Comments of Moung Ka
Munro, H. H. Short stories of Saki
Cousin Teresa
Munro, H. H. Short stories of Saki
Cross currents
Munro, H. H. Short stories of Saki
Cupboard of the yesterdays
Munro, H. H. Short stories of Saki
Defensive diamond
Munro, H. H. Short stories of Saki
Disappearance of Crispina Umberleigh
Munro, H. H. Short stories of Saki
"Down pens"
Munro, H. H. Short stories of Saki
The dreamer
Munro, H. H. Short stories of Saki

Munro, Hector H.—*Continued*

Dusk
  Munro, H. H. Short stories of Saki
Easter egg
  Munro, H. H. Short stories of Saki
The elk
  Munro, H. H. Short stories of Saki
Esmé
  Munro, H. H. Short stories of Saki
Excepting Mrs Pentherby
  Munro, H. H. Short stories of Saki
Fate
  Munro, H. H. Short stories of Saki
Feast of Nemesis
  Munro, H. H. Short stories of Saki
Filboid Studge, the story of a mouse that
    helped
  Munro, H. H. Short stories of Saki
For the duration of the war
  Munro, H. H. Short stories of Saki
Forbidden buzzards
  Munro, H. H. Short stories of Saki
Forewarned
  Munro, H. H. Short stories of Saki
Fur
  Munro, H. H. Short stories of Saki
Gabriel-Ernest
  Conklin, G. and Conklin, L. T. eds.
    Supernatural reader
  Munro, H. H. Short stories of Saki
Gala programme
  Munro, H. H. Short stories of Saki
The guests
  Munro, H. H. Short stories of Saki
The hedgehog
  Munro, H. H. Short stories of Saki
The hen
  Munro, H. H. Short stories of Saki
Hermann the Irascible—A story of the
    Great Weep
  Munro, H. H. Short stories of Saki
Holiday task
  Munro, H. H. Short stories of Saki
Hounds of Fate
  Munro, H. H. Short stories of Saki
Hyacinth
  Munro, H. H. Short stories of Saki
Image of the Lost Soul
  Munro, H. H. Short stories of Saki
Infernal Parliament
  Munro, H. H. Short stories of Saki
Innocence of Reginald
  Munro, H. H. Short stories of Saki
The interlopers
  Munro, H. H. Short stories of Saki
Jesting of Arlington Stringham
  Munro, H. H. Short stories of Saki
Judkin of the parcels
  Munro, H. H. Short stories of Saki
Laura
  Munro, H. H. Short stories of Saki
Lost sanjak
  Munro, H. H. Short stories of Saki
Louis
  Munro, H. H. Short stories of Saki
Louise
  Munro, H. H. Short stories of Saki
The lull
  Munro, H. H. Short stories of Saki
Lumber-room
  Munro, H. H. Short stories of Saki
Mapped life
  Munro, H. H. Short stories of Saki

Mark
  Munro, H. H. Short stories of Saki
Match-maker
  Munro, H. H. Short stories of Saki
Matter of sentiment
  Munro, H. H. Short stories of Saki
"Ministers of Grace"
  Munro, H. H. Short stories of Saki
Mrs Packletides tiger
  Blodgett, H. W. ed. Story survey. 1953
    ed.
  Cerf, B. A. and Moriarty, H. C. eds.
    Anthology of famous British stories
  Dachs, D. ed. Treasury of sports humor
  Munro, H. H. Short stories of Saki
Morlvera
  Munro, H. H. Short stories of Saki
The mouse
  Munro, H. H. Short stories of Saki
Music on the hill
  Munro, H. H. Short stories of Saki
Name-day
  Munro, H. H. Short stories of Saki
Occasional garden
  Munro, H. H. Short stories of Saki
Old town of Pskoff
  Munro, H. H. Short stories of Saki
On approval
  Munro, H. H. Short stories of Saki
Open window
  Bogorad, S. N. and Trevithick, J. eds.
    College miscellany
  Carrington, H. ed. Week-end book of
    ghost stories
  Christ, H. I. and Shostak, J. eds. Short
    stories
  Davenport, B. ed. Tales to be told in
    the dark
  Munro, H. H. Short stories of Saki
  Shaw, H. and Bement, D. Reading the
    short story
The oversight
  Munro, H. H. Short stories of Saki
Peace of Mowsle Barton
  Munro, H. H. Short stories of Saki
Peace offering
  Munro, H. H. Short stories of Saki
The penance
  Munro, H. H. Short stories of Saki
Phantom luncheon
  Munro, H. H. Short stories of Saki
Philanthropist and the happy cat
  Munro, H. H. Short stories of Saki
Purple of the Balkan Kings
  Munro, H. H. Short stories of Saki
Quail seed
  Munro, H. H. Short stories of Saki
The quest
  Munro, H. H. Short stories of Saki
Quince tree
  Munro, H. H. Short stories of Saki
The Recessional
  Munro, H. H. Short stories of Saki
Reginald
  Munro, H. H. Short stories of Saki
Reginald at the Carlton
  Munro, H. H. Short stories of Saki
Reginald at the theatre
  Munro, H. H. Short stories of Saki
Reginald in Russia
  Munro, H. H. Short stories of Saki
Reginald on besetting sins
  Munro, H. H. Short stories of Saki

Munro, Hector H.—*Continued*
  Reginald on Christmas presents
    Munro, H. H. Short stories of Saki
  Reginald on house-parties
    Munro, H. H. Short stories of Saki
  Reginald on tariffs
    Munro, H. H. Short stories of Saki
  Reginald on the Academy
    Munro, H. H. Short stories of Saki
  Reginald on worries
    Munro, H. H. Short stories of Saki
  Reginald's choir treat
    Munro, H. H. Short stories of Saki
  Reginald's Christmas revel
    Munro, H. H. Short stories of Saki
  Reginald's drama
    Munro, H. H. Short stories of Saki
  Reginald's peace poem
    Munro, H. H. Short stories of Saki
  Reginald's Rubaiyat
    Munro, H. H. Short stories of Saki
  Remoulding of Groby Lington
    Munro, H. H. Short stories of Saki
  Reticence of Lady Anne
    Munro, H. H. Short stories of Saki
  The romancers
    Munro, H. H. Short stories of Saki
  Saint and the Goblin
    Munro, H. H. Short stories of Saki
  Schartz-Metterklume method
    Munro, H. H. Short stories of Saki
  Secret sin of Septimus Brope
    Munro, H. H. Short stories of Saki
  Seven cream jugs
    Munro, H. H. Short stories of Saki
  Seventh pullet
    Munro, H. H. Short stories of Saki
  Sex that doesn't shop
    Munro, H. H. Short stories of Saki
  She-wolf
    Munro, H. H. Short stories of Saki
  The sheep
    Munro, H. H. Short stories of Saki
  Shock tactics
    Munro, H. H. Short stories of Saki
  Soul of Laploshka
    Munro, H. H. Short stories of Saki
  Square egg
    Munro, H. H. Short stories of Saki
  Sredni Vashtar
    Davenport, B. ed. Tales to be told in the dark
    Munro, H. H. Short stories of Saki
  The stake
    Munro, H. H. Short stories of Saki
  Stalled ox
    Munro, H. H. Short stories of Saki
  Stampeding of Lady Bastable
    Munro, H. H. Short stories of Saki
  Story of St Vespaluus
    Munro, H. H. Short stories of Saki
  Story-teller
    Munro, H. H. Short stories of Saki
    Schramm, W. L. ed. Great short stories
  The strategist
    Munro, H. H. Short stories of Saki
  Talking-out of Tarrington
    Munro, H. H. Short stories of Saki
  Tea
    Munro, H. H. Short stories of Saki
  The threat
    Munro, H. H. Short stories of Saki
  Tobermory
    Munro, H. H. Short stories of Saki
  Touch of realism
    Munro, H. H. Short stories of Saki
  Toys of peace
    Munro, H. H. Short stories of Saki
  Treasure-ship
    Munro, H. H. Short stories of Saki
  Unkindest blow
    Munro, H. H. Short stories of Saki
  Unrest-cure
    Munro, H. H. Short stories of Saki
  Way to the dairy
    Munro, H. H. Short stories of Saki
  Wolves of Cernogratz
    Munro, H. H. Short stories of Saki
  Wratislav
    Munro, H. H. Short stories of Saki
  Yarkand manner
    Munro, H. H. Short stories of Saki
  Young Turkish catastrophe
    Munro, H. H. Short stories of Saki
MURALS. See Paintings
The **murder.** Steinbeck, J.
Murder and the south wind. Rinehart, M. R.
Murder at City Hall. Carr, A. H. Z.
Murder at eleven. Milne, A. A.
Murder for two. Kirch, J. A.
Murder in the Fishing Cat. Millay, E. St V.
MURDER STORIES
  Akutagawa, R. In a grove
  Bergengruen, W. Concerning muskets
  Blish, J. Beanstalk
  Bradbury, R. Fruit at the bottom of the bowl
  Brown, F. Voice behind him
  Buckingham, N. Snake-eyes!!
  Burke, T. Hands of Mr Ottermole
  Clark, A. A. G. Amazing lady
  Clemens, S. L. Latest sensation (II)
  Cobb, I. S. Occurrence up a side street
  Cockburn, C. Total recall
  Collier, J. Another American tragedy
  Collier, J. Back for Christmas
  Collier, J. Midnight blue
  Collier, J. Touch of nutmeg makes it
  Collier, J. Wet Saturday
  Connelly, M. C. Coroner's inquest
  Dahl, R. Lamb to the slaughter
  De La Mare, W. J. Ideal craftsman
  De La Mare, W. J. Missing
  Dickens, C. Captain Murderer
  Ekbergh, I. D. Pink Ballerina
  Ellin, S. Orderly world of Mr Appleby
  Faulkner, W. Hand upon the waters
  Faulkner, W. The hound
  Faulkner, W. Tomorrow
  Forester, C. S. Bower of roses
  Gilmour, W. Danny Hagan's blind spot
  Glaspell, S. Jury of her peers
  Gordon, A. Alchemist's secret
  Goyen, W. White rooster
  Grau, S. A. Way of a man
  Hall, J. B. Estate and trespass
  Harvey, W. F. Vicar's web
  Hauptmann, G. J. R. Flagman Thiel
  Hawthorne, N. Mr Higginbotham's catastrophe
  Hergesheimer, J. Wild oranges
  Hume, S. T. Shake hands with a murderer
  Huxley, A. L. Gioconda smile

MURDER STORIES—*Continued*
 Johnston, N. F. Absolution
 Kafka, F. A fratricide
 Keene, D. Homicide House
 Kirch, J. A. Murder for two
 Klingsberg, H. M. Doowinkle, Attorney
 La Farge, O. The bystander
 Lagerlöf, S. O. L. The outlaws
 London, J. Make westing
 London, J. Moon-face
 Lord, J. The avenging
 Maugham, W. S. Before the party
 Maugham, W. S. Footprints in the jungle
 Maugham, W. S. Four Dutchmen
 Maugham, W. S. Happy couple
 Maugham, W. S. The letter
 Maugham, W. S. Man with a conscience
 Maugham, W. S. The mother
 Maugham, W. S. Official position
 Mystery Writers of America, inc. 20 great tales of murder; 19 stories
 O'Brien, F.-J. Diamond lens
 Poe, E. A. Cask of Amontillado
 Poe, E. A. Domain of Arnheim
 Poe, E. A. Imp of the perverse
 Poe, E. A. Tell-tale heart
 Porter, K. A. María Concepción
 Porter, W. S. Transformation of Martin Burney
 Porter, W. S. World and the door
 Post, M. D. Corpus delicti
 Queen, E. pseud. Driver's seat
 Queen, E. pseud. ed. Literature of crime; 26 stories
 Rinehart, A. Mirrored room
 Rinehart, M. R. The scandal
 Rowland, S. McGregor affair
 Sansom, W. One sunny afternoon
 Sansom, W. Various temptations
 Stevenson, R. L. Body-snatcher
 Stevenson, R. L. Markheim
 Turner, R. The gunny
 Van Doren, M. Roberts and O'Hara
 Verga, G. Mystery play
 Vickers, R. Little things like that
 Vickers, R. Man with the sneer
 Vickers, R. Million-to-one chance
 Welty, E. Flowers for Marjorie
 Wharton, E. N. J. A bottle of Perrier
 Winslow, T. S. Bronzes of Martel Greer
 Zola, E. Julien
  See also Crime and criminals; Mystery and detective stories
Murder tavern. Bloomfield, H.
Murder the bum! Fay, W.
MURDER TRIALS. See Trials
Murder without clues. Queen, E. pseud.
The **murderer**. Bradbury, R.
MURDERERS. *See* Crime and criminals; Murder stories; Mystery and detective stories
Murderer's luck. Clark, A. A. G.
Murders in the Rue Morgue. Poe, E. A.
Murdock, Richard M.
 Stop, look, listen
  Oberfirst, R. ed. 1952 anthology of best original short-shorts
Murphy, Alicia
 Portrait of a lady
  Thinker's digest (Periodical) Spoiled priest, and other stories

Murphy, Bud, 1920-
 Palomino
  Dennis, W. ed. Palomino and other horses
Murphy, Robert, 1902-
 You've got to learn
  Hazeltine, A. I. comp. Selected stories for teen-agers
Murrie, Pauline
 New beau
  Oberfirst, R. ed. 1954 anthology of best original short-shorts
Murtagh, Leo Dillon
 Hills of Donegal
  Story (Periodical) Story; no. 3
Museum piece. Carlson, E.
Musgrave ritual. Doyle, Sir A. C.
Mushrooms in Bronx Park. Gold, M.
MUSIC
 Gregutt, H. C. Jam session at Abby's
 Munro, H. H. The Chaplet
 Payne, L. V. Prelude
MUSIC, POPULAR (SONGS, ETC.)
  Writing and publishing
 Munro, H. H. Secret sin of Septimus Brope
The **music**. Waldo, E. H.
Music from Spain. Welty, E.
MUSIC HALLS (VARIETY THEATERS, CABARETS, ETC.)
 Brookhouser, F. She made the big town
 Munro, H. H. Cousin Teresa
Music lesson. Adamson, R.
Music on the hill. Munro, H. H.
MUSIC TEACHERS
 Adamson, R. Music lesson
 Babel', I. E. The awakening
 Gatty, L. Did he touch you?
 Gordimer, N. Commonplace story
 Guest, A. Barbèd rose
 McCullers, C. S. Madame Zilensky and the King of Finland
MUSICIANS
 Hardy, T. Absent-mindedness in a parish choir
 Wechsberg, J. New York is full of girls
 Welty, E. Powerhouse
  Composers
 Lardner, R. W. Some like them cold
 Paget, V. Wicked voice
 Platt, G. She shall have music
 Richter, C. Sinister journey
  Coronet players
 Foote, S. Ride out
 Saroyan, W. Cornet players
  Flute players
 Galsworthy, J. Ultima Thule
 Zola, É. Julien
  Harpists
 Whinery, M. First harpist
  Organists
 Van Paassen, P. Uncle Kees protests
  Pianists
 Davis, S. P. Christmas carol
 McCullers, C. S. Wunderkind
 Maugham, W. S. Alien corn

MUSICIANS—Pianists—*Continued*
　Pain, B. E. O. The doll
　Porter, W. S. Service of love
　Williams, T. Resemblance between a violin case and a coffin

Singers

　Eichelberger, R. K. On Christmas Eve
　Heimann, M. Message that failed
　MacMahon, B. Sing, Milo, sing
　Mansfield, K. Pictures
　Maugham, W. S. Voice of the turtle
　Paget, V. Wicked voice
　Porter, W. S. Matter of mean elevation
　See also Cantors

Trumpeters

　Davies, R. Boy with a trumpet

Violinists

　Burnett, W. Suffer the children
　Day, C. S. Noblest instrument
　Melville, H. The fiddler
　Williams, T. Resemblance between a violin case and a coffin
Mustang trail to glory. Loomis, N. M.
MUSTANGS. See Horses
Mutation. Carr, R. S.
MUTATION (BIOLOGY) See Evolution
Mute question. Ackerman, F. J.
Muten. Russell, E. F.
Mutineers be hanged. Hinternhoff, J. F.
MUTINY
　Bedford-Jones, H. Thirteen men
　Hinternhoff, J. F. Mutineers be hanged
　Jameson, M. White mutiny
　Melville, H. Benito Cereno
　Melville, H. Billy Budd, foretopman
　Nordhoff, C. B. and Hall, J. N. The mutiny
The mutiny. Nordhoff, C. B. and Hall, J. N.
Mutiny below. Mentiplay, C. R.
Mutt: the mongrel who knew no fear. Little, G. W.
Mutual superiority. Chekhov, A. P.
My Aunt Celia. Fischer, B.
My autumn courtship. Caldwell, E.
My beaver pal. Mills, E. A.
My bloody massacre (I) Clemens, S. L.
My boy, my boy. Li, G.-Y.
My brother down there. Frazee, S.
My brother Eliyahu's drink. Rabinowitz, S.
My brother who talked with horses. Thompson, M.
My brother's keeper. Pratt, F. and De Camp, L. S.
My brother's second funeral. Newhouse, E.
My brother's wife. Tucker, W.
My Christmas carol. Schulberg, B. W.
My cousin Dikran, the orator. Saroyan, W.
My da. O'Donovan, M.
My disciple. Lewis, W.
My double, and how he undid me. Hale, E. E.
My father and the circus. Brookhouser, F.
My father doesn't like me. Scott, W. R.
My fellow traveller to Oxford. Lewis, W.

My fey lady. Walsh, M.
My first deposit. Nadir, I. M.
My first love. Nadir, I. M.
My first Protestant. O'Donovan, M.
My friend Bingham. James, H.
My friend Flicka. Sture-Vasa, M. A.
My friend Joseph. Paterson, N.
My friend the doctor. Farrell, J. T.
My grandfather's eyes. Christowe, S.
My Grandmother Millard. Faulkner, W.
My grandmother's grandmother's Christmas candle. Butterworth, H.
My Julie. Newell, V. S.
My kind of a man. Gipson, F. B.
My kingdom for Jones. Schramm, W. L.
My lady love, my dove. Dahl, R.
My last book. Lipman, C. and Lipman, M.
My late senatorial secretaryship. Clemens, S. L.
My little boy. Ewald, C.
My little robins. Sansom, W.
My mother. Gide, A. P. G.
My mother's love story. Halper, A.
My Œdipus complex. O'Donovan, M.
My old man. Caldwell, E.
My old man. Hemingway, E.
My own brother. Cooke, A. A.
My own son. Cooke, A. A.
My own true ghost story. Kipling, R.
My Pinya. Adler, J.
My platonic sweetheart. Clemens, S. L.
My quarrel with Hersh Rasseyner. Grade, C.
"My queer Dean!"　Queen, E. pseud.
My sister Antonia. Valle-Inclán, R. del
My Tiare, good-bye. Tanzer, W.
My town. Schaefer, J. W.
My tree. Sansom, W.
My Uncle Sosthenes. Maupassant, G. de
Myers, Henry
　Pale sergeant
　　Queen, E. pseud. ed. Ellery Queen's awards: 9th ser.
Myers, Ruth Herrick
　Little ewe lamb
　　Story parade (Periodical) Adventure stories
MYNA BIRDS. See Mynahs
Myna birds. Queen, E. pseud.
Mynah birds. Michener, J. A.
MYNAHS
　Queen, E. pseud. Myna birds
MYSTERIES AND MIRACLE PLAYS
　Verga, G. Mystery play
Mysterious Chinese mandrake. Ekbergh, I. D.
Mysterious forest. Hudson, W. H.
Mysterious Kôr. Bowen, E.
Mysterious Madame Shanghai. Hughes, L.
Mysterious stranger. Clemens, S. L.
Mysterious villa
　Carrington, H. ed. Week-end book of ghost stories

Mystery. Claudy, C. H.

MYSTERY AND DETECTIVE STORIES

Best detective stories of the year—1950-1954; 61 stories
Blochman, L. G. Diagnosis: homicide; 8 stories
Bond, R. T. ed. Handbook for poisoners; 12 stories
Brown, F. Daymare
Brown, F. Mostly murder; 18 stories
Canning, V. The smuggler
Carr, J. D. Footprint in the sky
Charteris, L. Second Saint omnibus; 10 stories
Chesterton, G. K. Invisible man
Curtis, K. Drumbeaters Island
Davis, R. H. In the fog
Derleth, A. W. Memoirs of Solar Pons; 11 stories
Derleth, A. W. Three problems for Solar Pons; 3 stories
Furman, A. L. ed. Everygirls mystery stories; 10 stories
Futrelle, J. Problem of Cell 13
Green, A. K. The doctor, his wife, and the clock
Harrison, H. S. Miss Hinch
Kuttner, H. Private eye
MacDonald, P. Something to hide; 6 stories
Macfarlan, A. A. Loon laughs
Milne, A. A. Murder at eleven
Mystery Writers of America, inc. Butcher, baker, murder-maker; 20 stories
Mystery Writers of America, inc. Crooks' tour; 22 stories
Mystery Writers of America, inc. Maiden murders; 20 stories
Mystery Writers of America, inc. 20 great tales of murder; 19 stories
Peattie, D. C. and Peattie, L. R. Mystery in Four-and-a-Half Street
Queen, E. pseud. Murder without clues
Queen, E. pseud. ed. Queen's awards: 5th-9th ser; 76 stories
Queen, E. pseud. Queen's Bureau of Investigation; 18 stories
Queen, E. pseud. Sound of blackmail
Quentin, P. pseud. This looks like murder
Quentin, P. pseud. Town blonde, country blonde
White, W. A. P. ed. Four-&-twenty bloodhounds; 25 stories
Woolrich, C. Wait for me downstairs

Canada

Erskine, L. Y. Mystery at Moon Lake

England

Carr, J. D. The third bullet, and other stories; 7 stories
Chesterton, G. K. Father Brown omnibus; 51 stories
Chesterton, G. K. Hammer of God
Christie, A. M. Under dog, and other stories; 9 stories
Dickens, C. Hunted down
Doyle, Sir A. C. Adventure of the speckled band
Doyle, Sir A. C. Adventures of Sherlock Holmes; 50 stories
Doyle, Sir A. C. Book of Sherlock Holmes; 6 stories

Doyle, A. C. and Carr, J. D. Exploits of Sherlock Holmes; 12 stories
Dunsany, E. J. M. D. P. 18th baron. Two bottles of relish
Harvey, W. F. The lake
Harvey, W. F. Mishandled

France

LeBlanc, M. Invisible prisoner
Poe, E. A. Murders in the Rue Morgue
Poe, E. A. Mystery of Marie Roget
Poe, E. A. Purloined letter
Porter, W. S. Tracked to doom

United States

Gardner, E. S. Case of the irate witness
Poe, E. A. The gold-bug
Poe, E. A. "Thou art the man"
Porter, W. S. Adventures of Shamrock Jolnes
Porter, W. S. The sleuths
Porter, W. S. Theory and the hound
Porter, W. S. Tictocq
Queen, E. pseud. Calendar of crime; 12 stories
Rinehart, M. R. Burned chair
Rinehart, M. R. Frightened wife
Rinehart, M. R. Murder and the south wind
Stout, R. Triple jeopardy; 3 stories

Mystery at Moon Lake. Erskine, L. Y.
Mystery in Four-and-a-Half Street. Peattie, D. C. and Peattie, L. R.
Mystery of heroism. Crane, S.
Mystery of Kela Ouai. Canning, V.
Mystery of Marie Roget. Poe, E. A.
Mystery of Mike. Erskine, L. Y.
Mystery of the personal ad. Stribling, T. S.
Mystery of the Savage sump. Davis, S. P.
Mystery play. Verga, G.

MYSTICISM

Hesse, H. Within and without
Tolstoi, A. N. Graf. Fusty Devil

Myth of mankind. Lagerkvist, P. F.

MYTHICAL ANIMALS. See Animals, Mythical

MYTHOLOGY

Beaconsfield, B. D. 1st earl of. Ixion in heaven
See also Legends and folk tales

N

N.E.S.P.D.I.P. Parker, J. R.
N.R.A. for a dollar. Cooke, A. A.
The **NRACP.** Elliott, G. P.
Nadia Devereux. Eichrodt, J.
Nadir, Isaac Moishe, 1885-1943
Man who slept through the end of the world
  Howe, I. and Greenberg, E. eds. Treasury of Yiddish stories
My first deposit
  Ausubel, N. ed. Treasury of Jewish humor
My first love
  Howe, I. and Greenberg, E. eds. Treasury of Yiddish stories

Nadir, Isaac M.—*Continued*
  Nuttose and protose
    Ausubel, N. ed. Treasury of Jewish humor
  Ruined by success
    Ausubel, N. ed. Treasury of Jewish humor
Nadir, Moishe. See Nadir, Isaac Moishe
Na-Ha the fighter. Finger, C. J.
Nahman Ben Simḥah, of Bratzlav, 1770?-1810?
  A tale
    Leftwich, J. ed. Yisröel. 1952 ed.
Name-day. Munro, H. H.
Name for the city. Faulkner, W.
Name in the papers. Hughes, L.
Naming of names. Bradbury, R.
NANTUCKET. See Massachusetts—Nantucket
The nap. De La Mare, W. J.
NAPLES. See Italy—Naples
Narapoia. Nelson, A.
NARCOTICS
  Bowles, P. F. Under the sky
  Queen, E. pseud. Black Ledger
    See also Opium habit
Narrow escape. James, W.
NASHVILLE, TENNESSEE. See Tennessee—Nashville
Nason, Leonard Hastings, 1895-
  Rodney
    Cooper, A. C. ed. Modern short stories
Nasty Kupperman and the Ku Klux Klan. Berg, L.
NATCHEZ, MISSISSIPPI. See Mississippi—Natchez
NATCHEZ TRACE. See Mississippi—Natchez Trace
Nathan, Robert, 1894-
  Home is in the heart
    Brentano, F. ed. The word lives on
  Testing of Jonah
    Selden, R. ed. Ways of God and men
National honeymoon. Horgan, P.
NATIONAL SOCIALISM
  Kesten, H. Friend in the closet
  Shaw, I. Sailor off the Bremen
    See also Fascism
NATIONALISM
  Boyle, K. Effigy of war
NATIVE (TO GO NATIVE)
  Maugham, W. S. Fall of Edward Barnard
  Maugham, W. S. Force of circumstance
  Maugham, W. S. The pool
  Maugham, W. S. Red
  Porter, W. S. Helping the other fellow
Natives don't cry. Boyle, K.
Natural causes. Connolly, M.
NATURAL HISTORY MUSEUMS
  Maugham, W. S. Neil MacAdam
NATURE
  Burroughs, J. Sharp eyes
  Jefferies, R. Winds of heaven
  Slosson, A. T. Fishin' Jimmy
  Thoreau, H. D. Winter at Walden
Nature of the evidence. Sinclair, M.

NATURE STUDY. See Nature
Nature study. Kneale, N.
Naughty Saint Vitalis. Keller, G.
NAUSEA
  Adler, W. Other people
    See also Illness
NAVAHO INDIANS
  Clark, W. Van T. The anonymous
NAVAL LIFE. See subdivision Navy under various countries; e.g. Great Britain—Navy; United States—Navy
NAVAL MANEUVERS
  Divine, A. D. Thirty minutes to zero
NAVAL OFFICERS. See Great Britain—Navy; United States—Navy; etc.
Naval treaty. Doyle, Sir A. C.
Navy blue and bold. Curtis, M.
NAVY LIFE. See subdivision Navy under various countries, e.g. Great Britain—Navy; United States—Navy
NAZIS. See National socialism
Nearing, Homer, 1915-
  Hyperspherical basketball
    Magazine of fantasy and science fiction. Best from Fantasy and science fiction; 2d ser.
  Maladjusted classroom
    Magazine of fantasy and science fiction. Best from Fantasy and science fiction; 3d ser.
  Mathematical voodoo
    Magazine of fantasy and science fiction. Best from Fantasy and science fiction; [1st] ser.
Nearly perfect. Milne, A. A.
Neat strip. Runyon, D.
NEBRASKA
  Crane, S. Blue Hotel

Ranch life
    See Ranch life—Nebraska
NEBRASKA FARM LIFE. See Farm life—Nebraska
Necessity's child. Wilson, A.
Neck. Dahl, R.
The necklace. Maupassant, G. de
NECKLACES
  Blixen, K. The pearls
  Maupassant, G. de. The necklace
    See also Jewelry
The need. Coates, R. M.
Need to die. Berto, G.
NEGRO DIALECT STORIES. See Dialect stories—Negro
NEGRO FOLKLORE. See Legends and folk tales—Negro
Negro in the well. Caldwell, E.
NEGRO LAWYERS. See Law and lawyers
NEGRO SERVANTS. See Negroes as servants
NEGROES
  Allen, J. L. King Solomon of Kentucky
  Benét, S. V. Freedom's a hard-bought thing
  Berry, J. New shoes
  Betts, D. Sympathetic visitor

NEGROES—*Continued*
Boyd, J. Bloodhound
Boyd, J. Shiftless
Bradbury, R. Other feet
Buckingham, N. Death stalked the spring-stand!
Buckingham, N. Remember. . .
Caldwell, E. Big Buck
Caldwell, E. Blue Boy
Caldwell, E. Candy-Man Beechum
Caldwell, E. End of Christy Tucker
Caldwell, E. Kneel to the rising sun
Caldwell, E. Knife to cut corn bread with
Caldwell, E. Nine dollars' worth of mumble
Caldwell, E. People v. Abe Lathan, colored
Caldwell, E. Runaway
Conrad, J. The nigger of the Narcissus
Crane, S. The knife
Culver, M. Black water blues
Doughty, LeG. S. The firebird
Dreer, H. ed. American literature by Negro authors; 3 stories
Elliott, G. P. The NRACP
Faulkner, W. Dry September
Faulkner, W. That evening sun
Field, S. S. Good-by to Cap'm John
Foote, S. Ride out
Ford, N. A. and Faggett, H. L. eds. Best short stories by Afro-American writers; 40 stories
Gibbs, A. The test
Godchaux, E. Horn that called Bambine
Gordon, C. Her quaint honour
Grau, S. A. Black prince
Grau, S. A. Miss Yellow Eyes
Grau, S. A. Way of a man
Grau, S. A. White girl, fine girl
Haardt, S. P. Little white girl
Harris, J. C. Free Joe and the rest of the world
Howe, D. White kitten
Hughes, L. Laughing to keep from crying; 24 stories
Justice, D. The lady
Kidd, H. L. Low road go down
Laidlaw, C. Little black boys
Lincoln, V. E. In the garden
Melville, H. Benito Cereno
Noland, F. The whipping
Paul, L. No more trouble for Jedwick
Phillips, T. H. Shadow of an arm
Porter, W. S. Municipal report
Radford, M. Wm. Crane
Reynolds, M. and Brown, F. Dark interlude
Rice, A. C. H. Hoodooed
Sabin, E. L. Freedom
Schulberg, B. W. The one he called Winnie
Sellers, M. Something gay and foolish
Steele, W. F. Sooth
Taylor, P. H. What you hear from 'em?
Warren, R. P. Blackberry winter
Welty, E. Curtain of green
Welty, E. Keela, the outcast Indian maiden
Welty, E. Livvie
Welty, E. Livvie is back
Welty, E. Worn path

Willingham, C. Afternoon sun
Willingham, C. Excitement in Ergo
See also Slavery

Education
Calisher, H. Wreath for Miss Totten
NEGROES AS SERVANTS
Caldwell, E. The picture
Caldwell, E. Squire Dinwiddy
Faulkner, W. That evening sun
Johnson, J. W. The author
Lewis, E. G. Portrait
Steele, W. D. Can't cross Jordan by myself
Taylor, P. H. Bad dreams
Taylor, P. H. Cookie
Taylor, P. H. Wife of Nashville
See also Servants

Negro's head. Munby, A. N. L.

Neighbor Rosicky. Cather, W. S.

NEIGHBORS
Bojer, J. A letter to Klaus Brock
Canine, W. The clematis
Fitzgerald, F. S. K. Baby party
Gold, H. The witch
Grau, S. A. Girl with the flaxen hair
Munro, H. H. Blood-feud of Toad-Water
Rawlings, C. A. Flash of lightning

Neighbour Rosicky. Cather, W. S.

Neikirk, Mabel E.
Oscar on roller skates
Story parade (Periodical) Adventure stories
Oscar, the trained seal
Fenner, P. R. comp. Giggle box

Neil MacAdam. Maugham, W. S.

Ne'ilah in Gehenna. Peretz, I. L.

Neil's girl. Heathcott, M.

Neiman, Samuel, 1911-
Day papa died
American vanguard, 1950
Wine of one day
American vanguard, 1952

Neisloss, Myron, 1929-
The picnic
Wolfe, D. M. ed. Which grain will grow

Nelson, Alan, 1911-
Narapoia
Magazine of fantasy and science fiction. Best from Fantasy and science fiction; [1st] ser.

Nelson, Edna Deu Pree
St George ball
Story (Periodical) Story; no. 1
NELSON, HORATIO NELSON, VISCOUNT, 1758-1805
Melville, H. Billy Budd, foretopman

Nemerov, Howard, and Johnson, William R.
Exchange of men
Greene, J. I. and Abell, E. eds. Stories of sudden truth

The **nemesis.** Stafford, J.

Nemesis and the candy man. Porter, W. S.

Ne-nu-ka. Davis, R.

Neo-Hebrew poet. Zangwill, I.

NEPHEWS
Collier, J. Green thoughts
See also Uncles

NEPTUNE (PLANET)
Harris, C. W. and Breuer, M. J. Baby on Neptune
NERVOUS BREAKDOWN. See Neurasthenia
Nesbit, Edith. See Bland, Edith (Nesbit)
Nests in a stone image. Goyen, W.
Net nemesis. Coombs, C. I.
Net profit. Spiller, B. L.
NETHERLANDS

Amsterdam
Charteris, L. Amsterdam: The angel's eye
NETHERLANDS INDIES. See Dutch East Indies
NEURASTHENIA
Ketcham, P. The mistake
Moore, D. E. Portrait
Priestley, J. B. The statues
Purcell, D. Rider of the avalanche
White, A. Moment of truth
NEUROSES
Cather, W. S. Paul's case
NEUROTICS. See Neuroses
NEVADA
Clark, W. Van T. Indian well
Clark, W. Van T. Wind and the snow of winter
NEVADA

19th century
Emrich, D. ed. Comstock bonanza; 21 stories

Ranch life
See Ranch life—Nevada

Washoe County
Browne, J. R. Peep at Washoe
Wright, W. Washoe behemoth
Never a dull moment. Taber, G. B.
Never anything that fades. Steele, W. D.
Never bet the devil your head. Poe, E. A.
Never come mourning. Winchell, P.
Never room with a couple. Hughes, L.
Never trust a lady. Canning, V.
Never trust a woman. Newhouse, E.
Never trust the obvious. Chute, V.
Never underestimate. . . Waldo, E. H.
Nevermore without end. Sansom, W.

Neville, Kris
Bettyann
Healy, R. J. ed. New tales of space and time
Sloane, W. M. ed. Stories for tomorrow
Cold war
Astounding science fiction (Periodical)
Astounding science fiction anthology
Franchise
Sloane, W. M. ed. Stories for tomorrow
Hold back tomorrow
Bleiler, E. F. and Dikty, T. E. eds. Imagination unlimited
Old Man Henderson
Magazine of fantasy and science fiction. Best from Fantasy and science fiction; ｢1st｣ ser.
Underground movement
Merril, J. ed. Beyond human ken

New accelerator. Wells, H. G.
New advocate. Kafka, F.
New Atlantis. Bacon, F. viscount St Albans
New babes in old woods. Applegarth, M. T.
New beau. Murrie, P.
NEW BRUNSWICK. See Canada—New Brunswick
New cabin. Caldwell, E.
NEW CALEDONIA
Russell, J. Fourth man
New dress. Woolf, V. S.
NEW ENGLAND

17th century
Butterworth, H. My grandmother's grandmother's Christmas candle
Hawthorne, N. Endicott and the Red Cross

19th century
Jewett, S. O. Courting of Sister Wisby
NEW ENGLAND DIALECT. See Dialect stories—New England
NEW ENGLAND FARM LIFE. See Farm life—New England
New England nun. Freeman, M. E. W.
NEW FRANCE. See Canada
New girl. Van Doren, M.
NEW GUINEA
Cave, H. B. Peril of the river
Michener, J. A. The fossickers
Ullman, J. R. Am I blue?
New Guinea interlude. Valbor, K.
NEW HAMPSHIRE
Benét, S. V. Devil and Daniel Webster
Slosson, A. T. Fishin' Jimmy
New hat. Swinbank, G.
New house. Bowen, E.
New kid. Heyert, M.
NEW ORLEANS. See Louisiana—New Orleans
New police chief. Shneur, Z.
New reality. Harness, C. L.
New ritual. Seabright, I.
New shoes. Berry, J.
New suit. O'Flaherty, L.
New villa. Chekhov, A. P.
NEW YEAR
Bergengruen, W. Old Hussar
De Vries, P. Open house
Herbert, F. H. We were just having fun
Jackson, C. R. Boy who ran away
Mannix, E. New Year for Juicy
New Year for Juicy. Mannix, E.
New Year's Day. Newhouse, E.
NEW YEAR'S EVE. See New Year
New Year's Eve confession. Sudermann, H.
New York. Horwitz, J.
NEW YORK (CITY)
Johnson, R. B. Far below

19th century
Bunner, H. C. Story of a New York house
James, H. Washington Square

NEW YORK (CITY)—19th century—*Cont.*
O'Higgins, H. J. Big Dan Reilly
Porter, W. S. Complete works of O.
    Henry; 270 stories
Winslow, T. S. Cycle of Manhattan

20th century
Fitzgerald, F. S. K. May Day
Hauser, M. The mouse
Newhouse, E. Day before

Brooklyn
Fay, W. A nice, clean job
Gold, Z. Spring over Brooklyn
Heuman, W. There are broken hearts in
    Brooklyn
Horwitz, J. The roof
Wolfe, T. Only the dead know Brooklyn

East Side
Benson, T. In the fourth ward
Crane, S. Experiment in misery
Horwitz, J. Lunch

Greenwich Village
Malamud, B. The prison
Mitchell, J. Professor Sea Gull
Porter, W. S. Last leaf

Lower East Side
See New York (City)—East Side

Manhattan
Allan, G. Kentucky line-up
Connolly, M. Pigeon from St Barthol-
    omew's
Greenfield, R. Jonathan Harrow
Horwitz, J. The city
Horwitz, J. The island
Horwitz, J. New York
Horwitz, J. The street
Melville, H. Bartleby the scrivener
Porter, W. S. Cop and the anthem
Porter, W. S. Mammon and the archer
Porter, W. S. Rus in urbe

Zoological Park
Gold, M. Mushrooms in Bronx Park

NEW YORK (STATE)

18th century
Brick, J. The captives
Irving, W. Rip Van Winkle

19th century
Edmonds, W. D. Judge
Thompson, D. Once on Christmas

New York by camp fire light. Porter, W. S.

New York is full of girls. Wechsberg, J.

NEW ZEALAND

20th century
Michener, J. A. Until they sail

Newby, Percy Howard, 1918-
Crowning glory
    New writing (Periodical) Best stories

Newcomb, Covelle, 1908-
The challenge
    Fenner, P. R. comp. Cowboys, cowboys,
        cowboys
Grand prize
    Fenner, P. R. comp. Cowboys, cowboys,
        cowboys

Newcomb, Ellsworth
Two for the show
    American girl (Periodical) On my honor
Newell, Annie Salisbury
Grandpop comes home
    Oberfirst, R. ed. 1952 anthology of best
        original short-shorts
Newell, David McCheyne, 1898-
Into the web
    Best detective stories of the year—1951
Newell, Virginia Shaw
My Julie
    Oberfirst, R. ed. 1954 anthology of best
        original short-shorts

Newhouse, Edward, 1911-
All they do is talk
    Newhouse, E. Many are called
Billy the Bastard
    Newhouse, E. Many are called
Bronze thing
    Newhouse, E. Many are called
Choice of weapons
    Newhouse, E. Many are called
Close your eyes
    Newhouse, E. Many are called
Come again another day
    Newhouse, E. Many are called
Couple of old-timers
    Newhouse, E. Many are called
Day before
    Newhouse, E. Many are called
The eagle
    Newhouse, E. Many are called
Ever been to Brooklyn?
    Newhouse, E. Many are called
Four freedoms
    Newhouse, E. Many are called
Girl who had to get married
    Newhouse, E. Many are called
Gorgeous number
    Newhouse, E. Many are called
Hot time in the old town
    Newhouse, E. Many are called
I hope you'll understand
    Newhouse, E. Many are called
In time of calamity
    Newhouse, E. Many are called
Irving
    Newhouse, E. Many are called
Legs go first
    Newhouse, E. Many are called
Light across the hill
    Newhouse, E. Many are called
Magic hour
    Newhouse, E. Many are called
Major and Mrs Fletcher
    Newhouse, E. Many are called
The Mentocrats
    Newhouse, E. Many are called
My brother's second funeral
    Best American short stories, 1950
    Newhouse, E. Many are called
Never trust a woman
    Newhouse, E. Many are called
New Year's Day
    Newhouse, E. Many are called
Out where the West begins
    Newhouse, E. Many are called
Poker game
    Newhouse, E. Many are called
Position of the soldier
    Newhouse, E. Many are called

Newhouse, Edward—*Continued*
Pro and con
Newhouse, E. Many are called
Put yourself in my place
Newhouse, E. Many are called
The revolution
Newhouse, E. Many are called
Seventy thousand dollars
Newhouse, E. Many are called
Prize stories of 1950
Short visit to Naples
Newhouse, E. Many are called
Ten years on a desert island
Newhouse, E. Many are called
Time out
Newhouse, E. Many are called
Vacancy in Westchester
Newhouse, E. Many are called
The volcano
Newhouse, E. Many are called
Wacky afternoon
Newhouse, E. Many are called
War for Tony
Newhouse, E. Many are called
What do you do?
Newhouse, E. Many are called
With men it's different
Newhouse, E. Many are called
The wolf
Newhouse, E. Many are called

Newman, Frances, 1888-1928
Rachel and her children
Blodgett, H. W. ed. Story survey.
1953 ed.

Newman, Ruth S. 1909-
Delta interlude
American vanguard, 1952

News for the church. O'Donovan, M.

News from Troy. Putman, C.

NEWSBOYS
Saroyan, W. Mr Mechano
Saroyan, W. Resurrection of a life

NEWSPAPER LIFE. See Journalism

Newspaper man. Brier, H. M.

Newspaper story. Porter, W. S.

NEWSPAPER WORK. See Journalists

NEWSPAPERMEN. See Journalists

Newton, Dwight Bennett, 1916-
Mule tracks
Western Writers of America. Bad men
and good

Newton man. Coombs, C. I.

NEWTS
Calisher, H. Heartburn

Nexø, Martin Andersen, 1869-
Birds of passage
Neider, C. ed. Great short stories from
the world's literature

Next door to death. Stern, J.

"Next to reading matter." Porter, W. S.

A nice, clean job. Fay, W.

Nice fright. Benson, T.

Nice little girl. Grace, S.

NICHOLAS I, EMPEROR OF RUSSIA,
1796-1855
Bergengruen, W. Easter Greeting

NICHOLAS II, EMPEROR OF RUSSIA,
1868-1918
Gibbs, Sir P. H. Stranger in the village

Nicola, Helen B.
Two on trial
American girl (Periodical) On my
honor

NIECES
Auchincloss, L. Unholy three

Nigger of the Narcissus. Conrad, J.

Night at the Notch. Van Doren, M.

Night before Christmas. Aspinwall, M.

Night before prohibition. Aiken, C. P.

Night boat from Barcelona. Beck, V. J.

Night bus to Atlanta. Gill, B.

Night club. Brush, K. I.

NIGHT CLUBS
Brush, K. I. Night club

NIGHT COURTS. See Trials

Night he cried. Leiber, F.

Night in June. Williams, W. C.

Night in new Arabia. Porter, W. S.

Night in the warehouse. Peacock, W. S.

Night Mamma told a bald-faced lie.
Knox, J.

Night meeting. Bradbury, R.

Night my brother came home. Kaplan, R.

Night of the harvest festival. Sillanpää,
F. E.

Night on Don Jaime Street. Haycox, E.

Night riders of Northville. Calisher, H.

NIGHT SCHOOLS. See Evening and continuation schools

Night sequence. Priestley, J. B.

Night the bed fell. Thurber, J.

Night the world ended. Brown, F.

Night to howl. Alch, A. H.

Night visitor. Jackson, C. R.

Night watch. Heggen, T.

NIGHT WATCHMEN. See Watchmen

Night! Youth! Paris! And the moon. Collier, J.

Nightfall. Asimov, I.

Nightgown. Davies, R.

Nightmare Abbey. Peacock, T. L.

Nightmare brother. Nourse, A. E.

Nightmare face. Snow, W.

NIGHTMARES. See Dreams; Somnambulism

Nine billion names of God. Clarke, A. C.

Nine dollars' worth of mumble. Caldwell, E.

Nine-finger Jack. White, W. A. P.

Nine ladies vs. fate. Montross, L.

The Nistor, pseud. See Kahanovich, Pinchas

Nitro ship. Holder, W.

No admittance. Cicellis, K.

No body. Harvey, W. F.

No color. O'Rourke, F.

No competition. Lehr, W.

No connection. Asimov, I.

No continuing city. Beck, W.

The no-counts. Elkins, E.

No end to anything. Switzer, R.

No enemy of his. Gutman, C.

No evidence. Lincoln, V. E.

No fools, no fun. Lacy, M.

No forwarding address. Pratt, F. and De Camp, L. S.

No greater love. Schneider, G. W.

No greater love. Stewart, O.

No hero. Stuart, J.

No heroes wanted. Miers, E. S.

No Land of Nod. Springer, S.

No-man's Danny. Dinnis, E. M.

No meadow lark song. Thompson, E.

No moon for me. Miller, W. M.

No more the nightingales. Bates, H. E.

No more trouble for Jedwick. Paul, L.

No morning after. Clarke, A. C.

No motive. Du Maurier, D.

No, my darling daughter. La Farge, O.

No one believed me. Thompson, W.

No one can harm us. Undset, S.

No one my grief can tell. Hale, N.

No particular night or morning. Bradbury, R.

No peace with the sea. Longstreet, S.

No petty thief. Stuart, J.

No place for a woman. Williams, W. C.

No place for magic. Procter, M.

No room in her heart. Lull, R.

No room in the inn. Ford, N. A.

No-sided professor. Gardner, M.

No son, no gun, no streetcar. Seager, A.

No story. Porter, W. S.

No thunder, no lightning. Van Doren, M.

No time for dreams. Haycox, E.

No trip like this. Cawley, C. C.

No visitors. Benét, S. V.

No way down. Jenks, A.

No witchcraft for sale. Lessing, D. M.

No woman born. Moore, C. L.

NOAH
Meyouhas, J. Noah the prophet

Noah the Prophet. Meyouhas, J.

NOAH'S ARK
Milne, A. A. Before the flood

NOAH'S ARK (IMITATION)
Davies, R. Caleb's ark

NOBILITY. See Aristocracy

Noble guy. Farrell, J. T.

Noblest instrument. Day, C. S.

Nobody can beat Freidkin's meats. Kober, A.

"Nobody here but. . ." Asimov, I.

Nobody saw the ship. Jenkins, W. F.

Nobody say a word. Van Doren, M.

Nobody's business. Fischer, B.

Nogid's luck. Zevin, I. J.

Noise. Kuttner, H.

Noise in the night. Hodgson, W. H.

Noise level. Jones, R. F.

Noland, Felix
The whipping
Best American short stories, 1953

NOMADS
Enders, G. B. Kismet and the nomad woman

None but the fair. Paradis, M. B.

NONSENSE STORIES. See Humor

Noon wine. Porter, K. A.

Nordau, Max Simon, 1849-1923
Share in the hereafter
Leftwich, J. ed. Yisröel. 1952 ed.

Nordhoff, Charles Bernard, 1887-1947
I turn pearl-diver
Fenner, P. R. comp. Stories of the sea

Nordhoff, Charles Bernard, 1887-1947, **and Hall, James Norman,** 1887-1951
In pyjamas
Fenner, P. R. comp. Speed, speed, speed
The mutiny
Fenner, P. R. comp. Stories of the sea
School for combat
Jensen, P. ed. Fireside book of flying stories

Norling, Mary E.
Jade ring
Oberfirst, R. ed. 1952 anthology of best original short-shorts

Normandy joke. Maupassant, G. de

Norris, Frank, 1870-1902
Deal in wheat
Burrell, J. A. and Cerf, B. A. eds. Anthology of famous American stories

Norris, Hoke
Take her up tenderly
Best American short stories, 1950

Norris, Kathleen (Thompson) 1880-
Mother of Angela Hogan
Fremantle, A. J. ed. Mothers
What happened to Alanna
Thinker's digest (Periodical) Spoiled priest, and other stories

NORTH AFRICA. See Africa, North

NORTH CAROLINA
Boyd, J. Old pines, and other stories; 10 stories
Knox, J. Little Benders; 17 stories

NORTHWEST TERRITORIES. See Canada—Northwest territories

Norton, Browning
The panther
Queen, E. pseud, ed. The Queen's awards: 8th ser.

Norton, Henry A. 1906-
Man in the moon
Conklin, G. ed. Invaders of earth

NORWAY
Grimson, M. S. Norway

NORWEGIANS IN THE UNITED STATES
Hamsun, K. Wonderful new machine
Lewis, S. Young man Axelbrod

Nose for news. Coombs, C. I.

Nose of Don Aristide. Brown, F.

Nostalgia. Farrell, J. T.

Not a lick of sense. Gardiner, D.

Not a natural man. Van Doren, M.

Not a soul will come along. Parsons, E.
Not blotted. Claudy, C. H.
Not by bread alone. Benson, T.
Not final! Asimov, I.
Not fit for children. Smith, E. E.
Not for psychologists. Sykes, C.
Not my story. Walsh, M.
Not only dead men. Van Vogt, A. E.
Not quite Martin. Wilson, L.
Not that kind of a deal. Brookhouser, F.
Not to be opened. Young, R. F.
Not what she pretended. Madden, H. T.
Not with a bang. Knight, D.
Not with our fathers. Rothberg, A. A.
NOTARIES
    Clemens, S. L. Concerning notaries
NOTARY PUBLICS. See Notaries
Note on the literary life. Schulberg, B. W.
Notes from underground. Dostoevskiĭ, F. M.
Nothing can change it. Cooke, C.
Nothing ever breaks except the heart. Boyle,
    K.
Nothing happens in Brooklyn. Runyon, D.
"Nothing happens on the moon." Ernst, P.
Nothing new. O'Rourke, F.
Nothing overwhelms Giuseppe. Blue, E.
Nothing Sirius. Brown, F.
Nourse, Alan Edward
    High threshold
        Conklin, G. ed. Omnibus of science fic-
        tion
    Nightmare brother
        Sloane, W. M. ed. Space, space, space
    Tiger by the tail
        Conklin, G. ed. Science-fiction adven-
        tures in dimension
        Galaxy science fiction magazine. Second
        Galaxy reader of science fiction
Novás Calvo, Lino, 1903-
    Dark night of Ramón Yendía
        De Onís, H. ed. Spanish stories and
        tales
Novelette. Barker, A. L.
NOVELISTS. See Authors
The novitiate. Howarth, J.
Now and again now. Lincoln, V. E.
Now I lay me. Hemingway, E.
Now there is peace. Sherman, R.
Now we are broke, my dear. Balchin, N.
The Nowaks. Isherwood, C.
Noyes, Alfred, 1880-
    Log of the "Evening Star"
        Cerf, B. A. and Moriarty, H. C. eds.
        Anthology of famous British stories
    Uncle Hyacinth
        Cooper, A. C. ed. Modern short stories
Nuhn, Ferner, 1903-
    Ten
        Blodgett, H. W. ed. Story survey. 1953
        ed.
The nuisance. Lessing, D. M.
Null-P. Klass, P.
Number nine. Cartmill, C.

Number seventy-nine. Munby, A. N. L.
Number to remember. Stebel, S.
Nunc dimittis. Dahl, R.
NUNNERIES. See Convents
NUNS
    Connolly, M. Big red house on Hope
        Street
    Galsworthy, J. Salta pro nobis
    Hemingway, E. Gambler, the nun, and
        the radio
    Huxley, A. L. Nuns at luncheon
    McLaverty, M. Road to the shore
    MacMahon, B. Corn was springing
    McNulty, J. Can't slip any drugs to sis-
        ters on Fifth Avenue
    Pardo Bazán, E. condesa de. Sister
        Aparición
    Roberts, E. M. Sacrifice of the maidens
    Sansom, W. Little room
Nuns at luncheon. Huxley, A. L.
Nuns' holiday. Lieberman, R.
NUREMBERG. See Germany—Nurem-
    berg
NURSES AND NURSING
    Aiken, C. P. Bring! Bring!
    Aiken, C. P. Night before prohibition
    Bates, E. H. Time expired
    Fitzgerald, F. S. K. Alcoholic case
    Gordon, A. Old Ironpuss
    Harvey, W. F. Account rendered
    Harvey, W. F. Arm of Mrs Egan
    Harvey, W. F. Atmospherics
    Harvey, W. F. Chemist and druggist
    Harvey, W. F. Dark horses
    Harvey, W. F. Euphemia witchmaid
    Harvey, W. F. Flying out of Mrs Bar-
        nard Hollis
    Harvey, W. F. The lake
    Harvey, W. F. No body
    Harvey, W. F. Old masters
    Harvey, W. F. Ripe for development
    Keller, D. H. Psychophonic nurse
    Lardner, R. W. Zone of quiet
    Levine, T. M. Elaine's hope
    Parker, D. R. Horsie
    Scott, H. S. Sister
    Ullman, J. R. Between you and I
    Wilson, A. Mummy to the rescue
NUTS
    Hoffmann, E. T. A. History of Krakatuk
Nuttose and protose. Nadir, I. M.
NYANJA (AFRICAN TRIBE)
    Ullman, J. R. Am I blue?
Nye, Nelson Coral, 1907-
    Homecoming
        Western Writers of America. Holsters
        and heroes
    Rock bottom
        Western Writers of America. Bad men
        and good
NYGASSAS. See Nyanja (African tribe)

O

O city of broken dreams. Cheever, J.
O. Henry, pseud. See Porter, William Syd-
    ney
O. Henry Memorial awards. See First-prize
    stories, 1919-1954

O time in your flight. Cornier, V.

Oasis of gaiety. Taylor, E.

OBESITY. See Corpulence

OBJECTORS TO WAR. See Conscientious objectors

Oblinger, Michael
Jackpot vs. Yellowstrike
Dachs, D. ed. Treasury of sports humor

Oblong box. Poe, E. A.

O'Brien, Brian, 1898-
Pull, you lubbers!
Argosy (Periodical) Argosy Book of sea stories

O'Brien, Fitz-James, 1828-1862
Diamond lens
Burrell, J. A. and Cerf, B. A. eds. Anthology of famous American stories
Lost room
Conklin, G. and Conklin, L. T. eds. Supernatural reader

O'Brien, Jack. See O'Brien, John Sherman

O'Brien, John Sherman, 1898-1938
King and the Princess
Harper, W. comp. Dog show

OBSEQUIES. See Funeral rites and ceremonies

OBSERVATORIES, ASTRONOMICAL. See Astronomical observatories

Obsession. Winslow, T. S.

OBSTETRICS. See Childbirth

Obstinacy of Septimus Harding. Trollope, A.

Occasional garden. Munro, H. H.

Occurrence at Owl Creek bridge. Bierce, A.

Occurrence up a side street. Cobb, I. S.

OCEAN
Doyle, Sir A. C. Maracot Deep
Dunsany, E. J. M. D. P. 18th baron. Poltarnees, Beholder of Ocean
Elam, R. M. Project ocean floor
Knight, N. L. Crisis in Utopia

OCEAN TRAVEL
Aiken, C. P. Farewell! Farewell! Farewell!
Aiken, C. P. Mr Arcularis
Clark, W. Van T. Why don't you look where you're going
Dahl, R. Dip in the pool
De La Mare, W. J. Cape Race
De La Roche, M. Broken fan
Fitzgerald, F. S. K. Rough crossing
Maugham, W. S. Marriage of convenience
Maugham, W. S. Mr Know-All
Maugham, W. S. P. & O.
Maugham, W. S. Winter cruise
Michener, J. A. The jungle
Morley, C. D. The arrow
Poe, E. A. Oblong box
Tomlinson, H. M. The derelict
Wertenbaker, G. P. Ship that turned aside

OCEAN VOYAGES. See Ocean travel

Oceans are wide. Robinson, F. M.

O'Conaill, Domhnall
Lilacs out of the dead land
Burnett, W. and Burnett, H. S. eds. Sextet

O'Connell, Robert B.
You'll never mind
Hathaway, B. and Sessions, J. A. eds. Writers for tomorrow. 2d ser.

O'Connor, Flannery
Life you save may be your own
Prize stories, 1954

O'Connor, Frank, pseud. See O'Donovan, Michael

October and June. Porter, W. S.

OCTOGENARIANS. See Old age

OCTOPUS
Gordon, A. Sea devil
Hugo, V. M. comte. Combat with the octopus
White, R. Conflict is joined

Octopus marooned. Porter, W. S.

OCTOROONS. See Mulattoes

Odd chance. Haycox, E.

Odd old lady. Winslow, T. S.

Oddy and Id. Bester, A.

ODESSA. See Russia—Odessa

Odger, Charles
Johnnie Poothers
Joseph, M. ed. Best cat stories

O'Donnell, Lawrence, pseud. See Kuttner, Henry

O'Donnell, Mary (King). See King, Mary Paula

O'Donovan, Michael, 1903-
Babes in the wood
O'Donovan, M. Stories of Frank O'Connor [pseud]
Bridal night
O'Donovan, M. Stories of Frank O'Connor [pseud]
The cheapjack
O'Donovan, M. Stories of Frank O'Connor [pseud]
Christmas morning
O'Donovan, M. Stories of Frank O'Connor [pseud]
Counsel for Œdipus
O'Donovan, M. More stories by Frank O'Connor [pseud]
Custom of the country
O'Donovan, M. More stories by Frank O'Connor [pseud]
Darcy in the Land of Youth
O'Donovan, M. More stories by Frank O'Connor [pseud]
O'Donovan, M. Traveller's samples
Don Juan (Retired)
O'Donovan, M. More stories by Frank O'Connor [pseud]
Don Juan's temptation
O'Donovan, M. Stories of Frank O'Connor [pseud]
The drunkard
O'Donovan, M. Stories of Frank O'Connor [pseud]
O'Donovan, M. Traveller's samples
Eternal triangle
O'Donovan, M. More stories by Frank O'Connor [pseud]
Face of evil
O'Donovan, M. More stories by Frank O'Connor [pseud]

O'Donovan, Michael—*Continued*

Father and son
  O'Donovan, M. More stories by Frank O'Connor ₁pseud₎

First confession
  Greene, J. I. and Abell, E. eds. Stories of sudden truth
  O'Donovan, M. Stories of Frank O'Connor ₁pseud₎
  O'Donovan, M. Traveller's samples

First love
  O'Donovan, M. Stories of Frank O'Connor ₁pseud₎

Freedom
  O'Donovan, M. Stories of Frank O'Connor ₁pseud₎

Frying-pan
  O'Donovan, M. More stories by Frank O'Connor ₁pseud₎

Guests of the nation
  Gordon, C. and Tate, A. eds. House of fiction
  O'Donovan, M. More stories by Frank O'Connor ₁pseud₎

Holy door
  O'Donovan, M. Stories of Frank O'Connor ₁pseud₎

House that Johnny built
  O'Donovan, M. Stories of Frank O'Connor ₁pseud₎

The idealist
  O'Donovan, M. Stories of Frank O'Connor ₁pseud₎
  O'Donovan, M. Traveller's samples

In the train
  O'Donovan, M. Stories of Frank O'Connor ₁pseud₎
  O'Faoláin, S. The short story

Jerome
  O'Donovan, M. More stories by Frank O'Connor ₁pseud₎
  O'Donovan, M. Traveller's samples

Judas
  Davis, R. G. ed. Ten modern masters
  O'Donovan, M. More stories by Frank O'Connor ₁pseud₎

Lady of the sagas
  O'Donovan, M. More stories by Frank O'Connor ₁pseud₎
  O'Donovan, M. Traveller's samples

Legal aid
  O'Donovan, M. Stories of Frank O'Connor ₁pseud₎
  O'Donovan, M. Traveller's samples

Little mother
  O'Donovan, M. More stories by Frank O'Connor ₁pseud₎

Lonely rock
  O'Donovan, M. More stories by Frank O'Connor ₁pseud₎

Long road to Ummera
  O'Donovan, M. Stories of Frank O'Connor ₁pseud₎

The Luceys
  O'Donovan, M. Stories of Frank O'Connor ₁pseud₎

Mac's masterpiece
  Short, R. W. and Sewall, R. B. eds. Short stories for study. 1950 ed.

Mad Lomasneys
  O'Donovan, M. More stories by Frank O'Connor ₁pseud₎

Majesty of the law
  Davis, R. G. ed. Ten modern masters
  O'Donovan, M. Stories of Frank O'Connor ₁pseud₎
  Stauffer, R. M.; Cunningham, W. H. and Sullivan, C. J. eds. Adventures in modern literature

Man of the house
  O'Donovan, M. More stories by Frank O'Connor ₁pseud₎
  O'Donovan, M. Traveller's samples

Masculine principle
  O'Donovan, M. Stories of Frank O'Connor ₁pseud₎
  O'Donovan, M. Traveller's samples

Masculine protest
  O'Donovan, M. More stories by Frank O'Connor ₁pseud₎

The miracle
  O'Donovan, M. More stories by Frank O'Connor ₁pseud₎

The miser
  O'Donovan, M. Stories of Frank O'Connor ₁pseud₎

My da
  O'Donovan, M. Stories of Frank O'Connor nor

My first Protestant
  O'Donovan, M. More stories by Frank O'Connor ₁pseud₎
  O'Donovan, M. Traveller's samples

My Œdipus complex
  O'Donovan, M. Stories of Frank O'Connor ₁pseud₎

News for the church
  O'Donovan, M. Stories of Frank O'Connor ₁pseud₎

Old-age pensioners
  O'Donovan, M. Traveller's samples

Old faith
  O'Donovan, M. More stories by Frank O'Connor ₁pseud₎

Old fellows
  O'Donovan, M. Stories of Frank O'Connor ₁pseud₎

Orpheus and his lute
  O'Donovan, M. More stories by Frank O'Connor ₁pseud₎

Peasants
  Lynskey, W. C. ed. Reading modern fiction
  O'Donovan, M. Stories of Frank O'Connor ₁pseud₎

The pretender
  O'Donovan, M. Stories of Frank O'Connor ₁pseud₎

A romantic
  O'Donovan, M. More stories by Frank O'Connor ₁pseud₎

Sense of responsibility
  O'Donovan, M. More stories by Frank O'Connor ₁pseud₎

The sentry
  O'Donovan, M. More stories by Frank O'Connor ₁pseud₎
  O'Donovan, M. Traveller's samples

The shepherds
  O'Donovan, M. More stories by Frank O'Connor ₁pseud₎

Song without words
  Gable, M. Sister, ed. Many-colored fleece
  O'Donovan, M. Stories of Frank O'Connor ₁pseud₎

O'Donovan, Michael—*Continued*
Sorcerer's apprentice
  O'Donovan, M. More stories by Frank
    O'Connor ₍pseud₎
The thief
  O'Donovan, M. Traveller's samples
This mortal coil
  O'Donovan, M. Traveller's samples
Torrent damned
  O'Donovan, M. More stories by Frank
    O'Connor ₍pseud₎
Unapproved route
  O'Donovan, M. More stories by Frank
    O'Connor ₍pseud₎
Uprooted
  Davis, R. G. ed. Ten modern masters
  O'Donovan, M. Stories of Frank O'Con-
    nor ₍pseud₎
Vanity
  O'Donovan, M. More stories by Frank
    O'Connor ₍pseud₎

Odor of thought. Sheckley, R.

Odor of verbena. Faulkner, W.

Oesterreicher, A. 1863-
How Rezi baked motzas
  Leftwich, J. ed. Yisröel. 1952 ed.

Of love and joy. Rosegger, P.

Of our meeting with Cousin John. Oxenham, J.

Of shoes and ships. Marsland, A. M.

Of this time, of that place. Trilling, L.

Of time and Third Avenue. Bester, A.

O'Faoláin, Seán, 1900-
The bombshop
  Gordon, C. and Tate, A. eds. House of
    fiction
Lonely lives
  Blodgett, H. W. ed. Story survey.
    1953 ed.
Man who invented sin
  Felheim, M.; Newman, F. B. and Stein-
    hoff, W. R. eds. Modern short stories
Unholy living and half dying
  Gable, M. Sister, ed. Many-colored fleece

Off the face of the earth. Rawson, C.

OFFICE WORKERS. See Clerks

Officers' girl. Worden, W. L.

Official position. Maugham, W. S.

Official record. Pratt, F.

OFFICIALS. See Civil service

Offshore. Watkins, R. H.

O'Flaherty, Liam, 1897-
The bath
  O'Flaherty, L. Two lovely beasts, and
    other stories
The beggars
  O'Flaherty, L. Two lovely beasts, and
    other stories
The challenge
  Burnett, W. ed. World's best
  O'Flaherty, L. Two lovely beasts, and
    other stories
Child of God
  Fremantle, A. J. ed. Mothers
The eviction
  O'Flaherty, L. Two lovely beasts, and
    other stories
Flute-player
  O'Flaherty, L. Two lovely beasts, and
    other stories
Galway Bay
  O'Flaherty, L. Two lovely beasts, and
    other stories
Grey seagull
  O'Flaherty, L. Two lovely beasts and
    other stories
The lament
  O'Flaherty, L. Two lovely beasts and
    other stories
Life
  O'Flaherty, L. Two lovely beasts and
    other stories
Light
  O'Flaherty, L. Two lovely beasts and
    other stories
The mouse
  O'Flaherty, L. Two lovely beasts and
    other stories
New suit
  O'Flaherty, L. Two lovely beasts and
    other stories
Old hunter
  Cerf, B. A. and Moriarty, H. C. eds.
    Anthology of famous British stories
Old woman
  O'Flaherty, L. Two lovely beasts and
    other stories
The parting
  O'Flaherty, L. Two lovely beasts, and
    other stories
The seal
  O'Flaherty, L. Two lovely beasts, and
    other stories
The tide
  O'Flaherty, L. Two lovely beasts, and
    other stories
The touch
  O'Flaherty, L. Two lovely beasts, and
    other stories
Two lovely beasts
  O'Flaherty, L. Two lovely beasts, and
    other stories
The water hen
  O'Flaherty, L. Two lovely beasts, and
    other stories
The wedding
  O'Flaherty, L. Two lovely beasts, and
    other stories
Wild goat's kid
  Ungar, F. ed. To mother with love

Ogus, Aaron D. 1865-1943
The essrig
  Ausubel, N. ed. Treasury of Jewish
    humor
Shofar blower of Lapinishok
  Ausubel, N. ed. Treasury of Jewish
    humor

Oh joy, it's a boy. Scilken, M.

Oh, lovely land. Haycox, E.

"Oh, mirror, mirror." Kneale, N.

O'Hanlon, Debra M.
Life and death of a village
  Best Army short stories, 1950

O'Hara, John, 1905-
Do you like it here?
  Burrell, J. A. and Cerf, B. A. eds. An-
    thology of famous American stories
  Schorer, M. ed. The story

O'Hara, Mary, pseud. See Sture-Vasa, Mary (Alsop)

O'Higgins, Harvey Jerrold, 1876-1929
Big Dan Reilly
Burrell, J. A. and Cerf, B. A. eds. Anthology of famous American stories
His mother
Ungar, F. ed. To mother with love

OHIO
Anderson, S. I'm a fool
Anderson, S. Sophistication
Bromfield, L. Sugar camp

Frontier and pioneer life
See Frontier and pioneer life—Ohio

OIL WELLS. See Petroleum

OJIBWAY INDIANS. See Chippewa Indians

Okie. Blish, J.

Olaf the Magnificent. Sayres, W. C.

Olalla. Stevenson, R. L.

Old acquaintance. Collier, J.

Old acrobat and the ruined city. Putman, C.

OLD AGE
Aldrich, B. S. Bid the tapers twinkle
Aldrich, B. S. The dreams are real
Anderson, E. V. Old Tom O'Grady of Shay Ranch
Angoff, C. Alte Bobbe
Ashley, E. L. Aunt Lil
Auchincloss, L. Finish, good lady
Baum, V. Old house
Betts, D. End of Henry Fribble
Betts, D. Serpents and doves
Betts, D. Very old are beautiful
Boyd, J. Old pines
Burnet, D. Vision of Henry Whipple
Calisher, H. Box of ginger
Cather, W. S. Neighbor Rosicky
Chekhov, A. P. Tædium vitæ
Clark, W. Van T. Wind and the snow of winter
Collier, J. Little memento
Cooke, A. Christmas Eve
De La Roche, M. Death of a centenarian
Derleth, A. W. The telescope
Dreiser, T. Lost Phoebe
Elliott, H. S. Blue hat
Ferber, E. Old man Minick
Galsworthy, J. Ultima Thule
Grimson, M. S. Eighty years old
Hemingway, E. Clean, well-lighted place
Hemingway, E. Old man at the bridge
Humphrey, W. The Hardys
Jameson, M. Blind alley
Johnson, D. M. Laugh in the face of danger
Kandel, L. Boy with the innocent eyes
Karmel, I. Fru Holm
Lardner, R. W. Golden honeymoon
Munro, H. H. The cobweb
Newhouse, E. Couple of old-timers
Porter, K. A. Jilting of Granny Weatherall
Praag, S. E. van. Weesperstraat
Rosenfeld, J. Sick goose
Schaefer, J. W. Old Anse
Seager, A. Old man of the mountain
Suckow, R. Some others and myself; 7 stories

Tate, A. Immortal woman
Taylor, E. "Taking mother out"
Taylor, P. H. Their losses
Waugh, E. Bella Fleace gave a party
Welty, E. Old Mr Marblehall
Welty, E. Visit of charity
Welty, E. Worn path
West, J. Shivaree before breakfast

Old-age pensioners. O'Donovan, M.

Old Anse. Schaefer, J. W.

Old Calamity tries a bluff. Fishman, J. F.

Old century's river. La Farge, O.

Old Chief Mshlanga. Lessing, D. M.

Old crawdad. Wylie, P.

Old demon. Buck, P. S.

Old Doc Rivers. Williams, W. C.

Old Em's Kentucky home. Runyon, D.

Old faith. O'Donovan, M.

Old Faithful. Gallun, R. Z.

Old fellows. O'Donovan, M.

Old Gore. Stuart, J.

Old Hard. Beachcroft, T. O.

Old Hook 'n' Eye. Annixter, P. pseud.

Old house. Baum, V.

Old hunter. O'Flaherty, L.

Old Hussar. Bergengruen, W.

Old Ironpuss. Gordon, A.

Old John's place. Lessing, D. M.

OLD LADIES. See Old age

Old lady Mandle. Ferber, E.

Old maid. Balzac, H. de

Old maid. Wharton, E. N. J.

OLD MAIDS. See Spinsters

Old man. Du Maurier, D.

Old man. Faulkner, W.

Old man at the bridge. Hemingway, E.

Old man had four wives. Scheiner, F.

Old man Henderson. Neville, K.

Old man Isbell's wife. Davis, H. L.

Old man Minick. Ferber, E.

Old Man Mulligan. Miller, P. S.

Old man of the mountain. Seager, A.

Old man of the mountains. Gilbert, K.

Old man's bride. Byrd, S.

Old manuscript. Kafka, F.

Old masters. Harvey, W. F.

OLD MEN. See Old age

Old men. McCarthy, M. T.

Old men and boys. Jackson, C. R.

Old men's plans. La Farge, O.

Old Mr Marblehall. Welty, E.

Old mortality. Porter, K. A.

The old, old story. Street, J. H.

Old page. Kafka, F.

Old pal. Sullivan, R.

Old pastures. Foote, J. T.

Old people. Faulkner, W.

Old pines. Boyd, J.

Old ranch. Güiraldes, R.

Old Red. Gordon, C.

Old stock. Calisher, H.

Old time raid. Williams, W. C.

Old Tom O'Grady of Shay Ranch. Anderson, E. V.

Old town of Pskoff. Munro, H. H.

Old Turkey Neck. Lanning, G.

Old Well-Well. Grey, Z.

Old woman. Horwitz, J.

Old woman. Marshall, J.

Old woman. O'Flaherty, L.

Old Woodruff and his three wives. Moodie, S. S.

Old-world landowners. Gogol', N. V.

Olds, Helen (Diehl) 1895-
  Susan steps out
    Furman, A. L. ed. Everygirls career stories
  Vic's Orr kid
    Furman, A. L. ed. Everygirls career stories

Ole man Sanford. Foote, J. T.

The **oleander.** DeFord, M. A.

OLEANDERS
  DeFord, M. A. The oleander

O'Leary, John T.
  Protecting Mary
    Oberfirst, R. ed. 1952 anthology of best original short-shorts

Olesha, IUrii Karlovich, 1899-
  Envy
    Rahv, P. ed. Great Russian short novels

Olive, Harry
  Take it and like it
    Argosy (Periodical) Argosy Book of sports stories

Olive grove. Maupassant, G. de

Oliver, Chad, 1928-
  Ant and the eye
    Sloane, W. M. ed. Stories for tomorrow
  Any more at home like you?
    Star science fiction stories, no. 3
  Win the world
    Lesser, M. A. ed. Looking forward

Ollivant, Alfred, 1874-1927
  Shepherds' trophy
    Fenner, P. R. comp. Dogs, dogs, dogs

Olsen, Bob
  Four-dimensional roller-press
    Wollheim, D. A. comp. Every boy's book of science-fiction

Olsen, Dolores (Birk) See Hitchens, Dolores (Birk)

Olyesha, Yuri. See Olesha, IUrii Karlovich

O'Meara, Walter
  Bush medicine
    O'Meara, W. Tales of the two borders
  Child that walked at night
    O'Meara, W. Tales of the two borders
  Desert fire
    O'Meara, W. Tales of the two borders
  Lost child
    O'Meara, W. Tales of the two borders
  La Porcelaine Claire
    O'Meara, W. Tales of the two borders

  Red MacDonald
    O'Meara, W. Tales of the two borders
  To trouble the living
    O'Meara, W. Tales of the two borders

On account of a hat. Rabinowitz, S.

On (and off) the agenda. Kober, A.

On approval. Munro, H. H.

On behalf of the management. Porter, W. S.

On Christmas Day. Eggleston, M. W.

On Christmas Eve. Eichelberger, R. K.

On Greenhow Hill. Kipling, R.

On guard. Waugh, E.

On lying awake at night. White, S. E.

On presenting arms. Bergengruen, W.

On Ruegen Island. Isherwood, C.

On skating. Skinner, C. O.

On stony ground. Sansom, W.

On the brink. Yaffe, J.

On the day of the crucifixion. Andreev, L. N.

On the dodge. James, W.

On the drift. James, W.

On the great alkali plain. Doyle, Sir A. C.

On the harmful effects of tobacco; first version. Chekhov, A. P.

On the harmful effects of tobacco; final version. Chekhov, A. P.

On the heights. Corkery, D.

On the road. Chekov, A. P.

On the road. Hughes, L.

On the roof of the world. Roberts, Sir C. G. D.

On the verge. Sandoz, M. Y.

On the way. Gorky, M.

On the way home. Hughes, L.

On trial. Hoffman, E.

O'Nan, Jill, pseud. See O'Nan, Mildred (Cook)

O'Nan, Mildred (Cook) 1906-
  Table before me
    Gable, M. Sister, ed. Many-colored fleece

Once a cowboy. James, W.

Once-beautiful Ellie. Halladay, V.

Once on a Sunday. Wylie, P.

Once on Christmas. Thompson, D.

Once upon a crime. Cohen, O. R.

Once upon a time. Parker, J. R.

Once upon a train. Rice, C. and Palmer, S.

One. De Vries, P.

One-armed John finds a corpse. Hendryx, J. B.

One-armed John voices a threat. Hendryx, J. B.

One autumn night. Gorky, M.

One dollar's worth. Porter, W. S.

One for O'Brien. Morrill, G. P.

One for the team. Regli, A. C.

One Friday morning. Hughes, L.

One grave too few. Asquith, Lady C. M. E. C.

One guy, one gal, one island. Holder, W.

One he called Winnie. Schulberg, B. W.
One hour of glory. Rinehart, M. R.
One in a million. Brown, G.
One in three hundred. McIntosh, J. T.
One leg too many. Alexander, W.
One man's meat. Chekhov, A. P.
One mile of ice. Garner, H.
One minute longer. Terhune, A. P
One missing. Cooke, A. A.
One more inning. O'Rourke, F.
One morning they'll hang him. Allingham, M.
One named Jesus. Buck, P. S.
One night. Portor, L. S.
One night in Bradford. Bentley, P. E.
One night in Coffin Creek. Thompson, T.
One of hers. Van Doren, M.
One of the chosen. Calisher, H.
One of the Garretsons. Van Doren, M.
One of the missing. Bierce, A.
One of three others. Suckow, R.
One ounce of common sense. O'Rourke, F.
One phase of love. Maupassant, G. de
One ride too many. Bonham, F.
One summer. Grau, S. A.
One summer afternoon. Dann, L.
One sunny afternoon. Sansom, W.
One thousand dollars. Porter, W. S.
One, two, three little Indians. Garner, H.
One way of getting a hundred pounds. Kersh, G.
One-way street. Willis, A. A.
One way to victory. Ford, N. A.
The one who waits. Bradbury, R.
The onlooker. Isaacson, B. K.
Only love me. Terr, I.
Only the dead know Brooklyn. Wolfe, T.
Only the dead ride proudly. Fox, N. A.
Only thing we learn. Kornbluth, C. M.
ONTARIO, CANADA. See Canada—Ontario
Opatoshu, Joseph, 1886-1954
   Eternal wedding gown
      Howe, I. and Greenberg, E. eds. Treasury of Yiddish stories
   Horse thief
      Leftwich, J. ed. Yisröel. 1952 ed.
   May the Temple be restored!
      Howe, I. and Greenberg, E. eds. Treasury of Yiddish stories
Opatovsky, Joseph, pseud. See Opatoshu, Joseph
Open boat. Crane, S.
Open house. De Vries, P.
Open road. Farrell, J. T.
Open season. Lyle, D.
Open season. Summers, J. L.
Open secret. Kuttner, H.
Open, sesame! Grendon, S.
Open window. Munro, H. H.
Open winter. Davis, H. L.

Opening day with Mr Hardey's hounds. Surtees, R. S.
Opening day with the Duke of Tergiversation's hounds. Surtees, R. S.
Opening day with the Larkspur hounds. Surtees, R. S.
Opening doors. Shiras, W. H.
OPERA SINGERS. See Musicians—Singers
Operating instructions. Sheckley, R.
Operation pumice. Gallun, R. Z.
Operation RSVP. Piper, H. B.
OPERATIONS, SURGICAL. See Surgery
Opium eater. Keller, D. H.
OPIUM HABIT
   Maugham, W. S. Mirage
OPIUM TRADE
   Bowles, P. F. Señor Ong and Señor Ha
OPOSSUMS
   Annixter, P. pseud. White possum
Or else. Kuttner, H.
Oracle of the dog. Chesterton, G. K.
ORANG-UTANS
   Poe, E. A. Murders in the Rue Morgue
ORANGE
   Shneur, Z. Immortal orange
Orange room. Stuart, L.
ORATORS
   Saroyan, W. My cousin Dikran, the orator
Oratory contest. Farrell, J. T.
Orban twins. Bergengruen, W.
ORCHARDS
   Fuchs, A. M. Among the trees
ORCHESTRA
   Culver, M. Black water blues
   Rice, C. Goodbye forever
ORCHIDS
   Annixter, P. pseud. Orchids and crocodiles
   Collier, J. Green thoughts
   Wells, H. G. Strange orchid
Orchids and crocodiles. Annixter, P. pseud.
Ordeal in space. Heinlein, R. A.
Ordeal of Professor Klein. De Camp, L. S.
Orderly world of Mr Appleby. Ellin, S.
Orders. Jameson, M.
ORDERS, MONASTIC. See Monasticism and religious orders
Orders for Korea. Brown, M. F.
ORDNANCE
   Aldrich, T. B. How we astonished the Rivermouthians
   Bergengruen, W. Orban twins
      See also Arms and armor; Firearms
OREGON
   Davis, H. L. Team bells woke me; 13 stories
O'Reilly, John, 1907?-
   Sound of gunfire
      Meredith, S. ed. Bar 1 roundup of best western stories
O'Reilly, Tom
   60 ways to lose a horse bet
      Dachs, D. ed. Treasury of sports humor

Oreste. Shultz, W. H.
ORGANISTS. See Musicians—Organists
The **orgy:** an idyll. De La Mare, W. J.
Ornitz, Samuel, 1890-
  Yom Kipper fressers
    Ausubel, N. ed. Treasury of Jewish
      humor
O'Rourke, Frank, 1916-
  Argument with death
    O'Rourke, F. Ride west
  Battle royal
    O'Rourke, F. Ride west
  Best position
    O'Rourke, F. Greatest victory, and other
      baseball stories
  Cold water and cherry pie
    O'Rourke, F. Ride west
  Decision
    O'Rourke, F. Greatest victory, and other
      baseball stories
  Delayed decision
    O'Rourke, F. Greatest victory, and other
      baseball stories
  Easy going man
    O'Rourke, F. Ride west
  Flashing spikes
    O'Rourke, F. Greatest victory, and other
      baseball stories
  Greatest victory
    O'Rourke, F. Greatest victory, and other
      baseball stories
  Heavenly world series
    O'Rourke, F. Heavenly world series,
      and other baseball stories
  Home game
    O'Rourke, F. Greatest victory, and other
      baseball stories
  Impossible play
    O'Rourke, F. Heavenly world series,
      and other baseball stories
  Last accounting
    O'Rourke, F. Greatest victory, and other
      baseball stories
  Last out
    O'Rourke, F. Greatest victory, and other
      baseball stories
  Last pitch
    O'Rourke, F. Heavenly world series,
      and other baseball stories
  Last shot
    Meredith, S. ed. Bar 2
    O'Rourke, F. Ride west
  Last time around
    O'Rourke, F. Heavenly world series,
      and other baseball stories
  Last time up
    O'Rourke, F. Greatest victory, and other
      baseball stories
  Look for the kid with the guts
    O'Rourke, F. Heavenly world series,
      and other baseball stories
  Magic circle
    O'Rourke, F. Heavenly world series,
      and other baseball stories
  Man who sold himself
    O'Rourke, F. Ride west
  Moment of truth
    O'Rourke, F. Heavenly world series,
      and other baseball stories
  No color
    O'Rourke, F. Heavenly world series,
      and other baseball stories
  Nothing new
    O'Rourke, F. Greatest victory, and other
      baseball stories
  One more inning
    O'Rourke, F. Greatest victory, and other
      baseball stories
  One ounce of common sense
    O'Rourke, F. Heavenly world series,
      and other baseball stories
  Parade is ten minutes long
    O'Rourke, F. Ride west
  Right count
    O'Rourke, F. Ride west
  Twentieth game
    O'Rourke, F. Greatest victory, and other
      baseball stories
  Violence at sundown
    O'Rourke, F. Ride west
  Whippletree
    O'Rourke, F. Ride west
  Widow's peak
    O'Rourke, F. Ride west
ORPHANS
  Ballard, J. C. Mountain summer
  Benefield, B. Christmas Eve's Day
  Norris, K. T. Mother of Angela Hogan
  Paget, V. Dionea
  Ringwood, G. P. Little ghost
  Simak, C. D. Contraption
  Taylor, E. Hester Lilly
    See also Boys; Children; Girls
The **orphans.** Verga, G.
Orphans in uniform. Gilbreth, F. B. and
    Carey, E. M. G.
Orpheus and his lute. O'Donovan, M.
Orwell, George, 1903-1950
  Shooting an elephant
    New writing (Periodical) Best stories
Osage Girl. Curry, P. S.
Osborne, Maybelle Hinton
  Mrs Kochinsky and the problem child
    Seventeen (Periodical) Nineteen from
      Seventeen
Osborne, Robertson
  Action on Azura
    Greenberg, M. ed. Travelers of space
    Same as: Contact, incorporated
  Contact, incorporated
    Conklin, G. ed. Big book of science fic-
      tion
    Same as: Action on Azura
Osborne's revenge. James, H.
Oscar on roller skates. Neikirk, M. E.
Oscar, the trained seal. Neikirk, M. E.
Ospina, Carlos Wyld. See Wyld Ospina,
    Carlos
OSPREYS
  Roberts, Sir C. G. D. Fishers of the air
OSTLERS. See Stablemen
Other Diane. Balzac, H. de
Other foot. Bradbury, R.
Other Margaret. Trilling, L.
Other now. Jenkins, W. F.
Other one. Colette, S. G.
Other pebbles on the beach. Kober, A.
Other people. Adler, W.
Other people's misfortune. Chekhov, A. P.

Other people's troubles. Chekhov, A. P.
The other place. Priestley, J. B.
Other river. Bowen, R. O.
Other side. Kubilius, W.
Other side of the hedge. Forster, E. M.
Other son. Pirandello, L.
Other tracks. Sell, W.
Other two. Wharton, E. N. J.
Other Wise Man. Van Dyke, H.
Other woman. Winslow, T. S.
OTTERS
  Murphy, R. You've got to learn
Ounce of prevention. Carter, P.
Our advertisement brings a visitor. Doyle,
  Sir A. C.
Our country. Monn, A.
Our fair city. Heinlein, R. A.
Our father. Stern, J.
Our Felix. Rosenberg, E.
OUR LADY OF GUADALUPE.   See
  Guadalupe, Our lady of
Our lady's juggler. France, A.
Our last day with the Handley Cross. Sur-
  tees, R. S.
Our vegetable love. Putnam, C.
Our white deer. Schulberg, B. W.
Oursler, Fulton, 1893-1952
  Bargain in brimstone
    Thinker's digest (Periodical) Spoiled
    priest, and other stories
Oursler, Will. See Oursler, William Charles
Oursler, William Charles, 1913-
  Thread of life
    Mystery Writers of America, inc. 20
    great tales of murder
Out of Nazareth. Porter, W. S.
Out of sheer boredom. Chekhov, A. P.
Out of the night. Campbell, J. W.
Out of the past. Schaefer, J. W.
Out where the West begins. Newhouse, E.
Outcasts of Poker Flat. Harte, B.
OUTDOOR LIFE
  Andrews, R. C. ed. My favorite stories
    of the great outdoors; 35 stories
  Macfarlan, A. A. Moose boy
    See also Camping
Outer limit. Doar, G.
OUTER SPACE, VISITS TO OR FROM.
    See Interplanetary visitors; Inter-
    planetary voyages
The outlander. Jackson, C. R.
The outlaw. Ross, S.
The outlaw. Smith, E. C.
Outlaw trail. Mowery, W. B.
OUTLAWS
  Cheshire, G. Strangers in the evening
  Foster, B. Outlaws are in town
  Hendryx, J. B. Intrigue on Halfaday
    Creek; 28 stories
  Hinton, J. Mediators to the goatherd
  Johnson, D. M. Laugh in the face of
    danger
  Lagerlöf, S. O. L. The outlaws
  Loomis, N. M. The twilighters
  Nye, N. C. Rock bottom
  Porter, W. S. Caballero's way
  Porter, W. S. Chaparral Christmas gift
  Porter, W. S. Passing of Black Eagle
  Roper, W. Last cigarette
  Thompson, T. Silver saddle
  Welty, E. Still moment
    See also Brigands and robbers;
    Crime and Criminals
The outlaws. Lagerlöf, S. O. L.
Outlaws are in town. Foster, B.
Outlaw's boots. Thompson, T
An outlier from his tribe. Frankau, G.
The outstation. Maugham, W. S.
Oval portrait. Poe, E. A.
Over insurance. Collier, J.
Over the Green Mountains. Caldwell, E.
Over the line. Stevenson, C. L.
Over the mountain. Todd, R.
Over the top. Del Rey, L.
Over there. White, W.
The overcoat. Benson, S.
The overcoat. Gogol', N. V.
Overholser, Wayne D. 1906-
  Patriarch of Gunsight Flat
    Western Writers of America.. Holsters
    and heroes
OVERLAND JOURNEYS
  Browne, J. R. Peep at Washoe
  Chekhov, A. P. Across Siberia
  La Farge, O. Old man's plans
Overlooked lady. McNulty, J.
The oversight. Munro, H. H.
Overthrow. Cartmill, C.
Overture De Vries, P.
Owner's interest. Dingle, A. E.
OXEN
  Roberts, Sir C. G. D. Brothers of the
    yoke
  Schaefer, J. W. Takes a real man . . .
    See also Cattle
Oxenham, John, 1852-1941
  Of our meeting with Cousin John
    Brentano, F. ed. The word lives on
  Their first meeting
    Brentano, F. ed. The word lives on
OX-TEAMSTERS. See Teamsters
OYSTERS
  London, J. Raid on the oyster pirates
Oyved, Moysheh. See Good, Edward
OZARK MOUNTAINS
  Kantor, M. Life in her hands
  Mowery, W. B. Tales of the Ozarks; 9
    stories
    See also Mountain whites (Southern
    States

P

P. & O. Maugham, W. S.
P.G. Christmas. Hertlein, R.
Ph.D. Markfield, W.
Pa sees again. Dixon, E. S.

Pace, Jim
  Apple for Mom
    Furman, A L. ed. Teen-age horse stories
Pace that kills. Williams, W. C.
Pacing mustang. Seton, E. T.
Pack of troubles for one cent. Zevin, I. J.
Package of big bills. Hendryx, J. B.
Package tzoress. Vulfarts, M.
Packard, Frank Lucius, 1877-1942
  Man who confessed
    Moskowitz, S. ed. Great railroad stories
      of the world
The **pact.** Gainfort, P.
Padgett, Lewis, pseud. See Kuttner, Henry
PADUA. See Italy—Padua

Pagano, Jo, 1906-
  The disinherited
    Lass, A. H. and Horowitz, A. eds.
      Stories for youth
  Signor Santa
    Lohan, R. and Lohan, M. eds New
      Christmas treasury

Page, Norvell W.
  But without horns
    Greenberg, M. comp. Five science fic-
      tion novels

Page, Patricia K. 1916-
  The resignation
    Pacey, D. ed. Book of Canadian stories

Page, Thomas Nelson, 1853-1922
  Burial of the guns
    Scribner treasury
  Two little Confederates
    Fenner, P. R. comp. Yankee Doodle

Page and player. Bixby, J.

Page from the Song of Songs. Rabinowitz,
  S.

PAGEANTS
  Woolf, V. Between the acts

Pages from Cold Point. Bowles, P. F.

Paget, Violet, 1856-1935
  Amour dure
    Paget, V. Snake Lady, and other stories
  Dionea
    Paget, V. Snake Lady, and other stories
  Legend of Madame Krasinska
    Paget, V. Snake Lady, and other stories
  Prince Alberic and the Snake Lady
    Paget, V. Snake Lady, and other stories
  Seeker of pagan perfection
    Paget, V. Snake Lady, and other stories
  Virgin of the seven daggers
    Paget, V. Snake Lady, and other stories
  Wedding chest
    Paget, V. Snake Lady, and other stories
  Wicked voice
    Paget, V. Snake Lady, and other stories

Paid nurse. Williams, W. C.

Pail of air. Leiber, F.

Pain, Barry Eric Odell, 1864-1928
  The doll
    Cooper, A. C. ed. Modern short stories

PAIN. See Suffering

Painful case. Joyce, J.

PAINTERS
  Beck, V. J. Night boat from Barcelona
  Beck, W. Edge of doom
  Brenner, L. Discovery
  Collier, J. Witch's money
  Dahl, R. Skin
  De La Mare, W. J. The tree
  Horwitz, J. Generations of man
  Humphrey, W. The fauve
  Huxley, A. L. Tillotson banquet
  James, H. The liar
  Keller, D. H. Moon artist
  Lewis, E. G. Portrait
  McConnell, W. Totem
  Munro, H. H. The background
  Munro, H. H. The bull
  Munro, H. H. On approval
  Munro, H. H. Stalled ox
  Norling, M. E. Jade ring
  Paget, V. Seeker of pagan perfection
  Porter, W. S. Art and the bronco
  Porter, W. S. Day resurgent
  Porter, W. S. Madison Square Arabian
    night
  Porter, W. S. Masters of arts
  Porter, W. S. Service of love
  Schulberg, D. W. Passport to nowhere
  Stern, J. Idolater of Degas
  Ullman, J. R. Silver sword
  Van Doren, M. Like what?
  Waltari, M. T. Island of ice
  Waugh, E. Work suspended
  Werfel, F. Saverio's secret
PAINTINGS
  Bergengruen, W. Giorgio and Martino
  Bradbury, R. The smile
  Brenner, L. Merchant of art
  Fischer, B. My Aunt Celia
  Harvey, W. F. Old masters
  Lemelin, R. Stations of the Cross
  Lernet-Holenia, A. M. Mona Lisa
  Moore, D. E. Portrait
  Trilling, L. Other Margaret
  Wharton, E. N. J. The moving finger
A **pair.** Bottome, P.
The **pair.** Rabinowitz, S.
The **pair.** Van Doren, M.
Pair of Vikings. Aiken, C. P.
PAIUTE INDIANS
  Davis, S. P. Sage-brush chief

Pal: the dog who trained himself. Little,
  G. W.

Palacio Valdés, Armando, 1853-1938
  I Puritani
    De Onís, H. ed. Spanish stories and
      tales

Pale green fishes. Taylor, K.

Pale horse, pale rider. Porter, K. A.

Pale sergeant. Myers, H.

PALEONTOLOGISTS
  De Camp, L. S. Employment

PALESTINE

        Earliest to B.C. 63
  Zweig, A. Jerusalem delivered

        1st century
  Oxenham, J. Of our meeting with Cousin
    John

PALESTINE—*Continued*

Bethlehem

Goudge, E. Son-of-David

Jerusalem

Hirshbein, P. Tears on stones
Stinetorf, L. A. Refugee village
Palimpsest of St Augustine. Pratt, F. and De Camp, L. S.
PALIMPSESTS. See Manuscripts (Palimpsests)
Palm Beach Santa Claus. Runyon, D.
Palm Island plane factory. Chichester, F. C.
Palm Springs. Charteris, L.
Palm Sunday. Jackson, C. R.
Palma, Ricardo, 1833-1919
Two cooing doves
De Onís, H. ed. Spanish stories and tales
Palmer, Stuart, 1905-
Jinx man
Best detective stories of the year—1953
Riddle of the Black Museum
Mystery Writers of America, inc. Butcher, baker, murder-maker
Riddle of the dangling pearl
Mystery Writers of America, inc. Maiden murders
Riddle of the snafu murder
Mystery Writers of America, inc. 20 great tales of murder
Riddle of the tired bullet
Mystery Writers of America, inc. Four-&-twenty bloodhounds
Where angels fear to tread
Best detective stories of the year—1952
See also Rice, C. jt. auth.
Palo. Saroyan, W.
Palomino. Murphy, B.
PAMPAS
Güiraldes, R. Old ranch
PAN (GOD)
Beauclerk, H. De V. Miracle of the vineyard
Munro, H. H. Music on the hill
PANCAKES. See Griddle cakes
Pangborn, Edgar
Angel's egg
Conklin, G. ed. Invaders of earth
Mrrrar!
Queen, E. pseud, ed. Queen's awards: 8th ser.
Pick-up for Olympus
Conklin, G. and Conklin, L. T. eds. Supernatural reader
Singing stick
Queen, E. pseud. ed. Queen's awards: 7th ser.
The panther. Norton, B.
PANTHERS. See Leopards; Pumas
Paolo Uccello. Schwob, M.
Papa Pierre's pipe. Kantor, M.
Papa's going bye-bye. Harwood, K.
Papashvily, George, 1895?- and Papashvily, Helen (Waite) 1906-
Getting quick rich
Fenner, P. R. comp. Fun! Fun! Fun!

Papashvily, Helen (Waite) See Papashvily, G. jt. auth.
PARABLES
Grimson, M. S. When Dan came home
Parachute warning. Carter, R. G.
PARACHUTES
Carter, R. G. Parachute warning
Parade is ten minutes long. O'Rourke, F.
Paradis, Marjorie (Bartholomew)
None but the fair
American girl (Periodical) Christmas all year 'round
Red wagon
American girl (Periodical) Christmas all year 'round
PARADISE. See Eden
Paradise. Lagerkvist, P. F.
Paradise. Simak, C. D.
Paradise of bachelors. Melville, H.
Paradise of thieves. Chesterton, G. K.
Paradise street. Moore, C. L.
Paradise II. Sheckley, R.
Paradox lost. Brown, F.
PARAPSYCHOLOGY. See Thought-transference
Parasite planet. Weinbaum, S. G.
The parcel. Zweig, A.
Parcel of land. Skinner, C. O.
Pardo Bazán, Emilia, condesa de, 1852-1921
Sister Aparición
De Onís, H. ed. Spanish stories and tales
The pardon. Rawlings, M. K.
Pardon my mistake. Pratt, F.
Pardoner's tale. Chaucer, G.
PARENT AND CHILD
Gordimer, N. The defeated
O'Donovan, M. Masculine protest
Schorer, M. What we don't know hurts us

See also Fathers and sons

Parents and horses. Lewis, W.
PARIS. See France—Paris
Paris scene: 1931. Farrell, J. T.
Paris: The covetous headsman. Charteris, L.
The park. Bates, H. E.
Parker, C. W.
Flimsy walls
Stanford short stories, 1950
Parker, Daniel Francis, 1893-
Passing of the first floor back
Dachs, D. ed. Treasury of sports humor
Parker, Dorothy (Rothschild) 1893-
Big blonde
Burrell, J. A. and Cerf, B. A. eds. Anthology of famous American stories
First-prize stories, 1919-1954
Horsie
Fabricant, N. D. and Werner, H. eds. World's best doctor stories
Parker, Sir Gilbert, bart. 1862-1932
The flood
Pacey, D. ed. Book of Canadian stories

Parker, Glidden, 1913-
Bright and morning
Best American short stories, 1950
Parker, James Reid, 1909-
All the little jokers
Blaustein, A. P. ed. Fiction goes to court
Domino method
Parker, J. R. Open house
Down from the mountains
Parker, J. R. Open house
Estate of Alice V. Gregg
Parker, J. R. Open house
Hardy day
Parker, J. R. Open house
Hounds of spring
Parker, J. R. Open house
Intervention of providence
Parker, J. R. Open house
Joy, joy, joy!
Parker, J. R. Open house
Judgment of Paris
Parker, J. R. Open house
Katrina
Parker, J. R. Open house
Lower Mississippi is thicker than water
Parker, J. R. Open house
The millennium
Parker, J. R. Open house
Miss Ber
Parker, J. R. Open house
Mission to Massachusetts
Parker, J. R. Open house
Mr Gregg and the occult
Parker, J. R. Open house
Monks revel at Winkton
Parker, J. R. Open house
N.E.S.P.D.I.P.
Parker, J. R. Open house
Once upon a time
Parker, J. R. Open house
Red carpet
Parker, J. R. Open house
Robes et modes
Parker, J. R. Open house
Tenth Street idyll
Parker, J. R. Open house
Parkhurst, Genevieve
Payday
Harper, W. comp. Dog show
Parochial school. Doty, W. L.
PAROCHIAL SCHOOLS. See Church schools; Convent schools
PARODIES
De Vries, P. From there to infinity
De Vries, P. Requiem for a noun
De Vries, P. Touch and go
Leiber, F. Night he cried
See also Satire
PARRICIDE
Flaubert, G. Legend of St Julian the Hospitaller
Proust, M. Filial sentiments of a parricide
The **parrot.** Bowen, E.
The **parrot.** Duranty, W.
PARROTS
Annixter, P. pseud. Old Hook 'n' Eye
Bowen, E. The parrot
Collier, J. Bird of prey
Duranty, W. The parrot
The gift
Harvey, W. F. Ripe for development
Wetjen, A. R. Ship of silence
Parsley garden. Saroyan, W.
Parsons, Elizabeth, 1909-
Not a soul will come along
Prize stories of 1950
PARSONS. See Clergy
Part of the act. Alexander, S.
Part time hoopster. Coombs, C. I.
PARTIES
Emmons, B. Dance with the devil
Fitzgerald, F. S. K. Baby party
Hardy, T. Three strangers
Joyce, J. The dead
Mann, T. Disorder and early sorrow
Mansfield, K. Her first ball
Miller, J. D. Somebody else, not me
Saroyan, W. Cocktail party
Waugh, E. Bella Fleace gave a party
See also Birthdays; Children's parties; Dinners; Garden parties; House parties
The **parting.** O'Flaherty, L.
Parting at morning. Jackson, C. R.
PARTRIDGES
Seton, E. T. Redruff
Party dress. Winter, A. B.
Party to blackmail. Brandon, W.
Pasinetti, P. M.
Family history
Southern review. Anthology of stories from the Southern review
Passage in the life of Mr John Oakhurst. Harte, B.
Passage to Kentucky. Webber, E. M.
Passengers for Panama. Pease, H.
Passing of Black Eagle. Porter, W. S.
Passing of Poker Bill. Thompson, T.
Passing of the first floor back. Parker, D. F.
Passing through Fieldsville. Schneider, R.
Passion. Yuen Chin
Passion in the desert. Balzac, H. de
Passion of Lance Corporal Hawkins. Shaw, I.
Passos, John Rodgerigo dos. See Dos Passos, John Roderigo
PASSOVER
Bruggen, C. de H. van. Seder night
Heine, H. Seder night
Heine, H. Tale of olden time
Oesterreicher, A. How Rezi baked motzas
Rabinowitz, S. Passover guest
Rabinowitz, S. Passover in a village
Reisen, A. Rich poor man
See also Jews—Rites and ceremonies
Passover guest. Rabinowitz, S.
Passover in a village. Rabinowitz, S.
Passport to nowhere. Schulberg, B. W.
Past one at Rooney's. Porter, W. S.
PAST TIME. See Time
Paste. James, H.

Pasternak, Boris Leonidovich, 1890-
Letters from Tula
Guerney, B. G. comp. New Russian
stories
Pastor Dowe at Tacate. Bowles, P. F.
Pastorale. Sansom, W.
PASTORS. See Clergy
Pat Hobby himself: a patriotic short. Fitzgerald, F. S. K.
Pat Hobby himself: two old-timers. Fitzgerald, F. S. K.
Pat who was afraid of boys. Strain, F. B.
Patchouly. Morrison, J.
Patchy. Coatsworth, E. J.
PATENT MEDICINES. See Medicines,
Patent, proprietary, etc.
Paterson, Neil, 1915-
And Delilah
Paterson, N. China run
Black devil, mainly
Paterson, N. China run
China run
Paterson, N. China run
Crowning glory
Paterson, N. China run
Life and death of George Wilson who was
an extraordinary fine specimen
Paterson, N. China run
My friend Joseph
Paterson, N. China run
Portrait of Manuel
Paterson, N. China run
Scotch settlement
Paterson, N. China run
Paterson, Robert
Slowpoke
Strang, R. M. and Roberts, R. M. eds.
Teen-age tales v2
PATHOLOGY
Blochman, L. G. Kiss of Kandahar
Patient Griselda. Boccaccio, G.
Patient Miss Peel. De La Roche, M.
Patriarch of Gunsight Flat. Overholser,
W. D.
Patricia, Edith, and Arnold. Thomas, D.
PATRICIDE. See Parricide
Patrick, Joseph
Crowbar Captain
Bluebook (Periodical) Best sea stories
from Bluebook
Patrick Quentin, pseud. See Quentin,
Patrick, pseud.
Patrick will take over. Ready, W. B.
PATRIOTISM
Hale, E. E. Man without a country
Quiroga, H. The fatherland
PATROLS. See Guard duty
Patt, Esther, 1914-
The butcherbirds
Best American short stories, 1951
Prize stories of 1951
Patten, Gilbert, 1866-1946
Change of pitchers
Graber, R. S. ed. Baseball reader
End of the game
Graber, R. S. ed. Baseball reader

Game grows hotter
Graber, R. S. ed. Baseball reader
Hot finish
Graber, R. S. ed. Baseball reader
Patten, Lewis B.
Too good with a gun
Western Writers of America. Bad men
and good
Winter of his life
Western Writers of America. Holsters
and heroes
Patter of tiny feet. Kneale, N.
Pattern. Brown, F.
Patterson, Bob. See Patterson, Robert
Patterson, Elisabeth Gregg
Homecoming
Prize stories of 1951
Patterson, Robert
Babe
Esquire (Periodical) Girls from Esquire
Patterson, Thomas C.
Special assignment
Ford, N. A. and Faggett, H. L. eds.
Best short stories by Afro-American
writers (1925-1950)
Patton, Frances (Gray) 1906-
The game
Best American short stories, 1954
Let it rest
Jones, K. M. ed. New Confederate short
stories
Terrible Miss Dove
Bachelor, J. M.; Henry, R. L. and Salisbury, R. eds. Current thinking and
writing; 2d ser.
Pattullo, George, 1879-
Corazón
Peery, W. W. ed. 21 Texas short
stories
Pau. Ullman, J. R.
PAUL, SAINT, APOSTLE
Asch, S. "I will send thee"
Sienkiewicz, H. Keeper of the faith
PAUL I, EMPEROR OF RUSSIA, 1754-
1801
Tynîanov, I. N. Second Lieutenant Likewise
Paul, Herb
Angel with purple hair
Conklin, G. and Conklin, L. T. eds.
Supernatural reader
Paul, Louis, 1901-
No more trouble for Jedwick
First-prize stories, 1919-1954
Paul Farlotte. Scott, D. C.
Paul goes hunting. Rounds, G.
Paul's case. Cather, W. S.
Paul's mistress. Maupassant, G. de
PAUPERS. See Poverty
The **pause.** Asimov, I.
Pausodyne. Allen, G.
The **pavilion.** Bland, E. N.
Pavilion on the links. Stevenson, R. L.
PAWNBROKERS
Bergengruen, W. Eye cure
O'Donovan, M. Orpheus and his lute

Pay night. Wright, J. E.
Payday. Parkhurst, G.
Payment in full. Van Doren, M.
Payne, Lucile Vaughan
Prelude
Lass, A. H. and Horowitz, A. eds.
Stories for youth
Seventeen (Periodical) The Seventeen
reader
Sunday afternoon
Seventeen (Periodical) Nineteen from
Seventeen
Stowe, A. comp. It's a date
Payne, Pierre Stephen Robert, 1911-
Red mountain
Best American short stories, 1954
Payne, Robert. See Payne, Pierre Stephen
Robert
Payne, Stephen
Horse of her own
Furman, A. L. ed. Teen-age horse stories
With an O X herd
Boys' life (Periodical) Boys' life Ad-
venture stories
PEACE
Moore, W. Peacebringer
Peace of Mowsle Barton. Munro, H. H.
Peace offering. Munro, H. H.
Peacebringer. Moore, W.
The **Peacemaker.** Coppel, A.
The **peacemaker.** Dinnis, E. M.
PEACH
Porter, W. S. "Little speck in garnered
fruit"
Peach stone. Horgan, P.
Peacock, Thomas Love, 1785-1866
Nightmare Abbey
Connolly, C. ed. Great English short
novels
Peacock, Wilbur S.
Night in the warehouse
Best detective stories of the year—1952
Pearce, Dick. See Pearce, Richard Elmo
Pearce, John, 1913-
Things in common
American vanguard, 1953
Pearce, Richard Elmo, 1909-
Touch of sun tan
This week (Magazine) This week's
short-short stories
PEARL-FISHING
Nordhoff, C. B. I turn pearl-diver
PEARLS
Atherton, G. F. H. Pearls of Loreto
Blixen, K. The pearls
Heard, G. The collector
James, H. Paste
Maugham, W. S. Mr Know-All
Maugham, W. S. String of beads
The **pearls.** Blixen, K.
Pearls of Loreto. Atherton, G. F. H.
Pearson, Martin
Ajax of Ajax
Wollheim, D. A. comp. Flight into space

Pearson, Martin, and Corwin, Cecil
Mask of Demeter
Wollheim, D. A. ed. Prize science fic-
tion
PEASANT LIFE

France
Lewis, J. Wife of Martin Guerre

Russia
Bunin, I. A. Evening in spring
Chekhov, A. P. Peasants
Tolstoi, L. N. Graf. Three arshins of land

Sicily
Verga, G. Don Licciu Papa
Peasant Marey. Dostoevskiĭ, F. M.
Peasants. Chekhov, A. P.
Peasants. O'Donovan, M.
Pease, Howard, 1894-
Passengers for Panama
American boy (Periodical) American
boy anthology
Peattie, Donald Culross, 1898- **and Peattie,
Louise (Redfield)** 1900-
Mystery in Four-and-a-Half Street
American boy (Periodical) American
boy anthology
Weirwood marsh
Andrews, R. C. ed. My favorite stories
of the great outdoors
Peattie, Louise (Redfield) 1900- See Peat-
tie, D. C. jt. auth.
Peattie, Margaret (Rhodes)
Red Fox
Fenner, P. R. comp. Indians, Indians,
Indians
Pecos Bill. Malcolmson, A. B.
Peculiar people. Curtis, B.
PEDDLERS AND PEDDLING
Coppard, A. E. The higgler
Hawthorne, N. Mr Higginbotham's catas-
trophe
Libin, S. Schlemihlov's works
Patt, E. The butcherbirds
Porter, W. S. Nemesis and the candy man
Suhl, Y. With the aid of the one above
Peddler's cart. Coatsworth, E. J.
Peddler's nose. Williamson, J.
The **pedestrian.** Bradbury, R.
PEDLARS. See Peddlers and peddling
Peep at Washoe. Browne, J. R.
Peg. Kneale, N.
Peggety's parcel of shortcomings. Her-
sey, J. R.
The **pejemuller.** Household, G.
Pelican and the lyre bird. Arico, V.
PELOTA (GAME)
Sylvester, R. Last tanto
Pen pal. Lesser, M. A.
PENANCE. See Atonement
The **penance.** Munro, H. H.
Pendergast, Constance
The picnic
Best American short stories, 1953
The **pendulum.** Porter, W. S.

Penglase, Flo
  Strange house
    Furman, A. L. ed. Everygirls mystery
    stories
Pennies from heaven. Irwin, J. M.
Pennsylvania Station. Faulkner, W.
PENSIONS (BOARDING HOUSES) See
    Boarding houses
Pentecost, Hugh, pseud. See Phillips, Jud-
    son Pentecost
Pentecost. Douglas, L. C.
PEONIES
  Parker, J. R. Hounds of spring
People of the black circle. Howard, R. E.
People v. Abe Lathan, colored. Caldwell,
    E.
People's choice. Caldwell, E.
Perchance to dream. Robineau, L.
Percy Grimm. Faulkner, W.
Peretz, Isaac Loeb, 1851-1915
  Bontsha the Silent
    Howe, I. and Greenberg, E. eds. Treas-
    ury of Yiddish stories
  Cabalists
    Howe, I. and Greenberg, E. eds. Treas-
    ury of Yiddish stories
  Dead town
    Howe, I. and Greenberg, E. eds. Treas-
    ury of Yiddish stories
  Devotion without end
    Howe, I. and Greenberg, E. eds. Treas-
    ury of Yiddish stories
  The golem
    Howe, I. and Greenberg, E. eds. Treas-
    ury of Yiddish stories
  If not higher
    Howe, I. and Greenberg, E. eds. Treas-
    ury of Yiddish stories
  Little Hanukkah lamp
    Ausubel, N. ed. Treasury of Jewish
    humor
  Mad Talmudist
    Howe, I. and Greenberg, E. eds. Treas-
    ury of Yiddish stories
  Miracle on the sea
    Leftwich, J. ed. Yisröel. 1952 ed.
  Ne'ilah in Gehenna
    Howe, I. and Greenberg, E. eds. Treas-
    ury of Yiddish stories
  Pious cat
    Ausubel, N. ed. Treasury of Jewish
    humor
  Rabbi Yochanan the warden
    Howe, I. and Greenberg, E. eds. Treas-
    ury of Yiddish stories
Perfect day for bananafish. Salinger, J. D.
Perfect gentleman. McGregor, R. J.
Perfect host. Waldo, E. H.
Perfect murder. Gold, H. L.
Perfect secretary. Brannon, W. T.
Perforce to dream. Harris, J. B.
Perfumed garden. Keller, D. H.
PERFUMERY
  Ekbergh, I. D. Lure of perfume
Peril of the blue world. Abernathy, R.
Peril of the river. Cave. H. B.
Period piece. Coupling, J. J. pseud.

Period piece. Waugh, E.
PERIODICALS
  Porter, W. S. "Rose of Dixie"
Perishing of the pendragons. Chesterton,
    G. K.
Perl, Philip
  Man in Israel
    Ribalow, H. U. ed. These your children
Perpetua puts one over. Kent, C. G.
Perpetual motion. De Camp, L. S.
Perpetuum mobile. Chekhov, A. P.
Perrault, Ernest G. 1922-
  Silver King
    Weaver, R. and James, H. eds. Cana-
    dian short stories
Perry, George Sessions, 1910-
  The fourflusher
    Peery, W. W. ed. 21 Texas short stories
PERSECUTION
  Téllez, H. Ashes for the wind
Persephone. Le Sueur, M.
PERSIA
To 640 A.D.
  Meredith, G. Punishment of Shahpesh,
    the Persian, on Khipil, the builder
640-date
  Wall, J. W. The Kahn
Person, William Thomas, 1900-
  Any way race
    Owen, F. ed. Teen-age victory parade
  "I play basketball"
    Owen, F. ed. Teen-age winter sports
    stories
  Long-shot Porter
    Owen, F. ed. Teen-age winter sports
    stories
  Monster of Blue-Hole Lake
    Owen, F. ed. Teen-age victory parade
  Pony Porter swing
    Owen, F. ed. Teen-age victory parade
  Poor retriever
    Furman, A. L. ed. Teen-age dog stories
  Won by a tail
    Owen, F. ed. Teen-age victory parade
PERSONAL FINANCE. See Budgets, Per-
    sonal
Personal letter. Campbell, W. E. M.
PERSONALITY, DISORDERS OF
  Goodman, P. Iddings Clark
  Maclaren-Ross, J. This mortal coil
Pertwee, Roland, 1885-
  Fish are such liars
    Cerf, B. A. and Moriarty, H. C. eds.
    Anthology of famous British stories
PERU
  Palma, R. Two cooing doves
16th century
  Wassermann, J. Gold of Caxamalca
Peshkov, Alexis Maximovich. See Gorky,
    Maxim
The pest. Scott, W. R.
PESTILENCES. See Plagues
Pete. Knox, J.
Pete can fix it. Jones, R. F.

PETER, SAINT, APOSTLE
Douglas, L. C. Pentecost

Peterkins' Christmas tree. Hale, L. P.

Peter's Christmas present. Eggleston, M. W.

Petersen, Eric Jens
Who called you here?
Eaton, H. T. ed. Short stories

Peterson, Charles Alden
Dooley and the children's hour
Seventeen (Periodical) Nineteen from Seventeen

Peterson, G. M.
Sophomore forward
Owen, F. ed. Teen-age winter sports stories

Petite première in the Mont Blanc Massif. Knowlton, E.

Petracca, Joseph
Santa Lucia
Gable, M. Sister, ed. Many-colored fleece
Straight life
Collier's, the national weekly. Collier's best
See also Fenton, F. jt. auth.

Petrified man. Welty, E.

Petrified man (I-II) Clemens, S. L.

PETROLEUM
Crowell, C. T. The stoic
Sanford, W. M. Windfall

Petronius Arbiter, d. 66
Matron of Ephesus
Stegner, W. E.; Scowcroft, R. and Ilyin, B. eds. Writer's art

Petronius, Gaius. See Petronius Arbiter

Petrov, Vladimir, 1915-
"Get a horse, comrade"
This week magazine. This week's short-short stories

Peyton, Green, pseud. See Wertenbaker, Green Peyton

Phalanstery of Theleme. Rabelais, F.

PHANTASIES. See Fantasies

Phantom cry-baby. Blochman, L. G.

Phantom flivver. Mott, F. L.

Phantom Hall. Anderson, E. V.

Phantom luncheon. Munro, H. H.

Phantom of the bridge. Ware, L.

PHANTOM SHIPS. See Ghost ships

PHARAOHS. See Kings and rulers

PHARMACISTS
Bennett, S. Girls are so helpless
Bloomgarden, S. Share of paradise
Kipling, R. 'Wireless'

Pheasant hunter. Saroyan, W.

Phelps, Elizabeth Stuart. See Ward, Elizabeth Stuart (Phelps)

Philanthropist and the happy cat. Munro, H. H.

PHILANTHROPISTS
Porter, W. S. Chair of philanthromathematics

PHILANTHROPY. See Charity

PHILATELY. See Postage stamps

Philippa's fox-hunt. Somerville, E. A. O. and Martin, V. F.

Philistine in Bohemia. Porter, W. S.

Phillips, Alan, 1917-
Presence in the grove
Weaver, R. and James, H. eds. Canadian short stories

Phillips, Alexander Moore, 1907-
Death of the moon
Wollheim, D. A. comp. Flight into space

Phillips, James Atlee, 1915-
Fast break
Argosy (Periodical) Argosy Book of sports stories

Philips, Judson Pentecost, 1903-
Contradictory case
Queen, E. pseud. ed. Queen's awards: 6th ser.
Man who had no friends
Mystery Writers of America, inc. 20 great tales of murder
Room number twenty-three
Mystery Writers of America, inc. Maiden murders

Phillips, Peter, 1920-
At no extra cost
Best science fiction stories: 1952
Counter charm
Conklin, G. ed. Omnibus of science fiction
Dreams are sacred
Bleiler, E. F. and Dikty, T. E. eds. Imagination unlimited
Field study
Galaxy science fiction magazine. Galaxy reader of science fiction
Lost memory
Galaxy science fiction magazine. Second Galaxy reader of science fiction
Manna
Conklin, G. ed. Big book of science fiction
Plagiarist
Crossen, K. F. Future tense
She who laughs
Pohl, F. ed. Assignment in tomorrow
University
Galaxy science fiction magazine. Second Galaxy reader of science fiction
The warning
Merril, J. ed. Beyond the barriers of space and time

Phillips, Thomas Hal, 1922-
Shadow of an arm
Prize stories of 1951

Phillpotts, Eden, 1862-
"Hey diddle diddle, the cat. . ."
Cerf, B. A. and Moriarty, H. C. eds. Anthology of famous British stories

Phistairus. Lowry, R. J. C.

Phoebe. Porter, W. S.

Phoenix. Smith, C. A.

Phoenix on the sword. Howard, R. E.

PHONOGRAPH
Clark, W. Van T. Portable phonograph
Wendroff, Z. The gramophone

Phonograph and the graft. Porter, W. S.

The photograph. Kneale, N.

PHOTOGRAPHERS
Bradbury, R. Sun and shadow
Olds, H. D. Vic's Orr Kid
Leighton, M. C. Legacy of Canyon John

PHOTOGRAPHY. See Photographers

PHRENOLOGY
O'Donovan, M. Jerome

Physic. De La Mare, W. J.

PHYSICAL IMMORTALITY. See Immortality, Physical

PHYSICIANS
Allen, H. Surgery at Aquila
Balzac, H. de. Atheist's mass
Beachcroft, T. O. The eyes
Bergengruen, W. Eye cure
Bergengruen, W. Sand doctor
Blochman, L. G. Brood of evil
Blochman, L. G. Diagnosis: homicide; 8 stories
Blochman, L. G. Kiss of Kandahar
Boyle, K. White horses of Vienna
Bunner, H. C. Infidelity of Zenobia
Campbell, W. E. M. Bill's eyes
Cheever, J. Season of divorce
Chekhov, A. P. Enemies
Chekhov, A. P. La Cigale
Chekhov, A. P. Perpetuum mobile
Chekhov, A. P. Unpleasant incident
Chekhov, A. P. An unpleasantness
Collier, J. De mortuis
Collins, W. Dead hand
Ekbergh, I. D. Strange story
Farrell, J. T. My friend the doctor
Fitzgerald, F. S. K. Family in the wind
France, A. Manuscript of a village doctor
Gordimer, N. In the beginning
Grimson, M. S. Will and a way
Hart, A. Doctor Mallory
Harvey, W. F. Arm of Mrs Egan
Harvey, W. F. Long road
Hawthorne, N. Rappaccini's daughter
Hecht, B. Double exposure
Hecht, B. Miracle of the fifteen murderers
Herrick, R. Master of the inn
Horwitz, J. Just love, love, sweet love
Irwin, M. E. F. The doctor
James, H. Middle years
Kafka, F. Country doctor
Kuttner, H. Dream's end
McCoy, E. The cape
Marquis, D. Country
Maugham, W. S. Happy man
Medearis, M. Big Doc's girl
Millar, M. Couple next door
O'Donovan, M. The miracle
Pearce, R. E. Touch of sun tan
Pirandello, L. The fly
Poe, E. A. Facts in the case of M. Valdemar
Porter, W. S. Let me feel your pulse
Porter, W. S. The marionettes
Pratt, F. and De Camp, L. S. Love-nest
Samachson, J. Country doctor
Sansom, W. Eye man
Schulberg, B. W. Road to recovery
Strong, L. A. G. White cottage
Turgenev, I. S. District doctor
Van Doren, M. Payments in full
Watson, J. Story of Dr MacLure
Weiss, E. Cardiac suture

West, J. Horace Chooney, M. D.
Williams, W. C. Use of force
Woody, R. L. J. Cue for Connie
Wright, S. F. The rat
Young, F. B. Busman's holiday
See also Surgery

PHYSICISTS
Porges, A. The rats

Physiology of fear. Forester, C. S.

Pi in the sky. Brown, F.

PIANISTS. See Musicians—Pianists

PIANO
Davis, S. P. Christmas carol

The **piazza.** Melville, H.

Pick-up for Olympus. Panghorn, E.

Picket lines of Marton Hevessy. Household, G.

Picking cotton. Caldwell, E.

Pickles and pearls. Hall, D.

PICKPOCKETS. See Crime and criminals; Thieves

Pickthall, Marjorie Lowry Christie, 1883-1922
Worker in sandalwood
Pacey, D. ed. Book of Canadian stories

The **picnic.** Neisloss, M.

The **picnic.** Pendergast, C.

Picnic of Mores the cat. Brentano, C. M.

PICNICS
Pendergast, C. The picnic
Welty, E. Asphodel

The **picture.** Caldwell, E.

Pictures. Mansfield, K.

Pictures don't lie. MacLean, K.

Pictures in the fire. Collier, J.

Piece of linoleum. Keller, D. H.

Piece of news. Welty, E.

Piece of pie. Runyon, D.

Piece of steak. London, J.

Piece of string. Maupassant, G. de

Pierce, John Alvin
Invariant
Astounding science fiction (Periodical)
Astounding science fiction anthology

Pierre. Brookhouser, F.

Pierrot, George F.
Sheriton turnabout
American boy (Periodical) American boy anthology

PIETY. See Religion

Piffingcap. Coppard, A. E.

Pig and whistle. Gissing, G.

Pig Wisps. Sandburg, C.

The **pigeon.** Gustafson, R.

Pigeon cree. Chaplin, S.

Pigeon from St Bartholomew's. Connolly, M.

PIGEONS
Asch, S. Kola Road
Collier, J. Invisible dove dancer of Strathpheen Island

PIGEONS—*Continued*
  Gordimer, N. Kindest thing to do
  Gustafson, R. The pigeon
  Kalisman, H. H. The stray
  McLaverty, M. Pigeons
Pigeons. McLaverty, M.
PIGS
  Collier, J. Mary
  Grimson, M. S. Won and lost
  Still, J. Master time
  Weeks, R. Arkansas
PILATE, PONTIUS, 1st century
  France, A. Procurator of Judæa
  Komroff, M. Told in the stars
Pile of trouble. Kuttner, H.
The **Pilgrim.** Powell, D.
Pillar to post. Harris, J. B.
Pillars of society. Mallea, E.
The **pillows.** St Clair, M.
Pilnick, Boris, pseud. See Vogau, Boris
  Andreevich
Pilot and the bushman. Jacobs, S.
PILOTS, AIRPLANE. See Air pilots
Pimienta pancakes. Porter, W. S.
Pinch hitter. Cox, W. R.
Pincherle, Alberto, 1907-
  Back to the sea
    Horizon (Periodical) Golden Horizon
Pink and blue. Williams, W. C.
Pink ballerina. Ekbergh, I. D.
Pink medicine. Bottome, P.
Pink organdie. Albee, G. S.
Pinski, David, 1872-
  And then he wept
    Howe, I. and Greenberg, E. eds. Treas-
    ury of Yiddish stories
  It had to be
    Leftwich, J. ed. Yisröel. 1952 ed.
Pioneer city. Strachey, J.
PIONEER LIFE. See Frontier and pioneer
  life
Pious cat. Peretz, I. L.
Piper, H. Beam, 1904-
  He walked around the horses
    Pratt, F. ed. World of wonder
  Last enemy
    Astounding science fiction (Periodical)
    Astounding science fiction anthology
  Operation RSVP
    Pratt, F. ed. World of wonder
  Uller uprising
    Petrified planet
Piper pays. Ready, W. B.
PIPES, TOBACCO. See Tobacco pipes
PIRACY. See Pirates
Piracy preferred. Campbell, J. W.
Pirandello, Luigi, 1867-1936
  The fly
    Fabricant, N. D. and Werner, H. eds.
    World's best doctor stories
  Horse in the moon
    Neider, C. ed. Great short stories from
    the world's literature

House of agony
  Blodgett, H. W. ed. Story survey.
  1953 ed.
Other son
  Ungar, F. ed. To mother with love
Reserved coffin
  West, R. B. and Stallman, R. W. eds.
  Art of modern fiction
Pirate and the gamecock. Bloomfield, H.
Pirate gold. Coppock, C.
Pirate island. Crump, I.
PIRATES
  Allen, M. P. Two chests of treasure
  Coppel, A. The Peacemaker
  Crump, I. Pirate island
  Dunsany, E. J. M. D. P. 18th baron.
    Story of land and sea
  Fenner, P. R. comp. Pirates, pirates,
    pirates; 14 stories
      See also Sea stories
Pirates of Charles Town harbor. Holland,
  R. S.
Pit and the pendulum. Poe, E. A.
Pit in the jungle. Cottrell, D. W.
Pittsburgh special. Doty, W. L.
Pity the poor producer. Kaufman, W.
PIUTE INDIANS. See Paiute Indians
PIZARRO, FRANCISCO, 1475?-1538
  Wasserman, J. Gold of Caxamalca. 1952
  ed.
Place in the sun. Kober, A.
Place of one's own. Sitwell, Sir O. bart.
Placet is a crazy place. Brown, F.
Plagiarist. Phillips, P.
PLAGUE
  Dye, C. Syndrome Johnny
  Feuchtwanger, L. Mendel Hirsch
  Hofmannsthal, H. H. Edler von. Episode
    in the life of the Marshal de Bassom-
    pierre
  Jenkins, W. F. Plague
  London, J. Scarlet plague
  Poe, E. A. Masque of the Red Death
  White, H. C. Watch in the night
Plague-cart before horse. Sitwell, Sir O.
  bart.
The **plan.** Sulkin, S.
Plan goes wrong. Hendryx, J. B.
Planet passage. Wollheim, D. A.
PLANETARY ADVENTURES. See In-
  terplanetary voyages
Planetoid of doom. Colladay, M. M.
PLANETS
  Bloch, R. Fear planet
  Jacobi, C. Tepondicon
  Osborne, R. Contact, incorporated
      See also names of individual planets,
    e.g. Mars; Venus; etc.
The **plants.** Jenkins, W. F.
PLASTIC SURGERY. See Surgery, Plas-
  tic
Plato
  Plato's Atlantis
    Derleth, A. W. ed. Beyond time &
    space
Plato's Atlantis. Plato

Platt, George, 1919-
  Play the field alone
    Platt, G. Play the field alone, and
      other stories
  She shall have music
    Platt, G. Play the field alone, and other
      stories
  Touchdown for Rex
    Platt, G. Play the field alone, and other
      stories
  Very false alarm
    Platt, G. Play the field alone, and other
      stories
Plattner story. Wells, H. G.
Plautus in the convent. Meyer, C. F.
Play the field alone. Platt, G.
PLAYGROUNDS
  Enright, E. Apple seed and apple thorn
PLAYING CARDS. See Cards
Playing even for Obadiah. Van Loan, C. E.
PLAYWRIGHTS. See Dramatists
Pleasant dreams. Robin, R.
Please come home, My Lady. Street, J. H.
Please, Mr Patron. Stock, G. A.
Pleasures of the table. Davies, R.
The plot. Saroyan, W.
Plot backfires. Hendryx, J. B.
Plot is hatched. Hendryx, J. B.
Ploughing of the Leaca. Corkery, D.
Plum duff. Van Dresser, P.
Plum pudding and mince pie. Miller, A. D.
Plumb, Beatrice, 1886-
  Good-willer
    Elmquist, R. M. ed. Fifty years of
      Christmas
Plumbers. Claudy, C. H.
PLUTO (PLANET)
  Stone, L. F. Rape of the solar system
Plutonian drug. Smith, C. A.
Plutonian fire. Porter, W. S.
Plymouth Express. Christie, A. M.
PNEUMONIA
  Porter, W. S. Last leaf
POACHERS. See Poaching
POACHING
  Buckingham, N. Tight place
  Munro, H. H. The interlopers
Pod of a weed. Rosaire, F.
Poe, Edgar Allan, 1809-1849
  Angel of the odd
    Poe, E. A. Poe's stories and poems
  The assignation
    Poe, E. A. Tales. Dodd ed.
  Balloon-hoax
    Jensen, P. ed. Fireside book of flying
      stories
    Poe, E. A. Centenary Poe
    Poe, E. A. The gold bug, and other
      tales and poems
    Poe, E. A. Tales. Dodd ed.
  Berenice
    Poe, E. A. Tales. Dodd ed.
  Black cat
    Poe, E. A. Poe's stories and poems
    Poe, E. A. Tales. Dodd ed.

Bon-Bon
  Poe, E. A. Tales. Dodd ed.
Cask of Amontillado
  Blodgett, H. W. ed. Story survey.
    1953 ed.
  Bogorad, S. N. and Trevithick, J. eds.
    College miscellany
  Day, A. G. ed. Greatest American short
    stories
  Foerster, N. ed. American poetry and
    prose. 1952 ed.
  Poe, E. A. Centenary Poe
  Poe, E. A. Poe's stories and poems
  Poe, E. A. Tales. Dodd ed.
Colloquy of Monos and Una
  Poe, E. A. Centenary Poe
  Poe, E. A. Tales. Dodd ed.
Conversation of Eiros and Charmion
  Kuebler, H. W. ed. Treasury of science
    fiction classics
  Poe, E. A. Centenary Poe
  Poe, E. A. Tales. Dodd ed.
Descent into the maelström
  Poe, E. A. Centenary Poe
  Poe, E. A. The gold bug, and other
    tales and poems
  Poe, E. A. Poe's stories and poems
  Poe, E. A. Tales. Dodd ed.
Devil in the belfry
  Poe, E. A. Tales. Dodd ed.
Domain of Arnheim
  Poe, E. A. Centenary Poe
  Poe, E. A. Tales. Dodd ed.
Le Duc de L'Omelette
  Poe, E. A. Centenary Poe
Eleonora
  Poe, E. A. Tales. Dodd ed.
The elk
  Poe, E. A. Tales. Dodd ed.
Facts in the case of M. Valdemar
  Fabricant, N. D. and Werner, H. eds.
    World's best doctor stories
  Poe, E. A. Centenary Poe
  Poe, E. A. Tales. Dodd ed.
Fall of the House of Usher
  Foerster, N. ed. American poetry and
    prose. 1952 ed.
  Gordon, C. and Tate, A. eds. House of
    fiction
  Poe, E. A. Centenary Poe
  Poe, E. A. Poe's stories and poems
  Poe, E. A. Tales. Dodd ed.
Gold-bug
  Cody, S. ed. Greatest stories and how
    they were written
  Lamb, L. ed. Family book of best loved
    short stories
  Poe, E. A. Centenary Poe
  Poe, E. A. The gold bug, and other tales
    and poems
  Poe, E. A. Poe's stories and poems
  Poe, E. A. Tales. Dodd ed.
Hop-Frog
  Poe, E. A. Tales. Dodd ed.
Imp of the perverse
  Neider, C. ed. Great short stories from
    the world's literature
  Poe, E. A. Centenary Poe
  Poe, E. A. Tales. Dodd ed.
Island of the fay
  Poe, E. A. Tales. Dodd ed.
King Pest
  Poe, E. A. Tales. Dodd ed.

Poe, Edgar A.—*Continued*
Landor's cottage
Poe, E. A. Centenary Poe
Poe, E. A. Tales. Dodd ed.
Ligeia
Foerster, N. ed. American poetry and
prose. 1952 ed.
Poe, E. A. Centenary Poe
Poe, E. A. Tales. Dodd ed.
Loss of breath
Poe, E. A. Tales. Dodd ed.
Man of the crowd
Poe, E. A. Tales. **Dodd ed.**
Ms. found in a bottle
Poe, E. A. Centenary Poe
Poe, E. A. The gold bug, and other tales
and poems
Poe, E. A. Tales. Dodd ed.
Masque of the Red Death
Cuff, R. P. ed. American short story
survey
Poe, E. A. Centenary Poe
Poe, E. A. The gold bug, and other tales
and poems
Poe, E. A. Tales. Dodd ed.
Mellonta Tauta
Poe, E. A. Tales. Dodd ed.
Mesmeric revelation
Poe, E. A. Centenary Poe
Metzengerstein
Poe, E. A. Tales. Dodd ed.
Morella
Poe, E. A. Tales. Dodd ed.
Murders in the Rue Morgue
Burrell, J. A. and Cerf, B. A. eds. An-
thology of famous American stories
Poe, E. A. Centenary Poe
Poe, E. A. Poe's stories and poems
Poe, E. A. Tales. Dodd ed.
Mystery of Marie Rogêt
Poe, E. A. Centenary Poe
Poe, E. A. Tales. Dodd ed.
Never bet the devil your head
Poe, E. A. Poe's stories and poems
Oblong box
Poe, E. A. Tales. Dodd ed.
Oval portrait
Poe, E. A. Tales. Dodd ed.
Pit and the pendulum
Burrell, J. A. and Cerf, B. A. eds. An-
thology of famous American stories
Poe, E. A. Centenary Poe
Poe, E. A. The gold bug, and other tales
and poems
Poe, E. A. Poe's stories and poems
Poe, E. A. Tales. Dodd ed.
Premature burial
Poe, E. A. Tales. Dodd ed.
Purloined letter
Burrell, J. A. and Cerf, B. A. eds. An-
thology of famous American stories
Christ, H. I. and Shostak, J. eds. Short
stories
Day, A. G. ed. Greatest American short
stories
Foerster, N. ed. American poetry and
prose. 1952 ed.
Poe, E. A. Centenary Poe
Poe, E. A. The gold bug, and other
tales and poems
Poe, E. A. Poe's stories and poems
Poe, E. A. Tales. Dodd ed.

Shadow
Poe, E. A. Centenary Poe
Poe, E. A. Tales. Dodd ed.
Silence; a fable
Poe, E. A. Tales. Dodd ed.
The spectacles
Poe, E. A. Poe's stories and poems
Poe, E. A. Tales. Dodd ed.
The sphinx
Poe, E. A. Tales. Dodd ed.
System of Dr Tarr and Prof. Fether
Poe, E. A. Poe's stories and poems
Tale of the Ragged Mountains
Poe, E. A. The gold bug, and other
tales and poems
Poe, E. A. Tales. Dodd ed.
Tell-tale heart
Poe, E. A. Centenary Poe
Poe, E. A. Tales. Dodd ed.
Schramm, W. L. ed. Great short sto-
ries
Three Sundays in a week
Poe, E. A. Poe's stories and poems
"Thou art the man"
Poe, E. A. Tales. Dodd ed.
Thousand-and-second tale of Scheherazade
Derleth, A. W. ed. Beyond time &
space
Poe, E. A. Tales. Dodd ed.
Unparalleled adventure of one Hans Pfaall
Poe, E. A. Centenary Poe
William Wilson
Poe, E. A. Centenary Poe
Poe, E. A. Poe's stories and poems
Poe, E. A. Tales. Dodd ed.
X-ing a paragrab
Poe, E. A. Tales. Dodd ed.

About
Carr, J. D. Gentleman from Paris
The poet. Maugham, W. S.
Poet and the peasant. Porter, W. S.
Poet at home. Saroyan, W.
POETESSES. See Poets
POETRY
Heimann, M. Message that failed
Marsh, W. N. Beachhead in Bohemia
Munro, H. H. The Recessional
Munro, H. H. Reginald's peace poem
Munro, H. H. Reginald's Rubaiyat
POETS
Beck, W. Ask me no more
Brown, F. Greatest poem ever written
Carroll, J. W. At Mrs Farrelly's
Collier, J. Evening primrose
Collier, J. Possession of Angela Bradshaw
De La Mare, W. J. Willows
James, H. Aspern papers
Libin, S. Schlemihlov's works
Maugham, W. S. Colonel's lady
Maugham, W. S. The poet
Porter, W. S. Roads of destiny
Pratt, F. and De Camp, L. S. Gift of
God
Taylor, C. L. The envelope
Wang Chu. Poets' club
Zangwill, I. Neo-Hebrew poet
Poets' club. Wang Chu
Poets' excursion. Gurnard, J.
POGROMS. See Jews—Persecution
Point of a pin. Chesterton, G. K.

Point of departure. Calisher, H.
Point of honour. Maugham, W. S.
Point of view. Keith, S.
Poirier, Normand R.
  Teletype machine
    Hathaway, B. and Sessions, J. A. eds.
      Writers for tomorrow. 2d ser.
Poison. Dahl, R.
POISONING
  Grosskopf, E. K. Tea for Tamahara
POISONOUS PLANTS
  Hawthorne, N. Rappaccini's daughter
POISONS
  Bond, R. T. ed. Handbook for poisoners;
    12 stories
  Queen, E. pseud. Three widows
POKER (GAME)
  Davis, S. P. Carson poker incident
  Erin, B. Quiet morning
  Maugham, W. S. Portrait of a gentleman
  Maugham, W. S. Straight flush
  Newhouse, E. Poker game
Poker game. Newhouse, E.
POLAND
      1864-1918
  Asch, S. Kola Road
POLAR BEARS. See Bears
Polar night. Burke, N.
POLAR REGIONS. See Antarctic regions;
    Arctic regions
POLES IN ITALY
  Mann, T. Death in Venice
POLES IN THE UNITED STATES
  Farrell, J. T. Casual incident
POLICE
  Bruce, S. Farewell to crime
  Floherty, J. J. Duel at 70 miles an hour
  Frazee, S. Graveyard shift
  Snow, W. Fatal red hair
  Taylor, M. McGarry joins the Easter
    parade
      Ireland
  O'Donovan, M. Majesty of the law
      London
  Collins, W. Mr Policeman and the cook
      New York (City)
  Porter, W. S. According to their lights
  Porter, W. S. After twenty years
  Porter, W. S. Clarion call
      Russia
  Chekhov, A. P. Appropriate measures
  Shneur, Z. New police chief
      United States
  Algren, N. Captain is impaled
  Brown, F. Death of Riley
  Lardner, R. W. There are smiles
  Porter, W. S. Badge of policeman O'Roon
  Porter, W. S. Cop and the anthem
  Taubes, F. Trouble on 98th Street
POLICEWOMEN. See Police
POLISH SOLDIERS. See Soldiers, Polish
Politeness. Brown, F.
POLITICAL CAMPAIGNS. See Politics
POLITICAL PRISONERS. See Prisoners,
    Political

POLITICIANS. See Politics
POLITICIANS, ENGLISH. See Politics
    —England
POLITICIANS, FRENCH. See Politics—
    France
POLITICS
  Johnson, D. M. Man who shot Liberty
    Valance
  Moore, W. We the people
  Stuart, J. Governor Warburton's right-
    hand man
      Austria
  Boyle, K. White horses of Vienna
      England
  Maugham, W. S. Lord Mountdrago
  Munro, H. H. Canossa
  Munro, H. H. Forewarned
  Munro, H. H. Infernal Parliament
  Munro, H. H. "Ministers of Grace"
  Priestley, J. B. Leadington incident
      France
  Maugham, W. S. Appearance and reality
      Ireland
  Joyce, J. Ivy Day in the committee room
      Kentucky
  Fox, J. Knight of the Cumberland
      New York (City)
  Horwitz, J. The campaign
  O'Higgins, H. J. Big Dan Reilly
      Southern States
  Aswell, J. R. Shadow of evil
      Texas
  Porter, W. S. Art and the bronco
      United States
  Doty, W. L. Welcome home
  Porter, K. A. Day's work
      Wisconsin
  Miner, H. Due process
POLITICS, CORRUPTION IN. See Cor-
    ruption (in politics)
Polka dot dress. Adler, W.
POLO
  Miers, E. S. Bandy
Polonaise. Hoffmann, E.
Poltarnees, Beholder of Ocean. Dunsany,
    E. J. M. D. P. 18th baron
POLYNESIANS
  Michener, J. A. Povenaa's daughter
Polzunkov. Dostoevskiĭ, F. M.
Pommery 1921. Seager, A.
POMPEII. See Italy—Pompeii
Pompey and some peaches. Sitwell, Sir O.
    bart
The pond. Kneale, N.
PONTIUS PILATE. See Pilate, Pontius
PONY EXPRESS
  Garthwaite, M. H. Riding the Pony Ex-
    press
  Skelton, C. L. Mail starts
Pony Porter swing. Person, W. T.
Pooja. Marshall, E.

POOL (GAME)
McNulty, J. Yellow-ball-in-the-side
See also Billiards
The **pool**. Maugham, W. S.
POOL HALLS. See Poolrooms
Pool of adventure. Gilbert, K.
Pool of narcissus. Calisher, H.
Pool of the black one. Howard, R. E.
Pooler, James, 1905-
Herself
Greene, J. I. and Abell, E. eds. Stories
of sudden truth
POOLROOMS
Stegner, W. E. Blue-winged teal
THE POOR. See Poverty
Poor black sheep. Cousins, M.
Poor community. Reisin, A.
Poor Cousin Evelyn. Yaffe, J.
Poor man's pudding. Melville, H.
Poor people. Horwitz, J.
Poor retriever. Person, W. T.
Poor rule. Porter, W. S.
Poor superman. Leiber, F.
Pop's boy. Ashkenazy, I.
Porcelain cups. Cabell, J. B.
La **Porcelaine** Claire. O'Meara, W.
PORCUPINES
Gilbert, K. Pool of adventure
Reid, M. Battle of the marten and the
porcupine
Pore Perrie. Goyen, W.
Porges, Arthur, 1915-
The fly
Best science-fiction stories: 1953
Merril, J. ed. Beyond human ken
The rats
Best science fiction stories: 1952
Porky, the outboarder. Sherman, H. M.
PORT-AU-PRINCE. See Haiti—Port-au-
Prince
Portable phonograph. Clark, W. Van T.
Porte-cochere. Taylor, P. H.
Porter, Katherine Anne, 1894-
Day's work
Waite, H. O. and Atkinson, B. P. eds.
Literature for our time
Downward path to wisdom
Davis, C. B. ed. Eyes of boyhood
Flowering Judas
Heilman, R. B. ed. Modern short stories
Ludwig, J. B. and Poirer, W. R. eds.
Stories, British and American
Neider, C. ed. Great short stories from
the world's literature
West, R. B. and Stallman, R. W. eds.
Art of modern fiction
The grave
Peery, W. W. ed. 21 Texas short stories
Schorer, M. ed. The story
Jilting of Granny Weatherall
Fabricant, N. D. and Werner, H. eds.
World's best doctor stories
Gable, M. Sister, ed. Many-colored fleece
Schramm, W. L. ed. Great short stories

María Concepción
Burrell, J. A. and Cerf, B. A. eds. An-
thology of famous American stories
Foerster, N. ed. American poetry and
prose. 1952 ed.
Lynskey, W. C. ed. Reading modern
fiction
Noon wine
Ludwig, R. M. and Perry, M. B. eds.
Nine short novels
Old mortality
Gordon, C. and Tate, A. eds. House of
fiction
Southern review. Anthology of stories
from the Southern review
Pale horse, pale rider
Short, R. W. and Sewall, R. B. eds.
Short stories for study. 1950 ed.
That tree
Felheim, M.; Newman, F. B. and Stein-
hoff, W. R. eds. Modern short stories
Porter, William Sydney, 1862-1910
According to their lights
Porter, W. S. Complete works of O.
Henry
Adjustment of nature
Porter, W. S. Complete works of O.
Henry
The admiral
Porter, W. S. Complete works of O.
Henry
Adventures of Shamrock Jolnes
Porter, W. S. Complete works of O.
Henry
After twenty years
Porter, W. S. Complete works of O.
Henry
Porter, W. S. O. Henry's best stories
Afternoon miracle
Porter, W. S. Complete works of O.
Henry
Aristocracy versus hash
Porter, W. S. Complete works of O.
Henry
Art and the bronco
Peery, W. W. ed. 21 Texas stort stories
Porter, W. S. Complete works of
O. Henry
Assessor of success
Porter, W. S. Complete works of
O. Henry
At arms with Morpheus
Porter, W. S. Complete works of
O. Henry
Atavism of John Tom Little Bear
Porter, W. S. Complete works of
O. Henry
Babes in the jungle
Porter, W. S. Complete works of
O. Henry
Badge of policeman O'Roon
Porter, W. S. Complete works of
O. Henry
Best-seller
Porter, W. S. Complete works of
O. Henry
Between rounds
Porter, W. S. Complete works of
O. Henry
Bexar scrip no. 2692
Porter, W. S. Complete works of
O. Henry

Porter, William S.—*Continued*
  Bird of Bagdad
    Porter, W. S. Complete works of
      O. Henry
  Blackjack bargainer
    Burrell, J. A. and Cerf, B. A. eds. Anthology of famous American stories
    Porter, W. S. Complete works of
      O. Henry
  Blind man's holiday
    Porter, W. S. Complete works of
      O. Henry
  Brickdust row
    Porter, W. S. Complete works of
      O. Henry
  Brief début of Tildy
    Porter, W. S. Complete works of
      O. Henry
  Buried treasure
    Porter, W. S. Complete works of
      O. Henry
  Buyer from Cactus City
    Porter, W. S. Complete works of
      O. Henry
  By courier
    Porter, W. S. Complete works of
      O. Henry
  Caballero's way
    Porter, W. S. Complete works of
      O. Henry
  The cactus
    Porter, W. S. Complete works of
      O. Henry
  Caliph and the cad
    Porter, W. S. Complete works of
      O. Henry
  The caliph, cupid and the clock
    Porter, W. S. Complete works of
      O. Henry
  Call loan
    Porter, W. S. Complete works of
      O. Henry
  Call of the tame
    Porter, W. S. Complete works of
      O. Henry
  Calloway's code
    Porter, W. S. Complete works of
      O. Henry
  Caught
    Porter, W. S. Complete works of
      O. Henry
  The chair of philanthromathematics
    Porter, W. S. Complete works of
      O. Henry
  Champion of the weather
    Porter, W. S. Complete works of
      O. Henry
  Chaparral Christmas gift
    Porter, W. S. Complete works of
      O. Henry
  Chaparral prince
    Porter, W. S. Complete works of
      O. Henry
  Cherchez la femme
    Porter, W. S. Complete works of
      O. Henry
  Christmas by injunction
    Porter, W. S. Complete works of
      O. Henry
  Church with an overshot-wheel
    Porter, W. S. Complete works of
      O. Henry

City of dreadful night
    Porter, W. S. Complete works of
      O. Henry
Clarion call
    Porter, W. S. Complete works of
      O. Henry
    Porter, W. S. O. Henry's best stories
Comedy in rubber
    Porter, W. S. Complete works of
      O. Henry
    Porter, W. S. O. Henry's best stories
Coming-out of Maggie
    Porter, W. S. Complete works of
      O. Henry
Complete life of John Hopkins
    Porter, W. S. Complete works of
      O. Henry
Compliments of the season
    Porter, W. S. Complete works of
      O. Henry
Confessions of a humorist
    Porter, W. S. Complete works of
      O. Henry
Conscience in art
    Porter, W. S. Complete works of
      O. Henry
Cop and the anthem
    Eaton, H. T. ed. Short stories
    Porter, W. S. Complete works of
      O. Henry
    Porter, W. S. O. Henry's best stories
Cosmopolite in a café
    Porter, W. S. Complete works of
      O. Henry
Count and the wedding guest
    Porter, W. S. Complete works of
      O. Henry
Country of elusion
    Porter, W. S. Complete works of
      O. Henry
Cupid à la carte
    Porter, W. S. Complete works of
      O. Henry
Cupid's exile number two
    Porter, W. S. Complete works of
      O. Henry
Day resurgent
    Porter, W. S. Complete works of
      O. Henry
Day we celebrate
    Porter, W. S. Complete works of
      O. Henry
Defeat of the city
    Porter, W. S. Complete works of
      O. Henry
Departmental case
    Porter, W. S. Complete works of
      O. Henry
Detective detector
    Porter, W. S. Complete works of
      O. Henry
Diamond of Kali
    Porter, W. S. Complete works of
      O. Henry
Dicky
    Porter, W. S. Complete works of
      O. Henry
Dinner at—
    Porter, W. S. Complete works of
      O. Henry
Discounters of money
    Porter, W. S. Complete works of
      O. Henry

Porter, William S.—*Continued*

Dog and the playlet
  Porter, W. S. Complete works of
  O. Henry
Door of unrest
  Porter, W. S. Complete works of
  O. Henry
A double-dyed deceiver
  Porter, W. S. Complete works of
  O. Henry
Dougherty's eye-opener
  Porter, W. S. Complete works of
  O. Henry
The dream
  Porter, W. S. Complete works of
  O. Henry
The duel
  Porter, W. S. Complete works of
  O. Henry
Duplicity of Hargraves
  Porter, W. S. Complete works of
  O. Henry
Easter of the soul
  Porter, W. S. Complete works of
  O. Henry
Elsie in New York
  Porter, W. S. Complete works of
  O. Henry
Emancipation of Billy
  Porter, W. S. Complete works of
  O. Henry
Enchanted kiss
  Porter, W. S. Complete works of
  O. Henry
Enchanted profile
  Porter, W. S. Complete works of
  O. Henry
Ethics of pig
  Porter, W. S. Complete works of
  O. Henry
Exact science of matrimony
  Porter, W. S. Complete works of
  O. Henry
Extradited from Bohemia
  Porter, W. S. Complete works of
  O. Henry
Ferry of unfulfilment
  Porter, W. S. Complete works of
  O. Henry
Fickle fortune; or, How Gladys hustled
  Porter, W. S. Complete works of
  O. Henry
Fifth wheel
  Porter, W. S. Complete works of
  O. Henry
Flag paramount
  Porter, W. S. Complete works of
  O. Henry
Fog in Santone
  Porter, W. S. Complete works of
  O. Henry
The fool-killer
  Porter, W. S. Complete works of
  O. Henry
Foreign policy of Company 99
  Porter, W. S. Complete works of
  O. Henry
Fourth in Salvador
  Porter, W. S. Complete works of
  O. Henry
"Fox-in-the-morning"
  Porter, W. S. Complete works of
  O. Henry

Friendly call
  Porter, W. S. Complete works of
  O. Henry
Friends in San Rosario
  Porter, W. S. Complete works of
  O. Henry
From the cabby's seat
  Porter, W. S. Complete works of
  O. Henry
From each according to his ability
  Porter, W. S. Complete works of
  O. Henry
Furnished room
  Burrell, J. A. and Cerf, B. A. eds. Anthology of famous American stories
  Porter, W. S. Complete works of
  O. Henry
  Porter, W. S. O. Henry's best stories
  Schramm, W. L. ed. Great short stories
Georgia's ruling
  Porter, W. S. Complete works of
  O. Henry
Ghost of a chance
  Porter, W. S. Complete works of
  O. Henry
Gift of the Magi
  Day, A. G. ed. Greatest American short stories
  Lamb, L. ed. Family book of best loved short stories
  Porter, W. S. Complete works of
  O. Henry
  Porter, W. S. O. Henry's best stories
"Girl"
  Porter, W. S. Complete works of
  O. Henry
  Porter, W. S. O. Henry's best stories
Girl and the graft
  Porter, W. S. Complete works of
  O. Henry
Girl and the habit
  Porter, W. S. Complete works of
  O. Henry
Gold that glittered
  Porter, W. S. Complete works of
  O. Henry
Greater Coney
  Porter, W. S. Complete works of
  O. Henry
Green door
  Porter, W. S. Complete works of
  O. Henry
Guardian of the accolade
  Porter, W. S. Complete works of
  O. Henry
"Guilty party"
  Porter, W. S. Complete works of
  O. Henry
Halberdier of the Little Rheinschloss
  Porter, W. S. Complete works of
  O. Henry
The hand that riles the world
  Porter, W. S. Complete works of
  O. Henry
Handbook of Hymen
  Porter, W. S. Complete works of
  O. Henry
The harbinger
  Porter, W. S. Complete works of
  O. Henry
Harlem tragedy
  Porter, W. S. Complete works of
  O. Henry

Porter, William S.—*Continued*

He also serves
  Porter, W. S. Complete works of
    O. Henry
The head-hunter
  Porter, W. S. Complete works of
    O. Henry
Hearts and crosses
  Porter, W. S. Complete works of
    O. Henry
Hearts and hands
  Porter, W. S. Complete works of
    O. Henry
Helping the other fellow
  Porter, W. S. Complete works of
    O. Henry
Hiding of Black Bill
  Porter, W. S. Complete works of
    O. Henry
Higher abdication
  Porter, W. S. Complete works of
    O. Henry
Higher pragmatism
  Christ, H. I. and Shostak, J. eds. Short
    stories
  Porter, W. S. Complete works of
    O. Henry
Holding up a train
  Porter, W. S. Complete works of
    O. Henry
Hostages to Momus
  Porter, W. S. Complete works of
    O. Henry
Hygeia at the Solito
  Porter, W. S. Complete works of
    O. Henry
Hypotheses of failure
  Porter, W. S. Complete works of
    O. Henry
Indian summer of Dry Valley Johnson
  Porter, W. S. Complete works of
    O. Henry
Innocents of Broadway
  Porter, W. S. Complete works of
    O. Henry
Jeff Peters as a personal magnet
  Porter, W. S. Complete works of
    O. Henry
Jimmy Hayes and Muriel
  Porter, W. S. Complete works of
    O. Henry
Lady higher up
  Porter, W. S. Complete works of
    O. Henry
Last leaf
  Porter, W. S. Complete works of
    O. Henry
  Porter, W. S. O. Henry's best stories
Last of the troubadours
  Porter, W. S. Complete works of
    O. Henry
Law and order
  Porter, W. S. Complete works of
    O. Henry
Let me feel your pulse
  Porter, W. S. Complete works of
    O. Henry
Lickpenny lover
  Porter, W. S. Complete works of
    O. Henry
  Porter, W. S. O. Henry's best stories
Little local color
  Porter, W. S. Complete works of
    O. Henry

"Little speck in garnered fruit"
  Porter, W. S. Complete works of
    O. Henry
Little talk about mobs
  Porter, W. S. Complete works of
    O. Henry
Lonesome road
  Porter, W. S. Complete works of
    O. Henry
Lord Oakhurst's curse
  Porter, W. S. Complete works of
    O. Henry
Lost blend
  Porter, W. S. Complete works of
    O. Henry
Lost on dress parade
  Porter, W. S. Complete works of
    O. Henry
  Porter, W. S. O. Henry's best stories
Lotus and the bottle
  Porter, W. S. Complete works of
    O. Henry
Love-philtre of Ikey Schoenstein
  Porter, W. S. Complete works of
    O. Henry
Madame Bo-Peep, of the ranches
  Porter, W. S. Complete works of
    O. Henry
Madison Square Arabian night
  Porter, W. S. Complete works of
    O. Henry
Makes the whole world kin
  Porter, W. S. Complete works of
    O. Henry
Making of a New Yorker
  Porter, W. S. Complete works of
    O. Henry
Mammon and the archer
  Porter, W. S. Complete works of
    O. Henry
  Porter, W. S. O. Henry's best stories
Man about town
  Porter, W. S. Complete works of
    O. Henry
Man higher up
  Porter, W. S. Complete works of
    O. Henry
The marionettes
  Porter, W. S. Complete works of
    O. Henry
The Marquis and Miss Sally
  Porter, W. S. Complete works of
    O. Henry
Marry month of May
  Porter, W. S. Complete works of
    O. Henry
Masters of art
  Porter, W. S. Complete works of
    O. Henry
Matter of mean elevation
  Porter, W. S. Complete works of
    O. Henry
The memento
  Porter, W. S. Complete works of
    O. Henry
Memoirs of a yellow dog
  Porter, W. S. Complete works of
    O. Henry
Midsummer knight's dream
  Porter, W. S. Complete works of
    O. Henry
Midsummer masquerade
  Porter, W. S. Complete works of
    O. Henry

Porter, William S.—*Continued*
Missing chord
  Porter, W. S. Complete works of
    O. Henry
Modern rural sports
  Porter, W. S. Complete works of
    O. Henry
Moment of victory
  Porter, W. S. Complete works of
    O. Henry
Money maze
  Porter, W. S. Complete works of
    O. Henry
Municipal report
  Burrell, J. A. and Cerf, B. A. eds. Anthology of famous American stories
  Cuff, R. P. ed. American short story survey
  Porter, W. S. Complete works of
    O. Henry
Nemesis and the candy man
  Porter, W. S. Complete works of
    O. Henry
New York by camp fire light
  Porter, W. S. Complete works of
    O. Henry
Newspaper story
  Porter, W. S. Complete works of
    O. Henry
"Next to reading matter"
  Porter, W. S. Complete works of
    O. Henry
Night in new Arabia
  Porter, W. S. Complete works of
    O. Henry
No story
  Porter, W. S. Complete works of
    O. Henry
October in June
  Porter, W. S. Complete works of
    O. Henry
Octopus marooned
  Porter, W. S. Complete works of
    O. Henry
On behalf of the management
  Porter, W. S. Complete works of
    O. Henry
One dollar's worth
  Porter, W. S. Complete works of
    O. Henry
One thousand dollars
  Porter, W. S. Complete works of
    O. Henry
  Porter, W. S. O. Henry's best stories
Out of Nazareth
  Porter, W. S. Complete works of
    O. Henry
Passing of Black Eagle
  Porter, W. S. Complete works of
    O. Henry
Past one at Rooney's
  Porter, W. S. Complete works of
    O. Henry
The pendulum
  Porter, W. S. Complete works of
    O. Henry
Philistine in Bohemia
  Porter, W. S. Complete works of
    O. Henry
Phoebe
  Porter, W. S. Complete works of
    O. Henry

Phonograph and the graft
  Porter, W. S. Complete works of
    O. Henry
Pimienta pancakes
  Porter, W. S. Complete works of
    O. Henry
Plutonian fire
  Porter, W. S. Complete works of
    O. Henry
Poet and the peasant
  Porter, W. S. Complete works of
    O. Henry
Poor rule
  Porter, W. S. Complete works of
    O. Henry
Pride of the cities
  Porter, W. S. Complete works of
    O. Henry
Princess and the puma
  Porter, W. S. Complete works of
    O. Henry
Prisoner of Zembla
  Porter, W. S. Complete works of
    O. Henry
Proof of the pudding
  Porter, W. S. Complete works of
    O. Henry
Psyche and the pskyscraper
  Porter, W. S. Complete works of
    O. Henry
Purple dress
  Porter, W. S. Complete works of
    O. Henry
Queries and answers
  Porter, W. S. Complete works of
    O. Henry
Ramble in Aphasia
  Porter, W. S. Complete works of
    O. Henry
Ransom of Mack
  Porter, W. S. Complete works of
    O. Henry
Ransom of Red Chief
  Davis, C. B. ed. Eyes of boyhood
  Fenner, P. R. comp. Fun! Fun! Fun!
  Porter, W. S. Complete works of
    O. Henry
  Porter, W. S. O. Henry's best stories
The rathskeller and the rose
  Porter, W. S. Complete works of
    O. Henry
Red roses of Tonia
  Porter, W. S. Complete works of
    O. Henry
Reformation of Calliope
  Porter, W. S. Complete works of
    O. Henry
Remnants of the code
  Porter, W. S. Complete works of
    O. Henry
Renaissance at Charleroi
  Porter, W. S. Complete works of
    O. Henry
Retrieved reformation
  Porter, W. S. Complete works of
    O. Henry
  Porter, W. S. O. Henry's best stories
Roads of destiny
  Blodgett, H. W. ed. Story survey. 1953 ed.
  Porter, W. S. Complete works of
    O. Henry
  Pratt, F. ed. World of wonder

Porter, William S.—*Continued*
Roads we take
Porter, W. S. Complete works of
O. Henry
Robe of peace
Porter, W. S. Complete works of
O. Henry
Romance of a busy broker
Porter, W. S. Complete works of
O. Henry
Porter, W. S. O. Henry's best stories
"Rose of Dixie"
Porter, W. S. Complete works of
O. Henry
Roses, ruses and romance
Porter, W. S. Complete works of
O. Henry
Rouge et noir
Porter, W. S. Complete works of
O. Henry
Round the circle
Porter, W. S. Complete works of
O. Henry
Rubaiyat of a Scotch highball
Porter, W. S. Complete works of
O. Henry
Rubber plant's story
Porter, W. S. Complete works of
O. Henry
Ruler of men
Porter, W. S. Complete works of
O. Henry
Rus in urbe
Porter, W. S. Complete works of
O. Henry
Porter, W. S. O. Henry's best stories
Sacrifice hit
Porter, W. S. Complete works of
O. Henry
Schools and schools
Porter, W. S. Complete works of
O. Henry
Porter, W. S. O. Henry's best stories
Seats of the haughty
Porter, W. S. Complete works of
O. Henry
Service of love
Porter, W. S. Complete works of
O. Henry
Porter, W. S. O. Henry's best stories
Shamrock and the palm
Porter, W. S. Complete works of
O. Henry
Shearing the wolf
Porter, W. S. Complete works of
O. Henry
Ships
Porter, W. S. Complete works of
O. Henry
Shocks of doom
Porter, W. S. Complete works of
O. Henry
Shoes
Porter, W. S. Complete works of
O. Henry
Sisters of the golden circle
Porter, W. S. Complete works of
O. Henry
Skylight room
Porter, W. S. Complete works of
O. Henry
Porter, W. S. O. Henry's best stories

The sleuths
Porter, W. S. Complete works of
O. Henry
Smith
Porter, W. S. Complete works of
O. Henry
Snapshot at the President
Porter, W. S. Complete works of
O. Henry
Snow man
Porter, W. S. Complete works of
O. Henry
Social triangle
Porter, W. S. Complete works of
O. Henry
Sociology in serge and straw
Porter, W. S. Complete works of
O. Henry
Song and the sergeant
Porter, W. S. Complete works of
O. Henry
Sound and fury
Porter, W. S. Complete works of
O. Henry
Sparrows in Madison Square
Porter, W. S. Complete works of
O. Henry
Sphinx apple
Porter, W. S. Complete works of
O. Henry
Springtime à la carte
Porter, W. S. Complete works of
O. Henry
Porter, W. S. O. Henry's best stories
Squaring the circle
Porter, W. S. Complete works of
O. Henry
Strange story
Porter, W. S. Complete works of
O. Henry
Strictly business
Porter, W. S. Complete works of
O. Henry
Suite homes and their romance
Porter, W. S. Complete works of
O. Henry
Supply and demand
Porter, W. S. Complete works of
O. Henry
Tale of a tainted tenner
Porter, W. S. Complete works of
O. Henry
Technical error
Porter, W. S. Complete works of
O. Henry
Telemachus, friend
Porter, W. S. Complete works of
O. Henry
Tempered wind
Porter, W. S. Complete works of
O. Henry
Theory and the hound
Porter, W. S. Complete works of
O. Henry
Thimble, thimble
Porter, W. S. Complete works of
O. Henry
Thing's the play
Porter, W. S. Complete works of
O. Henry
Third ingredient
Porter, W. S. Complete works of
O. Henry
Porter, W. S. O. Henry's best stories

Porter, William S.—*Continued*
  Tictocq
    Porter, W. S. Complete works of O. Henry
  To him who waits
    Porter, W. S. Complete works of O. Henry
  Tobin's palm
    Porter, W. S. Complete works of O. Henry
  Tommy's burglar
    Porter, W. S. Complete works of O. Henry
  Tracked to doom
    Porter, W. S. Complete works of O. Henry
  Transformation of Martin-Burney
    Porter, W. S. Complete works of O. Henry
  Transients in Arcadia
    Porter, W. S. Complete works of O. Henry
  Trimmed lamp
    Porter, W. S. Complete works of O. Henry
    Porter, W. S. O. Henry's best stories
  Two recalls
    Porter, W. S. Complete works of O. Henry
  Two renegades
    Jones, K. M. ed. New Confederate short stories
    Porter, W. S. Complete works of O. Henry
  Two Thanksgiving Day gentlemen
    Porter, W. S. Complete works of O. Henry
  Ulysses and the dogman
    Porter, W. S. Complete works of O. Henry
  Unfinished Christmas story
    Porter, W. S. Complete works of O. Henry
  Unfinished story
    Porter, W. S. Complete works of O. Henry
    Porter, W. S. O. Henry's best stories
  Unknown quantity
    Porter, W. S. Complete works of O. Henry
  Unprofitable servant
    Porter, W. S. Complete works of O. Henry
  Vanity and some sables
    Porter, W. S. Complete works of O. Henry
  The venturers
    Porter, W. S. Complete works of O. Henry
  The vitagraphoscope
    Porter, W. S. Complete works of O. Henry
  Voice of the city
    Porter, W. S. Complete works of O. Henry
  "What you want"
    Porter, W. S. Complete works of O. Henry
  While the auto waits
    Porter, W. S. Complete works of O. Henry
    Porter, W. S. O. Henry's best stories
  Whirligig of life
    Porter, W. S. Complete works of O. Henry
    Porter, W. S. O. Henry's best stories
  Whistling Dick's Christmas stocking
    Porter, W. S. Complete works of O. Henry
  Witches' loaves
    Porter, W. S. Complete works of O. Henry
  World and the door
    Porter, W. S. Complete works of O. Henry

PORTERS. See Railroads—Employees

Portor, Laura Spencer
  One night
    Thinker's digest (Periodical) Spoiled priest, and other stories
  Spendthrifts
    Thinker's digest (Periodical) Spoiled priest, and other stories

Portrait. Lewis, E. G.

Portrait. Moore, D. E.

Portrait of a gentleman. Maugham, W. S.

Portrait of a lady. Murphy, A.

Portrait of Bascom Hawke. Wolfe, T.

Portrait of Lydia. Milne, A. A.

Portrait of Manuel. Paterson, N.

PORTRAITS
  Dahl, R. Nunc dimittis
  Poe, E. A. Oval portrait

PORTUGAL

Lisbon
  Saint Exupéry, A. de. Letter to a hostage
  Saroyan, W. The Assyrian

Poseidon's daughter. Sansom, W.

Position of the soldier. Newhouse, E.

Posse. Thompson, C. H.

Possession of Angela Bradshaw. Collier, J.

Possession on completion. Brooks, C.

Post, Melville Davisson, 1871-1930
  Corpus delicti
    Blaustein, A. P. ed. Fiction goes to court

Post mistress of Laurel Run. Harte, B.

Post-mortem murder. Lewis, S.

POSTAGE STAMPS
  Arthur, R. Postpaid to Paradise

POSTAL SERVICE
  Harte, B. Postmistress of Laurel Run
  Stock, G. A. Please, Mr Patron
  Zamîatin, E. I. God
    See also Pony Express

POSTMEN. See Postal service

Poston, Martha (Lee)
  Monkey spirit
    Story parade (Periodical) Adventure stories

Postpaid to Paradise. Arthur, R.

Pot Likker's first fox hunt. White, R.

Pot of gold. Cheever, J.

Poteen maker. McLaverty, M.

POULTRY
Dunsany, E. J. M. D. P. 18th baron. The hen
King, M. P. Chicken on the wind
Munro, H. H. Blood-feud of Toad-Water
See also Roosters

Pound of cure. Del Rey, L.

Povenaa's daughter. Michener, J. A.

POVERTY
Chekhov, A. P. A fragment
Crane, S. Experiment in misery
Crane, S. Men in the storm
Godchaux, E. Horn that called Bambine
Grinevskii, A. S. The ratcatcher
Heide, H. J. End of her rope
Krige, U. La Miseria
Melville, H. Poor man's pudding
Melville, H. Rich man's crumbs
Peretz, I. L. Bontsha the Silent
Pinski, D. And then he wept
Porter, W. S. Skylight room
Porter, W. S. Third ingredient
Reisen, A. Last hope
Reisen, A. Rich poor man
Swinbank, G. New hat
Verga, G. Black bread

Powder-white faces. Hughes, L.

Powell, Dawn, 1897-
Adam
Powell, D. Sunday, Monday and always
Artist's life
Powell, D. Sunday, Monday and always
Audition
Powell, D. Sunday, Monday and always
Blue hyacinths
Powell, D. Sunday, Monday and always
Cheerio
Powell, D. Sunday, Monday and always
The comeback
Powell, D. Sunday, Monday and always
Day after tomorrow
Powell, D. Sunday, Monday and always
Deenie
Powell, D. Sunday, Monday and always
Every day is ladies' day
Powell, D. Sunday, Monday and always
Feet on the ground
Powell, D. Sunday, Monday and always
The glads
Powell, D. Sunday, Monday and always
Grand march
Powell, D. Sunday, Monday and always
Here today, gone tomorrow
Powell, D. Sunday, Monday and always
Ideal home
Powell, D. Sunday, Monday and always
The Pilgrim
Powell, D. Sunday, Monday and always
The roof
Powell, D. Sunday, Monday and always
Such a pretty day
Powell, D. Sunday, Monday and always
You should have brought your mink
Powell, D. Sunday, Monday and always

Powell, Frances, 1935-
Black flag
Oberfirst, R. ed. 1954 anthology of best original short-stories

Powell, Jean
Lady walks
Stanford short stories, 1950

The **power.** Jenkins, W. F.

POWER BOATS. See Motorboats

Power of literature. Farrell, J. T.

Powerhouse. Bradbury, R.

Powerhouse. Welty, E.

Powers, Alfred
Hannibal's elephants
Fenner, P. R. comp. Elephants, elephants, elephants

Powers, James Farl, 1917-
Death of a favorite
Best American short stories, 1951
The forks
Heilman, R. B. ed. Modern short stories
He don't plant cotton
Lynskey, W. C. ed. Reading modern fiction
Lions, harts, leaping does
Gordon, C. and Tate, A. eds. House of fiction
Ludwig, J. B. and Poirier, W. R. eds. Stories, British and American
Prince of darkness
Best of the Best American short stories, 1915-1950
Thinker's digest (Periodical) Spoiled priest, and other stories
Valiant woman
Schorer, M. ed. The story

Powers, William T.
Meteor
Astounding science fiction (Periodical) Astounding science fiction anthology

Powys, Theodore Francis, 1875-1953
Christmas gift
Lohan, R. and Lohan, M. eds. New Christmas treasury

Praag, Siegfried Emanuel van, 1899-
Weesperstraat
Leftwich, J. ed. Yisröel. 1952 ed.

Practical joke. Farrell, J. T.

Practical joker. Simpson, M. E.

PRACTICAL JOKES. See Humor—Practical jokes

Prado, Pedro, 1894-
Laugh in the desert
Schramm, W. L. ed. Great short stories

Prairie kid. Johnson, D. M.

PRAIRIES
Garland, H. Under the lion's paw

Pratt, Fletcher, 1897-1956
Hormones
Star science fiction stories, no.2
Long view
Petrified planet
Official record
Pohl, F. ed. Assignment in tomorrow
Pardon my mistake
Derleth, A. W. ed. The outer reaches
Roger Bacon formula
Conklin, G. ed. Big book of science fiction
See also De Camp, L. S. jt. auth; Kubilius, W. jt. auth.

Pratt, Fletcher, 1897-1956, and De Camp, Lyon Sprague, 1907-
All that glitters
Pratt, F. and De Camp, L. S. Tales from Gavagan's bar
Ancestral amethyst
Pratt, F. and De Camp, L. S. Tales from Gavagan's bar
Beasts of Bourbon
Pratt, F. and De Camp, L. S. Tales from Gavagan's bar
Better mousetrap
Pratt, F. and De Camp, L. S. Tales from Gavagan's bar
Black ball
Pratt, F. and De Camp, L. S. Tales from Gavagan's bar
Caveat emptor
Pratt, F. and De Camp, L. S. Tales from Gavagan's bar
Corpus delectable
Pratt, F. and De Camp, L. S. Tales from Gavagan's bar
Dime brings you success
Pratt, F. and De Camp, L. S. Tales from Gavagan's bar
Elephas frumenti
Pratt, F. and De Camp, L. S. Tales from Gavagan's bar
Eve of St John
Pratt, F. and De Camp, L. S. Tales from Gavagan's bar
Gift of God
Pratt, F. and De Camp, L. S. Tales from Gavagan's bar
Gin comes in bottles
Pratt, F. and De Camp, L. S. Tales from Gavagan's bar
Green thumb
Pratt, F. and De Camp, L. S. Tales from Gavagan's bar
Here, Putzi!
Pratt, F. and De Camp, L. S. Tales from Gavagan's bar
The love-nest
Pratt, F. and De Camp, L. S. Tales from Gavagan's bar
More than skin deep
Pratt, F. and De Camp, L. S. Tales from Gavagan's bar
My brother's keeper
Pratt, F. and De Camp, L. S. Tales from Gavagan's bar
No forwarding address
Pratt, F. and De Camp, L. S. Tales from Gavagan's bar
Palimpsest of St Augustine
Pratt, F. and De Camp, L. S. Tales from Gavagan's bar
Rape of the lock
Pratt, F. and De Camp, L. S. Tales from Gavagan's bar
Stone of the sages
Pratt, F. and De Camp, L. S. Tales from Gavagan's bar
When the night winds howls
Pratt, F. and De Camp, L. S. Tales from Gavagan's bar
"Where to, please?"
Pratt, F. and De Camp, L. S. Tales from Gavagan's bar

Pratt, Fletcher, 1897-1956, and Ruby, B. F.
Thing in the woods
Conklin, G. ed. Omnibus of science fiction
PRAYERS
Saroyan, W. Be present at our table, Lord
Preacher goes to Texas. Thomason, J. W.
PREACHERS. See Clergy
Precinct captain. Farrell, J. T.
Prefect of discipline. Carroll, J. W.
Prefect of Jerusalem. Coolidge, O. E.
PREHISTORIC MAN. See Man, Prehistoric
PREHISTORIC TIMES
Bradbury, R. Sound of thunder
Chandler, A. B. False dawn
Wells, H. G. Story of the stone age
Williamson, J. In the scarlet star
PREJUDICES AND ANTIPATHIES
Keith, E. Children's hour
Trilling, L. Other Margaret
Yoss, N. Children learn so fast
Prelude. Payne, L. V.
Prelude. Smith, E. V.
Prelude to a pint of bitter. Zangwill, L.
PREMATURE BURIAL. See Burial, Premature
Premature burial. Poe, E. A.
Prentice, Helen
Billie's fire
Stanford short stories, 1952
Preparations for the night. De Jong, D. C.
Preposterous. Brown, F.
Presence in the grove. Phillips, A.
The **present.** Cohn, E. A.
Present for a good girl. Gordimer, N.
Present for Christmas. Foster, M.
Present for Elly. Cochran, R. G.
Present for Minna. Stern, R. G.
PRESENTS. See Gifts
PRESS AGENTS. See Publicity
Pressure. Rocklynne, R.
Preston, Betty Brown
Two Miss Koofers
Seventeen (Periodical) Nineteen from Seventeen
Presumed lost. Ullman, J. R.
PRESUMPTION OF DEATH. See Death, Apparent
The **pretender.** Clark, W. Van T.
The **pretender.** O'Donovan, M.
Pretending makes it so. Vandercook, J. W.
Prettiest girl in the room. Milne, A. A.
Pretty mouth and green my eyes. Salinger, J. D.
Prevost, Leona Elizabeth, 1922-
Rites of spring
Wolfe, D. M. ed. Which grain will grow
The **prey.** Cooke, A. A.
Price, Edith Ballinger, 1897-
Among those presents
American girl (Periodical) Christmas all year 'round

Price, Edith B.—*Continued*
Bobo and the Christmas spirit
American girl (Periodical) Christmas all year 'round
Merrie gentleman
American girl (Periodical) Christmas all year 'round
Price on hide-rack. Balch, G.
Prichard, Roy
Men and babies
Oberfirst, R. ed. 1954 anthology of best original short-shorts
Pride. Jameson, M.
PRIDE AND VANITY
Doty, W. L. College star
Doty, W. L. Man with the monocle
Winslow, T. S. Misses Grant
Pride in his holsters. Lowndes, R. W.
Pride of the cities. Porter, W. S.
Pride of Tony Colucci. Schulberg, B. W.
Priest and prophet at Bethel. Wilson, D. C.
Priest and the acolyte. Wilde, O.
Priest in the family. Kennedy, L.
Priestley, John Boynton, 1894-
Grey ones
Priestley, J. B. The other place, and other stories of the same sort
Guest of honour
Priestley, J. B. The other place, and other stories of the same sort
Leadington incident
Priestley, J. B. The other place, and other stories of the same sort
Look after the strange girl
Priestley, J. B. The other place, and other stories of the same sort
Mr Strenberry's tale
Kuebler, H. W. ed. Treasury of science fiction classics
Priestley, J. B. The other place, and other stories of the same sort
Night sequence
Priestley, J. B. The other place, and other stories of the same sort
The other place
Priestley, J. B. The other place, and and other stories of the same sort
The statues
Priestley, J. B. The other place, and other stories of the same sort
Uncle Phil on TV
Priestley, J. B. The other place, and other stories of the same sort
Primavera. Sitwell, Sir O. bart.
Priming the well. Caldwell, E.
Prince, Harold. See Prince, J. jt. auth.
Prince, Jerome, 1907- and Prince, Harold
Finger man
Mystery Writers of America, inc. Four-&-twenty bloodhounds
Man in the velvet hat
Mystery Writers of America, inc. Maiden murders
Prince Alberic and the Snake Lady. Paget, V.
Prince Godfrey frees mountain dwellers and little shepherds from a savage werewolf and from witches. Gorska, H.

Prince of darkness. Powers, J. F.
PRINCES
Paget, V. Prince Alberic and the Snake Lady
Princess and all the kingdom. Lagerkvist, P. F.
Princess and the puma. Porter, W. S.
Princess September. Maugham, W. S.
Princess who couldn't say yes. Van Doren, M.
PRINCESSES
Brophy, B. Crown princess
Coolidge, O. E. Luck charm
Street, J. L. Mr Bisbee's princess
Wilde, O. Birthday of the Infanta
PRINCETON UNIVERSITY
Boyd, J. Elms and Fair Oaks
Pringle. Barker, A. L.
PRINTERS AND PRINTING
Brown, F. Angelic angleworm
Brown, F. Etaoin Shrdlu
PRINTING. See Printers and printing
The **prism.** Van Doren, M.
The **prison.** Malamud, B.
PRISON SHIPS
Bedford-Jones, H. and Williams, L. B. Yellow Ship
The **prisoner.** Gordimer, N.
Prisoner of Zembla. Porter, W. S.
PRISONERS, CONDEMNED
Camus, A. Sentence of death
PRISONERS, POLITICAL
Bergengruen, W. Royal game
PRISONERS, RELEASED. See Ex-convicts
PRISONERS AND PRISONS
Benét, S. V. Blood of the martyrs
Brown, F. Cain
Eliot, G. pseud. In the prison
Maugham, W. S. Episode
Maugham, W. S. The kite
Maugham, W. S. Man with a conscience
Maugham, W. S. Official position
Michaëlis, K. Teacher Jensen
Munro, H. H. Lost sanjak
Poe, E. A. Pit and the pendulum
Schnabel, J. F. Journey for Wilbur
Steele, W. D. Renegade
Tucker, W. Exit
Van Doren, M. Episode at the Honeypot
Waugh, E. Love among the ruins

Italy
Mudford, W. Iron shroud

Russia
Dostoevskiĭ, F. M. Peasant Marey
PRISONERS OF WAR
Blackburn, E. R. Sunrise
Downey, H. Crispin's way
Farrell, J. T. Digging our own graves
O'Donovan, M. Guests of the nation
Saint Exupéry, A. de. Letter to a hostage
Sansom, W. How Claeys died
Sartre, J. P. The wall

Pritchett, Victor Sawdon, 1900-
  The ape
    Heilman, R. B. ed. Modern short stories
  The sailor
    New writing (Periodical) Best stories
  Story of Don Juan
    Asquith, Lady C. E. C. ed. Book of modern ghosts
Private eye. Kuttner, H.
Private hell. Westbrock, J. T.
Private—keep out. MacDonald, P.
PRIVATE SECRETARIES. See Secretaries
PRIVATEERING
  Adams, J. D. Cap'n Ezra, privateer
  Hinternhoff, J. F. Mutineers be hanged
Privilege of the limits. Thompson, E. W.
Prize cargo. England, G. A.
Prize corn chowder. Haywood, C.
PRIZE FIGHTERS. See Boxing
PRIZE FIGHTING. See Boxing
PRIZES
  De La Roche, M. The celebration
Pro and con. Newhouse, E.
Pro arte. Seager, A.
A **problem.** James, H.
Problem for Emmy. Townes, R. S.
Problem of Cell 13. Futrelle, J.
Problem on Balak. Aycock, R. D.
Process. Van Vogt, A. E.
Procter, Maurice
  Fox in the Pennine Hills
    Mystery Writers of America, inc. Crooks' tour
  No place for magic
    Mystery Writers of America, inc. Butcher, baker, murder-maker
Procurator of Judæa. France, A.
PRODUCERS, THEATRICAL. See Theatrical producers
Production test. Jones, R. F.
The **Professor.** Farrell, J. T.
Professor. Hughes, L.
Professor Sea Gull. Mitchell, J.
PROFESSORS. See Teachers
Professor's teddy-bear. Waldo, E. H.
Prohibition. Merochnik, M.
Project ocean floor. Elam, R. M.
PROJECTILES
  Arico, V. The rebel
The **promise.** Maugham, W. S.
The **promise.** Stewart, R.
Promised land. Moore, C. L.
PROMISES
  Maugham, W. S. The promise
The **promotion.** Arico, V.
Proof. Stubbs, H. C.
Proof of the pudding. Porter, W. S.
Propagandist. Jenkins, W. F.
Property. Verga, G.

Propes, Arthur
  All that glitters
    Ford, N. A. and Faggett, H. L. eds. Best short stories by Afro-American writers (1925-1950)
PROPHECIES
  Alarcón, P. A. de. The prophecy
  Harvey, W. F. August heat
  Hawthorne, N. Great Stone Face
  Heinlein, R. A. Life-line
  Komroff, M. Told in the stars
  Munro, H. H. Peace offering
  Whitley, C. M. Destiny strikes back
The **prophecy.** Alarcón, P. A. de
The **prophet.** Appet, N.
The **prophet.** McLaverty, M.
A **proposale.** Ashford, D.
PROSPECTORS
  Brandon, W. Ghost lode
  Clark, W. Van T. Indian well
  Clark, W. Van T. Wind and the snow of winter
  Grey, Z. Tappan's burro
  London, J. All-gold cañon
  Purcell, D. Rider of the avalanche
  Rogow, L. Laziest man in Texas
  Schaefer, J. W. Something lost
Prosper's "old mother." Harte, B.
PROSTITUTES
  Brement, M. Youth
  Gold, I. Change of air
  Hemingway, E. Light of the world
  Jackson, C. R. Old men and boys
  Waltari, M. T. Goldilocks
Protected species. Fyfe, H. B.
Protecting Mary. O'Leary, J. T.
PROTECTION OF GAME. See Game protection
Protégée of Jack Hamlin's. Harte, B.
PROTESTANTISM
  O'Donovan, M. My first Protestant
Prothalamion. Sheehy, E.
Proud robot. Kuttner, H.
The **Proudies** entertain. Trollope, A.
Proust, Marcel, 1871-1922
  Filial sentiments of a parricide
    Neider, C. ed. Great short stories from the world's literature
Proved by the sea. Marmur, J.
Proverbial murder. Carr, J. D.
The **provider.** Guiney, L. I.
Prowler on the hill. Hole, L. E.
Proxima centauri. Jenkins, W. F.
Prudence by name. Schaefer, J. W.
Prudent man. Walsh, M.
Prussian officer. Lawrence, D. H.
PRUSSIANS. See Soldiers, German
Psyche and the pskyscraper. Porter, W. S.
Psychiatrist of one's own. Gellhorn, M. E.
PSYCHIATRISTS
  Collier, J. Interpretation of a dream
  Kuttner, H. Dream's end
  Kuttner, H. and Moore, C. L. Wild surmise

PSYCHIATRISTS—*Continued*
Mauriac, F. Thérèse and the doctor
Rinehart, A. Mirrored room
Shiras, W. H. In hiding
Temple, W. F. Counter-transference
PSYCHIC PHENOMENA. See Supernatural phenomena
Psychical invasion. Blackwood, A.
PSYCHOANALYSIS. See Psychoanalysts
PSYCHOANALYSTS
Collier, J. Fallen star
Hecht, B. Double exposure
Horwitz, J. The voices
Maugham, W. S. Lord Mountdrago
Strasser, S. Case of the psychoanalyst
PSYCHOLOGISTS
Brandon, W. Party to blackmail
Coppel, A. The dreamer
Vonnegut, K. Report of the Barnhouse effect
PSYCHONEUROSES. See Neuroses
Psychopathic nurse. Keller, D. H.
Pu, Lien. See Lien Pu
Public eye. White, W. A. P.
Public enemies. Allen, E. and Kelley, F. B.
PUBLICITY
Beck, W. Men working
Porter, W. S. Girl and the graft
Porter, W. S. Rus in urbe
PUBLISHERS AND PUBLISHING
Porter, W. S. Sacrifice hit
Puck-eater. Kempton, K. P.
Pudding that broke up the preaching. Credle, E.
Pudney, John, 1909-
Kitty, kitty, kitty
Joseph, M. ed. Best cat stories
Pugh, Shirley Shapiro
Sensational type
Seventeen (Periodical) Nineteen from Seventeen
Pull, you lubbers! O'Brien, B.
PULLMAN PORTERS. See Railroads—Employees
Pulpit for Don. West, D.
Pultz, Constance
Good bye to Miss Stoddard's
Seventeen (Periodical) The Seventeen reader
PUMAS
Norton, B. The panther
Porter, W. S. Princess and the puma
Spofford, H. E. P. Circumstance
Stuart, J. Fight number twenty-five
Pump house key. Bonner, P. H.
PUNCH AND JUDY. See Puppets and puppet plays
Punishment of Shahpesh, the Persian, on Khipil, the builder. Meredith, G.
The **pupil.** James, H.
The **pupil.** Woolley, R.
PUPPETS AND PUPPET PLAYS
Metcalfe, J. The childish thing
Puppy business. Cavanna, B.

Pupsik. Bergengruen, W.
Purcell, Donald
Rider of the avalanche
Saturday evening post (Periodical) Saturday evening post stories, 1953
Purdy, Kenneth W. 1914?-
Change of plan
Best American short stories, 1953
Purification of Thelma Augenstern. Wolfson, V.
I **Puritani.** Palacio Valdés, A.
PURITANS
Hawthorne, N. Maypole of Merry Mount
Purloined letter. Poe, E. A.
Purple and fine linen. Edginton, H. M.
Purple dress. Porter, W. S.
Purple fields. Glemser, B.
Purple hat. Felder, D. F.
Purple hat. Welty, E.
Purple of the Balkan Kings. Munro, H. H.
Purple wig. Chesterton, G. K.
Pursuit of gloom. Willingham, C.
Pursuit of Mr Blue. Chesterton, G. K.
Pushcart man. Hughes, L.
Pushkin, Alexander. See Puskin, Alexandr Sergeevich
Pushkin, Alexandr Sergeevich, 1799-1837
The undertaker
Neider, C. ed. Great short stories from the world's literature
P'u Sung-Ling, 1640-1715
The bookworm
Lin, Y. ed. Famous Chinese short stories
Cricket boy
Lin, Y. ed. Famous Chinese short stories
Jojo
Lin, Y. ed. Famous Chinese short stories
Put on the spot. Howard, W.
Put yourself in my place. Newhouse, E.
Putman, Clay, 1925-
News from Troy
Prize stories, 1954
Old acrobat and the ruined city
Best American short stories, 1950
Stanford short stories, 1950
Our vegetable love
Best American short stories, 1953
The wounded
Prize stories of 1950
Stanford short stories, 1950
Young man of his time
Stanford short stories, 1951
Putting away of Uncle Quaggin. Kneale, N.
Puzo, Mario, 1920-
Last Christmas
American vanguard, 1950
Pygmalion. De Vries, P.
Pygmalion. Gilbreth, F. B. and Moller, E. C. G.

Pyle, Howard, 1853-1911
How the good gifts were used by two
Fenner, P. R. comp. Fools and funny
fellows
Tom Chist and his treasure box
Fenner, P. R. comp. Pirates, pirates,
pirates
Pyrénées-Orientales. See France, Provincial
and rural—Pyrénees-Orientales

Q

QUACKS AND QUACKERY
Caldwell, E. Medicine man
Phillips, P. Field study
QUADROONS. See Mulattoes
Quail for Mr Forester. Humphrey, W.
Quail seed. Munro, H. H.
QUAIL SHOOTING. See Hunting
QUAILS
Buckingham, N. Carry me back
QUAKERS. See Friends, Society of
Quality. Galsworthy, J.
Quality of mercy. Lipsky, E.
QUARRELING
Rabinowitz, S. Tit for tat
Scott, Sir W. Two drovers
QUARRIES AND QUARRYING
Van Doren, M. The quarry
The **quarry.** Van Doren, M.
Quarter section on Dullknife Creek. Haycox, E.
Quartet. De La Roche, M.
QUEBEC. See Canada—Quebec (Province)
Queen, Ellery, pseud.
Adventure of the Dauphin's doll
Queen, E. pseud. Calendar of crime
Adventure of the dead cat
Mystery Writers of America, inc. 20
great tales of murder
Queen, E. pseud. Calendar of crime
Adventure of the emperor's dice
Queen, E. pseud. Calendar of crime
Adventure of the fallen angel
Queen, E. pseud. Calendar of crime
Adventure of the Gettysburg bugle
Queen, E. pseud. Calendar of crime
Adventure of the ides of Michael Magoon
Queen, E. pseud. Calendar of crime
Adventure of the inner circle
Queen, E. pseud. Calendar of crime
Adventure of the medical finger
Queen, E. pseud. Calendar of crime
Adventure of the needle's eye
Queen, E. pseud. Calendar of crime
Adventure of the one-penny black
Mystery Writers of America, inc. Maiden murders
Adventure of the President's half disme
Queen, E. pseud. Calendar of crime
Adventure of the telltale bottle
Queen, E. pseud. Calendar of crime
Adventure of the three R's
Queen, E. pseud. Calendar of crime

Black ledger
Queen, E. pseud. Queen's Bureau of
Investigation
Child missing!
Queen, E. pseud. Queen's Bureau of
Investigation
Cold money
Queen, E. pseud. Queen's Bureau of
Investigation
Double your money
Queen, E. pseud. Queen's Bureau of
Investigation
Driver's seat
Queen, E. pseud. Queen's Bureau of
Investigation
Emperor's dice
Best detective stories of the year—1952
GI story
Queen, E. pseud. Queen's Bureau of
Investigation
Gambler's Club
Queen, E. pseud. Queen's Bureau of
Investigation
Gettysburg bugle
Mystery Writers of America, inc.
Butcher, baker, murder-maker
Ides of Michael Magoon
Mystery Writers of America, inc. Four-&-twenty bloodhounds
Lump of sugar
Queen, E. pseud. Queen's Bureau of
Investigation
Matter of seconds
Queen, E. pseud. Queen's Bureau of
Investigation
Miser's gold
Queen, E. pseud. Queen's Bureau of
Investigation
Money talks
Queen, E. pseud. Queen's Bureau of
Investigation
Murder without clues
Best detective stories of the year—1951
This week magazine. This week's short-short stories
"My queer Dean"
Best detective stories of the year—1954
Queen, E. pseud. Queen's Bureau of
Investigation
Myna birds
Queen, E. pseud. Queen's Bureau of
Investigation
Needle's eye
Mystery Writers of America, inc.
Crooks' tour
Question of honor
Queen, E. pseud. Queen's Bureau of
Investigation
Robber of Wrightsville
Queen, E. pseud. Queen's Bureau of
Investigation
Snowball in July
Queen, E. pseud. Queen's Bureau of
Investigation
Sound of blackmail
This week magazine. This week's short-short stories
Three widows
Queen, E. pseud. Queen's Bureau of
Investigation
Witch of Times Square
Queen, E. pseud. Queen's Bureau of
Investigation

Queen of the Black Coast. Howard, R. E.
Queenie: the gallant-hearted collie. Little,
    G. W.
"Queer." Anderson, S.
Queer feet. Chesterton, G. K.
Queer kind of sorrow. Sullivan, R.
Queiroz, Eça de. See Eça de Queiroz, José
    Maria
Quentin, Patrick, pseud.
    All the way to the moon
        Queen, E. pseud. ed. Queen's awards:
        6th ser.
    Boy's will
        Best detective stories of the year—1951
        Mystery Writers of America, inc.
        Crooks' tour
        Queen, E. pseud. ed. Queen's awards:
        5th ser.
    Fat cat
        Joseph, M. ed. Best cat stories
    Girl overboard
        Mystery Writers of America, inc. Four-
        &-twenty bloodhounds
    Love comes to Miss Lucy
        Mystery Writers of America, inc. 20
        great tales of murder
    This looks like murder
        This week magazine. This week's short-
        short stories
    Town blonde, country blonde
        This week magazine. This week's short-
        short stories
    Witness for the prosecution
        Mystery Writers of America, inc.
        Butcher, baker, murder-maker
Queries and answers. Porter, W. S.
The quest. Munro, H. H.
Quest for Saint Aquin. White, W. A. P.
Question of being businesslike. Yaffe, J.
Question of blood. Haycox, E.
Question of honor. Queen, E. pseud.
Quick one. Chesterton, G. K.
Quick shoots. Bonnaffon, A.
The quid pro quo. Danielson, R. E.
Quiet garden spot. Asch, S.
Quiet man. Walsh, M.
Quiet Mr Evans. Kneale, N.
Quiet morning. Erin, B.
Quiet one. Schuman, S.
A quiet wedding. Upson, W. H.
Quille, Dan de, pseud. See Wright, William
Quiller-Couch, Sir Arthur Thomas, 1863-
    1944
    Roll-call of the reef
        Cerf, B. A. and Moriarty, H. C. eds.
        Anthology of famous British stories
        Fenner, P. R. comp. Ghosts, ghosts,
        ghosts
Quince tree. Munro, H. H.
Quiroga, Horacio, 1879-1937
    The fatherland
        De Onís, H. ed. Spanish stories and
        tales
Quitandinha. Seager, A.

R

R.I.P. Trollope, A.
R. M. S. Titanic. Baldwin, H. W.
Rab and his friends. Brown, J.
Rabban Gamaliel. Cohn, E.
Rabbi and emperor. Cohn, E.
Rabbi and the siren. Spire, A.
Rabbi Itzik the fool. Steinberg, Y.
Rabbi Yochanan the warden. Peretz, I. L.
RABBIS
    Agnon, S. J. Story of the cantor
    Bergelson, D. In a backwoods town
    Bialik, H. N. Short Friday
    Bloch, J. R. Heresy of the water taps
    Cohn, E. Given years
    Cohn, E. Rabban Gamaliel
    Cohn, E. Rabbi and emperor
    Cohn, E. Remains of virtue
    Hamelin, Glückel of. A story
    Peretz, I. L. Cabalists
    Peretz, I. L. Devotion without end
    Peretz, I. L. If not higher
    Peretz, I. L. Rabbi Yochanan the warden
    Rabinowitz, S. Tit for tat
    Rappoport, S. Two great men
    Singer, I. J. Repentance
    Steinberg, Y. Rabbi Itzik the fool
    Werfel, F. V. Third commandment
    Zangwill, I. Neo-Hebrew poet
Rabbi's son. Babel', I. E.
RABBITS
    Caldwell, E. Molly-Cotton-Tail
    Cartmill, C. Number nine
    Seton, E. T. Raggylug
Rabchik, a Jewish dog. Rabinowitz, S.
Rabelais, Francois, 1490-1553?
    Phalanstery of Theleme
        Derleth, A. W. ed. Beyond time & space
RABIES. See Hydrophobia
Rabinowitz, Shalom, 1859-1916
    Dreyfus in Kasrilevke
        Howe, I. and Greenberg, E. eds. Treas-
        ury of Yiddish stories
    Eternal life
        Howe, I. and Greenberg, E. eds. Treas-
        ury of Yiddish stories
    Gy-ma-na-si-a
        Ausubel, N. ed. Treasury of Jewish hu-
        mor
    Hodel
        Howe, I. and Greenberg, E. eds. Treas-
        ury of Yiddish stories
    Menachem-Mendel, fortune hunter
        Ausubel, N. ed. Treasury of Jewish
        humor
    My brother Eliyahu's drink
        Ausubel, N. ed. Treasury of Jewish
        humor
    On account of a hat
        Howe, I. and Greenberg, E. eds. Treas-
        ury of Yiddish stories
    Page from the Song of Songs
        Howe, I. and Greenberg, E. eds. Treas-
        ury of Yiddish stories
    The pair
        Howe, I. and Greenberg, E. eds. Treas-
        ury of Yiddish stories

Rabinowitz, Shalom—*Continued*
Passover guest
Neider, C. ed. Great short stories from the world's literature
Passover in a village
Leftwich, J. ed. Yisröel. 1952 ed.
Rabchik, a Jewish dog
Ausubel, N. ed. Treasury of Jewish humor
The search
Howe, I. and Greenberg, E. eds. Treasury of Yiddish stories
Tit for tat
Neider, C. ed. Men of the high calling

RACCOONS
Gipson, F. B. My kind of a man
Peattie, D. C. and Peattie, L. R. Weirwood marsh
Roberts, Sir C. G. D. Black Swamp

Race in the wilderness. Coatsworth, E. J.

RACE PROBLEMS
Doty, W. L. Dark knight
Gibbs, A. The test
Hughes, L. One Friday morning
Mohler, C. Jesus complex
Tunis, J. R. Ronald leaves the Academy

RACES. See Automobile races; Boat racing; Horse racing; Running; Yacht racing

Rachel. Caldwell, E.

Rachel and her children. Newman, F.

Rachel's summer. Jackson, C. R.

RACIAL INTERMARRIAGES. See Interracial marriages

RACING. See Automobile races; Boat racing; Horse racing; Running; Yacht racing

RACKETEERS. See Gangsters

Rackowe, Alec, 1900-
Four-minute mile
Certner, S. and Henry, G. H. eds. Short stories for our times

Raddall, Thomas Head, 1903-
The amulet
Pacey, D. ed. Book of Canadian stories

Rader, Paul
Tabby cat
Best American short stories, 1951

Radford, Manson
Wm. Crane
Southern review. Anthology of stories from the Southern review

RADIATION POISONING. See Radioactivity

RADIO
Cheever, J. Enormous radio
Kipling, R. 'Wireless'
McNulty, J. The jackpot
Schulberg, B. W. Your Arkansas traveler

RADIO OPERATORS. See Radio

RADIOACTIVITY
Brown, F. The waveries
Browning, J. S. Burning bright

Raica, the bride of Cana. Gibran, K.

The raft. Rickenbacker, E. V.

Rag thing. Grinnell, D. pseud.

Raggylug. Seton, E. T.

RAIATEA (ISLAND)
Michener, J. A. Povenaa's daughter

The raid. Lewis, A.

Raid on the oyster pirates. London, J.

RAILROAD ACCIDENTS. See Railroads—Accidents

RAILROAD ENGINEERS
Wolfe, T. Far and the near

RAILROAD ENGINES. See Railroads—Trains

Railroad harvest. Household, G.

Railroad tangle. Cross, J. A.

RAILROADS
Boyd, J. Old pines
Cross, J. A. Hunch that clicked
Moskowitz, S. ed. Great railroad stories of the world; 13 stories
Mowery, W. B. Colonel Nat

Accidents
George, W. L. Ave, amor, morituri te salutant
Mann, T. Railway accident
Somerville, A. W. Tale of the old main line

Employees
Cohen, O. R. Toot for a toot
Cross, J. A. Railroad tangle
Davis, H. L. Flying switch
Dickens, C. Signal man
Hauptmann, G. J. R. Flagman Thiel
McLarn, J. C. Yardmaster
O'Donovan, M. Eternal triangle
O'Donovan, M. A romantic
Packard, F. L. Man who confessed

Models
Beck, W. Far whistle
Welch, D. Mrs Union Station

Spain
Marshall, B. Immodest maiden

Trains
Comstock, H. B. Fish wagon
Gordimer, N. Train from Rhodesia
Hayes, W. E. Big engine
James, M. Stolen railroad train
O'Donovan, M. In the train

Travel
Benson, T. A nice fright
Cousins, M. Uncle Edgar and the reluctant saint
Munro, H. H. The mouse
Munro, H. H. Name-day
Rabinowitz, S. On account of a hat
Vulfarts, M. Package tzoress
Winslow, T. S. Grandma

Railway accident. Mann, T.

RAILWAYS. See Railroads

Rain. Maugham, W. S.

Rain check. Kuttner, H.

The rainbow. Howard, W.

Rainmaker. Reese, J. H.

RAIN-MAKERS
Reese, J. Rainmaker

Raine, William MacLeod, 1871-1954
  Friend of Buck Hollister
    Western Writers of America. Bad men
    and good
Rainy day at Big Lost Creek. Stuart, J.
Rajah's Rock. Bonner, P. H.
Rakous, V. pseud. See Oesterreicher, A.
Ramble in Aphasia. Porter, W. S.
Rameau's nephew. Diderot, D.
Ramsay, Janet
  Miracle at Eastpoint
    American girl (Periodical) Christmas all
    year 'round
Ramsey, Harmon B. 1907-
  Mr Jones goes to Bethlehem
    Elmquist, R. M. ed. Fifty years to
    Christmas
RANCH LIFE
  Brand, M. pseud. Dust storm
  Cheshire, G. Bad year
  Miers, E. S. Black Bat
    See also Cowboys

      California
  Steinbeck, J. The chrysanthemums
  Steinbeck, J. The gift

      Mexico
  Bowles, P. F. At Paso Rojo

      Nebraska
  Jackson, C. T. Buffalo wallow

      Nevada
  Drago, H. S. Long winter

      Oregon
  Davis, H. L. Team bells woke me; 13
    stories

      Texas
  Burtis, T. Rope and the bulldog
  Porter, W. S. Hygeia at the Solito
  Porter, W. S. Law and order
  Porter, W. S. Madame Bo-Peep of the
    ranches
  Porter, W. S. Missing chord
Rancher of the hills. Booker, A. E.
Rancher's horse. Bennett, R. H.
Randall, Kenneth Charles, 1898-
  Wild hunter
    Fenner, P. R. comp. Dogs, dogs, dogs
Ramsom. Buck, P. S.
Ransom. Fyfe, H. B.
Ramsom note. Lord, M.
Ransom of Mack. Porter, W. S.
Ransom of Red Chief. Porter, W. S.
Ransom . . . $1,000,000. Runyon, D.
Rape of the lock. Pratt, F. and De Camp,
    L. S.
Rape of the solar system. Stone, L. F.
The **rapids.** Clark, W. Van T.
Rappaccini's daughter. Hawthorne, N.
Rappoport, Solomon, 1863-1920
  Moses Montefiore
    Leftwich, J. ed. Yisröel. 1952 ed.

Two great men
    Ausubel, N. ed. Treasury of Jewish
    humor
Rashomon. Akutagawa, R.
Rasmussen, Gladys Fuller
  Tea at Barnaby's
    Oberfirst, R. ed. 1952 anthology of best
    original short-shorts
The **rat.** Wright, S. F.
Rat race. De Courcy, D. and De Courcy, J.
Rat that could speak. Dickens, C.
The **ratcatcher.** Grinevskiĭ, A. S.
Rath, Ida Ellen, 1884-
  Longest day I live
    Oberfirst, R. ed. 1954 anthology of best
    original short-shorts
The **rathskeller** and the rose. Porter, W. S.
RATS
  De Courcy, D. and De Courcy, J. Rat
    race
  Dickens, C. The rat that could speak
  Muir, J. Pirate rat
  Porges, A. The rats
The **rats.** Porges, A.
The **rattle.** Devin, B.
Rattlesnake Trail. Fitts, H. K.
Rattling good yarn. Milne, A. A.
Rattner, Joan, 1922-
  Haitian incident
    American vanguard, 1953
Raw material. Maugham, W. S.
Rawlings, Charles A.
  Boy who gave his dog away
    Saturday evening post (Periodical). Sat-
    urday evening post stories, 1952
  Flash of lightning
    This week magazine. This week's short-
    short stories.
Rawlings, Marjorie (Kinnan) 1896-1953
  Benny and the bird-dogs
    Andrews, R. C. ed. My favorite stories
    of the great outdoors
  Gal young un
    First-prize stories, 1919-1954
  The pardon
    Blodgett, H. W. ed. Story survey. 1953
    ed.
Rawson, Clayton, 1906-
  Clues of the tattooed man & the broken
    legs
    Mystery Writers of America, inc. Four-
    &-twenty bloodhounds
  Off the face of the earth
    Mystery Writers of America, inc.
    Butcher, baker, murder-maker
Ready, William B. 1914-
  Angharad
    Ready, W. B. Great disciple, and other
    stories
  Barring the weight
    Gable, M. Sister, ed. Many-colored
    fleece
    Ready, W. B. Great disciple, and other
    stories
  Cattle raid on Cooley
    Ready, W. B. Great disciple, and other
    stories

Ready, William B.—*Continued*
  Coat for St Patrick's Day
    Ready, W. B. Great disciple, and other stories
  Coo-Cullen
    Ready, W. B. Great disciple, and other stories
  Coo-Cullen growing up
    Ready, W. B. Great disciple, and other stories
  Devlin
    Magazine of fantasy and science fiction. Best from Fantasy and science fiction; 3d ser.
  End of Coo-Cullen
    Ready, W. B. Great disciple, and other stories
  Giant Finn MacCool
    Ready, W. B. Great disciple, and other stories
  Great disciple
    Ready, W. B. Great disciple, and other stories
  Irish and the Jews and everybody else
    Ready, W. B. Great disciple, and other stories
  The Leprechauns
    Ready, W. B. Great disciple, and other stories
  Mother's meeting
    Ready, W. B. Great disciple, and other stories
  Patrick will take over
    Ready, W. B. Great disciple, and other stories
  Piper pays
    Ready, W. B. Great disciple, and other stories
  St Patrick's Day in the afternoon
    Ready, W. B. Great disciple, and other stories
  Solitary Dogan
    Ready, W. B. Great disciple, and other stories
  "Sufficient"
    Ready, W. B. Great disciple, and other stories
  Where falls not hail
    Ready, W. B. Great disciple, and other stories
Real customers. Gutman, C.
REAL ESTATE. See Real property
REAL ESTATE BUSINESS
  Herzl, T. Thumbling and Sapling
Real friend. Greco, E.
REAL PEOPLE. See names of individuals
REAL PROPERTY
  Skinner, C. O. Parcel of land
  Waugh, E. Englishman's home
Real thing. James, H.
Really important person. Chute, B. J.
Reaney, James Crerar, 1927-
  The bully
    Weaver, R. and James, H. eds. Canadian short stories
Reany, Colleen Thibaudeau. See Thibaudeau, Colleen
Reappearance. Birmingham, S. G.
Reason. Asimov, I.
Reason for Ann. Connolly, M.
Reb Anshel the golden. Steinberg, Y.
Rebbe and the rebbetsin. Shapiro, L.
The **rebel.** Arico, V.
Rebellion. Campbell, J. W.
Rebellion. Harnden, R. P.
Rebellious tree. Cohn, E.
Recent photograph. Bowen, E.
The **Recessional.** Munro, H. H.
Reck, Franklin Mering, 1896-
  Diving fool
    American boy (Periodical) American boy anthology
The **recluse.** Reisin, A.
Reconciliation. Brown, F.
Reconciliation. Landon, M. D. M.
Record-breaker. Temple, W. H.
Record of a man. Willingham, C.
Recovery. Cicellis, K.
Recruiting station. Van Vogt, A. E.
RECTORS. See Clergy
Rectory parlor. Doty, W. L.
Red. Maugham, W. S.
Red badge of courage. Crane, S.
Red carpet. Parker, J. R.
Red death of Mars. Williams, R. M.
Red dog. Maier, H.
Red Fox. Peattie, M. R.
Red-haired Miss Daintreys. Lehmann, R.
Red handkerchief. Gobineau, J. A. comte de
Red Hanrahan. Yeats, W. B.
Red hat. Brown, M. E.
Red head. Williams, W. C.
Red-Headed League. Doyle, Sir A. C.
Red leaves. Faulkner, W.
Red-letter day. Taylor, E.
Red Lodge. Wakefield, H. W.
Red MacDonald. O'Meara, W.
Red moon of Meru. Chesterton, G. K.
Red mountain. Payne, P. S. R.
Red nails. Howard, R. E.
Red necktie. Sinclair, J.
Red Pepper. Chute, B. J.
Red pony. Steinbeck, J.
Red Queen's race. Asimov, I.
Red rats of Plum Fork. Stuart, J.
Red roses of Tonia. Porter, W. S.
Red sands. Elam, R. M.
Red stocking. Eggleston, M. W.
Red Storm on Jupiter. Long, F. B.
Red wagon. Paradis, M. B.
Redman, Ben Ray, 1896-
  Ground mist
    Jensen, P. ed. Fireside book of flying stories
Redruff. Seton, E. T.
Red's education. Kjelgaard, J. A.
Reeder, left defense. Sherman, H. M.
Reelistic viewpoint. Wylie, P.

Rees, Gilbert
Rod of God
Burnett, W. and Burnett, H. S. eds.
Sextet
Reese, John Henry
Cat-eyed woman
Saturday evening post (Periodical)
Saturday evening post stories, 1953
Desert orchid
Saturday evening post (Periodical)
Saturday evening post stories, 1952
Last day at the office
Saturday evening post (Periodical)
Saturday evening post stories, 1951
Rainmaker
Heinlein, R. A. ed. Tomorrow, the stars
Reeve, Joel
Doubles or nothing
Argosy (Periodical) Argosy Book of
sports stories
Referent. Bradbury, R.
Reformation of Calliope. Porter, W. S.
Refuge for tonight. Williams, R. M.
The **refugee.** Rice, J.
Refugee village. Stinetorf, L. A.
REFUGEES
Connolly, M. Seminary Hill
Forester, C. S. The unbelievable
Karo, D. B. Carmi
Kristol, I. Adam and I
Saint Exupéry, A. de. Letter to a hostage
Schulberg, D. W. Passport to nowhere
The **refugees.** Yaffe, J.
Regarding monuments. Grimson, M. S.
REGENERATION
Moore, C. L. No woman born
Porter, W. S. Higher abdication
Wyld Ospina, C. Honor of his house
Reginald. Munro, H. H.
Reginald at the Carlton. Munro, H. H.
Reginald at the theatre. Munro, H. H.
Reginald in Russia. Munro, H. H.
Reginald on besetting sins. Munro, H. H.
Reginald on Christmas presents. Munro,
H. H.
Reginald on house-parties. Munro, H. H.
Reginald on tariffs. Munro, H. H.
Reginald on the Academy. Munro, H. H.
Reginald on worries. Munro, H. H.
Reginald's choir treat. Munro, H. H.
Reginald's Christmas revel. Munro, H. H.
Reginald's drama. Munro, H. H.
Reginald's peace poem. Munro, H. H.
Reginald's Rubaiyat. Munro, H. H.
Regli, Adolph Casper, 1896-
One for the team
Furman, A. L. ed. Teen-age stories of
the diamond
Southpaw switch
Furman, A. L. ed. Teen-age stories of
the diamond
Trouble on the range
Fenner, P. R. comp. Cowboys, cowboys,
cowboys

Regula Amrain and her youngest son.
Keller, G.
Reid, Constance Bowman
Yellow leaf
Story (Periodical) Story; no. 4
Reid, Forrest, 1876-1947
Courage
Carrington, H. ed. Week-end book of
ghost stories
Reid, Mayne, 1818-1883
Battle of the marten and the porcupine
Andrews, R. C. ed. My favorite stories
of the great outdoors
Reid, Thomas Mayne. See Reid, Mayne
Reigate squires. Doyle, Sir A. C.
Rein, Harold E.
Days and nights
American vanguard, 1950
Reingelder and the German flag. Kipling, R.
Reisen, Abraham. See Reisin, Abraham
Reisin, Abraham, 1876-1953
Avrom the cobbler
Ausubel, N. ed. Treasury of Jewish
humor
Big succeh
Howe, I. and Greenberg, E. eds. Treas-
ury of Yiddish stories
Last hope
Ausubel, N. ed. Treasury of Jewish
humor
The loan
Ausubel, N. ed. Treasury of Jewish
humor
Poor community
Howe, I. and Greenberg, E. eds. Treas-
ury of Yiddish stories
The recluse
Howe, I. and Greenberg, E. eds. Treas-
ury of Yiddish stories
Rich poor man
Leftwich, J. ed. Yisröel. 1952 ed.
Tuition for the rebbe
Howe, I. and Greenberg, E. eds. Treas-
ury of Yiddish stories
Reiss, Isaac. See Nadir, Isaac Moishe
REJUVENATION
Bradbury, R. Hail and farewell
Derleth, A. W. McIlvaine's star
Hawthorne, N. Dr Heidegger's experiment
Jameson, M. Blind alley
Simak, C. D. Second childhood
Wright, S. F. The rat
RELATIVES. See Family life; also specific
relative, e.g. Aunts; Brothers; etc.
RELAY RACES. See Running
The **relic.** Annett, W. S.
Relic of the Vikings. Mowery, W. B.
RELIGION
Betts, D. Mr Shawn and Father Scott
Gally, J. W. Spirits
Harte, B. Bell-ringer of Angel's
Schaefer, J. W. Emmet Dutrow
RELIGIOUS BELIEF. See Faith
RELIGIOUS LIBERTY
Hawthorne, N. Endicott and the Red
Cross
Reluctant dragon. Grahame, K.

Reluctant hangman. Dickinson, H.
Reluctant hero. McFee, W.
Reluctant heroes. Robinson, F. M.
Remains of virtue. Cohn, E.
Remarkable case of Davidson's eyes. Wells, H. G.
Remarque, Erich Maria, 1898-
  Darkness in Paris
    Burnett, W. ed. World's best
Remember. . . Buckingham, N.
Remember the night. Keene, D.
Remnants of the code. Porter, W. S.
The remorseful. Kornbluth, C. M.
Remoulding of Groby Lington. Munro, H. H.
Renaissance at Charleroi. Porter, W. S.
Renard, Jules, 1864-1910
  A romance
    Geist, S. ed. French stories and tales
  Spoiled cake
    Geist, S. ed. French stories and tales
Render unto Caesar. Schneider, G. W.
Rendezvous romance. Gulick, G. C.
Rendina, Laura (Jones) Cooper
  Biggest flounder
    McFarland, W. K. comp. Then it happened
The renegade. Farrell, J. T.
Renegade. Steele, W. D.
Rennie Peddigoe. Tarkington, B.
REPAIRING
  Jones, R. F. Tools of the trade
REPENTANCE
  Komroff, M. Alone the stranger passes
  Peretz, I. L. Devotion without end
Repentance. Singer, I. J.
Repetition. Van Vogt, A. E.
Report cards. Humphrey, W.
Report on the Barnhouse effect. Vonnegut, K.
Report to an academy. Kafka, F.
REPORTERS. See Journalists
Reporter's dream. Chekhov, A. P.
Repton, Humphrey, 1752-1818
  From a private mad-house
    Derleth, A. W. ed. Far boundaries
Requiem. Heinlein, R. A.
Requiem for a noun. De Vries, P.
Requiescat. Bowen, E.
Rescue. Van Doren, M.
Rescue at sea
  Carrington, H. ed. Week-end book of ghost stories
Rescuer extraordinary. Bruce, J. C.
RESCUES
  Conrad, J. Initiation
  Crane, S. Open boat
  Marmur, J. Proved by the sea
  Montague, C. E. Action
  Mowery, W. B. St Gabriel Zsbyski
  Porter, W. S. Chaparral prince
  Reynolds, J. M. and McCormick, H. P.
    Through Twelve-League Labyrinth

RESEARCH, MEDICAL. See Medical research
Resemblance between a violin case and a coffin. Williams, T.
Reserved coffin. Pirandello, L.
RESIDENCES. See Houses
Resident patient. Doyle, Sir A. C.
The resignation. Page, P. K.
Responsibility. Boyd, T. A.
RESTAURANTS, LUNCHROOMS, ETC.
  Brecht, H. W. Vienna roast
  De Vries, P. Different cultural levels eat here
  De Vries, P. If he hollers let him holler
  Gutman, C. Real customers
  Hemingway, E. The killers
  Kirch, J. A. Murder for two
Restless rest-house. Curling, J.
Restricted clientele. Crossen, K. F.
Resurgam. Zara, L.
Resurrection. Davies, R.
Resurrection of a life. Saroyan, W.
Resurrection of Father Brown. Chesterton, G. K.
Reticence of Lady Anne. Munro, H. H.
RETIREMENT
  Maugham, W. S. Lotus eater
  Taylor, P. H. Two ladies in retirement
Retreat to the stars. Brackett, L.
Retribution. Stone, W. J.
Retrieved reformation. Porter, W. S.
RETROSPECTIVE STORIES
  Angoff, C. Where did yesterday go?
  Galsworthy, J. The apple tree
  Gordon, C. Old Red
  Fiedler, L. A. Fear of innocence
  Hemingway, E. Snows of Kilimanjaro
  Humphrey, W. Fresh snow
  Maupassant, G. de. Minuet
  Toole, K. Short space
  West, R. B. Last of the grizzly bears
The return. Bowen, E.
The return. Corkery, D.
The return. Dunsany, E. J. M. D. P. 18th baron
The return. Glatstein, J.
Return. Matheson, R.
Return home. Rosenfeld, J.
Return of a hero. Sylvester, H.
Return of a legend. Gallun, R. Z.
Return of a private. Garland, H.
Return of Corporal Greene. Sarton, M.
Return of the native. Kober, A.
Return to Kansas City. Shaw, I.
Return to Lavinia. Caldwell, E.
Return to the Bronx. Markewich, R.
Returning good for evil. Cooke, A. A.
Reuben's courtship. Chase, M. E.
A reunion. Stafford, J.
Reunion at evening. Ballantyne, T. A.
REUNIONS
  Stafford, J. A reunion
  Van Doren, M. How bad? How long?

REUNIONS, FAMILY. See Family re-
      unions
REVENGE
      Clemens, S. L. Man that corrupted Had-
            leyburg
      Cohen, O. R. Law and the profits
      Cross, J. A. Hunch that clicked
      Haycox, E. Last draw
      Keller, D. H. The doorbell
      Kipling, R. Village that voted the earth
            was flat
      Maupassant, G. de. La Mère Sauvage
      Munro, H. H. Feast of Nemesis
      Munro, H. H. Lumber-room
      Munro, H. H. The penance
      O'Rourke, F. Last shot
      Paget, V. Wedding chest
      Poe, E. A. Cask of Amontillado
      Poe, E. A. Hop-Frog
      Porter, K. A. María Concepción
      Porter, W. S. Last of the troubadours
      Porter, W. S. One dollar's worth
      Russell, B. A. W. R. 3d earl. Guardians
            of Parnassus
      Schaefer, J. W. Out of the past
      Schnitzler, A. Bachelor's death
      Shaw, I. Sailor off the Bremen
      Van Doren, M. Mortimer
      Vickers, R. Million-to-one chance
Revenge. Schneur, Z.
Revenue Charlie. Weeks, R.
REVERE, PAUL, 1735-1818
      Benét, S. V. Tooth for Paul Revere
Reverend Father Gilhooley. Farrell, J. T.
Reverend John Smith prepares his sermon.
      Crockett, S. R.
Reverend Mother and the foolish decision.
      Lieberman, R.
REVERENDS. See Clergy
Reverse phylogeny. Long, A. R.
Revolt. Brenner, L.
Revolt of "Mother." Freeman, M. E. W.
Revolt of the pedestrians. Keller, D. H.
REVOLUTION, AMERICAN. See United
      States—18th century—Revolution
The revolution. Newhouse, E.
Revolution racket. Charteris, L.
Revolutionary etude. Schneider, G. W.
REVOLUTIONS
      Cicellis, K. Easy way
      Novás Calvo, L. Dark night of Ramón
            Yendía
      O'Donovan, M. Eternal triangle
      Porter, W. S. Caught
      Porter, W. S. "Fox-in-the-morning"
      Porter, W. S. Rouge et noir
      Porter, W. S. Smith
      Verga, G. Liberty
Reward of faith. Goudge, E.
Rex imperator. Wilson, A.
Rex of the Coast patrol. Johnson, M. S.
Rex v. Burnaby. Freeman, R. A.
Rey, Lester Del. See Del Rey, Lester

Reymont, Wladyslaw Stanislaw, 1868-1925
      Twilight
            Neider, C. ed. Great short stories from
            the world's literature
Reynolds, Helen Mary Greenwood (Camp-
      bell) 1884-
      Adventure on Lone Gulch Trail
            Story parade (Periodical) Adventure
            stories
Reynolds, J. M. and McCormick, H. P.
      Through Twelve-League Labyrinth
            Bluebook (Periodical) Best sea stories
            from Bluebook
Reynolds, Mack, 1918-
      Business, as usual
            Derleth, A. W. ed. Worlds of tomorrow
      Discord makers
            Conklin, G. ed. Invaders of earth
      Isolationist
            Conklin, G. ed. Big book of science
            fiction
      Man in the moon
            Lesser, M. A. ed. Looking forward
      Martians and the Coys
            Brown, F. and Reynolds, M. eds. Sci-
            ence-fiction carnival
Reynolds, Mack, 1918- and Brown, Fredric,
      1906-
      Dark interlude
            Best science fiction stories: 1952
            Galaxy science fiction magazine. Galaxy
            reader of science fiction
Reynolds, Quentin James, 1902-
      Glass of orange juice
            Ribalow, H. U. ed. World's greatest
            boxing stories
RHINE RIVER AND VALLEY
      Charteris, L. The Rhine: The Rhine
            maiden
The Rhine: The Rhine maiden. Charteris, L.
Rhodes, William Parle, 1902-
      Women will out
            Oberfirst, R. ed. 1954 anthology of best
            original short-shorts
RHODES
      Maugham, W. S. Human element
Rib steak. Anderson, E. V.
Rice, Alice Caldwell (Hegan) 1870-1942
      Hoodooed
            Summers, H. S. ed. Kentucky story
      Theater party
            Fenner, P. R. comp. Fun! Fun! Fun!
Rice, Craig, 1908-
      Goodbye forever
            Best detective stories of the year—1952
Rice, Craig, 1908- and Palmer, Stuart, 1905-
      Cherchez la frame
            Queen, E. pseud. ed. Queen's awards:
            6th ser.
      Once upon a train
            Queen, E. pseud. ed. Queen's awards:
            5th ser.
Rice, Jane
      The refugee
            Davenport, B. ed. Ghostly tales to be
            told

Rice, John Andrew, 1888-
Monday come home
Collier's, the national weekly. Collier's
best
Rich boy. Fitzgerald, F. S. K.
Rich man's crumbs. Melville, H.
RICH MEN. See Capitalists and financiers;
Wealth
Rich, poor, and indifferent. Van Doren, M.
Rich poor man. Reisin, A.
Richards, Dick
Training Alice and Congo
Fenner, P. R. comp. Elephants, ele-
phants, elephants
Richardson, Maurice Lane, 1907-
Way out in the continuum
Horizon (Periodical) Golden Horizon
Richardson, Robert Shirley, 1902-
Xi effect
Bleiler, E. F. and Dikty, T. E. eds.
Imagination unlimited
A richer dust. Coward, N. P.
Richter, Conrad, 1890-
Doctor Hanray's second chance
Saturday evening post (Periodical) Sat-
urday evening post stories, 1950
Marriage that couldn't succeed
Saturday evening post (Periodical) Sat-
urday evening post stories, 1952
Sinister journey
Saturday evening post (Periodical) Sat-
urday evening post stories, 1953
Rickenbacker, Edward Vernon, 1890-
The raft
McFee, W. ed. Great sea stories of
modern times
The riddle. De La Mare, W.
Riddle of the Black Museum. Palmer, S.
Riddle of the dangling pearl. Palmer, S.
Riddle of the snafu murder. Palmer, S.
Riddle of the tired bullet. Palmer, S.
RIDDLES
Hamelin, Glückel of. A story
Porter, W. S. Bird of Bagdad
Ride a pale ghost into night and time. Clay-
ton, J. B.
Ride 'im Chick Norris. Fleming, J. S.
Ride on the short dog. Still, J.
Ride out. Foote, S.
Ride the river. Haycox, E.
Rider of the avalanche. Purcell, D.
Rider on the pale horse. Eustis, H.
Riding. See Horsemanship
Riding the Pony Express. Garthwaite, M. H.
Rieseberg, Harry Earl
I dive for treasure
Fenner, P. R. comp. Stories of the sea
Rifleman's run. Brick, J.
Rig ship for diving. Bateman, A.
Right count. O'Rourke, F.
Right side. Collier, J.
Right thing. Lacy, E.
Right thing. Williams, W. C.

Rightful owner. Stuart, J.
RIGHTS OF WOMEN. See Woman—
Rights of women
Rigmarole. Callaghan, M. E.
Rilke, Rainer Maria, 1875-1926
How old Timofei died singing
Lange, V. ed. Great German short
novels and stories
Mirrored room
Fabricant, N. D. and Werner, H. eds.
World's best doctor stories
The stranger
Neider, C. ed. Great short stories from
the world's literature
Rinehart, Mary (Roberts) 1876-
Burned chair
Rinehart, M. R. Frightened wife, and
other murder stories
Frightened wife
Rinehart, M. R. Frightened wife, and
other murder stories
If only it were yesterday
Rinehart, M. R. Frightened wife, and
other murder stories
Murder and the south wind
Rinehart, M. R. Frightened wife, and
other murder stories
One hour of glory
Eaton, H. T. ed. Short stories
The scandal
Rinehart, M. R. Frightened wife, and
other murder stories
Ring around the redhead. MacDonald,
J. D.
RINGS
Norling, M. E. Jade ring
Ringstones. Wall, J. W.
Ringwood, Gwen (Pharis)
Little ghost
Weaver, R. and James, H. eds. Cana-
dian short stories
RIOTS
Asch, S. Kola Street
Rip Van Winkle. Irving, W.
Ripe for development. Harvey, W. F.
Ripeness of the time. Fonger, H.
Rise and fall of Mortimer Scrivens. Milne,
A. A.
Rise of Carthage. Williams, L.
Rise of Lorenzo Villari. Ferrone, J. R.
Ritchie, Lewis Anselm da Costa, 1886-
Some "Q" ships
McFee, W. ed. Great sea stories of
modern times
Rite, Eva, pseud. See Anderson, Esther
Victoria
Riter, Faye
Matter of vanity
Hathaway, B. and Sessions, J. A. eds.
Writers for tomorrow. 2d ser.
Sense of destination
Hathaway, B. and Sessions, J. A. eds.
Writers for tomorrow. 2d ser.
RITES AND CEREMONIES
Jews
See Jews—Rites and ceremonies
Rites of spring. Prevost, L. E.

Ritual. Sheckley, R.

The rivals. Davidson, S.

The river. Milne, A. A.

RIVER BOATS
Reese, J. H. Cat-eyed woman

River challenge. Coombs, C. I.

River dragon. Lane, C. D.

River, flow gently. Davies, R.

RIVER LIFE
Dunsany, E. J. M. D. P. 18th baron. Idle
days on the Yan
Reese, J. H. Cat-eyed woman

River pirates. Hobbs, A. K.

Rivers of Damascus. Byrne, D.

RIVIERA
Maugham, W. S. Gigolo and gigolette
Maugham, W. S. Happy couple
Maugham, W. S. Lion's skin
Maugham, W. S. Three fat women of
Antibes

Riviera renegade. Blochman, L. G.

ROACHES. See Cockroaches

Road number one. Stuart, J.

Road to recovery. Schulberg, B. W.

Road to the shore. McLaverty, M.

ROADS
Friend, O. J. Impossible highway
Heinlein, R. A. Roads must roll
Maugham, W. S. Mackintosh

Roads must roll. Heinlein, R. A.

Roads of destiny. Porter, W. S.

Roads we take. Porter, W. S.

Roark, Eldon, 1897-
Some heroes
Bloch, M. ed. Favorite dog stories

Robber of Wrightsville. Queen, E. pseud.

ROBBERIES
Queen, E. pseud. Robber of Wrightsville

ROBBERS. See Bank robbers; Brigands
and robbers; Grave robbers; Robberies; Theft; Thieves

Robbie. Asimov, I.

Robe and the sword. Voorhees, M. B.

Robe of peace. Porter, W. S.

Roberts, Sir Charles George Douglas, 1860-
1943
Bear that thought he was a dog
Roberts, Sir C. G. D. Thirteen bears
Black Swamp
Roberts, Sir C. G. D. Thirteen bears
Brothers of the yoke
Roberts, Sir C. G. D. Thirteen bears
Cabin door
Roberts, Sir C. G. D. Thirteen bears
Calling of the lop-horned bull
Roberts, Sir C. G. D. Thirteen bears
Fishers of the air
Roberts, Sir C. G. D. Thirteen bears
Gauntlet of fire
Roberts, Sir C. G. D. Thirteen bears
Ledge on Bald Face
Roberts, Sir C. G. D. Thirteen bears
Monarch of Park Barren
Roberts, Sir C. G. D. Thirteen bears
Mothers of the north
Roberts, Sir C. G. D. Thirteen bears

On the roof of the world
Roberts, Sir C. G. D. Thirteen bears
The trailers
Roberts, Sir C. G. D. Thirteen bears
With his back to the wall
Roberts, Sir C. G. D. Thirteen bears
"The young ravens that call upon him"
Pacey, D. ed. Book of Canadian stories

Roberts, David
Girl on the lake
Story (Periodical) Story; no. 2

Roberts, Elizabeth Madox, 1886-1941
Sacrifice of the maidens
Summers, H. S. ed. Kentucky story

Roberts, Morley, 1857-1942
Captain of the "Ullswater"
Cerf, B. A. and Moriarty, H. C. eds.
Anthology of famous British stories

Roberts, Ralph Myron, 1915-
Date with Janie
Strang, R. M. and Roberts, R. M. eds.
Teen-age tales v2
The fix
Strang, R. M. and Roberts, R. M. eds.
Teen-age tales v2
Follow that car
Strang, R. M. and Roberts, R. M. eds.
Teen-age tales v 1
Yellow convertible
Strang, R. M. and Roberts, R. M. eds.
Teen-age tales v 1

Roberts, Theodore Goodridge. See Goodridge Roberts, Theodore

Roberts and O'Hara. Van Doren, M.

Robertson, Frank Chester, 1890-
The guardian
Western Writers of America. Bad men
and good

Robertson, John Henry, 1909-
Back to the beginning
Asquith, Lady C. M. E. C. ed. Book of
modern ghosts

Robertson, Morgan, 1861-1915
Battle of the monsters
Derleth, A. W. ed. Beyond time & space

Robes et modes. Parker, J. R.

Robin, Ralph
Budding explorer
Magazine of fantasy and science fiction.
Best from Fantasy and science fiction;
2d ser.
Pleasant dreams
Conklin, G. ed. Omnibus of science fic-
tion

Robinc. White, W. A. P.

Robineau, Lisa
Perchance to dream
Queen, E. pseud. ed. Queen's awards:
6th ser.

Robinson, Frank M. 1926-
Fire and the sword
Bleiler, E. F. and Dikty, T. E. eds.
Imagination unlimited
Girls from Earth
Best science-fiction stories: 1953
Sloane, W. M. ed. Stories for tomorrow
Hunting season
Year's best science fiction novels, 1952

Robinson, Frank M.—*Continued*
Oceans are wide
Year's best science fiction novels, 1954
Reluctant heroes
Galaxy science fiction magazine. Galaxy reader of science fiction
Santa Claus planet
Best science fiction stories: 1951
Robinson, Gertrude, 1876-
Winged feet
Fenner, P. R. comp. Indians, Indians, Indians
Robinson, Leonard Wallace, 1912-
Ruin of soul
Prize stories of 1950
Robinson, Rosanne Smith
Mango tree
Best American short stories, 1954
ROBOTS. See Automata
Robots return. Williams, R. M.
Roche, Mazo de la. See De La Roche, Mazo
Roche, Roger Frison- See Frison-Roche, Roger
Rochlin, R. J.
Storm winds
Creamer, J. B. comp. Twenty-two stories about horses and men
The **rock.** Yemtzen, V.
Rock bottom. Nye, N. C.
Rock crystal. Stifter, A.
Rock-of-the-mass. Corkery, D.
The **rocket.** Bradbury, R.
Rocket man. Bradbury, R.
Rocket of 1955. Kornbluth, C. M.
ROCKET SHIPS
Bradbury, R. Golden apples of the sun
Bradbury, R. The rocket
Coppel, A. The dreamer
Gallun, R. Z. Operation Pumice
Grendon, E. Trip one
Hallstead, W. F. Space Lane cadet
Jenkins, W. F. Proxima centauri
Matheson, R. Shipshape home
Russell, E. F. Jay Score
Verne, J. Round the moon
See also Space ships
Rocket to the sun. Van Dresser, P.
Rocketeers have shaggy ears. Bennett, K.
Rocking-horse winner. Lawrence, D. H.
Rocklynne, Ross
Backfire
Conklin, G. ed. Omnibus of science fiction
Jaywalker
Galaxy science fiction magazine. Galaxy reader of science fiction
Pressure
Bleiler, E. F. and Dikty, T. E. eds. Imagination unlimited
Winner take all
Derleth, A. W. ed. Time to come
Rocky. Johnson, H.
ROCKY MOUNTAIN GOATS
Gilbert, K. Old man of the mountains
White, S. E. Climbing for goats

ROCKY MOUNTAINS
White, S. E. Climbing for goats
Rod of God. Rees, G.
RODEOS
Miers, E. S. Black Bat
Schaefer, J. W. Harvey Kendall
Wood, K. Workaday cowboy
See also Cowboys
Rodgers, Mary Augusta
Lover and his lass
Lantz, J. E. ed. Stories of Christian living
Rodney. Nason, L. H.
Rodney has a relapse. Wodehouse, P. G.
Roger Bacon formula. Pratt, F.
Roger Malvin's burial. Hawthorne, N.
Rogers, Joel Townsley
Moment without time
Startling stories (Periodical) Best from Startling stories
Rogers, Kay
Experiment
Magazine of fantasy and science fiction. Best from Fantasy and science fiction; 3d ser.
Rogow, Lee
Laziest man in Texas
This week magazine. This week's short-short stories
That certain flavor
This week magazine. This week's short-short stories
Rogue ship. Van Vogt, A. E.
ROGUES AND VAGABONDS
Kipling, R. Man who would be king
Rogues in the house. Howard, R. E.
Rojas, Manuel
Glass of milk
Bachelor, J. M.; Henry, R. L. and Salisbury, R. eds. Current thinking and writing; 2d ser.
Rokefort, K. D. pseud. See Woodward, George B.
Roll-call of the reef. Quiller-Couch, Sir A. T.
Rolland, Kermit
Mr Carmody's safari
Joseph, M. ed. Best cat stories
Roman fever. Wharton, E. N. J.
Roman holiday. Lewis, R.
Roman remains. Blackwood, A.
ROMAN SOLDIERS. See Soldiers, Roman
A **romance.** Renard, J.
Romance lingers, adventure lives. Collier, J.
Romance of a busy broker. Porter, W. S.
The **romancers.** Munro, H. H.
A **romantic.** O'Donovan, M.
Romantic boy. Goudsmit, S.
Romantic interlude in the life of Willie Collins. Farrell, J. T.
Romantic young lady. Maugham, W. S.
Romantically inclined. Caldwell, E.

ROME
B.C. 510-30
Wilder, T. N. From a journal-letter of Julius Caesar
B.C. 30-476 A.D.
Blackburn, E. R. Before the burning of Rome
ROME (CITY) See Italy—Rome (City)
Rome: The Latin touch. Charteris, L.
Romeo. Jackson, C. R.
Romney. Barker, A. L.
Ronald leaves the academy. Tunis, J. R.
The roof. Horwitz, J.
The roof. Powell, D.
Roof sitter. Eisenberg, F.
The rookie. Dailey, J.
The room. Sartre, J. P.
Room in the Dragon Volant. Le Fanu, J. S.
Room in the world. Zugsmith, L.
Room number twenty-three. Phillips, J. P.
Room without a telephone. Lewis, W.
ROOMERS. See Boarding houses
ROOMING HOUSES. See Boarding houses
Rooney, Frank, 1913-
Cyclists' raid
Best American short stories, 1952
Prize stories of 1951
Roos, Kelley, pseud.
Two over par
Mystery Writers of America, inc. Four-&-twenty bloodhounds
ROOSTERS
Benson, T. White cock
Goyen, W. White rooster
McLaverty, M. Game cock
Melville, H. Cock-a-doodle-doo!
Stuart, J. The champion
See also Cock fighting; Poultry
The rope. Baudelaire, C. P.
Rope and the bulldog. Burtis, T.
Rope enough. Collier, J.
Roper, Winniford, 1890-
Last cigarette
Oberfirst, R. ed. 1954 anthology of best original short-shorts
ROPING
James, W. Best riding and roping
Rosaire, Forrest, 1902-
Pod of a weed
Lass, A. H. and Horowitz, A. eds. Stories for youth
Rose for Emily. Faulkner, W.
"Rose of Dixie." Porter, W. S.
Rosegger, Peter, 1843-1918
Flight into Egypt
Selden, R. ed. Ways of God and men
Of love and joy
Brentano, F. ed. The word lives on
Rosenberg, Edgar, 1925-
Happy one
Hathaway, B. and Sessions, J. A. eds. Writers for tomorrow. 2d ser.
Our Felix
Stanford short stories, 1953

Rosenberg, Ethel (Clifford) 1915-
Aunt Esther's galoshes
Ausubel, N. ed. Treasury of Jewish humor
Mrs Rivkin grapples with the drama
Ausubel, N. ed. Treasury of Jewish humor
Ribalow, H. U. ed. These your children
Uncle Julius and the BMT
Ausubel, N. ed. Treasury of Jewish humor
Rosenfeld, Jonah, 1882-1944
Competitors
Howe, I. and Greenberg, E. eds. Treasury of Yiddish stories
Return home
Leftwich, J ed. Yisröel. 1952 ed.
Sick goose
Howe, I. and Greenberg, E. eds. Treasury of Yiddish stories
Roses, ruses and romance. Porter, W. S.
ROSH HA-SHANA
Reisin, A. Poor community
Rosinback. Young, J. M.
Rosmond, Babette, 1917- and Lake, Leonard M.
Are you run-down, tired—
Conklin, G. and Conklin, L. T. eds. Supernatural reader
Ross, Alberta L.
Something special for Jane
Oberfirst, R. ed. 1954 anthology of best original short-shorts
Ross, James, 1911-
Zone of interior
Collier's, the national weekly. Collier's best
Ross, Julian Maclaren- See Maclaren-Ross, Julian
Ross, Leonard Q. pseud. See Rosten, Leo Calvin
Ross, Martin, pseud. See Martin, Violet Florence
Ross, Sinclair, 1908-
Lamp at noon
Pacey, D. ed. Book of Canadian stories
The outlaw
Weaver, R. and James, H. eds. Canadian short stories
Rossiter, H. D.
Allan Franklin
Hathaway, B. and Sessions, J. A. eds. Writers for tomorrow. 2d ser.
Black bile
Hathaway, B. and Sessions, J. A. eds. Writers for tomorrow. 2d ser.
How dear to my heart
Hathaway, B. and Sessions, J. A. eds. Writers for tomorrow. 2d ser.
Rosten, Leo Calvin, 1908-
Mr K*A*P*L*A*N the Magnificent
Ribalow, H U. ed. This land, these people
The rot. Lewis, W.
ROTARY INTERNATIONAL
Milburn, G. The apostate
Roth, Cecil, 1899-
The martyr
Leftwich, J. ed. Yisröel. 1952 ed.

Rothberg, Abraham Alan, 1922-
Not with our fathers
Best American short stories, 1950
Ribalow, H. U. ed. These your childern
Rouge et noir. Porter, W. S
Rouge high. Hughes, L.
Rough crossing. Fitzgerald, F. S. K.
Rough green tree. Sullivan, R.
Round by round. Aiken, C. P.
Round dozen. Maugham, W. S.
ROUND TABLE. See Arthur, King
Round the circle. Porter, W. S.
Round the moon. Verne, J.
Round the world fliers. Williams, W. C.
Round trip. Sullivan, R.
The round up. Seredy, K.

Rounds, Glen, 1906-
Knute, the giant bullsnake
Fenner, P. R. ed. Fools and funny fellows
Paul goes hunting
Fenner, P. R. comp. Fun! Fun! Fun!
Uncle Torwal and Whitey go to town
Fenner, P. R. comp. Giggle box
Whitey's first round-up
Fenner, P. R. comp. Cowboys, cowboys, cowboys

Rousseau, Jean Jacques, 1712-1778
Isle of St Peter
Andrews, R. C. ed. My favorite stories of the great outdoors

ROWING
Shattuck, R. Workout on the river
See also Boat racing

Rowland, Sidney
McGregor affair
Mystery writers of America, inc. Butcher, baker, murder-maker

ROYAL CANADIAN MOUNTED POLICE. See Canada. Royal Canadian Mounted Police

Royal game. Bergengruen, W.

Rubaiyat of a Scotch highball. Porter, W. S.

RUBBER
Maugham, W. S. Back of beyond
Maugham, W. S. Flotsam and jetsam

RUBBER PLANTATIONS See Rubber

Rubber plant's story. Porter, W. S.

The rube. Grey, Z.

Rube and the racketeer. Mowery, W. B.

Ruby, B. F. See Pratt, F. jt. auth.

Rude awakening. Howard, W.

Rudnicki, Adolf, 1912-
Ascent to heaven
Rudnicki, A. Ascent to heaven
Crystal stream
Rudnicki, A. Ascent to heaven
Dying man
Rudnicki, A. Ascent to heaven
Great Stefan Konecki
Rudnicki, A. Ascent to heaven

Rudolph. Winslow, T. S.

Rugel, Miriam, 1911-
The flower
Abell, E. ed. American accent
Prize stories, 1954
The Ruggleses go to the Christmas party. Wiggin, K. D. S.
RUGS, HOOKED
Ross, A. L. Something special for Jane
Ruin of soul. Robinson, L. W.
Ruined by success. Nadir, I. M.
Rule of three. Waldo, E. H.
Ruler of men. Porter, W. S
RULERS. See Kings and rulers
The rulers. Van Vogt, A. E.
The Rull. Van Vogt, A. E.
Rum for dinner. Blochman, L. G.
The rumor. Caldwell, E.
Run for your life. Courtier, S. H.
Run, iron man. Herndon, B.
Runaround. Asimov, I.
Runaway. Caldwell, E.
The runaway. Zweig, S.
RUNAWAYS. See Hitchhikers
RUNAWAYS (CHILDREN)
Crane, S. His new mittens
Runbeck, Margaret Lee, 1905-
Dog for Miss Boo
Cavanna, B. ed. Pick of the litter
RUNNERS. See Running
RUNNING
Carter, R. G. Blue ribbon event
Farrell, J. T. Fastest runner on Sixty-First Street
Gartner, J. Jug Leg Kelley
Miers, E. S. Ghost runner
Miers, E. S. He who laughs last
Person, W. T Any way race
Strong, P. N. Anchor man
Sylvester, H. Last race
Tunis, J. R. Two-mile race

Running dark. Strong, P. N

Runyon, Damon, 1880-1946
All horse players die broke
Runyon, D. More guys and dolls
Barbecue
Runyon, D. More guys and dolls
Baseball Hattie
Graber, R. S. ed. Baseball reader
Runyon, D. More guys and dolls
Big Boy Blues
Blodgett, H. W. ed. Story survey. 1953 ed.
Runyon, D. More guys and dolls
Big shoulders
Runyon, D. More guys and dolls
Big umbrella
Runyon, D. More guys and dolls
Blonde mink
Runyon, D. More guys and dolls
Bred for battle
Ribalow, H. U. ed. World's greatest boxing stories
Broadway incident
Runyon, D. More guys and dolls
Burge McCall
Runyon, D. More guys and dolls

Runyon, Damon—*Continued*
Call on the President
Runyon, D. More guys and dolls
Cemetery bait
Runyon, D. More guys and dolls
Cleo
Runyon, D. More guys and dolls
Hold 'em Yale
Herzberg, M. J. comp. Treasure chest of sport stories
Idyll of Miss Sarah Brown
Runyon, D. More guys and dolls
Job for the Macarone
Runyon, D. More guys and dolls
Joe Terrace
Runyon, D. More guys and dolls
Johnny One-Eye
Runyon, D. More guys and dolls
Lacework Kid
Runyon, D. More guys and dolls
Leopard's spots
Runyon, D. More guys and dolls
Light in France
Runyon, D. More guys and dolls
Little Pinks
Runyon, D. More guys and dolls
Lonely heart
Runyon, D. More guys and dolls
Lou Louder
Runyon, D. More guys and dolls
Maybe a queen
Runyon, D. More guys and dolls
Melancholy Dane
Runyon, D. More guys and dolls
Neat strip
Runyon, D. More guys and dolls
Nothing happens in Brooklyn
Runyon, D. More guys and dolls
Old Em's Kentucky home
Runyon, D. More guys and dolls
Palm Beach Santa Claus
Runyon, D. More guys and dolls
Piece of pie
Christ, H. I. and Shostak, J. eds. Short stories
Runyon, D. More guys and dolls
Ransom . . . $1,000,000
Runyon, D. More guys and dolls
Sense of humor
Queen, E. pseud. ed. Literature of crime
Situation wanted
Runyon, D. More guys and dolls
Snatching of Bookie Bob
Dachs, D. ed. Treasury of sports humor
So you won't talk
Runyon, D. More guys and dolls
Tight shoes
Runyon, D. More guys and dolls
Too much pep
Runyon, D. More guys and dolls
Rupee. Willingham, C.
RURAL LIFE. See Farm life
Rus in urbe. Porter, W. S.

Rush hour. Benowitz, E.

Rush-hour romance. Crawford, E. and Dalmas, H.

Russell, Bertrand Arthur Willian Russell, 3d earl, 1872-
Benefit of clergy
Russell, B. A. W. R. 3d earl. Satan in the suburbs, and other stories
Corsican ordeal of Miss X
Russell, B. A. W. R. 3d earl. Satan in the suburbs, and other stories
Guardians of Parnassus
Russell, B. A. W. R. 3d earl. Satan in the suburbs, and other stories
The infra-redioscope
Russell, B. A. W. R. 3d earl. Satan in the suburbs, and other stories
Satan in the suburbs
Russell, B. A. W. R. 3d earl. Satan in the suburbs, and other stories

Russell, Eric Frank, 1905-
And then there were none
Sloane, W. M. ed. Stories for tomorrow
Year's best science fiction novels, 1952
Boomerang
Conklin, G. ed. Science-fiction thinking machines
Dear Devil
Conklin, G. ed. Big book of science fiction
Sloane, W. M. ed. Space, space, space
Fast falls the eventide
Best science-fiction stories: 1953
Glass eye
Merril, J. ed. Beyond human ken
Hobbyist
Astounding science fiction (Periodical) Astounding science fiction anthology
I am nothing
Best science-fiction stories: 1953
The illusionaries
Norton, A. M. ed. Space pioneers
Impulse
Conklin, G. ed. Invaders of earth
Jay Score
Heinlein, R. A. ed. Tomorrow, the stars
Late night final
Astounding science fiction (Periodical) Astounding science fiction anthology
Metamorphosite
Derleth, A. W. ed. Beachheads in space
Greenberg, M. ed. Journey to infinity
Muten
Brown, F. and Reynolds, M. eds. Science-fiction carnival
Test piece
Conklin, G. ed. Omnibus of science fiction
Timeless ones
Wollheim, D. A. ed. Prize science fiction
Ultima Thule
Lesser, M. A. ed. Looking forward

Russell, John, 1885-
Fourth man
Day, A. G. ed. Greatest American short stories
Jetsam
Shaw, H. and Bement, D. Reading the short story
Lost god
Grayson, C. ed. Fourth round

RUSSIA
Guerney, B. G. comp. New Russian stories; 16 stories
Munro, H. H. Old town of Pskoff

To 1800
Tynîanov, I. N. Second Lieutenant Likewise

RUSSIA—*Continued*
1800-1917
Bergengruen, W. Ali Baba and the forty horse-power
Bergengruen, W. Lykin's sleigh-ride
Bergengruen, W. Old Hussar
Chekhov, A. P. New villa
Chekhov, A. P. Peasants
Chekhov, A. P. Verotchka
Chekhov, A. P. The woman in the case, and other stories; 23 stories
Dostoevskiĭ, F. M. Father Zossima's duel
Dostoevskiĭ, F. M. White nights and other stories; 7 stories
Pushkin, A. S. The undertaker

1917-1945
Bergelson, D. Citizen Woli Brenner
Duranty, W. The parrot
Ehrenburg, I. G. The storm
Fraerman, R. I. The expedition
Frank, P. Those wily Americans
Gibbs, Sir P. H. Stranger in the village
Maugham, W. S. Mr Harrington's washing
Petrov, V. "Get a horse, comrade"
Sholokhov, M. A. Civil War
Yushkevich, S. S. In a Bolshevist marketplace

Army
Bergengruen, W. Ali Baba and the forty horse-power

Farm life
See Farm life—Russia

Leningrad
Dostoevskiĭ, F. M. White nights

Moscow
Wassermann, J. Lukardis

Odessa
Babel', I. E. In Odessa

Peasant life
See Peasant life—Russia

Ukraine
Yakovlev, A. S. The wizard

RUSSIAN COMMUNISM. See Communism—Russia

RUSSIAN SOLDIERS. See Soldiers, Russian

Russian who wanted to be friends. McKelway, St C.

RUSSIANS IN BORNEO
Maugham, W. S. Neil MacAdam

RUSSIANS IN CHINA
McCloy, H. Chinoiserie

RUSSIANS IN INDIA
Kipling, R. Man who was

RUSSIANS IN KIRGHIZ
Ivanov, V. V. The kid

RUSSIANS IN SWITZERLAND
Zweig, S. The runaway

Rust. Kelleam, J. E.

Rustling tree. Smith, J. C.

Rusty: the brave dog who lost his bark. Little, G. W.

RUTH (BIBLICAL CHARACTER)
Fineman, I. In the fields of Boaz
Knox, R. A. Ruth

Ruth, Babe. See Ruth, George Herman

RUTH, GEORGE HERMAN, 1894-1948
Considine, R. B. How Babe Ruth got his name

Ruth. Knox, R. A.

Ruth and Irma. Miller, M. B.

Rutt, Edwin
Canary from Cuba
Dachs, D. ed. Treasury of sports humor

Rydberg, Ernie
Caricature
American girl (Periodical) On my honor
Furman, A. L. ed. Everygirls mystery stories
Little genius
American girl (Periodical) Favorite stories

S

SRL ad. Matheson, R.

SABBATH
Agnon, S. J. Sabbathai
Bialik, H. N. Short Friday
Zangwill, I. Sabbath question in Sudminster
See also Sunday

Sabbath breaker. Zangwill, I.

Sabbath question in Sudminster. Zangwill, I.

Sabbathai. Agnon, S. J.

Sabin, Edwin Legrand, 1870-
Freedom
Bluebook (Periodical) Best sea stories from Bluebook

SABOTAGE
Bennett, K. Death at attention
Connolly, M. Seminary Hill
Lawrence, T. E. Blowing up a train

SABOTEURS. See Sabotage

Sabre in the hand. Spring, H.

The **Sack.** Morrison, W. S.

Sack of turnips. Caldwell, E.

Sacrament. Seager, A.

Sacred and the profane. Sykes, C.

Sacrifice hit. Porter, W. S.

Sacrifice of the maidens. Roberts, E. M.

Sad garden. Taylor, E.

Saga. Merochnik, M.

Saga of Sleepy Mugoon. Coombs, C. I.

Sage-brush chief. Davis, S. P.

Sagebrush champion. Drago, H. S.

SAHARA DESERT
Balzac, H. de. Passion in the desert

SAIL BOATS. See Boats and boating

SAILING VESSELS
Bloomfield, H. The trap
Hergesheimer, J. Wild oranges
Miers, E. S. Jimmy rides the seal herd
The **sailor**. Pritchett, V. S.
Sailor ashore. Hughes, L.
Sailor off the Bremen. Shaw, I.
Sailor! Sailor! Steele, W. D.
SAILORS. See Seamen
Sailor's pay. Carse, R.
Sailor's son. Williams, W. C.
St Clair, Margaret
Child of void
Conklin, G. ed. Invaders of earth
The gardener
Derleth, A. W. ed. Worlds of tomorrow
The pillows
Conklin, G. ed. Possible worlds of science fiction
Saint Exupéry, Antoine de, 1900-1944
Letter to a hostage
Neider, C. ed. Great short stories from the world's literature
SAINT ALBANS, VERMONT. See Vermont—Saint Albans
Saint and the Goblin. Munro, H. H.
Saint for Wessex. Bolton, I. M.
St Gabriel Zsbyski. Mowery, W. B.
Saint George. Sykes, C.
St George ball. Nelson, E. D. P.
Saint Joseph's ass. Verga, G.
Saint Manuel Bueno, martyr. Unamuno y Jugo, M. de
St Patrick's Day in the afternoon. Ready, W. B.
ST PETERSBURG. See Florida—St Petersburg
Saint Sammy. Mitchell, W. O.
Saintly simplicity. Chekhov, A. P.
SAINTS
Bowen, E. All saints
Flaubert, G. Legend of St Julian the Hospitaller
Munro, H. H. Saint and the Goblin
Unamuno y Jugo, M. de. Saint Manuel Bueno, Martyr
Saintsbury, Edward Bennett
Bread upon the waters
Oberfirst, R. ed. 1952 anthology of best original short-shorts
Saki, pseud. See Munro, Hector Hugh
Salad of Colonel Cray. Chesterton, G. K.
The **salesman**. Evans, T. M.
SALESMANSHIP. See Salesmen and salesmanship
Salesmanship. Chase, M. E.
SALESMEN AND SALESMANSHIP
Caldwell, E. Back on the road
Caldwell, E. Man who looked like himself
Chase, M. E. Salesmanship
De Vries, P. Through a glass darkly
Evans, T. M. The salesman
Herron, E. Hail fellow well met
Kafka, F. The metamorphosis

Kahler, H. M. The buckpasser
Porter, W. S. Lickpenny lover
Sansom, W. On stony ground
Upson, W. H. No rest for Botts; 12 stories
Welty, E. Death of a traveling salesman
Zevin, I. J. Pack of troubles for one cent
SALESWOMEN. See Salesmen and salesmanship
Salinger, Jerome David, 1919-
De Daumier-Smith's blue period
Salinger, J. D. Nine stories
Down at the dinghy
Salinger, J. D. Nine stories
For Esmé—with love and squalor
Prize stories of 1950
Salinger, J. D. Nine stories
Just before the war with the Eskimos
Salinger, J. D. Nine stories
Laughing man
Salinger, J. D. Nine stories
Perfect day for bananafish
Salinger, J. D. Nine stories
Pretty mouth and green my eyes
Burrell, J. A. and Cerf, B. A. eds. Anthology of famous American stories
Salinger, J. D. Nine stories
Teddy
Salinger, J. D. Nine stories
Uncle Wiggily in Connecticut
Salinger, J. D. Nine stories
Salisbury, Kathleen, pseud. See Morehouse, Kathleen (Moore)
Sally. Asimov, I.
Sally steps in. Cochran, R. G.
SALMON
Perrault, E. G. Silver King
SALOONS. See Hotels, taverns, etc.
Salt for the soul. Good, E.
Salt sea. Subercaseaux, B.
Salta pro nobis. Galsworthy, J.
SALVAGE
Munro, H. H. Treasure-ship
Salvage! Strong, P. N.
Salvation. Foote, J. T.
Salvatore. Maugham, W. S.
Salving of Pyack. Sullivan, A.
Sam and the dean. Foley, T.
Sam Hall. Anderson, P.
Sam Kravitz, that thief. Gold, M.
Sam Slick the clockmaker. Haliburton, T. C.
Samachson, Joseph, 1906-
Country doctor
Pohl, F. ed. Star science fiction stories
Model of a judge
Best science-fiction stories: 1954
SAMOA
Maugham, W. S. Mackintosh
Maugham, W. S. The pool
Maugham, W. S. Red
Pago Pago
Maugham, W. S. Rain
The **samovar**. Cournos, J.
Samuel. London, J.
Sanatorium. Maugham, W. S.

SANATORIUMS. See Hospitals and sana-
  toriums
Sanctification of the Name. Asch, S.
Sand. Singer, I. J.
Sand doctor. Bergengruen, W.
Sand fort. Miles, M. K.
Sandberg, Harold W. 1902-
  Captain Kidder
    Owen, F. ed. Teen-age winter sports
      stories
  Kid from Shingle Creek
    Owen, F. ed. Teen-age victory parade
Sandburg, Carl, 1878-
  Huckabuck family and how they raised
      popcorn in Nebraska and quit and
      came back
    Fenner, P. R. comp. Giggle box
  Pig Wisps
    Fenner, P. R. comp. Giggle box
The sandman. Hoffmann, E. T. A.
Sandoz, Mari, 1907-
  Lost school bus
    Saturday evening post (Periodical)
      Saturday evening post stories, 1951
  Sit your saddle solid
    Dennis, W. ed. Palomino and other
      horses
Sandoz, Maurice Yves, 1892-
  Mr Rabbi
    Sandoz, M. Y. On the verge
  On the verge
    Sandoz, M. Y. On the verge
  The trap
    Sandoz, M. Y. On the verge
  The tsantsa
    Sandoz, M. Y. On the verge
Sandy, Sue
  Black lie
    Oberfirst, R. ed. 1954 anthology of best
      original short-shorts
Sanford, Winifred Mahon, 1890-
  Windfall
    Peery, W. W. ed. 21 Texas short
      stories
Sangster, Margaret Elizabeth, 1894-
  Beautiful tree
    Elmquist, R. M. ed. Fifty years of
      Christmas
  For this is Christmas Day
    Lantz, J. E. ed. Stories of Christian
      living
  What Christmas brought the stranger
    Elmquist, R. M. ed. Fifty years of
      Christmas
Sanity. Leiber, F.
Sansom, William, 1912-
  Afternoon
    Sansom, W. South
  Bank that broke the man at Monte Carlo
    Sansom, W. South
  Boiler room
    Sansom, W. Something terrible, some-
      thing lovely
  Building alive
    Sansom, W. Something terrible, some-
      thing lovely
  Cat up a tree
    Joseph, M. ed. Best cat stories

  The cliff
    Sansom, W. Something terrible, some-
      thing lovely
  Crabfroth
    Sansom, W. Something terrible, some-
      thing lovely
  Death of Baldy
    Sansom, W. Passionate North
  Displaced persons
    Sansom, W. Something terrible, some-
      thing lovely
  Eye man
    Sansom, W. Something terrible, some-
      thing lovely
  From the water junction
    Sansom, W. Something terrible, some-
      thing lovely
  Girl on the bus
    Sansom, W. Passionate North
  Gliding gulls and going people
    Sansom, W. Passionate North
  Happy New Year
    Sansom, W. Passionate North
  How Claeys died
    Barrows, H. ed. 15 stories
    New writing (Periodical) Best stories
    Sansom, W. Something terrible, some-
      thing lovely
  In the morning
    Sansom, W. Something terrible, some-
      thing lovely
  Journey into smoke
    Sansom, W. Something terrible, some-
      thing lovely
  The kiss
    Sansom, W. Something terrible, some-
      thing lovely
  Landscape with figures
    Sansom, W. South
  Little fears
    Sansom, W. Something terrible, some-
      thing lovely
  Little room
    Sansom, W. Something terrible, some-
      thing lovely
  Miss Haines and the gondolier
    Story (Periodical) Story; no. 2
  My little robins
    Sansom, W. South
  My tree
    Sansom, W. Something terrible, some-
      thing lovely
  Nevermore without end
    Sansom, W. Passionate North
  On stony ground
    Ludwig, J. B. and Poirier, W. R. eds.
      Stories, British and American
  One sunny afternoon
    Sansom, W. Something terrible, some-
      thing lovely
  Pastorale
    Sansom, W. South
  Poseidon's daughter
    Sansom, W. South
  Saving grace
    Sansom, W. Something terrible, some-
      thing lovely
  Small world
    Sansom, W. Something terrible, some-
      thing lovely
  Something terrible, something lovely
    Sansom, W. Something terrible, some-
      thing lovely

Sansom, William—*Continued*
Street song
Sansom, W. South
Three dogs of Siena
Sansom, W. South
Time and place
Sansom, W. Passionate North
To Greenland, to Greenland
Sansom, W. Passionate North
Tutti frutti
Sansom, W. South
Various temptations
Sansom, W. Something terrible, something lovely
Vertical ladder
Sansom, W. Something terrible, something lovely
Waning moon
Sansom, W. Passionate North
A wedding
Sansom, W. Passionate North
The windows
Sansom, W. Something terrible, something lovely
World of glass
Sansom, W. Passionate North

SANTA CLAUS
Aldrich, B. S. Another brought gifts
Asimov, I. Christmas on Ganymede
Cooke, A. Christmas Eve
Cousins, M. Uncle Edgar and the reluctant saint
McLaverty, M. Father Christmas

Santa Claus and the Tenth Avenue kid. Cousins, M.

Santa Claus planet. Robinson, F. M.

Santa Lucia. Petracca, J.

Santee, Ross, 1889-
Fool about a horse
Dennis, W. ed. Palomino and other horses

Saphir, Moritz Gottlieb, 1795-1858
A conquest
Ausubel, N. ed. Treasury of Jewish humor
Gastronomy of the Jews
Ausubel, N. ed. Treasury of Jewish humor

Saratoga rain. Hughes, L.

"Sarban" pseud. See Wall, John W.

The **sardillion.** Enright, E.

Sargeson, Frank
Great day
New writing (Periodical) Best stories

Saroyan, William, 1908-
Ancient history and low hurdles
Lass, A. H. and Horowitz, A. eds. Stories for youth
The Assyrian
Saroyan, W. The Assyrian, and other stories
Be present at our table, Lord
Brentano, F. ed. The word lives on
Cocktail party
Saroyan, W. The Assyrian, and other stories
Cold day
Blodgett, H. W. ed. Story survey. 1953 ed.

Cornet players
Saroyan, W. The Assyrian, and other stories
Daring young man on the flying trapeze
Burrell, J. A. and Cerf, B. A. eds. Anthology of famous American stories
Fifty yard dash
Dachs, D. ed. Treasury of sports humor
The foreigner
Saroyan, W. The Assyrian, and other stories
Leaf thief
Saroyan, W. The Assyrian, and other stories
Mr Mechano
Waite, H. O. and Atkinson, B. P. eds. Literature for our time
My cousin Dikran, the orator
Greene, J. I. and Abell, E. eds. Stories of sudden truth
Palo
Best American short stories, 1952
Parsley garden
Saroyan, W. The Assyrian, and other stories
Pheasant hunter
Saroyan, W. The Assyrian, and other stories
The plot
Saroyan, W. The Assyrian, and other stories
Poet at home
Saroyan, W. The Assyrian, and other stories
Resurrection of a life
Best of the Best American short stories, 1915-1950
Summer of the beautiful white horse
Schramm, W. L. ed. Great short stories
Sunday zeppelin
Felheim, M.; Newman, F. B. and Steinhoff, W. R. eds. Modern short stories
Theological student
Saroyan, W. The Assyrian, and other stories
Third day after Christmas
Saroyan, W. The Assyrian, and other stories
Train going
Moskowitz, S. ed. Great railroad stories of the world

Sarton, May, 1912-
Return of Corporal Greene
Abell, E. ed. American accent

Sartre, Jean Paul, 1905-
Childhood of a leader
Sartre, J. P. Intimacy, and other stories
Erostratus
Sartre, J. P. Intimacy, and other stories
Intimacy
Sartre, J. P. Intimacy, and other stories
The room
Sartre, J. P. Intimacy, and other stories
The wall
Neider, C. ed. Great short stories from the world's literature
Sartre, J. P. Intimacy, and other stories
West, R. B. and Stallman, R. W. eds. Art of modern fiction

Sass, Herbert Ravenel, 1884-
  Affair at St Albans
    Jones, K. M. ed. New Confederate short
      stories
  Grey eagle
    Andrews, R. C. ed. My favorite stories
      of the great outdoors
SATAN. See Devil
Satan. Gibran, K.
Satan in the suburbs. Russell, B. A. W. R.
  3d earl
Satan's best girl. Van Doren, M.
SATIRE
  Bradbury, R. The exiles
  Brandon, W. College queen
  Broun, H. C. Fifty-first dragon
  Clemens, S. L. Latest sensation (II)
  Clemens, S. L. My bloody massacre (I)
  Collier, J. Another American tragedy
  Collier, J. Fancies and goodnights; 50
    stories
  Collier, J. Frog prince
  Collier, J. Pictures in the fire
  Elliott, B. Battle of the S . . . S
  Harte, B. Bell-ringer of Angel's
  Hsieh Liang. Wolf of Chungshan
  Jenkins, W. F. Fourth-dimensional dem-
    onstrator
  Lucian. True history
  Maugham, W. S. Appearance and reality
  Maugham, W. S. Closed shop
  Maugham, W. S. The luncheon
  Maugham, W. S. Mabel
  Milne, A. A. The barrister
  Monig, C. Love story
  Moore, W. We the people
  Morley, C. D. Home again
  Munro, H. H. Short stories of Saki; 134
    stories
  Peacock, T. L. Nightmare Abbey
  Porter, W. S. Comedy in rubber
  Porter, W. S. Dinner at—
  Porter, W. S. Elsie in New York
  Porter, W. S. The sleuths
  Porter, W. S. Tracked to doom
  P'u Sung-ling. The bookworm
  Russell, B. A. W. R. 3d earl. Benefit of
    clergy
  Russell, B. A. W. R. 3d earl. Infraredio-
    scope
  Russell, E. F. And then there were none
  Tucker, W. Able to Zebra
  Walsh, M. Take your choice
  Wang Chu. Poets' club
  Waugh, E. Love among the ruins
  Wharton, E. N. J. Xingu
  Wicklein, J. F. Mr Moody
  Zozulya, E. D. Studio of Love-Your-Fel-
    lowman
Saturday afternoon. Caldwell, E.
Saturday nocturne. Sullivan, R.
SATURN (PLANET)
  James, D. L. Moon of delirium
  Jones, N. R. Hermit of Saturn's ring
Saucer of loneliness. Waldo, E. H.
Savannah-la-mar. De Quincey, T.
Savannah River payday. Caldwell, E.
Saved. Maupassant, G. de

Saved by the sale. Suhl, Y.
Saverio's secret. Werfel, F.
Saving grace. Sansom, W.
Saviour John. Lagerkvist, P. F.
Saviour of the people. Franzos, K. E.
Saw gang. Stegner, W. E.
Sawyer, Ruth, 1880-
  Deserted mine
    Hazeltine, A. I. comp. Selected stories
      for teen-agers
  Fiddler, play fast, play faster
    Fenner, P. R. comp. Ghosts, ghosts,
      ghosts
  The flea
    Fenner, P. R. comp. Fools and funny
      fellows
Say that Jimmy kissed me. Brookhouser, F.
Sayers, Dorothy Leigh, 1893-
  Suspicion
    Bond, R. T. ed. Handbook for poisoners
Sayres, William C.
  Olaf the Magnificent
    Story (Periodical) Story; no. 1
Scalawag pup. Mowery, W. B.
The **scandal.** Rinehart, M. R.
Scandal at Mulford Inn. Wilson, N. C.
Scandal detectives. Fitzgerald, F. S. K.
Scandal in Bohemia. Doyle, Sir A. C.
Scandal of Father Brown. Chesterton, G. K.
The **scarab.** Gallun, R. Z.
The **scarecrow.** Farrell, J. T.
Sacred. Bauer, G. V.
Scarlet citadel. Howard, R. E.
Scarlet dream. Moore, C. L.
Scarlet letter. Hawthorne, N.
Scarlet plague. London, J.
Scars. Waldo, E. H.
Scars of honor. Johnson, D. M.
SCENARIOS. See Moving pictures
Scene. De Vries, P.
Scent of sarsaparilla. Bradbury, R.
SCEPTICISM. See Skepticism
Schaefer, Jack Warner, 1907-
  Cat nipped
    Schaefer, J. W. The pioneers
  Cooter James
    Schaefer, J. W. Big range
  Elvie Burdette
    Schaefer, J. W. Big range
  Emmet Dutrow
    Meredith, S. ed. Bar 3
    Schaefer, J. W. Big range
  General Pingley
    Schaefer, J. W. Big range
  Harvey Kendall
    Schaefer, J. W. The pioneers
  Hugo Kertchak, builder
    Schaefer, J. W. The pioneers
  Jeremy Rodock
    Schaefer, J. W. Big range
  Josiah Willett
    Schaefer, J. W. Big range
  Kittura Remsberg
    Schaefer, J. W. Big range
  Leander Frailey
    Schaefer, J. W. The pioneers

Schaefer, Jack W.—*Continued*
Major Burl
  Schaefer, J. W. Big range
Miley Bennett
  Schaefer, J. W. Big range
My town
  Schaefer, J. W. The pioneers
Old Anse
  Schaefer, J. W. The pioneers
Out of the past
  Schaefer, J. W. The pioneers
Prudence by name
  Schaefer, J. W. The pioneers
Sergeant Houck
  Meredith, S. ed. Bar 1 roundup of best
    western stories
  Schaefer, J. W. Big range
Something lost
  Schaefer, J. W. The pioneers
Takes a real man...
  Schaefer, J. W. The pioneers
That Mark horse
  Schaefer, J. W. The pioneers

Schafhauser, Charles
Gleeb for earth
  Galaxy science fiction magazine. Second
    Galaxy reader of science fiction

Schedule. Walton, H.

Scheffrin, Gladys R. 1928-
When you blow on a dandelion
  Wolfe, D. M. ed. Which grain will
    grow

Scheiner, Frank
Old man had four wives
  Ribalow, H. U. ed. This land, these
    people

Schiller, Johann Christoph Friedrich von,
  1759-1805
Sport of destiny
  Lange, V. ed. Great German short
    novels and stories

Schisgall, Oscar, 1901-
Eyes in the dark
  This week magazine. This week's short-
    short stories
"Take over, Bos'n!"
  This week magazine. This week's short-
    short stories

SCHIZOPHRENIA. See Insanity

Schlemihlov's work. Libin, S.

Schlichter, Etta W.
Big career
  Lantz, J. E. ed. Stories of Christian
    living

Schmidt, Carl F. 1923-
Ancestral voices
  Story (Periodical) Story; no. 4

Schmitt, Gladys, 1909-
David and Bathsheba
  Selden, R. ed. Ways of God and men

Schmitz, Ettore, 1861-1928
Generous wine
  Neider, C. ed. Great short stories from
    the world's literature

Schmitz, James H.
Caretaker
  Galaxy science fiction magazine. Second
    Galaxy reader of science fiction
End of the line
  Norton, A. M. ed. Space pioneers
Second night of summer
  Conklin, G. ed. Possible worlds of sci-
    ence fiction
We don't want any trouble
  Pohl, F. ed. Asignment in tomorrow
Witches of Karres
  Astounding science fiction (Periodical)
  Astounding science fiction anthology

Schnabel, James F.
Journey for Wilbur
  Best Army short stories, 1950

Schneider, George W. 1917-
Case of the southpaw spy
  Schneider, G. W. Clair de lune, and
    other stories
Clair de lune
  Schneider, G. W. Clair de lune, and
    other stories
Dove of God
  Schneider, G. W. Clair de lune, and
    other stories
For the want of a cigarette
  Schneider, G. W. Clair de lune, and
    other stories
Grandfather's tale
  Schneider, G. W. Clair de lune, and
    other stories
Iron cross, first class
  Schneider, G. W. Clair de lune, and
    other stories
Maestro's magic wand
  Schneider, G. W. Clair de lune, and
    other stories
Marche Militaire
  Schneider, G. W. Clair de lune, and
    other stories
No greater love
  Schneider, G. W. Clair de lune, and
    other stories
Render unto Caesar
  Schneider, G. W. Clair de lune, and
    other stories
Revolutionary etude
  Schneider, G. W. Clair de lune, and
    other stories
Shade of Omar
  Schneider, G. W. Clair de lune, and
    other stories
Sir Thomas
  Schneider, G. W. Clair de lune, and
    other stories
Star of Siam
  Schneider, G. W. Clair de lune, and
    other stories
What price genius
  Schneider, G. W. Clair de lune, and
    other stories
When titans meet
  Schneider, G. W. Clair de lune, and
    other stories

Schneider, Robert
Passing through Fieldsville
  Story (Periodical) Story; no. 2

Schneour, Salman. See Shneur, Zalman

Schneuer, Zalman. See Shneur, Zalman

Schnitzler, Arthur, 1862-1931
Bachelor's death
Pick, R. ed. German stories and tales
Same as: Death of a bachelor
Blind Geronimo and his brother
Blodgett, H. W. ed. Story survey. 1953 ed.
Death of a bachelor
Leftwich, J. ed. Yisröel. 1952 ed.
Same as: Bachelor's death
A farewell
Lange, V. ed. Great German short novels and stories

Schoenfeld, Bernard C.
Eagle and the cheetah
Story (Periodical) Story; no. 4

Schoenfeld, Howard
All of God's children got shoes
Queen, E. pseud. ed. Queen's awards: 8th ser.
Built up logically
Magazine of fantasy and science fiction. Best from Fantasy and science fiction, 1952
Tea pusher
Queen, E. pseud. ed. Queen's awards: 7th ser.

Scholz, Jackson Volney
Keystone feud
Fenner, P. R. comp. Crack of the bat
Furman, A. L. ed. Teen-age stories of the diamond

SCHOOL BUSES. See Motor buses

School for combat. Nordhoff, C. B. and Hall, J. N.

School life
Cassill, R. V. Larchmoor is not the world
Karchmer, S. "Hail, brother and farewell"
Kent, C. G. Perpetua puts one over
Lincoln, V. E. Glass wall

Canada
Reaney, J. C. The bully

England
Golding, L. Angels in Chayder
Hilton, J. The war years
Taylor, E. Hester Lilly

Germany
Mann, T. Masters of Buddenbrooks
Stafford, J. The nemesis
Zweig, S. Confusion of sentiment

Mexico
Brenner, L. Drunken lizard

Poland
Shapiro, L. Eating days

United States
Aldrich, B. S. Juno's swans
Auchincloss, L. Billy and the gargoyles
Brier, H. M. Yogi's dark horse
Calisher, H. Letitia, emeritus
Chute, B. J. Thank you Dr Russell
De Vries, P. Good boy
Doty, W. L. Parochial school
Erdman, L. G. Allen High's youth problem

Fitzgerald, F. S. K. Freshest boy
Goyen, W. Grasshopper's burden
Humphrey, W. Report cards
Johnson, O. M. Great pancake record
Johnson, O. M. Varmint tries dissipation
Knowles, J. Turn with the sun
O'Hara, J. Do you like it here?
Payne, L. V. Prelude
Saroyan, W. Ancient history and low hurdles
Stuart, J. Slipover sweater
Ullman, J. R. Visitation
White, M. To remember these things

SCHOOL PLAYS. See College and school drama

SCHOOL STORIES. See School life

SCHOOL TEACHERS. See Teachers

The schoolmistress. Chekhov, A. P.

SCHOOLS. See School life

Schools and schools. Porter, W. S.

The schooner. McLaverty, M.

Schorer, Mark, 1908-
Boy in the summer sun
Bogorad, S. N. and Trevithick, J. eds. College miscellany
Long in populous city pent
Cory, D. W. pseud. comp. 21 variations on a theme
What we don't know hurts us
Heilman, R. B. ed. Modern short stories

Schorr, Zygmunt
The appraisal
Ausubel, N. ed. Treasury of Jewish humor
Her rich American cousin
Ausubel, N. ed. Treasury of Jewish humor

Schramm, Wilbur Lang, 1907-
Horse that played third base for Brooklyn
Stauffer, R. M.; Cunningham, W. H. and Sullivan, C. J. eds. Adventures in modern literature
My kingdom for Jones
Creamer, J. B. comp. Twenty-two stories about horses and men
Dachs, D. ed. Treasury of sports humor

Schubert, Paul, 1899-
White Elk
This week magazine. This week's short-short stories

Schulberg, Budd Wilson, 1914-
All the town's talking
This week magazine This week's short-short stories
Breaking point
Esquire (Periodical) Girls from Esquire
Schulberg, B. W. Some faces in the crowd
Crowd pleaser
Ribalow, H. U. ed. World's greatest boxing stories
Schulberg, B. W. Some faces in the crowd
The dare
Schulberg, B. W. Some faces in the crowd
Enough
Schulberg, B. W. Some faces in the crowd

Schulberg, Budd W.—*Continued*
Ensign Weasel
Schulberg, B. W. Some faces in the crowd
Face of Hollywood
Schulberg, B. W. Some faces in the crowd
Foxhole in Washington
Schulberg, B. W. Some faces in the crowd
Legend that walks like a man
Schulberg, B. W. Some faces in the crowd
Meal ticket
Schulberg, B. W. Some faces in the crowd
Memory in white
Schulberg, B. W. Some faces in the crowd
My Christmas carol
Burrell, J. A. and Cerf, B. A. eds. Anthology of famous American stories
Schulberg, B. W. Some faces in the crowd
Note on the literary life
Schulberg, B. W. Some faces in the crowd
One he called Winnie
Schulberg, B. W. Some faces in the crowd
Our white deer
Schulberg, B. W. Some faces in the crowd
Passport to nowhere
Ribalow, H. U. ed. These your children
Pride of Tony Colucci
Schulberg, B. W. Some faces in the crowd
Road to recovery
Fabricant, N. D. and Werner, H. eds. World's best doctor stories
Short digest of a long novel
Schulberg, B. W. Some faces in the crowd
Table at Ciro's
Schulberg, B. W. Some faces in the crowd
Third nightcap, with historical footnotes
Schulberg, B. W. Some faces in the crowd
Typical gesture of Colonel Duggan
Schulberg, B. W. Some faces in the crowd
Your Arkansas traveler
Schulberg, B. W. Some faces in the crowd

Schulberg, Stuart
I'm really fine
Best American short stories, 1952

Schüler, Else Lasker- See Lasker-Schüler, Else

Schuman, Sylvie
Quiet one
McFarland, W. K. comp. Then it happened

Schuyler, William, 1912-
Back again
Stanford short stories, 1953

Schwartz, Delmore, 1913-
Bitter farce
Ribalow, H. U. ed. This land, these people

In dreams begin responsibilities
Schorer, M. ed. The story
Swallow, A. ed. Anchor in the sea
Schwartz, Max, 1919-
The victory
Ribalow, H. U. ed. These your children
Schwartz, Richard H.
Good people of Milton
Hathaway, B. and Sessions, J. A. eds. Writers for tomorrow. 2d ser.
Schwartz, Ruth A.
Shoes of bright green leather
American vanguard, 1950
Schwartz-Metterklume method. Munro, H. H.
Schwarz, Cynthia Johnson, 1923-
After the hay-makin'
American vanguard, 1952
Schwarz, Felix Conrad, 1906-
Serpent's tooth
Oberfirst, R. ed. 1954 anthology of best original short-shorts
Schweitzer, Gertrude, 1909-
Because she was like me
McFarland, W. K. comp. Then it happened
Kid brother
Strang, R. M. and Roberts, R. M. eds. Teen-age tales v2
The latchkey
Stowe, A. comp. It's a date
Little sisters are such pests
Lantz, J. E. ed. Stories of Christian living
Summer's end
Lantz, J. E. ed. Stories of Christian living
Schwob, Marcel, 1867-1905
Crates
Geist, S. ed. French stories and tales
Paolo Uccello
Geist, S. ed. French stories and tales
SCIENCE FICTION
Asimov, I. I, robot; 9 stories
Astounding science fiction (Periodical) Astounding science fiction anthology; 23 stories
Aycock, R. D. Unwelcome tenant
Best science fiction stories: 1950; 13 stories
Best science fiction stories: 1951; 18 stories
Best science fiction stories: 1952; 18 stories
Best science-fiction stories: 1953; 15 stories
Best science-fiction stories: 1954; 13 stories
Bleiler, E. F. and Dikty, T. E. eds. Imagination unlimited; 13 stories
Bleiler, E. F. and Dikty, T. E. eds. Science fiction omnibus: the best science fiction stories, 1949, 1950; 25 stories
Bradbury, R. Illustrated man; 19 stories
Brown, F. Angels and spaceships; 17 stories
Brown, F. Space on my hands; 9 stories
Brown, F. and Reynolds, M. eds. Science-fiction carnival; 13 stories
Campbell, J. W. Black star passes; 3 stories
Campbell, J. W. Cloak of Aesir; 7 stories

SCIENCE FICTION—*Continued*

Carr, R. S. Beyond infinity; 4 stories
Clarke, A. C. Expedition to earth; 11 stories
Conklin, G. ed. Big book of science fiction; 32 stories
Conklin, G. ed. Invaders of earth; 21 stories
Conklin, G. ed. Omnibus of science fiction; 42 stories
Conklin, G. ed. Possible worlds of science fiction; 22 stories
Conklin, G. ed. Science-fiction adventures in dimension; 23 stories
Conklin, G. ed. Science-fiction thinking machines; 20 stories
Conklin, G. and Conklin, L. T. eds. Supernatural reader; 27 stories
Crossen, K. F. ed. Adventures in tomorrow: 15 stories
Crossen, K. F. ed. Future tense; 14 stories
De Camp, L. S. Continent makers, and other tales of the Viagens; 8 stories
Del Rey, L., Matschat, C. H. and Carmer, C. L. eds. Year after tomorrow; 9 stories
Derleth, A. W. ed. Beachheads in space; 14 stories
Derleth, A. W. ed. Beyond time and space; 34 stories
Derleth, A. W. ed. Far boundaries; 20 stories
Derleth, A. W. ed. The outer reaches; 17 stories
Derleth, A. W. ed. Time to come; 12 stories
Derleth, A. W. ed. Worlds of tomorrow; 19 stories
Elam, R. M. Teen-age science fiction stories; 11 stories
Galaxy science fiction magazine. Galaxy reader of science fiction; 33 stories
Galaxy science fiction magazine. Second Galaxy reader of science fiction; 31 stories
Greenberg, M. comp. Five science fiction novels; 5 stories
Greenberg, M. ed. Journey to infinity; 12 stories
Greenberg, M. ed. Men against the stars; 12 stories
Greenberg, M. ed. Travelers of space; 14 stories
Hawthorne, N. Rappaccini's daughter
Healy, R. J. ed. New tales of space and time; 10 stories
Heinlein, R. A. Assignment in eternity; 4 stories
Heinlein, R. A. Green hills of earth; 10 stories
Heinlein, R. A. Man who sold the moon; 6 stories
Heinlein, R. A. Revolt in 2100; 3 stories
Howard, R. E. Coming of Conan; 7 stories
Howard, R. E. King Conan; 5 stories
Howard, R. E. Sword of Conan; 4 stories
Huxley, A. L. Education in the world state
Jameson, M. Bullard of the space patrol; 7 stories

Jenkins, W. F. ed. Great stories of science fiction; 12 stories
Jenkins, W. F. Sidewise in time, and other scientific adventures; 6 stories
Jones, R. F. The toymaker; 6 stories
Keller, D. H. Tales from Underwood; 23 stories
Kornbluth, C. M. The explorers; 9 stories
Kuebler, H. W. ed. Treasury of science fiction classics; 15 stories
Kuttner, H. Ahead of time; 10 stories
Kuttner, H. A gnome there was; 10 stories
Kuttner, H. Robots have no tails; 5 stories
Lesser, M. A. ed. Looking forward; 20 stories
Magazine of fantasy and science fiction. Best from Fantasy and science fiction; [1st ser]; 19 stories
Magazine of fantasy and science fiction. Best from Fantasy and science fiction; 2d ser; 17 stories
Magazine of fantasy and science fiction. Best from Fantasy and science fiction; 3d ser; 16 stories
Margulies, L. and Friend, O. J. eds. From off this world; 18 stories
Margulies, L. and Friend, O. J. eds. Giant anthology of science fiction; 10 stories
Matheson, R. Born of man and woman; 17 stories
Merril, J. ed. Beyond human ken; 21 stories
Merril, J. ed. Beyond the barriers of space and time; 19 stories
Miller, P. S. The titan; 8 stories
Moore, C. L. Judgment night; 5 stories
Moore, C. L. Shambleau, and others; 7 stories
Moskowitz, S. comp. Editor's choice in science fiction; 12 stories
Norton, A. M. ed. Space pioneers; 9 stories
Norton, A. M. ed. Space service; 10 stories
Petrified planet; 3 stories
Pohl, F. ed. Assignment in tomorrow; 16 stories
Pratt, F. ed. World of wonder; 19 stories
Pratt, F. and De Camp, L. S. No forwarding address
Pratt, F. and De Camp, L. S. Rape of the lock
Pratt, F. and De Camp, L. S. "Where to, please?"
Richardson, M. L. Way out in the continuum
Sheckley, R. Untouched by human hands; 13 stories
Simak, C. City; 8 stories
Star science fiction stories [no.1]; 15 stories
Star science fiction stories, no.2; 14 stories
Star science fiction stories, no.3; 10 stories
Startling stories (Periodical) Best from Startling stories; 11 stories
Tucker, W. Science-fiction subtreasury; 10 stories
Van Vogt, A. E. Away and beyond; 9 stories
Van Vogt, A. E. Destination: universe; 10 stories
Waldo, E. H. E pluribus unicorn; 13 stories

SCIENCE FICTION—*Continued*
Wells, H. G. Man who could work miracles
Wollheim, D. A. comp. Every boy's book of science-fiction; 10 stories
Wollheim, D. A. comp. Flight into space; 12 stories
Wollheim, D. A. ed. Prize science fiction; 12 stories
Year's best science fiction novels, 1952; 5 stories
Year's best science fiction novels, 1953; 5 stories
Year's best science fiction novels, 1954; 5 stories
　　See also Interplanetary visitors; Interplanetary voyages; Space ships; Future, Stories of the; Moon; Mars

Science of deduction. Doyle, Sir A. C.

Science teacher. Wiegand, W.

SCIENTIFIC EXPERIMENTS. See Experiments, Scientific

SCIENTIFIC STORIES. See Science fiction

SCIENTISTS
Barnard, L. G. Four men and a box
Benét, S. V. Blood of the martyrs
Forester, C. S. Physiology of fear
Jones, R. F. Stone and a spear
May, J. Dune roller
　　See also Anthropologists; Biologists; Chemists; Zoologists; etc.

Scilken, Marjorie, 1923-
Oh joy, it's a boy
American vanguard, 1953

The scoop. Farrell, J. T.

Score in the stands. Benchley, R. C.

The scorpion. Bowles, P. F.

SCOTCH DIALECT STORIES. See Dialect stories—Scotch

SCOTCH IN BORNEO
Maugham, W. S. Neil MacAdam
Maugham, W. S. Man from Glasgow
Skinner, C. L. Silent Scot
Tracy, D. Charity ward

Scotch settlement. Paterson, N.

SCOTLAND

19th century
Barrie, Sir J. M. bart. Courting of T'nowhead's Bell
Barrie, Sir J. M. bart. Farewell Miss Julie Logan
Scott, Sir W. Two drovers
Stevenson, R. L. Merry men
Strong, L. A. G. White cottage
Watson, J. Story of Dr MacLure

SCOTS. See Scotch

Scott, Duncan Campbell, 1862-1947
Paul Farlotte
Pacey, D. ed. Book of Canadian stories

Scott, Hugh Stowell, 1862-1903
Sister
Fabricant, N. D. and Werner, H. eds. World's best doctor stories

Scott, Virgil
Don't run, don't pass
Argosy (Periodical) Argosy Book of sports stories

Scott, Sir Walter, 1771-1832
Two drovers
Cerf, B. A. and Moriarty, H. C. eds. Anthology of famous British stories

Scott, William R. 1919?-
My father doesn't like me
Strang, R. M. and Roberts, R. M. eds. Teen-age tales v2
The pest
Collier's, the national weekly. Collier's best

SCOUNDRELS
Chekhov, A. P. Because of little apples

The scout. Mowery, W. B.

Scout detail. Haycox, E.

Scranton, Ruby R. pseud. See Jones, Ruby S.

Screaming skull. Crawford, F. M.

Screwball division. White, W. A. P.

SCRIBES. See Letter writers

SCRIVENERS. See Law and lawyers; Letter writers

Scrub cure. Miers, E. S.

SCULPTORS
Collier, J. Spring fever
Hameiri, A. Three Halutzot
Jade Goddess
James, H. Tree of knowledge
Winslow, T. S. Bronzes of Martel Greer
Zangwill, I. The luftmensch

Sculptors of life. West, W.

Scum of the earth. Cooke, A. A.

SEA. See Ocean

Sea afire. Floherty, J. J.

Sea anchor. Hill, M. Y.

SEA CAPTAINS. See Shipmasters

SEA DEVIL. See Octopus

Sea devil. Gordon, A.

Sea gypsy. Mayse, A.

Sea-horse of Grand Terre. Jackson, C. T.

Sea raiders. Wells, H. G.

SEA SCOUTS
Strong, P. N. Running dark

Sea serpent of Spoonville Beach. Helfer, H.

SEA-SERPENTS
Helfer, H. Sea serpent of Spoonville Beach
Jenkins, W. F. De profundis

SEA-SHORE
Mansfield, K. At the bay

SEA STORIES
Adams, B. M. The foreigner
Argosy (Periodical) Argosy Book of sea stories; 13 stories
Bluebook (Periodical) Best sea stories from Bluebook; 14 stories
Collins, W. 'Blow up with the brig!'
Connolly, J. B. The trawler
Conrad, J. Initiation
Conrad, J. Secret sharer
Conrad, J. Tales of land and sea; 12 stories
Conrad, J. Youth
Corkery, D. The awakening
Crane, S. Open boat

SEA STORIES—*Continued*
Dunsany, E. J. M. D. P. 18th baron.
  Story of land and sea
Fenner, P. R. comp. Stories of the sea;
  12 stories
Finger, C. J. Yankee captain in Patagonia
Forester, C. S. Mr Midshipman Horn-
  blower; 10 stories
Furman, A. L. ed. Teen-age sea stories;
  13 stories
Gilpatric, G. Last Glencannon omnibus;
  10 stories
Lindquist, W. Last-Light Channel
London, J. Make westing
McFee, W. ed. Great sea stories of mod-
  ern times; 12 stories
Martyr, W. Sleeping draft
Melville, H. Benito Cereno
Melville, H. Billy Budd, foretopman
Pease, H. Passengers for Panama
Poe, E. A. Ms. found in a bottle
Strong, P. N. Running dark
Subercaseaux, B. Salt sea
    See also Mutiny; Seamen

SEA VOYAGES. See Ocean travel

Seabright, Idris, 1911-
All problems are simple
Brightness falls from the air
  Best science fiction stories: 1952
Hole in the moon
  Magazine of fantasy and science fiction
  Best from Fantasy and science fic-
  tion; 2d ser.
Listening child
  Magazine of fantasy and science fiction.
  Best from Fantasy and science fiction;
  ⌐1st ser⌐
Man who sold rope to the gnoles
  Merril, J. ed. Beyond human ken
New ritual
  Magazine of fantasy and science fiction.
  Best from Fantasy and science fiction
  3d ser.

SEAFARING LIFE. See Sea stories

Seager, Allan, 1906-
All problems are simple
  Seager, A. Old man of the mountain,
  and seventeen other stories
Bang on the head
  Seager, A. Old man of the mountain,
  and seventeen other stories
Berkshire comedy
  Seager, A. Old man of the mountain,
  and seventeen other stories
The conqueror
  Seager, A. Old man of the mountain,
  and seventeen other stories
Flight south
  Seager, A. Old man of the mountain,
  and seventeen other stories
Fugue for harmonicas
  Seager, A. Old man of the mountain,
  and seventeen other stories
Game chickens
  Seager, A. Old man of the mountain,
  and seventeen other stories
Jersey, Guernsey, Alderney, Sark
  Seager, A. Old man of the mountain,
  and seventeen other stories
Kobold
  Seager, A. Old man of the mountain,
  and seventeen other stories

No son, no gun, no streetcar
  Seager, A. Old man of the mountain,
  and seventeen other stories
Old man of the mountain
  Seager, A. Old man of the mountain,
  and seventeen other stories
Pommery 1921
  Seager, A. Old man of the mountain,
  and seventeen other stories
Pro arte
  Seager, A. Old man of the mountain,
  and seventeen other stories
Quitandinha
  Seager, A. Old man of the mountain,
  and seventeen other stories
Sacrament
  Seager, A. Old man of the mountain,
  and seventeen other stories
Second wedding
  Cuff, R. P. ed. American short story
  survey
The street
  Seager, A. Old man of the mountain,
  and seventeen other stories
This town and Salamanca
  Seager, A. Old man of the mountain,
  and seventeen other stories
  Short, R. W. and Sewall, R. B. eds.
  Short stories for study. 1950 ed.
The unicorn
  Seager, A. Old man of the mountain,
  and seventeen other stories

The **seal.** O'Flaherty, L.

Seal hunting. Stefánsson, V.

SEALING
England, G. A. Prize cargo

SEALS (ANIMALS)
Finger, C. J. Na-Ha the fighter
Niekirk, M. E. Oscar, the trained seal
Stefánsson, V. Seal hunting

SEAMEN
Argosy (Periodical) Argosy Book of sea
  stories; 13 stories
Bowles, P. F. Fourth day out from Santa
  Cruz
Carroll, J. W. At Mrs Farrelly's
Collins, W. 'Blow up with the brig!'
Crane, S. Open boat
Dingle, A. E. Owner's interest
Dunsany, E. J. M. D. P. 18th baron. Idle
  days on the Yan
Dunsany, E. J. M. D. P. 18th baron.
  Three sailors' gambit
England, G. A. Prize cargo
Gilpatric, G. Last Glencannon omnibus;
  10 stories
Greene, F. S. Bunker Mouse
Kinau, R. Homesickness night
Maugham, W. S. Four Dutchmen
Melville, H. Billy Budd, foretopman
Schisgall, O. "Take over, bos'n!"

Search. Brown, F.

The **search.** Rabinowitz, S.

The **search.** Van Vogt, A. E.

The **search.** Woolley, R.

Search in the mist. Jenkins, W. F.

Search through the streets of the city.
  Shaw, I.

The **searchers.** Kuehn, S.

SEASHORE. See Sea-shore
SEASIDE RESORTS. See Summer resorts
Seasmiles. Winslow, A. G.
Season of divorce. Cheever, J.
Season of mists. Collier, J.
Seaton's aunt. De La Mare, W. J.
Seats of the haughty. Porter, W. S.
Seaver, Jon
    Kingdom in the corn
        Oberfirst, R. ed. 1954 anthology of best
        original short-shorts
SEAWEED GATHERING
    Trollope, A. Malachi's Cove
Seaworthy. Aronson, R.
The secession. Bowen, E.
Second act. Basch, M.
Second chance. Kubilius, W. and Pratt, F.
Second chance. Woody, R. L. J.
Second childhood. Simak, C. D.
Second Christmas. Booker, A. E.
Second dawn. Clarke, A. C.
Second death. Greene, G.
SECOND-HAND STORES
    Davis, L. R. Feeling for human interest
Second hut. Lessing, D. M.
Second Lieutenant Likewise. Tynĭanov,
    I. N.
Second Lieutenant, U.S.A. Res. Katz, S.
Second marriage. Williams, W. C.
Second night of summer. Schmitz, J. H.
Second pasture. Weston, C. G.
Second race. Allen, M. P.
Second sight of Dr Sam: Johnson. De La
    Torre, L.
Second solution. Van Vogt, A. E.
Second table. Weaver, J. D.
Second variety. Dick, P. K.
Second view of the family bosom. Harris,
    G. W.
Second wedding. Seager, A.
The secret. Donnelly, R.
The secret. Gregutt, H. C.
Secret closet. Aspinwall, M.
Secret garden. Chesterton, G. K.
Secret ingredient. Gallico, P. W.
Secret journal. Willingham, C.
Secret life of Walter Mitty. Thurber, J.
Secret miracle. Berges, J. L.
Secret of Coon Castle. Annixter, P. pseud.
Secret of Father Brown. Chesterton, G. K.
Secret of Flambeau. Chesterton, G. K.
Secret recipe. Hope, M. R.
SECRET SERVICE
    Blish, J. Beep
    Maugham, W. S. Giulia Lazzari
    Maugham, W. S. Hairless Mexican
    Maugham, W. S. Miss King
    Maugham, W. S. The traitor
        See also European War, 1914-1918—
    Secret service

Secret sharer. Conrad, J.
Secret sin of Septimus Brope. Munro,
    H. H.
Secret staircase. Lee, M. H.
Secret unattainable. Van Vogt, A. E.
Secret weapon of Joe Smith. Wallace, R.
SECRETARIES
    Aiken, C. P. Thistledown
    Clemens, S. L. My late senatorial secretaryship
    Gregutt, H. C. The secret
    Lawrence, D. H. Two blue birds
    Russell, B. A. W. R. 3d earl. Corsican
        ordeal of Miss X
    Waltari, M. T. Tie from Paris
Secrets of the heart. Gibran, K.
SEDATIVES
    Moore, W. Peacebringer
Seder night. Bruggen, C. de H. van
Seder night. Heine, H.
See you later. Kuttner, H.
Seed beneath the snow. Silone, I.
Seeds. Anderson, S.
Seeing eye dog. Fox, M. L.
Seeker of pagan perfection. Paget, V.
Seeker of the sphinx. Clarke, A. C.
The seekers. Williams, R. M.
Seely, Mabel (Hodnefield) 1903-
    House that Nella lived in
        Queen, E. pseud. ed. Queen's awards:
        7th ser.
The seesaw. Van Vogt, A. E.
Seforim, Mendele Mocher, pseud. See
    Abramowitz, Shalom Jacob
Seid, Ruth, 1913-
    Red necktie
        Ribalow, H. U. ed. This land, these
        people
Seide, Michael, 1911-
    Bad boy from Brooklyn
        Southern review. Anthology of stories
        from the Southern review
    Lady of my own
        Ribalow, H. U. ed. This land, these
        people
SELF-CENTERED PEOPLE. See Egoism
SELF-MADE MEN
    Cancela, A. Life and death of a hero
    Walsh, M. Son of a tinker
Self portrait. Wolfe, B.
SELF-SACRIFICE
    Cohn, E. Given years
    Crockett, S. R. Stickit minister
    Harte, B. Miggles
    Harte, B. Outcasts of Poker Flat
    Packard, F. L. Man who confessed
    Peretz, I. L. Devotion without end
    Russell, B. A. W. R. 3d earl. Corsican
        ordeal of Miss X
Seligsohn, I. J. 1924-
    The anchor
        Story (Periodical) Story; no. 4
Sell, William
    Other tracks
        Conklin, G. ed. Science-fiction adventures in dimension

Sellard, Dan
Jingle wears his spurs
Furman, A. L. ed. Teen-age horse stories
Sellars, Mary
Blessed event
Seventeen (Periodical) Nineteen from Seventeen
Something gay and foolish
McFarland, W. K. comp. Then it happened
Selver, Paul, 1888-
Well, I'm blowed
Leftwich, J. ed. Yisröel. 1952 ed.
Seminary Hill. Connolly, M.
SEMINOLE INDIANS
Dunsing, D. M. Vireo's song
SENECA INDIANS
Brick, J. The captives
'Seng hunter. Mowery, W. B.
Señor Ong and Señor Ha. Bowles, P. F.
SENSATION. See Senses and sensation
Sensational type. Pugh, S. S.
Sense of destination. Kensinger, F. R.
Sense of destination. Riter, F.
Sense of direction. Caspar, L.
Sense of humor. Betts, D.
Sense of humor. Runyon, D.
Sense of responsibility. O'Donovan, M.
Sense that in the scene delights. Demott, B. H.
SENSES AND SENSATION
Gold, H. L. Man with English
The **sensible** thing." Fitzgerald, F. S. K.
Sentence. Brown, F.
Sentence of death. Camus, A.
The **sentimentalists.** Jenkins, W. F.
The **sentinel.** Clarke, A. C.
SENTINELS. See Guard duty
SENTRIES. See Guard duty
The **sentry.** Bergengruen, W.
The **sentry.** O'Donovan, M.
Seraph in the apple tree. Coffin. R. P. T.
Seredy, Kate, 1896-
The round up
Fenner, P. R. comp. Cowboys, cowboys, cowboys
Sergeant Houck. Schaefer, J.
Sergîeev-Tsenskiĭ, Sergîeĭ Nikolaevich, 1876-
Man you couldn't kill
Blodgett, H. W. ed. Story survey. 1953 ed.
The **sermon.** Melville, H.
Sermon by Doctor Pep. Bellow, S.
SERMONS
Crockett, S. R. Reverend John Smith prepares his sermon
Street, J. H. The old, old story
Watson, J. His mother's sermon
SERPENT WORSHIP
Munro, H. H. Story of St Vespaluus
SERPENTS. See Snakes
Serpents and doves. Betts, D.
Serpent's tooth. Schwarz, F. C.

SERVANTS
Ade, G. Effie Whittlesy
Flaubert, G. Simple heart
Greene, G. Basement room
Parker, J. R. Intervention of Providence
Steele, W. D. Bubbles
Stein, G. Good Anna
Taylor, P. H. Bad dreams
Taylor, P. H. Two ladies in retirement
Taylor, P. H. Wife of Nashville
Trilling, L. Other Margaret
See also Negroes as servants

Butlers
Munro, H. H. The hen

Chauffeurs
O'Leary, J. T. Protecting Mary
Yaffe, J. Mr Feldman

Cleaning women
Grimson, M. S. It never fails

Companions
Auchincloss, L. Finnish, good lady
Auchincloss, L. Unholy three

Cooks
Collins, W. Mr Policeman and the cook
De Vries, P. Let 'em eat cook
Porter, W. S. "Girl"
Taylor, P. H. Wife of Nashville
Travers, P. L. Ah Wong

Hired girls
Maupassant, G. de. Story of a farm girl
Renard, J. A romance

Hired men
Strong, J. Hired man
Walsh, M. Thomasheen James and the dictation machine
Walsh, M. Thomasheen James goes to the dogs

Housekeepers
Collins, W. Mr Lepel and the housekeeper

Maids
Broch, H. Zerline, the old servant girl
Brush, K. I. Night club
Chou, S. Benediction
De La Roche, M. Patient Miss Peel
De Vries, P. Pygmalion
Ekbergh, I. D. Lady's maid
Flaubert, G. Simple heart
Gordimer, N. Ah, woe is me
Maugham, W. S. The treasure
Trilling, L. Other Margaret
Winslow, T. S. Sophie Jackson

Menservants
Lessing, D. M. No witchcraft for sale

Waiters
Hemingway, E. Clean, well-lighted place
Mann, T. Mario and the magician

Waitresses
Porter, W. S. Brief debut of Tildy

SERVANTS, NEGRO. See Negroes as servants

Service first. Keller, D. H.
Service of love. Porter, W. S.

Serviss, Garrett Putnam, 1851-1929
    Edison's conquest of Mars; excerpt
        Kuebler, H. W. ed. Treasury of science
        fiction classics
Seton, Ernest Thompson, 1860-1946
    Bingo; the story of my dog
        Seton, E. T. Wild animals I have
        known
    Coaly-bay the outlaw horse
        Dennis, W. ed. Palomino and other
        horses
    Lobo, the king of Currumpaw
        Seton, E. T. Wild animals I have known
    Pacing mustang
        Seton, E. T. Wild animals I have known
    Raggylug; the story of a cottontail rabbit
        Seton, E. T. Wild animals I have known
    Redruff; the story of the Don Valley
        partridge
        Seton, E. T. Wild animals I have known
    Silverspot: the story of a crow
        Andrews, R. C. ed. My favorite stories
        of the great outdoors
        Seton, E. T. Wild animals I have known
    Springfield fox
        Seton, E. T. Wild animals I have known
    Trail of the Sandhill Stag
        Scribner treasury
    Wully; the story of a yaller dog
        Seton, E. T. Wild animals I have known
Settlin'-down feelin'. Thompson, T.
Seven cream jugs. Munro, H. H.
Seventeen. Farrell, J. T.
Seventh pullet. Munro, H. H.
Seventh pup. Gates, D.
Seventh victim. Sheckley, R.
75,000. Chekhov, A. P.
Seventy thousand dollars. Newhouse, E.
SEVILLE. See Spain—Seville
Sex education. Fisher, D. F. C.
Sex opposite. Waldo, E. H.
SEX PROBLEMS
    Davies, R. Foolish one
Sex that doesn't shop. Munro, H. H.
SEXTONS
    Maugham, W. S. The verger
    Zevin, I. J. Nogid's luck
Sforim, Mendele Mocher, pseud. See Abram-
        owitz, Shalom Jacob
Shaara, Michael
    Soldier boy
        Conklin, G. ed. Science-fiction thinking
        machines
Shaatnez. Tchernichowski, S.
Shabbes-soup. Heijermans, H.
Shackleton, Sir Ernest Henry, 1874-1922
    Boat journey
        McFee, W. ed. Great sea stories of
        modern times
Shade of Omar. Schneider, G. W.
Shades of spring. Lawrence, D. H.
Shadow. Poe, E. A.
Shadow and the flash. London, J.
Shadow in the rose garden. Lawrence, D. H.
Shadow kingdom. Howard, R. E.

The shadow-line. Conrad, J.
Shadow of an arm. Phillips, T. H.
Shadow of evil. Aswell, J. B.
Shadow of the butte. Thompson, T.
Shadow of turning. Beck, W.
Shadow passes. Wodehouse, P. G.
Shadow play. Sitwell, Sir O. bart.
Shadows of the world. Taylor, E.
Shadowy third. Bowen, E.
Shake hands with a murderer. Hume, S. T.
SHAKESPEARE, WILLIAM, 1564-1616
    Benson, T. Shakespeare's elderly bore
    Irwin, I. H. Spring flight
Shakespeare's elderly bore. Benson, T.
Shall not perish. Faulkner, W.
Shallit, Joseph, 1915-
    Margie passes
        Story (Periodical) Story; no. 1
    Wonder child
        Best science-fiction stories: 1954
Shallit, Rebecca
    Initiation fee
        Seventeen (Periodical) Nineteen from
        Seventeen
Shambleau. Moore, C. L.
SHAME
    Anderson, S. "Queer"
Shame on you. Foote, J. T.
Shamrock and the palm. Porter, W. S.
SHANGHAI. See China—Shanghai
SHANTY BOATS. See House boats
Shantyboat pirate. Strong, P. N.
Shape. Sheckley, R.
Shape of light. Goyen, W.
Shape of things. Bradbury, R.
Shapiro, Irwin, 1911-
    How Old Stormalong captured Mocha
        Dick
        Fenner, P. R. comp. Fools and funny
        fellows
Shapiro, Lamed, 1878-1948
    Eating days
        Howe, I. and Greenberg, E. eds. Treas-
        ury of Yiddish stories
    Journeying through the milky way
        Leftwich, J. ed. Yisroël, 1952 ed.
    Rebbe and the rebbetsin
        Howe, I. and Greenberg, E. eds. Treas-
        ury of Yiddish stories
    Smoke
        Howe, I. and Greenberg, E. eds. Treas-
        ury of Yiddish stories
    White chalah
        Howe, I. and Greenberg, E. eds. Treas-
        ury of Yiddish stories
SHARE CROPPERS. See Tenant farming
Share in the hereafter. Nordau, M. S.
Share of paradise. Bloomgarden, S.
The sharers. Sullivan, R.
SHARKS
    Cottrell, D. W. The sharks were hungry
Sharks were hungry. Cottrell, D. W.

Sharp, D. D.
Eternal man
Margulies, L. and Friend, O. J. eds.
From off this world
Sharp, Margery, 1905-
London night's entertainment
Queen, E. pseud. ed. Literature of
crime
Winning sequence
Dachs, D. ed. Treasury of sports humor
Sharp eyes. Burroughs, J.
SHARPSHOOTERS
Brick, J. Rifleman's run
Shattered dream. Burnet, D.
Shattuck, Roger, 1923-
Workout on the river
Best American short stories, 1953
Shaw, Henrietta Otis
Lighted candles
American girl (Periodical) Christmas
all year 'round
Shaw, Irwin, 1913-
Act of faith
Burrell, J. A. and Cerf, B. A. eds. An-
thology of famous stories
Ribalow, H. U. ed. This land, these
people
The convert
Esquire (Periodical) Girls from Esquire
Eighty-yard run
Stegner, W. E.; Scowcroft, R. and Ilyin,
B. eds. Writer's art
Faith at sea
Fabricant, N. D. and Werner, H. eds.
World's best doctor stories
In the French style
Best American short sories, 1954
Main currents of American thought
Felheim, M.; Newman, F. B. and Stein-
hoff, W. R. eds. Modern short stories
Passion of Lance Corporal Hawkins
Lynskey, W. C. ed. Reading modern
fiction
Return to Kansas City
Ribalow, H. U. ed. World's greatest
boxing stories
Sailor off the Bremen
Heilman, R. B. ed. Secret life of Walter
Mitty
Search through the streets of the city
Best of the Best American short sto-
ries, 1915-1950
Triumph of justice
Blaustein, A. P. ed. Fiction goes to
court
Walking wounded
First-prize stories, 1919-1954
Shaw, Larry
Simworthy's circus
Brown, F. and Reynolds, M. eds. Sci-
ence-fiction carnival
SHAWNEE INDIANS
Kjelgaard, J. A. Wilderness road
She did not cry at all. Brookhouser, F.
She didn't like people. Cousins, M.
She made the big town! Brookhouser, F.
She never knew. Booker, S.
She shall have music. Platt, G.
She shall have music. Shulman, M.

She wanted a hero. Wylie, P.
She who laughs. Phillips, P.
She-wolf. Munro, H. H.
The **she**-wolf. Verga, G.
Shearing the wolf. Porter, W. S.
Sheckley, Robert, 1928-
The altar
Sheckley, R. Untouched by human
hands
Beside still waters
Sheckley, R. Untouched by human
hands
Cost of living
Sheckley, R. Untouched by human
hands
The demons
Sheckley, R. Untouched by human
hands
Impacted man
Sheckley, R. Untouched by human
hands
King's wishes
Sheckley, R. Untouched by human
hands
Last weapon
Star science fiction stories ₍no. 1₎
The monsters
Sheckley, R. Untouched by human
hands
Odor of thought
Star science fiction stories, no. 2
Operating instructions
Merril, J. ed. Beyond the barriers of
space and time
Paradise II
Derleth, A. W. ed. Time to come
Ritual
Sheckley, R. Untouched by human
hands
Seventh victim
Sheckley, R. Untouched by human
hands
Shape
Sheckley, R. Untouched by human
hands
Specialist
Galaxy science fiction magazine. Second
Galaxy reader of science fiction
Sheckley, R. Untouched by human
hands
Untouched by human hands
Sheckley, R. Untouched by human
hands
Warm
Galaxy science fiction magazine. Second
Galaxy reader of science fiction
Sheckley, R. Untouched by human
hands
The **shed.** Evans, E. E.
Sheehan, David Vincent
Get-away boy
Strang, R. M. and Roberts, R. M. eds.
Teen-age tales **v** 1
Sheehan, Patrick Augustine, 1852-1913
Incompatibility
Thinker's digest (Periodical) Spoiled
priest, and other stories
Spoiled priest
Thinker's digest (Periodical) Spoiled
priest, and other stories

Sheehy, Edward
Prothalmion
Gable, M. Sister, ed. Many-colored fleece
Sheener. Williams, B. A.
SHEEP
Davis, H. L. The homestead orchard
Davis, H. L. The stubborn spearmen
Warwick, J. Fire in the bush
The **sheep.** Munro, H. H.
SHEEP HERDERS. See Shepherds
SHEEP RAISING. See Sheep
Sheldon, Charles Monroe, 1857-1946
Stolen Christmas
Elmquist, R. M. ed. Fifty years of Christmas
Sheldon, Walt, 1917?-
Chore for a spaceman
Norton, A. M. ed. Space service
I, the unspeakable
Galaxy science fiction magazine. Galaxy reader of science fiction
The **shell.** Humphrey, W.
She'll be sorry. Johnson, H.
SHELL-FISH FISHERIES
Hobbs, A. K. River pirates
Shell of sense. Dunbar, O. H.
Shelton, Jerry
Culture
Conklin, G. ed. Big book of science fiction
Shen, Tsung-wen, 1905-
Little Flute
Story (Periodical) Story; no. 1
The **shepherd.** Hyman, M.
SHEPHERDS
Beachcroft, T. O. Erne from the coast
Dunsany, E. J. M. D. P. 18th baron. East and West
Gunnarson, G. Advent
Krige, U. Invisible shepherd
Oxenham, J. Their first meeting
Porter, W. S. Roads of destiny
The **shepherds.** O'Donovan, M.
Shepherd's boy. Middleton, R. B.
Shepherds' trophy. Ollivant, A.
Sheppard, Jerome
Black brassard
Best Army short stories, 1950
Sheraton mirror. Derleth, A. W.
SHERIFFS
Crane, S. Bride comes to Yellow Sky
Cunningham, J. M. Tin star
DeRosso, H. A. Bitter trail
Perry, G. S. The fourflusher
Raine, W. M. Friend of Buck Hollister
See also Western stories
Sheriton turnabout. Pierrot, G. F.
Sherlock Holmes gives a demonstration. Doyle, Sir A. C.
Sherman, Dulcie
Fifteen
Wolfe, D. M. ed. Which grain will grow

Sherman, Harold Morrow, 1898-
Fly chaser
Fenner, P. R. comp. Crack of the bat
Furman, A. L. ed. Teen-age stories of the diamond
A hot dog on ice
Furman, A. L. ed. Teen-age dog stories
Porky, the outboarder
Owen, F. ed. Teen-age victory parade
Reeder, left defense
American boy (Periodical) American boy anthology
Wild pitch
Furman, A. L. ed. Teen-age stories of the diamond
Sherman, Richard, 1906-
Life of Riley
Lass, A. H. and Horowitz, A. eds. Stories for youth
Now there is peace
Lass, A. H. and Horowitz, A. eds. Stories for youth
Sherred, T. L.
E for effort
Astounding science fiction (Periodical) Astounding science fiction anthology
Conklin, G. ed. Big book of science fiction
Sherwood, Robert Emmet, 1896-1955
"Extra! Extra!"
Shaw, H. and Bement, D. eds. Reading the short story
Shiloh's waters. Davis, H. L.
Shingle shack. Macdonald, Z. K.
Shingles for the Lord. Faulkner, W.
Shining fools. Bergengruen, W.
Ship from nowhere. Chandler, A. B.
Ship of silence. Wetjen, A. R.
Ship sails at midnight. Leiber, F.
Ship that turned aside. Wertenbaker, G. P.
SHIPMASTERS
Conrad, J. Secret sharer
Marmur, J. I will not abandon!
Marmur, J. Proved by the sea
Martyr, W. Sleeping draft
Patrick, J. Crowbar Captain
Roberts, M. Captain of the "Ullswater"
Strong, A. All on a winter's night
SHIPPING
Marmur, J. I will not abandon!
SHIPS
Fitzgerald, F. S. K. Rough crossing
Van Doren, M. The birds
Ships. Porter, W. S.
SHIPS, ABANDONED
Noyes, A. Log of the "Evening Star"
Steele, W. D. Yellow cat
SHIPS, GHOST. See Ghost ships
Ship's cat. Meigs, C. L.
Shipshape home. Matheson, R.
Shipwreck of Crunch and Des. Wylie, P.
SHIPWRECKS AND CASTAWAYS
Crane, S. Open boat
Farley, W. The storm
Hemingway, E. After the storm
Holder, W. One guy, one gal, one island
Lover, S. The gridiron

SHIPWRECKS & CASTAWAYS—*Cont.*
Marmur, J. Mad Island
Poe, E. A. Ms. found in a bottle
Quiller-Couch, Sir A. T. Roll-call of the reef
Schisgall, O. "Take over, bos'n!"
Shiras, Wilmar H. 1908-
In hiding
Bleiler, E. F. and Dikty, T. E. eds. Science fiction omnibus: the best science fiction stories, 1949, 1950
Jenkins, W. F. ed. Great stories of science fiction
Sloane, W. M. ed. Stories for tomorrow
Opening doors
Best science fiction stories: 1950
Bleiler, E. F. and Dikty, T. E. eds. Science fiction omnibus: the best science fiction stories, 1949, 1950
Shirley, Sylvia, 1919-
Slow journey
Prize stories of 1951
Shivaree before breakfast. West, J.
Shneour, Zalman. See Shneur, Zalman
Shneur, Zalman, 1887-
The girl
Howe, I. and Greenberg, E. eds. Treasury of Yiddish stories
Immortal orange
Ausubel, N. ed. Treasury of Jewish humor
Leftwich, J. ed. Yisröel. 1952 ed.
New police chief
Ausubel, N. ed. Treasury of Jewish humor
Revenge; extracts from a student's diary
Howe, I. and Greenberg, E. eds. Treasury of Yiddish stories
Shiftless. Boyd, J.
Shock. Kuttner, H.
Shock of doom. Porter, W. S.
Shock tactics. Munro, H. H.
Shock treatment. Stark, I.
SHOEMAKERS
Galsworthy, J. Quality
Maxtone Graham, J. A. Cobbler, cobbler, mend my shoe
Nexø, M. A. Birds of passage
Reisin, A. Avrom the cobbler
Singer, I. B. Little shoemakers
Van Doren, M. Little place
SHOE SHINERS. See Bootblacks
SHOES. See Boots and shoes
Shoes. Porter, W. S.
Shoes for breakfast. Treat, L.
Shoes of black green leather. See Schwartz, R. A. Shoes of bright green leather
Shoes of bright green leather. Schwartz, R. A.
SHOFAR. See Shophar
Shofar blower of Lapinishok. Ogus, A. D.
Sholokhov, Mikhail Aleksandrovich, 1905-
Civil War
Burnett, W. ed. World's best

SHOOTING
Bonner, P. H. The triumph
Saroyan, W. Pheasant hunter
Schaefer, J. W. My town
See also Hunting
The **shooting.** Caldwell, E.
Shooting an elephant. Orwell, G.
SHOPHAR
Ogus, A. D. Shofar blower of Lapinshok
SHOPKEEPERS. See Merchants
SHOPPING
De Vries, P. Household words
Munro, H. H. The dreamer
Munro, H. H. Sex that doesn't shop
Parker, J. R. Robes et modes
SHOPS, BEAUTY. See Beauty shops
Shore, Viola (Brothers) 1895-
'Bye, 'bye, Bluebeard
Queen, E. pseud. ed. Queen's awards: 6th ser.
Case of Karen Smith
Queen, E. pseud. ed. Queen's awards: 5th ser.
Shore for the sinking. Thompson, T.
Shores of Tripoli. Daniel, H.
Shorn lamb. Stafford, J.
Short digest of a long novel. Schulberg, B. W.
Short Friday. Bialik, H. N.
Short happy life of Francis Macomber. Hemingway, E.
Short space. Toole, K.
Short visit to Naples. Newhouse, E.
Shorty who wished he were taller. Strain, F. B.
SHOTGUNS. See Shooting
Shottle Bop. Waldo, E. H.
The **shout.** Graves, R.
Show window. Bradley, M. H.
SHOW WINDOWS
Blackburn, R. H. Clay dish
Shower of gold. Welty, E.
Shulman, Max, 1919-
Boy bites man
Shulman, M. The many loves of Dobie Gillis
Chance for adventure
This week magazine. This week's short-short stories
Everybody loves my baby
Shulman, M. The many loves of Dobie Gillis
Face is familiar but—
Shulman, M. The many loves of Dobie Gillis
King's English
Shulman, M. The many loves of Dobie Gillis
Love is a fallacy
Shulman, M. The many loves of Dobie Gillis
Love of two chemists
Shulman, M. The many loves of Dobie Gillis
Mock governor
Shulman, M. The many loves of Dobie Gillis

Shulman, Max—*Continued*
  She shall have music
    Shulman, M. The many loves of Dobie
    Gillis
  Sugar bowl
    Shulman, M. The many loves of Dobie
    Gillis
  Unlucky winner
    Shulman, M. The many loves of Dobie
    Gillis
  You think you got trouble?
    Shulman, M. The many loves of Dobie
    Gillis
Shultz, William Henry, 1913-
  Oreste
    Best American short stories, 1953
Shut a final door. Capote, T.
Shute, Henry Augustus, 1856-1943
  "Sequil"—or Things whitch aint finished
    in the first
    Davis, C. B. ed. Eyes of boyhood
Shylock in Czernowitz. Franzos, K. E.
SIAM. See Thailand
SIBERIA
  Chekhov, A. P. Across Siberia
SICILY
  Verga, G. Little novels of Sicily; 12
    stories
Sick bay to sea wall. White, R.
Sick child. Colette, S. G.
Sick goose Rosenfeld, J.
Sick horse. Caldwell, E.
Sidewise in time. Jenkins, W. F.
Siegel, Benjamin
  Little red jungle
    Seventeen (Periodical) Nineteen from
    Seventeen
Siegel, Larry
  Lay it down, Ziggy!
    Herzberg, M. J. comp. Treasure chest
    of sport stories
Sienkiewicz, Henryk, 1846-1916
  Keeper of the faith
    Brentano, F. ed. The word lives on
SIERRA NEVADA MOUNTAINS
  Breckenfeld, V. G. Touch of Arab
SIGHT
  McKenney, J. Skycaptain
    See also Blind
SIGHTSEEING BUSES
  Porter, W. S. Sisters of the golden rule
The sign. Dunsany, E. J. M. D. P. 18th
  baron
Sign of the broken sword. Chesterton, G. K.
Sign of the four. Doyle, Sir A. C.
The signal. Maupassant, G. de
Signal man. Dickens, C.
SIGNAL MEN, RAILROAD. See Rail-
  roads—Employees
Signed with his seal. Undset, S.
Signor Santa. Pagano, J.
SIKSIKA INDIANS
  Frazee, S. Great medicine
Silence. Poe, E. A.
Silence of Mr Prendegast. Cloete, S.

Silent Scot. Skinner, C. L.
Silent snow, secret snow. Aiken, C. P.
Silent wings. Coombs, C. I.
Silent woman. Kompert, L.
The silken-swift. Waldo, E. H.
Sillanpää, Frans Eemil, 1888-
  Night of the harvest festival
    Burnett, W. ed. World's best
Silly season. Kornbluth, C. M.
Silone, Ignazio, 1900-
  Mr Aristotle
    Neider, C. ed. Great short stories from
    the world's literature
  Seed beneath the snow; excerpts
    Burnett, W. ed. World's best
  The trap
    Blodgett, H. W. ed. Story survey.
    1953 ed.
Silver Blaze. Doyle, Sir A. C.
Silver cross. Doty, W. L.
Silver dollar. Thompson, T.
Silver King. Perrault, E. G.
SILVER MINES AND MINING
  Davis, S. P. Mystery of the Savage sump
  Hart, F. First Fourth in White Pine
Silver mounted. James, W.
Silver saddle. Thompson, T.
Silver spurs. Witham, E. C.
Silver sword. Ullman, J. R.
Silvers, Earl Reed, 1891-1948
  Stars in the sky
    Certner, S. and Henry, G. H. eds. Short
    stories for our times
Silverspot: the story of a crow. Seton, E. T.
Simak, Clifford Donald, 1904-
  Aesop
    Simak, C. D. City
  The answers
    Sloane, W. M. ed. Stories for tomorrow
  Asteroid of gold
    Wollheim, D. A. comp. Every boy's
    book of science-fiction
  Beachhead
    Derleth, A. W. ed. Beachheads in space
  Census
    Simak, C. D. City
  City
    Simak, C. D. City
  Contraption
    Star science fiction stories [no. 1]
  Courtesy
    Sloane, W. M. ed. Space, space, space
  Desertion
    Conklin, G. ed. Big book of science
    fiction
    Simak, C. D. City
  Eternity lost
    Astounding science fiction (Periodical)
    Astounding science fiction anthology
    Best science fiction stories: 1950
    Bleiler, E. F. and Dikty, T. E. eds. Sci-
    ence fiction omnibus: the best science
    fiction stories, 1949, 1950
  Good night, Mr James
    Derleth, A. W. ed. The outer reaches
    Galaxy science fiction magazine. Galaxy
    reader of science fiction

Simak, Clifford D.—*Continued*
Hobbies
Simak, C. D. City
Huddling place
Simak, C. D. City
Junkyard
Galaxy science fiction magazine. Second
Galaxy reader of science fiction
Limiting factor
Conklin, G. ed. Possible worlds of science fiction
Paradise
Simak, C. D. City
Second childhood
Galaxy science fiction magazine. Galaxy
reader of science fiction
Sloane, W. M. ed. Stories for tomorrow
Simple way
Simak, C. D. City
Skirmish
Conklin, G. ed. Science-fiction thinking machines

Simenon, Georges, 1903-
Château of missing men
Mystery Writers of America, inc.
Crooks' tour
Little house at Croix-Rousse
Mystery Writers of America, inc.
Maiden murders
Stan the killer
Mystery Writers of America, inc.
Butcher, baker, murder-maker

Simha of Worms. Cohn, E.

Simon's papa. Maupassant, G. de

Simple heart. Flaubert, G.

Simple way. Simak, C. D.

Simpson, Harriette Louisa. See Arnow, Harriette Louisa (Simpson)

Simpson, Maud Edith, 1897-
Practical joker
Oberfirst, R. ed. 1954 anthology of best original short-shorts

Simworthy's circus. Shaw, L.

SIN
Hawthorne, N. Minister's black veil
Sinclair, M. Where their fire is not quenched

SIN, UNPARDONABLE
Hawthorne, N. Ethan Brand

Sinai. Frischman, D.

Sinclair, Jo, pseud. See Seid, Ruth

Sinclair, John L. 1902-
The killer and the pit
Western Writers of America. Holsters and heroes

Sinclair, May, 1865?-1946
Nature of the evidence
Conklin, G. and Conklin, L. T. eds. Supernatural reader
Where their fire is not quenched
Davenport, B. ed. Ghostly tales to be told

Sing, Milo, sing. MacMahon, B.

SINGAPORE
Maugham, W. S. The letter

Singer, Israel Joshua, 1893-1944
Repentance
Howe, I. and Greenberg, E. eds. Treasury of Yiddish stories
Sand
Howe, I. and Greenberg, E. eds. Treasury of Yiddish stories

Singer, Isaac Bashevis, 1894-
Gimpel the fool
Howe, I. and Greenberg, E. eds. Treasury of Yiddish stories
Little shoemakers
Howe, I. and Greenberg, E. eds. Treasury of Yiddish stories

SINGERS. See Musicians—Singers

SINGING AND VOICE CULTURE
Fisher, D. F. C. As ye sow—

Singing stick. Pangborn, E.

Singmaster, Elsie, 1879-
Boy and a dog
Harper, W. comp. Dog show
Little and unknown
Brentano, F. ed. The word lives on

Sinister journey. Richter, C.

Sinister night. Chekhov, A. P.

SINN FEIN
Corkery, D. Unfinished symphony

Sins of Prince Saradine. Chesterton, G. K.

SIOUX INDIANS. See Dakota Indians

Sir Harry Scattercash's hounds: Mr Sponge carries the horn. Surtees, R. S.

Sir Harry's hounds again: Mr Sponge and Miss Lucy Glitters. Surtees, R. S.

Sir Louis dines out. Trollope, A.

Sir Rabbit. Welty, E.

Sir Thomas. Schneider, G. W.

Sire de Malétroit's door. Stevenson, R. L.

Siren of hope. Keith, S.

Sister. Humphrey, W.

Sister. Scott, H. S.

Sister Aparición. Pardo Bazán, E. condesa de

Sister Innocent and the useful miracle. Lieberman, R.

Sister superior. Wilson, A.

SISTERS
Curtis, M. Navy blue and bold
Davies, R. Resurrection
Davies, R. The sisters
Fleg, E. The adulteress
Gordimer, N. La vie Bohème
Horwitz, J. The burial
Horwitz, J. If God makes you pretty
Irwin, M. E. F. Where beauty lies
Johnson, D. M. Flame on the frontier
Lambert, J. Tall as the stars
Mansfield, K. Daughters of the late colonel
Marshall, E. Hill people
O'Donovan, M. Little mother
O'Donovan, M. Mad Lomasneys
Schuman, S. Quiet one
Stern, G. B. Cinderella's sister
Welty, E. Why I live at the P.O.
Wharton, E. N. J. Bunner sisters

SISTERS—*Continued*
  Wilson, A. Sister superior
  Winn, J. Hungry sister
  Winslow, A. G. Seasmiles
  Winslow, T. S. Misses Grant
The sisters. Davies, R.
The sisters. Jackson, C. R.
The sisters. Joyce, J.
SISTERS-IN-LAW
  Sansom, W. The windows
Sisters of the golden circle. Porter, W. S.
Sit your saddle solid. Sandoz, M.
SITTERS (CHILD CARE) See Baby sitters
SITTING BULL, DAKOTA CHIEF, 1837?-1890
  Mowery, W. B. Constable of Lone Sioux
Situation wanted. Runyon, D.
Sitwell, Sir Osbert, bart. 1892-
  Alive—alive oh!
    Sitwell, Sir O. bart. Collected stories
  Champagne for the old lady
    Sitwell, Sir O. bart. Collected stories
  Charles and Charlemagne
    Sitwell, Sir O. bart. Collected stories
  Dead heat
    Sitwell, Sir O. bart. Collected stories
  Death of a god
    Sitwell, Sir O. bart. Collected stories
  Defeat
    Sitwell, Sir O. bart. Collected stories
  Dumb-animal
    Sitwell, Sir O. bart. Collected stories
  Friendship's due
    Sitwell, Sir O. bart. Collected stories
  Glow-worm
    Sitwell, Sir O. bart. Collected stories
  The greeting
    Sitwell, Sir O. bart. Collected stories
  His ship comes home
    Sitwell, Sir O. bart. Collected stories
  Idyll through the looking-glass
    Sitwell, Sir O. bart. Collected stories
  Long journey
    Sitwell, Sir O. bart. Collected stories
  Love-bird
    Sitwell, Sir O. bart. Collected stories
  Lovers' meeting
    Sitwell, Sir O. bart. Collected stories
  Low tide
    Sitwell, Sir O. bart. Collected stories
  Machine breaks down
    Sitwell, Sir O. bart. Collected stories
  Man who drove Strindberg mad
    Sitwell, Sir O. bart. Collected stories
  The messenger
    Sitwell, Sir O. bart. Collected stories
  Place of one's own
    Sitwell, Sir O. bart. Collected stories
  Plague-cart before horse
    Sitwell, Sir O. bart. Collected stories
  Pompey and some peaches; a stereoscopic story in two parts
    Sitwell, Sir O. bart. Collected stories
  Primavera
    Sitwell, Sir O. bart. Collected stories
  Shadow play
    Sitwell, Sir O. bart. Collected stories

  Staggered holiday
    Sitwell, Sir O. bart. Collected stories
  That flesh is heir to. . .
    Sitwell, Sir O. bart. Collected stories
  Touching wood
    Sitwell, Sir O. bart. Collected stories
  Triple fugue
    Sitwell, Sir O. bart. Collected stories
  True lovers' knot
    Sitwell, Sir O. bart. Collected stories
  Woman who hated flowers
    Sitwell, Sir O. bart. Collected stories
  'You can carry it, Mrs Parkin'
    Sitwell, Sir O. bart. Collected stories
Six dollars. Steele, W. D.
Six months more to live. Gerahty, D. G.
Sixteen. Daly, M.
60 ways to lose a horse bet. O'Reilly, T.
Sizzling saboteur. Charteris, L.
Sjögren, Erik
  Death in the pass
    Saturday evening post (Periodical)
      Saturday evening post stories, 1950
SKATING
  Skinner, C. O. On skating
    See also Hockey
Skeedunk special. Miers, E. S.
Skeleton of Mr Nethersoul. Kloepfer, M.
Skelton, Charles L.
  Mail starts
    Fenner, P. R. comp. Cowboys, cowboys, cowboys
SKEPTICISM
  Caldwell, E. Yellow girl
Ski high. Chute, B. J.
SKIING. See Skis and skiing
Skin. Dahl, R.
SKIN DIVING
  Coombs, C. I. Four fathom fury
    See also Diving, Submarine
Skin game. Hendryx, J. B.
Skinner, Constance Lindsay, d. 1939
  Becky's Christmas turkey
    Fenner, P. R. comp. Indians, Indians, Indians
  Silent Scot
    Fenner, P. R. comp. Yankee Doodle
Skinner, Cornelia Otis, 1901-
  On skating
    Dachs, D. ed. Treasury of sports humor
  Parcel of land
    Blaustein, A. P. ed. Fiction goes to court
Skipper played it safe. Lott, D. N.
Skirmish. Simak, C. D.
SKIS AND SKIING
  Chute, B. J. Fall guy
  Chute, B. J. Ski high
  Coombs, C. I. Downhill dilemma
  Dodge, J. E. Headwall tempo
  Findlay, D. K. Suicide on skis
  Fitts, H. K. Rattlesnake Trail
  Miers, E. S. Christmas skis
  Purcell, D. Rider of the avalanche
  Schmidt, C. F. Ancestral voices
  Whittemore, C. W. Leap for two lives

The **skit**. Chekhov, A. P.
SKULLS
  Crawford, F. M. Screaming skull
Sky hook. Brier, H. M.
Sky line. Taylor, P. H.
Sky ride—a Tom Swift story. Appleton, V. pseud.
Skyblue lady. Lowry, R. J. C.
Skycaptain. McKenney, J.
Skylight Room. Porter, W. S.
SKYSCRAPERS
  McMorrow, T. Mr Murphy of New York
  Porter, W. S. Psyche and the pskyscraper
SLAUGHTERING AND SLAUGHTER-HOUSES
  Still, J. Master time
SLAVE SHIPS
  Melville, H. Benito Cereno
  Sabin, E. L. Freedom
SLAVE TRADE
  Melville, H. Benito Cereno
SLAVERY
  Benét, S. V. Freedom's a hard-bought thing
  Harris, J. C. Free Joe and the rest of the world
        Egypt
  Coolidge, O. E. The tree
        Fugitive slaves
  Faulkner, W. Was
Slay upon delivery. Kane, F.
Sleek sixteen. Curtis, M.
SLEEP
  Nadir, I. M. Man who slept through the end of the world
      See also Insomnia
SLEEP, PROLONGED
  Cohn, E. Honi ha-Meaggel
  Irving, W. Rip Van Winkle
SLEEP-WALKING. See Somnambulism
Sleeper awakened. Jackson, C. R.
Sleeping Beauty. Collier, J.
Sleeping draft. Martyr, W.
SLEEPLESSNESS. See Insomnia
Sleet storm. Lamberton, L.
SLEIGHT OF HAND. See Conjuring
Slesinger, Tess, 1905-1945
  Missis Flinders
    Gable, M. Sister, ed. Many-colored fleece
Sleuth-hound. Zoshchenko, M. M.
The **sleuths**. Porter, W. S.
Slice him down. Hughes, L.
Slightly crocked. McNulty, J.
Slipover sweater. Stuart, J.
Slipstream. Ford, C.
Slithering shadow. Howard, R. E.
Sloane, William Milligan, 1906-
  Let nothing you dismay
    Sloane, W. M. ed. Stories for tomorrow
Slosson, Annie (Trumbull) 1838-1926
  Fishin' Jimmy
    Scribner treasury

SLOT MACHINES. See Gambling
Slouch. Farrell, J. T.
Slow death. Caldwell, E.
Slow journey. Shirley, S.
Slowpoke. Paterson, R.
SLUM LIFE
  Crane, S. Maggie: a girl of the streets
Small, Sidney Herschel, 1893-
  Chinese dagger
    Best detective stories of the year—1951
  Stalking shadow
    Best detective stories of the year—1950
Small day. Caldwell, E.
Small homicide. Hunter, E.
SMALL TOWN LIFE
  Clemens, S. L. Man that corrupted Hadleyburg
  Crowell, C. T. The stoic
  Grau, S. A. Girl with the flaxen hair
  Lord, J. Boy who wrote 'no'
Small world. Cousins, M.
Small world. Sansom, W.
SMALLPOX
  Grimson, M. S. Story of Paula
Smell of smoke. Anderson, E. V.
The **smile**. Bradbury, R.
Smile box. Eggleston, M. W.
Smiling lady. Eggleston, M. W.
Smith, Clark Ashton, 1893-
  Beyond the Singing Flame
    Margulies, L. and Friend, O. J. eds. From off this world
  City of Singing Flame
    Margulies, L. and Friend, O. J. eds. From off this world
  Metamorphosis of earth
    Derleth, A. W. ed. Beachheads in space
  Phoenix
    Derleth, A. W. ed. Time to come
  Plutonian drug
    Derleth, A. W. ed. The outer reaches
  Voyage to Sfanomoë
    Derleth, A. W. ed. Beyond time & space
Smith, Edgar Valentine, 1875-1953
  Prelude
    First-prize stories, 1919-1954
    McFarland, W. K. comp. Then it happened
Smith, Edmund Ware, 1900-
  Underground episode
    Certner, S. and Henry, G. H. eds. Short stories for our times
Smith, Edward Elmer, 1890-
  Atlantis
    Greenberg, M. ed. Journey to infinity
Smith, Eugene Cadwallader, 1877-
  The outlaw
    Fenner, P. R. comp. Elephants, elephants, elephants
Smith, Evelyn E. 1927-
  Daxbr baxbr
    Derleth, A. W. ed. Time to come
  Not fit for children
    Galaxy science fiction magazine. Second Galaxy reader of science fiction

Smith, Evelyn E.—*Continued*
  Tea tray in the sky
    Galaxy science fiction magazine. Second
    Galaxy reader of science fiction
Smith, George Oliver, 1911-
  Cosmic jackpot
    Brown, F. and Reynolds, M. eds. Science-fiction carnival
Smith, J. Cameron
  Rustling tree
    Queen, E. pseud. ed. Queen's awards:
    5th ser.
Smith, James, 1737-1814
  Life among the Indians
    Andrews, R. C. ed. My favorite stories
    of the great outdoors
Smith, John Campbell, 1924-
  Who too was a soldier
    Prize stories of 1951
Smith, Joseph Emmett, 1932-
  Act of contrition
    American vanguard, 1953
Smith, Leslie
  Grass on the other side
    Stanford short stories, 1950
Smith, Logan Pearsall, 1865-1946
  'Ivanhoe'
    Horizon (Periodical) Golden Horizon
Smith, Sheila Kaye- See Kaye-Smith, Sheila
Smith. Chadwick, A.
Smith. Porter, W. S.
Smith and Jones. Aiken, C. P.
Smoke. Shapiro, L.
Smoke arm. Thompson, H.
Smoke ball kid. West, C.
Smoke tree. Mowery, W. B.
SMOKING
  Shapiro, L. Smoke
Smoky in the west. Haycox, E.
Smoky, the range colt. James, W.
Smoky: who twice saved his master's life.
    Little, G. W.
Smuggled atom bomb. Wylie, P.
The smuggler. Canning, V.
SMUGGLING
  Canning, V. Man who hated time
  Canning, V. The smuggler
  Gordon, A. Devil and Father Francisco
  Stern, R. G. Present for Minna
Smyth, Emily, 1911-
  The marvel
    Wolfe, D. M. ed. Which grain will
    grow
Snacker. Caldwell, E.
Snake dance. Ford, C.
Snake doctor. Cobb, I. S.
Snake-eyes!! Buckingham, N.
Snake of one's own. Steinbeck, J.
Snake woman and the preacher's wife.
    Brookhouser, F.
SNAKES
  Cobb, I. S. Snake doctor
  Dahl, R. Poison
  Doyle, Sir A. C. Adventure of the speckled
    band

  Holland, R. S. Cobra's hood
  Kipling, R. Reingelder and the German
    flag
  Mrs White
  Steinbeck, J. Snake of one's own
  Stuart, J. Dawn of remembered spring
Snapshot at the President. Porter, W. S.
Snarling Santa Claus. Wylie, P.
Snatching of Bookie Bob. Runyon, D.
Sneider, Vern J. 1916-
  Dumbest man in the army
    Saturday evening post (Periodical) Saturday evening post stories, 1952
  Long way from home
    Argosy (Periodical) Argosy Book of
    adventure stories
Snip; the dog that became a coyote. Franklin, G. C.
SNOBS AND SNOBBISHNESS
  Arnow, H. L. S. Washerwoman's day
  Maugham, W. S. The outstation
Snow, Walter
  Death—in the bag
    Mystery Writers of America, inc.
    Crooks' tour
  Fatal red hair
    Mystery Writers of America, inc.
    Butcher, baker, murder-maker
  Nightmare face
    Mystery Writers of America, inc. 20
    great tales of murder
Snow, William W. 1924-
  The ants
    Wolfe, D. M. ed. Which grain will grow
SNOW
  Aiken, C. P. Silent snow, secret snow
  Bantien, A. M. Emergency
Snow. Grove, F. P.
Snow man. Porter, W. S.
SNOW STORMS
  Garner, H. One mile of ice
  Harte, B. Outcasts of Poker Flat
  Munro, H. H. Name-day
Snowball effect. MacLean, K.
Snowball in July. Queen, E. pseud.
Snowbound Christmas. Aspinwall, M.
The snowfall. Garrigue, J.
Snows of Bardonechhia. Diamant, G.
Snows of Kilimanjaro. Hemingway, E.
Snowshoe Thompson. Fultz, D. M.
SNOWSTORMS. See Snow storms
Snulbug. White, W. A. P.
So help me. Algren, N.
So I'm home again. Walden, A. E.
So many years. Van Doren, M.
So much for the King. Verga, G.
So proudly we hail. Merril, J.
So you won't talk! Runyon, D.
Soap. Farrell, J. T.
Sobbin' women. Benét, S. V.
Sobol, Andreĭ Mikhailovich, 1888-1926
  Last expedition of Baron Feuhbel-Feuhtzenau
    Guerney, B. G. comp. New Russian
    stories

Social sense. Maugham, W. S.
Social triangle. Porter, W. S.
SOCIAL WORKERS
  Auchincloss, L. Edification of Marianne
SOCIALISM
  Fisher, D. F. C. Drop in the bucket
Sociology in serge and straw. Porter, W. S.
SOCRATES
  Alas, L. Cock of Socrates
Socrates. Christopher, J.
SOFAS
  Anderson, E. V. Tapestry extravaganza
Soft-boiled. Stewart, O.
SOFT DRINKS. See Carbonated beverages
Soft voice of the serpent. Gordimer, N.
The sojourner. McCullers, C. S.
Solar plexus. Blish, J.
Solarite. Campbell, J. W.
The soldier. Dahl, R.
Soldier boy. Shaara, M.
Soldier of the realm. Ullman, J. R.
Soldier ran away. Boyle, K.
SOLDIERS
  Bergengruen, W. On presenting arms
  Hemingway, E. Way you'll never be
  Ullman, J. R. Soldier of the realm
            American
  Arico, V. The promotion
  Boyd, T. A. Responsibility
  Boyle, K. Soldier ran away
  Brookhouser, F. The inn was perfect
  Brown, E. L. Hero
  Downey, H. The hunters
  Farrell, J. T. When boyhood dreams
    come true
  Hume, S. T. Shake hands with a murderer
  Landon, B. Advance party
  Lowry, R. J. C. Casualty
  Lowry, R. J. C. Happy New Year,
    kamerades!
  Salinger, J. D. For Esmé—with love and
    squalor
  Schaefer, J. W. Cat nipped
  Shaw, I. Act of faith
  Wasserman, N. A. Stars are black
  Whitmore, S. Lost soldier
  Winter, A. B. Party dress
            British
  Collier, J. Without benefit of Galsworthy
  Downey, H. The hunters
  Goldsmith, O. Disabled soldier
  Kipling, R. Incarnation of Krishna Mulvaney
  Kipling, R. 'Love-o'-women'
  Kipling, R. Man who was
  Kipling, R. On Greenhow Hill
  O'Donovan, M. Guests of the nation
  Shaw, I. Walking wounded
  Taylor, E. Oasis of gaiety
            Carthaginian
  Powers, A. Hannibal's elephants
            English
  See Soldiers—British
            Furloughs
  Lowry, R. J. Law and order
  Montague, M. P. England to America
            German
  Hebel, J. P. The hussar
  Lawrence, D. H. Prussian officer
            Hungarian
  Bergengruen, W. Stabenhaüser
            Polish
  Gellhorn, M. E. Voyage forme la jeunesse
            Roman
  Powers, A. Hannibal's elephants
            Russian
  Shapiro, L. White chalah
SOLDIERS, DISABLED. See Cripples
Soliloquy at dinner. Hutchins, M. P. M.
Solipsist. Brown, F.
Solitaire. Stern, J.
Solitary Dogan. Ready, W. B.
Solitude. Unamuno y Jugo, M. de
Solitude. Williams, B. A.
SOLOMON, KING OF ISRAEL
  Cohn, E. It looks like justice
  Fleg, E. Solomon the King
Solomon the King. Fleg, E.
Sol's little brother. Elam, R. M.
Soman, Florence Jane
  Your heart's out of order
    Stowe, A. comp. It's a date
"Some bum might mistook me for a wrestler." Mitchell, J.
Some can't take it. Fowler, B. B.
Some heroes. Roark, E.
Some like them cold. Lardner, R. W.
Some of father's adventures. Gannett, R. S.
Some "Q" ships. Ritchie, L. A. da C.
Somebody else, not me. Miller, J. D.
Someone like you. Dahl, R.
Somerville, Andrew W. 1900-
  Tale of the old main line
    Moskowitz, S. ed. Great railroad stories
    of the world
Somerville, Edith Anna Œnone, 1861-1949,
    and Martin, Violet Florence, 1865-1915
  Philippa's fox-hunt
    Cerf, B. A. and Moriarty, H. C. eds.
    Anthology of famous British stories
  Trinket's colt
    Creamer, J. B. comp. Twenty-two stories about horses and men
Something for December eighth. Zelver, A.
Something gay and foolish. Sellars, M.
Something green. Brown, F.
Something in common. Hughes, L.
Something lost. Schaefer, J. W.
Something special for Jane. Ross, A. L.
Something terrible, something lovely. Sansom, W.
Something to hide. MacDonald, P.
Something wrong. Stern, J.

Sometimes a man needs a friend. Taber, G. B.

Sommerfield, John
Above the clouds
New writing (Periodical) Best stories

SOMNAMBULISM
Maclaren-Ross, J. This mortal coil

Somnium: or the astronomy of the moon. Kepler, J.

Son of a tinker. Walsh, M.

Son-of-David. Goudge, E.

Son of the sun. London, J.

Song and the sergeant. Porter, W. S.

Song of the flying fish. Chesterton, G. K.

Song of the pewee. Grendon, S.

Song without words. O'Donovan, M.

SONG WRITERS. See Musicians—Composers

SONG WRITING. See Music, Popular (Songs, etc.)—Writing and publishing

SONGS
Bates, H. E. Christmas song

SONS. See Fathers and sons; Mothers and sons

Son's veto. Hardy, T.

Sooth. Steele, W. D.

The soothsayer. Bennett, K.

Sophie Jackson. Winslow, T. S.

Sophistication. Anderson, S.

Sophistication. Jackson, C. R.

Sophomore forward. Peterson, G. M.

Sophy's Christmas dinner. Bunn, H. F.

Sorcerer's apprentice. O'Donovan, M.

Sorcerer's son. Johnson, J. W.

SORCERY. See Magic; Witchcraft

SORORITIES. See Greek letter societies

Sorority. Hogan, A.

SORROW. See Joy and sorrow

Sorrows of Captain Schreiber. Stern, R. G.

Sorrows of Young Werther. Goethe, J. W. von

SOTO, HERNANDO DE, 1500?-1542
Wassermann, J. Gold of Caxamalca

Soul of Laploshka. Munro, H. H.

Soul that mice nibbled up. Kobrin, L.

SOUND
Recording and reproducing
Dahl, R. Sound machine

The sound. Van Vogt, A. E.

Sound and fury. Porter, W. S.

Sound machine. Dahl, R.

Sound of blackmail. Queen, E. pseud.

Sound of gunfire. O'Reilly, J.

Sound of murder. McGivern, W. P.

Sound of thunder. Bradbury, R.

Sound of waiting. Calisher, H.

SOUND PRODUCTION BY ANIMALS
White, S. E. On lying awake at night

SOUPS
Heijermans, H. Shabbes-soup

Source of irritation. Aumonier, S.

Source seven. Gilbert, M. F.

Souse of the border. Gilpatric, G.

THE SOUTH. See Southern States

SOUTH AFRICA. See Africa, South

SOUTH AMERICAN INDIANS. See Indians of South America

SOUTH CAROLINA

Charleston
Holland, R. S. Pirates of Charles Town harbor
Steele, W. D. Can't cross Jordan by myself

Sullivan's Island
Poe, E. A. The gold-bug

SOUTH SEA ISLANDS
Crump, I. Pirate island
London, J. Son of the sun
Maugham, W. S. Red
Morris, G. Back there in the grass

South toward home. Jackson, M. W.

SOUTHERN DIALECT. See Dialect stories—Southern

SOUTHERN STATES
Clayton, J. B. Ride a pale ghost into night and time
Faulkner, W. The bear
Faulkner, W. Rose for Emily
Fitzgerald, F. S. K. Ice palace
Gordon, C. Forest of the South
Gordon, C. Old Red
Harris, G. W. Sut Lovingood; 8 stories
Humphrey, W. Fresh snow
King, M. P. Honey house
Lytle, A. N. Jericho, Jericho, Jericho
Mohler, C. Jesus complex
Moody, M. H. Ghost of General Jackson
Patton, F. G. Let it rest
Porter, K. A. Old mortality
Porter, W. S. Two renegades
Street, J. H. I am not a stranger
Tolbert, F. X. Last rebel yell
See also names of individual Southern states

SOUTHERNERS. See Southern States

Southpaw switch. Regli, A. C.

Souto Alabarce, Arturo
Coyote 13
De Onís, H. ed. Spanish stories and tales

Space. Buchan, J. 1st baron Tweedsmuir

SPACE AND TIME
Asimov, I. Red Queen's race
Blish, J. Mistake inside
Buchan, J. 1st baron Tweedsmuir. Space
Heinlein, R. A. Elsewhen
Jenkins, W. F. Sidewise in time
See also Time

Space jockey. Heinlein, R. A.

Space Lane cadet. Hallstead, W. F.

Space rating. Berryman, J.

SPACE SHIPS
Bradbury, R. Kaleidoscope
Carr, R. S. Morning star
Jameson, M. Bullard of the space partol; 7 stories
Jenkins, W. F. First contact

SPACE SHIPS—*Continued*
  Jenkins, W. F. The journey
  Jones, R. F. Tools of the trade
  Sloane, W. M. Let nothing you dismay
  Van Vogt, A. E. Great engine
  Wilcox, D. Voyage that lasted six hundred years
    See also Rocket ships
SPACE STATIONS
  Del Rey, L. Idealist
SPACE TRAVEL. See Interplanetary voyages
SPACEMEN. See Air pilots
Spain, Nancy, 1917-
  Bewilderment of Snake McKoy
    Asquith, Lady C. M. E. C. ed. Book of modern ghosts
SPAIN
  Gunterman, B. L. Golden pitcher
    17th century
  Wilde, O. Birthday of the Infanta
    19th century
  Stevenson, R. L. Olalla
  Valle-Inclán, R. del. My sister Antonia
    20th century
  Charteris, L. Juan-les-Pins: the Spanish cow
  Hemingway, E. Capital of the world
    20th Century—Civil War, 1936-1939
  Bates, R. Forty-third division
  Lowry, R. J. C. Defense in University City
  Sartre, J. P. The wall
  Ullman, J. R. Chicken dinner
    Andalusia
  Maugham, W. S. Man from Glasgow
    Barcelona
  Spender, S. Burning cactus
    Granada
  Paget, V. Virgin of the Seven Daggers
    Seville
  Maugham, W. S. Happy man
  Maugham, W. S. The mother
  Maugham, W. S. Point of honour
  Maugham, W. S. Romantic young lady
    Toledo
  Cervantes Saavedra, M. de. Call of the blood
SPANIARDS IN CALIFORNIA
  Atherton, G. F. H. Pearls of Loreto
  Harte, B. Knight-errant of the foothills
Spanish blood. Hughes, L.
SPANISH CIVIL WAR. See Spain—20th century—Civil War, 1936-1939
SPANISH INQUISITION. See Inquisition
Sparrows in Madison Square. Porter, W. S.
Spawn. Miller, P. S.
SPEAKERS. See Orators
Speaking of characters. Dachs, D.
Special assignment. Patterson, T. C.
Special delivery. Collier, J.

Special story. Yaffe, J.
Specialist. Sheckley, R.
Specialty of the house. Ellin, S.
Speckled band. Doyle, Sir A. C.
The **spectacles.** Poe, E. A.
Spectator sport. MacDonald, J. D.
The **specter.** Maupassant, G. de
Specter general. Cogswell, T. R.
Spector, Mordecai, 1858-1925
  Meal for the poor
    Howe, I. and Greenberg, E. eds. Treasury of Yiddish stories
    Same as: Strike of the Schnorrers
  Strike of the Schnorrers
    Ausubel, N. ed. Treasury of Jewish humor
    Same as: Meal for the poor
SPECULATION
  Davis, S. P. Mystery of the Savage sump
  Norris, F. Deal in wheat
SPECULATION, LAND. See Land speculation
Speculations of Jefferson Thorpe. Leacock, S.
SPEECHES, ADDRESSES, ETC.
  Andrews, M. R. Perfect tribute
  Spring, H. Sabre in the hand
SPEED
  Fenner, P. R. comp. Speed, speed, speed; 12 stories
Spektor, Mordche. See Spector, Mordecai
Spelling bee. Chinn, L. C.
SPELLING BEES
  Chinn, L. C. Spelling bee
SPELLING REFORM
  Edwards, D. Meihem in ce klasrum
Spence cooperates. Caldwell, E.
Spencer, Gilmore
  Mulatto flair
    Ford, N. A. and Faggett, H. L. eds. Best short stories by Afro-American writers (1925-1950)
Spender, Stephen, 1909-
  Burning cactus
    Cory, D. W. pseud. comp. 21 variations on a theme
Spendthrifts. Portor, L. S.
Sperry, Armstrong, 1897-
  Black Falcon
    Fenner, P. R. comp. Pirates, pirates, pirates
  Buffalo and Injuns
    Fenner, P. R. comp. Indians, Indians, Indians
  Call it courage
    Fenner, P. R. comp. Stories of the sea
  Flying Cloud in the Roaring Forties
    Fenner, P. R. comp. Stories of the sea
Spettigue, Douglas, 1930-
  Asters for Teddie
    Weaver, R. and James, H. eds. Canadian short stories
The **sphinx.** Poe, E. A.
Sphinx apple. Porter, W. S.
Spider, spider. Aiken, C. P.
SPIDERS
  Porges, A. The fly
  Wells, H. G. Valley of spiders

Spiegel, Isaiah, 1906-
  Ghetto dog
    Howe, I. and Greenberg, E. eds. Treasury of Yiddish stories
SPIES
  Aumonier, S. Source of irritation
  Maugham, W. S. Giulia Lazzari
  Maugham, W. S. Hairless Mexican
  Maugham, W. S. His Excellency
  Maugham, W. S. Miss King
  Maugham, W. S. Mr Harrington's washing
  Maugham, W. S. The traitor
  Noyes, A. Uncle Hyacinth
  Silone, I. The trap
Spike. Bendrodt, J. C.
Spiller, Burton L.
  Net profit
    Dachs, D. ed. Treasury of sports humor
Spilo, Robert, 1925?-
  Big Ed
    American vanguard, 1953
SPINSTERS
  Anderson, S. Adventure
  Ashley, E. L. Aunt Lil
  Bowe, E. New house
  Brush, K. I. Good Wednesday
  De La Roche, M. Auntimay
  Fisher, D. F. C. Drop in the bucket
  Freeman, M. E. W. New England nun
  Goyen, W. Her breath upon the window-pane
  Mansfield, K. Daughters of the late colonel
  Maugham, W. S. Vessel of wrath
  Maugham, W. S. Winter cruise
  Singmaster, E. Little and unknown
  Sutro, A. Bread on the waters
  Welty, E. Asphodel
  Welty, E. Clytie
  Wilson, A. Little companion
  Winslow, T. S. Misses Grant
Spire, André, 1868-
  Rabbi and the siren
    Leftwich, J. ed. Yisröel. 1952 ed.
Spirit dope. Foote, J. T.
Spirits. Gally, J. W.
SPIRITUALISM
  Ford, J. L. Spiritualist's tale
  O'Brien, F.-J. Diamond lens
Spiritualist's tale. Ford, J. L.
SPITE. See Revenge
Splendid fellow. Bottome, P.
Split cherry tree. Stuart, J.
Split second. Du Maurier, D.
Spofford, Harriet Elizabeth (Prescott) 1835-1921
  Circumstance
    Cuff, R. P. ed. American short story survey
Spoiled cake. Renard, J.
Spoiled priest. Sheehan, P. A.
SPOILS SYSTEM. See Corruption (in politics)
Spooks of the valley. Jones, L. C.
Spooner. Farjeon, E.
SPOONERISMS
  Queen, E. pseud. "My queer Dean!"

Sport of destiny. Schiller, J. C. F. von
Sporting blood. Wylie, P.
SPORTS
  Argosy (Periodical) Argosy Book of sports stories; 20 stories
  Chute, B. J. Teen-age sports parade; 11 stories
  Coombs, C. L. Teen-age champion sports stories; 18 stories
  Dachs, D. ed. Treasury of sports humor; 36 stories
  Herzberg, M. J. comp. Treasure chest of sport stories; 19 stories
  Newhouse, E. Bronze thing
  Owen, F. ed. Teen-age victory parade; 13 stories
  Owen, F. ed. Teen-age winter sports stories; 16 stories
    See also Track athletics; and names of particular sports, e.g. Baseball, Golf; etc.
The sportsman. Bond, N. S.
Spot in history. Hall, J. B.
Spotted horses. Faulkner, W.
Sprague De Camp, Lyon. See De Camp, Lyon Sprague
Spring, Howard, 1889-
  Sabre in the hand
    Brentano, F. ed. The word lives on
SPRING
  Porter, W. S. Easter of the soul
SPRING CLEANING. See House cleaning
Spring evening. Farrell, J. T.
Spring fever. Collier, J.
Spring fever. Davis, D. S.
Spring flight. Irwin, I. H.
Spring over Brooklyn. Gold, Z.
Springer, Sherwood
  No Land of Nod
    Startling stories (Periodical) Best from Startling stories
Springfield fox. Seton, E. T.
Springtime à la carte. Porter, W. S.
Spruce Point mystery. Leighton, M. C.
Spry old character. Taylor, E.
Spur piece. Barr, J. pseud.
Spurs for Antonia. Eyre, K. W.
Square egg. Munro, H. H.
Squaring the circle. Porter, W. S.
The squash. Bergelson, D.
Squaw fever. Gulick, G. C.
Squire Dinwiddy. Caldwell, E.
Squires, James Radcliffe. See Squires, Radcliffe
Squires, Radcliffe, 1917-
  Baby buntings
    Story (Periodical) Story; no. 2
Squirrel who was scared. Tracy, D.
SQUIRRELS
  Tracy, D. Squirrel who was scared
Squirrels have bright eyes. Collier, J.
Squirt and the monkey. Stout, R.
Sredni Vashtar. Munro, H. H.
SRL ad. Matheson, R.
Stabbing in the streets. Lipsky, E.

Stabenhaüser. Bergengruen, W.
STABLEMEN
  Collins, W. Dream-woman
Stacey Bell. Van Doren, M.
Stafford, Jean, 1915-
  Between the porch and the altar
    Stafford, J. Children are bored on
    Sunday
  Bleeding heart
    Stafford, J. Children are bored on
    Sunday
  Children are bored on Sunday
    Stafford, J. Children are bored on
    Sunday
  Country love story
    Prize stories of 1951
    Stafford, J. Children are bored on
    Sunday
  Echo and the nemesis
    Stafford, J. Children are bored on
    Sunday
  Healthiest girl in town
    Best American short stories, 1952
  Home front
    Stafford, J. Children are bored on
    Sunday
  Interior castle
    Best of the Best American short stories,
    1915-1950
    Stafford, J. Children are bored on
    Sunday
  The maiden
    Stafford, J. Children are bored on
    Sunday
  Modest proposal
    Stafford, J. Children are bored on
    Sunday
  The nemesis
    Best American short stories, 1951
    Ludwig, J. B. and Poirier, W. R. eds.
    Stories, British and American
  A reunion
    Swallow, A. ed. Anchor in the sea
  Shorn lamb
    Best American short stories, 1954
    Prize stories, 1954
  Summer day
    Stafford, J. Children are bored on
    Sunday
  Winter's tale
    Aswell, M. L. W. ed. New short novels
STAGE-COACH LINES
  Harte, B. Dick Boyle's business card
  Harte, B. Ingénue of the Sierras
  Harte, B. Miggles
  Haycox, E. Stage to Lordsburg
STAGE LIFE. See Theater and stage life
Stage station. Haycox, E.
Stage to Lordsburg. Haycox, E.
Stage to Yuma. DeVries, M.
Staggered holiday. Sitwell, Sir O. bart.
STAGS. See Deer
Stair trick. Clingerman, M.
The stake. Munro, H. H.
Stalker & Co. Bonner, P. H.
Stalking shadow. Small, S. H.
Stalled ox. Munro, H. H.

Stallings, Laurence, 1894-
  Vale of tears
    Grayson, C. ed. Fourth round
Stampeding of Lady Bastable. Munro, H. H.
Stan the killer. Simenon, G.
Stancourt, Louis Joseph
  Vacant cross
    Thinker's digest (Periodical) Spoiled
    priest, and other stories
Stand-in. Wilson, B.
Stand to horse. Downey, F. D.
Standish, Burt L. pseud. See Patten, Gilbert
Standish, Robert, pseud. See Gerahty, Digby
  George
Stangland, A. G.
  Ancient brain
    Margulies, L. and Friend, O. J. eds.
    From off this world
Stanley, Dave, pseud. See Dachs, David
Stanley, Fay Grissom
  Last day of all
    Mystery Writers of America, inc. 20
    great tales of murder
Stanley, John Berchman, 1910-
  Matter of spelling
    Boys' life (Periodical) Boys' life Adven-
    ture stories
Stanley who was adopted. Strain, F. B.
Stanton, Will
  Barney
    Magazine of fantasy and science fiction.
    Best from Fantasy and science fiction;
    [1st ser]
  Town without a straight man
    Queen, E. pseud. ed. Queen's awards:
    8th ser.
Stapledon, Olaf. See Stapledon, William Olaf
Stapledon, William Olaf, 1886-
  Flying men
    Derleth, A. W. ed. Beyond time & space
  Last terrestrials
    Kuebler, H. W. ed. Treasury of science
    fiction classics
  The Martians
    Kuebler, H. W. ed. Treasury of science
    fiction classics
The Star. Keller, D. H.
The star. Wells, H. G.
Star begotten. Wells, H. G.
Star, Bright. Clifton, M.
Star buck. Kilcrin, I.
Star ducks. Brown, B.
Star dummy. White, W. A. P.
Star gypsies. Gresham, W. L.
Star light, star bright. Bester, A.
Star-linked. Fyfe, H. B.
Star mouse. Brown, F.
Star of Siam. Schneider, G. W.
Star producers. Charteris, L.
Star quality. Coward, N. P.
Starbride. White, W. A. P.
Stark, Irwin, 1912-
  Shock treatment
    Ribalow, H. U. ed. These your children

STARS
Brown, F. Pi in the sky
Derleth, A. W. McIlvaine's star
Porter, W. S. Phoebe

Stars are black. Wasserman, N.

Stars are the Styx. Waldo, E. H.

Stars in the sky. Silvers, E. R.

Start from scratch. Knipscheer, J. M. W.

Start in life. Kelly, R. G.

STARVATION
Saroyan, W. Daring young man on the flying trapeze

Starzl, R. F.
Hornets of space
Margulies, L. and Friend, O. J. eds. From off this world

STATE DEPARTMENT. See United States. State Department

State of mind. Aiken, C. P.

Statement of the case. Doyle, Sir A. C.

Stations of the Cross. Lemelin, R.

Statistics. Wendroff, Z.

STATUE OF LIBERTY, NEW YORK
Porter, W. S. Lady higher up

STATUES
Arico, V. Merchant's monument
Milton, M. E. Favor granted

The **statues.** Priestley, J. B.

Status quondam. Miller, P. S.

Steady like a rock. Bond, N. S.

STEALING. See Shoplifting; Theft; Thieves

Stebel, Sidney
Number to remember
Story (Periodical) Story; no. 3

Steel, Flora Annie (Webster) 1847-1929
Barber's clever wife
Fenner, P. R. comp. Fools and funny fellows

Steel brother. Dickson, G. R.

Steel cat. Collier, J.

STEEL WORKERS
Heyliger, W. Steelman's nerve

Steele, Flora Annie (Webster) See Steel, Flora Annie (Webster)

Steele, Wilbur Daniel, 1886-
Autumn bloom
Steele, W. D. Full cargo
Black road
Steele, W. D. Full cargo
Blue murder
Grayson, C. ed. Fourth round
Brother's keeper
Steele, W. D. Full cargo
Bubbles
First-prize stories, 1919-1954
By appointment
Steele, W. D. Full cargo
Can't cross Jordan by myself
First-prize stories, 1919-1954
Ching, Ching, Chinaman
Steele, W. D. Full cargo
Devil of a fellow
Steele, W. D. Full cargo
Fe-fi-fo-fum
Steele, W. D. Full cargo

For they know not what they do
Cuff, R. P. ed. American short story survey
Gray goose
Steele, W. D. Full cargo
How beautiful with shoes
Best of the Best American short stories, 1915-1950
Blodgett, H. W. ed. Story survey. 1953 ed.
Lady-killer
Queen, E. pseud. ed. Queen's awards: 5th ser.
Luck
Steele, W. D. Full cargo
Man and boy
Steele, W. D. Full cargo
Man who saw through heaven
Burrell, J. A. and Cerf, B. A. eds. Anthology of famous American stories
Never anything that fades
Steele, W. D. Full cargo
Renegade
Steele, W. D. Full cargo
Sailor! Sailor!
Steele, W. D. Full cargo
Six dollars
Steele, W. D. Full cargo
Sooth
Steele, W. D. Full cargo
The thinker
Steele, W. D. Full cargo
Two seconds
Steele, W. D. Full cargo
Way with women
Steele, W. D. Full cargo
Yellow cat
Shaw, H. and Bement, D. Reading the short story
Steele, W. D. Full cargo

Steelman's nerve. Heyliger, W.

STEEPLECHASING. See Horse racing

Stefánsson, Vilhjálmur, 1879-
Seal hunting
Andrews, R. C. ed. My favorite stories of the great outdoors

Stegner, Wallace Earle, 1909-
Balance his, swing yours
Stegner, W. E. Women on the wall
Berry patch
Stegner, W. E. Women on the wall
Beyond the glass mountain
Stegner, W. E. Women on the wall
Blue-winged teal
Abell, E. ed. American accent
First-prize stories, 1919-1954
Prize stories of 1950
Buglesong
Stegner, W. E. Women on the wall
Butcher bird
Stegner, W. E. Women on the wall
West, R. B. and Stallman, R. W. eds. Art of modern fiction
The Chink
Stegner, W. E. Women on the wall
Chip off the old block
Stegner, W. E. Women on the wall
The colt
Stegner, W. E. Women on the wall
Double corner
Stegner, W. E. Women on the wall

Stegner, Wallace E.—*Continued*
Goin' to town
  Stegner, W. E. Women on the wall
Hostage
  Stegner, W. E. Women on the wall
In the twilight
  Stegner, W. E. Women on the wall
Saw gang
  Stegner, W. E. Women on the wall
Sweetness of the twisted apples
  Stegner, W. E. Women on the wall
The traveler
  Best American short stories, 1952
Two rivers
  Stegner, W. E. Women on the wall
View from the balcony
  Stegner, W. E. Women on the wall
The volcano
  Stegner, W. E. Women on the wall
Women on the wall
  Best of the Best American short stories, 1915-1950
  Stegner, W. E. Women on the wall
  Stegner, W. E.; Scowcroft, R. and Ilyin, B. eds. Writer's art

Stein, Gertrude, 1874-1946
Bartholomew Arnold
  Stein, G. Mrs Reynolds, and five earlier novelettes
Brim Beauvais
  Stein, G. Mrs Reynolds, and five earlier novelettes
Good Anna
  Burrell, J. A. and Cerf, B. A. eds. Anthology of famous American stories
Hotel François Ier
  Stein, G. Mrs Reynolds, and five earlier novelettes
Marguerite
  Stein, G. Mrs Reynolds, and five earlier novelettes
What does she see when she shuts her eyes
  Stein, G. Mrs Reynolds, and five earlier novelettes

Stein, Mildred
First sad facts
  Wolfe, D. M. ed. Which grain will grow

Steinbeck, John, 1902-
The chrysanthemums
  Foerster, N. ed. American poetry and prose. 1952 ed.
The gift
  Stauffer, R. M.; Cunningham, W. H. and Sullivan, C. J. eds. Adventures in modern literature
Leader of the people
  Davis, C. B. ed. Eyes of boyhood
  Day, A. G. ed. Greatest American short stories
  Lamb, L. ed. Family book of best loved short stories
  Schramm, W. L. ed. Great short stories
  Shaw, H. and Bement, D. Reading the short story
  Short, R. W. and Sewall, R. B. eds. Short stories for study. 1950 ed.

Miracle of Tepayac
  Bachelor, J. M.; Henry, R. L. and Salisbury, R. eds. Current thinking and writing; 2d ser.
  Gable, M. Sister, ed. Many-colored fleece
  Grayson, C. ed. Fourth round
The murder
  Queen, E. pseud. ed. Literature of crime
Red pony
  Burrell, J. A. and Cerf, B. A. eds. Anthology of famous American stories
Snake of one's own
  Esquire (Periodical) Girls from Esquire

Steinberg, Yehudah, 1863-1908
Rabbi Itzik the fool
  Ausubel, N. ed. Treasury of Jewish humor
Reb Anshel the golden
  Ausubel, N. ed. Treasury of Jewish humor

Stendhal, De, pseud. See Beyle, Marie Henri

STENOGRAPHERS
Winslow, T. S. Obsession

STEPBROTHERS
Gaskell, E. C. S. Half-brothers

STEPFATHERS
Kaufman, A. Anchor me in mire

Stephens, James, 1882-1950
The horses
  Blodgett, H. W. ed. Story survey. 1953 ed.
Three lovers who lost
  Cerf, B. A. and Moriarty, H. C. eds. Anthology of famous British stories
The threepenny-piece
  Magazine of fantasy and science fiction. Best from Fantasy and science fiction; [1st ser]

Stephenson, Carl, 1886-
Leiningen versus the ants
  Certner, S. and Henry, G. H. eds. Short stories for our times

Stephenson, Carol, pseud. See Isaacson, Bernice Kavinoky

The stepmother. Jackson, M. W.
STEPMOTHERS
Jackson, M. W. The stepmother

Sterling, Stewart, pseud. See Winchell, Prentice

Stern, Daniel, 1928-
Conversation in Prague
  American vanguard, 1952

Stern, Gladys Browyn, 1890-
Cinderella's sister
  Leftwich, J. ed. Yisröel. 1952 ed.

Stern, James, 1904-
Broken leg
  Stern, J. Man who was loved
Face behind the bar
  Stern, J. Man who was loved
Idolater of Degas
  Stern, J. Man who was loved
Man who was loved
  Stern, J. Man who was loved
Next door to death
  New writing (Periodical) Best stories
  Stern, J. Man who was loved

Stern, James—*Continued*
Our father
Stern, J. Man who was loved
Solitaire
Stern, J. Man who was loved
Something wrong
Stern, J. Man who was loved
Travellers' tears
Stern, J. Man who was loved
Two men
Stern, J. Man who was loved
Under the beech tree
Stern, J. Man who was loved
Woman who was loved
Stern, J. Man who was loved

Stern, Richard G. 1928-
Present for Minna
This week magazine. This week's short-short stories
Sorrows of Captain Schreiber
Prize stories, 1954

Stettner, Stella, 1923-
Costa Rican counterpoint
American vanguard, 1952
Summer place
American vanguard, 1953

Steve and Sarah and Cyril. Willingham, C.

Stevens, James, 1892-
Jerkline
Grayson, C. ed. Fourth round

Stevenson, C. Leigh
Over the line
Ford, N. A. and Faggett, H. L. eds. Best short stories by Afro-American writers (1925-1950)

Stevenson, Robert Louis, 1850-1894
Beach of Falesá
Stevenson, R. L. Strange case of Dr Jekyll and Mr Hyde, and other stories
Body-snatcher
Stevenson, R. L. Strange case of Dr Jekyll and Mr Hyde, and other stories
Bottle imp
Stevenson, R. L. Strange case of Dr Jekyll and Mr Hyde, and other stories
Character of dogs
Andrews, R. C. ed. My favorite stories of the great outdoors
Isle of voices
Stevenson, R. L. Strange case of Dr Jekyll and Mr Hyde, and other stories
Lodging for the night
Blodgett, H. W. ed. Story survey. 1953 ed.
Cerf, B. A. and Moriarty, H. C. eds. Anthology of famous British stories
Lamb, L. ed. Family book of best loved short stories
Stevenson, R. L. Strange case of Dr Jekyll and Mr Hyde, and other stories
Markheim
Neider, C. ed. Great short stories from the world's literature
Queen, E. pseud. ed. Literature of crime
Stevenson, R. L. Strange case of Dr Jekyll and Mr Hyde, and other stories
Merry men
Stevenson, R. L. Strange case of Dr Jekyll and Mr Hyde, and other stories

Olalla
Stevenson, R. L. Strange case of Dr Jekyll and Mr Hyde, and other stories
Pavilion on the links
Stevenson, R. L. Strange case of Dr Jekyll and Mr Hyde, and other stories
Sire de Malétroit's door
Cerf, B. A. and Moriarty, H. C. eds. Anthology of famous British stories
O'Faoláin, S. The short story
Stevenson, R. L. Strange case of Dr Jekyll and Mr Hyde, and other stories
Strange case of Dr Jekyll and Mr Hyde
Stevenson, R. L. Strange case of Dr Jekyll and Mr Hyde, and other stories
Thrawn Janet
Stevenson, R. L. Strange case of Dr Jekyll and Mr Hyde, and other stories
Treasure of Franchard
Stevenson, R. L. Strange case of Dr Jekyll and Mr Hyde, and other stories
Will o' the mill
Stevenson, R. L. Strange case of Dr Jekyll and Mr Hyde, and other stories

STEWART, ALEXANDER TWINEY, 1803-1876
Benson, T. Bones of A. T. Stewart

Stewart, George Rippey, 1895-
Death of the glen
Bachelor, J. M.; Henry, R. L. and Salisbury, R. eds. Current thinking and writing; 2d ser.

Stewart, Ollie, 1906-
End of a dream
Ford, N. A. and Faggett, H. L. eds. Best short stories by Afro-American writers (1925-1950)
I shall not be moved
Ford, N. A. and Faggett, H. L. eds. Best short stories by Afro-American writers (1925-1950)
Leg man
Ford, N. A. and Faggett, H. L. eds. Best short stories by Afro-American writers (1925-1950)
No greater love
Ford, N. A. and Faggett, H. L. eds. Best short stories by Afro-American writers (1925-1950)
Soft-boiled
Ford, N. A. and Faggett, H. L. eds. Best short stories by Afro-American writers (1925-1950)

Stewart, Ramona, 1922-
The promise
Best American short stories, 1950

Stewart, Will, pseud. See Williamson, Jack

Stick up. French, F. C.

Stickit minister. Crockett, S. R.

Stifter, Adalbert, 1805-1868
Rock crystal
Pick, R. ed. German stories and tales
Talbot, D. ed. Treasury of mountaineering stories

Still, James, 1906-
Job's tears
Blodgett, H. W. ed. Story survey. 1953 ed.
Master time
Best American short stories, 1950
Mrs Razor
Summers, H. S. ed. Kentucky story

Still, James—*Continued*
Ride on the short dog
Abell, E. ed. American accent
Best American short stories, 1952
Still moment. Welty, E.
Still, still so. Van Doren, M.
Stinetorf, Louise (Allender) 1900-
Refugee village
Hazeltine, A. I. comp. Selected stories
for teen-agers
STINGINESS. See Misers
Stoakes, Harold R.
Turtles played the hares
Boys' life (Periodical) Boys' life Adventure stories
Stock, George A. 1897-
Please, Mr Patron
Oberfirst, R. ed. 1954 anthology of best
original short-shorts
STOCK BROKERS. See Brokers
Stock chapter. Davis, S. P.
STOCK EXCHANGE
Kornbluth, C. M. Dominoes
Stockbroker's clerk. Doyle, Sir A. C.
Stocker, Joseph
I rode a tornado
Fenner, P. R. comp. Speed, speed, speed
The **stocking.** Kneale, N.
Stockton, Frank Richard, 1834-1902
Christmas shadrach
Lohan, R. and Lohan, M. eds. New
Christmas treasury
Lady or the tiger?
Burrell, J. A. and Cerf, B. A. eds. Anthology of famous American stories
Day, A. G. ed. Greatest American short
stories
Lamb, L. ed. Family book of best loved
short stories
Scribner treasury
Tale of negative gravity
Derleth, A. W. ed. Beyond time &
space
Widow's cruise
Eaton, H. T. ed. Short stories
Stockwell, Joseph, 1925-
In the borderland
Stanford short stories, 1953
The **stoic.** Crowell, C. T.
Stolen bacillus. Wells, H. G.
Stolen body. Wells, H. G.
Stolen centuries. Kline, O. A.
Stolen Christmas. Sheldon, C. M.
Stolen letter. Collins, W.
Stolen railroad train. James, M.
Stolen white elephant. Clemens, S. L.
Stone, Leslie F.
Rape of the solar system
Wollheim, D. A. comp. Flight into space
Stone, Wilbur J. 1889-
Retribution
Oberfirst, R. ed. 1954 anthology of best
original short-shorts
STONE AGE. See Prehistoric times
Stone and a spear. Jones, R. F.

STONE-CUTTERS
Hawthorne, N. Ethan Brand
MacMahon, B. Corn was springing
Stone of the sages. Pratt, F. and De Camp,
L. S.
The **stones.** Corkery, D.
Stong, Philip Duffield, 1899-
Censored, the goat
Fenner, P. R. comp. Fun! Fun! Fun!
Stonier, George Walter, 1903-
Memoirs of a ghost
Asquith, Lady C. M. E. C. ed. Book of
modern ghosts
Stood up. Mason, T.
Stop, look, listen. Murdock, R. M.
Stop me if you've heard it. Coward, N. P.
Stop on the way to Texas. Dorrance, W. A.
Stop that fight! Katkov, N.
STOREKEEPERS. See Merchants
STORES
Anderson, S. "Queer"
Chekhov, A. P. History of a business enterprise
McNulty, J. Mrs Carmody's store
STORES, DEPARTMENT. See Department stores
STORKS
Thackeray, W. M. Sultan stork
Storm, Theodor, 1817-1888
Immensee
Lange, V. ed. Great German short
novels and stories
Veronika
Blodgett, H. W. ed. Story survey.
1953 ed.
The **storm.** Bowen, E.
The **storm.** Ehrenburg, I. G.
The **storm.** Farley, W.
The **storm.** Hearn, L.
The **storm.** Stuart, J.
Storm over second. Holder, W.
Storm struck. Corkery, D.
Storm warning. Wollheim, D. A.
Storm winds. Rochlin, R. J.
STORMALONG, ALFRED BULLTOP
Shapiro, I. How Old Stormalong captured
Mocha Dick
STORMS
Crane, S. Men in the storm
Harte, B. Outcasts of Poker Flat
Kuehn, S. The hunt
Lamberton, L. Sleet storm
Lane, G. C. Ensign Carson, USCGR
Lindquist, W. Last-Light Channel
Melville, H. Benito Cereno
Reynolds, J. M. and McCormick, H. P.
Through Twelve-League Labyrinth
Rochlin, R. J. Storm winds
Verga, G. Ugly weather
Vetter, M. M. Captain Kit
Welty, E. The winds
See also Hurricanes; Snow storms
A **story.** Hameln, Glückel of
The **story.** Michener, J. A.
Story coldly told. Benson, S.

Story of a farm girl. Maupassant, G. de
Story of a masterpiece. James, H.
Story of a New York house. Bunner, H. C.
Story of a piebald horse. Hudson, W. H.
Story of a year. James, H.
Story of Dr MacLure. Watson, J.
Story of Don Juan. Pritchett, V. S.
Story of Krespel. Hoffmann, E. T. A.
Story of land and sea. Dunsany, E. J. M. D. P. 18th baron
Story of Mathias. Barker, A. L.
Story of my cats. Fabre, J. H. C.
Story of my death. Bosis, L. de
Story of Paula. Grimson, M. S.
Story of Pompeii. Blackburn, E. R.
Story of St Vespaluus. Munro, H. H.
Story of the bald-headed man. Doyle, Sir A. C.
Story of the cantor. Agnon, S. J.
Story of the days to come. Wells, H. G.
Story of the just Casper and the fair Annie. Brentano, C. M.
Story of the Saint Joseph's ass. Verga, G.
Story of the stone age. Wells, H. G.
Story of Toby. Melville, H.
Story of Webster. Wodehouse, P. G.
Story-teller. Munro, H. H.
STORY-TELLING
  Munro, H. H. The story-teller
  Parker, J. R. Once upon a time
  Poe, E. A. Thousand-and-second tale of Scheherazade
STORY WITHIN A STORY
  Clemens, S. L. Celebrated jumping frog of Calaveras County
  Conrad, J. Heart of darkness
  Davis, R. H. In the fog
  Gally, J. W. Frozen truth
  Grimson, M. S. Faith, hope and charity
  Harvey, W. F. Vicar's web
  Horwitz, J. Poor people
  Jewett, S. O. Courting of Sister Wisby
  Kipling, R. Incarnation of Krishna Mulvaney
  Kipling, R. 'Love-o'-women'
  Kipling, R. On Greenhow Hill
  Lagerkvist, P. F. Eternal smile
  Maugham, W. S. Red
  Prado, P. Laugh in the desert
  Pratt, F. and De Camp, L. S. Tales from Gavagan's bar; 23 stories
  Priestley, J. B. The other place
  Rabinowitz, S. Tit for tat
  Salinger, J. D. Laughing man
  Sansom, W. Crabfroth
  Walsh, M. Thomasheen James and the dictation machine
  West, R. B. Last of the grizzly bears
Stoumen, Louis Clyde
  Blond dog
    Story (Periodical) Story; no. 1
Stout, Rex, 1886-
  The cop-killer
    Stout, R. Triple jeopardy
  Cop's gift
    Mystery Writers of America, inc. Butcher, baker, murder-maker

Home to roost
  Stout, R. Triple jeopardy
Squirt and the monkey
  Stout, R. Triple jeopardy
Stout gentleman. Irving, W.
STOWAWAYS
  Porter, W. S. Shamrock and the palm
  Pratt, F. Pardon my mistake
  Rocklynne, R. Jaywalker
  Subercaseaux, B. Salt sea
Strachey, Julia
  Pioneer city
    New writing (Periodical) Best stories
Straight flush. Maugham, W. S.
Straight life. Petracca, J.
Strain, Frances (Bruce)
  Babs and Phil who eloped
    Strain, F. B. "But you don't understand"
  Barney whose life was "all work and no play"
    Strain, F. B. "But you don't understand"
  Clumpy who was all arms and legs
    Strain, F. B. "But you don't understand"
  Cynthia who was afraid not to pet
    Strain, F. B. "But you don't understand"
  Jimmy who thought he "inherited bad blood"
    Strain, F. B. "But you don't understand"
  Josie who took things
    Strain, F. B. "But you don't understand"
  Linda who daydreamed
    Strain, F. B. "But you don't understand"
  Mitzie who was young for her age
    Strain, F. B. "But you don't understand"
  Pat who was afraid of boys
    Strain, F. B. "But you don't understand"
  Shorty who wished he were taller
    Strain, F. B. "But you don't understand"
  Stanley who was adopted
    Strain, F. B. "But you don't understand"
  Tommy who was overmanaged
    Strain, F. B. "But you don't understand"
Strange bed. Lieber, W. M.
Strange case of Dr Jekyll and Mr Hyde. Stevenson, R. L.
Strange case of John Kingman. Jenkins, W. F.
Strange crime of John Boulnois. Chesterton, G. K.
Strange event at St Brendan's. Lieberman, R.
Strange girl. Van Doren, M.
Strange harvest. Wandrei, D.
Strange house. Penglase, F.
Strange little piper. Bennett, R.
Strange men. Elam, R. M.
Strange moonlight. Aiken, C. P.
Strange notion. Helfer, H.

Strange orchid. Wells, H. G.
Strange story. Ekbergh, I. D.
Strange story. Porter, W. S.
Strange story of Jonathan Small. Doyle, Sir
  A. C.
The **stranger.** Haycox, E.
The **stranger.** Hughes, R. A. W.
The **stranger.** Rilke, R. M.
Stranger arrives on Halfaday. Hendryx,
  J. B.
Stranger in the village. Gibbs, Sir P. H.
Strangers and pilgrims. De La Mare, W. J.
Strangers in the evening. Cheshire, G.
Stranger's note
  Lin, Y. ed. Famous Chinese short stories
Strasser, Sheila
  Case of the psychoanalyst
    Story (Periodical) Story; no. 2
Stratagem of Joshua. Bradford, R.
The **strategist.** Munro, H. H.
STRAWBERRIES
  Caldwell, E. Strawberry season
Strawberry season. Caldwell, E.
Strawberry window. Bradbury, R.
The **strawstack.** Knister, R.
The **stray.** Kalisman, H. H.
The **stream.** Young, E. H.
STREAM OF CONSCIOUSNESS
  Aiken, C. P. By my troth, Nerissa!
  Aiken, C. P. Field of flowers
  Aiken, C. P. Gehenna
  Aiken, C. P. Man alone at lunch
  Aiken, C. P. State of mind
  Bellow, S. Sermon by Doctor Pep
  Bruggen, C. de H. van. Seder night
  Cicellis, K. Turn of the tide
  Hale, N. No one my grief can tell
  Parker, G. Bright and morning
  Porter, K. A. Jilting of Granny Weatherall
  Porter, K. A. Pale horse, pale rider
  Sansom, W. The cliff
  Saroyan, W. Resurrection of a life
  Scilken, M. Oh joy, it's a boy
  Shattuck, R. Workout on the river
  Woolf, V. S. New dress
The **streamliner.** Van Doren, M.
Street, James Howell, 1903-1954
  I am not a stranger
    Jones, K. M. ed. New Confederate short
    stories
  The old, old story
    Brentano, F. ed. The word lives on
  Please come home, My Lady
    Cavanna, B. ed. Pick of the litter
    Furman, A. L. ed. Teen-age dog stories
  They know how
    Grayson, C. ed. Fourth round
  Weep no more, My Lady
    Bloch, M. ed. Favorite dog stories
    Certner, S. and Henry, G. H. eds. Short
    stories for our times
    Cooper, A. C. ed. Modern short stories
    Lass, A. H. and Horowitz, A. eds.
    Stories for youth

Street, Julian Leonard, 1879-1947
  Mr Bisbee's princess
    First-prize stories, 1919-1954

The **street.** Horwitz, J.
The **street.** Seager, A.
Street song. Sansom, W.
Street that got mislaid. Waddington, P.
Street walker. Tucker, W.
Streeter, Edward, 1891-
  Letter to Mable
    Fenner, P. R. comp. Fun! Fun! Fun!
Strength of Gideon. Dunbar, P. L.
Strength of the strong. London, J.
Stribling, Thomas Sigismund, 1881-
  Mystery of the personal ad
    Queen, E. pseud. ed. Queen's awards:
    5th ser.
Strictly big league. Coombs, C. I.
Strictly business. Porter, W. S.
Strike of the Schnorrers. Spector, M.
STRIKES AND LOCKOUTS
  Munro, H. H. Byzantine omelette
  Munro, H. H. Unkindest blow
Strindberg, August, 1849-1912
  Autumn
    Blodgett, H. W. ed. Story survey.
    1953 ed.
The **string.** Maupassant, G. de
String of beads. Maugham, W. S.
Striving after the wind. Lindquist, W.
Stroke of thirteen. De La Torre, L.
Strong, Austin, 1881-
  All on a winter's night
    Cooper, A. C. ed. Modern short stories
Strong, Joan, 1923-
  Hired man
    Best American short stories, 1950
Strong, Leonard Alfred George, 1896-
  Danse Macabre
    Asquith, Lady C. M. E. C. ed. Book of
    modern ghosts
  Let me go
    Carrington, H. ed. Week-end book of
    ghost stories
  White cottage
    Cerf, B. A. and Moriarty, H. C. eds.
    Anthology of famous British stories
Strong, Paschal Neilson, 1901-
  Anchor man
    Owen, F. ed. Teen-age victory parade
  Behind the plate
    Fenner, P. R. comp. Crack of the bat
  Man on Stormrift Mountain
    American boy (Periodical) American
    boy Adventure stories
  Running dark
    Furman, A. L. ed. Teen-age sea stories
  Salvage!
    Furman, A. L. ed. Teen-age sea stories
  Shantyboat pirate
    Furman, A. L. ed. Teen-age sea stories
  Terror of Buccaneer Bay
    Fenner, P. R. comp. Stories of the sea
  Trail of the whiffle-poof
    Boys' life (Periodical) Boys' life Adven-
    ture stories

The **strudel.** Horwitz, J.

Struggle for life. Aldrich, T. B.

Struther, Jan, pseud. See Maxtone Graham,
  Joyce (Anstruther)

Struttin' with some barbecue. Duke, O.

Stuart, Jesse, 1907-
  Anglo-Saxons of Auxierville
    Stuart, J. Clearing in the sky & other stories
  Battle with the bees
    Stuart, J. Clearing in the sky & other stories
  The champion
    Stuart, J. Clearing in the sky & other stories
  Clearing in the sky
    Stuart, J. Clearing in the sky & other stories
  Coming down the mountain
    Stuart, J. Clearing in the sky & other stories
  Competition at Slush Creek
    Stuart, J. Clearing in the sky & other stories
  Dawn of remembered spring
    Best of the Best American short stories, 1915-1950
    Summers, H. S. ed. Kentucky story
  Evidence is high proof
    Stuart, J. Clearing in the sky & other stories
  Fight number twenty-five
    Lynskey, W. C. ed. Reading modern fiction
    Stuart, J. Clearing in the sky & other stories
  Governor Warburton's right-hand man
    Stuart, J. Clearing in the sky & other stories
  Horse-trading trembles
    Stuart, J. Clearing in the sky & other stories
  Hot-collared mule
    Stuart, J. Clearing in the sky & other stories
  Land of our enemies
    Stuart, J. Clearing in the sky & other stories
  No hero
    Stuart, J. Clearing in the sky & other stories
  No petty thief
    Stuart, J. Clearing in the sky & other stories
  Old Gore
    Stuart, J. Clearing in the sky & other stories
  Rainy day at Big Lost Creek
    Grayson, C. ed. Fourth round
  Red rats of Plum Fork
    Story (Periodical). Story; no. 3
  Rightful owner
    Lantz, J. E. ed. Stories of Christian living
  Road number one
    Stuart, J. Clearing in the sky & other stories
  Slipover sweater
    Stuart, J. Clearing in the sky & other stories
  Split cherry tree
    Certner, S. and Henry, G. H. eds. Short stories for our times
  The storm
    Stauffer, R. M.; Cunningham, W. H. and Sullivan, C. J. eds. Adventures in modern literature
  Testimony of trees
    Stuart, J. Clearing in the sky & other stories
  Thanksgiving hunter
    Hazeltine, A. I. comp. Selected stories for teen-agers
  Thirty-two votes before breakfast
    Stuart, J. Clearing in the sky & other stories
  To market, to market
    Stuart, J. Clearing in the sky & other stories
  When mountain men make peace
    Stuart, J. Clearing in the sky & other stories
  Woman in the house
    Southern review. Anthology of stories from the Southern review

Stuart, Lyle, 1922-
  Orange room
    American vanguard, 1952

Stubborn spearmen. Davis, H. L.

Stubbs, Harry Clement, 1922-
  Answer
    Conklin, G. ed. Science-fiction thinking machines
  Attitude
    Greenberg, M. ed. Travelers of space
  Cold front
    Greenberg, M. ed. Men against the stars
  Critical factor
    Star science fiction stories, no. 2
  Proof
    Conklin, G. ed. Possible worlds of science fiction

Student body. Wallace, F. L.

Student in economics. Milburn, G.

STUDENT LIFE. See School life

STUDENTS. See School life

Studio of Love-Your-Fellowman. Zozulya, E. D.

Studs. Farrell, J. T.

A **study** in scarlet. Doyle, Sir A. C.

Stuff of dreams. Boylston, H. D.

Stull, Paul
  Growing pains
    Oberfirst, R. ed. 1954 anthology of best original short-shorts

Sture-Vasa, Mary (Alsop) 1885-
  My friend Flicka
    Eaton, H. T. ed. Short stories

Sturgeon, Theodore, pseud. See Waldo, Edward Hamilton

Stutz and the tub. Whittemore, R.

Styron, William, 1925-
  Enormous window
    American vanguard, 1950

Subercaseaux, Benjamín, 1902-
  Salt sea
    De Onís, H. ed. Spanish stories and tales

Sublime vigil. Cuthberg, C. D.

SUBMARINE BOATS
  Bateman, A. Rig ship for diving
  Bateman, A. Submarine jitters
  Longstreet, S. No peace with the sea

SUBMARINE DIVING. See Diving, Submarine

Submarine jitters. Bateman, A.
Submarine plans. Christie, A. M.
SUBMARINE WARFARE
  Beach, E. L. Wahoo
  Lott, D. N. Skipper played it safe
SUBMARINES. See Submarine boats
Submissive wife. De La Roche, M.
Subterfuge. Bradbury, R.
Suburban frontiers. Young, R. F.
SUBURBAN LIFE
  De Vries, P. Life among the winesaps
  Humphrey, W. Last husband
Subway named Mobius. Deutsch, A. J.
SUBWAYS
  Adler, W. Other people
  Crawford, E. and Dalmas, H. Rush-hour
    romance
  Deutsch, A. J. Subway named Mobius
  Johnson, R. B. Far below
SUCCESS
  Maugham, W. S. The verger
  Verrinder, W. To a web begun
Success story. Barr, J. pseud.
Success story. Wodehouse, P. G.
SUCCESSION. See Inheritance and suc-
    cession
**SUCCOTH (FEAST OF TABER-
    NACLES)** See Sukkoth
Such a pretty day. Powell, D.
Such darling dodos. Wilson, A.
Suckow, Ruth, 1892-
  Auntie Bissel
    Suckow, R. Some others and myself
  Elegy for Alma's Aunt Amy
    Suckow, R. Some others and myself
  Eltha
    Suckow, R. Some others and myself
  Eminence
    Lohan, R. and Lohan, M. eds. New
      Christmas treasury
  Golden wedding
    Blodgett, H. W. ed. Story survey.
      1953 ed.
  A memoir
    Suckow, R. Some others and myself
  Memorial Eve
    Suckow, R. Some others and myself
  Merrittsville
    Suckow, R. Some others and myself
  Mrs Vogel and Ollie
    Suckow, R. Some others and myself
  One of three others
    Suckow, R. Some others and myself
Sudden attack of heartbreak. Lardner, J.
Sudden heart. Barlow, T.
Sudermann, Hermann, 1857-1928
  New Year's Eve confession
    Blodgett, H. W. ed. Story survey.
      1953 ed.
Suffer the little children. Burnett, W.
SUFFERING
  Elliott, G. P. Faq'
  Gordon, C. W. The canyon flowers
"Sufficient." Ready, W. B.
SUFFRAGE. See Woman—Suffrage
Sugar bowl. Shulman, M.

Sugar camp. Bromfield, L.
Sugar for the horse. Bates, H. E.
Suhl, Yuri, 1908-
  Saved by the sale
    Ausubel, N. ed. Treasury of Jewish
      humor
  With the aid of the One Above
    Ausubel, N. ed. Treasury of Jewish
      humor
    Ribalow, H. U. ed. This land, these
      people
SUICIDE
  Benson, T. To-morrow is another day
  Caldwell, E. After-image
  Calisher, H. In Greenwich there are many
    gravelled walks
  Collier, J. Bird of prey
  Collier, J. Halfway to Hell
  Connolly, M. Natural causes
  Coppel, A. The exile
  Du Maurier, D. No motive
  Hunt, F. C. Egg from the sky
  Marcus, P. Higher and higher
  Maugham, W. S. The pool
  Maugham, W. S. Rain
  Pincherle, A. Back to the sea
  Rinehart, A. Mirrored room
  Seligsohn, I. J. The anchor
SUICIDE, ATTEMPTED. See Suicide
Suicide on skis. Findlay, D. K.
Suite homes and their romance. Porter, W. S.
Suitor's white paper. Kober, A.
SUKKOTH
  Landa, M. J. Two legacies
  Reisin, A. Big succch
    See also Festivals
Sulkin, Sidney, 1918-
  The plan
    Ribalow, H. U. ed. These your children
Sullivan, Alan, 1868-
  Salving of Pyack
    Pacey, D. ed. Book of Canadian stories
Sullivan, Richard, 1908-
  Compline
    Sullivan, R. Fresh and open sky, and
      other stories
  The dispossessed
    Sullivan, R. Fresh and open sky, and
      other stories
  Dream of drums
    Sullivan, R. Fresh and open sky, and
      other stories
  Feathers
    Sullivan, R. Fresh and open sky, and
      other stories
  Fresh and open sky
    Sullivan, R. Fresh and open sky, and
      other stories
  Girl next door
    Sullivan, R. Fresh and open sky, and
      other stories
  Home fires
    Sullivan, R. Fresh and open sky, and
      other stories
  Honeymoon
    Sullivan, R. Fresh and open sky, and
      other stories
  In a glass darkly
    Sullivan, R. Fresh and open sky, and
      other stories

Sullivan, Richard—*Continued*
  Old pal
    Sullivan, R. Fresh and open sky, and
    other stories
  Queer kind of sorrow
    Sullivan, R. Fresh and open sky, and
    other stories
  Rough green tree
    Sullivan, R. Fresh and open sky, and
    other stories
  Round trip
    Sullivan, R. Fresh and open sky, and
    other stories
  Saturday nocturne
    Gable, M. Sister, ed. Many-colored fleece
  The sharers
    Sullivan, R. Fresh and open sky, and
    other stories
  Things past
    Sullivan, R. Fresh and open sky, and
    other stories
  The thread
    Sullivan, R. Fresh and open sky, and
    other stories
  Weight of the sky
    Sullivan, R. Fresh and open sky, and
    other stories
  The women
    Sullivan, R. Fresh and open sky, and
    other stories
  You're only young once
    Sullivan, R. Fresh and open sky, and
    other stories
SULLIVAN'S ISLAND. See South Caro-
  lina—Sullivan's Island
Sultan, Stanley
  And Jacob called
    Hathaway, B. and Sessions, J. A. eds.
    Writers for tomorrow. 2d ser.
  Fugue of the fig tree
    Best American short stories, 1953
Sultan stork. Thackeray, W. M.
Sum in addition. Campbell, W. E. M.
Sum of two angles. Willingham, C.
Summer. Baker, D. D.
Summer accident. Caldwell, E.
SUMMER COTTAGES. See Houses;
  Summer resorts
Summer day. Stafford, J.
Summer dream. Gallico, P. W.
Summer evening. Boyle, K.
Summer farmer. Cheever, J.
Summer morning in Dublin in 1938. Farrell,
  J. T.
Summer of the beautiful white horse. Saro-
  yan, W.
Summer people. Jackson, S.
Summer place. Stettner, S.
SUMMER RESORTS
  Jackson, C. R. The cheat
  Jackson, S. Summer people
  Mann, T. Mario and the magician
  Maugham, W. S. Round dozen
  Porter, W. S. Midsummer knights' dream
  Porter, W. S. Midsummer masquerade
SUMMER THEATER. See Theater and
  stage life

Summer tryout. Farrell, J. T.
SUMMER VACATIONS. See Vacations
Summer wear. De Camp, L. S.
Summers, James L. 1910-
  And now farewell
    Summers, J. L. Open season
  Boy in the mirror
    Seventeen (Periodical) The Seventeen
    reader
    Summers, J. L. Open season
  Decision for spring
    Summers, J. L. Open season
  Glass boy
    Summers, J. L. Open season
  I'll remember you
    Summers, J. L. Open season
  Like son
    Summers, J. L. Open season
  Long year
    Summers, J. L. Open season
  Open season
    Summers, J. L. Open season
  Tomorrow
    Summers, J. L. Open season
  Wait for me
    Summers, J. L. Open season
  Weren't you ever young!
    Summers, J. L. Open season
Summer's end. Schweitzer, G.
Summer's ending. Weeks, J.
SUN
  Bradbury, R. Golden apples of the sun
  Coblentz, S. A. Sunward
  Stubbs, H. C. Proof
Sun and shadow. Bradbury, R.
The sun and the hedge. Bentley, P. E.
Sun-Dog Trail. London, J.
Sun maker. William, J.
SUNDAY
  Babb, S. Wild flower
  Hawthorne, N. Sunday at home
    See also Sabbath
Sunday. Farrell, J. T.
Sunday afternoon. Payne, L. V.
Sunday at home. Hawthorne, N.
Sunday drive. Jackson, C. R.
Sunday evening. Bowen, E.
Sunday morning at the Compsons. Faulk-
  ner, W.
SUNDAY SCHOOLS
  Beck, W. Years brought to an end
Sunday zeppelin. Saroyan, W.
The sunfield. Caldwell, E.
Sung-Ling, P'u. See P'u Sung-ling
Sunley, Robert, 1917-
  Two ages of man
    Wolfe, D. M. ed. Which grain will grow
Sunnier side. Jackson, C. R.
Sunrise. Blackburn, E. R.
Sunrise on the veld. Lessing, D. M.
Sunset at sixteen. Fisher, D. C.
Sunward. Coblentz, S. A.
The superintendent. Cheever, J.
Superiority. Clarke, A. C.

SUPERNATURAL PHENOMENA

Barrie, Sir J. M. bart. Farewell Miss Julie Logan
Bierce, A. Damned thing
Ch'en Hsüan-yu. Chienniang
De La Mare, W. J. The creatures
De La Mare, W. J. The vats
Du Maurier, D. Monte Verità
Ekbergh, I. D. Strange story
Finney, J. I'm scared
Forster, E. M. Celestial omnibus
Heinlein, R. A. Lost legacy
Hodgson, W. N. Noise in the night
Irving, W. Adalantado of the Seven Cities
Irwin, M. E. F. Earlier service
James, M. R. The mezzotint
Jenkins, W. F. Little terror
Le Fanu, J. S. Room in the Dragon Volant
Maupassant, G. de. The Horla
Munby, A. N. L. Alabaster hand, and other stories; 14 stories
Noyes, A. Log of the "Evening Star"
Priestley, J. B. Guest of honour
Priestley, J. B. Leadington incident
Priestley, J. B. Look after the strange girl
Priestley, J. B. Night sequence
Priestley, J. B. The other place
Priestley, J. B. Uncle Phil on TV
P'u Sung-ling. Cricket boy
Rescue at sea
Richter, C. Sinister journey
Stevenson, R. L. Isle of voices
Valle-Inclán, R. del. My sister Antonia
Wall, J. W. Ringstones
Wells, H. G. Stolen body
See also Ghosts; Witchcraft

SUPERSTITION

Cobb, I. S. Snake Doctor
Kipling, R. Tomb of his ancestors
Pratt, F. and De Camp, L. S. Eve of St John
Rice, A. C. H. Hoodooed

Supply and demand. Porter, W. S.

Suppressed edition. Curle, R.

Surface tension. Blish, J.

Surface tension of molten metal. Willingham, C.

Surfman number nine. Detzer, K. W.

SURGEONS. See Physicians; Surgery

SURGERY

Benét, S. V. End to dreams
Brown, J. Rab and his friends
Gold, H. L. Matter of form
Herrick, R. Master of the inn
Kuttner, H. Dream's end
Stafford, J. Interior castle
Walsh, M. The bonesetter
Weiss, E. Cardiac suture
Wells, H. G. Under the knife

SURGERY, PLASTIC

Alpert, H. The change

Surgery at Aquila. Allen, H.

SURGICAL OPERATIONS. See Surgery

SURPRISE ENDINGS

Lever, C. J. Con Cregan's legacy

The **surrender.** Hendryx, J. B.

Surtees, Robert Smith, 1803-1864
Afternoon hunt with the Tantivity hounds
Surtees, R. S. Hunting scenes
Another quiet bye with Mr Jorrocks
Surtees, R. S. Hunting scenes
Bye-day with Mr Jorrocks
Surtees, R. S. Hunting scenes
Cat and Custard-pot day with the Handley Cross
Surtees, R. S. Hunting scenes
Children's day with Mr Jovey Jessop's hounds
Surtees, R. S. Hunting scenes
Cub-hunting with Mr Neville's hounds
Surtees, R. S. Hunting scenes
Day in Hit-im-and-Hold-im-shire
Surtees, R. S. Hunting scenes
Day with Hard-and-Sharp hounds
Surtees, R. S. Hunting scenes
Great run with the F.H.H.
Surtees, R. S. Hunting scenes
Heavyside Hunt: The new Master's first day
Surtees, R. S. Hunting scenes
Heavyside Hunt again: The lady whipper-in
Surtees, R. S. Hunting scenes
Larkspur again: A lawn meet at Rosemount Grange
Surtees, R. S. Hunting scenes
Larkspur hounds: A morning with a bagman
Surtees, R. S. Hunting scenes
Lord Scamperdale's finest day
Surtees, R. S. Hunting scenes
Mr Pomponius Ego out with the Handley Cross
Surtees, R. S. Hunting scenes
Mr Sponge's first day with the Flat Hat Hunt
Surtees, R. S. Hunting scenes
Mr Sponge's first day with the Hanby
Surtees, R. S. Hunting scenes
Opening day with Mr Hardey's hounds
Surtees, R. S. Hunting scenes
Opening day with the Duke of Tergiversation's hounds
Surtees, R. S. Hunting scenes
Opening day with the Larkspur hounds
Surtees, R. S. Hunting scenes
Our last day with the Handley Cross
Surtees, R. S. Hunting scenes
Sir Harry Scattercash's hounds: Mr Sponge carries the horn
Surtees, R. S. Hunting scenes
Sir Harry's hounds again: Mr Sponge and Miss Lucy Glitters
Surtees, R. S. Hunting scenes
Two days with Mr Neville's hounds
Surtees, R. S. Hunting scenes
With Mr Jorrocks in Pinch-me-near Forest
Surtees, R. S. Hunting scenes
With the Hit-im-and-Hold-im-shire: The sham day
Surtees, R. S. Hunting scenes

SURVEYING

Stuart, J. Testimony of trees

Survival. Canzoneri, R.

Survival. Harris, J. B.

SURVIVAL (AFTER AIRPLANE AC-
    CIDENTS, SHIPWRECKS, ETC)
  Bloomfield, H. The trap
  Carrighar, S. Marooned children
  Kubilius, W. Other side
  Mowat, F. Woman he left to die
  Russell, J. Fourth man
  Temple, W. F. Two shadows
Survival ship. Merril, J.
Susan steps out. Olds, H. D.
Susceptibility. MacDonald, J. D.
SUSPICION. See Skepticism
Suspicion. Sayers, D. L.
Sut and the Burns family. Harris, G. W.
Sut as a boy. Harris, G. W.
Sut meets the law. Harris, G. W.
Sut on the national scene. Harris, G. W.
Sut sets certain individuals right. Harris,
    G. W.
Sut takes on the whole world. Harris,
    G. W.
Sutro, Alfred, 1863-1933
  Bread on the waters
    Leftwich, J. ed. Yisröel. 1952 ed.
Sutton Place story. Cheever, J.
Svevo, Italo, pseud. See Schmitz, Ettore
Swados, Harvey B. 1920-
  The letters
    Best American short stories, 1952
SWALLOWS
  De La Roche, M. Come fly with me
SWAMPS
  Annixter, P. pseud. Dragon rider
  Peattie, D. C. and Peattie, L. R. Weir-
    wood marsh
Swan-moving. Taylor, E.
SWANS
  Boyle, K. Bridegroom's body
  Du Maurier, D. Old man
  Taylor, E. Swan-moving
Swanson, Neil Harmon, 1896-
  They kept the flag there
    American boy (Periodical) American
    boy Adventure stories
The swap. Heard, G.
Swaying elms. Blackburn, E. R.
SWEDEN
  Lagerkvist, P. F. Guest of reality
SWEDES IN THE UNITED STATES
  Caldwell, E. Country full of Swedes
Sweet girl graduate. Hutchins, M. P. M.
Sweetness of the twisted apples. Stegner,
    W. E.
Swell-looking girl. Caldwell, E.
Swenson, Eric Pierson, 1918-
  Lonely reef
    Fenner, P. R. comp. Stories of the sea
Swift, Jonathan, 1667-1745
  Laputa
    Derleth, A. W. ed. Beyond time & space
Swift Foot the hunter. Macfarlan, A. A.
Swift Thunder of the prairies. Maloy, L.
SWIMMING
  McKenney, R. Guinea pig
  Maugham, W. S. Friend in need

Swinbank, Gene, 1884-
  New hat
    Oberfirst, R. ed. 1952 anthology of best
    original short-shorts
SWINDLERS AND SWINDLING
  Bergengruen, W. Eye cure
  Charteris, L. Revolution racket
  Cozzens, J. G. Clerical error
  Curtis, K. The cameleers
  Danielson, R. E. The quid pro quo
  Dunsany, E. J. M. D. P. 18th baron.
    Memory machine
  Grimson, M. S. At the crossroads
  Hecht, B. Swindler's luck
  Hershman, M. Live bait
  Porter, W. S. Conscience in art
  Porter, W. S. Ethics of pig
  Porter, W. S. Exact science of matri-
    mony
  Porter, W. S. Gold that glittered
  Porter, W. S. Innocents of Broadway
  Porter, W. S. Jeff Peters as a personal
    magnet
  Porter, W. S. Man higher up
  Porter, W. S. Midsummer masquerade
  Porter, W. S. Modern rural sports
  Porter, W. S. On behalf of the manage-
    ment
  Porter, W. S. Poet and the peasant
  Porter, W. S. Shearing the wolf
  Porter, W. S. Tempered wind
  Queen, E. pseud. Double your money
Swindler's luck. Hecht, B.
SWINDLING. See Swindlers and swin-
    dling
SWINE. See Pigs
Swinnerton, Frank Arthur, 1884-
  The verdict
    Queen, E. pseud. ed. Literature of
    crime
Swinton, Allan
  A brotherhood
    American boy (Periodical) American
    boy Anthology
  Courage
    American boy (Periodical) American
    boy Adventure stories
SWISS ALPS. See Alps, Swiss
The switchboard. Martin, T. H.
Switzer, Robert
  Death of a prize fighter
    Prize stories of 1950
    Ribalow, H. U. ed. World's greatest
    boxing stories
  No end to anything
    Esquire (Periodical) Girls from Esquire
SWITZERLAND
  Rousseau, J. J. Isle of St Peter
  Welch, D. When I was thirteen
      Lucerne
  Charteris, L. Lucerne: The loaded tour-
    ist
      Zurich
  Jackson, C. R. Old men and boys
The sword. Betts, D.
Sword of tomorrow. Kuttner, H.
Sword of Welleran. Dunsany, E. J. M. D. P.
    18th baron
Sword of Yung Lo. Walsh, M.

SWORDFISH
Annixter, P. pseud. The swordsman
SWORDS
Dunsany, E. J. M. D. P. 18th baron.
Sword of Welleran
Walsh, M. Sword of Yung Lo
See also Arms and armor
The **swordsman.** Annixter, P. pseud.
Swordsmen of Varnis. Jackson, C.
Sydney and the green angel. Warnock,
J. D.

Sykes, Christopher, 1907-
Conflicting passions
Sykes, C. Character and situation
The interview
Sykes, C. Character and situation
Me and my brother
Sykes, C. Character and situation
Not for psychologists
Sykes, C. Character and situation
Sacred and the profane
Sykes, C. Character and situation
Saint George
Sykes, C. Character and situation

Sylvester, Harry, 1908-
Boxer: old
Ribalow, H. U. ed. World's greatest
boxing stories
Last race
Herzberg, M. J. comp. Treasure chest of
sport stories
Return of the hero
Eaton, H. T. ed. Short stories

Sylvester, Robert, 1907-
Last tanto
Grayson, C. ed. Fourth round

Symbiosis. Jenkins, W. F.

Symbol of courage. Hamilton, R. T.

Sympathetic visitor. Betts, D.

SYNAGOGUES
Kobrin, L. Milchiger Synagogue and the
blind preacher
Reisin, A. The recluse

Syndrome Johnny. Dye, C.

System of Dr Tarr and Prof. Fether. Poe,
E. A.

T

Taaffe, Michael. See Maguire, R. A.

Tabby cat. Rader, P.

Taber, Gladys (Bagg) 1899-
Best of breed
Taber, G. B. When dogs meet people
Champion comes home
Taber, G. B. When dogs meet people
Christmas gift
Taber, G. B. When dogs meet people
Honey and the home front
Cavanna, B. ed. Pick of the litter
Taber, G. B. When dogs meet people
Just a little havoc
Taber, G. B. When dogs meet people

Letter to the Dean
Shaw, H. and Bement, D. Reading the
short story
Little Goat
Taber, G. B. When dogs meet people
Man at the gate
Taber, G. B. When dogs meet people
Never a dull moment
Taber, G. B. When dogs meet people
Sometimes a man needs a friend
Taber, G. B. When dogs meet people
Top Hat goes to town
Taber, G. B. When dogs meet people
Unwanted one
Taber, G. B. When dogs meet people
You can't buy a dog
Taber, G. B. When dogs meet people
TABERNACLES, FEAST OF. See Suk-
koth

Tablanca, Luis
Country girl
Stauffer, R. M.; Cunningham, W. H.
and Sullivan, C. J. eds. Adventures
in modern literature
TABLE
Melville, H. Apple-tree table
Table at Ciro's. Schulberg, B. W.
Table before me. O'Nan, M. C.
Table near the band. Milne, A. A.
The **tablets** of the law. Hurston, Z. N.
Tabloid news. Bromfield, L.
Taboo. Leiber, F.
Tackle buster. Macfarlan, A. A.
Tact. Beer, T.
Tactical exercise. Waugh, E.
Tactical maneuver. Haycox, E.
Tædium vitæ. Chekhov, A. P.
Tagore, Sir Rabindranath, 1861-1941
Babus of Nayanjore
Cerf, B. A. and Moriarty, H. C. eds.
Anthology of famous British stories
The Cabuliwallah
Stauffer, R. M.; Cunningham, W. H. and
Sullivan, C. J. eds. Adventures in
modern literature
Hungry stones
Neider, C. ed. Great short stories from
the world's literature
TAHITI
Maugham, W. S. Fall of Edward Barnard
Michener, J. A. Povenaa's daughter
TAILOR SHOPS. See Tailors
TAILORS
Asch, S. Quiet garden spot
Favicchio, J. Three buttonholes
Frank, W. Under the dome
Tchernichowski, S. Shaatnez

Tain't so. Hughes, L.

The **taipan.** Maugham, W. S.

Take back your bay wreath. Mitchison,
N. M. H.

Take her up tenderly. Norris, H.

Take it and like it. Olive, H.

"Take over, Bos'n!"** Schisgall, O.

Take your choice. Walsh, M.

Takes a real man. . . Schaefer, J. W.
"**Taking** mother out." Taylor, E.
Taking the veil. Mansfield, K.
A **tale.** Hutchins, M. P. M.
A **tale.** Nahman Ben Simḥah, of Bratzlav
Tale of a chemist
  Derleth, A. W. ed. Far boundaries
Tale of a tainted tenner. Porter, W. S.
Tale of James Carabine. Byrne, D.
Tale of negative gravity. Stockton, F. R.
Tale of olden time. Heine, H.
Tale of Perez de Amorin. Zaferiou, S.
Tale of the old main line. Somerville, A. W.
Tale of the Ragged Mountains. Poe, E. A.
TALES. See Fables; Legends and folk tales
The **talisman.** De La Mare, W. J.
The **talisman.** Gordimer, N.
TALISMANS. See Charms
Talking about writers. Kaufman, W.
Talking-out of Tarrington. Munro, H. H.
Talking shop. Lewis, W.
Tall as the stars. Lambert, J.
Tall Bram of Little Pigeon. Wellman, M. W.
Tall hunter. Fast, H. M.
Tall men. Faulkner, W.
Tall one. Van Doren, M.
TALL STORIES. See Improbable stories
Tall story. Allingham, M.
Tall tale from the high hills. Credle, E.
TALL TALES. See Improbable stories
TAMERLANE, 1336-1405
  Gorky, M. Might of motherhood
Tangled hearts. Wodehouse, P. G.
Tanker man. Ward, M.
TANKS (MILITARY SCIENCE)
  Wells, H. G. Land ironclads
Tanner, Charles R.
  Angus MacAuliffe and the gowden tooch
    Conklin, G. and Conklin, L. T. eds.
    Supernatural reader

Tanzer, Ward
  My Tiare, good-bye
  Stanford short stories, 1951

Taper, Bernard, 1918-
  Kaddish
  Stanford short stories, 1953

TAPESTRY
  Anderson, E. V. Tapestry extravaganza

Tapestry extravaganza. Anderson, E. V.

Tappan's burro. Grey, Z.

Tarachow, Sidney. See Treat, L. jt. auth.

Tarkington, Booth, 1869-1946
  "Little gentleman"
    Burrell, J. A. and Cerf, B. A. eds. Anthology of famous American stories
  Little Orvie's new dog Ralph
    Furman, A. L. ed. Teen-age dog stories
  Rennie Peddigoe
    Tarkington, B. Three selected short novels
  Uncertain Molly Collicut
    Tarkington, B. Three selected short novels
  Walterson
    Tarkington, B. Three selected short novels
Tarnished gold. Glassman, B.
Tarpon! Bell, V. M.
TARPON FISHING
  Bell, V. M. Tarpon
Tarroo-ushtey. Kneale, N.
TARTARS. See Tatars
Tartarus of maids. Melville, H.
Tashrak, pseud. See Zevin, Israel Joseph
Taste. Dahl, R.
Taste of command. Hail, S.
TATARS
  Chekhov, A. P. In exile
Tate, Allen, 1899-
  Immortal woman
    Summers, H. S. ed. Kentucky story
TATTOOING
  Bradbury, R. The illustrated man
  Dahl, R. Skin
  Friedman, B. H. As I am, you will be
  Munro, H. H. The background
  Porter, W. S. Double-dyed deceiver
Taubes, Frank
  Trouble on 98th Street
    Best detective stories of the year—1951
Tavern at Powell's Ferry. Haycox, E.
TAVERNS. See Hotels, taverns, etc.
TAX COLLECTORS. See Taxation
TAXATION
  Herbert, Sir A. P. Board of Inland Revenue v. Haddock
TAXES. See Taxation
TAXI DRIVERS. See Cab drivers
TAXICAB DRIVERS. See Cab drivers
TAXICABS
  Aiken, C. P. Hey, taxi!
Taylor, C. Lindsay
  The envelope
    Thinker's digest (Periodical) Spoiled priest, and other stories
Taylor, Elizabeth, 1912-
  Beginning of a story
    Taylor, E. Hester Lilly, and twelve short stories
  First death of her life
    Ludwig, J. B. and Poirier, W. R. eds. Stories, British and American
    Taylor, E. Hester Lilly, and twelve short stories
  Hester Lilly
    Taylor, E. Hester Lilly, and twelve short stories
  I live in a world of make-believe
    Taylor, E. Hester Lilly, and twelve short stories
  Idea of age
    Taylor, E. Hester Lilly, and twelve short stories
  Light of day
    Taylor, E. Hester Lilly, and twelve short stories

Taylor, Elizabeth—*Continued*
Oasis of gaiety
Taylor, E. Hester Lilly, and twelve short stories
Red-letter day
Taylor, E. Hester Lilly, and twelve short stories
Sad garden
Taylor, E. Hester Lilly, and twelve short stories
Shadows of the world
Taylor, E. Hester Lilly, and twelve short stories
Spry old character
Taylor, E. Hester Lilly, and twelve short stories
Swan-moving
Taylor, E. Hester Lilly, and twelve short stories
"Taking mother out"
Taylor, E. Hester Lilly, and twelve short stories

Taylor, Katharine Haviland, d. 1941
The failure
Certner, S. and Henry, G. H. eds. Short stories for our times

Taylor, Kressmann
Pale green fishes
Best American short stories, 1954
McGarry and the television frame-up
Best detective stories of the year—1951

Taylor, Matt
McGarry joins the Easter parade
This week magazine. This week's short-short stories
Megelhoffer theory
Dachs, D. ed. Treasury of sports humor

Taylor, Peter Hillsman, 1917-
Bad dreams
Taylor, P. H. Widows of Thornton
Cookie
Taylor, P. H. Widows of Thornton
Dark walk
Taylor, P. H. Widows of Thornton
Fancy woman
Southern review. Anthology of stories from the Southern review
Porte-cochere
Taylor, P. H. Widows of Thornton
Sky line
Gordon, C. and Tate, A. eds. House of fiction
Their losses
Prize stories of 1950
Taylor, P. H. Widows of Thornton
Two ladies in retirement
Taylor, P. H. Widows of Thornton
What you hear from 'em?
Taylor, P. H. Widows of Thornton
Wife of Nashville
Best American short stories, 1950
Best of the Best American short stories, 1915-1950

Taylor, Samuel Woolley, 1907-
Last voyage of the Unsinkable Sal
Bluebook (Periodical) Best sea stories from Bluebook

Tazewell, Charles, 1912-
After-hours visitor
Saturday evening post (Periodical) Saturday evening post stories, 1952

Tchekhov, Anton. See Chekhov, Anton
Tchernichovsky, Saul. See Tchernichowski, Saul
Tchernichowski, Saul, 1875-1943
Shaatnez
Leftwich, J. ed. Yisröel. 1952 ed.
Tea. Munro, H. H.
Tea at Barnaby's. Rasmussen, G. F.
Tea for Tamahara. Grosskopf, E. K.
Tea from the brigantine. Carter, R. G.
Tea on the mountain. Bowles, P. F.
Tea pusher. Schoenfeld, H.
Tea tray in the sky. Smith, E. E.
TEACH, EDWARD, d. 1718
Malcolmson, A. B. Blackbeard
Teacher Jensen. Michaëlis, K.
TEACHERS
Aldrich, B. S. Welcome home, Hal!
Bowen, E. Daffodils
Calisher, H. Wreath for Miss Totten
Cassill, R. V. Larchmoor is not the world
Chekhov, A. P. The schoolmistress
Daudet, A. Last class
De Vries, P. Good boy
Gardner, M. Island of five colors
Garrigue, J. The snowfall
Goodman, P. Iddings Clark
Harte, B. Idyll of Red Gulch
Harte, B. M'liss
Heinlein, R. A. Elsewhen
Henderson, Z. Ararat
Henderson, Z. You know what, teacher?
Hole, L. E. Prowler on the hill
Irving, W. Legend of Sleepy Hollow
Irwin, J. M. Pennies from heaven
Karchmer, S. "Hail, brother and farewell"
McCarty, M. B. Your long black hair
McLaverty, M. Poteen maker
Michaëlis, K. Teacher Jensen
O'Donovan, M. The frying-pan
O'Donovan, M. Lady of the sagas
O'Donovan, M. Unapproved route
Paget, V. Amour dure
Patton, F. G. Terrible Miss Dove
Priestley, J. B. Mr Strenberry's tale
Queen, E. pseud. "My queer Dean!"
Rosaire, F. Pod of a weed
Russell, E. F. Timeless ones
Saroyan, W. Ancient history and low hurdles
Scott, D. C. Paul Farlotte
Selver, P. Well, I'm blowed
Shattuck, R. Workout on the river
Stafford, J. Winter's tale
Trilling, L. Of this time, of that place
Wexler, J. I am Edgar
Wiegand, W. The science teacher
Yates, E. Enshrined in the heart
Zweig, S. Confusion of sentiment
See also College life; Governesses; Music teachers; School life; Tutors
Team bells woke me. Davis, H. L.
Team man. Bent, J. F.
TEAMSTERS
Gally, J. W. Big Jack Small
Tears on stones. Hirshbein, P.
TEAS (PARTIES)
De La Roche, M. Death of a centenarian

Technical error. Porter, W. S.
Technical expert. Katz, L.
Technical slip. Harris, J. B.
Technique. Winslow, T. S.
Teddy. Salinger, J. D.
TEEN-AGERS. See Adolescence
TEETH
   Andreev, L. N. On the day of the cruci-
     fixion
   Poe, E. A. Berenice
Teething ring. Causey, J.
Telemachus, friend. Porter, W. S.
TELEPATHY. See Thought-transference
TELEPHONE OPERATORS. See Tele-
   phone workers
TELEPHONE WORKERS
   Ward, E. S. P. Chief operator
The **telescope.** Derleth, A. W.
Telescope and the umbrella. Mevorach, J.
TELETYPE
   Poirier, N. R. Teletype machine
Teletype machine. Poirier, N. R.
TELEVISION
   Carver, C. Twenty floors up
   Grimson, M. S. When TV came to the
     backwoods
   Hatch, E. Channel 10
   Priestley, J. B. Uncle Phil on TV
   Schulberg, B. W. Your Arkansas traveler
Television helps, but not very much. Mc-
   Nulty, J.
Tell it to the Marines! Litten, F. N.
Tell-tale heart. Poe, E. A.
Téllez, Hernando, 1908-
   Ashes for the wind
     De Onís, H. ed. Spanish stories and
     tales
Temperate zone. Enright, E.
Tempered wind. Porter, W. S.
The **tempest.** Gibran, K.
Temple, Willard Henry, 1912-
   Most unusual season
     Dachs, D. ed. Treasury of sports hu-
     mor
   Record-breaker
     Owen, F. ed. Teen-age winter sports
     stories

Temple, William Frederick, 1914-
   Counter-transference
     Best sceince-fiction stories: 1953
   Date to remember
     Conklin, G. ed. Invaders of earth
   Forget-me-not
     Best science fiction stories: 1951
   Two shadows
     Best science fiction stories: 1952
   Way of escape
     Conklin, G. ed. Science-fiction adven-
     tures in dimension
Temple first. Melville, H.
Temple second. Melville, H.
Temptation of Reb Mottel. Kobrin, L.
Ten. Nuhn, F.
TEN COMMANDMENTS. See Command-
   ments, Ten

Ten thousand blueberry crates. Caldwell,
   E.
Ten years on a desert island. Newhouse,
   E.
TENANT. See Landlord and tenant
TENANT FARMING
   Betts, D. Gentle insurrection
   Caldwell, E. Kneel to the rising sun
   Faulkner, W. Barn burning
   Godchaux, E. Horn that called Bambine
Tender to the ship. Goldsmith, G.
TENEMENT HOUSES
   Babikoff, V. Day of rest
Tenn, William, pseud. See Klass, Philip
TENNESSEE
   Buckingham, N. Hallowed years
   Taylor, P. H. Widows of Thornton; 8
     stories
           Farm life
     See Farm life—Tennessee
           Nashville
   Porter, W. S. Municipal report
   Taylor, P. H. Wife of Nashville
Tennessee's partner. Harte, B.
TENNIS
   Chute, B. J. Double fault
   Chute, B. J. Doubles or nothing
   Chute, B. J. The winner
   Coombs, C. I. Net nemesis
   Maugham, W. S. Facts of life
   Miers, E. S. Weary Willie
   Reeve, J. Doubles or nothing
   Taylor, M. Megelhoffer theory
TENNIS PLAYERS. See Tennis
Tennison, Jack, pseud. See Jackson, Charles
   Tenney
Tennyson, Hallam, 1921-
   Appendicitis
     Tennyson, H. Wall of dust, and other
     stories
   Armistice
     Tennyson, H. Wall of dust, and other
     stories
   Home leave
     Tennyson, H. Wall of dust, and other
     stories
   In the desert
     Tennyson, H. Wall of dust, and other
     stories
   Land of my fathers
     Tennyson, H. Wall of dust, and other
     stories
   Wall of dust
     Tennyson, H. Wall of dust, and other
     stories
Tenth Street idyll. Parker, J. R.
Tenting tonight. Jackson, C. R.
Tepondicon. Jacobi, C.
Teresa. Charteris, L.
Terhune, Albert Payson, 1872-1942
   Coming of Lad
     Fenner, P. R. comp. Dogs, dogs, dogs
   The "critter"
     Bloch, M. ed. Favorite dog stories
   Hero
     Strang, R. M. and Roberts, R. M. eds.
     Teen-age tales v 1

Terhune, Albert P.—*Continued*
  One minute longer
    Eaton, H. T. ed. Short stories
  Yule miracle
    Furman, A. L. ed. Teen-age dog stories
TERMITES
  Kruse, C. B. Dr LuMie
Terr, Irma
  Only love me
    Wolfe, D. M. ed. Which grain will
    grow
Terrible Miss Dove. Patton, F. G.
Terribly strange bed. Collins, W.
Terror of Buccaneer Bay. Strong, P. N.
The **test.** Appet, N.
The **test.** Gibbs, A.
The **test.** Witherow, J. M.
Test piece. Russell, E. F.
TESTIMONY. See Witnesses
Testimony of trees. Stuart, J.
Testing of Jonah. Nathan, R.
Tête-à-tête. Kober, A.
TEXAS
  McDaniel, R. Coroner de luxe
  Perry, W. W. ed. 21 Texas short stories;
    21 stories

          19th century
  Porter, W. S. Hiding of Black Bill

          20th century
  Humphrey, W. Quail for Mr Forester

          Houston
  Goyen, W. Her breath upon the window-
    pane
          Ranch life
  See Ranch life—Texas
Texas Christmas 1872. Fletcher, G. N.
TEXAS RANGERS
  Cunningham, E. Bar-Nothing's happy
    birthday
  Porter, W. S. Jimmy Hayes and Muriel
Thackeray, William Makepeace, 1811-1863
  Sultan stork
    Cerf, B. A. and Moriarty, H. C. eds.
    Anthology of famous British stories
THAILAND
  Landon, M. D. M. Reconciliation
Thang. Gardner, M.
Thank you, Dr Russell. Chute, B. J.
THANKSGIVING DAY
  Porter, W. S. Two Thanksgiving Day
    gentlemen
Thanksgiving hunter. Stuart, J.
Thanksgiving spirit. Farrell, J. T.
That brute Simmons. Morrison, A.
That certain flavor. Rogow, L.
That evening sun. Faulkner, W.
That evening sun go down. Faulkner, W.
That flesh is heir to. . . Sitwell, Sir O. bart.
That Greek dog. Kantor, M.
That lovely green boat. Berge, B.
That Mark horse. Schaefer, J. W.
That mighty contact. White, H. C.

That only a mother. Merril, J.
That others might live. Booker, A. E.
That pig of a Morin. Maupassant, G. de
That share of glory. Kornbluth, C. M.
That spot. London, J.
That tree. Porter, K. A.
That will be fine. Faulkner, W.
That's my boy. Brondfield, J.
That's picture business. Kaufman, W.
That's what happened to me. Fessier, M.
THEATER AND STAGE LIFE
  Coward, N. P. Star quality
  Farrell, J. T. Summer tryout
  Franzos, K. E. Shylock in Czernowitz
  Kaufman, W. Call me Nate; 11 stories
  Melville, H. Temple second
  Munro, H. H. Reginald at the theatre
  Rosenberg, E. C. Mrs Rivkin grapples
    with the drama
  Winslow, T. S. The actress
  Winslow, T. S. Technique
Theater party. Rice, A. C. H.
THEATERS. See Theater and stage-life
THEATRICAL PRODUCERS
  Ullman, J. R. Hello darling
THEFT
  Cuevas, E. Lock the doors, lock the win-
    dows
  Davis, S. P. Christmas carol
  Norling, M. E. Jade ring
  Rabinowitz, S. The search
  Saroyan, W. Parsley garden
Their first meeting. Oxenham, J.
Their kingdom. Frison-Roche, R.
Their losses. Taylor, P. H.
Theological student. Saroyan, W.
THEOLOGY
  Saroyan, W. Theological student
Theory and the hound. Porter, W. S.
There are broken hearts in Brooklyn. Heu-
    man, W.
There are smiles. Lardner, R. W.
There isn't time now. Gregutt, H. C.
There shall be darkness. Moore, C. L.
There was a queen. Faulkner, W.
There was a star. Erdman, L. G.
There will always be hope. Williams, C.
There will come soft rains. Bradbury, R.
There's something about you. Lansing, E.
    C. H.
Thérèse and the doctor. Mauriac, F.
Thériault, Yves, 1915-
  Jeannette
    Weaver, R. and James, H. eds. Cana-
    dian short stories
Theseus. Gide, A. P. G.
They. Heinlein, R. A.
'**They.**' Kipling, R.
They also sit. De Vries, P.
They grind exceeding small. Williams, B. A.
They kept the flag there. Swanson, N. H.
They know how. Street, J. H.
They shall inherit the earth. Kober, A.
They shoot horses, don't they? McCoy, H.

They weren't going to die. Boyle, K.

They're scared, Mr Bradlaugh. Kneale, N.

Thibaudeau, Colleen, 1925-
  City underground
    Weaver, R. and James, H. eds. Canadian short stories

The **thief.** Eggleston, M. W.

The **thief.** O'Donovan, M.

THIEVES
  Aiken, C. P. Impulse
  Bruce, S. Farewell to crime
  Canning, V. Never trust a lady
  Chaucer, G. Pardoner's tale
  Cohen, O. R. Toot for a toot
  Cooke, A. A. Scum of the earth
  De Vries, P. If the shoe hurts
  Doty, W. L. Mr Dee and the middleman
  Doyle, Sir A. C. Blue carbuncle
  Edginton, H. M. Purple and fine linen
  Harte, B. Ingénue of the Sierras
  Kobrin, L. Milchiger Synagogue and the blind preacher
  Malamud, B. The prison
  Moroso, J. A. Tierney meets a millionaire
  Murdock, R. M. Stop, look, listen
  Porter, W. S. Assessor of success
  Porter, W. S. Clarion call
  Porter, W. S. Makes the whole world kin
  Porter, W. S. The marionettes
  Porter, W. S. Retrieved reformation
  Porter, W. S. Tommy's burglar
  Rabinowitz, S. Passover guest
  Reid, C. B. Yellow leaf
  Stevenson, R. L. Lodging for the night
  Stuart, J. No petty thief
  Walsh, M. Thomasheen James goes to the dogs
    See also Theft

Thimble, thimble. Porter, W. S.

Thing in the cellar. Keller, D. H.

Thing in the pond. Ernst, P.

Thing in the woods. Fletcher, P. and Ruby, B. F.

Thing in their hearts. Wolfe, E.

Thing of beauty. Lieberman, E.

Things. Lawrence, D. H.

Things in common. Pearce, J.

Things of distinction. Crossen, K. F.

Things pass by. Jenkins, W. F.

Things past. Sullivan, R.

Thing's the play. Porter, W. S.

The **thinker.** Steele, W. D.

THINKING MACHINES. See Automata

Third Avenue medicine. McNulty, J.

The **third** bullet. Carr, J. D.

Third commandment. Werfel, F. V.

Third day after Christmas. Saroyan, W.

Third from the sun. Matheson, R.

Third guest. Traven, B. pseud.

Third ingredient. Porter, W. S.

Third level. Finney, J.

Third nightcap, with historical footnotes. Schulberg, B. W.

Thirteen at table. Dunsany, E. J. M. D. P. 18th baron

Thirteen men. Bedford-Jones, H.

Thirteen o'clock. Kornbluth, C. M.

Thirty minutes to zero. Divine, A. D.

Thirty seconds—thirty days. Clarke, A. C.

Thirty trips to Washington. McKay, M. C.

Thirty-two votes before breakfast. Stuart, J.

This is the house. Kuttner, H.

This is the land. Bond, N. S.

This looks like murder. Quentin P. pseud.

This mortal coil. Maclaren-Ross, J.

This mortal coil. O'Donovan, M.

This star shall be free. Jenkins, W. F.

This time to-morrow. Coward, N. P.

This town and Salamanca. Seager, A.

This way out. Brown, F.

Thistledown. Aiken, C. P.

Thomas, David, pseud. See Furman, Abraham Loew

Thomas, Dylan, 1914-1953
  Patricia, Edith, and Arnold
    Barrows, H. ed. 15 stories

Thomas, Ruth
  Crip, come home!
    Bachelor, J. M.; Henry, R. L. and Salisbury, R. eds. Current thinking and writing; 2d ser.

Thomasheen James and the dictation machine. Walsh, M.

Thomasheen James goes to the dogs. Walsh, M.

Thomason, John William, 1893-1944
  Mating of a stamp collector
    Jones, K. M. ed. New Confederate short stories
  Preacher goes to Texas
    Neider, C. ed. Men of the high calling
    Peery, W. W. ed. 21 Texas short stories

Thompson, C. Hall, 1923-
  Posse
    Meredith, S. ed. Bar 1 roundup of best western stories

Thompson, Dorothy, 1894-
  Once on Christmas
    Lohan, R. and Lohan, M. eds. New Christmas treasury

Thompson, Edward William, 1849-1924
  Privilege of the limits
    Pacey, D. ed. Book of Canadian stories

Thompson, Elizabeth
  No meadow lark song
    Stanford short stories, 1950

Thompson, Harlan
  Cliff dance
    Fenner, P. R. comp. Cowboys, cowboys, cowboys
  Indian fighter
    Furman, A. L. ed. Teen-age horse stories
  Smoke arm
    Furman, A. L. ed. Teen-age stories of the diamond

Thompson, Lorena
  Grasshopper a burden
    Oberfirst, R. ed. 1954 anthology of best original short-shorts

Thompson, Morton, 1907?-1953
  My brother who talked with horses
    Creamer, J. B. comp. Twenty-two stories about horses and men

Thompson, Robert Emmett, 1924-
It's a nice day—Sunday
Prize stories of 1951
Same as: It's such a nice day—Sunday
It's such a nice day—Sunday
Stanford short stories, 1952
Same as: It's a nice day—Sunday
Thompson, Thomas, 1913-
Burdick's last battle
Thompson, T. They brought their guns
Chico and the badman
Thompson, T. They brought their guns
Doctors of death
Thompson, T. They brought their guns
Empty holster
Thompson, T. They brought their guns
Gun job
Thompson, T. They brought their guns
Jolly
Southern review. Anthology of stories
from the Southern review
Memento
Thompson, T. They brought their guns
One night in Coffin Creek
Thompson, T. They brought their guns
Outlaw's boots
Thompson, T. They brought their guns
Passing of Poker Bill
Thompson, T. They brought their guns
Settlin'-down feelin'
Meredith, S. ed. Bar 3
Shadow of the butte
Meredith, S. ed. Bar 2
Shore for the sinking
Peery, W. W. ed. 21 Texas short
stories
Silver dollar
Thompson, T. They brought their guns
Silver saddle
Western Writers of America. Bad men
and good
Valley for Martha
Thompson, T. They brought their guns
Thompson, Will, 1900?-1949
No one believed me
Merril, J. ed. Beyond the barriers of
space and time
Thoreau, Henry David, 1817-1862
Winter at Walden
Andrews, R. C. ed. My favorite stories
of the great outdoors
Thorne, Anthony, 1904-
Dark red chrysanthemum
New writing (Periodical) Best stories
Thoroughbred. Brier, H. M.
Those men from Mars. Carr, R. S.
Those wily Americans. Frank, P.
"**Thou** art the man." Poe, E. A.
Thou good and faithful. Brunner, K. H.
Though dreamers die. Del Rey, L.
THOUGHT-TRANSFERENCE
Bates, H. Death of a sensitive
Bradbury, R. The veldt
Clifton, M. Star, Bright
Harvey, W. F. Flying out of Mrs Barn-
ard Hollis
Heinlein, R. A. Lost legacy
MacLean, K. Defense mechanism
Matheson, R. Lover, when you're near me
Miller, W. M. Command performance
Shultz, W. H. Oreste
Tucker, W. Job is ended

Thousand-and-second tale of Scheherazade.
Poe, E. A.
Thousand days for Mokhtar. Bowles, P. F.
Thousand-dollar bill. Komroff, M.
THRASHERS
Thomas, R. Crip, come home!
Thrawn Janet. Stevenson, R. L.
The **thread.** Sullivan, R.
Thread of life. Oursler, W. C.
The **threat.** Munro, H. H.
Three Annas. Chekhov, A. P.
Three arshins of land. Tolstoĭ, L. N. Graf
Three Bears Cottage. Collier, J.
Three buttonholes. Favicchio, J.
Three carpenters. Van Doren, M.
Three-day blow. Hemingway, E.
Three deaths. Tolstoĭ, L. N. Graf
Three dogs of Siena. Sansom, W.
Three dollars. Claudy, C. H.
Three dreams of Mr Findlater. Milne, A. A.
Three fat women of Antibes. Maugham,
W. S.
Three friends. De La Mare, W. J.
Three gray men. Goudge, E.
Three Halutzot. Hemeiri, A.
Three hermits. Tolstoĭ, L. N. Graf
Three hours between planes. Fitzgerald,
F. S. K.
Three hundred innings. Meader, S. W.
Three kings. Household, G.
Three links. Cooke, A. A.
Three lovers who lost. Stephens, J.
Three men on a nickel. Kaufman, W.
Three minute novel. Mann, H.
Three players of a summer game. Williams,
T.
Three sailors' gambit. Dunsany,
E. J. M. D. P. 18th baron
Three secrets of human flight. Lange-
wiesche-Brandt, W. E.
Three Skeleton Key. Toudouze, G. G.
Three sneezes. Duvoisin, R. A.
Three strangers. Hardy, T.
Three-strips of flesh. Canaday, J. E.
Three Sundays in a week. Poe, E. A.
Three tools of death. Chesterton, G. K.
Three widows. Queen, E. pseud.
THREE WISE MEN. See Magi
The **threepenny**-piece. Stephens, J.
Threnody. White, W. A. P.
The **threshold.** McKelvey, L.
Through a glass darkly. De Vries, P.
Through channels. Matheson, R.
Through the purple cloud. Williamson, J.
Through Twelve-League Labyrinth. Rey-
nolds, J. M. and McCormick, H. P.
Throwback. DeFord, M. A.
Thumbling and Sapling. Herzl, T.
Thunder and roses. Waldo, E. H.
Thunder and the wise guy. Hallstead,
W. F.

Thunder Road. Gault, W. C.
Thundering Hurd. Aspinwall, M.
Thunderstorm. Caldwell, E.
Thurber, James, 1894-
  Catbird seat
    Best of the Best American short stories,
      1915-1950
    Grayson, C. ed. Fourth round
    Queen, E. pseud. ed. Literature of crime
    Schorer, M. ed. The story
  Greatest man in the world
    Jensen, P. ed. Fireside book of flying
      stories
  More alarms at night
    Burnett, W. ed. World's best
  Night the bed fell
    Fenner, P. R. comp. Fun! Fun! Fun!
  Secret life of Walter Mitty
    Burrell, J. A. and Cerf, B. A. eds. An-
      thology of famous American stories
    Day, A. G. ed. Greatest American short
      stories
    Heilman, R. B. ed. Modern short sto-
      ries
    Shaw, H. and Bement, D. Reading the
      short story
    Stauffer, R. M.; Cunningham, W. H. and
      Sullivan, C. J. eds. Adventures in
      modern literature
    Waite, H. O. and Atkinson, B. P. eds.
      Literature for our time
  The whip-poor-will
    Davenport, B. ed. Tales to be told in
      the dark
  You could look it up
    Graber, R. S. ed. Baseball reader
THURSDAY ISLAND
  Maugham, W. S. French Joe
Thus I refute Beelzy. Collier, J.
Tictocq. Porter, W. S.
TIDAL WAVES
  Hearn, L. The storm
  Maugham, W. S. Yellow streak
The **tide.** Alabaster, M. E.
The **tide.** O'Flaherty, L.
Tie from Paris. Waltari, M. T.
Tierney meets a millionaire. Moroso, J. A.
The **tiger.** Li Fu-yen
Tiger by the tail. Nourse, A. E.
Tiger cat. Keller, D. H.
TIGERS
  Annixter, P. pseud. Loose tiger
  Bottome, P. Henry
  Li Fu-yen. The tiger
  Marshall, E. Heart of Little Shikara
  Munro, H. H. Mrs Packletide's tiger
Tight place. Buckingham, N.
Tight shoes. Runyon, D.
Till death do us part. Kirch, J. A.
Tillotson banquet. Huxley, A. L.
TIMBER. See Lumber industry
Timber. Galsworthy, J.
TIMBER WOLF. See Wolves
TIME
  Abernathy, R. Heritage
  Allen, G. Pausodyne
  Anderson, P. Flight to forever
  Bates, H. Alas, all thinking!

  Bradbury, R. Scent of sarsaparilla
  Clarke, A. C. All the time in the world
  Conklin, G. ed. Science-fiction adventures
    in dimension; 23 stories
  Dell, D. Biography project
  Fenton, F. and Petracca, J. Tolliver's
    travels
  Harris, J. B. The chronoclasm
  Locke R. D. Demotion
  Miller, P. S. Status quondam
  Missing one's coach
  Priestley, J. B. Look after the strange girl
  Reynolds, M. and Brown, F. Dark inter-
    lude
  Wells, H. G. New accelerator
  White, W. A. P. Chronokinesis of Jona-
    than Hull
Time and place. Sansom, W.
TIME AND SPACE. See Space and time
Time expired. Bates, H. E.
Time for a change. Howard, Q. R.
Time for silence. Felder, D. F.
Time is out of joint. Kober, A.
Time is the traitor. Bester, A.
Time locker. Kuttner, H.
Time machine. Wells H. G.
TIME MACHINES
  Asimov, I. Red Queen's race
  Bradbury, R. Sound of thunder
  Harris, J. B. The chronoclasm
  Jenkins, W. F. Life-work of Professor
    Muntz
  Kuttner, H. Shock
  Wells, H. G. Time machine
Time out. Newhouse, E.
Time the tiger. Lewis, W.
Time to rest. Harris, J. B.
TIME TRAVEL. See Time
TIME, TRAVELS IN
  Anderson, P. and Dickson G. Trespass
  Bradbury, R. Fox in the forest
Timeless ones. Russell, E. F.
Timperley, Rosemary
  Christmas meeting
    Asquith, Lady C. M. E. C. ed. Book of
      modern ghosts
TIMUR. See Tamerlane
Tin star. Cunningham, J. M.
Ting-a-ling. Gray, D.
The **tinkler.** Anderson, P.
Tiny and the monster. Waldo, E. H.
Tip in time. Foote, J. T.
Tip the green earth. Marcus, P.
Tippett, James Sterling, 1885-
  Magic at midnight
    Story parade (Periodical) Adventure
      stories
Tiptoe all the way. Kelly, R. G.
Tirol: The golden journey. Charteris, L.
Tit for tat. Rabinowitz, S.
The **Titan.** Miller, P. S.
To a web begun. Verrinder, W.
To be given to God. Forester, C. S.
To build a fire. London, J.
To entertain strangers. Claudy, C. H.

To fall asleep. Williams, W. C.
To fit the crime. Matheson, R.
To follow knowledge. Long, F. B.
To Greenland, to Greenland. Sansom, W.
To have and to lose. Galbraith, N. F.
To him who waits. Kirk, R. G.
To him who waits. Porter, W. S.
To live is to return. Lincoln, V. E.
To market, to market. Stuart, J.
To people a new world. Bond, N. S.
To punish the offender. Arico, V.
To remember these things. White, M.
To serve man. Knight, D.
To the limit. Haycox, E.
To the new world. Metzker, I.
To the ringing of bells. Lieberman, R.
To trouble the living. O'Meara, W.
TOADS. See Frogs; Horned toads
TOASTERS. See Household appliances
TOBACCO
Gordon, C. Her quaint honour
Mabry, T. D. Indian feather
TOBACCO INDUSTRY. See Tobacco
TOBACCO PIPES
Auerbach, B. Hansjorg and his pipe
Tobermory. Munro, H. H.
Tobias Gregson shows what he can do.
Doyle, Sir A. C.
Tobin, Richard Lardner, 1910-
Act of God
Story (Periodical) Story; no. 1
Tobin's palm. Porter, W. S.
TOBOGGANING
Coombs, C. I. Brake happy
Today and today. De Vries, P.
Todd, Ruthven, 1914-
Man who wasn't there
Mystery Writers of America, inc.
Crooks' tour
Over the mountain
Talbot, D. ed. Treasury of mountaineering stories
Tods' amendment. Kipling, R.
Toine. Maupassant, G. de
Toland, Stewart
The letter
McFarland, W. K. comp. Then it happened
Tolbert, Frank X. 1912-
Last Rebel yell
Jones, K. M. ed. New Confederate short stories
Told in the stars. Komroff, M.
TOLEDO. See Spain—Toledo
TOLERATION
Coffin, R. P. T. Seraph in the apple tree
Toll bridge. Haycox, E.
Tolliver's travels. Fenton, F. and Petracca, J.
Tolstoĭ, Alexseĭ Nikolaevich, Graf, 1882-1945
Fusty Devil
Guerney, B. G. comp. New Russian stories

Tolstoĭ, Alexis Nicholaievich. See Tolstoĭ, Aleksei Nikolaevich
Tolstoĭ, Lev Nikolaevich, Graf, 1828-1910
Death of Iván Ilých
Neider, C. ed. Short novels of the masters
Hadji Murad
Rahv, P. ed. Great Russian short novels
Three arshins of land
West, R. B. and Stallman, R. W. eds. Art of modern fiction
Three deaths
Gordon, C. and Tate, A. eds. House of fiction
Three hermits
Neider, C. ed. Great short stories from the world's literature
Neider, C. ed. Men of the high calling
Tolstoy, Leo Nikolaevich. See Tolstoĭ, Lev Nikolaevich, Graf
Tom Chist and his treasure box. Pyle, H.
Tom: the friend of all boys. Little, G. W.
Tomato Cain. Kneale, N.
Tomb of his ancestors. Kipling, R.
Tombling day. Bradbury, R.
Tomboy. Hodkin, R. E.
Tomlinson, Henry Major, 1873-
The derelict
Cerf, B. A. and Moriarty, H. C. eds. Anthology of famous British stories
Tommy who was overmanaged. Strain, F. B.
Tommy's burglar. Porter, W. S.
Tomorrow. Faulkner, W.
Tomorrow. Summers, J. L.
To-morrow is another day. Benson, T.
Tomorrow you're sentenced. Arico, V.
Tone of time. James, H.
Tongue of beast. Claudy, C. H.
Tonight will be different. Howland, R.
Tonio Kröger. Mann, T.
Tony Kytes, the arch-deceiver. Hardy, T.
Too big a dream. White, W.
Too close to nature. Chute, B. J.
Too good with a gun. Patten, L. B.
Too late for murder. Crossen, K. F.
Too many brides. Wilson, R.
Too many crooks. Heyliger, W.
Too much gold. London, J.
Too much horse. Butler, E. P.
Too much Hugo. Bosher, E. F.
Too much pep. Runyon, D.
Too young to have a gun. Lowrey, P. H.
Toole, Kathleen
Short space
Swallow, A. ed. Anchor in the sea
Tools of the trade. Jones, R. F.
Toomai of the elephants. Kipling, R.
Toot for a toot. Cohen, O. R.
TOOTH. See Teeth
The tooth. Dewey, G. G.
Tooth for Paul Revere. Benét, S. V.
Tooth, the whole tooth, and nothing but the tooth. Benchley, R. C.

TOOTHACHE. See Teeth

Tootie and the cat licenses. Kneale, N.

Toozee the puss. Ekbergh, I. D.

The **top.** Albee, G. S.

Top Hat goes to town. Taber, G. B.

Top man. Ullman, J. R.

Top secret. Grinnell, D.

Topley Place sale. Munby, A. N. L.

TOPOLOGY
    Gardner, M. Island of five colors
    Gardner, M. No-sided professor

Torch song. Cheever, J.

Tornado. Vaughn, G.

TORNADOES
    Fitzgerald, F. S. K. Family in the wind
    Vaughn, G. Tornado

TORONTO. See Canada—Toronto

Torrent damned. O'Donovan, M.

Torrid zone. Flora, F.

TORTURE
    Poe, E. A. Pit and the pendulum

Total recall. Helvick, J. pseud.

Total stranger. Cozzens, J. G.

Totem. McConnell, W.

The **touch.** O'Flaherty, L.

Touch and go. De Vries, P.

Touch of Arab. Breckenfeld, V. G.

Touch of nutmeg makes it. Collier, J.

Touch of psychology. Lansing, E. C. H.

Touch of realism. Munro, H. H.

Touch of sun tan. Pearce, R. E.

Touchdown crazy. Fay, W.

Touchdown for Rex. Platt, G.

Touching wood. Sitwell, Sir O. bart.

Toudouze, George Gustave, 1877-
    Three Skeleton Key
       McFee, W. ed. Great sea stories of
       modern times

Tough little Christmas story. Mathews, M.

TOURIST TRADE
    Annett, W. S. The relic
    Goldsmith, G. Tender to the ship

Tourist trade. Tucker, W.

TOURISTS. See Tourist trade

Tournament star. Farrell, J. T.

TOURNAMENTS
    Fox, J. Knight of the Cumberland

Tower of the Elephant. Howard, R. E.

Town blonde, country blonde. Quentin, P. pseud.

Town in eastern Oregon. Davis, H. L.

Town mouse. Becker, S. D.

Town wanted. Brown, F.

Town without a straight man. Stanton, W.

Townes, Robert Sherman
    Problem for Emmy
       Conklin, G. ed. Science-fiction thinking
       machines

TOWNS. See Cities and towns

The **toymaker.** Jones, R. F.

TOYS
    Klass, P. Child's play
    Munro, H. H. Toys of peace

Toys of peace. Munro, H. H.

TRACK ATHLETICS
    Carter, R. G. Blue ribbon event
    Chute, B. J. Magnificent merger
    Chute, B. J. Red Pepper
    Chute, B. J. Triple threat
    Coombs, C. I. Varsity vaulter
    Fessier, M. That's what happened to me
    Person, W. T. Any way race
    Saroyan, W. Fifty yard dash
    Scott, W. R. My father doesn't like me
    Strong, P. N. Anchor man
    Verran, R. Lesson for Flying Goat
      See also Running

Tracked to doom. Porter, W. S.

Trackside grave. McLarn, J. C.

Tractor hoarder. Upson, W. H.

TRACTORS
    Upson, W. H. I'm in a hurry

Tracy, Don, 1905-
    Charity ward
       Saturday evening post (Periodical) Saturday evening post stories, 1950
    Squirrel who was scared
       Saturday evening post (Periodical) Saturday evening post stories, 1951
       Strang, R. M. and Roberts, R. M. eds. Teen-age tales v 1

TRADE UNIONS
    Williamson, J. Breakdown

Tradition of 1804. Hardy, T.

Tragedy at the Baths. Hughes, L.

Tragedy of Pondicherry Lodge. Doyle, Sir A. C.

Tragedy of two ambitions. Hardy, T.

Trail blazer. Gallun, R. Z.

Trail hand. Ernenwein, L. C.

Trail of the Sandhill Stag. Seton, E. T.

Trail of the whiffle-poof. Strong, P. N.

TRAILERS. See Automobiles—Trailers

The **trailers.** Roberts, Sir C. G. D.

Train, Arthur Cheney, 1875-1945
    Dog Andrew
       Blaustein, A. P. ed. Fiction goes to court
    Mr Tutt collects a bet
       Dachs, D. ed. Treasury of sports humor

Train from Rhodesia. Gordimer, N.

Train going. Saroyan, W.

TRAIN ROBBERS. See Brigands and robbers

TRAIN TRIPS. See Railroads—Travel

TRAINED NURSES. See Nurses and nursing

Training Alice and Congo. Richards, D.

TRAINING OF ANIMALS. See Animals—Training

Trainload of soldiers; excerpt from "Rufus M." Estes, E.

TRAINS, RAILROAD. See Railroads—Trains

The **traitor**. Hart, J. S.
The **traitor**. Maugham, W. S.
TRAITORS
 Maugham, W. S. The traitor
  See also Treason
Tramp, the sheep dog. Lang, D.
TRAMPS
 Chekhov, A. P. Drowning
 Huckabay, M. B. Ghost of Sam Bates
 Newhouse, E. Billy the Bastard
 Newhouse, E. The girl who had to get
  married
 Newhouse, E. Out where the West begins
 Nexø, M. A. Birds of passage
 O'Connor, F. Life you save may be your
  own
 Porter, W. S. The caliph, cupid and the
  clock
 Porter, W. S. Cop and the anthem
 Porter, W. S. Higher abdication
 Porter, W. S. Shocks of doom
 Warren, R. P. Blackberry winter
Transfer point. White, W. A. P.
TRANSFORMATION. See Metamorphosis
Transformation of Martin Burney. Porter,
 W. S.
Transience. Clarke, A. C.
Transients. Evans, T. M.
Transients in Arcadia. Porter, W. S.
TRANSMIGRATION
 Kipling, R. 'Finest story in the world'
 Poe, E. A. Ligeia
  See also Reincarnation
TRANSMUTATION. See Metamorphosis
The **trap**. Bloomfield, H.
The **trap**. Sandoz, M. Y.
The **trap**. Silone, I.
Trap is set. Hendryx, J. B.
TRAPPERS
 Edmonds, W. D. Judge
 Gulick, G. C. Rendezvous romance
 Gulick, G. C. Waters of Manitou
Trapper's mates. Williamson, H.
TRAVEL
 Chekhov, A. P. Across Siberia
 Collier, J. Incident on a lake
 Shulman, M. Chance for adventure
 Waugh, E. Cruise
  See also Ocean travel; Railroads—
  Travel
The **traveler**. Stegner, W.
TRAVELERS, COMMERCIAL. See Com-
 mercial travelers
TRAVELING SALESMEN. See Salesmen
 and salesmanship
The **traveller**. Crémieux, B.
The **traveller**. Matheson, R.
Traveller from the West and the traveller
 from the East. Warner, S. T.
Travellers' tears. Stern, J.
TRAVELS IN TIME. See Time, Travels
 in
Traven, B. pseud.
 Third guest
  Best American short stories, 1954

Travers, Pamela L. 1906-
 Ah Wong
  Bachelor, J. M.; Henry, R. L. and Salis-
  bury, R. eds. Current thinking and
  writing; 2d ser.
TRAVESTIES. See Parodies
The **trawler**. Connolly, J. B.
TREASON
 Gellhorn, M. E. Honeyed peace
  See also Traitors
The **treasure**. Lumpkin, G.
The **treasure**. Maugham, W. S.
Treasure of Franchard. Stevenson, R. L.
Treasure of Tranicos. Howard, R. E.
Treasure-ship. Munro, H. H.
TREASURE-TROVE
 Allen, M. P. Two chests of treasure
 Calahan, H. A. Back to Treasure Island
 Coppock, C. Pirate gold
 Curtis, K. Cruises in the sun
 Delavigne, J. F. C. Up the garret stairs
 Dobie, J. F. Midas on a goatskin
 Munro, H. H. Treasure-ship
 Poe, E. A. The gold-bug
 Pyle, H. Tom Chist and the treasure box
 Queen, E. pseud. Needle's eye
 Wells, H. G. Mr Brisher's treasure
TREASURER
 Caldwell, E. The rumor
Treasures of the sea. Gordimer, N.
Treat, Lawrence, 1903-
 Shoes for breakfast
  Mystery Writers of America, inc. Maiden
  murders
Treat, Lawrence, 1903- **and Tarachow, Sid-
 ney**
 Wire brush
  Mystery writers of America, inc. Crooks'
  tour
The **tree**. Coolidge, O. E.
The **tree**. De La Mare, W. J.
A **tree**. A rock. A cloud. McCullers, C. S.
Tree for two. Marker, W. D.
Tree men of Potu. Holberg, L. baron
Tree of knowledge. James, H.
Tree of life. Moore, C. L.
Tree toad. Davis, R. H.
TREES
 Bjørnson, B. How the mountain was clad
 Cohn, E. Rebellious tree
 Coolidge, O. E. The tree
 De La Mare, W. S. The tree
 Holberg, L. baron. Tree men of Potu
 Kuttner, H. Hard-luck diggings
 Sansom, W. My tree
Tree's wife. Counselman, M. E.
Tregannet book of hours. Munby, A. N. L.
Tregarthen, John Coulson, 1854-1933
 Great run
  Andrews, R. C. ed. My favorite stories
  of the great outdoors
Trends. Asimov, I.
Trenton in thirty minutes. Felsen, G.
Très Jolie. Foote, J. T.

Trespass. Anderson, P. and Dickson, G.

The trial. Forster, E. M.

Trial by fire. Kirtland, A.

Trial of John Nobody. Carr, A. H. Z.

TRIALS
  Algren, N. Captain is impaled
  Benét, S. V. Devil and Daniel Webster
  Bergengruen, W. Concerning muskets
  Blish, J. Beanstalk
  Carr, A. H. Z. Trial of John Nobody
  Cobb, I. S. Boys will be boys
  Connelly, M. C. Coroner's inquest
  Davis, R. H. Wasted day
  Duranty, W. The parrot
  Faulkner, W. Tomorrow
  Gally, J. W. Hualapi
  Galsworthy, J. The juryman
  Harte, B. Colonel Starbottle for the plaintiff
  Harte, B. Tennessee's partner
  Hurston, Z. N. Conscience of the court
  Klingsberg, H. M. Doowinkle, Attorney
  Lewis, J. Wife of Martin Guerre
  Millar, K. Wild goose chase
  Milne, A. A. The barrister
  O'Donovan, M. Counsel for Œdipus
  Post, M. D. Corpus delicti
  Shaw, I. Triumph of justice
  Swinnerton, F. A. The verdict
  Train, A. C. Dog Andrew

India
  Forster, E. M. The trial

Trials of a ballplayer's wife. Broun, H. C.

TRICKERY. See Hoaxes

Trickster and the old witch
  Pacey, D. ed. Book of Canadian stories

Trigger tide. Guin, W.

Trilling, Lionel, 1905-
  Of this time, of that place
    Felheim, M.; Newman, F. B. and Steinhoff, W. R. eds. Modern short stories
    Waite, H. O. and Atkinson, B. P. eds. Literature for our time
  Other Margaret
    Ludwig, J. B. and Poirier, W. R. eds. Stories, British and American
    West, R. B. and Stallman, R. W. eds. Art of modern fiction

Trimmed lamp. Porter, W. S.

TRINITY COLLEGE. See Cambridge, England. University

Trinket's colt. Somerville, E. A. O. and Martin, V. F.

Trip one. Grendon, E.

Trip to Czardis. Cranberry, E. P.

Triple fugue. Sitwell, Sir O. bart.

Triple threat. Chute, B. J.

TRIPOLITAN WAR. See United States—19th century—Tripolitan War, 1801-1805

The triumph. Bonner, P. H.

Triumph of justice. Shaw, I.

Triumph with bells and laughter. Brookhouser, F.

Trivulzio and the King. Bergengruen, W.

Trixie: the dog who did her duty. Little, G. W.

Trollope, Anthony, 1815-1882
  Bailiffs at Framley
    Trollope, A. Bedside Barsetshire
  Bartsetshire
    Trollope, A. Bedside Barsetshire
  Bartsetshire worthy—Archdeacon Grantly
    Trollope, A. Bedside Barsetshire
  Bishop sends his inhibition
    Trollope, A. Bedside Barsetshire
  Caleb Thumble returns to Barchester
    Trollope, A. Bedside Barsetshire
  Crosbie starts his honeymoon
    Trollope, A. Bedside Barsetshire
  Dr Fillgrave refuses a fee
    Trollope, A. Bedside Barsetshire
  The Duke entertains
    Trollope, A. Bedside Barsetshire
  Frank takes a brother's privilege
    Trollope, A. Bedside Barsetshire
  Grace Crawley and the Archdeacon
    Trollope, A. Bedside Barsetshire
  Johnny Eames does well
    Trollope, A. Bedside Barsetshire
  Josiah Crawley at the Palace
    Trollope, A. Bedside Barsetshire
  Josiah Crawley charged with theft
    Trollope, A. Bedside Barsetshire
  Love scene
    Trollope, A. Bedside Barsetshire
  Malachi's Cove
    Cerf, B. A. and Moriarty, H. C. eds. Anthology of famous British stories
  Mark Robarts is adamant
    Trollope, A. Bedside Barsetshire
  Mark Robarts signs a bill
    Trollope, A. Bedside Barsetshire
  Mary comes into money
    Trollope, A. Bedside Barsetshire
  Mesdames Grantly and Proudie get together
    Trollope, A. Bedside Barsetshire
  Mr Slope vanquished
    Trollope, A. Bedside Barsetshire
  Mrs Proudie goes too far
    Trollope, A. Bedside Barsetshire
  Mrs Proudie intervenes
    Trollope, A. Bedside Barsetshire
  Mrs Proudie vanquished
    Trollope, A. Bedside Barsetshire
  Obstinacy of Septimus Harding
    Trollope, A. Bedside Barsetshire
  The Proudies entertain
    Trollope, A. Bedside Barsetshire
  R.I.P.
    Trollope, A. Bedside Barsetshire
  Sir Louis dines out
    Trollope, A. Bedside Barsetshire

Trouble in St Brendan's. Lieberman R.

Trouble on 98th Street. Taubes, F.

Trouble on Tantalus. Miller, P. S.

Trouble on the range. Regli, A. C.

Trouble with the angels. Hughes, L.

Trouble with the union. Harrington, D.

Troubled water. English, T.

TROUSERS
  Caldwell, E. Corduroy pants

Trout widows. Ford, C.

TRUCK DRIVERS
  Porter, W. S. Caliph and the cad

True history. Lucian

True lovers' knot. Sitwell, Sir O. bart.

True relation of the apparition of one Mrs
    Veal. Defoe, D.
The **trumpet.** De La Mare, W. J.
"Trumpet" comes to Pickeye! Goodman,
    J. T.
Trusting snakes. Arico, V.
TRUTH
    Munro, H. H. Reginald on besetting sins
Truth about Pyecraft. Wells, H. G.
Truth about Sylvanus. Van Doren, M.
TRUTHFULNESS AND FALSEHOOD
    Crane, S. The knife
    Dickson, G. R. Lulungomeena
    Gally, J. W. Frozen truth

Tryout. Barr, J. pseud.

The tsantsa. Sandoz, M. Y.

Tsung-Wen, Shen. See Shen, Tsung-wen

T'uan Ch'engshih, d. 863
    Cinderella
        Lin, Y. ed. Famous Chinese short sto-
        ries

TUBERCULOSIS
    Maugham, W. S. Sanatorium
    Porter, W. S. Fog in Santone
    Porter, W. S. Hygeia at the Solito
    Waltari, M. T. Island of ice

Tucker, Bob, pseud. See Tucker, Wilson

Tucker, Louis
    Cubic city
        Margulies, L. and Friend, O. J. eds.
        From off this world

Tucker, Wilson, 1914-
    Able to Zebra
        Tucker, W. Science-fiction subtreasury
    Exit
        Moskowitz, S. comp. Editor's choice in
        science fiction
        Tucker, W. Science-fiction subtreasury
    Gentlemen—the Queen!
        Tucker, W. Science-fiction subtreasury
    Home is where the wreck is
        Tucker, W. Science-fiction subtreasury
    The job is ended
        Tucker, W. Science-fiction subtreasury
    The mountaineer
        Tucker, W. Science-fiction subtreasury
    My brother's wife
        Tucker, W. Science-fiction subtreasury
    "MCMLV"
        Tucker, W. Science-fiction subtreasury
    Street walker
        Tucker, W. Science-fiction subtreasury
    Tourist trade
        Best science fiction stories: 1952
        Heinlein, R. A. ed. Tomorrow, the stars
    Wayfaring strangers
        Tucker, W. Science-fiction subtreasury

Tudor chimney. Munby, A. N. L.

TUGBOATS
    Strong, P. N. Salvage

Tuition for the rebbe. Reisin, A.

Tu Kwang-t'ing, 850-933
    Curly-beard
        Lin, Y. ed. Famous Chinese short sto-
        ries

Tulip. De Vries, P.

Tunis, John Roberts, 1889-
    Ronald leaves the academy
        Hazeltine, A. I. comp. Selected stories
        for teen-agers
    Two-mile race
        Herzberg, M. J. comp. Treasure chest
        of sport stories
    Unpredictable Dodgers
        Fenner, P. R. comp. Crack of the bat

Tunkel, Joseph, 1881-1950
    From what a Litvak makes a living
        Ausubel, N. ed. Treasury of Jewish
        humor
    The gift
        Ausubel, N. ed. Treasury of Jewish
        humor
    Glass of tea
        Ausubel, N. ed. Treasury of Jewish
        humor

Tunkeler, Der. See Tunkel, Joseph

TUNNELS AND TUNNELING
    Benson, T. Man from the tunnel
    Maltz, A. Man on a road

Turgenev, Ivan Sergeevich, 1818-1883
    Byézhin Meadow
        Gordon, C. and Tate, A. eds. House of
        fiction
        Same as: Bezhin Meadow; Byezhin
        Prairie
    District doctor
        Blodgett, H. W. ed. Story survey.
        1953 ed.
        Neider, C. ed. Great short stories from
        the world's literature
    First love
        Rahv, P. ed. Great Russian short novels

TURKEY
Constantinople
    Bergengruen, W. Orban twins

Turkey-red. Wood, F. G.

TURKEYS
    Buckingham, N. Comin' twenty-one

TURKISH BATHS. See Baths, Turkish

Turn and turn about. Holland, R. S.

Turn of the screw. James, H.

Turn of the tide. Cicellis, K.

Turn off the moon. Hause, M.

Turn with the sun. Knowles, J.

Turnabout. Faulkner, W.

Turner, Robert
    The gunny
        Meredith, S. ed. Bar 3

TURTLES
    Keith, S. Point of view

Turtles played the hares. Stoakes, H. R.

TUTORS
    James, H. The pupil
    Wall, J. W. Ringstones

Tutti frutti. Sansom, W.

"Twa kings." De La Roche, M.

Twain, Mark, pseud. See Clemens, Samuel
    Langhorne

Twentieth floor. Van Doren, M.

Twentieth game. O'Rourke, F.

Twenty-five bucks. Farrell, J. T.

Twenty floors up. Carver, C.

Twenty-six and one. Gorky, M.
Twilight. Reymont, W. S.
Twilight of the wise. Hilton, J.
The twilighters. Loomis, N. M.
TWINS
Bergengruen, W. Orban twins
Collier, J. Season of mists
Cooke, A. A. Two peas in a pod
Lewis, S. Willow walk
Pratt, F. and De Camp, L. S. My brother's keeper
Walsh, M. Sword of Yung Lo
Wilson, H. L. Wrong twin
Twisted branch. Cicellis, K.
Two ages of man. Sunley, R.
Two anecdotes
Davenport, B. ed. Tales to be told in the dark
Two-bits of traffic C. Crump, I.
Two blue birds. Lawrence, D. H.
Two bottles of relish. Dunsany, E. J. M. D. P. 18th baron
Two brothers
Lohan, R. and Lohan, M. eds. New Christmas treasury
Two brothers. Farrell, J. T.
Two chests of treasure. Allen, M. P.
Two churches of 'Quawket. Bunner, H. C.
Two cooing doves. Palma, R.
Two Daumiers. Krige, U.
Two days with Mr Neville's hounds. Surtees, R. S.
Two drovers. Scott, Sir W.
Two face. Long, F. B.
Two-faced promise. Gulick, G. C.
Two for a ride. Moore, G. M.
Two for the show. Newcomb, E.
Two friends. Davies, R.
Two friends. Maupassant, G. de
Two great men. Rappaport, S.
Two in one. Chekhov, A. P.
Two infants. Gibran, K.
Two ladies in retirement. Taylor, P. H.
Two legacies. Landa, M. J.
Two legs for the two of us. Jones, J.
Two little Confederates. Page, T. N.
Two little soldiers. Maupassant, G. de
Two lovely beasts. O'Flaherty, L.
Two men. Stern, J.
Two men confer with Cuter Malone. Hendryx, J. B.
Two-mile race. Tunis, J. R.
Two miracles. Deledda, G.
Two Miss Koofers. Preston, B. B.
Two of a kind. Chekhov, A. P.
Two on trial. Nicola, H. B.
Two over par. Roos, K. pseud.
Two peas in a pod. Cooke, A. A.
Two pillars blight. Claudy, C. H.
Two pleasures. Wendroff, Z.
Two recalls. Porter, W. S.

Two renegades. Porter, W. S.
Two ringers. Foote, J. T.
Two rivers. Stegner, W. E.
Two seconds. Steele, W. D.
Two shadows. Temple, W. F.
Two sisters. Farrell, J. T.
Two soldiers. Faulkner, W.
Two strangers came to town. Dick, I. M.
Two Thanksgiving Day gentlemen. Porter, W. S.
Two were left. Cave, H. B.
Two wishes. Gibran, K.
Two wrongs. Fitzgerald, F. S. K.
The Twonky. Kuttner, H.
Tyger! Tyger! Carr, A. H. Z.
Tynîanov, ÎUrii Nikolaevich, 1894-1943
Second Lieutenant Likewise
Guerney, B. G. comp. New Russian stories
Tynyanov, Yuri Nicholaievich. See Tynîanov, ÎUrii Nikolaevich
Typhoon. Conrad, J.
Typical gesture of Colonel Duggan. Schulberg, B. W.
TYPISTS
Porter, W. S. Springtime à la carte
TYRANNY. See Despotism
TYROL
Charteris, L. Tirol: The golden journey
Tzagan. Wood, C.
Tzensky, Sergîeï Sergeev-. See Sergîeev-Tsenskiï, Sergîeï Nikolaevich

U

UCCELLO, PAOLO DI DONO, KNOWN AS, 1396?-1475
Schwob, M. Paolo Uccello
UGANDA. See Congo, Belgian—Uganda
Ugly. Maupassant, G. de
Ugly sister. Maxtone Graham, J. A.
Ugly weather. Verga, G.
UKRAINE. See Russia—Ukraine
Uller uprising. Piper, H. B.
Ullman, James M.
Anything new on the strangler?
Queen, E. pseud. ed. Ellery Queen's awards: 9th ser.
Ullman, James Ramsey, 1907-
Am I blue?
Ullman, J. R. Island of the blue macaws, and sixteen other stories
Between you and I
Ullman, J. R. Island of the blue macaws, and sixteen other stories
Chicken dinner
Ullman, J. R. Island of the blue macaws, and sixteen other stories
Deadly north face
Saturday evening post (Periodical) Saturday evening post stories, 1951

Ullman, James R.—*Continued*
  Diversion
    Ullman, J. R. Island of the blue macaws, and sixteen other stories
  Easy day for a lady
    Ullman, J. R. Island of the blue macaws, and sixteen other stories
  Girl on horseback
    Ullman, J. R. Island of the blue macaws, and sixteen other stories
  Hello darling
    Ullman, J. R. Island of the blue macaws, and sixteen other stories
  I seen 'em go
    Ullman, J. R. Island of the blue macaws, and sixteen other stories
  Island of the blue macaws
    Ullman, J. R. Island of the blue macaws, and sixteen other stories
  Mountains of the Axis
    Ullman, J. R. Island of the blue macaws, and sixteen other stories
  Pau
    Ullman, J. R. Island of the blue macaws, and sixteen other stories
  Presumed lost
    Ullman, J. R. Island of the blue macaws, and sixteen other stories
  Silver sword
    Ullman, J. R. Island of the blue macaws, and sixteen other stories
  Soldier of the realm
    Ullman, J. R. Island of the blue macaws, and sixteen other stories
  Top man
    Talbot, D. ed. Treasury of mountaineering stories
    Ullman, J. R. Island of the blue macaws, and sixteen other stories
  Visitation
    Ullman, J. R. Island of the blue macaws, and sixteen other stories
  White night
    Ullman, J. R. Island of the blue macaws, and sixteen other stories
Ullman, Victor
  Message for Harold
    Ribalow, H. U. ed. This land, these people
Ultima Thule. Galsworthy, J.
Ultima Thule. Russell, E. F.
Ulysses and the dogman. Porter, W. S.
Umbilical cord. Gordimer, N.
The **umbrella.** Maupassant, G. de
Unamuno, Miguel de. See Unamuno y Jugo, Miguel de
Unamuno y Jugo, Miguel de, 1864-1936
  Saint Manuel Bueno, martyr
    De Onís, H. ed. Spanish stories and tales
  Solitude
    Neider, C. ed. Great short stories from the world's literature
Unapproved route. O'Donovan, M.
The **unbelievable.** Forester, C. S.
The **unbeliever.** Johnson, D. M.
Unborn ghosts. Cardoz, N.
Uncertain flowering. Laurence, M.
Uncertain Molly Collicut. Tarkington, B.

Uncertain weapon. Eliot, G. F.
Uncle Charlie. Ketchum, P.
Uncle David's Christmas. Eggleston, M. W.
Uncle Edgar and the reluctant saint. Cousins, M.
Uncle Henry's love nest. Caldwell, E.
Uncle Hyacinth. Noyes, A.
Uncle Jeff. Caldwell, E.
Uncle Julius and the BMT. Rosenberg, E. C.
Uncle Kees protests. Van Paassen, P.
Uncle Phil on TV. Priestley, J. B.
Uncle Sod's birthday social. Knox, J.
Uncle Torwal and Whitey go to town. Rounds, G.
Uncle Wiggily in Connecticut. Salinger, J. D.
Uncle Willy. Faulkner, W.
UNCLES
  Ballard, J. C. Mountain summer
  Betts, D. Family album
  Burt, M. S. Each in his generation
  Carlson, E. Museum piece
  Collier, J. Another American tragedy
  Melville, H. Happy failure
  Rosenberg, E. C. Uncle Julius and the BMT
  Waltari, M. T. Moonscape
The **unconquered.** Maugham, W. S.
Under dog. Christie, A. M.
Under dogs. Azuela, M.
Under the beech tree. Stern, J.
Under the dome. Frank, W. D.
Under the dome: Aleph. Frank, W. D.
Under the greenwood tree. Williams, W. C.
Under the knife. Wells, H. G.
Under the lion's paw. Garland, H.
Under the sky. Bowles, P. F.
Underground episode. Smith, E. W.
Underground movement. Neville, K.
UNDERGROUND RAILROAD
  Benét, S. V. Freedom's a hard-bought thing
  Coatsworth, E. J. Peddler's card
The **understanding.** Lincoln, V. E.
The **undertaker.** Pushkin, A. S.
UNDERTAKERS
  Davies, R. Gents only
  Pratt, F. and De Camp, L. S. Corpus delectable
  Pushkin, A. S. The undertaker
Undset, Sigrid, 1882-1949
  No one can harm us
    Thinker's digest (Periodical) Spoiled priest, and other stories
  Signed with his seal
    Thinker's digest (Periodical) Spoiled priest, and other stories
UNEMPLOYED
  Bondarenko, W. C. Job well done
  Caldwell, E. Dorothy
  Caldwell, E. Slow death
  Maltz, A. Happiest man on earth
  Pagano, J. The disinherited
  Zugsmith, L. Room in the world

Unexpected reunion. Hebel, J. P.
UNFAITHFULNESS. See Marriage problems
Unfinished Christmas story. Porter, W. S.
UNFINISHED STORIES
  Chekhov, A. P. De-compensation
Unfinished story. Porter, W. S.
Unfinished symphony. Corkery, D.
Unholy living and half dying. O'Faoláin, S.
Unholy three. Auchincloss, L.
Unholy trio. Hendryx, J. B.
The **unicorn.** Seager, A.
Unite and conquer. Waldo, E. H.
UNITED STATES

To 1776
Carter, R. G. Tea from the brigantine

18th century—Revolution
Brick, J. Rifleman's run
Erskine, L. Y. After school
Forbes, E. "Disperse, ye rebels!"
Hale, E. E. General Washington's pig
Skinner, C. L. Silent Scot

18th century—Revolution— Prisoners and Prisons
Brick, J. Rifleman's run

19th century—Tripolitan War, 1801-1805
Daniel, H. Shores of Tripoli

19th century—War of 1812
Swanson, N. H. They kept the flag there

19th century—Civil War
Allen, H. Surgery at Aquila
Bierce, A. Occurrence at Owl Creek bridge
Bierce, A. One of the missing
Boyd, J. Elms and Fair Oaks
Brick, J. Message for Uncle Billy
Clayton, J. B. Ride a pale ghost into night and time
Cozzens, J. G. Men running
Crane, S. Gray sleeve
Crane, S. Mystery of heroism
Danielson, R. E. Corporal Hardy
Dowdey, C. Bugles blow retreat
James, M. Stolen railroad train
Page, T. N. Burial of the guns
Page, T. N. Two little Confederates
Porter, W. S. Two renegades
Sass, H. R. Affair at St Albans
Street, J. H. They know how
Toland, S. The letter
Welty, E. The burning

19th century—Civil War— Prisoners and Prisons
Brick, J. Message for Uncle Billy

19th century—War of 1898
Crane, S. Episode of war

Army
Best Army short stories, 1950; 12 stories
Chase, F. General from the Pentagon
Cozzens, J. G. Men running
Haycox, E. Dispatch to the general
Haycox, E. Scout detail
Newhouse, E. Major and Mrs Fletcher
Newhouse, E. Position of the soldier
Newhouse, E. Time out
Porter, W. S. Moment of victory
Shaw, I. Act of faith
Tennyson, H. In the desert

Army—Recruiting, enlistment, etc.
Wilson, B. Stand-in

Army Air Forces
Gordon, A. Kiss for the Lieutenant

Coast Guard
Detzer, K. W. Surfman number nine

Naval Academy, Annapolis
White, R. Sick bay to sea wall

Navy
Auchincloss, L. Fall of a sparrow
Auchincloss, L. Loyalty up and loyalty down
Auchincloss, L. Wally
Burnet, D. Why did he leave me?
Faulkner, W. Turnabout
Hale, E. E. Man without a country
Heggen, T. Night watch
Schulberg, B. W. Ensign Weasel
White, R. An eye for an eye

State Department
Acheson, E. G. Big shot
UNIVERSE
  Hamilton, E. Fessenden's worlds
Universe is not really expanding. Willingham, C.
University. Phillips, P.
UNIVERSITY OF MOSCOW. See Moscow. University
UNJUST ACCUSATION. See False accusation
Unkindest blow. Munro, H. H.
Unknown Chekhov. Chekhov, A. P.
Unknown quantity. Porter, W. S.
UNKNOWN SOLDIER
  Dos Passos, J. R. Body of an American
Unlucky number. Coombs, C. I.
Unlucky winner. Shulman, M.
Unparalleled adventure of one Hans Pfaall. Poe, E. A.
UNPARDONABLE SIN. See Sin, Unpardonable
Unpleasant incident. Chekhov, A. P.
An **unpleasantness.** Chekhov, A. P.
Unpredictable Dodgers. Tunis, J. R.
Unprofitable servant. Porter, W. S.
Unquiet spirit. Coolidge, O. E.
Unready to wear. Vonnegut, K.
Unrest-cure. Munro, H. H.
The **unsaid** prayer. Van Paassen, P.
Unseen collection. Zweig, S.
Unspoiled reaction. McCarthy, M. T.
Untermeyer, Louis, 1885-
  Donkey of God
    Lohan, R. and Lohan, M. eds. New Christmas treasury

Until they sail. Michener, J. A.

Untimely toper. De Camp, L. S. and Pratt, F.

Untouched by human hands. Sheckley, R.

Unturned card. Marshall, E.

Unwanted one. Taber, G. B.

Unwelcome tenant. Aycock, R. D.

Up from the depths. Wodehouse, P. G.

Up in a balloon. Ekbergh, I. D.

Up the garret stairs. Delavigne, J. F. C.

Uprooted. O'Donovan, M.

Upshaw, Helen, 1928-
  The harvest
    American vanguard, 1950
  Love smelled of vanilla
    American vanguard, 1952

Upson, William Hazlett, 1891-
  Alexander Botts goes underground
    Upson, W. H. No rest for Botts
  Alexander Botts vs. the income tax
    Upson, W. H. No rest for Botts
  Botts and the brink of disaster
    Upson, W. H. No rest for Botts
  Botts and the jet-propelled tractor
    Upson, W. H. No rest for Botts
  Botts bogs down
    Upson, W. H. No rest for Botts
  Botts cleans out the parts department
    Upson, W. H. No rest for Botts
  Botts discovers uranium
    Upson, W. H. No rest for Botts
  Botts gets a new job
    Upson, W. H. No rest for Botts
  Botts makes magic
    Upson, W. H. No rest for Botts
  Expensive Mr Botts
    Upson, W. H. No rest for Botts
  Frank and honest
    Upson, W. H. No rest for Botts
  I'm in a hurry
    Cuff, R. P. ed. American short story
     survey
  A quiet wedding
    Dachs, D. ed. Treasury of sports humor
  Tractor hoarder
    Upson, W. H. No rest for Botts

Upturned face. Crane, S.

URANUS (PLANET)
  Bond, N. S. Day we celebrate
  Wollheim, D. A. Planet passage

Use of force. Williams, W. C.

USURERS. See Pawnbrokers

Utility. Jones, R. F.

Utopia. More, Sir T.

UTOPIAS
  Bacon, F. viscount St Albans. New At-
    lantis
  Blish, J. Okie
  Campanella, T. City of the sun
  Goldsmith, O. Asem
  More, Sir T. Utopia
  Richter, C. Sinister journey
  Russell, E. F. And then there were none

V

Vacancy in Westchester. Newhouse, E.

Vacant cross. Stancourt, L. J.

Vacation houses. See Summer resorts

VACATIONS
  Garland, H. Mrs Ripley's trip
  Hesse, H. Youth, beautiful youth
  Miller, C. Gentle season
  Young, E. H. The stream

VACCINATION
  Kipling, R. Tomb of his ancestors

A vagabond. Maupassant, G. de

VAGABONDS. See Tramps

VAGRANTS. See Tramps

Vain beauty. Maupassant, G. de

Valbor, Kirsten, 1919-
  New Guinea interlude
    American vanguard, 1952

Valdés, Armando Palacio. See Palacio
  Valdés, Armando

Vale of tears. Stallings, L.

Valiant lady. Bendrodt, J. C.

Valiant woman. Powers, J. F.

Valle-Inclán, Ramón del, 1870-1936
  My sister Antonia
    De Onís, H. ed. Spanish stories and
    tales

Valley for Martha. Thompson, T.

Valley of dreams. Weinbaum, S. G.

Valley of great wells. Van Doren, M.

Valley of spiders. Wells, H. G.

Valley of the beasts. Blackwood, A.

Value of the dollar. Gordon, E. E.

Vampire of the village. Chesterton, G. K.

Van Bruggen, Carry. See Bruggen, Carry
  (de Haan) van

Vance, Carol
  Captive heart
    Lantz, J. E. ed. Stories of Christian
    living

Vance, Jack, pseud. See Kuttner, Henry

Vandercook, John Womack, 1902-
  The challenge
    Queen, E. pseud. ed. Queen's awards:
    7th ser.
  Pretending makes it so
    Saturday evening post (Periodical)
    Saturday evening post stories, 1951

Van de Water, Frederic Franklyn, 1890-
  Eve enters
    Cavanna, B. ed. Pick of the litter

Van Doren, Mark, 1894-
  Bad corner
    Van Doren, M. Short stories
  Big enough for a horse
    Van Doren, M. Short stories
  Birdie, come back
    Van Doren, M. Short stories
  The birds
    Van Doren, M. Short stories
  Brown cap
    Van Doren, M. Nobody say a word,
    and other stories

Van Doren, Mark—*Continued*
  The butterfly
    Van Doren, M. Nobody say a word,
      and other stories
  The combination
    Van Doren, M. Short stories
  Consider courage
    Van Doren, M. Short stories
  Courage and the power
    Van Doren, M. Short stories
  Dollar bill
    Van Doren, M. Short stories
  The dream
    Van Doren, M. Nobody say a word,
      and other stories
  Engine and the flare
    Van Doren, M. Short stories
  Episode at the Honeypot
    Queen, E. pseud. ed. Queen's awards:
      7th ser.
    Van Doren, M. Nobody say a word,
      and other stories
  Facts about the hyacinthes
    Van Doren, M. Nobody say a word,
      and other stories
  Father O'Connell
    Van Doren, M. Nobody say a word,
      and other stories
  Fisk Fogle
    Van Doren, M. Short stories
  Four brothers
    Van Doren, M. Nobody say a word,
      and other stories
  God has no wife
    Van Doren, M. Nobody say a word,
      and other stories
  Good thing to know
    Van Doren, M. Short stories
  Grandison and son
    Van Doren, M. Nobody say a word,
      and other stories
  Great deal of weather
    Van Doren, M. Nobody say a word,
      and other stories
  Honeymoon
    Van Doren, M. Nobody say a word,
      and other stories
  How bad? How long?
    Van Doren, M. Nobody say a word,
      and other stories
  I, Tobit
    Van Doren, M. Nobody say a word,
      and other stories
  Imp of string
    Van Doren, M. Short stories
  In what far country
    Van Doren, M. Short stories
  The key
    Van Doren, M. Short stories
  Lady over the wall
    Van Doren, M. Nobody say a word,
      and other stories
  Like what?
    Van Doren, M. Nobody say a word,
      and other stories
  Little place
    Van Doren, M. Nobody say a word,
      and other stories
  Lucky Murdock
    Van Doren, M. Short stories
  Man who had died a lot
    Van Doren, M. Short stories

  Many are called
    Van Doren, M. Short stories
  Miss Swallow
    Van Doren, M. Short stories
  Mr Hasbrouck
    Van Doren, M. Short stories
  Mrs Lancey
    Van Doren, M. Nobody say a word,
      and other stories
  Mortimer
    Van Doren, M. Nobody say a word,
      and other stories
  New girl
    Van Doren, M. Short stories
  Night at the Notch
    Van Doren, M. Short stories
  No thunder, no lightning
    Van Doren, M. Short stories
  Nobody say a word
    Best American short stories, 1952
    Van Doren, M. Nobody say a word,
      and other stories
  Not a natural man
    Van Doren, M. Short stories
  One of hers
    Van Doren, M. Nobody say a word,
      and other stories
  One of the Garretsons
    Van Doren, M. Short stories
  The pair
    Van Doren, M. Nobody say a word,
      and other stories
  Payment in full
    Van Doren, M. Short stories
  Princess who couldn't say yes
    Van Doren, M. Nobody say a word,
      and other stories
  The prism
    Van Doren, M. Nobody say a word,
      and other stories
  The quarry
    Van Doren, M. Nobody say a word,
      and other stories
  Rescue
    Van Doren, M. Short stories
  Rich, poor, and indifferent
    Van Doren, M. Nobody say a word,
      and other stories
  Roberts and O'Hara
    Van Doren, M. Short stories
  Satan's best girl
    Van Doren, M. Short stories
  So many years
    Van Doren, M. Nobody say a word,
      and other stories
  Stacey Bell
    Van Doren, M. Short stories
  Still, still so
    Best American short stories, 1953
    Van Doren, M. Nobody say a word,
      and other stories
  Strange girl
    Van Doren, M. Short stories
  The streamliner
    Van Doren, M. Short stories
  Tall one
    Van Doren, M. Nobody say a word,
      and other stories
  Three carpenters
    Van Doren, M. Nobody say a word,
      and other stories

Van Doren, Mark—*Continued*
Truth about Sylvanus
Van Doren, M. Nobody say a word,
and other stories
Twentieth floor
Van Doren, M. Nobody say a word,
and other stories
Valley of great wells
Van Doren, M. Nobody say a word,
and other stories
Wander's world
Van Doren, M. Short stories
The watchman
Van Doren, M. Short stories
Wild wet place
Van Doren, M. Short stories
Witch of Ramoth
Van Doren, M. Nobody say a word,
and other stories

Van Dresser, Peter
By virtue of circumference
Del Rey, L.; Matschat, C. H. and Car-
mer, C. L. eds. Year after tomorrow
Plum duff
Del Rey, L.; Matschat, C. H. and Car-
mer, C. L. eds. Year after tomorrow
Rocket to the sun
Del Rey, L.; Matschat, C. H. and Car-
mer, C. L. eds. Year after tomorrow

Vandy, Vandy. Wellman, M. W.

Van Dyke, Henry, 1852-1933
First Christmas tree
Scribner treasury
Lost boy
Selden, R. ed. Ways of God and men
Other Wise Man
Lohan, R. and Lohan, M. eds. New
Christmas treasury
Wedding ring
Thinker's digest (Periodical) Spoiled
priest, and other stories

Vanina Vanini. Beyle, M. H.

Vanishing of Vaudrey. Chesterton, G. K.

Vanishing wolf. Davis, H. L.

VANITY. See Pride and vanity

Vanity. Corkery, D.

Vanity. O'Donovan, M.

Vanity and some sables. Porter, W. S.

Vanka. Chekhov, A. P.

Van Loan, Charles Emmett, 1876-1919
Cure for lumbago
Dachs, D. ed. Treasury of sports humor
Levelling with Elisha
Creamer, J. B. comp. Twenty-two stories
about horses and men
Mister Conley
Graber, R. S. ed. Baseball reader
Herzberg, M. J. comp. Treasure chest of
sport stories
Playing even for Obadiah
Creamer, J. B. comp. Twenty-two stories
about horses and men

Van Luik, Carmen, 1918-
Green tendrils
Wolfe, D. M. ed. Which grain will grow

Van Ness, Lilian
Give my love to Maggie
Prize stories of 1950

Van Paassen, Pierre, 1895-
Uncle Kees protests
Burnett, W. ed. World's best
The unsaid prayer
Brentano, F. ed. The word lives on

Van Vechten, Carl, 1880-
Feathers
Joseph, M. ed. Best cat stories

Van Vogt, Alfred Elton, 1912-
Asylum
Van Vogt, A. E. Away and beyond
Automaton
Crossen, K. F. ed. Adventures in to-
morrow
Can of paint
Van Vogt, A. E. Destination: universe!
The chronicler
Greenberg, M. comp. Five science fiction
novels
Co-operate—or else
Derleth, A. W. ed. The outer reaches
Dear Pen Pal
Derleth, A. W. ed. Far boundaries
Van Vogt, A. E. Destination: universe!
Defense
Van Vogt, A. E. Destination: universe!
Dormant
Startling stories (Periodical) Best from
Startling stories
Van Vogt, A. E. Destination: universe!
Enchanted village
Conklin, G. ed. Possible worlds of sci-
ence fiction
Van Vogt, A. E. Destination: universe!
Far Centaurus
Greenberg, M. ed. Men against the stars
Van Vogt, A. E. Destination: universe!
Film library
Van Vogt, A. E. Away and beyond
Final command
Greenberg, M. ed. Robot and the man
Fulfillment
Healy, R. J. ed. New tales of space and
time
Great engine
Van Vogt, A. E. Away and beyond
Great judge
Van Vogt, A. E. Away and beyond
The harmonizer
Van Vogt, A. E. Away and beyond
Heir unapparent
Van Vogt, A. E. Away and beyond
The monster
Van Vogt, A. E. Destination: universe!
Not only dead men
Conklin, G. ed. Invaders of earth
Process
Best science fiction stories: 1951
Recruiting station
Conklin, G. ed. Omnibus of science
fiction
Repetition
Derleth, A. W. ed. Beachheads in space
Rogue ship
Margulies, L. and Friend, O. J. eds.
Giant anthology of science fiction
The rulers
Van Vogt, A. E. Destination: universe!
The Rull
Greenberg, M. ed. Travelers of space
The search
Van Vogt, A. E. Destination: universe!

Van Vogt, Alfred E.—*Continued*
Second solution
Van Vogt, A. E. Away and beyond
Secret unattainable
Van Vogt, A. E. Away and beyond
The seesaw
Derleth, A. W. ed. Beyond time & space
The sound
Van Vogt, A. E. Destination: universe!
Vault of the beast
Astounding science fiction (Periodical)
Astounding science fiction anthology
Van Vogt, A. E. Away and beyond
Variation on a theme. Collier, J.
Variations on a theme of rain. Barker, A. L.
VARIETY THEATERS. See Music halls
(Variety theaters, cabarets, etc)
Various temptations. Sansom, W.
Varmint tries dissipation. Johnson, O. M.
Varsity vaulter. Coombs, C. I.
The **vats.** De La Mare, W. J.
Vaughn, Gertrude
Tornado
Oberfirst, R. ed. 1954 anthology of best
original short-shorts
Vault of the beast. Van Vogt, A. E.
Vega. Cheever, J.
VEILS
Hawthorne, N. Minister's black veil
The **veldt.** Bradbury, R.
Velia. Bonner, P. H.
The **vendetta.** Maupassant, G. de
Venerated bones. Lagerkvist, P. F.
VENEZUELA
Hudson, W. H. Mysterious forest
VENGEANCE. See Revenge
VENICE. See Italy—Venice
VENTRILOQUISTS
Collier, J. Spring fever
The **venturers.** Porter, W. S.
VENUS (PLANET)
Bennett, K. Rocketeers have shaggy ears
Bradbury, R. Long rain
Brown, F. Politeness
Carr, R. S. Morning star
Elam, R. M. Venusway
Jameson, M. Blind man's bluff
Jameson, M. Lilies of life
Kuttner, H. Clash by night
Kuttner, H. Iron standard
Lesser, M. Black Eyes and the daily grind
Long, F. B. The critters
MacLean, K. The fittest
Moore, C. L. There shall be darkness
Neville, K. Franchise
Pratt, F. Roger Bacon formula
Van Vogt, A. E. Can of paint
Weinbaum, S. G. Lotus eaters
Weinbaum, S. G. Parasite planet
The **Venus.** Williams, W. C.
Venus and the seven sexes. Klass, P.
Venus ascendant. Gellhorn, M. E.
Venus is a man's world. Klass, P.

VENUSIANS
Crossen, K. P. Ambassadors from Venus
Oliver, C. Win the world
White, W. A. P. Nine-finger Jack
Venusway. Elam, R. M.
VERA CRUZ. See Mexico—Vera Cruz
Verbal transcription: 6 A.M. Williams, W. C.
The **verdict.** Swinnerton, F. A.
Verdict of innocence. Beck, W.
Verdun Belle. Woollcott, A.
Verga, Giovanni, 1840-1922
Across the sea
Verga, G. Little novels of Sicily
Black bread
Verga, G. Little novels of Sicily
Cavalleria rusticana
Verga, G. Cavalleria rusticana, and other
narratives
Don Licciu Papa
Verga, G. Little novels of Sicily
The gentry
Verga, G. Little novels of Sicily
His Reverence
Verga, G. Cavalleria rusticana, and other
narratives
Verga, G. Little novels of Sicily
Home tragedy
Verga, G. Cavalleria rusticana, and other
narratives
Liberty
Verga, G. Little novels of Sicily
Malaria
Verga, G. Little novels of Sicily
Mystery play
Verga, G. Cavalleria rusticana, and other
narratives
Verga, G. Little novels of Sicily
The orphans
Verga, G. Little novels of Sicily
Property
Verga, G. Cavalleria rusticana, and other
narratives
Verga, G. Little novels of Sicily
Saint Joseph's ass
Verga, G. Cavalleria rusticana, and
other narratives
Same as: Story of the Saint Joseph's ass
The she-wolf
Verga, G. Cavalleria rusticana, and
other narratives
So much for the King
Verga, G. Little novels of Sicily
Story of the Saint Joseph's ass
Verga, G. Little novels of Sicily
Same as: Saint Joseph's ass
Ugly weather
Verga, G. Cavalleria rusticana, and
other narratives
The **verger.** Maugham, W. S.
VERGERS. See Sextons
Verlaine, Paul Marie, 1844-1896
Charles Husson
Cory, D. W. pseud. comp. 21 variations
on a theme
VERMONT
Fisher, D. F. C. Flint and fire
Fisher, D. F. C. Witch doctor

VERMONT—*Continued*

Farm life

See Farm life—Vermont

Saint Albans

Sass, H. R. Affair at St Albans

Vernam, Glenn
If you weel permit me
  Fenner, P. R. comp. Cowboys, cowboys, cowboys

Verne, Jules, 1828-1905
Dr Ox's experiment
  Derleth, A. W. ed. Beyond time & space
In the year 2889
  Conklin, G. ed. Big book of science fiction
Round the moon
  Kuebler, H. W. ed. Treasury of science fiction classics

Verner, Clara, 1900-
Meddlin' Papa
  Oberfirst, R. ed. 1954 anthology of best original short-shorts

Veronika. Storm, T.

Verotchka. Chekhov, A. P.

Verral, Charles Spain
Itch to win
  Fenner, P. R. comp. Speed, speed, speed

Verran, Roger
Lesson for Flying Goat
  Owen, F. ed. Teen-age winter sports stories

Verrinder, W.
To a web begun
  Oberfirst, R. ed. 1952 anthology of best original short-shorts

Verse on the window. Boyd, J.

Vertical ladder. Sansom, W.

Very false alarm. Platt, G.

Very late spring. Caldwell, E.

Very mischief. Frost, L.

Very old are beautiful. Betts, D.

Very sharp for jagging. Clay, R.

Vessel of wrath. Maugham, W. S.

Veteran ballplayer. Wolfe, T.

VETERANS (CIVIL WAR)
Danielson, R. E. Corporal Hardy
Garland, H. Return of a private
  See also Soldiers, American

VETERANS (EUROPEAN WAR, 1914-1918
Hemingway, E. In another country
Munro, H. H. Square egg
Nason, L. H. Rodney

VETERANS (IRELAND)
Walsh, M. Butcher to the Queen

VETERANS (WORLD WAR, 1939-1945)
Barker, A. L. Novelette
Beck, W. No continuing city
Galbraith, N. F. To have and to lose
Jones, J. Two legs for the two of us
Karchmer, S. "Hail, brother and farewell"
Purcell, D. Rider of the avalanche
Rothberg, A. A. Not with our fathers
Sarton, M. Return of Corporal Greene
Schwartz, R. H. Good people of Milton

VETERANS, DISABLED. See Cripples

Vetter, Marjorie (Meyn)
Captain Kit
  American girl (Periodical) Favorite stories
Fool dog
  American girl (Periodical) On my honor
Holiday house party
  American girl (Periodical) Christmas all year 'round
Let the wind blow
  American girl (Periodical) On my honor

VICARS. See Clergy

Vicar's web. Harvey, W. F.

Vickers, Roy
Double image
  Queen, E. pseud. ed. Ellery Queen's awards: 9th ser.
Hair shirt
  Queen, E. pseud. ed. Queen's awards: 6th ser.
Little things like that
  Best detective stories of the year—1954
Man with the sneer
  Best detective stories of the year—1952
Million-to-one chance
  Best detective stories of the year—1950
Miss Paisley's cat
  Queen, E. pseud. ed. Queen's awards: 8th ser.

Vic's Orr kid. Olds, H. D.

The **victim.** Lowry, R. J. C.

Victim no. 5. Keeler, H. S.

Victory. Faulkner, W.

Victory. Gregutt, H. C.

The **victory.** Schwartz, M.

Victory unintentional. Asimov, I.

La **vie** Bohème. Gordimer, N.

Vienna roast. Brecht, H. W.

View from the balcony. Stegner, W. E.

Vigny, Alfred Victor, comte de, 1797-1863
Malacca cane
  Dupee, F. W. ed. Great French short novels

VIKINGS
Mowery, W. B. Relic of the Vikings

Village Elder. Chekhov, A. P.

Village that voted the earth was flat. Kipling, R.

Villain as a young boy. Barker, A. L.

Villiers de l'Isle-Adam, Jean Marie Mathias Philippe Auguste, comte de, 1838-1889
Desire to be a man
  Geist, S. ed. French stories and tales

VILLON, FRANCOIS, b. 1431
Stevenson, R. L. Lodging for the night

Vineland's burning. Justice, D.

Vines, Howell, 1899-
Ginsing gatherers
  Southern review. Anthology of stories from the Southern review

Vint. Chekhov, A. P.

Violence at sundown. O'Rourke, F.

Violent interlude. Haycox, E.

VIOLINISTS. See Musicians—Violinists

Vireo's song. Dunsing, D. M.

Virgin of the seven daggers. Paget, V.

Virginians are coming. Farrell, J. T.

Virtue. Maugham, W. S.

Virtuoso. Goldstone, H.

The **vise.** Magnes, W. D.

Vision. Corkery, D.

Vision of Henry Whipple. Burnet, D.

Vision of Mirzah. Addison, J.

VISIONS. See Dreams

Visit of charity. Welty, E.

Visit to a neighbor. Cicellis, K.

Visit to friends. Chekhov, A. P.

Visit to the fair. Williams, W. C.

Visitation. Ullman, J. R.

VISITING
Betts, D. Sympathetic visitor
Chekhov, A. P. Visit to friends
Gellhorn, M. E. Week end at Grimsby
Jackson, C. R. Parting at morning
Rosenberg, E. C. Aunt Esther's galoshes
Welty, E. Visit of charity

Visiting fire-eater. Wylie, P.

The **visitor.** Bowen, E.

The **visitor.** Bradbury, R.

The **visitor.** Caldwell, E.

The **visitor.** Horwitz, J.

VISITORS. See Guests

VISITORS, INTERPLANETARY. See
Interplanetary visitors

The **vitagraphoscope.** Porter, W. S.

VOCATIONAL STORIES
Furman, A. L. ed. Everygirls career stories; 12 stories

Vogau, Boris Andreevich, 1894-
Big heart
Guerney, B. G. comp. New Russian stories

Voice behind him. Brown, F.

VOICE CULTURE. See Singing and voice culture

Voice of Bugle Ann. Kantor, M.

Voice of the city. Porter, W. S.

Voice of the lobster. Kuttner, H.

Voice of the turtle. Maugham, W. S.

The **voices.** Horwitz, J.

The **volcano.** Newhouse, E.

The **volcano.** Stegner, W. E.

VOLCANOES
Ullman, J. R. Silver sword

Von Hagen, Christine Inez (Brown) 1912-
Dueña for a day
American girl (Periodical) Favorite stories
Katti's Galápagos Christmas
American girl (Periodical) Christmas all year 'round

Von Hameln, Glückel. See Hameln, Glückel of

Vonnegut, Kurt, 1922-
Big trip up yonder
Pohl, F. ed. Assignment in tomorrow
Report on the Barnhouse effect
Heinlein, R. A. ed. Tomorrow, the stars
Unready to wear
Galaxy science fiction magazine. Second Galaxy reader of science fiction

VOODOOISM
Maugham, W. S. Honolulu
Maugham, W. S. P. & O.
Nearing, H. The mathematical voodoo

Voorhees, Melvin B.
Robe and the sword
Best Army short stories, 1950

Voyage forme la jeunesse. Gellhorn, M. E.

Voyage that lasted six hundred years. Wilcox, D.

Voyage to Sfanomoë. Smith, C. A.

VOYAGES, OCEAN. See Ocean travel

Vries, Peter de. See De Vries, Peter

Vulfarts, M.
Package tzoress
Ausubel, N. ed. Treasury of Jewish humor

W

W. S. Hartley, L. P.

The **wabbler.** Jenkins, W. F.

Wacky afternoon. Newhouse, E.

Waddell, Richie
You'd better be right!
Strang, R. M. and Roberts, R. M. eds. Teen-age tales v2

Waddington, Patrick
Street that got mislaid
Weaver, R. and James, H. eds. Canadian short stories

The **wager.** Corkery, D.

WAGERS
Betting Scotchman
Chekhov, A. P. The bet
Clemens, S. L. Celebrated jumping frog of Calaveras County
Corkery, D. The wager
Dahl, R. Man from the south
Dahl, R. Taste
Faulkner, W. Was
Maugham, W. S. Mr Know-All
Munro, H. H. Matter of sentiment
O'Donovan, M. Don Juan (Retired)
Poe, E. A. Never bet the Devil your head
Pratt, F. and De Camp, L. S. Ancestral amethyst
Runyon, D. Piece of pie

Wages of synergy. Waldo, E. H.

Wagstaff pearls. Eberhart, M. G.

Wahl, Betty
Gingerbread
Gable, M. Sister, ed. Many-colored fleece

Wahoo. Beach, E. L.

Wailing precipice. Bates, R.

WAILING WALL. See Palestine—Jerusalem—20th century

Wait for me. Summers, J. L.

Wait for me downstairs. Woolrich, C.

WAITERS. See Servants—Waiters

The **wake.** Hicks, M. A.

Wake of Patsy McLaughlin. Farrell, J. T.

Wakefield, Henry W.
Red Lodge
Carrington, H. ed. Week-end book of ghost stories

Wakefield, Herbert Russell, 1889-
Gorge of the Churels
Derleth, A. W. ed. Night's yawning peal

Wakefield. Hawthorne, N.

WAKEFULNESS. See Insomnia

Wakelee, Lee
Angela was eighteen
Stowe, A. comp. It's a date

Waker dreams. Matheson, R.

WAKES. See Funeral rites and ceremonies

Waldeck, Theodore J. 1894-
Evil one
Fenner, P. R. comp. Elephants, elephants, elephants
Igongo elephants
Fenner, P. R. comp. Elephants, elephants, elephants

Walden, Amelia Elizabeth
So I'm home again
American girl (Periodical) Favorite stories

Waldo, Edward Hamilton, 1918-
Bianca's hands
Waldo, E. H. E pluribus unicorn
Cellmate
Waldo, E. H. E pluribus unicorn
Chromium helmet
Jenkins, W. F. ed. Great stories of science fiction
The clinic
Star science fiction stories, no. 2
Completely automatic
Conklin, G. ed. Possible worlds of science fiction
Die, Maestro, die!
Waldo, E. H. E pluribus unicorn
Farewell to Eden
Derleth, A. W. ed. The outer reaches
Fluffy
Waldo, E. H. E pluribus unicorn
Golden egg
Conklin, G. ed. Science-fiction thinking machines
The hurkle is a happy beast
Best science fiction stories: 1950
Bleiler, E. F. and Dikty, T. E. eds. Science fiction omnibus: the best science fiction stories, 1949-1950
It wasn't syzygy
Waldo, E. H. E pluribus unicorn
Martian and the moron
Derleth, A. W. ed. Worlds of tomorrow
Memory
Crossen, K. F. ed. Adventures in tomorrow
Mewhu's jet
Conklin, G. ed. Big book of science fiction
Minority report
Derleth, A. W. ed. Beyond time & space
Mr Costello, hero
Pohl, F. ed. Assignment in tomorrow
The music
Waldo, E. H. E pluribus unicorn
Never underestimate. . .
Conklin, G. ed. Omnibus of science fiction
Perfect host
Merril, J. ed. Beyond human ken
Professor's teddy-bear
Waldo, E. H. E pluribus unicorn
Rule of three
Galaxy science fiction magazine. Galaxy reader of science fiction
Saucer of loneliness
Galaxy science fiction magazine. Second Galaxy reader of science fiction
Waldo, E. H. E pluribus unicorn
Scars
Waldo, E. H. E pluribus unicorn
Sex opposite
Waldo, E. H. E pluribus unicorn
Shottle Bop
Conklin, G. and Conklin, L. T. eds. Supernatural reader
The silken-swift
Waldo, E. H. E pluribus unicorn
Stars are the Styx
Galaxy science fiction magazine. Galaxy reader of science fiction
Thunder and roses
Astounding science fiction (Periodical) Astounding science fiction anthology
Tiny and the monster
Conklin, G. ed. Invaders of earth
Unite and conquer
Greenberg, M. ed. Journey to infinity
Wages of synergy
Startling stories (Periodical) Best from Startling stories
Way of thinking
Waldo, E. H. E pluribus unicorn
What dead men tell
Bleiler, E. F. and Dikty, T. E. eds. Imagination unlimited
World well lost
Waldo, E. H. E pluribus unicorn
Yesterday was Monday
Conklin, G. ed. Science-fiction adventures in dimension

Waldron, D.
Evensong
Best American short stories, 1952

Waldron, Webb, 1883-1945
If Lincoln had yielded
Jones, K. M. ed. New Confederate short stories

WALES
Davies, R. Boy with a trumpet, and other selected short stories; 20 stories

Farm life
See Farm life—Wales

Walk for me. Blackburn, E. R.

Walk in the dark. Clarke, A. C.

Walker, Augusta
Day of the cipher
Prize stories, 1954
Walker, David Harry, 1911-
Bait for a tiger
Saturday evening post (Periodical)
Saturday evening post stories, 1952
Walker, Turnley, 1913-
Wonderful automobile
Story (Periodical) Story; no. 1
WALKING
Bowen, E. Human habitation
Keller, D. H. Revolt of the pedestrians
Saroyan, W. Leaf thief
See also Hitchhikers
Walking corpse. Lipman, C. and Lipman, M.

Walking wounded. Shaw, I.

Wall, John W.
Calmahain
Wall, J. W. Ringstones, and other
curious tales
Capra
Wall, J. W. Ringstones, and other
curious tales
Christmas story
Wall, J. W. Ringstones, and other
curious tales
The Khan
Wall, J. W. Ringstones, and other
curious tales
Ringstones
Wall, J. W. Ringstones, and other
curious tales
The **wall.** Sartre, J. P.

Wall around the world. Cogswell, T. R.

Wall of darkness. Clarke, A. C.

Wall of dust. Tennyson, H.

Wall of fire. Kirkland, J.

Wallace, F. L.
Student body
Galaxy science fiction magazine. Second Galaxy reader of science fiction
Wallace, John F.
Bound for the bottom
Argosy (Periodical) Argosy Book of
sea stories
Jonah curse
Argosy (Periodical) Argosy Book of
sea stories
Wallace, Robert
Secret weapon of Joe Smith
Prize stories, 1954
Wallace, W. J.
Dead run
Best detective stories of the year—1954
WALLS
Bradbury, R. Golden kite, the silver wind

Wally. Auchincloss, L.

Walnut hunt. Caldwell, E.

Walpole, Sir Hugh, 1885-1941
The life and death of a crisis
Brentano, F. ed. The word lives on
Mr Huffam
Lohan, R. and Lohan, M. eds. New
Christmas treasury
Mr Oddy
Cerf, B. A. and Moriarty, H. C. eds.
Anthology of famous British stories

WALRUSES
Roberts, Sir C. G. D. Mothers of the
north
Walsh, Maurice, 1879-
The bonesetter
Walsh, M. Son of a tinker
Butcher to the queen
Walsh, M. Son of a tinker
Come back, my love
Saturday evening post (Periodical)
Saturday evening post stories, 1953
Walsh, M. Take your choice
A dialogue
Walsh, M. Son of a tinker
Heather wine
Walsh, M. Son of a tinker
Honest fisherman
Walsh, M. Take your choice
Mission sermon
Walsh, M. Son of a tinker
My fey lady
Walsh, M. Son of a tinker
Not my story
Walsh, M. Son of a tinker
Prudent man
Walsh, M. Son of a tinker
Quiet man
Walsh, M. Take your choice
Son of a tinker
Walsh, M. Son of a tinker
Sword of Yung Lo
Walsh, M. Take your choice
Take your choice
Walsh, M. Take your choice
Thomasheen James and the dictation machine
Walsh, M. Take your choice
Thomasheen James goes to the dogs
Walsh, M. Take your choice
Walsh, Thomas, 1908-
Blonde nurse
Mystery Writers of America, inc.
Butcher, baker, murder-maker
Waltari, Mika Toimi, 1908-
Before the twilight of the gods
Waltari, M. T. Moonscape, and other
stories
Goldilocks
Waltari, M. T. Moonscape, and other
stories
Island of ice
Waltari, M. T. Moonscape, and other
stories
Moonscape
Waltari, M. T. Moonscape, and other
stories
Tie from Paris
Waltari, M. T. Moonscape, and other
stories
Walterson. Tarkington, B.

Walton, Harry
Episode on Dhee Minor
Greenberg, M. ed. Travelers of space
Schedule
Greenberg, M. ed. Men against the
stars
Wan Lee, the pagan. Harte, B.

Wanderer. Boyle, K.

The **wanderers.** Welty, E.

Wandering Gentile. Forester, C. S.

WANDERING JEW
Porter, W. S. Door of unrest
Wander's world. Van Doren, M.
Wandrei, Donald, 1908-
Blinding shadows
Derleth, A. W. ed. Beachheads in space
Colossus
Derleth, A. W. ed. Beyond time &
space
Finality unlimited
Derleth, A. W. ed. The outer reaches
Infinity zero
Derleth, A. W. ed. Far boundaries
Strange harvest
Derleth, A. W. ed. Worlds of tomorrow
Wang Chu, 997-1057
Poets' club
Lin, Y. ed. Famous Chinese short
stories
Waning moon. Sansom, W.
Wanted: a chauffeur. Farrell, J. T.
Wanted—an enemy. Leiber, F.
WAR
Crane, S. Upturned face
Kubilius, W. and Pratt, F. Second chance
Rosenfeld, J. Return home
Russell, E. F. I am nothing
Ullman, J. R. Soldier of the realm

Casualties
Crane, S. Episode of war
Howells, W. D. Editha
Stallings, L. Vale of tears
War against the moon. Maurois, A.
WAR AND CHILDREN
Lagerkvist, P. F. Children's campaign
WAR CORRESPONDENTS
Krige, U. Two Daumiers
See also Journalists
War for Tony. Newhouse, E.
War in the air. Cassill, R. V.
WAR OF 1812. See United States—19th
century—War of 1812
War passed over us. Berto, G.
War shirt. Johnson, D. M.
WAR VETERANS. See Veterans
The **war** years. Hilton, J.
Ward, Elizabeth Stuart (Phelps) 1844-1911
Chief operator
Cooper, A. C. ed. Modern short stories
Ward, Frank
Kill and run
Best detective stories of the year—1954
Ward, Millard, 1904-
Tanker man
Furman, A. L. ed. Teen-age sea stories
Ward no. 6. Chekhov, A. P.
Ward 'O' 3 (b) Lewis, A.
Ward of Colonel Starbottle's. Harte, B.
Ware, Edmund, pseud. See Smith, Edmund
Ware
Ware, Leon
Phantom of the bridge
Saturday evening post (Periodical)
Saturday evening post stories, 1951
WARFARE. See War
Warm. Sheckley, R.

Warm hand. Gonzalez, N. V. M.
Warm river. Caldwell, E.
Warner, Charles Dudley, 1829-1900
A-hunting of the deer
Andrews, R. C. ed. My favorite stories
of the great outdoors
Calvin, the cat
Joseph, M. ed. Best cat stories
Warner, Sylvia Townsend, 1893-
Traveller from the West and the traveller
from the East
Joseph, M. ed. Best cat stories
The **warning.** Phillips, P.
Warnock, J. D.
Sydney and the green angel
Stanford short stories, 1952
Warren, Billy. See Warren, William
Stephen
Warren, Robert Penn, 1905-
Blackberry winter
Summers, H. S. ed. Kentucky story
When the light gets green
Gordon, C. and Tate, A. eds. House of
fiction
Southern review. Anthology of stories
from the Southern review
Warren, William Stephen, 1882-
The branding
Fenner, P. R. comp. Cowboys, cow-
boys, cowboys
Warrior's exile. Johnson, D. M.
WARS, INTERPLANETARY. See Inter-
planetary wars
Warwick, James
Fire in the bush
Christ, H. I. and Shostak, J. eds. Short
stories
Was. Faulkner, W.
Was it a dream? Maupassant, G. de
Was it murder? Claudy, C. H.
Was it too late? Booker, A. E.
Wash. Faulkner, W.
Wash-tub. Maugham, W. S.
Washerwoman's day. Arnow, H. L. S.
WASHINGTON, D.C.
Acheson, E. G. Big shot
Washington Square. James, H.
Washoe behemoth. Wright, W.
WASHOE COUNTY. See Nevada—Wa-
shoe County
Wasserman, Norman, 1924-
Stars are black
American vanguard, 1950
Wassermann, Jakob, 1873-1934
Gold of Caxamalca
Leftwich, J. ed. Yisröel. 1952 ed.
Lukardis
Pick, R. ed. German stories and tales
Wasted day. Davis, R. H.
A **wasted** life. Cooke, A. A.
Watch in the night. White, H. C.
Watcher of the dead. Gordimer, N.
The **watchers.** Calisher, H.
WATCHES. See Clocks and watches
Watchful gods. Clark, W. Van T.

Watching baseball. Benchley, R. C.
The watchman. Van Doren, M.
WATCHMEN
    O'Donovan, M. Eternal triangle
    Van Doren, M. I, Tobit
Water broncs. Douglas, J. S.
Water bug. Coombs, C. I.
Water canteen. Arico, V.
Water ghost of Harrowby Hall. Bangs,
    J. K.
The water hen. O'Flaherty, L.
Water hole. Haycox, E.
Water is for washing. Heinlein, R. A.
WATERMELONS
    Upshaw, H. The harvest
The waters of Bethesda. Bauer, F. A. M.
Waters of Manitou. Gulick, G. C.
Waters of Shiloah. Cohn, E.
WATERSPOUTS
    Holland, R. S. Cobra's hood
Watkins, Richard Howells
    Offshore
        Bluebook (Periodical) Best sea stories
        from Bluebook
Watson, John, 1850-1907
    His mother's sermon
        Brentano, F. ed. The word lives on
        Neider, C. ed. Men of the high calling
    Story of Dr MacLure
        Cerf, B. A. and Moriarty, H. C. eds.
        Anthology of famous British stories
Watson, John Cherry, 1909-
    Benny and the Tar-Baby
        Peery, W. W. ed. 21 Texas short
        stories
Waugh, Alec, 1898-
    Wed, my darling daughter
        This week magazine. This week's short-
        short stories
Waugh, Evelyn, 1903-
    Bella Fleace gave a party
        Cerf, B. A. and Moriarty, H. C. eds.
        Anthology of famous British stories
        Waugh, E. Tactical exercise
    Cruise
        Waugh, E. Tactical exercise
    Curse of the horse race
        Waugh, E. Tactical exercise
    Englishman's home
        Waugh, E. Tactical exercise
    Excursion in reality
        Waugh, E. Tactical exercise
    Love among the ruins
        Waugh, E. Tactical exercise
    Mr Loveday's little outing
        Waugh, E. Tactical exercise
    On guard
        Waugh, E. Tactical exercise
    Period piece
        Waugh, E. Tactical exercise
    Tactical exercise
        Waugh, E. Tactical exercise
    Winner takes all
        Waugh, E. Tactical exercise
    Work suspended
        Waugh, E. Tactical exercise
Wave of Osiris. Lagerkvist, P. F.
The waveries. Brown, F.

WAX MUSEUMS. See Waxworks
The waxwork. Burrage, A. M.
WAXWORKS
    Burrage, A. M. The waxwork
Way of a man. Grau, S. A.
Way of a traitor. Greenfield, R.
Way of all fish. Wylie, P.
Way of escape. Temple, W. F.
Way of thinking. Waldo, E. H.
Way out in the continuum. Richardson,
    M. L.
Way to the dairy. Munro, H. H.
Way with women. Steele, W. D.
Way you'll never be. Hemingway, E.
Wayfaring strangers. Tucker, W.
"We also walk dogs." Heinlein, R. A.
We are looking at you, Agnes. Caldwell, E.
We don't know. De Vries, P.
We don't want any trouble. Schmitz, J. H.
We kill people. Kuttner, H.
We the people. Moore, W.
We, too, are bidden. Broun, H. C.
We were just having fun. Herbert, F. H.
We won't be needing you, Al. Young, S.
WEALTH
    Auchincloss, L. Finish, good lady
    Balchin, N. Now we are broke, my dear
    Fitzgerald, F. S. K. Diamond as big as
        the Ritz
    Fitzgerald, F. S. K. Rich boy
    Graham, M. C. Face of the poor
    Porter, W. S. Mammon and the archer
    Porter, W. S. Trimmed lamp
    Steinberg, Y. Reb Anshel the golden
    Zevin, I. J. Nogid's luck
Weaning of Laura Wade. Hayes, N.
The weapon. Brown, F.
WEAPONS. See Arms and armor
Weary hour. Mann, T.
Weary Willie. Miers, E. S.
WEATHER
    Van Doren, M. Great deal of weather
    Wollheim, D. A. Storm warning
Weaver, John Downing, 1912-
    Second table
        Collier's, the national weekly. Collier's
        best
Webb, Richard Wilson, and Wheeler, Hugh
    Callingham. See Quentin, Patrick,
    pseud.
Webber, Everett M.
    Passage to Kentucky
        Argosy (Periodical) Argosy Book of
        adventure stories
Weber, Lenora (Mattingly) 1895-
    Christmas thaw
        American girl (Periodical) Christmas
        all year 'round
        American girl (Periodical) On my
        honor
WEBSTER, DANIEL, 1782-1852
    Benét, S. V. Devil and Daniel Webster
Wechsberg, Joseph, 1907-
    New York is full of girls
        Esquire (Periodical) Girls from Es-
        quire

Wed, my darling daughter. Waugh, A.

The **wedding.** Matheson, R.

The **wedding.** O'Flaherty, L.

Wedding. Sansom, W.

WEDDING ANNIVERSARIES
Aiken, C. P. The anniversary
Aldrich, B. S. Will the romance be the
same?
Suckow, R. Golden wedding

Wedding at Cushing's Fort. Hendryx, J. B.

Wedding bells will ring so merrily. Farrell,
J. T.

Wedding chest. Paget, V.

WEDDING CHESTS. See Hope chests

Wedding dance. Daguio, A. T.

Wedding ring. Van Dyke, H.

WEDDINGS
Babel', I. E. The King
Caldwell, E. Over the Green Mountains
Fitzgerald, F. S. K. Stories of F. Scott
Fitzgerald
Schmitz, E. Generous wine
Schorr, Z. The appraisal
Spector, M. Meal for the poor
Spector, M. Strike of the Schnorrers

Sweden
Lagerkvist, P. F. Marriage feast

Wedekind, Frank, 1864-1918
Burning of Egliswyl
Lange, V. ed. Great German short
novels and stories

The **weeds.** McCarthy, M. T.

Week end at Grimsby. Gellhorn, M. E.

Week of roses. Wesley, D.

Weekend at Grimsby. Gellhorn, M. E.

Weeks, Edward, 1898-
Mickey
Harper, W. comp. Dog show

Weeks, Jack
Summer's ending
Collier's, the national weekly. Collier's
best

Weeks, Raymond, 1863-1954
Arkansas
Certner, S. and Henry, G. H. eds. Short
stories for our times
Cooper, A. C. ed. Modern short stories
Brigands in Snuggletop Woods
Fenner, P. R. comp. Fun! Fun! Fun!
Mosquitoes of Arkansas
Fenner, P. R. comp. Fun! Fun! Fun!
Revenue Charlie
Fenner, P. R. comp. Fun! Fun! Fun!

Weep no more, My Lady. Street, J. H.

Weesperstraat. Praag, S. E. van

Weichert, Ernst
The mother
Fremantle, A. J. ed. Mothers

Weidman, Jerome, 1913-
The Kinnehórrah
Ribalow, H. U. ed. This land, these
people
Man inside
This week magazine. This week's short-
short stories

Weight of command. Haycox, E.

Weight of the sky. Sullivan, R.

Weinbaum, Stanley Grauman, 1902-1935
Lotus eaters
Derleth, A. W. ed. Beyond time &
space
Martian odyssey
Margulies, L. and Friend, O. J. eds.
From off this world
Parasite planet
Wollheim, D. A. comp. Flight into
space
Valley of dreams
Margulies, L. and Friend, O. J. eds.
From off this world

Weirwood marsh. Peattie, D. C. and Peattie, L. R.

Weiss, Ernst, 1884-1940
Cardiac suture
Pick, R. ed. German stories and tales

Weissenberg, Isaac Meier, 1881-1937
Father and the boys
Howe, I. and Greenberg, E. eds. Treas-
ury of Yiddish stories
Mazel tov
Howe, I. and Greenberg, E. eds. Treas-
ury of Yiddish stories

Welch, Denton
Judas tree
New writing (Periodical) Best stories
When I was thirteen
Cory, D. W. pseud. comp. 21 variations
on a theme

Welch, Douglas, 1906-
Mrs Union Station
Moskowitz, S. ed. Great railroad stories
of the world

Welcome home. Doty, W. L.

Welcome home, Hal! Aldrich, B. S.

We'll always have Christmas. Wuorio, E.-L.

Well, I'm blowed. Selver, P.

Well of angel. Lewis, M.

Well of the star. Goudge, E.

Well-oiled machine. Fyfe, H. B.

Well, that's that. Farrell, J. T.

Wellman, Manly Wade, 1905-
Desrick on Yandro
Magazine of fantasy and science fiction.
Best from Fantasy and science fiction;
2d ser.
Dhoh
Derleth, A. W. ed. Night's yawning
peal
Island in the sky
Margulies, L. and Friend, O. J. eds.
Giant anthology of science fiction
Men against the stars
Greenberg, M. ed. Men against the
stars
Tall Bram of Little Pigeon
Boys' life (Periodical) Boys' life Ad-
venture stories
Vandy, Vandy
Magazine of fantasy and science fiction.
Best from Fantasy and science fiction;
3d ser.
Where angels fear
Davenport, B. ed. Ghostly tales to be
told

Wells, Herbert George, 1886-1946
  Æpyornis Island
    Wells, H. G. 28 science fiction stories
  Argonauts of the air
    Wells, H. G. 28 science fiction stories
  Country of the blind
    Cerf, B. A. and Moriarty, H. C. eds.
      Anthology of famous British stories
    Stauffer, R. M.; Cunningham, W. H.
      and Sullivan, C. J. eds. Adventures
      in modern literature
    Wells, H. G. 28 science fiction stories
  Crystal egg
    Wells, H. G. 28 science fiction stories
  Dream of Armageddon
    Wells, H. G. 28 science fiction stories
  Empire of the ants
    Wells, H. G. 28 science fiction stories
  Filmer
    Wells, H. G. 28 science fiction stories
  In the abyss
    Wells, H. G. 28 science fiction stories
  In the Avu observatory
    Wells, H. G. 28 science fiction stories
  Inexperienced ghost
    Christ, H. I. and Shostak, J. eds. Short
      stories
  Land ironclads
    Wells, H. G. 28 science fiction stories
  Late Mr Elvesham
    Wells, H. G. 28 science fiction stories
  Little mother up the Mörderberg
    Talbot, D. ed. Treasury of mountain-
      eering stories
  Magic shop
    Wells, H. G. 28 science fiction stories
  Man who could work miracles
    Schramm, W. L. ed. Great short stories
    Wells, H. G. 28 science fiction stories
  Mr Brisher's treasure
    Queen, E. pseud. ed. Literature of
      crime
  Mr Britling writes until sunrise
    Brentano, F. ed. The word lives on
  New accelerator
    Derleth, A. W. ed. Beyond time &
      space
    Wells, H. G. 28 science fiction stories
  The Plattner story
    Wells, H. G. 28 science fiction stories
  Remarkable case of Davidson's eyes
    Wells, H. G. 28 science fiction stories
  Sea raiders
    Wells, H. G. 28 science fiction stories
  The star
    Kuebler, H. W. ed. Treasury of science
      fiction classics
    Wells, H. G. 28 science fiction stories
  Star begotten
    Wells, H. G. 28 science fiction stories
  Stolen bacillus
    Wells, H. G. 28 science fiction stories
  Stolen body
    Wells, H. G. 28 science fiction stories
  Story of the days to come
    Wells, H. G. 28 science fiction stories
  Story of the stone age
    Wells, H. G. 28 science fiction stories
  Strange orchid
    Wells, H. G. 28 science fiction stories
  Time machine
    Kuebler, H. W. ed. Treasury of science
      fiction classics

  Truth about Pyecraft
    Wells, H. G. 28 science fiction stories
  Under the knife
    Wells, H. G. 28 science fiction stories
  Valley of spiders
    Wells, H. G. 28 science fiction stories

Wells, John, pseud. See Kaplan, Alvin
  Harold

WELLS
  Van Doren, M. Valley of great wells

WELSH FARM LIFE. See Farm life—
  Wales

Welshimer, Helen, 1901-
  Father comes home
    Elmquist, R. M. ed. Fifty years of
      Christmas

Welty, Eudora, 1909-
  Asphodel
    Welty, E. Selected stories
  At the landing
    Welty, E. Selected stories
  The burning
    Davis, R. G. ed. Ten modern masters
    Prize stories of 1951
  Clytie
    Welty, E. Selected stories
  Curtain of green
    Best of the Best American short stories,
      1915-1950
    Welty, E. Selected stories
  Death of a travelling salesman
    Schorer, M. ed. The story
    Waite, H. O. and Atkinson, B. P. eds.
      Literature for our time
    Welty, E. Selected stories
  First love
    Lynskey, W. C. ed. Reading modern
      fiction
    Welty, E. Selected stories
  Flowers for Marjorie
    Welty, E. Selected stories
  The hitch-hikers
    Burrell, J. A. and Cerf, B. A. eds. An-
      thology of famous American stories
    Welty, E. Selected stories
  June recital
    Welty, E. Golden apples
  Keela, the Outcast Indian Maiden
    Ludwig, J. B. and Poirier, W. R. eds.
      Stories, British and American
    Welty, E. Selected stories
  The key
    Welty, E. Selected stories
  Lily Daw and the three ladies
    Welty, E. Selected stories
  Livvie
    Welty, E. Selected stories
    Same as: Livvie is back
  Livvie is back
    First-prize stories, 1919-1954
    Greene, J. L. and Abell, E. eds. Stories
      of sudden truth
    Same as: Livvie
  A memory
    Ludwig, J. B. and Poirier, W. R. eds.
      Stories, British and American
    Welty, E. Selected stories
  Moon Lake
    Welty, E. Golden apples
  Music from Spain
    Welty, E. Golden apples

Welty, Eudora—*Continued*
Old Mr Marblehall
Welty, E. Selected stories
Petrified man
Davis, R. G. ed. Ten modern masters
Millett, F. B. ed. Reading fiction
Southern review. Anthology of stories
from the Southern review
Welty, E. Selected stories
Piece of news
Welty, E. Selected stories
Powerhouse
Welty, E. Selected stories
West, R. B. and Stallman, R. W. eds.
Art of modern fiction
Purple hat
Welty, E. Selected stories
Shower of gold
Felheim, M.; Newman, F. B. and Stein-
hoff, W. R. eds. Modern short stories
Welty, E. Golden apples
Sir Rabbit
Welty, E. Golden apples
Still moment
Welty, E. Selected stories
Visit of charity
Welty, E. Selected stories
The wanderers
Welty, E. Golden apples
The whistle
Welty, E. Selected stories
Whole world knows
Welty, E. Golden apples
Why I live at the P.O.
Gordon, C. and Tate, A. eds. House of
fiction
Welty, E. Selected stories
Wide net
First-prize stories, 1919-1954
Welty, E. Selected stories
The winds
Welty, E. Selected stories
Worn path
Barrows, H. ed. 15 stories
Davis, R. G. ed. Ten modern masters
Heilman, R. B. ed. Modern short
stories
Welty, E. Selected stories
The **Wendigo**. Blackwood, A.
Wendroff, Zalman, 1879-
The gramophone
Ausubel, N. ed. Treasury of Jewish
humor
Statistics
Ausubel, N. ed. Treasury of Jewish
humor
Two pleasures
Ausubel, N. ed. Treasury of Jewish
humor

Wendrowsky, Zalman. See Wendroff, Zalman

Weren't you ever young! Summers, J. L.

WEREWOLVES. See Werwolves

Werfel, Franz V. 1890-1945
Jeremiah: the voice without and within
Selden, R. ed. Ways of God and men
Saverio's secret
Leftwich, J. ed. Yisröel. 1952 ed.
Third commandment
Neider, C. ed. Men of the high calling
Same as: Thou shalt not take the name
of the Lord thy God in vain

Wertenbaker, Green Peyton, 1907-
Ship that turned aside
Conklin, G. ed. Big book of science
fiction
WERWOLVES
Kipling, R. Mark of the beast
Munro, H. H. Gabriel-Ernest
Munro, H. H. She-wolf
Rice, J. The refugee
White, W. A. P. Compleat werewolf
Wesley, Donald, 1922-
Week of roses
Best American short stories, 1953
West, Anne
Pulpit for Don
Lantz, J. E. ed. Stories of Christian
living
Wonder in Willow Hill
Lantz, J. E. ed. Stories of Christian
living
West, Cy
Smoke ball kid
Owen, F. ed. Teen-age victory parade
West, Jessamyn
Battle of Finney's Ford
Greene, J. I. and Abell, E. eds. Stories
of sudden truth
Breach of promise
Abell, E. ed. American accent
Prize stories, 1954
Child's day
Swallow, A. ed. Anchor in the sea
Homer and the lilies
Thinker's digest (Periodical) Spoiled
priest, and other stories
Horace Chooney, M.D.
Stegner, W. E.; Scowcroft, R. and Ilyin,
B. eds. Writer's art
The illumination
Brentano, F. ed. The word lives on
Thinker's digest (Periodical) Spoiled
priest, and other stories
Lead her like a pigeon
Thinker's digest (Periodical) Spoiled
priest, and other stories
Shivaree before breakfast
Heilman, R. B. ed. Modern short
stories
West, Michael Philip
Hector
Derleth, A. W. ed. Night's yawning
peal
West, Ray Benedict, 1908-
The ascent
Talbot, D. ed. Treasury of mountain-
eering stories
Last of the grizzly bears
Best American short stories, 1951
West, Wallace
Sculptors of life
Conklin, G. ed. Science-fiction thinking
machines
THE WEST
Harte, B. Bret Harte's stories of the old
West; 11 stories
Harte, B. Outcasts of Poker Flat
Johnson, D. M. Indian country; 11 stories
Schubert, P. White Elk

See also Western stories

Farm life
See Farm life—The West

Westbrock, John T. 1918-
　Private hell
　　American vanguard, 1950
Western islands. Masefield, J.
WESTERN STORIES
　Brand, M. pseud. Wine on the desert
　DeVries, M. Stage to Yuma
　Haycox, E. By rope and lead; 9 stories
　Haycox, E. Outlaw; 10 stories
　Haycox, E. Pioneer loves; 9 stories
　Haycox, E. Rough justice; 9 stories
　Hendryx, J. B. Intrigue on Halfaday
　　Creek; 28 stories
　Hendryx, J. B. Murder on Halfaday
　　Creek; 30 stories
　Meredith, S. ed. Bar 1 roundup of best
　　western stories; 12 stories
　Meredith, S. ed. Bar 2; 12 stories
　Meredith, S. ed. Bar 3; 11 stories
　O'Rourke, F. Ride west; 11 stories
　Porter, W. S. Hearts and crosses
　Schaefer, J. W. Big range; 10 stories
　Thompson, T. They brought their guns;
　　11 stories
　Western Writers of America. Bad men
　　and good; 14 stories
　Western Writers of America. Holsters
　　and heroes; 12 stories
　　　See also Cowboys; Ranch life

Westfield House. Miller, C.

Westmacott, Mary, pseud. See Christie,
　Agatha (Miller)

Weston, Christine (Goutiere) 1904-
　Forest of the night
　　Best American short stories, 1953
　Loud sing cuckoo
　　Best American short stories, 1952
　Man in gray
　　Best American short stories, 1954
　Second pasture
　　Collier's, the national weekly. Collier's
　　best

Wet Saturday. Collier, J.

Wetjen, Albert Richard, 1900-1948
　Ship of silence
　　Bluebook (Periodical) Best sea stories
　　from Bluebook

Wexler, Jerry, 1917-
　I am Edgar
　　Story (Periodical) Story; no. 2

Whaler 'round the Horn. Meader, S. W.
WHALES
　Davies, W. M. Battle with a whale
WHALING
　Carmer, C. L. Mr Sims and Henry
　Davies, W. M. Battle with a whale
　Marmur, J. Below Cape Horn
　Meader, S. W. Whaler 'round the Horn
　　　See also Sea stories

The wharf. De La Mare, W. J.

Wharton, Edith Newbold (Jones) 1862-
　1937
　After Holbein
　　Wharton, E. N. J. Edith Wharton
　　treasury
　Autre temps
　　Wharton, E. N. J. Edith Wharton
　　treasury

Bottle of Perrier
　Wharton, E. N. J. Edith Wharton
　treasury
Bunner sisters
　Wharton, E. N. J. Edith Wharton
　treasury
The choice
　Foerster, N. ed. American poetry and
　prose. 1952 ed.
Lady's maid's bell
　Wharton, E. N. J. Edith Wharton
　treasury
Madame de Treymes
　Scribner treasury
　Wharton, E. N. J. Edith Wharton
　treasury
Mission of Jane
　Burrell, J. A. and Cerf, B. A. eds. An-
　thology of famous American stories
Moving finger
　Wharton, E. N. J. Edith Wharton
　treasury
Old maid
　Wharton, E. N. J. Edith Wharton
　treasury
Other two
　Wharton, E. N. J. Edith Wharton
　treasury
Roman fever
　Wharton, E. N. J. Edith Wharton
　treasury
Xingu
　Wharton, E. N. J. Edith Wharton
　treasury

What Christmas brought the stranger.
　Sangster, M. E.
What dead men tell. Waldo, E. H.
What do hippos eat? Wilson, A.
What do you do? Newhouse, E.
What does she see when she shuts her eyes.
　eyes. Stein, G.
What happened to Alanna. Norris, K. T.
What have I done? Clifton, M.
What if. . . Asimov, I.
What is a miracle? Komroff, M.
What is rape? Willingham, C.
What John Rance had to tell. Doyle, Sir
　A. C.
What price genius. Schneider, G. W.
"What so proudly we hail. . ." Keene, D.
What thin partitions. Clifton, M. and Apos-
　tolides, A.
What time is it? Elam, R. M.
What Vasile saw. Marie, consort of Ferdi-
　nand I, King of Rumania
What we don't know hurts us. Schorer, M.
What you hear from 'em? Taylor, P. H.
What you need. Kuttner, H.
"What you want." Porter, W. S.
Whatever happened to Corporal Cuckoo?
　Pohl, F. ed.
What's in a corner. Horton, P.
What's in two names. Hutchins, M. P. M.
What's it like out there? Hamilton, E.
WHEAT
　Norris, F. Deal in wheat
Wheel of time. Arthur, R.

Wheeler, Hugh Callingham. See Quentin, Patrick, pseud.

When boyhood dreams come true. Farrell, J. T.

When Dan came home. Grimson, M. S.

When day is done. Cawley, C. C.

When I was thirteen. Welch, D.

"When in doubt—wash." Gallico, P. W.

When in Rome— James, W.

When mountain men make peace. Stuart, J.

When Riga was evacuated. Bergengruen, W.

When Santa helped. Eggleston, M. W.

When shadows fall. Hubbard, L. R.

When the aliens left. Meyer, E. L.

When the bough breaks. Kuttner, H.

When the earth lived. Kuttner, H.

When the green star waned. Dyalhis, N.

When the light gets green. Warren, R. P.

When the night wind howls. Pratt, F. and De Camp, L. S.

"When the season cometh round." Yaffe, J.

"When time who steals our years away!" Buckingham, N.

When titans meet. Schneider, G. W.

When TV came to the backwoods. Grimson, M. S.

When worlds collide. Balmer, E. and Wylie, P.

When you blow on a dandelion. Scheffrin, G. R.

Where angels fear. Wellman, M. W.

Where angels fear to tread. Palmer, S.

Where are your guns? Fast, H. M.

Where beauty lies. Irwin, M. E. F.

Where did yesterday go? Angoff, C.

Where early fa's the dew. Gilpatric, G.

Where falls not hail. Ready, W. B.

Where Teetee Wood lies cold and dead. Chapman, W.

Where the girls were different. Caldwell, E.

Where the grass, they say, is blue. McNulty, J.

Where their fire is not quenched, Sinclair, M.

"Where to, please?" Pratt, F. and De Camp, L. S.

While the auto waits. Porter, W. S.

WHIMSICAL STORIES. See Fantasies

Whinery, Marion. See Casey, Marian (Whinery)

The whip-poor-will. Thurber, J.

The whipping. Noland, F.

Whippletree. O'Rourke, F.

Whirligig of life. Porter, W. S.

WHIRLPOOLS
Poe, E. A. Descent into the maelström

The whistle. Doremus, J.

The whistle. Welty, E.

Whistle and the heroes. Wilner, H.

Whistler, Laurence, 1912-
Captain Dalgety returns
Asquith, Lady C. M. E. C. ed. Book of modern ghosts

Whistling Dick's Christmas stocking. Porter, W. S.

White, Antonia, 1901-
Moment of truth
Horizon (Periodical) Golden Horizon

White, Edward Lucas, 1866-1934
House of the nightmare
Davenport, B. ed. Ghostly tales to be told

White, Helen Constance, 1896-
Francis cures the leper
Thinker's digest (Periodical) Spoiled priest, and other stories
That mighty contact
Thinker's digest (Periodical) Spoiled priest, and other stories
Watch in the night
Thinker's digest (Periodical) Spoiled priest, and other stories

White, Leslie Turner, 1903-
Bayou bait
Argosy (Periodical) Argosy Book of sea stories

White, Milton
To remember these things
Lass, A. H. and Horowitz, A. eds. Stories for youth
Yellow turtleneck sweater
Seventeen (Periodical) Nineteen from Seventeen
Stanford short stories, 1950

White, Robb, 1909-
Conflict is joined
Boys' life (Periodical) Boys' life Adventure stories
Dog in the double bottoms
Furman, A. L. ed. Teen-age dog stories
An eye for an eye
Furman, A. L. ed. Teen-age sea stories
Pot Likker's first fox hunt
Fenner, P. R. comp. Dogs, dogs, dogs
Sick bay to sea wall
American boy (Periodical) American boy anthology

White, Stewart Edward, 1873-1946
Climbing for goats
Talbot, D. ed. Treasury of mountaineering stories
On lying awake at night
Andrews, R. C. ed. My favorite stories of the great outdoors

White, Will
Over there
Hathaway, B. and Sessions, J. A. eds. Writers for tomorrow. 2d ser.
Too big a dream
Hathaway, B. and Sessions, J. A. eds. Writers for tomorrow. 2d ser.

White, William Anthony Parker, 1911-
The ambassadors
Crossen, K. F. Future tense
Anomaly of the empty man
Mystery Writers of America, inc. Crooks' tour
Chronokinesis of Jonathan Hull
Jenkins, W. F. ed. Great stories of science fiction
Compleat werewolf
Merril, J. ed. Beyond human ken
Conquest
Star science fiction stories, no. 2

White, William A. P.—*Continued*
Ghost of me
Merril, J. ed. Beyond the barriers of space and time
Girl who married a monster
Mystery Writers of America, inc. Butcher, baker, murder-maker
Greatest Tertian
Conklin, G. ed. Invaders of earth
Nine-finger Jack
Best science fiction stories: 1952
Mystery Writers of America, inc. 20 great tales of murder
Public eye
Best detective stories of the year—1953
Quest for Saint Aquin
Healy, R. J. ed. New tales of space and time
Robinc
Greenberg, M. ed. Robot and the man
Screwball division
Mystery Writers of America, inc. Four-&-twenty bloodhounds
Snulbug
Magazine of fantasy and science fiction. Best from Fantasy and science fiction; 3d ser.
Star dummy
Conklin, G. ed. Omnibus of science fiction
Starbride
Sloane, W. M. ed. Stories for tomorrow
Threnody
Mystery Writers of America, inc. Maiden murders
Transfer point
Crossen, K. F. ed. Adventures in tomorrow
White army. Dresser, D.
White chalah. Shapiro, L.
White circle. Clayton, J. B.
White cock. Benson, T.
White cottage. Strong, L. A. G.
White Elk. Schubert, P.
White girl, fine girl. Grau, S. A.
White heron. Jewett, S. O.
White horses of Vienna. Boyle, K.
White kid gloves. Cousins, M.
White kitten. Howe, D.
White leopard. Fletcher, I. C.
White light. Dovbish, B.
White mare. McLaverty, M.
White monkey
Lin, Y. ed. Famous Chinese short stories

WHITE MOUNTAINS
Hawthorne, N. Ambitious guest
Hawthorne, N. Great Stone Face

White mustang. McCourt, E. A.
White mutiny. Jameson, M.
White night. Ullman, J. R.
White nights. Dostoevskiĭ, F. M.
White people. Machen, A.
White pinnacle. Jacobi, C.
White possum. Annixter, P. pseud.
White powder. Machen, A.

White rooster. Goyen, W.
White sack. Munby, A. N. L.
White sea monkey. Benson, T.
White shadow. Kenig, L.
White silk gloves. Ekbergh, I. D.
White wolf. Goodridge Roberts, T.
White wolf. Maupassant, G. de
Whitehill, Joseph
Day of the last rock fight
Queen, E. pseud. ed. Ellery Queen's awards: 9th ser.
Whiter than snow. Feeney, T. B.
Whitewash. Macaulay, R.
Whitey's first round-up. Rounds, G.
Whitley, Clifton M.
Destiny strikes back
Best Army short stories, 1950
Whitmore, Stanford, 1925-
Bontemps
Abell, E. ed. American accent
Stanford short stories, 1953
Lost soldier
Prize stories, 1954
Love affair
Stanford short stories, 1952
Whitney, Phyllis Ayame, 1903-
Delicate female
McFarland, W. K. comp. Then it happened
Lucky 'leven
American girl (Periodical) Favorite stories
Whittemore, Charles W. 1894-
Leap for two lives
Owen, F. ed. Teen-age winter sports stories
Whittemore, Reed, 1919-
Stutz and the tub
Prize stories, 1954
Who called you here? Petersen, E. J.
Who is my neighbor? Grimson, M. S.
Who—me, signor? Kneale, N.
Who too was a soldier. Smith, J. C.
Whole world knows. Welty, E.
Who's cribbing? Lewis, J.
Who's passing for who? Hughes, L.
Why Adonis laughed. Millin, S. G. L.
Why did he leave me? Burnet, D.
Why don't you look where you're going? Clark, W. Van T.
Why I live at the P.O. Welty, E.
Why, you reckon? Hughes, L.
Wibberley touch. Milne, A. A.
Wicked cousin. Charteris, L.
Wicked voice. Paget, V.
Wicklein, John F.
Mr Moody
Story (Periodical) Story; no. 4
Wide net. Welty, E.
Widow and her son. Gibran, K.
Widow Cruse. De La Roche, M.
Widow Flynn's apple tree. Dunsany, E. J. M. D. P. 18th baron
Widow in waiting. Masur, H. Q.
Widow voyage. Wylie, P.

WIDOWERS
  Betts, D. End of Henry Fribble
  McNulty, J. Television helps, but not very much
  Maugham, W. S. The dream
  Verga, G. The orphans
WIDOWS
  Aiken, C. P. Spider, spider
  Benson, T. Bones of A. T. Stewart
  Bowen, E. Requiescat
  Breuer, B. Home is a place
  Chastity
  Chou, S. Benediction
  Harte, B. Postmistress of Laurel Run
  Horwitz, J. The roof
  Kantor, M. Life in her hands
  Lincoln, V. E. To live is to return
  Maugham, W. S. The escape
  Maugham, W. S. Jane
  Queen, E. pseud. Three widows
  Rasmussen, G. F. Tea at Barnaby's
  Steele, W. D. Autumn bloom
  Stockton, F. R. Widow's cruise
  Taylor, P. H. Dark walk
  Winslow, T. S. Lamb chop for the little dog

Widow's cruise. Stockton, F. R.

Widow's peak. O'Rourke, F.

Wiechert, Ernst
  The mother
    Ungar, F. ed. To mother with love
Wiegand, William, 1928-
  Science teacher
    Story (Periodical) Story; no. one
Wife of his youth. Chesnutt, C. W.

Wife of Martin Guerre. Lewis, J.

Wife of Nashville. Taylor, P. H.

Wiggin, Kate Douglas (Smith) 1856-1923
  The Ruggleses go to the Christmas party
    Fenner, P. R. comp. Giggle box
Wilbur, Richard, 1921-
  Game of catch
    Abell, E. ed. American accent
    Prize stories, 1954
Wilby spirit. Willingham, C.

Wilcox, Don
  Voyage that lasted six hundred years
    Lesser, M. A. ed. Looking forward
WILD ANIMALS. See Animals

WILD BOARS. See Boars

WILD CATS. See Pumas

Wild duck's nest. McLaverty, M.

Wild flower. Babb, S.

Wild flowers. Caldwell, E.

Wild goat's kid. O'Flaherty, L.

Wild goose chase. Millar, K.

Wild hunter. Randall, K. C.

Wild Jack Rhett. Haycox, E.

Wild oranges. Hergesheimer, J.

Wild pitch. Sherman, H. M.

Wild surmise. Kuttner, H. and Moore, C. L.

Wild wet place. Van Doren, M.

WILDCATS. See Pumas

Wilde, Oscar, 1854-1900
  Birthday of the Infanta
    Cerf, B. A. and Moriarty, H. C. eds. Anthology of famous British stories
  Priest and the acolyte
    Cory, D. W. pseud. comp. 21 variations on a theme
Wilder, Thornton Niven, 1897-
  From a journal-letter of Julius Caesar
    Burnett, W. ed. World's best
WILDERNESS. See Outdoor life

The **wilderness.** Bradbury, R.

Wilderness champion. Lippincott, J. W.

Wilderness road. Kjelgaard, J.

Wildy's secret revealer. Anderson, E. V.

Wilkins, Mary E. See Freeman, Mary Eleanor (Wilkins)

Will and a way. Grimson, M. S.

Will o' the mill. Stevenson, R. L.

Will the romance be the same? Aldrich, B. S.

"Will you walk a little faster?" Klass, P.

Willard, Harriet W.
  Just for you
    American girl (Periodical) On my honor
Wm. Crane. Radford, M.

William Henry VanBuren. Hendryx, J. B.

William the conqueror. Kipling, R.

William Wilson. Poe, E. A.

Williams, Barbara
  Hey wait for me
    Seventeen (Periodical) Nineteen from Seventeen
Williams, Ben Ames, 1889-1953
  Mine enemy's dog
    Bloch, M. ed. Favorite dog stories
  Sheener
    Certner, S. and Henry, G. H. eds. Short stories for our times
  Solitude
    Grayson, C. ed. Fourth round
  They grind exceeding small
    Thinker's digest (Periodical) Spoiled priest, and other stories
Williams, Colleen
  There will always be hope
    Dreer, H. ed. American literature by Negro authors
Williams, Henry Lionel
  Gold mine in the sky
    Story parade (Periodical) Adventure stories
Williams, James Howard
  Elephant intelligence
    Fenner, P. R. comp. Elephants, elephants, elephants
Williams, L. B. See Bedford-Jones, H. jt. auth.

Williams, Lawrence, 1915-
  Rise of Carthage
    Collier's, the national weekly. Collier's best
Williams, Ralph
  Emergency landing
    Conklin, G. ed. Big book of science fiction

Williams, Ralph—*Continued*
Head hunters
Conklin, G. ed. Omnibus of science
fiction
Sloane, W. M. ed. Stories for tomor-
row

Williams, Robert E. 1926-
Feminine wiles
Oberfirst, R. ed. 1954 anthology of
best original short-shorts

Williams, Robert Moore, 1907-
Castaway
Conklin, G. ed. Invaders of earth
Red death of Mars
Del Rey, L.; Matschat, C. H. and Car-
mer, C. L. eds. Year after tomorrow
Greenberg, M. ed. Men against the
stars
Refuge for tonight
Best science fiction stories: 1950
Bleiler, E. F. and Dikty, T. E. eds.
Science fiction omnibus: The best
science fiction stories, 1949, 1950
Robots return
Greenberg, M. ed. Robot and the man
The seekers
Wollheim, D. A. comp. Flight into
space

Williams, Roger, 1604?-1683
Hawthorne, N. Endicott and the Red
Cross

Williams, Tennessee, 1914-
Resemblance between a violin case and a
coffin
Best American short stories, 1951
Three players of a summer game
Best American short stories, 1953

Williams, William Carlos, 1883-
Above the river
Williams, W. C. Make light of it
The accident
Williams, W. C. Make light of it
Ancient gentility
Williams, W. C. Make light of it
At the front
Williams, W. C. Make light of it
The buffalos
Williams, W. C. Make light of it
Burden of loveliness
Williams, W. C. Make light of it
Cold world
Williams, W. C. Make light of it
Colored girls of Passenack—old and new
Williams, W. C. Make light of it
Comedy entombed: 1930
Williams, W. C. Make light of it
Country rain
Williams, W. C. Make light of it
Danse pseudomacabre
Williams, W. C. Make light of it
Dawn of another day
Williams, W. C. Make light of it
Descendant of kings
Williams, W. C. Make light of it
Difficult man
Williams, W. C. Make light of it
Face of stone
Williams, W. C. Make light of it
Final embarrassment
Williams, W. C. Make light of it

Four bottles of beer
Williams, W. C. Make light of it
Frankie the newspaperman
Williams, W. C. Make light of it
Girl with a pimply face
Williams, W. C. Make light of it
Good-natured slob
Williams, W. C. Make light of it
Good old days
Williams, W. C. Make light of it
Hands across the sea
Williams, W. C. Make light of it
In northern waters
Williams, W. C. Make light of it
Inquest
Williams, W. C. Make light of it
The insane
Williams, W. C. Make light of it
Jean Beicke
Williams, W. C. Make light of it
Knife of the times
Cory, D. W. pseud. comp. 21 varia-
tions on a theme
Williams, W. C. Make light of it
Lena
Williams, W. C. Make light of it
Life along the Passaic River
Williams, W. C. Make light of it
Lucky break
Williams, W. C. Make light of it
Mind and body
Williams, W. C. Make light of it
Night in June
Williams, W. C. Make light of it
No place for a woman
Williams, W. C. Make light of it
Old Doc Rivers
Williams, W. C. Make light of it
Old time raid
Williams, W. C. Make light of it
Pace that kills
Williams, W. C. Make light of it
Paid nurse
Williams, W. C. Make light of it
Pink and blue
Williams, W. C. Make light of it
Red head
Williams, W. C. Make light of it
Right thing
Williams, W. C. Make light of it
Round the world fliers
Williams, W. C. Make light of it
Sailor's son
Williams, W. C. Make light of it
Second marriage
Williams, W. C. Make light of it
To fall asleep
Williams, W. C. Make light of it
Under the greenwood tree
Williams, W. C. Make light of it
Use of force
Greene, J. I. and Abell, E. eds. Stories
of sudden truth
Heilman, R. B. ed. Modern short
stories
Schorer, M. ed. The story
Williams, W. C. Make light of it
The Venus
Williams, W. C. Make light of it
Verbal transcription: 6 A.M.
Williams, W. C. Make light of it
Visit to the fair
Williams, W. C. Make light of it

Williams, William C.—*Continued*
World's end
Williams, W. C. Make light of it
The zoo
Williams, W. C. Make light of it

Williamson, Henry, 1897-
Trapper's mates
Cerf, B. A. and Moriarty, H. C. eds.
Anthology of famous British stories

Williamson, Jack, 1908-
Breakdown
Greenberg, M. ed. Journey to infinity
Crucible of power
Greenberg, M. comp. Five science fiction novels
Guinevere for everybody
Star science fiction stories, no. 3
Happiest creature
Star science fiction stories, no. 2
Hindsight
Astounding science fiction (Periodical)
Astounding science fiction anthology
In the scarlet star
Wollheim, D. A. comp. Every boy's book of science-fiction
Man from outside
Derleth, A. W. ed. Beachheads in space
Lesser, M. A. ed. Looking forward
Peddler's nose
Pohl, F. ed. Assignment in tomorrow
Sun maker
Margulies, L. and Friend, O. J. eds. Giant anthology of science fiction
Through the purple cloud
Margulies, L. and Friend, O. J. eds. From off this world

Willie Collins. Farrell, J. T.

Willie craves action. Hendryx, J. B.

Willingham, Calder, 1922-
Afternoon sun
Willingham, C. Gates of hell
Bird life
Willingham, C. Gates of hell
Career of Augurt Nimrodtk
Willingham, C. Gates of hell
Drop of pure liquid
Willingham, C. Gates of hell
Eternal rectangle
Willingham, C. Gates of hell
Eupepsia
Willingham, C. Gates of hell
Excitement in Ergo
Willingham, C. Gates of hell
Farewell, hon
Willingham, C. Gates of hell
Guardian angel
Willingham, C. Gates of hell
James A. Dukes
Willingham, C. Gates of hell
Jane
Willingham, C. Gates of hell
Little Bubo
Willingham, C. Gates of hell
Little dreams of Mr Morgan
Willingham, C. Gates of hell
Love on toast
Willingham, C. Gates of hell
Mathematics of intelligence
Willingham, C. Gates of hell
Pursuit of gloom
Willingham, C. Gates of hell

Record of a man
Willingham, C. Gates of hell
Rupee
Willingham, C. Gates of hell
Secret journal
Willingham, C. Gates of hell
Steve and Sarah and Cyril
Willingham, C. Gates of hell
Sum of two angles
Willingham, C. Gates of hell
Surface tension of molten metal
Willingham, C. Gates of hell
Universe is not really expanding
Willingham, C. Gates of hell
What is rape?
Willingham, C. Gates of hell
Wilby spirit
Willingham, C. Gates of hell

Willis, Anthony Armstrong, 1897-
One-way street
Best detective stories of the year—1953

Willman, Paula
Labyrinth
Wolfe, D. M. ed. Which grain will grow

The **willow.** Etnier, E. J.

Willow walk. Lewis, S.

Willows. De La Mare, W. J.

WILLS
Bennett, A. Mary with the high hand
Bernstein, H. Greatest funeral in the world
Collins, W. Mr Lepel and the housekeeper
Kneale, M. Putting away of Uncle Quaggin
Lever, C. J. Con Cregan's legacy
Parker, J. R. Estate of Alice V. Gregg

See also Inheritance and succession

Wilner, Herbert
Whistle and the heroes
Prize stories, 1954

Wilsey, Russell G. 1928-
For men only
Wolfe, D. M. ed. Which grain will grow

Wilson, Angus, 1914?-
Christmas Day in the workhouse
Wilson, A. Such darling dodos and other stories
Heart of elm
Wilson, A. Such darling dodos and other stories
Learning's little tribute
Wilson, A. Such darling dodos and other stories
Little companion
Wilson, A. Such darling dodos and other stories
Mummy to the rescue
Ludwig, J. B. and Poirier, W. R. eds. Stories, British and American
Wilson, A. Such darling dodos and other stories
Necessity's child
Wilson, A. Such darling dodos and other stories
Rex imperator
Wilson, A. Such darling dodos and other stories

Wilson, Angus—*Continued*
Sister superior
Wilson, A. Such darling dodos and
other stories
Such darling dodos
Wilson, A. Such darling dodos and
other stories
What do hippos eat
Wilson, A. Such darling dodos and
other stories

Wilson, Ben
Stand-in
Strang, R. M. and Roberts, R. M. eds.
Teen-age tales v2

Wilson, Dorothy (Clarke) 1904-
Priest and prophet at Bethel
Brentano, F. ed. The word lives on

Wilson, Edward
Men from the boys
Stanford short stories, 1951

Wilson, Ethel, 1890-
Hurry, hurry!
Pacey, D. ed. Book of Canadian stories
Mrs Golightly and the first convention
Weaver, R. and James, H. eds. Canadian short stories

Wilson, Harry Leon, 1867-1939
Wrong twin
Davis, C. B. ed. Eyes of boyhood

Wilson, John Walter, 1920-
Grass grow again
Peery, W. W. ed. 21 Texas short stories

Wilson, Leon, 1913-
Not quite Martin
Fenner, P. R. comp. Ghosts, ghosts, ghosts

Wilson, Neill Compton, 1889-
Scandal at Mulford Inn
Saturday evening post (Periodical)
Saturday evening post stories, 1952

Wilson, Richard
Back to Julie
Pohl, F. ed. Assignment in tomorrow
Friend of the family
Star science fiction stories, no. 2

Wilson, Robert McNair, 1882-
Cyprian bees
Bond, R. T. ed. Handbook for poisoners

Wilson, Ruth
Too many brides
Mystery Writers of America, inc.
Maiden murders

Win the world. Oliver, C.

Wincelberg, Simon, 1924-
The conqueror
Best American short stories, 1953
Honeymoon
Story (Periodical) Story; no. 2

Winchell, Prentice, 1895-
Devil on wheels
Argosy (Periodical) Argosy Book of sports stories
Never come mourning
Mystery Writers of America, inc. Four-&-twenty bloodhounds

WIND. See Winds

Wind and the snow of winter. Clark, W. Van T.

Wind blows. Mansfield, K.

The **windfall.** Caldwell, E.

Windfall. Sanford, W. M.

WINDOW DRESSING. See Show windows

WINDOWS
Dunsany, E. J. M. D. P. 18th baron. Wonderful window

The **windows.** Sansom, W.

WINDS
Mansfield, K. Wind blows

The **winds.** Welty, E.

Winds of heaven. Jefferies, R.

WINE AND WINE MAKING
Daudet, A. Father Gaucher's elixir
De Vries, P. Life among the winesaps
Walsh, M. Heather wine

Wine of one day. Neiman, S.

Wine on the desert. Brand, M. pseud.

Wing walker. Gilpatric, G.

Winged feet. Robinson, G.

Wingless victory. Heard, G.

Wings. Clemens, S. L.

Wings of an angel. Kaufman, W.

Wings of night. Del Rey, L.

Winn, Josephine
Hungry sister
Abell, E. ed. American accent

The **winner.** Chute, B. J.

Winner lose all. Kuttner, H.

Winner take all. Rocklynne, R.

Winner takes all. Waugh, E.

Winner's money. Litten, F. N.

Winning pitcher. Worthington, J.

Winning sequence. Sharp, M.

Winslow, Anne (Goodwin)
Seasmiles
Prize stories of 1950

Winslow, Thyra (Samter) 1893-
The actress
Winslow, T. S. Sex without sentiment
Angie Lee's fortune
Winslow, T. S. Sex without sentiment
Bronzes of Martel Greer
Winslow, T. S. Sex without sentiment
Cycle of Manhattan
Burrell, J. A. and Cerf, B. A. eds. Anthology of famous American stories
Ribalow, H. U. ed. These your children
Dear Sister Sadie
Winslow, T. S. Sex without sentiment
Fur flies
Winslow, T. S. Sex without sentiment
Girls in black
Winslow, T. S. Sex without sentiment
Grandma
Leftwich, J. ed. Yisröel. 1952 ed.
Ungar, F. ed. To mother with love
Hotel dog
Winslow, T. S. Sex without sentiment

Winslow, Thyra S.—*Continued*
  Interview
    Winslow, T. S. Sex without sentiment
  Lamb chop for the little dog
    Winslow, T. S. Sex without sentiment
  Misses Grant
    Winslow, T. S. Sex without sentiment
  Mrs Wilson's husband goes for a swim
    Winslow, T. S. Sex without sentiment
  More like sisters
    Winslow, T. S. Sex without sentiment
  Obsession
    Winslow, T. S. Sex without sentiment
  Odd old lady
    Winslow, T. S. Sex without sentiment
  Other woman
    Winslow, T. S. Sex without sentiment
  Rudolph
    Winslow, T. S. Sex without sentiment
  Sophie Jackson
    Winslow, T. S. Sex without sentiment
  Technique
    Winslow, T. S. Sex without sentiment

Winston, Harry
  Greater love
    Ford, N. A. and Faggett, H. L. eds.
      Best short stories by Afro-American
      writers (1925-1950)
  Life begins at forty
    Ford, N. A. and Faggett, H. L. eds.
      Best short stories by Afro-American
      writers (1925-1950)

Winter, Arthur B.
  Party dress
    Oberfirst, R. ed. 1954 anthology of best
      original short-shorts

Winter, J. A.
  Expedition polychrome
    Norton, A. M. ed. Space service

WINTER
  Clark, W. Van T. Wind and the snow of
    winter
  Enright, E. Temperate zone
  Thoreau, H. D. Winter at Walden

Winter at Walden. Thoreau, H. D.

Winter cruise. Maugham, W. S.

Winter detail. Denicoff, M.

Winter dreams. Fitzgerald, F. S. K.

Winter in July. Lessing, D. M.

Winter months in a cow camp. James, W.

Winter of his life. Patten, L. B.

Winterbotham, Russell Robert, 1904-
  Fourth dynasty
    Conklin, G. ed. Omnibus of science fic-
    tion

Winters, Emmanuel, pseud. See Horowitz,
  Emmanuel

Winters, Yvor, 1900-
  Brink of darkness
    Swallow, A. ed. Anchor in the sea

Winter's tale. Stafford, J.

Wire brush. Treat, L. and Tarachow, S.

'Wireless.' Kipling, R.

WISCONSIN

          19th century
  Garland, H. Return of a private

WISCONSIN POLITICS. See Politics—
  Wisconsin

WISE MEN. See Magi

Wise men of Holmola. Bowman, J. C. and
  Bianco, M. W.

Wise men of Trehenna. Locke, W. J.

The **wish.** Dahl, R.

Wish book. Milburn, G.

WISHES
  Rossiter, H. D. How dear to my heart

The **wishbone.** Macauley, R.

Wister, Owen, 1860-1938
  Journey in search of Christmas
    Lohan, R. and Lohan, M. eds. New
      Christmas treasury

WIT AND HUMOR. See Humor

The **witch.** Gold, H.

Witch doctor. Fisher, D. F. C.

WITCH DOCTORS. See Witchcraft

Witch of Ramoth. Van Doren, M.

Witch of Times Square. Queen, E. pseud.

Witch war. Matheson, R.

WITCHCRAFT
  Barker, A. L. Jane Dore—dear childe
  Bradbury, R. Invisible boy
  Brenner, L. Moon magic
  Brentano, C. M. Picnic of Mores the cat
  Collier, J. Lady on the grey
  Dunsany, E. J. M. D. P. 18th baron.
    Widow Flynn's apple tree
  Hawthorne, N. Young Goodman Brown
  Irwin, M. E. F. Monsieur seeks a wife
  Jenkins, W. F. The power
  Keller, D. H. The bridle
  Keller, D. H. Opium eater
  King-Hall, S. By one, by two, and by
    three
  Munro, H. H. Peace of Mowsle Barton
  Paget, V. Dionea
  Pratt, F. and De Camp, L. S. Caveat
    emptor

WITCHES. See Witchcraft

Witches' loaves. Porter, W. S.

Witches money. Collier, J.

Witches of Karres. Schmitz, J. H.

With an O X herd. Payne, S.

With his back to the wall. Roberts, Sir
  C. G. D.

With men it's different. Newhouse, E.

With Mr Jorrocks in Pinch-me-near Forest.
  Surtees, R. S.

With the aid of the One Above. Suhl, Y.

With the fog. Morehouse, K. M.

With the greatest of ease. Annixter, P.
  pseud.

With the Hit-im-and-hold-im-shire: The
  sham day. Surtees, R. S.

With these hands. Kornbluth, C. M.

Witham, E. C.
  Silver spurs
    Queen, E. pseud. ed. Queen's awards:
    8th ser.

Witherow, James Milling, 1867-1934
The test
Thinker's digest (Periodical) Spoiled
priest, and other stories
Within and without. Hesse, H.
Without benefit of clergy. Kipling, R.
Without benefit of Galsworthy, Collier, J.
Witness for the prosecution. Quentin, P.
pseud.
WITNESSES
Chekhov, A. P. Women make trouble
Witnesses. Claudy, C. H.

WIVES. See Husband and wife

Wives of the dead. Hawthorne, N.

The **wizard.** Yakovlev, A. S.

Wodehouse, Pelham Grenville, 1881-
Birth of a salesman
Wodehouse, P. G. Nothing serious
Bramley is so bracing
Wodehouse, P. G. Nothing serious
Excelsior
Wodehouse, P. G. Nothing serious
Feet of clay
Wodehouse, P. G. Nothing serious
How's that, umpire
Wodehouse, P. G. Nothing serious
Jeeves and the song of songs
Cerf, B. A. and Moriarty, H. C. eds.
Anthology of famous British stories
Rodney has a relapse
Wodehouse, P. G. Nothing serious
Shadow passes
Wodehouse, P. G. Nothing serious
Story of Webster
Joseph, M. ed. Best cat stories
Success story
Wodehouse, P. G. Nothing serious
Tangled hearts
Wodehouse, P. G. Nothing serious
Up from the depths
Wodehouse, P. G. Nothing serious

Wohl, Sam
The bride
Ribalow, H. U. ed. These your children

Wolf, Mari
Homeland
Sloane, W. M. ed. Stories for tomorrow

The **wolf.** Newhouse, E.

Wolf of Chungshan. Hsieh Liang

Wolf pack. Miller, W. M.

Wolfe, Bernard, 1915-
Self portrait
Galaxy science fiction magazine. Second
Galaxy reader of science fiction
Greenberg, M. ed. Robot and the man

Wolfe, Elizabeth
Thing in their hearts
Stanford short stories, 1950

Wolfe, Thomas, 1900-1938
The far and the near
Moskowitz, S. ed. Great railroad stories
of the world
Lost boy
Stegner, W. E.; Scowcroft, R. and
Ilyin, B. eds. Writer's art
Waite, H. O. and Atkinson, B. P. eds.
Literature for our time

Only the dead know Brooklyn
Blodgett, H. W. ed. Story survey. 1953
ed.
Portrait of Bascom Hawke
Burrell, J. A. and Cerf, B. A. eds. An-
thology of famous American stories
Veteran ballplayer
Graber, R. S. ed. Baseball reader
World Series and a small town
Graber, R. S. ed. Baseball reader

About
Bradbury, R. Forever and the earth

Wolfert, Ira, 1908-
'Git or git got'
Jensen, P. ed. Fireside book of flying
stories
The indomitable blue
Best American short stories, 1952

Wolfson, Victor
Purification of Thelma Augenstern
Ribalow, H. U. ed. This land, these
people

Wollheim, Donald A.
Disguise
Sloane, W. M. ed. Stories for tomorrow
Planet passage
Wollheim, D. A. comp. Flight into
space
Storm warning
Conklin, G. ed. Invaders of earth

Wolson, Morton
The attacker
Best detective stories of the year—
1954

WOLVES
Annixter, P. pseud. Last lobo
Chekhov, A. P. Hydrophobia
Davis, H. L. The vanishing wolf
Gilbert, K. Old man of the mountains
Goodridge Roberts, T. White wolf
Hsieh Liang. Wolf of Chungshan
Kipling, R. Mowgli's brothers
Munro, H. H. Wolves of Cernogratz
Roberts, Sir C. G. D. With his back to
the wall
Seton, E. T. Lobo, the king of Cur-
rumpaw

Wolves of Cernogratz. Munro, H. H.
WOMAN

Relation to other women
Glaspell, S. Jury of her peers
Maugham, W. S. Romantic young lady
Maugham, W. S. Three fat women of
Antibes
Palma, R. Two cooing doves
Taylor, E. Hester Lilly
Welty, E. The winds
Winslow, T. S. Girls in black

Rights of women
Graham, R. B. C. Faith

Social and moral questions
De Ford, M. A. Throwback
Maugham, W. S. Rain

Suffrage
Munro, H. H. Gala programme
Munro, H. H. Hermann the Irascible
Munro, H. H. The threat
Munro, H. H. Young Turkish catastrophe

Woman from Twenty-One. Fitzgerald, F. S. K.

Woman he left to die. Mowat, F.

Woman hunt no good. La Farge, O.

Woman in love. Household, G.

Woman in the case. Chekhov, A. P.

Woman in the house. Caldwell, E.

Woman in the house. Stuart, J.

Woman of fifty. Maugham, W. S.

A woman of virtue. Field, R. L.

WOMAN SUFFRAGE. See Woman—Suffrage

Woman taken in adultery. Eça de Queiroz, J. M.

Woman who hated flowers. Sitwell, Sir O. bart.

Woman who was everybody. Calisher, H.

Woman who was loved. Stern, J.

Woman with a past. Fitzgerald, F. S. K.

The women. Sullivan, R.

WOMEN AS AUTHORS
Aiken, C. P. Your obituary, well written

WOMEN AS HUNTERS
Collier, J. Squirrels have bright eyes

WOMEN AS LAWYERS
Eichrodt, J. Nadia Devereux

WOMEN AS MURDERERS
Du Maurier, D. Kiss me again, stranger

WOMEN AS RANCHERS
Thompson, T. Shadow of the butte

WOMEN IN BUSINESS
Winslow, T. S. Girls in black

Women make trouble. Chekhov, A. P.

Women on the wall. Stegner, W. E.

WOMEN VOTERS. See Woman—Suffrage

Women will out. Rhodes, W. P.

WOMEN'S CLUBS
Wharton, E. N. J. Xingu

Won and lost. Grimson, M. S.

Won by a tail. Person, W. T.

Won by inches! Campbell, Sir M.

Wonder child. Shallit, J.

Wonder in Willow Hill. West, A.

Wonderful automobile. Walker, T.

Wonderful new machine. Hamsun, K.

Wonderful Tar-Baby story. Harris, J. C.

Wonderful window. Dunsany, E. J. M. D. P. 18th baron

Wood, Clement, 1888-1950
Tzagan
Denis, W. ed. Palomino and other horses

Wood, Frances (Gilchrist) 1859-1944
Turkey-red
Cooper, A. C. ed. Modern short stories

Wood, Kerry, 1907-
Workaday cowboy
Fenner, P. R. comp. Cowboys, cowboys, cowboys
Owen, F. ed. Teen-age victory parade

WOOD CARVING
Caldwell, E. Handy

Wood-for-the-trees. MacDonald, P.

Wood smoke. Chidester, A.

WOODCHOPPERS. See Woodcutters

WOODCUTTERS
Traven, B. pseud. Third guest
Van Doren, M. Tall one

Woods, William
Free man
Story (Periodical) Story; no. 4

Woodward, George B.
College marriage
Oberfirst, R. ed. 1952 anthology of best original short-shorts

Woody, Regina Llewellyn (Jones)
Cue for Connie
Furman, A. L. ed. Everygirls career stories
Second chance
American girl (Periodical) Favorite stories

Woolf, Virginia (Stephen) 1882-1941
Between the acts
Connolly, C. ed. Great English short novels
Duchess and the jeweller
Neider, C. ed. Great short stories from the world's literature
Kew Gardens
Felheim, M.; Newman, F. B. and Steinhoff, W. R. Modern short stories
New dress
Heilman, R. B. ed. Modern short stories

Woollcott, Alexander, 1887-1943
Moonlight sonata
Davenport, B. ed. Ghostly tales to be told
Verdun Belle
Cavanna, B. ed. Pick of the litter

Woolley, Rollo
The pupil
Horizon (Periodical) Golden Horizon
The search
New writing (Periodical) Best stories

Woolrich, Cornell, 1903-
Blue ribbon
Ribalow, H. U. ed. World's greatest boxing stories
Wait for me downstairs
Cuff, R. P. ed. American short story survey

Word for Coffey. De La Roche, M.

Worden, William L.
Officers' girl
Saturday evening post (Periodical) Saturday evening post stories, 1951

Words for John Willie. Higbee, A. R.

Work suspended. Waugh, E.

Workaday cowboy. Wood, K.

Worker in sandalwood. Pickthall, M. L. C.

Workout in the park. Farrell, J. T.

Workout on the river. Shattuck, R.

Works of God. Berto, G.

WORLD; END OF THE. See End of the world

World and the door. Porter, W. S.

World is mine. Kuttner, H.

World of glass. Sansom, W.

World of little doves. Davis, H. L.

World outside. Maier, H.

World Series and a small town. Wolfe, T.

World the children made. Bradbury, R.

WORLD WAR, 1939-1945
Karchmer, S. N. Fistful of Alamo heroes
Newhouse, E. I hope you'll understand
Newhouse, E. What do you do?
Saint Exupéry, A. de. Letter to a hostage

Aerial operations
Bates, H. E. Colonel Julian
Gallico, P. W. The bombardier
Newhouse, E. Short visit to Naples

Africa, North
Krige, U. Death of the Zulu
Krige, U. Two Daumiers

Children
Asch, S. Duty to live
Blue, E. Nothing overwhelms Giuseppe

Collaborationists
See Treason

Egypt
Shaw, I. Walking wounded

England
O'Donovan, M. Darcy in the Land of
  Youth
Van Paassen, P. The unsaid prayer

France
Boyle, K. Defeat
Boyle, K. They weren't going to die
Brookhouser, F. Triumph with bells and
  laughter
Downey, H. The hunters
Kantor, M. Papa Pierre's pipe
Macfarlan, A. A. Danger by candlelight
Maugham, W. S. The unconquered
Remarque, E. M. Darkness in Paris

Germany
Forester, C. S. The nightmare; 10 stories
Waltari, M. T. Before the twilight of the
  gods

Italy
Berto, G. Works of God and other sto-
  ries; 4 stories
Krige, U. Charcoal burners
Ullman, J. R. Diversion

Jews
Schulberg, B. W. Enough

Medical and sanitary affairs
Krige, U. Christmas box
Ullman, J. R. Between you and I
Ullman, J. R. Presumed lost

Naval operations
Auchincloss, L. Fall of a sparrow
Eliot, G. F. Uncertain weapon

Naval operations—Submarine
Beach, E. L. Archerfish
Holmes, W. J. Action off Formosa
Taylor, S. W. Last voyage of the Un-
  sinkable Sal
Yates, T. Living torpedo

Norway
Petersen, E. J. Who called you here?

Pacific Ocean
Arico, V. Water canteen
Heatter, B. Island happy

Poland
Gronowicz, A. Mania-head-in-the-clouds

Prisoners and prisons
Downey, H. Crispin's way
Krige, U. Charcoal burners

United States
Johnson, D. M. Scars of honor

**WORLD WAR AMBULANCE DRIV-
ERS.** See World War, 1939-1945—
  Medical and sanitary affairs

World well lost. Waldo, E. H.

World without. Herbert, B.

WORLDS, NEW. See Future, Stories of
the

World's end. Williams, W. C.

The **worm.** Keller, D. H.

WORMS
Keller, D. H. The worm

Worn path. Welty, E.

WORRY
Munro, H. H. Reginald on worries

Worse and worse. Chekhov, A. P.

Worst crime in the world. Chesterton, G. K.

Worthington, Jay
Box score battle
  Furman, A. L. ed. Teen-age stories of
    the diamond
Winning pitcher
  Furman, A. L. ed. Teen-age stories of
    the diamond

Worthington, Rex
Kind of scandal
  Prize stories, 1954

The **wounded.** Putman, C.

WOUNDED IN BATTLE. See War—
  Casualties

Wratislav. Munro, H. H.

Wreath for Miss Totten. Calisher, H.

WRECKS, RAILROAD. See Railroad—
  Accidents

WRESTLING
Komroff, M. Light of the moon
Mitchell, J. "Some bum might mistook
  me for a wrestler"
Olive, H. Take it and like it
Upson, W. H. Quiet wedding

Wretched old capitalist. Hallack, C.

Wright, Frances (Fitzpatrick) 1897-
Best foot forward
  American girl (Periodical) On my
    honor
Declaration of independence
  American girl (Periodical) Favorite
    stories
Let nothing you dismay
  American girl (Periodical) Christmas
    all year 'round
Miracles still happen
  American girl (Periodical) Christmas
    all year 'round

Wright, Hamilton
Lenore and the boys
Story (Periodical) Story; no. 2
Wright, J. Ernest, 1897-
Pay night
American vanguard, 1952
Wright, Katharine O.
Christmas at Thunder Gap
American girl (Periodical) Christmas
all year 'round
Wright, Sewell Peaslee
The infra-medians
Wollheim, D. A. comp. Every boy's
book of science-fiction
Wright, Sydney Fowler, 1874-
Automata: I
Conklin, G. ed. Science-fiction thinking
machines
Automata: II
Conklin, G. ed. Science-fiction thinking
machines
Automata: III
Conklin, G. ed. Science-fiction thinking
machines
The rat
Kuebler, H. W. ed. Treasury of science fiction classics
Wright, William, 1829-1898
Washoe behemoth
Emrich, D. ed. Comstock bonanza
Wrist watch and some ants. Marshall, R. D.
Wrists on the door. Fish, H.
Writ of divorcement. Lewisohn, L.
WRITERS. See Authors
WRITING, AUTOMATIC
Jenkins, W. F. Other now
Wrong guy. Mahoney, W. B.
Wrong problem. Carr, J. D.
Wrong shape. Chesterton, G. K.
Wrong twin. Wilson, H. L.
Wully. Seton, E. T.
Wunderkind. McCullers, C. S.
Wuorio, Eva-lis
We'll always have Christmas
American girl (Periodical) Christmas
all year 'round
Wyckoff, James
Door between
Story (Periodical) Story; no. one
Wyld Ospina, Carlos, 1881-
Honor of his house
De Onís, H. ed. Spanish stories and
tales
Wylie, Philip, 1902-
Bait for McGillicudy
Wylie, P. Best of Crunch and Des
Crazy over horse mackerel
Wylie, P. Best of Crunch and Des
Crunch catches one
Wylie, P. Best of Crunch and Des
Des takes a holiday
Wylie, P. Best of Crunch and Des
Eve and the sea serpent
Wylie, P. Best of Crunch and Des
Experiment in crime
Wylie, P. Three to be read
The expert
Wylie, P. Best of Crunch and Des

Fifty-four, forty and fight
Wylie, P. Best of Crunch and Des
Fish bites man
Wylie, P. Best of Crunch and Des
Hooky line and sinker
Wylie, P. Best of Crunch and Des
Hull down
Wylie, P. Best of Crunch and Des
Light tackle
Wylie, P. Best of Crunch and Des
Man who had been around
Wylie, P. Best of Crunch and Des
Old crawdad
Wylie, P. Best of Crunch and Des
Once on a Sunday
Wylie, P. Best of Crunch and Des
Reelistic viewpoint
Wylie, P. Best of Crunch and Des
She wanted a hero
Wylie, P. Best of Crunch and Des
Shipwreck of Crunch and Des
Wylie, P. Best of Crunch and Des
Smuggled atom bomb
Wylie, P. Three to be read
Snarling Santa Claus
Wylie, P. Best of Crunch and Des
Sporting blood
Wylie, P. Three to be read
Visiting fire-eater
Wylie, P. Best of Crunch and Des
Way of all fish
Dachs, D. ed. Treasury of sports humor
Wylie, P. Best of Chunch and Des
Widow voyage
Wylie, P. Best of Chunch and Des
See also Balmer, E. jt. auth.
Wyndham, John, pseud. See Harris, John
Beynon
Wynne, Anthony, pseud. See Wilson, Robert McNair

X

X-ing a paragrab. Poe, E. A.
**XERXES I, KING OF PERSIA, B.C. 519-
465**
Fineman, I. Interview with Ahashuerus
Xi effect. Robinson, R. S.
Xingu. Wharton, E. N. J.

Y

YACHT RACING
Crump, I. Little guy
Yaffe, James, 1927-
Aunt Rose's ghost story
Yaffe, J. Poor Cousin Evelyn
Encounter with the Queen of Bothnya
Yaffe, J. Poor Cousin Evelyn
Mr Birnbaum's little joke
Yaffe, J. Poor Cousin Evelyn
Mr Feldman
Ribalow, H. U. ed. These your children
Yaffe, J. Poor Cousin Evelyn

Yaffe, James—*Continued*
  Mom in the spring
    Queen, E. pseud. ed. Ellery Queen's
      awards: 9th ser.
  Mom knows best
    Queen, E. pseud. ed. Queen's awards:
      7th ser.
  Mom makes a bet
    Best detective stories of the year—
      1953
  On the brink
    Queen, E. pseud. ed. Queen's awards:
      8th ser.
  Poor Cousin Evelyn
    Yaffe, J. Poor Cousin Evelyn
  Question of being businesslike
    Yaffe, J. Poor Cousin Evelyn
  The refugees
    Yaffe, J. Poor Cousin Evelyn
  Special story
    Yaffe, J. Poor Cousin Evelyn
  "When the season cometh round"
    Yaffe, J. Poor Cousin Evelyn
Yakovlev, Alexsandr Stepanovich, 1886-
  The wizard
    Guerney, B. G. comp. New Russian
      stories
Yam gruel. Akutagawa, R.
Yamamoto, H.
  Yoneko's earthquake
    Best American short stories, 1952
Yankee captain in Patagonia. Finger, C. J.
Yankee exodus. Goldsmith, R. M.
YAQUI INDIANS
  Davis, H. L. World of little doves
Yardmaster. McLarn, J. C.
YARDMASTERS. See Railroads—Em-
  ployees
Yarkand manner. Munro, H. H.
Yates, Elizabeth, 1905-
  Enshrined in the heart
    Brentano, F. ed. The word lives on
Yates, Tom
  Living torpedo
    Saturday evening post (Periodical)
      Saturday evening post stories, 1951
Yea, he did fly. Kantor, M.
Year day. Kuttner, H.
Year of the jackpot. Heinlein, R. A.
Years before anger. Kolins, W. F.
Years brought to an end. Beck, W.
"The years draw nigh." Del Rey, L.
Yeast men. Keller, D. H.
Yeats, William Butler, 1865-1939
  Red Hanrahan
    Cerf, B. A. and Moriarty, H. C. eds.
      Anthology of famous British stories
    Short, R. W. and Sewall, R. B. eds.
      Short stories for study. 1950 ed.
Yegor's story. Chekhov, A. P.
Yehoash, pseud. See Bloomgarden, Solomon
Yehudi principle. Brown, F.
Yellow-ball-in-the-side. McNulty, J.
Yellow cat. Steele, W. D.
Yellow convertible. Roberts, R. M.
Yellow dog. Harte, B.

Yellow face. Doyle, Sir A. C.
Yellow girl. Caldwell, E.
Yellow leaf. Reid, C. B.
Yellow Ship. Bedford-Jones, H. and Wil-
  liams, L. B.
Yellow streak. Maugham, W. S.
Yellow turtleneck sweater. White, M.
Yellow wall-paper. Gilman, C. P. S.
Yente Telebende. Adler, J.
Yentzen, Vurrell, 1919-
  The rock
    Best American short stories, 1954
Yes-girl. Benson, T.
Yesterday and today. Gibran, K.
Yesterday was Monday. Waldo, E. H.
Yezierska, Anzia, 1885-
  Fat of the land
    Fremantle, A. J. ed. Mothers
    Leftwich, J. ed. Yisröel. 1952 ed.
  Hunger
    Ribalow, H. U. ed. These your chil-
      dren
Yisgadal. Klein, J. M.
Ylla. Bradbury, R.
YOGA
  Exbergh, I. D. Hindu Yogi Science of
    Breath
Yogi's dark horse. Brier, H. M.
Yoicks—and away. Marquand, J. P.
Yom Kipper fressers. Ornitz, S.
YOM KIPPUR
  Ornitz, S. Yom Kipper fressers
  Peretz, I. L. Miracle on the sea
  Rabinowitz, S. The search
Yoneko's earthquake. Yamamoto, H.
Yoo hoo! Mudhen! Allen, M. P.
YORKSHIRE. See England, Provincial
  and rural—Yorkshire
Yoss, Norman, 1910-
  Children learn so fast
    Oberfirst, R. ed. 1952 anthology of best
      original short-shorts
You aim so high. Brookhouser, F.
You and who else? De Vries, P.
You are not I. Bowles, P. F.
'You can carry it, Mrs Parkin.' Sitwell,
  Sir O. bart.
You can't buy a dog. Taber, G. B.
You can't do that. Marquand, J. P.
You can't say that. Cartmill, C.
You could look it up. Thurber, J.
You know what, teacher? Henderson, Z.
You should have brought your mink.
  Powell, D.
You think you got trouble? Shulman, M.
Youd, Christopher
  Christmas tree
    Greenberg, M. ed. Travelers of space
You'd better be right! Waddell, R.
You'll never mind. O'Connell, R. B.
Young, Emily Hilda, 1880-1949
  The stream
    Talbot, D. ed. Treasury of mountain-
      eering stories

Young, Francis Brett, 1884-1954
Busman's holiday
Cerf, B. A. and Moriarty, H. C. eds.
Anthology of famous British stories
Young, James Martin
Rosinback
Collier's, the national weekly. Collier's
best
Young, Roger Flint
Not to be opened
Best science fiction stories: 1951
Suburban frontiers
Conklin, G. ed. Science-fiction adventures in dimension
Young, Scott
Dangerous ice
Argosy (Periodical) Argosy Book of
sports stories
Maloney's last stand
Argosy (Periodical) Argosy Book of
sports stories
We won't be needing you, Al
Herzberg, M. J. comp. Treasure chest
of sport stories
Young Archimedes. Huxley, A. L.
Young Goodman Brown. Hawthorne, N.
Young man Axelbrod. Lewis, S.
Young man from yesterday. Brookhouser, F.
Young man of his time. Putman, C.
Young Mari Li. MacMahon, B.
"The **young** ravens that call upon him."
Roberts, Sir C. G. D.
Young Turkish catastrophe. Munro, H. H.
Your Arkansas traveler. Schulberg, B. W.
Your heart's out of order. Soman, F. J.
Your long black hair. McCarty, M. B.
Your obituary, well written. Aiken, C. P.
You're only young once. Sullivan, R.
YOUTH
Anderson, S. Sophistication
Elias, A. Jarka
Fitzgerald, F. S. K. Jelly-bean
Neville, K. Hold back tomorrow
Payne, L. V. Prelude
Strang, R. M. and Roberts, R. M. eds.
Teen-age tales; 35 stories
Waugh, A. Wed, my darling daughter
See also Adolescence; Boys; Girls
Youth. Brement, M.
Youth. Conrad, J.
Youth, beautiful youth. Hesse, H.
YOUTH, ETERNAL. See Rejuvenation
Youth from Vienna. Collier, J.
You've got to learn. Murphy, R.
Yüan Chên. See Yuen Chin
Yuen Chin, 779-831
Passion (or the Western room)
Lin, Y. ed. Famous Chinese short stories
YUKON TERRITORY
Hendryx, J. B. Intrigue on Halfaday
Creek; 28 stories
Hendryx, J. B. Murder on Halfaday
Creek; 30 stories

London, J. All-gold cañon
London, J. At the rainbow's end
London, J. Love of life
London, J. To build a fire
Yule miracle. Terhune, A. P.
YUM KIPPUR. See Yom Kippur
Yushkevich, Semion Solomonovich, 1868-
1927
Algebra
Guerney, B. G. comp. New Russian
stories
In a Bolshevist market-place
Leftwich, J. ed. Yisröel. 1952 ed.
Yushkewitch, Simeon. See Yushkevich,
Semion Solomonovich

Z

Zachary Crebbin's angel. Kneale, N.
Zaferiou, Socrates, 1925-
Tale of Perez de Amorin
American vanguard, 1952
Zaimis. Bendrodt, J. C.
Zamiatin, Eugene Ivanovich. See Zamiâtin,
Evgeniĭ Ivanovich
Zamiâtin, Evgeniĭ Ivanovich, 1884-1937
God
Guerney, B. G. comp. New Russian
stories
Zangwill, Israel, 1864-1926
The luftmensch
Ausubel, N. ed. Treasury of Jewish
humor
Neo-Hebrew poet
Ausubel, N. ed. Treasury of Jewish
humor
Sabbath breaker
Leftwich, J. ed. Yisröel. 1952 ed.
Sabbath question in Sudminster
Ausubel, N. ed. Treasury of Jewish
humor
Zangwill, Louis, 1869-1938
Prelude to a pint of bitter
Leftwich, J. ed. Yisröel. 1952 ed.
Zara, Louis, 1910-
The citizner
Certner, S. and Henry, G. H. eds. Short
stories for our times
Resurgam
Ribalow, H. U. ed. This land, these
people
Zarapore beat. Blochman, L. G.
Zelver, Al
Something for December eighth
Stanford short stories, 1951
Zelver, Patricia Farrell, 1923-
Long hot day
Stanford short stories, 1950
Zeritsky's law. Griffith, A.
Zerline, the old servant girl. Broch, H.
Zero hour. Bradbury, R.
Zevin, Israel Joseph, 1872-
Nogid's luck
Ausubel, N. ed. Treasury of Jewish
humor

Zevin, Israel J.—*Continued*
Pack of troubles for one cent
Ausubel, N. ed. Treasury of Jewish humor
Zhabotǐnskiǐ, Vladimir Evgen'evich, 1880-1940
Edmée
Leftwich, J. ed. Yisröel. 1952 ed.
ZIPPORAH (BIBLICAL CHARACTER)
Hazaz, C. Bridegroom of blood
Zola, Émile, 1840-1902
Captain Burle
Dupee, F. W. ed. Great French short novels
Julien
Geist, S. ed. French stories and tales
Zone of interior. Ross, J.
The **zoo.** Williams, W. C.
ZOOLOGICAL GARDENS
Richards, D. Training Alice and Congo
ZOOLOGISTS
Bloomgarden, S. Zoology
Zoology. Bloomgarden, S.
Zoshchenko, Mikhail Mikhaǐlovich, 1895-
The aristocrat
Stauffer, R. M.; Cunningham, W. H. and Sullivan, C. J. eds. Adventures in modern literature
Sleuth-hound
Guerney, B. G. comp. New Russian stories

Zostchenko, Mikhail. See Zoshchenko, Mikhail Mikhaǐlovich
Zozulya, Ephim Davidovich, 1891-
Studio of Love-Your-Fellowman
Guerney, B. G. comp. New Russian stories
Zugsmith, Leane, 1903-
Room in the world
Summers, H. S. ed. Kentucky story
ZULUS
Krige, U. Death of the Zulu
ZURICH. See Switzerland—Zurich
Zweig, Arnold, 1887-
Jerusalem delivered
Leftwich, J. ed. Yisröel. 1952 ed.
The parcel
Blodgett, H. W. ed. Story survey. 1953 ed.
Zweig, Stefan, 1881-1942
Confusion of sentiment
Cory, D. W. pseud. comp. 21 variations on a theme
Invisible collection
Schramm, W. L. ed. Great short stories
West, R. B. and Stallman, R. W. eds. Art of modern fiction
Same as: Unseen collection
The runaway
Stauffer, R. M.; Cunningham, W. H. and Sullivan, C. J. eds. Adventures in modern literature
Unseen collection
Leftwich, J. ed. Yisröel. 1952 ed.
Same as: Invisible collection

PART II

List of Collections Indexed

An author and title list of collections indexed, with their various editions.

Abell, Elizabeth, 1906-
(ed.) American accent; fourteen stories by authors associated with the Bread Loaf Writers' Conference; with a foreword by Theodore Morrison. Ballantine. 1954 193p
See also Greene, J. I. jt. ed.

Adventure stories, Boys' life. Boys' life (Periodical)

Adventure stories from Story parade. Story parade (Periodical)

Adventures in modern literature. Stauffer, R. M.; Cunningham, W. H. and Sullivan, C. J. eds.

Adventures in tomorrow. Crossen, K. F. ed.

Adventures of Sherlock Holmes. Doyle, Sir A. C.

Ahead of time. Kuttner, H.

Aiken, Conrad Potter, 1889-
Short stories. Duell 1950 416p

Akutagawa, Ryūnosuke, 1892-1927
Rashomon, and other stories; tr. by Takashi Kojima; introduction by Howard Hibbett; illus. by M. Kuwata. Liveright 1952 119p illus

Alabaster hand, and other ghost stories. Munby, A. N. L.

Aldrich, Bess (Streeter) 1881-
The Bess Streeter Aldrich reader. Appleton 1950 467p
Analyzed for short stories only

Aleichem, Sholom, pseud. See Rabinowitz, Shalom

American accent. Abell, E. ed.

American boy (Periodical)
American boy Adventure stories; selected by Cecile Matschat and Carl Carmer; illus. by Norman Guthrie Rudolph. Winston 1952 367p illus
American boy anthology; comp. by Franklin M. Reck; illus. by Clifford Geary. Crowell 1951 488p illus

American boy Adventure stories. American boy (Periodical)

American boy anthology. American boy (Periodical)

American dream girl. Farrell, J. T.

American girl (Periodical)
Christmas all year 'round; ed. by Marjorie Vetter; twenty-five Christmas stories. Abelard-Schuman 1952 320p
Favorite stories; selected and ed. by Marjorie Vetter and Ruth Baker Bowman. Nelson 1950 224p
On my honor; twenty stories from the American girl; selected and ed. by Marjorie Vetter. Longmans 1951 229p

American literature by Negro authors. Dreer, H. ed.

American short story survey. Cuff, R. P. ed.

American vanguard, 1950; ed. by Charles I. Glicksberg. . . [Pub. for the] New School for Social Research [by] Cambridge Pub. Co. 1950 314p

American vanguard, 1952; ed. by Don M. Wolfe. [Pub. for the] New School for Social Research [by] Greenberg 1952 325p
Analyzed for short stories only

American vanguard, 1953; ed. by Charles I. Glicksberg and Brom Weber. . . [Pub. for the] New School for Social Research [by] Dial Press 1953 314p
Analyzed for short stories only

Anchor in the sea. Swallow, A. ed.

Anderson, Esther Victoria, 1892-
Six tales for the family, by Eva Rite [pseud]. Pageant Press 1951 71p

Anderson, Quentin
(ed.) James, H. Selected short stories

Andrews, Roy Chapman, 1884-
(ed.) My favorite stories of the great outdoors; nature lover's treasury; selected, and with an introduction. Greystone 1950 404p

Angels and spaceships. Brown, F.

Ann Lee's. Bowen, E. See Bowen, E. Early stories

Annixter, Paul, pseud.
Brought to cover; 15 outdoor tales of action and adventure. Wyn 1951 247p

Anthology of famous American stories. Burrell, J. A. and Cerf, B. A. eds.

Anthology of famous British stories. Cerf, B. A. and Moriarty, H. C. eds.

Anthology of stories from the Southern review. Southern review

Argosy (Periodical)
Argosy Book of adventure stories; ed. by Rogers Terrill. Barnes, A.S. 1952 311p
Argosy Book of sea stories; ed. by Rogers Terrill. Barnes, A.S. 1953 328p
Argosy Book of sports stories; ed. by Rogers Terrill. Barnes, A.S. 1953 340p

Argosy Book of adventure stories. Argosy (Periodical)

Argosy Book of sea stories. Argosy (Periodical)

Argosy Book of sports stories. Argosy (Periodical)

Arico, Victor, 1912-
The knight returns, and other stories; a collection of thirteen works. William-Frederick Press 1952 82p

Arm of Mrs Egan. Harvey, W. F.

Art of modern fiction. West, R. B. and Stallman, R. W. eds.

Artist grows up in Mexico. Brenner, L.

Ascent to heaven. Rudnicki, A.

Asimov, Isaac, 1920-
I, robot. Gnome Press 1950 253p

Asquith, Lady Cynthia Mary Evelyn (Charteris) 1887-
(ed.) Book of modern ghosts. Scribner 1953 236p

Assignment in eternity. Heinlein, R. A.

Assignment in tomorrow. Pohl, F. ed.

The **Assyrian,** and other stories. Saroyan, W.

Astounding science fiction (Periodical)
Astounding science fiction Anthology; selected and with an introduction by John W. Campbell, jr. Simon & Schuster 1952 585p

Astounding science fiction Anthology. Astounding science fiction (Periodical)

Aswell, Mary Louise (White) 1902-
(ed.) New short novels, by Jean Stafford [and others]. . . . Ballantine 1954 188p

At the crossroads, and other stories and sketches. Grimson, M. S.

Atkinson, Peter, 1917- See Waite, H. O. jt. ed.

Auchincloss, Louis, 1917-
Injustice collectors. Houghton 1950 248p
Romantic egoists. Houghton 1954 210p

Ausubel, Nathan, 1899-
(ed.) A treasury of Jewish humor. Doubleday 1951 xxvii, 735p
Analyzed for short stories only

Away and beyond. Van Vogt, A. E.

B

Bachelor, Joseph Morris, 1889-1947; Henry, Ralph Ledyard, 1895- and Salisbury, Rachel
(eds.) Current thinking and writing; 2d ser. Appleton 1951 316p
Analyzed for short stories only

Bad men and good. Western Writers of America

Baker, Frank, 1908-
Blessed are they; eight stories. Newman Press 1951 178p

Ballad of the sad café. McCullers, C. S.

Bar 1 roundup of best western stories. Meredith, S. ed.

Bar 2. Meredith, S. ed.

Bar 3. Meredith, S. ed.

Barker, A. L. 1919-
Novelette; with other stories. Scribner 1951 239p

Barr, James, pseud.
Derricks. Greenberg 1951 230p

Barrows, Herbert
(ed.) 15 stories. Heath 1950 211p

Baseball reader. Graber, R. S. ed.

Bates, Herbert Ernest, 1905-
Colonel Julian, and other stories. Little 1952 240p

Beachheads in space. Derleth, A. W. ed.

Beck, Warren
Far whistle, and other stories. Antioch Press 1951 224p

Bedside Barsetshire. Trollope, A.

Beguile. Cooke, A. A.

Bella, Bella kissed a fella. Kober, A.

Bement, Douglas, 1898-1943. See Shaw, H. jt. ed.

Bendrodt, James Charles
Of men, dogs and horses. Greenberg 1952 126p illus

Bennett, Ethel Hume (Patterson) 1881-
(ed.) Roberts, Sir C. G. D. Thirteen bears

Benson, Theodora, 1906-
  Man from the tunnel, and other stories. Appleton 1950 271p

Bentley, Phyllis Eleanor, 1894-
  Panorama; tales of West Riding. Macmillan 1952 287p

Bergengruen, Werner, 1892-
  Last Captain of Horse; a portrait of chivalry. [Tr. from the German language edition by Eric Peters] Thames (N.Y.) 1953 303p
    Analyzed for short stories only

Bernhard, Emil, pseud. See Cohn, Emil Bernhard

Berto, Giuseppe
  Works of God, and other stories; tr. from the Italian by Angus Davidson. New Directions 1950 224p

The **Bess** Streeter Aldrich reader. Aldrich, B. S.

Best American short stories, 1950-1954; and the Yearbook of the American short story; ed. by Martha Foley, assisted by Joyce F. Hartman. Houghton 1950-54 5v

Best Army short stories, 1950. Rinehart 1950 243p

Best cat stories. Joseph, M. ed.

Best detective stories of the year—1950-1954. Ed. by David C. Cooke. Dutton 1950-54 5v

Best from Fantasy and science fiction. Magazine of fantasy and science fiction

Best from Startling stories. Startling stories (Periodical)

Best of Bret Harte. Harte, B.

Best of Crunch and Des. Wylie, P.

Best of Hawthorne. Hawthorne, N.

Best of the Best American short stories, 1915-1950; ed. by Martha Foley. Houghton 1952 364p

Best science fiction stories: 1950-1954. Ed. by Everett F. Bleiler and T. E. Dikty. Fell 1950-54 5v (Fell's science fiction lib)

Best short stories by Afro-American writers (1925-1950) Ford, N. A. and Faggett, H. L. eds.

Best stories from New writing. New writing (Periodical)

Betts, Doris
  Gentle insurrection, and other stories. Putnam 1954 274p

Beyond human ken. Merril, J.

Beyond infinity. Carr, R. S.

Beyond the barriers of space and time. Merril, J. ed.

Beyond time & space. Derleth, A. W. ed.

Big book of science fiction. Conklin, G. ed.

Big range. Schaefer, J. W.

Black prince, and other stories. Grau, S. A.

Black star passes. Campbell, J. W.

Blackburn, Ernest Richard, 1926-
  The swaying elms, and other stories. Moody Press 1950 255p (Provident books)

Blaustein, Albert P. 1921-
  (ed.) Fiction goes to court; favorite stories of lawyers and the law, selected by famous lawyers. Holt 1954 303p
    Analyzed for short stories only

Bleiler, Everett Franklin, 1920-
  (ed.) Best science fiction stories. See Best science fiction stories
  (ed.) Year's best science fiction novels. See Year's best science fiction novels

Bleiler, Everett Franklin, 1920- **and Dikty, Thaddeus Eugene**
  (ed.) Imagination unlimited; science-fiction and science. Farrar, Straus 1952 430p
  (ed.) Science fiction omnibus: the best science fiction stories, 1949, 1950. Introduction by Melvin Korshak. Garden City Bks. 1952 2v in 1

Blessed are they. Baker, F.

Bloch, Marguerite
  (ed.) Favorite dog stories; illus. by Robert Doremus. World Pub. 1950 250p illus

Blochman, Lawrence Goldtree, 1900-
  Diagnosis: homicide; the casebook of Dr Coffee. Lippincott 1950 (Main line mysteries) 217p

Blodgett, Harold William, 1900-
  (ed.) Story survey. Rev. ed. Lippincott 1953 825p

Bloodstock, and other stories. Irwin, M. E. F.

Bluebook (Periodical)
  Best sea stories from Bluebook; ed. by Horace Vondys; with an introduction and notes by Donald Kennicott. McBride Co. 1954 359p

Bogorad, Samuel Nathaniel, 1917- **and Trevithick, Jack,** 1909-
  (eds.) College miscellany; ed. with introductions. Rinehart 1952 621p
    Analyzed for short stories only

Bond, Raymond Tostevin, 1893-
  (ed.) Handbook for poisoners. . . Rinehart 1951 311p

Bonner, Paul Hyde, 1893-
  Glorious mornings; stories of shooting and fishing. Scribner 1954 228p

Book of Canadian stories. Pacey, D. ed.

Book of cowboy stories, Will James'. James, W.

Book of modern ghosts. Asquith, Lady C. M. E. C. ed.

Book of Sherlock Holmes. Doyle, Sir A. C.

Booker, Adria E.
Was it too late? & other stories. Meador 1954 85p front

Bottome, Phyllis, 1884-
Man and beast; illus. by W. T. Mars. Harcourt [1954] 118p illus

Boucher, Anthony, pseud. See White, William Anthony Parker

Bowen, Elizabeth, 1899-
Early stories; <Encounters & Ann Lee's>. Knopf 1951 364p

Bowles, Paul Frederic, 1911-
Delicate prey, and other stories. Random House 1950 307p

Boy in the house, and other stories. De La Roche, M.

Boy with a trumpet, and other selected short stories. Davies, R.

Boyd, James, 1888-1944
Old pines, and other stories. Univ. of N.C. Press 1952 165p

Boyle, Kay, 1903-
Smoking mountain; stories of postwar Germany. McGraw 1951 273p

Boys' life (Periodical)
Boys' life Adventure stories; ed. by Irving Crump; jacket and front. by Reynold Brown. Nelson 1950 224p

Boys' life Adventure stories. Boys' life (Periodical)

Bradbury, Ray, 1920-
Golden apples of the sun; drawings by Joe Mugnaini. Doubleday 1953 250p illus
Illustrated man. Doubleday 1951 251p

Brenner, Leah, 1915-
Artist grows up in Mexico; with illus. by Diego Rivera. Beechhurst Press 1953 144p illus

Brentano, Frances
(ed.) The word lives on; a treasury of spiritual fiction; introduction by Halford E. Luccock. Doubleday 1951 355p
Analyzed for short stories only

Bret Harte's stories of the old West. Harte, B.

Brick, John, 1922-
They ran for their lives. Doubleday 1954 287p

Brickell, Herschel, 1889-1952
(ed.) Prize stories. See Prize stories

Brookhouser, Frank, 1912-
She made the big town! And other stories. Univ. of Kan. City Press 1952 251p

Brooks, Cleanth, 1906-
(ed.) Anthology of stories from the Southern review. See Southern review. Anthology of stories from the Southern review

Brophy, Brigid, 1929-
Crown princess & other stories. Viking 1953 252p

Brought to cover. Annixter, P. pseud.

Brown, Fredric, 1906-
Angels and spaceships. Dutton 1954 224p
Mostly murder; eighteen stories. Dutton 1953 247p
Space on my hands. Shasta Pubs. 1951 224p

Brown, Fredric, 1906- **Reynolds, Mack,** 1918-
(eds.) Science-fiction carnival; ed. and with introductions. Shasta Pubs. 1953 315p

Buckingham, Nash, 1880-
Hallowed years. Stackpole Co. 1953 209p
Analyzed for short stories only

Bullard of the space patrol. Jameson, M.

Burger, Knox
(ed.) Collier's, the national weekly. Collier's best

Burnett, Hallie (Southgate) 1908-
See Burnett, W. jt. ed.

Burnett, Whit, 1899-
(ed.) Story (Periodical) Story; no. 1-4
(ed.) World's best; stories, humor, drama, biography, history, essays, poetry. Dial Press 1950 1186p
Analyzed for short stories only

Burnett, Whit, 1899- **and Burnett, Hallie (Southgate)** 1908-
(eds.) Sextet; six story discoveries in the novella form... McKay 1951 246p

Burrell, John Angus, 1890- **and Cerf, Bennett Alfred,** 1898-
(eds.) Anthology of famous American stories. Modern Lib. 1953 1340p

"But you don't understand." Strain, F. B.

Butcher, baker, murder-maker. Mystery Writers of America, inc.

By rope and lead. Haycox, E.

C

Caldwell, Erskine, 1903-
Complete stories. Duell; Little 1953 664p
Courting of Susie Brown. Duell; Little 1952 202p

Caldwell, Erskine—*Continued*
Humorous side of Erskine Caldwell; an anthology, ed. with an introduction by Robert Cantwell. Duell 1951 xxxiii, 253p

Calendar of crime. Queen, E. pseud.

Calico shoes. Farrell, J. T. See Farrell, J. T. Short stories

Calisher, Hortense, 1911-
In the absence of angels; stories. Little 1951 243p

Call me Nate. Kaufman, W.

Campbell, John Wood, 1910-
(ed.) Astounding science fiction (Periodical) Astounding science fiction anthology
Black star passes. Fantasy Press 1953 254p
Cloak of Aesir. Shasta Pubs. 1952 255p

Campfire adventure stories. Macfarlan, A. A.

Can all this grandeur perish? Farrell, J. T. See Farrell, J. T. Short stories

Canadian short stories. Weaver, R. and James, H. eds.

Canny Mr Glencannon. Gilpatric, G. See Gilpatric, G. Last Glencannon omnibus

Carmer, Carl, 1893-
(ed.) American boy (Periodical) American boy Adventure stories

Carr, John Dickson, 1905-
The third bullet, and other stories. Harper 1954 213p

Carr, Robert Spencer, 1909-
Beyond infinity. Fantasy Press 1951 236p

Carrington, Hereward, 1880-
(ed.) Week-end book of ghost stories. Washburn 1953 280p

Cast a cold eye. McCarthy, M. T.

Cavalleria rusticana, and other narratives. Verga, G.

Cavanna, Betty, 1909-
(ed.) Pick of the litter; Betty Cavanna's favorite dog stories. Westminster Press 1952 222p

Cawley, Clifford Comer
No trip like this, and other stories. House of Edinboro 1951 238p

Celeste & other stories. Merochnik, M.

Centenary Poe. Poe, E. A.

Cerf, Bennett Alfred, 1898- **and Moriarty, Henry Curran**
(eds.) Anthology of famous British stories. Modern Lib. 1952 xxii, 1233p
Original Random House edition pub. 1940 is entered in the main catalog under title: Bedside book of famous British stories
See also Burrell, J. A. jt. ed.

Certner, Simon, and Henry, George H.
(eds.) Short stories for our times. Houghton 1950 470p illus

Character and situation. Sykes, C.

Charteris, Leslie, 1907-
The Saint in Europe. Doubleday 1953 191p
Second Saint omnibus. Doubleday 1951 336p

Cheever, John, 1912-
Enormous radio, and other stories. Funk 1953 237p

Chekhov, Anton Pavlovich, 1860-1904
Unknown Chekhov; stories and other writings hitherto untranslated; tr. with an introduction by Avrahm Yarmolinsky. Noonday 1954 316p
Woman in the case, and other stories; tr. by April FitzLyon and Kyril Zinovieff, and with an introduction by Andrew G. Colin. British Bk. Centre 1953 189p

Chesterton, Gilbert Keith, 1874-1936
Father Brown omnibus. . . New and rev. ed. Dodd 1951 993p
"Including The innocence of Father Brown; The incredulity of Father Brown; The scandal of Father Brown; The wisdom of Father Brown; The secret of Father Brown; The vampire of the village." Subtitle

Children are bored on Sunday. Stafford, J.

China run. Paterson, N.

Christ, Henry Irving, 1915- **and Shostak, Jerome**
(eds.) Short stories; a collection for high school students. Oxford Bk. Co. 1948 429p illus

Christian herald (Periodical) See Elmquist, R. M. ed. Fifty years of Christmas

Christie, Agatha (Miller) 1891-
Under dog, and other stories. Dodd 1951 248p (Red badge detective)

Christmas all year 'round. American girl (Periodical)

Christmas books. Dickens, C.

Christmas Eve. Cooke, A.

Christmas gift. Cousins, M.

Christmas stories. Dickens, C.

Chute, Beatrice Joy, 1913-
Teen-age sports parade; illus. by William B. Ricketts. Grosset 1949 255p illus

Cicellis, Kay
Easy way; with a foreword by V. Sackville-West. Scribner 1950 237p

The **city**. Horwitz, J.

City. Simak, C. D.

Clair de lune, and other stories. Schneider, G. W.

Clark, Walter Van Tilburg, 1909-
Watchful gods, and other stories. Random House 1950 306p

Clarke, Arthur Charles, 1917-
Expedition to earth; eleven science-fiction stories. Ballantine 1953 165p

Claudy, Carl Harry, 1879-
These were brethren. **Temple** Pubs. 1947 279p

Clearing in the sky & other stories. Stuart, J.

Cloak of Aesir. Campbell, J. W.

Cody, Sherwin, 1868-
(ed.) Greatest stories and how they were written; selected by W. E. Henley; with a series of introductions on the art of short story writing. Re-edited ed. Sherwin Cody Associates 1950 442p

Cohn, Emil, 1881-1948
Stories and fantasies from the Jewish past; tr. from the German manuscript by Charles Reznikoff. Jewish Pub. 1951 262p

Colette, Sidonie Gabrielle, 1873-1954
Short novels of Colette; with an introduction by Glenway Wescott. Dial Press 1951 lvii, 733p

Collected stories. Faulkner, W.

Collected stories. Sitwell, Sir O. bart.

Collected tales. De La Mare, W. J.

College miscellany. Bogorad, S. N. and Trevithick, J. eds.

Collier, John, 1901-
Fancies and goodnights. Doubleday 1951 364p

Collier's, the national weekly
Collier's best; a selection of short stories from the magazine with an introduction and notes by Knox Burger. Harper 1951 299p

Collier's best. Collier's, the national weekly

Collins, Wilkie, 1824-1889
Tales of suspense; ed. by Robert Ashley and Herbert van Thal. Lithographs by Anne Scott. Lib. Pubs. 1954 255p illus

Colonel Julian, and other stories. Bates, H. E.

Coming of Conan. Howard, R. E.

Complete short stories. Maugham, W. S.

Complete stories. Caldwell, E.

Complete works of O. Henry. Porter, W. S.

Comstock bonanza. Emrich, D. ed.

Conklin, Groff, 1914-
(ed.) Big book of science fiction; ed. with an introduction. Crown 1950 545p
(ed.) Invaders of earth. Vanguard 1952 333p
(ed.) Omnibus of science fiction; ed. with an introduction by Groff Conklin. Crown 1952 562p
(ed.) Possible worlds of science fiction. Vanguard 1951 372p
(ed.) Science-fiction adventures in dimension. Vanguard 1953 354p
(ed.) Science-fiction thinking machines: robots, androids, computers. Vanguard 1954 367p
Analyzed for short stories only

Conklin, Groff, 1904- and Conklin, Lucy Tempkin
(eds.) Supernatural reader. Lippincott 1953 349p

Connolly, Cyril, 1903-
(ed.) Great English short novels; ed. and with an introduction, by Cyril Connolly. Dial Press 1953 879p
Analyzed for short stories only
(ed.) Horizon (Periodical) Golden Horizon

Connolly, Myles, 1897-
Reason for Ann, and other stories. McMullen 1953 231p

Conrad, Joseph, 1857-1924
Tales of land and sea; introduction by William McFee; illus. by Richard M. Powers. Hanover House 1953 695p

Continent makers, and other tales of the Viagens. De Camp, L. S.

Cooke, Alistair, 1908-
Christmas Eve; illus. by Marc Simont. Knopf 1952 56p illus

Cooke, Arthur A.
Beguile; an assortment of short stories. House of Edinboro 1949 317p

Cooke, David Coxe, 1917-
(ed.) Best detective stories of the year. See Best detective stories of the year

Coolidge, Olivia E.
Egyptian adventures; illus. by Joseph Low. Houghton 1954 209p illus

Coombs, Charles Ira, 1914-
Teen-age champion sports stories; illus. by William B. Ricketts. Lantern Press 1950 254p

Cooper, Alice Cecilia, 1895-
(ed.) Modern short stories. Globe Bk. 1949 376p illus

Corkery, Daniel, 1878-
The wager, and other stories; illus. with wood engravings by Elizabeth Rivers. Devin-Adair 1950 192p illus

Cory, Donald Webster, pseud.
(comp.) 21 variations on a theme. Greenberg 1953 436p
Analyzed for short stories only

Courting of Susie Brown. Caldwell, E.

Cousins, Margaret, 1905-
Christmas gift. Doubleday 1952 219p

Coward, Noël Pierce, 1899-
Star quality; six stories by Noel Coward. Doubleday 1951 308p

Cowboys, cowboys, cowboys. Fenner, P. R. comp.

Coxe, George Harmon, 1901-
(ed.) Mystery Writers of America, inc. Butcher, baker, murder-maker

Crack of the bat. Fenner, P. R. comp.

Crane, Stephen, 1871-1900
Stephen Crane; an omnibus; ed. with introduction and notes by Robert Wooster Stallman. Knopf 1952 703p front
Analyzed for short stories only

Creamer, Jack B.
(comp.) Twenty-two stories about horses and men; comp. with an introduction by Jack B. Creamer; with decorations by Ned King. Coward-McCann 1953 309p illus
Analyzed for short stories only

Crooks' tour. Mystery writers of America, inc.

Crossen, Kendall Foster, 1910-
(ed.) Adventures in tomorrow. Greenberg 1951 278p
(ed.) Future tense; new and old tales of science fiction. Greenberg 1952 364p

Crown princess & other stories. Brophy, B.

Cruises in the sun. Curtis, K.

Crump, Irving, 1887-
(ed.) Boys' life (Periodical) Boys' life Adventure stories

Crunch and Des, Best of. Wylie, P.

Cuff, Roger Penn, 1899-
(ed.) American short story survey. Stackpole Co. 1953 427p

Cunningham, William Hayes. See Stauffer, R. M. jt. auth.

Current thinking and writing; second series. Bachelor, J. M.; Henry, R. L. and Salisbury, R. eds.

Curtis, Kent
Cruises in the sun. Seymour 1950 287p illus

D

Dachs, David, 1922-
(ed.) Treasury of sports humor, ed. by Dave Stanley [pseud]; introduction by Ted Husing. Grosset 1946 487p illus

Dahl, Roald, 1916-
Someone like you. Knopf 1953 359p

Dannay, Frederic, 1905- and Lee, Manfred Bennington, 1905- See Queen, Ellery, pseud.

Davenport, Basil, 1905-
(ed.) Ghostly tales to be told; a collection of stories from the great masters, arranged for reading and telling aloud. Dodd 1950 317p
(ed.) Tales to be told in the dark; a selection of stories from the great authors, arranged for reading and telling aloud. Dodd 1953 335p

Davies, Rhys, 1903-
Boy with a trumpet, and other selected short stories; with an introduction by Bucklin Moon. Doubleday 1951 304p

Davis, Clyde Brion, 1894-
(ed.) Eyes of boyhood. Lippincott 1953 xxiii, 323p
Analyzed for short stories only

Davis, Harold Lenoir, 1896-
Team bells woke me, and other stories. Morrow 1953 300p

Davis, Robert Gorham, 1908-
(ed.) Ten modern masters; an anthology of the short story. Harcourt 1953 510p

Day, Arthur Grove, 1904-
(ed.) Greatest American short stories; twenty classics of our heritage. McGraw 1953 359p

De Camp, Lyon Sprague, 1907-
Continent makers, and other tales of the Viagens. Twayne 1953 272p
See also Pratt, F. jt. auth.

De La Mare, Walter John, 1873-1956
Collected tales; chosen, and with an introduction, by Edward Wagenknecht. Knopf 1950 467p

De La Roche, Mazo, 1885-
Boy in the house, and other stories. Little 1952 244p

Delicate prey, and other stories. Bowles, P. F.

Del Rey, Lester, 1915- Matschat, Cecile (Hulse) and Carmer, Carl Lamson, 1893-
(eds.) Year after tomorrow; an anthology of science fiction stories; foreword by Lester Del Rey; illus. by Mel Hunter. Winston 1954 339p illus

Dennis, Wesley, 1903-
(ed.) Palomino and other horses; ed. and illus. by Wesley Dennis. World Pub. 1950 249p illus

De Onís, Harriet, 1899-
(ed.) Spanish stories and tales. Knopf 1954 270p
 Analyzed for short stories only

Derleth, August William, 1909-
(ed.) Beachheads in space; ed. and with an introduction. Pellegrini & Cudahy 1952 320p
(ed.) Beyond time & space; selected with an introduction. Pellegrini & Cudahy 1950 643p
(ed.) Far boundaries; 20 science-fiction stories. Pellegrini & Cudahy 1951
Memoirs of Solar Pons; with an introduction by Ellery Queen. Mycroft & Moran 1951 245p
(ed.) Night's yawning peal; a ghostly company, selected and with a foreword. Arkham House 1952 280p
(ed.) The outer reaches; favorite science-fiction tales chosen by their authors. Pellegrini & Cudahy 1951 342p
Three problems for Solar Pons. Mycroft & Moran 1952 112p
(ed.) Time to come; science-fiction stories of tomorrow. Farrar, Straus 1954 311p
(ed.) Worlds of tomorrow; science-fiction with a difference. Pellegrini & Cudahy 1953 251p

Derricks. Barr, J. pseud.

Destination: universe! Van Vogt, A. E.

De Vries, Peter
No but I saw the movie. Little 1952 248p

Diagnosis: homicide. Blochman, L. G.

Dickens, Charles, 1812-1870
Christmas books . . . with plates and illus. by John Leech. Macdonald & Co. 1953 449p illus (Macdonald illustrated classics)
Christmas stories; A Christmas carol, The chimes, The cricket on the hearth. Illus. by Howard Simon; introduction by May Lamberton Becker. World Pub. 1946 319p illus (Rainbow classics)

Dikty, Thaddeus Eugene. See Bleiler, E. F. jt. ed.

Dog show. Harper, W. comp.

Dogs, dogs, dogs. Fenner, P. R. comp.

Dostoevskiĭ, Fedor Mikhaĭlovich, 1821-1881
White nights, and other stories; tr. from the Russian by Constance Garnett. Macmillan 1950 288p

Doty, William Lodewick, 1919-
Stories for discussion. Wagner, J. F. 1951 168p

Doyle, Adrian Conan, 1910-1955, and Carr, John Dickson, 1905-
Exploits of Sherlock Holmes. Random House 1954 388p

Doyle, Sir Arthur Conan, 1859-1930
Adventures of Sherlock Holmes . . . Heritage 1950 764p illus
Book of Sherlock Holmes; illus. by Charlotte Ross; introduction by May Lamberton Becker. World Pub. 1950 320p illus (Rainbow classics)
Sherlock Holmes; selected stories. With an introduction by S. C. Roberts. Oxford 1954 435p

The dream and the desert. Krige, U.

Dreer, Herman, 1889-
(ed.) American literature by Negro authors. Macmillan 1950 334p illus
 Analyzed for short stories only

Du Maurier, Daphne, 1907-
Kiss me again, stranger; a collection of eight stories long and short; drawings by Margot Tomes. Doubleday 1952 319p

Dunsany, Edward John Moreton Drax Plunkett, 18th baron, 1878-
Sword of Welleran, and other tales of enchantment, by Lord Dunsany; with line drawings by Robert Barrell. Devin-Adair 1954 181p illus

Dupee, Frederick Wilcox, 1904-
(ed.) Great French short novels. Dial Press 1952 717p

E

E pluribus unicorn. Waldo, E. H.

Early stories. Bowen, E.

Earthly creatures. Jackson, C. R.

Easy way. Cicellis, K.

Eaton, Harold Thomas, 1894-
(ed.) Short stories. Am. Bk. 1951 xxxi, 342p

Edel, Leon
(ed.) James, H. Selected fiction

Edith Wharton treasury. Wharton, E. N. J.

Editor's choice in science fiction. Moskowitz, S. comp.

Eggleston, Margaret (White) 1878-
Red stocking, and other Christmas stories. Harper 1937 153p illus

Egyptian adventures. Coolidge, O. E.

Eight uncollected tales. James, H.

Ekbergh, Ida Diana
Mysterious Chinese mandrake, and other stories. Pageant Press 1954 52p

Elam, Richard M.
Teen-age science fiction stories; introduction by Burr W. Leyson; illus. by Charles H. Geer. Lantern Press 1952 254p illus

Elephants, elephants, elephants. Fenner, P. R. comp.

Ellery Queen's awards. Queen, E. pseud. ed.

Elmquist, Ruth M.
(ed.) Fifty years of Christmas; an anthology of stories, poems and short pieces from the Christian herald; introduction by Daniel A. Poling. Rinehart 1951 300p
Analyzed for short stories only

Emrich, Duncan, 1908-
(ed.) Comstock bonanza; western Americana of J. Ross Browne [and others]. . . Vanguard 1950 363p
Analyzed for short stories only

Encore. Maugham, W. S.

Encounters. Bowen, E. See Bowen, E. Early stories

Engle, Paul, 1908- **and Martin, Hansford**
(eds.) Prize stories 1954. See Prize stories 1954

Enormous radio, and other stories. Cheever, J.

Esquire (Periodical)
Girls from Esquire; introduction by Frederic A. Birmingham. Random House 1952 308p illus
Analyzed for short stories only

Eternal smile, and other stories. Lagerkvist, P. F.

Evans, Thomas M. 1881-
Gentlemen of valor, and other stories. Exposition 1951 221p

Every boy's book of science-fiction. Wollheim, D. A. comp.

Everygirls career stories. Furman, A. L. ed.

Everygirls mystery stories. Furman, A. L. ed.

Expedition to earth. Clarke, A. C.

Exploits of Sherlock Holmes. Doyle, A. C. and Carr, J. D.

The **explorers.** Kornbluth, C. M.

F

Fabricant, Noah Daniel, 1904- **and Werner, Heinz,** 1901-
(eds.) World's best doctor stories. Garden City Bks. 1951 276p

Faggett, Harry Lee, 1911- See Ford, N. A. jt. ed.

Family book of best loved short stories. Lamb, L. ed.

Famous Chinese short stories. Lin, Y.

Fancies and goodnights. Collier, J.

Far boundaries. Derleth, A. W. ed.

Far whistle, and other stories. Beck, W.

Farrell, James Thomas, 1904-
American dream girl. Vanguard 1950 302p
Further short stories. Sun Dial 1948 313p
At head of title: When boyhood dreams come true
Analyzed for short stories only
Short stories. Vanguard [1951, c1934] xxxvi, 534p
Published separately and entered in the main catalog under titles: Calico shoes; Guillotine party; Can all this grandeur perish?

Father Brown omnibus. Chesterton, G. K.

Faulkner, William, 1897-
Collected stories. Random House 1950 900p
Faulkner reader; selections from the works of William Faulkner. Random House 1954 682p
Analyzed for short stories only

Faulkner reader. Faulkner, W.

Favorite dog stories. Bloch, M. ed.

Favorite stories. American girl (Periodical)

Felheim, Marvin, 1914- **Newman, Franklin B. and Steinhoff, William R.**
(eds.) Modern short stories. Oxford 1951 448p

Fenner, Phyllis Reid, 1899-
(comp.) Cowboys, cowboys, cowboys; stories of roundups & rodeos, branding & bronco-busting. Illus. by Manning deV. Lee. Watts, F. 1950 287p illus
(comp.) Crack of the bat. Knopf 1952 160p
(comp.) Dogs, dogs, dogs; stories of challengers and champions, heroes and hunters, warriors and workers; illus. by Manning deV. Lee. Watts, F. 1951 270p illus
(comp.) Elephants, elephants, elephants; stories of rogues and workers, tuskers and trekkers, jungle trails of circus tanbark; illus. by Manning deV. Lee. Watts, F. 1952 303p illus
(comp.) Fools and funny fellows; more "Time to laugh" tales; illus. by Henry C. Pitz. Knopf 1947 185p illus

Fenner, Phyllis R.—*Continued*

(comp.) Fun! Fun! Fun! Stories of fantasy and farce, mischief and mirth, whimsy and nonsense; illus. by Joseph J. Zabinski. Watts, F. 1953 283p illus

(comp.) Ghosts, ghosts, ghosts; stories of spooks and spirits, haunts and hobgoblins, werewolves and will-o'-the-wisps. Illus. by Manning deV. Lee. Watts, F. 1952 281p illus

(comp.) Giggle box; pictures by William Steig. Knopf 1950 144p illus

(comp.) Indians, Indians, Indians; stories of tepees and tomahawks, wampum belts & war bonnets, peace pipes & papooses; illus. by Manning deV. Lee. Watts, F. 1950 287p illus

(comp.) Pirates, pirates, pirates; stories of cutlasses and corsairs, buried treasure and buccaneers, ships and swashbucklers. Illus. by Manning deV. Lee. Watts, F. 1951 287p illus

(comp.) Speed, speed, speed; stories of races and chases in hot rods and jets, trains and planes, submarines and speedboats; illus. by William Lohse. Watts F. 1954 246p illus
Analyzed for short stories only

(comp.) Stories of the sea; illus. by Kurt Werth. Knopf 1953 178p illus

(comp.) Yankee Doodle; stories of the brave and the free. Illus. by John Alan Maxwell. Knopf 1951 214p illus

Fiction goes to court. Blaustein, A. P. ed.

15 stories. Barrows, H.

Fifty years of Christmas. Elmquist, R. M. ed.

Fireside book of flying stories. Jensen, P. ed.

First-prize stories, 1919-1954; from the O. Henry Memorial awards; introduction by Harry Hansen. Hanover House 1954 495p

Fischer, Bruno, 1908-
(ed.) Mystery Writers of America, inc. Crooks' tour

Fitzgerald, Francis Scott Key, 1896-1940
Stories of F. Scott Fitzgerald; a selection of 28 stories; with an introduction by Malcolm Cowley. Scribner 1951 473p

Five science fiction novels. Greenberg, M. comp.

Flight into space. Wollheim, D. A. comp.

Flying Officer. See Bates, Herbert Ernest

Foerster, Norman
(ed.) Poetry and prose; shorter ed. prepared with supplementary notes by William Charvat. Houghton 1952 924p
Analyzed for short stories only

Foley, Martha
(ed.) Best American short stories. See Best American short stories
(ed.) Best of the Best American short stories

Foley, Martha, and Hartman, Joyce F.
(ed.) Best American short stories, 1953

Fools and funny fellows. Fenner, P. R. comp.

Foote, John Taintor, 1881-1950
Hoofbeats; the great horse stories. Appleton 1950 243p illus
Also available from Grosset

Ford, Nick Aaron, 1904- **and Faggett, Harry Lee,** 1911-
(eds.) Best short stories by Afro-American writers (1925-1950) Meador 1950 307p

Forester, Cecil Scott, 1899-
Mr Midshipman Hornblower. Little 1950 310p
The nightmare. Little 1954 242p

Four-&-twenty bloodhounds. Mystery Writers of America, inc.

Fourth round. Grayson, C.

Fremantle, Anne (Jackson) 1909-
(ed.) Mothers; a Catholic treasury of great stories; with 8 half-tone reproductions; ed. with an introduction. Daye [1951] 383p illus
Analyzed for short stories only

French stories and tales. Geist, S. ed.

Fresh and open sky, and other stories. Sullivan, R.

Friend, Oscar Jerome, 1897- See Margulies, L. jt. ed.

Frightened wife, and other murder stories. Rinehart, M. R.

From off this world. Margulies, L. and Friend, O. J. eds.

Full cargo. Steele, W. D.

Fun! Fun! Fun! Fenner, P. R. comp.

Furman, Abraham Loew, 1902-
(ed.) Everygirls career stories. Lantern Press 1954 221p illus
(ed.) Everygirls mystery stories; illus. by Albert L. Lake. Lantern Press 1954 222p illus
(ed.) Teen-age dog stories, ed. by David Thomas [pseud]; illus. by Richard N. Osborne. Grosset 1949 256p illus

Furman, Abraham L.—*Continued*
  (ed.) Teen-age horse stories; ed. by David Thomas [pseud]; illus. by Richard Osborne. Lantern Press 1950 252p illus
    Also available from Grosset
  (ed.) Teen-age sea stories, by David Thomas [pseud]. Grosset 1948 252p illus
  (ed.) Teen-age stories of the diamond, ed. by David Thomas [pseud]; illus. by William B. Ricketts. Lantern Press 1950 253p illus
    Also available from Grosset

Further short stories. Farrell, J. T.

Future tense. Crossen, K. F. ed.

G

Gable, Mariella, Sister, 1899-
  (ed.) Many-colored fleece. Sheed 1950 xxxii, 336p

Galaxy reader of science fiction. Galaxy science fiction magazine

Galaxy science fiction magazine
  Galaxy reader of science fiction; ed. and with an introduction by H. L. Gold. Crown 1952 566p
  Second Galaxy reader of science fiction; ed. and with an introduction by H. L. Gold. Crown 1954 504p

Game cock, and other stories. McLaverty, M.

Gates of hell. Willingham, C.

Geist, Stanley
  (ed.) French stories and tales. Knopf 1954 326p

Gellhorn, Martha Ellis, 1908-
  Honeyed peace; stories. Doubleday 1953 253p

Gentle insurrection and other stories. Betts, D.

Gentlemen of valor, and other stories. Evans, T. M.

German stories and tales. Pick, R. ed.

Ghost and flesh. Goyen, W.

Ghostly tales to be told. Davenport, B. ed.

Ghosts, ghosts, ghosts. Fenner, P. R. comp.

Giant anthology of science fiction. Margulies, L. and Friend, O. J. eds.

Gibran, Kahlil, 1886-1931
  Treasury of Kahlil Gibran; ed. by Martin L. Wolf; tr. from the Arabic by Anthony Rizcallah Ferris. Citadel 1951 417p
    Analyzed for short stories only

Giggle box. Fenner, P. R. comp.

Gilpatric, Guy, 1896-1950
  Canny Mr Glencannon
    Gilpatric, G. Last Glencannon omnibus v 1
  Last Glencannon omnibus; including The canny Mr Glencannon and Mr Glencannon ignores the war; with an introduction by Barnaby Conrad. Dodd 1953 2v in 1
  Mr Glencannon ignores the war
    Gilpatric, G. Last Glencannon omnibus v2

Girls from Esquire. Esquire (Periodical)

Glicksberg, Charles Irving, 1901-
  (ed.) American vanguard

Glorious mornings. Bonner, P. H.

Gnome there was, and other tales of science fiction and fantasy. Kuttner, H.

Gold, Horace L.
  (ed.) Galaxy science fiction magazine. Galaxy reader of science fiction
  (ed.) Galaxy science fiction magazine. Second Galaxy reader of science fiction

The **gold** bug, and other tales and poems. Poe, E. A.

Golden apples. Welty, E.

Golden apples of the sun. Bradbury, R.

Gordimer, Nadine
  Soft voice of the serpent, and other stories. Simon & Schuster 1952 244p

Gordon, Caroline, 1895- **and Tate, Allen,** 1899-
  (eds.) House of fiction; an anthology of the short story, with commentary. Scribner 1950 649p

Goudge, Elizabeth, 1900-
  Reward of faith; illus. by Nora Unwin. Coward-McCann 1951 186p illus

Gough, Lionel
  (ed.) Surtees, R. S. Hunting scenes

Goyen, William, 1918-
  Ghost and flesh; stories and tales. Random House 1952 183p

Graber, Ralph Schultz
  (ed.) Baseball reader. Barnes, A.S. 1951 302p
    Analyzed for short stories only

Grau, Shirley Ann
  Black prince, and other stories. Knopf 1954 293p

Grayson, Charles, 1905-
  (ed.) Fourth round; an anthology. Holt 1952 374p
    At head of title: Stories for men

Great disciple, and other stories. Ready, W. B.

Great English short novels. Connolly, C. ed.

Great French short novels. Dupee, F. W. ed.

Great German short novels and stories. Lange, V. ed.

Great railroad stories of the world. Moskowitz, S. ed.

Great Russian short novels. Rahv, P. ed.

Great sea stories of modern times. McFee, W. ed.

Great short stories. Neider, C. ed.

Great short stories. Schramm, W. L. ed.

Great short stories from the world's literature. Neider, C. ed.

Great stories of science fiction. Jenkins, W. F. ed.

Greatest American short stories. Day, A. G. ed.

Greatest stories and how they were written. Cody, S. ed.

Greatest victory, and other baseball stories. O'Rourke, F.

Green hills of earth. Heinlein, R. A.

Greenberg, Eliezer, 1896- See Howe, I. jt. ed.

Greenberg, Martin, 1918-
(comp.) Five science fiction novels. Gnome Press 1952 382p
(ed.) Journey to infinity; introduced by Fletcher Pratt. Gnome Press 1951 381p
(ed.) Men against the stars; introduced by Willy Ley. Gnome Press 1950 351p
(ed.) Robot and the man ₁by₁ John D. MacDonald ₁and others₁. Gnome Press 1953 251p
(ed.) Travelers of space; introduced by Willy Ley; illus. by Edd Cartier. Gnome Press 1951 400p illus

Greene, Joseph Ingham, 1897- and Abell, Elizabeth, 1906-
(eds.) Stories of sudden truth. Ballantine 1953 255p

Grimson, Marie S.
At the crossroads, and other stories and sketches. Exposition 1953 125p

Guerney, Bernard Guilbert, 1894-
(comp.) New Russian stories; selected and tr. by Bernard Guilbert Guerney. New Directions 1953 240p

Guillotine party. Farrell, J. T. See Farrell, J. T. Short stories

H

Halliday, Bret, pseud. See Dresser, Davis

Hallowed years. Buckingham, N.

Handbook for poisoners. Bond, R. T. ed.

Happy New Year, kamerades! Lowry, R. J. C.

Harper, Wilhelmina, 1884-
(comp.) Dog show; a selection of favorite dog stories; with portraits of real dogs by Marie C. Nichols. Houghton 1950 182p illus
(ed.) Harte, B. Bret Harte's stories of the old West

Harris, George Washington, 1814-1869
Sut Lovingood; ed. with an introduction by Brom Weber. Grove 1954 262p

Harte, Bret, 1836-1902
Best of Bret Harte; selected by Wilhelmina Harper and Aimée M. Peters; illus. by Paul Brown. Houghton 1947 434p illus
Bret Harte's stories of the old West; selected by Wilhelmina Harper and Aimée M. Peters; illus. by Paul Brown. Wilcox & Follett 1940 322p illus
Analyzed for short stories only

Harvey, William Fryer, 1885-1937
Arm of Mrs Egan, and other strange stories. Dutton 1952 256p

Hathaway, Baxter, 1909- and Sessions, John A.
(eds.) Writers for tomorrow; 2d ser. A collection of fiction by writers of tomorrow for readers of today. Cornell Univ. Press 1952 227p

Hawthorne, Nathaniel, 1804-1864
Best of Hawthorne; ed. with introduction and notes, by Mark Van Doren. Ronald 1951 436p
Analyzed for short stories only

Haycox, Ernest, 1899-1950
By rope and lead. Little 1951 174p
Outlaw. Little 1953 179p
Pioneer loves. Little 1952 177p
Rough justice. Little 1950 177p

Hazeltine, Alice Isabel, 1878-
(comp.) Selected stories for teenagers; for pleasure and understanding. Abingdon 1952 240p illus
Analyzed for short stories only

Headley, Elizabeth (Cavanna) See Cavanna, Betty

Healy, Raymond J.
(ed.) New tales of space and time; introduction by Anthony Boucher ₁pseud₁. Holt 1951 294p

Heaven is so high. Lieberman, R.

Heavenly world series, and other baseball stories. O'Rourke, F.

Heilman, Robert Bechtold, 1906-
(ed.) Modern short stories; a critical anthology. Harcourt 1950 438p

Heinlein, Robert Anson, 1907-
  Assignment in eternity; four long science fiction stories. Fantasy Press 1953 255p
  Green hills of earth; Rysling and the adventure of the entire solar system! With an appreciation by Mark Reinsberg. Shasta Pubs. 1951 256p
  Man who sold the moon; Harriman and the escape from the earth to the moon! Introduction by John W. Campbell, jr. Shasta Pubs. 1950 288p
  Revolt in 2100; the prophets and the triumph of reason over superstition! With an introduction by Henry Kuttner. Shasta Pubs. 1953 317p
  (ed.) Tomorrow, the stars; a science fiction anthology; ed. and with an introduction by Robert A. Heinlein. Doubleday 1952 249p

Hemingway, Ernest, 1898-
  Hemingway reader; selected with a foreword and twelve brief prefaces by Charles Poore. Scribner 1953 xx, 652p
    Analyzed for short stories only

Hemingway reader. Hemingway, E.

Hendryx, James Beardsley, 1880-
  Intrigue on Halfaday Creek. Doubleday 1953 186p
  Murder on Halfaday Creek. Doubleday 1951 191p

Henry, George H. See Certner, S. jt. ed.

Henry, O. pseud. See Porter, William Sydney

Henry, Ralph Ledyard, 1895- See Bachelor, J. M. jt. ed.

Herzberg, Max John, 1886-
  (comp.) Treasure chest of sport stories. Messner 1951 231p

Hester Lilly, and twelve short stories. Taylor, E.

Hoffmann, Ernst Theodor Amadeus, 1776-1822
  Tales from Hoffmann; tr. by various hands ed. and with an introduction by J. M. Cohen; with illus. by Gavarni. Coward-McCann 1951 314p illus

Holsters and heroes. Western Writers of America

Home leave. Tennyson, H.

Honeyed peace. Gellhorn, M. E.

Hoofbeats. Foote, J. T.

Horizon (Periodical)
  Golden Horizon; ed. together with an introduction by Cyril Connolly. British Bk. Centre 1953 596p
    Analyzed for short stories only

Horowitz, Arnold. See Lass, A. H. jt. ed.

Horwitz, Julius, 1920-
  The city. World Pub. 1953 219p

House of fiction. Gordon, C. and Tate, A. eds.

Household, Geoffrey, 1900-
  Tales of adventurers. Little 1952 247p

Howard, Robert Ervin, 1906-1936
  Coming of Conan. Gnome Press 1953 224p
    Analyzed for short stories only
  King Conan: The Hyborean age. Gnome Press 1953 255p
  The sword of Conan: the Hyborean age. Gnome Press 1952 251p

Howard, Wendell, 1891?-
  Last refuge of a scoundrel, and other stories. Exposition 1952 85p

Howe, Irving, 1920- and Greenberg, Eliezer, 1896-
  (eds.) Treasury of Yiddish stories; with drawings by Ben Shahn. Viking 1954 630p illus
    Analyzed for short stories only

Hughes, Langston, 1902-
  Laughing to keep from crying. Holt 1952 206p

Humorous side of Erskine Caldwell. Caldwell, E.

Humphrey, William, 1924-
  Last husband, and other stories. Morrow 1953 239p

Hunting scenes. Surtees, R. S.

Hutchins, Maude Phelps (McVeigh)
  Love is a pie. New Directions 1952 223p
    Analyzed for short stories only

I

I, robot. Asimov, I.

Illustrated man. Bradbury, R.

Ilyin, Boris, 1918- See Stegner, W. E. jt. ed.

Imagination unlimited. Bleiler, E. F. and Dikty, T. E. eds.

In the absence of angels. Calisher, H.

Incredulity of Father Brown. Chesterton, G. K. See Chesterton, G. K. Father Brown omnibus

Indian country. Johnson, D. M.

Indians, Indians, Indians. Fenner, P. R. comp.

Injustice collectors. Auchincloss, L.

Innocence of Father Brown. Chesterton, G. K. See Chesterton, G. K. Father Brown omnibus

Intimacy, and other stories. Sartre, J. P.

Intrigue on Halfaday Creek. Hendryx, J. B.

Invaders of earth. Conklin, G. ed.

Irwin, Margaret Emma Faith
Bloodstock, and other stories. Harcourt 1953 206p

Island of the blue macaws, and sixteen other stories. Ullman, J. R.

It's a date. Stowe, A. comp.

Ivens, Bryna
(ed.) Seventeen (Periodical) Nineteen from Seventeen
(ed.) Seventeen (Periodical) The Seventeen reader

J

Jackson, Charles Reginald, 1903-
Earthly creatures; ten stories. Farrar, Straus 1953 222p
Sunnier side; twelve Arcadian tales. Farrar, Straus 1950 311p

James, Helen. See Weaver, R. jt. ed.

James, Henry, 1843-1916
Eight uncollected tales; ed. and with an introduction by Edna Kenton. Rutgers Univ. Press 1950 314p
Selected fiction; ed. with an introduction and notes by Leon Edel. Dutton 1953 609p (Everyman's lib)
Analyzed for short stories only
Selected short stories; ed. with an introduction by Quentin Anderson. Rinehart 1950 317p (Rinehart editions)

James, Will, 1892-1942
Will James' Book of cowboy stories; illus. by Will James. Scribner 1951 242p illus

Jameson, Malcolm, 1891-1945
Bullard of the space patrol; ed. by Andre Norton [pseud]. World Pub. 1951 255p

Jenkins, William Fitzgerald, 1896-
(ed.) Great stories of science fiction ed. by Murray Leinster [pseud]; introduction by Clifton Fadiman. Random House 1951 xxvii, 321p
Sidewise in time, and other scientific adventures, by Murray Leinster [pseud]. Shasta Pubs. 1950 211p

Jensen, Paul
(ed.) Fireside book of flying stories. . . Simon & Schuster 1951 464p
Analyzed for short stories only

Johnson, Dorothy Marie, 1905-
Indian country; with a foreword by Jack Schaefer. Ballantine 1953 197p

Jones, Katharine M. 1900-
(ed.) New Confederate short stories. Univ. of S.C. Press 1954 202p

Jones, Raymond F. 1915-
The toymaker. Fantasy 1951 287p

Jorrocks, John, pseud. See Surtees, Robert Smith

Joseph, Michael, 1897-
(ed.) Best cat stories; ed. with an introduction by Michael Joseph; illus. by Eileen Mayo. Bentley 1953 270p illus
Analyzed for short stories only

Journey to infinity. Greenberg, M. ed.

Judgment night. Moore, C. L.

K

Kafka, Franz, 1883-1924
Selected short stories of Franz Kafka; tr. by Willa and Edwin Muir; introduction by Philip Rahv. Modern Lib. 1952 328p

Kaufman, Wolfe
Call me Nate; introduction by Elliot Paul; illus. by Irma Selz. Exposition 1951 143p illus

Keller, David Henry, 1880-
Tales from Underwood. Pellegrini & Cudahy 1952 322p

Kenton, Edna, 1875-
(ed.) James, H. Eight uncollected tales

Kentucky story. Summers, H. S. ed.

The kid who beat the Dodgers, and other sports stories. Miers, E. S.

King Conan. Howard, R. E.

Kipling, Rudyard, 1865-1936
Maugham's choice of Kipling's best; sixteen stories selected and with an introductory essay by W. Somerset Maugham. Doubleday 1953 xxviii, 324p

Kiss me again, stranger. Du Maurier, D.

Kneale, Nigel
Tomato Cain, and other stories; with a foreword by Elizabeth Bowen. Knopf 1950 300p

Knight returns, and other stories. Arico, V.

Knox, Joe
Little Benders. Lippincott 1952 255p

Kober, Arthur, 1900-
Bella, Bella kissed a fella. Random House 1951 206p

Kornbluth, Cyril M. 1923-
The explorers; short stories. Ballantine 1954 145p

Krige, Uys, 1910-
The dream and the desert. Houghton 1954 223p
Analyzed for short stories only

Kuebler, Harold W.
(ed.) Treasury of science fiction classics. Hanover House 1954 694p

Kuttner, Henry, 1914-
Ahead of time; ten stories of science fiction and fantasy. Ballantine 1953 177p
Gnome there was, and other tales of science fiction and fantasy, by Lewis Padgett ₁pseud₁. Simon & Schuster 1950 276p
Robots have no tails ₁by₁ Lewis Padgett ₁pseud₁. Gnome Press 1952 224p

L

Lagerkvist, Pär Fabian, 1891-
Eternal smile, and other stories; tr. by Alan Blair ₁and others₁. Random House 1954 389p
Analyzed for short stories only

Lamb, Lawrence
(ed.) Family book of best loved short stories, ed. by Leland W. Lawrence ₁pseud₁. Hanover House 1954 498p

Lange, Victor, 1908-
(ed.) Great German short novels and stories; ed. with an introduction by Victor Lange. Modern Lib. 1952 486p
Revision of the title originally ed. by B. A. Cerf, entered in the main catalog

Lantz, John Edward
(ed.) Stories of Christian living; foreword by Martha Foley. Assn. Press 1950 293p

Lass, Abraham Harold, 1907- **and Horowitz, Arnold,** 1913-
(eds.) Stories for youth. Harper 1950 374p

Last Captain of Horse. Bergengruen, W.

Last Glencannon omnibus. Gilpatric, G.

Last husband, and other stories. Humphrey, W.

Last refuge of a scoundrel, and other stories. Howard, W.

Laughing to keep from crying. Hughes, L.

Lawrence, Leland W. pseud. See Lamb, Lawrence

Lee Vernon, pseud. See Paget Violet

Leftwich, Joseph, 1892-
(ed.) Yisröel; the first Jewish omnibus. ₁Rev. ed.₁ Beechhurst Press 1952 723p

Lehmann, John, 1907-
(ed.) New writing (Periodical) Best stories

Leinster, Murray, pseud. See Jenkins, William Fitzgerald

Lesser, Milton, A. 1918-
(ed.) Looking forward; an anthology of science fiction. Beechhurst Press 1953 400p

Lessing, Doris May, 1919-
This was the Old Chief's country; stories. Crowell 1952 256p

Lewis, Wyndham, 1886-
Rotting Hill. Regnery 1952 265p

Lieberman, Rosalie
Heaven is so high. Bobbs 1950 283p

Lin, Yu-t'ang, 1895-
(ed.) Famous Chinese short stories; retold by Lin Yutang. Day 1952 299p

Lincoln, Victoria Endicott, 1904-
Wild honey; some pilgrims and vagrants going our way. Rinehart 1953 238p
Analyzed for short stories only

Literature for our time. Waite, H. O. and Atkinson, B. P. eds.

Literature of crime. Queen, E. pseud. ed.

Little, George Watson
True stories of heroic dogs; with an introduction by Mrs Albert Payson Terhune. Grosset 1951 256p illus

Little Benders. Knox, J.

Little novels of Sicily. Verga, G.

Lohan, Robert, 1889-1953, **and Lohan, Maria**
(eds.) New Christmas treasury; with more stories for reading aloud. Daye 1954 406p
Analyzed for short stories only

London, Jack, 1876-1916
Sun-Dog Trail and other stories. World Pub. 1951 251p

Looking forward. Lesser, M. A. ed.

Love is a pie. Hutchins, M. P. M.

Love stories of India. Marshall, E.

Lowry, Robert James Collas, 1919-
Happy New Year, kamerades! 11 stories. Drawings by the author. Doubleday 1954 256p illus
Analyzed for short stories only

Ludwig, Jack Barry, and Poirier, W. Richard
(eds.) Stories, British and American. Houghton 1953 505p
Analyzed for short stories only

Ludwig, Richard M. 1920- **and Perry, Marvin B.** 1918-
(eds.) Nine short novels. Heath 1952 li, 571p

Lynskey, Winifred C. 1905-
(ed.) Reading modern fiction; 30 stories with study aids. Scribner 1952 485p

M

McCarthy, Mary Therese, 1912-
Cast a cold eye. Harcourt 1950
212p

McCloy, Helen
(ed.) Mystery Writers of America, inc. 20 great tales of murder

McComas, J. Francis
(ed.) Best from Fantasy and science fiction; 2d ser.

McCullers, Carson (Smith) 1917-
Ballad of the sad café; the novels and stories of Carson McCullers. Houghton 1951 791p
Analyzed for short stories only

MacDonald, Philip
Something to hide. Doubleday 1952 220p

Macfarlan, Allan A.
Campfire adventure stories; illus. by Paulette Jumeau. Assn. Press 1952 225p illus

McFarland, Wilma K. 1890-
(comp.) Then it happened—stories of unforgettable moments. Watts, F. 1952 320p

McFee, William, 1881-
(ed.) Great sea stories of modern times; ed. with original material and an introduction. McBride Co 1953 346p

McLaverty, Michael
Game cock, and other stories; with illus. by Sister Irena Uptegrove. Devin-Adair 1947 192p illus

McNulty, John, 1895-1956
Man gets around. Little 1951 280p

Magazine of fantasy and science fiction
Best from Fantasy and science fiction [1st]-3d ser. ed. by Anthony Boucher [pseud] and J. Francis McComas. Little 1952-1954 3v
2d ser. analyzed for short stories only

Maiden murders. Mystery Writers of America, inc.

Make light of it. Williams, W. C.

Man and beast. Bottome, P.

Man from the tunnel, and other stories. Benson, T.

Man gets around. McNulty, J.

Man who sold the moon. Heinlein, R. A.

Man who was loved. Stern, J.

Many are called. Newhouse, E.

Many-colored fleece. Gable, M. Sister, ed.

The **many** loves of Dobie Gillis. Shulman, M.

Margulies, Leo, 1900- and Friend, Oscar Jerome, 1897-
(eds.) From off this world. Gems of science fiction chosen from "Hall of Fame classics." Merlin 1949 430p
(eds.) Giant anthology of science fiction; 10 complete short novels. Merlin 1954 580p

Marshall, Edison, 1894-
Love stories of India. Farrar, Straus 1950 307p

Martin, Hansford
(ed.) Prize stories 1954. See Prize stories 1954

Matheson, Richard, 1926-
Born of man and woman; tales of science fiction and fantasy; introduction by Robert Bloch. Chamberlain Press 1954 252p

Matschat, Cecile (Hulse)
(ed.) American boy (Periodical) American boy Adventure stories

Maugham, William Somerset, 1874-
Complete short stories. Doubleday 1952 2v
Encore; original stories by W. Somerset Maugham; screenplays by T. E. B. Clarke, Arthur Macrae [and] Eric Ambler. Doubleday 1952 156p
Analyzed for short stories only
Trio; original stories by W. Somerset Maugham; screenplays by W. Somerset Maugham, R. C. Sherriff [and] Noel Langley. Doubleday 1950 156p
Analyzed for short stories only
(ed.) Kipling, R. Maugham's choice of Kipling's best

Maugham's choice of Kipling's best. Kipling, R.

Maupassant, Guy de, 1850-1893
Selected tales; ed. with an introduction by Saxe Commins; illus. by Adolf Dehn. Random House 1950 334p illus

Melville, Herman, 1819-1891
Selected tales and poems; ed. with an introduction by Richard Chase. Rinehart 1950 417p
Analyzed for short stories only
Selected writings. . . Random House 1952 903p
Analyzed for short stories only

Memoirs of Solar Pons. Derleth, A. W.

Men against the stars. Greenberg, M. ed.

Men of the high calling. Neider, C. ed.

Meredith, Scott, 1923-
(ed.) Bar 1 roundup of best western stories; selected and with introductions, by Scott Meredith. Dutton 1952 256p
(ed.) Bar 2; roundup of best western stories; selected and with introductions by Scott Meredith. Dutton 1953 256p
(ed.) Bar 3; roundup of best western stories; selected and with introductions by Scott Meredith. Dutton 1954 223p

Merochnik, Minnie, 1887-
Celeste & other stories. Storm 1950 247p

Merril, Judith, 1923-
(ed.) Beyond human ken; twenty-one startling stories of science fiction and fantasy; with an introduction by Fletcher Pratt. Random House 1952 334p
(ed.) Beyond the barriers of space and time; with an introduction by Theodore Sturgeon. Random House 1954 294p front

Michener, James Albert, 1907-
Return to Paradise. Random House 1951 437p
Analyzed for short stories only

Miers, Earl Schenck, 1910-
The kid who beat the Dodgers, and other sports stories; illus. by Paul Galdone. World Pub. 1954 190p illus

Miller, Peter Schuyler, 1912-
The Titan. Fantasy Press 1952 252p

Millett, Fred Benjamin, 1890-
(ed.) Reading fiction: a method of analysis with selections for study. Harper 1950 269p
Analyzed for short stories only

Milne, Alan Alexander, 1882-1956
Table near the band. Dutton 1950 249p

Mines, Samuel
(comp.) Startling stories (Periodical) Best from Startling stories

Miriam, Sister, 1886-
(ed.) Thinker's digest (Periodical) Spoiled priest, and other stories

Mr Glencannon ignores the war. Gilpatric, G. See Gilpatric, G. Last Glencannon omnibus

Mr Midshipman Hornblower. Forester, C. S.

Mrs Reynolds, and five earlier novelettes. Stein, G.

Modern short stories. Cooper, A. C. ed.

Modern short stories. Felheim, M.; Newman, F. B. and Steinhoff, W. R. eds.

Modern short stories. Heilman, R. B. ed.

Moonscape, and other stories. Waltari, M. T.

Moore, Catherine Lucile, 1911-
Judgment night; a selection of science fiction. Gnome Press 1952 344p
Shambleau, and others. Gnome Press 1953 224p

More guys and dolls. Runyon, D.

More stories. O'Donovan, M.

Moskowitz, Samuel
(comp.) Editor's choice in science fiction. McBride 1954 285p
(ed.) Great railroad stories of the world; ed. with notes by Samuel Moskowitz; introduction by Freeman H. Hubbard. McBride Co. 1954 331p
Analyzed for short stories only

Mostly murder. Brown, F.

Mothers. Fremantle, A. J. ed.

Mowery, William Byron, 1899-
Sagas of the Mounted Police; illus. by Carl Kidwell. Bouregy 1953 256p illus
Tales of the Ozarks; illus. by Mario Cooper. Bouregy 1954 253p illus

Munby, Alan Noel Latimer
Alabaster hand, and other ghost stories. Macmillan 1950 192p

Munro, Hector Hugh, 1870-1916
Short stories of Saki [pseud]; with an introduction by Christopher Morley. Modern Lib. 1951 718p (Modern lib. of the world's best bks)
Analyzed for short stories only

Murder on Halfaday Creek. Hendryx, J. B.

My favorite stories of the great outdoors. Andrews, R. C. ed.

Mysterious Chinese mandrake, and other stories. Ekbergh, I. D.

Mystery Writers of America, inc.
Butcher, baker, murder-maker, by members of the Mystery Writers of America; ed. and with an introduction by George Harmon Coxe. Knopf 1954 341p
Crooks' tour, by members of the Mystery Writers of America; ed. by Bruno Fischer. Dodd 1953 301p
Four-&-twenty bloodhounds. . . Ed. and with introductions by Anthony Boucher [pseud]. Simon & Schuster 1950 406p
Maiden murders; introduction by John Dickson Carr. Harper 1952 302p

Mystery Writers of America, inc.
—*Continued*
20 great tales of murder, by experts of the Mystery Writers of America; ed. by Helen McCloy and Brett Halliday ₁pseud₁. Preface by Baynard Kendrick. Random House 1951 336p
Analyzed for short stories only

N

Neider, Charles, 1915-
(ed.) Great short stories from the world's literature. Rinehart 1950 502p
(ed.) Men of the high calling. Abingdon 1954 238p
(ed.) Short novels of the masters; ed. with an introduction. Rinehart 1948 643p

New Christmas treasury. Lohan, R. and Lohan, M. eds.

New Confederate short stories. Jones, K. M. ed.

New Russian stories. Guerney, B. G. comp.

New short novels. Aswell, M. L. W. ed.

New tales of space and time. Healy, R. J. ed.

New writing (Periodical)
Best stories; ed. by John Lehmann. Harcourt 1951 351p

Newhouse, Edward, 1911-
Many are called; forty-two short stories. Sloane 1951 384p

Newman, Franklin B. See Felheim, M. jt. ed.

The **nightmare.** Forester, C. S.

Night's yawning peal. Derleth, A. W. ed.

Nine short novels. Ludwig, R. M. and Perry, M. B. eds.

Nine stories. Salinger, J. D.

1954 anthology of best original short-shorts. Oberfirst, R. ed.

1952 anthology of best original short-shorts. Oberfirst, R. ed.

Nineteen from Seventeen. Seventeen (Periodical)

No but I saw the movie. De Vries, P.

No rest for Botts. Upson, W. H.

No trip like this, and other stories. Cawley, C. C.

Nobody say a word, and other stories. Van Doren, M.

Norton, Alice Mary
(ed.) Space pioneers; ed. with an introduction and notes by Andre Norton ₁pseud₁. World Pub. 1954 294p

(ed.) Space service; ed. with an introduction and notes, by Andre Norton ₁pseud₁. World Pub. 1953 277p

Nothing serious. Wodehouse, P. G.

Novelette; with other stories. Barker, A. L.

O

O. Henry, pseud. See Porter, William Sydney

O. Henry's best stories. Porter, W. S.

Oberfirst, Robert
(ed.) 1952 anthology of best original short-shorts. Humphries 1953 169p
(ed.) 1954 anthology of best original short-shorts; including Technique sells the short-short. Oberfirst Publications 1954 319p
Analyzed for short stories only

O'Connor, Frank, pseud. See O'Donovan, Michael

O'Donovan, Michael, 1903-
More stories by Frank O'Connor ₁pseud₁. Knopf 1954 385p
Stories of Frank O'Connor ₁pseud₁. Knopf 1952 367p
Traveller's samples; stories and tales, by Frank O'Connor ₁pseud₁. Knopf 1951 238p

Of men, dogs and horses. Bendrodt, J. C.

O'Faoláin, Séan, 1900-
The short story. Devin-Adair 1951 370p
Analyzed for short stories only

O'Flaherty, Liam, 1897-
Two lovely beasts, and other stories; with illus. by John H. De Pol. Devin-Adair 1950 274p illus

Old man of the mountain, and seventeen other stories. Seager, A.

Old pines, and other stories. Boyd, J.

O'Meara, Walter
Tales of the two borders. Bobbs 1952 197p

Omnibus of science fiction. Conklin, G. ed.

On my honor. American girl (Periodical)

On the verge. Sandoz, M. Y.

Onís, Harriet de. See De Onís, Harriet

Open house. Parker, J. R.

Open season. Summers, J. L.

O'Rourke, Frank, 1916-
Greatest victory, and other baseball stories. Barnes, A.S. 1950 206p

O'Rourke, Frank—*Continued*
Heavenly world series, and other baseball stories. Barnes, A.S. 1952 192p
Ride west. Ballantine 1953 182p
The **other** place, and other stories of the same sort. Priestley, J. B.
The **outer** reaches. Derleth, A. W. ed.
Outlaw. Haycox, E.
Owen, Frank, 1893-
(ed.) Teen-age victory parade; illus. by William B. Ricketts. Lantern Press 1950 255p illus
Also available from Grosset
(ed.) Teen-age winter sports stories. Grosset 1949 256p

P

Pacey, Desmond, 1917-
(ed.) Book of Canadian stories; with an introduction and notes. ₁Rev. ed₁ Ryerson Press 1950 310p
Padgett, Lewis, pseud. See Kuttner, Henry
Paget, Violet, 1856-1935
Snake Lady, and other stories ₁by₁ Vernon Lee ₁pseud₁. Ed. and with an introduction by Horace Gregory. Grove 1954 288p
Palomino and other horses. Dennis, W.
Panorama. Bentley, P. E.
Parker, James Reid, 1909-
Open house; illus. by Leonard Shorthall. Doubleday 1951 219p illus
Passionate North. Sansom, W.
Paterson, Neil, 1915-
China run; a book of stories. Random House 1951 247p
Peery, William Wallace, 1910-
(ed.) 21 Texas short stories. Univ. of Tex. Press 1954 264p
Perry, Marvin B. See Ludwig, R. M. jt. ed.
Petrified planet; with an introduction by John Clark. Twayne 1952 263p
Pick, Robert, 1898-
(ed.) German stories and tales. Knopf 1954 371p
Pick of the litter. Cavanna, B. ed.
Pioneer loves. Haycox, E.
The **pioneers.** Schaefer, J. W.
Pirates, pirates, pirates. Fenner, P. R. comp.
Platt, George, 1919-
Play the field alone, and other stories. Vantage 1954 51p
Play the field alone, and other stories. Platt, G.

Poe, Edgar Allan, 1809-1849
Centenary Poe; tales, poems, criticism, marginalia and Eureka; ed. and with an introduction by Montagu ·Slater. McBride Co. 1950 559p
Analyzed for short stories only
The gold bug, and other tales and poems; illus. by Jacob Landau. Macmillan 1953 225p illus
Analyzed for short stories only
Poe's stories and poems; stories adapted by Ollie Depew; ed. by Herbert Spencer Robinson; illus. by Thomas G. Fraumeni. Globe Bk. 1951 257p illus
Analyzed for short stories only
Tales; with sixteen full-page illus. of the author, his family and environment and reproductions from previous editions together with an introductory biographical sketch and captions by Laura Benét. Dodd 1952 666p illus
Poe's stories and poems. Poe, E. A.
Poetry and prose. Foerster, N. ed.
Pohl, Frederik, 1919?-
(ed.) Assignment in tomorrow; an anthology; ed. and with an introduction by Frederik Pohl. Hanover House 1954 317p
(ed.) Star science fiction stories. See Star science fiction stories, no. 1-3
Poirier, W. Richard. See Ludwig, J. B. jt. ed.
Poor Cousin Evelyn. Yaffe, J.
Porter, William Sydney, 1862-1910
Complete works of O. Henry ₁pseud₁; foreword by Harry Hansen. Doubleday 1953 2v
Analyzed for short stories only
O. Henry's best stories; ed. by Lou P. Bunce. Globe Bk. 1953 297p
Possible worlds of science fiction. Conklin, G. ed.
Powell, Dawn, 1897-
Sunday, Monday and always. Houghton 1952 213p
Pratt, Fletcher, 1897-1956
(ed.) World of wonder; an introduction to imaginative literature; foreword by Edith Mirrielees. Twayne 1951 445p
Pratt, Fletcher, 1897-1956, **and De Camp, Lyon Sprague,** 1907-
Tales from Gavagan's bar; illus. by Inga. Twayne 1953 228p illus
Priestley, John Boynton, 1894-
The other place, and other stories of the same sort. Harper 1953 265p

Prize science fiction. Wollheim, D. A. ed.

Prize stories, 1919-1954. See First-prize stories, 1919-1954

Prize stories of 1950: the O. Henry awards; selected and ed. by Herschel Brickell. Doubleday 1950 325p

Prize stories of 1951: the O. Henry awards; selected and ed. by Herschel Brickell. Doubleday 1951 xxvi, 325p
  No volumes issued for 1952-1953

Prize stories 1954: the O. Henry awards; selected and ed. by Paul Engle and Hansford Martin. Doubleday 1954 318p

Q

Queen, Ellery, pseud.
  Calendar of crime. Little 1951 248p
  (ed.) Literature of crime; stories by world-famous authors. Little 1950 405p
  (ed.) Queen's awards: 5th-9th; the winners of the . . . annual detective short-story contest; sponsored by Ellery Queen's Mystery magazine. Little 1950-1954 5v
    Ninth series has title: Ellery Queen's awards
  Queen's Bureau of Investigation. Little 1954 228p

Queen's awards. Queen, E. pseud. ed.

Queen's Bureau of Investigation. Queen, E. pseud.

Quinn, Arthur Hobson, 1875-1944
  (ed.) Wharton, E. N. J. Edith Wharton treasury

R

Rahv, Philip, 1908-
  (ed.) Great Russian short novels; ed. with an introduction by Philip Rahv. Dial Press 1951 774p

Rashomon, and other stories. Akutagawa, R.

Reading fiction. Millett, F. B. ed.

Reading modern fiction. Lynskey, W. C. ed.

Reading the short story. Shaw, H. and Bement, D.

Ready, William B. 1914-
  Great disciple, and other stories. Bruce Pub. 1951 158p

Reason for Ann, and other stories. Connolly, M.

Reck, Franklin Mering, 1896-
  (comp.) American boy (Periodical) American boy Anthology

Red stocking, and other Christmas stories. Eggleston, M. W.

Return to Paradise. Michener, J. A.

Revolt in 2100. Heinlein, R. A.

Reward of faith. Goudge, E.

Rey, Lester del. See Del Rey, Lester

Reynolds, Mack, 1918- See Brown, F. jt. ed.

Ribalow, Harold Uriel, 1919-
  (ed.) These your children; ed. with an introduction by Harold U. Ribalow. Beechhurst Press 1952 429p
  (ed.) This land, these people ⌊by Howard Fast and others⌋ with an introduction by the editor. Beechhurst Press 1950 302p
  (ed.) World's greatest boxing stories. Twayne 1952 309p

Ride west. O'Rourke, F.

Rinehart, Mary (Roberts) 1876-
  Frightened wife, and other murder stories. Rinehart 1953 280p

Ringstones, and other curious tales. Wall, J. W.

Rite, Eva, pseud. See Anderson, Esther Victoria

Roberts, Sir Charles George Douglas, 1860-1943
  Thirteen bears; chosen and ed. by Ethel Hume Bennett; illus. by John A. Hall. Ryerson Press 1947 254p illus

Roberts, Ralph Myron, 1915- See Strang, R. M. jt. ed.

Robot and the man. Greenberg, M. ed.

Robots have no tails. Kuttner, H.

Roche, Mazo de la. See De La Roche, Mazo

Romantic egoists. Auchincloss, L.

Rotting Hill. Lewis, W.

Rough justice. Haycox, E.

Rudnicki, Adolf, 1912-
  Ascent to heaven; tr. by H. C. Stevens. Roy Pubs. 1951 204p illus

Runyon, Damon, 1880-1946
  More guys and dolls; thirty-four of the best short stories by Damon Runyon, with an introduction by Clark Kinnaird. Garden City Bks. 1951 401p

Russell, Bertrand Arthur William Russell, 3d earl, 1872-
  Satan in the suburbs, and other stories; illus. by Asgeir Scott. Simon & Schuster 1953 148p illus

S

Sagas of the Mounted Police. Mowery, W. B.

The Saint in Europe. Charteris, L.

Saki, pseud. See Munro, Hector Hugh

Salinger, Jerome David, 1919-
Nine stories. Little 1953 302p

Salisbury, Rachel. See Bachelor, J. M. jt. ed.

Sandoz, Maurice Yves, 1892-
On the verge; illus. by Salvador Dali. Doubleday 1950 127p illus 127p illus

Sansom, William, 1912-
Passionate North. Harcourt 1953 249p
Something terrible, something lovely. Harcourt 1954 231p
South; aspects and images from Corsica, Italy, and Southern France. Harcourt 1950 198p

"Sarban," pseud. See Wall, John W.

Saroyan, William, 1908-
The Assyrian, and other stories. Harcourt 1950 xxxix, 276p

Sartre, Jean Paul, 1905-
Intimacy, and other stories; tr. by Lloyd Alexander. New Directions 1948 270p

Satan in the suburbs, and other stories. Russell, B. A. W. R. 3d earl

Saturday evening post (Periodical)
Saturday evening post stories, 1950-1953 Random House 1950-53 4v

Saturday evening post stories, 1950-1953. Saturday evening post (Periodical)

Scandal of Father Brown. Chesterton, G. K. See Chesterton, G. K. Father Brown omnibus

Schaefer, Jack Warner, 1907-
Big range. Houghton 1953 203p
The pioneers. Houghton 1954 193p

Schneider, George W. 1917-
Clair de lune, and other stories. Vantage 1951 99p

Schorer, Mark, 1908-
(ed.) The story; a critical anthology. Prentice-Hall 1950 606p

Schramm, Wilbur Lang, 1907-
(ed.) Great short stories. Harcourt 1950 536p

Schulberg, Budd Wilson, 1914-
Some faces in the crowd; short stories. Random House 1953 308p

Science-fiction adventures in dimension. Conklin, G. ed.

Science-fiction carnival. Brown, F. and Reynolds, M. eds.

Science fiction omnibus: the best science fiction stories, 1949, 1950. Bleiler, E. F. and Dikty, T. E. eds.

Science-fiction subtreasury. Tucker, W.

Science-fiction thinking machines. Conklin, G. ed.

Scowcroft, Richard, 1916- See Stegner, W. E. jt. ed.

Scribner treasury; 22 classic tales, by Mary Raymond Shipman Andrews ᵣand othersᵢ . . . introduction and notes by J. G. E. Hopkins. Scribner 1953 689p

Seager, Allan, 1906-
Old man of the mountain, and seventeen other stories. Simon & Schuster 1950 278p

Second Galaxy reader of science fiction. Galaxy science fiction magazine

Second Saint omnibus. Charteris, L.

Secret of Father Brown. Chesterton, G. K. See Chesterton, G. K. Father Brown omnibus

Selden, Ruth
(ed.) Ways of God and men; great stories from the Bible in world literature; ed. with an introduction. Daye 1950 403p

Selected fiction. James, H.

Selected short stories. James, H.

Selected short stories of Franz Kafka. Kafka, F.

Selected stories for teen-agers. Hazeltine, A. I. comp.

Selected tales and poems. Melville, H.

Selected writings. Melville, H.

Sessions, John A. See Hathaway, B. jt. ed.

Seton, Ernest Thompson, 1860-1946
Wild animals I have known; and 200 drawings by Ernest Seton Thompson. . . Scribner 1926 298p illus

Seventeen (Periodical)
Nineteen from Seventeen; stories from Seventeen magazine selected by Bryna Ivens. Lippincott 1952 239p
The Seventeen reader; stories and articles from Seventeen magazine; selected and ed. by Bryna Ivens. Lippincott 1951 310p illus
Analyzed for short stories only

The **Seventeen** reader. Seventeen (Periodical)

Sewall, Richard Benson. See Short, R. W. jt. ed.

Sex without sentiment. Winslow, T. S.

Sextet. Burnett, W. and Burnett, H. S. eds.

Shambleau, and others. Moore, C. L.

Shaw, Harry, 1905- **and Bement, Douglas,** 1898-1943
(eds.) Reading the short story. 2d ed. ᵣbyᵢ Harry Shaw. Harper 1954 396p

She made the big town! And other stories. Brookhouser, F.

Sheckley, Robert, 1928-
Untouched by human hands; thirteen stories. Ballantine 1954 169p

Sherlock Holmes. Doyle, Sir A. C.

Short, Raymond Wright, 1903- **and Sewall, Richard Benson**
(eds.) Short stories for study; an anthology. Rev. ed. Holt 1950 602p

Short novels by Colette. Colette, S. G.

Short novels of the masters. Neider, C. ed.

Short stories. Aiken, C. P.

Short stories. Christ, H. I. and Shostak, J. eds.

Short stories. Eaton, H. T. ed.

Short stories. Farrell, J. T.

Short stories. Van Doren, M.

Short stories for our times. Certner, S. and Henry, G. H. eds.

Short stories for study. Short, R. W. and Sewall, R. B. eds.

Short stories of Saki. Munro, H. H.

The **short** story. O'Faoláin, S.

Shostak, Jerome. See Christ, H. I. jt. ed.

Shulman, Max, 1919-
The many loves of Dobie Gillis; eleven campus stories. Doubleday 1951 223p

Sidewise in time, and other scientific adventures. Jenkins, W. F.

Simak, Clifford D. 1904-
City. Gnome Press 1952 224p

Sitwell, Sir Osbert, bart. 1892-
Collected stories. Harper 1952 540p map

Six tales for all the family. Anderson, E. V.

Sloane, William Milligan, 1906-
(ed.) Space, space, space; stories about the time when men will be adventuring to the stars; selection, introduction and commentaries by William Sloane. Watts, F. 1953 288p
(ed.) Stories for tomorrow; an anthology of modern science fiction; selection and prefaces by William Sloane. Funk 1954 628p

Smoking mountain. Boyle, K.

Snake Lady, and other stories. Paget, V.

Soft voice of the serpent, and other stories. Gordimer, N.

Some faces in the crowd. Schulberg, B. W.

Some others and myself. Suckow, R.

Someone like you. Dahl, R.

Something terrible, something lovely. Sansom, W.

Something to hide. MacDonald, P.

Son of a tinker. Walsh, M.

South. Sansom, W.

Southern review
Anthology of stories from the Southern review; ed. by Cleanth Brooks and Robert Penn Warren. La. State Univ. Press 1953 435p

Space on my hands. Brown, F.

Space pioneers. Norton, A. M. ed.

Space service. Norton, A. M. ed.

Space, space, space. Sloane, W. M. ed.

Spanish stories and tales. De Onís, H. ed.

Speed, speed, speed. Fenner, P. R. comp.

Spoiled priest, and other stories. Thinker's digest (Periodical)

Stafford, Jean, 1915-
Children are bored on Sunday. Harcourt 1953 252p

Stallman, Robert Wooster, 1911-
See West, R. B. jt. ed.

Stanford short stories, 1950-1953... Stanford Univ. Press 1950-53 4v

Stanley, Dave, pseud. See Dachs, David

Star quality; six stories. Coward, N. P.

Star science fiction stories, [no. 1]-3; ed. by Frederik Pohl. Ballantine 1953-54 3v

Startling stories (Periodical)
Best from Startling stories; comp. by Samuel Mines; with an introduction by Robert A. Heinlein. Holt 1953 301p

Stauffer, Ruth Matilda, 1885- **Cunningham, William Hayes,** 1887- **and Sullivan, Catherine J.**
(eds.) Adventures in modern literature. 3d ed. Harcourt 1951 747p illus
Analyzed for short stories only

Steele, Wilbur Daniel, 1886-
Full cargo; more stories. Doubleday 1951 369p

Stegner, Wallace Earle, 1909-
Women on the wall. Houghton 1950 277p
(ed.) Stanford short stories. See Stanford short stories

Stegner, Wallace Earle, 1909- **Scowcroft, Richard,** 1916- **and Ilyin, Boris,** 1918-
(eds.) Writer's art; a collection of short stories. Heath 1950 358p

Stein, Gertrude, 1874-1946
Mrs Reynolds, and five earlier novelettes; with a foreword by Lloyd Frankenberg. Yale Univ. Press 1952 378p

Steinhoff, William R. See Felheim, M. jt. ed.

Stephen Crane: an omnibus. Crane, S.

Stern, James, 1904-
Man who was loved. Harcourt 1951 234p

Stevenson, Robert Louis, 1850-1894
Strange case of Dr Jekyll and Mr Hyde, and other stories; illus. by W. Stein. Coward-McCann 1950 525p illus

Stewart, Beach, 1899-
(ed.) This week (Periodical) This week's short-short stories

Stories and fantasies from the Jewish past. Cohn, E.

Stories, British and American. Ludwig, J. B. and Poirier, W. R. eds.

Stories for discussion. Doty, W. L.

Stories for tomorrow. Sloane, W. M.

Stories for youth. Lass, A. H. and Horowitz, A. eds.

Stories of Christian living. Lantz, J. E. ed.

Stories of F. Scott Fitzgerald. Fitzgerald, F. S. K.

Stories of Frank O'Connor. O'Donovan, M.

Stories of sudden truth. Greene, J. I. and Abell, E. eds.

Stories of the sea. Fenner, P. R. comp.

Story (Periodical)
Story; the magazine of the short story in book form, number one-four; ed. by Whit Burnett and Hallie Burnett. McKay 1951-53 4v

The story. Schorer, M. ed.

Story; number one-four. Story (Periodical)

Story parade (Periodical)
Adventure stories from Story parade; outstanding stories of adventure. Winston 1950 314p

Story survey. Blodgett, H. W. ed.

Stout, Rex, 1886-
Triple jeopardy. Viking 1952 216p

Stowe, Aurelia
(comp.) It's a date; boy-girl stories for the teens; illus. by Eleanor Dart. Random House 1950 214p illus

Strain, Frances (Bruce)
"But you don't understand"; a dramatic series of teen-age predicaments. Appleton 1950 217p
Analyzed for short stories only

Strang, Ruth May, 1895- and Roberts, Ralph Myron, 1915-
(eds.) Teen-age tales. Heath 1954 2v illus
Analyzed for short stories only

Strange case of Dr Jekyll and Mr Hyde, and other stories. Stevenson, R. L.

Stuart, Jesse, 1907-
Clearing in the sky & other stories; woodcuts by Stanley Rice. McGraw 1950 262p illus

Sturgeon, Theodore, pseud. See Waldo, Edward Hamilton

Such darling dodos and other stories. Wilson, A.

Suckow, Ruth, 1892-
Some others and myself; seven stories and a memoir. Rinehart 1952 281p

Sullivan, Catherine J. See Stauffer, R. M. jt. ed.

Sullivan, Richard, 1908-
Fresh and open sky, and other stories. Holt 1950 210p

Summers, Hollis Spurgeon, 1916-
(ed.) Kentucky story; a collection of short stories. Univ. of Ky. Press 1954 247p

Summers, James L. 1910-
Open season. Doubleday 1951 182p

Sun-Dog Trail and other stories. London, J.

Sunday, Monday and always. Powell, D.

Sunnier side. Jackson, C. R.

Supernatural reader. Conklin, G. and Conklin, L. T. eds.

Surtees, Robert Smith, 1803-1864
Hunting scenes; selected by Lionel Gough; with an introduction by Siegfried Sassoon. British Bk. Centre 1954 253p

Sut Lovingood. Harris, G. W.

Swallow, Alan, 1903-
(ed.) Anchor in the sea; an anthology of psychological fiction. Morrow 1947 255p

The swaying elms, and other stories. Blackburn, E. R.

The sword of Conan. Howard, R. E.

Sword of Welleran, and other tales of enchantment. Dunsany, E. J. M. D. P. 18th baron

Sykes, Christopher, 1907-
Character and situation; six short stories; introduction by Evelyn Waugh. Knopf 1950 240p

T

Taber, Gladys (Bagg) 1899-
When dogs meet people. Macrae Smith Co. 1952 237p illus

Table near the band. Milne, A. A.

Tactical exercise. Waugh, E.

Take your choice. Walsh, M.

Talbot, Daniel
(ed.) Treasury of mountaineering stories. Putnam 1954 337p

Tales. Poe, E. A.

Tales from Gavagan's bar. Pratt, F. and De Camp, L. S.

Tales from Hoffmann. Hoffmann, E. T. A.

Tales from Underwood. Keller, D. H.

Tales of adventurers. Household, G.

Tales of land and sea. Conrad, J.

Tales of suspense. Collins, W.

Tales of the Ozarks. Mowery, W. B.

Tales of the two borders. O'Meara, W.

Tales to be told in the dark. Davenport, B. ed.

Tarkington, Booth, 1869-1946
  Three selected short novels. Doubleday 1947 341p

Tate, Allen, 1899- See Gordon, C. jt. ed.

Taylor, Elizabeth, 1912-
  Hester Lilly, and twelve short stories. Viking 1954 210p

Taylor, Peter Hillsman, 1917-
  Widows of Thornton. Harcourt 1954 310p
    Analyzed for short stories only

Team bells woke me, and other stories. Davis, H. L.

Teen-age champion sports stories. Coombs, C. I.

Teen-age dog stories. Furman, A. L. ed.

Teen-age horse stories. Furman, A. L. ed.

Teen-age science fiction stories. Elam, R. M.

Teen-age sea stories. Furman, A. L. ed.

Teen-age sports parade. Chute, B. J.

Teen-age stories of the diamond. Furman, A. L. ed.

Teen-age tales. Strang, R. M. and Roberts, R. M. eds.

Teen-age victory parade. Owen, F. ed.

Teen-age winter sports stories. Owen, F. ed.

Ten modern masters. Davis, R. G. ed.

Tennyson, Hallam, 1921-
  Wall of dust, and other stories. Viking 1948 188p

Terrill, Rogers
  (ed.) Argosy (Periodical) Argosy Book of adventure stories
  (ed.) Argosy (Periodical) Argosy Book of sea stories
  (ed.) Argosy (Periodical) Argosy Book of sports stories

Then it happened. McFarland, W. K. comp.

These were brethren. Claudy, C. H.

These your children. Ribalow, H. U. ed.

They brought their guns. Thompson, T.

They ran for their lives. Brick, J.

Thinker's digest (Periodical)
  Spoiled priest, and other stories; an anthology of short stories and sketches from the Thinker's digest; introduction by N. Elizabeth Monroe. Kenedy 1950 284p

The third bullet, and other stories. Carr, J. D.

Thirteen bears. Roberts, Sir C. G. D.

This land, these people. Ribalow, H. U. ed.

This was the Old Chief's country. Lessing, D. M.

This week magazine
  This week's short-short stories; ed. with an introduction and an essay "How to write a short-short story," by Stewart Beach. Random House 1953 307p

This week's short-short stories. This week magazine

Thomas, David, pseud. See Furman, Abraham Loew

Thompson, Thomas, 1913-
  They brought their guns. Ballantine 1953 162p

Three problems for Solar Pons. Derleth, A. W.

Three selected short novels. Tarkington, B.

Three to be read. Wylie, P.

Time to come. Derleth, A. W. ed.

The Titan. Miller, P. S.

To mother with love. Ungar, F. ed.

Tomato Cain, and other stories. Kneale, N.

Tomorrow, the stars. Heinlein, R. A. ed.

The toymaker. Jones, R. F.

Travelers of space. Greenberg, M. ed.

Traveller's samples. O'Donovan, M.

Treasure chest of sport stories. Herzberg, M. J. comp.

A treasury of Jewish humor. Ausubel, N. ed.

Treasury of Kahlil Gibran. Gibran, K.

Treasury of mountaineering stories. Talbot, D. ed.

Treasury of science fiction classics. Kuebler, H. W. ed.

Treasury of sports humor. Dachs, D. ed.

Treasury of Yiddish stories. Howe, I. and Greenberg, E. eds.

Trio. Maugham, W. S.

Triple jeopardy. Stout, R.

Trollope, Anthony, 1815-1882
  Bedside Barsetshire; comp. by Lance O. Tingay; illus. by Gwen Raverat. Knopf 311p illus
    Analyzed for short stories only

True stories of heroic dogs. Little, G. W.

Tucker, Wilson, 1914-
Science-fiction subtreasury. Rinehart 1954 240p
28 science-fiction stories. Wells, H. G.
20 great tales of murder. Mystery Writers of America, inc.
21 Texas short stories. Peery, W. W. ed.
21 variations on a theme. Cory, D. W. pseud. comp.
Twenty-two stories about horses and men. Creamer, J. B. comp.
Two lovely beasts, and other stories. O'Flaherty, L.

U

Ullman, James Ramsey, 1907-
Island of the blue macaws, and sixteen other stories. Lippincott 1953 320p
Under dog and other stories. Christie, A. M.
Ungar, Frederick
(ed.) To mother with love; a tribute in great stories; with eight halftone reproductions. Ed. with an introduction by Frederic Ungar. Daye 1951 379p illus
Analyzed for short stories only
Untouched by human hands. Sheckley, R.
Upson, William Hazlett, 1891-
No rest for Botts; Earthworms make the world go round. Rinehart 1951 279p

V

Vampire of the village. Chesterton, G. K. See Chesterton, G. K. Father Brown omnibus
Van Doren, Mark, 1894-
Nobody say a word, and other stories. Holt 1953 276p
Short stories. Abelard-Schuman 1950 394p
(ed.) Hawthorne, N. Best of Hawthorne
Van Vogt, Alfred Elton, 1912-
Away and beyond. Pellegrini & Cudahy 1952 309p
Destination: universe! Pellegrini & Cudahy 1952 295p
Verga, Giovanni, 1840-1922
Cavalleria rusticana, and other narratives [selected by J. I. Rodale] Illus. by Aldren Watson. (Story classics) Rodale 1950 173p illus
Analyzed for short stories only
Little novels of Sicily; tr. by H. D. Lawrence. Grove 1953 226p
Vetter, Marjorie (Meyn)
(ed.) American girl (Periodical) Christmas all year 'round

(ed.) American girl (Periodical) Favorite stories
(ed.) American girl (Periodical) On my honor
Vondys, Horace
(ed.) Bluebook (Periodical) Best sea stories from Bluebook
Vries, Peter de. See De Vries, Peter

W

The **wager,** and their stories. Corkery, D.
Waite, Harlow O. and Atkinson, Benjamin Peter, 1917-
(eds.) Literature for our time; an anthology for college students. Rev. ed. Holt 1953 998p illus
Earlier edition ed. by L. S. Brown, H. O. Waite and B. P. Atkinson, analyzed in main catalog
Analyzed for short stories only
Waldo, Edward Hamilton, 1918-
E pluribus unicorn; a collection of short stories of Theodore Sturgeon [pseud]. Abelard Press 1953 276p
Wall, John W.
Ringstones, and other curious tales, by "Sarban" [pseud.] Coward-McCann 1951 283p
Wall of dust, and other stories. Tennyson, H.
Walsh, Maurice, 1879-
Son of a tinker. Lippincott 1951 245p
Take your choice. Lippincott 1954 187p
Waltari, Mika Toimi, 1908-
Moonscape, and other stories; tr. by Naomi Walford. Putnam 1954 310p
Was it too late? & other stories. Booker, A. E.
Watchful gods, and other stories. Clark, W. Van T.
Waugh, Evelyn
Tactical exercise. Little 1954 289p
Ways of God and men. Selden, R. ed.
Weaver, Robert, and James, Helen
(eds.) Canadian short stories. Oxford 1952 248p
Weber, Brom, 1917-
(ed.) American vanguard, 1953
See also Glicksberg, C. I. jt. ed.
Week-end book of ghost stories. Carrington, H. ed.
Wells, Herbert George, 1886-1946
28 science fiction stories. Dover 1952 915p
Analyzed for short stories only
Welty, Eudora, 1909-
Golden apples. Harcourt 1949 244p

Welty, Eudora—*Continued*
Selected stories; containing all of A curtain of green, and other stories, and The wide net, and other stories; with an introduction by Katherine Anne Porter. Modern Lib. 1954 2v in 1

Werner, Heinz, 1901- See Fabricant, N. D. jt. ed.

West, Ray Benedict, 1908- **and Stallman, Robert Wooster,** 1911-
(eds.) Art of modern fiction. Rinehart 1949 652p
Analyzed for short stories only

Western Writers of America
Bad men and good; a roundup of western stories by members of the Western Writers of America; with a foreword by Luke Short [pseud]. Dodd 1953 240p
Holsters and heroes; stories from the Western Writers of America; with a preface by Noel M. Loomis. Macmillan 1954 207p

Wharton, Edith Newbold (Jones) 1862-1937
Edith Wharton treasury; ed. and with an introduction by Arthur Hobson Quinn. Appleton 1950 xxxi, 581p
Analyzed for short stories only

When boyhood dreams come true. See Farrell, J. T. Further short stories

When dogs meet people. Taber, G. B.

Which grain will grow. Wolfe, D. M.

White, William Anthony Parker, 1911-
(ed.) Magazine of fantasy and science fiction. Best from Fantasy and science fiction
(ed.) Mystery Writers of America, inc. Four-&-twenty bloodhounds

White nights, and other stories. Dostoevskii, F. M.

Widows of Thornton. Taylor, P. H.

Wild animals I have known. Seton, E. T.

Wild honey. Lincoln, V. E.

Will James' Book of cowboy stories. James, W.

Williams, William Carlos, 1883-
Make light of it; collected stories. Random House 1950 342p

Willingham, Calder, 1922-
Gates of hell. Vanguard 1951 190p

Wilson, Angus, 1914?-
Such darling dodos and other stories. Morrow 1950 187p

Winslow, Thyra Samter, 1893-
Sex without sentiment. Abelard-Schuman 1954 312p

Wisdom of Father Brown. Chesterton, G. K. See Chesterton, G. K. Father Brown omnibus

Wodehouse, Pelham Grenville, 1881-
Nothing serious. Doubleday 1951 222p

Wolf, Martin L.
(ed.) Gibran, K. Treasury of Kahlil Gibran

Wolfe, Don Marion, 1902-
(ed.) Which grain will grow; stories and sketches of childhood [by] Adler [and others]. Cambridge Pub. Co. 1950 205p
Analyzed for short stories only
(ed.) American vanguard, 1952. See American vanguard, 1952

Wollheim, Donald A.
(comp.) Every boy's book of science-fiction; comp. and ed. by Donald A. Wollheim. Fell 1951 254p
(comp.) Flight into space; great science-fiction stories of interplanetary travel. Fell 1950 251p
(ed.) Prize science fiction; ed. with an introduction by Donald A. Wollheim. McBride Co. 1953 230p

Woman in the case, and other stories. Chekhov, A. P.

Women on the wall. Stegner, W. E.

The **word** lives on. Brentano, F. ed.

Works of God, and other stories. Berto, G.

World of wonder. Pratt, F. ed.

World's best. Burnett, W. ed.

World's best doctor stories. Fabricant, N. D. and Werner, H. eds.

World's greatest boxing stories. Ribalow, H. U. ed.

Worlds of tomorrow. Derleth, A. W. ed.

Writer's art. Stegner, W. E.; Scowcroft, R. and Ilyin, B. eds.

Writers for tomorrow. Hathaway, B. and Sessions, J. A.

Wylie, Philip, 1902-
Best of Crunch and Des. Rinehart 1954 404p
Three to be read. . . Rinehart 1951 312p

Y

Yaffe, James, 1927-
Poor Cousin Evelyn. Little 1951 269p

Yankee Doodle. Fenner, P. R. comp.

Year after tomorrow. Del Rey, L.; Matschat, C. H. and Carmer, C. L. eds.

Year's best science fiction novels, 1952-1954; ed. and with an introduction by Everett F. Bleiler and T. E. Dikty. Fell 1952-54 3v

Yisröel. Leftwich, J. ed.

Directory of Publishers

Abelard-Schuman. Abelard-Schuman, Inc, 404 4th Av, N.Y. 16

Abingdon. Abingdon Press, Hdqrs, 810 Broadway, Nashville 2, Tenn.

Am. Bk. American Book Company, 55 5th Av, N.Y. 3

Antioch Press, Yellow Springs, Ohio

Appleton. Appleton-Century-Crofts, Inc, 35 W 32d St, N.Y. 1

Arkham House, Sauk City, Wis.
    Associated imprint: Mycroft & Moran

Assn. Press. Association Press (Nat. Council of Y.M.C.A's) 291 Broadway, N.Y. 7

Ballantine. Ballantine Books, Inc, 101 5th Av, N.Y. 3

Barnes, A.S. A. S. Barnes & Company, 232 Madison Av, N.Y. 16

Beechhurst Press. Beechhurst Press, Inc, 11 E 36th St, N.Y. 16

Bentley. Robert Bentley, Inc, 8 Ellery St, Cambridge 38, Mass.

Bobbs. The Bobbs-Merrill Company, Inc, 724-730 N Meridian St, Indianapolis 7

Bouregy. Bouregy & Curl, Inc, 22 E 60th St, N.Y. 22

British Bk. Centre. British Book Centre, Inc, 122 E 55th St, N.Y. 22

Bruce Pub. Bruce Publishing Company, 400 N Broadway, Milwaukee 1

Cambridge Pub. Co. Cambridge Publishing Company, 315 E 69th St, N.Y. 21

Chamberlain Press. The Chamberlain Press, Inc, P.O. Box 7713, Philadelphia

Citadel. Citadel Press, 222 4th Av, N.Y. 3

Cornell Univ. Press. Cornell University Press, 124 Roberts Pl, Cornell Heights, Ithaca, N.Y.

Coward-McCann. Coward-McCann, Inc, 210 Madison Av, N.Y. 16

Crowell. The Thomas Y. Crowell Company, 432 4th Av, N.Y. 16

Crown. Crown Publishers, 419 4th Av, N.Y. 16

Day. John Day Company, Inc, 210 Madison Av, N.Y. 16

Daye. Stephen Daye Press, Inc, N.Y. See Ungar

Devin-Adair. The Devin-Adair Company, 23-25 E 26th St, N.Y. 10

Dial Press. Dial Press, Inc, 461 4th Av, N.Y. 16

Dodd. Dodd, Mead & Company, Inc, 432 4th Av, N.Y. 16

Doubleday. Doubleday & Company, Inc, 575 Madison Av, N.Y. 22

Dover. Dover Publications, Inc, 920 Broadway, N.Y. 10

Duell. Duell, Sloan & Pearce, Inc, 124 E 30th St, N.Y. 16

Dutton. E. P. Dutton & Company, Inc, 300 4th Av, N.Y. 10

Exposition. The Exposition Press, Inc, 386 4th Av, N.Y. 16

Fantasy. Fantasy Publishing Company Inc, 8318-8320 Avalon Blvd, Los Angeles 3

Fantasy Press. Fantasy Press, Box 159, Reading, Pa.

Farrar, Straus. Farrar, Straus & Cudahy, Inc, 101 5th Av, N.Y. 3
    Purchased Pellegrini & Cudahy

Fell. Frederick Fell, Inc, Inc, 386 4th Av, N.Y. 16

Follett. Follett Publishing Company, 1000 W Washington Blvd, Chicago 7

Funk. Funk & Wagnalls Company, 153 E 24th St, N.Y. 10

Garden City Bks. Garden City Books, 575 Madison Av, N.Y. 22
    Also use imprint: Hanover House: Sun Dial

Globe Bk. Globe Book Company, Inc, 175 5th Av, N.Y. 10

Gnome Press. Gnome Press, 80 E 11th St, N.Y. 3

Greenberg. Greenberg Publisher, 201 E 57th St, N.Y. 22

Greystone. Greystone Corporation (Greystone Press) Publishers, 100 6th Av, N.Y. 13

Greystone Press. See Greystone

Grosset. Grosset & Dunlap, Inc, 1107 Broadway, N.Y. 10

Grove. Grove Press, 795 Broadway, N.Y. 3

Hanover House. See Garden City Bks.

Harcourt. Harcourt, Brace & Company, Inc, 383 Madison Av, N.Y. 17

Harper. Harper & Brothers (Pleiad Press Imprint) 49 E 33d St, N.Y. 16

Heath. D. C. Heath & Company, 285 Columbus Av, Boston 16

Heritage. Heritage Press, 595 Madison Av, N.Y. 22
    Refer orders to Dial Press

Holt. Henry Holt & Company, Inc, 383 Madison Av, N.Y. 17

Houghton. Houghton Mifflin Company (Riverside Press, Cambridge) 2 Park St, Boston 7

House of Edinboro. House of Edinboro Publishers, 21 Edinboro St, Boston 11

Humphries. Bruce Humphries, Inc, Publishers, 48 Melrose St, Boston

Jewish Pub. The Jewish Publication Society of America, 222 N 15th St, Philadelphia 2

Kenedy. P. J. Kenedy & Son, 12 Barclay St, N.Y. 8

Knopf. Alfred A. Knopf, Inc, 501 Madison Av, N.Y. 22

La. State Univ. Press. Louisiana State University Press, University Station, Baton Rouge 3, La.

Lantern Press. Lantern Press, Inc, 257 4th Av, N.Y. 10

Lib. Pubs. Library Publishers, Inc, 8 W 40th St, N.Y. 18

Lippincott. J. B. Lippincott Company, 227-231 S 6th St, Philadelphia 5

Little. Little, Brown & Company, 34 Beacon St, Boston 6

Liveright. Liveright Publishing Corporation 386 4th Av, N.Y. 16

Longmans. Longmans, Green & Company, Inc, 55 5th Av, N.Y. 3

McBride. Medill McBride Company. See Crown

McBride Co. The McBride Company, Inc, 200 E 37th St, N.Y. 16

MacDonald & Co. MacDonald & Company (Publishers) Ltd, 16 Maddox St, London W 1

McGraw. McGraw-Hill Book Company, Inc, 330 W 42d St, N.Y. 36

McKay. David McKay Company, Inc, 55 5th Av, N.Y. 3

Macmillan. The Macmillan Company, 60 5th Av, N.Y. 11

McMullen. The Declan X McMullen Company, Inc, 839 Stewart Av, Garden City, N.Y.

Macrae Smith Co. Macrae Smith Company, Lewis Tower Bldg, 225 S 15th St, Philadelphia 2

Meador. Meador Publishing Company, 324 Newbury St, Boston 15

Merlin. Merlin Press, Inc, 250 W 57th St, N.Y. 19
 Books distributed by Greenberg

Messner. Julian Messner, Inc, Publishers, 8 W 40th St, N.Y. 18

Modern Lib. Modern Library, Inc, 457 Madison Av, N.Y. 22

Moody Press. The Moody Press (The Moody Bible Institute of Chicago) 820 N LaSalle St, Chicago 10

Morrow. William Morrow & Company, Inc, 425 4th Av, N.Y. 16

Mycroft & Moran. See Arkham House

Nelson. Thomas Nelson & Sons, Copewood & Davis Sts, Camden, N.J.

New Directions, Norfolk, Conn.

Noonday. Noonday Press, 80 E 11th St, N.Y. 3

Oberfirst Pblns. Oberfirst Publications, Ocean City, N.J.

Oxford. Oxford University Press, 16-00 Pollitt Drive, Fair Lawn, N.J.

Oxford Bk. Co. Oxford Book Company, 222 4th Av, N.Y. 3

Pageant Press. Pageant Press, Inc, 130 W 42d St, N.Y. 36

Pamphlet Distributing. The William-Frederick Press Pamphlet Distributing Company, 313-315 W 35th St, N.Y.

Pellegrini & Cudahy. See Farrar, Straus

Prentice-Hall. Prentice-Hall, Inc, Route 9W, Englewood Cliffs, N.J.

Putnam. G. P. Putnam's Sons, 210 Madison Av, N.Y. 16

Random House. Random House, Inc, Promotion Dept, 457 Madison Av, N.Y. 22

Regnery. Henry Regnery Company, Publishers, 20 W Jackson Blvd, Chicago 4

Rinehart. Rinehart & Company, Inc, 232 Madison Av, N.Y. 16

Rodale. Rodale Books, Inc, 6th & Minor Sts, Emmaus, Pa.

Ronald. The Ronald Press Company, 15 E 26th St, N.Y. 10

Roy Pubs. Roy Publishers, 30 E 74th St, N.Y. 21

Rutgers Univ. Press. Rutgers University Press, New Brunswick, N.J.

Ryerson Press. Ryerson Press (United Church Publishing House) 299 Queen St, W. Toronto 2B

Scribner. Charles Scribner's Sons, 597-599 5th Av, N.Y. 17

Seymour. Ralph Fletcher Seymour, 410 S Michigan Av, Chicago 5

Shasta Pubs. 5525 S Blackstone, Chicago 37

Sheed. Sheed & Ward, Inc, 840 Broadway, N.Y. 3

Sherwin Cody Associates, Dobbs Ferry, N.Y.

Simon & Schuster. Simon & Schuster, Inc, 630 5th Av, N.Y. 20
 Distribute Greystone Press Bks.

Sloane. William Sloane Associates, Inc, 425 4th Av, N.Y. 16

Stackpole Co. Stackpole Company, Telegraph Press Bldg, Cameron & Kelker, Harrisburg, Pa.

Stanford Univ. Press. Stanford University Press, Stanford, Calif.

Storm. Storm Publishers, Inc, 80 E 11th St, N.Y. 3

Sun Dial. Sun Dial Press, N.Y. See Garden City Bks.

Temple Pubs. Temple Publishers, McLachlen Bldg, 10th & G Sts, NW, Washington, D.C.

Thames (N.Y.) Thames & Hudson Publishers, Inc, 424 Madison Av, N.Y. 17
 Refer orders to Vanguard

Twayne. Twayne Publishers, Inc, 31 Union Sq, W, N.Y. 3

Ungar. Freedrick Ungar Publishing Company, 105 E 24th St, N.Y. 10
 Purchased Stephen Daye, Inc

Univ. of Kan. City Press. University of Kansas City Press, Kansas City 4, Mo.
 Books distributed and also published jointly by Twayne

Univ. of Ky. Press. University of Kentucky Press, McVey Hall, Lexington 29, Ky.

Univ. of N.C. Press. University of North Carolina Press, Box 510, Chapel Hill, N.C.

Univ. of S.C. Press. University of South Carolina Press, Columbia 1, S.C.

Univ. of Tex. Press. University of Texas Press, Austin 12, Tex.

Vanguard. Vanguard Press, Inc, 424 Madison Av, N.Y. 17

Vantage. Vantage Press, Inc, 120 W 31st St, N.Y. 1

Viking. The Viking Press, Inc, 18 E 48th St, N.Y. 17

Wagner, J.F. Joseph F. Wagner, Inc, 53 Park Pl, N.Y. 7

Washburn. Ives Washburn, Inc, Publishers, 55 5th Av, N.Y. 3

Watts, F. Franklin Watts, Inc, 699 Madison Av, N.Y. 21

Westminster Press. Westminster Press, Witherspoon Bldg, Philadelphia 7

Wilcox & Follett. See Follett

William-Frederick Press. See Pamphlet Distributing

Winston. John C. Winston Company, 1006-1020 Arch St, Philadelphia 7

World Pub. The World Publishing Company, 2231 W 110th St, Cleveland 2

Wyn. A. A. Wyn, Inc, 23 W 47th St, N.Y. 36

Yale Univ. Press. Yale University Press, 143 Elm St, New Haven 7, Conn.